Frommer's®

Harvey -

Scandinavia

22nd Edition

by Darwin Porter & Danforth Prince

Here's what the critics say about Frommer's:

"Amazingly easy to use. Very portable, very complete."
—*Booklist*

"Detailed, accurate, and easy-to-read information for all price ranges."
—*Glamour Magazine*

"Hotel information is close to encyclopedic."
—*Des Moines Sunday Register*

"Frommer's Guides have a way of giving you a real feel for a place."
—*Knight Ridder Newspapers*

BICENTENNIAL
1807
WILEY
2007
BICENTENNIAL

Wiley Publishing, Inc.

Published by:

Wiley Publishing, Inc.

111 River St.
Hoboken, NJ 07030-5774

ISBN: 978-0-470-10059-2

Editor: Anuja Madar
Production Editor: Michael Brumitt
Cartographers: Dorit Kreisler and Andrew Dolan
Photo Editor: Richard Fox
Anniversary Logo Design: Richard Pacifico
Production by Wiley Indianapolis Composition Services

Front cover photo: Denmark, Hillerod: Frederiksborg Slot across Slotso Lake
Back cover photo: Finland, Helsinki: Commercial Center for modern Finnish design

For information on our other products and services or to obtain technical support, please
contact our Customer Care Department within the U.S. at 800/762-2974, outside the
U.S. at 317/572-3993 or fax 317/572-4002.

Wiley also publishes its books in a variety of electronic formats. Some content that
appears in print may not be available in electronic formats.

Manufactured in the United States of America

5 4 3 2 1

Contents

4 Introducing Copenhagen 61

5 Exploring Copenhagen 97

6 Exploring the Danish Countryside 153

7 The Best of Norway 212

List of Maps

An Invitation to the Reader

In researching this book, we discovered many wonderful places—hotels, restaurants, shops, and more. We're sure you'll find others. Please tell us about them, so we can share the information with your fellow travelers in upcoming editions. If you were disappointed with a recommendation, we'd love to know that, too. Please write to:

Frommer's Scandinavia, 22nd Edition
Wiley Publishing, Inc. • 111 River St. • Hoboken, NJ 07030-5774

An Additional Note

Please be advised that travel information is subject to change at any time—and this is especially true of prices. We therefore suggest that you write or call ahead for confirmation when making your travel plans. The authors, editors, and publisher cannot be held responsible for the experiences of readers while traveling. Your safety is important to us, however, so we encourage you to stay alert and be aware of your surroundings. Keep a close eye on cameras, purses, and wallets, all favorite targets of thieves and pickpockets.

About the Authors

A team of veteran travel writers, **Darwin Porter** and **Danforth Prince** have produced numerous titles for Frommer's, including best-selling guides to Italy, France, the Caribbean, England, and Germany. Porter, a former bureau chief of *The Miami Herald,* is also a Hollywood biographer, providing inside looks at the private lives of such stars as Humphrey Bogart, Katherine Hepburn, and aviator Howard Hughes. His latest bio is *Brando Unzipped.* Formerly of the Paris bureau of *The New York Times,* Prince is also president of Blood Moon Productions and other media-related firms.

Other Great Guides for Your Trip:

Frommer's Denmark

Frommer's Norway

Frommer's Sweden

Frommer's Europe

Frommer's Europe from $85 a Day

Frommer's European Cruises & Ports of Call

Frommer's Gay & Lesbian Europe

Frommer's Europe by Rail

Frommer's Star Ratings, Icons & Abbreviations

Every hotel, restaurant, and attraction listing in this guide has been ranked for quality, value, service, amenities, and special features using a **star-rating system.** In country, state, and regional guides, we also rate towns and regions to help you narrow down your choices and budget your time accordingly. Hotels and restaurants are rated on a scale of zero (recommended) to three stars (exceptional). Attractions, shopping, nightlife, towns, and regions are rated according to the following scale: zero stars (recommended), one star (highly recommended), two stars (very highly recommended), and three stars (must-see).

In addition to the star-rating system, we also use **seven feature icons** that point you to the great deals, in-the-know advice, and unique experiences that separate travelers from tourists. Throughout the book, look for:

Finds	Special finds—those places only insiders know about
Fun Fact	Fun facts—details that make travelers more informed and their trips more fun
Kids	Best bets for kids and advice for the whole family
Moments	Special moments—those experiences that memories are made of
Overrated	Places or experiences not worth your time or money
Tips	Insider tips—great ways to save time and money
Value	Great values—where to get the best deals

The following **abbreviations** are used for credit cards:

AE   American Express   DISC   Discover   V   Visa
DC   Diners Club   MC   MasterCard

Frommers.com

Now that you have this guidebook to help you plan a great trip, visit our website at **www. frommers.com** for additional travel information on more than 3,500 destinations. We update features regularly to give you instant access to the most current trip-planning information available. At Frommers.com, you'll find scoops on the best airfares, lodging rates, and car rental bargains. You can even book your travel online through our reliable travel booking partners. Other popular features include:

- Online updates of our most popular guidebooks
- Vacation sweepstakes and contest giveaways
- Newsletters highlighting the hottest travel trends
- Online travel message boards with featured travel discussions

What's New in Scandinavia

Many of the old towns and villages remain relatively the same year after year, but in the four capitals of Scandinavia, the pulse beats faster, and changes are being made so these great cities can remain on the cutting edge.

COPENHAGEN **Accommodations** In the past year or so, Copenhagen has seen the opening of more hotels than in its entire history. Old "dragons" are being spruced up to meet the competition, hotels are opening in completely new buildings, and former hotels are being recycled into something better.

That virtual landmark, the Sophie Amalie, has shed its skin and emerged as the new **Front Hotel Copenhagen,** Skt. Annæ Plads 21, P.O. Box 9076, DK-1022 Copenhagen K (© **33-13-34-00;** www.front.dk; p. 73), one of the finest addresses in the capital outfitted in Danish modern with chic furnishings such as trendy black leather.

During the life of this edition, the staid old **Le Meridien Palace Hotel,** Rådhuspladsen 57, DK-1550 Copenhagen (© **33-14-40-50;** www.palace-hotel.dk; p. 75), is being vastly restored and redesigned, beginning with the opening of "The Night Wing" in the autumn of 2006. More changes are in the air, although this 1910 hotel will remain open during the renovations.

After a major overhaul and many changes, the Park Hotel has become **Hotel Fox,** Jarmers Plads 3, DK-1551 Copenhagen (© **33-13-30-00;** www.hotelfox.dk; p. 78). The owners hired 21 separate designers from all over Europe to strut their stuff—and so they did, turning the Fox into one of the most avant-garde of all Danish modern hotels in Copenhagen. Each room is a work of art.

Dining Enjoying a love affair with the press is that bastion of Nordic cuisine, **NOMA,** Strandgade 93 (© **32-96-32-97;** p. 87). Many of its specialties are plucked from the chilling waters of the North Atlantic. Fish, the house specialty, is poached, grilled, pickled, smoked, or salted according to old Nordic traditions.

ROSKILDE In a move that made headlines around the world, the remains of the czarina Maria Feodorovna, the mother of the last emperor of Russia, were removed from **Roskilde Cathedral,** Domkirkestræde 10, in 2006 and returned to St. Petersburg. She married Alexander and bore him six children, one of whom, Nicholas II, was executed at the time of the Russian Revolution. See p. 148.

SKAGEN On the north coast of Jutland, there is no more acclaimed place to stay or dine than the new **Ruth's Hotel,** Hans Ruths Vej 1 (© **98-44-11-24;** www.ruths-hotel.dk; p. 210), which lies among the sand dunes of this artists' colony and summer resort. The on-site spa is the best in Jutland, and the restaurant, Ruth's Gourmet, is acclaimed as one of the top five in the country outside Copenhagen.

OSLO   More changes are occurring in fast-moving Oslo than anywhere else in Norway. One thing you can always count on is a change in pricing, which is frequently on the rise. As the center of a North Sea oil empire, Oslo is one of the world's costliest cities.

Accommodations   The Best Western showcase, **Hotel Bastion,** Skippergaten 7 (© **800/528-1234** or 22-47-77-00; www.hotelbastion.no; p. 248), was also taken over by Clarion in 2006. Under its new owners, this hotel has moved up to become one of the most sophisticated in Oslo, supporting a chic designer decor.

The biggest news was generated by the Thon chain, which moved aggressively in 2006 to take over the moderately priced Rainbow chain hotels. Thon today runs some of the best hotels in Oslo in the reasonably priced field. If one is fully booked, a reservation can be made in another comparably priced establishment.

Thon's new hotels, where improvements are anticipated during the life of this edition, include **Thon Hotel Cecil,** Stortingsgata 8 (© **23-31-48-00;** www.thonhotels.no; p. 251), and **Thon Hotel Stefan,** Rosenkrantzgate 1 (© **23-31-55-00;** www.thonhotels.no; p. 251).

Attractions   World headlines were generated at the **Munch Museet,** Tøyengate 53 (© **23-49-35-00;** p. 276), when Edvard Munch's world famous *The Scream* (one of four versions) was recovered. It had been stolen in February 1994 and reclaimed from thieves with little damage. Valued at $75 million, the painting was uninsured at the time of its theft.

BERGEN   The hot new hotel address in this capital of the west is the **Clarion Collection Hotel Havnekontoret,** Slottsgaten 1 (© **55-60-11-00;** p. 310), which opened in 2006 right along the Bryggen harborfront. An antique transportation hub was recycled into a first-class hotel of grace and charm, the architects respecting the style of the building while installing state-of-the-art facilities and plumbing.

In other hotel news, the long-standing and cost-conscious Hotel Ambassadeur has been given a new lease on life as the **P Hotel Bergen,** Vestre Torvgate 9 (© **55-90-08-90;** p. 315). Even though minor upgrades have been made, the hotel remains one of the most affordable in high-priced Bergen.

GEILO   Of all the resorts between Oslo and Bergen, the most excitement was generated by the revamping of the **Nye Vestlia Resort,** N-3580 Geilo (© **32-08-72-00;** p. 348), which has the best spa facilities in central Norway. One of the country's best known interior architects, Helene Hennie, was hired to bring new life into this long-existing resort. An avant-garde structure has added 24 luxurious suites and 22 elegant doubles to the existing room count.

HAMMERFEST   For those adventurous travelers making their way to the North Cape, the **Skansen Mat og Vinstue** has opened at the Rica Hotel Hammerfest, Sørøygata 15 (© **78-41-13-33;** p. 334). The chef promises to imbue his diners with "a touch of the Arctic." The small, intimate restaurant has an open kitchen and a fireplace.

TRONDHEIM   Buying out the Rainbow chain, the aggressive Thon chain has taken over some of the most affordable hotels in Trondheim and improved them for a new generation of visitors. The most significant takeover is the landmark **Thon Hotel Gildevangen,** Søndre Gate 22B (© **73-87-01-30;** www.thonhotels.no; p. 354), which has been a hotel since 1930. Renovations throughout much of 2006 and early 2007 have erased all traces of a devastating fire that swept over this structure in 2005.

Near the market square, the old Tulip Inn Rainbow has now become the **Thon**

Hotel Trondheim, Kongens Gate 15 (© 73-50-50-50; www.thonhotels.no; p. 354). During the life of this edition, Thon plans to reduce the number of rooms to make the existing accommodations larger.

STOCKHOLM Dining One of the members of ABBA has opened the chic **Bistro Rival** in the Hotel Rival, Maria-torget 3 (© 08/545-789-00; p. 411). This had become the hippest dining spot in town, offering market-fresh and tantalizing cuisine to the see-and-be-seen circuit. Like the clientele, the food is international.

GOTHENBURG In Sweden's second city, the hotel scene has remained relatively sleepy, but there's been an explosion of restaurants. Though no rival of Stockholm, Gothenburg is increasingly taken seriously by discerning foodies. One of the most hip and appealing drinking and dining spots is **Bliss Resto,** Magasins-gatan 3 (© 031/138555; p. 467), which serves an ambitious menu featuring delectable tapas among other international offerings.

Dispensing a French and Swedish cuisine, **Cyrano's,** Prinsgatan 7 (© 031/143110; p. 467), is one of the city's justifiably popular new bistros, featuring, among other selections, some of the most savory pizzas in town. The setting evokes Provence in the south of France.

Named after a district in New York, **Soho,** Östra Larmgatan 16 (© 031/13-33-26; p. 468), is a cozy place for dining on international specialties and sipping something from the exceptional wine bar, which carries 40 reds and 40 whites sold by the glass.

Finally, **Wasa Allé & Wasa Källare,** Vasagatan 24 (© 031/31-31-91; p. 469), roams the planet for inspiration—not only Sweden, but France, Brazil, and the countries of Asia. A former pharmacy has been converted into this fashionable

rendezvous, which now serves some of the best cuisine in the city. It also contains an inexpensive cellar cafe where you can place your order at the counter.

MALMÖ Sweden's third city is exploding with new developments in the wake of a spectacular bridge spanning the Öresund, linking southern Sweden with Denmark. Copenhagen is only a short drive away. Nothing is more dazzling on the Malmö skyline than the avant-garde **"Turning Torso,"** Sweden's tallest building, an apartment house rising 190km (624 ft.) with 54 floors and a 90-degree twist from the base to the top.

In hotels, **Scandic Hotel Kramer,** Stortorget 7 (© 040/693-54-00; www.scandic-hotels.com; p. 501), in the center of town, was growing a bit stale until a top-to-bottom refurbishment made it once again one of the finest addresses in Malmö.

In dining, Malmö is undergoing a revolution. Now that it's linked to the Continent, more and more restaurants are opening with exotic menus. One of the best of these is **Lemongrass,** Grunbod-gatan 9 (© 40/30-69-79; p. 503), which brings Thai cuisine to Malmö, and also offers Chinese and Japanese specialties, including sushi.

LUND In one of Scandinavia's greatest university centers, the ancient city of Lund, **Hotel Lundia,** Knut den Stores Gata 2 (© 046/280-65-00; www.lundia.se; p. 510), has emerged as a choice address for overnighting. This long-established hotel near the railway station has been given a new lease on life, drawing upon the traditions of Swedish modernism and Japanese simplicity. Much of the elegance of the past has been retained, including white-marble sheathing, but everything has been given a fresh look with the use of curved birch furnishings and other natural materials.

The preferred address for dining is **The Living Room,** Knut den Stores Gata 2 (© **046/280-65-000;** p. 511), installed in the just recommended Hotel Lundia. Finely tuned Swedish and international cuisine, using market-fresh ingredients, attracts serious foodies.

As night falls, **Slagthuset,** Jörgen Köcksgatan 7A (© **040/10-99-31;** p. 505), has become the city's hippest and most appealing dance club. The setting is a former 19th-century slaughterhouse for cattle and hogs, lying directly behind the railway station. It's the largest and most energetic dance club in Scandinavia.

KIRUNA In Swedish Lapland, Kiruna is the largest city in the world in terms of geography, covering 4,848 sq. km (1,872 sq. miles), but you better get there before it moves. In an astonishing announcement, the Swedish government has announced that the city will have to relocate, since it's in danger of sliding down a vast crater left by the iron-ore mines underneath the city. In the years to come, many buildings will be loaded onto large trailers and transported to a safer location. See p. 545.

HELSINKI Accommodations The old hotel Hesperia has been taken over and turned into the **Crowne Plaza Helsinki,** Mannerheimintie 50, FIN-00260 Helsinki (© **09/2521-0000;** www.crowneplaza-helsinki.fi; p. 583), and is now better than ever under its new managers. All the bedrooms and public facilities have been renovated at this nine-floor palace, a bastion of comfort and convenience.

Back in the 1950s, this site was the headquarters for a chain of hardware stores, but today it's the **Klaus K. Hotel,** Bulevardi 2-4, FIN-00120 Helsinki (© **020/770-4700;** www.klauskhotel.com; p. 586), a 139-room hotel that manages to look cozy in spite of its size. It's known for its series of restaurants and bars, plus a nightclub. In its expensive price range, it's the most activity-filled hotel in Helsinki.

Under new management, the **Seurahuone Helsinki;** Kaivokatu 12, FIN-00100 Helsinki (© **09/691-41;** www.hotelliseurahuone.fi; p. 588), was extensively upgraded in 2006, but still retains its five-floor Art Nouveau format on its exterior. Across the street from the rail station, it has been enlarged to 118 rooms with the addition of a new wing.

Dining Helsinki continues to grow more sophisticated in its nighttime diversions as evoked by the opening of **Teatteri Ravintola** in the Svenska Theater Pohjoisesplanadi 2 (© **09/681-11-36;** p. 598). Compared to a Caribbean cruise ship, it is a complex of bars, nightclubs, and restaurants, of which Teatteri, with its international cuisine, is the best choice. Because there's so much happening at this one address, you can make an evening of it.

The best bargain lunch in town is found at **The Bank Lunch Club,** Unioninkatu 20 (© **09/1345-6260;** p. 598). The lunch buffet is one of the best in town in addition to a staggering array of food choices, including wok-fried dishes prepared to order in front of you.

At **Filmitähti Bar & Restaurant,** Erottajankatu 4 (© **020/770-4712;** p. 598), you get a preview of both fine international food and Finnish film. Against a backdrop of a candy-cane decor, you are served such treats juicy burgers, meal-size salads, and reindeer sausages.

1

Suggested Itineraries for Scandinavia

Vacations are getting shorter, and a "lean-and-mean" schedule is called for if you want to experience the best of Scandinavia in a relatively small amount of time.

If you're a time-pressed traveler, as most of us are, you may find the first two itineraries helpful in organizing your time and picking and choosing among the many tempting destinations, which range from Denmark to Finland, but also take in the highlights of Norway and Sweden. Of all the driving tours we've previewed, none is more dramatic than the "Western Fjord Country" of Norway, hailed as one of the most beautiful sightseeing attractions on earth—perhaps *the* most beautiful.

1 Scandinavia (Denmark) in 1 Week

After a visit of 2 or 3 days to **Copenhagen,** Denmark's capital, you can set out to explore more of the island of Zealand on which Copenhagen sits. The highlights of North Zealand, both of which can be visited in a day, include the **Louisiana Museum of Modern Art** and **Kronborg Slot,** the legendary castle that's popularly called "Hamlet's Castle."

After an overnight, you can continue on to the cathedral city of **Roskilde** for another night before crossing the bridge onto the neighboring island of **Funen,** where you can spend 2 nights in its capital, **Odense,** birthplace of Hans Christian Andersen. Later you can head south for a night in the port city of **Svendborg** before a car ferry to the island of Ærø, the most beautiful in the Danish archipelago.

Day ❶: Louisiana Museum ✸✸✸ & Helsingør ✸

On **Day 1** of our driving tour, after wrapping up your visit to Copenhagen and renting a car, head north in the morning to the town of Humlebaek, 32km (20 miles) north of Copenhagen, for a morning visit to the **Louisiana Museum of Modern Art** (p. 138), which opens at 10am. This is one of the greatest art museums of Scandinavia, and you'll want to give it at least 1½ hours.

From Copenhagen, follow coastal road #152, known as Strandvej. Depending on traffic, the scenic drive takes some 45 minutes. After a visit, continue north from Humlebaek into Helsingør, a distance of 14km (8½ miles), following the same Strandvej route. Once in Helsingør, you can check into a hotel for the night, but if you don't want to change hotels so often, you can use Copenhagen as your base and return there for the night.

There are many attractions in Helsingør, but the one magnet for most visitors is **Kronborg Slot** (p. 144), fabled as "Hamlet's Castle" even though Shakespeare presumably never visited it and Hamlet may never have existed. Allow at least 1½ hours for an afternoon visit here after lunch in Helsingør.

Day ❷: The Cathedral City of Roskilde ☆☆

On the morning of **Day 2,** leave Helsingør (or Copenhagen if you spent the night there) for a drive west to Roskilde. The distance is 32km (20 miles) west of Copenhagen, or 72km (45 miles) southwest of Helsingør. From Copenhagen, head west on the E-21 express highway; from Helsingør, follow Route 6 southwest.

If you're on Route 6 from Helsingør, you can stop off for a morning visit to **Hillerød,** a distance of 25km (15 miles) southwest of Helsingør, or 35km (22 miles) north of Copenhagen. This town possesses one of the great treasures of Denmark, the **Frederiksborg Castle** (p. 140), which has been called "the Danish Versailles." Surrounded by a moat, it's the most beautiful royal residence in Denmark and the setting for the Museum of National History, with one of Denmark's greatest collections of historical paintings. Allow at least 1½ hours for a visit.

From Hillerød, continue along Route 6 southwest into Roskilde, where you can check into a hotel for the night. In the afternoon, visit the **Roskilde Domkirke** (p. 148) and try to take a 90-minute tour boat of the **Roskilde Fjord** (p. 149). If you can't schedule a visit to the fjord, then call on the **Lejre Research Center** (p. 150), which in spite of its dull name is actually a reconstructed Iron Age village.

Days ❸ & ❹: Odense ☆☆ & H. C. Andersen

On the morning of **Day 3,** leave Zealand altogether and drive west to the neighboring island of Funen, whose capital is **Odense,** lying 134km (83 miles) to the west of Roskilde. From Roskilde, take Route 14 southwest to the express highway E-20, continuing west to the port of Korsør, where you cross the Great Belt Bridge into Funen, entering the island through its gateway city of Nyborg. Once on land in Funen, continue west along E20 until you see the cutoff arteries leading north into the center of Odense. Once here, book into a hotel for a 2-night stay.

After lunch you can take in some of the major sights of the city, including **H. C. Andersen's Childhood Home** (p. 160). If it's summer, you might even hook up with a 2-hour walking tour, taking in all the highlights. Check with the tourist office.

On the morning of **Day 4,** visit **Funen Village** (p. 160), an open-air regional museum depicting life in Denmark in the 1700s and 1800s. In a busy afternoon you can visit both **Egeskov Castle** (p. 161), one of the grandest in Denmark, as well as **Ladbyskibet** (p. 162), 19km (12 miles) northeast of Odense, to see the ruins of a 10th-century Viking ship.

Day ❺: Svendborg ☆: Favorite Port for Yachties

On the morning of **Day 5,** check out of your hotel in Odense and drive 43km (27 miles) south to the port city of Svendborg, following Route 9. Once in Svendborg, check into a hotel for the night and set out to see the rather minor sights in town, including **Anne Hvides Gård** (p. 165), **St. Jørgen's Church** (p. 165), and **St. Nicolai Church** (p. 177). After lunch you can explore nearby islands, each linked to Svendborg by a bridge. These include the horseshoe-shaped **Thurø,** called "The Garden of Denmark," and **Tåsinge** (p. 167), where you can visit several attractions such as the church tower at **Bregninge Kirke**

(p. 171) for its panoramic views. After a call on the 17th-century **Valdemars Slot** (p. 168), you can spend the rest of the afternoon just exploring at random. Since the island is so small, it's almost impossible to get lost. Return to Svendborg for the night.

Days ⑥ & ⑦: Ærø ⭐⭐: Denmark's Most Beautiful Island

On the morning of **Day 6,** leave Svendborg by driving to the port, where you can board a car ferry heading for the island of **Ærø,** 29km (18 miles) across the water south of Svendborg. Check into a hotel in the picture-postcard capital of Ærøskøbing for 2 nights, and set out to explore the island.

Start by walking the cobblestone streets of this most enchanting of Danish villages, saving the driving tour of the island for the following day. The main attraction of the town is Ærøskøbing itself, although there are specific sights of minor interest, including the **Ærø Museum** (p. 172) and an 18th-century church **Ærøskøbing** (p. 172). Dine in an old *kro* (inn), and later walk down by the water to watch the yachts and other boats bobbing in the harbor at night.

On the morning of **Day 7,** while still based in Ærøskøbing, set out on a leisurely motor tour of the island, stopping at random to enjoy anything that fascinates you. We'd head east to the "second city" on **Marstal,** really just a little port town. After a 2-hour visit here you can take the southern road all the way to the little port **Søby** in the northwest. From Søby, you can drive southeast back to Ærøskøbing for the night.

The following morning you can take the ferryboat back to Svendborg, where you can drive north once again toward Odense, linking with the E20 to carry you east across the Great Belt Bridge to Zealand and back to Copenhagen, where you can make air or rail connections to your next destination.

2 Scandinavia (Sweden) in 2 Weeks

After a whirlwind 1-week tour of Denmark (see above), many visitors extend their Scandinavian trip for another week with a tour of Sweden. You can, of course, drive between Copenhagen and Stockholm, but that's a long haul. Our suggestion is to take a shuttle flight. After a 2-or 3-day visit based in the Swedish capital, you can rent another car for a final look at Sweden during week 2, exploring some of the southern tier of the country. If you move fast enough, you'll be able to see the highlights of **Stockholm** in just 2 days, and take a 1-day trip to visit two ancient cities—**Sigtuna** and **Uppsala,** the latter the site of one of Scandinavia's greatest universities. The itinerary also calls for 2 days on the island of **Gotland,** highlighted by the medieval walled city of **Visby.** Back on the mainland, you'll still have 2 days left to explore the old port of **Kalmar** to see its famous castle and to go shopping in the **glassworks district** of Sweden.

Days ❽ & ❾: Stockholm ⭐⭐⭐: Gateway to Sweden

You've spent the first 7 days exploring Denmark, so on **Day 8,** arrive in **Stockholm** as early as you can so you will have more time for sightseeing. After checking into a hotel for 2 or 3 nights, set out to explore the capital of Sweden.

There is no better introduction to the city's highlights than to take our 3-hour walking tour of **Gamla Stan** (Old Town; coverage begins on p. 422). After lunch in an Old Town tavern, head for the **Royal Palace** (p. 422), which is the official address of the king and queen of Sweden.

In the afternoon, explore Scandinavia's top attraction, the 17th-century man-of-war, the *Royal Vasa* (p. 427), pulled from the bottom of the sea. For a night of fun, go to **Skansen** on Djurgården (p. 428), which is an open-air museum with a vast array of attractions. It stays open until 10pm in summer.

On the morning of **Day 9,** set out to see all the highlights you missed on Day 8.

The two greatest attractions that remain are both outside the city. If you work out the transportation details, you can see the first sight, **Drottningholm Palace and Theater** (p. 430), in the late morning and the second attraction, **Millesgården** (p. 430), by the end of the afternoon. For your final evening in Stockholm, head to **Gröna Lunds Tivoli** (p. 439), an amusement park for family fun. It's not as great as the original Tivoli in Copenhagen, but visitors still enjoy it.

Day ❿: Sigtuna ⭐ & Uppsala ⭐⭐⭐

On the morning of **Day 10,** you can still use Stockholm as your base, returning that evening, or else you can check out and stay in Uppsala.

Head northwest of Stockholm for 48km (30 miles) to visit the ancient town of **Sigtuna** on a north arm of Lake Mälaren. This is Sweden's oldest town, founded at the beginning of the 11th century. To reach it, drive north on the express highway, E-4, until you reach the turnoff leading west into the center of

Sigtuna. Spend 2 hours wandering its old streets before returning to the E4 for the final lap to **Uppsala,** 68km (42 miles) northwest of Stockholm.

Have lunch in this old university city. In the afternoon, visit **Uppsala Domkyrka** (p. 448), the largest cathedral in Scandinavia; the **Linnaeus Garden and Museum** (p. 447), founded by the world's most famous botanist; and end the day at **Gamla Uppsala** (p. 449) to see what remains of Old Uppsala, founded 15 centuries ago as the capital of the Svea kingdom.

Days ⓫ & ⓬: Gotland ✿✿ & Visby ✿✿✿

On the morning of **Day 11,** leave Stockholm, or Uppsala as the case may be, and

drive 219km (136 miles) south of Stockholm to catch the car ferry at Nynäshamn for the 3-hour journey to the island of Visby.

After disembarking, visit the medieval walled city of **Visby** for a 2-night stopover. Spend the rest of the afternoon exploring its medieval streets (coverage begins on p. 531).

On the morning of **Day 12,** set out to discover the island on your own wheels, having armed yourself with a detailed map from the tourist office. Return to Visby by nightfall.

Day ⓭: Kalmar ✿: The Key to Sweden

On the morning of **Day 13,** check out of your hotel in Visby, driving to the embarkation point for the Swedish mainland. Take a ferry that goes from Visby to the eastern coast port of Oskarshamn. Once here, follow **E66** south to the port of **Kalmar,** 409km (254 miles) from Stockholm. You can arrive in Kalmar in time for a late lunch.

In the afternoon, visit **Kalmar Slott,** a castle founded in the 12th century and once called "the key to Sweden" because of its strategic position. In the fading afternoon, wander Kalmar's warren of cobblestone streets and market squares, most of them a holdover from the 17th century. Check into a hotel in Kalmar for the night.

Day ⑭: Växjö & the Kingdom of Crystal ★★★

On the morning of **Day 14,** your final day in Sweden, leave Kalmar in the morning and drive 110km (68 miles) to **Växjö,** the capital of the so-called "Kingdom of Crystal," or the glassworks district. From Kalmar, head west on Route 25.

Once in Växjö, check into a hotel for the night. If your ancestors came from this district, you'll want to visit the **House of Emigrants** (p. 381). If not, you can spend the rest of the day visiting the glass factories, the best of which are **Boda Glasbruk, Orrefors Glasbruk,** and **Kosta Glasbruk.** Feel free to skip one or two of these if you become "glassed out." Our coverage of the attractions in the glassworks district begins on p. 435.

After an overnight at Växjö, you can head back north to Stockholm the following morning for transportation links to your next destination.

3 Western Fjord Country in 1 Week

This driving tour of the fjords of western Norway, one of the world's greatest tourist attractions, is far more scenic than the environs of Oslo. Of course, one of the grandest parts of it may be by boat—not by car—traversing the most scenic of the fjords such as Sognefjord.

If all the fjords were laid out in a straight line, they would measure 21,347km (13,264 miles), the distance between the north and south poles. Throw in Europe's largest glacier, little fjordside farming villages, and jagged snowcapped peaks, and you've got beauty galore. The Ice Age did a good job in carving out this wonderland of nature.

Day ❶: Ålesund ★★: Top of the Fjord Country

Spread over three islands and opening onto two bright blue fjords, **Ålesund** is a good launch pad for a driving tour of the fjord country, lying 1,186km (737 miles) northwest of Oslo. Since it is such a long distance from Oslo, it's best to fly here and rent a car before setting out. There are no rail lines to Ålesund.

Before heading out from Ålesund, you can explore the rebuilt Art Nouveau town, including its most important attraction, the **Sunnmøre Museum,** one of the fjord country's best open-air museums.

Day ❷: Åndalsnes & Romsdalsfjord ★

Leave Ålesund on the morning of **Day 2,** driving east to the resort of **Åndalsnes,** a distance of 127km (79 miles), following A69. Once here check into a hotel for the night. At Åndalsnes, try to hook up with a summer excursion, especially one involving a hike thought the **Romsdalen Alps** enveloping Åndalsnes. The summit of **Nesaksla Mountain** towers over Åndalsnes at 715m (2,345 ft.). You can ask about the boat trips on **Romsdalsfjord,** one of the most beautiful in western Norway.

Western Fjord Country in 1 Week

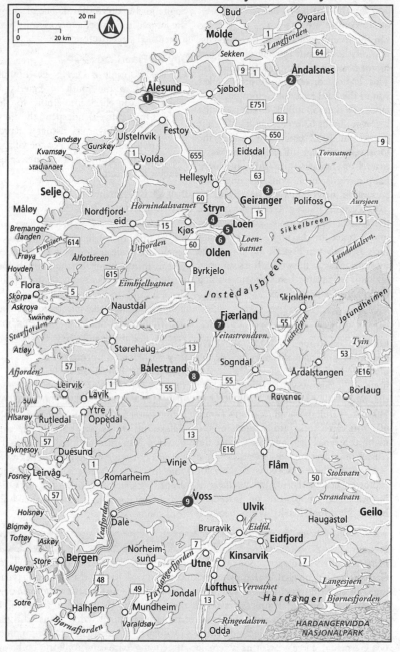

Day ❸: The Trollstigvein ⭐
to Geirangerfjord ⭐⭐⭐

On the morning of **Day 3,** leave Åndalsnes and head south on one of the great motor drives in Norway, the **Trollstigvein.** This 20-hour drive along Route 63 takes you to the fjord resort of **Geiranger,** a distance of 85km (53 miles). At one point the highway climbs 620m (2,034 ft). When it opened in 1952 (and even today), the **Ørnevein,** or Eagle's Road, section was a marvel of engineering. Nearly one dozen hairpin turns await you, opening onto panoramic views over **Geirangerfjord.**

Once at the resort of **Geiranger,** explore the area in the afternoon after checking into a hotel for the night. Its waterfalls, such as the **Seven Sisters,** are among the most dramatic in the world. If it's summer, and you arrive late, there's also an evening tour of the Geirangerfjord.

**Day ❹: A Trio of Resorts: Stryn,
Loen & Olden**

On the morning of **Day 4,** leave Geiranger and take the ferry across the Geirangerfjord to Hellesylt, a scenic hour's boat ride away. At Hellesylt, follow the signs south to **Stryn,** a distance of 50km (30 miles), traveling along Route 60. You can check into a hotel for the night at Stryn, Loen, or Olden, since the cluster of resorts are close together.

Each of these resorts is a base for exploring one of the natural wonders of Norway, the ice plateau of **Jostedalsbreen National Park,** lying between

Sognefjord and Nordfjord. The glacier is the largest in Europe, and you must have a qualified guide to tour it.

Day ❺: Fjaerland ⭐⭐

On the morning of **Day 5,** head 60km (37 miles) to the south to **Fjaerland,** where you can check into a hotel for the night. Once at Fjaerland, spend the afternoon touring **Bøyaøyri Estuary,** a protected nature reserve north of the village, and visit the exhibits at the **Norwegian Glacier Museum.**

Day ❻: Balestrand ⭐⭐ **&
the Sognefjord** ⭐⭐⭐

On the morning of **Day 6,** leave Fjaerland and journey by car ferry to **Balestrand,** a scenic boat ride taking only 45 minutes. Check into a hotel for the night before setting out to explore one of the world's deepest and most beautiful fjords, the famous **Sognefjord.** This fjord stretches for 205km (127 miles), and a scenic boat ride on it will consume your afternoon.

Day ❼: Voss: ⭐ **Summer Fun
in a Winter Playground**

On **Day 7,** it's just a 90km (56 mile) drive south to Voss, where you can check into a hotel for the night. Route 13 links Balestrand to Voss, but the section between Vangsnes and Balestrand is by car ferry. A wide range of activities await you in Voss. It's also a good "escape" point back to either Bergen or Oslo, which can be your transportation hubs for leaving Norway.

4 Denmark for Families in 1 Week

Denmark offers many attractions that kids enjoy, none more notable than the Tivoli Gardens in Copenhagen. Perhaps your main concern with having children along is pacing yourself with museum time. Our suggestion is to explore **Copenhagen** for 2 days, spend Day 3 visiting "Hamlet's Castle" in the north, and then head to the island of Funen, centering at its capital, **Odense,** birthplace of famed writer Hans Christian Andersen. Finally, we go to Jutland, which is Denmark's mainland link to the continent (via Germany). Here we visit its two major attractions, **Århus** and **Aalborg,** both containing Tivoli-like amusement parks of their own, plus numerous other attractions.

Days ❶ & ❷: Arrival in Copenhagen 🐱🐱🐱

Before renting a car to explore the countryside, you can take in the glories of Copenhagen itself, the most kid-friendly of all Scandinavian capitals. After you've checked into a hotel for 2 nights, take one of the bus and boat tours to get oriented. See "Organized Tours" (p. 123). Follow this up with a guided tour of **Amalienborg Palace** (p. 102), where Queen Margrethe II lives with her royal family. After lunch, descend on the **Tivoli Gardens** (p. 128), where you and your kids can wander for hours and grab dinner.

On the morning of **Day 2,** visit **Den Lille Havfrue** (p. 104), "The Little Mermaid," the most photographed statue in Scandinavia. After that, explore **Ny Carlsberg Glyptotek** (p. 98), one of the greatest art museums in Europe. If your child is older, he or she will enjoy the art here, which includes a prehistoric sculpture of a hippopotamus. In the afternoon, visit **Frilandsmuseet** (p. 113), an open-air museum and reconstructed village that evokes life in the 19th century, lying at Lyngby on the fringe of Copenhagen.

When you return to Copenhagen, you can do as many families do and pay a final visit to **Tivoli Gardens,** or else you can visit another amusement park, **Bakken** (p. 115), on the northern fringe of the city. If you like merry-go-rounds and roller coasters, Bakken is even more fun than the carefully manicured Tivoli.

Day ❸: Helsingør 🟊 & Roskilde 🟊🟊

On the morning of **Day 3,** check out of your hotel and drive 40km (25 miles) north of Copenhagen, taking the E-4 express highway. Once at Helsingør you can pay a morning visit to the Dutch-Renaissance-style **Kronborg Castle,** legendary home of Shakespeare's fictional Hamlet. Kids may think that Walt Disney created this dank, spooky place, which is surrounded by a deep moat.

After a visit of 1½ hours, you can head for our final destination of the day—the cathedral city of **Roskilde,** 72km (45 miles) southwest. It's reached by following Route 6 all the way. Check into a hotel in Roskilde for the day, and set about to explore this ancient city. Call first at the **Roskilde Domkirke** (p. 148). Kids delight in seeing the 16th-century clock, where a tiny sculpted St. George on horseback marks the hour by charging a dragon. Afterward, drive 20km (12 miles) north of Roskilde to see the **Viking Ship Museum** (p. 149), displaying the remains of five wrecked Viking-era ships. Return to Roskilde for the night.

Days ❹ & ❺: H. C. Andersen's Odense 🟊🟊

On the morning of **Day 4,** drive west from Roskilde for 134km (83 miles) until you reach Odense. To do so, you have to cross the Great Belt Bridge into Nyborg, lying west on the Funen side. From Nyborg, E-20 will carry you to Odense, where you can check into a hotel for 2 nights. In Odense, follow the same family-friendly itinerary as outlined in Days 3 and 4 under "Scandinavia (Denmark) in 1 Week," earlier.

Days ❻ & ❼: Denmark's Beautiful Island of Ærø 🟊🟊🟊

Leave Odense on the morning of **Day 6,** driving south to Svendborg, a distance of 43km (27 miles), following Route 9. Once at Svendborg, take a car ferry over to the island of Ærø, 29km (18 miles) from Svendborg. Once here, check into a hotel in the tiny island's capital, **Ærøskøbing,** for 2 nights and set about to explore this Lilliputian town with a driving tour of the island to follow on Day 7.

Use the same family-friendly itinerary as outlined under Days 6 and 7 under "Scandinavia (Denmark) in 1 Week," earlier.

After a visit to Ærø, you can easily return to Copenhagen the following day, using a bridge and a ferry boat. Copenhagen lies a distance of 176km (110 miles) to the east of Ærø.

5 Sweden for Families in 1 Week

Our suggestion is to limit **Stockholm** to 2 days, **Gothenburg** to 1 day, and combine a visit to the "third city" of **Malmö** and the university city of **Lund** on your seventh and final day. The entire family can enjoy a drive across Sweden, bypassing the **Göta Canal** and spending the night in the ancient town of **Mariestad.**

Days ❶ & ❷: Stockholm: 🟊🟊🟊 Family Fun in the Capital

On the morning of **Day 1,** set out to explore **Stockholm** by taking our 3-hour walking tour of **Gamla Stan** (Old Town; p. 422). Have lunch in the Old Town and follow with a visit to the **Kungliga Slottet** (p. 422), the royal palace. Kids also enjoy seeing the **Changing of the Royal Guard** (p. 422), but that can be difficult to schedule. The palace is such a vast complex that children always find lots of attractions here to interest them. After a stroll through, head for the **Vasamuseet** (*Royal Vasa;* p. 427), the 17th-century man-of-war that sank on its

maiden voyage. Spend your first night in Stockholm at **Gröna Lunds Tivoli** (p. 439), a vast amusement park that will be the highlight of the Swedish capital for many kids.

On the morning of **Day 2,** set out to see many of the highlights of **Stockholm** you didn't have time for on Day 1. Begin the day by taking in the vast compound of **Skansen** (p. 428), Sweden's greatest open-air museum. This vast parkland has old workshops and some 150 antique buildings. Expect to spend the entire morning here. To cap your afternoon, the whole family will enjoy one of the **canal cruises** offered by Stockholm Sightseeing (p. 431). No doubt your kids will demand to be taken back to **Gröna Lunds Tivoli** (p. 439) for their final night in Stockholm.

Day ❸: Mariestad ⊕ & The Göta Canal ⊕⊕⊕

The **Göta Canal** is the most scenic water route in Sweden, linking Stockholm in the east with the "second city" of Gothenburg in the west. In all, it's a journey of 560km (347 miles), which can be comfortably broken up into 2 days of driving. Leave Stockholm on the morning of **Day 3,** taking the E-3 expressway west all the way to the town of **Mariestad.** In the first day you'll need to cover 318km (197 miles). Mariestad is the best center for taking cruises on **Lake Vänern,** which, with its 20,000 small islands and islets, is the world's largest freshwater archipelago. Try to get as early a start in Stockholm as you can so you'll arrive in Mariestad in time to take one of the cruises. Check with the tourist office as soon as you arrive in Mariestad to see what's available.

Days ❹ & ❺: Arrival in Gothenburg ✮✮✮

On the morning of **Day 4,** leave Mariestad and continue in a southwest direction 180km (112 miles) along E-3 to the capital of the west coast of Sweden, the maritime city of **Gothenburg.** Some kids we've encountered traveling in Sweden with their families have told us they like Gothenburg more than Stockholm.

On your first day, take the classic **Paddan boat ride** (see p. 457), traveling through the moat and canal out to the harbor and the giant dockland. Return for a stroll along the **Avenyn,** the main street of Gothenburg and the scene of an active street life.

As the afternoon fades, head for **Liseberg Park** (p. 472), the largest amusement park in Scandinavia. You can spend the evening here, as it's open until 10pm or 11pm in summer. Dozens of restaurants, including fast-food joints, await you. Return to your hotel where you will need a 2-night booking to take in the highlights of Gothenburg.

On the morning of **Day 5,** get up early to visit the **fish auction** at the harbor, beginning at 7am (p. 470). After seeing **Feskekörka** (p. 470), the "fish church," take tram 6 to the **Guldhedens Vattentorn** (p. 470), a water tower, for the most panoramic view of Gothenburg. Later, go to the **Götaplatsen** (p. 470) in the center of Gothenburg to gaze upon the **Poseidon Fountain,** sculptured by Carl Milles, Sweden's greatest sculptor. This is a great place for a family photo.

Later in the afternoon, explore **Botaniska Trädgården** (p. 473), with its array of natural amusements. In the late afternoon or early evening, nearly all families return to **Liseberg Park** (p. 472) for another night of fun.

Day ❻: Helsingborg: Gateway to Denmark

On the morning of **Day 6,** leave Gothenburg and drive south for 230km (143 miles) to **Helsingborg** at the narrowest point of the Öresund, a body of water that separates Sweden and Denmark. At this point the two countries are only 5km (3 miles) apart, and Denmark lies a 25-minute ferry ride from Helsingborg. From Gothenburg, drive south on the E-6 to reach Helsingborg.

After checking into a hotel for the night, set about to explore the attractions of Helsingborg, including the **Fredriksdal Open-Air Museum and Botanical Garden** (p. 489) and the **Sofiero Slott** (p. 490), a former royal residence lying 5km (3 miles) north of Helsingborg.

In the midafternoon you can cross over on the ferry to **Helsingør** in Denmark to visit the so-called "Hamlet's Castle." Return to Helsingborg for the night.

Day ❼: Lund ✮✮ & Malmö ✮✮

On the morning of **Day 7,** your final day in Sweden, leave Helsingborg in the morning and drive along E-6 in the direction of **Malmö.** At the junction with Route 66, make a detour north to the university and cathedral city of **Lund.** Lund is 56km (35 miles) from Helsingborg.

At Lund, entice your child to accompany you to the **Domkyrkan** (p. 508), or Cathedral of Lund. The 14th-century astronomical clock here is sure to enchant with its Middle Age–style tournament compete with clashing knights and the blare of trumpets. Before the morning fades, you can also visit the **Kulturen** (p. 508), an open-air museum of old houses, complete with a kid-pleasing carriage museum. After lunch in Lund, head on to Malmö for the night, where you can check into a hotel. Malmö lies only 18km (11 miles) south of Lund; take Route 66.

With the time remaining in the afternoon, you can visit **Malmöhus Slott** (p. 497), the old Malmö castle that has so many museums and galleries that everyone will find something of interest here. After dinner, reward your kids with a visit to **Folkets Park** (p. 506), a People's Park filled with Tivoli-like amusements, including a playhouse just for kids.

The following morning it will be just a short drive over Öresund Bridge and into **Copenhagen,** where transportation arrangements can be made to most parts of the world.

2

The Best of Denmark

Denmark presents visitors with an embarrassment of riches—everything from exciting Copenhagen and historic castles to unusual offshore islands and quaint villages. To help you decide how best to spend your time, we've compiled a list of our favorite experiences and discoveries. In the following pages, you'll find the kind of candid advice we'd give our close friends.

1 The Best Travel Experiences

- **A Day (and Night) at Tivoli Gardens:** These 150-year-old pleasure gardens are worth the airfare to Copenhagen all by themselves. They offer a little bit of everything: open-air dancing, restaurants, theaters, concert halls, an amusement park . . . and, oh yes, gardens as well. From the first bloom of spring until the autumn leaves start to fall, they're devoted to lighthearted fun. The gardens are worth a visit any time but are especially pleasant at twilight, when the lights begin to glint among the trees. See chapter 5.

- **A Week Down on the Farm:** The best way to see the heart of Denmark and meet the Danes is to spend a week on one of their farms. Nearly 400 farms around the country take in paying guests. Stick a pin anywhere on a map of Denmark away from the cities and seacoast, and you'll find a thatched and timbered farm, or perhaps a more modern homestead. Almost anyplace makes a good base from which to explore the rest of the country on day trips. Although there's no official agency to arrange such holidays, many visitors seeking this kind of offbeat accommodation

often surf the Internet for farms that advertise their willingness to receive guests. Another way to hook up is to decide what part of Denmark you'd like to visit and then contact the nearest tourist office for a list of farms willing to accept paying guests.

- **On the Trail of the Vikings:** Renowned for 3 centuries of fantastic exploits, the Vikings explored Greenland to the north, North America to the west, and the Caspian Sea to the south and east from roughly A.D. 750 to 1050. Their legacy lives on in Denmark. Relive the age at the **Nationalmuseet** in Copenhagen, which displays burial grounds of the Viking period, along with the largest and richest hoards of treasure, including relics from the "Silver Age." Even Viking costumes are exhibited. See p. 109. At Roskilde, explore the **Viking Ship Museum,** containing five vessels found in a fjord nearby, the largest of which was built in Ireland around 1060 and manned by 60 to 100 warriors. See p. 149. If you're in Ribe, check out the **Museum of the Viking Age,** where a multimedia room, "Odin's Eye," introduces the visitor to the world of the Vikings

Scandinavia

through a vivid sound and vision experience. See chapters 5 and 6.

- **In the Footsteps of Hans Christian Andersen:** To some visitors, this storyteller is the very symbol of Denmark. The fairy tale lives on in Odense, on the island of Funen, where Andersen was born the son of a shoemaker in 1805. His childhood home, a small half-timbered house on

Munkemøllestræde, where he lived from 1807 to 1817, has been turned into a museum. You can also visit the H. C. Andersen's Hus, where much of his memorabilia is stored (including his walking stick and top hat), and take a few moments to listen to his tales on tape. But mostly you can wander the cobblestone streets that he knew so well, marveling at the life of this man—and his works—that, in the words of his obituary, struck "chords that reverberated in every human heart," as they still do today. See p. 158.

2 The Best Scenic Towns & Villages

- **Dragør:** At the very doorstep of Copenhagen, this old seafaring town once flourished as a bustling herring port on the Baltic. Time, however, passed it by, and for that we can be grateful, because it looks much as it used to, with half-timbered ocher and pink 18th-century cottages topped with thatch or red-tile roofs. The entire village is under the protection of the National Trust of Denmark. A 35-minute ride from the Danish capital will take you back 2 centuries. See "Side Trips from Copenhagen" in chapter 5.

- **Ærøskøbing:** This little village on the country's most charming island (Ærø) is storybook Denmark. A 13th-century market town, Ærøskøbing is a Lilliputian souvenir of the past, complete with little gingerbread houses. You expect Hansel and Gretel to arrive at any moment. See "Across the Water to Ærø" in chapter 6.

- **Odense:** The birthplace of Hans Christian Andersen is visited by thousands of the storyteller's fans every year. Denmark's third-largest city still has a medieval core, and you can walk its cobblestone streets and admire its half-timbered houses, including H. C. Andersen's Hus. Other than its associations with the writer, Odense is a worthwhile destination in its own right, filled with attractions (including St. Canute's Cathedral). On the outskirts you can explore everything from the 1554 Renaissance castle, Egeskov, to a 10th-century Viking ship at Ladby. See "Odense: Birthplace of Hans Christian Andersen" in chapter 6.

- **Ribe:** Located on the island of Jutland, this is the best-preserved medieval town in Denmark—known for its narrow cobblestone lanes and crooked, half-timbered houses. An important trading center during the Viking era, it's known today as the town where the endangered stork—the subject of European myth and legend—nests every April. The National Trust protects the medieval center. From April to mid-September a night watchman circles Ribe, spinning tales of the town's legendary days and singing traditional songs. See "Ribe" in chapter 6.

- **Ebeltoft:** On Jutland, this well-preserved town of half-timbered buildings is the capital of the Mols hill country. It's a town of sloping row houses, crooked streets, and local handicraft shops. The Town Hall looks as if it had been erected for kindergarten children; in Ebeltoft you can also visit the 1860 frigate *Jylland*, the oldest man-of-war in Denmark. See "Ebeltoft" in chapter 6.

3 The Best Active Vacations

- **Biking:** A nation of bikers, Denmark has organized the roads to suit the national sport. A network of bike routes and paths is protected from heavy traffic, and much of the terrain is flat. Bicycling vacations are available as inclusive tours that cover bike rental, ferry tickets, and accommodations en route. Some deluxe tours transport your luggage from one hotel to the next. For more information, contact the **Danish Cycling Federation,** Rømersgade 5, DK-1362 Copenhagen (© **33-32-31-21;** www.dcf.dk).

- **Camping:** With about 550 officially sanctioned campgrounds, Denmark has one of the highest numbers, per capita, of campgrounds of any nation in the world, and living in a tent or a pop-up trailer in the great outdoors is something of a national obsession. There are plenty of campsites near the city limits of Copenhagen, and many more are located around the country in areas of scenic or historic interest, some near the sea. The official website and address of the **Danish Camping Federation** is www.camping raadet.dk. For information about the nation's campsites, visit the website, call, or write at Campingrådet, Mosedalsvej 15, DK 2500 Valby (© **39-27-88-44**). Other sources of information about camping are available at www.visitdenmark.com (the official website of the Danish Tourist Board), or an equivalent site, www dk-camp.dk, which lists more than 300 campsites that are privately owned. You can obtain a free *DK Camping Danmark* catalog at all DK-CAMPing grounds, tourist offices, and many service stations.

- **Fishing:** For centuries, much of Denmark relied on the sea and whatever the country's fishermen could pull out of it for its diet. Since then, no *smørrebrød* buffet has been complete without a selection of shrimp, herring, and salmon. The preparation of plaice, cod, eel, perch, and trout are culinary art forms. The seas off Funen, especially within the Great Belt, have yielded countless tons of

seafood, and that tradition has encouraged anglers and sport enthusiasts to test their luck in the rich waters of the Baltic. Many outfitters can introduce you to the mysteries of fresh and saltwater fishing. One of the most consistently reliable is **Ole Dehn,** Søndergard 22, Lohals, DK-5953 Tranekær (© **62-55-17-00**), on the island of Langeland, south of Funen. Its most popular offering involves half-day deep-sea fishing tours on the Great Sound, which cost 250DKK (US$43/£20) per person.

- **Golf:** There are about 130 golf courses scattered across the flat, sandy, and sometimes windy landscapes of Denmark, many of them landscaped around the sand dunes, ponds, forests, and rocky outcroppings for which the country is well known. Most of the clubs welcome visitors, although in some cases you might be asked to present a membership card from your club at home. Local tourism offices are usually well versed in steering golfers to worthwhile courses, but for some insight into what's available, visit www.golf online.dk.

- **Horseback Riding:** Riding schools throughout Denmark rent horses, and local tourist offices can hook you up with a stable if one is available in their area. Our favorite place for riding is **Krogbækgaard,** Læso, DK-9940 (© **98-49-15-05;** www.rideferie.dk). It is situated on Langeland, a long and narrow tidal barrier off the southern coast of Funen. The stable houses 120 Islandic ponies, a sturdy breed that survives well in the harsh climate and scrub-covered landscape of this windswept island.

4 The Best Festivals & Special Events

- **July 4th Festival** (Rebild, near Aalborg): This is one of the few places outside the United States that celebrates U.S. independence. Each year Danes and Danish Americans gather for picnic lunches, outdoor entertainment, and speeches. See chapter 3.
- **Fire Festival Regatta** (Silkeborg): This is the country's oldest and biggest festival, with nightly cruises on the lakes and illumination provided by thousands of candles onshore. The fireworks display on the final night is without equal in Europe, and Danish artists provide the entertainment at a large fun fair. Usually held the first week in August. See chapter 3.
- **Aalborg Carnival:** Celebrated in late May, this is one of the country's great

spring events. Happy revelers in colorful costumes fill the streets. Almost 10,000 people take part in the celebration, honoring the victory of spring over winter. See chapter 6.
- **Copenhagen Jazz Festival:** One of the finest jazz festivals in Europe takes place in July. During this festival, you can find some of the best musicians in the world jamming here in the Danish capital. Indoor and outdoor concerts—many of them free—are presented. See chapter 3.
- **Viking Festival** (Frederikssund): During this annual festival (mid-June to early July), bearded Vikings revive Nordic sagas in an open-air theater. After each performance, there's a traditional Viking banquet. See chapter 5.

5 The Best Castles & Palaces

- **Christiansborg Palace** (Copenhagen): The queen receives official guests here in the Royal Reception Chamber, where you must don slippers to protect the floors. The complex also holds the Parliament House and the Supreme Court. From 1441 until the fire of 1795, this was the official residence of Denmark's monarchy. You can tour the richly decorated rooms, including the Throne Room and banqueting hall. Below you can see the well-preserved ruins of the 1167 castle of Bishop Absalon, founder of Copenhagen. See chapter 5.
- **Rosenborg Castle** (Copenhagen): Founded by Christian IV in the 17th century, this redbrick Renaissance castle remained a royal residence until the early 19th century, when the building was converted into a museum. It still houses the crown jewels, and its collection of costumes

and royal memorabilia is unequaled in Denmark. See chapter 5.
- **Kronborg Slot** (Helsingør): Shakespeare never saw this castle, and Hamlet (if he existed at all) lived centuries before it was ever built. But Shakespeare did set his immortal play here. Intriguing secret passages and casemates fill its cannon-studded bastions, and it often serves as the backdrop for modern productions of *Hamlet.* The brooding statue of Holger Danske sleeps in the dungeon, but, according to legend, this Viking chief will rise again to defend Denmark if the country is endangered. See chapter 5.
- **Frederiksborg Castle** (Hillerød): Known as the Danish Versailles, this moated *slot* (castle) is the most elaborate in Scandinavia. It was built in the Dutch Renaissance style of red brick with a copper roof, and its oldest

parts date from 1560. Much of the castle was constructed under the direction of the "master builder," Christian IV, from 1600 to 1620. Fire ravaged the castle in 1859, and the structure had to be completely restored. It is now a major national history museum. See chapter 5.

- **Egeskov Castle** (Kværndrup): On the island of Funen, this 1554 Renaissance "water castle" is set amid splendid gardens. The most romantic example of Denmark's fortified manors, the castle was built in the middle of a moat, surrounded by a park. The best-preserved Renaissance castle of its type in Europe, it has many attractions on its grounds, including airplane and vintage automobile museums. See chapter 6.

6 The Best Offbeat Experiences

- **Cycling Around Ærø:** Regardless of how busy our schedule, we always like to devote at least 1 sunny day on what we view as the greatest cycling trip in Denmark: A slow, scenic ride around the island of Ærø, lying off the coast of Funen. The island, relatively flat, its countryside dotted with windmills, evokes the fields of Holland, but is unique unto itself. Country roads will take you across fertile fields and into villages of cobbled streets and half-timbered houses. You'll think Hans Christian Andersen planned the island just for you. This is small-town Denmark at its best. Yes, you'll even pass a whistling postman in red jacket and gold-and-black cap looking like an extra in a 1940s film. See p. 169.

- **Journeying Back to the 1960s:** If you're nostalgic for the counterculture of the 1960s, it lives on in Christiania, a Copenhagen community located at the corner of Prinsessegade and Badsmandsstræde on Christianshavn. Founded in 1972, this anarchists' commune occupies former army barracks; its current residents preach a gospel of drugs and peace. Christiania's residents have even organized their own government and passed laws, for example, to legalize drugs. They're not complete anarchists, however, since they venture into the city at least once a month to pick up their social welfare checks. Today you can wander about their community, which is complete with a theater, cafes, grocery stores, and even a local radio station. See chapter 5.

- **Exploring Erotica:** In 1968, Denmark was the first country ever to "liberate" pornography, and today, the **Erotica Museum,** at Købmagergade 24 (© **33-12-03-11**), in Copenhagen is devoted to the subject. Learn about the sex lives of such famous figures as Nietzsche, Freud, and even Duke Ellington. Founded by a photographer of nudes, the museum has exhibits ranging from the tame to the tempestuous—everything from Etruscan drawings to pictures of venereal skin disease. See p. 109.

- **Calling on Artists & Craftspeople:** West Jutland has many open workshops where you can see craftspeople in action; you can meet the potter, the glassblower, the painter, the textile designer, and even the candlestick maker. Local tourist offices can tell you which studios are open to receive guests in such centers as Tønder, Ribe, and Aero.

7 The Best Buys

- **Danish Design:** It's worth making a shopping trip to Denmark. The simple but elegant style that became fashionable in the 1950s has made a comeback. Danish modern chairs, glassware, and even buildings have returned. Collectors celebrate "old masters" such as Arne Jacobsen, Hans Wegner, and Poul Kjærhom, whose designs from the 1940s and 1950s are sold in antiques stores. Wegner, noted for his sculptured teak chairs, for example, is now viewed as the grand old man of Danish design. Younger designers have followed in the old masters' footsteps, producing carefully crafted items for the home—everything from chairs and desks to table settings and silverware. For the best display of Danish design today, walk along the pedestrian-only Strøget, the major shopping street of Copenhagen. The best single showcase for modern Danish design may be **Illums Bolighus,** Amagertorv 10 (© **33-14-19-41**).

- **Crystal & Porcelain:** Holmegaard crystal and Royal Copenhagen porcelain are household names, known for their beauty and craftsmanship. These items cost less in Denmark than in the United States, although signed art glass is costly everywhere. To avoid high prices, you can shop for seconds, which are discounted by 20% to 50% (sometimes the imperfection can be detected only by an expert). The best center for these collectors' items in Copenhagen is **Royal Copenhagen Porcelain,** Amagertorv 6 (© **33-13-71-81**).

- **Silver:** Danish designers have made a name for themselves in this field. Even with taxes and shipping charges, you can still save about 50% when purchasing silver in Denmark as compared with in the United States. If you're willing to consider "used" silver, you can get some remarkable discounts. The big name in international silver—and you can buy it at the source—is **Georg Jensen,** Amagertorv 6, Copenhagen (© **33-11-40-80**).

8 The Best Hotels

- **Hotel d'Angleterre** (Copenhagen; © **800/44-UTELL** in the U.S., or 33-12-00-95; www.remmen.dk): Some critics rate this as the finest hotel in Denmark. As it drifted toward mediocrity a few years back, a massive investment was made to save it. Now the hotel is better than ever—housing a swimming pool and a nightclub. Behind its Georgian facade, much of the ambience is in the traditional English mode. Service is among the finest in Copenhagen. See p. 69.

- **Falsled Kro** (Falsled; © **62-68-11-11**): Not only does this house Funen Island's finest accommodations, but it's the quintessential Danish inn, with origins dating from the 1400s. This Relais & Châteaux property has elegant furnishings as well as a top-quality restaurant, rivaling the best in Copenhagen. See p. 169.

- **Hotel Hesselet** (Nyborg; © **65-31-30-29**): This stylish modern hotel on Funen Island occupies a woodland setting in a beech forest. The spacious rooms are artfully decorated, often with traditional furnishings. A library, Oriental rugs, and an open fireplace add graceful touches to the public areas. Many Copenhagen residents come here for a retreat, patronizing the hotel's gourmet restaurant at night. See p. 157.

- **Hotel Dagmar** (Ribe; © 75-42-00-33): Jutland's most glamorous hotel was converted from a private home in 1850, although the building itself dates back to 1581. This half-timbered hotel encapsulates the charm of the 16th century, with such adornments as carved chairs, sloping wood floors, and stained-glass windows. Many bedrooms are furnished with antique canopy beds. A fine restaurant, serving both Danish and international dishes, completes the picture. See p. 188.

- **Phoenix Copenhagen** (Copenhagen; © 33-95-95-00; www.phoenix copenhagen.com): The Danish Communist Party used to have its headquarters here, but the "Reds" of the Cold War era wouldn't recognize this pocket of posh today. It reeks of capitalistic excess and splendor, from its dazzling public rooms with French antiques to its rooms with dainty Louis XVI styling. See p. 72.

9 The Best Restaurants

- **Era Ora** (Copenhagen; © 32-54-06-93): This 20-year-old restaurant has the best Italian food in Denmark and is the domain of two Tuscan-born partners who have delighted some of the most discerning palates in Copenhagen. Denmark's superb array of fresh seafood, among other produce, is given a decidedly Mediterranean twist at this citadel of refined cuisine. See p. 85.

- **Falsled Kro** (Falsled; © 62-68-11-11): Even if you don't stay here, consider stopping for a meal. A favorite among well-heeled Europeans, this restaurant produces stellar French-inspired cuisine and often uses seasonal produce from its own gardens. The succulent salmon is smoked on the premises in one of the outbuildings, and the owners breed quail locally. Such care and attention to detail make this one of Denmark's top restaurants. See p. 169.

- **Godt** (Copenhagen; © 33-15-21-22): Even the queen of Denmark dines at this superb restaurant, celebrated locally for its international cuisine. The best and freshest of produce and various ingredients at the market are fashioned into the most pleasing and quintessential of international dishes. See p. 85.

- **Marie Louise** (Odense; © 66-17-92-95): Glittering with crystal and silver, this dining room on a pedestrian street is one of the finest on the island of Funen. In an antique house, this Danish/Franco alliance offers a cuisine that's the epitome of taste, preparation, and service. Seafood and fish are the favored dishes. See p. 164.

- **The Paul** (Copenhagen; © 33-75-07-75): Winning a coveted Michelin star, this is the best restaurant among the deluxe dining rooms of the famous Tivoli Gardens. Drawing gourmet diners with its carefully crafted international menu, it offers an inspired cuisine among beautiful gardens. There is a daring and innovation here that you won't find in any other Tivoli restaurant. See p. 84.

3

Planning Your Trip to Denmark

In the following pages, we've compiled the practical advice you'll need—airline information, what things cost, a calendar of events—so that you may plan your trip to Denmark with ease.

1 The Regions in Brief

ZEALAND Home to Denmark's capital, **Copenhagen,** Zealand draws more visitors than any other region. It's the largest island and the wealthiest, most densely populated section. Other cities include **Roskilde,** 32km (20 miles) west of Copenhagen, which is home to a landmark cathedral (burial place of many kings) and a collection of Viking vessels discovered in a fjord. In the medieval town of **Køge,** witches were burned in the Middle Ages. One of the most popular attractions on the island is **Helsingør** ("Elsinore," in English), about 40km (25 miles) north of Copenhagen, where visitors flock to see "Hamlet's castle." Off the southeast corner of the island lies the island of **Møn,** home to Møns Klint, an expanse of white cliffs that rises sharply out of the Baltic.

JUTLAND The peninsula of Jutland links the island nation of Denmark with Germany. Jutland has miles of coastline, with some of northern Europe's finest sandy beaches. Giant dunes and moors abound on the west coast, whereas the interior has rolling pastures and beech forests. Jutland's more interesting towns and villages include **Jelling,** heralded as the birthplace of Denmark and the ancient

seat of the Danish kings; here you can see an extensive collection of Viking artifacts excavated from ancient burial mounds. The Viking port of **Ribe** is the oldest town in Denmark. It's known throughout the world as the preferred nesting ground of numerous endangered storks. The resort of **Fanø,** with its giant dunes, heather-covered moors, and forests, is an excellent place to bird-watch or view Denmark's varied wildlife. The university city of **Århus** is Jutland's capital and second only to Copenhagen in size. **Aalborg,** founded by Vikings more than 1,000 years ago, is a thriving commercial center in northern Jutland. It lies close to Rebild National Park and the Rold Forest.

FUNEN With an area of 1,850 sq. km (1,150 sq. miles), Funen is Denmark's second-largest island. Called the "garden of Denmark," Funen is known to the world as the birthplace of Hans Christian Andersen. Its rolling countryside is dotted with orchards, stately manors, and castles. **Odense,** Andersen's birthplace, is a mecca for fairy-tale writers and fans from around the world. Nearby stands Egeskov Castle, Europe's best-preserved Renaissance castle, resting on oak columns in the middle of a small lake.

Denmark

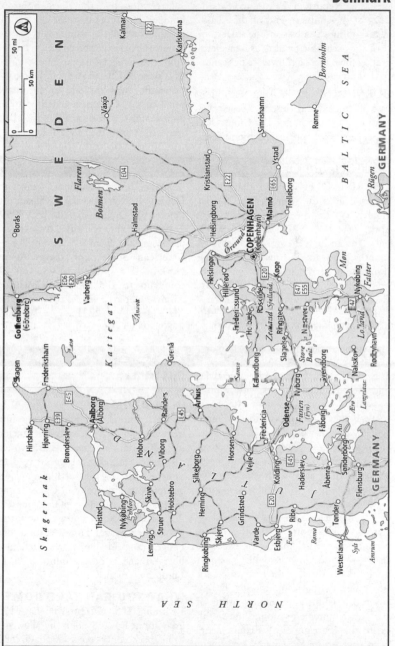

Funen has a number of bustling ports, including **Nyborg** in the east and **Svendborg** at the southern end of the island. **Ærøskøbing,** nearby on the island of Ærø and accessible by ferry, is a medieval market town that's a showplace of Scandinavian heritage.

BORNHOLM   In the Baltic Sea, southeast of Zealand and close to Sweden, lies the island of Bornholm. The countryside is peppered with prehistoric monuments and runic stones, and numerous fishing villages dot the shoreline. Some of Europe's largest castle-ruins are in this region. The town of **Rønne** is the site of Denmark's oldest regional theater; it stages numerous concerts and shows year-round. The island of **Christiansø,** off the coast of Bornholm, was the site of Denmark's penal colony. Criminals sentenced to life imprisonment were deported to the island, where they spent their lives in slavery.

2 Visitor Information

TOURIST OFFICES   In the **United States,** contact the **Scandinavian Tourist Board,** 655 Third Ave., 18th floor, New York, NY 10017 (© **212/885-9700;** www.goscandinavia.com), at least 3 months in advance for maps, sightseeing information, ferry schedules, or more. You can also try the **Danish Tourist Board,** 655 Third Ave., 18th floor, New York, NY 10017 (© **212/885-9700;** www.visitdenmark.com).

In the **United Kingdom,** contact the **Danish Tourist Board,** 55 Sloane St., London SW1X 9SY (© **020/7259-5959**).

If you get in touch with a **travel agent,** make sure the agent is a member of the **American Society of Travel Agents (ASTA).** If a problem arises, you can complain to the society's **Consumer Affairs Department,** 1101 King St., Alexandria, VA 22314 (© **703/739-2782;** www.astanet.com).

3 Entry Requirements

U.S., Canadian, U.K., Irish, Australian, and New Zealand citizens with a **valid passport** don't need a visa to enter Denmark if they don't expect to stay more than 90 days or work there. If after entering Denmark you want to stay more than 90 days, you can apply for a permit for an extra 90 days at your home country's consulate, which as a rule is granted immediately.

For information on how to get a passport, go to "Passports" in the "Fast Facts" section of this chapter—the websites listed provide downloadable passport applications as well as the current fees for processing passport applications. For an up-to-date country-by-country listing of passport requirements around the world, go to the "Foreign Entry Requirement" Web page of the U.S. State Department at **http://travel.state.gov**.

CUSTOMS
WHAT YOU CAN BRING INTO DENMARK
Foreign visitors can bring along most items for personal use duty-free, including fishing tackle, a pair of skis, two tennis rackets, a baby carriage, two hand cameras with 10 rolls of film, and 400 cigarettes or a quantity of cigars or pipe tobacco not exceeding 500 grams (1.1 lb.). There are strict limits on importing alcoholic beverages. However, for alcohol bought tax-paid, limits are much more liberal than in other countries of the European Union.

WHAT YOU CAN TAKE HOME
Returning **U.S. citizens** who have been away for at least 48 hours are allowed to bring back, once every 30 days, $800 worth of merchandise duty-free. You'll be

Tips **Passport Savvy**

Allow plenty of time before your trip to apply for a passport; processing normally takes 3 weeks but can take longer during busy periods (especially spring). And keep in mind that if you need a passport in a hurry, you'll pay a higher processing fee. When traveling, safeguard your passport in an inconspicuous, inaccessible place such as a money belt, and keep a copy of the critical pages with your passport number in a separate place. If you lose your passport, visit the nearest consulate or embassy of your native country as soon as possible for a replacement.

charged a flat rate of 10% duty on the next $1,000 worth of purchases. Be sure to have your receipts handy. On mailed gifts, the duty-free limit is $200. You cannot bring fresh foodstuffs into the United States; tinned foods, however, are allowed. For specifics on what you can bring back, download the invaluable free pamphlet *Know Before You Go* online at **www.cbp.gov**. (Click on "Travel" and then on "Know Before You Go! Online Brochure.") Or contact the **U.S. Customs & Border Protection (CBP),** 1300 Pennsylvania Ave. NW, Washington, DC 20229 (© **877/287-8667**) and request the pamphlet. For a clear summary of Canadian rules, request the book *I Declare* from **The Canada Border Services Agency,** 1730 St. Laurent Blvd., Ottawa, K1G 4KE (© **800/461-9999** in Canada, or 204/983-3500; www.cbsa-asfc.gc.ca). **Citizens of the U.K.** who are **returning from a European Union (E.U.)**

country will go through a separate Customs Exit (called the "Blue Exit") especially for E.U. travelers. In essence, there is no limit on what you can bring back from an E.U. country, as long as the items are for personal use (this includes gifts), and you have already paid the necessary duty and tax. For more information, contact **HM's Customs and Excise office,** National Advice Service, Dorset House, Stamford Street, London SE1 9PY (© **0845/010-9000**; www.hmce.gov.uk). A helpful brochure available from Australian consulates or Customs offices is *Know Before You Go.* For more information, call the **Australian Customs Service** at © **1300/363-263,** or log on to www.customs.gov.au. New Zealanders should contact **New Zealand Customs,** The Customhouse, 17–21 Whitmore St., Box 2218, Wellington (© **0800/428-786** or 04/473-6099; www.customs.govt.nz).

4 Money

Although Denmark is a member of the European Union, a majority of Danes rejected the euro as their form of currency in September 2000. They continue to use the **krone** (crown), which breaks down into 100 øre. The plural is **kroner.** The international monetary designation for the Danish kroner is "DKK." (The Swedish currency is the kronor, but note the different spelling.)

CURRENCY EXCHANGE

Many hotels in Denmark simply do not accept a dollar- or pound-denominated personal check; those that do will certainly charge for making the conversion. In some cases, a hotel may accept countersigned traveler's checks or a credit or charge card.

If you're making a deposit on a hotel reservation, it's cheaper and easier to pay

The Danish Krone

For American Readers   At this writing, $1 = approximately 5.9 kroner. (Danish kroner are identified throughout this guidebook as DKK.) Stated differently, 1DKK = approximately 17¢. This was the rate of exchange used to calculate the dollar values given throughout this edition. Bear in mind that throughout the context of this book, dollar amounts less than $10 are rounded to the nearest nickel, and dollar amounts greater than $10 are rounded to the nearest dollar.

For British Readers   At this writing, £1 = approximately 11DKK, or, stated differently, 1DKK = approximately 9p. This was the rate of exchange used to calculate the pound values in the table below.

Regarding the Euro   At the time of this writing, 1DKK = .134€. Stated differently, 1€ = approximately 7.46DKK. These rates can and probably will change during the lifetime of this edition. For updates on these currency conversions, check an up-to-date source at the time of your arrival in Denmark.

DKK	US$	UK	Euro	DKK	US$	UK	Euro
1	0.17	0.09	0.13	75.00	12.75	6.75	10.05
2	0.34	0.18	0.27	100.00	17.00	9.00	13.40
3	0.51	0.27	0.40	125.00	21.25	11.25	16.75
4	0.68	0.36	0.54	150.00	25.50	13.50	20.10
5	0.85	0.45	0.67	175.00	29.75	15.75	23.45
6	1.02	0.54	0.80	200.00	34.00	18.00	26.80
7	1.19	0.63	0.94	225.00	38.25	20.25	30.15
8	1.36	0.72	1.07	250.00	42.50	22.50	33.50
9	1.53	0.81	1.21	275.00	46.75	24.75	36.85
10	1.70	0.90	1.34	300.00	51.00	27.00	40.20
15	2.55	1.35	2.01	350.00	59.50	31.50	46.90
20	3.40	1.80	2.68	400.00	68.00	36.00	53.60
25	4.25	2.25	3.35	500.00	85.00	45.00	67.00
50	8.50	4.50	6.70	1000.00	170.00	90.00	134.00

with a check drawn on a Danish bank. This can be arranged by a large commercial bank or by a specialist such as **Ruesch International,** 700 11th St. NW, 4th floor, Washington, DC 20001 (© **800/ 424-2923** or 202/408-1200; www. ruesch.com). It performs a wide variety of conversion-related tasks, usually for about $15 per transaction.

If you need a check payable in a Danish currency, call Ruesch's toll-free number, describe what you need, and write down the transaction number. Mail your dollar-denominated personal check (payable to Ruesch International) to the Washington, D.C., office. When it's received, the company will mail you a check denominated in the requested currency for the specified amount, minus the $3 charge. The company can also help you with wire transfers, as well as the conversion of VAT (value-added tax) refund checks. Information is mailed upon request.

In England, contact Ruesch International Ltd., Lower Cookham Road, Maidenhead, Berkshire SL6 8XY (© 0845/880-0400).

ATMs

The easiest and best way to get cash away from home is from an ATM (automated teller machine). The **Cirrus** (© 800/424-7787; www.mastercard.com) and **PLUS** (© 800/843-7587; www.visa.com) networks span the globe: look at the back of your bank card to see which network you're on, and then call or check online for ATM locations at your destination. Be sure you know your personal identification number (PIN) before you leave home and be sure to find out your daily withdrawal limit before you depart. Also keep in mind that many banks impose a fee every time a card is used at a different bank's ATM, and that fee can be higher for international transactions (up to $5 or more) than for domestic ones (where they're rarely more than $1.50). On top of this, the bank from which you withdraw cash may charge its own fee. To compare banks' ATM fees within the U.S., use www.bankrate.com. For International withdrawal fees, ask your bank.

TRAVELER'S CHECKS

Traveler's checks are something of an anachronism from the days before the ATM made cash accessible at any time. Traveler's checks used to be the only sound alternative to traveling with dangerously large amounts of cash. They were as reliable as currency, but, unlike cash, could be replaced if lost or stolen.

You can get traveler's checks at almost any bank. **American Express** offers denominations of $20, $50, $100, $500, and (for cardholders only) $1,000. You'll pay a service charge ranging from 1% to 4%. You can also get American Express traveler's checks over the phone by calling © 800/221-7282; Amex gold

and platinum cardholders who use this number are exempt from the 1% fee.

Visa offers traveler's checks at banks nationwide. The service charge ranges between 1.5% and 2%; checks come in denominations of $20, $50, $100, $500, and $1,000. Call © 800/732-1322 for information. AAA members can obtain Visa checks for a $9.95 fee (for checks up to $1,500) at most AAA offices or by calling © 866/339-3378. **MasterCard** also offers traveler's checks. Call © 800/223-9920 for a location near you.

Foreign currency traveler's checks are useful if you're traveling to one country, or to the euro zone; they're accepted at locations such as bed-and-breakfasts where dollar checks may not be, and they minimize the amount of math you have to do at your destination. **American Express, Thomas Cook, Visa,** and **MasterCard** offer foreign currency traveler's checks. You'll pay the rate of exchange at the time of your purchase (so it's a good idea to monitor the rate before you take the plunge), and most companies charge a transaction fee per order (and a shipping fee if you order online).

If you choose to carry traveler's checks, be sure to keep a record of their serial numbers separate from your checks in the event that they are stolen or lost. You'll get a refund faster if you know the numbers.

CREDIT CARDS

Credit cards are a safe way to carry money: They also provide a convenient record of all your expenses, and they generally offer relatively good exchange rates. You can also withdraw cash advances from your credit cards at banks or ATMs, provided you know your PIN. If you've forgotten yours, or didn't even know you had one, call the number on the back of your credit card and ask the bank to send it to you. It usually takes 5 to 7 business days, though some banks will provide the number over the phone if you tell them

What Things Cost in Copenhagen	US$	UK£
Train from the airport to the city center	$4.60	£2.45
Subway from the Central Station to outlying suburbs	$3.05	£1.60
Double room, without private bathroom, at the Hotel Nebo (inexpensive)	$117.00	£62.00
Double room, with bathroom, at the Hotel Kong Arthur (moderate)	$258.00	£137.00
Double room at the Hotel d'Angleterre (very expensive)	$442.00	£234.00
Lunch for one at Café Zeze (inexpensive)	$26.00	£14.00
Lunch for one at the Restaurant Els (moderate)	$34.00	£18.00
Dinner for one, without wine, at Nyhavns Faergekro (inexpensive)	$32.00	£17.00
Dinner for one, without wine, at Copenhagen Corner (moderate)	$44.00	£23.00
Dinner for one, without wine, at Kommandanten (very expensive)	$112.00	£59.00
Pint of beer (draft pilsner or lager)	$8.50	£4.50
Cup of coffee in a cafe or bar	$4.70–$6.50	£2.50–£3.40
Coca-Cola in a cafe or bar	$5.10	£2.70
Admission to the Tivoli Gardens	$12.75	£6.75
Movie ticket	$11.00	£5.85
Ticket to the Royal Theater	$12–$114	£6.30–£60

your mother's maiden name or some other personal information. Keep in mind that when you use your credit card abroad, most banks assess a 2% fee above the 1% fee charged by Visa, MasterCard, or American Express for currency conversion on credit charges. But credit cards still may be the smart way to go when you factor in things like exorbitant ATM fees and higher traveler's check exchange rates (and service fees).

For tips and telephone numbers to call if your wallet is stolen or lost, go to "Lost & Found" in the "Fast Facts" section of this chapter.

5 When to Go

CLIMATE

Denmark's climate is mild for a Scandinavian country—New England farmers experience harsher winters. Summer temperatures average between 61°F and 77°F (16°C–25°C). Winter temperatures seldom go below 30°F (–1°C), thanks to the warming waters of the Gulf Stream. From the weather perspective, mid-April to November is a good time to visit.

Denmark's Average Daytime Temperatures

	Jan	Feb	Mar	Apr	May	June	July	Aug	Sept	Oct	Nov	Dec
°F	32	32	35	44	53	60	64	63	57	49	42	37
°C	0	0	2	7	12	15	18	17	14	9	6	3

HOLIDAYS

Danish public holidays are: January 1 (New Year's Day), Maundy Thursday, Good Friday, Easter Sunday, Easter Monday, May 1 (Labor Day), Common Prayers Day (4th Fri after Easter), Ascension Day (mid-May), Whitsunday (late May), Whitmonday, June 5 (Constitution Day), December 25 (Christmas Day), and December 26 (Boxing Day).

DENMARK CALENDAR OF EVENTS

Note: Exact dates below apply for 2007. Should you be using this guide in 2008, check with local tourist boards for exact dates.

May

Ballet and Opera Festival (Copenhagen). Classical and modern dance and two operatic masterpieces are presented at the Old Stage of the Royal Theater in Copenhagen. For tickets, contact the Royal Theater, Box 2185, DK-1017 København (© **33-69-69-69**; www.kgl-teater.dk). Mid-May to June.

Aalborg Carnival. This is one of the country's great spring events. The streets fill with people in colorful costumes. Thousands take part in the celebration, which honors the victory of spring over winter. For information, call © **98-13-72-11**; www.karneval aalborg.dk. Late May.

Carnival in Copenhagen. A great citywide event that includes a children's carnival. For information, call © **33-38-85-04**; www.karneval.dk. Mid-May.

June

Viking Festival (Frederikssund, 13km/8 miles southwest of Hillerød). For almost a month every summer, "bearded Vikings" present old Nordic sagas in an open-air setting. After each performance, a traditional Viking meal is held. Call © **47-31-06-85** or visit www.vikingespil.dk for more information. Late June to early July.

Midsummer's Night (throughout the country). This age-old event is celebrated throughout Denmark and is the longest day of the year. Festivities throughout the tiny nation begin at around 10pm with bonfires and celebrations along the myriad coasts. June 21.

July

Funen Festival. This annual musical extravaganza frequently draws big, international headliners such as U2. The festival's music is often hard-core rock, but gentler, classical melodies are presented as well. It takes place in the city of Odense, on the island of Funen. For more information, call the Odense tourist bureau (© **66-12-75-20**; www.visitodense.com). Early July.

Roskilde Festival. Europe's biggest rock festival has been going strong for more than 3 decades, now bringing about 90,000 revelers each year to the central Zealand town. Beside major rock concerts, which often draw "big names," scheduled activities include theater and film presentations. For more information, call © **46-36-66-13**, or visit www.roskilde-festival.dk. Early July.

July 4th (Rebild). Rebild National Park, near Aalborg, is one of the few places outside the United States to honor American Independence Day. For more information, contact the Aalborg Tourist Office, Østerågade 8, DK-9000 Aalborg (© **99-30-60-90;** www.aalborg-tourist.dk). July 4th.

Copenhagen Jazz Festival. International jazz musicians play in the streets, squares, and theaters. Pick up a copy of *Copenhagen This Week* to find the venues. For information, call © **33-93-20-13,** or visit www.jazzfestival.dk. Early July.

Sønderborg Tilting Festival. Dating from the Middle Ages, the "tilting at the ring" tradition has survived only in the old town of Sønderborg on the island of Als in southern Jutland. While riding at a gallop, a horseman uses his lance to see how many times (in 24 attempts) he can take the ring. Parades, music, and entertainment are included. For more information, contact the Turistbureau, Rådhustorvet 7, DK-6400 Sønderborg (© **74-42-35-55**). Early July.

August

Fire Festival Regatta (Silkeborg). Denmark's oldest and biggest festival features nightly cruises on the lakes, with thousands of candles illuminating the shores. The fireworks display on the last night is the largest and most spectacular in northern Europe. Popular Danish artists provide entertainment at a large fun fair. For more information, contact the Turistbureau, Godthåbsuej 4, DK-8600 Silkeborg (© **86-85-31-55;** www.ildregatta.dk). Mid-August.

Fall Ballet Festival (København). The internationally acclaimed Royal Danish Ballet returns home to perform at the Old Stage of the Royal Theater just before the tourist season ends. For tickets, contact the Royal Theater, Box 2185, DK-1017 København (© **33-69-69-69;** www.kgl-teater.dk). Mid-August to September.

Århus Festival Week ✦. This is the largest cultural festival in Scandinavia and includes a wide range of cultural activities such as opera, jazz, classical and folk music, ballet, and theater. Sporting activities and street parties abound as well. For more information, call © **89-40-91-85,** or visit www.aarhusfestival.dk. Late August to early September.

6 The Active Vacation Planner

BEACHES

With some 8,000km (5,000 miles) of coastline, Denmark has many long strips of sandy beaches, which are largely protected from sea winds by dunes. Most of these beaches are relatively unspoiled, and the Danes like to keep them that way (any polluted beaches are clearly marked). Many Danes like to go nude at the beach. Nudist beaches aren't clearly identified; often you'll see bathers with and without clothing using the same beach. The best beach resorts are those on the north coast of Zealand and the southern tip of the island of Bornholm. Beaches on the east coast of Jutland are also good, often attracting Germans from the south. Funen also has a number of good beaches, especially in the south.

BIKING

A nation of bikers, Denmark has organized its roads to suit this national sport. Bikers can pedal along a network of biking routes and paths protected from heavy traffic. The Danish landscape is made for this type of vacation. Most tourist offices publish biking tour suggestions for their own district; it's a great way to see the sights and get in shape at the same time. The **Dansk Cyklist Forbund** (Danish Cycling Federation), Rømersgade 7, DK-1362 Copenhagen (© **33-32-31-21;** www.dcf.dk), publishes excellent guides covering the whole country and can also provide information about a number of prepackaged biking vacations.

FISHING

Since no place in Denmark is more than 56km (35 miles) from the sea, fishing is a major pastime. Denmark also has well-stocked rivers and lakes, including fjord waters around the Limfjord. Anglers between the ages of 18 and 67 must obtain a fishing permit from the **Danish Ministry of Fisheries** (www.fisketeen.dk) for 30DKK ($5.10/£2.70) for 1 day or 90DKK ($15/£8.10) for 1 week; these are available at any post office. Jutland is known for its good trout fishing; salmon is also available, but it is found more readily in Norway. Anglers who fish from the beach can catch eel, mackerel, turbot, sea trout, plaice, and flounder. For more information about fishing in Denmark, contact **Sportfiskerforbund,** Worsåesgade 1, DK-7100 Vejle (© **75-82-06-99**).

GOLF

Denmark's undulating landscape is ideal for the construction of golf courses. Prospective golfers should bring a valid golf club membership card from home.

For information on the best courses near where you're staying, contact local tourist offices.

HANG GLIDING & PARAGLIDING

Although Denmark is a relatively flat country, good possibilities for practicing paragliding do exist. **The Danish Union of Windgliders** provides information about suitable locations. As a rule, the union has arranged with local landowners that a slope or some other suitable place may be used. Since equipment cannot be rented in Denmark, clients must bring their own. More information is available from **Dansk Drageflyver Union** (© **46-14-15-09;** www.danskdrageflyverunion.dk).

SAILING

Denmark has about 600 harbors, both large and small, including the island of Bornholm. Those who like to sail have many opportunities to do so, especially in the open waters of the Baltic or in the more sheltered waters of the South Funen Sea between Lolland/Falster and Zealand. The Limfjord in North Jutland is also ideal for sailing. Many sailing boats are available for rent, as are cruisers. For information, contact the tourist offices.

WALKING

About 100 pamphlets have been published describing short and long walks in Danish forests. Twenty of these are printed in English and are available from local tourist offices.

7 Travel Insurance

Since Denmark is far from home for most of us, and a number of things could go wrong—lost luggage, trip cancellation, a medical emergency—consider the following types of insurance.

Check your existing insurance policies and credit card coverage before you buy travel insurance. You may already be covered for lost luggage, canceled tickets, or medical expenses.

The cost of travel insurance varies widely, depending on the cost and length of your trip, your age and health, and the type of trip you're taking, but expect to pay between 5% and 8% of the vacation itself.

Travel in the Age of Bankruptcy

Airlines go bankrupt, so protect yourself by **buying your tickets with a credit card.** The Fair Credit Billing Act guarantees that you can get your money back from the credit card company if a travel supplier goes under (and if you request the refund within 60 days of the bankruptcy). **Travel insurance** can also help, but make sure it covers against "carrier default" for your specific travel provider. And be aware that if a U.S. airline goes bust midtrip, a 2001 federal law requires other carriers to take you to your destination (albeit on a space-available basis) for a fee of no more than $25, provided you rebook within 60 days of the cancellation.

TRIP-CANCELLATION INSURANCE Trip-cancellation insurance helps you get your money back if you have to back out of a trip, if you have to go home early, or if your travel supplier goes bankrupt. Allowed reasons for cancellation can range from sickness to natural disasters. Insurance policy details vary, so read the fine print—and make sure that your airline or cruise line is on the list of carriers covered in case of bankruptcy.

For more information, contact one of the following recommended insurers: **Access America** (© 866/807-3982; www.accessamerica.com); **Travel Guard International** (© 800/826-4919; www.travelguard.com); **Travel Insured International** (© 800/243-3174; www.travelinsured.com); and **Travelex Insurance Services** (© 888/457-4602; www.travelex-insurance.com).

MEDICAL INSURANCE For travel overseas, most health plans (including Medicare and Medicaid) do not provide coverage, and the ones that do often require you to pay for services upfront and reimburse you only after you return home. Even if your plan does cover overseas treatment, most out-of-country hospitals make you pay your bills up front and send you a refund only after you've returned home and filed the necessary paperwork with your insurance company.

As a safety net, you may want to buy travel medical insurance, particularly if you're traveling to a remote or high-risk area where emergency evacuation is a possible scenario. If you require additional medical insurance, try MEDEX Assistance (© **800/732-5309** or 410/453-6300; www.medexassist.com) or Worldwide Assistance (© **800/777-8710;** www.worldwideassistance.com). This latter company is the oldest and most experienced travel-assistance network in the world.

LOST-LUGGAGE INSURANCE On international flights (including U.S. portions of international trips), baggage coverage is limited to approximately $9.07 per pound, up to approximately $635 per checked bag. If you plan to check items more valuable than the standard liability, see if your valuables are covered by your homeowner's policy, or get baggage insurance as part of your comprehensive travel-insurance package. Don't buy insurance at the airport, as it's usually overpriced.

If your luggage is lost, immediately file a lost-luggage claim at the airport, detailing the luggage contents. For most airlines, you must report delayed, damaged, or lost baggage within 4 hours of arrival. The airlines are required to deliver luggage, once found, directly to your house or destination free of charge.

8 Health & Safety

STAYING HEALTHY

Denmark is viewed as a "safe" destination, although problems, of course, can and do occur anywhere. You don't need to get shots, most foodstuff is safe, and the water in cities and towns potable. If you're concerned, order bottled water. It's easy to get a prescription filled in towns and cities, and nearly all places throughout Denmark contain hospitals with English-speaking doctors and well-trained medical staffs.

Before you go, contact the **International Association for Medical Assistance to Travelers (IAMAT; ℭ 716/754-4883,** or 416/652-0137 in Canada; www.iamat.org) for tips on travel and health concerns in the countries you're visiting, and lists of local, English-speaking doctors. The United States **Centers for Disease Control and Prevention** (ℭ **800/311-3435;** www.cdc.gov) provides up-to-date information on health hazards by region or country and offers tips on food safety.

In Canada contact **Health Canada** (ℭ **613/957-2991;** www.hc-sc.gc.ca). The website **www.tripprep.com,** sponsored by a consortium of travel medicine practitioners, may also offer helpful advice on traveling abroad. You can find listings of reliable clinics overseas at the **International Society of Travel Medicine** (www.istm.org). Any foreign consulate can provide a list of area doctors who speak English.

WHAT TO DO IF YOU GET SICK AWAY FROM HOME

Nearly all doctors in Scandinavia speak English. If you get sick, consider asking your hotel concierge to recommend a local doctor—even his or her own. You can also try the emergency room at a local hospital. Many hospitals also have walk-in clinics for emergency cases that are not life-threatening; you may not get immediate attention, but you won't pay the high price of an emergency room visit. We list hospitals and emergency numbers under "Fast Facts," in the various cities such as Copenhagen.

If you worry about getting sick away from home, consider purchasing **medical travel insurance,** and carry your ID card in your purse or wallet. In most cases, your existing health plan will provide the coverage you need. See the section on Insurance, above, for more information.

If you suffer from a chronic illness, consult your doctor before you depart. For conditions such as epilepsy, diabetes, or heart problems, wear a **Medic Alert Identification Tag** (ℭ **888/633-4298;** www.medicalert.org), which will immediately alert doctors to your condition and give them access to your records through Medic Alert's 24-hour hot line.

Pack **prescription medications** in your carry-on luggage and keep them in their original containers, with pharmacy labels—otherwise they won't make it through airport security. Also, bring

---

Healthy Travels to You

The following government websites offer up-to-date health-related travel advice.

- **Australia:** www.dfat.gov.au/travel
- **Canada:** www.hc-sc.gc.ca/index_e.html
- **U.K.:** www.dh.gov.uk/PolicyAndGuidance/HealthAdviceForTravellers/fs/en
- **U.S.:** www.cdc.gov/travel

along copies of your prescriptions in case you lose your pills or run out. Carry the generic name of prescription medicines, in case a local pharmacist is unfamiliar with the brand name. Don't forget an extra pair of contact lenses or prescription glasses.

STAYING SAFE

Denmark has a relatively low crime rate with rare, but increasing, instances of violent crime. Most crimes involve the theft of personal property from cars, residences, or in public areas. Pickpockets and purse-snatchers often work in pairs or groups with one distracting the victim while another grabs valuables. Often they operate in or near major rail stations in Copenhagen. Hotel breakfast rooms and lobbies attract professional, well-dressed thieves who blend in with guests and target purses and briefcases left unguarded by unsuspecting tourists and business travelers. Valuables should not be left unguarded in parked vehicles.

The loss or theft abroad of a U.S. passport should be reported immediately to the local police and the nearest U.S. Embassy or Consulate. If you are the victim of a crime while overseas, in addition to reporting to local police, contact the nearest U.S. Embassy or Consulate for assistance.

U.S. citizens may refer to the Department of State's pamphlet, *A Safe Trip Abroad,* for ways to promote a trouble-free journey. The pamphlet is available by mail from the **Superintendent of Documents, U.S. Government Printing Office,** Washington, DC 20402, via the Internet at www.gpoaccess.gov, or via the Bureau of Consular Affairs home page at http://travel.state.gov.

9 Specialized Travel Resources

TRAVELERS WITH DISABILITIES

Most disabilities shouldn't stop anyone from traveling. There are more options and resources out there than ever before.

In general, Denmark's trains, airlines, ferries, and department stores and malls are accessible. For information about wheelchair access, ferry and air travel, parking, and other matters, contact the **Danish Tourist Board** (see "Visitor Information," earlier).

Useful information for people with disabilities is provided by *De Samvirkende Invalideorganisationer* (**Danish Disability Council,** abbreviated in Denmark as DSI), Bredgade 25, DK-1260 Copenhagen, Denmark (© 33-11-10-44; www.dch.dk). Established in 1934, it organizes 29 smaller organizations, each involved with issues of concern to physically challenged people, into one coherent grouping that represents the estimated 300,000 persons with disabilities living in Denmark today. For the best overview of what this organization does, visit their website at www.handicap.dk.

Many travel agencies offer customized tours and itineraries for travelers with disabilities. **Flying Wheels Travel** (© 507/451-5005; www.flyingwheelstravel.com) offers escorted tours and cruises that emphasize sports and private tours in minivans with lifts. **Access-Able Travel Source** (© 303/232-2979; www.access-able.com) offers extensive access information and advice for traveling around the world with disabilities. **Accessible Journeys** (© 800/846-4537 or 610/521-0339; www.disabilitytravel.com) caters specifically to slow walkers and wheelchair travelers and their families and friends.

Organizations that offer assistance to travelers with disabilities include **Moss-Rehab** (www.mossresourcenet.org), which provides a library of accessible-travel resources online; **SATH** (Society for

Accessible Travel & Hospitality; © 212/ 447-7284; www.sath.org; annual membership fees: $45 adults, $30 seniors and students), which offers a wealth of travel resources for all types of disabilities and informed recommendations on destinations, access guides, travel agents, tour operators, vehicle rentals, and companion services; and the **American Foundation for the Blind** (AFB; © 800/232-5463; www.afb.org), a referral resource for the blind or visually impaired that includes information on traveling with Seeing Eye dogs.

For more information specifically targeted to travelers with disabilities, the community website **iCan** (www.ican online.net/channels/travel/index.cfm) has destination guides and several regular columns on accessible travel. Also check out the quarterly magazine *Emerging Horizons* (www.emerginghorizons.com); and *Open World* magazine, published by SATH.

FOR BRITISH TRAVELERS

The **Royal Association for Disability and Rehabilitation (RADAR)**, Unit 12, City Forum, 250 City Rd., London EC1V 8AF (© 020/7250-3222; www. radar.org.uk), publishes three vacation "fact packs." Another good resource is **Holiday Care Service,** 7th floor, Sunley House, 4 Bedford Park, Croydon, Surrey CR0 2AP (© 0845/124-9971; www.holidaycare.org.uk), a national charity advising on accessible accommodations for the elderly and persons with disabilities.

GAY & LESBIAN TRAVELERS

In general, Denmark is one of the most gay-friendly countries in Europe and was one of the first to embrace same-sex marriages. Antidiscrimination laws have been in effect since 1987. Most Danes are exceptionally friendly and tolerant of lifestyles of either sexual preference.

Obviously, an urban center such as Copenhagen will have a more openly gay life than rural areas. In many ways, the Erotic Museum in Copenhagen, which documents the history of hetero- and homosexual pleasure in an unprejudiced manner, illustrates the city's attitudes toward sex.

The **Danish National Association for Gays and Lesbians** (Landsforeningen for Bøsser og Lesbiske, abbreviated as LBL) maintains its headquarters at Teglgaard stræde 13, 1007 Copenhagen (© 33-13-19-48; www.lbl.dk), with branches in at least four of the larger cities of Denmark. You might find it hard to reach a live body on their telephone line (their hours of operation are very limited), but they maintain one of the most informative and user-friendly websites of any gay organization in Europe, complete with maps on how to reach whichever of the gay and lesbian venues they describe on their site.

The **International Gay and Lesbian Travel Association (IGLTA;** © 800/448-8550 or 954/776-2626; www. iglta.org) is the trade association for the gay and lesbian travel industry, and offers an online directory of gay- and lesbian-friendly travel businesses; go to their website and click on "Members."

Many agencies offer tours and travel itineraries specifically for gay and lesbian travelers. **Above and Beyond Tours** (© 800/397-2681; www.abovebeyond tours.com) is the exclusive gay and lesbian tour operator for United Airlines. **Now, Voyager** (© 800/255-6951; www. nowvoyager.com) is a well-known San Francisco–based gay-owned and -operated travel service.

Olivia Cruises & Resorts (© 800/631-6277; www.olivia.com) charters entire resorts and ships for exclusive lesbian vacations, and offers smaller group experiences for both gay and lesbian travelers.

The following travel guides are available at most travel bookstores and gay and lesbian bookstores, or you can order them online: *Frommer's Gay & Lesbian Europe,* an excellent travel resource; *Spartacus International Gay Guide* (Bruno Gmünder Verlag; www.spartacus world.com/gayguide) and *Odysseus: The International Gay Travel Planner* (Odysseus Enterprises Ltd.), both good, annual English-language guidebooks focused on gay men; and the **Damron** guides (www.damron.com), with separate, annual books for gay men and lesbians.

SENIOR TRAVEL

Mention the fact that you're a senior citizen when you make your travel reservations. Although all of the major U.S. airlines except America West have canceled their senior discount and coupon book programs, many hotels still offer discounts for seniors. In most cities, people over the age of 60 qualify for reduced admission to theaters, museums, and other attractions, as well as discounted fares on public transportation.

Members of **AARP** (formerly known as the American Association of Retired Persons), 601 E St. NW, Washington, DC 20049 (© **888/687-2277**; www. aarp.org), get discounts on hotels, airfares, and car rentals.

Many reliable agencies and organizations target the 50-plus market. **Elderhostel** (© **877/426-8056**; www.elder hostel.org) arranges study programs for those age 55 and over (and a spouse or companion of any age) in the U.S. and in more than 80 countries around the world. Most courses last 5 to 7 days in the U.S. (2–4 weeks abroad), and many include airfare, accommodations in university dormitories or modest inns, meals, and tuition. **ElderTreks** (© **800/ 741-7956**; www.eldertreks.com) offers small-group tours to off-the-beaten-path or adventure-travel locations, restricted to travelers 50 and older.

INTRAV (© **800/456-8100**; www. intrav.com) is a high-end tour operator that caters to the mature, discerning traveler, not specifically seniors, with trips around the world that include guided safaris, polar expeditions, private-jet adventures, and small-boat cruises down jungle rivers.

Recommended publications offering travel resources and discounts for seniors include the quarterly magazine *Travel 50 & Beyond* (www.travel50andbeyond. com); *Travel Unlimited: Uncommon Adventures for the Mature Traveler* (Avalon); *101 Tips for Mature Travelers,* available from Grand Circle Travel (© **800/221-2610** or 617/350-7500; www.gct.com); and *Unbelievably Good Deals and Great Adventures That You Absolutely Can't Get Unless You're Over 50* (McGraw-Hill), by Joann Rattner Heilman.

FAMILY TRAVEL

The family vacation is a rite of passage for many households, one that in a split second can devolve into a *National Lampoon* farce. But as any veteran family vacationer will assure you, a family trip can be among the most pleasurable and rewarding times of your life.

Most Danish hoteliers will let children 12 and under stay in a room with their parents for free; others do not. Sometimes this requires a little negotiation at the reception desk.

Danes like kids but don't offer a lot of special amenities for them. For example, a kids' menu in a restaurant is a rarity. You can, however, order a half portion, and most waiters will oblige.

At attractions—even if it isn't specifically posted—inquire if a kids' discount is available. European Community citizens under 18 are admitted free to all state-run museums.

Traveling with Minors

It's always wise to have plenty of documentation when traveling in today's world with children. For changing details on entry requirements for children traveling abroad, keep up-to-date by going to the U.S. State Department website: http://travel.state.gov. To prevent international child abduction, E.U. governments have initiated procedures at entry and exit points. These often (but not always) include requiring documentary evidence of relationship and permission for the child's travel from the parent or legal guardian not present. Having such documentation on hand, even if not required, facilitates entries and exits. All children must have their own passport. To obtain a passport, the child *must* be present—that is, in person—at the center issuing the passport. Both parents must be present as well. If not, then a notarized statement from the parents is required. Any questions parents or guardians might have can be answered by calling the **National Passport Information Center** at © 877/487-2778 Monday to Friday 8am to 8pm Eastern Standard Time.

To locate those accommodations, restaurants, and attractions that are particularly kid-friendly, refer to the "Kids" icon throughout this guide.

Familyhostel (© 800/733-9753; www.learn.unh.edu/familyhostel) takes the whole family, including kids ages 8 to 15, on moderately priced domestic and international learning vacations. Lectures, field trips, and sightseeing are guided by a team of academics.

Recommended family travel Internet sites include **Family Travel Forum** (www.familytravelforum.com), a comprehensive site that offers customized trip planning; **Family Travel Network** (www.familytravelnetwork.com), an award-winning site that offers travel features, deals, and tips; **Traveling Internationally with Your Kids** (www.travelwithyourkids.com), a comprehensive site offering sound advice for long-distance and international travel with children; and **Family Travel Files** (www.thefamilytravelfiles.com), which offers an online magazine and a directory of off-the-beaten-path tours and tour operators for families.

STUDENT TRAVEL

When planning to travel outside the U.S., you'd be wise to arm yourself with an **International Student Identity Card (ISIC),** which offers substantial savings on rail passes, plane tickets, and entrance fees. It also provides you with basic health and life insurance and a 24-hour help line. The card is available for $22 from **STA Travel** (© 800/781-4040 in North America; www.sta.com or www.statravel.com), the biggest student travel agency in the world. If you're no longer a student but are still under 26, you can get an **International Youth Travel Card (IYTC)** for the same price from the same people, which entitles you to some discounts (but not on museum admissions). **Travel CUTS** (© 800/667-2887 or 416/614-2887; www.travelcuts.com) offers similar services for both Canadians and U.S. residents. Irish students may prefer to turn to **USIT** (© 01/602-1600; www.usitnow.ie), an Ireland-based specialist in student, youth, and independent travel.

SINGLE TRAVELERS

Single travelers are often hit with a "single supplement" to the base price. To avoid it, you can agree to room with other single travelers on the trip, or you can find a compatible roommate before you go from one of the many roommate locator agencies.

Travel Buddies Singles Travel Club
(© 800/998-9099; www.travelbuddies worldwide.com), based in Canada, runs small, intimate, single-friendly group trips and will match you with a roommate free and save you the cost of single supplements. **TravelChums** (© 212/787-2621; www.travelchums.com) is an Internet-only travel-companion matching service with elements of an online personals-type site, hosted by the respected New York–based Shaw Guides travel service. **The Single Gourmet Club** (www.singlegourmet.com/chapters.php) is an international social, dining, and travel club for singles of all ages, with club chapters in 21 cities in the U.S. and Canada. Annual membership fees vary from city to city.

Many reputable tour companies offer singles-only trips. **Singles Travel International** (© 877/765-6874; www.singlestravelintl.com) offers singles-only trips to places such as London, Fiji, and the Greek Islands. **Backroads** (© 800/462-2848; www.backroads.com) offers more than 160 active-travel trips to 30 destinations worldwide, including Denmark and Norway.

10 Planning Your Trip Online

The most popular online travel agencies are **Travelocity** (www.travelocity.com or www.travelocity.co.uk); **Expedia** (www.expedia.com, www.expedia.co.uk, or www.expedia.ca); and **Orbitz** (www.orbitz.com).

In addition, most airlines now offer online-only fares that even their phone agents know nothing about. For the websites of airlines that fly to and from your destination, go to "Getting There," p. 45.

Other helpful websites for booking airline tickets online include:

- www.biddingfortravel.com
- www.cheapflights.com
- www.hotwire.com
- www.kayak.com
- www.lastminutetravel.com
- www.opodo.co.uk
- www.priceline.com
- www.sidestep.com
- www.site59.com
- www.smartertravel.com

SURFING FOR HOTELS

In addition to **Travelocity, Expedia, Orbitz, Priceline,** and **Hotwire** (see above), the following websites will help you with booking hotel rooms online:

- www.hotels.com
- www.quickbook.com
- www.travelaxe.net
- www.travelweb.com
- www.tripadvisor.com

It's a good idea to **get a confirmation number** and **make a printout** of any online booking transaction.

SURFING FOR RENTAL CARS

For booking rental cars online, the best deals are usually found at rental-car company websites, although all the major online travel agencies also offer rental-car reservations services. Priceline and Hotwire work well for rental cars, too; the only "mystery" is which major rental company you get, and for most travelers the difference between Hertz, Avis, and Budget is negligible.

TRAVEL BLOGS & TRAVELOGUES

To read a few blogs about Scandinavia, try:

- www.travelblog.com
- www.travelblog.org
- www.worldhum.com
- www.writtenroad.com

Frommers.com: The Complete Travel Resource

For an excellent travel-planning resource, we highly recommend **Frommers.com** (www.frommers.com), voted Best Travel Site by *PC Magazine*. We're a little biased, of course, but we guarantee that you'll find the travel tips, reviews, monthly vacation giveaways, bookstore, and online-booking capabilities to be thoroughly indispensable. Special features include our popular **Destinations** section, where you can access expert travel tips, hotel and dining recommendations, and advice on the sights to see in more than 3,500 destinations around the globe; the **Frommers.com Newsletter,** with the latest deals, travel trends, and money-saving secrets; and our **Travel Talk** area featuring **Message Boards,** where Frommer's readers post queries and share advice, and where our authors sometimes show up to answer questions. Once you finish your research, the **Book a Trip** area can lead you to Frommer's preferred online partners' websites, where you can book your vacation at affordable prices.

11 The 21st-Century Traveler

INTERNET ACCESS AWAY FROM HOME

Travelers have any number of ways to check their e-mail and access the Internet on the road. Of course, using your own laptop—or even a PDA (personal digital assistant) or electronic organizer with a modem—gives you the most flexibility. But even if you don't have a computer, you can still access your e-mail and even your office computer from cybercafes.

WITHOUT YOUR OWN COMPUTER

It's hard nowadays to find a city that *doesn't* have a few cybercafes. Although there's no definitive directory for cybercafes—these are independent businesses, after all—two places to start looking are at **www.cybercaptive.com** and **www.cybercafe.com**.

Aside from formal cybercafes, most **youth hostels** have at least one computer you can get to the Internet on. And most **public libraries** across the world offer Internet access free or for a small charge.

Avoid **hotel business centers** unless you're willing to pay exorbitant rates.

Most major airports now have **Internet kiosks** scattered throughout their gates. The kiosks' clunkiness and high price mean they should be avoided whenever possible.

WITH YOUR OWN COMPUTER

More and more hotels, cafes, and retailers are signing on as Wi-Fi (wireless fidelity) "hotspots." Mac owners have their own networking technology: Apple AirPort. **Boingo** (www.boingo.com) and **Wayport** (www.wayport.com) have set up networks in airports and high-class hotel lobbies. iPass providers (see below) also give you access to a few hundred wireless hotel lobby setups. To locate other hotspots that provide **free wireless networks** in cities around the world, go to **www.personaltelco.net/index.cgi/WirelessCommunities**.

For dial-up access, most business-class hotels throughout the world offer dataports for laptop modems, and a few thousand

Online Traveler's Toolbox

Veteran travelers usually carry some essential items to make their trips easier. Following is a selection of handy online tools to bookmark and use.

- **Airplane Seating and Food.** Find out which seats to reserve and which to avoid (and more) on all major domestic airlines at www.seatguru.com. And check out the type of meal (with photos) you'll likely be served on airlines around the world at www.airlinemeals.com.
- **Foreign Languages for Travelers** (www.travlang.com). Learn basic terms in more than 70 languages, and click on any underlined phrase to hear what it sounds like.
- **Intellicast** (www.intellicast.com) and **Weather.com** (www.weather.com). Gives weather forecasts for all 50 states and for cities around the world.
- **Mapquest** (www.mapquest.com). This best of the mapping sites lets you choose a specific address or destination, and in seconds, it will return a map and detailed directions.
- **Subway Navigator** (www.subwaynavigator.com). Download subway maps and get savvy advice on using subway systems in dozens of major cities around the world.
- **Time and Date** (www.timeanddate.com). See what time (and day) it is anywhere in the world.
- **Universal Currency Converter** (www.xe.com/ucc). See what your dollar or pound is worth in more than 100 other countries.
- **Visa ATM Locator** (www.visa.com), for locations of PLUS ATMs worldwide, or **MasterCard ATM Locator** (www.mastercard.com), for locations of Cirrus ATMs worldwide.

hotels in the U.S. and Europe now offer free high-speed Internet access. In addition, major Internet service providers (ISPs) have **local access numbers** around the world, allowing you to go online by placing a local call. The **iPass** network also has dial-up numbers around the world. You'll have to sign up with an iPass provider, who will then tell you how to set up your computer for your destination(s). For a list of iPass providers, go to www.ipass.com, and click on "Individuals Buy Now." One solid provider is **i2roam** (© **866/811-6209** or 920/235-0475; www.i1roam.com).

Wherever you go, bring a **connection kit** of the right power and phone adapters, a spare phone cord, and a spare Ethernet network cable—or find out whether your hotel supplies them to guests.

USING A CELLPHONE
OUTSIDE THE U.S.

The three letters that define much of the world's **wireless capabilities** are GSM (Global System for Mobiles), a big, seamless network that makes for easy cross-border cellphone use throughout Europe and dozens of other countries worldwide. In the U.S., T-Mobile, AT&T Wireless, and Cingular use this quasi-universal system; in Canada, Microcell and some Rogers customers are GSM, and all Europeans and most Australians use GSM.

If your cellphone is on a GSM system, and you have a world-capable multiband phone such as many Sony Ericsson, Motorola, or Samsung models, you can make and receive calls across civilized areas on much of the globe, from Andorra to Uganda. Just call your wireless operator and ask for "international roaming" to be activated on your account. Unfortunately, per-minute charges can be high—usually $1 to $1.50 in western Europe and up to $5 in places such as Russia and Indonesia.

While you can rent a phone from any number of overseas sites, including kiosks at airports and at car-rental agencies, we suggest renting the phone before you leave home. North Americans can rent one before leaving home from **InTouch USA** (✆ **800/872-7626;** www.intouch global.com) or **RoadPost** (✆ **888/290-1606** or 905/272-5665; www.roadpost. com). InTouch will also, for free, advise you on whether your existing phone will work overseas; simply call ✆ **703/222-7161** between 9am and 4pm EST, or go to **http://intouchglobal.com/travel.htm**.

12 Getting There

BY PLANE

Flying in winter—Scandinavia's off-season—is cheapest; summer is the most expensive. Spring and fall are in between. In any season, midweek fares (Mon–Thurs) are the lowest.

THE MAJOR AIRLINES

FROM NORTH AMERICA SAS (Scandinavian Airlines Systems; ✆ **800/221-2350** in the U.S., or 0870/6072-7727 in the U.K.; www.Scandinavian. net) has more nonstop flights to Scandinavia from more North American cities than any other airline, and it has more flights to and from Denmark and within Scandinavia than any other airline in the world. From Seattle and Chicago, SAS offers nonstop flights to Copenhagen daily in midsummer and almost every day in winter; from Newark, New Jersey, there are daily flights year-round to Copenhagen. SAS's agreement with United Airlines, the "Star Alliance," connects other U.S. cities (such as Dallas/Fort Worth, Denver, Houston, Los Angeles, Minneapolis/St. Paul, New York, San Francisco, and Washington, D.C.) to the three U.S. gateway cities.

Nonstop flights to Copenhagen from the greater New York area take about 7½ hours; from Chicago, around 8½ hours; from Seattle, 9¼ hours.

FROM THE U.K. British Airways (✆ **800/AIRWAYS,** or 0870/850-9850 in the U.K.; www.britishairways.com) offers convenient connections through Heathrow and Gatwick to Copenhagen. The price structure (and discounted prices on hotel packages) sometimes makes a stopover in Britain less expensive than you might have thought. **SAS** offers five daily nonstop flights to Copenhagen from Heathrow (1¾ hr.), two daily nonstops from Glasgow (2 hr.), and three daily nonstops from Manchester (2 hr., 20 min.). Other European airlines with connections

Tipping the Scales

Effective September 2006, SAS is imposing a maximum weight allowance of 50 pounds per bag for economy passengers flying to or from the U.S. If any piece of baggage exceeds this weight, it must be repacked or sent as cargo.

through their home countries to Copenhagen include **Icelandair** (② **800/ 223-5500** in the U.S., or 0870/787-4020 in the U.K.; www.icelandair.com), **KLM** (② **800/225-2525** in the U.S., or 0870/507-4074 in the U.K.; www. klm.com), and **Lufthansa** (② **800/ 645-3880** in the U.S., or 0870/8377-747 in the U.K.; www.lufthansa.com). Be aware, however, that unless you make all your flight arrangements in North America before you go, you might find some of these flights prohibitively expensive.

FLYING FOR LESS: TIPS FOR GETTING THE BEST AIRFARE

Passengers sharing the same airplane cabin rarely pay the same fare. Travelers who need to purchase tickets at the last minute, change their itinerary at a moment's notice, or fly one-way often get stuck paying the premium rate. Here are some ways to keep your airfare costs down.

- Passengers who can book their ticket **long in advance,** can **stay over Saturday night,** or **fly midweek** or **at less-trafficked hours** may pay a fraction of the full fare. If your schedule is flexible, say so, and ask if you can secure a cheaper fare by changing your flight plans.
- You can also save on airfares by keeping an eye out in local newspapers for **promotional specials** or **fare wars,** when airlines lower prices on their most popular routes. You rarely see fare wars offered for peak travel times, but if you can travel in the off months, you may snag a bargain.
- Search **the Internet** for cheap fares (see "Planning Your Trip Online," earlier).
- **Consolidators,** also known as bucket shops, are great sources for international tickets, although they usually can't beat the Internet on fares within North America. Start by looking in Sunday newspaper travel sections; U.S. travelers should focus on the *New York Times, Los Angeles Times,* and *Miami Herald.* For less-developed destinations, small travel agents who cater to immigrant communities in large cities often have the best deals. *Beware:* Bucket shop tickets are usually nonrefundable or rigged

---

Tips Getting through the Airport

- Arrive at the airport 1 hour before a domestic flight and 2 hours before an international flight; if you show up late, tell an airline employee, and he or she will probably whisk you to the front of the line.
- Beat the ticket-counter lines by using airport electronic kiosks or even online check-in from your home computers, from where you can print out boarding passes in advance. Curbside check-in is also a good way to avoid lines.
- Bring a current, government-issued photo ID such as a driver's license or passport. Children under 18 do not need government-issued photo IDs for flights within the U.S., but they do for international flights to most countries.
- Speed up security by removing your jacket and shoes before you're screened. In addition, remove metal objects such as big belt buckles. If you've got metallic body parts, a note from your doctor can prevent a long chat with the security screeners.
- Use a TSA-approved lock for your checked luggage. Look for Travel Sentry certified locks at luggage or travel shops and Brookstone stores (or online at www.brookstone.com).

Tips New Security Measures

Because of increased security measures, the Transportation Security Administration has made changes to the prohibited items list. All liquids and gels—including shampoo, toothpaste, perfume, hair gel, suntan lotion and all other items with similar consistency—**are limited** within your carry-on baggage and the security checkpoint. Check the **Transportation Security Administration** site, www.tsa.gov, for the latest information.

---

with stiff cancellation penalties, often as high as 50% to 75% of the ticket price, and some put you on charter airlines, which may leave at inconvenient times and experience delays. Several reliable consolidators are worldwide and available online. **STA Travel** (© **800/781-4040;** www.sta. com) is now the world's leader in student travel, thanks to its purchase of Council Travel. It also offers good fares for travelers of all ages. **ELTExpress** (Flights.com; © **800/TRAV-800;** www.eltexpress.com) started in Europe and has excellent fares worldwide, but particularly to that continent. It also has "local" websites in 12 countries. **FlyCheap** (© **800/FLY-CHEAP;** www.1800flycheap.com) is owned by package-holiday megalith MyTravel and so has especially good access to fares for sunny destinations. **Air Tickets Direct** (© **800/778-3447;** www.airticketsdirect.com) is based in Montreal and leverages the currently weak Canadian dollar for low fares.

• Join **frequent-flier clubs.** Accrue enough miles, and you'll be rewarded with free flights and elite status. It's free, and you'll get the best choice of seats, faster response to phone inquiries, and prompter service if your luggage is stolen, if your flight is canceled or delayed, or if you want to change your seat. You don't need

to fly to build frequent-flier miles—**frequent-flier credit cards** can provide thousands of miles for doing your everyday shopping.

BY CAR

You can easily drive to Denmark from Germany. Many people drive to Jutland from Hamburg, Bremerhaven, and Lübeck. A bridge links Jutland and the central island of Funen. In 1998, a bridge opened that goes across the Great Belt from Funen to the island of Zealand, site of the city of Copenhagen. The bridge lies near Nyborg, Denmark. Once in West Zealand, you'll still have to drive east across the island to Copenhagen.

Car-ferry service to Denmark from the United Kingdom generally leaves passengers at Esbjerg, where they must cross from Jutland to Copenhagen. From Germany, it's possible to take a car ferry from Travemünde, northeast of Lübeck, which will deposit you at Gedser, Denmark. From here, connect with E55, an express highway north to Copenhagen.

BY TRAIN

If you're in Europe, it's easy to get to Denmark by train. Copenhagen is the main rail hub between Scandinavia and the rest of Europe. For example, the London-Copenhagen train—through Ostende, Belgium, or Hook, Holland—leaves four times daily and takes 22 hours. About 10 daily express trains run from Hamburg to Copenhagen (5½ hr.). There are also intercity trains on the Merkur route from Karlsruhe, Germany, to Cologne to Hamburg to Copenhagen. The Berlin-Ostbahnhof-Copenhagen train (8½ hr.) connects with Eastern European trains. Two daily express trains make this run.

Thousands of trains run from Britain to the Continent, and at least some of them go directly across or under the Channel, through France or Belgium and Germany into Denmark. For example, a train leaves London's Victoria Station daily at 9am and arrives in Copenhagen the next day at 8:25am. Another train leaves London's Victoria Station at 8:45pm and arrives in Copenhagen the next day at 8:20pm. Both go through Dover-Ostende, or with a connection at Brussels. Once you're in Copenhagen, you can make rail connections to Norway, Finland, and Sweden. Because of the time and distances involved, many passengers rent a couchette (sleeping berth), which costs around £18 ($34) per person. Designed like padded benches stacked bunk-style, they're usually clustered six to a compartment.

If you plan to travel extensively on European and/or British railroads, it would be worthwhile for you to get a copy of the latest edition of the *Thomas Cook European Timetable of Railroads*. It's available online at www.thomascook timetables.com.

RAIL PASSES FOR NORTH AMERICAN TRAVELERS

EURAILPASS If you plan to travel extensively in Europe, the **Eurailpass** might be a good bet. It's valid for first-class rail travel in 18 European countries. With one ticket, you travel whenever and wherever you please; more than 100,000 rail miles are at your disposal. Here's how it works: The pass is sold only in North America. A Eurailpass good for 15 days costs $605, a pass for 21 days is $785, a 1-month pass costs $975, a 2-month pass

is $1,378, and a 3-month pass goes for $1,703. Children under 4 travel free if they don't occupy a seat; all children under 12 who take up a seat are charged half price. If you're under 26, you can buy a **Eurail Youthpass,** which entitles you to unlimited second-class travel for 15 days ($394), 21 days ($510), 1 month ($634), 2 months ($896), or 3 months ($1,108). Travelers considering buying a 15-day or 1-month pass should estimate rail distance before deciding whether a pass is worthwhile. To take full advantage of the tickets for 15 days or a month, you'd have to spend a great deal of time on the train. Eurailpass holders are entitled to substantial discounts on certain buses and ferries as well. Travel agents in all towns and railway agents in such major cities as New York, Montreal, and Los Angeles sell all of these tickets. For information on Eurailpasses and other European train data, call **RailEurope** at © **877/272-RAIL**, or visit **www.raileurope.com**.

Eurail Saverpass offers a 15% discount to each person in a group of three or more people traveling together between April and September, or two people traveling together between October and March. The price of a Saverpass, valid all over Europe for first class only, is $513 for 15 days, $668 for 21 days, $828 for 1 month, $1,173 for 2 months, and $1,450 for 3 months. Even more freedom is offered by the **Saver Flexipass,** which is similar to the Eurail Saverpass, except that you are not confined to consecutive-day travel. For travel over any 10 days within 2 months, the fare is $608; for any 15 days over 2 months, the fare is $800.

Eurail Flexipass allows even greater flexibility. It's valid in first class and offers the same privileges as the Eurailpass. However, it provides a number of individual travel days over a much longer period of consecutive days. Using this pass makes it possible to stay longer in one city and not lose a single day of travel.

There are two Flexipasses: 10 days of travel within 2 months for $715, and 15 days of travel within 2 months for $940.

With many of the same qualifications and restrictions as the Eurail Flexipass, the **Eurail Youth Flexipass** is sold only to travelers under age 25. It allows 10 days of travel within 2 months for $465 and 15 days of travel within 2 months for $611.

SCANRAIL PASS If your visit to Europe will be primarily in Scandinavia, the Scanrail pass may be better and cheaper than the Eurailpass. This pass allows its owner a designated number of days of free rail travel within a larger time block. (Presumably, this allows for days devoted to sightseeing scattered among days of rail transfers between cities or sites of interest.) You can choose a total of any 5 days of unlimited rail travel during a 2-month period, 10 days of rail travel within a 2-month period, or 21 days of unlimited rail travel. The pass, which is valid on all lines of the state railways of Denmark, Finland, Norway, and Sweden, offers discounts or free travel on some (but not all) of the region's ferry lines as well. The pass can be purchased only in North America. It's available from any office of **RailEurope** (© **800/848-7245** in the U.S., or 800/361-RAIL in Canada) or **ScanAm World Tours,** 108 N. Main St., Cranbury, NJ 08512 (© **800/545-2204;** www.scandinaviantravel.com).

Depending on whether you choose first- or second-class rail transport, 5 days out of 2 months costs $149 to $298; 8 days out of 2 months costs $180 to $360, 10 days out of 2 months costs $200 to $400, and 21 consecutive days of unlimited travel costs $232 to $463. Seniors get an 11% discount, and students receive a 30% discount.

EURAIL DENMARK PASS For those who plan to travel only in Denmark, a series of cost-cutting passes are offered. The major one is the **Eurail Denmark Pass,** offering both first- and second-class unlimited travel on Denmark's national rail network. For travel any 3 or 7 days within a 1-month period, the 3-day pass costing $77 to $166 for adults (first and second class) or $39 to $58 for children (ages 4–11). The 7-day pass goes for $116 to $181 for adults, or $58 to $91 for children.

Two or more passengers traveling together can take advantage of the **Eurail Denmark Saverpass,** offering unlimited travel in first and second class. On this deal, you get 3 days of travel in 1 month for $64 to $103 for adults, or $32 to $52 for children. For 7 days in 1 month, the cost ranges from $103 to $155 for adults, or $52 to $78 for children.

A better deal for passengers under 26 is the **Eurail Denmark Youthpass,** costing $51 for 3 days in 1 month or $90 for 7 days.

RAIL PASSES FOR BRITISH TRAVELERS

If you plan to do a lot of exploring, you may prefer one of the three rail passes designed for unlimited train travel within a designated region during a predetermined number of days. These passes are sold in Britain and several other European countries.

An **InterRail Pass** is available to passengers of any nationality, with some restrictions—they must be under age 26 and able to prove residency in a European or North African country (Morocco, Algeria, and Tunisia) for at least 6 months before buying the pass. It allows unlimited travel through Europe, except Albania and the republics of the former Soviet Union. Prices are complicated and vary depending on the countries you want to include. For pricing purposes, Europe is divided into eight zones; the cost depends on the number of zones you include. The most expensive option £277 ($499) allows 1 month of unlimited travel in all eight zones and is known to BritRail staff as a "global." The least expensive option of £140 ($252) allows 16 days of travel within only one zone.

Passengers age 25 and older can buy an **InterRail 26-Plus Pass** that, unfortunately, is severely limited geographically. It is, however, accepted for travel throughout Denmark, Finland, Norway, and Sweden. Second-class travel with the pass costs £206 ($371) for 12 days or £393 ($707) for 1 month. Passengers must meet the same residency requirements that apply to the InterRail Pass (described above).

For information on buying individual rail tickets or any of the just-mentioned passes, contact **National Rail Inquiries,** Victoria Station, London (② **08705/ 848-848**). Tickets and passes are also available at any of the larger railway stations, as well as selected travel agencies throughout Britain and the rest of Europe.

BY SHIP & FERRY

It's easy to travel by water from several ports to Denmark. Liners carrying cars and passengers operate from England, Germany, Poland, Norway, and Sweden.

Check with your travel agent about these cruises.

FROM BRITAIN DFDS Seaways (② **0870/252-0524;** www.dfdsseaways. com) runs vessels year-round between Harwich, England, and Esbjerg in West Jutland. The crossing takes 16 to 20 hours. The same line also sails from Newcastle upon Tyne to Esbjerg, but only in the summer, as part of a 22-hour passage. Overnight cabins and space for cars are available on both routes.

FROM NORWAY & SWEDEN The **Norwegian Coastal Voyage, Inc.** (② **800/323-7436** or 212/319-1300 in the U.S.; www.coastalvoyage.com), operates vessels from Oslo to Hirtshals in North Jutland.

Stena Line (② **02-01-0;** www.stena line.com) runs popular sea links from Oslo to Frederikshavn, North Jutland (11½ hr.), and from Gothenburg, Sweden, to Frederikshavn (3 hr.). For information, schedules, and fares, contact **Stena Line UK, Ltd.** (② **08705/70-70-70;** www. stenaline.co.uk). For 24-hour updates on sailing, call ② **08705/755-755.**

13 Packages for the Independent Traveler

For travelers who feel more comfortable if everything is prearranged—hotels, transportation, sightseeing excursions, luggage handling, tips, taxes, and even meals—a package tour is the obvious choice, and it may even help save money.

A reliable tour operator is **Scantours, Inc.,** 3439 Wade St., Los Angeles, CA 90006 (② **800/223-7226** or 310/636-4656; www.scantours.com).

BUS TOURS ScanAm World Tours (② **800/545-2204;** www.scanamtours. com) offers a tour through the "Heart of Fairy Tale Denmark." You can choose a 5-day, 4-night trip through Hans Christian Andersen country, including a visit to

Odense (his birthplace) and an excursion to Legoland. Tours begin at $485 per person.

SELF-DRIVE TOURS Several companies offer self-drive tours, which usually include accommodations, rental cars, and customized itineraries. **Scantours, Inc.** (② **800/545-2204;** www.scantours.com), features the 5-day "A Taste of Danish Castles," which is available year-round. Prices begin at $685 per person. The company also sponsors a tour of Danish inns. The 4-day self-drive tour includes accommodations, breakfast, car rental, and an itinerary. Prices start at $370 per person.

BICYCLE TOURS An excellent way to explore the flat, rolling Danish countryside is on a bicycle. Numerous organizations (including Scantours, Inc., and ScanAm Tours) sponsor bike tours through various regions of the country. You can choose one that covers the castles, beaches, and fjords of northern Denmark; the southern Funen islands; the beaches and marshland of western Jutland; or the lake country in eastern Jutland. **Blue Marble Travel** (© 215/923-3788; www. bluemarble.org) offers 7-day excursions to Hans Christian Andersen country and several small islands in the Baltic for $1,850 per person. **Dansk Cyklist Forbund,** Rømersgade 7, DK-1362 Copenhagen (© 33-32-31-21; www.dcf.dk), can provide the latest information on cycling tours in Denmark.

ADVENTURE TRAVEL OPERATORS

In North America, a few companies offer adventure trips to Denmark. **Crossing Latitudes,** 420 W. Koch St., Bozeman, MT 59715 (© 800/572-8747; fax 406/585-5356; www.crossinglatitudes. com), offers sea kayaking and backpacking expeditions throughout the region; and **Blue Marble Travel,** 350 Ramapo Valley Rd., Suite 18-131, Oakland, NJ 07436 (© 215/923-3788; www.blue marble.org), features reasonably priced biking and hiking trips in Denmark and Norway.

IN THE U.K.

The oldest travel agency in Britain, **Cox & Kings,** Gordon House 10, Greencoat Place, London SW1P 1PH (© 020/ 7873-5000; www.coxandkings.co.uk), was established in 1758. Today the company specializes in unusual, if pricey, holidays. Its offerings in Scandinavia include cruises through the spectacular fjords and waterways, bus and rail tours through sites of historic and aesthetic interest, and visits to the region's best-known sites.

To cycle through the splendors of Scandinavia, you can join Britain's oldest and largest association of bicycle riders, the **Cyclists' Touring Club,** Cotterell House, 69 Meadrow, Godalming, Surrey GU7 3HS (© 0870/873-0060; www. ctc.org.uk). Founded in 1878, it charges £31 ($50) a year for membership, which includes information, maps, a subscription to a newsletter packed with practical information and morale boosters, plus recommended cycling routes through virtually every country in Europe. The organization's information bank on scenic routes through Scandinavia is especially comprehensive. Membership can be arranged over the phone with a credit card (such as MasterCard, Visa, Access, or Barclaycard).

LEARNING VACATIONS

Danish Cultural Institute (Det Danske Kultur Institutu), Kultorvet 2, DK-1175 København (© 33 13 54 48; fax 33 15-10-91; www.dankultur.dk), offers summer seminars in English, including a course in Danish culture. Credit programs are available, but many courses are geared toward professional groups from abroad.

Another good source of information about courses in Denmark is the **American Institute for Foreign Study (AIFS),** River Plaza, 9 W. Broad St., Stamford, CT 06902 (© 866/906-2437; www. aifs.org). This organization can set up transportation and arrange for summer courses, with bed and board included.

The largest organization dealing with higher education in Europe is the **Institute of International Education (IIE),** 809 United Nations Plaza, New York, NY 10017 (© 800/445-0443 or 212/ 883-8200; www.iie.org). A few of its booklets are free; for $47, plus $6 for postage, you can buy the more definitive *Vacation Study Abroad.* The Information Center in New York is open to the public

Tuesday through Thursday from 11am to 4pm. The institute is closed on major holidays.

One well-recommended clearinghouse for academic programs throughout the world is the **National Registration Center for Study Abroad (NRCSA)**, 823 N. 2nd St., P.O. Box 1393, Milwaukee, WI 53203 (© **414/278-0631;** www.nrcsa.com). The organization maintains language study programs throughout Europe.

HOME STAYS

Friendship Force International (FFI), 34 Peachtree St. NW, Suite 900, Atlanta, GA 30303 (© **404/522-9490;** www. friendshipforce.org), is a nonprofit organization that encourages friendship among people worldwide. Dozens of branch offices throughout North America arrange visits, usually once a year. Because of group bookings, the airfare to the host country is usually less than the cost of individual APEX tickets. Each participant spends 2 weeks in the host country, one as a guest in the home of a family and the second traveling in the host country.

Servas, 1125 16th St., Suite 201, Arcata, CA 95521 (© **707/825-1714;** www.usservas.org), is an international nonprofit, nongovernmental, interfaith network of travelers and hosts whose goal is to help promote world peace, goodwill, and understanding. (Its name means "to serve" in Esperanto.) Servas hosts offer travelers hospitality for 2 days. Travelers pay an $85 annual fee and a $25 list deposit after filling out an application and being approved by an interviewer (interviewers are located across the United States). They then receive Servas directories listing the names and addresses of Servas hosts.

HOME EXCHANGES

One of the most exciting breakthroughs in modern tourism is the home exchange. Sometimes the family automobile is included. Of course, you must be comfortable with the idea of having strangers in your home, and you must be content to spend your vacation in one place.

Home exchanges cut costs. You don't pay hotel bills, and you can also save money by shopping in markets and eating in. One potential problem, though, is that you may not get a home in the area you request.

Heritage—The Search for Roots

More than 12 million North Americans have Scandinavian roots, many in Denmark. To help you trace your ancestry, Danish consulates can furnish fact sheets. Many original Danish records are available on microfilm from **The Family History Library**, 35 N. West Temple, Salt Lake City, UT 84150 (© **801/240-2331**).

Established in 1992, the **Danish Immigrant Museum,** Elk Horn, Iowa (© **712/764-7001**; www.dkmuseum.org), is devoted to telling the story of Scandinavian migration to the United States. It also collects and preserves a vital chapter in Danish-American history.

In Denmark itself, the major archives concerning immigration are held at **Det Danske Udvandrerarkiv** (Danes' Worldwide Archives), Arkivstraede 1, P.O. Box 1731, DK-9100 Aalborg (© **99-31-42-20**; fax 98-10-22-48; www. emiarch.dk).

Intervac, U.S., 30 Corte San Fernando, Tiburon, CA 94920 (© **800/756-HOME** or 415/435-3497; www.intervacus.com), is part of the largest worldwide exchange network. It publishes four catalogs a year, containing more than 10,000 homes in more than 36 countries. Members contact each other directly. The cost is $86 plus postage, which includes the purchase of three of the company's catalogs (which will be mailed to you), plus the inclusion of your own listing in whichever one of the three catalogs you select.

The Invented City, 41 Sutter St., Suite 1090, San Francisco, CA 94104 (© **415/486-7588;** www.invented-city.com), publishes home-exchange listings three times a year. For the $50 membership fee, you can list your home with your own written descriptive summary.

Home Link (© **800/638-3841;** www.homelink.org) will send you five directories a year—in one of which you're listed—for $80.

14 Getting Around

BY PLANE

The best way to get around Scandinavia is to take advantage of air passes that apply to the whole region. If you're traveling extensively in Europe, special European passes are also available.

SAS'S VISIT SCANDINAVIA PASS The vast distances encourage air travel between Scandinavia's far flung points. One of the most worthwhile promotions is SAS's **Visit Scandinavia Pass.** Available only to travelers who fly SAS across the Atlantic, it includes up to six coupons, each of which is valid for any SAS flight within or between Denmark, Norway, and Sweden. Each coupon costs $80, a price that's especially appealing when you consider that an economy-class ticket between Stockholm and Copenhagen can cost as much as $250 each way. The pass is especially valuable if you plan to travel to the far northern frontiers of Sweden or Norway; in that case, the savings over the price of a regular economy-class ticket can be substantial. For information on buying the pass, call **SAS** (© **800/221-2350;** www.scandinavian.net).

WITHIN DENMARK For those in a hurry, **SAS** (© **32-32-00-00** in Copenhagen) operates daily service between Copenhagen and points on Jutland's mainland. From Copenhagen it takes about 40 minutes to fly to Aalborg, 35 minutes to Århus, and 30 minutes to Odense's Beldringe Airport.

Fares to other Danish cities are sometimes included in a transatlantic ticket at no extra charge, as long as the additional cities are specified when the ticket is written.

BY TRAIN

Low-lying Denmark, with its hundreds of bridges and absence of mountains, has a large network of railway lines that connect virtually every hamlet with the largest city, Copenhagen. For **information, schedules, and fares** anywhere in Denmark, call © **70-13-14-15.** Waiting times for a live person on this telephone line range from long to very long. Alternatively, you can check the **Danish National Railways** website, **www.dsb.dk,** for schedules and prices, and to reserve space on specific trains.

A word you're likely to see and hear frequently is *Lyntog* ("Express Trains"), which are the fastest trains presently operational in Denmark. Be warned in advance that the most crowded times on Danish trains are Fridays, Sundays, and national holidays, so plan your reservations accordingly.

On any train within Denmark, children between the ages of 4 and 15 are charged half-price if they're accompanied by an adult, and up to two children under 4 can travel for free with any adult on any train in Denmark. Seniors (age 65 or older) receive a discount of between 20% for travel on Fridays, Sundays, and holidays, and discounts of 45% every other day of the week. No identification is needed when you buy your ticket, but the conductor who checks your ticket might ask for proof of age.

The Danish government offers dozens of discounts on the country's rail networks—depending on the type of traveler, days or hours traveled, and destination. Because discounts change often, it's always best to ask for a discount based on your age and the number of days (or hours) you intend to travel.

BY BUS

By far the best way to visit rural Denmark is by car, but if you want or need to travel by bus, be aware that you'll probably get your bus at the railway station. (In much of Scandinavia, buses take passengers to destinations not served by the train; therefore, the bus route often originates at the railway station.) The arrival of trains and departure of buses are usually closely timed.

For seniors (ages 65 and over), round-trip bus tickets are sometimes offered at one-way prices (excluding Sat, Sun, and peak travel periods around Christmas and Easter). Most discounts are granted only to seniors who are traveling beyond the city limits of their point of origin.

BY CAR

RENTALS Avis, Budget, and Hertz offer well-serviced, well-maintained fleets of cars. You may have to reserve and pay for your rental car in advance (usually 2 weeks, but occasionally as little as 48 hr.) to get the lowest rates. Unfortunately, if your trip is canceled or your arrival date changes, you might have to fill out a lot of forms to arrange a refund. All three companies may charge slightly higher rates to clients who reserve less than 48 hours in advance and pay at pickup. The highest rates are charged to walk-in customers who arrange their rentals after they arrive in Denmark.

Before you rent, you should know that the Danish government imposes a whopping 25% tax on all car rentals. Agencies that encourage prepaid rates almost never collect this tax in advance—instead, it's imposed as part of a separate transaction when you pick up the car. Furthermore, any car retrieved at a Danish airport is subject to a one-time supplemental tax of 255DKK ($43/£23); you might prefer to pick up your car at a downtown location. Membership in certain travel clubs or organizations (such as AAA or AARP) might qualify you for a modest discount.

Note: Reserve in North America. Walk-in customers are charged a considerably higher rate.

Avis (© **800/331-1212** in the U.S. and Canada; www.avis.com), maintains four offices in Copenhagen: two at the arrivals hall of the airport, one at Landgreven 10 (© **70-24-77-64**), and another at Kampmannsgade 1 (© **70-24-77-07**).

Budget (© **800/527-0700** in the U.S., or 800/472-3325 in Canada; www.budget.com) has two rental locations in Copenhagen. The larger branch is at the Copenhagen airport (© **35-53-39-00**), and the other office is at Vesterfarimagsgade 7 (© **33-55-70-00**).

Hertz (© **800/654-3001** in the U.S. and Canada; www.hertz.com) has two offices in Copenhagen, one at the airport (© **33-17-90-20**); and the other at Ved Vesterport 3 (© **33-17-90-20**).

Also consider using a small company. **Kemwel** (© **800/678-0678** in the U.S.; www.kemwel.com) is the North American representative for two Denmark-based car companies, Van Wijk and Hertz. It may be able to offer attractive rental prices to North Americans who pay in full at least 10 days before their departure. Seniors and members of AAA get a 5% discount.

15 Tips on Accommodations

There are other alternatives, but chances are most visitors to Denmark will check into a hotel. Accommodations range from the most basic, perhaps lacking private bathrooms, to the most deluxe. Outside of Copenhagen, you are likely to encounter first class in the top category instead of *luxe* accommodations. The one thing you'll not find is a truly cheap hotel. Even the most inexpensive hotels might be considered a bit pricey in some parts of the world. To compensate, many hotels, especially chain members, offer discounted rates on weekends when hotels lose their most reliable client—the commercial traveler.

Our accommodation listings include service charges and taxes so you won't be shocked when the time comes to pay the bill and a lot of extras are added on, as is the situation in many European countries.

Denmark classifies its hotels by stars ranging from one (the most basic) to five (deluxe). A hotel without a restaurant is called Hotel *Garni*. One-star hotel rooms have a hand basin with hot and cold running water and at least one bathroom per 10 rooms for communal use; two-star hotels have at least 30% of the units with private bathrooms; three-star hotels offer rooms with their own private bathroom (such hotels also have an elevator if there are more than two floors). Moving up, four-star hotels offer around-the-clock reception, an a la carte restaurant, room service, minibars, laundry service, and a bar. The best hotels in Denmark are five stars, with luxuriously appointed rooms, often indoor pools, professionally staffed fitness centers, air conditioning, safes in the rooms, and around-the-clock room service, among other luxuries.

If you have not booked a room prior to your arrival in Copenhagen, you can go to **Wonderful Copenhagen Tourist Information** at Bernstorffsgade 1, opposite the Central Station next to Tivoli. A handling fee of $9 is charged. There is also a booking desk, charging the same handling fee, at the **Copenhagen Airport Arrival Hall.**

Advance booking online is possible through **Wonderful Copenhagen Tourist Information & Booking Center,** Gammel Kongevej 1, DK 1610 Copenhagen (© **70-22-24-42;** www.visitcopenhagen.dk). Outside Copenhagen, bookings can be made online at www.danishhotels.dk and www.visitdenmark.com, through local tourist offices, or directly with the hotel.

ALTERNATIVE ACCOMMODATIONS

If you'd like to avoid a stay in a hotel, consider these other options:

Bed & Breakfast: Dansk Bed & Breakfast publishes a catalogue of guest houses throughout Denmark that receive visitors for overnight stays, fortifying them the next morning with a hearty Danish breakfast. A typical B&B, of several possibilities, might be a century-old farmhouse built of granite and half-timbering, dating from the 18th century, and standing on 3.2 hectares (8 acres) of land with a small lake and an ecological vegetable garden. Contact **Dansk Bed & Breakfast** at Sankt Peders Stræde 41, DK-1453 Copenhagen (© **39-61-04-05;** www.bedandbreakfast.dk).

The best and densest concentration of B&Bs is found on the Hans Christian Andersen island of Funen. There is a separate organization handling these bookings: **Nyborg Tourist Office,** Torvey 9, DK-5800 Nyborg (℃ **65-31-02-80;** www.bed-breakfast-fyn.dk). The typical overnight price for a double room in a B&B is 170DKK ($29/£15).

Castles & Manor Houses   Denmark is riddled with old manor houses and even a few small castles that receive paying guests all year. In our view, this type of lodging is the most exciting way to stay in Denmark because of the grandeur of the buildings. You get to feel like a king (or queen), or at least a prince and princess for the night. Some of the establishments in this category are more like country homes than castles or manors. By taking in boarders, many of the owners of these privately owned estates are preserving Denmark's cultural heritage. For more information, contact **Danish Castles & Manor Houses,** Sankt Leonis Stræde 1A, DK-8800 Viborg (℃ **86-60-38-44;** www.slotte-herregaarde.dk).

Danish Inns   Nearly 100 atmospheric and often old-world accommodations spread across the country have formed an association, offering accommodations in old inns (called *kros*) and hotels often hundreds of years old. The bedrooms, however, are mostly renovated in the modern style. You get atmosphere and comfort, and most often good, solid food, both regional dishes but in many cases French specialties as well. For this type of accommodation, book through **Danska Kroer og Hoteller,** Vejlevej 16, DK-8700 Horsens (℃ **75-64-87-00;** www.krohotel.dk).

Farm Vacations   Some 110 farms all over Denmark receive paying guests. To get close to the heart of the country and to meet the Danes, there's no better way than spending a week on one of these farms. In addition to an atmospheric stay, you can enjoy good country cooking with fresh

vegetables, newly laid eggs, and rich butter. You stay on a farm as the guest of the family, joining members and other guests for meals. Often lodgings are in a small apartment on the grounds or even a cottage near the main building. In many cases you do your own housekeeping. Prices average around $30 per person, including a full Danish breakfast. You can book with the farm directly or else go through **Landsforeningen for Landboturisme,** Lerbakken 7, DK-8410 Rønde. (℃ **87-37-39-00;** www.bondegaardsferie.dk).

Vacation Homes   Yes, it's possible to rent your own house—most often a seaside cottage—throughout Denmark. The houses may be a snug retreat for two or else spacious enough to accommodate 10 to 12 guests. Some of these vacation homes are within a 30-minute drive of Copenhagen. They are available all year, and prices begin at around $500 per week, the rates depending on the season, size, and location. Naturally, seaside vacation homes are the most sought after and most expensive in July and August. Many of the best homes are found on the west coast of Jutland, often with an indoor swimming pool and sauna. To book one of these homes contact one of the following organizations: **Dansommer** (℃ **86-17-61-22;** www.dansommer.com); **Navasol AS** (℃ **73-75-66-11;** www.novasol.com); and **Sol og Strand** (℃ **99-44-44-44;** www.sologstrand.com).

Chain Hotels & Discounts   The most prevalent chain hotel in Denmark is **Best Western** (℃ **800/WESTERN;** www. bestwestern.com). It offers a Best Western Advance Card that allows you to take advantage of special "summer low" or "winter special promotion" rates, and grants such privileges as allowing one child under the age of 12 to stay free in a room shared with parents.

16 Recommended Books

HISTORY & PHILOSOPHY *A Kierkegaard Anthology*, edited by Robert Bretall (Princeton University Press), explores the work of the Copenhagen-born philosopher who developed an almost pathological sense of involvement in theology. A representative selection of some of his more significant works is included.

Copenhagen, A Historical Guide, by Torben Ejlersen (published by Høst & Søn in Denmark, and available at most bookstores there), an 88-page guide, takes you on a brief tour of the city that began as a ferry landing and became one of the most important capitals of Europe.

Of Danish Ways, written by two Danish Americans, Ingeborg S. MacHiffic and Margaret A. Nielsen (Harper & Row, 1984), a delightful account of a land and its people, has a little bit of everything: history, social consciousness, customs, food, handicrafts, art, music, and theater.

BIOGRAPHY & LITERATURE *Andersen's Fairy Tales*, by H. C. Andersen (New American Library), and *The Complete Hans Christian Andersen Fairy Tales* (Crown) are anthologies that include all of his most important works such as *The Little Mermaid, The Tinderbox*, and *The Princess and the Pea*.

Danish Literature: A Short Critical Guide, by Paul Borum (Nordic Books), is a well-written review that explores Danish literature from the Middle Ages to the 1970s.

Out of Africa (Modern Library), *Letters from Africa* (University of Chicago Press), and *Seven Gothic Tales* (Random House) are all by Karen Blixen (who wrote under the name Isak Dinesen), one of the major authors of the 20th century who gained renewed fame with the release of the 1985 movie *Out of Africa*, with Meryl Streep and Robert Redford. *Isak Dinesen*, by Judith Thurman (St. Martin's Press), chronicles Blixen's amazing life from an unhappy childhood in Denmark and marriage to Baron Blixen to immigration to Kenya and her passionate love affair with Denys Finch Hatton.

FAST FACTS: Denmark

Area Code The country code for Denmark is **45**. It precedes any call made to Denmark from another country. There are no city area codes. Every telephone number has eight digits.

Business Hours Most **banks** are open Monday through Friday from 9:30am to 4pm (Thurs to 6pm), but outside Copenhagen, banking hours vary. **Stores** are generally open Monday through Thursday from 9am to 5:30pm, Friday 9am to 7 or 8pm, and Saturday noon to 2pm; most are closed Sunday.

Doctors Most areas have doctors on duty 24 hours a day on Saturdays, Sundays, and holidays; weekday emergency hours are 4pm to 7:30am. Every doctor speaks English.

Drug Laws Penalties for the possession, use, purchase, sale, or manufacturing of drugs are severe. The quantity of the controlled substance is more important than the type of substance. Danish police are particularly strict with cases involving the sale of drugs to children.

Electricity Voltage is generally 220 volts AC, 50 to 60 cycles. In many camping sites, 110-volt power plugs are also available. Adapters and transformers may be purchased in Denmark. It's always best to check at your hotel desk before using an electrical outlet.

Embassies All embassies are in Copenhagen. The embassy of the **United States** is at Dag Hammärskjölds Allé 24, DK-2100 København (© 33-41-71-00). Other embassies are the **United Kingdom,** Kastelsvej 40, DK-2100 København (© 35-44-52-00); **Canada,** Kristen Berniskows Gade 1, DK-1105 København K (© 33-48-32-00); **Australia,** Dampfaergevej 26, DK-2100 København (© 70-26-36-76); and **Ireland,** Østbanegade 21, DK-2100 København (© 35-42-32-33).

Emergencies Dial © **112** for the fire department, the police, or an ambulance, or to report a sea or air accident. Emergency calls from public telephone kiosks are free (no coins needed).

Holidays See "When to Go," earlier in this chapter.

Language Danish is the national tongue. English is commonly spoken, especially among young people. You should have few, if any, language barriers. The best phrase book is *Danish for Travellers* (Berlitz).

Liquor Laws To consume alcohol in Danish bars, restaurants, or cafes, customers must be 18 or older. There are no restrictions on children under 18 who drink at home or, for example, from a bottle in a public park. Danish police tend to be lenient unless drinkers become raucous or uncontrollable. There is no leniency, however, in the matter of driving while intoxicated. It's illegal to drive with a blood-alcohol level of 0.8% or more, which could be produced by two drinks. If the level is 1.5%, motorists pay a serious fine. If it's more than 1.5%, drivers can lose their license. If the level is 2.0% or more (usually produced by six or seven drinks), a prison term of at least 14 days might follow. Liquor stores in Denmark are closed on Sunday.

Mail Most post offices are open Monday through Friday from 9 or 10am to 5 or 6pm and Saturday from 9am to noon; they're closed Sunday. All mail to North America is sent airmail without extra charge. Mailboxes are painted red and display the embossed crown and trumpet of the Danish Postal Society.

Maps The best map for touring Denmark is part of the series published by Hallwag. It's for sale at all major bookstores in Copenhagen, including the most centrally located one, **Boghallen,** Rådhuspladsen 37 (© **33-47-25-60**), in the Town Hall Square.

Newspapers & Magazines English-language newspapers are sold at all major news kiosks in Copenhagen but are much harder to find in the provinces. London papers are flown in for early-morning delivery, but you may find the *International Herald Tribune* or *USA Today* more interesting. Pick up a copy of *Copenhagen This Week,* printed in English, which contains useful information.

Passports **For residents of the United States:** Whether you're applying in person or by mail, you can download passport applications from the U.S. State Department website at **http://travel.state.gov**. For general information, call the **National Passport Agency** (© **202/647-0518**). To find your regional passport office, either check the U.S. State Department website or call the **National Passport Information Center** toll-free number (© **877/487-2778**) for automated information.

For residents of Canada: Passport applications are available at travel agencies throughout Canada or from the central **Passport Office,** Department of Foreign Affairs and International Trade, Ottawa, ON K1A 0G3 (℃ **800/567-6868;** www.ppt.gc.ca).

For residents of the United Kingdom: To pick up an application for a standard 10-year passport (5-year passport for children under 16), visit your nearest passport office, major post office, or travel agency, contact the **United Kingdom Passport Service** at ℃ **0870/521-0410,** or search its website at www.ukpa.gov.uk.

For residents of Ireland: You can apply for a 10-year passport at the **Passport Office,** Setanta Centre, Molesworth Street, Dublin 2 (℃ **01/671-1633;** www.irlgov.ie/iveagh). Those under age 18 and over 65 must apply for a €12 3-year passport. You can also apply at 1A South Mall, Cork (℃ **021/272-525)** or at most main post offices.

For residents of Australia: You can pick up an application from your local post office or any branch of Passports Australia, but you must schedule an interview at the passport office to present your application materials. Call the **Australian Passport Information Service** at ℃ **131-232,** or visit the government website at www.passports.gov.au.

For residents of New Zealand: You can pick up a passport application at any New Zealand Passports Office or download it from their website. Contact the **Passports Office** at ℃ **0800/225-050** in New Zealand, or 04/474-8100, or log on to www.passports.govt.nz.

Police In an emergency, dial ℃ **90-000** anywhere in the country.

Pharmacies They're known as *apoteker* in Danish and are open Monday through Thursday from 9am to 5:30pm, Friday 9am to 7pm, and Saturday 9am to 1pm.

Police Dial ℃ **112** for police assistance.

Radio & TV No English-language radio or TV stations broadcast from Denmark. Only radios and TVs with satellite reception can receive signals from countries such as Britain. News programs in English are broadcast Monday through Saturday at 8:30am on Radio Denmark, 93.85 MHz. Radio 1 (90.8 MHz VHF) features news and classical music. Channels 2 and 3 (96.5/93.9 MHz) include some entertainment, broadcast light news items, and offer light music. Most TV stations transmit from 7:30am to 11:30pm. Most films (many of which are American) are shown in their original languages, with Danish subtitles.

Restrooms All big plazas, such as Town Hall Square in Copenhagen, have public lavatories. In small towns and villages, head for the marketplace. Hygienic standards are usually adequate. Sometimes men and women patronize the same toilets (signs read TOILETTER or WC). Otherwise, men's rooms are marked HERRER or H, and women's rooms are marked DAMER or D.

Safety Denmark is one of the safest European countries for travelers. Copenhagen, the major population center, naturally experiences the most crime. Muggings have been reported in the vicinity of the railway station, especially late at night, but crimes of extreme violence are exceedingly rare. Exercise the usual precautions you would when traveling anywhere.

Taxes The 25% VAT (value-added tax) on goods and services is known in Denmark as *moms* (pronounced *mumps*). Special tax-free exports are possible, and many stores will mail goods home to you, circumventing *moms*. If you want to take your purchases with you, look for shops displaying Danish tax-free shopping notices. Such shops offer tourists tax refunds for personal export. This refund applies to purchases of at least 300DKK ($51) for U.S. and Canadian visitors. Danish Customs must stamp your tax-free invoice when you leave the country. You can receive your refund at Copenhagen's Kastrup International Airport when you depart. If you go by land or sea, you can receive your refund by mail. Mail requests for refunds to Danish Tax-Free Shopping A/S, H. J. Holstvej 5A, DK-2605 Brøndby, Denmark. You'll be reimbursed by check, cash, or credit or charge card credit in the currency you want.

For the refund to apply, the 300DKK must be spent in one store, but not necessarily at the same time. Some major department stores allow purchases to be made over several days or even weeks, at the end of which receipts will be tallied. Service and handling fees are deducted from the total, so actual refunds come up to about 19%. Information on this program is available from the Danish Tourist Board (see "Visitor Information," earlier).

A 25% *moms* is included in hotel and restaurant bills, service charges, entrance fees, and repair bills for foreign-registered cars. No refunds are possible on these items.

Telephone The country code for Denmark is **45**. It should precede any call made to Denmark from another country.

Danish phones are fully automatic. Dial the eight-digit number; there are no city area codes. Don't insert any coins until your party answers. At public telephone booths, use two 50-øre coins or a 1-krone or 5-krone coin only. You can make more than one call on the same payment if your time hasn't run out. Emergency calls are free.

Time Denmark operates on Central European Time—1 hour ahead of Greenwich Mean Time and 6 hours ahead of Eastern Standard Time. Daylight saving time is observed from the end of March to the end of September.

Tipping Tips are seldom expected, but when they are, you should give only 2DKK or 3DKK (35¢–50¢/20p–30p). Porters charge fixed prices, and tipping is not customary for hairdressers or barbers. Service is built into the system, and hotels, restaurants, and even taxis include a 15% service charge in their rates. Because of the service charge, plus the 25% *moms,* you'll probably have to pay an additional 40% for some services!

Consider tipping only for special services—some Danes would feel insulted if you offered them a tip.

Water Tap water is safe to drink throughout Denmark.

4

Introducing Copenhagen

Denmark may be small, but it packs a powerful punch. Its capital, Copenhagen, seems to be the seat of everything Danish—artistic, financial, and political.

The Frommer's guides have long maintained their loyalty to promoting the glories of Copenhagen, and we continue that long-ago commitment. In his first guide, *Europe on $5 A Day,* Arthur Frommer wrote, "After Copenhagen, the rest of Europe will become a footnote." An exaggeration, of course, but after all these decades, Copenhagen remains the "fun" capital of Scandinavia—and also the most affordable—and the Danes continue to practice their own *joie de vivre.* There is an enthusiasm for life here that always sweeps us up in its spell.

The city continues to change. Middle Eastern restaurants now compete with old-fashioned eateries serving food that Danish grandmothers used to cook. Internet cafes have become the rendezvous point of choice for young Danes instead of the traditional sudsy taverns beloved by their parents. The city isn't as safe as it used to be: Crime and drugs are on the rise. In other words, welcome to the modern world.

But some things never change. Many Copenhageners still bike to work along the city's canals. We still join the locals who follow their noses to the cafes where the smell of freshly baked bread lures us in for a morning Danish and a cup of freshly brewed coffee. Along the way, we still pass that little old shopkeeper out soaping down his glass windows.

"We are a bit unconventional but affable," a former mayor told us. "We have big hearts and can accommodate all lifestyles and persuasions. There's also a rebellious streak of independence in us . . . But we wouldn't be Danes if we didn't exercise our freedoms."

Copenhagen, the capital of Denmark, got its name from the word *køben-havn,* which means "merchants' harbor." It grew in size and importance because of its position on the Øresund (the Sound), the body of water between Denmark and Sweden, guarding the strategic passage of all maritime traffic heading into or out of the Baltic.

From its humble beginnings, Copenhagen has become the largest city in Scandinavia, home to 1.8 million people, and seat of one of the oldest kingdoms in the world.

Over the centuries, Copenhagen has suffered more than its share of invasions and disasters. In the 17th century, the Swedes repeatedly besieged it, and in the 18th century, it endured the plague and two devastating fires. The British attacked twice during the Napoleonic wars in the early 1800s. In 1940, the Nazis invaded Denmark and held onto Copenhagen until 1945, when the British army moved in again, this time as liberators.

Copenhagen is a city with much charm, as reflected in its canals, narrow streets, and old houses. Its most famous resident was Hans Christian Andersen, whose memory lives on. Another of Copenhagen's world-renowned inhabitants was

Søren Kierkegaard, who used to take long morning strolls in the city, planning his next addition to the collection of essays that eventually earned him the title "father of existentialism."

In 2000, the Øresund Bridge was officially opened, physically linking Sweden and Denmark for the first time. Today there's a 16km (10-mile) car and train link between Zealand (the eastern part of Denmark, the island on which Copenhagen sits) and Skane, the southern part of Sweden. If you'd like to link a visit with Copenhagen to Malmö, Copenhagen's fast-growing counterpart across the border in Sweden, or perhaps visit some of the châteaux of southern Sweden, just drive across the bridge.

Copenhagen still retains some of the characteristics of a village. If you ignore the suburbs, you can cover most of the central belt on foot. It's almost as if the city were designed for strolling, as reflected by its Strøget, the longest and oldest pedestrians-only street in Europe.

1 Orientation

ARRIVING

BY PLANE   You arrive at **Kastrup Airport** (© 32-31-32-31; www.cph.dk), 12km (7½ miles) from the center of Copenhagen. Air-rail trains link the airport with the Central Railway Station in the center of town. The ride takes 13 minutes and costs 27DKK ($4.60/£2.45). Located right under the airport's arrivals and departures halls, the Air Rail Terminal is a short escalator ride from the gates. You can also take an SAS bus to the city terminal; the fare is 26DKK ($4.35/£2.30) A taxi to the city center costs between 150DKK and 200DKK ($26–$34/£14–£18).

BY TRAIN   Trains arrive at the **HovedBanegården** (Central Railroad Station; © 70-13-14-15 for rail information), in the center of Copenhagen, near Tivoli Gardens and the Rådhuspladsen. The station operates a luggage-checking service, but room bookings are available only at the tourist office (see "Visitor Information," below).

From the Central Railroad Station, you can connect with the **S-tog,** a local train; trains depart from platforms in the terminal itself. The information desk is near tracks 5 and 6.

BY BUS   Buses from Zealand and elsewhere pull into the Central Railroad Station. For bus information, call © 36-13-14-15 daily 7am to 9:30pm.

BY CAR   If you're driving from Germany, a car ferry will take you from Travemünde to Gedser in southern Denmark. From Gedser, get on E-55 north, an express highway that will deliver you to the southern outskirts of Copenhagen. If you're coming from Sweden via the Øresund Bridge, it will deposit you on the city's eastern outskirts, close to Kastrup Airport. From here, it's a short drive to the center.

VISITOR INFORMATION

The **Copenhagen Tourist Information Center,** Vesterbrogade 4A (© 70-22-24-42; www.VisitCopenhagen.com), adjacent to the main entrance of Tivoli, dispenses information. It's open in July and August Monday to Saturday 9am to 8pm; May and June Monday to Saturday 9am to 6pm; September to April Monday to Friday 9am to 4pm and Saturday 9am to 2pm.

CITY LAYOUT

MAIN ARTERIES & STREETS   The heart of Old Copenhagen is a warren of pedestrian streets, bounded by Nørreport Station to the north, Rådhuspladsen (Town

Hall Square) to the west, and Kongens Nytorv, a busy square that's positioned at the top of the Nyhavn Canal, to the east. **Strøget,** the longest continuous pedestrians-only route in Europe, goes east from Town Hall Square to Kongens Nytorv, and is made up of five interconnected streets: Frederiksberggade, Nygade, Vimmelskaftet, Amagertorv, and Østergade. Strøget is lined with shops, bars, restaurants, pizza parlors, and, in summer, sidewalk cafes. **Pistolstræde** contains a maze of galleries, restaurants, and boutiques, housed in restored 18th-century buildings.

Fiolstræde (Violet St.), a dignified street with antiques shops and bookshops, cuts through the university (Latin Quarter). If you turn into Rosengaarden at the top of Fiolstræde, you'll come to **Kultorvet** (Coal Square) just before you reach Nørreport Station. Here you join the third main pedestrian street, **Købmagergade** (Butcher St.), which winds around and finally meets Strøget at Amagertorv.

At the end of Strøget you approach **Kongens Nytorv** (King's Square). This is the site of the Royal Theater and Magasin, the largest department store in Copenhagen. This will put you at the beginning of **Nyhavn,** the former seamen's quarter that has been gentrified into an upmarket area of expensive restaurants, apartments, cafes, and boutiques.

The government of Denmark has been centered for the past 800 years on the small and very central downtown island of **Slotsholmen,** which is connected to the center by eight different bridges. The island's most immediately visible attraction is the imperial-looking granite mass of Christiansborg Castle, home of the Danish Parliament, the Prime Minister's offices, the country's Supreme Court, and several museums.

The center of Copenhagen is **Rådhuspladsen** (Town Hall Square). From here it's a short walk to the Tivoli Gardens, the city's major attraction, the Central Railroad Station, and the bus station. **Vesterbrogade,** a wide, densely trafficked boulevard, passes by Tivoli en route to the Central Railroad Station. **H. C. Andersens Boulevard,** another major avenue, named after Denmark's most famous writer, runs beside the Rådhuspladsen and Tivoli Gardens.

FINDING AN ADDRESS All even numbers are on one side of the street, all odd numbers on the other. Buildings are listed in numerical order. A, B, or C is often inserted after the street number.

NEIGHBORHOODS IN BRIEF

Tivoli Gardens Steeped in nostalgia, these amusement gardens were built in 1843 on the site of former fortifications in the heart of Copenhagen, on the south side of Rådhuspladsen. Some 160,000 flowers and 110,000 electric lights set the tone, and a collection of restaurants, dance halls, theaters, beer gardens, and lakes attract many thousands of visitors every year.

Strøget This pedestrians-only urban walkway stretches between Rådhuspladsen and Kongens Nytorv, two of the city's most visible and busiest plazas. En route along its trajectory are two spectacular, although smaller, squares, Gammeltorv and Nytorv, "old" and "new" squares, which seem to blossom during the warm weather months with outdoor seating—extensions of the many restaurants which line its edges. The word "Strøget" usually doesn't appear on any maps. Instead, Strøget encompasses five interconnected streets: Frederiksberggade, Nygade, Villelskaftet, Amagertorv, and Østergade.

Nyhavn/Kongens Nytorv Originally conceived in the 1670s by the Danish king as a shelter from the storms of the North and Baltic Sea, and as a means of hauling building supplies into central Copenhagen, Nyhavn (New Harbor) today is the site of a denser concentration of restaurants than any other neighborhood in Copenhagen. Moored beside its granite embankments you'll see old or even antique fishing boats, some of which remain in place to preserve the sense of old-fashioned nostalgia. For many generations, Nyhavn was the haunt of sailors looking for tattoos, cheap drinks, and other diversions. Nowadays it's one of the most obviously gentrified sections of the city, with outdoor terraces, which are mobbed during warm-weather months with chattering, sometimes hard-drinking Danes on holiday. At the top or western terminus of the Nyhavn canal is the five-sided Kongens Nytorv (King's New Market), site of the deluxe Hotel d'Angleterre and the Royal Theater.

Indre By This is the Old Town, the heart of Copenhagen. Once filled with monasteries, it's a maze of streets, alleyways, and squares. The neighborhood around Gammeltorv and Nørregade, sometimes called "The Latin Quarter," contains many buildings linked with the university. The **Vor Frue Kirke** (cathedral of Copenhagen) and **Rundetårn** (Round Tower) are here.

Slotsholmen This island, site of Christiansborg Palace, was where Bishop Absalon built Copenhagen's first fortress in 1167. Today it's the seat of the Danish parliament and home of Thorvaldsen's Museum. Bridges link Slotsholmen to Indre By. You can also visit the Royal Library (site of a recent hypermodern new wing described later in this guidebook as "The Black Diamond"), the Theater Museum, and the Royal Stables. The 17th-century Børsen (stock exchange) is also here.

Christianshavn Set on the opposite side of Copenhagen's harbor from the rest of the city, this was the "new town" ordered by master builder King Christian IV in the early 1500s. The town was originally constructed in the Dutch Renaissance style to house workers in the shipbuilding industry. Visitors come today mainly to see the Danish Film Museum on Store Søndervoldstræde and **Vors Frelsers Kirke**, on the corner of Prinsessegade and Skt. Annæ Gade. Sightseers can climb the spire of the old church for a panoramic view. Within the Christianshavn district is the offbeat community of **Christiania.** In 1971, many young and homeless people moved in, without the city's permission, proclaiming Christiania a "free city" (i.e., partially exempt from the rules and regulations of the Danish government) within the orbit of Greater Copenhagen. It has been a freewheeling and controversial place ever since. Once filled with barracks for soldiers, Christiania is within walking distance of Vor Frelsers Kirke at Christianshavn. You can enter the area on Prinsessegade. The craft shops and restaurants here are fairly cheap because the residents refuse to pay Denmark's crippling 25% sales tax.

Vesterbro Once a slum loaded with junkies and prostitutes, Vesterbro would be comparable to the East Village in New York City. Its main street, **Istedgade,** runs west from the Central Railway Station. Don't come here for monuments or museums, but for hip cafes, bars, music, and ethnic restaurants. No longer a slum, Vesterbro's sense of newfound hip centers on the cafes and bars around the Halmtorvet, Vesterbro's main square. Expect gentrification but also cultural diversity such as Turkish-Kurdish gift shops, food markets loaded with fruits you might not immediately recognize, barbers from Istanbul, and, from time to time, a sex shop like those that proliferated here during the 1970s and 1980s.

Nørrebro Adjacent to Vesterbro (see above), Nørrebro takes the immigrant overflow and is also rich in artisan shops and ethnic restaurants, especially Turkish and Pakistani. This area has been a blue-collar neighborhood since the middle of the 19th century. The original Danish settlers have long since departed, replaced by immigrants who are not always greeted with a friendly reception in Copenhagen. The area also abounds with trend-conscious artists, students, and musicians who can't afford the high rents elsewhere. Numerous secondhand clothing stores—especially around Sankt Hans Torv—give Nørre-bro the flavor of a Middle Eastern bazaar. Antiques shops (believe us, many of the furnishings and objets d'art aren't authentic) also fill the area. Most of these "antiques" stores lie along Ravnsborgade. The district is also home to a historic cemetery, Assistens Kirkegård, burial ground of both Hans Christian Andersen and Søren

Kirkegård, just to the west of Nørrebro-gade. If you're looking for the two dens-est concentrations of the nightlife for which the district has become famous, head for either **Sankt Hans Torv** or Blågårdsgade.

Frederiksberg Heading west of the inner city along Vesterbrogade, you will reach the residential and business dis-trict of Frederiksberg. It grew up around **Frederiksberg Palace,** con-structed in the Italianate style with an ocher facade. A park, Frederiksberg Have, surrounds the palace. To the west of the palace is the **Zoologisk Have,** one of the largest zoos in Europe.

Dragør Dragør is a fishing village south of the city that dates from the 16th century. Along with Tivoli, this seems to be everybody's favorite leisure spot. It's especially recommended for those who want to absorb the aura of an 18th-century Danish village but only have time to see the Copenhagen area. Walk its cobblestone streets and enjoy its 65 old red-roofed houses, des-ignated as national landmarks.

2 Getting Around

BY PUBLIC TRANSPORTATION

A joint zone fare system includes Copenhagen Transport buses; State Railway, Metro, and S-tog trains in Copenhagen and North Zealand; plus some private railway routes within a 40km (25-mile) radius of the capital, enabling you to transfer from train to bus and vice versa with the same ticket.

BASIC FARES A *grundbillet* (basic ticket) for both buses and trains costs 18DKK ($3.05/£1.60). Up to two children ages 11 and under ride for half fare when accom-panied by an adult. For 105DKK ($18/£9.45) you can purchase a ticket allowing 24-hour bus and train travel through nearly half of Zealand; it's half-price for children 7 to 11, and free for children 6 and under.

DISCOUNT PASSES The **Copenhagen Card** entitles you to free and unlimited travel by bus and rail throughout the metropolitan area (including North Zealand), 25% to 50% discounts on crossings to and from Sweden, and free admission to many sights and museums. The card is available for 1 or 3 days and costs 199DKK ($34/£18) and 429DKK ($73/£39), respectively. Up to 2 children under the age of 10 are allowed to go free with each adult card. If you have 3 or more children, a 50%

Impressions

What strikes me now most as regards Denmark is the charm, beauty, and independence of the women.

—Arnold Bennett, *Journal 1913*

discount is granted. Buy the card at tourist offices, the airport, train stations, and most hotels. For more information, contact the Copenhagen Tourist Information Center (see "Orientation," above) or visit www.CPHCard.com.

For information about low-cost train, ferry, and plane trips, go to **Wasteels,** Skoubogade 6 (© **33-14-46-33**), in Copenhagen. It's open Monday to Friday 9am to 5pm and Saturday 10am to 3pm.

Eurailpasses (which must be purchased in the U.S.) and **Nordturist Pass** tickets (which can be purchased at any train station in Scandinavia) can be used on local trains in Copenhagen. (For a more complete discussion of the cost/use of these passes, see p. 48.)

BY BUS   Copenhagen's well-maintained buses are the least expensive method of getting around, and most buses leave from Rådhuspladsen in the heart of the city. A basic ticket allows 1 hour of travel and unlimited transfers within the zone where you started your trip. For information, call © **36-13-14-15.**

BY METRO   In 2002, Copenhagen launched its first Metro line, taking passengers from east to west across the city or vice versa. Operating 24 hours, the Metro runs as far west as Vanlose or as far south as Vestmager. Nørreport is the transfer station to the **S-tog** system, the commuter rail link to the suburbs. Metro trains run every 2 minutes during rush hours and every 15 minutes at night. Fares are integrated into the existing zonal systems (see "Basic Fares," above).

BY S-TOG   The S-tog connects the heart of Copenhagen, most notably the Central Station, with the city's suburbs. Use of the tickets is the same as on buses (see "Basic Fares," above). You can transfer from a bus line to an S-tog train on the same ticket. Eurailpass holders generally ride free. For more information, call © **70-13-14-15.**

BY CAR

Because of the widespread availability of traffic-free walkways in Copenhagen and its many parks, gardens, and canal-side promenades, the Danish capital is well suited to pedestrian promenades. It's best to park your car in any of the dozens of city parking lots and then retrieve it when you're ready to explore the suburbs or countryside. Many parking lots are open 24 hours, but a few close between 1 and 7am; some close on Saturday afternoon and on Sunday when traffic is generally lighter. The cost ranges from 23DKK to 25DKK ($3.90–$4.25/£2.05–£2.25) per hour, or 240DKK ($41/£22) for 24 hours. Two centrally located parking lots are **Industriens Hus,** H. C. Andersens Blvd. 18 (© **33-91-21-75**), open Monday to Thursday 7am to midnight, Saturday 9am to 1am, and Sunday 9am to midnight; and **Park City,** Israels Plads (© **70-22-92-20**), open daily from 6am to midnight for entry. (You can exit from this facility any time, 24 hr. a day.)

BY TAXI

Watch for the FRI (free) sign or green light to hail a taxi, and be sure the taxis are metered. **Taxa 4x35** (© **35-35-35-35**) operates the largest fleet of cabs. Tips are included in the meter price: 19DKK to 32DKK ($3.25–$5.45/£1.70–£2.90) at the drop of the flag and 12DKK ($2.05/£1.10) per kilometer thereafter, Monday to Friday 7am to 4pm. From 6pm to 6am, and all day Saturday and Sunday, the cost is 15DKK ($2.55/£1.35) per kilometer. Many drivers speak English.

BY BICYCLE

To reduce pollution from cars (among other reasons), many Copenhageners ride bicycles. In her younger days, even the queen of Denmark could be seen cycling around just like her subjects. You can rent a bike at **Copenhagens Cyklebors,** Gothersgade 157 (© **33-14-07-17**). Depending on the bike, daily rates range from 60DKK to 150DKK ($10–$26/£5.40–£14) with deposits from 200DKK to 300DKK ($34–$51/£18–£27). Hours are Monday to Friday 8:30am to 5:30pm and Saturday 10am to 1:30pm.

FAST FACTS: Copenhagen

American Express Amex is represented throughout Denmark by **Nyman & Schultz,** Nørregade 7A (© **33-13-11-81**; bus: 34 or 35), with a branch in Terminal 3 of the Copenhagen Airport. Fulfilling all the functions of American Express except for foreign exchange services, the main office is open Monday to Thursday 8:30am to 4:30pm, and Friday 8:30am to 4pm. The airport office remains open until 8:30pm Monday to Friday. On weekends and overnight on weekdays, a recorded message, in English, will deliver the phone number of a 24-hour Amex service in Stockholm. This is useful for anyone who has lost a card or traveler's checks.

Bookstores One of the best and most centrally located is **Politikens Boghallen,** Rådhuspladsen 37 (© **33-47-25-60**; bus: 2, 8, or 30), offering more English titles than its competitors. Hours are Monday to Friday 10am to 7pm, and Saturday 10am to 4pm.

Business Hours Most **banks** are open Monday to Friday 10am to 4pm (to 6pm Thurs). **Stores** are generally open Monday to Thursday 9am to 6pm, Friday 9am to 7 or 8pm, and Saturday 9am to 2pm; most are closed Sunday. **Offices** are open Monday to Friday 9 or 10am to 4 or 5pm.

Currency Exchange Banks give better rates than currency kiosks. The main branch of Den Danske Bank (The Danish Bank), Holmens Kanal, 2-12 (© **33-44-00-00**), is open Monday to Friday from 10am to 4pm (to 5:30pm Thurs). When banks are closed, you can exchange money at **Forex** (© **33-11-29-05**) in the Central Railroad Station, daily 8am to 10pm, or at the **Change Group,** Østergade 61 (© **33-93-04-55**; bus: 9 or 10), daily 8:30am to 8:15pm.

Dentists During regular business hours, ask your hotel to call the nearest English-speaking dentist. For emergencies, go to **Tandlægevagten,** Oslo Plads 14 (© **35-38-02-51**; bus: 6 or 9), near Østerport Station and the U.S. Embassy. It's open Monday to Friday 8am to 9:30pm and Saturday, Sunday, and holidays 10am to noon. Be prepared to pay in cash.

Doctors To reach a doctor, dial © **38-11-40-00** 24 hours a day (www.copenhagen doctors.dk). The doctor's fee is payable in cash and visits cost 120DKK ($20/£11) per visit from Monday to Friday 8am to 4pm and 160DKK ($27/£14) all other times. The doctor will arrive within 45 minutes and provide most medication. Language is hardly a problem in Denmark where virtually all doctors speak English.

Emergencies Dial 🕻 **112** to report a fire or call the police or an ambulance. State your phone number and address. Emergency calls from public telephones are free (no coins needed).

Hospitals In cases of illness or accident, even foreigners are entitled to free medical treatment in Denmark. One of the most centrally located hospitals is **Rigshospitalet,** Blegdamsvej 9 (🕻 **35-45-35-45;** bus: 10).

Internet Access To check your e-mail or to send messages, go to **Copenhagen Hovebibliotek,** Krystalgade 15 (🕻 **33-73-60-60;** bus: 5, 14, or 16), open Monday to Friday 10am to 7pm, Saturday 10am to 2pm. Cost is 25DKK to 30DKK ($4.25–$5.10/£2.25–£2.70)

Lost Property The Lost and Found Property office at Slotsherrensvej 113, 2720 Vanløse (🕻 **38-74-88-22;** bus: 12 or 22), is open Monday, Wednesday, and Friday 9am to 2pm, Tuesday and Thursday 9am to 5:30pm.

Luggage Storage & Lockers Luggage can be stored in lockers at Central Railroad Station. Lockers are available Monday to Saturday 5:30am to 1am and Sunday 6am to 1am. The cost is between 25DKK ($4.25/£2.25) and 35DKK ($5.95/£3.15) for 24 hours, depending on the size of your luggage

Newspapers Foreign newspapers, particularly the *International Herald Tribune* and *USA Today,* are available at the Central Railroad Station in front of the Palladium movie theater on Vesterbrogade, at many newspaper kiosks on Strøget, and at the newsstands of big hotels. Foreign fashion and lifestyle magazines are also widely sold.

Pharmacies An *apotek* (pharmacy) open 24 hours a day is **Steno Apotek,** Vesterbrogade 6C (🕻 **33-14-82-66;** bus: 6), lying opposite the central rail station.

Police In an emergency, dial 🕻 **112.** For other matters, go to the police station at Halmtorvet 20 (🕻 **33-25-14-48**).

Post Office For information about the Copenhagen post office, phone 🕻 **80-20-70-30.** The main post office, where your *poste restante* (general delivery) letters can be picked up, is located at Tietgensgade 37, DK-1704 Copenhagen (🕻 **80-20-70-30;** bus: 10 or 46). It's open Monday to Friday 11am to 6pm and Saturday 10am to 1pm. The post office at the Central Railroad Station is open Monday to Friday 8am to 9pm, Saturday 9am to 4pm, and Sunday 10am to 4pm.

Restrooms Public toilets are at Rådhuspladsen (Town Hall Square), the Central Railroad Station, and at all terminals. Look for the signs TOILETTER, WC, DAMER (women), or HERRER (men). There is no charge.

Safety Compared with other European capital cities, Copenhagen is relatively safe. However, since the early 1990s, with the increase of homelessness and unemployment, crime has risen. Guard your wallet, purse, and other valuables as you would when traveling in any big city.

Taxes Throughout Denmark you'll come across MOMS on your bills, a government-imposed value-added tax of 25%. It's included in hotel and restaurant bills, service charges, entrance fees, and repair of foreign-registered cars. No refunds are given on these items.

Transit Information Day or night, phone © **70-13-14-15** for bus, Metro, and S-tog information.

3 Where to Stay

High season in Denmark is May to September, which pretty much coincides with the schedule at Tivoli Gardens. Once Tivoli closes for the winter, lots of rooms become available. Make sure to ask about winter discounts and if breakfast is included (usually it isn't).

Nearly all doubles come with a private bathroom. Find out, though, whether this means a shower or a tub. At moderate and inexpensive hotels, you can save money by requesting a room without a bathroom. Keep in mind that in most moderate and nearly all of the inexpensive hotels, bathrooms are cramped, and there's never enough room to spread out all of your stuff. Many were added to older buildings that weren't designed for bathrooms. Also, towels are much thinner than you might like, so packing one from home might not be a bad idea.

Several moderately priced hotels in Copenhagen are known as **mission hotels;** they were originally founded by a temperance society, but now about half of them are fully licensed to serve alcohol. They tend to cater to middle-class families.

RESERVATIONS SERVICE At Bernstorffsgade 1, across from the Tivoli's main entrance, the Tourist Information Center maintains a useful hotel-booking service, **Værelsænvisningen** (© **70-22-24-42**). In person, the charge, whether you book into a private home, hostel, or luxury hotel, is 100DKK ($17/£9) per person. This fee is waived when booking by telephone or Internet. You'll also be given a city map and bus directions. This particular office doesn't accept advance reservations; it can arrange private accommodations if the hotels in your price range are already full. The office is open April 19 to September 30, daily 9am to 9pm, and October to April 18, Monday to Friday 9am to 5pm and Saturday 9am to 2pm. In the same building is the **Hotel Booking Service** (© **70-22-24-42**), which will reserve hotel rooms in advance.

NYHAVN & KONGENS NYTORV
VERY EXPENSIVE

Hotel d'Angleterre ✹✹✹ *Kids*   If hotels were crowned like the queen of Denmark, the coronation would surely place the gem-studded crown on this bastion of elegance, deluxe comfort, and sophistication. "Don't even consider any other choice—they're all dumps," Marlene Dietrich, appearing at the Tivoli Gardens, once wrote. The world of politicians, rock stars, and even crowned heads must have taken the advice of the Blue Angel. Although they weren't exactly seen strolling through the lobby arm in arm, both the Baroness Margaret Thatcher and Madonna have also checked in. A recent guest was Michael Jackson who, when the staff refused to sell him a suit of armor from the public rooms, threatened to buy the entire hotel.

Where to Stay in Copenhagen

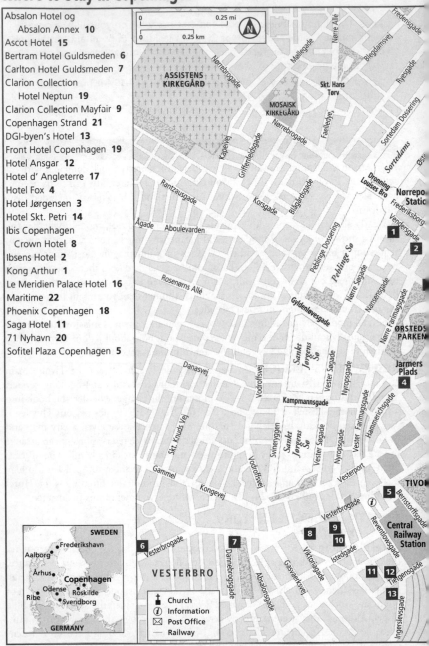

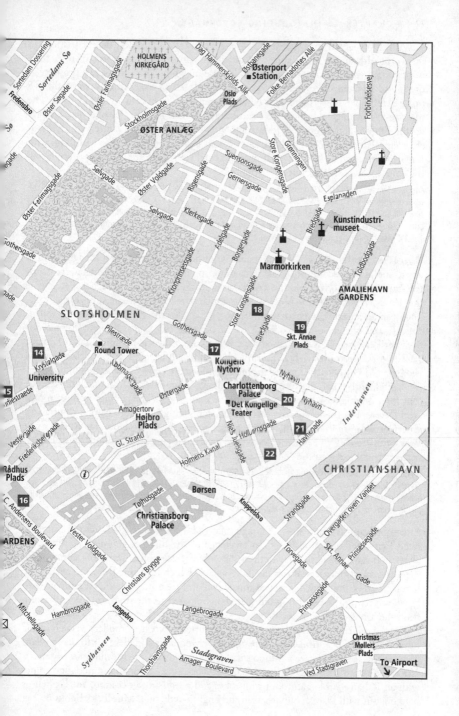

With 250 years of history, the d'Angleterre is one of the oldest deluxe bastions in the world, although it's kept abreast of the times with modern comforts. Its royal suite is, of course, fit for a king (or queen as the case may be). The seven-story property at the top of Nyhavn is a member of the Leading Hotels of the World. It was built as a private club for English merchants before its transformation into a hotel in 1805. The midsize-to-spacious bedrooms are beautifully furnished in a medley of styles. We prefer the Empire and Louis XVI rooms, though you may opt for a conservatively modern room. Each high-ceilinged bedroom comes with a private marble bathroom with robes, phone, and a tub/shower combo. The deluxe rooms are in front; those facing the courtyard are smaller but more tranquil.

Kongens Nytorv 34, DK-1050 Copenhagen. ⓒ 800/44-UTELL in the U.S., or 33-12-00-95. Fax 33-12-11-18. www.remmen.dk. 123 units. 2,450DKK–2,950DKK ($417–$502/£221–£266) double; from 5,000DKK ($850/£450) suite. AE, DC, MC, V. Parking 175DKK ($30/£16). Bus: 1, 6, or 9. **Amenities:** Restaurant; bar; indoor heated pool; fitness center; spa; sauna; 24-hr. room service; babysitting; laundry service/dry cleaning; nonsmoking rooms. In room: A/C, TV, dataport, minibar, hair dryer, safe, Wi-Fi.

Hotel Skt. Petri ℱℱℱ

If your name is Johnny Depp (traveling incognito) or if you're the playboy-columnist Taki Theodoracopulos, perhaps the d'Angleterre is just too staid for you, so you join the world's fashionistas and interior designers here. Since the 1930s, the site of this hotel was the much loved department store Dalle Valle. Today, in an amazing reincarnation, it's become one of the grandest hotels in Copenhagen—and our personal favorite. Modern Danish design, as interpreted by interior designer Per Arnoldi, is showcased here. Rooms are individually done in a minimalist yet elegant style, with bright, cheerful colors and such touches as Mondrian-inspired headboards. The beds are among the most comfortable we've encountered in the Danish capital, with down mattress pads, soft pillows, Angora blankets, and comfy duvets. Opt for a double with terrace on the fifth or sixth floors. The ceilings in most rooms are a bit low, but the lobby rises three floors, embracing an atrium garden. Musicians, artists, and designers are among those we've seen in the fashionable **Bar Rouge** or in **Brasserie Bleu.** If you don't believe us when we tell you how fabulous this place is, perhaps you'll listen to the "talking elevator."

Krystalgade 22, DK-1172 Copenhagen. ⓒ 33-45-91-00. Fax 33-45-91-10. 268 units. 998DKK–2,695DKK ($170–$458/£90–£243) double; from 3,395DKK ($577/£306) suite. AE, DC, MC, V. Parking 195DKK ($35/£18). S-tog: Nørreport. **Amenities:** Restaurant; bar; fitness room; 24-hr. room service; laundry service/dry cleaning; nonsmoking rooms; rooms for those with limited mobility. In room: A/C, TV, dataport, minibar, hair dryer, safe, Wi-Fi.

Phoenix Copenhagen ℱℱ

Though it falls a bit short of its goal, this government-rated four-star hotel poses a serious challenge to the discreet grandeur of the d'Angleterre. It saw the light of day in the 1680s when it was constructed to accommodate the aristocratic courtiers of Amalienborg Palace, which is visible from the rear of the hotel. In 1847 the guest house was torn down and rebuilt as a luxury Victorian-style hotel, attracting the English nobility. It was compared to the mythical phoenix rising from the ashes—hence, its name.

Tons of white and colored marble were imported to create a modern version of the Louis XVI style. Beautiful wool carpeting and chandeliers add glamour to the standard guest rooms, but many are a bit too small for our tastes. If you're willing to pay more, opt for one of the business-class rooms or perhaps a suite. Each accommodation comes with an Italian marble bathroom with robes and a tub/shower combo. You'll catch us hanging out with Danish publishers in the English-style pub, Murdock's Books & Ale, devouring beer and *smørrebrød* against a backdrop of mahogany and brass, later dining from an international menu in the Restaurant Von Plessen, named to honor the original owner of the hotel.

Bredgade 37, DK-1260 Copenhagen. (C) **33-95-95-00.** Fax 33-33-98-33. www.phoenixcopenhagen.com. 213 units. 1,850DKK–2,890DKK ($315–$491/£167–£260) double; 2,190DKK–3,600DKK ($372–$612/£197–£324) suite. AE, DC, MC, V. Parking 113DKK ($19/£10). Bus: 1, 6, 9, or 10. **Amenities:** Restaurant; bar; car rental; 24-hr. room service; babysitting; laundry service/dry cleaning; nonsmoking rooms. *In room:* A/C, TV, dataport, minibar, hair dryer, iron, safe, trouser press (in some), Wi-Fi.

EXPENSIVE

Clarion Collection Hotel Neptun *☆*   The dream of this place never quite came true. Founded in 1854, the hotel was meant to be the gathering place for the bohemian and literati set. These days, commercial clients, a scattering of tourists, and even tour groups dominate the client list, but the main lounge still evokes an upper-crust living room in an English country house, with its traditional furnishings and even a chess table.

Many of the bedrooms open onto two covered interior courtyards, adding a little glamour to the joint. Ask for one of the bedrooms that open onto a courtyard, as they are the brightest during the day and the most tranquil in the evening. Bedrooms are tastefully furnished in a modern style, and most of them are either small or midsize. The tiled bathrooms, though modest in size, are well equipped and maintained, each with a tub-shower combo. Another feature of the hotel is an outdoor terrace on the sixth floor, where you can order drinks in the summer. Some bright young chefs operate the hotel's restaurant, The Gendarmen, next door, which offers a seasonally adjusted menu that respects traditional Danish recipes but prepares many of them with a lighter touch.

Skt. Annæ Plads 18–20, DK-1250 Copenhagen. (C) **800/654-6200** in the U.S., or 33-96-20-00. Fax 33-96-20-66. www.choicehotels.dk. 133 units. 1,290DKK–1,925DKK ($219–$327/£116–£173) double; 2,095DKK–2,595DKK ($356–$441/£189–£234) suite. Breakfast 125DKK ($23/£11). AE, DC, MC, V. Parking 125DKK ($23/£11) per night. Bus: 1, 6, 9, or 19. **Amenities:** Restaurant; bar; room service (noon–9pm); babysitting; laundry service/dry cleaning; nonsmoking rooms. *In room:* A/C, TV, dataport (in some), minibar, hair dryer, safe.

Front Hotel Copenhagen *☆*   From the outside, this boxy-looking building might remind you of the rash of angular modern construction that blossomed throughout central Europe during the Cold War. On the inside, however, it's one of the hottest and most appealing recently opened hotels in town. It originated in 1964 as a hotel. After several different configurations, most recently a radical upgrade in 2005, it now enjoys a link with the nearby Hotel d'Angleterre, one of the most elegant and most expensive in town, and a location close to the very central Nyhavn Canal. Throughout, the decor is minimalist and somewhat self-consciously linked to the Spartan-looking heyday of Denmark's modern design movement. In fact, it's so minimalist that some parts of it, including the lobby area, might remind you of a college dormitory, except for the snazzily uniformed and endearingly cheerful staff. Bedrooms benefit from very large windows, high-quality Danish modern furniture, lots of sunlight, and panoramic views, and are accessible via the hotel's only really visible drawback—small, awkwardly configured elevators that are simply too cramped for the amount of use they get. Bedrooms contain furniture, some of it upholstered with black leather, that evokes the best in postmillennium design.

Skt. Annæ Plads 21, P.O. Box 9076, DK-1022 Copenhagen K. (C) **33-13-34-00.** Fax 33-11-77-07. 31 units. 1,590DKK–2,790DKK ($284–$498/£143–£251) double. AE, DC, MC, V. Metro: Kongens Nytorv. **Amenities:** Restaurant; bar; health club and exercise area; laundry/dry cleaning. *In room:* A/C, TV, minibar, Wi-Fi.

71 Nyhavn 𝒞𝒞   Few people dream of sleeping in a warehouse until they check in here. Back in 1804 this building, on the corner between the harbor and Nyhavn Canal, housed everything from bales of cotton from America to live chickens from the Danish countryside. Today the massively restored red-brick structure, converted into a hotel in 1971, is one of the most successful examples of recycling in the Danish capital. The smell of spices from the Far East has long faded, but the architects wisely kept the Pomeranian fir beams for atmosphere. That the building is standing at all today is something of a miracle because an 1807 British bombardment destroyed most of the surrounding structures.

We like to wake up in the morning here, pulling back the draperies for a view of the old ships anchored at Nyhavn. If there's a downside, it's the smallness of most of the bedrooms, though each comes with a tiled bathroom with a tub/shower combo. "Don't say that our rooms are tiny," the assistant manager told us. "We prefer the word *cozy*." And they are, with crisscrossing timbers, soft leather furniture, and dark wood accents. Gastronomic evenings are a daily event in the on-site Pakhuskælderen, where the menu is seasonally adjusted.

Nyhavn 71, DK-1051 Copenhagen. 𝒞 **33-43-62-00**. Fax 33-43-62-01. www.71nyhavnhotel.com. 150 units. Mon–Thurs 1,885DKK–2,500DKK ($336–$445/£170–£225) double, 3,135DKK–5,235DKK ($559–$934) suite; Fri–Sun 1,430DKK–1,840DKK ($255–$328/£129–£166) double, 3,900DKK–5,200DKK ($696–$928/£351–£468) suite. Rates include breakfast (weekends only). AE, DC, MC, V. Free parking. S-tog: Kongens Nytorv. **Amenities:** Restaurant; bar; car rental; room service (7am–10:30pm); babysitting; laundry service/dry cleaning; nonsmoking rooms. *In room:* A/C, TV, dataport, minibar, hair dryer, trouser press, iron, safe, Wi-Fi.

MODERATE

Copenhagen Strand 𝒞 (Value)   This hotel is rated only three stars by the government, but, frankly, we think that only its lack of a restaurant keeps it from four-star status. In 2002, two 18th-century brick-and-timber warehouses were recycled into a hotel at a site only a 5-minute walk from Nyhavn. Because of its harborfront location, the snug lobby has a maritime theme with pictures of ships on the walls and chic brown leather sofas. Many of the old-fashioned architectural details of the building have been retained, and there is a certain nautical gloss here, with varnished wood, brass hardware, and marine artifacts. We like to drop in at the bar in the lobby, where the reception staff works double time mixing drinks and pulling pints.

The medium-size rooms are cozy but predictably less richly decorated than the lobby. For the most part, they are small, cozy, and both tastefully and comfortably furnished in Danish modern. Each unit comes with a sparkling bathroom with tub-shower combo. The best accommodations, if you can afford them, are 16 double executive rooms, plus junior suites and deluxe suites, each of which opens onto a panoramic view of the harbor.

Havnegade 37, DK-1058 Copenhagen K. 𝒞 **33-48-99-00**. Fax 33-48-99-01. www.copenhagenstrand.dk. 174 units. Mon–Thurs 1,670DKK–2,360DKK ($298–$421/£150–£212) double, 2,875DKK–3,290DKK ($513–$587/£259–£296) suite; Fri–Sun 1,330DKK–1,875DKK ($237–$334/£120–£169) double, 2,085DKK–3,115DKK ($372–$556/£188–£280) suite. Rates include buffet breakfast. AE, DC, MC, V. Parking 210DKK ($37/£19). Tram: 1 or 6. **Amenities:** Breakfast room; bar; car rental; business center; 24-hr. room service; babysitting; laundry service/dry cleaning; nonsmoking rooms. *In room:* TV, dataport (in most units), minibar, hair dryer, trouser press, iron, Wi-Fi.

INEXPENSIVE

Maritime   This hotel on a tranquil street near the waterfront has some expensive neighbors, such as the d'Angleterre, but it keeps its prices more affordable. For its location near Nyhavn Canal, it's a recommendable choice. We used to be put off by the staff's rigid attitude, although on our last visit we found them far more helpful and cooperative. The hotel has benefited from some refurbishing and updating, while keeping to its maritime theme. Even though the building itself is a century old—maybe older—all the well-furnished, midsize bedrooms are up to date and comfortably and tastefully furnished. Each unit comes with a well-kept private bathroom with a shower. Even if you want a sandwich and a drink at 4 o'clock in the morning, one is available 24 hours a day in the lobby.

Peder Skrams Gade 19, DK-1054 Copenhagen. (© 33-13-48-82. Fax 33-15-03-45. www.hotel-maritime.dk. 64 units. 925DKK–1,700DKK ($164–$303/£83–£153) double; 1,350DKK–2,200DKK ($241–$392/£122–£198) triple. Rates include breakfast. AE, DC, DISC, MC, V. Bus: 1, 6, or 9. **Amenities:** Restaurant; bar; lounge; laundry service/dry cleaning; non-smoking rooms. *In room:* TV, dataport, hair dryer.

NEAR RÅDHUSPLADSEN (TOWN HALL)
VERY EXPENSIVE

Le Meridien Palace Hotel 🏵🏵   Opened in 1910 and declared a historic landmark in 1985, the Palace Hotel has been a respite for countless camera-shy celebrities. Although the hotel has tried to keep abreast of the times, it's no longer the front-runner it once was. That will change, however, during the lifetime of this edition, thanks to an ongoing renovation that will soon bring the hotel from government-rated, four-star to five-star status. The transformation of the accommodations had already begun in the fall of 2006, with the opening of "The Night Wing," with all new interiors, carpets, draperies, and plumbing. The decor in this wing is individually designed and, as its name suggests, inspired by the "mystical hues of night." The other contemporary-looking rooms are attractively furnished in an updated version of the Danish modern style — elegant, simple, and comfortable. Most bathrooms are cramped, but they do have tub/shower combos. The best rooms are on the top floor, away from street noises. If you're assigned a room on floors 2 and 3, you are still in luck—they have high ceilings and tasteful furnishings and appointments. Notice the soaring tower associated with this hotel—it rivals that of Town Hall, which lies almost immediately next door. The reception staff is especially helpful in arranging theater tickets, tours, and transportation. Be careful not to confuse this hotel, by the way, with the Sofitel Plaza, which is a radically different entity somewhat closer to the railway station. It's an easy error to make, and one with which the desk staff is all too familiar.

Rådhuspladsen 57, DK-1550 Copenhagen. (© 800/448-8355 in the U.S., or 33-14-40-50. Fax 33-14-52-79. www. palace-hotel.dk. 162 units. 2,150DKK ($384/£194) double; 3,300DKK ($589/£297) suite. 20% discount may be available on weekends and in midwinter, depending on occupancy. AE, DC, MC, V. Parking 250DKK ($45/£23). Bus: 2, 30, 32, 33, 34, or 35. **Amenities:** Restaurant; bar; 24-hr. room service; massage; babysitting; laundry service/dry cleaning; nonsmoking rooms. *In room:* TV, minibar, hair dryer, safe, trouser press.

EXPENSIVE

Bertram Hotel Guldsmeden 🏵   This is the newer and more elegant twin of the also-recommended Carlton Hotel Guldsmeden. Both lie within about 270m (900 ft.) of one another, on a wide and busy boulevard that runs into the rear of Copenhagen's Central Railway station, within about 10-minute walk. Rising six stories, the hotel originated in 2006, after a 19th-century townhouse was radically restored, with special emphasis on the landscaping within the building's central courtyard. Rooms overlook either the courtyard, the noisy Vesterbrogade, or the quieter neighborhood in back. Furniture in the bedrooms was imported from Indonesia and includes four-poster beds and the heavy, artfully simple lines in natural wood that go well with the concepts of Danish modern design and the bright pastel colors in which the rooms are painted. We are especially delighted with the organic breakfast buffet, with excellent grainy breads, homemade yogurt, charcuterie, and French cheese—all served on hand-decorated Mexican crockery. Staff is friendly and accommodating, and overall, the hotel is viewed as a well-chosen, well-conceived middle-bracket choice within a rapidly gentrifying neighborhood loaded with bars, cafes, and increasingly distant memories of the porno shops and sex-industry staples that used to flourish here.

Vesterbrogade 107, 1620 Copenhagen V. (C) **33-25-04-05.** Fax 33 25 04 02. www.hotelguldsmeden.dk. 47 units. 1,497DKK ($267/£135) double; 1,695DKK ($302/£153) suite. Rates include breakfast buffet. AE, DC, MC, V. Parking 75DKK ($13/£6.75) per night. Bus: 6A. **Amenities:** Restaurant; bar; limited room service; babysitting; laundry service/dry cleaning; nonsmoking rooms. *In room:* TV, minibar, hair dryer, safe, Wi-Fi.

Sofitel Plaza Copenhagen 🏵🏵   The likes of Keith Richards and Tina Turner have checked in here, and though the hotel is still going strong, it's actually past its heyday. Commissioned by King Frederik VIII in 1913, it once hosted its share of big-name celebrities to Copenhagen, even royalty. Today queens and kings stay elsewhere, although rock stars find it suits them just fine, especially its location opposite the Tivoli Gardens and near the Central Railway Station.

Still imbued with a turn-of-the-20th-century atmosphere, it has been successfully overhauled for first-class comfort without losing its ambience. As befits the age and era of this hotel, guest rooms come in various sizes and configurations, many evoking an English country house. Antiques, double-glazed windows, and views of the cityscape make this a winning choice. For a kind of Paris garret atmosphere, book one of the top floor rooms with dormered windows, among the coziest in Copenhagen, especially if you're a romantic duo on an off-the-record weekend. Bathrooms are generous in size, completely tiled, and contain tub/shower combos and makeup mirrors. The hotel's Library Bar is our favorite place for a drink in town.

Bernstorffsgade 4, DK-1577 Copenhagen. (C) **800/221-4542** in the U.S., or 33-14-92-62. Fax 33-93-93-62. www.accorhotel.dk. 93 units. 2,150DKK ($365/£195) double; 6,695DKK ($1194/£603) suite. 1 child stays free in parent's room. AE, DC, MC, V. Parking 165DKK ($29/£15). Bus: 1 or 6. **Amenities:** Restaurant; bar; fitness center; car rental; 24-hr. room service; babysitting; laundry service/dry cleaning; nonsmoking rooms. *In room:* A/C, TV, dataport, minibar, hair dryer, safe.

MODERATE

Ascot Hotel 🏵 *Value*   The word ascot, because of its British associations, usually suggests elegance—but not so here. This is one of the best small hotels in Copenhagen, despite the perception that it's in need of a partial renovation and sprucing up. On a side street about a 2-minute walk from Town Hall Square, the inn of personality and charm was built in 1902 (on 492 wooden pilings rescued from a medieval fortification that had previously stood on the site). In 1994, the hotel annexed an adjacent building designed in the 19th century as a bathhouse; its black-marble columns and interior bas-reliefs are historically notable. Martin Nyrop, who designed the landmark Town Hall, also was the architect for the bath house. The furniture is rather standard, and the finest units open onto the street. Nevertheless, the units in the rear get better air circulation and more light. The tiled bathrooms are generous in size and equipped with tub/shower combos.

Studiestræde 61, DK-1554 Copenhagen. (C) **33-12-60-00.** Fax 33-14-60-40. www.ascothotel.dk. 120 units. 1,090DKK–1,480DKK ($194–$265/£98–£133) double; 1,695DKK–2,560DKK ($302–$456/£153–£230) suite. Rates include buffet breakfast. Winter discounts available. AE, DC, MC, V. Parking 85DKK ($14/£7.65). Bus: 14 or 16.

Amenities: Restaurant; bar; fitness center; room service (7am–11pm); laundry service/dry cleaning; nonsmoking rooms. *In room:* TV, dataport, hair dryer.

Carlton Hotel Guldsmeden ✿ (Finds   Housed in a much-renovated 19th century townhouse in the heart of the rapidly gentrifying Vesterbro neighborhood, within a 15-minute walk west from Tivoli and the Central Railway Station, this is a government-rated three-star hotel offering good value and occasional doses of genuine charm. The structure might be old, but the bedrooms are contemporary-looking and up-to-date, ranging from small to midsize. Each is handsomely decorated in a vaguely French colonial style with high ceilings, wood paneling, and four-poster beds imported from Indonesia. The best rooms contain such luxuries as fireplaces, balconies with summer furniture, and claw-footed bathtubs instead of showers. The place is made more homelike and inviting by the original art decorating the walls and a judicious use of elegant teak furnishings, along with carpets from Pakistan and pottery from Mexico. Its newer sister hotel, Bertram's Hotel Guldsmeden, is more charming and a bit more plush, and unlike the Carlton, it contains its own restaurant.

Vesterbrogade 66, DK-1620 Copenhagen. ✆ 33-22-15-00. Fax 33-22-15-55. www.hotelguldsmeden.dk. 64 units. 1,375DKK ($245/£124) double; 1,695DKK ($302/£153) junior suite. Rates include buffet breakfast. AE, DC, MC, V. Bus: 6A. Parking 75DKK ($13/£6.75). **Amenities:** Breakfast room; bar; limited room service; laundry service; bike rental; nonsmoking rooms. *In room:* TV, dataport, minibar, hair dryer, safe, Wi-Fi.

DGI-byen's Hotel ✿ (Finds   There's no hotel like this one in all of Copenhagen. Right behind the Central Station and convenient to most public transportation, this government-rated three-star hotel attracts sports lovers to its precincts, which contain a bowling alley, gigantic swim center, spa, "climbing wall," shooting range, and, oh yes, a hotel. (The "DGI" within its name translates as "Danish Gymnastics Association.") This is a dynamic, flexible so-called multicenter attracting schoolchildren, sports clubs, company executives, and regular visitors. Bedrooms, midsize to large, reflect the presuppositions and tenets of Danish modern design. Interiors are simple yet tasteful and comfortable with dark wood furnishings and blond-wood floors. Swimming is free to hotel guests within the public indoor pool, located a short distance from the hotel, but access to the spa costs extra. The on-site restaurant, serving good and reasonably priced food, was created from an old cattle market that stood here in 1870.

Tietgensgade 65, DK-1704 Copenhagen. ✆ 33-29-80-70. Fax 33-29-80-59. www.dgi-byen.dk. 104 units. 925DKK–1,595DKK ($165–$284/£84–£144) double. AE, DC, MC, V. Parking 130DKK ($23/£12). **Amenities:** Restaurant; bar; lounge; 5 indoor heated pools; sports center; spa; Jacuzzi; sauna; babysitting; laundry service/dry cleaning; nonsmoking rooms; rooms for those with limited mobility; solarium. *In room:* TV, hair dryer, dataport.

Kong Arthur ✿ (Kids (Value   Most guests checking in here think this hotel was named after England's legendary King Arthur. Actually, the Arthur in its name comes from Arthur Frommer, one of the early owners of this hotel and the founding father of the Frommer's guides. Right by the Copenhagen lakes and close to Rosenborg Palace, Kong Arthur is a government-rated four-star hotel just a 15-minute walk from the Tivoli Gardens. Charm, high-quality comfort, and a welcoming atmosphere greet you today, but back in 1882, things were a bit more rawboned here. The building was once a home for Danish orphans leading a Dickens-like existence. We like to go down to breakfast since it's served in a large greenhouselike room that's flooded with light on sunny days. Bedrooms range from midsize to spacious, and each is tastefully and comfortably furnished with carpets and large, tiled bathrooms with tub/shower combos.

Nørre Søgade 11, DK-1370 Copenhagen. ℂ **33-11-12-12.** Fax 33-32-61-30. www.kongarthur.dk. 117 units. 1,520DKK–1,720DKK ($271–$307/£137–£155) double; from 3,020DKK ($539/£272) suite. Rates include buffet breakfast. AE, DC, MC, V. Free parking. Bus: 5, 7, or 16. **Amenities:** 4 restaurants; bar; sauna; car rental; 24-hr. room service; massage; babysitting; laundry service/dry cleaning; nonsmoking rooms. *In room:* TV, dataport, minibar, hair dryer, safe, trouser press.

INEXPENSIVE

Hotel Fox 🐾 *Finds*   In 2005, one of Copenhagen's most unusual and trend-conscious hotels opened within the premises of what until then been a staid and predictable staple (the Park Hotel) on the Copenhagen hotel scene. The new owners solicited the talents of 21 separate designers from throughout Europe, each of whom submitted plans for new interior decors that reflected their individual whims and priorities. The result is a small-scale hotel that really appreciates the concept of "design" and that, in the opinion of some detractors, has carried it to levels that are almost overwhelming. Its white-painted facade carries renditions of street graffiti that might be almost too artful or too "carefully rehearsed." Each room is a highly idiosyncratic work of art, ranging from tongue-in-cheek enclaves of camp to rigorously streamlined case studies for postindustrial minimalism. Unless you've already requested a particular theme in advance, a computer at the reception desk will show you the visuals of where you're about to sleep. Choices, among many others, include a room dominated by a boxing theme, a unit filled with taurine (bull-inspired) souvenirs, an accommodation with syrupy reminders of Heidi, and one devoted to an all-American theme featuring extrawide beds for fullbacks and their Brünhildes. On site, the Fox Kitchen and Bar is self-consciously trendy.

Jarmers Plads 3, DK-1551 Copenhagen. ℂ **33-13-30-00.** Fax 33-14-30-33. www.hotelfox.dk. 61 units. Doubles 920DKK–1,620DKK ($164–$289/£83–£146). Rates include breakfast. AE, DC, MC, V. Parking 150DKK ($27/£14) nearby, 12DKK ($2.15/£1.10) per hour on street. Bus: 14 or 16. **Amenities:** Restaurant; bar; laundry service/dry cleaning. *In room:* TV, hair dryer, safe.

Ibis Copenhagen Crown Hotel *Value*   When you see the name Ibis at some 650 hotels on the Continent or in Scandinavia, you'll know that the price is right. In business for more than a century, this welcoming hotel is only a short walk from the Tivoli Gardens and the main train station. You enter through a tranquil, beautiful courtyard, evoking a Copenhagen of long ago. The traffic-clogged Vesterbrogade is a short distance away, but once you enter, you feel that this is a well-maintained, safe, and quiet haven. The midsize bedrooms are classically and tastefully decorated, some of them opening onto Vesterbrogade, the rest onto the courtyard. Each accommodation comes with a full bathroom with tub/shower combo. The most attractive feature of this hotel is its rooftop restaurant, where a varied Scandinavian breakfast buffet is served overlooking the rooftops of the city.

Vesterbrogade 41, DK-1620 Copenhagen. ℂ **33-21-21-66.** Fax 33-21-00-66. www.accorhotels.com. 80 units. 625DKK–850DKK ($111–$152/£56–£77) double. Rates include breakfast. AE, DC, MC, V. Bus: 6. **Amenities:** Restaurant; bar; laundry service/dry cleaning; nonsmoking rooms. *In room:* TV, dataport, minibar, hair dryer.

INDRE BY
MODERATE

Clarion Collection Mayfair 🐾   The Clarion Collection people, a hotel chain known for creating havens of charm and comfort, have moved in on the long-established Mayfair 2 blocks west of the Central Station to give it a new lease on life. Rated three stars by the government, the hotel isn't as well known as it should be, but has enjoyed

Family-Friendly Hotels

Hotel Ansgar (p. 80) This hotel rents out a dozen large rooms spacious enough to house up to six overnight guests, which makes the Ansgar ideal for families traveling with children.

Hotel d'Angleterre (p. 69) This elegant hotel contains a swimming pool and in-house video; both help keep children entertained.

Ibsens Hotel (p. 80) This hotel caters to families on a budget, since many of its triple rooms are large enough to house mom, dad, and one or two kids. There are no other special features for kids, however.

Kong Arthur (p. 77) Once a home for Danish orphans, this is a safe haven in a residential section near tree-lined Peblinge Lake.

refurbishing and redecorating, making it a choice address in Copenhagen. In some of its furnishings and decor, it evokes a well-heeled private home in England. Bedrooms come in a wide range of sizes, but each is tastefully furnished and comfortable, with full marble bathrooms with tub/shower combos. The best accommodations here have small sitting areas, so you don't feel you're living in a "box." The district around the hotel is becoming increasingly trendy, with the opening of new shops, cocktail lounges, and restaurants.

Helgolandsgade 3, DK 1653 Copenhagen V. ☎ 077/424-6423 in the U.S., or 70-12-17-00. Fax 33-23-96-86. www.choicehotels.com. 105 units. 1,095DKK ($186/£99) double; from 2,330DKK ($396/£210) suite. AE, DC, MC, V. Bus: 6, 16, 28, 29, or 41. **Amenities:** Breakfast room; bar; lounge; bicycle rental; babysitting; laundry service/dry cleaning; nonsmoking rooms. *In room:* TV, fax, dataport, minibar, hair dryer, iron, safe, trouser press.

INEXPENSIVE

Absalon Hotel og Absalon Annex ⋆ *Value* In the increasingly gentrified Vesterbro area, the Absalon traces its origins to a love story that unfolded at the nearby railroad station. Shortly after the yet-to-be father of the present owners began his first job as a porter at a neighboring hotel, he was asked to go to the station to pick up a new babysitter who had just arrived from Jutland. They fell in love, married, and bought the first of the buildings that became the hotel. Two of their children were born in room no. 108. This family-run lodging, one of the best-managed hotels in the neighborhood, consists of four townhouses that were joined into one building and became a hotel in 1938. It has a spacious blue-and-white breakfast room and an attentive staff directed by third-generation owners. The first generation was on hand to welcome first-time tourists carrying a dog-eared book called *Europe on $5 a Day.* The guest rooms are simple and modern, and come in various sizes ranging from cramped to spacious. We find that those on the fifth floor have the most character. These rooms get the most light and are elegantly furnished in a modified Louis XIV or classical English style, with marble bathrooms with tubs. Overflow guests are housed in one of the rather functional rooms in the Absalon Annex. Bathrooms are equipped with tub/shower combos. For years we have been impressed with the thoughtful extras provided by this hotel—for example, they set aside a luggage room where they will store your bags for free if you'd like to travel lighter into the Danish countryside.

Helgolandsgade 15, DK-1653 Copenhagen. ℂ **33-24-22-11.** Fax 33-24-34-11. www.absalon-hotel.dk. 262 units. 900DKK–1,150DKK ($153–$196/£81–£104) double; 1,100DKK–1,300DKK ($187–$221/£99–£117) triple; 1,260DKK–1,810DKK ($214–$308/£113–£163) suite. Rates include buffet breakfast. AE, DC, MC, V. Bus: 6, 10, 16, 27, or 28. **Amenities:** Breakfast room; lounge; laundry service/dry cleaning; nonsmoking rooms. *In room:* TV, dataport (in some), hair dryer (in some), trouser press.

Hotel Ansgar *Kids*   Just when we were about to drop this tired old workhorse from the guide, it burst into bloom again, with renovated and modernized bedrooms. Decorating magazines may not be too impressed, but you get tasteful rooms that are comfortably plain in Danish modern. No clutter here. Although its prices have risen, the hotel is still good value and has been ever since it opened in 1885 in a five-story structure. Think of the rooms as cozy instead of small—it's better that way. Two dozen large rooms can accommodate up to six (that's a bit crowded) and are suitable for families. The bedrooms contain well-kept bathrooms with Danish modern shower units (no great compliment). Guests arriving at Kastrup Airport can take the SAS bus to the Air Terminal at the Central Railroad Station, walk through the station, and be inside the hotel in less than 4 minutes.

Colbjørnsensgade 29, DK-1652 Copenhagen. ℂ **33-21-21-96.** Fax 33-21-61-91. www.ansgar-hotel.dk. 81 units. 850DKK–1,250DKK ($145–$213/£77–£113) double. Rates include buffet breakfast. Extra bed 200DKK ($34/£18). AE, DC, MC, V. Bus: 6, 10, 28, or 41. **Amenities:** Breakfast room; lounge; room service (7am–10pm); laundry service/dry cleaning; nonsmoking rooms. *In room:* TV.

Saga Hotel   In 1947, two developers purchased two late-19th-century apartment buildings that had survived the Nazi occupation and set out to gut them and turn them into hotel rooms. One of the owners told the press at the time, "We predicted that many tourists would return to Denmark after the war years and many of them would need a clean, respectable, but affordable place to stay." Those long-ago words still ring true today. As trendy boutique hotels rise up almost yearly, the Saga is rather like it was when it was created, although it has kept up with the times with improvements such as Internet access. The five-story building still has no elevator and many of its rooms are still without private bathrooms. As such, it attracts groups of international visitors in summer and Danish student and convention groups in winter. The rooms are small to midsize, each furnished in a Danish modern style, and most equipped with a private bathroom with tub/shower combo. The hotel is especially attractive to families in that it offers some very spacious units with three, four, or even five beds. A generous Scandinavian buffet breakfast is another temptation, and the hotel will also allow you to use its storage facilities at no extra charge.

Colbjørnsensgade 18–20, DK-1652 Copenhagen. ℂ **33-24-49-44.** Fax 33-24-60-33. www.sagahotel.dk. 79 units, 31 with bathroom. 480DKK–750DKK ($82–$128/£43–£68) double without bathroom, 600DKK–950DKK ($102–$162/£54–£86) double with bathroom. Rates include breakfast. Extra bed 150DKK ($26/£14). Modest winter discounts. AE, DC, MC, V. Bus: 6, 10, 16, 28, or 41. **Amenities:** Breakfast room; lounge; nonsmoking rooms. *In room:* TV, Wi-Fi.

NEAR NØRREPORT STATION
MODERATE
Ibsens Hotel *Kids Finds*   The family owners, the Brøchner-Mortensen family, succeed in combining an old-fashioned nostalgia with all the modern amenities today's traveler demands. A charming, government-rated three-star hotel in the Nansensgade area, right by the lakes, the hotel is convenient for trips to both Rosenborg Palace and the Tivoli Gardens. In an area filled with cafes and trendy restaurants, the hotel first

opened its doors in 1906, surviving wars, occupation, and changing tastes, and somehow keeping abreast of it all. The guest rooms are comfortably and tastefully furnished, each well maintained and containing private bathrooms that are a bit cramped but have tub/shower combos. These cozy rooms open onto a beautiful courtyard. We like the way the hotel offers you a choice of decor on each floor. One floor, for example, showcases Danish modern, whereas another floor has more of a bohemian aura and is filled with antiques. "If you're a modernist and your tastes a minimalist, we have a bed awaiting you," said a member of the reception staff. "But if you're the more exuberant type—wildly romantic—we can also provide a nest for your poetic soul."

Vendersgade 23, DK-1363 Copenhagen. ✆ **33-13-19-13.** Fax 33-13-19-16. www.ibsenshotel.dk. 118 units. 1,220DKK–1,420DKK ($207–$241/£110–£128) double; 2,200DKK ($374/£198) suite. Rates include buffet breakfast. AE, DC, MC, V. Bus: 5, 14, or 16. **Amenities:** 2 restaurants; bar; car rental; babysitting; laundry service/dry cleaning; nonsmoking rooms. *In room:* TV, Wi-Fi.

INEXPENSIVE

Hotel Jørgensen   When this hotel first opened in 1984, it became Denmark's first gay hotel, and many of its guests thought (incorrectly) it'd been named in honor of a former American GI, George, who later, after a little surgery, became famous as the transgendered Christine Jorgensen, making headlines around the world with her sex change. In a stucco-fronted building that opened in 1906 as the headquarters of a publishing house, the hotel has changed over the decades. Located on a busy boulevard in central Copenhagen, it now caters to a conventional mix of clients of all sexual persuasions. Many of its guests are backpackers drawn to its cheap lodgings in dormitory rooms segregated by genders and holding between 6 and 12 beds. Although clients over age 35 are aggressively discouraged from renting any of the dormitory rooms, they're welcome within the conventional bedrooms. The hotel is reasonably well maintained, prices are more or less affordable, and the small rooms are conventional and well organized. Bathrooms, in those units that have them, are well kept and contain tub/shower combos.

Rømersgade 11, DK-1362 Copenhagen. ✆ **33-13-81-86.** Fax 33-15-51-05. 24 units; 13 dorm rooms (150 beds). 700DKK ($119/£63) double; 140DKK ($24/£13) per person in dorm. Rates include breakfast. MC, V. Parking 90DKK ($15/£8.10). Bus: 14 or 16. **Amenities:** Breakfast room; lounge. *In room:* TV.

4 Where to Dine

It's estimated that Copenhagen has more than 2,000 cafes, snack bars, and restaurants, and a higher number of Michelin-starred restaurants than any other city in Europe in 2006. Of those, 10 restaurants had at least one Michelin star, each within a rectangular area measuring 2km (1¼ mile) on each side. The most convenient restaurants are either in Tivoli Gardens or around Rådhuspladsen (Town Hall Square), around the Central Railroad Station, or in Nyhavn. Others are in the shopping district, on streets off of Strøget.

You pay for the privilege of dining in Tivoli; prices are always higher. Reservations are not usually important, but it's best to call in advance. Nearly everyone who answers the phone at restaurants speaks English.

TIVOLI GARDENS

Prices at the restaurants in the Tivoli are about 30% higher than elsewhere. To compensate, skip dessert and buy something less expensive (perhaps ice cream or pastry)

Where to Dine in Copenhagen

Atlas Bar/
  Restaurant Flyvefisken **6**
Axelborg Bodega **2**
Bøf & Ost **15**
Café Lumskebugten **26**
Café Sorgenfri **17**
Café Zeze **9**
Copenhagen Corner **20**
Domhus Kælderen **19**
Era Ora **22**
Godt **5**
Kommandanten **11**
Kong Hans Kælder **12**
Krogs Fiskerestaurant **13**
NOMA **23**
Nørrebro Bryghus **4**
Nyhavns Færgekro **24**
Pasta Basta **14**
Peder Oxe's Restaurant/
  Vinkælder Wine Bar **16**
Pierre André **10**
Pussy Galore's Flying Circus **1**
Restaurant Els **25**
St. Gertruds Kloster **7**
Søren K **21**
Sult **8**
Tivoli Gardens Restaurants **3**
  Café Ketchup
  Færgekroen
  La Crevette
  The Paul
TyvenKokkenHansKoneog-
  HendesElsker **18**

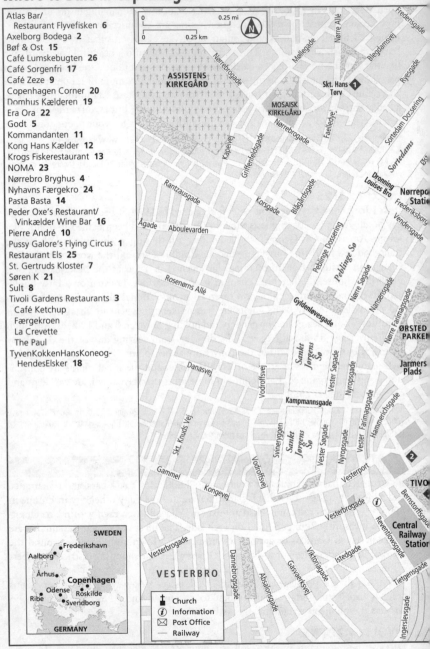

later at one of the many stands in the park. Take bus no. 1, 6, 8, 16, 29, 30, 32, or 33 to reach the park and any of the following restaurants.

Note: Most of these restaurants are open only from May to mid-September.

VERY EXPENSIVE

The Paul *ÆÆÆ* INTERNATIONAL   Winning a coveted Michelin star, the first for a restaurant in the Tivoli Gardens, this is one of the three or four most sought-after culinary landmarks in town. Enough Danish and European journalists have written about this place to have almost guaranteed its fame, one that's supplemented by its location within one of the most famous architectural experiments in Tivoli—the Glassalen—a greenhouse-style building once used as a concert hall and designed by Poul Henningsen as a statement of Danish pride immediately after World War II. The mastermind behind this sophisticated venue is British-born chef Paul Cunningham, whose stated desire is to provide Tivoli revelers "with an intense gourmet experience." The experience you'll have might strike you because of its originality and, according to some diners, its amused sense of eccentricity.

The staff might not even bring table settings to your table until they (or Paul himself) engages you in a dialogue about what the kitchen can offer on any given night—a selection that will invariably be spectacular. And if you chafe at the idea of spending too much time at any particular table, no one will mind if you ask for the third, or fifth course, for example, to be served at a table with, say, a different view. Come here for superb food, a sense of international and very hip whimsy, and a creative and upbeat sense of fun. When we last visited, we asked Paul to serve us what Bill Clinton had tasted on his visit. What arrived was hardly bubba food but a divine free-range chicken from the island of Bornholm served with a confit of veal sweetbreads. We also tasted a perfect butter-roasted Dover sole with corn, capers, and chanterelles. The rhubarb and vanilla terrine for dessert brought an enchantment to the already enchanted setting of the Tivoli.

Vesterbrogade 3. ⓒ **33-75-07-75.** Reservations recommended. Fixed-price menu with wine. 700DKK–800DKK ($119–$136/£63–£72). AE, DC, MC, V. Mon–Sat noon–2pm and 6–8pm. Closed Oct–Mar.

EXPENSIVE

La Crevette *Æ* SEAFOOD/DANISH   This restaurant has been around for so long that it's a cliché of Tivoli dining, but as the manager rightly protests, "You shouldn't ignore us just because we're not new and trendy like Paul. Our food is as good or better than it always was, and you don't have to rob a bank to dine with us—only a mere convenience store." This exclusive restaurant offers more varied seafood dishes than any of its Tivoli competitors. Housed in a 1909 pavilion, it has an outdoor terrace, modern dining room, and well-trained staff. The seafood is fresh, flavorful, and prepared in innovative ways—slices of pickled salmon come with oyster flan and egg cream with chives, and a bisque of turbot is served with veal bacon and quail's eggs. Meat and poultry courses are extremely skimpy on the menu, but you don't come here for that. Finish your repast with a selection of cheese from France, Denmark, and Italy (served with marinated prunes, a nice touch), or the fresh pastries of the day. The restaurant has its own confectionery.

Vesterbrogade 5, Tivoli. ⓒ **33-14-60-03.** Reservations recommended. Main courses 255DKK–315DKK ($43–$54/£23–£28); 4-course fixed-price dinner 455DKK ($77/£41). AE, DC, MC, V. Daily noon–midnight.

MODERATE

Færgekroen DANISH   If you like honest, straightforward fare, without a lot of trimmings, and don't like to spend a lot of money, this might be the place for you.

Nestled in a cluster of trees at the edge of the lake, this restaurant resembles a pink half-timbered Danish cottage. In warm weather, try to sit on the outside dining terrace. The menu offers drinks, snacks, and full meals. The latter might include an array of omelets, beef with horseradish, fried plaice with melted butter, pork chops with red cabbage, curried chicken, and fried meatballs. The food, prepared according to old recipes, is similar to what you might get down on a Danish farm. A pianist provides singalong music from Tuesday to Saturday starting at 8pm. The owners of this place recently invested in their own on-site microbrewery, which produces two kinds of beer, both of which taste wonderful.

Vesterbrogade 3, Tivoli. © **33-12-94-12.** Main courses 110DKK–205DKK ($19–$35/£9.90–£18). AE, DC, MC, V. Daily 11am–midnight (hot food until 9:45pm).

NYHAVN & KONGENS NYTORV
VERY EXPENSIVE

Era Ora ✶✶✶ ITALIAN   A Danish friend confided that whenever his wife discovers he'd been cheating on her, he always takes her for dinner here—"and all is forgiven." This reminder of Denmark's golden age *(Era Ora)* is on virtually everyone's list as the very best Italian restaurant in Denmark and is one of the best restaurants in Copenhagen. Established in 1982 by Tuscan-born partners Edelvita Santos and Elvio Milleri, it offers an antique-looking dining room, with additional seating for parties up to 12 in the wine cellar. You're likely to find some chic people dining here, including members of Denmark's royal family, lots of politicians, and well-known Danish writers and artists. The cuisine is based on Tuscan and Umbrian models, with sophisticated variations inspired by Denmark's superb array of fresh seafood and produce. Time plays a key role in the success of this restaurant, whose chefs believe that quality food takes dedication, so nothing is rushed—neither the food nor the guests. Traditional favorites include a platter of 10 types of antipasti, arguably the best version of these Italian hors d'oeuvres in the country. The menu offers a mouth-watering array of classics combined with more imaginative dishes created by the produce of the season and the inspiration of the highly skilled chefs. Dishes have subtle flavorings and "sing" in harmony when ingredients are mixed. The chefs continue to invent and reinvent flavor combinations with a wizardry that's nothing short of staggering.

Their homemade pastas with the town's most savory Italian sauces are made fresh daily. In autumn, the rack of venison is justifiably praised by food critics, and the veal dishes are the best we've sampled in Copenhagen. The chefs also do wonders with the fresh fish and shellfish caught off Danish coasts. Desserts are dreamy concoctions, and the clever sommelier guides diners through an impressive cellar with some of the Continent's greatest vintages.

Overgaden Neden Vandet 33B. © **32-54-06-93.** Reservations required. Fixed-price menus 700DKK–2,300DKK ($119–$391/£63–£207). AE, DC, MC, V. Mon–Sat 7pm–1am. Bus: 2 or 8.

Godt ✶✶✶ INTERNATIONAL   Its cuisine is as haute as ever, but Godt's reputation has been eclipsed by trendier and more newsworthy restaurants that are just as good. Nonetheless, it still remains a favorite of ours. A consistent small-scale choice that's known to everyone in the neighborhood, including the queen, this very formal restaurant offers two floors of minimalist and modern decor that never exceeds more than 20 diners at a time. Food is prepared fresh every day, based on what's best at the market. The chefs have prodigious talent and imagination, and the dishes are constantly changing. The sauces are sublime, as are the herbs and seasonings. Certain dishes appear frequently on the menu, such as the sautéed Norwegian redfish with a purée of celery and watercress sauce, which is an example of the chef's prowess. Using hand-picked ingredients, the chef turns out a perfectly roasted rack of hare with fresh cranberries and roasted chanterelles. Desserts are a high-flying trip to Valhalla, especially the fresh figs marinated with black currant liqueur, wrapped in phyllo pastry, and served with a coulis of pears and a velvety chocolate mousse.

Gothersgade 38. ℂ **33-15-21-22**. Reservations required. Fixed-price menus 480DKK–600DKK ($82–$102/£43–£54). Tues–Sat 6am–midnight. Closed July and Dec 23–Jan 3. Bus: 6, 10, or 14.

Kommandanten 𝄞𝄞𝄞 INTERNATIONAL   Some of our most savvy food-wise friends in Copenhagen insist that this is the country's best restaurant, and we always like to argue the point over a bottle of wine, citing our other recommendations that also richly earn their three stars. Praise has included, "If God were to visit Denmark, this is where he'd dine." Other critics, such as *Time Out,* have attacked not the cuisine but the patrons, citing "stern, fat men with equally fat cigars and even fatter expense accounts." On our latest rounds, the Armani-clad patrons didn't seem especially fat, but they did carry American Express platinum cards and gazed at the menu when not taking in a trio of Andy Warhol originals of Margrethe II in the downstairs dining room.

To date, this is the only Michelin restaurant in Copenhagen to have received two coveted stars, a rating it has held since 1997. Although a restaurant has stood on this historic street for 75 years, it only reached levels of haute cuisine in 1990. The 1698 burger's house, in which the restaurant is encased, contains numerous small rooms on several levels, evocative of Copenhagen at the time of the author Ludvig Holberg.

The cuisine reflects the seasons and features the very finest products and high-quality ingredients that the country offers. The aim of the chefs is simplicity, and natural flavors are never subdued. The menu, changed every 2 weeks, offers both classical dishes and innovative selections, such as spring chicken with rhubarb set off zestily with an orange and lemon verbena sauce. The luminously fresh halibut comes with smoked eel, fresh peas, and elderflower, a first-rate taste sensation. At last we learned the secret of cooking lobster *à la nage*—anise seed.

Ny Adelgade 7. ℂ **33-12-09-90**. Reservations required. Main courses 330DKK–400DKK ($56–$68/£30–£36); fixed-price 5-course menu 790DKK ($134/£71). AE, DC, MC, V. Mon–Sat 5:30–10pm. Bus: 1 or 6.

Kong Hans Kælder 𝄞𝄞𝄞 FRENCH/DANISH/ASIAN   This vaulted Gothic cellar, once owned by King Hans (1455–1513), not only lies in the oldest building in Copenhagen, it's also the site of the best restaurant. Only Kommandanten (see above) gives it serious competition. Five centuries ago the site of the restaurant was a vineyard, a tradition still honored by the name of the street—Vingårdsstræde. Grapes were an ingredient in many of the dishes of the time.

Hans Christian Andersen once lived upstairs, writing *Love in the Nicola Tower.* In *Only a Minstrel,* he wrote of his little garret, claiming that even though the rich folks who lived on the floors below had "the whole of the merry street to themselves," he had "the great vista of the heavens where the stars shone in the clear evening."

Chef Thomas Rode Andersen has turned the cellar into a *Relais Gourmands* (a member of the exclusive society of gourmet restaurants), and he creates dishes that might have plated by an inspired impressionist painter.

The chef is mainly inspired by the classic traditions of French gastronomy, though he feels free to draw upon the cuisines and raw materials of other countries. He doesn't believe in drowning a dish but in allowing its natural flavor to shine through. In autumn, fresh partridge and pigeon arrive from the fields, the same place where the mushrooms are gathered. He even smokes his own salmon on site for 36 hours in an antique oven. Blue lobsters are yanked from a tank, and other freshly caught fish and shellfish come from harbors nearby. The menu is inventive, delicious, sublime, and full of flavor, with market-fresh ingredients decisively seasoned and appearing in combinations perhaps unknown to you. Take, for example, foie gras with dried wild goose breast and beet stalks, followed by breast of duck with bigarade sauce (a classic duck sauce made with oranges and wine). For dessert, nothing can beat plum ice cream with Armagnac.

Vingårdsstræde 6. ⓒ **33-11-68-68**. Reservations required. Main courses 260DKK–390DKK ($44–$66/£23–£35); fixed-price menu 735DKK–925DKK ($125–$157/£66–£83). AE, DC, DISC, MC, V. Mon–Sat 6–10pm. Closed July 20–Aug 10 and Dec 24 26. Bus: 1, 6, or 9.

NOMA ⭒⭒⭒ NORDIC   With a certain testosterone-driven enthusiasm, the chefs here celebrate the cuisine of the cold North Atlantic. In fact, the name of the restaurant is short for *nordatlantiskl mad*, or North Atlantic food. During its relatively short life, this showcase of Nordic cuisine has received greater amounts of favorable press than virtually any other restaurant in Denmark. Positioned within an antique, stone-sided warehouse in Christianshavn, it makes it an almost religious duty to import ultra-fresh fish and shellfish three times a week from Greenland, Iceland, and the Faroe Islands. Chef Rene Redzepi concocts platters where fish is poached, grilled, pickled, smoked, or salted according to old Nordic traditions, and then served in ways that are sometimes more elaborately decorated, and more visually flamboyant by far, than the decor of the white, rather bare setting in which they are served. Come here for crayfish, lobsters, halibut in a foamy wasabi-flavored cream sauce, and any other creature that thrives in the cold waters of Nordic Europe, and expect to see celebrities from throughout northern Europe, including members of the Danish royal family.

Strandgade 93. ⓒ **32-96-32-97**. Reservations recommended. Main courses 295DKK–350DKK ($50–$60/£27–£32); set price menus 550DKK 650DKK ($94 $111/£50 £59). AE, DC, MC, V. Mon–Fri noon–2pm and Mon–Sat 6–10pm. Bus: 2 or 8.

Pierre André ⭒⭒⭒ FRENCH   Pierre André is viewed as "no longer on the cutting edge" by the fickle local media, and to some extent, that is true. While there is a stiffness and formality here, what is overlooked is that Pierre André chefs are still among the finest in Copenhagen for their take on a classic French cuisine. Named after the two sons of the Danish/French couple that owns the place, this restaurant is painted a warm shade of terra-cotta and is close to Nyhavn and the Hotel d'Angleterre. Menu items are elegant and stylish, as shown by a house specialty of carpaccio of foie gras "Emilia-Romagna," served with shaved Parmesan and truffles. Other winning starters include a salad of curried lobster with broccoli; braised filet of turbot with mushrooms, leeks, and mango sauce; wild venison with a bitter chocolate sauce, corn, and cranberries; and a chocolate cake specialty whose center is partially liquefied in a gooey but delectable concoction that runs onto your plate. Everything we've sampled has been a burst of flavor, ranking with the top restaurants of Paris or London. The chefs have considerable talent to create imaginative dishes packed with robust flavors, but nothing that's overpowering.

Ny Østergade 21. ⓒ **33-16-17-19**. Reservations required. Main courses 275DKK–395DKK ($47–$67/£25–£36); fixed-price menus 400DKK–755DKK ($68–$128/£36–£68). AE, DC, MC, V. Tues–Sat noon–2pm and 6–10pm. Closed 3 weeks July–Aug. Bus: 6, 10, or 14.

MODERATE

Café Lumskebugten ℛ *Finds* DANISH   This spick-and-span, well-managed bastion of Danish charm has an unpretentious elegance that's admired throughout the capital. A now-legendary matriarch named Karen Marguerita Krog established it in 1854 as a tavern for sailors. As the tavern's reputation grew, aristocrats, artists, and members of the Danish royal family came to dine. Today, a tastefully gentrified version of the original beef hash is still served.

Antique ship models decorate two glistening white dining rooms, and in summer, service spills onto the tables on the outdoor terraces. The food is excellent, but be prepared for a long experience here, as the staff tends to move politely but slowly through the service rituals, sometimes making meals here more lengthy and drawn out than you might have wanted. The selection of dishes takes you back to the way Danes ate in the 1950s, and that's not meant as a putdown by us. Danes like their own version of soul food. In this case it means fried platters of herring or Danish fish cakes with mustard sauce and minced beets. The sugar-marinated salmon with a mustard cream sauce remains one of the delights of the Danish kitchen, as does a "symphony" of fish with saffron sauce and new potatoes. You might order the classic herb-flavored tartare of salmon as a starter.

Esplanaden 21. 𝐂 33-15-60-29. Reservations recommended. Main courses 175DKK–275DKK ($30–$47/£16–£25); 5-course fixed-price dinner 545DKK ($93/£49). AE, DC, MC, V. Mon–Fri 11:30am–10pm; Sat 5–10pm. Bus: 1, 6, or 9.

Restaurant Els DANISH/FRENCH   This former coffeehouse is one of the most charming and upscale restaurants in Nyhavn, and certainly the one with the best decor. Meticulously preserved since it was installed in 1854, it's lined with murals that feature maidens in diaphanous dresses cavorting beneath trellises in a mythical garden. Dripping with Art Nouveau grace notes, they're believed to be the work of 19th-century muralist Christian Hitsch, who adorned parts of the interior of the Danish Royal Theater. Hans Christian Andersen was a regular here, and just before our arrival, novelist John Irving was here discussing the European marketing for one of his novels

Each day there's a different fixed-price menu, as well as a la carte. Most dishes are perfectly prepared, including pepper-pickled salmon served with fresh herbs and watercress; lobster soup; grilled scallops with chestnuts and a confit of tomatoes; grilled calf's liver with onion marmalade, tomatoes, and thyme; breast of chicken roasted with honey and ginger, served with vermouth sauce; and saddle of lamb with a compote of plums and red onions. You might follow all this by black-currant sorbet with cassis.

Store Strandstræde 3 (off Kongens Nytorv). 𝐂 33-14-13-41. Reservations recommended. Main courses 158DKK–265DKK ($27–$45/£14–£24); sandwiches (lunch only) 50DKK–85DKK ($8.50–$14/£4.50–£7.65); fixed-price 2-course lunch 200DKK ($34/£18); fixed-price 3-course lunch 225DKK ($38/£20); fixed-price 5-course dinner 495DKK ($84/£45). AE, DC, MC, V. Mon–Sat noon–3pm; daily 5:30–10pm. Closed July. Bus: 1, 6, or 10.

INEXPENSIVE

Café Zeze CONTINENTAL   On some days, if you have an ambitious sightseeing agenda, only a cafe will do to get you in and out quick. Set in a neighborhood with a dense collection of shops and offices, this hip bistro and cafe has a reputation for good food and brisk service. You'll find a cheerful-looking setup with a high ceiling, mirrors, and a mostly yellow interior. Noise levels can get a bit high, especially late at night, when more folk seem to be drinking than eating, but overall the place can be a lot of fun. Menu items change frequently, but expect a well-prepared medley of dishes.

The menu is better than some fast-food joint, and the cooks use market-fresh ingredients to create old favorites such as grilled chicken breast with fresh mushrooms or filet of lamb with shiitake mushrooms. Sometimes they even use their imaginations, dressing up a sautéed turkey breast with coconut and chile sauce or else roasted guinea fowl with fresh shrimp and braised arugula.

Ny Østergade 20. ℂ 33-14-23-90. Reservations recommended. Main courses 75DKK–92DKK ($13–$16/£6.75–£8.30) at lunch, 100DKK–175DKK ($17–$30/£9–£16) at dinner. AE, DC, MC, V. Mon–Sat 11:30am–4:30pm and 5:30–10pm (last order). Bar and cafe Mon–Thurs 9am–midnight; Fri–Sat 9am–3am. Bus: 350 F.

Nyhavns Færgekro 𝒦 *Finds* DANISH/FRENCH   The "Nyhavn Ferry Inn" near the harbor has a long tradition and many loyal fans, of which we include ourselves. The house is old, dating from the final years of the 18th century. On the popular summer terrace, diners enjoy not only their food but a view of the surrounding 18th-century houses and the canal. Inside, the decor is unusual, with a spiral stairway from an antique tram and a black-and-white "checkerboard" marble floor. Lights serve as call buttons to summon the staff when you want service.

The kitchen prepares a daily homemade buffet of 10 types of herring in different styles and sauces, including fried, *rollmops* (rolled or curled herring), and smoked. Some people make a full meal of the herring. You can also order *smørrebrød*— everything from smoked eel with scrambled eggs to chicken salad with bacon. A true Dane, in the tradition of Nyhavn, orders a schnapps or aquavit at lunch. Denmark has a tradition of making spicy aquavit from the herbs and plants of the land— Saint-John's-wort from Tisvilde Hegn, sloe-leaf from the wild moors, green walnuts from the south of Funen, and many other varieties. Dinners here are relatively limited, usually configured as a set-price menu, with main courses including a choice of either grilled salmon or grilled entrecote—nothing particularly imaginative but perfectly adequate and well-prepared.

Nyhavn 5. ℂ 33-15-15-88. Reservations required. Lunchtime herring buffet 89DKK ($15/£8). Fixed-price dinner 109DKK ($32/£17). DC, MC, V. Daily 11.30am–4pm and 5–11.30pm. Closed Jan 1 and Dec 24–25. Bus: 1, 6, or 9.

NEAR RÅDHUSPLADSEN
EXPENSIVE

Sult 𝒦 DANISH/FRENCH   If you, like us, were turned on by the novel, *Sult,* by Norwegian author Knut Hamsun, you might want to try out the restaurant whose moniker pays homage to the book. This fashionable, trendy eatery is inside the Danish Film Institute's center and is both a cultural and a gourmet experience. The setting is like a modern museum with wood floors, towering windows, and high lofty ceilings. Chef Fredrik Ohlsson has traveled the continent for his culinary inspiration, although he specializes in French cuisine. Using market-fresh ingredients, he often elevates his food to the sublime. Just describing the rather simple dishes does not suggest their artfulness in seasonings and natural flavors. The chef will take a grilled tuna or a

---

 Family-Friendly Restaurant

Copenhagen Corner (p. 91)   A special children's menu features such dishes as shrimp cocktail and grilled rump steak.

filet of lamb, even oven-baked lemon sole, and make something special out of it. If you don't want to make decisions, opt for one of the fixed-price menus, which are innovative and engaging to the palate. The wine list is impressive but rather high priced.

Vognmagergade 8B. © 33-74-34-17. Reservations recommended. 185DKK ($31/£17) all main courses. Fixed-price menus 240DKK–425DKK ($41–$72/£22–£38). AE, DC, MC, V. Tues–Sat noon–midnight, Sun 11am–10pm. S-tog: Nørreport.

TyvenKokkenHansKoneog-HendesElsker *Finds* ★★ INTERNATIONAL/ FRENCH   In the old days, these headquarters were the seat of the most famous brothel in Copenhagen, advertising that there was no lust that could not be satisfied here. Today the demands of most customers can be satisfied just by offering a finely honed cuisine. The restored 18th-century townhouse near Rådhuspladsen (Town Hall Square) is one of the city's most unusual and one of its best restaurants. Its bizarre name comes from Peter Greenaway's cannibalistic *The Cook, The Thief, His Wife and Her Lover,* a brilliant film with macabre feast scenes. The two-story restaurant offers tables with a view over old Copenhagen from upstairs. The chefs here are inspired in their selection of an innovative fixed-price menu, which we find to be among the best in Copenhagen. The menu changes weekly, but we enjoy the "Lobstermenu" with champagne, beginning with grilled lobster's claw and turbot with green peas and pearl onions, proceeds to encompass risotto with lobster fragments and fresh chanterelles, and follows with lobster tail with seared foie gras. Everything is good here, even something simple but sublime such as entrecôte with fresh vegetables. Finish off with a luscious dessert or a platter of various European farm cheeses.

Magstræde 16. © 33-16-12-92. Reservations recommended. Main courses 180DKK–375DKK ($31–$64/£16–£34); 6-course menu 600DKK ($102/£54). AE, DC, MC, V. Wed–Sat 6pm–2am.

MODERATE

Atlas Bar/Restaurant Flyvefisken DANISH/THAI/INTERNATIONAL   This joint has always been a darling of local hipsters, and you may want to join them for a slice of Copenhagen life often not seen by the casual visitor. The cuisine at these two restaurants (prepared in the same kitchen) include lots of vegetarian food inspired by the fare of Thailand, Mexico, and India, with a Danish overview toward tidiness and coziness. On the street level, the cramped, cozy Atlas Bar serves a busy lunchtime crowd, but slackens off a bit at night, when the wood-sheathed Flyvefisken (Flying Fish) opens for dinner upstairs, where you can expect a bit more emphasis on Thai cuisine and its fiery flavors, including lemongrass, curries, and several of the hot, spicy fish soups native to Bangkok. Although the authenticity of the Thai cuisine has lost a bit of its zest in the long jump from Thailand, it's still a change of pace from typical Danish fare.

Lars Bjørnstræde 18. © 33-14-95-15. Reservations recommended. Main courses 75DKK–140DKK ($13–$24/ £6.75–£13) at lunch, 110DKK–200DKK ($19–$34/£9.90–£18) at dinner. AE, DC, MC, V. Atlas Bar Mon–Sat noon–10pm. Restaurant Flyvefisken Mon–Sat 5:30–10pm. Bus: 5 or 6A.

Café Ketchup INTERNATIONAL   Set within the direct sightline of Tivoli's biggest stage, and loaded with contented or animated drinkers during concerts, this is the most consistently popular middle-bracket restaurant in Tivoli, the grounds of which are loaded with worthy competitors. It radiates outward like the spokes of a wheel from a central Beaux-Arts core, a glass-ceilinged pavilion ringed with covered terraces, a boon whenever it rains. If there's a trendy lounge-bar within Tivoli that's favored by the young, the beautiful, and the restless, this is it. Some paparazzi hang out here in summer, hoping to catch a visiting celebrity picking his (or her) nose. In fact, it might remind you of the postmodern hip of a tuckaway bar in such newly fashionable outlying districts as Nørrebro, but with more flowers and an enhanced sense of whimsy. There's a nearly hallucinogenic collection of cocktails offered (martinis, sours, juleps, and more). The cuisine is competent without being great. The best food items include Brittany oysters with lemon and shallot-flavored vinegar; mussels in a Pernod-flavored cream sauce with fennel and summer onions; miso-baked halibut with spinach and garlic-flavored potatoes; venison with sautéed foie gras; and pear-flavored sorbet with Danish raspberries and cream.

In Tivoli. (C) 33-75-07-57. Reservations not necessary. Main courses 150DKK–355DKK ($26–$60/£14–£32). AE, DC, MC, V. Daily noon–4pm and 5–10pm. Bar remains open till midnight. When Tivoli is closed, this restaurant shuts down.

Copenhagen Corner *Kids* INTERNATIONAL/FRENCH   This is no doubt the most convenient place for a good meal in the heart of Copenhagen. It's an especially good choice if you're going to the Tivoli nearby and don't want to pay the inflated food prices charged there. Set amid some of the heaviest pedestrian traffic in Copenhagen, this deeply entrenched landmark restaurant opens onto Rådhuspladsen, around the corner from the Tivoli Gardens. Outfitted with some of the accessories of a greenhouse-style conservatory for plants, it offers well-prepared, unpretentious meals to dozens of city residents throughout the day and evening. The menu, which offers many Danish favorites, will place you deep in the heart of Denmark, beginning with three kinds of herring or freshly peeled shrimp with dill and lemon. There's even a carpaccio of filet of deer for the most adventurous palates. The soups are excellent, such as the consommé of white asparagus flavored with chicken and fresh herbs. The fish is fresh and beautifully prepared, especially the steamed Norwegian salmon with a "lasagna" of potatoes, or the baked halibut with artichokes. Meat and poultry courses, although not always equal to the fish, are tasty and tender, especially the veal liver Provençal.

H. C. Andersens Blvd. 1A. (C) 33 91 45 45. Reservations recommended. Main courses 128DKK–233DKK ($22–$43/£12–£23); 3-course fixed-price menu 375DKK ($64/£34). AE, DC, MC, V. Daily 11:30am–11pm. Bus: 1, 6, or 8.

Søren K *(F)* INTERNATIONAL/FRENCH   Named after Denmark's most celebrated philosopher, this is an artfully minimalist dining room that's on the ground floor of "The Black Diamond," the ultramodern, intensely angular addition to the Royal Library. It has the kind of monochromatic gray and flesh-toned decor you might find in Milan, and glassy, big-windowed views that stretch out over the nearby canal. Menu items change frequently, but the chef never cooks with butter, cream, or high-cholesterol cheese, making a meal here a low-cholesterol as well as a savory experience. In a land known for its "butter-and-egg men," this type of cooking is heresy. Some Danes boycott it, but foreign visitors, especially those watching their waistlines, flock here for a superb meal. Your taste buds will love the velvety foie gras, a carpaccio of veal, and a truly superb oyster soup. Attention to detail and a proud professionalism distinguish such main dishes as veal chops served with lobster sauce and a half-lobster and roasted venison with nuts and seasonal berries with a marinade of green tomatoes. To reach this place, you'll have to enter the library and pass through the lobby of the new Black Diamond Wing.

On the ground floor of the Royal Library's Black Diamond Wing, Søren Kierkegaards Plads 1. (C) 33-47-49-50. Reservations recommended. Main courses 92DKK–145DKK ($16–$25/£8.30–£13) at lunch, 195DKK–225DKK ($33–$38/£18–£20) at dinner; fixed-price 3-course dinner 395DKK ($67/£36); 6-course tasting menu 495DKK ($84/£45). AE, DC, MC, V. Mon–Sat 11am–10:30pm. Bus: 1, 2, 5, 8, or 9.

Quick Bites

Copenhagen has many hot dog stands, chicken and fish grills, and *smørrebrød* counters that serve good, fast, inexpensive meals.

Hot dog stands, especially those around Rådhuspladsen, offer *polser* (steamed or grilled hot dogs) with shredded onions on top and *pommes frites* (french fries) on the side.

The *bageri* or *konditori* (bakery), found on almost every block, sells fresh bread, rolls, and Danish pastries.

Viktualiehandler (small food shops), found throughout the city, are the closest things to a New York deli. You can buy roast beef with free *log* (fried onions); Bornholmer, a large, boneless sardine from the Danish island of Bornholm; and *røgost,* a popular and inexpensive smoked cheese. The best buy is smoked fish, and yogurt fans will be delighted to know that the Danish variety is cheap and tasty. It's available in small containers—just peel off the cover and drink it right out of the cup as the Danes do. *Hytte ret* (cottage cheese) is also good and cheap.

The favorite lunch of Scandinavians, particularly Danes, is *smørrebrød.* The purest form is made with dark rye bread, called *rugbrød.* Most taverns and cafes offer *smørrebrød,* and many places serve it as takeout food.

You can picnic in any of the city parks in the town center. Try Kongsgarten near Kongens Nytorv, the Kastellet area near *The Little Mermaid* statue, Botanisk Have (site of the Botanical Gardens), the lakeside promenades in southeastern Copenhagen, and the old moat at Christianshavn. Remember not to litter.

INEXPENSIVE

Axelborg Bodega DANISH   Since 1912, this cafe, across from Benneweis Circus and near Scala and the Tivoli, has served down-home cooking, Danish style. In fair weather you can sit out and enjoy a brisk Copenhagen evening and people watching. Most regulars here opt for the *dagens ret* or daily special, which is the equivalent of the old blue plate special served at diners throughout America in the 1940s. Typical Danish dishes are featured on those specials, invariably *frikadeller* (Ping-Pong-ball-size meatballs) and the inevitable pork chops, which was the favorite dish of the Nazi occupation forces in the early 1940s. A wide selection of open-faced Danish sandwiches (*smørrebrød*) are also available, costing 52DKK to 76DKK ($8.85–$13/£4.70–£6.85) each. Although the atmosphere is somewhat impersonal, this is a local favorite; diners enjoy the dishes from Grandma's recipe box.

Axeltorv 1. ⓒ **33-11-06-38.** Reservations recommended. Main courses 95DKK–148DKK ($16–$25/£8.55–£13). AE, DC, MC, V. Restaurant daily 11am–9pm. Bar daily 11am–2am. Bus: 1 or 6.

Café Sorgenfri *(Value* SANDWICHES   The English translation for this place means "without sorrows." Should you have any, however, you can drown them in your beer here in the antique interior of this cafe, sheltered in a house from 1796. Don't come here expecting grand cuisine, or even a menu with any particular variety. This place has thrived for 150 years selling beer, schnapps, and a medley of *smørrebrød* that appeals to virtually everyone's sense of workaday thrift and frugality. With only about 50 seats, the joint is likely to be crowded around lunch hour, with somewhat more space during the midafternoon. Everything inside reeks of old-time Denmark, from the potted shrubs that adorn the facade to the well-oiled paneling that has witnessed many generations of Copenhageners selecting and enjoying sandwiches. Between two and four of them might compose a reasonable lunch, depending on your appetite. You'll find this place in the all-pedestrian shopping zone in the commercial heart of town.

Brolæggerstræde 8. ✆ **33-11-58-80.** Reservations recommended for groups of 4 or more. *Smørrebrød* 45DKK–75DKK ($7.65–$13/£4.05–£6.75). AE, DC, MC, V. Daily 11am–9pm. Bus: 5 or 6.

Domhus Kælderen DANISH/INTERNATIONAL   For some reason this eatery seems to attract a lot of foreign visitors, especially English hipsters. Its good food, and a location across the square from City Hall, also guarantees a large number of lawyers and their clients. This is a bustling and old-fashioned emporium of Danish cuisine. The setting is a half-cellar room illuminated with high lace-draped windows that shine light down on wooden tables and 50 years of memorabilia. Menu items at lunch might include *frikadeller* and heaping platters of herring, Danish cheeses, smoked meats and fish, salads, and a worthy assortment of open-faced sandwiches (*smørrebrød*). The dinner menu is more ambitious, calling for a harder effort on the part of the kitchen staff, who turn out pickled salmon and several fine cuts of beef—our favorite choices— served either with a béarnaise or pepper sauce. Also look for the catch of the day, prepared in virtually any way you like. The food is typically Danish and well prepared, and while you get no culinary surprises here, you are rarely disappointed.

Nytorv 5. ✆ **33-14-84-55.** Reservations recommended. Main courses 68DKK–148DKK ($12–$25/£6.10–£13) at lunch, 128DKK–198DKK ($22–$34/£12–£18) at dinner; set menus 225DKK–275DKK ($38–$47/£20–£25). AE, DC, MC, V. Daily 11am–4pm and 5–10pm. Bus: 5.

INDRE BY
VERY EXPENSIVE

St. Gertruds Kloster 🏵🏵🏵 *Finds* INTERNATIONAL   Surely this is how the medieval kings of Denmark must have dined, with Hamlet pondering the question in the background. It is the most romantic restaurant in Denmark, a great place to pop the question or tell your spouse you want a divorce. There's no electricity in the labyrinth of 14th-century underground vaults, and the 1,500 flickering candles, open grill, iron sconces, and rough-hewn furniture create an elegant ambience. Enjoy an aperitif in the darkly paneled library. The chefs display talent and integrity, their cuisine reflecting precision and sensitivity. Every flavor is fully focused, each dish balanced to perfection. Try the fresh, homemade foie gras with black truffles, lobster served in a turbot bouillon, venison (year-round) with green asparagus and truffle sauce, or a fish-and-shellfish terrine studded with chunks of lobster and salmon. These dishes range from merely being good to being sublime. Because of the high prices, you're likely to find a higher-than-usual percentage of foreign visitors, and not too many native Copenhageners.

Hauser Plads 32. ✆ **33-14-66-30.** Reservations required. Main courses 250DKK–320DKK ($43–$54/£23–£29); fixed-price menu 488DKK–528DKK ($83–$90/£44–£48). AE, DC, MC, V. Daily 5–11pm. Closed Dec 25–Jan 1. Bus: 4E, 7E, 14, or 16.

MODERATE

Bøf & Ost DANISH/FRENCH   Even if the food weren't good, we'd like to come here on a summer evening to occupy a cafe-style table overlooking "Grey Friars Square." We consider this eatery the best people-watching place in Copenhagen. This neighborhood favorite created a bit of a buzz when it first opened in a 1728 building constructed over cellars from a medieval monastery. But that buzz has long died down as fickle foodies have found newer places other than "Beef & Cheese" to pamper their stomachs. But, even though abandoned by the media in search of something new, the place still turns out food as good as the day it opened. The lobster soup wins us over, and we often follow with some of the best beef tenderloin steaks in town. After all, Bøf & Ost has to live up to its namesake. The cheese in its name is justified when a platter with six different selections of the best cheese in the countryside arrives for you to devour with crusty, freshly baked bread. One local diner confided in us: "The food is not worthy of God's own table, but it's so good for me I come here once a week."

Gråbrødretorv 13. Ⓒ **33-11-99-11.** Reservations required. Main courses 149DKK–199DKK ($25–$34/£13–£18); fixed-price lunch menu 118DKK ($20/£11). DC, MC, V. Mon–Sat 11:30am–10:30pm. Closed Jan 1. Bus: 5.

Peder Oxe's Restaurant/Vinkælder Wine Bar 🍴 DANISH   The setting alone has a certain romance, as in the Middle Ages it was the site of a monastery for gray-robed friars who couldn't own anything and were forced to beg for a living. Selections from the salad bar cost 35DKK ($5.95/£3.15) when accompanied by a main course, but the offerings are so tempting that many prefer to enjoy salad alone for 79DKK ($13/£7.10) per person. Although fresh-salad buffets are commonplace in the U.S., the idea had never been introduced into Denmark until Peder Oxe pioneered the concept. It was an immediate success. The restaurant continues to this day to select its mesclun, arugula, escarole, watercress, iceberg, spinach, and other popular lettuce greens, and it also uses fine raw materials for its classic dishes, turning to the entire world kitchen for inspiration.

The cooks serve only beef from free-range cattle along with freshly caught fish and shellfish. Game from the Danish countryside appears on the menu in autumn, and Danish lamb, among the best in Europe, is a standard feature. Other dishes include a tantalizing lobster soup and those tiny Danish bay shrimp we like to devour. You can also drop in for lunch at any time of the day to order lighter fare such as open-faced sandwiches or even a Danish hamburger. ("Do you want chile mayonnaise with that?")

We have found that the chefs cook the best fried herring in all of Copenhagen here, and we'll let you in on their secret. They coat filet of the fish with Dijon mustard, grated fresh horseradish, and even caviar before rolling them in rye flour and pan frying them in Danish country butter. The smoked eel is prepared on the premises, and don't be surprised if the waiter, assuming you are familiar with the varieties available, asks if you want silver eel, broad-headed eel, or point-headed eel. All are smoked with juniper berries and are delicious, but that silver eel wins our hearts.

Gråbrødretorv 11. Ⓒ **33-11-00-77.** Reservations recommended. Main courses 89DKK–189DKK ($15–$32/£8–£17); fixed-price lunch menu 67DKK–118DKK ($11–$20/£6.05–£11). DC, MC, V. Daily 11:30am–midnight. Bus: 5.

INEXPENSIVE

Pasta Basta *Value* ITALIAN   When the kroner in your pocket becomes the jangle of coins—not the rustle of paper—head here for a great deal on dining. This restaurant's main attraction is a table loaded with cold antipasti and salads, one of the best deals in town. With more than nine selections on the enormous buffet, it's sometimes called the "Pasta Basta Table." For 79DKK ($13/£7.10), you can partake of all that you can eat, plus unlimited bread. The restaurant is divided into half a dozen cozy dining rooms, each decorated in the style of ancient Pompeii, and is located on a historic cobblestone street off the main shopping boulevard, Strøget. Its fans and devotees praise it for its policy of staying open late—usually several hours later than most of the other restaurants in town—something that might come in useful on one of those long midsummer nights when you've miscalculated how late it really is, and suddenly can't find a restaurant that's still serving dinner.

Every day the chefs prepare 15 different homemade pastas. You can, if you wish, go with our favorite—saffron-flavored fettuccine in a white wine sauce with grilled salmon strips and a garnish of salmon caviar. Other menu choices include carpaccio served with olive oil and basil, a platter with three kinds of Danish caviar (whitefish, speckled trout, and vendace), thin-sliced salmon with a cream-based sauce of salmon roe, and Danish suckling lamb with fried spring onions and tarragon. Dessert offerings include an assortment of Danish, French, and Italian cheeses, crème brûlée, and *tartufo*, an Italian ice cream treat.

Valkendorfsgade 22. © **33-11-21-31.** Reservations recommended. Main courses 98DKK–169DKK ($17–$29/ £8.80–£15). DC, MC, V. Sun–Sat 11:30am–2am. Bus: 5.

SLOTSHOLMEN
EXPENSIVE

Krogs Fiskerestaurant *ƒƒƒ* SEAFOOD   Orson Welles claimed that this fish restaurant was the only place north of the Riviera that knew how to make a bouillabaisse. The great actor/director and gourmet/gourmand was just one of the celebrities who has praised this seafood restaurant, one of the oldest in Copenhagen, dating from 1910. Only a short walk from Christiansborg Castle, the restaurant stands in a historic district of 19th-century houses, and its building dates from 1789, when it opened as a fish shop. The canal side plaza where fishermen moored their boats is now the site of the restaurant's outdoor terrace. The walls of the high-ceilinged restaurant are covered with gold-plated mirrors and paintings from the 1800s, the work of a Danish artist, Valdemar Andersen.

Even for inveterate quibblers like us, it's hard to find something to fault in the fish dishes served here, as they are among the freshest in Copenhagen. The chefs strike a studied balance between modernized traditional dishes and updated haute cuisine classics—all at celestial prices. The caviar is the city's finest and comes from unlikely places such as Iran. With the main courses, "nouvelle" cuisine here is something served at the turn of the 20th century, including a divine plaice meunière with lemon, parsley, and brown butter. The Dover sole is even prepared at the table, and the shellfish selection, served hot or cold, is without equal in Copenhagen. This is a most engaging restaurant, especially if you're over 50—the "sweet young things" of Copenhagen dine at trendier joints. Before the waiter arrives with the bill, make sure you've taken your heart medication.

Gammel Strand 38. © **33-15-89-15.** Reservations required. Main courses 328DKK–585DKK ($56–$99/£30–£53); fixed-price 5-course menu 750DKK ($128/£68). AE, DC, MC, V. Mon–Sat 6–11pm. Bus: 1 or 2.

IN NØRREBRO
INEXPENSIVE

Nørrebro Bryghus *ƒ finds* DANISH   This is the best and most appealing restaurant in the Nørrebro district, a big-time, big-city brewery that dwarfs almost every other restaurant in the neighborhood. Occupying two floors of what was originally built in 1857 as a metal foundry, it brews between 10,000 and 20,000 liters of beer per month, as many as 10 different kinds, all of which are dispensed in copious amounts. In addition, many of the dishes served here are braised, fried, or stewed in beer. And if you're interested in how the fruit of the hops is actually concocted, you can sign up for any of the free brewery tours conducted here every Monday to Thursday from 5 to 6pm (Danish-language versions) and from 6 to 7pm (English-language versions). Menu items change with the season and with whatever beer happens to have been brewed within the previous week or so. Examples include crisp-fried whitefish served with roasted and glazed fennel in Pacific Pale Ale in a coriander *beurre blanc* and tarragon sauce; cold tomato consommé flavored with Çeske Böhmer beer, smoked shrimps, scallops and shellfish oil; poached filet of beef served with mangetout peas, new carrots, and green beans, served with sage sauce flavored with La Granja Stout; and raspberry feuilleté with milk foam. One of the genuinely sought-after facets of this place involves prereserving the "brewmaster's table" for a specially composed seven- or eight-course meal, each course liberally soused with a different beer, with a minimum of eight diners needed for the full-fledged experience.

Ryesgade 3. ℂ **35-30-05-30.** Reservations not necessary. Lunch platters 78DKK–155DKK ($13–$26/£7–£14); Dinner main courses 189DKK–198DKK ($32–$34/£17–£18). Set-price menus 235DKK–398DKK ($40–$68/£21–£36). AE, DC, MC, V. Sun-Wed 11:30am–3pm and 5:30–10pm, with bar staying open till midnight; Thurs–Sat 11:30am–3pm and 5:30–10:30pm, with bar staying open till 2am. Bus: 3A.

Pussy Galore's Flying Circus ℱ INTERNATIONAL   No restaurant in Copenhagen has such an amusing name. Named after the James Bond character, this eatery is in trendy Nørrebro. From inexpensive fresh salads to some of the juiciest burgers in town, it's a great place to eat, drink, and check out the scene. The location is a bit away from the center, but that doesn't seem to bother one of its patrons, Prince Frederik, the playboy heir to the throne. Media types also flock here.

In summer, tables overflow onto the sidewalk. Many books that review the world's best bars, including one by "Black Bush Whiskey," list this place among the globe's best watering holes. As an attractive waiter confided to us, "Café Ketchup gets the young and beautiful; we get the younger and more beautiful." Against a 1990s minimalist decor, with Arne Jacobsen chairs, partake of great cocktails (especially the mojitos). Many regulars drop in every morning for eggs and bacon, returning in the evening for, perhaps, a wok-fried delight.

Sankt Hans Torv 30. ℂ **35-24-53-00.** Reservations not accepted. Main courses 70DKK–115DKK ($12–$20/£6.30–£10). AE, DC, MC, V. Mon–Fri 8am–2am; Sat–Sun 9am–2am. Bus: 3A.

Exploring Copenhagen

There is talk of a renaissance in Copenhagen, as Denmark moves deeper into the 21st century. Much of the city, with its copper-domed landmarks, is cutting edge. A sea of change is sweeping across Copenhagen as tired, seedy old buildings are restored—many turned into boutique hotels. At trendy restaurants, young Danes are reinventing the cuisine of their ancestors, too long dominated by the Danish pig.

Museums are becoming more user-friendly, and even the queen is appearing on the streets in scarlet red. The culture and charm of old Copenhagen is still here, but in a word the city has become "cool."

A dynamic new life, spurred in part by the young and the changes brought by newly arriving immigrants, has made this venerable old city more vibrant than it's ever been in its history.

"You couldn't be bored here if you tried," a visiting dancer from London told us. He was referring to the around-the-clock summer fun offered in the Danish capital, everything from a free-love-and-drug commune to beer breweries, baroque palaces, art-filled museums, and even an erotica museum.

On a summer evening, there is no greater man-made attraction in all of Scandinavia than the Tivoli pleasure gardens, which seems to have emerged intact from the days when the world was young . . . and so were we. The Danes love childhood too much to abandon it forever—no matter how old they get—so Tivoli keeps alive the magic of fairy lights and the wonder of yesteryear.

Although many visitors arrive in Copenhagen just to attend the Tivoli, there's a lot more going on here. The city is proud of its vast storehouse of antiquities and holds its own with most other capitals of Europe, although dwarfed, of course, by London, Paris, and Rome.

People come to Copenhagen for various reasons—some to absorb the city's art, others merely to have fun. Copenhagen hasn't become another Hamburg yet, but it still peddles miles of porno and sex toys, for which it became infamous in the 1970s. Several annual summer festivals take place here, and live bands—some of the best in Europe—appear in parks to keep Copenhagen rocking around the clock when the sun shines. One actor who settled into Copenhagen found it an "orgy" of boats, bikes, joggers, in-line skaters, and beer.

Shopping is another reason visitors show up here, as the city is famous for its beautifully designed wares for the home, including porcelain by Bing & Grøndahl and Royal Copenhagen, and sterling silver by Georg Jensen, among other big names. Strøget remains one of the most fabled shopping streets of Europe.

Some Danes endorse all that "Wonderful, Wonderful Copenhagen" tourist propaganda. "Tell your readers we have everything," said a tourist official. "We even attract transsexual wannabes who want to change their gender. As you know, we became famous for that way back in the '50s."

Other disgruntled "natives" resent those tourist brochures, and some cynical individual, every now and then, goes and chops off the head of *The Little Mermaid* in protest.

"We don't think Copenhagen is so wonderful," said a squatter at the commune of Christiania. "In fact, we think it sucks." That's why she and others created an illegal, self-governed and "free living" community called Christiania back in 1971. In spite of police interference, it's still going strong right in the heart of Copenhagen.

On the community's "pusher street," vendors sell their hard drugs.

The summer sun may not set until 11pm, but in winter expect cold, cloudy, dark, rainy weather. "We brood like Hamlet then," said a local. "But winter or summer, we're super friendly and welcoming . . . and in English too."

After years of traveling to Denmark, we heartily agree with that assessment.

1 In & Around the Tivoli Gardens

Louis Tussaud Wax Museum   Now a part of Tivoli, the Louis Tussaud Wax Museum (he was the great-grandson of Madame Tussaud) offers a sense of kitschy fun and the opportunity to get "scared witless" in the dungeon. As such, it's a campy but major attraction in Copenhagen, featuring more than 200 wax figures—everybody from Danish kings and queens to Leonardo da Vinci. Some of these wax effigies, frankly, are way off the mark, whereas other likenesses are right on target. We applaud the museum for including famous figures from Denmark instead of just concentrating on more fabled international stars and legends. Children can visit the Snow Queen's Castle, or watch Frankenstein and Dracula guard the monsters and vampires. We always head here thinking the attraction will be just too corny for us, but end up finding effigies that enthrall us.

H. C. Andersens Blvd. 22. ⓒ **33-11-89-00.** www.tussaud.dk. Admission 80DKK ($14/£7.20) adults, 35DKK ($5.95/£3.15) children 5–9, 59DKK ($10/£5.30) children 10–15. Apr 16–Sept 13 daily 10am–11pm; Sept 14–Apr 15 daily 10am–6pm. Last entry 1 hr. before closing. Bus: 1, 2, 16, 28, 29, or 41.

Ny Carlsberg Glyptotek ✸✸✸   Talk about putting sudsy beer money to good use. The Glyptotek, behind Tivoli, is one of the great art museums of Europe. Founded by the 19th-century art collector Carl Jacobsen, Mr. Carlsberg himself, the museum includes modern art and antiquities. It reopened in June 2006 after a 3-year closing and the expenditure of 100 million DKK ($17 million/£9 million), part of which was spent for the construction of a wing called "The Ancient Mediterranean World."

The modern section has both French and Danish art, mainly from the 19th century. Sculpture, including works by Rodin, is on the ground floor, and works of the Impressionists and related artists, including van Gogh's *Landscape from St. Rémy* ✸, are on the upper floors. Egyptian, Greek, and Roman antiquities are on the main floor; Etruscan, Greek, and Cypriot on the lower floor. The **Egyptian collection** ✸✸ is outstanding; the most notable piece is a prehistoric rendering of a hippopotamus. Fine Greek originals (headless Apollo, Niobe's tragic children) and Roman copies of Greek bronzes (4th-c. Hercules) are also displayed, as are some of the noblest Roman busts—Pompey, Virgil, Augustus, and Trajan. The **Etruscan collection** ✸✸✸—sarcophagi, a winged lion, bronzes, and pottery—is a favorite of ours and the best such collection outside Italy.

In 1996 the Ny Glyptotek added a French masters' wing. Constructed of white marble and granite, it's in the inner courtyard, which can be reached only through the conservatory. In a climate- and light-controlled environment, you'll find an extensive collection of French masterpieces including works by Manet, Monet, Degas, and Renoir, as well as an impressive collection of French sculpture, such as Rodin's *The Burghers of Calais*, plus 30 of his other works. The display features Cézanne's famous *Portrait of the Artist* 𝖆𝖆, as well as about **35 paintings** 𝖆𝖆 by former Copenhagen resident Paul Gauguin. Consider dropping into the museum's restaurant, Café Glyptoteket, which some locals find so appealing that they come here for its sake alone, with no intention of visiting the museum.

Dantes Plads 7. ☎ **33-41-81-41.** www.glyptoteket.dk. Admission 50DKK ($8.50/£4.50) adults, free for children, free for everyone Wed and Sun. Tues–Sun 10am–4pm. Bus: 1, 2, 5, 6, 8, or 10.

Rådhus (Town Hall) and World Clock

We have never been able to work up much enthusiasm for this towering monument, the City Hall of Copenhagen. It was said to have been inspired by the main tower at the Piazza del Campo in Siena. The original is magnificent, the one in Copenhagen a bit dull. The architect, Martin Nyrop, wanted to create a building that would "give gaiety to everyday life and spontaneous pleasure to all." We're not so sure he succeeded, but check it out anyway. Statues of Hans Christian Andersen and Niels Bohr (the Nobel Prize–winning physicist) are worth a look. Jens Olsen's **World Clock** is open for viewing Monday to Friday 10am to 4pm and Saturday at 1pm. Frederik IX set the clock on December 15, 1955. The clockwork is so exact that it's accurate to within half a second every 300 years. Climb the tower for an impressive view, but it's not for the faint of heart—300 steps with no elevator.

To the east of the Rådhus is one of Copenhagen's most famous landmarks, the **Lurblæserne** (Lur Blower Column), topped by two Vikings blowing an ancient trumpet called a *lur*. There's a bit of artistic license taken here. The *lur* actually dates from the Bronze Age (ca. 1500 B.C.), while the Vikings lived some 1,000 years ago. But it's a fascinating sight anyway.

Rådhuspladsen. ☎ **33-66-25-82.** Admission to Rådhus 30DKK ($5.10/£2.70); 5DKK (10¢/45p) children. Guided tour of Rådhus 30DKK ($5.10/£2.70) Mon–Fri 3pm; Sat 3pm. Guided tour of tower Oct–May Mon–Sat noon; June–Sept Mon–Fri 10am, noon, and 2pm, Sat noon. Bus: 1, 6, or 8.

Tivoli Gardens 𝖆𝖆𝖆 *Moments*

Created in 1843, the Tivoli gardens gave Walt Disney an idea, and look what he did with it. The original is still here, standing in an 8-hectare (20-acre) garden in the center of Copenhagen. Its greatest admirers call it a pleasure park or flower garden; its critics suggest that it's one giant beer garden. Michael Jackson, after appearing here, tried to buy the entire complex but was turned down, as were interests from Disney. The Tivoli is the virtual symbol of Denmark, and no Dane wants to see it go to foreigners.

Let's face it: The Tivoli is filled with schmaltz, but somehow with its glitz, glamour, and gaiety it manages to win over hardened cynics. Children prefer it during the day, but adults tend to like it better at night when more than 100,000 specially made soft-glow light bulbs and at least a million regular bulbs are turned on—what an electric bill.

It features thousands of flowers, a merry-go-round of tiny Viking ships, games of chance and skill (pinball arcades, slot machines, shooting galleries), and a Ferris wheel of hot-air balloons and cabin seats. The latest attraction at Tivoli, "The Demon," is the biggest roller coaster in Denmark. Passengers whiz through three loops on the thrill ride, reaching a top speed of 80kmph (50 mph). There's also a playground for children.

An Arabian-style fantasy palace, with towers and arches, houses more than two dozen expensive restaurants, from a lakeside inn to a beer garden. Take a walk around the edge of the tiny lake with its ducks, swans, and boats.

Copenhagen Attractions

Amalienborg Palace 13
Assistens Kirkegård 1
Botanisk Have 5
Christiansborg Palace 23
Davids Samling 9
Den Hirschsprungske Samling 6
Erotica Museum 15
Frederikskirche
  (Marble Church) 14
Frihedsmuseet 11
Holmens Kirke 24
Københavns Bymuseum &
  Søren Kirkegård
  Samlingen 2
Kongelige Bibliotek 25
Kunstindustrimuseet 12
The Little Mermaid 10
Louis Tussaud Wax Museum 4
Nationalmuseet 21
Ny Carlsberg Glyptotek 20
Orlogsmuseet 27
Rådhus and World Clock 18
Rosenborg Castle 8
Rundetårn (Round Tower) 16
Statens Museum for Kunst 7
Thorvaldsens Museum 22
Tivoli Gardens 19
Tøjhusmuseet 26
Tycho Brahe Planetarium 3
Vor Frelsers Kirken 28
Vor Frue Kirken 17

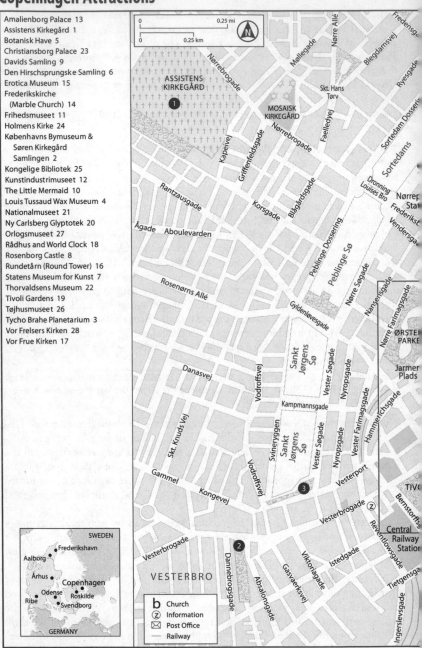

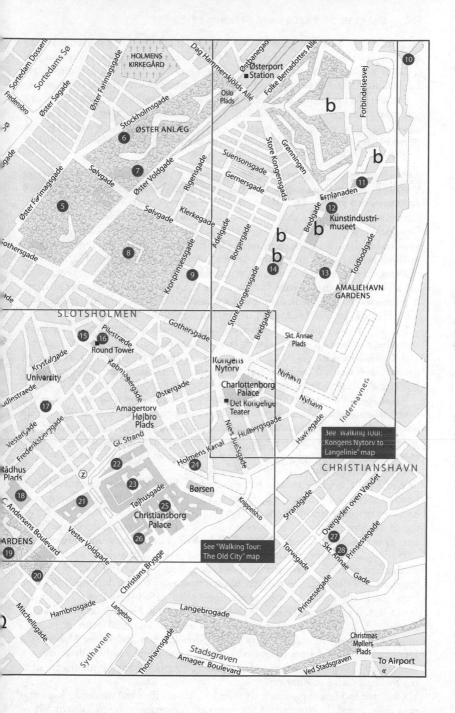

HOLMENS KIRKEGÅRD

Dag Hammerskjölds Allé

Østbanegad

Østerport
■ Station

Oslo
Plads

Folke Bernadottes Allé

Forbindelsesvej

b

b

10

Sortedam Dossen

Fredensbro

Sortedams Sø

Øster Søgade

Øster Farimagsgade

Stockholmsgade

ØSTER ANLÆG

6

7

Øster Voldgade

Suensonsgade

Store Kongensgade

Grønningen

Gernersgade

11

b

Øster Farimagsgade

Sølvgade

Øster Farimagsgade

5

Rigensgade

Sølvgade

Klerkegade

Adelgade

Borgergade

Store Kongensgade

Esplanaden

Bredgade

12

Kunstindustri-
museet

b

Gothersgade

8

Kronprinsessegade

9

14

b

13

b

Toldbodgade

AMALIEHAVN
GARDENS

SLOTSHOLMEN

15

16

Round Tower

Pilestræde

Gothersgade

Krystalgade

University

Studiestræde

17

Købmagergade

Østergade

Amagertorv
Højbro
Plads

Vestergade

Frederiksberggade

Gl. Strand

Z

22

Holmens Kanal

Store Kongensgade

Bredgade

Kongens
Nytorv

Charlottenborg
Palace
■ Det Kongelige
Teater

Niels Juelsgade

Nyhavn

Nyhavn

Holbergsgade

Skt. Annae
Plads

Havnegade

Indiehavnen

See "Walking Tour:
Kongens Nytorv to
Langelinie" map

Rådhus
Plads

18

21

23

Tøjhusgade

25

Christiansborg
Palace

26

H.C. Andersens Boulevard

Vester Voldgade

GARDENS

19

20

Mitchellsgade

Hambrosgade

Langebro

Christians Brygge

Børsen

Knippelsbro

See "Walking Tour:
The Old City" map

CHRISTIANSHAVN

Strandgade

Overgaden oven Vandet

27

Torvegade

28

Skt. Annae
Gade

Prinsessegade

Langebrogade

Prinsessegade

Sydhavnen

Thorshavnsgade

Stadsgraven

Amager Boulevard

Ved Stadsgraven

Christmas
Møllers
Plads

To Airport

A parade of the red-uniformed Tivoli Boys Guard takes place on weekends at 5:20 and 7:20pm (also on Wed at 5pm), and their regimental band gives concerts on Saturday at 3pm on the open-air stage. The oldest building at Tivoli, the Chinese-style Pantomime Theater with its peacock curtain, offers pantomimes in the evening.

For more on the nighttime happenings in Tivoli—fireworks, bands, orchestras, discos, variety acts—see "Copenhagen After Dark," later in this chapter.

Vesterbrogade 3. ℂ 33-15-10-01. www.tivoligardens.com. Admission 75DKK ($13/£6.75) adults, 40DKK ($8.15/£4.30) children 3–11, free kids under 2. For all rides 200DKK ($34/£18) adults, 150DKK ($26/£14) children 3–11. Family ticket (2 adults, 2 kids) 575DKK ($98/£52). Closed mid-Sept to mid-Apr. Bus: 1, 16, or 29.

2 Amalienborg Palace & Environs

Amalienborg Palace 🕂🕂   If the beloved *Dronning,* Queen Margrethe II, is in residence, a swallowtail flies from the roof of this palace. The queen became the ruler of Denmark in 1953, only after the laws of succession were changed to allow a woman to ascend to the throne. The daughter of King Frederik IX and Queen Ingrid was born in 1940 during one of her country's darkest hours, the Nazi takeover of Denmark.

She studied at universities in London and the Sorbonne in Paris before becoming a member of the Women's Flying Corps and the WAAF in England. After her marriage to a French diplomat, Henri Comte de Laborade de Monpezat, in 1967, she had two sons, Frederik, born in 1968, and Joachim, born in 1969.

She has turned out to be a hardworking, progressively modern royal who is more accessible and beloved by her subjects than her counterpart, the queen of England. The Danes love their queen, despite being a very liberal people with a tradition of democratic equality. A survey revealed one of the reasons why. "She puffs cigars like a smokestack," claim her admirers.

These four 18th-century French-style rococo mansions—opening onto one of the most attractive squares in Europe—have been the home of the Danish royal family since 1794, when Christiansborg burned. Visitors flock to see the changing of the guard at noon, when the royal family is in residence. This has been called Copenhagen's greatest photo opportunity, but it doesn't impress us as much as the changing of the guard at London's Buckingham Palace.

The Royal Life Guard in black bearskin busbies (like the hussars) leaves Rosenborg Castle at noon and marches along Gothersgade, Nørre Voldgade, Frederiksberggade, Købmagergade, Østergade, Kongens Nytorv, Bredgade, Skt. Annæ Plads, and Amaliegade, to Amalienborg. After the event, the Guard, still accompanied by the band, returns to Rosenborg Castle via Frederiksgade, Store Kongensgade, and Gothersgade.

In 1994, some of the official and private rooms in Amalienborg were opened to the public. The rooms, reconstructed to reflect the period 1863 to 1947, all belonged to members of the royal family, the Glücksborgs, who ascended the throne in 1863. The highlight is the period devoted to the long reign (1863–1906) of Christian IX (1818–1906) and Queen Louise (1817–98). The items in his study and her drawing room—gifts from their far-flung children—reflect their unofficial status as "parents-in-law to Europe." Indeed, the story of their lives has been called "the Making of a Dynasty." Both came from distant sides of the then-heirless royal family to create a "love match." The verses for their 1842 wedding song (a Danish tradition) were written by Hans Christian Andersen.

Christian and Louise gave their six children a simple (by royal standards) but internationally oriented upbringing. One daughter, Alexandra, married Edward VII of

Frommer's Favorite Copenhagen Experiences

Sitting at an Outdoor Cafe. Because of Copenhagen's long gray winters, sitting outdoors and drinking beer or eating is a favorite, savored summer pastime. The best spot is at Nyhavn (New Harbor), beginning at Kongens Nytorv. Enjoy ice cream while admiring the tall ships moored in the canal.

Going to the Tivoli. This is the quintessential summer adventure, a tradition since 1843. It's an amusement park with a difference—even the merry-go-rounds are special, using a fleet of Viking ships instead of the usual horses.

Strolling Strøget. The Danish word *strøget* means "to stroll"—and that's exactly what shopping addicts do along this nearly 1.2km (¾-mile) stretch, from Rådhuspladsen to Kongens Nytorv.

Exploring Alternative Lifestyles. Not for everybody, but worth a look, is a trip to the Free City of Christiania, on the island of Christianshavn (take bus no. 8 from Rådhuspladsen). Since 1971, some 1,000 squatters have taken over 130 former army barracks (spread across 8 hectares/20 acres) and declared themselves a free city. You can shop, dine, and talk to the natives about the experimental community, which has its own doctors, clubs, and stores. It even flies its own flag. Exercise caution here, however.

England; another, Dagmar, wed Czar Alexander III of Russia. The crown prince, later Frederik VIII, married Louise of Sweden-Norway; another son became king of Greece, and yet another declined the throne of Bulgaria. In 1905 a grandson became king of Norway.

In the 1880s, members of the Danish royal family, numbering more than 50, got together regularly each summer at the Fredensborg Palace, north of Copenhagen. The children, now monarchs in their own right, brought Christian IX and Louise presents—works of art from the imperial workshops and from jewelers such as Fabergé—as well as souvenirs, embroideries, and handicrafts made by the grandchildren. All became treasures for the aging king and queen, and many are exhibited in the museum rooms today.

Also open to the public are the studies of Frederik VIII and Christian X. Thanks to his marriage to Louise of Sweden-Norway, the liberal-minded Frederik VIII (1843–1912), who reigned from 1906 to 1912, had considerable wealth, and he furnished Amalienborg Palace sumptuously. The king's large study, decorated in lavish neo-Renaissance style, testifies to this.

The final period room in the museum is the study of Christian X (1870–1947), the grandfather of current queen Margrethe II, who was king from 1912 to 1947. He became a symbol of national resistance during the German occupation of Denmark during World War II. Along with the period rooms, a costume gallery and a jewelry room are open to the public. The Amalienborg Museum rooms compose one of two divisions of the Royal Danish Collections; the other is at Rosenborg Palace in Copenhagen.

Christian VIII's Palace. © **33-40-10-10.** www.rosenborgslot.dk. Admission 50DKK ($8.50/£4.50) adults, 30DKK ($5.10/£2.70) students, 15DKK ($2.55/£1.35) children 5–12, free for children 4 and under. May–Oct daily 10am–4pm; Nov–Apr daily 11am–4pm. Closed Mon. Bus: 1, 6, 9, or 10.

Den Lille Havfrue (The Little Mermaid) ℛ *(Moments*   The statue *everybody* wants to see in Copenhagen is the slightly smaller-than-life-size bronze of *Den Lille Havfrue,* inspired by Andersen's famous fairy tale *The Little Mermaid.* Edvard Eriksen sculpted the statue, unveiled in 1913. It rests on rocks right off the shoreline of the seagoing entrance to Copenhagen's harbor, close to Kastellet and the Langelinie cruise piers.

In spite of its small size, the statue is as important a symbol to Copenhageners as the Statue of Liberty is to New Yorkers. Tragedy struck on January 6, 1998, when an anonymous tipster called a freelance television cameraman in the middle of the night to check out the 1.2m (4-ft.) bronze Mermaid. She'd lost her head. Most of the city responded with sadness. "She is part of our heritage, like Tivoli, the queen, and stuff like that," said local sculptor Christian Moerk.

The Mermaid had also been decapitated in 1964. The culprits at that time were never discovered, and the head was never recovered. In the early 1920s some unknown party or parties cut off her arm. The original mold exists, so it's possible to recast the bronze and weld back missing body parts. The arm was replaced.

Although not taking blame for the last attack in 1998, the Radical Feminist Faction sent flyers to newspapers to protest "the woman-hating, sexually fixated male dreams" allegedly conjured by the statue's bronze nudity. After the last decapitation, the head turned up at a TV station, delivered by a masked figure. In the spring, welders put her head back on, making the seam invisible. Today, *The Little Mermaid*—head, fishy tail, and all—is back to being the most photographed nude woman in Copenhagen.

Because of all these attacks, the statue, seen by about a million visitors a year, may actually be moved out of the reach of both vandals and tourists to a safer, more secure place. City officials are considering such a proposal. At present, many visitors claim they can't see the statue because throughout the day other tourists are constantly climbing all over her to have their picture taken.

In 2006 another Little Mermaid sculpture was unveiled, a "genetically modified sister," lying 396m (1,320 ft.) from the original. The new bronze is by Bjørn Nørgaard, a professor at the Royal Danish Academy of Fine Arts. Like the original, Nørgaard's mermaid also sits on a rock, but her features are twisted and her limbs exaggeratedly long and skeletal. Nørgaard created the sculpture for the Danish Pavilion at Expo 2002, the World's Fair held in Hanover, Germany.

Near *The Little Mermaid* statue is **Gefion Springvandet** (Gefion Fountain), sculpted by Anders Bundgaard. Gefion was a Scandinavian goddess who plowed Zealand away from Sweden by turning her sons into oxen.

Also in the area is **Kastellet** at Langelinie (ℂ **33-11-22-33**), a pentagon-shaped citadel, replete with moats, constructed by King Frederik III in the then virtually impregnable style of the 1660s. Some of Copenhagen's original ramparts still surround the structure. Although today the site is brightened with beds of seasonal flowers and statues honoring prominent Danes, the Citadel functioned as the capital's first line of defense from seagoing invasion until the 18th century. During the Nazi occupation of Copenhagen, the Germans made it their headquarters. Today the Danish military occupies the buildings. You can, however, explore the beautiful grounds of Churchill-parken surrounding Kastellet. At the entrance to the park stands St. Albans, the English church of Copenhagen. You can still see the double moats built as part of Copenhagen's defense in the wake of the Swedish siege of the capital on February 10, 1659. The ruined citadel can be explored daily from 6am to sunset. Admission is free.

Langelinie on the harbor. Bus: 1, 6, or 9.

Frihedsmuseet (Museum of Danish Resistance, 1940–45) ☞ As World War II buffs, we always pay at least one visit here on every trip to Copenhagen. There's always some new piece of information to learn. In 1942, Hitler sent King Christian X a birthday greeting. The response was terse. In retaliation, Hitler sent Werner Best, one of the architects of the Gestapo, to rule Denmark. Hitler used Denmark mainly as a "larder" to feed his Nazi armies during the war. The Danes resisted at every turn, including rounding up 7,000 Danish Jews and shipping them off to neutral Sweden before they could be deported to Germany. This museum also reveals the tools of espionage and sabotage that the Danes used to throw off the Nazi yoke in World War II. Beginning softly with peace marches in the early days of the war, the resistance movement grew from a fledgling organization into a highly polished and skilled underground that eventually electrified and excited the Allied world. "Danes Fighting Germans!" blared the headlines.

The museum highlights the workings of the outlaw press, the wireless communications equipment and illegal films, relics of torture and concentration camps, British propaganda leaflets dropped in the country, satirical caricatures of Hitler, information about Danish Jews and, conversely, about Danish Nazis, and material on the paralyzing nationwide strikes. In all, this moment in history is graphically and dramatically preserved. An armed car, used against Danish Nazi informers and collaborators, is displayed on the grounds.

Churchillparken. ☎ 33-13-77-14. www.frihedsmuseet.dk. Free admission. May–Sept 15 Tues–Sat 10am–4pm, Sun 10am–5pm; Sept 16–Apr Tues–Sat 11am–3pm, Sun 11am–4pm. Bus: 1, 6, or 9.

Kunstindustrimuseet (Museum of Decorative and Applied Art) ☞ Admittedly, this museum of decorative and applied art is for aficionados and is not everyone's "cuppa," but for what it is, it is the finest such museum in Scandinavia. With more than 300,000 decorative objects on view, it's a lot to digest and worth at least 2 hours of your time.

The rococo building itself is one of the historic landmarks of Copenhagen, containing four wings surrounding a garden. It was part of the Royal Frederik Hospital, built from 1752 to 1757 during the reign of King Frederik V, and it was here in a hospital bed that Søren Kierkegaard drew his last breath in 1855.

Allowed to rot and grow seedy, the building was taken over by the city in thee 1920s, restored, and turned into a series of rooms, which are arranged in chronological order and trace living rooms from the Middle Ages to the 20th century.

Pride of place is given to furniture, tapestries, other textiles, pottery, porcelain, glass, and silver, and there are many exhibits focusing on the innovative role of Danish modern design—mostly furniture and fabrics—since the 1930s. There are also rare collections of Chinese and Japanese art and handicrafts. The library contains around 65,000 books and periodicals dealing with arts and crafts, architecture, costumes, advertising, photography, and industrial design. The gardens surrounding the museum are open during museum hours. In summer, theatrical performances are staged here for both adults and children, and the museum cafe offers al fresco cafe-style tables when the weather is fair. We find these gardens, with their manicured grounds and beautiful old linden trees, as well as strategically placed sculptures, one of the most charming of the outdoor spaces of Copenhagen, an ideal place to "take a break."

Bredgade 68. ☎ 33-18-56-56. www.kunstindustrimuseet.dk. Admission to museum 40DKK ($6.80/£3.60) adults, free for children under 18. Free admission to library. Museum Tues–Fri 10am–4pm; Sat–Sun noon–4pm. Library Tues–Sat 10am–4pm. S-tog: Østerport. Bus: 1, 6, or 9.

Impressions

There is nothing of Hamlet in their character.
—R. H. Bruce Lockhart, *My Europe*, 1952

Copenhagen is the best-built city of the north.
—William Coxe, *Travels*, 1792

Davids Samling ⊕ *(Finds)*   When we first climbed the stairs to the top floor of this museum, we were astonished to discover an unheralded surprise—the Nordic world's greatest collection of art from the **World of Islam** ⊕⊕⊕, dating from the 7th to the 19th centuries and looted from such distant points as Spain and West India. An astonishing array of pottery, weaponry, glassware, silverware, texts, and textiles, among other exhibits, await you.

Originally, Christian Ludvig David, a lawyer in the Danish High Court, began this collection with his wide-ranging tastes. He died in 1960, leaving his carefully chosen treasure trove to the city, and since that time the museum has added to his bequests.

It's true that most visitors ignore the barrister's collection as they rush to take in the wonders of Rosenborg Slot or the Statens Museum for Kunst, both of which are nearby, but the Sambling collection deserves at least 1½ hours of your time. In addition to those Islamic treasures, the museum includes floors devoted to European fine and applied art from the 18th to the 20th centuries. Regrettably, the museum will be closed for renovations until June 2008.

David's other major bequest was his summer villa in the northern suburbs of Copenhagen at Marienborg, reserved for the Danish prime minister's use.

Kronprinsessegade 30. © **33-13-55-64.** Free admission. Tues–Sun 1–4pm. Bus: 1, 6, 9, 10, 19, 29, 31, 42, or 43.

3 Rosenborg Castle, Botanical Gardens & Environs

Rosenborg Castle ⊕⊕⊕   "It's cool in a Robin Leach kinda way," wrote an American student after viewing this palace, the greatest and purest (its facade hasn't changed since 1633) Renaissance structure in Denmark. It has survived fires and wars, and stands to delight us today, or at least those of us who have 2 hours to spare.

Christian IV conceived of the palace in 1606, but it began with **Kongens Have** ⊕, the King's Garden, which still surrounds the palace today, and is one of the more delightful places in Copenhagen for a stroll. The king liked the place so much he built a summer pavilion here, which eventually led to the creation of this monumental red brick "slot," inspired by the Dutch Renaissance style, and today one of the most beautiful and evocative monuments of Denmark.

It houses everything from narwhal-tusked and ivory coronation chairs to Frederik VII's baby shoes—all artifacts from the Danish royal family, who for many generations relegated this elegant building to the role of a storage bin for royal artifacts. Officially, its biggest draws are the dazzling **crown jewels and regalia** ⊕⊕⊕ in the basement Treasury, which houses a lavishly decorated coronation saddle from 1596 and other treasures. Try to see the **Knights Hall** ⊕ in Room 21, with its coronation seat, three silver lions, and relics from the 1700s. Room 3 was used by founding father Christian IV (lucky in love, unlucky in war), who died in this bedroom decorated with Asian lacquer art and a stucco ceiling.

Øster Voldgade 4A. ⓒ **33-15-32-86**. www.rosenborgslot.dk. Admission 65DKK ($11/£5.85) adults, 40DKK ($6.80/
£3.60) students and seniors, free for children under 17. Palace and treasury (royal jewels) Jan–Apr Tues–Sun
11am–2pm; May and Sept–Oct daily 10am–4pm; June–Aug daily 10am–5pm; Nov–Dec 17 Tues–Sun 11am–2pm.
S-tog: Nørreport. Bus: 5, 10, 14, 16, 31, 42, 43, 184, or 185.

Botanisk Have (Botanical Gardens) 🐾

Cacti, orchids, and palm trees always
draw us to the most splendid 10 hectares (25 acres) in all of Denmark. Planted from
1871 to 1874—and still around to thrill us to this day—these botanical gardens are
on a lake that was once part of the city's defensive moat around Rosenborg Slott,
which fronts the gardens. In fact, after a visit to Rosenborg, we always like to come
here to wind down after devouring so many royal treasures. Greenhouses grow both
tropical and subtropical plants, none finer than the **Palm House** 🐾🐾, which appears
even more exotic this far north. Retreat here on a rainy day, and imagine you're in the
tropics. An alpine garden also contains mountain plants from all over the world.

Gothersgade 128. ⓒ **35-32-22-40**. www.botanic-garden.ku.dk. Free admission. May–Sept daily 8:30am–6pm;
Oct–Apr Tues–Sun 8:30am–4pm. S-tog: Nørreport. Bus: 5A, 14, 40, 42, or 43. Closed Dec 24 and Jan 1.

Statens Museum for Kunst (Royal Museum of Fine Arts) 🐾🐾🐾 Kids

We could
spend an entire day here and always find some new artistic discovery. If you can't
afford so much time, give it at least 2 hours, even more if you can spare it. The largest
museum in Denmark houses painting and sculpture from the 13th century to the
present, the collection originally acquired by the kings of Denmark.

The old museum building dates from 1896, the creation of architect Wilhelm
Dahlerup, but it has been greatly extended by modern wings. In 1750 Frederik V
launched the collection by purchasing vast art from the continent, especially Flemish
and Dutch paintings, but also Italian and German works. Bruegel, Rubens,
Rembrandt, and Memling are just some of the artists waiting to dazzle you. Of all
these works, we are drawn to a masterpiece by Andrea Mantegna, *Christ as the*
Suffering Redeemer 🐾🐾🐾.

The so-called Danish golden age of painting from the 19th century forms one of
the greatest treasures of the museum. Except for Edvard Munch from Norway, most
of these Scandinavian artists will not be known to the general public. One of the
best treats here is a mighty symbolist work, *Christ in the Kingdom of Death* 🐾🐾 by
P. C. Skovgaard, representing a milestone in Danish art. Nearly all the Danish masters
of the era are exhibited, including the famous Skagen and Funen painters.

Generous donations or long-term loans have beefed up the former royal collection
of paintings and sculptures. In 1928 Johannes Rump donated a huge collection of
early French modernists. The predictable Braque and Picasso works are here, but there
is a stunning collection of **25 paintings by Henri Matisse** 🐾🐾.

The **Italian school** 🐾🐾 is also a rich trove of art, with works by Filippino Lippi,
Titian, and Tintoretto. The museum also contains one of the world's oldest collections
of **European prints and drawings** 🐾🐾🐾, including contributions from Giacometti,
Rembrandt, Degas, and Toulouse-Lautrec. Some of these copper prints, drawings,
etchings, watercolors, and lithographic works date from the 1400s. The German
painter Albrecht Dürer claims that he gave the king "the best pieces of all my prints."

Also on site is a **Children's Museum** on the ground floor, with hands-on displays.
At a workshop held daily from 2 to 4pm, kids can draw, paint, and sculpt. If you want
to take a break, head for the stylish cafe on site, decorated by artist Viera Collaro and
offering a view of the greenery of Østre Anlæg, a park and a lake.

Sølvgade 48–50. © **33-74-84-94**. www.smk.dk. Free admission. Tues and Thurs–Sun 10am–5pm; Wed 10am–8pm. Bus: 10, 14, 26, 40, 43, 184, or 185.

Den Hirschsprungske Samling (Hirschsprung Collection) ⊛   The setting for the museum is romantic, as it's beautifully situated in the green parklands of Østre Anlæg on the old ramparts of Copenhagen. Never have the "dancing light and sparkling waters" of the Danish seashore and countryside been so evocatively captured as they are in this highly personal collection of art from Denmark's so-called golden age of painting (1800–50), when naturalism was not just in bloom, but flowering at its zenith.

You may not even recognize the names of any of the artists on parade, but you can still have a visual treat for 1 to 1½ hours by wandering through, focusing on whatever captures your fancy. The collection was financed by the smoking of tobacco. Heinrich Hirschsprung (1836–1908), a tobacco manufacturer, bequeathed his treasures to the Danish state, which housed them in a neoclassical building constructed in 1911 in back of the Fine Arts Museum.

Just as long as the painters were Danish, Hirschsprung collected their art over a period of 40 years—paintings, drawings, and sculptures, including the Skagen artists, the Symbolists, and the *Fynboerne* ("Natives of Funen"). We feel a great intimacy was created here by the museum's wise decision to exhibit beautiful interiors featuring furniture from the homes and studios of many of the artists. Captivating us were such artists as Eckersberg, Købke, and Lundbye, and on the Skagen painters P. S. Krøyer and Anna and Michael Ancher.

Stockholmsgade 20. © **35-42-03-36**. www.hirschsprung.dk. Admission 35DKK ($5.95/£3.15) adults, free for children under 16, free to all Wed. Wed–Mon 11am–4pm. Bus: 6A, 14, 40, 42, or 43.

4 Christiansborg Palace & Environs

Christiansborg Palace ⊛⊛⊛   Over the centuries Christiansborg Castle has led a rough life ever since the founding father of Copenhagen, Bishop Absalon, completed the first Slott here in 1167. That castle burned down—and so did the next two palaces.

Christiansborg Slot was a royal residence beginning in 1416, when Erik of Pomerania moved in. The royals lived here until fleeing to more comfortable quarters at Amalienborg Slott in 1794. Christian VI ordered that the entire castle be torn down in 1732: he didn't like Frederik IV's aesthetic tastes, finding Christiansborg "an eyesore." But his new place burned down on the night of February 26, 1794.

What is left standing today is a granite-and-copper palace from 1928. It stands on Slotsholmen, a small island in the center of Copenhagen that has been the seat of political power in Denmark for 800 years. Today it houses the Danish Parliament, the Supreme Court, this prime minister's offices, and the Royal Reception Rooms. A guide will lead you through richly decorated rooms, including the Throne Room, Banqueting Hall, and the Queen's Library. Before entering, you'll be asked to put on soft overshoes to protect the floors.

Under the palace, visit the well-preserved ruins of the 1167 castle of Bishop Absalon.

You can also see **Kongelige Stalde & Kareter** ⊛, Christiansborg Ridebane 12 (© **33-40-10-10**), the royal stables and coaches. Elegantly clad in riding breeches and jackets, riders exercise the royal horses. Vehicles include regal coaches and "fairy-tale" carriages, along with a display of harnesses in use by the royal family since 1778.

Admission is 10DKK ($1.70/90p) for adults, free for children under 12. The site can be visited May to October Saturday to Sunday 2 to 4pm.

Christiansborg Slotsplads. © **33-92-64-92.** Guided tour of Royal Reception Rooms 60DKK ($10/£5.40) adults, 25DKK ($4.25/£2.25) children 4–17. Admission to castle ruins 40DKK ($6.80/£3.60) adults, 15DKK ($2.55/£1.35) children 4–17. Free admission to parliament. Guided tours of Reception Rooms May–Sept daily at 11am, 1pm, and 3pm; Oct–Apr Tues–Sun at 3pm. Ruins May–Sept daily 10am–4pm; Oct–Apr Tues–Sun 10am–4pm. English-language tours of parliament daily 11am, 1pm, and 3pm year-round. Bus: 1, 2, 5, 8, or 9.

Nationalmuseet (National Museum) 🎭🎭🎭 *Kids* The nucleus of this museum started out as Frederik II's "Royal Chamber of Curiosities" in 1650. It continued to grow and is now the Nordic world's greatest repository of anthropological artifacts. Housed in a sumptuous once-royal palace, the museum is "not just for students," as one bored critic noted.

There's something here for everyone, even for kids who gravitate to the on-site Children's Museum geared to ages 4 to 12. You never know what you'll come upon, including the *lur* horn, a Bronze Age instrument that is among the oldest of its kind in Europe. It still makes music. The world-famous **Sun Chariot** 🎭🎭🎭 is an elegant Bronze Age piece of pagan art. Dating from around 1,200 B.C., the rare find was unearthed by a farmer while plowing his ground in 1902.

The museum is divided into five different departments, beginning with the Pre-historic Wing on the ground floor with artifacts from the reindeer stalkers of the Ice Age to the Vikings, with runic stones, helmets, and fragments of battle gear. This department will reopen in May 2008.

In the Runic Stone Hall, the **Hjortespring Boat** 🎭🎭 dates from around 300 B.C. This "war canoe" is the oldest plank-built boat unearthed in the north of Europe. One of the most stunning displays in this hall is the **Golden Age Room** 🎭🎭🎭, with its dazzling display of gold objects, some dating from 1,000 B.C.

One of the richest sections of the museum lies upstairs in the Medieval and Renaissance Departments, covering both the pre- and post-Reformation eras. Naturally exhibits are strong in ecclesiastical art, but also well represented in the decorative art accumulated by a trio of Danish Renaissance kings, including Christian III and IV, as well as Frederik II. A rare treasure here Frederik II's tapestries made for the Great Hall of Kronborg Slot.

The Peoples of the World Department is one of the oldest ethnographical collections in the world, with artifacts ranging from Papua New Guinea to Central America. This section also displays artifacts of the Eskimo culture that still flourishes in Greenland, which is under the control of Denmark. The **Royal Collection of Coins and Medals** 🎭🎭 lies in one of the loveliest rooms (#146) in Copenhagen, with views over Christiansborg Slot. The salon displays various coins from antiquity. The **Collection of Antiquities** 🎭🎭🎭 has been called "the British Museum in miniature." It contains everything from two fragments from the Parthenon, stolen by a Danish naval officer in 1687, to Holy Roman cups depicting Homeric legends.

Ny Vestergade 10. © **33-13-44-11.** www.natmus.dk. Free admission. Tues–Sun 10am–5pm. Closed Dec 24–25 and Dec 31. Bus: 1, 2, 5, 6, 8, 10, or 41.

Erotica Museum Everything you ever wanted to know about sex will be revealed to you here, although we could skip those vivid depictions of venereal skin diseases. All age groups are represented here, from teenagers to octogenarians. This is perhaps the only museum in the world where you can go to learn about the sex lives of such

famous people as Freud, Nietzsche, and Duke Ellington. Founded by Ole Ege, a well-known Danish photographer of nudes, it's within walking distance of Tivoli and the Central Railroad Station. In addition to providing a glimpse into the sex lives of the famous, the exhibits present a survey of erotica from around the world as well as through the ages.

The exhibits range from the tame to the tempestuous—everything from Etruscan drawings and Chinese paintings to Greek vases depicting a lot of sexual activity. On display are remarkable lifelike tableaux created by craftspeople from Tussaud's Wax Museum, as well as a collection of those dirty little postcards Americans tried to sneak home through Customs back in the 1920s and 1930s.

As you ascend the floors of the museum, the more explicit the exhibits become. By the time you reach the fourth (top) floor, a dozen video monitors are showing erotic films, featuring everything from black-and-white films from the 1920s—all made underground—to today's triple X-rated releases.

Købmagergade 24. Ⓒ 33-12-03-11. Admission 109DKK ($19/£9.80). Visitors under 15 must be accompanied by an adult. May–Sept daily 10am–11pm; Oct–Apr Sun–Thurs 11am–8pm, Fri–Sat 10am–10pm. S-tog: Nørreport.

Tøjhusmuseet (Royal Arsenal Museum) ⚔ If in your darkest soul, you have a bloody heart and want to see the weapons that man has used to kill his fellow man over the centuries, you've come to the gruesome doorstep. Actually, the long Arsenal Hall on the ground floor is an architectural curiosity, the longest arched hall in Europe, with its cross vaults supported by 16 heavy center pillars. Displayed here are an armada of weapons, some 350 historical guns, mortars, and howitzers, with artillery equipment ranging from 1500 to the present day. The Armory Hall upstairs was once a storehouse for hand weapons, and today has 7,000 of these killers, some dating from 1300. Christian IV's original arsenal building was constructed between 1589 and 1604 with the thickest walls in Copenhagen, measuring 4m (13 ft.). The most beautiful weapons—if such a word can be used in this context—are the ivory-inlaid pistols and muskets. The royal suits of armor are almost works of art unto themselves. Here is where we'll go out on a limb: this arsenal museum is the finest of its kind in the world.

Tøjhusgade 3. Ⓒ 33-11-60-37. www.thm.dk. Admission 40DKK ($6.80/£3.60) adults, 20DKK ($3.40/£1.80) students and seniors, free for children under 18. Tues–Sun noon–4pm. Closed Jan 1, Dec 23–26, and Dec 31. Bus: 1, 2, 5, 8, and 9.

Thorvaldsens Museum ⚔ This is the oldest art gallery in Denmark, having opened on September 18, 1848. This museum on Slotsholmen, next door to Christiansborg, houses the greatest collection of the works of Bertel Thorvaldsen (1770–1844), the biggest name in neoclassical sculpture. Thorvaldsen's life represented the romanticism of the 18th and 19th centuries: He rose from semipoverty to the pinnacle of success in his day. He's famous for his most typical, classical, restrained works, taken from mythology: Cupid and Psyche, Adonis, Jason, Hercules, Ganymede, Mercury—all of which are displayed at the museum. *Jason* was one of his first works and remains one of our favorites. It brought fame and success to him throughout Europe, and set him off on a long career after its completion in 1803. In addition to the works of this latter-day exponent of Roman classicism, the museum also contains Thorvaldsen's personal, and quite extensive, collection, everything from the Egyptian relics of Ptolemy to the contemporary paintings he acquired during his lifetime *(Apollo Among the Thessalian Shepherds)*. After many years of self-imposed exile in Italy, Thorvaldsen returned in triumph to his native Copenhagen, where he died a national figure and was buried here in the courtyard of his own personal museum.

Bertel Thorvaldsens Plads 2. ℂ **33-32-15-32**. www.thorvaldsensmuseum.dk. Admission 20DKK ($3.40/£1.80) adults, free for children under 18, free to all Wed. Tues–Sun 10am–5pm. Closed Jan 1, Dec 24–25, and Dec 31. Bus: 1A, 2, 15, 26, 29, or 650S.

5 In the Old Town (Indre By)

Rundetårn (Round Tower)   For the most **panoramic view** ℱℱℱ of the city of Copenhagen, climb the spiral ramp (no steps) leading up to the top of this tower, which was built in 1642. The spiral walk to the top is unique in European architecture, measuring 209m (67 ft.) and winding itself 7½ times around the hollow core of the tower, forming the only link between the individual parts of the building complex. Obviously not wanting to walk, Peter the Great, in Denmark on a state visit, galloped up the ramp on horseback, preceded by his carriage-drawn czarina. Rundetårn is also the oldest functioning observatory in Europe, in use until 1861 by the University of Copenhagen. Now anyone can observe the night sky through the astronomical telescope in the winter months.

Købmagergade 52A. ℂ **33-73-03-73**. www.rundetaarn.dk. Admission 25DKK ($4.25/£2.25) adults, 5DKK (85¢/45p) children 5–15. Tower June–Aug Mon–Sat 10am–8pm, Sun noon–8pm; Sept–May Mon–Sat 10am–5pm, Sun noon–5pm. Observatory Oct 15–Mar 22 only Tues–Wed 7–10pm; June 20–Aug 10 only Sun 1–4pm. Bus: 5, 7E, 14, 16, or 42.

Vor Frue Kirke (Copenhagen Cathedral)   For such an important European capital as Copenhagen, the cathedral of the Danish capital is relatively modest. The reason that it's so lacking in art and treasures was because of a fanatical attack by Lutheran zealots during the darkest days of the Reformation. They came through here destroying precious treasures that should have been saved for future generations to appreciate.

The cathedral was designed by C. F. Hansen, the third such building erected here. The original Gothic structure was destroyed by fire in 1728, and the second cathedral damaged by British bombardments in 1807.

The church is often used for funerals of the country's greatest men and women—the funeral of Hans Christian Andersen took place here in 1875 and that of Søren Kierkegaard in 1855.

We like to come here mainly to listen to certain musical events (ask at the tourist office for details) and to see several sculptures by the great Thorvaldsen, including his majestic *Christ and the Apostles* ℱℱ.

Nørregade. ℂ **33-14-41-28**. Free admission. Mon–Fri 8am–5pm. Bus: 5 or 6A.

6 More Museums

Kongelige Bibliotek (Royal Library) ℱ   The Danish Royal Library, dating from the 1600s, is the largest and most impressive in the Norse countries. The classical building, with its high-ceilinged reading rooms, is a grand and impressive place. The library owns original manuscripts by such Danish writers as H. C. Andersen and Karen Blixen (Isak Dinesen). In 1998, sorely in need of more storage space for its many historically important records, the library was expanded with the addition of a gargantuan and sharply angular granite annex, the Black Diamond, which extended the venerable antique structure out and over the waterfront traffic artery, expanding it in a dazzling (and dizzying) study in architectural contrasts. *Tip:* If you have the time, don't suffer from any kind of vertigo, and aren't stopped by a security guard, consider taking the elevator to the highest floor of the echoing interior spaces of the Black Diamond. Because of locked doors and security codes on that level, you'll probably remain within the hallways and not within any of the *"Sanctum sanctorums."* But even from the catwalks and walkways of the top floor, the sense of height, interplay of sunlight and shadows, and the perspectives can be both terrifying and awe-inspiring. An irony? In keeping with the Black Diamond's role as a repository for books, its floors, as designated by the elevators inside, are labeled as Levels "A, B, and C" rather than the more conventional designations as "1, 2, or 3." Likened to Sydney's Opera House for its evocative and enigmatic appearance, the Black Diamond's progressive but boxy-looking design adds to the monumentality of the waterfront promenade—by the harbor between the bridges Langebro and Knippelsbro. A myriad of dazzling, reflective slabs of black granite from Zimbabwe cover the facade, and its exterior walls slant sharply at disconcerting angles. Along with space for 200,000 books, the Black Diamond features a bookshop, an upscale restaurant (The Søren K), six reading rooms, a courtyard for exhibitions, and a 600-seat concert hall. After viewing the interiors of both the old and new sections of the library, you can wander through its formal gardens, past the fishpond and statue of philosopher Søren Kierkegaard.

Søren Kierkegaards Plads 1. ℂ 33-47-47-47. www.kb.dk. Free admission. Mon–Fri 10am–5pm. Bus: 1, 2, 5, 6, 8, or 9.

Orlogsmuseet (Royal Naval Museum)   Do you ever lie awake at night wondering what happened to the propeller from the German U-boat that sank the *Lusitania?* Look no further: It's here at this former naval hospital in Søkvasthuset, opening onto the Christianshavn Kanal. That's not all that's here, as you can follow the history of Denmark, a maritime nation, through the exhibits of its royal navy. Although there are a lot of artifacts that won't interest you, many will. More than 300 model ships, many based on designs that date from as early as 1500, are on view, and some of them were designed and constructed by naval engineers, serving as prototypes for the construction of actual ships that ventured into the cold dark waters of the North Sea. The models are wide ranging—some are fully "dressed," with working sails, whereas others are cross-sectional with their frames outlined. You get a vast array of other naval artifacts too, including an intriguing collection of figureheads, some of which are artworks themselves. For us, nothing is as glamorous or splendid as an ornate state barge from 1780.

Overgaden Oven Vandet 58. ℂ 33-11-60-37. www.orlogsmuseet.dk. Admission 40DKK ($6.80/£3.60) adults, free for children under 16. Tues–Sun noon–4pm. Bus: 2, 19, or 350S.

7 The Churches of Copenhagen

For information on the Copenhagen Cathedral, refer to "In the Old Town (Indre By)," above.

Frederikskirke (Marble Church) ☆   In many ways, this landmark church is more richly decorated and impressive than Copenhagen's cathedral, Vor Frue Kirke. Instead of Frederikskirke, Danes often call this building "Marmorkirken" or the Marble Church. Lying just a short walk from Amalienborg Palace, it began unsuccessfully in 1749. The original plan was to use "quarries" of expensive Norwegian marble. The treasury dried up in 1770, and work came to a halt. It wasn't resumed until late in the

19th century when an industrialist, C. F. Tietgen, put up the money for its completion. This time a cheaper Danish marble was used instead. The original design was for
neo-classical revival, but in the end the church was constructed in the Roman baroque
style, opening in 1894. Inspired by Michelangelo's dome for St. Peter's in Rome, the
Danish church was crowned with a copper dome, measuring 46m (151 ft.), making
it one of the largest in the world.

Frederiksgade 4. ℂ 33-15-01-44. Free admission to church. Free admission. Church Mon–Thurs 10am–5pm; Fri–Sun
noon–5pm. Dome June 15–Aug 31 daily 1 and 3pm; Sept–June 14 Sat–Sun 1 and 3pm. Bus: 1, 6, or 9.

Holmens Kirke   This Lutheran church became world famous in 1967 when Queen
Margrethe II married Prince Henrik here. Built in 1619, this royal chapel and naval
church lies across the canal from Slotsholmen, next to the National Bank of Denmark.
Although the structure was converted into a church for the Royal Navy in 1619, its
nave was built in 1562 as an anchor forge. By 1641 the ever-changing church was renovated to its current, predominantly Dutch Renaissance style. The so-called "royal
doorway" was brought from Roskilde Cathedral in the 19th century. Inside, the
extraordinary feature of this church is its ostentatious **baroque altar** 𝕱𝕱 of unpainted
oak, a carved pulpit by Abel Schrøder the Younger that extends right to the roof. In
the burial chamber are the tombs of some of Denmark's most towering naval figures,
including Admiral Niels Juel, who successfully fought off a naval attack by Swedes in
1677 in the Battle of Køge Bay. Peder Tordenskjold, who defeated Charles XII of Sweden during the Great Northern War in the early 1700s, is also entombed here.

Holmens Kanal. ℂ 33-13-61-78. Free admission. Mon–Sat 9am–2pm; Sat 9am–noon. Bus: 1, 2, 6, 8, 9, 10, 31, 37,
or 43.

Vor Frelsers Kirken   The architect of the 1752 staircase of the "Church of Our
Savior" (its English name) was Laurids de Thurah. A legend still persists about him.
It is said that he constructed the staircase encircling the building the wrong way.
Climbing to the top, and belatedly realizing what he'd done, he jumped to his death.
A good story, but it's not true. According to more reliable reports, he died poverty
stricken in his sleep in his own bed in 1759. The green-and-gold tower of this Gothic
structure is a Copenhagen landmark, dominating the Christianshavn area. Inside,
view the splendid baroque altar, richly adorned with a romp of cherubs and other figures. There are also a lovely font and an immense three-story organ from 1698. Four
hundred vertigo-inducing steps will take you to the top, where you'll see a gilded figure of Christ standing on a globe and a **panoramic view** 𝕱𝕱𝕱 of the city. *Warning:*
Those steps grow narrower as they reach the pinnacle.

Skt. Annæ Gade 29. ℂ 32-57-27-98. Free admission to church. Admission to tower 20DKK ($3.40/£1.80) adults,
10DKK ($1.70/90p) children. Apr–Aug Mon–Sat 11am–4:30pm, Sun noon–4:30pm; Sept–Oct Mon–Sat
11am–3:30pm, Sun noon–3:30pm; Nov–Mar daily 11am–3:30pm. Metro: Christianshavn. It is possible to visit the
tower only Apr–Oct.

8 A Glimpse into the Past Outside Copenhagen

Frilandsmuseet (Open-Air Museum) 𝕱𝕱𝕱   Your schedule may allow you to visit
only Copenhagen with no time for the Danish countryside. But there is a way out of
that—call it a look at "Denmark in a Nutshell." At one of the largest and oldest (1897)
open-air museums in the world, you can wander into a time capsule of long ago—a sort
of Danish version of the Scottish Brigadoon—and return to a town that still lives on in

the 19th century, when Hans Christian Andersen was writing all those fairy tales. This reconstructed village in Lyngby, on the fringe of Copenhagen, recaptures Denmark's one-time rural character. The "museum" is nearly 36 hectares (89 acres), a 3km (1¾-mile) walk around the compound, and includes more than 50 re-created buildings—farmsteads, windmills, and fishermen's cottages. Exhibits include a half-timbered 18th-century farmstead from one of the tiny windswept Danish islands, a primitive longhouse from the remote Faroe Islands, thatched fishermen's huts from Jutland, tower windmills, and a potter's workshop from the mid-19th century. Folk dancers in native costume perform, and there are demonstrations of lacemaking and loom-weaving.

Adjacent to the open-air museum stands **Brede Vaerk** ☆, an intact industrial plant that gives a complete picture of a former factory community, which closed in 1956. The Nationalmuseet moved to preserve it as a reminder of Denmark's past. Still intact are the cottages of the working-class families, even the houses of the foremen. Their former eating house has been turned into a restaurant today, and there is even an orphanage and nursery garden. The old factory buildings house exhibitions illustrating "The Cradle of Industry." Our delight here is touring **Brede House** ☆☆, a neoclassical manor dating from 1795. The owner of the mill, Peter van Hemert, lived here with his family before he went bankrupt in 1805. He pictured himself a fanciful decorator, decking his halls like he was Louis XVI.

The park is about 14km (8⅔ miles) from the Central Railroad Station. There's an old-style restaurant at the entryway to the museum.

Kongevejen 100. © **33-13-44-11.** www.natmus.dk. Free admission. Tues–Sun 10am–5pm. Closed Mon, except Apr 17–June 5 and Oct. 16 Closed Dec 24–25 and Dec. 31. S-tog: Sorgenfri (leaving every 20 min. from Copenhagen Central Station). Bus: 184 or 194.

9 Literary Landmarks

Fans of **Hans Christian Andersen** may want to seek out the various addresses where he lived in Copenhagen, including Nyhavn 18, Nyhavn 20, and Nyhavn 67. He also lived for a time at Vingårdsstræde 6.

Assistens Kirkegård (Assistens Cemetery) ☆   Dating from 1711, and the largest burial ground in Copenhagen, this is the liveliest cemetery we've ever encountered in Europe. Instead of a tranquil "rest-in-peace" kind of place, it's been turned into a public park. Families come here for picnics, and aspirant rock bands use it as an open-air venue to perform before a live, captive audience. Sunbathers don't seem to mind stripping down for a "bath" on the grave of the dear departed.

It also contains the graves of the two towering literary figures of Denmark, both Hans Christian Andersen and Søren Kierkegaard. Both of these men were rivals in life, but in this graveyard they are at peace with one another. Many critics today believe both men were latent homosexuals. Martin Andersen Nexø, a famous novelist of his time who depicted the struggles of the working class, is also buried here, as are many other famous Danes, a sort of "Who Was Who." Even the brewer who still keeps half of Denmark drunk at night, Carlsberg patriarch Christen Jacobsen, is also interred here.

Nørrebrogade/Kapelvej 4. © **35-37-19-17.** Free admission. Jan–Feb 8am–5pm; Mar–Apr 8am–6pm; May–Aug 8am–8pm; Sept–Oct 8am–6pm; Nov–Dec 8am–4pm. Bus: 5, 7E, or 16.

Københavns Bymuseet & Søren Kierkegaard Samlingen   We come here not to see the city museum exhibits, but to learn more about one of Denmark's most enigmatic authors, Søren Kierkegaard. A section of the museum is devoted to the "Father of Existentialism," his life illustrated by personal belongings, drawings, letters, books, and old photographs. Born in Copenhagen on May 3, 1813, he eventually died in his beloved city in October 1855 when he collapsed on the street. He was only 42. As a hedonist youth he indulged himself—not in liquor like some writers but in the consumption of pastry. His pastry bill in 1836 was said to equal the annual wage of a typical Danish family. His most famous work was created in 1843 when he wrote his philosophical novel *Enten/Eller (Either/Or)*. From an early age, when he learned to think and reason, Kierkegaard proclaimed himself a "genius"—and so he was.

If you hang around, you can check out some of the city museum collections. Unless you're interested in sewers and gas pipes, we'd suggest you skip the "Underground Exhibition." The section on old shop fronts evoking Copenhagen of yesterday is more intriguing if you'd like to see "the way it was."

Vesterbrogade 59. ⒞ **33-21-07-72.** www.kbhbymuseum.dk. Admission 20DKK ($3.40/£1.80) adults, free for children under 18, free to all Fri. Thurs–Mon 10am–4pm; Wed 10am–9pm. Bus: 6, 16, 27, or 28.

10 Of Artistic Interest

Arken Museum of Modern Art ✿ *Finds*   Of the major modern art museums of Copenhagen, this one is the most undiscovered because it lies in the dreary suburb of Ishøj, just a 15-minute train ride from the center of Copenhagen. Constructed of white concrete and steel, and evoking the hull of a beached ship, the museum was built in 1996 to celebrate Copenhagen's designation as the European City of Culture for that year. Architectural critics were appalled when a 25-year-old student, Søren Robert Lund, was selected while still a student at the Royal Danish Academy of Fine Arts. But in time, Lund has won over some of his attackers, especially when the building won a major award for the best design for a new gallery in Europe. But that wasn't until 1997.

Artists who show their works here remain almost universal in their condemnation of Lund, feeling that the frame—with its curious "marine architecture"—competes with the picture; that is, the art exhibited inside. The museum owns some 300 works of art (not all on exhibit at once), but it supplements this trove with temporary exhibitions devoted to, say, the works of Picasso. In addition to gallery space, the museum has a concert hall, sculpture courtyards, and a restaurant.

Ishøj Strandpark, Skovvej 100. ⒞ **43-54-02-22.** www.arken.dk. Admission 40DKK ($6.80/£3.60) adults, children under 18 free. Tues–Sun 10am–5pm; Wed 10am–9pm. Train: E or A to Ishøj Station, and then bus 128.

11 Especially for Kids

Copenhagen is a wonderful place for children, and many so-called adult attractions (except the Erotic Museum) also appeal to kids. **Tivoli** is an obvious choice, as is the statue of *Den Lille Havfrue (The Little Mermaid)* at Langelinie. Try to see the changing of the Queen's Royal Life Guard at **Amalienborg Palace,** including the entire parade to and from the royal residence. Kids also enjoy **Frilandsmuseet,** the open-air museum. (For details on these sights, see listings earlier in this chapter.) Other attractions great for kids include the following:

Bakken Amusement Park   This is the Tivoli on a bad day, but a lot of fun if you don't like your amusement parks too manicured. On the northern edge of Copenhagen, about 12km (7½ miles) from the city center, this amusement park was created 35 years before the Pilgrims landed at Plymouth Rock. It's a local favorite, featuring roller coasters, dancing, a tunnel of love, and a merry-go-round. Open-air restaurants are plentiful, as are snack bars and ice cream booths. Some individual attractions—100 or so rides—charge a separate admission fee (proceeds support this unspoiled natural preserve). We like to see the singing girls and cabaret at **Bakkens Hvile** 食食. They rival the Rockettes at New York City's Radio City Music Hall and remain the most popular revue show in Denmark. There are no cars in the park—only bicycles and horse-drawn carriages are allowed.

Dyrehavevej 62, Klampenborg. ℂ **39-63-73-00**. www.bakken.dk. Free admission; rides cost 10DKK–50DKK ($1.70–$8.50/90p–£4.50) each. Summer daily noon–midnight. Closed mid-Sept to late Mar. S-tog: Klampenborg (about 20 min. from Central Railroad Station); then walk through the Deer Park or take a horse-drawn cab.

Danmarks Akvarium

Opened in 1939, a year before the Nazi invasion of Denmark, this is not among the world-class aquariums such as the one that opened in Atlanta, Georgia. However, it's worth a look if you happen to be visiting the grounds of **Charlottenlund Slot** (Palace) at Hellerup, a coastal suburb of Copenhagen. After walking through the grounds (the palace is not open), site of a royal residence since 1690, drop in at the zoo. Although it was enlarged in 1974, it still features only 90 or so tanks of the usual marine "suspects"—sharks, turtles, piranhas, and both the fish that can survive in the North Sea and those from more tropical waters.

Strandvejen, in Charlottenlund Fort Park, Charlottenlund. ℂ **39-62-32-83**. www.akvarium.dk. Admission 85DKK ($14/£7.65) adults, 45DKK ($7.65/£4.05) children. May–Aug daily 10am–6pm; Sept–Oct and Feb–Apr daily 10am–5pm; Nov–Jan daily 10am–4pm. S-tog: Charlottenlund. Bus: 14 or 166.

Eskperimentarium (Hands-On Science Center) 食食

It is said that curators from all over the world come here to plan the science museums of the 21st century. This is the most interactive museum in the Nordic world. In the old mineral water-bottling hall of Tuborg breweries 5km (3 miles) north of Copenhagen in Hellerup, this museum has a hands-on approach to science. Visitors engage all five of their senses as they participate in some 300 interactive exhibitions and demonstrations divided into three themes: "Man," "Nature," and "The Interaction Between Man and Nature." Visitors hear what all the world's languages sound like, make a wind machine blow up to hurricane force, check their skin to test how much sun it can take, dance in an "inverted" disco, program a robot, gaze enthralled at an optical illusion, experience a human-size gyroscope, or visit a slimming machine. Families can work as a team to examine enzymes, make a camera from paper, or test perfume. Exhibitions change frequently, and from what we've seen, thrill adults almost more than the kids.

Tuborg Havnevej 7, Hellerup. ℂ **39-27-33-33**. www.experimentarium.dk. Admission 120DKK ($20/£11) adults, 75DKK ($13/£6.75) children 3–11, free for children under 3. Mon and Wed–Fri 9:30am–5pm; Tues 9:30am–9pm; Sat–Sun 11am–5pm. Closed Dec 23–25, Dec 31, and Jan 1. S-tog: Hellerup or Svanemøllen. Bus: 1, 14, or 21.

Tycho Brahe Planetarium

When ET makes his first real earth landing—that is, not in a film—he'll no doubt set down here first to honor the famed Danish astronomer Tycho Brahe (1546–1601). Of course, Brahe got a lot of things wrong—after all, he disagreed with Copernicus and still believed that Earth stood at the center of the universe. But he did some things right, including mapping the position of more than 1,000 fixed stars—and he did all this with the naked eye since Galileo didn't emerge with his telescope until 1610. And, long before plastic surgery was all the rage, Brahe sported a silver nose (the original fell to the ground after a duel in Rostock).

On a dome-shaped screen, IMAX films are shown, creating the marvel of the night sky, with its planets, galaxies, star clusters, and comets. The permanent exhibition, "The Active Universe," doesn't quite answer all the questions of the mysteries of space,

THE TRAVELOCITY GUARANTEE

...THAT SAYS EVERYTHING YOU BOOK WILL BE RIGHT, OR WE'LL WORK WITH OUR TRAVEL PARTNERS TO MAKE IT RIGHT, RIGHT AWAY.

*To drive home the point,
we're going to use the word "right" in every single sentence.*

Let's get right to it. Right to the meat! Only Travelocity guarantees everything about your booking will be right, or we'll work with our travel partners to make it right, right away. Right on!

Here's a picture taken smack dab right in the middle of Antigua, where the Guarantee also covers you.

The Guarantee covers all but one of the items pictured to the right.

For example, what if the ocean view you booked actually looks out at a downright ugly parking lot? You'd be right to call – we're there for you. And no one in their right mind would be pleased to learn the rental car place has closed and left them stranded. Call Travelocity and we'll help get you back on the right track.

Now, you may be thinking, "Yeah, right, I'm so sure." That's OK; you have the right to remain skeptical. That is until we mention help is always right around the corner. Call us right off the bat, knowing our customer service reps are there for you 24/7. Righting wrongs. Left and right.

Now if you're guessing there are some things we can't control, like the weather, well you're right. But we can help you with most things – to get all the details in righting,* visit travelocity.com/guarantee.

*Sorry, spelling things right is one of the few things not covered under the Guarantee.

I'd give my right arm for a guarantee like this, although I'm glad I don't have to.

You'll never roam alone.

but exhibitions on natural science and astronomy may just leave you with a lingering desire for space travel.

Gammel Kongevej 10. ℭ **33-12-12-24.** Admission 25DKK ($4.25/£2.25) adults, 15DKK ($2.55/£1.35) children; OMNIMAX films 95DKK ($16/£8.55) adults, 65DKK ($11/£5.85) children. Mon–Fri 9:30am–9pm; Sat–Sun 10:30am–9pm. Bus: 1 or 14.

Zoologisk Have (Copenhagen Zoo)   This zoo has come a long way since 1859,

when it opened with stuffed birds, a seal in a bathtub, and a turtle in a bucket. Today, at its location in Frederiksberg, west of the center of Copenhagen, it is home to 3,300 animals and 264 species. The zoo, in fact, is a window to the wilds of the world, with animals from the icy snowfields of Greenland to the hot, dusty savannahs of Africa. You get to see everything from the musk oxen and reindeer of the far north to the hungry lions of Kenya. Expect the usual apes and elephants from a Tarzan movie, but enjoy a close encounter with a polar bear, a now threatened species. The world is filled with ragtag children's zoos, but the one here is exceptional. Kids can pet beasts that are "not too wild." The highlight for the kiddies is an Eiffel-like tower that rises 40m (131 ft.), dating from 1905. *Warning:* The zoo is mobbed on a summer Sunday.

Roskildevej 32, Frederiksberg. ℭ **72-20-02-00.** www.zoo.dk. Admission 100DKK ($17/£9) adults, 60DKK ($10/£5.40) children. Jan–Feb and Nov–Dec daily 9am–4pm; Mar Mon–Fri 9am–4pm, Sat–Sun 9am–5pm; Apr–May and Sept Mon–Fri 9am–5pm, Sat–Sun 9am–6pm; June–Aug daily 9am–6pm; Oct daily 9am–5pm. S-tog: Valby. Bus: 4A, 6A, 26, or 832.

12 Copenhagen on Foot: Walking Tours

WALKING TOUR 1   THE OLD CITY

Start:	Rådhuspladsen.
Finish:	Tivoli Gardens.
Time:	1½ hours.
Best Time:	Any sunny day.
Worst Times:	Rush hours (weekdays 7:30–9am and 5–6:30pm).

Start at:

❶ Rådhuspladsen (Town Hall Square)

Pay a visit to the bronze statue of Hans Christian Andersen, the spinner of fairy tales, which stands near a boulevard bearing his name. Also on this square is a statue of two *lur* horn players that has stood here since 1914.

Bypassing the *lur* horn players, walk east along Vester Voldgade onto a narrow street on your left:

❷ Lavendelstræde

Many houses along here date from the late 18th century. At Lavendelstræde 1, Mozart's widow (Constanze) lived with

her second husband, Georg Nikolaus von Nissen, a Danish diplomat, from 1812 to 1820.

The little street quickly becomes:

❸ Slutterigade

Courthouses rise on both sides of this short street, joined by elevated walkways. Built between 1805 and 1815, this was Copenhagen's fourth town hall, now the city's major law courts. The main courthouse entrance is on Nytorv.

Slutterigade will lead to:

❹ Nytorv

In this famous square, you can admire fine 19th-century houses. Philosopher

Søren Kierkegaard (1813–55) lived in a house adjacent to the courthouse.

Cross Nytorv, and veer slightly west (to your left) until you reach Nygade, part of the:

⑤ Strøget

At this point, this traffic-free shopping street has a different name. (It actually began at Rådhuspladsen and was called Frederiksberggade.) The major shopping street of Scandinavia, Strøget is a stroller's and a shopper's delight, following a 1.2km (¾-mile) trail through the heart of Copenhagen.

Nygade is one of the five streets that compose Strøget. Head northeast along this street, which becomes winding and narrow Vimmelskaftet, and then turns into Amagertorv. Along Amagertorv, on your left, you'll come across the:

⑥ Helligåndskirken (Church of the Holy Ghost)

Complete with an abbey, Helligåndskirken is the oldest church in Copenhagen, founded at the beginning of the 15th century. Partially destroyed in 1728, it was reconstructed in 1880 in a neoclassical style. Some of the buildings on this street date from 1616. The sales rooms of the Royal Porcelain Factory are at Amagertorv 6.

Next you'll come to Østergade, the last portion of Strøget. You'll see Illum's department store on your left. Østergade leads to the square:

⑦ Kongens Nytorv

Surrounding Copenhagen's largest square, with an equestrian statue of Christian IV in the center, are many restored antique buildings. The statue is a bronze replica of a 1688 sculpture.

At Kongens Nytorv, head right until you come to Laksegade. Then go south along this street until you reach the intersection with Nikolajgade. Turn right. This street will lead to the:

⑧ Nikolaj Kirke

The building dates from 1530 and was the scene of the thundering sermons of Hans Tausen, a father of the Danish Reformation.

TAKE A BREAK
A mellow spot for a pick-me-up, either a refreshing cool drink or an open-faced sandwich, **Cafeen Nikolaj**, Nikolaj Plads 12 (© **33-11-63-13**), attracts both older shoppers and young people. You can sit and linger over a cup of coffee, and no one is likely to hurry you. You can visit anytime in the afternoon, perhaps making it your luncheon stopover. The setting is within the interior of (during cold weather) or in the shadow of (during warm weather) this charming and antique red-brick church.

After seeing the church, head left down Fortunstræde to your next stop, a square off Gammel Strand:

⑨ Højbro Plads

You'll have a good view of Christiansborg Palace and Thorvaldsens Museum on Slotsholmen. On Højbro Plads is an equestrian statue honoring Bishop Absalon, who founded Copenhagen in 1167. Several old buildings line the square.

Continue west along:

⑩ Gammel Strand

From this waterfront promenade—the name means "old shore"—the former edge of Copenhagen, you'll have a panoramic look across to Christiansborg Palace. A number of antique buildings line this street, and at the end you'll come upon the Ministry of Cultural Affairs, occupying a former government pawnbroking establishment, dating from 1730.

To the right of this building, walk up:

⑪ Snaregade

This old-fashioned provincial street is one of the most evocative of the old city. Walk until you reach Knabrostræde. Both streets boast structures built just after the great fire of 1795. Where the streets intersect, you'll see the Church of Our Lady.

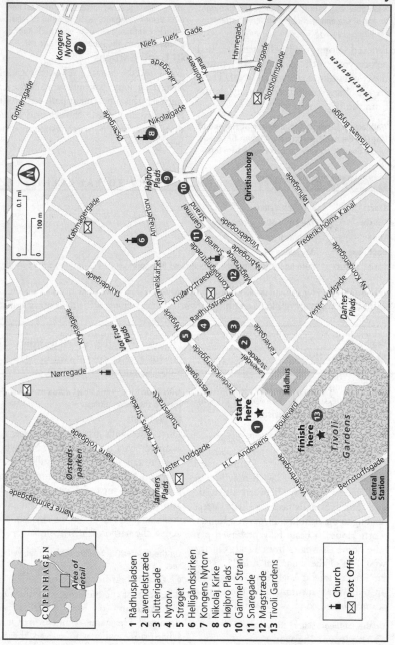

COPENHAGEN

Area of detail

1 Rådhuspladsen
2 Lavendelstræde
3 Slutterigade
4 Nytorv
5 Strøget
6 Helligåndskirken
7 Kongens Nytorv
8 Nikolaj Kirke
9 Højbro Plads
10 Gammel Strand
11 Snaregade
12 Magstræde
13 Tivoli Gardens

✝■ Church
⊠ Post Office

Make your way back to Snaregade, and turn right to one of Copenhagen's best-preserved streets:

⑫ Magstræde

Proceed along to Rådhusstræde. Just before you reach Rådhusstræde, notice the two buildings facing that street. These are the oldest structures in the city, dating from the 16th century.

Walk across Vandkunsten, a square at the end of Magstræde, and then turn right down Gasegade, which doesn't go very far before you turn left

along Farvergade. At this street's intersection with Vester Voldgade, you'll come to the Vartov Church. Continue west until you reach Rådhuspladsen. Across the square, you'll see the:

⑬ Tivoli Gardens

You'll find the entrance at Vesterbrogade 3. Attracting some 4.5 million visitors every summer, this amusement park has 25 different entertainment choices and attractions, and just as many restaurants and beer gardens.

WALKING TOUR 2	KONGENS NYTORV TO LANGELINIE

Start:	Kongens Nytorv.
Finish:	*The Little Mermaid.*
Time:	1½ hours.
Best Time:	Any sunny day.
Worst Times:	Rush hours (weekdays 7:30–9am and 5–6:30pm).

Although the Nyhavn quarter, once a boisterous sailors' town, has quieted down, it's still a charming part of old Copenhagen, with its 1673 canal and 18th-century houses.

Begin at:

❶ Kongens Nytorv

The "King's New Market" dates from 1680. It contains Magasin, the biggest department store in the capital, plus an equestrian statue of Christian IV.

On the northeast side of the square is:

❷ Thott's Mansion

Completed in 1685 for a Danish naval hero and restored in 1760, it now houses the French Embassy. Between Bredgade and Store Strandstræde, a little street angling to the right near Nyhavn, is Kanneworff House, a beautifully preserved private home that dates from 1782. On the west side of the square, at no. 34, is the landmark Hotel d'Angleterre. Also here is an old anchor memorializing the Danish seamen who died in World War II.

On the southeast side of the square is:

❸ The Royal Theater

Founded in 1748, the theater presents ballet, opera, and plays. Statues of famous

Danish dramatists are out front. The present theater, constructed in 1874, has a neo-Renaissance style.

With your back to the Hotel d'Angleterre, walk toward the water along:

❹ Nyhavn

Once filled with maritime businesses and seamen's bars and lodgings, Nyhavn is now "restaurant row." First, walk along its north (left) side. In the summer, cafe tables border the canal, giving it a festive atmosphere. At the port end of the canal, you can see the Naval Dockyards and, across the harbor, Christianshavn.

On the quieter (south) side of the canal, you can see:

❺ Charlottenborg Palace

The style of the building, now the Danish Academy of Fine Arts, is pure baroque. The name comes from Queen Charlotte Amalie, who moved there in 1700. Beautiful old homes, antiques shops, and more restaurants line the

Walking Tour: Kongens Nytorv to Langelinie

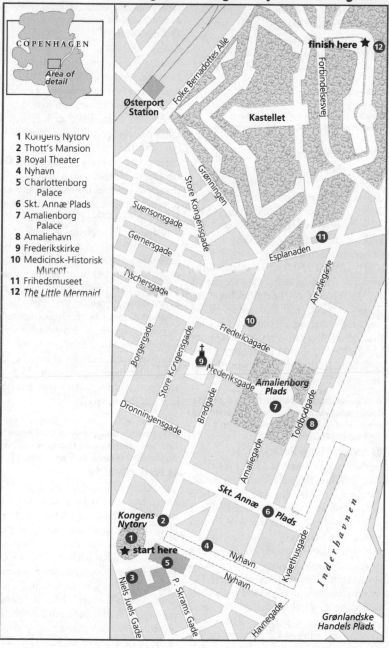

COPENHAGEN

Area of detail

1 Kongens Nytorv
2 Thott's Mansion
3 Royal Theater
4 Nyhavn
5 Charlottenborg Palace
6 Skt. Annæ Plads
7 Amalienborg Palace
8 Amaliehavn
9 Frederikskirke
10 Medicinsk-Historisk Museet
11 Frihedsmuseet
12 The Little Mermaid

finish here ★ 12

Østerport Station

Kastellet

Folke Bernadottes Allé

Forbindelsesvej

Grønningen

Store Kongensgade

Suensonsgade

Gernersgade

Dischersgade

Borgergade

Store Kongensgade

Dronningensgade

Bredgade

Frederiksgade

Fredericiagade

Esplanaden

Amaliegade

10

9

11

Amalienborg Plads

7

8

Toldbodgade

Amaliegade

Skt. Annæ 6 Plads

Kongens 2 Nytorv

1

★ start here

5

3

4

Nyhavn

Nyhavn

Niels Juels Gade

P. Skrams Gade

Havnegade

Kvæthusgade

Inderhavnen

Grønlandske Handels Plads

southern bank. Nyhavn was the home of Hans Christian Andersen at various times. He lived at no. 20, where he wrote his first fairy tales, in 1835, and at no. 67 from 1845 to 1864. He spent the last 2 years of his life at no. 18, where he died in 1875.

Walk back to the harbor end of Nyhavn, and turn left onto Kvæsthusgade, which will take you to:

⑥ Skt. Annæ Plads

Before the radical transformation of Copenhagen's harborfront, ferries used to depart from piers here for other destinations in Scandinavia, including Oslo. Now, however, the harborfront, and the back of this desirable long and narrow square, is the site of one of the biggest urban transformations in the city's history. The ferryboat terminals have moved to the commercial neighborhood of Nordhavn, and the city seems to be watching what will eventually emerge from this site, just a short walk from Nyhavn and its rows of restaurants. Many consulates, two hotels, and fine old buildings open onto it.

Walk inland along the plads, and turn right onto Amaliegade, which leads under a colonnade into symmetrical majesty of the cobble-covered Amalienborg Plads, site of:

⑦ Amalienborg Palace

In the square's center is a statue of Frederik V. When the queen is in residence, the changing of the guard takes place here daily at noon. The palace is the official residence of the queen and her French prince, but sections of it are open to visitors. The palace is actually composed of a quartet of nearly identical baroque mansions, each interconnected with galleries or subterranean passages, and each positioned at cardinal points of the same octagon-shaped courtyard. The queen lives in the wing that's adjacent to the neoclassical colonnade.

Between the square and the harbor are the gardens of:

⑧ Amaliehavn

Among the most beautiful in Copenhagen, these gardens were laid out by Jean Delogne, who made lavish use of Danish granite and French limestone. The bronze pillars around the fountain were the work of Arnaldo Pomodoro, an Italian sculptor. From this point, look across the harbor at the most exciting recently constructed building in town, the **Danish Opera House,** with a soaring rooftop that evokes the reinforced concrete structures of Le Corbusier, and a design that evokes the outspread wings of a dove. It was designed by Henning Larsen, "The House Architect of Copenhagen," with perfect acoustics and "chandeliers that might have been inspired by a show palace in Las Vegas." From your waterfront vantage, notice the way that the location of the Opera House repeats the rectilinear layout of Amalienborg Palace and the nearby Marble Church. The buildings each line up along the same lines, a brilliant combination of baroque and postmodern architecture combined into a coherent whole.

After viewing the waterfront gardens, walk away from the water, crossing Amalienborg Plads and emerging onto Frederiksgade. Continue along this street until you reach:

⑨ Frederikskirke

This church is often called the *Marmorkirken,* or "marble church." Construction began in 1740, but had to stop in 1770 because of the costs. The church wasn't completed until 1894—using Danish marble instead of more expensive Norwegian marble. The church was modeled on and intended to rival St. Peter's in Rome; indeed, it ended up with one of the largest church domes in Europe. Supported on a dozen towering piers, the dome has a diameter of 32m (105 ft.).

Facing the church, turn right and head north along Bredgade, passing at no. 22 the:

⑩ Medicinsk-Historisk Museet (Medical History Museum)

The collection is gruesome, with fetuses, dissected heads, and the like.

TAKE A BREAK
Before you approach *The Little Mermaid*, consider tea and a snack at Café **Lumskebugten,** Esplanaden 21 (📞 **33-15-60-29**; see "Where to Dine," in chapter 4). Dating from 1854, and permeated with a sense of the cozy, old-fashioned Denmark of long ago, this cafe offers a cold plate served throughout the afternoon. There are five specialties: beef tartare, fish cakes with mustard sauce, marinated salmon, baked cod, and shrimp.

Bredgade ends at Esplanaden, which opens onto Churchillparken, a green belt bordering the water. Turn right and walk along Esplanaden until you come to Churchillparken and the:

⑪ Frihedsmuseet

The Danish Resistance museum commemorates the struggle against the Nazis from 1940 to 1945.

After leaving the museum, walk toward the water along Langelinie, where signs point the way to:

⑫ *The Little Mermaid*

Perched on rocks just off the harbor bank, *Den Lille Havfrue*, the most photographed statue in Scandinavia, dates from 1913. The bronze figure, by Edvard Eriksen, was modeled after the figure of prima ballerina Ellen Price. In time, this much-attacked and abused statue became the symbol of Copenhagen.

13 Organized Tours

BUS & BOAT TOURS   The boat and bus sightseeing tours in Copenhagen range from get-acquainted jaunts to in-depth excursions. Either of the following tours can be arranged through **Copenhagen Excursions** (📞 **32-54-06-06**) or **Vikingbus** (📞 **32-66-00-00**). Inexpensive bus tours depart from the *lur* blowers' statue at Town Hall Square, and boat trips leave from Gammel Strand (the fish market) or Nyhavn.

For orientation, hop on a bus for the 1½-hour **City Tour,** which covers scenic highlights such as *The Little Mermaid,* Rosenborg Castle, and Amalienborg Palace. Tours depart from the City Hall Square daily at 9:30am, 11:30am, and 1:30pm May 15 to September 30. They cost 130DKK ($22/£12) for adults and 65DKK ($11/£5.85) for children under 12.

We heartily recommend the **City and Harbor Tour,** a 2½-hour trip by launch and bus that departs from Town Hall Square. The boat tours the city's main canals, passing *The Little Mermaid* and the Old Fish Market. It operates May 15 to September 30 daily at 9:30am, 11:30am, and 1:30pm. It costs 175DKK ($30/£16) for adults and 90DKK ($15/£8.10) for children under 12.

Shakespeare buffs may be interested in an afternoon excursion to the castles of North Zealand. The 7-hour tour explores the area north of Copenhagen, including Kronborg (Hamlet's castle), a brief visit to Fredensborg, the queen's residence, and a stopover at Frederiksborg Castle and the National Historical Museum. Tours depart from Town Hall Square, running February to April and October to December Wednesday and Sunday at 9:30am; May to September Wednesday, Saturday, and Sunday at 9:30am. The cost is 430DKK ($73/£39) for adults and 225DKK ($38/£20) for children under 12.

For more information about these tours and the most convenient place to buy tickets in advance, call **Vikingbus** or **Copenhagen Excursions.** You can also visit www.sightseeing.dk.

GUIDED WALKS THROUGH COPENHAGEN   Staff members of the Copenhagen Tourist Information Office conduct 2-hour guided walking tours of the city every Monday and Friday to Sunday at 10am between May and September. The price is 80DKK ($13/£7.20) for adults and 25DKK ($4.20/£2.25) for children. For information, contact the **Copenhagen Tourist Information Center,** Vesterbrogade 4A ((© **70-22-24-42;** www.visitcopenhagen.com).

A VISIT TO COPENHAGEN'S MOST FAMOUS BREWERY   Carlsberg is the most famous beer in Denmark and the country's best known brand internationally. Much of it is produced within an old-fashioned brewery constructed in 1847, which was enlarged in 2005 with the addition of a spanking-new microbrewery that's devoted to the production of at least four "affiliated" brews, which are being marketed under the brand name of "Jacobsen." Jointly, the brewery turns out at least three million bottles of beer a day. From within the newly redesigned visitor center, you can take a self-guided tour of both sides of the brewery, walking around an observation gallery whose English-language signs and flickering video screens will explain the brewing process. The factory is open for visits Tuesday to Sunday 10am to 4pm. Entrance (and access to the self-guided tours) costs 45DKK ($7.65/£4.05) per person (there's no discount for children), and each adult visitor is given a free beer at the end of the tour with the option of buying more at the on-site pub. The entrance to the brewery is graced with a pair of sculpted elephants, each with armored regalia that includes a swastika. That doesn't mean the company was a Nazi sympathizer—Carlsberg used the symbol as part of its image long before Hitler. Take bus no. 26 from Copenhagen Central Station or from the Town Hall Square in Copenhagen to **Carlsberg Brewery,** Gamle Carlsberg Vej 11 ((© **33-27-13-14**).

14 Active Sports

BICYCLING   The absence of hills and the abundance of parks and wide avenues with bicycle lanes make cycling the best way to explore Copenhagen. Bike-rental shops and stands are scattered throughout the city. Two suggestions are **Københavns Cyker,** Reventlowsgade 11 ((© **33-33-86-13;** bus: 6 or 10), and **Dan Wheel,** Colbjørnsensgade 3 ((© **33-21-22-27;** bus: 28 or 41). A deposit of 500DKK ($85/£45) is required. Alternatively, **City Bike** is a great way to get around central Copenhagen. Bike racks are located throughout the city center. The service is free, and you unlock your bike with a 20DKK ($3.40/£1.80) deposit. When you return the bike, your deposit is returned (in the same way as with a supermarket cart). The bikes are available from May to December (www.bycyklen.dk).

FITNESS   **Form & Fitness,** Øster Allé 42E ((© **35-55-00-78;** bus: 9 or 10), offers a day pass for 150DKK ($26/£14). Aerobics, weights, and fitness machines are available Monday to Thursday 6:30am to 11pm, Friday 6:30am to 9pm, and Saturday and Sunday 8am to 6pm.

GOLF   Denmark's best-known golf course, and one of its most challenging to golfers around the world, is at the **Rungsted Golf Klub,** Vestre Stationsveg 16, Rungsted ((© **45-76-85-82;** bus: 3, 16, or 45). It's in the heart of Denmark's "Whisky Trail," a string of homes and mansions known for their allure to retirees, about 21km (13 miles) north of Copenhagen. Some degree of competence is required, so beginners and intermediate golfers might want to hold off. If you're an advanced golfer, call for information and to arrange a tee time. Greens fees run 350DKK to 550DKK ($60–$94/£32–£50) for a full day's use of the club's 18 holes. To play, you must present evidence of a 21 handicap on Saturday and Sunday, or 25 on weekdays. With advance notice, you can rent clubs for 250DKK ($43/£23). No carts are allowed on the ecologically fragile course, which is open year-round, except when it is snowing.

JOGGING   The many parks (known to locals as "green lungs") of Copenhagen provide endless routes for joggers. Our favorite, just west of the city center, circles Lakes Sortedams, St. Jorgens, and Peblinge. The paths that wind through the Frederiksborg gardens are also well suited for joggers.

SWIMMING   In spite of an often bone-chilling climate, swimming is a favorite Danish pastime. The **Frederiksborg Svømmehal,** Helgesvej 29 (© **38-14-04-04;** bus: 6 or 18), is open to the public Monday to Friday 7am to 9pm, Saturday 9am to 4pm, and Sunday 9am to 4pm. Tickets cost 30DKK ($5.10/£2.70). You can also try **Sundby Swimming Pool,** Sundbyvestervej 50 (© **32-58-55-68;** bus: 30 or 31), or **Kildeskovshallen,** Adolphsvej 25 (© **39-77-44-00;** bus: 165).

TENNIS   Visitors usually pay a large fee to play tennis at hotels and clubs in Copenhagen. There's a high hourly rate, and courts must be reserved in advance. At the **Hotel Mercur,** Vester Farimagsgade 17 (© **33-12-57-11;** bus: 40 or 46), visitors pay 130DKK ($22/£12) for the first hour, 100DKK ($17/£9) for each additional hour. Another club is **Københavns Boldklub,** Peter Bangs Vej 147 (© **38-71-41-50;** bus: 1); this club is in Frederiksberg, a neighborhood west of central Copenhagen.

15 The Shopping Scene

Copenhagen is in the vanguard of shopping in Europe, and much of the action takes place on **Strøget,** the pedestrian street in the heart of the capital. Strøget begins as Frederiksberggade, north of Rådhuspladsen, and winds to Østergade, which opens onto Kongens Nytorv. The jam-packed street is lined with stores selling everything from porcelain statues of *Youthful Boldness* and open-faced sandwiches piled high with Greenland shrimp to pizza slices and some of the most elegant porcelain in Europe. There are also high-volume outlets of both McDonald's and Burger King.

Between stops, relax with a drink at an outdoor cafe, or just sit on a bench and people-watch.

In two nearby walking areas—**Gråbrødretorv** and **Fiolstræde**—you can browse through antiques shops and bookshops.

Bredgade, beginning at Kongens Nytorv, is the antiques district, where prices tend to be very high. **Læderstræde** is another shopping street that competes with Bredgade in antiques.

BEST BUYS   In a country famed for its designers and craftspeople, the best buys are in stainless steel, porcelain, china, glassware, toys, functionally designed furniture, textiles, and jewelry, particularly silver jewelry set with semiprecious stones.

In addition to the centers described below, for excellent buys in Scandinavian merchandise, as well as tax-free goods, we recommend the **shopping center at the airport.** A VAT-refund office is located nearby.

SHIPPING IT HOME & RECOVERING VAT   Denmark imposes a 25% tax on goods and services, a "value-added tax" known in Denmark as *moms* (pronounced *mumps* and every bit as painful). Tax-free exports are possible. Many stores will mail goods to your home so you can avoid paying the tax. If you want to take your purchases, look for shops displaying Danish tax-free shopping notices. Such shops offer tourists tax refunds for personal export. This refund applies to purchases of more than 300DKK ($51/£27) for visitors from the United States and Canada—spent at the same store, but not necessarily all at once. For more information, see "Taxes" in "Fast Facts: Denmark," in chapter 3. For answers to tax refund questions, call **Global Refund** (© **32-52-55-66**).

STORE HOURS In general, shopping hours are 9:30am or 10am to 5:30pm Monday to Thursday, to 7pm or 8pm on Friday, and to 2pm on Saturday. Most shops are closed Sunday, except the kiosks and supermarket at the Central Railroad Station. Here you can purchase food until 10pm or midnight. The Central Railroad Station's bakery is open until 9pm, and one kiosk at Rådhuspladsen, which sells papers, film, and souvenirs, is open 24 hours.

SHOPPING A TO Z
AMBER
The Amber Specialist The owners, known to customers as the "Amber Twins," will sell you "the gold of the north." This petrified resin originated in the large coniferous forests that covered Denmark some 35 million years ago. The forest disappeared, but the amber lasted and is now used to create handsome jewelry. This shop carries a large collection of stunning amber set in 14-karat gold. Frederiksberggade 28. © **33-11-88-03.** Bus: 28, 29, or 41.

ART GALLERIES & AUCTION HOUSES
Bruun Rasmussen Established shortly after World War II, this is Denmark's leading auction house. July is usually quiet, although the premises remain open for appraisals and purchases. The season begins in August, with an auction of paintings and fine art. Viewing time is allowed before auctions, which are held about once a month. There are also auctions of art, wine, coins, books, and antique weapons. Bredgade 33. © **33-13-69-11.** Bus: 1, 6, 9, or 10.

Galerie Asbaek This modern-art gallery has a permanent exhibit of the best local artists, along with changing shows by Scandinavian and foreign artists. A bookshop and cafe serving French-inspired Danish food is on the premises. Graphics and posters are for sale. Bredgade 20. © **33-15-40-04.** Bus: 1, 6, 9, 10, 28, 29, or 41.

BOOKS
Boghallen This big store at Town Hall Square carries many books in English, as well as a wide selection of travel-related literature, including maps. It stocks books in English on Danish themes, such as the collected works of Hans Christian Andersen. Rådhuspladsen 37. © **33-47-25-60.** Bus: 2, 8, or 30.

DEPARTMENT STORES
Illum One of Denmark's top department stores, Illum is on Strøget. Take time to browse through its vast store of Danish and Scandinavian design. There are a restaurant and a special export cash desk at street level. Østergade 52. © **33-14-40-02.** Bus: 1, 6, 9, or 10.

Magasin An elegant department store, Magasin is the biggest in Scandinavia. It offers a complete assortment of Danish designer fashion, a large selection of glass and porcelain, and souvenirs. Goods are shipped abroad tax-free. Kongens Nytorv 13. © **33-11-44-33.** Bus: 1, 6, 9, or 10.

FURS

Birger Christensen   This is one of Scandinavia's leading fur shops. It has its own designer line, two well-stocked floors of inventory, and furs and fashions by some of the world's leading designers, including Valentino and Oscar de la Renta. You can also purchase—cheaper than the furs—a selection of cashmere or wool blended coats with fur lining and fur trim, and conventional (non-fur) sportswear from Chanel, Yves St-Laurent, Marc Jacobs, and Prada. This is swank shopping and very, very expensive. Østergade 38. ✆ **33-11-55-55.** Bus: 1, 6, 9, 10, 19, 29, 31, 42, or 43.

GLASSWARE, PORCELAIN & CRYSTAL

Rosenthal Studio-Haus ✪✪✪   You'll find an array of ceramic works here, especially by well-known Danish artist Bjørn Wiinblad, whose figures we find whimsical and delightful. You can also get some good buys on Orrefors crystal, including some stunning bowls. The sculptural reliefs, handmade in lead crystal, range from miniatures to giant animals in limited world editions of 199 pieces. They often depict the animals of the far north. Frederiksberggade 21. ✆ **33-14-21-01.** Bus: 28, 29, or 41.

Royal Copenhagen Porcelain ✪✪✪   Royal Copenhagen's trademark, three wavy blue lines, has come to symbolize quality. Founded in 1775, the factory was a royal possession for a century before passing into private hands in 1868. Royal Copenhagen's Christmas plates are collectors' items. The factory has turned out a new plate each year since 1908, most of the designs depicting the Danish countryside in winter. There's a huge selection of seconds on the top floor, and unless you're an expert, you probably can't tell the difference. Visitors are welcome at the factory at Søndre Fasanvej 5 ((✆ **38-14-48-48**), where tours are given Monday to Friday from 9am to 3pm. (These tours, which occur at a location about 15km/9⅓ miles west of Copenhagen, can be arranged, along with transportation from central Copenhagen by contacting the Royal Copenhagen store at the phone number listed above.) Purchases cannot be made at the factory.

There are also various porcelain and silver retailers in this same location, as well as the Royal Copenhagen Antiques shop, which specializes in buying and selling antique Georg Jensen, Royal Copenhagen, Bing & Grøndahl Porcelain, and Michelson Christmas Spoons. In November 2006, the showrooms of this place were radically renovated into a pale blue and white design that include plays of both natural and artificial light, sound, and perfume. In the Royal Scandinavia retail center, Amagertorv 6 (Strøget). ✆ **33-13-71-81.** www.royalcopenhagen.com. Bus: 1, 2, 6, 8, 28, 29, or 41 for the retail outlet; 1 or 14 for the factory.

HOME FURNISHINGS

Illums Bolighus ✪✪✪   A center for modern Scandinavian and Danish design, this is one of Europe's finest showcases for household furnishings and accessories. It stocks furniture, lamps, rugs, textiles, bedding, glassware, kitchenware, flatware, china, jewelry, and ceramics. The store also sells women's and men's clothes and accessories, and there's even a gift shop. Amagertorv 10 (Strøget). ✆ **33-14-19-41.** www.illumsbolighus.com. Bus: 28, 29, or 41.

Lysberg, Hansen & Therp   This major interior-decorating center offers fabrics, carpets, and furniture. The model apartments are furnished in impeccable taste. The company manufactures its own furniture in traditional design and imports fabrics, usually from Germany or France. The gift shop has many hard-to-find creations. Bredgade 77. ✆ **33-14-47-87.** Bus: 1, 6, 9, or 10.

Paustian ☆☆☆ Copenhagen's leading furniture showroom, in the somewhat distant industrial Nordhavn section, will ship anywhere in the world. The finest of Scandinavian design is on display, along with reproductions of the classics. There's a well-recommended adjoining restaurant. Kalkbrænderiløbskaj 2. ℭ **39-16-65-65.** www.paustian.dk. S-tog: Nordhavn.

JEWELRY

Hartmann's Selected Estate Silver & Jewelry ☆ *Finds* This shop buys silver and jewelry from old estates and sells it at reduced prices. Ulrik Hartmann, the store's owner, launched his career as a 10-year-old trading at a local flea market, but went on to greater things. The shop is near Kongens Nytorv. While in the neighborhood, you can walk for hours, exploring the auction rooms, jewelry shops, and art galleries in the vicinity. Bredgade 4. ℭ **33-33-09-63.** Bus: 1, 6, 9, or 10.

Kaere Ven One of the city's oldest diamond dealers, in business for more than 100 years, this outlet advertises itself as offering "prices from another century." That's a gross exaggeration, but you can often find bargains in antique jewelry, even old Georg Jensen silver. An array of rings, earrings, necklaces, and bracelets are sold, along with other items. A few items in the store are sold at 50% off competitive prices, but you have to shop carefully and know what you're buying. Star Kongens Gade 30. ℭ **33-11-43-15.** Bus: 1, 6, 9, or 10.

MUSIC

Axel Musik One of the best-stocked music stores in the Danish capital, Axel also has another branch in the city's main railway station. In Scala Center (ground floor), Axeltorv 2. ℭ **33-14-05-50.** Bus: 1, 6, or 8.

PEWTER & SILVER

Georg Jensen ☆☆☆ Georg Jensen is legendary for its silver. On display is the largest and best collection of Jensen hollowware in Europe. The store also features gold and silver jewelry in traditional and modern Danish designs. In the Royal Scandinavia retail center, Amagertorv 6 (Strøget). ℭ **33-11-40-80.** www.georgjensen.com. Bus: 1, 6, 8, 9, or 10.

16 Copenhagen After Dark

Danes know how to party. A good night means a late night, and on warm weekends, hundreds of rowdy revelers crowd Strøget until sunrise. Merrymaking in Copenhagen is not just for the younger crowd; jazz clubs, traditional beer houses, and wine cellars are routinely packed with people of all ages. Of course, the city has a more highbrow cultural side as well, exemplified by excellent theaters, operas, ballets, and one of the best circuses in Europe.

To find out what's happening at the time of your visit, pick up a free copy of *Copenhagen This Week* at the tourist information center. The section marked "Events Calendar" has a week-by-week roundup of the "hottest" entertainment and sightseeing events in the Danish capital.

TIVOLI GARDENS

In the center of the gardens, the large **open-air stage** books vaudeville acts (tumbling clowns, acrobats, aerialists) who give performances every Friday night at 10pm, and on an arbitrary, oft-changing schedule that varies from week to week and summer to summer. Spectators must enter through the turnstiles for seats, but there's an unobstructed view from outside if you prefer to stand. Jazz and folklore groups also perform here during the season. Admission is free.

The 150-year-old outdoor **Pantomime Theater,** with its Chinese stage and peacock curtain, is near the Tivoli's Vesterbrogade 3 entrance and presents shows Tuesday to Thursday at 6:15pm and 8:15pm; Friday at 7:30pm and 9pm; Saturday at 8:15pm and 8:30pm; and Sunday at 4:30pm and 6:30pm. The repertoire consists of 16 different commedia dell'arte productions featuring the entertaining trio Pierrot, Columbine, and Harlequin—these are authentic pantomimes that have been performed continuously in Copenhagen since 1844. Admission is free.

The modern **Tivolis Koncertsal** (concert hall) is a great place to hear top artists and orchestras, led by equally famous conductors. Opened in 1956, the concert hall can seat 2,000, and its season—which begins in late April and lasts for more than 5 months—has been called "the most extensive music festival in the world." Performances of everything from symphony to opera are presented Monday to Saturday at 7:30pm, and sometimes at 8pm, depending on the event. Good seats are available at prices ranging from 200DKK to 700DKK ($34–$119/£18–£63) when major artists are performing, but most performances are free. Tickets are sold at the main booking office on Vesterbrogade 3 (℃ **33-15-10-12** or 45-70-15-65) or online at www.billetnet.dk.

Tivoli Glassalen (℃ **33-15-10-12** for information and/or ticket sales) is housed in a century-old octagonal gazebo-like building with a glass, gilt capped canopy. Shows are often comedic/satirical performances by Danish comedians in Danish and usually don't interest non-Danish audiences. A noteworthy exception to this are the annual Christmas programs, presented in November and December, in English. There are also musical reviews, with a minimum of any spoken language, presented throughout the year. Tickets range from 200DKK to 400DKK ($34–$68/£18–£36).

THE PERFORMING ARTS

Note: For tickets to most of the musical, cultural, and sports-themed entertainment venues of Denmark, check out **Billetnet** (℃ **45/70-15-15-65;** www.Billetnet.dk), a local branch of Ticketmaster that sells tickets to credit card holders.

For **discount seats** (sometimes as much as 50% off), go to a ticket kiosk at the corner of Fiolstræde and Nørre Voldgade, across from the Nørreport train station. Discount tickets are sold the day of the performance and may be purchased Monday to Friday noon to 5pm and Saturday noon to 3pm.

Copenhagen Opera House ✮✮✮   Opened by Queen Margrethe, this $441-million, 1,700-seat opera house is the luxurious home of the Royal Danish Opera. The opera house is the gift of the AP Møller and Chastine McKinney Møller Foundation, which is headed by Mærsk McKinney-Møller, one of the wealthiest men in the country. Prior to his donation of the Opera House, he had already received, directly from the Queen, Denmark's highest honor—the coveted and intensely prestigious Order of the Elephant. Designed by Danish architect Henning Larsen, the opera house uses precious stones and metals, including 105,000 sheets of gold leaf and chandeliers that outshine anything in Las Vegas. In addition to the international artists, the opera house also showcases the works of such Danish composers as Carl Nielsen and Poul Ruders. You can dine at the on-site **Restauranten** before curtain time, with a three-course menu costing 425DKK ($72/£38). In addition there is an **Opera Café,** serving sandwiches, salads, and light Danish specialties. The season runs from mid-August until the beginning of June. During that period, tours of the building are offered daily on a frequently changing schedule, which usually requires a phone call as a means of hammering out its schedule. Ekuipagemesteruej 10. ℂ **33-69-69-33.** Tickets standing-room space 70DKK ($12/£6.30); seats 200DKK–400DKK ($34–$68/£18–£36). Box office (ℂ **33-69-69-69;** Mon–Sat noon–6pm).

Det Kongelige Teater (Royal Theater)   Performances by the world-renowned **Royal Danish Ballet** 𝔊𝔊𝔊 and **Royal Danish Opera** 𝔊𝔊𝔊, dating from 1748, are major winter cultural events in Copenhagen. Because the arts are state-subsidized in Denmark, ticket prices are comparatively low, and some seats may be available at the box office the day before a performance. The season runs August to June. Kongens Nytorv. ℂ **33-69-69-69.** www.kgl-teater.dk. Tickets 70DKK–670DKK ($12–$114/£6.30–£60), half-price for seniors over 66 and people under 26. Bus: 1, 6, 9, or 10.

THE CLUB & MUSIC SCENE
DANCE CLUBS

Den Røde Pimpernel   Throughout most of the day, this place functions as a lively dining and drinking emporium within the heart of Tivoli, whose walls are painted a vivid shade of red in honor of its gallant 17th-century namesake *The Scarlet Pimpernel.* Every evening after 10pm, however, its tables are moved, creating a wide-open dance floor. If you arrive prior to 10pm, admission is free, with the understanding that you've already paid the admission to get into Tivoli. If you arrive after 10pm, admission costs 60DKK ($10/£5.40). Know in advance that the youngest clients, those in their 30-somethings, tend to appear on Thursday and Sunday; other nights, the patrons are a bit more staid, aged anywhere from 30 to a youthful 50-ish. It's open daily noon to 4am. Bernstorffsgade 3, Tivoli. ℂ **33-75-07-60.** Bus: 2, 8, or 30.

NASA   Its name has changed several times in the past decade, but even so, this is the most posh of three less impressive nightclubs that occupy three respective floors of the same building. The late-night crowd of 25- to 40-year-olds includes many avid fans of whatever musical innovation has just emerged in London or Los Angeles. The decorative theme includes lots of white, lots of mirrors, and lots of artfully directed spotlights. Don't be surprised to see a room full of expensively, albeit casually, dressed Danes chatting away in a cacophony of different languages. Technically, the site is a private club, but polite and presentable newcomers can usually gain access. It's open Friday and Saturday midnight to 6am. Gothersgade 8F, Bolthensgaard. ℂ **33-93-74-15.** Cover 100DKK ($17/£9) for nonmembers. Bus: 1, 6, or 9.

The Rock   Thanks to an armada of designers who developed it and a self-appointed role as a "Design Disco," its interior is more artfully outfitted than any other in Copenhagen. Expect lots of postmodern gloss, references to the California rave movement, an occasional emphasis on dance music of the 1980s, a small corner outfitted like a cozy beer hall, and a clientele that seems familiar with the music and ambience of some very hip clubs in Europe and the United States. Part of its interior was based on a waiting room of a 1970s Scandinavian airport, complete with then-innovative streamlined design that's been associated with Denmark ever since. It's open Friday and Saturday 11pm till at least 5:30am. Skindergade 45. ℂ **33-13-26-25.** Cover 60DKK ($10/£5.40). Bus: 1 or 6.

Rust   Rust sprawls over a single floor in the Nørrebro district, where the clientele is international and high energy. Since 1989 faithful patrons have been flocking to its restaurant, several bars, a dance floor, and a stage where live musicians perform every Thursday night beginning around 9pm. Meals are served Wednesday to Saturday 5:30pm to around midnight, and at least someone will begin to boogie on the dance floor after 9:30pm, as drinks flow. The setting is dark and shadowy, "a great place to feel up your partner—or someone else's," one of the patrons told us. There are places to sit, but none so comfortable that you'll stay in one spot for too long. No one under age 21 is admitted, but you'll see very few over age 45. Open 9pm to at least 5am Wednesday to Saturday. Guldbergsgade 8. © **35-24-52-00.** Cover 50DKK–110DKK ($8.50–$19/£4.50–£9.90) Wed–Sat. Bus: 5 or 6.

Vega   Consider this brick-built circular 19th-century monument as the closest thing in town to an old hippie be-in, where you'll enter a multi-faceted, multi-purpose environment. At least two of the venues inside are devoted to live concerts that begin, according to a baffling and oft-changing schedule, anytime between 8 and 11pm, depending on the inclinations of the musicians, and for which entrance usually varies from 100DKK to 180DKK ($17–$31/£9–£16). And when the concert ends, you'll still find at least three other dining and drinking emporiums inside, some with live music of their own, and each with a distinctly different ambience. And on nights when there happens not to be any live music, the smaller bars and dining areas inside are likely to be rocking and rolling the night away. Most venues inside require a minimum age of 20, and except for the concerts whose prices are noted above, entrance to each of the bars and restaurants inside is free. It lies in Vesterbro, behind the railway station. Phones may or may not ring, depending on the whim of who's tending house. Enghavevej 40. © **33-26-09-51** or 33-25-70-11. For schedules of the concerts coming up, visit www.vega.dk. Bus: 1, 6, 9, or 19.

JAZZ, ROCK & BLUES
Copenhagen JazzHouse ⭐   The decor is modern and uncomplicated, and serves as a consciously simple foil for the music and noise. This club hosts more performances by non-Danish jazz artists than any other jazz bar in town. Shows begin relatively early, at around 8:30pm, and usually finish early, too. Around midnight on Friday and Saturday, the club is transformed from a live concert hall into a disco (it's open until 5am). It's closed Mondays; otherwise, it keeps a confusing schedule that changes according to the demands of the current band. Niels Hemmingsensgade 10. © **33-15-26-00.** Cover 65DKK–280DKK ($11–$48/£5.85–£25) when live music is performed, depending on the artist. Bus: 10.

La Fontaine   This is a dive that hasn't changed much since the 1950s, but it's the kind of dive that—if you meet the right partner, or if you really groove with the music—can be a lot of fun. Small and cozy to the point of being cramped, it functions mostly as a bar, every Tuesday to Saturday 8pm to 6am or even 8am. Sunday hours are 9pm to 1am. Live music is performed on Friday and Saturday, when freeform jazz artists play starting around 11:30pm. Kompagnistræde 11. © **33-11-60-98.** Cover 50DKK ($8.50/£4.50) Fri–Sat. Bus: 5 or 10.

Mojo Blues Bar   Mojo is a candlelit drinking spot that offers blues music, 90% of which is performed by Scandinavian groups. This grubby but strangely appealing joint is open daily 8pm to 5am. Løngangstræde 21C. © **33-11-64-53.** Cover 50DKK ($8.50/£4.50) Fri–Sat. Bus: 2, 8, or 30.

THE BAR SCENE
PUBS
Café Zirup Set on a street that's packed with worthy competitors, this cafe and bar is loaded with people who seem fun, charming, and engaged with life and the well-being of their companions. Its name translates as "syrup," and throughout, the venue is youthful and hip. Salads, sandwiches, and platters cost from 89DKK to 99DKK ($15–$17/£8–£8.90). Open Monday to Thursday 10am to midnight, Friday and Saturday 10am to 2am. Læderstræde 32. ℂ **33-13-50-60.** Bus: 1, 6, 9, or 10.

Le Coq Rouge Cozy, traditional, and radically reconfigured in 2006 into a replica of a Parisian brasserie, this maintains the kind of bar where a businessperson could feel at home after a transatlantic flight. It's on the ground floor of one of Copenhagen's most legendary (and discreet) hotels, and its platters of French and Danish food go for 120DKK to 200DKK ($20–$34/£11–£18) each. Open Monday to Saturday from noon to midnight. Beer costs 45DKK ($7.65/£4.05); drinks begin at 52DKK ($8.85/£4.70). In the Kong Frederik Hotel, Vester Voldgade 25. ℂ **33-12-48-48.** Bus: 26, 250S, 5A, and 6A.

Library Bar Frequently visited by celebrities and royalty, the Library Bar was once rated by the late Malcolm Forbes as one of the top five bars in the world. In a setting of antique books and works of art on the lobby level of the Hotel Plaza, you can order everything from a cappuccino to a cocktail. The bar was originally designed and built as the hotel's library, Oregon pine was used for the paneling, and hundreds of books line the walls. It's open daily from noon till midnight (till 2am Fri–Sat). Beer costs 50DKK ($8.50/£4.50); drinks cost from 68DKK to 78DKK ($12–$13/£6.10–£7). In the Hotel Plaza, Bernstorffsgade 4. ℂ **33-14-92-62.** Bus: 10, 15, or 26.

Nyhavn 17 This is the last of the honky-tonk pubs that used to make up the former sailors' quarter, and even this bastion has seen a rapid gentrification in recent years. The cafe is a short walk from the patrician Kongens Nytorv, and in summer you can sit outside. It's open Sunday to Thursday 10am to 2am and Friday and Saturday to 3am. Beer costs 46DKK ($7.80/£4.15), and drinks start at 60DKK ($10/£5.40). Nyhavn 17. ℂ **33-12-54-19.** Bus: 1, 6, 27, or 29.

A WINE BAR
Hvids Vinstue Built in 1670, this old wine cellar is a dimly lit safe haven for an eclectic crowd, many patrons—including theatergoers, actors, and dancers—drawn from the Royal Theater across the way. In December only, a combination of red wine and cognac is served. It's open Monday to Saturday 10am to 1am; Sunday from 10am to 8pm. Beer costs 38DKK ($6.45/£3.40); wine costs 29DKK ($4.95/£2.60). Open-faced sandwiches run 55DKK ($9.35/£4.95) and include a free beer. Kongens Nytorv 19. ℂ **33-15-10-64.** Bus: 1, 6, 9, or 10.

GAY & LESBIAN CLUBS
Boiz Bar Two hundred years ago, the antique and richly beamed interior of this place was used to shelter cattle. Today, in a much-sanitized format, it's a whimsically outfitted men's bar and restaurant contained within one large room with a cozy annex bar a few paces away. There are at least three separate bars/drinking areas within this establishment, a cluster of tables in the center of the larger of the two rooms, with leather upholsteries and the kind of lighting that makes the crowd of mostly gay men aged between 20 to 50 look dramatic. Main courses in the restaurant cost from

129DKK to 169DKK ($22–$29/£12–£15), and a glass of beer costs 36DKK ($6.10/£3.25). Most of the time this place functions as a flamboyant version of an old Danish *kro* (inn), but every Friday and Saturday beginning at 10pm, there's a drag show, with artists imported from London, followed by high energy on a dance floor that's active till around 5am. Hours are Sunday to Thursday 4pm to 2am, Friday and Saturday 4pm to 5am. Magstræde 12-14. ✆ **33-14-52-70.** Bus: 6A.

Centralhjornet This is the oldest gay bar in Copenhagen, having attracted a clientele as far back as the early 20th century. Old-fashioned, wood-paneled, and cozy, it's absolutely mobbed with gay and to a lesser extent, lesbian, tourists during the Christmas holidays. It's open every day of the year from 2pm till midnight. Between October and May, there's a drag show presented every Thursday night beginning around 10pm. Kattesundet 18. ✆ **33-11-85-49.** Bus: 14 or 16.

Cosy Bar It runs a fine line between a crowd that favors leather and what you'd expect from a working crew of men performing manual labor down by the harborfront. Popular and cruisy, it's open daily 11pm till 8am, dispensing ample amounts of schnapps and suds during the course of a working night. Studiestræde 24. ✆ **33-12-74-27.** Bus: 6 or 29.

Jailhouse Copenhagen Set amid the densest concentration of gay men's bars in town, about a block from its nearest competitor (the also-recommended Men's Bar, which attracts something of the same clientele), this is the bar most quickly cited as an amicable and amenable watering hole for the leather, bear, and S&M community. The name of the place influences its decor: Imagine a large, shadowy space with a prominent, beer-soaked bar, battered walls and floors, and iron bars that subdivide the space into a series of simulated jail cells. If you're in the mood for a meal, there's a restaurant upstairs, where crisp white napery contrasts with simulations of cellblocks. Food is Danish and Scandinavian, with specialties that focus on old-fashioned, tried-and-true comfort food, with some modern and somewhat experimental twists. Overall, food is a lot better than what you might have expected in jail. The bar is open from 2pm to 2am (Thurs–Fri until 5am). The entrance is free, with a beer costing 35DKK ($5.95/£3.15). The restaurant is open only Thursday to Saturday 6 to 11pm, with a set-price three-course meal going for 230DKK ($39/£21). Studiestræde 12. ✆ **33-15-22-55.** Bus: 2, 8, or 30.

The Men's Bar This is the only leather bar in town, filled with a bemused collection of uniforms, leather, Levi's, and gay-icon memorabilia. Amicable and fraternal, it showcases a framed portrait, in full military uniform, of "The cutest prince in Europe," Crown Prince Frederik, happily and recently married to "that woman." Note that if it's a particularly hot day, someone might encourage you to take off your shirt, in exchange for which, if you're a newcomer, the bartender is likely to give you a free glass of schnapps. It's open daily 3pm to 2am. A beer will set you back 20DKK ($3.40/£1.80). Teglgaardstræde 3. ✆ **33-12-73-03.** Bus: 2, 8, or 30.

Pan Club This nationwide organization was established in 1948 for the protection and advancement of gay and lesbian rights. It's headquarters is a 19th-century yellow building off of the Strøget, and a dance club occupies three of its floors, while a modern cafe is on the ground level. Every night is gay night, although a lot of straights come here for the music. The cafe is open Thursday 9pm to 4pm; Friday and Saturday 10pm to 5am. The dance club is open Friday 10pm to 5am and Saturday 10pm to 6am. Knabrostræde 3. ✆ **33-11-19-50.** Cover 60DKK ($10/£5.40) for the dance club. Bus: 28, 29, or 41.

XXX COPENHAGEN

The heady "boogie nights" of the 1970s, when pornography aficionados flocked to Copenhagen to purchase X-rated materials, are long gone. Copenhagen is no longer the capital of sex, having long ago lost out to Hamburg and Amsterdam, but many city residents can quote the year when a landmark ruling from Denmark's supreme court made printed pornography legal (1967). Despite the fact that pornographic Copenhagen is not as cutting edge or raunchy as it was, it's still possible to take a walk on the wild side any night of the week. Two of the densest concentrations of porno and the sex industry still lie on **Istedgade** and **Helgolandsgade,** both of them near the rail terminus in the center of the city. Ironically, the sex shops peddling magazines and X-rated films stand virtually adjacent to decent and well-recommended family hotels.

GAMBLING

Casino Copenhagen   Let the dice roll. Danish authorities allowed the country's first fully licensed casino to open in the first-class SAS Scandinavia Hotel in 1990. Today gamblers play such popular games as roulette, baccarat, blackjack, slot machines, and poker. The whole operation is overseen by Casinos of Austria, the largest casino operator in Europe. It's open daily 2pm to 4am. Jackets (but not neckties) are required for men, and presentation of a valid ID (passport or driver's license) is necessary. In the SAS Scandinavia Hotel, Amager Blvd. 70. © **33-96-59-65.** Cover 85DKK ($14/£7.65), but entrance is free every Wednesday from 5–7pm. Bus: 5A, 250.

17 Side Trips from Copenhagen

BEACHES

Locals and visitors are flocking to a newly created beach, **Amager Beach Park** 𝕲, which opened in 2006, just a 15-minute drive from the center of Copenhagen, 5km (3 miles). The beach lies on the Øresund coastline with a view of Sweden and the Øresund Bridge, which now links Denmark with Sweden. You can swim, sunbathe, scuba dive, race boats, or just admire the ships on the Øresund Sound while having a cup of coffee. Off the existing Amager Beach, a completely new island was created with wide, sandy beaches and bathing jetties. Tons of sand was brought in to create the island beach, which is 2km (1¼ miles) long and 50m (164 ft.) wide. In a newly dug lagoon are paddling beaches for children. By the time you read this, three Metro stations should be open right by the beach, which will make it easy to zip over here from Copenhagen if the sun's out. For more information, check with **www.amager-strand.dk**.

The beach closest to Copenhagen is **Bellevue** (S-tog: Klampenborg), but the water is not recommended for swimming. Klampenborg, the community that's adjacent to Bellevue Beach, can provide distractions in addition to a beach: It's the site of the "White City" or "White Town," a residential community designed in the 1930s by modernist master Arne Jacobsen, and revered by Danes as a prime example of the workability of Danish architecture and design.

If you don't mind traveling farther afield, take a trip (by train or car) to the beaches of North Zealand—**Gilleleje, Hornbæk, Liseleje,** and **Tisvildeleje.** Although these are family beaches, minimal bathing attire is worn.

To reach any of these beaches, take the train to Helsingør, and then continue by bus. Or you can make connections by train to Hillerød and switch to a local train; check at the railroad station for details. If you drive, you may want to stay for the evening discos at the little beach resort towns dotting the north coast of Zealand.

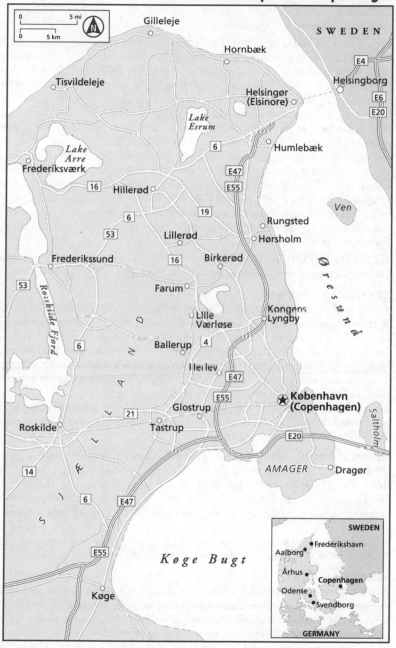

DRAGØR

5km (3 miles) S of Copenhagen's Kastrup Airport

Even if you have to skip the rest of Denmark, head to this little fishing port to see what an idyllic Danish village would look like if Walt Disney had created it. Though we don't mean to put it down, the Frilandsmuseet (p. 113) was an artificially created site—and a grand one at that—but Dragør is the real thing. Young professionals are flocking here from Copenhagen to purchase homes, as they're within an easy commute of the city.

This old seafaring town on the island of Amager is filled with well-preserved half-timbered ocher and pink 18th-century cottages with steep red-tile or thatch roofs, many of which are under the protection of the National Trust.

Dragør (pronounced *Drah*-wer) was a busy port on the herring-rich Baltic Sea in the early Middle Ages, and when fishing fell off, it became a sleepy little waterfront village. After 1520, Amager Island and its villages—Dragør and Store Magleby—were inhabited by the Dutch, who brought their own customs, Low-German language, and agricultural expertise to Amager, especially their love of bulb flowers. In Copenhagen you still see wooden-shoed Amager locals selling their hyacinths, tulips, daffodils, and lilies in the streets.

GETTING THERE   By Bus   Take bus nos. 30, 33, or 73E from Rådhuspladsen (Town Hall Square) in Copenhagen (trip time: 35 min.).

SEEING THE SIGHTS

Amager Museum   This museum is only of passing interest and could be skipped in favor of spending more time walking the streets of Dragør. But if you do duck into it, you'll learn how strong the influence of the Dutch used to be here, ever since farmers from Holland settled Dragør in the 16th century. The interiors of a Dutch house reveal how they decorated their homes and lived in modest comfort, and the Amager Dutch, as they were known, live again in the exhibits of their rich textiles, fine embroidery, and such artifacts as silver buckles and buttons.

Hovedgaden 4–12, Store Magleby. ⓒ 32-53-93-07. www.amagermuseet.dk. Admission 30DKK ($5.10/£2.70) adults, 10DKK ($1.70/90p) children. May–Sept Tues–Sun noon–4pm; Oct–Mar Wed and Sun noon–4pm. Closed in Apr. Bus: 30, 33, or 350S.

Dragør Museum   As you're wandering along Dragør's harborfront, you can spend 20 minutes or so looking inside the town's oldest fisherman's cottage, dating from 1682. The exhibits are modest, but reveal how the Amager Dutch lived when they settled Dragør. Pictures and artifacts reveal that their lives were devoted to farming, goose breeding, seafaring, fishing, ship piloting, and salvaging the cargo of ships wrecked off the coast.

Havnepladsen 2–4. ⓒ 32-53-41-06. www.dragoermuseum.dk. Admission 20DKK ($3.40/£1.80) adults, 10DKK ($1.70/90p) children. May–Sept Tues–Sun and holidays noon–4pm. Closed Oct–Apr. Bus: 30, 32, or 350S.

WHERE TO STAY

Dragør Badehotel   In 1907, a railway line was extended from Copenhagen to this fishing hamlet, and this government-rated three-star hotel opened that same year to greet visitors. The rail line is long gone, but the much-improved and modernized hotel still remains. Restoration in recent years has brought much-needed change, but the old style that prevailed around the turn of the 20th century was respected. The mid-size bedrooms are furnished in a Nordic modern with exceedingly comfortable beds, and maintenance is top rate. Most of the accommodations come with a view of the sea, and the most desirable units open onto their own private balconies. Traditional Danish cuisine is served in the main restaurant, or else you can dine on the open-air terraces in summer. Nonguests are welcome to enjoy the hotel's restaurant. There are six different preparations of herring to get you going, followed by a "Dragør Plate" of mixed meats and pâtés, tender schnitzels, homemade soups, and a selection of *smørrebrød* (open-face sandwiches) at lunch.

Drogdensvej 43, DK-2791 Dragør. ⓒ **32-53-05-00.** Fax 32-53-04-99. www.badehotellet.dk. 34 units. 795DKK–995DKK ($135–$169/£72–£90) double. AE, DC, MC, V. Bus: 30, 33, or 73E. **Amenities:** Restaurant; lounge; laundry service; nonsmoking rooms; rooms for those w/limited mobility. *In room:* TV, minibar.

WHERE TO DINE
The Dragør Badehotel (see above) also offers an excellent cuisine.

Restaurant Beghuset DANISH Even on the most rushed of visits, we like to schedule at least one meal at this old-fashioned dining room, which not only serves good, home-cooked food, but is a nostalgic reminder of the Denmark of yesterday. This cafe and restaurant on a cobblestone street in the center of town looks like an idyllic cottage. To reach the restaurant section, walk through the cafe. Although the menu changes every 2 to 3 months to accommodate seasonal items, a weary traveler in search of sustenance will be tempted by selections such as fish soup, Swedish caviar, and fresh oysters. Main courses include a divinely cooked guinea fowl braised in red wine served with bacon of veal (their own invention) and herbs, and Dragør plaice roasted in butter and served with either parsley sauce or a bacon thyme sauce.

Strandgade 14. ⓒ **32-53-01-36.** Reservations recommended. 1-platter lunch 169DKK–198DKK ($29–$34/£15–£18); 2-course lunch 198DKK (US$34/£18); 3-course lunch 225DKK–275DKK ($38–$47/£20–£25); dinner main courses 178DKK–218DKK ($30–$37/£16–£20); 3-course fixed-price dinner 358DKK ($61/£32); 4-course fixed-price dinner 398DKK ($68/£36). AE, DC, MC, V. Tues–Sun noon–3pm and 6–9pm. Bus: 30, 33, or 73E.

Strandhotel ⓚ DANISH In spite of its name, this establishment no longer accepts overnight guests, but is one of the finest restaurants in Dragør, offering a more imaginative cuisine than the more standard, yet good, Danish fare featured at the Beghuset (see above). Strandhotel is still going strong, but it's been a long time since Frederik III used to drop by for a bowl of the chef's eel soup. Even Søren Kierkegaard used to come here to brood (apparently about his confused sexuality).

At lunchtime an ample spread of *smørrebrød* is served, although other offerings include filet of pork in paprika sauce, a savory smoked filet of eel, and a delectable trout with almonds. At dinner the chefs tempt you with such dishes as grilled tuna with raspberries or oven-baked whitefish served in a banana leaf with saffron cream sauce.

Strandlinbyn 9, Havnen. ⓒ **32-53-00-75.** Reservations recommended. Main courses 158DKK–196DKK ($27–$33/£14–£18); lunch *smørrebrød* 78DKK–188DKK ($13–$32/£7–£17); "quick lunch" 188DKK ($32/£17). AE, DC, MC, V. Daily 9am–9:30pm. Closed Nov–Mar. Bus: 350S.

HUMLEBÆK (LOUISIANA MUSEUM)
32km (20 miles) N of Copenhagen

The area running along the coast north of Copenhagen is called both the Danish Riviera and Millionaire's Row. Some of the wealthiest people in Denmark live in palatial homes between Copenhagen and the town of Humlebæk. But the only reason most visitors come to this former fishing village, unless they have a private invitation, is to visit the world-famous Louisiana Museum, our favorite art center in all of Denmark.

ESSENTIALS

GETTING THERE **By Train** Humlebæk is on the Copenhagen-Helsingør train line; there are two trains per hour that leave Copenhagen's main railway station heading toward Humlebæk (trip time: 40 min.). Once you reach Humlebæk, the Louisiana Museum is a 10-minute walk.

By Bus Take the S-tog train, line A or B, to Lyngby station. From there, take bus no. 388 along the coast road. There's a bus stop at the museum.

By Car Follow the Strandvej (coastal road no. 152) from Copenhagen. The scenic drive takes about 45 minutes.

SEEING THE SIGHTS

Louisiana Museum of Modern Art ★★★ *Kids* A lot of Americans think this museum for some odd reason was named for the state of Louisiana, but the museum's name came from the fact that the first owner of the estate here, Alexander Brun, had three wives, each named Louise. In a spacious old park with a panoramic view across Øresund to Sweden, this is one of the greatest museums of modern art in the Nordic world. The modest collection of Scandinavian art that opened here in 1954 has grown and grown with bequests and donations, and future architects have added more galleries onto the existing 19th-century villa.

The museum opened with works by the COBRA group, the name of artists from the cities of *CO*penhagen, *BR*ussels, and *A*msterdam. These original works are displayed along with some of the finest paintings and sculpture by international artists such as Calder, Dubuffet, Max Ernst, Giacometti, Picasso, and Andy Warhol.

The museum has one of the largest exhibition spaces in Europe, and major exhibitions of contemporary art are staged here. There is also an extensive program of concerts, lectures, films, author discussions, and public debates. Children find their own haven here, especially at the **Børnehuset,** or children's house, and the **Søhaven,** or Sea Garden. The museum's cafe is on a terrace with Alexander Calder's sculptures.

Gl. Strandvej 13. ⓒ **49-19-07-19.** Admission 80DKK ($14/£7.20) adults, 70DKK ($12/£6.30) students free for children 18 and under. Wed 10am–10pm; Thurs–Tues 10am–5pm. Closed Dec 24–25 and Dec 31.

WHERE TO DINE

Louisiana Café DANISH Since 1772 there has been an inn on this spot, feeding wayfarers of yore who took a horse and carriage along the coast heading for Helsingør. Today much of yesterday has been swept away, and what remains is this cafe-restaurant, which is the best and also the most convenient place for lunch, just only a short walk from the museum. If you're so enthralled with the museum and are around at dinnertime, you can also dine here before heading back to the heart of Copenhagen.

We've always found the food satisfying in an old-fashioned sort of way, although we never feel we have to call the editors of *Gourmet* magazine on our cellphones. At lunch most diners dig into a range of open-faced sandwiches—usually three is enough to satisfy. At night you can partake of recipes based on tried-and-true dishes such as a platter-size Wiener schnitzel. Veal comes in medallions with a rich morel sauce, and herring is dressed up with a sherry sauce.

Gl. Strandvej 13. ⓒ **49-19-07-19.** Reservations recommended. Main courses 178DKK–225DKK ($30–$38/£16–£20). AE, DC, MC, V. Daily 10am–9:30pm.

HILLERØD

35km (22 miles) NW of Copenhagen

We don't expect you to fall in love with Hillerød, since unless you've consumed a lot of Danish beer, it can be a bit dull. We come here not only because it's a transport hub for North Zealand, especially for those connecting to trains heading for the north shore beaches, but to see its sprawling castle of Frederiksborg.

After a fire swept over it in 1859, even the royal family found the repairs too costly. They gave it up to the Carlsberg beer baron, J. C. Jacobsen, and he spearheaded the move to create the extravagant palace you see today.

You can spend at least 1½ hours here wandering through its chambers before falling in love with the baroque gardens out back.

Even if you don't like palaces and gardens, the ideal time to arrive here is in summer for the Viking Festival (see below).

If you, like us, are into long walks, you've come to the right place. Hillerød, in the heart of North Zealand, is surrounded by some of the most beautiful and extensive woodlands in the country. Christian IV used to ride through here in 1602, and you can follow his trails. Though we can't tell you about all the best walks and trails to follow, the tourist office can give you a leaflet outlining "the best of the best."

To the south sprawl the woodlands of **Store Dyrehave,** but we prefer the northern stretch of **Gribskov,** the second largest forest in Denmark. The woodlands are still rich in game, and we take delight in spotting one of the pale, tailless roe deer. It's estimated there are some 800 fallow deer here, each distinguished by its white-speckled hide.

If you don't like to walk, you can also ask the tourist office for another leaflet, "Bicycle Routes in North Zealand." Routes drawn on the map follow the most scenic paths, roads, and forest trails.

The forests of Gribskov front our favorite North Zealand lake, **Esrum Sø.** If you like bathing in admittedly chilly waters, sailing a boat, or fishing, you've come to the right place. The parklands of Fredensborg Slot (Fredensborg Palace; see below) lie on the eastern shore of the lake, where chances are good in summer that you can hook up with one of the concessions featuring sailing trips on this gorgeous lake.

ESSENTIALS

GETTING THERE   The S-tog from Copenhagen arrives every 10 minutes throughout the day (trip time: 40 min.).

By Train   Trains link Hillerød with Helsingør in the east, and there are also rail links with Gilleleje and Tisvildeleje.

By Bus   Hillerød has good bus connections with the major towns of North Zealand: bus no. 305 from Gilleleje; bus nos. 306, 336, and 339 from Hornbæk; and bus nos. 336 and 339 from Fredensborg.

By Car   From Copenhagen, take Route 16 north.

VISITOR INFORMATION   The **tourist office,** Cristiansgade 1 (© **48-24-26-26;** www.hillerodturist.dk), is open Monday to Wednesday 10:30am to 5:30pm and Thursday to Friday 10:30am to 4:30pm.

SPECIAL EVENTS   Every summer some 250 men, women, and children don their Viking costumes and go on a rampage, re-creating the drama of the Viking age when the mere expression, "the Vikings are coming," sent terror throughout a land about to be conquered. **Frederikssund Vikingspil** (Viking Festival) ✪✪✪ is the biggest event of the Danish summer. If possible, try to adjust your schedule to take in the fun.

Frederikssund is a town 13km (8 miles) southwest of Hillerød and 48km (30 miles) northwest of Copenhagen. It stages a 2-week festival in mid-June. Nordic sagas are revived—and the record is set straight about who "discovered" America 5 centuries before Christopher Columbus. The festival features a series of plays, medieval and modern, about the Vikings.

The traditional play is performed nightly at 8pm, and a Viking banquet follows. Tickets for the festival are 125DKK ($21/£11) adults and 40DKK ($6.80/£3.60) children 5 to 12 (it's not suitable for children 4 and under). The dinner costs 159DKK ($27/£14) adults and 95DKK ($16/£8.55) children 5 to 12. Trains depart for Frederikssund at 20-minute intervals from Copenhagen's Central Railroad Station (trip time: 50 min.), and there are enough trains back to Copenhagen after the spectacle ends to allow commutes from the capital. From the station at Frederikssund, it's a 20-minute walk to the site of the pageant. For details, contact the tourist information office in Copenhagen, or phone the Frederikssund Tourist Office (© **47-31-06-85**).

EXPLORING THE TOWN
Det Nationalhistoriske Museum på Frederiksborg (Frederiksborg Castle) ✪✪✪

We don't like giving labels to places that are designed to mislead. Don't fall for that hype about Frederiksborg Castle being "the Danish Versailles." Versailles, it isn't, but it *is* the most beautiful royal residence in Denmark. Surrounded by a moat, the *slot* (castle) was constructed on three islands in a lake. Like Kronborg, it was built in Dutch Renaissance style (red brick, copper roof, sandstone facade). The oldest parts date from 1560 and the reign of Frederik II. His more extravagant son, Christian IV, erected the main part of the castle from 1600 to 1620. Danish monarchs used it for some 2 centuries. From 1671 to 1840, Danish kings were crowned in Christian IV's chapel, which is still used as a parish church. Since 1693 it has been a chapel for the knights of the Order of the Elephant and of the Grand Cross of Danneborg. Standing in the gallery is an old organ built by Esaias Compenius in 1610. Every Thursday from 1:30 to 2pm, the chapel organist plays for museum visitors.

Since 1878 the castle has housed the Museum of National History. Founded by the brewer J. C. Jacobsen as part of the Carlsberg Foundation, it encompasses the Great Hall and the former Audience Chamber of Danish monarchs. The museum contains the best collection of portraits and historical paintings in the country. You can explore 70 of its rooms, each with paintings, gilded ceilings, and tapestries covering entire walls. The 20th-century collection on the third floor is a bit livelier, with its chronologically arranged exhibits. There are portraits and paintings here, but somehow the photographs are even more intriguing.

The castle is a 15-minute walk or a short taxi ride from the train station.

In Frederiksborg Slot. © **48-26-04-39**. Admission 60DKK ($10/£5.40) adults, 15DKK ($2.55/£1.35) children 6–15, free for children under 6. Nov–Mar daily 11am–3pm; Apr–Oct daily 10am–5pm. Bus: 701 from Hillerød Station.

Frederiksborg Castle Garden ✪✪ For decades these gardens were used by three kings of Denmark, including Frederik IV, Christian VI, and Frederik V. They were designed by Johan Cornelius Krieger from 1720 to 1725. In a flight of fancy, he got carried away, creating a cascade with water canals and fountains, along with promenades, groves of trees, and even a parterre sporting royal monograms to flatter the egos of his patrons.

Sadly, during his reign, Christian VII (1766–1808) wasn't in the mood for a baroque romp, and the tightwad king, preoccupied with military matters, felt the gardens had grown out of style and were too expensive for his royal purse to maintain. By 1933, the gardens had decayed. But in recent times, monies were found to re-create the gardens as they were in their baroque heyday. As many as 65,000 box plants and 166 pyramid-shaped yews have been planted in the parterre, while 375 limes and 7,000 hornbeam plants create the avenues and groves. The cascade floor consists of nearly half a kilometer (¼ mile) of dressed granite stones. During the summer, the Frederiksborg Castle Garden forms the venue for several recurring concerts, maypole celebrations, and other cultural events.

Rendelæggerbakken 3. ℭ 48-26-04-39. Free admission. May–Aug daily 10am–9pm; Sept and Apr daily 10am–7pm; Oct and Mar daily 10am–5pm; Nov–Feb daily 10am–4pm. Bus: 701 from Hillerød Station.

WHERE TO STAY

Hotel Hillerød   This is the town's best choice for an overnight stay. Okay, so its low-slung design and features might remind you of a motel on the outskirts of a large American city. Even so, the hotel is furnished both sensibly and comfortably, and all the bedrooms are well maintained with Danish modern pieces and neatly kept bathrooms with shower units. Most of the accommodations come with a small kitchenette, as well as a private terrace. Breakfast is the only meal served and, even if there are any shortcomings here, the attentive staff makes up for it. The location is a 3-minute walk from the town's commercial center.

Milnersvej 41, DK-3400 Hillerød. ℭ 48-24-08-00. Fax 48-24-08-74. www.hotelhillerod.dk. 74 units, 63 with kitchenette. 1,110DKK ($189/£100) double. Rates include breakfast. AE, DC, MC, V. **Amenities:** Breakfast room; lounge; laundry service; dry cleaning; nonsmoking rooms, rooms for those w/limited mobility. *In room:* TV, minibar, coffeemaker, hair dryer, trouser press, safe.

WHERE TO DINE

Slotskroen ⍟ DANISH   This place been going strong since it opened its doors in 1795. Though it's the oldest tavern in town, it's also kept abreast of the times in both its menu selections and its decor. Nowadays, food is served only at lunchtime (although on rare occasions, dinner is offered). Within a trio of cozy and historic-looking dining rooms, some of whose windows open onto direct views of the nearby castle, you can enjoy access to a smörgåsbord that's laden with tasty hot and cold dishes, several kinds of open-face Danish sandwiches, *frikadeller* (meatballs), and fresh salads. Otherwise, fixed-price menus might include any of several kinds of herring, a buttery Wiener schnitzel, and a well-flavored version of beefsteak. There's also an outdoor terrace for use during warm weather.

Slotsgade 67. ℭ 48-20-18-00. Smörgåsbord buffet 169DKK ($29/£15). AE, DC, MC, V. Daily noon–5pm.

Spisestedet Leonora ⍟ DANISH   Since the 1970s this well-managed tavern has flourished in the former Frederiksborg Castle stables. Don't panic—the original smell is long gone. It's the most sought-after dining spot in town for anyone visiting the castle, partly because of its array of carefully crafted open-face sandwiches. The place also serves succulent grilled meats, especially Danish lamb, fresh salads, and platters of warm, homemade food, which are big enough to make a meal unto themselves.

In Frederiksborg Slot. ℭ 48-26-75-16. Main courses 55DKK–145DKK ($9.35–$25/£4.95–£13); lunch plate 98DKK ($17/£8.80); *smørrebrød* 42DKK–98DKK ($7.15–$17/£3.80–£8.80). DC, MC, V. Daily 10am–5pm. Closed 1 week at Christmas. Bus: 701 or 702.

FREDENSBORG

9.5km (6 miles) W of Helsingør, 40km (25 miles) N of Copenhagen

The best time to visit is in July, when the queen graciously opens the doors of Fredensborg Slot (palace) to visitors from around the world. Elizabeth II of England has a lot more money, a lot more paintings, and many more precious furnishings, but the Danish queen's summer abode is impressive as well, though not as grand as Frederiksborg Slot, with which it is often confused.

On the southeast shore of Esrum Sø, the country's second largest lake, Fredensborg is more than a royal palace. Many visitors rush through, visiting the palace and then departing immediately. However, you can stay and dine in the area and enjoy a number of other attractions as well (see below).

The first inhabitants of the town were people who helped serve the royal court. But over the years others moved in, and today the town is a lively little place even when the Queen isn't in residence. To Denmark, it occupies a position somewhat similar to Windsor in England and is home to some 40 specialty shops.

The palace is a major backdrop for events in the life of the royal family—weddings, birthday parties, and the like. Heads of states from many of the countries of the world are received here when they pay state visits, and foreign ambassadors present their credentials to the monarch here as well.

ESSENTIALS

GETTING THERE   By Train   From Copenhagen's Central Railroad Station, frequent trains run to Fredensborg, but there are no buses.

By Car   From Copenhagen, head north on the E55 toward Helsingør, turning west on Route 6.

VISITOR INFORMATION   The **Fredensborg Turistinformation,** Slotsgade 2 (© **48-48-21-00**), is open Monday to Friday noon to 4pm.

SEEING THE SIGHTS

Fredensborg Slot ⑆   This is the summer residence of the Danish royal family. Once it was called the palace of "the parents-in-law" of Europe. King Christian IX and Queen Louise had sons and daughters sitting on thrones in many of the royal houses of Europe, and they would gather in the summer months to catch up on royal gossip. Although the palace has been added on to many times, it still retains its baroque, rococo, and classic features.

When the queen is in residence today, visitors assemble at noon to watch the changing of the guard, but don't expect this ceremony to match that of Buckingham Palace in London. On Thursdays, except in July, the queen often appears to acknowledge a regimental band concert in her honor.

The Danish architect J. D. Krieger built the palace for King Frederik IV. Originally there was only the main building with a Cupola Hall, but over the years the palace was extended with such additions as the Chancellery House and the Cavaliers Wing. Though hardly one of the impressive royal palaces of Europe, it has its own charm, especially in the Domed Hall and the Garden Room.

The palace opens onto a 275-year-old **baroque garden** ⑆⑆. A public part of the palace garden is open year-round, but the private, reserved royal garden is open only in July, Sunday to Friday 9am to 5pm. The orangery in the royal garden is also open in July, daily 1 to 4:30pm. These are some of the largest and best-preserved gardens in Denmark. Note how strictly symmetrical and geometrical the shapes are. Drawing on Italian designs for their inspiration, Frederik IV and J. C. Krieger laid out the palace gardens in the 1720s. In the 1760s Frederik V redesigned the garden, adding elements from French baroque horticulture.

Slottet. © **33-40-31-87.** Admission 40DKK ($6.80/£3.60) adults, 15DKK ($2.55/£1.35) children. Palace July daily 1–5pm. Joint ticket for the Palace and the Orangery and Herb Garden: 40DKK ($6.80/£3.60) for adults and 15DKK ($2.55/£1.35) for children.

HELSINGØR (ELSINORE): IN SEARCH OF HAMLET ⚐

40km (25 miles) N of Copenhagen, 24km (15 miles) NE of Hillerød, 72km (45 miles) NE of Roskilde

Does it really matter to the pilgrims flocking to this town that Hamlet never existed? Or that William Shakespeare never visited Helsingør? To the pilgrims wanting to see "Hamlet's Castle," the power of legend is what really matters.

After arriving, make your way through the noisy, congested crowds and the fast-food stalls, and move deeper into Helsingør, where you'll find that it has a certain charm, with a market square, medieval lanes, and old half-timbered and brick buildings, many constructed by ships' captains in the heyday of the 19th-century shipping industry.

In 1429, King Erik of Pomerania ruled that ships passing Helsingør had to pay a toll for sailing within local waters. The town quickly developed into the focal point for international shipping, bringing in a lot of revenue. King Erik also constructed the Castle of Krogen, later rebuilt by Christian IV as the Castle of Kronborg. For a while Helsingør prospered and grew so much that it was the second-largest town in the country.

Today much of the town's prosperity depends on those free-spending Hamlet devotees and that sliver of water between Denmark and Sweden, with ferries leaving frequently for Helsingborg.

ESSENTIALS

GETTING THERE By Train   There are frequent trains from Copenhagen (trip time: 50 min.).

By Car   Take E-4 north from Copenhagen.

By Ferry   Ferries ply the waters of the narrow channel separating Helsingør (Denmark) from Helsingborg (Sweden) in less than 25 minutes. They're operated around the clock by **Scandlines** (© **33-15-15-15;** www.scandlines.dk), which charges 21DKK ($3.55/£1.90) each way for a pedestrian without a car, and 254DKK ($43/£23) each way for a car with up to nine persons inside. Between 6am and 11pm, departures are every 20 minutes; 11pm to 6am, departures are timed at intervals of 40 to 80 minutes. The process is simple and straightforward: You simply drive your car onboard and wait in your car. Border formalities during the crossing between Denmark and Sweden are perfunctory, and although you should carry a passport, you might not even be asked for it.

VISITOR INFORMATION   The **tourist office,** Havnepladsen 3 (© **49-21-13-33;** www.visithelsingor.dk), is open Monday to Friday 10am to 4pm and Saturday 10am to 1pm; June 20 to August 31 Monday to Friday 10am to 5pm, and Saturday 10am to 3pm.

SEEING THE SIGHTS

Kronborg Slot ✦✦✦ There is no evidence that Shakespeare, as mentioned, ever saw this sandstone-and-copper Dutch Renaissance–style castle, full of intriguing secret passages, but he made it famous in *Hamlet*. If Hamlet had really lived, it would have been centuries before Kronborg was built (1574–85).

The castle, on a peninsula jutting out into Øresund, was restored in 1629 by Christian IV after it had been gutted by fire. Other events in its history include looting, bombardment, occupation by Swedes, and use as a barracks (1785–1922). The facade is covered with sandstone, and the entire castle is surrounded by a deep moat—but no dragon. You approach the castle via a wooden bridge and by going through Mørkeport, a gate from the 16th century. This will lead you to the main courtyard of Kronborg.

Note: Instead of entering the castle at once, you can walk around the moat to the waterfront, where you can view a spectacular vista of the Swedish coast. At the platform—backed by massive bronze guns—Hamlet is said to have seen the ghost of his father, shrouded in pea-soup fog.

The starkly furnished Great Hall is the largest in northern Europe. Originally 40 tapestries portraying 111 Danish kings were hung around this room on special occasions. They were commissioned by Frederik II and produced around 1585. Only seven remain at Kronborg; the rest have disappeared except for seven in the Nationalmuseet in Copenhagen. The church, with its original oak furnishings and the royal chambers, is worth exploring. The bleak and austere atmosphere adds to the drama. Holger Danske, a mythological hero who is believed to assist Denmark whenever the country is threatened, is said to live in the basement. That "hero" didn't emerge when Nazi storm-troopers invaded Denmark on Hitler's orders, but the legend, like the legend of Hamlet, still persists. Also on the premises is the **Danish Maritime Museum** (© **49-21-06-85**), which explores the history of Danish shipping. Unless you're really nautical, you might skip this if you're rushed for time. However, that would mean you'd miss seeing the world's oldest surviving ship's biscuit, dating from 1852. There are also an impressive collection of model ships and other sailors' memorabilia. More intriguing are relics of Denmark's colonial past in the West Indies (Caribbean), West Africa, Greenland, and even India.

Guided tours are given every half-hour October to April. In summer you can walk around on your own. The castle is less than a kilometer (about ½ mile) from the rail station. In 2000, Kronborg was added to UNESCO's World Heritage List.

Kronborg. © **49-21-30-78**. www.kronborgcastle.com. Admission 60DKK ($10/£5.40) adults, 15DKK ($2.55/£1.35) children 6–14, free for children under 6. Joint ticket for the castle and the Danish Maritime Museum 75DKK ($13/£6.75) adults, 60DKK ($10/£5.40) children. May–Sept daily 10:30am–5pm; Apr and Oct Tues–Sun 11am–4pm; Nov–Mar Tues–Sun 11am–3pm. Closed Dec 25.

Skt. Mariæ Kirke ✦ Too often neglected by those Hamlet-crazed visitors, this former Carmelite monastery is one of the best preserved in the North of Europe. The church was built between 1430 and 1500, and much of its original architecture remains. You can see the newly renovated organ that was used by the famous baroque composer, Dietrich Buxtehude, from 1660 to 1668. Murals dating from the 1480s have also been restored, and there is an impressive altarpiece from 1637. The interior contains two galleries, a royal gallery and a rococo gallery, dating from the 17th and 18th centuries. After the Reformation, the monastery was dissolved and converted into an old people's home. Inside the walls of the ecclesiastical compound is the **Karmeliterklosteret Monastery** ✿, which can be visited on a guided tour. After the monks were booted out, this building was turned into a hospital specializing in brain surgery. The monastery lies near the intersection of Havnegade and Kronborgvej.

Skt. Annagade 38. ✆ **49-21-17-74**. Free admission. Thurs 4–6pm; Mon–Sat 9am–noon. Guided tours May 16–Sept 15 Mon–Fri at 2pm, 20DKK ($3.40/£1.80) adults, 5DKK (85¢/45p) children.

Sankt Olai's Kirke   If you have time after visiting the monastery above, you can walk nearby to see this church, which is actually the cathedral of Helsingør. It was named after the patron saint, St. Olai, the Norwegian king, Olav (spelled differently), who died in 1030. Throughout the church are illustrations of this saintly king slaying the dragon of paganism.

The present building dates from 1559, constructed on the site of a small Romanesque church from the 1200s.

At the dawn of the 21st century, restorers opened many of the burial chambers here, discovering very well-preserved mummies. After studying these long-dead corpses, they were sealed away once more and buried beneath a floor of concrete and tile to "safeguard the peace of the dead now and forever."

Architecturally, the christening chapel and the baptistery of this spired church are worth a brief inspection. Also take in the ornately decorated altar. The Sankt Olai takes up a city block between Stengade and Sankt Olai Gade.

Skt. Annagade 12. ✆ 49 21-04-43. Free admission. May–Aug Mon–Sat 10am–4pm; Sept–Apr daily 10am–2pm.

Helsingør Bymuseet   This Renaissance townhouse, built in 1520 by Carmelite friars as a hospital for foreign sailors, suffering from diseases, has erased that sad history. Today it's the "attic" of Helsingør, a magnificent Renaissance townhouse filled with the city's relics. Children, or at least little girls, gravitate to the collection of 200 antique dolls. There is also a fine-scale model of Helsingør in 1801. The banquet hall on the main floor is filled with the chief goodies, artifacts left over from the golden age of Helsingør when it was a major shipping center. As for some of those portraits, they evoke the type you hide in your own family attic. In the basement are relics of the Middle Ages, best left undisturbed in our view.

Helsingørsgade 65. ✆ **49-28-18-00**. Admission 15DKK (US$2.55/£1.35) adults, free for children. May–Oct Tues–Sun 11am–4pm.

Danmarks Tekniske Museet (Technical Museum of Denmark) ✿ *Finds*   Did you know that rich Danes were driving an automobile, the Hammelvognen, back in 1888? They were, and it's on display here, in addition to the world's first typewriter and the world's first electromagnetic sound recorder (tape recorder). Steam engines, antique electric appliances, bicycles, vintage cars, and the oldest Danish airplanes are on display here.

Although there are many exhibits, including a pewter workshop, we are most intrigued by the 30 or so airplanes, ranging from gyrocopters to helicopters. Our favorite is called the "Danish Edison," an invention of J. C. Ellhammer. Danes will tell you he made the first flight in Europe in 1906. Regrettably, if this is true, his feat was never recorded. The museum is in the southern part of town in a former iron foundry.

Fabriksvej 25. ✆ **49-22-26-11**. Admission Jan 2–Apr 30 and Oct 1–Dec 30 50DKK ($8.50/£4.50) adults, 25DKK ($4.25/£2.25) children; May–Sept 65DKK ($11/£5.85) adults, 25DKK ($4.25/£2.25) children. Tues–Sun 10am–5pm.

WHERE TO STAY

Hotel Marienlyst 𝕲   This hotel, on the western outskirts of town beyond the castle, is about as close to Las Vegas as you'll get in Denmark. Even if you don't like its flashy neon aggressiveness, it's the best and most comfortable place to stay in town. Composed of three buildings, its headquarters and oldest core were built around 1850, while the largest of its annexes went up in the mid-1970s. With a panoramic view over the gray sea toward Sweden, this hotel contains a glossy outbuilding with one of only six gambling casinos in Denmark. Rooms are a study in sleek Nordic styling—comfortable and beautifully maintained. The bathrooms are neatly kept, with tub/shower combinations. Many rooms have balconies or terraces, and 86 have a view of the sound. The suites and apartments have a kitchen and dishwasher.

Nordre Strandvej 2, DK-3000 Helsingør. ℭ **49-21-40-00.** Fax 49-21-49-00. www.marienlyst.dk. 222 units. 1,120DKK–1,825DKK ($190–$310/£101–£164) double; 2,175DKK–2,775DKK ($370–$472/£196–£250) suite. Rates include breakfast. AE, DC, MC, V. Bus: 340. **Amenities:** 2 restaurants; bar; water park; indoor heated pool; sauna; room service (7am–11pm); babysitting; laundry service; dry cleaning; nonsmoking rooms; rooms for those w/limited mobility; casino. *In room:* TV, dataport, hair dryer.

WHERE TO DINE

Typical Danish hot meals, such as *hakkebof* (hamburger steak), *frikadeller* (Danish rissoles or meatballs), rib roast with red cabbage, cooked or fried flounder or herring, and *æggekage* (egg cake) with bacon, are served in the local restaurants. In Helsingør you'll also find many fast-food places, and you won't want to miss the celebrated ice-cream wafers.

Ophelia Restaurant DANISH/FRENCH   Naturally, in the town of Hamlet, some enterprising owner had to come up with a touristy name to lure visitors. Ophelia is one of the most appealing restaurants in town and cooks using market-fresh ingredients. In the elegantly rustic dining room, photos of *Hamlet* productions from around the world line the brick walls. Specialties of the house include "Hamlet veal steak" and calorie-rich desserts. Lunches cost half as much as dinner. Although not overly imaginative, the cookery is very competent, with dish after tasteful dish emerging from the kitchen.

In the Hotel Hamlet, Bramstræde 5. ℭ **49-21-05-91.** Reservations recommended. Main courses 90DKK–190DKK ($15–$32/£8.10–£17). AE, DC, MC, V. Daily noon–9:30pm. Bus: 801 or 802.

San Remo DANISH   A down-to-earth self-service establishment that nevertheless sports crystal chandeliers, the San Remo offers 35 different meals, including *frikadeller* and potatoes. The fare is robust, filling, and cheap—nothing more. The cafeteria is set in a traffic-free shopping mall half a block from the harbor in a Dutch-inspired building dating from 1904.

Stengade 53 (at Bjergegade). ℭ **49-21-00-55.** Main courses 32DKK–95DKK ($5.45–$16/£2.90–£8.55). MC, V. June–July daily 9am–9pm; Aug–May daily 11am–6pm. Bus: 801 or 802.

ROSKILDE 𝕲𝕲
32km (20 miles) W of Copenhagen

If you have only 1 day for North Zealand, we'd skip the highly touted and touristy "Hamlet's Castle" and make the trek to Roskilde instead.

Next to Copenhagen, this is Zealand's second-largest town, with one of its longest histories, dating from 998. It's true that much of this thriving town is devoted to industry, but there are many remnants of its illustrious past as a royal residence in the

10th century and the spiritual capital not only of Denmark but of northern Europe in the 12th century. The Vikings used Roskilde Fjord to sail in from the open sea after one of their conquests.

Royal tombs, Viking boats, and one of northern Europe's biggest open-air rock festivals keep the visitors coming.

Roskilde, once a great ecclesiastical seat, was Denmark's leading city until the mid–15th century. Today the twin spires of **Roskilde Cathedral** stand out from the Danish landscape like elegantly tapered beacons. These towers are the first landmark you see when approaching the city.

Roskilde may be centuries past its peak, but it's no sleepy museum town. It's filled with a dynamic student community, boutique-filled streets, several landmarks and major sights, and a population of more than 52,000 people.

Toward the end of the first millennium (A.D.), the Vikings settled the area, drawn, no doubt, by its sinuous coastline, where they could launch their ships. In 1957, divers in the Roskilde Fjord came upon shards of wood and reported their findings. Their discovery turned out to be bigger than anyone imagined. Here, sunken and mud-preserved, were five Viking ships that presumably had been put there to block the passage of enemy ships.

Archaeologists began the painstaking job of building a watertight dam and draining that section of the fjord, while keeping the chunks of splinters of wood wet enough so as not to cause them to disintegrate. Splinter by splinter they began the reconstruction and reassembly of the boats—a process that continues today. You can see their efforts on display at the **Viking Ship Museum** (see below).

Between A.D. 990 and A.D. 1000, Roskilde's prominence grew, becoming the home of the royal residence. By the 11th century, a Catholic church and a Bishop's Seat resided at Roskilde, which was to remain Denmark's capital until the Reformation in 1536.

At that time all the parish churches were abolished and the Catholic hierarchy disappeared. The government and the monarchy moved to Copenhagen. Nonetheless, at its peak, Roskilde's importance was expressed in its architecture. By 1150, it was surrounded by an embankment and a moat, inside of which stood 12 churches and a cathedral. In 1170, Bishop Absalon built a new church on the site where Harald Bluetooth had erected his church 2 centuries before. Though it took 300 years to construct, and was subsequently burned, destroyed, ravaged, and rebuilt, Absalon's cathedral laid the foundation for the existing Roskilde Cathedral or Domkirke, which today is a UNESCO World Heritage Site.

ESSENTIALS

GETTING THERE   By Train   Trains leave three times an hour from Copenhagen's Central Railroad Station on the 35-minute trip to Roskilde.

By Bus   Buses depart from Roskilde several times daily from Copenhagen's Central Railroad Station.

By Car   Take the E-21 express highway west from Copenhagen.

VISITOR INFORMATION   The **Roskilde-Egnens Turistbureau,** Gullandsstræde 15 (© **46-31-65-65**), provides pamphlets about the town and the surrounding area. The office is open January 1 through March 31 and August 23 to December 31 Monday to Thursday 9am to 5pm, Friday 9am to 4pm, and Saturday 10am to 1pm; April 1 to June 27 Monday to Friday 9am to 5pm and Saturday 10am to 1pm; June 28 to August 22 Monday to Friday 9am to 6pm and Saturday 10am to 2pm. While at the tourist office inquire about a Roskilde card, which costs 185DKK ($31/£17) adults or 95DKK ($16/£8.55) children 10 to 15; free for 9 and under. The card admits you to the 10 attractions in the area and is valid for 7 days from the date of issue. Without the card, it would cost 439DKK ($75/£40) to visit these same attractions.

SPECIAL EVENTS　The **Roskilde Festival** 👀 (© **46-36-66-13;** www.roskilde-festival.dk) is northern Europe's best outdoor concert. It is held outdoors June 29 to July 2 on a large grassy field and attracts fans of rock and techno music. To get information on the festival—dates and performances—call the above number, or contact the Roskilde-Egnens Turistbureau (see "Visitor Information," above).

SEEING THE SIGHTS
Roskilde Domkirke 👀👀　There's no church in Copenhagen, or anywhere else in Denmark for that matter, to rival this towering edifice. This cathedral made Roskilde the spiritual capital of Denmark and northern Europe. Today it rises out of a modest townscape like a mirage—a cathedral several times too big for the town surrounding it. Construction started in 1170 when Absalon was bishop of Roskilde. Work continued into the 13th century, and the building's original Romanesque features gave way to an early Gothic facade. The twin towers weren't built until the 14th century.

Today the cathedral's beauty goes beyond a single architectural style, providing almost a crash course in Danish architecture. Although damaged by a fire in 1968, the cathedral has been restored, including its magnificent altarpiece.

The Domkirke is the final abode of 38 Danish monarchs whose tombs are here, ranging from the modest to the eccentric. Not surprisingly, the tomb of Christian IV, the builder king who was instrumental in the construction of nearly all of Copenhagen's famous towers and castles, is interred in a grandiose chapel here with a massive painting of himself in combat, a bronze likeness by the Danish sculptor, Bertel Thorvaldsen. In humble contrast is a newer addition, from 1972, of the simple brick chapel of King Frederik IX, which stands outside the church. This chapel is octagonal in shape and decorated with hand-painted tiles designed by the architects Johannes and Inger Exner and Vilhelm Wohlert. Other notable tombs include the white marble sarcophagus of Queen Margrethe I.

In King Christian I's Chapel, which dates from the 15th century, there is a column marked with the heights of several kings. The tallest monarch was Christian I, at 2.1m (6 ft., 9 in.). This, no doubt, was an exaggeration, as his skeleton measures only 1.9m (6 ft., 2 in.). A large, bright cupola graces the late-18th- and early-19th-century chapel of King Frederik V. Note also the Gothic choir stalls, each richly and intricately carved with details from both the Old and New Testaments.

The gilded winged altar in the choir was made in Antwerp in the 1500s and was originally intended for Frederiksborg Castle. Pictures on the wings of the altar depict scenes from the life of Jesus, ranging from the Nativity to the Crucifixion.

For us, the most charming aspect of the cathedral is its early-16th-century clock, poised on the interior south wall above the entrance. A tiny St. George on horseback marks the hour by charging a dragon.

Note: Free concerts on the cathedral's pipe organ, which dates from the 1500s, are often presented at 8pm on Thursdays in summer. They are featured less frequently throughout the rest of the year. Check with the tourist office.

Domkirkestræde 10. © **46-35-16-24.** www.roskildedomkirke.dk. Admission 25DKK ($4.25/£2.25) adults, 15DKK ($2.55/£1.35) children. Apr–Sept Mon–Fri 9am–4:45pm, Sat 9am–noon, Sun 12:30–4:45pm; Oct–Mar Tues–Sat 10am–3:45pm, Sun 12:30–3:45pm. Bus: 602, 603, or 604.

Viking Ship Museum (Vikingeskibshallen) 🕊🕊 If the cathedral weren't reason enough to visit Roskilde, the Viking ships displayed here certainly are. These ships sailed to England, to Hamburg on the German coast, and—dare we speculate?—even to the east coast of North America. Displayed here are five vessels found in Roskilde Fjord and painstakingly pieced together from countless fragments of wreckage. It's presumed that the crafts were deliberately sunk about 20km (12 miles) north of Roskilde at the narrowest section of the fjord to protect the settlement from a sea attack. The discovery was relatively unprotected and unpublicized until 1957, when the Danish National Museum carried out a series of underwater excavations.

A merchant cargo ship used by the Vikings, a small ferry or fishing boat, and a Danish Viking warship similar to the ones portrayed in the Bayeux Tapestry are also displayed, and a "longship," a Viking man-of-war that terrorized European coasts, was also discovered. Copies of Viking jewelry may be purchased in the museum gift shop, and there's also a cafeteria.

To understand the attraction better, the museum shows a short film, *The Ships of the Vikings,* about the excavation and preservation of the ships and the building and navigation of *Roar Ege,* a Viking ship replica.

In 1997, the Viking Ship Museum opened a museum harbor for its collection of Nordic vessels, including *Roar Ege,* plus another Viking ship replica, *Helge Ask.* The museum's restored sloop, *Ruth,* is also moored here. And workshops where you can try your hand at old maritime crafts, such as rope- and sail-making, woodwork, and other activities, are located opposite the Boat Yard.

Vindeboder 12. © **40-30-02-00.** www.vikingeskibsmuseet.dk. Admission May–Sept 80DKK ($14/£7.20) adults, 200DKK ($34/£18) family ticket; Oct–Apr 50DKK ($8.50/£4.50) adults, 130DKK ($22/£12) family ticket; free for children under 17. Daily 10am–5pm. Bus: 216 or 607.

Roskilde Museum Located 90m (295 ft.) from the Town Square, this museum, in a former merchant's house, features exhibits of the celebrated Hedebo embroidery and regional costumes. Displays also include an *aurochs* (an ancient European ox) skeleton, a unique Viking tomb, and a large number of medieval finds from the town. Take the strange-looking pictures that satirist Gustav Wied took of his family, for example, or what passed for children's toys in the Middle Ages. The museum also has a grocer's courtyard, with the shop in operation.

Skt. Ols Gade 15–18. © **46-31-65-00.** www.roskildemuseum.dk. Admission 30DKK ($5.10/£2.70) adults, free for children under 12. Daily 11am–4pm. Closed Dec 24–25 and Dec 31–Jan 1. Bus: 601, 602, 603, or 605.

Museet for Samtidskunst (Museum of Contemporary Art) This is the artistic center of Roskilde. Invariably, there's always a presentation of interest to "culture vultures." In a beautiful palace from the 18th century, this museum of modern art has frequently changing exhibitions, together with performances, film shows, and dance and classical-music concerts. It also houses a screening room presenting programs with Danish and foreign artists. "The Palace Collections" are also housed here, displaying objets d'art and paintings that rich Roskilde merchants and their families collected in the 18th and 19th centuries.

Stændertorvet 3D. © **46-31-65-70.** Admission 30DKK ($5.10/£2.70) adults, 15DKK ($2.55/£1.35) seniors, free for children. Tues–Fri 11am–5pm; Sat–Sun noon–4pm. Bus: 601, 602, 603, or 605.

MORE ATTRACTIONS

The **St. Jørgensbjerg quarter** was originally a small fishing village, and a number of old, half-timbered houses, some with thatch roofs, remain. These houses cluster around **Skt. Jørgensbjerg Kirke,** Kirkegade, which stands on the top of a hill with a panoramic view of Roskilde Fjord. This is one of the oldest and best-preserved stone buildings in Denmark. The nave and choir of the church date from the beginning of the 12th century, but the walled-up north door is even older, possibly dating from 1040. Slender billets, found only in wooden churches, are in the corners of the church and in the center of the nave. A model of a *kogge,* a medieval merchant vessel, has been engraved in a wall. The church is open only June 22 to August 31, Monday to Friday 10am to noon. To get here from Roskilde, take bus no. 607 toward Boserup.

The same bus will deliver you to **Skt. Ibs Kirke** ("The Church of St. James"), Skt. Ibs Vej (© **46-35-29-66**), also in the north of Roskilde. Although no longer in use as a church, this ruin dates from around 1100. Abolished as a church in 1808, it was later a field hospital and a merchant's warehouse. Regrettably, the merchant destroyed the tower, the chancel, the porch, and the church vaults of this medieval relic, but spared the nave. It is open for visits April 4 to October 17, from sunup to sundown.

NEARBY ATTRACTIONS

Ledreborg Park Og Slot ❆   One of the last remaining aristocratic families of Denmark, the Holstein-Ledreborgs, still live in this castle and are willing to share their treasures with you in fair weather. A baroque manor house and French/English-style park 7km (4⅓ miles) southwest of Roskilde and 43km (27 miles) west of Copenhagen, Ledreborg is one of the best-preserved monuments in Denmark. Built by Johan Ludwig Holstein, a minister to Christian IV, this 33-room house has a landscaped garden and 88-hectare (217-acre) park. The Holstein-Ledreborg family has owned it for eight generations. Between 1741 and 1757, it was turned from a farmhouse into a baroque manor. Inside are a collection of 17th- and 18th-century antiques and a gallery of Danish paintings. It's approached by a 6km (3¾-mile) alley of lime trees, some 2 centuries old. Near the manor is a grave dating from the late Stone Age, approximately 3000 B.C.

Allé 2, Lejre. © **46-48-00-38.** Admission 75DKK ($13/£6.75) adults, 45DKK ($7.65/£4.05) children 3–14. Mid-June to Aug daily 11am–5pm; May to mid-June and Sept Sun 11am–5pm. Closed Oct–Apr. From Copenhagen's Central Railroad Station, take the direct train to Lejre, which leaves hourly and takes 35 min.; from Lejre station, take the 3-min. bus 233 to the castle and park. From Roskilde, there are frequent buses to Lejre, followed by the short bus ride to the castle and park. Combined ticket for Ledreborg Park Og Slot and Lejre Research Center (see below) 130DKK ($22/£12) adults, 70DKK ($12/£6.30) children.

Lejre Research Center ❆ *Kids*   Imagine being able to wander back into a village reconstructed from the Iron Age and seeing workers, wearing the *couture* of the era, going about their daily chores, with which you can help. Such a thing is possible if you head here and have some 2 hours to spare. Eight kilometers (5 miles) west of Roskilde, this archaeological research center, Lejre Research Center, is the site of a reconstructed Iron Age community on 10 hectares (25 acres) of woodland. The main feature is clay-walled and thatch houses built with tools just as they were some 2,000 years ago. Staffers re-create the physical working conditions as they thatch Iron Age huts, work fields with *ards* (oxen-pulled plows), weave, and make pottery by an open fire. They also sail in dugout canoes, grind corn with a stone, and bake in direct fire. Visitors can take part in these activities. Jutland black pottery is produced here, and handicrafts and books are for sale at the gift shop. There are tables where you can enjoy a picnic lunch.

Slagealléen 2, Lejre. © **46-48-08-78**. Admission 95DKK ($16/£8.55) adults, 55DKK ($9.35/£4.95) children. Tues–Fri 10am–4pm; Sat–Sun 11am–5pm. Closed mid-Sept to Apr. Take the train from Copenhagen to Lejre; then bus 233 to the center. From Roskilde, there are frequent buses to Lejre; then take bus 233.

WHERE TO STAY

Hotel Prindsen ⓡ   The Prindsen has been an enduring favorite for 100 years, and we have found that it has kept up with the times, even though its foundations date from 1695. Today it offers medium-size, smartly furnished rooms with bathrooms containing tub/shower combinations. Though a bit small, all in all the rooms are cozy nests. We prefer the five rooms on the top floor, which have a view of the fjord. All the guest rooms in the newer wing are decorated in a Nordic style with wooden floors. Those in the older section are furnished in a more classic style. Take your choice, as rooms in both sections are equally comfortable. Our favorite pocket of posh here is the extremely spacious and elegant Hans Christian Andersen suite.

Algade 13, DK-4000, Roskilde. © **46-30-91-00**. Fax 46-30-91-50. www.hotelprindsen.dk. 77 units. 1,325DKK–1,525DKK ($225–$259/£119–£137) double; from 2,150DKK ($366/£194) suite. Rates include breakfast. AE, DC, MC, V. Bus: 602 or 603. **Amenities:** Restaurant; bar; sauna; 24-hr. room service; laundry service; dry cleaning; nonsmoking rooms. *In room:* TV, dataport, minibar, hair dryer, trouser press.

WHERE TO DINE

La Brasserie ⓡ STEAK/DANISH/INTERNATIONAL   We've always found this first-rate restaurant, in the previously recommended hotel, to be one of the best places in town for dining. The food is well prepared with market-fresh ingredients. The staff is perhaps the friendliest and most helpful in town, and the decor is in the stylish bistro decor often found in modern Paris. Everything is prepared from scratch, and hand-picked Danish raw materials are used whenever possible. The chefs get their butter from a special dairy; their herring is cured for 8 months in Iceland, and their virgin olive oil comes from a small privately owned farm near Madrid.

We love the simple grilled entrecôte with baked herb butter, baked potato, and grilled tomatoes, and for a hefty, succulent meal, opt for the sirloin steak cut from Angus beef. In fair weather, you can dine outside.

Algade 13. © **46-30-91-00**. Reservations recommended. Main courses 138DKK–248DKK ($23–$42/£12–£22). AE, DC, MC, V. Daily noon–10pm.

Raadhuskælderen ⓡ DANISH   Savvy foodies will often direct you to one of the oldest restaurant venues in Roskilde, a dining room at the street level of a building erected in 1430 across the street from the town's cathedral. Although it's tempting to remain within the vaulted interior, there's also an outdoor terrace that is pleasant during midsummer, especially because of its view of the cathedral. Menu items are carefully prepared using very fresh ingredients. Some of the chef's best dishes include salmon steak with tartar sauce and rack of lamb delectably roasted and served with a sauce made from fresh summer berries.

Stændertorvet, Fondens Bro 1. © **46-36-01-00**. Reservations recommended. Main courses 148DKK–218DKK ($25–$37/£13–£20); lunch menu 128DKK–168DKK ($22–$29/£12–£15). DC, MC, V. Mon–Sat 11am–11pm.

Restaurant Toppen DANISH   Both a good view and good food can be had at Toppen. At the top of a 1961 water tower, 84m (276 ft.) above sea level, Restaurant

Toppen offers a panoramic view of the whole town, the surrounding country, and Roskilde Fjord—all from the dining room. Begin with a shrimp cocktail served with dill and lemon. Main dishes include sirloin of pork a la Toppen with mushrooms and a béarnaise sauce. For dessert, try the chef's nut cake with fruit sauce and sour cream. The cookery has much improved, and there is a finesse and consistency that wasn't here before. The restaurant is less than 1.5km (1 mile) east of the town center between Vindingevej and Københavnsvej. The water tower doesn't revolve electronically, but some clients, in the words of the management, "get the feeling that it's turning if they drink enough." There's a free elevator to the top.

Bymarken 37. © 46-36-04-12. Reservations recommended. Main courses 69DKK–125DKK ($12–$21/£6.20–£11). DC, MC, V. Mon–Fri 3:30–10pm; Sat–Sun noon–10pm. Bus: 601.

Exploring the Danish Countryside

Denmark, a relatively flat country with good roads, is easy to explore on your own in several driving tours. To reach Bornholm from Copenhagen and Zealand, you'll need to rely on ferry connections. A new bridge links Funen and Zealand. Another bridge connects Funen and Jutland, which is linked to the mainland of Europe.

If you have time for only one destination outside Copenhagen, make it **Funen**. It's the most visited island, mainly because of its capital, **Odense,** the birthplace of Hans Christian Andersen and home to some of northern Europe's best-preserved castles.

Denmark's western peninsula, **Jutland** (also called Jylland), is the only part of the country that's connected to the European mainland; its southern border touches Germany.

Bornholm, "the pearl of the Baltic," can be reached only by plane or boat. Inhabited since the Iron Age, the island is quite different from the rest of Denmark. A visit is a good choice if you're looking for something offbeat.

1 Funen

After visiting Copenhagen and "Hamlet's Castle" in North Zealand, nearly all visitors head for **Odense,** the capital of the island of Funen (*Fyn* in Danish), lying to the west of Zealand. While Hans Christian Andersen was born in Odense, and houses and memorabilia associated with him are the big attractions, there is so much more here, including the most fantastic island in Scandinavia, little old "time-warp" Ærø of the southern coast. Hop gardens, Viking runic stones, orchards of fruit trees, busy harbors, market towns, swan ponds, thatch-roof houses, once-fortified castles, and stately manor homes invite exploration by car.

Funen has some 1,125km (700 miles) of coastline, with wide sandy beaches in some parts, and woods and grass that grow all the way to the water's edge in others. Steep cliffs provide sweeping views of the Baltic or the Kattegat.

Although ferryboats have plied the waters between the islands and peninsulas of Denmark since ancient times, recent decades have seen the development of a network of bridges. In 1934 the first plans were developed for a bridge over the span of water known as the **Storebælt** (Great Belt), the 19km (12-mile) silt-bottomed channel that separates Zealand (and Copenhagen) from Funen and the rest of continental Europe. After many delays caused by war, technical difficulties, and lack of funding, and after the submission of 144 designs by engineers from around the world, construction began in 1988 on an intricately calibrated network of bridges and tunnels.

On June 14, 1998, her majesty, Queen Margrethe II, cut the ribbon shortly before driving across the Great Belt Bridge. The project incorporated both railway and road traffic divided between a long underwater tunnel and both low and high bridges. (The rail link has operated since 1997.) Only some aspects of the Chunnel between England and France are on par with the staggering scale of this project.

Visitors can view exhibitions about the bridge at the **Great Belt Exhibition Center** (© **58-35-01-00**), located at the entrance to the bridge. It's open July to August, Wednesday to Monday 11am to 4pm, and admission is free.

NYBORG: GATEWAY TO FUNEN
130km (81 miles) W of Copenhagen, 34km (21 miles) E of Odense

One of the oldest towns in Denmark, founded 7 centuries ago, Nyborg lies at the western terminus of the Storebælt Bridge and is the easternmost town on the island of Funen. Local residents thought the opening of the bridge would boost tourism, but that has happened only marginally. Most motorists, especially tourists, rush through town en route to Odense to pay their respects to the memory of Hans Christian Andersen.

That's a shame, really, because Nyborg deserves at least 2 hours of your time, which will allow you to visit its old Torvet, the market square in the center, the ruins of a medieval castle, and some old cross-timbered houses. Like so many other cities or towns of Denmark, Nyborg was more strategic in the Middle Ages than it is today.

Its location in the middle of the trade route between Zealand in the east and Jutland in the west helped boost its importance. In medieval times, about 1200 to 1413, Nyborg was the capital of Denmark. Medieval buildings and well-preserved ramparts are testaments to that era. Nyborg's town square, the **Torvet,** was created in 1540, when a block of houses was demolished to make room for the royal tournaments of Christian III.

In summer, Denmark's oldest open-air theater, **Nyborg Voldspil,** is the setting for an annual musical or operetta under the leafy beeches on the old castle ramparts. Throughout the summer, classical music concerts (featuring international soloists) are performed in the castle's Great Hall. Inquire at the tourist office (see "Essentials," below) for further details.

Dating from the mid-1600s, the Tattoo is an ancient military ceremony with musical accompaniment. This old custom has been revived to honor the corps who played an important role in the Schleswig wars in 1848 and again in 1864. In tribute to the old corps, the present-day Tattoo participants wear a green uniform with its characteristic cap, or *chakot.* The corps marches through the center of town at 9pm each year on June 30, thereafter every Tuesday in July and August.

ESSENTIALS
GETTING THERE   By Train or Bus   You can reach Nyborg by train or bus (via ferry). Trains leave Copenhagen every hour, and there's frequent bus service from Copenhagen as well. From Odense, east-bound trains arrive 2 times an hour.

VISITOR INFORMATION   The **Nyborg Turistbureau,** Torvet 9 (© **65-31-02-80;** www.nyborgturist.dk), is open June 15 to August, Monday to Friday 9am to 5pm and Saturday 9:30am to 2pm; September to June 14, Monday to Friday 9am to 4pm and Saturday 9:30am to noon.

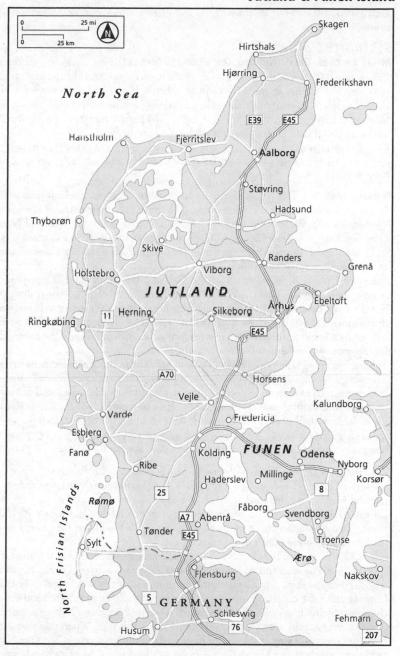

GETTING AROUND   Bus nos. 1, 3, and 4 serve all in-town destinations listed below.

SEEING THE SIGHTS

Mads Lerches Gård (Nyborg Og Omegns Museet) ✦   Of all the places in

Funen, this 1601 house, the former home of the town mayor, provides the best insight into what life was like in the 17th century—that is, if you had some money in the bank. The house, painted a reddish pink, is filled with exhibitions on local history, but far more intriguing than that are the antique-filled period chambers spread over 30 rooms on two floors. There's even a small brewery on site.

Slotsgade 11. ℂ **65-31-02-07**. www.museer-nyborg.dk. Admission 30DKK ($5.10/£2.70) adults, 15DKK ($2.55/£1.35) children 6–14, free for children under 6. July–Aug daily 10am–4pm; Apr–May and Sept–Oct daily 10am–3pm. Closed Nov–June. Bus: 1, 3, or 4.

Nyborg Slot ✦   This hardly compares to Windsor Castle in England, but to the

Danes it's just as important. Dating from 1170, this is one of the oldest of Denmark's royal castles. Originally it was built to defend the country from the Wends of North Germany. King Erik Glipping signed Denmark's first constitution in this moated castle in 1282, and Nyborg became the seat of the Danish Parliament, the Danehof, until 1413 when Copenhagen took over.

In a regrettable decision, much of the Slot was demolished in 1722 to provide building materials for Odense Castle. Nevertheless, parts of the original ramparts remain. From these bastions, Danes rained down hot tar on their invaders. If you walk these ramparts today, you'll have a **panoramic view** ✦ of Nyborg and the sea. The terrace in front is still lined with bronze guns facing the town center, and the town gate, **Landporten** ✦, can be seen just north of the castle.

Most intriguing is the still remaining **Danehof** ✦, the hall where Parliament met. The walls are painted with geometric murals, and there is an extensive collection of armaments such as guns and swords, suits of armor (rather impressive), and old royal paintings (not too impressive). Other rooms open to view include the King's Room, the Knights' Hall, and even the apartment once occupied by the royal kids.

Slotspladen. ℂ **65-31-02-07**. www.museer-nyborg.dk. Admission 30DKK ($5.10/£2.70) adults, 15DKK ($2.55/£1.35) children. July–Aug daily 10am–4pm; Sept–Oct daily 10am–3pm. Closed Nov–June. Bus: 1, 2, or 3.

Vor Frue Kirke   The Church of Our Lady, as it's called in English, is still a place of

worship even though it dates from the Middle Ages. Unfortunately restorers and decorators descended on the church in 1870 and completely changed it, so we're not allowed to see the purity of its original simple architectural details. Even so, it's still a worthy place to wander about for 30 to 45 minutes. We found that the greatest treasure here is a **baroque pulpit** ✦ in stunning detail.

The Gothic spire of the church is a landmark for miles around, and the interior is split into a trio of aisles and endowed with woodcarvings, carved old epitaphs, candelabra, and model ships. The elegant wrought-iron gate you see was forged in 1649 by Casper Fincke, the court-appointed craftsman to King Christian IV. The most evocative aspect of the church, which we discovered while strolling about Nyborg one night, is that at 9:45pm the Watchman's Bell from 1523 is still rung, a tradition that dates back for centuries. Lying at the end of Kongegade in the town center, Vor Frue Kirke can be entered through its south door. Nearby at Adelgade and Korsbrodregade stands a large stone-built house, **Korsbrodregården,** dating from 1396. This was the Chapter House of the Order of St. John, its vaulted cellar converted today into a gift shop. Adelgade. ✆ 65-31-16-08. Free admission. Daily 9am–6pm.

WHERE TO STAY
Hotel Hesselet ✿✿✿   Such an elegant hotel of high international standard comes as a surprise in this sleepy, provincial town. One of the most stylish hotels in Funen, outclassing most of those in Odense itself, is idyllically set among beech trees, opening onto a view of the Great Belt with its Storebæltsbro suspension bridge. Request a room with a view of this sea spectacle, or else you'll be assigned an accommodation opening onto a forest.

Inside, the hotel creates a glamorous aura in its public lounges with Asian artifacts and plush Oriental carpets, a large fireplace, sunken living rooms, and a cozy library lined with leather-bound volumes. Bedrooms are sumptuously furnished and spacious, each with tasteful appointments and the best bathrooms of any hotel along the east coast of Funen, with granite floors, double wash basins, bathtubs, and separate shower cabins, plus plenty of toiletries.

Even if you're not a guest, consider a meal here preceded by an aperitif on the patio or by the open fireplace in cold weather. A first-rate chef, Tina Møhring Madsen, composes her dishes incorporating fresh seasonal produce.

Christianslundsvej 119, DK-5800 Nyborg. ✆ **65-31-30-29.** Fax 65-31-29-58. www.hesselet.dk. 47 units. Mon–Thurs 1,580DKK–1,780DKK ($269–$303/£142–£160) double; Fri–Sun 1,280DKK–1,680DKK ($218–$286/£115–£151) double; 2,400DKK–2,800DKK ($408–$476/£216–£252) suite. Rates include breakfast. AE, DC, MC, V. Free parking. **Amenities:** Restaurant; bar; indoor heated pool; 2 tennis courts; sauna; room service (7am–10pm); babysitting; laundry service/dry cleaning; rooms for those w/limited mobility; nonsmoking rooms; solarium. *In room:* TV, dataport, minibar, hair dryer, safe.

WHERE TO DINE
Central Cafeen ✿ DANISH/FRENCH   When we first discovered this restaurant many years ago, we were put off by its name of "Central Café." Only after dining here did we discover that this is one of the finest restaurants along the east coast of Funen, set directly across the street from City Hall in a 1787 house that has contained some kind of restaurant here since 1854. With a sense of local history and a deep-seated pride, it offers four separate, cozy dining rooms, each outfitted with sepia-toned photographs of four generations of Danish monarchs, plus a quirky collection of ladies' hats tucked museum-style in glass cases.

The composition of the set-price menus changes every month to take advantage of seasonal produce. First-rate ingredients are used, often shrimp and lobster. Begin with a bowl of the creamy lobster bisque, going on to the fried plaice with a lobster-and-shrimp sauce. Roasted salmon appears with fresh spinach, and meat-eaters gravitate to the fried pork cutlets in a parsley sauce. The sumptuous desserts are made daily, and there is an impressive but pricey wine list to back up the cuisine.

Nørregade 6. ✆ **65-31-01083.** Reservations recommended. Main courses 128DKK–198DKK ($22–$34/£12–£18). Set-price menus 208DKK ($35/£19) and 238DKK ($40/£21) 3-courses. AE, DC, MC, V. Mon–Sat 11am–9:30pm. Bus: 1, 3, or 4.

Restaurant Østervemb ✿ DANISH/FRENCH   The down-home Danish cooking here is as heart-warming as that provided by a nourishing Danish aunt, although the chefs get a bit fancy at times and "Frenchify" some of their more elegant offerings.

In the east of Nyborg, Østervemb has been feeding locals since 1924. The market-fresh fish is one of the culinary attractions here, as we realized when we dived into a platter piled high with three different preparations of herring. The main courses are carefully wrought and the ingredients married well, as evoked by the breast of Danish hen served with fresh spinach and mushrooms. The curried chicken salad was given extra flavor by crispy bacon bits, and a grilled beef tenderloin, tender and moist, came with a tarragon-flavored glaze and a fricassee of oyster mushrooms. As elsewhere in Denmark, desserts are predictably good.

Mellemgade. ℭ **65-30-10-70.** Reservations recommended. Lunch platters 190DKK ($32/£17); dinner main courses 187DKK–235DKK ($32–$40/£17–£21); fixed-price 2-course menu 280DKK ($48/£25), 3 course 328DKK ($56/£30). DC, MC, V. Tues–Sat noon–2:30pm and 5:30–10:30pm.

ODENSE: BIRTHPLACE OF HANS CHRISTIAN ANDERSEN ★★

156km (97 miles) W of Copenhagen, 34km (21 miles) W of Nyborg, 43km (27 miles) NW of Svendborg

Many people make their living off Hans Christian Andersen and all the visitors his memory brings to Odense. But the town never seemed to appreciate the boy until the world discovered his writing. In some respects, he was treated like Salzburg treated Mozart. Actually, the storyteller had a very unhappy childhood in Odense and left as soon as he was old enough to make his way to Copenhagen.

His cobbler father was always out of money and had been forced to marry Hans's ill-tempered, peasant mother when she was 7 months pregnant. The Andersen grandmother was insane and, as noted by Andersen himself, a "pathological liar."

But those unpleasant memories are long gone today, and Odense is proud of its world-famous son, hawking souvenirs and dusting off the writer's memorabilia to each new generation. This ancient town, the third largest in Denmark, has changed greatly since Andersen walked its streets, but its historic core still evokes the fairy-tale town that Andersen knew so well.

Odense is in the heart of Funen and home to more than 185,000 inhabitants. It's one of the oldest cities in the country, with a history stretching back some 1,000 years. The city's name stems from two words—*Odins Vi* (Odin's shrine), suggesting that the god Odin must have been worshipped here in pre-Christian times. Long before Odense became a pilgrimage center for fans of Andersen, it was an ecclesiastical center and site of religious pilgrimage in the Middle Ages.

Odense today is not just a fairy-tale town, but an industrial might in Denmark, its harbor linked by a canal to the Odense Fjord and thus the Great Belt. It's a center of electro-technical, textile, steel, iron, and timber production.

In summer Odense takes on a festive air, with lots of outdoor activities, including music and theater taking place on its squares and in its piazzas. Cafes and pubs are lively day and night.

ESSENTIALS

GETTING THERE   By Train or Bus   You can easily reach Odense by train or bus from Copenhagen, as about 12 trains or buses a day leave Copenhagen's Central Railroad Station for Odense (trip time: 3 hr.).

By Car   From Nyborg, head west on E-20 to Allerup, and then follow Route 9 north to Odense.

VISITOR INFORMATION   Odense Tourist Bureau is at Rådhuset, Vestergade 2A (ℭ **66-12-75-20;** www.visitodense.com). It's open mid-June to August, Monday to Friday 9am to 6pm, Saturday and Sunday 10am to 3pm; September to mid-June, Monday to Friday 9:30am to 4:30pm, Saturday 10am to 1pm.

Besides helping you arrange excursions, the tourist bureau sells the **Odense Adventure Pass,** giving you access to 16 of the city's museums, the Odense Zoo, six indoor swimming pools, and unlimited free travel on the city buses and DSB trains within the municipality. It also entitles you to discounts on river cruises and admission to the summer-only presentation of the city's Hans Christian Andersen plays (see "Seeing the Sights," below). Passes are valid for 1 or 2 days. A 1-day pass is 125DKK ($21/£11) for adults, 65DKK ($11/£5.85) for children under 14; 2-day passes cost 160DKK for adults ($27/£14) and 85DKK ($14/£7.65) for kids.

GETTING AROUND   By Bus   Bus no. 2 serves all in-town destinations listed below.

SEEING THE SIGHTS

The Odense Tourist Bureau (see above) offers a 2-hour **walking tour** conducted in July and August, every Tuesday, Wednesday, and Thursday at 11am, from a meeting place behind its office. Covering the town's major sites, it costs 50DKK ($8.50/£4.50) adults and 25DKK ($4.25/£2.25) children, and reservations are recommended.

Also at the tourist office, you can get information about the **Hans Christian Andersen plays,** which are presented every year mid-July to mid-August. The plays are given on an outdoor stage in the Funen Village, where members of the audience sit on blankets on the grass (if it's dry) or stand. Even if you don't understand Danish, there's lots of entertainment value in the visuals. Plays begin every day at 4pm, last around 90 minutes, cost 70DKK ($12/£6.30) adults and 45DKK ($7.65/£4.05) children, and are usually mobbed with H. C. Andersen fans.

Less than a kilometer (½ mile) west of the city center is **Superbowl,** Grøneløkkenvej (© **70-11-11-55;** bus: 91 or 92), a complex of amusements and diversions that are entirely devoted to popular American culture. It incorporates facilities for indoor go-cart racing, an indoor version of American-style miniature golf, several bowling alleys, and a small-scale collection of rides and games inspired by the theme parks of Florida. Each individual attraction within the park maintains its own hours and entrance policies, but the best way to appreciate this site's activities is to head here anytime daily between 10am and 6pm, when for an all-inclusive fee of 80DKK ($14/£7.20), you'll have unlimited access to all of them.

Carl Nielsen Museet   At the Odense Concert Hall, you can learn about the life and music of Denmark's greatest composer, Carl August Nielsen (1865–1931).

This towering musician developed a unique polytonal and contrapuntal musical form, his operas including *Saul and David* in 1903 and *Maskerade* in 1906. He also composed symphonies, concertos, and choral and chamber music. Nielsen singlehandedly "woke up" Danish music after its sleepy decline of decades. In the museum you can listen to some of his greatest works, even a polka he penned as a child before joining the Odense Military Band as a trumpet player at the tender age of 14.

A biographical slide show brings to life the cultural icon, whose six symphonies, several operas, hymns, and popular songs (many of which are patriotic) are still played around the world today.

Nielsen married a famous sculptor, Anne Marie Carl-Nielsen, strangely keeping her husband's first name in her full name. Although hardly as well known as her husband, she created works still on view in Denmark, including her equestrian statue of Christian IX that stands outside the Royal Stables in Copenhagen.

Claus Bergsgade 11. ② 65-51-46-01. www.odmus.dk. Admission 25DKK ($4.25/£2.25) adults; free children 16 and under. Tues and Fri 4–8pm; Sun noon–4pm.

Danmarks Jernbanemuseum (Railway Museum) ⓐ ⓚ*ids*   This is one of the best transportation museums in Scandinavia, appropriately located adjacent to the Odense train station. It's a very active museum and not some dull depot of long-abandoned locomotives, although there are those here too, the best of which is a **royal carriage** ⓐ that once carried his majesty, King Christian IX.

The history of locomotives and carriages, from the first train in Denmark, dating from 1847, until more modern times, is on display, including a "B-Machine," a moving vehicle from 1869. A replica of a 19th-century train depot is on view along with two dozen engines and various saloon cars. Model ferries, buses, model railway tracks, and even Wagons-Lits restaurant cars and ferries are on view. The entire family can go on the mini-trains and take a simulated ride in a large diesel locomotive.

Dannebrogsgade 24. ② 66-13-66-30. www.jernbanemuseum.dk. Admission 48DKK ($8.15/£4.30) adults, 20DKK ($3.40/£1.80) children. Daily 10am–4pm.

Funen Village/Den Fynske Landsby ⓐⓐ ⓚ*ids*   If Hans Christian Andersen were to come back to life, he'd feel that the world had never changed if he were to land in this village. This is the Danish version of Scotland's mystical "Brigadoon," where some 30 buildings, dating from the 17th to the 19th centuries, keep alive the village milieu of yesterday, with half-timbered houses, flower gardens, a grazing cow (or goat), and a communal pond.

In a scenic setting in the Hunderup Woods, these old buildings include a tollhouse, weaver's shop, windmill, farming homestead, vicarage, village school, brickworks, and the inevitable jail. Each was reassembled on this site and authentically furnished. You can visit workshops to see craftspeople, including a basket maker, spoon cutter, weaver, and the village blacksmith.

As an added treat, plays and folk dances are staged at the on-site Greek-style theater. The best way to get here is to take a boat from Munke Mose in Odense down the river to Erik Boghs Sti. After disembarking, it's a 15-minute scenic walk to the museum. A one-way fare is 40DKK ($6.80/£3.60) for adults or 30DKK ($5.10/£2.70) for children 15 and under.

Sejerskovvej 20. ② 65-51-46-01. Admission 55DKK ($9.35/£4.95) adults, 15DKK ($2.55/£1.35) children 15 and under. Mid-June to mid-Aug daily 9:30am–7pm; Apr to mid-June and mid-Aug to mid-Oct Tues–Sun 10am–5pm; mid-Oct to Mar Sun 11am–3pm. Bus: 21 or 22 from Flakhaven.

H. C. Andersens Barndomshjem (H. C. Andersen's Childhood Home) ⓚ*ids* Visit Andersen's humble childhood abode, where the fairy-tale writer lived from 1807 to 1819. From what is known of Andersen's childhood, his mother was a drunken, superstitious washerwoman, and Andersen was a gawky boy, lumbering and graceless, the victim of his fellow urchins' cruel jabs. However, all is serene at the cottage today; in fact, the little house with its tiny rooms has a certain unpretentious charm, and the "garden still blooms," as in *The Snow Queen*. The museum is only mildly diverting, worth no more than 15 or 20 minutes of your time.

Munkemøllestraede 3. ② 65-51-46-01. www.odmus.dk. Admission 25DKK ($4.25/£2.25) adults, free children 18 and under. June–Aug daily 10am–4pm; Sept–May daily 11am–3pm.

H. C. Andersens Hus ⟨★★⟩ *Kids*   Though not the rival of the Shakespeare properties in Stratford-upon-Avon, the object of most Funen pilgrimages is to the house of the greater spinner of fairy tales himself, Hans Christian Andersen. When it opened in 1908, it became one of the first writer museums in the world focusing on the life and work of a single author. In various memorabilia, such as hundreds of documents, manuscripts, and reprints of his books in 100 languages (including Zulu), you learn of the writer's life from his birth as the son of a poor cobbler in Odense, to his hard times in Copenhagen, until his eventual debut upon the world stage.

We even learn about some aspects of his love life, as when he fell for Jenny Lind, "the Swedish Nightingale," who did not return his affection. Letters to such fellow famous writers as Charles Dickens are also on exhibit. The storyteller lives again as you get to see some of his "props," such as his famous walking stick, Fred Astaire–like top hat, and battered portmanteau.

Bangs Boder 29. ⟨✆⟩ **65-51-46-01.** Admission 55DKK ($9.35/£4.95) adults, free for under 17. June 16–Aug daily 9am–7pm; Sept–June 15 Tues–Sun 10am–4pm.

NEARBY ATTRACTIONS

Egeskov Castle ⟨★★★⟩   This moated Renaissance castle is the best preserved of its type in Europe. Plan to spend at least a morning or an afternoon here. Constructed in 1554, it is still privately owned and inhabited by the descendants of Henrik Bille, who purchased the castle in 1784. The location of Denmark's most splendid fortified manor is outside of the town of Kvaerndrup, lying 18 miles (29km) south of Odense.

The castle was built on oak pillars in the middle of a moat or small lake, for which thousands of oak trees in the neighboring forests were cut down.

The most dramatic story in the castle's history is about an unfortunate maiden, Rigborg, who was seduced by a young nobleman and bore him a child out of wedlock. Banished to the castle, she was imprisoned by her father in a tower from 1599 to 1604.

Because of the private living quarters, only some of the castle is open to view, including the restored **Great Hall** ⟨★★⟩, which is now a venue for chamber music concerts on 10 summer Sundays beginning in late June and starting at 5pm. The inhabitants of this castle were great hunters, and you can visit a hunting room with some of their most prized trophies, including elephant tusks and the heads of tigers. You can also view precious antiques and classical paintings.

For us the spectacular **gardens** ⟨★★★⟩ in the 12-hectare (30-acre) park are even more beautiful than the interior. Laid out in the 1730s, the gardens are among the most dramatic in Denmark. The **Fuchsia Garden** ⟨★★★⟩ contains the largest collection of fuchsias in Europe with about 75 different species. The English Garden with its tree-studded green lawns sweeps down to the streams and the castle lake. In summer the rose beds are a delight to behold, the prize flower being the pink "Egeskov Rose." The site also includes a kiosk where you can purchase rose jelly; a museum of antique cars, old airplanes, and horse-drawn carriages; and the world's largest maze, which is made of cut beech hedges and is several centuries old.

Egeskovgade 18, Kvaerndrup. ⟨✆⟩ **62-27-10-16.** www.egeskov.dk. Admission including castle, park, and maze 150DKK ($26/£14) adults, 77DKK ($13/£6.95) children 4–12; park, maze, and museum 77DKK ($13/£6.95) adults, 52DKK ($8.85/£4.70) children 4–12. Free for children under 4. July park daily 10am–8pm, castle daily 10am–7pm; June and Aug park daily 10am–6pm, castle daily 10am–5pm; May and Sept park and castle daily 10am–5pm. Closed Oct–Apr. Train: From Odense or Svendborg every hour. Bus: 920 from Nyborg.

Ladbyskibet   Admittedly, the ruins of a 10th-century Viking ship, discovered in 1935, doesn't compare to those discovered in the Oslofjord and displayed on Oslo's Bygdøy peninsula. But if you're not going on to Oslo, this is your best shot at seeing what one of those ships looked like.

This is the only Viking ship discovered to date in Denmark. Archaeologists are puzzled why more Viking ships haven't been unearthed in Denmark because they were used as coffins for burying chieftains. In this one, the corpse of the pagan chieftain buried was never found, just the bones of nearly a dozen horses and dogs. Other utensils, believed to be of use in Valhalla, were also interred with the corpse. Remains of the ship are displayed in a burial mound along with replicas from the excavation (the originals are in the National Museum of Copenhagen).

Vikingevej 123, Ladby. ⓒ 65-32-16-67. www.kert-mus.dk. Admission 40DKK ($6.80/£3.60) adults, free for children under 15. May 15–Sept 14 daily 10am–5pm; Mar–May 14 and Sept 15–Oct daily 10am–4pm; Nov–Feb Wed–Sun 11am–3pm. Bus: 482 from Kerteminde. Lies 19km (12 miles) northeast of Odense.

SHOPPING

Inspiration Zinch ✦, Vestergade 82–84 (ⓒ **66-12-96-93**), offers the widest selection of Danish design and handicrafts on the island of Funen. All the big names are here, everything from Royal Copenhagen to Georg Jensen, but you will also come across younger and more modern designers. In the heart of the old town, opposite Hans Christian Andersen's house, you'll find a display of Danish crafts and Christmas decorations in a typical atmosphere of Old Funen at **Klods Hans,** Hans Jensens Stræde 34 (ⓒ **66-11-09-40**). Another outlet is **Smykker,** 3 Klaregade (ⓒ **66-12-06-96**), which offers museum copies of Bronze Age, Iron Age, and Viking jewelry—all made in gold, sterling silver, and bronze in the outlet's own workshop. **College Art,** Grandts Passage 38 (ⓒ **66-11-35-45**), has assembled a unique collection of posters, lithographs, silk-screens, original art, and cards. The best gallery for contemporary art is **Galleri Torso,** Hasselvej 25 (ⓒ **66-13-44-66**). Finally, if none of the above shops has what you want, head for **Rosengårdcentret** at Munkerisvej and Ørbaekvej. It's Denmark's biggest shopping center, with nearly 110 stores under one roof.

WHERE TO STAY

Clarion Hotel Plaza ✦✦✦   This is Odense's classiest address, with far more personality, atmosphere, and glamour than its closest rival, the also-recommended Radisson SAS (see below). One of Funen's most alluring hostelries, the Plaza lies less than half a kilometer (¼ mile) outside of the town center, and only a 5-minute walk from the train station. A stately place to stay, it fronts the city's finest and leafiest park, Kongens Have.

After checking in and inspecting the formal lounges, an old-fashioned early-20th-century elevator takes you to the midsize-to-spacious bedrooms, many of which evoke life in an English country home, opening onto scenic views. The rooms are handsomely decorated, often with antique reproductions, and they escape the curse of too much Danish modern, each coming with a tiled bathroom with tub/shower combos. The hotel's terrace overlooks the park and a garden. A first-class cuisine of both Danish and international specialties is served in the Plaza's formal restaurant, known for its attentive service and impressive wine *carte*.

Østre Stationsvej 24, DK-5000 Odense. ⓒ **877/424-6423** in the U.S., or 66-11-77-45. Fax 66-14-41-45. www.hotel-plaza.dk. 68 units. July–Aug 925DKK ($157/£83) double, 1,840DKK ($313/£166) suite; Sept–June 1,350DKK ($230/£122) double, 1,845DKK ($314/£166) suite. Rates include breakfast. AE, DC, MC, V. Free parking. Bus: 31, 33, 35, or 36. **Amenities:** Restaurant; bar; 24-hr. room service; laundry service/dry cleaning; nonsmoking rooms. *In room:* TV, dataport, minibar, hair dryer, safe.

Hotel Ansgar *Kids*   When this hotel opened in 1902 it attracted clean-living, non-drinking Christians. Today, those associations are gone, and there's even a bar on site. Just a 5-minute walk from the train depot, behind a brick-and-stone facade, the hotel has been considerably renovated, with the installation of modern furniture and double-glaze windows to cut down on the traffic noise. As befits the style of the hotel's era, the rooms range from small to spacious, each comfortably furnished with Italian pieces and well-kept bathrooms with tub/shower combos. The staff does much in summer to attract the family trade, even giving kids a coupon for free ice cream. A wide range of dishes from both the Danish and international kitchen is served, and one of the best food values in town is the restaurant's two-course fixed-price dinner at 150DKK ($26/£14).

Østre Stationsvej 32, DK-5000 Odense. ⓒ **66-11-96-93.** Fax 66-11-96-75. www.hotel-ansgar.dk. 64 units. June–Aug 750DKK ($128/£68) double; Sept–May 1,050DKK ($179/£95) double. Rates include breakfast. Extra bed 150DKK ($26/£14). AE, DC, MC, V. Free parking. Bus: 31, 33, 35, or 36. **Amenities:** Restaurant; bar; kids playroom; laundry service/dry cleaning; nonsmoking rooms. *In room:* TV, dataport, minibar, hair dryer, Wi-Fi.

Radisson SAS H. C. Andersen Hotel *Kids Kids*   It may lack the nostalgic charm of the Plaza, but commercial travelers find this first-class hotel more convenient and livelier, with a roster of facilities that includes a casino. In summer, fans of Andersen from abroad fill its 1960s Nordic-style bedrooms, since it's near a former Hans Christian Andersen residence in the heart of the city. This red-brick hotel, one of the finest on the island of Funen, welcomes you into a plant-filled lobby and a glass-roofed reception area, where you encounter the most efficient staff in Odense.

The tasteful, conservatively decorated, and comfortably appointed bedrooms come in a variety of sizes—some large, others, especially the singles, a bit cramped, with the most tranquil rooms opening onto the interior. Each of the bathrooms, though small, is well equipped with thoughtful extras such as makeup mirrors along with tub/shower combos.

Overlooking the market square, the hotel's formal restaurant is known for catering to special requests, such as vegetarian or other diets. It serves a refined international and Danish cuisine and does so exceedingly well, using market-fresh ingredients.

Claus Bergs Gade 7, DK-5000 Odense. ⓒ **800/333-3333** in the U.S., or 66-14-78-00. Fax 66-14-78-90. www. radissonsas.com. 145 units. 850DKK–1,665DKK ($145–$283/£77–£150) double. Rates include breakfast. AE, DC, MC, V. Bus: 4 or 5. **Amenities:** Restaurant; bar; fitness center; sauna; room service (7am–10pm); laundry service/dry cleaning; nonsmoking rooms; rooms for those w/limited mobility; solarium; casino. *In room:* TV, dataport, minibar, hair dryer, safe, Wi-Fi.

WHERE TO DINE

Den Gamle Kro *Kids* DANISH/FRENCH   For all we know, Hans Christian Andersen used to drop into this place—after all, it's been serving food and drink to the locals since 1683. Set a 5-minute walk from the city center, it is unusual architecturally in that it was constructed within the courtyards of several antique buildings, but has been modernized with its time-worn stone capped by a sliding glass roof.

A cellar-level bar is lined with antique masonry, and the street-level restaurant rests under centuries-old beams. The food has remained consistently good over the years, and we've dropped in for lunch for some of the best *smørrebrød* selections in town, including shrimp and dill stacked on top of freshly baked bread.

If you return for dinner, you'll find some of the best fixed-price meals in town. There's nothing you're served here that you haven't tasted before, including beef tenderloin flavored with herbs or herb-sprinkled trout sautéed in butter, but the ingredients are market fresh and skillfully prepared by the kitchen staff, which also creates yummy, freshly made desserts.

Overgade 23. ⓒ **66-12-14-33**. Reservations recommended. Main courses 179DKK–278DKK ($30–$47/£16–£25); fixed-price meals 298DKK–358DKK ($51–$61/£27–£32). AE, DC, MC, V. Mon–Sat 11am–10:30pm; Sun 11am–9:30pm. Bus: 2.

Marie Louise ✯✯✯ FRENCH/INTERNATIONAL   You'd have to return to Copenhagen to order French food as fine as what's served in this antique house, which shelters one of the smallest, most exclusive, and best restaurants in Odense.

Its dining room is a white walled re-creation of an old-fashioned country tavern, although closer inspection reveals a decidedly upscale slant to the furnishings, accessories, silver, and crystal. A polished staff serves well-planned dishes based mainly on French recipes, with more and more international recipes appearing on recent menus.

The chef prepares dishes with a certain precision and sensitivity to food, as evoked by such delectable specialties as a salmon-and-dill mousse with shrimp sauce. Most savvy diners order the fresh fish dishes of the day, perhaps turbot in Riesling or a champagne sauce. The chef gets an extra point for that divine lobster he served us in Danish country butter. An array of enticing desserts is laid out like works of art for your selection.

Lottrups Gaard, Vestergade 70–72. ⓒ **66-17-92-95**. Reservations recommended. Main courses 318DKK–387DKK ($54–$66/£29–£35); fixed-price menu 345DKK–565DKK ($59–$96/£31–£51). V. Mon–Sat noon–midnight. Closed July. Bus: 2.

Under Lindetraeet ✯ DANISH/INTERNATIONAL   This inn, located across the street from the H. C. Andersen museum, has been a landmark and a local favorite since the 1960s, and it is the most popular restaurant in town. It's one of the finest restaurants in town, with a menu based on fresh, first-class ingredients. Skillfully prepared dishes include tender Danish lamb, filet of plaice with butter sauce, *escalope* of veal in sherry sauce, fried herring with new potatoes, and an upscale version of *skipperlabskovs*, the famed sailors' hash. The atmosphere is Old World, and in summer, meals and light refreshments are served outside under linden trees.

Ramsherred 2. ⓒ **66-12-92-86**. Reservations required. Main courses 225DKK–495DKK ($38–$84/£20–£45); fixed-price menus 395DKK–595DKK ($67–$101/£36–£54). AE, DC, MC, V. Mon–Fri 11am–11pm; Sat–Sun 6–11pm. Closed July 4–24. Bus: 2.

SVENDBORG

43km (27 miles) S of Odense, 147km (91 miles) W of Copenhagen

Svendborg is the second biggest town in Funen (with 42,000 residents), it's a major commercial and tourist hub for South Funen, and it has none of the fairytale overlay that Odense hypes. It's a sailors' town and has had a long history as a maritime center. Until 1915, it was the home port for a big fleet of sailing ships because of its position on the beautiful Svendborg Sound, which provides convenient access to Baltic ports.

Although shipbuilding is a ghost of itself, there are a couple of shipyards that still construct wood-hulled ships and are around to repair visiting yachts plying the waters off the coast of South Funen.

Frankly, we'd spend only a night here, as the islands of Ærø and Tåsinge (see below) are more alluring. But if you give Svendborg a day, you'll find much to do.

Svendborg is a lively modern town, with museums, constantly changing art exhibits, and sports. It has swimming pools, beaches, and a yachting school. Its best beach, **Christiansminde,** is one of several in Funen flying the blue flag indicating nonpolluted waters.

Svendborg is also a market town, and on Sunday morning, you can visit the cobblestone central plaza where flowers and fish are sold. Wander through the many winding streets where brick and half-timbered buildings still stand. On **Ragergade** you'll see the old homes of early seafarers. **Møllergade,** a pedestrian street, is one of the oldest streets in town, with about 100 different shops.

Literary buffs know that the German writer Bertolt Brecht lived at Skovsbo Strand, west of Svendborg, from 1933 to 1939, but he left at the outbreak of World War II. During this period he wrote *Mother Courage and Her Children,* which is still performed around the world.

ESSENTIALS
GETTING THERE   By Train   You can take a train from Copenhagen to Odense, where you can get a connecting train to Svendborg, with frequent service throughout the day.

By Car   From our last stopover in Odense, head south on Route 9, following the signs into Svendborg.

VISITOR INFORMATION   Contact the **Svendborg Tourist Office,** Centrumpladsen (© **62-21-09-80;** www.visitsydfyn.dk), open June 20 to August 21, Monday to Friday 9:30am to 6pm and Saturday 9:30am to 3pm; January 2 to June 19 and August 22 to December 30, Monday to Friday 9:30am to 5pm, and Saturday 9:30am to 12:30pm (closed Dec 23–Jan 1). Biking routes and maps are available at this office. Bike rentals for hotel guests, at 60DKK ($10/£5.40) per day, can be obtained at the Hotel Svendborg, Centrumpladsen 1 (© **62-21-17-00;** bus: 200 or 204).

GETTING AROUND   By Bus   Bus no. 200 serves all in-town destinations listed below, except for Vester Skerninge Kro, for which you need a car.

SEEING THE SIGHTS
Anne Hvides Gård   This cross-timbered house, in the center of the Torvet, the old market square, looks like it's had too much to drink. Actually it's the oldest secular house in Svendborg, dating from 1558 and operated today as a branch of the County Museum. This is another one of those "let's-raid-the-attic-to-see-what-we-can-see" type of museums. Its most dramatic features are the re-creations of interiors from the 18th and 19th centuries, and there are plenty of silver objects, glassware, copper and brass utensils, and the inevitable faience. Temporary cultural exhibitions are also presented here.

Fruestraede 3. © **62-21-34-57.** www.svendborgmuseum.dk. Admission 25DKK ($4.25/£2.25) adults, 15DKK ($2.55/£1.35) seniors, free for children when accompanied by an adult. Apr–Sept Tues–Sun 10am–5pm; off season by arrangement with the main office.

Skt. Jørgen's Kirke   Only the Church of St. Nicolai (see below) exceeds the beauty of St. George's church, whose origins date from the 12th century, when it was originally a chapel for lepers who were forced to live outside the town in an attempt to control spread of the disease. The church was named for that fearless knight, St. George, patron of lepers. The core of the church is a Gothic longhouse with a three-sided chancel from the late 13th century. During restoration of the church in 1961, an archaeological dig of the floor disclosed traces of a wooden building believed to be a predecessor of the present house of worship.

Strandvej 97. © **62-21-14-73.** Free admission. Mon–Fri 8am–4pm.

Skt. Nicolai Kirke   Svendborg's oldest church is situated among a cluster of antique houses off Kyseborgstræde, in the vicinity of Gerrits Plads just south of the market square. The brick church was built in the Romanesque style before 1200, and last restored in 1892. Inside you'll find a fine altarpiece by Joachim Skovgaard and magnificent **stained-glass windows** ⚘, which were designed by Kraesten Iversen during the Nazi occupation of Denmark from 1940 to 1945. Nearby you can admire a statue by Kai Nielsen (1820–1924), a native son who went on to greater glory and became a famous sculptor.

Skt. Nicolajgade 2B. ⓒ **62-21-28-54.** Free admission. May–Aug daily 10am–3pm; Sept–Apr daily 10am–noon.

Viebaeltegård   We view this museum as being of such minor interest that we rarely give it more than 30 or 40 minutes. If the day is sunny, we prefer to come here to enjoy a picnic lunch in the museum garden. The headquarters for the county museum is housed in a former poorhouse/workhouse from 1872, the only one of its kind still existing in Denmark. The complex of "social welfare" buildings has been converted into museums of history, displaying artifacts from ancient times to the Middle Ages, including so-called "finds" from fields around Svendborg and South Funen. More intriguing is the crafts workshops on site, where you can watch goldsmiths, potters, and printers at work. There's also an on-site museum shop that has some wonderful crafts for sale.

Grubbemøllevej 13 (near Dronningemaen). ⓒ **62-21-02-61.** www.svendborgmuseum.dk. Admission 40DKK ($6.80/£3.60) adults, free for children 18 and under when accompanied by an adult. Open year-round Tues–Sun 10am–4pm.

WHERE TO STAY

Hotel Svendborg ⚘   Built in the 1950s (not a great decade for architecture), this stylish hotel offers the best accommodations in Svendborg, with the rooms spread across four floors above the commercial core of town. It's never been our favorite, as we prefer more evocative or romantic addresses, but during the 2 nights we spent here we were exceedingly comfortable and found the British staff helpful and informative. Bedrooms range from small to spacious, and each is furnished in a tasteful Scandinavian modern design with excellent bathrooms with tub/shower combos. The eight apartments, each with kitchen, can be rented to one to four guests. On site is the firstclass restaurant, Krinsten, serving a menu based on the season.

Centrumpladsen 1, DK-5700 Svendborg. ⓒ **62-21-17-00.** Fax 62-21-90-12. www.hotel-svendborg.dk. 133 units. 995DKK–1,245DKK ($169–$212/£90–£112) double; 1,750DKK–2,300DKK ($298–$391/£158–£207) suite; 1,450DKK ($247/£131) apt for 2; 1,750DKK ($298/£158) apt for 4. Rates include breakfast. AE, DC, MC, V. Free parking. Bus: 200 or 204. **Amenities:** Restaurant; bar; room service (7am–10pm); laundry service/dry cleaning; rooms for those w/limited mobility; nonsmoking rooms. *In room:* TV, dataport, minibar, hair dryer, safe, Wi-Fi.

Missionshotellet Stella Maris ⚘ *Value*   A Danish countess with a staff of 18 servants once occupied this 1904 estate, naming it Stella Maris, meaning "Star of the Sea," because of its location southwest of the city in a lovely old-fashioned seaside villa. In time it became part of a Christian hotel chain, maintaining both a smoke- and alcoholfree atmosphere.

This old-fashioned world of charm and nostalgia is today one of the undiscovered allures of Svendborg, with its English-style drawing room (with piano), overstuffed chairs, and antiques. Surrounded by well-landscaped gardens, it offers midsize-tospacious bedrooms, each with an individual color scheme, or else rose wallpaper and white-lace curtains. The rooms in front opening onto Svendborg Sound are the more expensive options, and you can follow a private path leading directly to the water.

Kogtvedvaenget 3, DK-5700 Svendborg. © **62-21-38-91**. Fax 62-22-41-74. www.stellamaris.dk. 26 units, 19 with bathroom. 680DKK ($116/£61) double without bathroom; 750DKK–900DKK ($128–$153/£68–£81) double with bathroom. Rates include breakfast. DC, MC, V. Bus: 202. From Svendborg head west along Kogtvedvej. **Amenities:** Breakfast room. *In room:* No phone.

WHERE TO DINE

Restaurant Marco Polo 🎇 ITALIAN   Housed in a former ironmonger's smithy, this appealing and congenial restaurant serves the best food in town. Chef and owner, Mr. Nikolaj, attracts foodies to his dining room at the edge of Svendborg's harbor with Italian, not Danish, cuisine. To get you going, the chef might tempt with his ravioli and a freshly made pesto and tomato sauce; golden brown roasted chicken with a Gorgonzola sauce; delectable fettuccini with strips of salmon; or grilled lamb entrecôte in a whiskey sauce.

Kullinggade 1B. © **62-22-92-11**. Reservations recommended. Main courses 99DKK–159DKK ($17–$27/£8.90–£14). MC, V. Mon–Sat 5–10pm.

Svendborgsund DANISH/FRENCH   Many Danes, often sailors and visiting yachties, come here just to drink in the separate bar area, but the food in the restaurant is good and wholesome, the cooks following traditional recipes. In summer, the terrace is a magnet, and you can sit out taking in a picture-postcard view of all the ferryboats, trawlers, and yachts in the harbor. The waterfront restaurant is the oldest in town, built of white-painted stone in the 1830s and lying about a 5-minute walk south of the center of town. The food is for the meat-potatoes-and-onion crowd—in fact, that is the most popular dish to order here and is called *biksemad* in Danish. The chef specializes in fresh fish, and does so exceedingly well, and also prepares tasty pork chops and tender Danish lamb.

Havnepladsen 5A. © **62-21-07-19**. Reservations recommended. Main courses 100DKK–188DKK ($17–$32/£9–£17); lunch *smørrebrød* 60DKK–100DKK ($10–$17/£5.40–£9). MC, V. Daily 11am–10pm.

NEARBY ATTRACTIONS ON TÅSINGE

Ærø is the major tourist attraction of Funen, outside Odense, but the lesser known island of Tåsinge is for lovers, the most romantic hideaway in all of Denmark. Although sleepy, it is still the largest island in the South Funen archipelago, and it's been connected to Funen by the Svendborg Sound Bridge since 1966. The location is only 3km (2 miles) south of Svendborg via the bridge, but a distance of 43km (27 miles) south of Odense.

Route 90, which is the main road, crisscrosses the island, but we'll let you in on a secret. When you see a signpost marked Tåsinge, take it to the northeastern sector of the island. Once here, you'll find the "skipper town" of **Troense** 🎇🎇, one of the best preserved and most idyllic villages in all of Denmark. Many half-timbered houses still stand on **Badstuen** and **Gronnegade** 🎇, the latter declared by many makers of landscape calendars as "the prettiest street in Denmark." While exploring Troense, you can dart in for a quick look at the town's maritime museum, **Sofartssamlingerne I Troense** (p. 168) and visit **Valdemars Slot** nearby (see below).

The island was the setting for a famous tragic love story depicted in the 1967 film *Elvira Madigan*. After checking out of a hotel in Svendborg, Danish artist Elvira Madigan and her lover, Sixten Sparre, a Swedish lieutenant, crossed by ferry to Tåsinge, where together they committed suicide. The Romeo and Juliet of Denmark were buried in the Landet Kirkegård, Elvira Madigansvej, at Landet, in the middle of Tåsinge, where many brides, even today, throw their wedding bouquets on their graves.

The island is best explored by car—follow Route 9 and drive over the causeway—or you could take local bus no. 980. You can also take the vintage steamer MS *Helge* (© **62-21-09-80** for information), which departs several times daily from the harbor at Svendborg. The steamer operates from May 7 to September 5. A one-way ticket costs 35DKK ($5.95/£3.15); a round-trip, 70DKK ($12/£6.30). Tickets are sold onboard or at the Svendborg Tourist Office (see above).

Sofartssamlingerne I Troense   Funen sailors once traversed the trade routes from Scandinavia to China and East India. Along the way, they picked up rare curiosities of all shapes and sizes (some of which are too erotic to put on display), and many of those artifacts, often from the early 19th century, have been put on display here. It's a flotsam and jetsam type of ships-in-a-bottle museum that has such mismatched exhibits as Sunderland china, rope-work art, and Staffordshire figures, along with model ships and figureheads. This Maritime Museum, a branch of the County Museum, is housed in a 1790s school, with a rooftop belfry.

Strandgade 1, Troense. © **62-22-52-32**. Admission 25DKK ($4.25/£2.25) adults, free for children. May–Oct daily 10am–5pm. Cross the causeway to Tåsinge, turn left and then left again, heading down Bregingevej toward the water; turn right at Troensevej and follow the signs to the old port of Troense and to the village school (now the museum) on Strandgade.

Valdemars Slot 𝄞𝄞 *(Kids*   Although not quite as stellar attraction as Egeskov (p. 161), this palace is our second favorite on Funen, and it looms large in history, having been given to naval hero Niels Juel for his third victory over the Swedes in 1678. The castle was built between 1639 and 1644 by Christian IV for his son, Valdemar, in a romantic style, and it is still occupied today by a charming, handsome couple, Caroline and Rory Fleming, who welcome guests (some groups) to stay overnight.

You can eat here after enjoying one of four museums, including a big-game trophy room, a toy museum, and a yachting museum. Children take special delight in the toy museum, whose collection covers the past 125 years. Along with several thousand toys, there are books, comics, and model cars. By far the most intriguing are the room interiors themselves, filled with artifacts and antiques. Guests today treat the property better than the Swedish soldiers who once occupied it, sending the copper roof back home to Sweden to make bullets and stabling their horses in the church.

Valdemars Castle Church, in the south wing, was consecrated in 1687 and has been used for worship ever since. Two stories high, it's overarched by three star vaults and illuminated by Gothic windows.

Slotsalléen 100, Troense. © **62-22-50-04**. www.valdemarsslot.dk. Admission 90DKK ($15/£8.10) adults, 45DKK ($7.65/£4.05) children. Apr–June and Aug daily 10am–5pm; July daily 10am–6pm; Sept Tues–Sun 10am–5pm; Oct 1–19 Sat–Sun 10am–5pm. Take the MS *Helge* from Svendborg Harbor. By car, from Troense, follow Slotsalléen to the castle.

WHERE TO STAY & DINE

Det Lille Hotel 𝄞 *(Finds*   Beside the harbor in the center of Troense, this is one of the most appealing small hotels in the district. The half-timbered building with a straw roof was built 150 years ago to house a family that worked at a nearby castle (Valdemars Slot). The hotel's quirky old age and the kindness of its owner, Birgit Erikssen, more than compensate for the lack of private bathrooms. Rooms are cramped but comfortable, and very likable. Other than breakfast, the only meals served are those prepared by Ms. Erikssen, which are priced at 170DKK ($29/£15) each, but only if you announce your intention of dining in-house several hours in advance.

Badstuen 15, Troense, Tåsinge, DK-5700 Svendborg. © **62-22-53-41**. Fax 62-22-52-41. www.detlillehotel.dk. 8 units, none with bathroom. 590DKK ($100/£53) double. Rates include breakfast. AE, DC, MC, V. **Amenities:** Breakfast room; lounge. *In room:* No phone.

Restaurant Slotskaelderen DANISH/FRENCH   Inside the thick stone walls of Valdemars Slot, this restaurant is divided into an unpretentious Danish bistro and an upscale French restaurant. The bistro serves such "down-home" dishes as schnitzels, *lobscouse* (hash), and roulades of beef with Danish beer and aquavit. The views over the tidal flats and sea are better from the restaurant, but most visitors prefer the informality and lower prices of the bistro. For more elegant dining, with formal place settings, you can enjoy haute cuisine like that served in the best of Paris's *luxe* restaurants, feasting on venison, delicate foie gras, and velvety lobster bisque.

In Valdemars Slot, Slotsalléen Troense. © **62-22-59-00**. Restaurant main courses 68DKK–398DKK ($12–$68/ £6.10–£36); bistro main courses 158DKK ($27/£14). MC, V. June to mid-Sept daily 11:30am–5pm; Apr–May and mid-Sept to mid-Dec Tues–Sat 11am–9pm. Closed mid-Dec to Mar.

NEARBY AT MILLINGE

The epitome of Danish roadside lodging, the following 15th-century smugglers' inn has been converted into a premier hotel, the finest in Funen, just 40km (24 miles) from Odense and 42km (25 miles) from Svendborg.

Falsled Kro ✦✦✦   The epitome of a Danish roadside inn, this former 15th-century smuggler's inn has been converted into a premier Relais & Château, the finest hotel in Funen, lying west of Faaborg on Route 329. Perhaps our most delightful memory of a stay here is when the owner allowed mushroom gatherers with their baskets to come onto the property and pick wild mushrooms, including cèpes, horns of plenty, chanterelles—some with an apricot aroma—and field mushrooms tasting of aniseed. The most delectable of all morels are available as early as April

The *kro* (inn) offers tradition and quality in its colony of beautifully furnished thatched buildings clustered around a cobblestone courtyard with a fountain. The spacious rooms are often furnished with antiques, and some of the units are in converted outbuildings or cottages across the road. Regardless of your room assignment, expect the comfort to be equal. The inn is filled with grace notes such as stone fireplaces, and, as a piece of enchantment, a lovely garden leads to the water and the yacht harbor. The *kro* is better than anything in Odense and also offers the island's premier restaurant.

Assensvej 513, Falsled, DK-5642 Millinge. © **62-68-11-11**. Fax 62-68-11-62. www.falsledkro.dk. 20 units. 1,350DKK–2,450DKK ($230–$417/£122–£221) double; 2,675DKK–2,900DKK ($455–$493/£241–£261) suite. AE, DC, MC, V. Bus: 930. **Amenities:** Restaurant; bar; 24-hr. room service; babysitting; laundry service; dry cleaning. *In room:* TV, dataport (in suites), minibar, hair dryer.

ACROSS THE WATER TO ÆRØ ✦✦✦

29km (18 miles) S of Svendborg, 74km (46 miles) S of Odense, 177km (110 miles) SW of Copenhagen

If this small Danish island, off the southern coast of Funen, didn't exist, Hans Christian Andersen would have invented it. Its capital, Ærøskøbing, is a Lilliputian souvenir of the past and is awash in a rainbow of colors.

Many of Denmark's offshore islands are dull and flat with red-brick market towns best passed through hurriedly. But Ærø is a place at which you'll want to linger, wandering its sleepy one-lane roads, walking the cobblestone streets of its hamlets, or merely spending a day at the beach. The best sands are along the northern and eastern coastlines, and chances are, even in July, you'll end up with a strip of sand all to yourself.

The place is small so it's easy to get around—30km (8 miles) long and 8km (5 miles) at its widest point. The number of windswept "souls" is also small, no more than 7,000 hearty islanders, with less than a thousand in the capital of Ærøskøbing.

There are only three towns that could even be called that. If time is fleeting, explore only **Ærøskøbing,** the best preserved town of 18th-century Denmark. The largest town is the ancient seaport of **Marstal,** where mariners once set out to conquer the Seven Seas. Though its maritime glory is a distant memory, there's still a bustling marina and a shipyard that makes wooden vessels as they did in Viking days. Yachts sail into **Søby,** the third town with a still active shipyard and a sizable fishing fleet.

Small fishing harbors, wheat fields, storybook hamlets of half-timbered houses, a dilapidated church or two from the Middle Ages, beer gardens, old windmills, and yacht-filled marinas make Ærø the kind of island you search for—but rarely find—in all of Scandinavia. Sure, Ærø is all cliché charm, but a cliché wouldn't be that unless it existed once upon a time.

ESSENTIALS

GETTING THERE   By Ferry   The only way to reach Ærø is by ferry; car ferries depart Svendborg six times daily (trip time: 1 hr.). For a schedule, contact the tourist office or the ferry office at the harbor in Svendborg. Bookings are made through **Det Ærøske Faergegraf-Ikselskab** in Ærøskøbing (℅ **62-52-40-00**).

GETTING AROUND   By Bus   It's best to take a car on the ferry since there's limited bus service on Ærø (℅ **62-53-10-10** in Ærøskøbing for bus information). Bus no. 990 runs every hour on the hour in the afternoon between Ærøskøbing, Marstal, and Søby, but there's only limited morning service. The tourist bureau (see below) provides bus schedules, which change seasonally. Tickets are 62DKK ($10/£5.60) for the day and can be bought on the bus.

If you'd like to take a bus tour of the island, call **Jesper "Bus" Jensen** (℅ **62-58-13-13**). His bus holds 12 to 14 passengers and costs 50DKK ($8.50/£4.50) per person.

VISITOR INFORMATION   The **Ærøskøbing Turistbureau,** Vestergade 1 (℅ **62-52-13-00**), is open June 15 to August, Monday to Friday 10am to 3:30pm, Saturday 10am to 3pm; September to June 14, Monday to Friday 10am to 3pm, Saturday 10am to 1pm.

CYCLING AROUND THE ISLAND

Ærø is one of the best islands in Denmark for cycling because of its low-lying terrain and scenic paths. Local tourist offices provide maps outlining routes for 15DKK ($2.55/£1.35), which can also be used for walks. Numbers 90, 91, and 92 mark cycle trails around the coast. Bike rentals cost 45DKK ($7.65/£4.05) a day, and rentals in Ærøskøbing are available at the **Ærøskøbing Vandrerhjem,** Smedevejen 15 (℅ **62-52-10-44**); at Marstal at **Nørremark Cykelforretning,** Møllevejen 77 (℅ **62-53-14-77**); and at **Søby Cykelforretning,** Langebro 4A (℅ **62-58-18-42**).

The road continues west to Tranderup, where you can visit **Tranderup Kirke,** a Romanesque building with Gothic vaulting. Inside, the large carved figure depicting Mary and the infant Jesus dates from around the 14th century and is one of the oldest ecclesiastical pieces on the island. The triptych is from around 1510, and the large mural over the chancel arch reveals the date of its execution in 1518. Originally, the spires of Tranderup resembled those of Bregninge (see below), but they were rebuilt in a neoclassical style in 1832; the largest bell was cast in 1566 and is still in use.

After a visit, follow the signs west to the village of **Vodrup,** which was founded in the 13th century and is mentioned for the first time in 1537 as "Wuderup." The village disappeared in the 17th century when the land became part of Vodrup Estate. When the estate was dissolved, the village came back.

The cliffs at Vodrup, **Vodrup Klint** 𝄞𝄞, have an unusual geology: Large blocks of land have slipped down and resemble huge steps. The soil lies on top of a layer of gray clay, which can be seen at the base of the cliffs by the beach. The layer of clay is full of snail and cockle shells, left here by the sea. Water seeping down through the earth is stopped by the clay. When the clay absorbs enough water, it becomes so "movable" that it acts as a sliding plane for the layers above. The last great landslide here occurred in 1834.

Vodrup Klint is one of the most southerly points in Denmark, attracting creatures such as lizards and many species of plants—the carline thistle grows on these cliffs, blooming from July to September. An unusual characteristic of the cliffs is a proliferation of springs, where water bubbles out by the foot of the slopes. When the cattle need water, farmers need only push a pipe into the cliff face and let the water collect in a pool.

Fyn County has bought the cliffs, roughly 35 hectares (86 acres), and set them aside for public use. Animals are allowed to graze the fields in the summer months, and you can walk on all areas of the land. Cycle trail 91 runs right past Vodrup Klint, so it's often a stopover for bikers.

The route continues west to Bregninge and **Bregninge Kirke,** a 13th-century building with grandiose vaults that were added during the late 15th century. Its impressive spire shows the influence of east Schleswig (Germany) building traditions and is roofed with oak tiles. The murals inside date from around 1510—one, for example, depicts the Passion of Christ, another, the life of John the Baptist. The magnificent **triptych** ✦ dates from shortly before the Reformation and was made by the German sculptor Claus Berg. The crucifix in the nave is from the latter Middle Ages, and the 1612 pulpit was executed in the Renaissance style.

After visiting the southern part of Ærø, you can continue northwest into Søby.

EXPLORING THE ISLAND

The neat little village of **Ærøskøbing** 𝄞𝄞 was a 13th-century market town that came to be known as a skippers' town in the 17th century. Called "a Lilliputian souvenir of the past," few Scandinavian towns have retained their heritage as much as Ærøskøbing. In the heyday of the windjammer, nearly 100 commercial sailing ships made this their home port.

The ferry from Fåborg docks at **Søby,** in the northwest part of the island. Before you rush to Ærøskøbing, visit a mellow manorial property, **Søbygård.** Now in ruins, this manor house in the center of Søby is complete with a moat and dank dungeons.

Marstal, a thriving little port on the east coast of Ærø, has had a reputation in sailors' circles since the days of the tall ships. The harbor, protected by a granite jetty, is still busy. It has a shipyard that produces steel and wooden vessels, an engine factory, a ferry terminal, and one of Denmark's biggest yacht basins. The street names attest to Marstal's seafaring background—Skonnertvej, Barkvej, and Galeasevej (Schooner, Bark, and Ketch roads); Danish naval heroes such as Rasmus Minor and Christen Hansen; and Seven Ferry Lanes.

Visit the **seamen's church,** with the spire and illuminated clock, in the town center. Inside are ship models and an altarpiece that depicts Christ stilling the tempest at sea.

Twice a day, a mail boat takes a limited number of passengers on a 45-minute trip to tiny **Birkholm Island** for swimming and exploration. There are no cars on Birkholm. Reservations on the mail boat can be made at the Marstal Tourist Office.

SEEING THE SIGHTS

Ærøskøbing Kirke   This church was built between 1756 and 1758 as a replacement for a rather dilapidated church from the Middle Ages. In its present state, the 13th-century font and the pulpit stem from the original structure, and were donated by Duke Philip of Lyksborg in 1634, the year he bought Gråsten County on the island of Ærø. The altarpiece is a copy of Eckersberg's picture, which hangs in Vor Frue Kirke in Svendborg. The colors selected for the interior of the church, along with the floral motifs, were the creation of Elinar V. Jensen in connection with an extensive restoration project carried out in 1950. Søndergade 43. © 62-52-11-72. Free admission. Daily 8am–5pm.

Ærø Museum   This is the best local museum, found at the corner of Nørregade and Brogade. In the old days it was inhabited by the bailiff, but today you'll find a rich exhibit of the island's past. The collection includes antiques and paintings from the mid-1800s. Brogade 35 (at the corner of Nørregade). © 62-52-29-50. Admission is 20DKK ($3.40/£1.80). Mar–Oct 10am–4pm; Nov–Feb Mon–Fri 10am–1pm.

Flaskeskibssamlingen *(Finds*   This museum commemorates the seafaring life documented by Peter Jacobsen's ships in bottles. Upon his death in 1960 at the age of 84, this former cook, nicknamed "Bottle Peter," had crafted more than 1,600 bottled ships and some 150 model sailing vessels built to scale, earning him the reputation in Ærøskøbing of "the ancient mariner." The museum also has Ærø clocks, furniture, china, and carved works by sculptor H. C. Petersen. Smedegade 22. © 62-52-29-51. Admission is 25DKK ($4.25/£2.25) adults, 10DKK ($1.70/90p) children 10–15, free 9 and under. Daily 10am–5pm.

WHERE TO STAY
In Ærøskøbing

Hotel Ærøhus *⟨⚘⟩*   Cozy intimacy and nostalgia are combined at this classic Danish inn, where many traditional features from its past, such as copper kettles and glowing lamps, mix with modern amenities. An old-fashioned lounge, a typical Danish courtyard, and a luxuriant garden are part of the allures of this place.

The midsize-to-spacious bedrooms are traditionally furnished in a vaguely French boudoir style for the most part, and most of them come with private bathrooms with shower, some units lack facilities, and guests share the adequate corridor bathrooms. The good island cooking, based on fresh produce, is a reason to stay here, and tables are placed on the terrace in summer. (We like to hang out on a summer evening at the barbecue grill.) Offering live music on most summer weekends, the inn is just a 3-minute walk from the harbor.

Vestergade 38, DK-5970 Ærøskøbing. © 62-52-10-03. Fax 62-52-21-23. www.aeroehus.dk. 30 units, 18 with bathroom. 700DKK ($119/£63) double without bathroom; 1,190DKK ($202/£107) double with bathroom. Rates include breakfast. MC, V. Free parking. **Amenities:** Restaurant; bar *In room:* TV, dataport, hair dryer, safe.

Pension Vestergade 44 *⟨⚘⟩ (Value*   One of the most historically appealing buildings of Ærøskøbing is in the center of the village, 183m (600 ft.) from the ferryboat piers, within an antique (built in 1784) half-timbered structure that the Danish historical authority considers almost sacrosanct. This allegiance to maintaining the building in its pristine original condition has restricted its owner, English-born Susanna Greve, from adding private bathrooms to its venerable interior. But because of its history and atmosphere, the guests don't seem to mind. This enormous apricot-colored building was built by a local sea captain for each of his two daughters, and it's divided into almost exactly equal halves. Only half of the house is occupied by this B&B. (The other half is the home of a local doctor and is not open for view.) Within Susanna's half, you'll find scads of Danish and English antiques, substantial and bracing breakfasts, midafternoon coffee that's served every day, and a distinctive (and rather philosophical) sense of humor. Local fire codes demand an absolute no-smoking policy on the building's upper floors. As for plumbing issues, know in advance that the inn maintains five bathrooms, each opening onto corridors and public areas, for six accommodations, more than most other B&Bs in Denmark. Susanna knows the ins and outs of virtually every tourist facility in town and is generous about transmitting information about local restaurants and bike-rental facilities to her guests. There's a communal TV in one of the public areas.

Vestergade 44. DK-5970, Ærøskøbing. © **62-52-22-98.** www.pension-vestergade44.dk. 6 units, none with private bathroom. 680DKK–780DKK ($116–$133/£61–£70) double. No credit cards. *In room:* Dataport, no phone.

In Marstal

Hotel Ærø Strand ⨋   Surrounded by sea grass and sweeping vistas of the water, this first-class hotel is the largest and most up-to-date on the island, a 5-minute walk from the center, and less than half a kilometer (¼ mile) from the beach. The hotel is about the only place on Ærø that could be called a holiday resort, offering midsize-to-spacious bedrooms, each decorated in Danish modern set against pastel-colored walls, and each containing a sleek tiled bathroom with tub/shower combo. The suites are twice the size of the regular rooms and worth the extra money if you can afford it. The restaurant is right by the harbor, and during the day fishermen can be seen bringing in the catch. In winter you can retreat to one of the cozy nooks inside, and in summer dine close to the giant heart-shaped swimming pool.

Egehovedvej 4, DK-5960 Marstal. © **62-53-33-20.** Fax 62-53-31-50. 100 units. 925DKK ($157/£83) double; 1,295DKK ($220/£117) suite. Rates include breakfast. DC, MC, V. Free parking. Closed Dec 20–Jan 2. Bus: 990 to Marstal. **Amenities:** Restaurant; bar; disco; indoor heated pool; sauna; Jacuzzi; solarium; tennis court. *In room:* TV.

WHERE TO DINE

Ærøskøbing Røgeri *(Value* SEAFOOD   The setting is anything but glamorous, and the food you order will be served on paper plates with plastic knives and forks. And if you're looking for wine to accompany your meal, forget it, as the beverage of choice is beer. Nevertheless, this is one of the most popular places in town, a culinary landmark that patrons describe with nostalgia and affection. Set beside the harbor in a raffish-looking house built in the old Ærø style, it serves only fresh fish that has been smoked (usually that morning) in electric and wood-fired ovens on the premises. You specify what kind of fish you want (salmon, herring, filet or whole mackerel, trout, or shrimp) and which of a half-dozen seasonings you want (dill, parsley, pepper, paprika, garlic, or "Provençal"). Then, carry your plate to the outdoor seating area overlooking the harbor, or haul it back to wherever you're staying. The most expensive thing on the menu is a slab of fresh-smoked salmon accompanied with bread, butter, and a portion of potato salad; the least expensive is a make-it-yourself *smørrebrød* that includes a smoked herring, a slice of rough-textured bread, and Danish butter.

Havnen 15. © **62-52-40-07.** Platters 19DKK–26DKK ($3.25–$4.40/£1.70–£2.35). No credit cards. Daily 10am–6pm (until 8pm mid-June to mid-Aug). Closed Sept–Apr.

Restaurant Mumm 👁 AMERICAN/INTERNATIONAL   In a simple house whose foundation dates from 1780, this restaurant enjoys a reputation for well-prepared dishes that sometimes carry a North American (or at least an international) flavor (a former owner was a chef at a Florida resort). There is a copious salad buffet, well-flavored steaks, and an abundance of seafood (most of which comes from local waters), including filet of plaice, grilled salmon with hollandaise sauce, and various preparations of shrimp and snails. Inside you'll find a pair of dining rooms; the less formal one offers a view into a very busy kitchen. There's also a garden terrace, where parasols and candles usually adorn the outdoor tables.

Søndergade 12. 📞 **62-52-12-12.** Ærøskøbing. Main courses 120DKK–188DKK ($20–$32/£11–£17). AE, DC, MC, V. June–Sept daily 11:30am–2:30pm and 6–9:30pm; May and Sept Tues–Sun 11:30am–2:30pm and 6–9:30pm. Closed Oct–Apr.

2 Bornholm ★★

153km (95 miles) E of Copenhagen

We had discovered all of Denmark before getting around to Bornholm, writing it off as a Baltic island where Danish families who can't afford a Mediterranean holiday go to romp on the sandy beaches in summer. But after coming to know Bornholm in greater depth, we eventually succumbed to its peculiar charm.

The most hurried visitor to Denmark will still pass it by, and it's damn hard to get an accommodation in July and August unless you make reservations well in advance. Most of the holiday flats want a full week's booking, and very few visitors, except perhaps the Germans, have so much time to devote to Bornholm.

We like to skip the overcrowded summers altogether and visit either in the late spring or early fall, when Bornholm appears at its most dramatic seasonal change. Of course, that means you'll have to forego beach life, but the waters, even in July or August, are just too cold for us.

Surrounded by the Baltic Sea, astride the important shipping lanes that connect St. Petersburg with Copenhagen and the Atlantic, Bornholm sits only 37km (23 miles) off the coast of Sweden, and about 153km (95 miles) east of Copenhagen and the rest of Denmark. Prized as a strategic Baltic military and trading outpost since the early Middle Ages (but sadly the site of many bloody territorial disputes among the Danes, Germans, and Swedes), Bornholm is home to 45,000 year-round residents. An additional 450,000 visitors arrive during the balmy months of summer. Besides tourism, which is growing rapidly, the economy relies on trade, fishing, herring processing, agriculture, and the manufacture of ceramics, which, thanks to the island's deep veins of clay, has been a major industry since the 1700s.

Covering a terrain of granite and sandstone is a thin but rich layer of topsoil; the island's rock-studded surface is made up of forests and moors. The unusual topography and surprisingly temperate autumn climate—a function of the waters of the Baltic—promotes the verdant growth of plants: figs, mulberries, and enough lavish conifers to create the third-largest forest in Denmark (right in the center of the island). This forest, Almindingen, has the only rocking stone that still rocks. Rocking stones are giant erratic boulders weighing up to 40 tons that were brought to Bornholm by the advancing glaciers during the last Ice Age. In addition, one of Denmark's largest waterfalls, Døndalen, lies in the north of Bornholm in a rift valley and is best viewed from spring through fall.

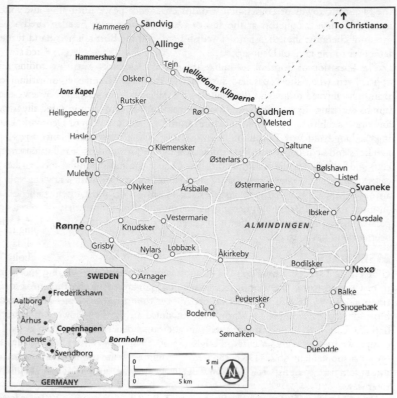

Bornholm

The island covers 945 sq. km (365 sq. miles), and most of the inhabitants live along 140km (87 miles) of coastline. Not only do the flora and fauna differ in many respects from the rest of Denmark, but its geology is unique as well. The island is divided into two geologic zones: 1,500-million-year-old bedrock to the north and a 550-million-year-old layer of sandstone to the south.

Bornholmers traditionally have been fishermen and farmers. Today their villages are still idyllic, evocative of the old way of life in their well-kept homesteads, as are fishing hamlets with their characteristic smokehouse chimneys, often used for smoking herring.

The island is still sparsely populated. Grand Canary, a Spanish island off the coast of Africa, for example, is the same size as Bornholm, but while that resort hosts some two million residents in high season, the greatest number of people ever seen on Bornholm at one time is 100,000.

The best beaches of Bornholm lie in the southwestern section of the island, between the towns of Balka and the main beach town of Dueodde.

Because of its location at the crossroads of warring nations, Bornholm has had a turbulent history, even as recently as 1945. Strongholds and fortified churches protected local inhabitants when the island was a virtual plaything in the power struggle between royal and religious forces. It was plundered by pirate fleets, noblemen, and the Hanseatic towns of Pomerania. It didn't experience peace until after it revolted against Swedish conquerors at the end of Denmark's war with Sweden in 1658. A group of liberators shot the island's Swedish Lord, and the Bornholmers handed their land over to the king of Denmark.

The liberation of Bornholm—unlike the rest of Denmark—was slow to come in 1945. Even when the Nazis had surrendered, the local German commandant on Bornholm refused to give up the island to the Allies. In response, the Soviets rained bombs down on Rønne and Nexø (the two main towns), and then invaded the island and occupied it for several months before returning it to the crown of Denmark. During the long Cold War, Bornholm became one of NATO's key surveillance bases.

The island's cuisine is obviously influenced by the surrounding sea. Baltic herring, cod, and salmon are the traditional dishes. One of the most popular local dishes is called *Sun over Gudhjem,* a specialty of smoked herring topped with a raw egg yolk in an onion ring. It's served with coarse salt and chives, or, most often, radishes. In autumn, the small Bornholm herring are caught and used for a variety of spiced and pickled dishes. Another local dish is salt-fried herring served on dark rye bread with beetroot and hot mustard.

ESSENTIALS

GETTING THERE   By Ferry   The most popular means of reaching the island from Copenhagen is the 7-hour ferryboat ride. Maintained by the **Bornholmstraffiken** (© **56-95-18-66**), these ferries depart year-round from the pier at Kvæsthusbroen once per evening at 11:30pm, with scheduled arrival the following morning at 6:30am. Late-June to mid-August there's an additional departure at 8:30am every day except Wednesday. Passage costs 33DKK ($5.60/£3) per person each way, plus an optional supplement of 221DKK ($38/£20) to rent a private cabin. These ferries are most often used to transport a car from Copenhagen, which costs 174DKK ($30/£16) each way.

Bornholm Ferries, Havnen, at Rønne (© **56-95-18-66**), operates 2½-hour ferries from Ystad on the southern coast of Sweden, with up to four departures daily. These ferries have tax-free shops onboard. A car with a maximum of five passengers costs 164DKK ($28/£15) each way. You can also travel from Sassnitz-Mukran (Rügen) in north Germany for a 3½-hour crossing to Bornholm, arriving at Rønne. Tax-free shopping is also found onboard on this crossing. From Germany, one-way passage for a car with a maximum of five passengers is 1,275DKK ($217/£115). Each of these ferries has a restaurant or bistro featuring a buffet with Danish and Bornholm specialties.

By Plane   Cimber Air (© **70-10-12-18** for reservations and information) has about nine flights a day from Copenhagen to Bornholm's airport, 5.5km (3½ miles) south of Rønne. Depending on restrictions, round-trip fares range from 567DKK to 1,680DKK ($96–$286/£51–£151).

VISITOR INFORMATION   The tourist office, **The Bornholm Welcome Center,** Kystvej 3, Rønne (© **56-95-95-00**), is open June to August daily 10am to 5:30pm; April, May, September, and October Monday to Friday 9am to 4pm, Saturday 10am to 1pm; November to March Monday to Friday 9am to 4pm.

GETTING AROUND   By Car   The best place on the island for car rentals is **Europcar,** Nodre Kystvej 1 in Rønne (© **877/940-6900** in the U.S., or 84-331-133). Its least expensive rentals begin at 2,750DKK ($468/£248) per week, including unlimited mileage and insurance coverage, as well as the government tax. In addition, **Avis** is located at Snellemark 19, in Rønne (© **800/230-4898** in the U.S., or 56-95-22-08).

By Bicycle   During sunny weather, biking around the island is almost as popular as driving. If you want to do as the Danes do, rent a bike; the prices are pretty much the same throughout the island—about 60DKK ($10/£5.40) a day. A suggested bike-rental company in Rønne is **Bornholms Cykleudleijning,** Nordre Kystvej 5 (© **56-95-13-59**). Open daily 8am to 4pm and 8:30 to 9pm.

EXPLORING THE ISLAND

Even if you have a car available, you might want to bike the tour we've outlined in this chapter. Ask at any tourist office for a map of the island's more than 190km (118 miles) of bicycle trails, and divide this tour into several days, hitting the highlights mentioned below at your own pace.

The tour begins at Rønne, but you could join in at almost any point; the route goes counterclockwise around the island's periphery. Be aware that Bornholm's highways do not have route numbers; even though some maps show the main east-west artery as Route 38, local residents call it "the road to Nexø."

RØNNE

Your arrival point is Rønne, the capital of the island, but there are far more rewarding targets away from the main town, which lies on the western coast facing the island of Zealand and is the site of the major harbor and airport.

But, once here, you'll find Rønne has a certain charm as you walk its historic Gamle Stan, or Old Town, with its cobblestone streets flanked by cross-timbered houses, many of them brightly painted in colors such as yellow and orange.

The best streets for seeing Bornholm as it used to be are **Laksegade** and **Storegade,** plus the triangular sector lying between **Store Torv** and **Lille Torv.** You'll find even more charm in many of the island's smaller towns or hamlets.

Because of Soviet aerial attacks in 1945, most of Rønne was left in shambles, so what you see today is essentially a modern town with a population of some 15,000. The parents of today's inhabitants rebuilt Rønne wisely in the postwar years, opting for an old-fashioned architectural look, which makes most of the houses look older than they actually are.

If you arrive by ferry, you'll notice **St. Nicolai Church,** dedicated to the patron saint of seafarers, on Harbour Hill, towering over the small South Boat Harbor just below. It wasn't until the 18th century that locals moved ahead with plans for a large trading harbor here, and even today the harbor is expanding to service ferries and the many cruise ships that call at Rønne in increasing numbers.

Should you experience a rare hot day in Denmark, you'll find that vast stretches of sand lie both south and north of Rønne. These beaches are popular with Danish families, many from Copenhagen, in summer.

SEEING THE SIGHTS

Bornholms Museum (Museum of Bornholm) ✦   To open this museum, islanders raided their attics for any curiosities that might be of interest to the general public and came up with a number of objects, ranging from antique toys from the 19th century to gold objects discovered by farmers who were plowing their fields. Installed in what used to be the major hospital on the island, the museum traces the history of Bornholm's unique position in the Baltic through displays on archaeology, folkloric costumes, ethnology, and seafaring and agrarian traditions. Several rooms are outfitted with 19th-century antique furniture, island-made silverware, and accessories. Of special interest is the collection of Bornholm-made clocks, copied from a shipment of English clocks that was salvaged from a Dutch shipwreck in the late 1700s. Since Bornholm is known for its ceramics and glassware, it's no surprise that there are nearly 5,000 pieces of glassware and handcrafted ceramics.

Skt. Mortensgade 29. © 56-95-07-35. www.bornholmsmuseum.dk. Admission 40DKK ($6.80/£3.60); free for kids 12 and under. Mid-May to mid-Oct Mon–Sat 10am–5pm; mid-Oct to mid-May Mon–Sat 1–4pm.

Forsvarsmuseet   Today this museum attracts World War II buffs, but originally the citadel was built in 1650 for defensive purposes in the southern part of town. With its massive round tower, this old castle is like an armed fortress, with guns, blades, weapons, war maps, and models of fortification. There are even military uniforms of the men who fought each other, plus a rare collection of antique armaments. By far the most intriguing exhibitions depict the Nazi occupation of the island from 1940 to 1945.

Kastellet Galløkken. © 56-95-65-83. Admission 30DKK ($5.10/£2.70) adults, 10DKK ($1.70/90p) children 6–12, free for children under 6. June–Oct Tues–Sun 11am–5pm.

Hjorth's Fabrik (Bornholm Ceramic Museum) ⋆   Bornholm has long been famed for its beautiful ceramics, and this working ceramics museum showcases the craft better than any other place on the island. In 1858, a small-scale factory, Hjorth's Ceramics, was established to make pottery from the island's rich deposits of clay, surviving until 1993. In 1995, this museum was established in the company's original factory. Inside, you'll find an intriguing hybrid between an art gallery and an industrial museum. You'll see the island's best examples of the dark-brown, yellow, and gray pottery that was produced in abundance beginning in the 1700s; samples of the dishes and bowls made by the Hjorth company over the years; and some of the work of Bornholm's modern-day potters. Throughout the year several ceramic artists maintain studios inside, casting, spinning, or glazing pots in full view of visitors. The museum shop sells modern-day replicas of Hjorth ceramics, and many exhibits trace the production process from start to finish.

Krystalgade 5. © 56-95-01-60. Admission mid-Apr to mid-Oct 35DKK ($5.95/£3.15) adults, 10DKK ($1.70/90p) children 10–15, free 9 and under; mid-Oct to mid-Apr 10DKK ($1.70/90p) adults, free for children. May–Oct Mon–Fri 10am–5pm, Sat 10am–2pm; Nov–Apr Mon–Fri 10am–5pm, Sat 10am–1pm.

WHERE TO STAY

Hotel Griffen ⋆ *Kids*   Last time we checked in here, the manager offered to help us rent a bike (the island trail starts right in front of the hotel) and pack a picnic lunch for the trip. This kind of assistance makes us vote the staff here as the most helpful on island. This hotel is the largest on Bornholm, and though it falls a few notches below the Radisson Hotel Fredensborg (see below), it's one of the most inviting.

Though it was constructed in the dull architectural era of the 1970s, the hotel's buildings have a certain style, designed to evoke 18th-century hip-roofed manor houses. Two of the four buildings contain the bedrooms, which are separated from the dining, drinking, and convention facilities in the other structures.

Lying in the heart of Rønne, a 5-minute walk to the beach and the town center, the hotel is also close to a busy summer marina. We especially like the way the architects added plenty of windows so guests can take in views of the Baltic in many directions. Some rooms have floor-to-ceiling windows and glass doors.

The small-to-midsize bedrooms are furnished in a modern but minimalist style, each comfortable and tasteful with well-appointed private tiled bathrooms with tub/shower combos. We are especially fond of their "Sunset Menu," served every evening between 5 and 9pm, and based on the "freshest and best" found at the market that day, most often seafood from Baltic waters.

Ndr. Kystvej 34, DK-3700 Rønne. ℂ 56-95-51-11. Fax 56-95-52-97. www.hotelgriffen.dk. 140 units. 1,125DKK ($191/£101) double; 1,715DKK ($292/£154) suite. AE, DC, MC, V. **Amenities:** Restaurant; bar; indoor heated pool; kids' pool; sauna; use of tennis courts at Radisson; room service (7am–9pm). *In room:* TV, hair dryer.

Radisson Hotel Fredensborg 𝒢𝒢 *Kids* There are hotels on Bornholm with more atmosphere and charm, but this chain hotel is clearly the market leader for international luxury. However, what passes for *luxe* living on Bornholm wouldn't make the grade in Copenhagen. One of the few hotels on island to remain open all year, Fredensborg lies in a wooded, tranquil location adjacent to a beach and less than a kilometer (about ½ mile) south of Rønne harbor. Its Danish modern style from the 1960s wouldn't win architectural awards, but its midsize-to-spacious bedrooms are the island's best appointed, each comfortable and tasteful with a private balcony or terrace overlooking the Baltic. Bathrooms are small with sleek tiles, modern plumbing, and a tub/shower combo. The suites are really apartments with full kitchens, most often rented to families with small children. Some of the best food in Rønne is served at the hotel's well-reputed Di 5 Stâuerna restaurant (see below), specializing in Danish/French cuisine. Guests are allowed to use the pool at the previously recommended Griffen.

Strandvejen 116, DK-3700 Rønne. ℂ 800/333-3333 in the U.S., or 56-95-44-44. Fax 56-95-03-14. www.bornholm hotels.dk. 72 units. 1,195DKK–1,395DKK ($203–$237/£108–£126) double; 1,495DKK–1,795DKK ($254–$305/£135–£162) suite. Rates include buffet breakfast. AE, DC, MC, V. **Amenities:** Restaurant; bar; tennis court; sauna; room service (7am–10pm); babysitting; laundry service/dry cleaning; nonsmoking rooms. *In room:* TV, dataport, minibar, hair dryer.

WHERE TO DINE
Di 5 Stâuerna 𝒢𝒢 DANISH/FRENCH/INTERNATIONAL This is the best and most upscale restaurant on island, with a clientele that tends to select it for celebratory meals and family gatherings. Its name translates as "the five rooms," each of which is outfitted in a Danish country style. There's always a platter of the fish of the day, which is usually fried in butter and served with new potatoes—a style that Bornholmers have enjoyed since their childhood. Other more elaborate options include Hereford beefsteak prepared *cordon bleu*-style, with salted cured ham and Emmenthaler cheese; tournedos of beef flambéed in Calvados and served with apples and onions; and our favorite: Bornholm lamb served with a sauce concocted from rosemary, olive oil, and tarragon.

In the Radisson Hotel Fredensborg, Strandvejen 116. ℂ 56-95-44-44. Reservations recommended. Main courses 75DKK–210DKK ($13–$36/£6.75–£19); fixed-price tasting menu 265DKK ($45/£24). AE, DC, MC, V. Daily 11:30am–9:30pm.

Rådhuskroen 𝒢 *Finds* DANISH This is the most visible and, in its own way, most charming restaurant in Rønne, although it doesn't use the pricey ingredients or employ the expensive chefs hired by the previously recommended Di 5 Stâuerna. It's situated in the cellar of the Town Hall, a 140-year-old building with a long history of feeding island residents—and feeding them well. Wall sconces cast romantic shadows over a collection of antique furniture and accessories, and a well-trained service staff serves fresh and well-prepared dishes such as filet of salmon in a "summer sauce" of fresh tomatoes, chives, and herbs, and two sizes of tender and well-prepared beefsteak.

Nørregade 2. ℭ **56-95-00-69.** Reservations recommended on weekends. Main courses 10DKK–171DKK ($1.70–$29/90p–£15). AE, DC, MC, V. Mon–Sat noon–3pm and 5–9pm.

FROM RØNNE TO NEXØ

From Rønne, drive east along the island's modern highway, A-38, following the signs toward Nexø. Stop in **Nylars** (about 5km/3 miles from Rønne), a town that's known as the site of the best-preserved of Bornholm's four round churches. The **Nylarskirke** (ℭ **56-97-20-13**), built around 1250 and rising prominently from the center of a community with no more than about 50 buildings, contains frescoes that depict the Creation and the expulsion of Adam and Eve from the Garden of Eden. The cylindrical nave has three floors, the uppermost of which was a watchman's tower in the Middle Ages. You can also view two fragments of a runic stone. From Rønne, you can take bus no. 6 if you don't have a car; the bike path from Rønne to Åkirkeby also passes by the church. Admission free. Open May to October 20, Monday to Friday 9am to 5pm.

Continue driving another 5km (3 miles) east until you reach **Åkirkeby,** the only inland settlement of any size and Bornholm's oldest (the town charter dates from 1346) The little town was important in medieval times when islanders had to move inland to avoid attacks from enemies at sea.

Åkirkeby is also home to the island's oldest and largest church, **Åkirke,** Torvet (ℭ **56-97-41-03**), originally built around 1250. This church isn't as eccentric as some of the others. It's a sandstone-fronted monument built with defense in mind, as you'll note from the small windows. Inside, a Romanesque baptismal font is incised with runic inscriptions believed to be carved by the master craftsman Sigraf on the island of Gotland. Other runic inscriptions appear on the cloverleaf-shaped arches. The church is open daily 10am to 4pm, charging 6DKK ($1/55p) for visitors.

Åkirkeby is a good point to cut inland if you wish to see some of Bornholm's woodlands, among the densest in Denmark, with forests filled with oak, hemlock, fir, spruce, and beech trees. The tourist office in Rønne (see "Visitor Information," above) will give you a map outlining the best of the trails that cut through Bornholm's largest forest, **Almindingen,** in the center of the island. It can be reached by following a marked road north from Åkirkeby. The forest is also the location of the island's highest point, **Rytterknægten,** a 160m (525-ft.) hill with a lookout tower, Kongemindet, with a staircase you can climb for a panoramic view of the dense woodlands.

You can also pick up information at a minor, rarely used tourist office that's much less visible than the island's main office in Rønne. It's the **Sydbornholms Turistbureau,** Torvet 2 (ℭ **56-97-45-20**), at Åkirkeby. Mid-May to mid-September, it's open Monday through Friday 9am to 6pm and Saturday 8am to 1pm. The rest of the year, hours are Monday to Friday 10am to 6:30pm and closed Saturday and Sunday.

A minor museum for devoted automobile fans is the **Bornholms Automobilmuseum,** Grammegardsvej 1 (ℭ **56-97-45-95**), displaying vintage cars and motorcycles, plus some farm equipment and tractors that highlight the 20th century's advances in agrarian science. Antique cars and tractors derive from such manufacturers as Delahaye, Opel, Ford, Adler, Singer, Jaguar, and Fiat. It's open May to October, Monday to Saturday 10am to 5pm. The rest of the year it's closed, and admission costs 30DKK ($5.10/£2.70) per person.

From Åkirkeby, cut southeast for 4.5km (2¾ miles), following the signs to **Pedersker,** a hamlet with only three shops (which close down during the cold-weather months). Six kilometers (4 miles) later you'll reach **Dueodde,** the name of both a raff-ish beachfront community and the entire region around the southernmost tip of the island. The village of Dueodde marks the southern edge of a stretch of coastline that is the finest beach on the island. The oceanfront bounty—and the best beaches on the island—stretch northward and eastward to the town of **Balka,** 5km (3 miles) beyond, encompassing stretches of white sand whose grains are so fine that they were used for generations to fill hourglasses. The towns are little more than backdrops for seasonal kiosks and a scattering of holiday homes for mainland Danes and Swedes. Most of the landscape is a virtual wilderness of pine and spruce trees, salt-tolerant shrubs, and sand dunes, some of which rise more than 12m (39 ft.) above the nearby sea.

The focal point of this southeastern coastline is the **Dueodde Fyr** (Dueodde Light-house), the tallest lighthouse on the island, built in 1962 to warn ships away from the extreme southern tip of the island. Weather permitting, you can climb to its top dur-ing daylight hours May to October for a fee of 5DKK (85¢/45p), which you pay directly to the lighthouse keeper. For information, call the tourist office in Dueodde (© 56-49-70-79).

From Dueodde, continue along the coast in a northeasterly direction, passing through the unpretentious fishing hamlets of **Snogebæk** and **Balka.** Immediately north of Balka the road will deliver you north to Nexø, the second major town of the island after Rønne, opening onto the eastern coast facing Sweden.

WHERE TO STAY & DINE
Hotel Balka Strand   This is the only hotel along Bornholm's beach-fringed eastern coast that remains open year-round, so it stays busy even in midwinter, usually with conferences. Originally built in the 1970s and doubled in size in 1992, the hotel's exterior could easily fit into any number of towns in America's heartland. There's nothing particularly Bornholmian about it; rather it's imbued with a more interna-tional aura. The government gives it four stars, based more on comfort and facilities than any particular winning atmosphere. Nonetheless, the hotel staff is helpful and personal in their welcome, and the building is laid out in a one-story format about 150m (490 ft.) from one of the island's best bathing beaches adjoining a protected nature preserve ideal for walks or hikes. The neatly kept midsize bedrooms, with a bathroom with tub/shower combo, are comfortably and tastefully furnished in Dan-ish modern. Standard but good cuisine is served in a big-windowed dining room, where most Danish-style dinners conclude with live music, dancing, or some form of entertainment.

Boulevarden 9, DK-3730 Nexø. © 56-49-49-49. Fax 56-49-49-48. 95 units, half with kitchenettes. 975DKK–1,095DKK ($166–$186/£88–£99) double without kitchenette; 1,050DKK–1,315DKK ($179–$224/£95–£118) double with kitch-enette. Rates include breakfast and dinner. MC, V. From Nexø, drive 2.5km (1½ miles) south along the coastal road, following the signs to Balka and Dueodde. **Amenities:** Restaurant; bar; outdoor heated pool; tennis court; sauna; 24-hr. room service; laundry service/dry cleaning; nonsmoking rooms; rooms for those w/limited mobility. *In room:* TV, dataport, hair dryer.

FROM NEXØ TO ALLINGE
Nexø, with a year-round population of 3,900, is the island's largest fishing port. It's home to excellent replicas of the privately owned 17th- and 18th-century buildings that were considered architectural highlights of the island before World War II. In

May 1945, several days after the rest of Denmark had been liberated from the Nazis, the Russians bombed Nexø heavily for 2 days. It had been a final holdout of Nazi soldiers during the closing days of the war. (Bornholm was also the last area of Denmark to get rid of its Soviet "liberators," who didn't completely evacuate until 1946.)

One of the town's more eccentric monuments is the **Nexø Museum,** Havnen (© **56-49-25-56**), open daily May to October 10am to 4pm. For an entrance fee of 35DKK ($5.95/£3.15), you'll see displays of fishing-related equipment that has sustained the local economy, and memorabilia of the Danish author Martin Andersen (1869–1954)—better known as Martin Andersen Nexø, a pen name he adopted in honor of his native village. His novel *Pelle the Conqueror,* set in Bornholm and later made into an Oscar-winning film, revealed how Danish landowners in the early 20th century exploited Swedish newcomers to the island. Admittedly, this is hardly a subject that interests most people, and you may want to pass it by in favor of outdoor fun, which is what Bornholm is all about.

Continue 5.5km (3½ miles) north along the coastal road, following the signs to **Svaneke.** Denmark's easternmost settlement has fewer than 1,200 year-round residents. It bears some resemblance to eastern regions of the Baltic with which it has traded, and it has many 17th- and 18th-century cottages along cobblestone streets leading to the harbor. Many writers, sculptors, and painters buy homes in Svaneke, an idyllic retreat from the urban life of Copenhagen. Svaneke is the most photogenic town on Bornholm; in 1975 it won the European Gold Medal for town preservation.

From Svaneke, leave the Baltic coastline and head inland through the northern outskirts of the third largest forest in Denmark, the **Almindingen.** Dotted with creeks and ponds, and covered mostly with hardy conifers, it's known for its wildflowers—especially lilies-of-the-valley—and well-designated hiking trails. Then, head for **Østermarie,** a village of about 40 relatively nondescript buildings. Three kilometers (2 miles) northwest of Østermarie is the more culturally significant **Østerlars,** home to the largest of the island's distinctive round churches, the **Østerlarskirke,** Gudhjemsveg 28 (© **56-49-82-64;** bus: 9 from Gudhjem). It's open early April to mid-October, Monday to Saturday 9am to 5pm, charging 10DKK ($1.70/90p) adults (free for children) to enter. The Vikings originally built it around 1150, using rocks, boulders, and stone slabs. The church was dedicated to St. Laurence and later enlarged with chunky-looking buttresses; it was intended to serve in part as a fortress against raids by Baltic pirates. Inside are several wall paintings that date from around 1350, depicting scenes from the life of Jesus.

From Østerlars, drive 3.2km (2 miles) north, following the signs to **Gudhjem (God's Home),** a steeply inclined town that traded with the Hanseatic League during the Middle Ages. Most of its population died of the plague in 1653 and 1654, but the town was repopulated some years later by Danish guerrilla fighters and sympathizers following territorial wars with Sweden. You'll find a town with many fig and mulberry trees and steep slopes that give it a vaguely Mediterranean flavor.

SEEING THE SIGHTS IN GUDHJEM

Especially charming are Gudhjem's 18th-century half-timbered houses and the 19th-century smokehouses, known for their distinctive techniques of preserving herring with alderwood smoke. Its harbor, blasted out of the rocky shoreline in the 1850s, is the focal point for the town's 1,200 permanent residents.

Gudhjem Museum   Frankly, we find the temporary art exhibits and the outdoor sculptures more intriguing than the permanent collection of locomotives and other rail-related memorabilia housed here. Its exhibits depict the now-defunct rail line that once crisscrossed the island.

Stationsvej 1. ⓒ **56-48-54-62.** Admission 25DKK ($4.25/£2.25), 10DKK ($1.70/90p) children. Mid-May to mid-Sept Mon–Sat 10am–5pm; Sun 2–5pm. Closed mid-Sept to mid-May.

Landsbrugs Museum (Bornholm Agricultural Museum)   Inside a timbered, thatch-roof farmhouse originally built in 1796, you're taken in the world of Bornholm farmers, a sort of Ma and Pa Kettle exhibition with pigs, goats, cows, and barnyard fowl similar to those that were bred on the island a century ago. The farmhouse and its surrounding garden is a journey back in time. You can see the brightly colored interior of the house as it was in the 19th century, complete with farm implements. Among the Danish woolen sweaters and wooden spoons made locally and sold on site is the best homemade mustard we've ever tasted in Denmark.

Melstedvej 25 (1km/½ mile south of Gudhjem). ⓒ **56-48-55-98.** Admission 30DKK ($5.10/£2.70) adults, 10DKK ($1.70/90p) children. Mid-May to mid-Oct Tues–Sun 10am–5pm. Closed mid-Oct to mid-May.

CONTINUING ON TO ALLINGE

To get to Allinge (15km/9 miles) from Gudhjem, proceed west along the coastal road, enjoying dramatic vistas over granite cliffs and sometimes savage seascapes. The entire coastline is known as **Helligdoms Klipperne (Cliffs of Sanctuary)**, for the survivors of the many ships that foundered along this granite coastline over the centuries.

Midway along the route you'll see the island's newest museum, the **Bornholms Kunstmuseet (Art Museum of Bornholm)**, Helligdommen (ⓒ **56-48-43-86**), which opened in 1993 and contains the largest collection of works by Bornholm artists. It's open June to August daily 10am to 5pm; April, May, September and October, Tuesday to Sunday 10am to 5pm; November to March, Tuesday and Thursday 1 to 5pm, Sunday 10am to 5pm. Admission is 50DKK ($8.50/£4.50) adults, free for children ages 15 and under. From the rocky bluff where the museum sits, you can see the isolated island of **Christiansø** (see below), about 11km (7 miles) offshore, home to about 120 year-round residents, most of whom make their living from the sea.

Continue driving northwest until you reach the twin communities of **Allinge** and **Sandvig.** Allinge's architecture is noticeably older than that of Sandvig. The 200- and 300-year-old half-timbered houses were built for the purveyors of the herring trade, and the smokehouses preserved the fish for later consumption or for export abroad. The newer town of Sandvig, to the northwest, flourished around the turn of the 20th century, when many ferries connected it with Sweden, and became a stylish beach resort. The woods that surround the twin communities are known as the **Trolleskoe (Forest of Trolls),** home to wart-covered and phenomenally ugly magical creatures that delight in brewing trouble, mischief, and the endless fog that sweeps over this end of the island.

From Allinge, detour inland (southward) for about 4km (2½ miles) to reach **Olsker,** site of the **Olskirke (Round Church of Ols),** Lindesgordsvej (ⓒ **56-48-05-29**). Built in the 1100s, it's the smallest of the island's round churches and was painstakingly restored in the early 1950s. Dedicated to St. Olav (Olav the Holy, king of Norway, who died in 1031), it looks something like a fortress—an image the original architects wanted very much to convey.

Now double back to Allinge and head north toward Sandvig, a distance of about a kilometer (less than a mile). You'll soon see **Madsebakke,** a well-signposted open-air site that contains the largest collection of Bronze Age rock carvings in Denmark. There's no building, enclosed area, or even curator. Simply follow the signs beside the main highway. The carvings include 11 depictions of high-prowed sailing ships of unknown origin. The carvings were made in a smooth, glacier-scoured piece of bedrock close to the side of the road.

From here, proceed just over a mile to the island's northernmost tip, **Hammeren,** for views that—depending on the weather—may extend all the way to Sweden. Here you'll see the island's oldest lighthouse, **Hammerfyr** (1871).

WHERE TO STAY IN SANDVIG

Strandhotellet *(Finds* Though it was originally built as a house of stables in 1896, it was converted a decade later into the largest and most stylish hotel in Bornholm. That glory is long gone, but the venerable old hotel is a worthy detour for diners who drive from other parts of the island, and the three floors of spartan accommodations, with exposed birch wood and (in most cases) sea views, offer well-maintained bathrooms with tub/shower combos.

Strandpromenaden 7, DK-3770 Sandvig. ⓒ 56-48-03-14. Fax 56-48-02-09. 49 units. 650DKK–950DKK ($111–$162/£59–£86) double; 900DKK–1,400DKK ($153–$238/£81–£126) suite. AE, DC, MC, V. **Amenities:** Restaurant; bar; sauna. *In room:* TV.

WHERE TO DINE IN SANDVIG

Strandhotellet Restaurant DANISH/SEAFOOD   Today's hotel dining room, attracting both residents and visitors to the island, grew out of a 1930s dance hall and supper club that once flourished here. The chefs have to import a lot of their produce, but use whatever is fresh at the local markets. The smoked filet of wild salmon with a savory tomato tapenade got us off to a fine start and was followed by a platter of various fish, the actual dish varying depending on the catch of the day. The meat lovers will enjoy the beef medallions with a ragout of fresh vegetables.

Strandpromenaden 7, Sandvig. ⓒ 56-48-03-14. Main courses 59DKK–69DKK ($10–$12/£5.30–£6.20) at lunch, 93DKK–130DKK ($16–$22/£8.40–£12) at dinner. AE, DC, MC, V. Daily noon–10pm.

FROM ALLINGE & SANDVIG BACK TO RØNNE

For your final adventure, turn south, following the signs pointing to Rønne. After less than a kilometer (½ mile) you'll see the rocky crags of a semiruined fortress that Bornholmers believe is the most historically significant building on the island—the **Hammershus Fortress** *(*, begun in 1255 by the archbishop of Lund (Sweden). He planned this massive fortress to reinforce his control of the island. Since then, however, the island has passed from Swedish to German to Danish hands several times; it was a strategic powerhouse controlling what was then a vitally important sea lane. The decisive moment came in 1658, when the Danish national hero Jens Kofoed murdered the Swedish governor and sailed to Denmark to present the castle (and the rest of the island) to the Danish king.

Regrettably, the fortress's dilapidated condition was caused by later architects, who used it as a rock quarry to supply the stone used to construct some of the buildings and streets (including Hovedvagten) of Rønne, as well as several of the structures on Christiansø, the tiny island 11km (6¾ miles) northeast of Bornholm. The systematic destruction of the fortress ended in 1822, when it was "redefined" as a Danish national treasure. Much of the work that restored the fortress to the eerily jagged condition you'll see today was completed in 1967. Hammershus escaped the fate of the second-most-powerful fortress on the island, Lilleborg. Set deep in Bornholm's forests, Lilleborg was gradually stripped of its stones for other buildings after its medieval defenses became obsolete.

Some 4km (2½ miles) south of Hammershus—still on the coastal road heading back to Rønne—is a geological oddity called **Jons Kapel** (Jon's Chapel); it can be seen by anyone who'd like to take a short hike (less than 1km/½ mile) from the highway. The rocky bluff has a panoramic view over the island's western coast, where, according to ancient legend, an agile but reclusive hermit, Brother Jon, preached to the seagulls and crashing surf below. To get here, follow the signs from the highway.

To get back to Rønne, continue southward another 13km (8 miles), passing through the hamlet of **Hasle** en route.

3 Jutland

Dramatically different from the rest of Denmark, Jutland ("Jylland" in Danish) is a peninsula of heather-covered moors, fjords, farmland, lakes, and sand dunes. Besides its major tourist centers—Ribe in the south, Århus and Aalborg (Ålborg) in the north—it has countless old inns and undiscovered towns.

Jutland borders the North Sea, the Skagerrak, and the Kattegat. It extends 400km (250 miles) from the northern tip, Skagen, to the German border in the south. The North Sea washes up on many kilometers of sandy beaches, making this a popular vacation spot.

The meadows are filled with rich bird life and winding rivers; nature walks are a popular pastime. The heart of Jutland is mainly beech forest and lake country, sprinkled with modest-size towns and light industry. Steep hills surround the deep fjords of the east coast. Gabled houses in the marshlands of southern Jutland add to the peninsula's charm. Two of the most popular vacation islands are Rømø and Fanø, off the southwest coast. Here, many traditional homes of fishermen and ship captains have been preserved.

Our driving tour of Jutland begins at Ribe. If you're arriving in east Jutland from Copenhagen, take Route 32 west. From mainland Europe, take Route 11 from Tønder. Esbjerg is connected to Ribe by Route 24, which joins Route 11 south.

RIBE 𝒜𝒜

32km (20 miles) S of Esbjerg, 300km (186 miles) W of Copenhagen

This is one of Denmark's oldest towns, and if you have to miss all the other cities of Jutland, spend a night here, where local residents ask, "Will the storks return on April 1?" Every year some wood storks—now an endangered species—fly to Ribe to build their huge nests on top of the red-roofed, medieval, half-timbered, and crooked houses, which flank the narrow cobblestone lanes.

One of New York's most legendary citizens, Jacob A. Riis, was born in Ribe. When "the town's prettiest girl" broke his heart, he headed for New York in 1870. Once here, he was shocked by the city's inhumane slums, which he wrote about in his first book in 1890, *How the Other Half Lives*. A friend of Theodore Roosevelt, Riis was offered the job of mayor of the city, but turned it down to pursue his efforts to get a million people off the streets and into decent housing. For such work, he became known as "the most beneficial citizen of New York." In time, he returned to Ribe where "the prettiest girl" said yes this time. His former residence lies at the corner of Skolegade and Grydergade, a plaque marking his former abode.

As a former port, Ribe was an important trading center during the Viking era (around A.D. 900) and became an Episcopal seat in 948, when one of the first Christian churches in Denmark was established here. It was also the royal residence of the ruling Valdemars around 1200.

In medieval days, sea-trade routes to England, Germany, Friesland, the Mediterranean, and other ports linked Ribe, but then its waters receded. Today it's surrounded by marshes, much like a landlocked Moby Dick. On a charming note, the town watchman still makes his rounds—armed with his lantern and trusty staff—since the ancient custom was revived in 1936.

ESSENTIALS

GETTING THERE   By Train & Bus   There's hourly train service from Copenhagen (via Bramming). The schedules of both trains and buses are available at the tourist office.

By Car   From Kolding, head west across Jutland on the motorway (E-20), and cut southwest when you reach Route 32, which will carry you into Ribe.

VISITOR INFORMATION   The **Ribe Turistbureau,** Torvet 3 (© **75-42-15-00;** www.ribetourist.dk), is open June 15 to August, Monday to Saturday 9:30am to 5:30pm, and Sunday 10am to 2pm; April to June 14 and September to October, Monday to Friday 9am to 5pm and Saturday 10am to 1pm; and November to March, Monday to Friday 9:30am to 4:30pm and Saturday 10am to 1pm.

GETTING AROUND   By Bicycle   If you'd like to bike your way around the area, you can rent bikes for 60DKK ($10/£5.40) at **Ribe Vandrerhjem** (Youth Hostel), Skt. Pedersgade 16 (© **75-42-06-20**).

SEEING THE SIGHTS

Det Gamle Rådhus (Town Hall Museum)   Originally built in 1496, the Town Hall Museum today houses some rather unimpressive artifacts and archives off Ribe's illustrious past. These include a 16th-century gruesome executioner's axe, ceremonial swords, the town's money chest, antique tradesmen's signs, and a depiction of the "iron hand," still a symbol of police authority. Perhaps the most exciting thing to look is storks building a nest on the top of the building.

Von Støckends Plads. © **79-89-89-55**. Admission 15DKK ($2.55/£1.35) adults, 5DKK (85¢/45p) children 7–14, free for children under 7. June–Aug daily 1–3pm; May and Sept Mon–Fri 1–3pm. Closed Oct–Apr.

Ribe Domkirke ✮✮   Denmark's earliest wooden church, built around A.D. 860, once stood on this spot. In 1150 it was rebuilt in the Romanesque style, opening onto the main square of town, but over the years has been remodeled and altered considerably. The **south portal** ✮ remains a rare example of Danish Romanesque sculpture and is known for its carved tympanum depicting the *Descent of Christ from the Cross*. Most of the *kirke* was built of a soft porous rock (tufa) found near the German city of Cologne and shipped north along the Rhine River. It took 100 years for the Dom to be completed. The church features a wide nave flanked by aisles, a dome roof, and gothic arches. The interior holds treasures from many eras, including mosaics, stained glass, and frescoes in the eastern apse by the artist Carl-Henning Pedersen, who created them in the 1980s. Older treasures include an organ from the 1600s and an elaborate altar from 1597.

The Devil, or so it is said, used to enter the Domkirke through the **"Cat's Head Door"** 𝔊𝔊, once the principal entryway into the church, found at the south portal of the transept. The triangular pediment depicts Valdemar II and his queen, Dagmar, positioned at the feet of Mary and her infant son. Daily at noon and 3pm the cathedral bell still tolls in mourning of Dagmar's death during childbirth.

For the most **panoramic view** 𝔊𝔊 of Ribe and the surrounding marshes, climb the 248 steps to the cathedral tower. A watchman once stood here on the lookout for floods, which frequently inundated Ribe.

Torvet (in the town center off Sønderportsgade). © **75-42-06-19.** www.ribe-domkirke.dk. Admission 12DKK ($2.05/£1.10) adults, 5DKK (85¢/45p) children. June–Aug daily 10am–5:30pm; May and Sept daily 10am–5pm; Oct–Apr Mon–Sat 11am–3pm, Sun 1–3pm.

Ribe Kunstmuseet
Of minor interest, this museum, with its more than 600 paintings and sculptures, is dedicated to acquiring art from various epochs in Danish history, from 1750 to 1940. There are masterpieces from artists from all the major eras in Danish painting—the Golden Age, the Realistic Period, the Skagen and Funen artists, Modernism, and the period "between the wars." The museum is housed in a stately villa in a garden on the Ribe River, the former resident of a factory owner.

Skt. Nicolai Gade 10. © **75-42-03-62.** Admission 40DKK ($6.80/£3.60) adults, free for children under 16. Sept–June Tues–Sun 11am–4pm; July–Aug Tues–Sun 11am–5pm. Closed Jan 1–Feb 11.

Ribes Vikinger (Museum of the Viking Age and the Middle Ages in Ribe)
This museum showcases Ribe in both its Viking era and its medieval epoch. Beginning in the year of 700, when a marketplace was established on the banks of the Ribe River, thousands of archaeological finds have been dug up to reveal how the Vikings lived and traded with Europe to the south. Pottery and skeletons are exhibited from the Middle Ages, and the re-created Debtors' Prison reveals how harsh justice was, with its spiked maces, thumbscrews, and executioner's swords. Most bizarre of all is a multimedia room, Wodan's Eye, where you can explore the Viking age via computer, lights, and sound.

Odins Plads. © **76-88-11-22.** www.ribesvikinger.dk. Admission 60DKK ($10/£5.40) adults, free children 14 and under, family ticket 130DKK ($22/£12). Apr–June and Sept–Oct daily 10am–4pm; July–Aug Thurs–Tues 10am–6pm, Wed 10am–9pm; Nov–Mar Tues–Sun 10am–4pm.

Skt. Catharine Kirke 𝔊
The Spanish Black Friars (Dominicans) came to Ribe in 1228 and began constructing a church and chapter house (the east wing of a monastery). Parts of the original edifice can still be seen, particularly the southern wall. The present church, near Dagmarsgade, with nave and aisles, dates from 1400 to 1450, the tower from 1617. Only the monks' stalls and the Romanesque font remain from the Middle Ages, with the delicately carved pulpit dating from 1591, the ornate altarpiece from 1650. The brothers were kicked out in 1536 at the time of the Reformation, and in time the complex became both an asylum for the mentally ill and later a wartime field hospital. You can walk through the cloisters and see ship models and religious paintings hanging in the southern aisle. Tombstones of Ribe citizens from the Reformation and later can be seen along the outer walls of the church.

Skt. Catharine's Plads. © **75-42-05-34.** Free admission to church; cloisters 5DKK (85¢/45p) adults, 1DKK (17¢/9p) children under 14. May–Sept daily 10am–noon and 2–5pm; Oct–Apr daily 10am–noon and 2pm–4pm. Closed during church services.

A SIDE TRIP TO RØMØ ⊛

Rømø, the largest Danish island in the North Sea, is about 9km (5½ miles) long and 6.5km (4 miles) wide. It has a certain appeal because of its wild, windswept appearance. In the summer it attracts lots of tourists (especially Germans), possibly because of the nude sunbathing. In the off season it's one of the sleepiest places in Europe, making it great for rest and relaxation.

To reach Rømø, take the 9.5km (6-mile) stone causeway from mainland Jutland. Or take a bus south from Ribe to Skaerbaek, and then bus no. 29 across the tidal flats.

WHERE TO STAY

Den Gamle Arrest ⊛⊛ *Finds*   No other hotel on Jutland's peninsula has done a better job of spinning its old life into something new. This previous town jail is now a charming hotel, made from the same bricks as the town's more prestigious addresses. Located on the main town square, the hotel's former life is evident in a few of the cramped "jail cells" and the brick wall on the grounds that bears the prisoners' inscriptions. However, the ground floor boasts a bridal suite with four-poster bed and a garden with roses, fountains, and stone sculptures.

Torvet 11, DK-6760 Ribe. ℂ 75-42-37-00. Fax 75-42-37-22. www.dengamlearrest.dk. 12 units, 2 with bathroom. 565DKK–765DKK ($96–$130/£51–£69) double without bathroom; 855DKK–965DKK ($145–$164/£77–£87) double with bathroom. Rates include breakfast. No credit cards. **Amenities:** Restaurant; bar. *In room:* TV (in some), no phone.

Hotel Dagmar ⊛⊛⊛   The most famous hotel in Denmark outside Copenhagen is also the oldest in the country, dating from 1581. Converted from a private home in 1850, it's also the most glamorous hotel in South Jutland, taking its name from the medieval Danish queen. The bedrooms have been carefully restored, respecting the hotel's age while adding modern conveniences. Most of the units, as befits a building of this vintage, have low ceilings, sloping floors, and windows with deep sills. Textiles are in autumnal colors, and the walls are decorated with original paintings. Each bedroom is also individually decorated and comes in various shapes and sizes. Some of the rooms are equipped with shower-only bathrooms, while others may have old-fashioned bathtubs with sitz baths or phones in the bathrooms. Dagmar also offers the best food in Ribe (see "Where to Dine," below).

Torvet 1, DK-6760 Ribe. ℂ 75-42-00-33. Fax 75-42-36-52. www.hoteldagmar.dk. 50 units. 1,125DKK–1,525DKK ($191–$259/£101–£137) double. Rates include breakfast. AE, DC, MC, V. **Amenities:** 3 restaurants; bar; room service (7am–10pm); laundry service/dry cleaning; nonsmoking rooms. *In room:* TV, minibar, hair dryer, safe.

Hotel Fru Mathies *Value*   For those who like to travel the B&B route, this is one of the best—and most affordable—choices in town. Set behind a bright yellow stucco facade, a very short walk from the city's pedestrian zone, this hotel was named after its present guardian and supervisor, Fru (Mrs.) Inga Mathies. There's a shared TV/living room on the premises, and the small bedrooms are simple but cozy affairs, each with a bathroom equipped with a tub/shower combo and modest numbers of old-fashioned accessories. Breakfast is the only meal served, and it's generous and satisfying.

Saltgade 15, DK-67660 Ribe. ℂ 75-42-34-20. 6 units, 4 with bathroom. 590DKK ($100/£53) double without bathroom; 640DKK ($109/£58) double with bathroom. Rates include breakfast. AE, DC, MC, V. **Amenities:** Breakfast room; bar; lounge. *In room:* TV, minibar, no phone.

WHERE TO DINE

Restaurant Backhaus DANISH   This place has served as a restaurant or an inn for as long as anyone in Ribe can remember. Today, steaming platters of all-Danish food arrive in generous portions at reasonable prices. Menu specialties include a Danish platter containing artfully arranged presentations of herring, cheeses, and vegetables that taste wonderful with the establishment's earthy, rough-textured bread. Tomato soup with sour cream comes with a surprising but refreshing dab of horseradish. The chef tells us that the most frequently ordered dish is tender pork schnitzels with boiled potatoes and braised red cabbage. However, we found that the sautéed strips of beef tenderloin with fried onions hit the spot on a cold, windy, rainy day. Dessert might be a hazelnut pie with vanilla ice cream.

On the premises are seven simple rooms, stripped down but comfortable and well maintained. With breakfast included, doubles cost 500DKK ($85/£45). With the exception of about a week every year at Christmas, the hotel is open year-round.

Grydergade 12, DK-6760 Ribe. ℂ **75-42-11-01.** Reservations recommended. Main courses 100DKK–170DKK ($17–$29/£9–£15). MC, V. Daily 11am–9:30pm.

Restaurant Dagmar ✿✿ DANISH/INTERNATIONAL

Honoring a beloved medieval queen, this restaurant opposite the cathedral is a major address and stopover for those making the gastronomic tour of Denmark. Its four dining rooms are a 19th-century "dream" of ornate furnishings and objets d'art, a tribute to the heyday of the Belle Epoque era. In such fancy surroundings, they could get away with ordinary food, but the chefs showcase a varied cuisine that is refreshingly authentic and based on the best of market-fresh ingredients in any season. Care, craftsmanship, and a concern for your palate go into every dish served by the best waitstaff in town.

We usually opt for one of the two fresh North Sea fish dishes of the day, but we also like the scallops topped with a sweet-potato crisp, and in autumn we go for the sautéed stuffed quail with mushrooms accompanied by a *beurre blanc* sauce. We feel the chefs shine brighter with their regional cuisine, but they also borrow freely from international larders, serving tender veal tenderloin with one of the tastiest Shallow Mousse we've ever sampled and a delectable port wine sauce.

In the Hotel Dagmar, Torvet 1. ℂ **75-42-00-33.** Reservations required. Main courses 165DKK–265DKK ($28–$45/£15–£24); fixed-price lunch 200DKK ($34/£18). AE, DC, MC, V. Daily noon–10pm.

Restaurant Saelhunden ✿ DANISH/INTERNATIONAL

One of the most evocative and cheerful restaurants in Ribe occupies a venerable but cozy brick building whose history dates from 1634. Set beside the river that flows through the city, the restaurant has flourished since 1969 and has a staff that, like the menu, comes from throughout Europe. The cuisine is based on fresh ingredients and, for the most part, sticks to tried-and-true favorites so beloved by the Danish palate, including smoked salmon or platters of Ping-Pong sized meatballs. The dish that most locals seem to order is the fried filets of plaice with boiled potatoes. Other items include at least three kinds of steaks that feature T-bone, French-style entrecôte, and something known as "English steak." A local delicacy is smoked and fried dab, a flat fish not unlike flounder that flourishes in the local estuaries. No one will mind if you come here just for a beer or a simple snack. In summertime, it mirrors a beer garden in Hamburg with an outdoor terrace.

Skibbroen 13. ℂ **75-42-09-46.** Reservations recommended. Main courses 136DKK–210DKK ($23–$36/£12–£19). MC, V. Daily 11am–10pm. Beer served till 11pm.

Weis Stue ✿ DANISH

For old-fashioned dining in a mellow atmosphere, there is no better place in Ribe than this small, charming, brick-and-timber inn on the market square near the cathedral and the Hotel Dagmar, which owns it. The food in this ground-floor restaurant is plentiful and well prepared, based on the best from field, air, and stream. We like the marinated herring with raw onions and the always divine little shrimp they served with mayonnaise. For something more substantial, we feast on smoked Greenland halibut with scrambled eggs, a local favorite, as is the liver paste with mushrooms. For more standard dishes, you can order a very good filet of beef flavored with onions. We end with a selection of Danish cheese.

The inn also has four guest rooms that are cozy, but don't have private bathrooms. A double costs 645DKK ($110/£58), including breakfast.

Torvet 2, DK-6760 Ribe. © 75-42-07-00. Reservations recommended. Main courses 140DKK–195DKK ($24–$33/£13–£18); 2-course fixed-price menu 158DKK ($27/£14). AE, DC, MC, V. Daily 11am–10pm.

FANØ 🐦🐦
47km (29 miles) NW of Ribe, 283km (176 miles) W of Copenhagen

Off the coast of South Jutland, Fanø, at least in our view, is the most beautiful of all North Sea islands—and we've sailed to all of them. It is the one place in Denmark which we most prefer for some R&R. Come here to enjoy the outdoors and nature, ducking into the man-made attractions only if it's a rainy day.

Consisting of a landmass of some 54 sq. km (21 sq. miles), with a population of 3,500, Fanø is known for its white sandy beaches, which have made it a popular summer resort. Set against a backdrop of dunes heath, the best beaches are in the northwest, mostly in and around the hamlets of Rindby Strand and Fanø Bad.

Nordby, where the ferry arrives, is a logical starting point for exploring the island. Here you'll find heather-covered moors, windswept sand dunes, fir trees, wild deer, and bird sanctuaries. From Ribe, Fanø makes for a great day's excursion (or longer if there's time).

Sønderho, on the southern tip, and only 14km (8½ miles) from Nordby, with its memorial to sailors drowned at sea, is our favorite spot—somewhat desolate, but that's its charm.

It was a Dutchman who launched Denmark's first bathing resort at Nordby in 1851. It consisted of a raft on which some bathing huts had been set up. The bathers entered the huts, undressed, put on different clothes, pulled down an awning to the water's surface, and bathed under the awning. How modest of them.

Until 1741 Fanø belonged to the king, who, when he ran short of money, sold the island at an auction. The islanders themselves purchased it, and the king then granted permission for residents to build ships, which led to its prosperity. From 1741 to 1900, some 1,000 sailing vessels were constructed here, with the islanders often manning them as well. Inhabitants built many beautiful houses on Fanø with monies earned, and some of these charming, thatched homes still stand today. There are some in the northern settlement of Nordby, but more gems are found in the south at Sønderho.

Although Nordby and Sønderho are the principal settlements, beach lovers head for the seaside resort of **Fanø Bad,** which is also a popular camping area. From Fanø Bad the beach stretches almost 4km (2½ miles) to the north. Bathing here is absolutely safe as a sandy bottom slopes gently into the North Sea, and there are no ocean holes or dangerous currents.

Fanø adheres to old island traditions more than any other island in Denmark, with the exception of Ærø. As late as the 1960s, some of the elderly women on Fanø still wore the "Fanø costume," which originally consisted of five skirts, but today's costumes are likely to have only three. When the skirt was to be pleated, it was wet, laced up, and sent to the baker, who steamed it in a warm oven. Today you'll see it only at special events and festivals.

ESSENTIALS

GETTING THERE **By Car & Ferry** From Ribe, head north on Route 11 to Route 24. Follow Route 24 northwest to the city of Esbjerg, where you can board a ferry operated by **Scandlines** (☎ **70-10-17-44;** www.scandlines.dk for information and schedules). May to October, ferries depart Esbjerg every 20 minutes during the day (trip time: 12 min.). In winter, service is curtailed, with departures during the day every 45 minutes. A round-trip ticket costs 30DKK ($5.10/£2.70) adults or 15DKK ($2.55/£1.35) children, and one average-size car, along with five passengers, is carried for 340DKK ($58/£31) round-trip.

VISITOR INFORMATION The **Fanø Turistbureau,** Færgevej 1, Nordby (☎ **75-16-26-00**), is open Monday to Friday 9am to 4pm, Saturday 9am to 1pm, and Sunday 11am to 1pm, except from June 6 to August 23, when hours are Monday to Friday 9am to 6pm, Saturday 9am to 7pm, and Sunday 9am to 5pm.

WHERE TO STAY & DINE

Hotel Fanø Badeland *(Kids* This hotel takes no chances with the likely possibility that fog or rain might ruin the swimming. Although it sits on Fanø's western edge, close to one of the best beaches on the island, it has the added benefit of a glass-enclosed complex of indoor pools creating. Located 3.2km (2 miles) south of the hamlet of Nordby, the hotel was built amidst windswept scrubland. The midsize rooms are urban-looking, minimalist, and angular, with well-kept shower-only bathrooms and small kitchenettes nestled into the corners of the living rooms. Each has either one or two bedrooms outfitted with simple, durable furniture and no-nonsense accessories. The atmosphere is rather impersonal, but it's perfectly suited for families who want to spend most of their time outdoors. You'll pay an additional 65DKK ($11/£5.85) per person for a package containing sheets and towels; otherwise, bring your own.

Strandvejen 52–56, DK-6720 Fanø. ☎ **75-16-60-00.** Fax 75-16-60-11. www.fanoebadeland.dk. 126 units, each with kitchenette. 820DKK–945DKK ($139–$161/£74–£85) 1-bedroom unit for up to 4 occupants; 925DKK–1,225DKK ($157–$208/£83–£110) 2-bedroom unit for up to 6 occupants. Discounts offered for stays of 5 nights or more. MC, V. Bus: 631. **Amenities:** Restaurant; bar; swimming complex; tennis court; fitness center; sauna; room service (8am–10pm); laundry service/dry cleaning. *In room:* TV.

Sønderho Kro *(Kids Kids Kids* Dating from 1722, hosts Niels and Birgt Steen Sørensen run one of Denmark's oldest and most charming inns. A Relais & Châteaux lodging, the thatch-roof inn in the heart of the village of Sønderho is the best we've ever encountered in South Jutland.

The building is under the protection of the National Museum, which closely supervised its expansion in 1977. Each of the bedrooms comes in a different shape and size, and each is individually decorated in a tasteful way, complete with a modern private bathroom with tub/shower combo. The windows open onto views over a nearby dike, the marshlands, and the North Sea. Lace curtains, lovely tapestries, and four-poster beds add to the old-fashioned allure.

Guests congregate in the first-floor lounge, opening onto views of tidal flats, or in the beautiful garden. The inn lies 13km (8 miles) south of the Nordby ferry dock, where a bus carries nonmotorists the final distance into Sønderho.

Kropladsen 11, Sønderho, DK-6720 Fanø. ℂ **75-16-40-09.** Fax 75-16-43-85. www.sonderhokro.dk. 13 units. 1,030DKK–1,410DKK ($175–$240/£93–£127) double. Rates include full breakfast. AE, DC, MC, V. Free parking. **Amenities:** Restaurant; lounge; room service (7am–10pm); laundry service/dry cleaning. *In room:* TV, hair dryer.

ÅRHUS ⍟

160km (99 miles) NE of Fanø, 175km (109 miles) W of Copenhagen

It's "the world's smallest city," but happens to be the second largest city in Denmark and the capital of Jutland. Because Copenhagen is so far to the east, Århus has also been called "the capital of the West." A large student population makes for a vast cultural life, which reaches its peak in late summer when visitors flock here for an arts festival.

There is a lot to see and do here, and rather than spent time in man-made attractions we like to visit the city's bars, the best in Jutland, and its sidewalk cafes. There are sandy beaches nearby and a number of museums, but the best way to experience Århus life is by walking its cobblestone streets and having a picnic at one of the city parks.

The city's current economic growth is based on communications, the food industry, electronics, textiles, iron and steel, and Danish design, as well as the harbor, which is now the second most important in Denmark, rivaled only by Copenhagen.

Originally Århus was a Viking settlement, founded as early as the 10th century; its original name, Aros, meaning estuary, comes from its position at the mouth of a river, Århus Å. The town experienced rapid growth, and by 948 it had its own bishop. An Episcopal church was built here in 1060, and a cathedral was started at the dawn of the 13th century. This prosperity came to a temporary end in the late Middle Ages, when the town was devastated by the bubonic plague. The Reformation of 1536 also slowed the growth of Århus. But the coming of the railway in the 19th century renewed prosperity, which continues to this day. Try to plan at least a full day and night here—or two if you can spare the time.

ESSENTIALS

GETTING THERE   By Plane   Århus Airport is in Tirstrup, 43km (27 miles) northeast of the city. **SAS** (ℂ **800/221-2350** in North America, or 70-10-20-00 in Århus; www.aar.dk) operates some 12 flights a day from Copenhagen, Monday to Friday, and about six on Saturday and Sunday. SAS also operates an afternoon flight most days between Århus and London. An airport bus runs between the train depot at Århus and the airport, meeting all major flights. The cost of a one-way ticket is 85DKK ($14/£7.65).

By Train   About five or six trains a day travel between Århus and Copenhagen (trip time: 4½ hr.). Some 20 trains a day connect Aalborg with Århus (1 hr., 40 min.). From Frederikshavn, the North Jutland port and ferry-arrival point from Norway, some 20 trains a day run to Århus (3 hr.).

By Bus   Two daily buses make the run to Århus from Copenhagen (4 hr.).

By Car   From the east, cross Funen on the E-20 express highway, heading north at the junction with the E-45. From the north German border, drive all the way along the E-45. From Frederikshavn and Aalborg in the north, head south along the E-45.

VISITOR INFORMATION   The tourist office, **Tourist Århus,** Bancgårdspladsen 20 (ℂ **87-31-50-10;** www.visitaarhus.com), is open June 26 to September 10 Monday to Friday 9:30am to 6pm, Saturday 9:30am to 5pm, and Sunday 9:30am to 1pm; September 11 to April 30, Monday to Friday 9am to 4pm, Saturday 10am to 1pm; May 1 to June 26 Monday to Friday 9:30am to 5pm and Saturday 10am to 1pm.

GETTING AROUND A regular bus ticket, valid for one ride, can be purchased on the rear platform of all city buses for 17DKK ($2.90/£1.55). You can buy a **tourist ticket** for 50DKK ($8.50/£4.50) at the tourist office or at newsstands throughout the city center. The 24-hour ticket covers an unlimited number of rides within the central city and includes a 2½-hour guided tour of Århus.

SEEING THE SIGHTS

For the best introduction to Århus, head for the town hall's tourist office, where a 2½-hour **sightseeing tour** leaves daily at 10am June 24 to August 31, costing 80DKK ($14/£7.20) per person.

In addition to the major museums listed below, you can also visit two museums on the grounds of Århus University, Nordre Ringgade. They include **Steno Museet,** C. F. Møllers Allé (© **89-42-39-75;** www.stenomuseet.dk.; bus: 2, 3, or 4), which displays exhibits documenting natural science and medicine. You'll see beautiful 19th-century astronomical telescopes, a 1920s surgical room, and some of the first computers made in Denmark in the 1950s. Posters, models, and do-it-yourself experiments, including tests of Galileo's demonstrations of gravity and of electromagnetism, are also on display. In addition, you can walk through an herbal garden with some 250 historical medicinal herbs. There is also a Planetarium, with daily shows Tuesday to Sunday at 11am, 1pm, and 2pm, or Saturday and Sunday at noon and 2pm. Hours for the museum are Tuesday to Sunday 10am to 4pm (until 7pm Oct–Mar). Admission is 45DKK ($7.65/£4.05) and free for ages 17 and under.

Also at the university is a **Naturhistorisk Museum,** Block 210, Universitetsparken (© **86-12-97-77;** www.naturhistoriskmuseum.dk; bus: 2 or 3), filled with mounted animals from all over the world, some of which are displayed in engaging dioramas. The collection of Danish animals, especially birds, is unique within Denmark. Skeletons, minerals, and a display devoted to the evolution of life are some of the other exhibits. It's open daily 10am to 4pm (to 5pm July–Aug). It's closed on Mondays November to March. Admission is 40DKK ($6.80/£3.60) adults, and free for those 17 and under.

Århus Domkirke (Cathedral of St. Clemens) ✦ As European city cathedrals go, the Domkirke at Århus is low on the totem pole. When it was built in 1201 in the Romanesque style, it probably had greater style. But in the 1400s, after a fire, it was rebuilt in the Gothic style, with a soaring 96m (315-ft.) white-washed nave (the longest in Denmark), practically as deep as its spire is tall. The interior is relatively plain, except for one of the few pre-Reformation survivors, a grand **tripartite altarpiece** ✦✦. Behind the altar is a painted glass window, the creation of Emmanuel Vigeland, brother of the more celebrated Gustav Vigeland of Norway. Chalk frescoes from medieval times depict scenes from the Bible in lavender and black, among other colors. Our favorite is a depiction of St. George slaying a dragon to save a princess in distress. Also depicted is the namesake of the church, St. Clement, who drowned with an anchor around his neck, making him the patron saint of sailors. Before you leave, climb the tower for a **panoramic view** ✦✦ over Århus and its surrounding area. (After the cathedral, we suggest a visit to the nearby medievalesque **arcade** at Vestergade 3, with half-timbered buildings, a rock garden, an aviary, and antique interiors.)

Bispetorvet. © **86-20-54-00.** Free admission. May–Sept Mon–Sat 9:30am–4pm; Oct–Apr Mon–Sat 10am–3pm. Bus: 3, 11, 54, or 56.

Den Gamle By ✦✦✦ *Kids* Outside of Copenhagen, this is Denmark's only government-rated three-star museum, a journey back to yesterday that takes you through a

Danish market town as it appeared in olden days. More than 75 historic buildings, many of them half-timbered, were uprooted from various locations throughout the country and placed here to illustrate Danish life from the 16th to the 19th centuries in a re-created botanical garden. The open-air museum differs from similar attractions near Copenhagen and Odense in that the Århus museum focuses more on rural life. Visitors walk through the authentic-looking workshops of bookbinders, carpenters, hatters, and other craftspeople. There is also a pharmacy, a school, and an old-fashioned post office. A popular attraction is the Burgomaster's House, a wealthy merchant's antiques-stuffed, half-timbered home, built at the end of the 16th century. Be sure to see the textile collection and the Old Elsinore Theater, erected in the early 19th century. The museum also houses a collection of china, clocks, delftware, and silverware. Summer music programs are staged, and there's a restaurant, tea garden, bakery, and beer cellar. Many activities and programs are designed especially for kids.

Viborgvej 2. ℭ **86-12-31-88**. www.dengamleby.dk. Admission 80DKK ($14/£7.20) adults. Free children 16 and under. Sept–Oct and Apr–May daily 10am–5pm; Nov–Dec and Feb–Mar daily 10am–4pm; Jan daily 11am–3pm; June–Aug daily 9am–6pm. Bus: 3, 14, or 25.

Rådhuset (Town Hall)   Just before the outbreak of World War II, Arne Jacobsen, one of Denmark's greatest designers, drew up the plans for this Town Hall. Built between 1936 and 1941 to commemorate the 500th anniversary of the Århus charter, it's been the subject of controversy ever since. The outer skeleton of the building evokes scaffolding that was abandoned, although the interior has light, open spaces and plenty of glass. It can be seen only on a guided tour. An elevator (and 346 steps) runs to the top of the 59m (194-ft.) tower, where a carillon occasionally rings. *Note:* The guided tour at 11am includes the tower. The elevator and stairs are open three times a day: 11am, noon, and 2pm.

Rådhuspladsen. ℭ **89-40-20-00**. Admission to tower 5DKK (85¢/45p); guided tour 10DKK ($1.70/90p). Guided tours Mon–Fri 11am. Tower 11am, noon, and 2pm. Closed Sept–June 23. Bus: 3, 4, 5, or 14.

THE MANOR HOUSES OF EAST JUTLAND

Clausholm 🏰🏰   Seventeenth-century Clausholm is a splendid baroque palace, one of the earliest in Denmark. It was commissioned by Frederik IV's chancellor, whose adolescent daughter, Anna Sophie, eloped with the king. When Frederik died, his son by his first marriage banished the queen to Clausholm, where she lived with her court until her death in 1743.

The rooms are basically unaltered, but few of the original furnishings remain. The salons and ballroom feature elaborate stucco ceilings and decorated panels, and an excellent collection of Danish rococo and Empire furnishings has replaced the original pieces. The Queen's Chapel, where Anna Sophie and her court worshipped, is unchanged and contains the oldest organ in Denmark. In 1976, the Italian baroque gardens were reopened, complete with a symmetrically designed fountain system.

Clausholm is about 13km (8 miles) southeast of Randers and 31km (19 miles) north of Århus.

Voldum, Hadsten. ℭ **86-49-16-55**. www.clausholm.dk. Admission (including guided tour) 70DKK ($12/£6.30) adults, free for children under 14. Castle (open only in July) daily 11am–4pm. Park (May–Sept) daily 11am–4pm. Bus: 221 from Randers.

The Museums at Gammel Estrup 🏰   One of the most elegant Renaissance manors in Central Jutland lies 39km (24 miles) northeast of Århus. Today this compound of buildings is the site of the **Jutland Manor House Museum,** complete with a great Hall, a chapel, and richly decorated stucco ceilings, and the **Danish Agricultural Museum,** which celebrates the role of Danish farming over the past thousand years. The entire compound dates from the 14th century, but the structures you see were extensively rebuilt and remodeled in the early 1600s. Expect a glimpse into medieval fortifications, baronial furnishings, the changing nature of tools and machines used during Danish plantings and harvests, and an enormous sense of pride in Denmark and its traditions.

Jyllands Herregårdsmuseum, Randersvej 2, Auning. ⓒ **86-48-30-01.** www.gl-estrup.dk. Admission 70DKK ($12/£6.30) adults, or free ages 17 and under. Agricultural Museum Jan–Mar and Nov–Dec Tues–Sun 10am–3pm; Apr–June and Sept–Oct daily 10am–5pm; July–Aug daily 10am–6pm. Manor House Museum Apr–June and Sept–Oct daily noon–4:30pm; July–Aug daily noon–4:30pm. Bus: 119. From Randers, take Rte. 16 east to Auning.

Rosenholm Slot 𝒢   One of Jutland's stateliest Renaissance manors was built in 1559 on a small island in the middle of a lake. Stone lions guard the bridge that leads to the castle where the Rosenkrantz family has lived for more than 4 centuries. The four-winged castle is encircled by 14 hectares (35 acres) of landscaped parkland. We find Rosenholm far more impressive than the queen's more modest digs at Marselisbourg. The Great Hall is graced with a portrait of King Frederik V, and most of the other salons and galleries are furnished and decorated in a Moorish-inspired Spanish style—or else with rococo adornments (a bit much at times). The Winter Room is walled with leather, and French and Flemish tapestries, some 3 centuries old, adorn the Tower Room and the Corner Room. The location is 21km (13 miles) north of Århus and 1km (½ mile) north of the village of Hornslet.

Hornslet. ⓒ **86-99-40-10.** www.rosenholmslot.dk. Admission 60DKK ($10/£5.40) adults, free for children under 6. June 1–19 Sat–Sun 11am–4pm; June 20–Aug 31 daily 11am–4pm. Closed Sept–May. Bus: 119 or 121 from Århus.

SHOPPING

Århus is the biggest shopping venue in Jutland, with some 400 specialty stores, each of them tightly clustered within an area of about 1¼ sq. km (½ sq. mile). The centerpiece of this district is the Strøget, whose terminus is the Store Torv, dominated by the Århus Domkirke. You might try a large-scale department store first. One of the best is **Salling,** Søndergade 27 (ⓒ **86-12-18-00**), with some 30 specialty boutiques, all under one roof. A wide range of articles for the whole family is sold here, including body-care items, clothing, gifts, toys, music, and sports equipment. **Magasin du Nord,** Immervad 2–8 (ⓒ **86-12-33-00**), is the largest department store in Scandinavia, in business for more than 125 years. The staff will assist visitors with tax-free purchases.

Since 1866, **Georg Jensen,** Søndergade 1 (ⓒ **86-12-01-00**), has been known for style and quality, producing unique silver and gold jewelry, elegant clocks and watches, and stainless steel cutlery, among other items. A leading goldsmith, **Hingelberg,** Store Torv 3 (ⓒ **86-13-13-00**), is the licensed Cartier outlet and offers a wide selection of top-quality designer jewelry.

Galleri Bo Bendixen, Store Torv 14 (ⓒ **86-12-67-50**), offers the brilliant, colored, top-quality designs of Bo Bendixen, the famous Danish graphic artist. The shop also sells a wide range of gifts and garments for children and adults. **Volden 4 Kunsthåndværk,** Volden 4 (ⓒ **86-13-21-76**), specializes in top-quality applied art and glass made by some of the leading artisans of the country. Silver, copper, and brass ornaments are for sale, as are exclusive bronze candlesticks.

Bülow Duus Glassblowers, Studsgade 14 (© **86-12-72-86**), is a working glass-blowing shop that's open to the public. Drinking glasses, candlesticks, bowls, and other items are for sale. For traditional Danish pottery, head for **Favlhuset,** Møllestien 53 (© **86-13-06-32**).

If you still haven't found what you're looking for, head for **Inspiration Buus,** Ryesgade 2 (© **86-12-67-00**), which sells top-quality gifts, kitchenware, tableware, and toiletry articles, much of it of Danish design.

WHERE TO STAY

Low-cost accommodations in this lively university city are limited. Those on a modest budget should check with the tourist office in the Rådhuset (© **87-31-50-10**) for bookings in **private homes.**

Depending on the day of the week or the time of the year you check in, rooms in many of the hotels labeled inexpensive aren't inexpensive at all, but more moderate in price.

Hotel La Tour *(Kids* If you're not too demanding, this is quite a good choice, especially for families on a holiday. Since its construction in 1956 and its rebuilding in 1986, this hotel has followed a conscious policy of downgrading (yes, downgrading) its accommodations and facilities from a once lofty status to a middle-brow formula. The result is a hotel that's far from being the best in town—viewed, we imagine, as a great success by the management. The hotel, housed in an unimaginative two-story building, is 3.5km (2¼ miles) north of Århus center. It offers well-maintained, simple bedrooms with small bathrooms containing tub/shower combos. There is a patio-style restaurant serving competently prepared Danish and international food, a bar, and a children's playroom (open May–Sept only).

Randersvej 139, DK-8200 Århus. © 86-16-78-88. Fax 86-16-79-95. www.latour.dk. 101 units. 825DKK ($140/£74) double; 1,045DKK ($178/£94) suite. Rates include breakfast. AE, DC, MC, V. Bus: 2, 3, or 11. **Amenities:** Restaurant; bar; room service (7am–10pm); laundry service/dry cleaning. *In room:* TV, minibar, hair dryer, safe.

Hotel Royal *(★★★* If you're looking for the best modern facilities, check into the Radisson SAS (see below). But for traditional extravagance and royal luxury, this is the most glamorous accommodation in town, attracting celebs such as Madonna and Sting. The gilt date on its neobaroque facade commemorates the hotel's establishment in 1838. There have been numerous additions and upgrades since. The Royal stands close to the city's symbol, its cathedral. A vintage elevator takes you to the guest rooms, many of them quite spacious. They're modern, with good-size bathrooms containing tub/shower combos. Beds are refurbished and accommodations are fitted with high-quality furniture, carpeting, and fabrics. The ground floor houses the Royal Scandinavian Casino and night club, offering such games of chance as international roulette, black jack, and seven-card stud poker.

Stove Torv 4, DK-8000 Århus. © 86-12-00-11. Fax 86-76-04-04. www.hotelroyal.dk. 102 units. 1,595DKK ($271/£144) double; 1,995DKK ($339/£180) suite. Rates include breakfast. AE, DC, MC, V. Parking 150DKK ($26/£14). Bus: 56 or 58. **Amenities:** Restaurant; bar; sauna; room service (7am–10pm); babysitting; laundry service/dry cleaning; nonsmoking rooms; casino. *In room:* TV, dataport, minibar, hair dryer, beverage maker, Wi-Fi.

Radisson SAS Scandinavia Hotel Århus *(★★★* This is one of the most modern and dynamic hotels in Denmark, and a place that municipal authorities show off to visiting dignitaries. It was built in 1995 above the largest convention facilities in Jutland

and is the most popular convention hotel in the region. Of course, for that reason, we like it less. However, should you arrive when a convention isn't taking place, the hotel can be a honey. Bedrooms occupy floors 4 to 11 of a glass-and-stone-sheathed tower that's visible from around the city. Lower floors contain check-in, dining, drinking, and convention facilities. The standard bedrooms are outfitted in plush upholstery with bright colors. Each has a tasteful decor that's different from its immediate neighbor, incorporating Scandinavian, English, Japanese, or Chinese themes, and each has large-windowed views over the city and a well-kept bathroom with a tub/shower combo. Costing more money are the upgraded business-class rooms, with newspaper delivery, turndown service, and free entrance to the fitness suite.

Margrethepladsen 1, DK-8000 Århus C. ☎ 800/333-3333 in the U.S., or 86-12-86-65. Fax 86-12-86-75. www.radissonsas.com/aarhus.dk. 234 units. 1,540DKK–1,685DKK ($262–$286/£139–£152) double; from 2,260DKK ($384/£203) suite. Rates include breakfast. AE, DC, MC, V. Bus: 1, 2, 6, or 16. **Amenities:** Restaurant; bar; fitness center; sauna; 24-hr. room service; massage; babysitting; laundry service/dry cleaning; nonsmoking rooms; rooms for those w/limited mobility. *In room:* TV, dataport, minibar, hair dryer, safe, trouser press, Wi-Fi.

Scandic Plaza ⊛ *(Kids)* The massive bulk of this chain-run hotel rises imposingly in the heart of the city, and we think it's most reliable and comfortable choice for overnighting, without reaching the pinnacle scaled by the Radisson SAS. It's vastly improved and enlarged since that time since it opened in 1930, but the hotel has never escaped the "chain format" of its bedroom decor. However, furnishings are first class and the decoration is tasteful, with well-maintained private bathrooms with tub/shower combos. The on-site Restaurant Brazil comes as a surprise with its Latin cuisine. Before dinner, head for the cozy bar, where six exotic cocktails await your selection every evening along with the standard beer and liquors. This is one of the best hotels for families traveling with children, as it offers a playroom with games, toys, books, a wood train, and crayons.

Banegårdspladsen 14, DK-8100 Århus C. ☎ 87-32-01-00. Fax 87-32-01-99. www.scandichotels.com/aarhus. 162 units. 1,025DKK–1,695DKK ($174–$288/£92–£153) double; from 1,865DKK ($317/£168) suite. Rates include breakfast. DC, MC, V. Bus: 3, 17, 56, or 58. **Amenities:** Restaurant; bar; fitness center; kids playroom; Jacuzzi; sauna; room service (7:30am–10:30pm); laundry service/dry cleaning; nonsmoking rooms. *In room:* TV, dataport, minibar, hair dryer, iron, safe, Wi-Fi.

WHERE TO DINE

Hotel Philip Restaurant ⊛⊛⊛ DANISH/FRENCH In the most exclusive hotel in Århus, a delightful restaurant is imbued with a romantic atmosphere and serves quality food prepared with the best and freshest of ingredients—an unbeatable combination. Tables are placed on beautiful hardwood floors, are elegantly set, and are lit by brass candleholders. The ceiling is adorned with a metal tapestry in the Art Nouveau style, and the walls are painted dark but brightened with summery yellow ornaments.

Inventiveness goes hand in hand with solid technique, and the kitchen also takes full advantage of the region's riches, with seafood predominating. We like the way the chefs seasonally adjust the menu to take advantage of the best produce—fresh asparagus in late spring, the finest of game dishes in the autumn, and the freshest catch of the day. We can't recommend specific dishes because they are forever changing, but take that standby cannelloni, which the chef stuffs with Serrano ham, seafood, and Danish cheese, and serves with truffles.

Åboulevarden 28. ☎ 87-32-14-44. Reservations required. Main courses 160DKK–200DKK ($27–$34/£14–£18). DC, MC, V. Mon–Sat noon–10:30pm.

Prins Ferdinand (R(R(R DANISH/INTERNATIONAL　This is the only restaurant in town to give Philip (see above) a run for its *kroner*. Its name is actually a reference to the notorious carousing Prince Frederik (1792–1863), who spent most of his nights in Århus gambling or pursuing wine and women. On the edge of Århus's historic center in a former tea salon, this is one of the city's finest restaurants. It was established in 1988 by different owners, but is run today by the hospitable Tonny Hansen and Martin Lemvig, who welcome the local business community and the most discerning of visiting foodies into their lovely *luxe* restaurant. In two pink-toned dining rooms laden with flickering candles and flowers, you can order a platter of fresh smoked salmon served with tartare of salmon and pepper-cream sauce; turbot with Russian caviar and a drizzle of olive oil; or boneless pigeon stuffed with fresh goose liver served with a raspberry sauce. For dessert, we recommend the pears cooked with elderberries and served with vanilla ice cream, nougat, and almonds. The restaurant also has the most unusual array of dessert cheeses in Jutland, which include artisan creations produced by small farmers.

Viborgvej 2. © **86-12-52-05.** Reservations recommended. Main courses 140DKK–175DKK ($24–$30/£13–£16) at lunch, 160DKK–250DKK ($27–$43/£14–£23) at dinner; fixed-price menus 175DKK–235DKK ($30–$40/£16–£21) at lunch, 395DKK–995DKK ($67–$169/£36–£90) at dinner. AE, DC, MC, V. Tues–Sat noon–3pm and 6–9pm. Bus: 3.

Restaurant Margueritten (R *Finds* DANISH/FRENCH/ITALIAN　One of the town's better restaurants was carved out of what used to be stables for horses. This is a cozy place for lunch and an ideal venue for a romantic dinner. Old Danish stripped furniture and beamed ceilings enhance the ambience, and in summer a beautiful little garden in the rear is open. This menu is modern and always uses the freshest regional produce. Chefs offer such dishes as guinea fowl with a stuffing of tiger shrimp; the distinctive flavor comes from the marinade of yogurt and tandoori spices. Some of the best dishes we found on the menu included filet of wild pork with a balsamic chocolate sauce, medallion of beef in a cognac sauce with mixed vegetables, and a tangy breast of duck with a raspberry sauce and fresh plums that have been marinated in port. The English-speaking waitstaff is polite and helpful.

Guldsmedgade 20. © **86-19-60-33.** Reservations required. 1-course fixed-price menu 159DKK ($27/£14), 2 courses 179DKK ($30/£16), 3 courses 209DKK ($36/£19). AE, MC, V. Mon–Sat 11:30am–11pm.

Teater Bodega DANISH　Originally established at a different address in 1907, Teater Bodega moved across the street from both the Århus Dramatic Theater and the Århus Cathedral in 1951. It offers an amusing dining ambience for local actors and theater-goers, its walls covered with illustrations of theater costumes and other thespian memorabilia. The food is solid and flavorful in the Danish country style. Various kinds of Danish hash, including *biksemad,* are served along with regular or large portions of Danish roast beef. Although the beef dishes are good, a waiter assured us that most locals go for a platter of the freshly caught plaice or flounder.

Skolegade 7. © **86-12-19-17.** Reservations recommended. Main courses 89DKK–198DKK ($15–$34/£8–£18); lunch *smørrebrød* 48DKK–89DKK ($8.15–$15/£4.30–£8); 3-course fixed-price lunch or dinner 258DKK ($44/£23). DC, MC, V. Mon–Sat 11am–11:30pm. Bus: 6.

SILKEBORG
44km (27 miles) W of Århus, 280km (174 miles) W of Copenhagen

In the heart of the Danish lake district, this town of 35,000 opens onto the waters of Lake Longsø, where we like to go for a stroll at night to see the largest color fountain in Scandinavia. If you don't like the lake (highly unlikely), there's always the Gudenå River, the longest in Denmark. The Danes themselves come here to go canoeing, hiking through the surrounding hills, or boating on the lake. Silkeborg has some notable attractions, but its natural beauty is just as appealing.

In 1845, Michael Drewsen, whose statue is seen in the heart of town on the Torvet main square, built a paper mill on the east side of the river, and in time other industries sprouted up, leading to great prosperity for the town. Unlike some little towns of Denmark, with their narrow cobblestone streets, Silkeborg is spaciously laid out. A progressive town, it is scenic, historic yet modern, with a vast shopping district of 200 specialty stores, the largest marketplace in Central Jutland, a multiplex cinema, dozens of restaurants, and a convention center.

ESSENTIALS
GETTING THERE   From Århus, follow Route 15 west to Silkeborg. If you aren't driving, there's frequent train service from Copenhagen via Fredericia.

VISITOR INFORMATION   The **Silkeborg Turistbureau** is at Godthåbsvej 4 (© **86-82-19-11;** www.silkeborg.com). It's open June 15 to August, Monday to Friday 9am to 5pm, Saturday and Sunday 10am to 2pm; September, October, and April to June 14, Monday to Friday 9am to 4pm, Saturday 10am to 1pm; November to March, Monday to Friday 10am to 3pm. In December the office is also open Saturday 10am to 1pm.

GETTING AROUND   Numerous bus routes service the city; all local buses depart from the stop on Fredensgade. There's no number to call for information. Tickets cost 20DKK ($3.40/£1.80) per individual ride, or 23DKK ($3.90/£2.10) if you need a transfer.

SEEING THE SIGHTS
Although we can never resist the charms of "The Tollund Man" (see below), the greatest adventure for us is to sail aboard the world's last coal-fired paddle steamer, the *Hjejlen* ✸✸✸, which has been sailing since 1861. It follows the route of the Gudenå River, going along a waterway of 161km (100 miles) through Jutland's wonder lake district. Himmelbjerget, or "Sky Mountain," is the major attraction along the route. Departures are daily from Silkeborg harbor at 10am and again at 2pm from mid-June to mid-August, with a roundtrip costing 117DKK ($20/£11) for adults or half price for children 4 to 11 (3 and under free). For schedules and more information, call **Hjejlen Co., Ltd.,** Havnen (© **86-82-07-66;** www.hjejlen.com).

Silkeborg Museum   One of the world's greatest human treasures from antiquity is the world-famous and much-photographed **"Tollund Man"** ✸✸✸. Discovered in a peat bog in 1950, he is the most perfectly preserved human being to have survived the ages. When he lived during the Iron Age (roughly 500 B.C.–A.D. 500), the great city of Athens was in decline, the second Punic War was being fought, the finishing touches were being put on the Great Wall of China, and Hannibal was trying to get those damn elephants to cross the Alps.

The Tolland Man is so well preserved that when his body was discovered, locals called the police, thinking it was a recent murder. You can even see the wrinkles in his forehead. His head capped by fur, the Tollund Man was strangled by a plaited leather string, probably as part of a ritual sacrifice for a successful peat harvest. He was also a vegetarian, as scientists have determined, his last meal consisting of flax, barley, and oats.

Sleeping near the Tollund Man for centuries is the **Elling Woman** ✸✸, whose body was discovered in 1938 about 60m (200 ft.) from where the Tollund Man was later discovered. Wrapped in a sheepskin cape, she had been hanged with a leather thong, the V-shaped furrow still visible around her neck today. Scientists estimate that she was about 25 years old when she died in 210 B.C., probably the result of another ritual sacrifice.

After seeing these rather gruesome sights, you can admire the setting of the museum in a manor house by the Gudenå River, directly east of the Torvet or market square. The building itself dates back to 1767 and is the oldest structure in Silkeborg.

The museum also displays exhibits devoted to regional history and local handcrafts, including an antique glass collection, the renowned **Sorring ceramics** ✸. The museum carries a special exhibition of a clog maker's workshop, a collection of stone implements, antique jewelry, and artifacts from the ruins of Silkeborg Castle. In the handicraft and Iron Age markets, artisans use ancient techniques to create iron, jewelry, and various crafts.

Hovedgaardsvej 7. © **86-82-14-99**. www.silkeborgmuseum.dk. Admission 45DKK ($7.65/£4.05); free 17 and under. May to mid-Oct daily 10am–5pm; mid-Oct to Apr Sat–Sun noon–4pm. Bus: 10.

WHERE TO STAY

The Silkeborg Turistbureau (see above) can book you into nearby **private homes.**

Hotel Dania ✸   If you want modernity and facilities, check into the Radisson SAS (see below). But if you desire tradition, you could find no better choice than the town's oldest hotel, dating from 1848. Much improved over the years, it's been modernized without losing its charm. The bedrooms either overlook the lake or the Torvet, the main town square. Antiques fill the corridors and reception lounge, but the midsize-to-spacious guest rooms have been decorated in Danish modern, each unit containing a neatly kept bathroom with tub/shower combo. Outdoor dining on the square is popular in the summer, and the **Underhuset** restaurant serves typical Danish food along with Scandinavian and French dishes. The hotel's dining room measures as one of the longest restaurants in Denmark.

Torvet 5, DK-8600 Silkeborg. © **86-82-01-11**. Fax 86-82-20-04. www.hoteldania.dk. 49 units. 1,069DKK–1,478DKK ($182–$251/£96–£133) double; 1,675DKK–2,405DKK ($285–$409/£151–£216) suite. Rates include breakfast. AE, DC, MC, V. Free parking. Bus: 3. **Amenities:** Restaurant; bar; room service (7am–10pm); babysitting; laundry service/dry cleaning; nonsmoking rooms. *In room:* TV, minibar, hair dryer, safe, trouser press.

Radisson SAS Hotel ✸✸✸   This 150-year-old former paper factory is now the most modern hotel in the area. The location is not quite as central as the Dania, but the Radisson rises right by the harbor, a short walk from attractions, shops, and restaurants. The chain hotel is also a favorite venue in Silkeborg for conferences, as the town's convention center, Jyst Musik & Teaterhus, lies nearby. The hotel offers the finest and most modern doubles and suites in Greater Silkeborg, successfully combining Danish modern with traditional styling, including state-of-the-art bathrooms with tub/shower combos. When it's snowing outside, the lobby bar fireplace is the best place to be in Silkeborg. During fair weather, the restaurant, with its spacious terrace offering panoramic views of the Remstrup River, is a favorite spot.

Papirfabrikken 12, DK-8600 Silkeborg. © **88-82-22-22**. Fax 88-82-22-23. www.radissonsas.com. 86 units. 1,205DKK–1,345DKK ($205–$229/£108–£121) double; 1,945DKK–2,260DKK ($331–$384/£175–£203) suite. Rates include continental breakfast. AE, DC, MC, V. **Amenities:** Restaurant; bar; Jacuzzi (in suites); sauna; 24-hr. room service; laundry service/dry cleaning; nonsmoking rooms; rooms for those w/limited mobility. *In room:* A/C, TV, dataport, minibar, fridge, hair dryer, iron, Wi-Fi.

WHERE TO DINE

Spiesehuset Christian VIII 🌶🌶 DANISH/FRENCH   The best restaurant in Silkeborg, this establishment was founded in 1992 in what was originally a private house built in the late 1700s. It seats only 30 people in a dining room painted in what the owners describe as the color of heaven (cerulean blue), accented with modern paintings. We like dishes such as lobster ravioli, carpaccio of marinated sole and salmon with a saffron sauce, filet of beef with truffle sauce, flavored medallions of veal stuffed with a purée of wild duck and herbs, and classics such as tender rack of Danish lamb with garlic sauce.

Christian VIII Vej 54. © 86-82-25-62. Reservations required. Main courses 170DKK–260DKK ($29–$44/£15–£23). AE, DC, MC, V. Mon–Sat 4–10pm.

EBELTOFT 🌶

97km (60 miles) E of Silkeborg, 53km (33 miles) NE of Århus, 336km (209 miles) W of Copenhagen

Wandering the cobblestone streets of Ebeltoft is like going back to a town 200 years ago. This town of half-timbered houses had a long slumber of about 2 centuries, when it economically stagnated. When it woke up in the 1960s, it found its old buildings and streets had become a tourist attraction. So instead of tearing down buildings, locals restored them with their increased prosperity.

Ebeltoft, "apple orchard" in Danish, is the capital of the Mols hill country, an area of great scenic beauty in Central Jutland. Allow at least 3 hours to wander its streets—in some cases, hidden-away lanes—and to explore its old inns. Sometimes a ruddy-faced fisherman will consent to have his picture taken, assuring you that he is still following the same profession as his grandfather.

Ebeltoft's Viking age wooden "dragon boats" have given way to expensive yachts in the harbor. Life at Ebeltoft developed around this beautiful harbor and its scenic bay, Ebeltoft Vig.

In the Middle Ages, Ebeltoft was a thriving port, enjoying trade with Germany, Sweden, and, of course, Copenhagen. However, after a dispute in 1659, the Swedish army invaded, sacking the port and setting fire to the merchant fleet. Ebeltoft never really recovered from this almost fatal blow until it became a tourist destination in the 1960s. Ironically, it was Swedish tourists who first discovered the antique charms of Ebeltoft, with its timber-framed buildings topped with red tile roofs.

ESSENTIALS

GETTING THERE   By Train & Bus   There's no direct train service to Ebeltoft. From Copenhagen, take the train (via Fredericia) to Århus; at Århus Central Station, board bus no. 123 for Ebeltoft.

By Car   From Silkeborg head east on Route 15 through Århus, and continue around the coast, following Route 21 south to Ebeltoft.

VISITOR INFORMATION   Contact the **Ebeltoft Turistbureau,** Strandvejen 2 (© **86-34-14-00;** www.ebeltoftturist.dk), open June 15 to August, Monday to Saturday 10am to 6pm and Sunday 11am to 4pm; and September to June 14, Monday to Friday 9am to 4pm and Saturday 10am to 1pm.

SEEING THE SIGHTS

Det Gamle Rådhus   This is the smallest town hall in Denmark and looks like something erected just for kindergarten children to play in. The 1789 building has blackened half-timbering, a red-brick and timbered facade, and a bell tower. Its museum houses an ethnographic collection from Thailand and artifacts from the town's history. It's in the town center north of Strandvejen.

Torvet. © **86-34-55-99.** Admission 25DKK ($4.25/£2.25); free ages 17 and under. Apr–Aug daily 10am–5pm; Sept–Oct Tues–Sun 11am–3pm; Nov–Mar Sat–Sun 11am–3pm.

Fregatten Jylland ⊛ Moored at the harbor, the *Jylland* is the oldest man-of-war in Denmark (1860) and the world's longest wooden ship at 71m (233 ft.). The vessel is an impressive monument to Ebeltoft's maritime heyday, and the restoration of the three-masted ship was financed by Mærsk McKinney Møller, a local shipping tycoon. Stand on the bridge and gun deck, imagining the harbor 2 centuries ago, and, down below, check out the captain's room and the galley with several miniature sea battle scenarios on display.

Strandvejen 4. © **86-34-10-99.** www.fregatten-jylland.dk. Admission 80DKK ($14/£7.20) adults, 40DKK ($6.80/£3.60) children. Jan 2–Mar 21 and Oct 25–Dec 30 daily 10am–4pm; Mar 22–June 13 and Aug 23–Oct 24 daily 10am–5pm; June 14–Aug 22 daily 10am–7pm.

WHERE TO STAY & DINE

Hotel Ebeltoft Strand ⊛ *Kids* This hotel is the best choice in the town center, although summer visitors will find the swanky Molskroen (see below) along the coast more inviting. Constructed in 1978, the comfortable, well-furnished guest rooms often have a private balcony or terrace, overlooking Ebeltoft Bay or the Mol hills. Each of the units, painted in pastel-like Nordic colors, comes with a well-kept bathroom with tub/shower combo. Family rooms can be composed by joining another room, with an extra bed for kids (providing they are under the age of 18), for 1,295DKK ($220/£117) for four guests. Kids have their own room but with a connecting door leading to where their parents sleep. In winter, guests retreat to a cozy lounge with a fireplace, but in summer the terrace with a view of the water is preferred. The restaurant serves the best lunch buffet in town, and the chef relies on the fresh produce of the season to create an enticing menu. The location is a 5-minute drive from the ferry dock and a 15-minute jaunt from Tirstrup Airport.

Nordre Strandvej 3, DK-8400 Ebeltoft. © **86-34-33-00.** Fax 86-34-46-36. www.ebeltoftstrand.dk. 72 units. 1,195DKK ($203/£108) double. Rates include buffet breakfast. AE, DC, MC, V. Free parking. Bus: 123 from Århus. **Amenities:** Restaurant; bar; indoor heated pool; kids' playroom; 24-hr. room service; laundry service/dry cleaning; nonsmoking rooms; rooms for those w/limited mobility. *In room:* TV, dataport, minibar, hair dryer, safe.

Molskroen ⊛ *Finds* Perched northwest of Ebeltoft on the coast, this half-timbered structure began life in 1923 as a private manor, but has been expanded and altered over the years. This hotel was vastly upgraded, and its prices have risen dramatically. Nevertheless, it's the best place to stay in the area. Many rooms have terraces overlooking Mols Hills, and a fine white sandy beach is only 100m (328 ft.) away. The *kro* is in the center of an area of summer houses mostly built in the 1920s and 1930s. The medium-size guest rooms are now sleek, functional, and comfortable, with freshly tiled bathrooms equipped with tub/shower combos. Ten of the bedrooms are found in the annex, a red-brick building with a tiled roof. Accommodations here are every bit as good in the main building. Nine of these annex accommodations are individually furnished junior suites set on two floors, with four beds in each room, making them suitable for families. Even if you're not a guest, consider a stopover at the on-site French restaurant, which offers the most imaginative cuisine in the area, the specialty being roast duck filled with dates, apricots, and figs. Note the four original Warhol prints of famous queens, including Denmark's own Queen Margrethe. In winter, when the terrace closes down, you can sit and enjoy your brandy in front of a fireplace.

Hovegaden 16, Femmøller Strand, DK-8400 Ebeltoft. © **86-36-23-00**. Fax 86-36-23-00. www.molskroen.dk. 18 units. 1,380DKK–1,680DKK ($235–$286/£124–£151) double; 2,300DKK–3,500DKK ($391–$595/£207–£315) suite. Rates include breakfast. AE, DC, V. Free parking. Closed Dec 24–Jan 8. Bus: 123 from Århus. **Amenities:** Restaurant; bar; room service (7am–10pm); babysitting; laundry service/dry cleaning; 1 room for those w/limited mobility. *In room:* TV, fax, dataport, minibar, hair dryer, safe.

AALBORG ⚇

132km (82 miles) NW of Ebeltoft, 383km (238 miles) W of Copenhagen

We won't pretend that Aalborg is our favorite city in Jutland (Århus is), but you can have a great time if you explore the attractions, especially some of those in the environs. We like to stand at Aalborg harbor, watching ships head out for sea, sailing to Britain and Ireland, faraway Iceland and even the Faroe islands.

The largest city in northern Jutland, Aalborg (Ålborg) opens onto the Limfjord and is known worldwide for its aquavit. Although essentially a shipping town and commercial center, Aalborg makes a good base for sightseers, with its many hotels and attractions, more than 300 restaurants, and diverse nightlife.

History is a living reality in Aalborg. The city was founded 1,000 years ago when the Viking fleets assembled in these parts before setting off on their predatory expeditions. The city's historic atmosphere has been preserved in its old streets and alleys. Near the Church of Our Lady are many beautifully restored and reconstructed houses, some of which date from the 16th century.

Denmark's largest forest, **Rold,** where robber bandits once roamed, is just outside town. **Rebild National Park** is the site of the annual American Fourth of July celebration.

Not far from Aalborg, on the west coast of northern Jutland, some of the finest beaches in northern Europe stretch from Slettestrand to Skagen. The beach resort towns of **Blokhus** and **Løkken** are especially popular with Danes, Germans, and Swedes.

ESSENTIALS

GETTING THERE   By Plane   You can fly from Copenhagen to Aalborg; the **airport** (© **98-17-11-44;** www.aal.dk) is 6.5km (4 miles) from the city center.

By Train   There is frequent train service from Copenhagen by way of Fredericia to Århus; there you can connect with a train to Aalborg, a 90-minute ride.

By Bus   Aalborg's bus station is the transportation center for northern Jutland and is served from all directions. For all bus information in northern Jutland, call **Nordjyllands Trafikselskab** (© **98-11-11-11**).

By Car   From Ebeltoft, follow Route 21 north until you reach the junction with Route 16. Drive west on Route 16 until you come to E-45, which runs north to Aalborg.

VISITOR INFORMATION   The **Aalborg Tourist Bureau** is at Østerågade 8 (© **99-30-60-90;** www.visitaalborg.dk). It's open June to August, Monday to Friday 9am to 6pm, Saturday 10am to 1pm; September to June, Monday to Friday 9am to 4:30pm, Saturday 10am to 1pm. In July it is open Monday to Friday 9am to 5:30pm, Saturday 10am to 4pm.

GETTING AROUND   For bus information, call © **98-11-11-11.** Most buses depart from Østerågade and Nytorv in the city center. A typical fare costs 16DKK

($2.70/£1.45), although you can buy a 24-hour tourist pass for 110DKK ($19/£9.90) to ride on all the city buses for a day. Information about bus routes is available from the *Aalborg Guide,* which is distributed free by the tourist office.

SPECIAL EVENTS   The **Aalborg Carnival,** scheduled each year on May 25 and 26, is one of the major events of spring in Jutland. Streets are filled with festive figures in colorful costumes strutting in a parade. Up to 100,000 people participate in this annual event, marking the victory of spring over winter's darkness. The whole city seems to explode in joy. There's also the **Aalborg Jazz and Blues Festival** August 13 to 19. Jazz fills the whole city at dozens of clubs, although most activity centers on C. W. Obels Plads. Every year on the Fourth of July, Danes and Danish Americans meet to celebrate America's **Independence Day** in the lovely hills of Rebild.

SEEING THE SIGHTS

Aalborgtårnet   Whenever we visit a city or town with a lookout point, we always head there first for a panoramic overview. In Aalborg, that perfect view (that is, if it's a clear day) is seen from this tower, rising 100m (328 ft.) in the air. Reached by stairs or elevator, its view takes in everything from the smokestacks to the beautiful Limfjord. Weather permitting, you can see the North Sea and even Rold Forest in the south. The tower itself is no beauty, but it does have its reward, including its location on a hill in back of the Nordjyllands Kunstmuseum and at the border of Mølleparken, the best woodland for walking or hiking in the area.

Søndre Skovvej, at Skovbakken. ⓒ 98-77-05-11. www.aalborgtaarnet.com. Admission 25DKK ($4.25/£2.25) adults, 15DKK ($2.55/£1.35) children 3–14, free for children under 3. Apr–July daily 10am–5pm; July daily 10am–7pm; Aug daily 10am–5pm. Closed Sept–Mar. Bus: 11, 14, or 16.

Aalborg Zoologiske Have *(★ (Kids*   We've seen bigger and better zoos in our lives, but this remains one of our favorites because of its success in the breeding of near-extinct animals such as the Siberian tiger. More than 1,300 animals are housed here, including crocs, zebras, tigers, giraffes, polar bears, and orangutans. Apes and beasts of prey are kept under minimal supervision. They live in such simulated conditions as an African savannah or a rain forest from South America. With the opening of a large playground, Oasen, kids can romp around like the resident monkeys. Other adventures include a river bank for crocs, a pampa for anteaters, and a forest full of bears.

Mølleparkvej 63. ⓒ 96-31-29-29. www.aalborg-zoo.dk. Admission 95DKK ($16/£8.55) adults, 50DKK ($8.50/£4.50) children 3–11, free for children under 3. Jan–Feb and Nov–Dec daily 10am–2pm; Mar daily 10am–3pm; Apr and Sept–Oct daily 10am–4pm; May–Aug daily 9am–6pm. Last ticket is sold 1 hr. before closing. Bus: 11. Lies 4km (2½ miles) south of Aalborg.

Budolfi Domkirke   Even if you don't visit this church, you'll be made aware of its presence. A carillon makes beautiful music daily every hour from 9am to 10pm. This elaborately decorated and whitewashed cathedral is dedicated to St. Botolph, patron saint of sailors. The baroque spire of the church is Aalborg's major landmark. The church you see today is the result of 800 years of rebuilding and expansion. On the south wall is a fresco depicting St. Catherine of Alexandria and some small grotesque centaurs. Look for the altarpiece from 1689 and the pulpit from 1692—both carved by Lauridtz Jensen. The marble font from 1727 was a gift to the church. Also note the gallery in the north aisle, with its illustrations of the Ten Commandments. A similar gallery in the south aisle illustrates the suffering of Christ and also bears the names of a number of prominent Aalborg citizens from around the mid–17th century. A series of cocks "crow the hour" from four matching clock faces on the church's tower.

Algade. (C) **98-12-46-70.** Free admission. June–Aug Mon–Fri 9am–4pm, Sat 9am–2pm; Sept–May Mon–Fri 9am–3pm, Sat 9am–noon. Bus: 3, 5, 10, or 11.

Helligåndsklostret (Monastery of the Holy Ghost)   This site was the secret head-quarters of the "Churchill Club," which was the first Resistance group established in Denmark to fight the Nazis. This vine-covered monastery is the oldest social-welfare institution in Denmark, as well as the oldest building in Aalborg. Built near the heart of town in 1431 and designed with step-shaped gables, it contains a well-preserved rectory, a series of vaulted storage cellars—some of which occasionally functioned as prisons—a whitewashed collection of cloisters, and a chapter house whose walls in some areas are decorated with 16th-century frescoes. The complex can be visited only as part of a guided tour.

C. W. Obels Plads (call the tourist office for information). Guided tour 40DKK ($6.80/£3.60) adults, 10DKK ($1.70/90p) children. Guided tour late June to mid-Aug Mon–Fri 1:30pm. Bus: 1.

Jens Bang's Stenhus (*K*   This is the finest example of Renaissance domestic archi-tecture in the north of Europe. This six-floor mansion, built in 1624 in a glittering Renaissance style, once belonged to a wealthy merchant, Jens Bang. Bang was gifted but also argumentative and obstinate. He deliberately made his house rich with orna-mentation and ostentation as a "challenge" to the other good citizens of the town. It was rumored that he sought revenge on enemies by caricaturing them in the many grotesque carvings on the facade of the house. In spite of his wealth, he was never made a member of the town council, and to this day his image is depicted on the south facade sticking his tongue out at the Town Hall. The historic wine cellar, Duus Vinkjaelder, is the meeting place of the Guild of Christian IV. On the ground floor is an old apothecary shop. The mansion is still privately owned and is not open to the public.

Østeragade 9. Bus: 3, 5, 10, or 11.

Nordjyllands Kunstmuseet (Museum of Modern and Contemporary Art) (*K* (*Kids*   This building is a prime example of modern Scandinavian architecture. Built from 1968 to 1972, it was designed as a showplace for 20th-century Danish and international art. The nucleus of the collection dates from 1850, but it's been added to over the years with purchases and bequests. The Carlsberg Foundation, those beer barons, have donated some of the most notable works, including William Scharff's *Nocturne Series* and J. F. Willumsen's *War Invalids*. We find that the museum's most romantic picture is Harald Slott-Møller's *Spring* (1901). The greatest treasure trove of art came from two dental technologists, Anna and Kresten Krestensen, who amassed a notable collection of Danish and international art from 1920 to 1950. In later years, as funds became available, the museum purchased works by great international artists including Fernand Léger, Max Ernst, and Wassily Kandinsky. Many events are staged for children, including picture hunts, family tours, and children's museum exhibits. Ask about musical concerts frequently staged here all year. On the ground floor is a good cafe overlooking the sculpture park. In 1994, artist Paul Gernes decorated the walls of the cafe, which serves a light lunch menu and open sandwiches.

Kong Christians Allé 50. (C) **98-13-80-88.** www.nordjyllandsjunstmuseum.dk. Admission 40DKK ($6.80/£3.60) adults, free for children. Free admission Dec. Tues–Sun 10am–5pm. Tues Feb–Apr and Sept–Nov until 9pm. Bus: 15 or 16.

WHERE TO STAY

The **Aalborg Tourist Bureau** (see above) can book a room for you in a private Danish home—double or single—with access to a shower. Bed linen is included in the price, and all rooms are situated within the city limits and reached by bus. In July and August, the peak tourist months, Helnan Phønix slashes its rates and becomes a moderately priced choice because it's primarily a business hotel, and for them, high tourist season is their low season. Although many rooms at the Limsford Hotel are labeled expensive, the hotel also rents dozens of more affordable accommodations.

Helnan Phønix Hotel ✦✦✦   In the town's most sumptuous mansion, you'll find the oldest, largest, most historic, and most prestigious hotel in Aalborg, lying close to the bus station. It originated in 1783 on the main street of town as the private home of the Danish brigadier general assigned to protect Aalborg from assault by foreign powers. In 1853, it was converted into a hotel. Today, it appears deceptively small from Aalborg's main street, and very imposing if you see its modern wings from the back. Bedrooms are tastefully and elegantly appointed with dark wood furnishings. Some of the rooms have exposed ceiling beams, and all of them are equipped with neatly tiled bathrooms with tub/shower combos. The hotel's restaurant, Brigadieren, serves a sophisticated Danish and international cuisine.

Vesterbro 77, DK-9000 Aalborg. ✆ **98-12-00-11.** Fax 98-10-10-20. www.helnan.dk. 244 units. Summer 955DKK ($162/£86) double, 2,500DKK ($425/£225) suite; winter 1,180DKK ($200/£106) double, 2,500DKK ($425/£225) suite. AE, DC, MC, V. **Amenities:** Restaurant; bar; gym; Jacuzzi; sauna; room service (7am–10pm); massage; laundry service/dry cleaning; nonsmoking rooms; solarium. *In room:* TV, dataport, minibar, hair dryer, safe.

Hotel Hvide Hus ✦   If you're willing to forego the antique charms of the Phønix and prefer a more modern "high rise" address, then this Best Western hotels is one of the most viable candidates. The first-rate "White House Hotel" is in Kilde Park, about a 12-minute walk from the heart of Aalborg and close to the bus station. Many international businesspeople now stay here instead of at the traditional Phønix. In cooperation with well-known galleries, the hotel is decorated with works by some of Denmark's leading painters. The guest rooms are well furnished in fresh Scandinavian modern style; all have private balconies with a view of Aalborg. Each unit is also equipped with a well-maintained bathroom with a tub/shower combo. The restaurant **Kilden** and the bar **Pejsebar** are both located on the 15th floor, from where there is a view of the city.

Vesterbro 2, DK-9000 Aalborg. ✆ **800/780-7234** in the U.S. and Canada, or 98-13-84-00. Fax 98-13-51-22. www.hotelhvidehus.dk. 198 units. Sat–Sun 925DKK ($157/£83) double, 1,860DKK ($316/£167) suite; Mon–Fri 1,325DKK–1,495DKK ($225–US$254/£119–£135) double; 2,430DKK ($413/£207) suite. Rates include buffet breakfast. AE, DC, MC, V. Free parking. **Amenities:** Restaurant; bar; room service (7am–11pm); massage; babysitting; laundry service/dry cleaning; nonsmoking rooms. *In room:* TV, minibar, hair dryer, trouser press.

Radisson SAS Limfjord Hotel ✦✦   This is the most avant-garde hotel in town—a five-story yellow-brick structure with huge expanses of glass in a streamlined Danish modern layout. In the center of town, a 3-minute walk east of the cathedral, the hotel opens onto the famous Limsjorden Canal. It's near Jomfru Anegade, a street packed with bars and restaurants. The public rooms are sparsely furnished with modern, streamlined furniture. Many of the midsize-to-spacious bedrooms overlook the harbor, and each is well maintained with tasteful, comfortable furnishings. All rooms have a tub/shower combo, the suites blessed with a Jacuzzi. The hotel offers some of the best drinking and dining facilities in town, and its casino is a hub of nighttime activity.

Ved Stranden 14–16, DK-9000 Aalborg. © **800-333-3333** in the U.S., or 98-16-43-33. Fax 98-16-17-47. www. radissonsas.com. 188 units. 995DKK–1,615DKK ($169–$274/£90–£145) double; 2,215DKK ($376/£199) suite. Rates include breakfast. AE, DC, MC, V. Parking 75DKK ($13/£6.75). Bus: 1, 4, 40, or 46. **Amenities:** Restaurant; pizzeria; bar; fitness center; sauna; 24-hr. room service; laundry service/dry cleaning; nonsmoking rooms; rooms for those w/limited mobility; casino. *In room:* TV, dataport, minibar, hair dryer, trouser press, Wi-Fi.

WHERE TO DINE

Jomfru Anegade is the most famous restaurant-filled street in Jutland. If you can't find good food here, you didn't try. It's got something for most palates and pocketbooks.

Kniv og Gaffel ◌◌ FRENCH/DANISH   This is a romantic choice for dining, housed in the oldest preserved citizen's house, dating from 1552, in Aalborg. The street takes its name from Maren Turis, a woman who lived here in the 16th century and was accused of witchcraft, tried, and proven innocent. Those terrifying memories are long erased today, and you'll experience only lots of atmosphere and wonderful food served by candlelight. Its old oak tables fill up every night, and the wood floors are buckled and slanted with age. The house specialty is thick steaks, the best in Aalborg, although you can order an array of other dishes prepared with first-rate ingredients plucked from the markets that very morning. On our most recent rounds, we enjoyed fresh Norwegian salmon baked with mushrooms and served with a béarnaise sauce. The chicken breast platter is delectably cooked with homemade basil and tomato sauce, and served with a garden salad and baked potato.

Maren Turis Gade 10. © **98-16-69-72.** Reservations recommended. Main courses 42DKK–160DKK ($7–$27/£3.80–£14). DC, MC, V. Mon–Sat noon–midnight. Bus: 1, 3, or 5.

Mortens Kro ◌◌◌ FRENCH/DANISH   This artful restaurant is the domain of Morten Nealsen, the most gifted chef in Aalborg, and is the best place to dine in the city. The chef wanted a "New York look with a Parisian ambience," the latter evoked by the champagne bar. Well-rehearsed rules of cooking technique and the classic school of French cuisine have been beautifully blended with Danish flavors. Appetizers include a seafood plate with a sauté of mint- and lemon-flavored rice noodles. For a main course, try the filet of sea wolf marinated with chili and lemon, served with a golden saffron risotto. The fresh lobster is divine, boiled to perfection and served with a lemon-flavored homemade mayonnaise that's so good we wanted to bottle it. The desserts are excellent, especially the passion-fruit sorbet with pieces of rose hip served in a meringue "nest" with rose hip syrup. DJs entertain during the weekends.

Mølleå 4-6, Mølleå Arkaden. © **98-12-48-60.** Reservations recommended. Main courses 138DKK–228DKK ($23–$39/£12–£21). Fixed-price menu 298DKK–648DKK ($51–$110/£27–£58). DC, MC, V. Mon–Sat 5:30–10pm. Bus: 3, 5, 10, or 11.

SKAGEN ◌
105km (65 miles) NE of Aalborg, 488km (303 miles) W of Copenhagen

Since the 19th century, Skagen (pronounced *Skane*) has been the leading artists' colony of Denmark. As is inevitable in such cases, hordes of tourists followed in the footsteps of the artists to discover the northernmost tip of Jutland on its east coast. A sort of "bony finger" of land points into the North Sea at the second biggest fishing port in Denmark.

We find the combination today of Nordic sailors—Skagen has been a fishing port for centuries—and a colony of artists an intriguing mix. The early artists were more isolated here, but the coming of the railway in 1890 opened up Skagen to the world with its link to the terminus of Frederikshavn.

We've spent hours here in both September and October wandering the heather-covered moors, the undulating stretches of dunes, and some of the best, but not the warmest, beaches in Europe. We particularly like to stand at the point where the North Sea meets the Baltic, the subject of countless landscape paintings. It's not unknown to have visitors applaud the spectacular sunsets here. By the end of July, the visitors are in retreat, and Skagen happily reverts to the locals again.

ESSENTIALS

GETTING THERE   By Car   Take E-45 northeast to Frederikshavn. From there, head north on Route 40 to Skagen.

By Train   Several trains a day run from Copenhagen to Århus, where you connect with another train to Frederikshavn. From Frederikshavn there are 12 daily trains to Skagen.

VISITOR INFORMATION   The **Skagen Turistbureau** is at Skt. Laurentiivej 22 (© 98-44-13-77; www.skagen-tourist.dk). Open January 3 to March 31 and November 1 to December 23, Monday to Friday 10am to 4pm, Saturday 10am to 1pm; April, May and August 29 to October 30, Monday to Friday 9am to 4pm, Saturday 10am to 2pm; June 1 to 26 and August 1 to 28, Monday to Saturday 9am to 5pm, Sunday 10am to 2pm, and June 27 to July 31, Monday to Saturday 9am to 6pm, Sunday 10am to 4pm.

SEEING THE SIGHTS

Since it opened in 1907, **Skagen Havn (Skagen Harbor)** ✿ has been one of the major attractions in town. It's seen at its best when the boats come back to land their catches (times vary). For early risers, the fish auction "at the rack of the morning" is a popular attraction. Mid-May to mid-October, the oldest part of the harbor is a haven for the boating crowds centered around one of the marinas. Many yachting people in Jutland use Skagen as their favorite harbor haven.

Gammel Skagen (Old Town) ✿ lies 2.5km (1½ miles) from Skagen Havn. Signs point the way. Originally Gammel Skagen was the fishing hamlet—that is, until Skagen Havn opened in 1907. Today, Gammel Skagen is a little resort town with large beach hotels that are mainly timeshares.

An attraction worth exploring is **Rådjerg Mile,** a migrating dune moving at the rate of about 11m (36 ft.) annually. Located 16km (10 miles) south of town, it can be reached via Kandestederne. This dune was formed on the west coast in the 16th century during the great sand drift that characterized the landscape until the 20th century. The dune continues to move yearly, eastward toward the forest.

Den Tilsandede Kirke   This church buried in sand dunes 1.5km (1 mile) south of town is an amusing curiosity. The only part that's visible is the upper two-thirds of the tower. When Hans Christian Andersen visited in 1859, he called the church "The Pompeii of Skagen." The only things hidden under the dunes are the remnants of a wall, the old floor, and perhaps the baptismal font. By 1775, the church had fallen into disrepair and was used by fewer and fewer members. By 1795 it was closed down, and in 1810 it was partly demolished, the stones sold to people in the area as building materials for their private houses. Today red stakes in the ground indicate the placing and extent of the nave and vestry.

© **98-44-43-71.** Admission 10DKK ($1.70/90p) adults, 5DKK (85¢/45p) children. June–Sept 1 daily 11am–5pm; winter Sat–Sun 11am–5pm.

Skagen By- & Egnsmuseum   This museum, a 15-minute stroll from the train depot, is evocative of a time long gone. The lifesaving station here reminds us of how the seas sometimes violently clash in the depths of winter, as demonstrated by the dramatic photographs of ships and men in distress. In this open-air museum, the homes of both well-to-do fishermen as well as their poorer cousins were moved here to demonstrate how life was lived in Skagen from 1830 to 1880. A maritime museum is filled with nautical memorabilia, and an original Dutch windmill is all that's left of the many that used to dot the landscape.

Fortidsminderne, P. K. Nielsensvej. (C) **98-44-47-60**. Admission 35DKK ($5.95/£3.15) adults, free for children ages 17 and under. May–June and Aug–Sept Mon–Fri 10am–4pm; Sat–Sun 11am–4pm; July Mon–Fri 10am–5pm, Sat–Sun 11am–4pm; Mar–Apr and Oct Mon–Fri 10am–4pm; Nov–Feb Mon–Fri 11am–3pm.

Skagens Museum *Finds*   The glory days of the artists of Skagen school of painting come alive at this impressive museum of their work. The apogee of their art was created from the beginning of the 1870s until the turn of the 20th century. The Skagen artists were inspired by naturalism and open-air painting, their favorite motif being quaint cottages or the fishermen working on local beaches. The artists came to celebrate the North Sea landscapes, everything bathed in that special light that seems to exist in Skagen.

The major artists of this period included Michael Ancher (1849–1909) and his wife, Anna (1859–1935). You'll also see works by another of the school's leading painters, P. S. Krøyer (1851–1909), plus many more—the entire collection consists of 1,800 paintings, sculptures, drawings, and graphic works.

Brøndumsvej 4. (C) **98-44-64-44**. www.skagensmuseum.dk. Admission 60DKK ($10/£5.40) adults, free for children ages 17 and under. May–Sept daily 10am–5pm; Apr and Oct Tues–Sun 11am–4pm; Nov–Mar Wed–Fri 1–4pm, Sat 11am–4pm, Sun 11am–3pm.

Nordsømuseet   The main attraction of this two-story oceanarium in Hirtshals is the giant aquarium itself, containing some 4.5 million liters of seawater. Visitors can gaze upon an 8m-high (26-ft.) column of water, or view the "ocean" through an aquarium window, the thickest in the world.

The large aquarium has been designed to house schools of fish of the North Sea, including herring, mackerel, garfish, and horse mackerel. Among the large creatures, several species of North Sea sharks can be viewed. Each day divers feed the shoal fish and the sharks, and describe life in the aquarium to visitors.

The original museum is devoted to modern Danish sea fishing, detailing man's exploitation of the North Sea—for better or worse. Displays of the daily lives of fishermen, equipment, and vessels are placed alongside exhibits depicting the resources of the North Sea. Seals are common along the coast of Denmark, but you seldom spot them. However, in the on-site seal pool, you can observe the animals at close range—above as well as underwater. Feeding times for the seals are daily at 11am and again at 3pm.

Willemoesvej at Hirtshals. (C) **98-94-44-44**. Admission 110DKK ($19/£9.90) adults, 55DKK ($9.35/£4.95) children 3–11, free for children under 3. July–Aug daily 10am–6pm; Sept–June daily 10am–5pm. From Skagen take Rte. 40 south to the junction with Rte. 597 heading west into Hirtshals, a distance of 30 miles (48km).

WHERE TO STAY

Color Hotel Skagen *Finds*   This is more of a place to settle in for 2 or 3 days for a beach holiday, exploring the North Sea coast, than an overnight stopover at a motel. Southwest of Skagen, beside the only road leading into town from the rest of Jutland, this sprawling, one-story hotel lies 2km (1¼ miles) from the sea. Here, alone on sandy flatlands, it possesses an almost otherworldly sense of isolation. Unlike many of its competitors, which cater to families with children, this place appeals mostly to couples. Built in 1969, the hotel has a formal restaurant. The spacious, attractively furnished guest rooms contain hardwood floors, padded armchairs, and big windows. Each unit also contains neatly kept bathrooms with tub/shower combos. Of the accommodations, 45 are listed as apartments, which are rented only for 3 days at a time except during midsummer, when they are rented per week.

Gammel Landevej 39, DK-9990 Skagen. ⓒ 98-44-22-33. Fax 98-44-21-34. www.skagenhotel.dk. 153 units. 950DKK–1,395DKK ($162–$237/£86–£126) double; 1,695DKK–2,395DKK ($288–$407/£153–£216) suite; 6,500DKK–9,900DKK ($1,105–$1,683/£585–£891) apt. per week. AE, DC, MC, V. From Skagen, drive 2km (1¼ miles) southwest of town along Rte. 40. **Amenities:** Restaurant; bar; outdoor heated pool; fitness center; sauna; 24-hr. room service; nonsmoking rooms; rooms for those w/limited mobility. *In room:* TV, dataport, hair dryer, safe.

Finns Hotel Pension

Originally built in 1909 in a style that the owner refers to as "a Norwegian wood house," this old-fashioned Danish homestead is designed like houses that Scandinavian immigrants made popular during the 19th century in American states such as Minnesota. In a residential neighborhood of Skagen, a 10- to 15-minute walk northeast of the city center and a 3-minute walk from the beach, it's furnished with old furniture and antiques. Many rooms have beamed ceilings and a charming but vaguely claustrophobic allure. Our only warning involves a rigidity on the part of the hardworking managers and staff, who establish very clear-cut rules for new arrivals, who aren't noted for their flexibility, and who maintain an aggressive "take it or leave it" approach. If you give advance notice, they'll prepare a three-course evening meal, which is served only to residents, for a price of 300DKK ($51/£27) per person. If you agree to this, on pain of severe reproach, don't be late for dinner. Children 14 and under are not accepted.

Østre Strandvej 63, DK-9990 Skagen. ⓒ 98-45-01-55. Fax 98-45-05-55. www.finnshotelpension.dk. 6 units, 3 with bathroom. 950DKK ($162/£86) double with bathroom, 675DKK–825DKK ($115–$140/£61–£74) double without bathroom. Rates include breakfast. MC, V. Closed Oct–Mar. **Amenities:** Dining room. *In room:* No phone.

Ruth's Hotel ⭐⭐⭐

This is both a bastion of comfort and gastronomy—its restaurant, in fact, is one of the greatest outside Copenhagen. Located in the sand dunes of Old Skagen, it stands by the beach just 4km (2½ miles) from the center of modern Skagen. It takes its name from its founders, Emma and Hans Christian Ruth. The bedrooms are superior to anything at the resort, beautifully furnished and designed, exuding spaciousness and light. Each comes with a private tiled private bathroom with a tub/shower combo, and some units even have a Jacuzzi. A private balcony or terrace opens onto a view of the sea.

The spa is one of the best in Jutland, complete with solarium, sauna, Turkish baths, therapy pool, and gym. The hotel restaurant, Ruth's Gourmet, is one of the top five in the country outside of Copenhagen, yet we hesitate to recommend it because it requires reservations a month in advance. If you're lucky enough to get a table, you'll be rewarded with Chef Michel Michaud's repertoire of sublime dishes, which embrace the best of fine French cuisine and tradition, with a carefully chosen wine *carte.* You stand a better chance of dining on the airy, sunlit terrace of the on-site brasserie, where the food is watched over by Chef Michaud himself.

Hans Ruths Vej 1 ⓒ 98-44-11-24. Fax 98-45-08-75. www.ruths-hotel.dk. 26 units. 1,625DKK–1,975DKK ($154–$352/£146–£178) double; from 1,875DKK ($334/£169) suite. AE, DC, MC, V. **Amenities:** Restaurant; brasserie; bar; heated indoor pool; gym; spa; limited room service; laundry service. *In room:* TV, hair dryer, Wi-Fi.

Strandhotellet/Strandhuset ✦   This hotel at Gamle Skagen is for wild romantics who like the wind from the North Sea blowing through their hair. Built in 1912 as a holiday home, it's only a stone's throw from the sea and incorporates the dunes and buildings of a historic farm into the main building. The compound also contains four other outbuildings, each with an individual atmosphere. The newest addition is Strandhuset which was built in the 1990s with a prominent hip roof. The suites with kitchens within Strandhuset are evocative of a tasteful private summer home. These suites have tub/shower combos, the regular doubles coming with only a shower. Everything has a warm, cozy atmosphere, helped along with the original art work on the walls, and the wicker and the painted wood furnishings. Breakfast is served within a greenhouse-style extension at one end of the house.

Jeckelsvej, Gammel Skagen, DK-9990 Skagen. ℂ **98-44-34-99.** Fax 98-44-59-19. www.strandhotellet.glskagen.dk. 14 units, 6 with kitchenette. 1,000DKK–1,700DKK ($170–$289/£90–£153) double; 1,200DKK–1,950DKK ($204–$331/£108–£176) junior suite; 1,600DKK–2,850DKK ($272–$484/£144–£257) senior suite. AE, DC, MC, V. 4km (2½ miles) south of Skagen center. **Amenities:** Restaurant (summer only); bar; room service (7am–10pm). *In room:* TV, hair dryer, iron, Wi-Fi.

WHERE TO DINE

Skagen Fiske Restaurant ✦ SEAFOOD   One of the best-known fish restaurants in Jutland occupies the red-sided premises of a gable-roofed building that was erected directly beside the harborfront in 1907. You'll enter a bar on the establishment's street level, where the floor is composed of the actual beachfront—nothing more than sand. Climb to the nautically decorated dining room one floor above street level for meals. Lunches usually include flavorful platters that might contain fish cakes, Norwegian lobster, peel-your-own-shrimp, three different preparations of herring, or grilled filets of sole with lemon sauce. Dinners are more elaborate, consisting of whatever fish has been hauled in that day by local fishermen, prepared any way you specify, with virtually any sauce that's reasonably available.

Fiskehuskai 13. ℂ **98-44-35-44.** Reservations recommended. Lunch platters 58DKK–73DKK ($9.90–$12/£5.20–£6.60); dinner main courses 255DKK–288DKK ($43–$49/£23–£26). Fixed price menus 395DKK–495DKK ($67–$84/£36–£45) AE, DC, MC, V. Daily 6–10:30pm. Closed: Jan–Feb.

7

The Best of Norway

From snowcapped mountains to fjords warmed by the Gulf Stream, Norway is a land of stunning contrasts. Although the "Land of the Midnight Sun" is a modern, industrial nation, it's equally a world of remote towns and villages, with a population devoted to outdoor activities. So you won't have to exhaust yourself making difficult decisions, we've searched out the best deals and once-in-a-lifetime experiences in the country.

1 The Best Travel Experiences

- **Enjoying Nature:** Norway is one of the last major countries of the world where you can experience nature on an exceptional level. It's a land of contrasts, with soaring mountains, panoramic fjords, ice-blue glaciers, deep-green forests, fertile valleys, and rich pastures. The glowing red midnight sun reflects off snow-covered mountains, and the northern lights have fired the imaginations of artists and craftspeople for centuries.

- **Experiencing Norway in a Nutshell:** One of Europe's great train rides, this 12-hour excursion is Norway's most exciting. Tours leave from the Bergen train station. If you have limited time but want to see the country's most dramatic scenery, take this spectacular train trip. See chapter 10.

- **Visiting the North Cape:** For many, a trip to one of the northernmost inhabited areas of the world will be the journey of a lifetime. Accessible by ship, car, or air, the North Cape holds a fascination that outweighs its bleakness. Hammerfest, the world's northernmost town of significant size, is an important port of call for North Cape steamers. See chapter 11.

- **Exploring the Fjord Country:** Norway's fjords are stunningly serene and majestic, some of the world's most awe-inspiring sights. Bergen can be your gateway; two of the country's most famous fjords, the Hardangerfjord and the Sognefjord, can easily be explored from there. See chapter 11.

- **Seeing the Midnight Sun at the Arctic Circle:** This is one of the major reasons visitors flock to Norway. The Arctic Circle marks the boundary of the midnight sun of the Arctic summer and the sunless winters of the north. The midnight sun can be seen from the middle of May until the end of July. The Arctic Circle cuts across Norway south of Bodø. Bus excursions from that city visit the circle. The adventurous few who arrive in the winter miss the midnight sun, but are treated to a spectacular display of the aurora borealis (northern lights), the flaming spectacle of the Arctic winter sky. In ancient times, when the aurora could be seen farther south, people thought it was an omen of disaster. See chapter 11.

2 The Best Scenic Towns & Villages

- **Fredrikstad:** Founded in 1567 at the mouth of the River Glomma, Fredrikstad preserved its Old Town, which had become a fortress by 1667. Today Fredrikstad (about 97km/60 miles south of Oslo) offers a glimpse of what a Norwegian town looked like several hundred years ago. The old buildings in the historic district have been converted into studios for craftspeople and artisans, while maintaining their architectural integrity. After a visit here, you can drive along Oldtidsveien (the "highway of the ancients"), the most concentrated collection of archaeological monuments in Norway. See chapter 9.

- **Tønsberg:** On the western bank of the Oslofjord, this is Norway's oldest town. It was founded in A.D. 872, a year before King Harald Fairhair united parts of Norway. This Viking town became a royal coronation site. Its hill fortress is sometimes called "the Acropolis of Norway." Its ancient district, Nordbyen, is filled with well-preserved homes, and the folk museum houses a treasure trove of Viking-era artifacts. See chapter 9.

- **Bergen:** The gateway to Norway's fjord country, this town is even more scenic than the capital, Oslo. It was the capital of Norway for 6 centuries and a major outpost of the medieval Hanseatic merchants. The town's biggest tourist event is the Bergen International Music Festival, but there are also many year-round attractions. Many visitors come to explore Bergen's museums (including Edvard Grieg's former home) and its varied environs—fjords galore, mountains, and waterfalls. See chapter 10.

- **Trondheim:** Norway's third-largest city traces its history to 997, when the Vikings flourished. Norway's kings are crowned at the ancient cathedral, Nidaros Domen; Scandinavia's largest medieval building, it was erected over the grave of St. Olaf (also spelled Olav), the Viking king. Trondheim is the popular stopover for travelers from Oslo to destinations north of the Arctic Circle. See chapter 11.

- **Bodø:** Lying 1,306km (811 miles) north of Oslo, this far northern seaport, the terminus of the Nordland railway, is the gateway to the Arctic Circle, which lies just south of this breezy town. Another excellent place to observe the midnight sun from June 1 to July 13, Bodø is the capital of Nordland. From here you can also explore the environs, filled with glaciers and "bird islands." Bodø is also a gateway to the remote Lofoten Islands. See chapter 11.

3 The Best Active Vacations

- **Fishing:** The cold, clear waters of Norway's freshwater streams are renowned for their salmon and trout, and the storm-tossed seas off the coast have traditionally provided enough cod and mackerel to satisfy most of the nation's population. Serious anglers sometimes end up losing themselves in the majesty of the scenery. Tips on fishing in and around the Norwegian fjords are provided by the **Bergen Sportsfiskere (Bergen Angling Association),** Fosswinckelsgate 37, Bergen (© **55-32-11-64**), and the tourist information offices in Oslo and Bergen. Rural hotels throughout the nation can also give pointers to likely spots. For a truly unusual fishing experience, **Borton Overseas** (© **800/843-0602;** www.bortonoverseas.com) can arrange treks and accommodations in old-fashioned fishermen's cottages in the isolated Lofoten Islands. The rustic-looking, fully renovated cottages are adjacent to the sea. Rentals are for 3 days and include bed linens, maid service, boat rentals, and fishing equipment. The most popular seasons are March, when cod abounds, and June through August, when the scenery and weather are particularly appealing. For our specific "fishing hole" recommendations in Scandinavia, refer to "Fishing," under "Outdoor Activities," throughout this book.

- **Hiking:** The woods (Marka) around Oslo are ideal, as there are thousands of kilometers of trails, hundreds of which are lit. If you don't want to leave the city, Frogner Park also has many paths. Any Norwegian regional tourist bureau can advise you about hiking and jogging. In Bergen, for example, refer to the **Bergen Touring**

Club (p. 325), whose members have spent years hiking through the western fjord country and can advise about the best trails.

- **Skiing:** This is the undisputed top winter sport in Norway, attracting top-notch skiers and neophytes from around the world. Norway is a pioneer in promoting skiing as a sport for persons with disabilities. Modern facilities comparable to those in Europe's alpine regions dot the landscape. If you're a serious skier, consider the best winter resorts in Voss, Geilo, and Lillehammer (site of the 1994 Winter Olympics). See chapters 9 and 11.

- **Mountain Climbing:** Local tourist offices can offer advice, but what we like best are guided hikes to the archaeological digs of the 8,000-year-old Stone Age settlements near the Hardangerjøkulen (Hardanger Glacier). The digs are about an hour's drive north of the mountain resort of Geilo. For information, contact the **Turistinformasjonen** (© **32-09-59-00**). See chapter 11.

4 The Best Festivals & Special Events

- **Bergen International Festival:** This European cultural highlight, which takes place in late May and early June, ranks in importance with the Edinburgh and Salzburg festivals. Major artists from all over the world descend on the small city to perform music, drama, opera, ballet, folkloric presentations, and more. The works of Bergen native Edvard Grieg dominate the festival, and daily concerts are held at his former home, Troldhaugen. Contemporary plays are also performed, but the major focus is on the works of Ibsen. See chapter 8.

- **Molde International Jazz Festival:** In this "City of Roses," Norway's

oldest jazz festival is held every summer, usually around mid-July. Some of the best jazz artists in the world fly in for this event. People stay up most of the night listening to music and drinking beer. Sometimes the best concerts are the impromptu jam sessions in smoky little clubs. See chapter 8.

- **Holmenkollen Ski Festival:** This large ski festival takes place in March at the Holmenkollen Ski Jump, on the outskirts of Oslo. The agenda is packed with everything from international ski-jumping competitions to Norway's largest cross-country race for amateurs. See chapter 8.

5 The Best Museums

- **Viking Ship Museum** (Oslo): Three stunning burial vessels from the Viking era were excavated on the shores of the Oslofjord and are now displayed in Bygdøy, Oslo's "museum island." The most spectacular is the *Oseberg*, from the 9th century, a 19m-long (64-ft.) dragon ship with a wealth of ornaments. See chapter 9.
- **Edvard Munch Museum** (Oslo): Here you'll find the most significant collection of the work of Edvard Munch (1863–1944), Scandinavia's most noted artist. It was his gift to the city, and it's a staggering treasure trove: 1,100 paintings, 4,500 drawings, and about 18,000 prints. See chapter 9.
- **Norwegian Folk Museum** (Oslo): Some 140 original buildings from all over Norway were shipped here and reassembled on 14 hectares (35 acres) at Bygdøy. Although Scandinavia is known for such open-air museums,

this one is the best. The buildings range from a rare, stave church constructed around 1200 to one of the oldest wooden buildings still standing in Norway. See chapter 9.
- **Vigelandsparken** (Oslo): This stunning park in western Oslo displays the lifetime work of Gustav Vigeland, the country's greatest sculptor. In the 30-hectare (75-acre) Frogner Park, you can see more than 200 sculptures in granite, bronze, and iron. Included is the "Angry Boy," his most celebrated work, and the most recognizable. See chapter 9.
- **Det Hanseatiske Museum** (Bergen): Depicting commercial life on the wharf in the early 18th century, this museum is housed in one of the city's best-preserved wooden buildings. German Hanseatic merchants lived in similar medieval houses near the harbor. See chapter 10.

6 The Best Buys

Most of the products mentioned below are available at better shops in Oslo and Bergen; see "Shopping" in chapters 9 and 10.

- **Ceramics:** In the 1960s and 1970s, Norway earned a reputation among potters and stoneware enthusiasts for its chunky, utilitarian pottery. The trend today is to emulate the fragile, more decorative designs popular in France, England, and Germany, so Norwegian ceramists are producing thinner, more delicate, and more ornate forms. The best selection is found at **Tibords Interiør Bergen Storsenter** (© **55-55-33-41;** p. 326) in Bergen.
- **Costumes:** Norway boasts more than 450 regional costumes, especially in

the coastal communities. The original fishermen's sweater was knit of naturally colored wool (beige, brown, black, or off-white) in a deliberately large size and then was washed in hot water so that it shrank. The tightly woven sweater could then resist water. Modern versions of these sweaters are known for their nubby texture, sophisticated patterns, and varying shades. The best purveyor of Norwegian costumes and folk dress from both north and south is **Heimen Husflid** in Oslo (© **22-41-40-50;** p. 289).
- **Crystal:** In Norway you can buy flawless crystal that's as clear as a Nordic iceberg. Norwegian tastes lean toward the clean, uncluttered

look, stressing line, form, and harmony. Crystal is sold at many stores, especially in Bergen and Oslo, but we have been consistently impressed with the selection on display at the prestigious **Norway Designs** (© 23-11-45-10; p. 288) in Oslo.

- **Knitwear:** Many visitors eagerly seek Norwegian knitwear. Among the best buys are hand-knit or "half-handmade" garments. The latter, knit on electric looms, are so personalized and made in such small quantities that only an expert can tell that they aren't completely handmade. Beautifully made Norwegian knitwear is on sale at **Norway Designs** (© 23-11-45-10; p. 288) in Oslo, and there is also an especially large selection at the **Oslo Sweater Shop** (© 22-42-42-45; p. 290), also in Oslo.

7 The Best Hotels

- **Grand Hotel,** Karl Johans Gate 31, N-0159 Oslo (© **800/223-5652** in the U.S., or 23-21-20-00; www.grand.no; p. 244): This is Norway's premier hotel, the last of Oslo's classic old-world palaces. It opened in 1874 and is still going strong. Ibsen and Munch were regular visitors. Constant renovations keep the hotel up to date and in great shape. The opulent suites house the Nobel Peace Prize winner every year.

- **Hotel Bristol,** Kristian IV's Gate 7, N-0164 Oslo 1 (© **22-82-60-00;** www.bristol.no; p. 248): Inspired by Edwardian-era British taste, the interior design here is the most lavish and ornate in Oslo. You enter a world of rich paneling, leather chairs, glittering chandeliers, and carved pillars. The most inviting area is the bar off the lobby, decorated in a library motif. The guest rooms boast painted classic furnishings and rich fabrics.

- **Radisson SAS Hotel Norge,** Nedre Ole Bulls Plass 4, N-5807 Bergen (© **800/333-3333** in the U.S., or 55-57-30-00; www.radissonsas.com; p. 311): This grand hotel on Norway's west coast is sleek, modern, and cosmopolitan. The center of Bergen's major social events, the hotel is both traditional and handsomely up-to-date. It's also equipped with all the amenities guests expect in a deluxe hotel. The service is highly professional.

- **Dr. Holms Hotel,** N-3580 Geilo (© **32-09-57-00;** www.drholms.com; p. 347): One of Norway's most famous resort hotels, this establishment was opened by Dr. Holms in 1909. It still stands for elegance, comfort, and tradition, all of which are especially evident during the winter ski season. After its face-lift in 1989, the hotel offers beautifully furnished rooms with classic styling, and two new wings with a swimming complex. Famed musical artists often perform here.

- **Clarion Collection Hotel Grand Olav,** Kjøpmannsgata 48, N-7010 Trondheim (© **73-80-80-80;** www.choicehotels.no; p. 352): This is the most stylish hotel in Norway's medieval capital, a tasteful enclave of comfort and good living. Located next to the city's concert house, the property is modern, filled with amenities, and imaginatively decorated.

8 The Best Restaurants

- **Bagatelle** (Bygdøy Allé 3, Oslo; ℰ **22-44-63-97**; p. 262): Competitors come and go, but this French restaurant in the West End of the city still reigns supreme as the finest dining room in Oslo. Known for its market-fresh ingredients and its imaginative cookery, the restaurant adjusts its menus to take advantage of every season.

- **Oro** (Tordenskioldsgate 6A, Oslo; ℰ **23-01-02-40**; p. 253): A hyperstylish restaurant, Oro is as good as it gets in Norway's capital, ranking right up there with anything Norway has to offer. The continental cuisine at this first-class dining citadel evokes the best of the restaurants of Paris.

- **Statholdergaarden** (Rådhusgata 11, Oslo; ℰ **22-41-88-00**; p. 259): Gourmets from all over Norway flock here to sample chef Bent Stiansen's interpretation of modern Norwegian cooking. Stiansen is almost fanatically tuned to what's best in any season, and he serves some of the capital's finest dishes. He uses great imagination and widely varied ingredients—everything from Arctic char to a rare vanilla bean imported from Thailand.

- **Restaurant Julius Fritzner** (Karl Johans Gate 31, Oslo; ℰ **23-21-20-00**; p. 256): One of the most impressive dining establishments to make its debut in Norway in the mid-1990s, this restaurant in the Grand Hotel is still getting rave reviews. The chef uses only the finest Scandinavian ingredients in contemporary and traditional dishes; the emphasis is on enhancing and balancing flavors rather than creating surprises.

- **Finnegaardstuene** (Rosenkrantzgate 6, Bergen; ℰ **55-55-03-00**; p. 316): In a converted Hanseatic League warehouse, this Norwegian-French restaurant is one of the finest in western Norway. The cuisine revolves around only the freshest ingredients, especially fish. The kitchen uses classical French preparation methods to create such delectable items as lime-marinated turbot in caviar sauce or breast of duck in lime and fig sauce.

- **Enhjørningen** (Bryggen, Bergen; ℰ **55-32-79-19**; p. 316): At "The Unicorn" (its English name), some of this port's best seafood is served on the ancient Hanseatic wharf set within one of the historic structures of this far western port city. In an old-fashioned setting, you'll be served some of the freshest and most savory fish and seafood dishes in the area, from the town's best bowl of fish soup to cognac-marinated salmon.

8

Planning Your Trip to Norway

This chapter contains many of the details you'll need to plan your trip to Norway. See chapter 3, "Planning Your Trip to Denmark," which includes information pertaining to Scandinavia as a whole.

1 The Regions in Brief

WESTERN NORWAY Western Norway is fabled for its fjords, saltwater arms of the sea that stretch inland. Many date from the end of the last Ice Age. Some fjords cut into mountain ranges as high as 990m (3,300 ft.). The longest fjord in western Norway is the Sognefjord, north of Bergen, which penetrates 177km (110 miles) inland. Other major fjords in the district are the Nordfjord, Geirangerfjord, and Hardangerfjord. The capital of the fjord district is **Bergen,** the largest city on the west coast. **Lofthus,** a collection of farms extending along the slopes of Sørfjorden, offers panoramic views of the fjord and the **Folgefonn Glacier.** The area north of the **Hardangerfjord** is a haven for hikers and is home to Hardangervidda National Park, which is on Europe's largest high-mountain plateau and home to Norway's largest herd of wild reindeer. The town of **Voss,** birthplace of American football great Knute Rockne, is surrounded by glaciers, fjords, rivers, and lakes.

CENTRAL NORWAY Fjords are also common in central Norway; the two largest are the Trondheimsfjord and Narnsfjord. It's not unusual for roads to pass waterfalls that cascade straight down into fjords. Many thick forests and snow-capped peaks fill central Norway. The town of **Geilo,** halfway between Bergen and Oslo, is one of Norway's most popular ski resorts. It boasts more than 130km (80 miles) of cross-country trails. **Trondheim,** central Norway's largest city, is home to Nidaros Domen, the 11th-century cathedral that was once the burial place for kings. **Røros** is a well-preserved 18th-century mining town. The medieval city of **Molde,** Norway's capital during World War II, plays host to one of Europe's largest jazz festivals. **Geiranger,** site of the Seven Sisters waterfall, is one of Norway's most popular resorts.

EASTERN NORWAY On the border with Sweden, eastern Norway is characterized by clear blue lakes, rolling hills, and green valleys. In some ways it's the most traditional part of the country. Because of its many fertile valleys, it was one of the earliest areas to be settled. Some of the biggest valleys are Valdres, Østerdal, Hallingdall, Numedal, and Gudbrandsdalen. Campers and hikers enjoy the great forests of the Hedmark region, site of Norway's longest river, the Glomma (Gløma), which flows about 580km (360 miles). The area has many ski resorts, notably **Lillehammer,** site of the 1994 Winter Olympics. Norway's most visited destination is the capital, **Oslo,** which rises from the shores of the Oslofjord. The city of **Fredrikstad,** at the mouth of the Glomma, was once the

Norway

0   100 mi
0   100 km

*Norwegian
Sea*

Vesterålen Islands

Lofoten Islands

North Cape
Honningsvåg   Vardø
                   Vadsø
Hammerfest
                   Kirkenes
              Lakselv
         Alta E6
              Karasjok
    Tromsø
         Kautokeino

Harstad
              Abisko   FINLAND
Svolvær Narvik
              Kiruna
Skutvik

Bodø
    Fauske

Svartisen

ARCTIC CIRCLE
         Mo I Rana   Luleå
         E6

A T L A N T I C   O C E A N

S W E D E N

         E6

              Umeå

Trondheim
Kristiansund
         Røros   Sundsvall
Molde
    Oppdal
Ålesund
    Åndalsnes
      Geiranger E6

Balestrand Beitostølen   Gävle
         E68 Lillehammer
    Flåm   Hamar
Voss Ulvik Gjøvik
    Geilo   Uppsala
Bergen Utne
    Eidfjord
    Kinsarvik Oslo   *Stockholm
Lofthus
         Tønsberg Karlstad
Haugesund
    Skien   *Baltic Sea*
Stavanger Sandefjord
         Fredrikstad
*North   Skara
Sea* Arendal E6
    E18   Gotland
    Kristiansand Gothenburg

Gulf of Bothnia

RUSSIA

*North
Sea*

marketplace for goods entering the country. Its 17th-century Kongsten Fort was designed to defend Norway from Sweden. **Tønsberg,** Norway's oldest town, dates from the 9th century. This area is also the site of the **Peer Gynt Road,** of Ibsen fame, and the mountainous region is home to numerous ski resorts.

SOUTHERN NORWAY

Southern Norway is sometimes referred to as "the Riviera" because of its unspoiled and uncrowded—but chilly—beaches. It's also a favorite port of call for the yachting crowd. **Stavanger,** the oil capital of Norway, is the largest southern city and also quite popular. There is much to explore in this Telemark region, which is filled with lakes and canals popular for summer canoeing and boating. **Skien,** birthplace of the playwright Henrik Ibsen (1828–1906), is primarily an industrial town. In Skien, you can board a lake steamer to travel through a series of canals. The southern part of **Kristiansand** links Norway with continental Europe. Close by is **Hamresanden Beach,** one of the longest (10km/6-mile) uninterrupted beaches in Europe. Along the western half of the district are more fjords, notably the Lysefjord, Sandefjord, and Vindefjord.

NORTHERN NORWAY

The "Land of the Midnight Sun" is a region of craggy cliffs that descend to the sea and deep, fertile valleys along deserted moors. It has islands with few, if any, inhabitants, where life has remained relatively unchanged for generations. The capital of the Nordland region is **Bodø,** which lies just north of the Arctic Circle; it's a base for Arctic fishing trips and visits to the wild Glomfjord. Norway's second-largest glacier, **Svartisen,** is also in this region, as is the city of **Narvik,** a major Arctic port and the gateway to the **Lofoten Islands.** The islands, which have many fishing villages, make up one of the most beautiful areas of Norway. Visitors come here from all over the world for sport fishing and bird-watching.

TROMS

The main city in this region is **Tromsø,** from which polar explorations launch. A key attraction is the world's northernmost planetarium. Troms contains one of Norway's most impressive mountain ranges, the Lyngs Alps, which attract winter skiers and summer hikers. **Alta,** site of the Altafjord, is reputed to have the best salmon-fishing waters in the world.

FINNMARK

At the top of Norway is the Finnmark region, home of the Sami (erroneously called Lapps). Settlements here include **Kautokeino** (the Sami town) and **Hammerfest,** the world's northernmost town. Most tourists come to Finnmark to see the **North Cape,** Europe's northernmost point and an ideal midnight-sun viewing spot. **Vardø** is the only Norwegian mainland town in the Arctic climate zone. In the 17th century it was the site of more than 80 witch burnings. The town of **Kirkenes** lies 274km (170 miles) north of the Arctic Circle, close to the Russian border.

2 Visitor Information

TOURISM BOARDS

In the **United States,** contact the **Scandinavian Tourist Board,** 655 Third Ave., Suite 1810, New York, NY 10017 (© 212/885-9700; www.goscandinavia. com), at least 3 months in advance for maps, sightseeing pointers, ferry schedules, and other information.

In the **United Kingdom,** contact the **Norwegian Tourist Board,** a division of the Scandinavian Tourist Board, Charles House, 5 Lower Regent St., London SW1Y 4LR (© 0207/839-6255, calls cost 50p per min.). You might also try the tourist board's official website: **www.visitnorway.com.**

ENTRY REQUIREMENTS

Citizens of the United States, Canada, Ireland, Australia, and New Zealand, and British subjects need a valid **passport** to enter Norway. Visas are only required if you want to stay more than 3 months.

A British Visitor's Passport is also valid for holidays and some business trips of less than 3 months. The passport can include your spouse and is valid for 1 year. Apply in person at a main post office in the British Isles, and the passport will be issued that day.

Your current domestic **driver's license** is acceptable in Norway. An international driver's license is not required.

3 Money

For a general discussion of changing money, using credit and charge cards, and other money matters, see "Money," in chapter 3.

The Norwegian Krone

For American Readers   At this writing, $1 = approximately 6.5 kroner. (Norwegian kroner are identified throughout this guidebook as NOK). Stated differently, 1NOK = approximately 15¢. This was the rate of exchange used to calculate the dollar values given throughout this edition. Bear in mind that throughout the context of this book, dollar amounts less than $10 are rounded to the nearest nickel, and dollar amounts greater than $10 are rounded to the nearest dollar.

For British Readers   At this writing, £1 = approximately 12.37NOK, or, stated differently, 1NOK = approximately 8p. This was the rate of exchange used to calculate the pound values in the table below.

Regarding the Euro   At the time of this writing, 1NOK = approximately .12€. Stated differently, 1€ = approximately 8.36NOK. These rates can and probably will change during the lifetime of this edition. For updates on these currency conversions, check an up-to-date source at the time of your arrival in Norway.

NOK	US$	UK	Euro	NOK	US$	UK	Euro
1.00	0.15	0.08	0.12	75.00	11.55	6.00	9.00
2.00	0.31	0.16	0.24	100.00	15.40	8.00	12.00
3.00	0.46	0.24	0.36	125.00	19.25	10.00	15.00
4.00	0.62	0.32	0.48	150.00	23.10	12.00	18.00
5.00	0.77	0.40	0.60	175.00	26.95	14.00	21.00
6.00	0.92	0.48	0.72	200.00	30.80	16.00	24.00
7.00	1.08	0.56	0.84	225.00	34.65	18.00	27.00
8.00	1.23	0.64	0.96	250.00	38.50	20.00	30.00
9.00	1.39	0.72	1.08	275.00	42.35	22.00	33.00
10.00	1.54	0.80	1.20	300.00	46.20	24.00	36.00
15.00	2.31	1.20	1.80	350.00	53.90	28.00	42.00
20.00	3.08	1.60	2.40	400.00	61.60	32.00	48.00
25.00	3.85	2.00	3.00	500.00	77.00	40.00	60.00
50.00	7.70	4.00	6.00	1000.00	154.00	80.00	120.00

What Things Cost in Norway	US$	UK£
Taxi from Gardermoen Airport to the city center	$92.00	£48.00
Bus from Gardermoen Airport to the city center	$15.40	£8.00
Double room at the Cochs Pensjonat (inexpensive)	$98.00	£51.20
Double room at the Rainbow Hotel Cecil (moderate)	$134.00	£69.60
Double room at the Grand Hotel (very expensive)	$323.00	£168.00
Lunch for one at Mamma Rosa (inexpensive)	$30.00	£16.00
Lunch for one at A Touch of France (moderate)	$39.00	£20.00
Dinner for one, without wine, at Friskeport Vegeta Vertshus (inexpensive)	$23.00	£12.00
Dinner for one, without wine, at 3 Brødre (moderate)	$45.00	£23.20
Dinner for one, without wine, at Babette's Gjestehus (expensive)	$77.00	£40.00
Pint of beer (draft pilsner) in a bar	$8.50	£4.40
Coca-Cola in a restaurant	$4.30	£2.25
Cup of coffee in a bar or cafe	$3.70	£1.95
Admission to the Viking Ship Museum	$6.20	£3.20
Movie Ticket	$11.60	£6.00
Theater Ticket (at National Theater)	$31.00–$62.00	£16.00–£32.00

CURRENCY   The Norwegian currency is the *krone* (plural: *kroner*), written as "NOK." There are 100 *øre* in 1 krone. Bank notes are issued in denominations of 50, 100, 200, 500, and 1,000 *kroner*. Coins are issued in denominations of 50 *øre*, 1 *krone*, and 5, 10, and 20 *kroner*.

4 When to Go

CLIMATE

In the summer, the average temperature in Norway ranges from 57°F (14°C) to 65°F (18°C). In January, it hovers around 27°F (–3°C), ideal for winter sports. The Gulf Stream warms the west coast, where winters tend to be temperate. Rainfall, however, is heavy.

Above the Arctic Circle, the sun shines night and day from mid-May until late July. For about 2 months every winter, the North Cape is plunged into darkness.

THE MIDNIGHT SUN   In the summer, the sun never fully sets in northern Norway, and even in the south, the sun may set around 11pm and rise at 3am. Keep in mind that although the sun shines at midnight, it's not as strong as at midday. Bring a warm jacket or sweater.

HOLIDAYS

Norway celebrates the following public holidays: New Year's Day (Jan 1), Maundy Thursday, Good Friday, Easter, Labor Day (May 1), Ascension Day (mid-May), Independence Day (May 17), Whitmonday (late May), Christmas (Dec 25), and Boxing Day (Dec 26).

Norway's Average Daytime Temperatures

		Jan	Feb	Mar	Apr	May	June	July	Aug	Sept	Oct	Nov	Dec
Oslo	Temp (°F)	25	26	32	41	51	60	64	61	53	42	33	27
	Temp (°C)	−4	−3	0	5	11	16	18	16	12	6	1	−3
Bergen/	Temp (°F)	35	35	38	41	40	55	59	58	54	47	42	38
Stavanger	Temp (°C)	2	2	3	5	4	13	15	14	12	8	6	3
Trondheim	Temp (°F)	27	27	31	38	47	53	58	57	50	42	35	31
	Temp (°C)	−3	−3	−1	3	8	12	14	14	10	6	2	−1

NORWAY CALENDAR OF EVENTS

Dates are approximate. Check with the local tourist office before making plans to attend a specific event.

January

Northern Lights Festival, Tromsø. Classical and contemporary music performances by musicians from Norway and abroad. For more information, call *ⓒ* **77-68-90-70,** or visit www.nordlys festivalen.no. Late January.

February

Kristiansund Opera Festival. Featuring Kristiansund Opera's productions of opera and ballet, plus art exhibitions, concerts, and other events. For more information, call *ⓒ* **71-58-99-60,** or visit www.oik.no. Early February.

March

Holmenkollen Ski Festival *ⓐ*, Oslo. One of Europe's largest ski festivals, with World Cup Nordic skiing and biathlons, international ski-jumping competitions, and Norway's largest cross-country race for amateurs. Held at Holmenkollen Ski Jump on the outskirts of Oslo. To participate, attend, or request more information, contact Skiforeningen, Kongeveien 5, Holmenkollen, N-0787 Oslo 3 (*ⓒ* **22-92-32-00;** www.skiforeningen.no). Early March.

Narvik Winter Festival. Sports events, carnivals, concerts, and opera performances highlight this festival dedicated to those who built the railway across northern Norway and Sweden. For more information, contact the festival (*ⓒ* **76-94-87-00;** www.vinterfestuka. no). Second week of March to mid-April.

Birkebeiner Race, Rena to Lillehammer. This historic international ski race, with thousands of participants, crosses the mountains between Rena and Lillehammer, site of the 1994 Olympics. It's a 53km (33-mile) cross-country trek. For more information, call *ⓒ* **41-77-29-00,** or visit www.birkebeiner.no. Mid-March.

April

Vossa Jazz Festival. Three days of jazz and folk music performances by European and American artists. *ⓒ* **56-52-99-11.** www.vossajazz.no. First week of April.

May

Bergen International Festival (Bergen Festspill) *ⓐⓐ*. A world-class music event, featuring artists from Norway and around the world. This is one of the largest annual musical events in Scandinavia. Held at various venues in Bergen. For information, contact the Bergen

International Festival, Vågsallmenningen 1, 4055, Dreggen N-5835 Bergen (℃ 55-21-06-30; www.festspillene.no). Late May to early June.

June

Faerder Sailing Race. Some 1,000 sailboats participate in this race, which ends in Borre, by the Oslofjord. ℃ 23-27-56-00. www.kns.no. Mid-June.

North Cape March. This trek from Honningsvåg to the North Cape is one of the world's toughest. The round-trip march is 68km (42 miles). Contact the North Cape Tourist Office for information (℃ 78-47-68-60; www.northcape.no). Mid-June.

Emigration Festival, Stavanger. Commemoration of Norwegian immigration to North America, with exhibitions, concerts, theater, and folklore. Contact Stavanger Tourist Information (℃ 51-85-92-00; www.regionstavanger.com). Mid-June.

Midsummer Night, nationwide. Celebrations and bonfires all over Norway. For information, contact the **Scandinavian Tourist Board** (℃ 212/885-9700; www.goscandinavia.com). June 23.

Emigration Festival, Kvinesdal. Commemorates the Norwegian immigration to the United States. For information, contact the Kvinesdal Tourist Information (℃ 38-35-13-06; www.visitsydvest.no). Late June to early July.

Midnight Sun Marathon, Tromsø. The marathon in northern Norway starts at midnight. ℃ 77-67-33-63. www.msm.no. Mid-June.

July

Kongsberg International Jazz Festival ℛ. International artists participate in one of the most important jazz festivals in Scandinavia, with open-air concerts. ℃ 32-73-31-66. www.kongsberg-jazz festival.no. Early July.

Exxon Mobil Bislett Games, Oslo. International athletic competitions "are staged in Oslo, with professional participants from all over the world. ℃ 22-59-17-59. www.bislettgames.com. Mid-July.

Molde International Jazz Festival ℛ. The "City of Roses" is the site of Norway's oldest jazz festival. It attracts international stars from both sides of the Atlantic every year. Held at venues in Molde for 6 days. For details, contact the Molde Jazz Festival, Box 415, N-6401 Molde (℃ 71-20-31-50; www.moldejazz.no). Mid-July.

Norway Cup International Youth Soccer Tournament, Oslo. The world's largest youth soccer tournament attracts 1,000 teams from around the world to Oslo. For information, call ℃ 22-28-90-57, or visit www.norwaycup.no. Late July to early August.

Telemark International Folk Music Festival, Bø. An international festival of folk music and folk dance takes place in the home of many famous fiddlers, dancers, and singers. For information, call ℃ 35-95-19-19, or visit www.telemarkfestivalen.no. July 30 to August 2.

August

Peer Gynt Festival, Vinstra. Art exhibitions, evenings of music and song, parades in national costumes, and other events honor Ibsen's fictional character. For information, call ℃ 61-29-47-70, or visit www.peergynt.no. Early August.

Oslo Jazz Festival. This annual festival features music from the earliest years of jazz (1920–25), as well as classical concerts, opera, and ballet. Contact the Oslo tourist Bureau (℃ 81-53-05-55; www.oslojazz.no). Second week of August.

Chamber Music Festival, Oslo. Norwegian and foreign musicians perform at Oslo's Akershus Castle and Fortress, which dates from A.D. 1300. For information, call © **23-10-07-30,** or visit www.oslokammermusikkfestival.no. Mid-August.

World Cup Summer Ski Jumping, Marikollen. This event takes place in Marikollen, Raelingen, just outside the center of Oslo. Mid-August.

September

International Salmon Fishing Festival, Suldal. Participants come from Norway and abroad to the Suldalslagen River, outside Stavanger in western Norway. For information, call © **57-74-75-05,** or visit www.vestkysten.no. Dates vary.

Oslo Marathon. This annual event draws some of Norway's best long-distance runners. For information, call © **47-23-33-18-00,** or visit www.oslo maraton.no. Mid-September.

December

Nobel Peace Prize Ceremony, Oslo. This major event attracts world attention. Held at Oslo City Hall. Attendance is by invitation only. For information, contact the Nobel Institute, Henrik Ibsen Gate 51, N-0255 Oslo 2 (© **22-12-93-00;** www.nobel. se). December 10.

5 The Active Vacation Planner

BICYCLING   Bikes can be rented in just about every town in Norway. Inquire at your hotel or the local tourist office. The Norwegian Mountain Touring Association (see "Hiking," below) provides inexpensive lodging for those who take overnight bike trips. For suggestions on tours, maps, and brochures, contact **Den Rustne Eike,** Vestbaneplassen 2, N-0458 Oslo (© **22-44-18-80;** www.denrustne eike.no).

BIRD-WATCHING   Some of Europe's noteworthy bird sanctuaries are on islands off the Norwegian coast or on the mainland. Rocky and isolated, the sanctuaries offer ideal nesting places for millions of seabirds that vastly outnumber the local human population during certain seasons. Foremost among the sanctuaries are the **Lofoten Islands**—particularly two of the outermost islands, Vaerøy and Røst—and the island of Runde. A .4km (¼-mile) bridge (one of the longest in Norway) connects **Runde** to the coastline, a 2½-hour drive from Ålesund. Runde's year-round human population is about 150, and the colonies of puffins, cormorants,

razor-billed auks, guillemots, gulls, and eider ducks number in the millions. Another noteworthy bird sanctuary is at **Fokstumyra,** a national park near Dombås.

The isolated island of **Lovund** is a 2-hour ferry ride from the town of Sandnesjøen, south of Bodø. Lovund ("the island of puffins") has a human population of fewer than 270 and a bird population in the hundreds of thousands. You can visit Lovund and the other famous Norwegian bird-watching sites on your own, or sign up for one of the organized bird-watching tours sponsored by such highly recommended companies as **Borton Overseas,** 5412 Lyndale Ave., Minneapolis, MN 55419 (© **800/843-0602** or 612/882-4640; www.bortonoverseas. com).

Brochures and pamphlets are available from the tourist board **Destination Lofoten** (© **76-06-98-00**).

FISHING   Norway has long been famous for its salmon and trout fishing. The best months for salmon are June and July, and the season extends into August.

Sea trout fishing takes place from June to September and is best in August. The brown trout season varies with altitude.

Fishing in the ocean is free. To fish in lakes, rivers, or streams, anyone over 16 must have a fishing license. A license to fish in a lake costs from 95NOK ($15/£7.60); in a river, 190NOK ($29/£15). National fishing licenses can be purchased at local post offices. For more information, contact the **Bergen Angling Association,** Fosswinckelsgate 37, Bergen (© **55-32-11-64**).

A U.S.-based company that can arrange fishing (as well as hunting) excursions anywhere within Norway and the rest of Scandinavia is **Five Stars of Scandinavia,** 13104 Thomas Rd., KPN, Gig Harbor, WA 98329 (© **800/722-4126;** www.5stars-of-scandinavia.com). For a truly unusual fishing experience, they can arrange rentals of old-fashioned fishermen's cottages in the isolated Lofoten Islands. The rustic-looking, fully renovated cottages each lie adjacent to the sea and evoke 19th-century isolation in a way that you'll find either wondrous or terrifying, depending on your point of view.

One of the most qualified fishing outfitters in Bergen spends part of its time delivering food, tools, and spare parts to the thousands of fishermen who make their living in boats and isolated fjords along the western coast of Norway. **Camperlan,** P.O. Box 11, Strandkaien 2, N-5083 Bergen (© **55-32-34-72**), and its president and founder, Capt. Dag Varlo, will take between two and four passengers out for deep-sea fishing excursions in the teeming seas off the country's western coast. Although the boats go out in all seasons, midsummer is the most appealing because of the extended daylight hours.

GOLFING Many golf clubs are open to foreign guests. Greens fees tend to be moderate. Our two favorite clubs are the **Oslo Golf Klubb** (18 holes) at Bogstad,

Oslo (© **22-51-05-60;** www.oslogk.no), and the 18-hole **Meland Golf Club,** Meland/Frekhaug, 36km (22 miles) north of Bergen (© **56-17-46-00;** www.melandgolf.no).

HIKING The mountains and wilderness make hiking a favorite pastime. The **Norwegian Mountain Touring Association,** Storgata 3, N-0101 Oslo 1 (© **22-82-28-22;** www.dntoa.no), offers guided hikes that last 5 to 8 days. They cost $501 to $578, including meals and lodging.

HORSEBACK RIDING Many organizations offer horseback tours of Norway's wilderness, enabling visitors to see some of the more spectacular scenery. Tours can range from a few hours to a full week and are available all over the country. Luggage is transported by car. One tour organizer is **Borton Overseas,** 5412 Lyndale Ave., Minneapolis, MN 55419 (© **800/843-0602** or 612/882-4640; www.bortonoverseas.com).

SAILING Norway's long coast can be a challenge to any yachting enthusiast. The most tranquil havens are along the southern coast. To arrange rafting or boat trips, along with boat rentals and evening parasailing, call **SeaAction** (© **94-36-85-14** or 33-33-69-93; www.seaaction.com).

SCUBA DIVING Excellent diving centers provide scuba-diving trips and instruction. There are a number of shipwrecks along Norway's extensive coastline and fjords. Diving information is available from **Dykkernett** (© **22-02-31-39;** www.dykkernett.no).

SKIING Norway's skiing terrain is world class. The optimum months are February and March (the first half of Apr also tends to be good). Two of the principal resorts, **Geilo** and **Voss,** lie on the Oslo-Bergen rail line. The most famous and easily accessible resort is **Lillehammer,** north of Oslo. In and around the Norwegian capital skiing is common; the

Tracing Your Norwegian Roots

If you're of Norwegian ancestry, you can get information on how to trace your family history from the nearest Norwegian consulate. In Norway, contact the **Norwegian Emigration Center,** Strandkaien 31, N-4005 Stavanger (© 51-53-88-60; www.emigrationcenter.com), for a catalog of information about Norwegian families who emigrated to the United States.

In the United States, the **Family History Library of the Church of Jesus Christ of Latter-day Saints,** 35 N. West Temple, Salt Lake City, UT 84150 (© 801/240-2331; www.familysearch.org), has extensive records of Norwegian families that emigrated to the United States and Canada. The library is open to the public without charge for genealogical research. Mormon churches in other cities have listings of materials available in Salt Lake City; for a small fee you can request pertinent microfilms, which you can view at a local church.

famous ski jump, **Holmenkollen,** with its companion ski museum, is minutes from the heart of Oslo. Its yearly ski championship attracts ace skiers from all over Europe and North America every March.

Norwegian ski resorts are known for their informality, which is evident in the schools and the atmosphere. The emphasis is on simple pleasures, not the sophistication often found at alpine resorts. (Incidentally, the word *ski* is an Old Norse word, as is *slalom.*)

Much of Norwegian skiing is cross-country—perfect for the amateur—and there are lots of opportunities for downhill skiing. Other winter sports include curling, sleigh rides, and skating. All major centers have ski lifts, and renting equipment in Norway is much cheaper than in some luxury resorts.

Norway also offers summer skiing, both downhill and cross-country, at summer ski centers near glaciers. You can get more information from the **Stryn Sommerskisenter,** N-6880 Stryn (© 57-87-40-40; www.strynefjellet.com).

WHALE-WATCHING   In Norway you can catch a glimpse of 19m-long (65-ft.), 39,600-kilogram (88,000-lb.) sperm whales, the largest toothed whales in the world. You can also see killer whales, harbor porpoises, minke whales, and white-beaked dolphins. Whale researchers conduct 6-hour whale-watching tours in the Arctic Ocean.

For information and bookings, contact **Passage Tours of Scandinavia,** 239 Commercial Blvd., Fort Lauderdale, FL 33308 (© 800/548-5960 or 954/776-7070; www.passagetours.com). Whale-watching in the Lofoten Islands can be arranged by **Borton Overseas,** 5412 Lyndale Ave., Minneapolis, MN 55419 (© 800/843-0602 or 612/882-4640; www.bortonoverseas.com).

6 Health & Insurance

For general information, see "Travel Insurance" in chapter 3.

Put your essential medicines in your carry-on luggage and bring enough prescription medications to last through your stay. In Norway, pharmacists cannot legally honor a prescription written outside the country; if you need more of your medications, you'll have to see a doctor and have a new prescription written.

Norway's national health plan does not cover American or Canadian visitors.

Medical expenses must be paid in cash. Medical costs are generally more reasonable than elsewhere in western Europe.

7 Tips for Travelers with Special Needs

A number of resources and organizations in North America and Britain can assist travelers with special needs in trip planning. For details, see "Specialized Travel Resources" in chapter 3.

FOR TRAVELERS WITH DISABILITIES   Scandinavian countries have been in the vanguard of providing services for people with disabilities. In general, trains, airlines, ferries, and department stores and malls are accessible. For information about wheelchair access, ferry and air travel, parking, and other matters, contact the Norwegian Tourist Board (see "Visitor Information," earlier).

The **Norwegian Association of the Disabled,** Schweigaardsgt #12, 9217 Grønland, 0185 Oslo (© **24-10-24-00;** www.nhf.no), provides useful information.

FOR GAY & LESBIAN TRAVELERS Call **Gay/Lesbian Visitor Information,** St. Olavs Plass 2, N-0165 Oslo (© **22-11-05-09**). An English-speaking

representative will give you up-to-date information on gay and lesbian life in Oslo and let you know which clubs are currently in vogue. In Norway, gays and lesbians have the same legal status as heterosexuals, with the exception of adoption rights. Legislation passed in 1981 protects gays and lesbians from discrimination. In 1993, a law was passed recognizing the "partnerships" of homosexual couples—in essence, a recognition of same-sex marriages. The age of consent for both men and women in Norway is 16 years of age.

FOR SENIORS   Mention the fact that you're a senior citizen when you first make your travel reservations. All major airlines and many Norwegian hotels offer discounts for seniors.

In Norway, people over age 67 are entitled to 50% off the price of first- and second-class train tickets. Ask for the discount at the ticket office.

8 Getting There

BY PLANE

For more information on plane travel options, see "Getting There" in chapter 3.

All transatlantic flights from North America land at Oslo's Fornebu Airport. **SAS** (© **800/221-2350** in the U.S.; www.scandinavian.net) flies nonstop daily from Newark to Oslo.

If you fly to Norway on another airline, you'll be routed through a gateway city in Europe and sometimes continue on a different airline. **British Airways** (© **800/AIRWAYS** in the U.S.; www. britishairways.com), for example, has dozens of daily flights from many North American cities to London, and you

can continue to Oslo. **Icelandair** (© **800/223-5500** in the U.S.; www. icelandair.com) can be an excellent choice, with connections through Reykjavik. **KLM** (© **800/347-7747** in the U.S.; www.nwa.com) serves Oslo through Amsterdam.

For passengers from the U.K., **British Airways** (© **0870/850-9850** in the U.K.) operates at least four daily nonstops to Oslo from London. **SAS** (© **0870/ 6072-7727** in the U.K.) runs four daily flights from Heathrow to Oslo. Flying time from London to Oslo on any airline is around 2 hours.

Summer (generally June–Sept) is the peak season and the most expensive. Norway's off-season is winter (about Nov 1–Mar 21). Shoulder season (spring and fall) is in between. In any season, midweek fares (Mon–Thurs) are lowest.

BY CAR

If you're driving from the Continent, you must go through Sweden. From **Copenhagen,** take the E-47/55 express highway north to Helsingør, and catch the car ferry to Helsingborg, Sweden. From there, E-6 runs to Oslo. From **Stockholm,** drive across Sweden on E-18 to Oslo.

BY TRAIN

Copenhagen is the main rail hub for service between Scandinavia and the rest of Europe. There are three daily trains from Copenhagen to Oslo. All connect with the Danish ferries operating either to Norway through Helsingør or Hirtshals.

Most rail traffic from Sweden into Norway follows the main corridors between Stockholm and Oslo and between Gothenburg and Oslo.

Thousands of trains run from Britain to the Continent, and at least some of them go directly across or under the Channel, through France or Belgium and Germany into Denmark, where connections can be made to Norway. Because of the time and distances involved, many passengers rent a couchette (sleeping berth), which costs around 222NOK ($38/£18) per person. Couchettes are designed like padded benches, stacked bunk-style, and are usually clustered six to a compartment.

BY SHIP & FERRY

FROM DENMARK The trip from Frederikshavn at the northern port of Jutland in Denmark to Oslo takes 11 hours. **Stena Line** (✆ **96-20-02-00;** www. stenaline.com, for general reservations 24 hr.) operates the service.

FROM SWEDEN From Strømstad, Sweden, in the summer, the daily crossing to Sandefjord, Norway, takes 2½ hours. Bookings can be made through **Color Line,** Tollbugata 5, N-3210 Sandefjord (✆ **810-00-811;** www.colorline.com).

FROM ENGLAND **Sea Europe Holidays,** 6801 Lake Worth Rd., suite 107, Lake Worth, FL 33467 (✆ **800/533-3755** in the U.S.; www.seaeurope.com).

BY CRUISE SHIP

Norway's fjords and mountain vistas are among the most spectacular panorama in the world. Many ship owners and cruise lines offer excursions along the Norwegian coast.

One of the most prominent lines is **Cunard** (✆ **800/7-CUNARD** in the U.S. and Canada; www.cunard.com). Eleven- and 5-day cruises on the new Cunard flagship, *Queen Mary 2,* are available. This new vessel re-creates the grandeur of those old queen liners, *Queen Mary* and *Queen Elizabeth,* but overall is more modern and larger. The 150,000-ton ship carries a total of 2,620 passengers.

Departing from Southampton, England, the ship calls at Oslo and Bergen, and cruises the North Sea. En route it also stops at the most frequently visited fjords. Prices for the 5-day cruise include round-trip airfare to London on British Airways from 79 gateway cities throughout the world.

9 Special Interest Tours

One of the best ways to see Norway's wilderness is by organized tour. The following are just a few of the many tours that are available. Check with your travel agent for other options or a custom-designed tour. All prices in this section are per person with double occupancy.

Norway's brisk waters are known for the abundance and quality of their salmon, with a season lasting from June 1 to August 31. The best salmon-fishing tours are arranged in central Norway, especially along the Guala River, one of the country's best-known salmon-fishing rivers. Week-long fishing tours are offered in Trondheim by **Ursus Major** (© **99-22-49-60;** www.ursus-major.no).

In July and August, 6-day **bike trips** run through the Lofoten Islands. They offer moderately rolling terrain, dramatic scenery, traditional *rorbuer* (fishing cottage) lodging, and hearty regional cuisine. Prices begin at 18,868NOK ($3,198/£1,509). Tours are offered by **Backroads** (© **800/ GO-ACTIVE;** www.backroads.com).

10 Getting Around

BY PLANE

The best way to get around Norway is to take advantage of air passes that apply to the whole region. If you're traveling extensively, special European passes are available.

WITHIN NORWAY Norway has excellent air service. In addition to SAS, two independent airways, Braathens and Wideroe Flyveselskap, provide quick and convenient ways to get around a large country with many hard-to-reach areas. All three airlines offer reduced rates (known as "minifares") available when booked outside Norway.

BRAATHENS In a partnership with SAS, Braathens (© **91-50-54-00** in Oslo, or 55-23-55-23 in Bergen; www.braathens. no) carries more passengers on domestic routes than any other airline in Norway. It has regularly scheduled flights inside Norway, linking major cities as well as more remote places not covered by other airlines. Its air routes directly link Oslo with all major Norwegian cities; it also offers frequent flights along the coast, from Oslo to Tromsø and to Longyearbyen on the island of Spitsbergen.

OTHER AIRLINES Linked to the SAS reservations network, **Wideroe** (© **81-00-12-00;** www.wideroe.no) specializes in STOL (short takeoff and landing) aircraft. It services rarely visited fishing communities on offshore islands, isolated fjord communities, and destinations north of the Arctic Circle. For more information or tickets, contact SAS or local travel agents in Norway.

BY TRAIN

Norway's network of electric and diesel-electric trains runs as far as Bodø, 100km (62 miles) north of the Arctic Circle. (Beyond that, visitors must take a coastal steamer, plane, or bus to Tromsø and the North Cape.) Recently upgraded express trains (the fastest in the country) criss-cross the mountainous terrain between Oslo, Stavanger, Bergen, and Trondheim. For information and reservations, log on to the Norwegian State Railways (NSB; © 81-50-08-88; www.nsb.no).

On express and other major trains, you must reserve seats at the train's starting station. Sleepers are priced according to the number of berths in each compartment. Children 4 to 15 years of age and seniors pay 50% of the regular adult fare. Group and midweek tickets are also available.

EURAIL NORWAY PASS A restricted rail pass applicable only to the state railway lines, the Eurail Norway Pass is available for 3 to 8 days of unlimited rail travel in 1 month. It's suitable for anyone who wants to cover the long distances that separate Norwegian cities. The pass is available in North America through **Rail Europe** (© **800/848-7245;** www.raileurope.com). The cost is $227 for adults in second class for any 3 days in 1 month. For 4 days of travel in 1 month, second class cost is $268. For 5 days of travel in 1 month, second class cost is $310. For 6 days of travel in 1 month, second class cost is $351. For 7 days of travel in 1 month, second class cost is $393. For 8 days of travel in 1 month, second class is $435. Children 4 to 15 years of age pay half the adult fare, and those under 4 ride free.

MINIPRIS TICKETS   NSB's regional trains offer unlimited travel for 199NOK to 299NOK ($31–$46/£16–£24), no matter what your destination: Geilo, Tronheim, even Bodø in the north. The offer is valid for a limited number of seats. You can purchase the ticket by logging on to www.nsb.no. Tickets are often sold out, so make reservations as soon as possible. At this price, tickets are not refundable, and a change of reservation is not possible. A 50NOK fee ($7.70/£4) will grant you access to the NSB "Komfort Class" section.

BY BUS

Trains or coastal steamers may not go directly to your destination, but passengers can usually continue on a scenic bus ride. Norway's bus system is excellent, linking remote villages along the fjords. Numerous all-inclusive motorcoach tours, often combined with steamer travel, leave from Bergen and Oslo in the summer. The train ends in Bodø; from there you can get a bus to Fauske (63km/39 miles east). From Fauske, the Polar Express bus spans the entire distance along the Arctic Highway, through Finnmark (Lapland) to Kirkenes near the Russian border and back. The segment from Alta to Kirkenes is open from June to October, but there's year-round service from Fauske to Alta. Passengers are guaranteed hotel accommodations along the way.

Buses have air-conditioning, toilets, adjustable seats, reading lights, and a telephone. Reservations are not accepted on most buses, and payment is made to the driver on board. Fares depend on the distance traveled. Children under 4 travel free, and children 4 to 16 and seniors pay half price. For the Oslo-Sweden-Hammerfest "Express 2000," a 30-hour trip, reservations must be made in advance.

For more information about bus travel in Norway, contact **NOR-WAY Busseks-press AS,** Karl Johans Gate (© **81-54-44-44;** www.nor-way.no) in Oslo, or **Passage Tours of Scandinavia** (© **800/548-5960** in the U.S.; www.passagetours.com).

BY CAR & FERRY

Dazzling scenery awaits you at nearly every turn. Some roads are less than perfect (often dirt or gravel), but passable. Most mountain roads are open by May 1; the so-called motoring season lasts from mid-May to the end of September. In western Norway hairpin curves are common, but if you're willing to settle for doing less than 240km (about 150 miles) a day, you needn't worry. The easiest and most convenient touring territory is in and around Oslo and south to Stavanger. However, you can drive to the North Cape.

Bringing a car into Norway is relatively uncomplicated. If you own the car you're driving, you must present your national driver's license, car registration, and proof that the car is insured. (This proof usually takes the form of a document known as a "Green Card," which customs agents will refer to specifically.) If you've rented a car in another country and want to drive it into Norway, be sure to verify at the time of rental that the registration and insurance documents are in order.

If you're driving through any of Norway's coastal areas, you'll probably have to traverse one or many of the country's famous fjords. Although more and more bridges are being built, Norway's network of privately run ferries is essential for transporting cars across hundreds of fjords and estuaries. Motorists should ask the tourist bureau for the free map "Norway by Car," and a timetable outlining the country's dozens of car ferry services. The cost for cars and passengers is low.

RENTALS   Avis, Budget, and Hertz offer well-serviced, well-maintained fleets of rental cars in Norway. Prices and terms tend to be more favorable for those who reserve vehicles in North America before their departure and who present evidence of membership in such organizations as AAA or AARP. The major competitors' prices tend to be roughly equivalent, except for promotional deals scheduled from time to time. Prices should include the 23% government tax. It pays to ask questions before you commit to a prepaid reservation. Each company maintains an office at the Oslo airport, in the center of Oslo, and at airports and city centers elsewhere around the country. Contact **Budget** (© **800/527-0700** in the U.S. and Canada; www.budget.com); **Hertz** (© **800/654-3001** in the U.S.; www.hertz.com); or **Avis** (© **800/331-1212** in the U.S.; www.avis.com).

INSURANCE   Rates include nominal insurance coverage, which is probably enough for most drivers and most accidents. However, if you did not buy additional insurance and you have a mishap, your responsibility depends on the car-rental firm. At some companies, without additional insurance, you might be held responsible for the car's full value. No matter what type of insurance you choose, remember that driving after having consumed even a small amount of alcohol is punishable by heavy fines, imprisonment, or both.

11 Recommended Books

HISTORY & MYTHOLOGY   *The Vikings,* by Johannes Brøndsted (Penguin), is one of the most enjoyable and best-written documents of the age of the Vikings.

Quisling: A Study in Treason, by Oddvar K. Hoidal (Oxford University Press), studies the world's most famous traitor, Quisling, who was executed by the Norwegians for running the Nazi puppet government.

The Vinland Sagas: The Norse Discovery of America was translated by Magnus Magnusson and Hermann Palsson (Penguin). Viking fans will not be able to put down this incredible chronicle, detailing how Norwegian Vikings sailed in their long ships to the eastern coast of "Vinland" (America) as early as the 10th century.

LITERATURE & THEATER   *The Governor's Daughter,* by Camilla Collett (several editions), was published in 1854 and is often called the first modern Norwegian novel.

Ibsen Plays: One to Six, by Henrik Ibsen (Heinemann Educational), presents the works of Norway's greatest playwright, including *A Doll's House* and *Hedda Gabler.*

The Ferry Crossing, by Edvard Hoem (Garland), was a success in 1989 and depicts a tiny Norwegian coastal village in an unorthodox story form.

FAST FACTS: Norway

Area Code   The international country code for Norway is **47**. If you're calling from outside the country, the city code is **2** for Oslo and **5** for Bergen. Inside Norway, no area or city codes are needed. Phone numbers have eight digits.

Business Hours Most **banks** are open Monday to Friday from 8:15am to 3:30pm (on Thurs to 5pm) and are closed Saturday and Sunday. The bank at Fornebu Airport is open daily from 7am to 10:30pm, and there's another bank at Gardermoen Airport, open Monday to Saturday from 6:30am to 8pm, and Sunday from 7am to 8pm. Most **businesses** are open Monday to Friday from 9am to 4pm. **Stores** are generally open Monday to Friday from 9am to 5pm (many stay open on Thurs until 6 or 7pm) and Saturday 9am to 1 or 2pm. Sunday closings are observed.

Dentists For emergency dental services, ask your hotel or host for the nearest dentist. Most Norwegian dentists speak English.

Doctors If you become ill or injured while in Norway, your hotel can refer you to a local doctor, nearly all of whom speak English. If you don't stay at a hotel, call ℂ **113,** the national 24-hour emergency medical number.

Drugstores Drugstores, called *apotek,* are open during normal business hours.

Electricity Norway uses 220 volts, 30 to 50 cycles, AC, and standard continental two-pin plugs. Transformers and adapters will be needed with Canadian and American equipment. Always inquire at your hotel before plugging in any electrical equipment.

Embassies & Consulates In case you lose your passport or have some other emergency, contact your embassy in Oslo. The embassy of the **United States** is at Henrik Ibsensgate 48, N-0244 Oslo (ℂ 22-44-85-50); **United Kingdom,** Thomas Heftyes Gate 8, N-0244 Oslo (ℂ 23-13-27-00); and **Canada,** Wergelandsveien 7, N-0244 Oslo (ℂ 22-99-53-00). The **Irish Embassy** is at Haakon VII's gate 1, N-0244 Oslo (ℂ 22-01-72-00). The **Australian Embassy** is closed in Oslo; contact the Australian Consulate, Strandveien 20, Lysaker N-1324 (ℂ 67-58-48-48). The **New Zealand Embassy** is also closed in Oslo; contact the **New Zealand Consulate,** Strandveien 50, Lysaker, N1324 (ℂ 67-11-00-33). There is a British consulate in Bergen at Carl Konowsgate 34 (ℂ 55-36-78-10).

Emergencies Throughout Norway, call ℂ **112** for the **police,** ℂ **110** to report a **fire,** or ℂ **113** to request an **ambulance.**

Laundry & Dry Cleaning Most hotels provide these services. There are coin-operated launderettes and dry cleaners in most Norwegian cities.

Liquor Laws Most restaurants, pubs, and bars in Norway are licensed to serve liquor, wine, and beer. The drinking age is 18 for beer and wine, and 20 for liquor.

Mail Airmail letters or postcards to the United States and Canada cost 10.50NOK ($1.60/85p) for up to 20 grams (7/10 oz.). Airmail letters take 7 to 10 days to reach North America. The principal post office in Norway is Oslo Central Post Office, Dronningensgate 15, N-0101 Oslo. Mailboxes are vibrant red, embossed with the trumpet symbol of the postal service. They're found on walls, at chest level, throughout cities and towns. Stamps can be bought at the post office, at magazine kiosks, or at some stores.

Only the post office can weigh, evaluate, and inform you of the options for delivery time and regulations for sending parcels. Shipments to places outside Norway require a declaration on a printed form stating the contents and value of the package.

Maps Many tourist offices supply free maps of their district. You can also contact the Norwegian Automobile Club, Storgata 2, N-0155 Oslo 1 ((C) 22-34-14-00), which offers free or inexpensive road maps. Most visitors find it quicker and more convenient to buy a detailed road map; this is the best approach for anyone who plans to tour extensively outside the major cities. Some of Norway's most reliable maps are published by Cappelen.

Passports Refer to "Fast Facts" in chapter 3.

Police Dial (C) 112 nationwide.

Radio & TV Radio and television broadcasts are in Norwegian. However, Norwegian National Radio (NRK) has news summaries in English several times weekly.

Restrooms All terminals, big city squares, and the like have public lavatories. In small towns and villages, head for the marketplace. Hygiene standards are usually adequate. If you patronize the toilets in a privately run establishment (such as a cafe), it's polite to buy at least a small pastry or coffee.

Taxes Norway imposes a 19.4% value-added tax (VAT) on most goods and services, which is figured into your final bill. If you buy goods in any store bearing the tax-free sign, you're entitled to a cash refund of up to 18.5% on purchases costing more than 310NOK ($48/£25). Ask the shop assistant for a tax-free shopping check, and show your passport to indicate that you're not a resident of Scandinavia. You may not use the articles purchased before leaving Norway, and they must be taken out of the country within 3 months of purchase. Complete the information requested on the back of the check you're given at the store; at your point of departure, report to an area marked by the tax-free sign, not at customs. Your refund check will be exchanged there in *kroner* for the amount you are owed. Refunds are available at airports, ferry and cruise-ship terminals, borders, and train stations.

Telephone & Telegrams Direct-dial long-distance calls can be made to the United States and Canada from most phones in Norway by dialing (C) 00 (double zero), then the country code (1 for the U.S. and Canada), followed by the area code and phone number. Check at your hotel's front desk before you place a call. Norwegian coins of 1NOK (15¢/8p), 5NOK (75¢/4p), and 10NOK ($1.55/8p) are used in the increasingly rare pay phones.

Telegrams can be sent from private or public phones by dialing (C) 0138.

Time Norway operates on Central European Time—1 hour ahead of Greenwich Mean Time and 6 hours ahead of Eastern Standard Time. Norway goes on summer time—1 hour earlier—from the end of March until around the end of September.

Tipping Hotels add a 10% to 15% service charge to your bill, which is sufficient unless someone has performed a special service. Most bellhops get at least 15NOK ($2.30/£1.20) per suitcase. Nearly all restaurants add a service charge of up to 15% to your bill. Barbers and hairdressers usually aren't tipped, but toilet attendants and hatcheck people expect at least 3NOK (4¢/25p). Don't tip theater ushers. Taxi drivers don't expect tips unless they handle heavy luggage.

Water Tap water is generally safe to drink throughout Norway. Never drink from a mountain stream, fjord, or river, regardless of how clean it might appear.

9

Oslo

We've watched Oslo, the capital of Norway, grow from a sprawling country town into the sophisticated metropolis it is today. Fueled by oil money from the "black gold" of the North Sea, Oslo today is permeated with a Nordic *joie de vivre* in contrast to its staid, dull reputation of yesterday, when locals preferred a bowl of hot porridge at dinner instead of a sizzling steak.

"We have become Eurochic," the mayor of Oslo told us. "Today when one of the local Oslovians comes into my office, I no longer expect to be greeted by a blond Viking. Although still wed to our Nordic roots, we are now ethnically diverse. I might be extending my hand to a refugee from Somalia, or an aging Vietnam veteran."

Oslo has some of the greatest museums of northern Europe, but still manages, in spite of its growing population, to have more greenbelts than any other European capital. There are still virgin forests in Oslo and zillions of hiking trails that lead to fjords or mountains.

"We've never lost our love of nature," said writer Bente Hamsun, "but we are now cosmopolitan. We're so cosmopolitan, in fact, that we even drink cosmopolitans. Stockholm and Copenhagen may have more nightlife and cultural events than us, but we're getting there."

The only problem is that Oslo is one of the most expensive cities in Europe. Proceed with caution if you're on a strict budget.

Oslo was founded in the mid–11th century by a Viking king and became the capital around 1300 under Haakon V. In the course of its history, the city burned down several times; fire destroyed it in 1624. The master builder Christian IV, king of Denmark and Norway, ordered the town rebuilt near the Akershus Castle. He named the new town Christiania (after himself), its official name until 1924, when the city reverted to its former name.

In 1814, Norway separated from Denmark and united with Sweden, a union that lasted until 1905. During that period the Royal Palace, the House of Parliament, the old university, the National Theater, and the National Gallery were built.

After World War II, Oslo grew to 454 sq. km (175 sq. miles); it now has 530,000 inhabitants. It is one of the largest of world capitals in acreage—not in population.

Oslo is also one of Europe's most heavily forested cities, and its citizens relish this standing. Oslovians love nature in both summer and winter. When the winter snows fall, they bundle up and take to their nearby ski slopes. During their brief summer, they're quick to shed their clothes and head to the pine-covered hills in the north for long hikes and picnics, or else for sails on the blue waters of Oslofjord to the south. After a long winter slumber, the fjord suddenly becomes clogged with hundreds of sailboats, motorboats, Windsurfers, and dozens of sunbathers taking in the few precious days of summer sun Oslovians are granted.

1 Orientation

ARRIVING

BY PLANE   Planes from all over the world fly into **Oslo International Airport** in Gardermoen (© **81-55-02-50**), about 50km (31 miles) east of downtown Oslo, a 45-minute drive from the center. All domestic and international flights coming into Oslo arrive through this much-upgraded airport, including aircrafts belonging to SAS, British Airways, and Icelandair.

There's frequent bus service, departing at intervals of between 15 and 30 minutes throughout the day, into downtown Oslo. Bus service is maintained by **SAS** (© **22-80-49-71**; www.flybussen.no), whose buses deliver passengers to the Central Railway station and to most of the SAS hotels within Oslo. The cost is 100NOK ($15/£8) per person. There's also a high-speed railway service between Gardermoen and Oslo's main railway station, requiring a transit time of only 20 minutes, priced at 110NOK ($17/£8.80) per person each way. If you want to take a taxi, be prepared for a lethally high charge of around 600NOK to 700NOK ($92–$108/£48–£56) for up to four passengers plus their luggage. If you need a "maxi-taxi," a minivan that's suitable for between 5 and 15 passengers plus their luggage, you'll be charged 900NOK ($139/£72).

BY TRAIN   Trains from the Continent, Sweden, and Denmark arrive at **Oslo Sentralstasjon,** Jernbanetorget 1 (© **81-50-08-88** for train information), located at the beginning of Karl Johans Gate, in the center of the city. The station is open daily from 4:30am to 1am. From the Central Station, trains leave for Bergen, Stavanger, Trondheim, Bodø, and all other rail links in Norway. You can also take trams to all major parts of Oslo. Lockers and a luggage office are available at the station, where you can exchange money if needed.

BY CAR   If you're driving from mainland Europe, the fastest way to reach Oslo is to take the car ferry from Frederikshavn, Denmark. From Frederikshavn, car ferries run to several towns near Oslo and to Gothenburg, Sweden. You can also take a car ferry from Copenhagen to several points in western Sweden, or from Helsingør, Denmark, to Helsingborg, Sweden. Highway E-6 runs the length of Sweden's western coast from Malmö through Helsingborg and Gothenburg, right up to Oslo. If you're driving from Stockholm to Oslo, take E-3 west to Örebro, where it connects with E-18 to Oslo. Once you're near the outskirts of Oslo from any direction, follow the signs into the Sentrum.

BY FERRY   Ferries from Europe arrive at the Oslo port, a 15-minute walk (or a short taxi ride) from the center. From Denmark, Scandinavia's link with the Continent, ferries depart for Oslo from Copenhagen, Hirtshals, and Frederikshavn.

From Strømstad, Sweden, in the summer the daily crossing to Sandefjord, Norway, takes 2½ hours; from Sandefjord, it's an easy drive or train ride north to Oslo.

Tips **High-Speed Link from Stockholm**

The first high-speed train between Stockholm and Oslo has reduced travel time to 4 hours and 50 minutes between these Scandinavian capitals. Depending on the day, there are two to three trains daily in each direction, and this high-speed train now competes directly with air travel.

VISITOR INFORMATION

Assistance and information for visitors are available at the **Tourist Information Office,** Fridtjof Nansens Plass 5, N-0160 Oslo (© **24-14-77-00;** www.visitoslo.com). Free maps, brochures, sightseeing tickets, and guide services are available. The office is open from June to August daily 9am to 7pm; April to May and September Monday to Saturday 9am to 5pm; and October to March Monday to Friday 9am to 4pm.

The information office at the **Oslo Sentralstasjon (Central Station),** Jernbanetorget 1, is open daily from May to September 8am to 11pm and October to April daily 8am to 5pm. There's no phone.

CITY LAYOUT

MAIN ARTERIES & STREETS   Oslo is at the mouth of the Oslofjord, which is 97km (60 miles) in length. Opening onto the harbor is **Rådhusplassen (City Hall Square),** dominated by the modern City Hall, a major attraction. Guided bus tours leave from this point, and the launches that cruise the fjords depart from the pier facing the municipal building. You can catch Bygdøy-bound ferries from the quay at Rådhusplassen. On a promontory to the east is **Akershus Castle.**

Karl Johans Gate, Oslo's main street (especially for shopping and strolling), is north of City Hall Square. This boulevard begins at Oslo Sentralstasjon (Central Station) and stretches all the way to the 19th-century Royal Palace at the western end.

A short walk from the palace is the famed **Studenter Lunden (Students' Grove),** where seemingly everybody gathers on summer days to socialize. The University of Oslo is nearby. Dominating this center is the National Theater, guarded by statues of Ibsen and Bjørnson, the two greatest names in Norwegian theater. South of the theater, near the harbor, is **Stortingsgata,** another shop-filled street.

The main city square is **Stortorvet,** although it's no longer the center of city life, which has shifted to Karl Johans Gate.

At a subway stop near the National Theater, you can catch an electric train to **Tryvannstårnet,** the loftiest lookout in Scandinavia, and to the **Holmenkollen Ski Jump.**

FINDING AN ADDRESS   Street numbers begin on the southern end of streets running north-south and on the eastern end of streets running east-west. Odd numbers are on one side of the street, and even numbers on the other. Where large buildings hold several establishments, different addresses are designated with A, B, and C.

STREET MAPS   Maps of Oslo are distributed free at the tourist office (see "Visitor Information," above). For extensive exploring, especially of some back streets, you may need a more detailed map. Opt for a pocket-size map with a street index that can be opened and folded like a wallet. Such maps are sold at most newsstands in the central city. If you can't find a map, go to the city's most central bookstore, **Tanum Karl Johan,** Karl Johans Gate 43 (© **22-41-11-00**).

NEIGHBORHOODS IN BRIEF

Oslo is made for walking—in fact, you can walk from the Central Station all the way to the Royal Palace (Slottet) in a straight line. Except for excursions to the museum-loaded Bygdøy peninsula and the Holmenkollen Ski Jump, most attractions can be covered on foot.

Oslo is not neatly divided into separate neighborhoods or districts. It consists mainly of **central Oslo,** with the Central Station to the east of the city center and the Royal Palace to the west. Karl Johans Gate, the principal street, connects these two points. Central Oslo is the heart of the city, the most crowded and traffic-congested, but also the most convenient place to stay. Those on the most rushed of schedules—the average visitor spends only 2 days in Oslo—will book an accommodation in the center. It's not a real neighborhood, but it's the core of the city, as Piccadilly Circus is to London. Most Oslo hotels and restaurants are here, as are almost 50 museums and galleries—enough to fill many a rainy day. The best of the lot include Akershus Castle, the Historical Museum, and the National Gallery.

The streets Drammensveien and Frognerveien lead northwest to Frogner Park (Frognerparken), whose main entrance is on Kirkeveien. This historical area is the site of the Vigeland Sculpture Park, which displays some of Gustav Vigeland's masterpieces.

The **Old Town** (or Gamlebyen) lies south of the Parliament Building (the Stortinget) and Karl Johans Gate. This section contains some of the city's old-fashioned restaurants, along with the Norwegian Resistance Museum and the Old Town Hall. A stay here is the same as staying in central Oslo (see above). The only difference is that the streets of the Old Town have more old-fashioned Norwegian flavor than the more modern parts of central Oslo.

Aker Brygge is Oslo's newest neighborhood, and while it's an excellent place for dining and diversions, it is sadly lacking in hotels. For sights along the waterfront, it's the best place for long walks to take in the port life. It emerged near the mouth of the Oslofjord in the old wharf area formerly used for shipbuilding yards. Fueled by oil wealth, steel-and-glass buildings now rise from what had been a relatively dilapidated section. Some of the best shops, theaters, restaurants, and cultural attractions are here, along with apartments for such well-heeled owners as Diana Ross.

The main attractions in **eastern Oslo** are the Botanisk Hage (Botanic Garden), the Zoological Museum, and the Munch Museum in Tøyen—little more is worth seeing here. Unless you're interested in seeing those sights mentioned, you might skip eastern Oslo. However, thousands of visitors head here just to see the Munch Museum (p. 276).

The **West End** is a chic residential area graced with some of the city's finest hotels and restaurants. It's a more tranquil setting than the center and only 15 minutes away by public transportation. Many visitors who stay here don't mind the short commute and prefer this area to the more traffic-clogged center. However, for walking and sightseeing, central Oslo and its port are more alluring. There is little to see in the West End unless you like walking up and down pleasant residential streets.

Farther west—6km (about 4 miles) by car but better reached by car ferry—is the **Bygdøy** peninsula. Here you'll find such attractions as the Norwegian Folk Museum, the Viking ships, the polar ship *Fram,* and the *Kon-Tiki* Museum. Break up your sightseeing venture with a meal here, but plan to stay elsewhere.

The suburb of **Frogner** begins .8km (½ mile) west of Oslo's center and stretches for a mile or so. Unless you specifically have business here, you might skip this section of the city.

Lying behind the S-station, the main rail station for Oslo, is the **Grønland district,** where many Oslovians go for ethnic dining. There are large Pakistani and Indian communities here, but the town's best Indian and Pakistani restaurants lie within more upscale neighborhoods. Come here for affordable dining, not for long, leisurely walks. On a hurried visit, you could afford to skip Grønland entirely without suffering any cultural loss.

At last, once-staid Oslo has grown big and diverse enough to have its own trendy, counterculture district. Lying in east Oslo is trendy **Grünerløkka,** which most of its inhabitants refer to affectionately as "Løkka." This once-run-down sector of Oslo traditionally was known as the worker's district. Today many professional Oslovians are moving in to restore apartments, and the district is the site of several fashionable cafes and restaurants. Those seeking nightlife options can check out some of the establishments in this area.

Many Oslo neighborhoods lie along the **Oslofjord,** which stretches more than 97km (60 miles) north from the Skagerrak to Oslo. Basins dotted with islands fill the fjord. (There are 40 islands in the immediate Oslo archipelago.) Chances are you won't be staying or dining along the fjord, but might consider a boat trip along the water, as it's a grand attraction on a summer day.

Nearly all visitors want to see **Holmenkollen,** a wooded range of hills northwest of the city rising to about 226m (1,740 ft.). You can reach it in 35 minutes by electric train from the city center. Skiers might want to stay here in winter, lodging at the Holmenkollen Park Hotel Rica. Otherwise, come for the view and perhaps make it a luncheon stopover; then head back to the historic core.

Marka, Oslo's forest, is a sprawling recreation area with hiking, bicycling, skiing, fishing, wild-berry picking, jogging trails, and more. It contains 343 lakes, 500km (310 miles) of ski trails, 623km (387 miles) of trails and roads, 11 sports chalets, and 24 ski jumps and alpine slopes. If you like to go for long walks on summer days, Marka's the spot for you. It's also one of the best places in Greater Oslo for a picnic.

2 Getting Around

BY PUBLIC TRANSPORTATION

Oslo has an efficient citywide network of buses, trams (streetcars), and subways. Buses and electric trains take passengers to the suburbs; from mid-April to October, ferries to Bygdøy depart from the harbor in front of the Oslo Rådhuset (City Hall).

DISCOUNT PASSES   The **Oslo Pass** can help you become acquainted with the city at a fraction of the usual price. It allows free travel on public transportation, free admission to museums and other top sights, discounts on sightseeing buses and boats, a rebate on your car rental, and special treats in restaurants. You can purchase the card at hotels, fine stores, and tourist information offices, from travel agents, and in the branches of Sparebanken Oslo Akershus. Adults pay 210NOK ($32/£17) for a 1-day card, 300NOK ($46/£24) for 2 days, and 390NOK ($60/£31) for 3 days. Cards for kids 4 to 15 cost 90NOK ($14/£7.20), 110NOK ($17/£8.80), and 140NOK ($22/£11); 3 and under free.

BY BUS, TRAM & SUBWAY   Jernbanetorget is Oslo's major **bus and tram** terminal stop. Most buses and trams passing through the heart of town stop at Wessels Plass, next to the Parliament, or at Stortorvet, the main marketplace. Many also stop at the National Theater or University Square on Karl Johans Gate, as well as stopping through Oslo's suburbs.

The **subway (T-banen)** has four branch lines to the east. The Western Suburban route (including Holmenkollen) has four lines to the residential sections and recreation grounds west and north of the city. Subways and trains leave from near the National Theater on Karl Johans Gate.

For schedule and fare information, call Trafikanten (© **81-50-01-76;** www.trafikanten.no). The ticket is valid for one ride. When you put it into the machine, it punches it, which invalidates it for any future use after your ride is over. Drivers sell single-trip tickets for 30NOK ($4.60/£2.40); children 4 to 15 travel for half fare; 3 and under are free. An eight-coupon Flexi card costs 160NOK ($25/£13) and is half price for children. Maxi cards can be used for unlimited transfers for 1 hour from the time the ticket is stamped.

BY TAXI

If you need a taxi, call © **23-23-23-23,** available 24 hours a day. Reserve at least an hour in advance.

Hiring a taxi is very expensive in Oslo. Tariffs start at 30NOK ($4.60/£2.40) for hailed taxis in the streets, or at 50NOK ($7.70/£4) if you summon one in advance. In addition to regular fares, there are lethal surcharges between 5 and 10pm costing 110NOK ($17/£8.80), or between 10pm and 4am costing 210NOK ($32/£17). All taxis have meters, and Norwegian cab drivers are generally honest. When a cab is available, a roof light goes on. Taxis can be hailed on the street, provided they're more than 91m (300 ft.) from a taxi stand. The most difficult time to hail a taxi is Monday to Friday from 8:30 to 10am and 3 to 5pm, and Saturday from 8:30 to 10am.

BY CAR

Driving is not a practical way to get around Oslo because parking is limited. The efficient public transportation system makes a private car unnecessary. You can reach even the most isolated areas by public transportation.

Among the multistory parking lots in the city center, the best is **Vestre Vika Bilpark,** Dronning Mauds Gate (© **22-83-35-35**). The cost of parking a car in a public garage is 48NOK ($7.40/£3.85) per hour or 175NOK ($27/£14) for 24 hours. Illegally parked cars are towed away. For car problems, call the **NAF Alarm Center** (© **22-34-14-00**), available 24 hours a day.

BY FERRY

Beginning in mid-April, ferries depart for Bygdøy from Pier 3 in front of the Oslo Rådhuset. For schedules, call **Båtservice** (© **23-35-68-90**). The ferry or bus to Bygdøy is a good choice, because parking there is limited. Other ferries leave for various parts of the Oslofjord. Inquire at the **Tourist Information Office,** Fridtjof Nansens Plass 5, N-0160 Oslo (© **24-14-77-00**).

BY BICYCLE

Den Rustne Eike, Vestbaneplassen 2 (© **22-83-52-08**), rents bikes at moderate rates, complete with free maps of interesting routes in Oslo and its environs. The cost is 270NOK to 280NOK ($42–$43/£22–£23) per day, or 900NOK ($139/£72) per week, with a 1,000NOK ($154/£80) deposit required. It's open May to October daily 9am to 9pm; in the off season, it's open Monday to Friday 10am to 6pm.

FAST FACTS: Oslo

American Express American Express Reisebyrå, Karl Johans Gate 33 (© 22-98-37-00), is open Monday to Friday 9am to 6pm, Saturday 10am to 4pm.

Area Code The country code for Norway is **47**. If you're calling from outside the country, the city code for Oslo is **2**. Inside Norway, no area or city codes are needed. Telephone numbers have eight digits.

Babysitters Hotels can often enlist the help of a housekeeper for "child-minding." Give at least a day's notice, or two if you can. You can also contact the tourist office (see "Visitor Information," above), which keeps a list of available sitters on file.

Bookstores Oslo has many bookstores. The most central and one of the best stocked is **Tanum Karl Johan,** Karl Johans Gate 43 (© **22-41-11-00**).

Currency Exchange **Banks** will exchange most foreign currencies or cash traveler's checks. Bring your passport for identification. If banks are closed, try automated machines at the Oslo Sentralstasjon to exchange currency. You can also exchange currency at the **Bureau de Change** at the main Oslo post office, Dronningensgatan 15 (© **23-14-90-00**).

Dentists Oslo is home to many excellent dentists, and many of them will rearrange their schedules on short notice to handle a foreign visitor who is in dental pain. If you're having a dental emergency, you can contact either of these organizations at extended hours, usually 24 hours a day, for the address of a dentist who can take a new client on short notice: **Volvat Medisinske Senter (Volvat Medical Center),** Borgenveien 2A (© **22-95-75-00**); and **Oslo Legevakt (Oslo Emergency Hospital),** Storgten 40 (© **22-11-80-80;** ask for emergency services).

Doctors Some larger hotels have arrangements with doctors in case a guest becomes ill, or try the 24-hour **Oslo Akuttetaten (Emergencies),** Storgata 40 (© **22-93-22-93**). A privately funded alternative is **Oslo Akutten,** Nedre Vollgate 8 (© **22-00-81-60**). For more routine medical assistance, you can contact the biggest hospital in Oslo, **Ullaval,** Kirkeveien 166 (© **22-11-80-80**). To consult a private doctor (nearly all of whom speak English), check the telephone directory, or ask at your hotel for a recommendation.

Drugstores A 24-hour pharmacy is **Jernbanetorvets Apotek,** Jernbanetorget 4A (© **22-41-24-82**).

Embassies & Consulates See "Fast Facts: Norway," in chapter 8.

Emergencies Dial the Oslo **police** at © **112;** to report a **fire,** call © **110;** call an **ambulance** at © **113.**

Eyeglass Repair **Ulf Jacobsen Optiker,** Karl Johans Gate 20 (© **22-00-83-10**), is a big eyeglass supplier. Most contact lenses are in stock, too. Unusual prescriptions take about 2 days. Hours are Monday and Wednesday to Friday 9am to 5pm, Tuesday 9am to 6pm, and Saturday 10am to 3pm.

Internet Access You can tap in free at the Rådhuset, the City Hall on Rådhusplassen (© **23-46-16-00**). There is also free service at the library (see below), where you must sign up for slots.

Laundry & Dry Cleaning Washing and drying can usually be completed in an hour. You must have your coins ready to put in the machines. Dry cleaning is extremely expensive in Oslo, and many establishments take more than a week to return clothing. Try **American Lincoln Norge,** Østmarkv 25 (© **22-27-24-50**), which promises 24-hour service.

Libraries The Oslo municipal library, **Diechmann Library,** Henrik Ibsens Gate 1 (© **23-43-29-00**; T-banen: Stortinget), is the largest in Norway. It has many English-language volumes, a children's department, and a music department. Hours are Monday to Friday 10am to 8pm (to 6pm June to August), Saturday 9am to 2pm (11am to 2pm June to August).

Lost Property It's uncertain—even in law-abiding Norway—whether someone will actually return a valuable object that you've lost, but the two most obvious places to begin your search are the Lost Property office at Gardermoen Airport (© **64-81-34-77**), which is open daily 7am to 6pm; and the Lost Property office at the Central Railway Station (© **23-15-40-47**), open Monday to Friday midnight to 5pm.

Luggage Storage & Lockers Facilities for luggage storage are available at the **Oslo Sentralstasjon,** Jernbanetorget 1 (© **81-50-08-88**). It's open daily 4:30am to 1am. Lockers cost 30NOK to 60NOK ($4.60–$9.25/£2.40–£4.80) per day, depending on size.

Newspapers & Magazines English-language newspapers and magazines are sold—at least in the summer months—at newsstands throughout Oslo. International editions, including the *International Herald Tribune* and *USA Today,* are always available, as are the European editions of *Time* and *Newsweek.*

Photographic Needs Try **Preus Photo,** Karl Johans Gate 33 (© **22-42-98-04**), for supplies, including black-and-white and color film. Film can be developed in 1 hour. It's open Monday to Friday 9am to 5pm, and Saturday 10am to 3pm.

Police Dial © **112.**

Post Office The **Oslo General Post Office** is at Dronningensgatan 15 (© **23-14-90-00** for information). Enter at the corner of Prinsensgate. It's open Monday to Friday 8am to 5pm and Saturday 9am to 2pm; it's closed Sunday and public holidays. You can arrange for mail to be sent to the main post office c/o General Delivery. The address is Poste Restante, P.O. Box 1181-Sentrum, Dronningensgatan 15, N-0101 Oslo, Norway. You must show your passport to collect it.

Radio & TV The biggest broadcaster is the Norwegian government, which owns and controls programming on the NRK station. Oslo receives many broadcasts from other countries, including BBC programs from London, on 9410kHz.

Restrooms Clean public toilets can be found throughout the city center, in parks, and at all bus, rail, and air terminals. For a detailed list, contact the Tourist Information Office.

Safety Of the four Scandinavian capitals, Oslo is widely considered the safest. However, don't be lulled into a false sense of security. Be careful, and don't carry your wallet visibly exposed or sling your purse over your shoulder.

Taxes Oslo has no special city taxes. You'll pay the same value-added tax throughout the country (see "Fast Facts: Norway" in chapter 8).

Taxis See "Getting Around," above.

Transit Information For information about tram and bus travel, call **Trafikan-ten** (**(℃ 81-50-01-76**), located in front of the Central Station. For information about train travel, go to the Central Station, or call **(℃ 81-50-08-88**.

Weather See the temperature chart in section 5, "When to Go," in chapter 8.

3 Where to Stay

By the standards of many U.S. and Canadian cities, hotels in Oslo are very expensive. If you're from London, you'll feel right at home. If the prices make you want to cancel your trip, read on. Oslovian hotels lose most of their business travelers, their main revenue source, during the peak tourist months in midsummer. July is always a month for discounts. Some hotels' discounts begin June 21. Regular pricing usually resumes in mid-August. For exact dates of discounts, which often change from year to year, check with the hotel.

Hotels also slash prices on weekends—usually Friday and Saturday—and sometimes Sunday. Again, hotels often change their policies, so it's best to check when you make your reservations. Don't always expect a discount—a quickly arranged conference could lead hotels to increase their prices.

The most economy-minded visitors can cut costs by staying at one of the old-fashioned hotels that offer a number of rooms without private bathrooms. Sometimes a room has a shower but no toilet. In most cases, corridor toilets and bathrooms are plentiful. Even the rooms without bathrooms usually have a sink with hot and cold running water.

HOTEL RESERVATIONS The worst months for finding a place to stay in Oslo are May, June, September, and October, when many business conferences are held. July and August are better, even though that's the peak time of the summer tourist invasion.

If you happen to arrive in Oslo without a reservation, head for the **Oslo Tourist Information Office,** Fridtjof Nansens Plass 5 (**(℃ 24-14-77-00**), which can find you a room in your price category. The minimum stay is 2 days. Don't try to phone—the service is strictly for walk-ins who need a room on the night of their arrival.

Note: Rates quoted below include the service charge and tax. Breakfast—usually a generous Norwegian buffet—is almost always included. Unless otherwise indicated, all our recommended accommodations come with bathrooms.

CENTRAL OSLO
VERY EXPENSIVE

Grand Hotel *(★★★) (Kids)* Famous guests still arrive at the leading hotel of Norway, but perhaps none as celebrated as guests of yore, who include Henrik Ibsen, Gen. Dwight Eisenhower, and Charlie Chaplin. Today you are likely to see CEOs, Nobel Peace Prize winners, and movie stars.

Tradition and style still reign supreme, as it did when the Grand opened its doors in 1874 in a Louis XVI revival style building imbued with Art Nouveau. Constant modernization has not managed to erase its original character. The hotel stands on the wide boulevard that leads to the Royal Palace. The stone-walled hotel with its mansard gables and copper tower is now one of the most distinctive landmarks of Oslo. Guest rooms are in the 19th-century core or in one of the tasteful modern additions. Newer rooms contain plush facilities and electronic extras, and the older ones have been completely modernized. Most of the old-fashioned bathrooms are done in marble or tile and have tub/shower combinations. An eight-story extension contains larger, brighter doubles.

The hotel has several restaurants that serve international and Scandinavian food. The Palmen, the Julius Fritzner (p. 256), and the Grand Café (p. 257), the most famous cafe in Oslo, offer live entertainment. The Hotel Bristol and Hotel Continental are less pretentious, but many well-heeled families prefer the Grand. Children enjoy the indoor pool, and the reception staff keeps a list of kid-friendly activities going on in the city.

Karl Johans Gate 31, N-0159 Oslo. (C) 800/223-5652 in the U.S., or 23-21-20-00. Fax 23-21-21-00. www.grand.no. 289 units. Summer 1,500NOK ($231/£120) double, from 2,580NOK ($397/£206) suite; fall, winter, spring 2,100NOK ($323/£168) double, from 2,990NOK ($460/£239) suite. Rates include buffet breakfast. AE, DC, MC, V. Parking 200NOK ($31/£16). T-banen: Stortinget. **Amenities:** 3 restaurants; 2 bars; nightclub; indoor heated pool; fitness center; health club; sauna; solarium; shopping arcade; 24-hr. room service; babysitting; massage; laundry service/dry cleaning; nonsmoking rooms; rooms for those w/limited mobility. *In room:* A/C, TV, dataport, minibar, hair dryer, safe, trouser press.

Hotel Continental (★★★ It's not the Grand, but this deluxe hotel is beautifully appointed and more fun, attracting a big entertainment industry crowd. Although it's been around since 1900 and is still one of Norway's grand old hotels, it has a more modern aura than the Grand, is the only Norwegian member of the Leading Hotels of the World, and is the only major hotel in Oslo that's still mostly owned by an individual family. It's cozy, a bit inbred, and thoroughly welcoming in its approach to virtually everything. Expect lots of personalized touches, such as a masterful collection of framed original lithographs and woodcuts by Edvard Munch in a salon near the reception area. Bedrooms are plush and intensely well decorated, often with wallpaper and an unerring upper-crust touch, sometimes evoking comfortable bedrooms in private homes. Bathrooms are tiled or clad in marble, each with a tub/shower combination. The suites absolutely rival those at the Grand, including the Abel Suite named after the famous Norwegian mathematician Niels Henrik Abel.

Stortingsgaten 24-26, Oslo N-0117. (C) 22-82-40-00. Fax 22-42-96-89. www.hotel-continental.no. 154 units. Sun–Thurs 2,390NOK–2,900NOK ($368–$447/£191–£232) double, from 3,800NOK ($585/£304) suite; Fri–Sat 1,350NOK–2,150NOK ($208–$331/£108–£172) double, from 2,650NOK ($408/£212) suite. Rates include breakfast buffet. AE, DC, MC, V. Parking 240NOK ($37/£19). T-banen: Nationaltheatret. **Amenities:** 2 restaurants; 2 bars; 2 cafes; 24-hr. room service; babysitting; laundry service/dry cleaning; nonsmoking rooms. *In room:* A/C, TV, dataport, minibar, hair dryer, safe, trouser press.

EXPENSIVE

Clarion Hotel Royal Christiania (★ Opposite the main train station, this is one of the leading business and leisure hotels in Oslo, though not where we like to check in. In fairness, it is fine in every way—very convenient—and it has its devotees. Because it's such a mammoth pile, it doesn't have the personalized service of the Grand or Continental. This is the second-largest hotel in Norway, a soaring 14-story tower built to house athletes and administrators during the 1952 Winter Olympics. Extensively upgraded in the 1990s, with the addition of two nine-story wings, today it's a luxury hotel that is comparable to the nearby Radisson SAS Plaza Hotel, but without so much drama. This modern hotel and the surrounding high-traffic neighborhood

Where to Stay in Oslo

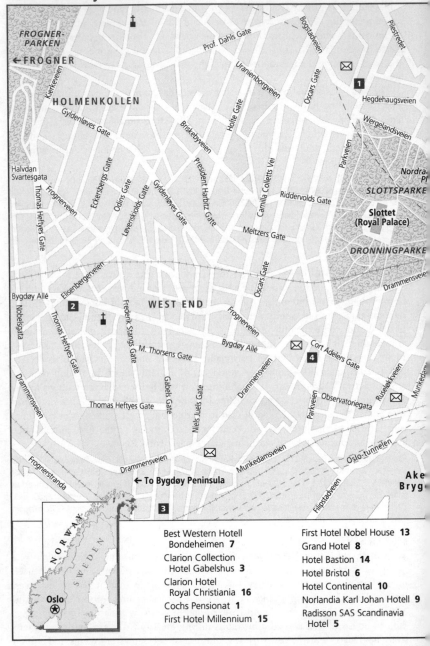

Best Western Hotell
Bondeheimen **7**

Clarion Collection
Hotel Gabelshus **3**

Clarion Hotel
Royal Christiania **16**

Cochs Pensionat **1**

First Hotel Millennium **15**

First Hotel Nobel House **13**

Grand Hotel **8**

Hotel Bastion **14**

Hotel Bristol **6**

Hotel Continental **10**

Norlandia Karl Johan Hotell **9**

Radisson SAS Scandinavia
Hotel **5**

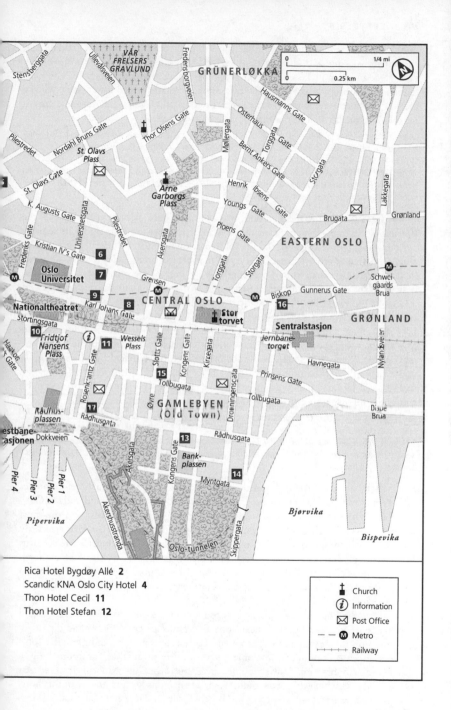

Rica Hotel Bygdøy Allé **2**
Scandic KNA Oslo City Hotel **4**
Thon Hotel Cecil **11**
Thon Hotel Stefan **12**

✝ Church
ⓘ Information
✉ Post Office
— Ⓜ — Metro
├─┼─┼─┤ Railway

don't evoke old-fashioned Norway, but you will find comfort, efficiency, good design, and a hardworking staff. The medium-size guest rooms are as quiet, conservatively decorated, and blandly tasteful as you'd expect from an international chain. The well-maintained bathrooms have tub/shower combinations and heated towel racks. We like the way the hotel stays abreast of the times, even installing a first-rate Japanese restaurant, Fuji, though you'll find a French restaurant as well.

Biskop Gunnerus' Gate 3, N-0106 Oslo. © 23-10-80-00. Fax 23-10-80-80. www.choicehotels.no. 503 units. Sun–Thurs 930NOK–1,440NOK ($143–$222/£74–£115) double, from 2,500NOK ($385/£200) suite; Fri–Sat and June 15–Aug 1 1,195NOK ($184/£96) double, 1,780NOK ($274/£142) suite. Rates include breakfast. AE, DC, MC, V. Parking 225NOK ($35/£18). Bus: 30, 31, or 41. **Amenities:** 4 restaurants; bar; indoor pool; fitness center; sauna; business center; limited room service; massage; laundry service/dry cleaning; nonsmoking rooms; rooms for those w/limited mobility. *In room:* TV, dataport, minibar, coffeemaker, hair dryer.

Hotel Bastion ★★ *Finds*   In 2006, this boutique hotel became a member of the Clarion Collection, a chain of small hotels with personal touches. Under its reincarnation, it is the closest rival to the Bristol (see below), which still has an edge up. The owner, Morten Mørch, personally selected the furniture, fabrics, and art. Of course, he got a little assistance from Anemone W. Våge, one of the best known Norwegian designers (she even decorated the apartments of the royal family nearby). In the Old Town of Oslo, within walking distance of Karl Johans Gate, this is a warm, inviting, residential-style property, a "bastion" of comfort. The midsize-to-spacious bedrooms have style, taste, and comfort, yet are also intimate and unpretentious. If you want to go upmarket, you can ask for one of the junior or deluxe suites, among the best in the capital. Bathrooms are deluxe, with tubs big enough to be shared by a loving couple and a view of the in-bathroom TV. In the better suites, the bathrooms have separate showers and Jacuzzis. Guests can frequent the chic lobby bar for drinks or dinner, or gather the following morning in the lounge for a bountiful breakfast buffet.

Skippergaten 7, N-0152 Oslo. © 800/528-1234 or 22-47-77-00. Fax 22-33-11-80. www.hotelbastion.no. 99 units. Mon–Thurs 1,150NOK ($177/£92) double, 2,200NOK ($339/£176) suite; Fri–Sun 795NOK ($122/£64) double, 1,700NOK ($262/£136) suite. AE, DC, MC, V. T-banen: Jernbanetorget. **Amenities:** Breakfast lounge; lobby bar; fitness center; room service (3–10pm); laundry service; nonsmoking rooms. *In room:* A/C, TV, dataport, minibar, iron, beverage maker, trouser press.

Hotel Bristol ★★★ *Kids*   Imbued with character, this 1920s-era hotel competes aggressively and gracefully with two other historic properties, the Grand and the Continental. Of the three, the Bristol consistently emerges as the hippest and the most accessible. To show that it believes in keeping up with the times, it added a security wing with bulletproof windows. Film stars, pop stars, writers, and musicians select this hotel as their favorite in Norway. Set in the commercial core of Oslo, 1 block north of Karl Johans Gate, the Bristol is warm, rich with tradition, and comfortable. It also isn't as formal as either the Grand or the Continental, attracting the media, arts, and showbiz communities with a sense of playfulness.

In 2001, the hotel almost doubled its room count, thanks to the annexation and conversion of an office building next door. Bedrooms are comfortable and dignified, but not as plush or as intensely "decorated" as the rooms in either of its grander competitors. Each accommodation comes with a tiled or marble bathroom with a tub/shower combination. Lavish public areas still evoke the Moorish-inspired Art Deco heyday in which they were built. There's enormous life and energy in this hotel thanks to active restaurants, such as the Bristol Grill (p. 256), and piano bars.

Kristian IV's Gate 7, N-0164 Oslo 1. © **22-82-60-00**. Fax 22-82-60-01. www.bristol.no. 252 units. Mon–Fri 2,000NOK ($308/£160) double; Sat–Sun 1,000NOK–1,300NOK ($154–$200/£80–£104) double, 4,000NOK–7,580NOK ($616–$1,167/£320–£606) suite. Rates include breakfast buffet. AE, DC, MC, V. Tram: 10, 11, 17, or 18. **Amenities:** 2 restaurants; 2 bars; live pianist in the lobby; nightclub/dance bar; small-scale exercise room and fitness center; spa; limited room service; laundry service/dry cleaning; nonsmoking rooms. *In room:* A/C, TV, dataport, minibar, hair dryer, trouser press.

Radisson SAS Scandinavia Hotel 🦁
As the sun sets over Oslo, we like to gather with friends at Summit 21 on the 21st floor for one of the grandest vistas of Oslo. This black, angular hotel doesn't quite escape the impersonal curse of its 1975 construction, but it tries nobly and succeeds rather well on its interior. Thanks to aggressive, seasonal price adjustments and an appealing setting, this "grandfather" of Oslo's modern hotels boasts an average occupancy rate of 73%, as opposed to the Norwegian national average of only 54%. With 22 floors, this is Oslo's third-biggest hotel (after the Radisson SAS Plaza Hotel and the Clarion Hotel Royal Christiana), the second-tallest building, and the first hotel that most Oslovians think of when they hear the name "SAS Hotel." It also has a wider range of amenities than much of its younger competition. Bedrooms are relatively large and very comfortable, and come in about a dozen different styles, including Scandinavian, Japanese, ersatz "rococo," Art Deco, and, the latest, a nautical style inspired by the maritime traditions of Norway.

Holbergsgate 30, N-0166 Oslo. © **23-29-30-00**. Fax 23-29-30-01. www.radissonsas.com. 488 units. 1,195NOK–2,095NOK ($184–$323/£96–£168) double; from 3,500NOK ($539/£280) suite. Rates include breakfast. AE, DC, MC, V. Parking 180NOK ($28/£14). T-banen: Nationaltheatret. **Amenities:** 3 restaurants; bar; indoor pool; fitness room; sauna; underground shopping arcade; laundry service/dry cleaning; nonsmoking rooms; rooms for those w/limited mobility. *In room:* A/C, TV, dataport, minibar, coffeemaker, safe.

MODERATE

Best Western Hotell Bondeheimen *(Value*
You won't find Madonna roaming the hallways, but you'll meet fellow guests who are more interested in value than in frills. In the city center, a short block from the Students' Grove at Karl Johans Gate, the Bondeheimen was built in 1913 and translates as "farmers' home." A cooperative of farmers and students established this hotel, now a Best Western, to provide affordable, teetotalist-friendly accommodations when they visited Oslo from the countryside. Although small, the compact rooms are comfortably furnished, often with Norwegian pine pieces. Bedrooms are larger than standard with tasteful furniture, and the bathrooms, although small and mostly without tubs, contain shower units and heated floors. On site is a Kaffistova restaurant, dispensing reasonably priced food that's just a cut above typical cafeteria fare.

Rosenkrantzgate 8 (entrance on Kristian IV's Gate), N-0159 Oslo 1. © **800/633-6548** in the U.S., or 23-21-41-00. Fax 23-21-41-01. www.bondeheimen.com. 127 units. Mon–Thurs 1,390NOK ($214/£111) double; Fri–Sun 1,090NOK ($168/£87) double. Rates include breakfast. AE, DC, MC, V. Parking 140NOK ($22/£11). Tram: 7 or 11. **Amenities:** Restaurant; boutique; laundry service/dry cleaning; nonsmoking rooms; rooms for those w/limited mobility. *In room:* TV, dataport, minibar, coffeemaker, hair dryer, iron.

First Hotel Millennium 🦁🦁 *(Kids*
Since there are two "First" hotels in Oslo, a choice has to be made. If you're given one of the better rooms, we prefer the Millennium, as it is one of the "personality" hotels of Oslo, known for its cozy atmosphere and character. As reflected by the price, rooms are standard and superior. The standard rooms are comfortable in every way, but the superior ones among the most spacious in town, with many Art Deco touches in the furnishings and designs. On the top floor

are a dozen accommodations with their own large balconies opening onto cityscape views, and naturally these are booked first. Family rooms are also very spacious, with a separate bedroom and living area. All the bedrooms have wood floors and bathrooms equipped with a shower. The First Lady Room is filled "with everything a woman needs" such as a large, comfortable robe, slippers, a vanity kit, and more. Rising nine floors behind a pale pink facade, the hotel is noted for a stylish kind of minimalism, and the location is central to everything from Akershus Fortress to the fashionable shops along Karl Johans Gate. Primo & Ciao, the on-site restaurant, offers first-rate Mediterranean and Italian specialties.

Tollbugate 25, N-0157 Oslo. © 21-02-28-00. Fax 21-02-28-30. www.firsthotels.com. 112 units. 1,145NOK–1,545NOK ($176–$238/£92–£124) double. AE, DC, MC, V. T-banen: Stortinget. **Amenities:** Restaurant; bar; limited room service; babysitting; laundry service/dry cleaning; nonsmoking rooms; room for those w/limited mobility. *In room:* TV, minibar, hair dryer, Wi-Fi.

First Hotel Nobel House 🕸 *Kids*   Even though it often plays "second fiddle" to the Millennium (see above), this is nonetheless a desirable address. Each room comes with a small kitchenette, and family suites are decorated in a fairytale theme, making this a favorite with families. This elegant boutique hotel—whose lobby has a seven-story glassed-in atrium with Oriental carpets, columns, and a fireplace—has a personalized feel. A member of a Sweden-based hotel chain, the hotel has a polite staff and a lot of idiosyncratic style. This is one of the few hotels where we prefer the regular rooms to the oddly laid-out, curiously spartan suites, where lots of room might be devoted, say, to an interior hallway. Each of the suites is thematically decorated, based on the life of a famous Scandinavian, usually with photographic tributes to such opera and ballet personalities as Kirsten Flagstad, Ingrid Bjoner, and Indra Lorentzen. Rooms and suites are accessible via a labyrinthine path of stairs and many angled hallways, and are sometimes a bit hard to find unless if you're being escorted by a staff member. Each unit has some kind of original art and, in many cases, exposed brick. Regardless of your room assignment, expect an immaculate tiled bathroom with a tub/shower combo.

Kongensgate 5, N-0153 Oslo. © 23-10-72-00. Fax 23-10-72-10. 72 units. Mon–Thurs 1,556NOK ($240/£124) double, from 2,400NOK ($370/£192) suite; Fri–Sun 1,420NOK ($219/£114) double, from 1,800NOK ($277/£144) suite. Rates include breakfast. AE, DC, MC, V. Parking 155NOK ($24/£12) per night. T-banen: Stortinget. **Amenities:** Outdoor Jacuzzi on roof terrace; fitness room; sauna; laundry service/dry cleaning; nonsmoking rooms. *In room:* A/C, TV, minibar, iron.

Norlandia Karl Johan Hotell 🕸🕸   It is regrettable that this hotel was built across the street from the grander Grand, to which it is often compared unfavorably. However, if you forget that for a moment, you'll find a winning address with charm and grace. As you wander about its stylish public rooms, taking in the stained glass and circular staircase, you'll think you've stumbled into Belle Epoque Paris. The five-story hotel is in a renovated building that dates from the late 18th century, when it opened to acclaim on the main parade street of Oslo, Karl Johan. The owners have done much to imbue the hotel with character, filling the rooms with Norwegian folk art and installing antiques in every room, both public and private. The reception area sets the tone, with mirrors, marble, Asian rugs, and antiques. The medium-size bedrooms have a classic decor with excellent fabrics, double glazing on the windows to cut down on the noise outside, and tiny but marble-clad bathrooms with tub/shower combinations. We prefer the rooms that open onto the front and contain French windows from which you get a panoramic view of the central city.

Karl Johans Gate 33, N-0162 Oslo. © **23-16-17-00.** Fax 22-42-05-19. www.norlandia.no. 111 units. Mon–Fri 1,595NOK ($246/£128) double, from 2,000NOK ($308/£160) suite; Sat–Sun 1,000NOK ($154/£80) double. Rates include breakfast. AE, DC, MC, V. Parking 140NOK ($22/£11) in nearby public garage. T-banen: Nationaltheatret or Stortinget. **Amenities:** Laundry service/dry cleaning; nonsmoking rooms; rooms for those w/limited mobility. *In room:* TV, minibar, hair dryer, iron, trouser press, Wi-Fi.

Thon Hotel Cecil &_{Value} On our last visit, we sat downstairs talking to three guests, each a member of the nearby Norwegian Parliament. One member assured us that this hotel, a member of the Thon chain, represents great value—"comfortable yet affordable, an unbeatable combination." This contemporary hotel enjoys a central location, and many restaurants, sights, and shops lie within a short walk of the main entrance. Dating from 1989, it was constructed on the site of a previous hotel destroyed by fire. As if inspired by a much grander Hyatt, most of its rooms are built to open onto a central atrium. Only four rooms on each of the eight floors overlook the street (the sometimes rowdy—at least at night—Rosenkrantzgate). The well-maintained rooms are cozy and contain neatly kept bathrooms with tub/shower combinations. Expect relatively simple styling with none of the trappings of more expensive nearby competitors—there's no health club, sauna, or full-fledged room service.

Stortingsgata 8 (entrance on Rosenkrantzgate), N-0130 Oslo. © **23-31-48-00.** Fax 23-31-48-50. www. thonhotels.no. 111 units. 870NOK–1,445NOK ($134–$223/£78–£130) double. AE, DC, MC, V. Parking 160NOK ($25/£14). T-banen: Stortinget. **Amenities:** Laundry service/dry cleaning; nonsmoking rooms; rooms for those w/limited mobility. *In room:* A/C, TV, minibar, coffeemaker, hair dryer, Wi-Fi.

Thon Hotel Stefan _{Value} As "Thons" go, this is the low man on our totem pole, but is a recommendable choice if its siblings are fully booked. We've seen bigger and better hotels in Oslo, but very few that offer such comfort at these affordable rates. In an excellent location in the center of the city, this unpretentious hotel never claims to be better than it is. Built in 1952, it has been modernized and much improved over the years. The color-coordinated guest rooms are traditional in style and well furnished and maintained, with small but adequate bathrooms containing tub/shower combinations. From May until September 1, weekend rates are granted only to those who make reservations less than 48 hours before arrival.

Rosenkrantzgate 1, N-0159 Oslo 1. © **23-31-55-00.** Fax 23-31-55-55. www.thonhotels.com. 139 units. Mon–Thurs 870NOK–1,345NOK ($134–$207/£78–£121) double; Fri–Sat 670NOK ($103/£60) double. Rates include breakfast. AE, DC, MC, V. Parking 182NOK ($28/£16). Tram: 10, 11, 17, or 18. **Amenities:** Coffee shop/bar; laundry service/dry cleaning; nonsmoking rooms; rooms for those w/limited mobility. *In room:* A/C, TV, minibar, coffeemaker, hair dryer, safe, Wi-Fi.

INEXPENSIVE

Cochs Pensjonat _{Value} Cochs is the most famous and most enduring boarding house in Oslo, having been launched in 1927 by the Coch sisters. It's been greatly expanded over the years, and the policy of "resident bachelors," two or three sharing a bathless room, is long gone. This is a clean, well-conceived, inexpensive hotel that represents excellent value. The building has an ornate facade that curves around a bend in a boulevard that banks the northern edge of the Royal Palace. This is a comfortable but simple lodging whose newer rooms are high-ceilinged, spartan but pleasant, and outfitted with birch wood furniture. We infinitely prefer "the Royal Rooms," which were created in 1996 when a large apartment was incorporated into the guesthouse, looking out onto Slottsparken. You'll climb a flight of antique steps from the ground floor to reach the second-floor lobby. Rooms—including a communal TV lounge that's sometimes packed with residents—rise for two additional floors above that. Expect very few, if any, amenities and services at this hotel—rooms are without telephones. Breakfast is served at KafeCaffé in Parkveien 21.

Parkveien 25, N-0350 Oslo. (℃) **23-33-24-00.** Fax 23-33-24-10. www.cochspensjonat.no. 88 units. Rooms with bathroom, TV, and kitchenette 640NOK ($91/£58) double, 795NOK ($113/£72) triple, 940NOK ($133/£85) quad. Rooms without kitchenette and without private bathroom 540NOK ($77/£49) double, 675NOK ($96/£61) triple, 820NOK ($116/£74) quad. MC, V. Tram: 11 or 12. *In room:* TV, kitchenette (in some), no phone.

Scandic KNA Oslo City Hotel
This hotel looks deceptively new, thanks to a futuristic-looking mirrored facade that was added in the 1970s to an older core that was originally built in the 1940s by the Norwegian Auto Club. The hotel also underwent a recent renovation in 2004. Inside, you'll find a cozy lobby-level bar and restaurant serving Norwegian food, a deeply entrenched kind of informality, and a reception staff that's a bit inexperienced. Bedrooms are simple, clean, and a bit spartan-looking. The small bathrooms are shower-only. Room rates rise steeply in winter, but if you come in summer, it's a real bargain. The low summer prices and a neighborhood that's calm, quiet, and close to the Royal Palace make up for the shortcomings. If you're a self-motivated kind of traveler with a clear idea of what you want to see and where you want to go in Oslo, without much need for attention or advice from the staff, this might be an appropriate choice.

Parkveien 68, N-0254 Oslo. (℃) **23-15-57-00.** Fax 23-15-57-11. www.scandic-hotels.com/KNA. 189 units. Sept–May Sun–Thurs 895NOK–1,654NOK ($138–$255/£81–£149) double, Fri–Sat 831NOK–1,095NOK ($128–$169/£75–£99) double; June–Aug 970NOK–1,350NOK ($149–$208/£87–£122) double. No discounts on weekends June–Aug. AE, DC, MC, V. Tram: 12 or 15. **Amenities:** Restaurant; bar; health club; sauna; 24-hr. room service. *In room:* TV, minibar, trouser press.

WEST END
MODERATE
Clarion Collection Hotel Gabelshus ★ *Finds*
This Clarion Collection chain member may not be as first class as the previously recommended chain members (see earlier), but in some ways we prefer it because of its location. It's a brisk 15-minute walk from the city center on a tree-lined street. Since its opening as a guesthouse back in 1912, it has greatly expanded in a take-over of an adjoining building. Discreetly conservative, it looks like an English manor house, laced with climbing ivy. The public rooms are filled with antiques, art, burnished copper, and working fireplaces. Guest rooms are decorated with tasteful colors and textiles, and some have terraces. Go for one of those, of course. Choose between Scandinavian modern furniture or traditional styling. The accommodations are well maintained and equipped with double-glazed windows. Bathrooms are small but immaculate, with tub/shower combinations.

Gabels Gate 16, N-0272 Oslo 2. (℃) **23-27-65-00.** Fax 23-27-65-60. www.choicehotels.no. 114 units. Fri–Sun yearround 990NOK ($152/£89) double, rest of year 1,500NOK ($231/£135) double; 2,000NOK ($308/£180) suite. Rates include buffet breakfast. AE, DC, MC, V. Free parking. Tram: 10. **Amenities:** Breakfast room; lounge; sauna; laundry service/dry cleaning; sauna; nonsmoking rooms. *In room:* TV, minibar, hair dryer, Wi-Fi.

Rica Hotel Bygdøy Allé ★ *Finds*
This hotel is better equipped than the Gabelshus, but you'll pay more for the privilege. This intimate, charming hotel, the smallest in the Rica chain, has the air of an artsy boutique hotel. Its designers shoehorned it into the framework of a late-19th-century Flemish-revival brick structure in Oslo's well-heeled West End. Each of the bedrooms is different in its layout, corresponding to the already-existing towers and gables of the older structure. Room nos. 206, 214, 406,

and 414 are among the most sought-after because of their Victorian-era curved walls and bay windows. Other than that, the decor is conservative and predictably upscale—and a bit bland, usually in tones of pale blue. Each unit comes with a small bathroom with shower. Within the hotel is one of the finest restaurants in the West End, the Magma Bar & Restaurant, offering an exquisite cuisine based on the finest market-fresh ingredients. The chef, Sonja Lee, is justifiably acclaimed.

Bygdøy Allé 53, N-0265 Oslo. ℭ **23-08-58-00.** Fax 23-08-58-08. www.rica.no. 57 units. Sun–Thurs 1,360NOK–1,650NOK ($209–$254/£122–£149) double; Fri–Sat 960NOK–1,260NOK ($148–$194/£86–£113) double. Rates include breakfast. AE, DC, MC, V. Tram: 10. Bus: 30, 31, 32, or 33. **Amenities:** Restaurant; bar; limited room service; laundry service/dry cleaning; nonsmoking rooms. *In room:* TV, minibar, hair dryer, trouser press.

4 Where to Dine

You can now "dine around the world" without leaving the city of Oslo. The biggest concentration of restaurants is at Aker Brygge. This former shipbuilding yard on the harborfront is now the smartest dining and shopping complex in Norway.

The influx of immigrants in recent years has led to the growth of Mexican, Turkish, Moroccan, Chinese, Greek, and other international restaurants. Among European cuisines, French and Italian are the most popular. Many restaurants offer American-style food.

Not all restaurants in Oslo are new. Some have long been associated with artists and writers—the Grand Café, for example, was the stomping ground of Henrik Ibsen and Edvard Munch.

At nearly all restaurants recommended below a 15% service charge and the 20% value-added tax are included in the bill. No further tipping is required, although it's customary to leave some small change if the service has been satisfactory.

Wine and beer can be lethal to your final bill, so be careful.

CENTRAL OSLO
VERY EXPENSIVE

Oro 🟎🟎🟎 CONTINENTAL/MEDITERRANEAN   Oro is among our top five choices in Oslo. Gallons of ink have been used in the Norwegian press to describe this hyperstylish restaurant, winner of a Michelin star. Norwegian-born chef Mads Larsson directs the kitchen of a three-faceted establishment that includes a European gourmet restaurant, a separate but still very glamorous tapas bar, and a boutique-style deli (open Mon–Fri 11:30am–3pm). The restaurant and the tapas bar are curvaceous, slick-looking testimonials to the appeal of stainless steel and warm-toned hardwoods. We recommend the fixed-price menus, although be warned that each of them will be prepared only for every member of the table at the same time. The 995NOK ($153/£90) menu includes nine different courses, each of them composed differently every day, according to the availability of the ingredients and the whims of the chef. Other options include a three-course vegetarian menu at 450NOK ($69/£41). Representative dishes, each one delectable, include lobster ravioli, glazed scallops with Serrano ham, a platter that combines three different versions of foie gras (grilled, *en terrine*, and *en brioche*), and spit-roasted pigeon stuffed with foie gras.

Tordenskioldsgate 6A (entrance on Kjeld Stubs Gate). ℭ **23-01-02-40.** Reservations required. Main courses 300NOK–347NOK ($46–$53/£27–£31); fixed-price menus 450NOK–995NOK ($69–$153/£41–£90). AE, DC, MC, V. Mon–Sat 6–10pm. T-banen: Stortinget.

Where to Dine in Oslo

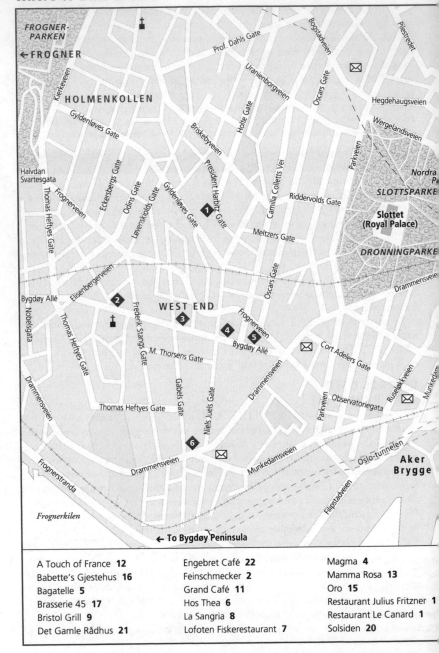

A Touch of France **12**
Babette's Gjestehus **16**
Bagatelle **5**
Brasserie 45 **17**
Bristol Grill **9**
Det Gamle Rådhus **21**

Engebret Café **22**
Feinschmecker **2**
Grand Café **11**
Hos Thea **6**
La Sangria **8**
Lofoten Fiskerestaurant **7**

Magma **4**
Mamma Rosa **13**
Oro **15**
Restaurant Julius Fritzner **1**
Restaurant Le Canard **1**
Solsiden **20**

Statholderens Krostue 23
Statholdergaarden 23
Stortorvets Gjæstgiveri 10
Terra Bar & Restaurant 14
Theatercafeen 18
3 Brødre 17

Vegeta Vertshus 19
Village Tandoori 3

† Church
ⓘ Information
⊠ Post Office
--- Ⓜ Metro
+++ Railway

Restaurant Julius Fritzner ✹✹ NORWEGIAN/CONTINENTAL   Its name-sake, Julius Fritzner, opened the Grand Hotel in 1874, so it's only fitting that the present-day owners of the hotel have named its deluxe restaurant in his honor. One of the best and most impressive restaurants in Oslo, it opened in 1995 to rave reviews, and the accolades never stopped. One floor above street level in Norway's most prestigious hotel, the venue is conservative, with a battalion of impeccably trained waiters who maintain their humor and personal touch despite the sophisticated setting. The dishes, all made with the finest Scandinavian ingredients, change with the season and the chef's inspiration. Some of the best dishes we've sampled are pan-fried turbot, lobster and caviar sauce, crispy fried cod with sautéed vegetables, poached halibut with vermouth sauce, and a tender roast saddle of lamb with aromatic fresh rosemary. Desserts, which are delicious and occasionally theatrical, include a terrine of chocolate with a compote of peaches and sorbet flavored with basil and cinnamon.

In the Grand Hotel, Karl Johans Gate 31. ✆ **23-21-20-00.** Reservations recommended. Main courses 220NOK–366NOK ($34–$56/£20–£33); 3-course fixed-price menu 480NOK ($74/£43); 4-course fixed-price menu 550NOK ($85/£50); 6-course fixed-price menu 640NOK ($99/£58). AE, DC, MC, V. Mon–Sat 5–10pm. T-banen: Stortinget.

EXPENSIVE

Babette's Gjestehus ✹ *Finds* SCANDINAVIAN/FRENCH   Visiting Babette's is not the cheapest thing to do in Oslo, but we never came away regretting the *kroner* dumped here. The tiny place is hidden away in a shopping arcade by the City Hall. Named for the heroine of the film *Babette's Feast*—which almost every Scandinavian has seen at least once—this restaurant is decorated in the style of a turn-of-the-20th-century Norwegian home. The walls are blue, the antiques are genuine, the curtains are lace, and there's a scattering of old paintings dotting the walls. The masterful chefs use seasonal products to produce reliable, superb-tasting food all year. Menu items include filets of reindeer with lingonberries, steamed brill with mustard sauce and stewed tomatoes, and pan-fried breast of duck with creamed cabbage.

Rådhuspassasjen, Roald Amundsensgate 6. ✆ **22-41-64-64.** Reservations recommended. Main courses 250NOK–310NOK ($39–$48/£23–£28); 6-course fixed-price menu 760NOK ($117/£68). AE, DC, MC, V. Mon–Sat 5–11pm. T-banen: Sentrum.

MODERATE

Bristol Grill ✹✹ CONTINENTAL   Every time we come into this dining room, we think we're entering an elegant gentleman's club in London, only women are welcomed too. This is the premier dining room of the Hotel Bristol (p. 248), one of Oslo's most prestigious hotels. You'll find old-world courtliness, formal service without a lot of flash or frenzy, and elegant decor that evokes a baronial hunting lodge from around 1924, the year the restaurant was founded. At that time, it was an all-male smoking, drinking, and dining club. A few years later, it evolved into the dining venue you'll see today, with an allure that eventually welcomed such entertainers as Frank Sinatra. You'll pass through a cozy, woodsy-looking piano bar to reach the restaurant. The culinary focus has been radically improved, and the menu continues to be one of the finest in the Norwegian capital because it is beautifully adjusted to take advantage of the best ingredients of the seasons. There's a spectacular version of bouillabaisse, prepared with Nordic fish and seasoned with saffron, which can be ordered as either a starter or a main course. We've followed this with one of the chef's most successful specialties: medallions of venison sautéed with vanilla and bacon, served on a bed of mushrooms with a terrine of potatoes.

In the Hotel Bristol, Kristian IV's Gate 7. (C) **22-82-60-00.** Reservations recommended especially at night. Main courses 210NOK–285NOK ($32–$44/£19–£26). AE, DC, MC, V. Daily 4–11pm. Tram: 10, 11, 17, or 18.

Grand Café ★★ NORWEGIAN   Over the decades, this 1874 cafe was the living and dining room for the elite of Kristiania (the old name for Oslo). The country's greatest artists have dined here with foreign diplomats, kings, and explorers. Of course, it's not as chic as it once was, but we're still loyal to it and view a night here as part of our Norwegian experience. A large mural on one wall depicts Ibsen and Edvard Munch along with other, less famous, former patrons. Pick up a postcard, sold at the reception desk, if you care to find out more about the mural's subjects. The atmosphere and tradition here are sometimes more compelling than the cuisine, but if you like solid, honest flavors, this is the place to eat. The menu relies on Norwegian country traditions (how many places still serve elk stew?). You can also order everything from a napoleon with coffee to a full meal with fried stingray or reindeer steaks.

In the Grand Hotel, Karl Johans Gate 31. (C) **23-21-20-00.** Reservations recommended. Main courses 155NOK–320NOK ($24–$49/£14–£29). AE, DC, MC, V. Mon–Sat 11am–11pm; Sun noon–11pm. T-banen: Stortinget.

La Sangria ★ *Finds* SPANISH   If you, like much of the world, believe that a day without tapas is a day in hell, you may be reluctant to visit Norway with its boiled cauliflower and reindeer steaks. However, here you can enjoy all those old tapas favorites—snails in garlic butter, fried Spanish chorizo sausage, sautéed chicken in garlic. Established in 1992 in a location across the street from the Radisson SAS Scandinavia Hotel (p. 249), within a dining room sheathed with roughly textured stucco and hand-painted Iberian porcelain, this is the best Spanish restaurant in Oslo. It was launched by two hardworking brothers (Fernando and Juan-Carlos) from Madrid, whose appreciation for both bullfighting and soccer, especially the Real Madrid team, is obvious by the posters, memorabilia, and photos displayed. Menu items evoke the flavors of Iberia and include at least two versions of paella; Serrano ham with Manchego cheese and chorizo sausage; and *bacalhau* (cod) alla Vizcaina. Our favorite dishes are bone-free chicken stuffed with ham and cheese in a white-wine sauce or (in the same sauce) bone-free slices of tender, lean lamb flavored with fresh garlic.

Holbergsgate 19. (C) **22-11-63-15.** Reservations recommended. Main courses 175NOK–200NOK ($27–$31/£14–£16). AE, DC, MC, V. Mon–Sat 3–11pm; Sun 3–10pm. Closed Dec 23–Jan 2. Tram: 11 or 19.

Terra Bar & Restaurant MEDITERRANEAN   For us, this dining venue, a three-in-one affair, fulfills a number of purposes. On site is an informal tapas bar, Terra Tapas. The tapas here are traditional and well crafted, though we find those served at La Sangria (see above) more authentic. There is also a formal stylish restaurant overlooking the Parliament and a modern wine bar in the cellar. Against the backdrop of a minimalist decor, this restaurant and bar attracts many Norwegian politicians at lunch. During the evening, a younger crowd predominates. Nearly 250 different wines are on the menu, and you can eat and drink entirely in the bar area.

   About a third of the menu here is devoted to seafood, and there are enough vegetarian dishes to satisfy the hungriest of nonmeat eaters. Menu items change, sometimes radically, with the season. Winter dishes focus on hearty beefs, hot soups, and generous cuts of beef, lamb, poultry, and game. Summer fare is lighter, with such dishes as mussels in white-wine sauce; fish that includes tuna and catfish, sometimes in a fresh dill-weed sauce; tenderloin of beef with fresh asparagus; and chicken breasts with risotto and red-wine sauce. The pastry chef is justifiably proud of the homemade Italian ice creams and sorbets.

Stortingsgaten 2. ⓒ **22-40-55-20**. Reservations recommended. Lunch salads, sandwiches, and platters 70NOK–175NOK ($11–$27/£5.60–£14); dinner main courses 200NOK–260NOK ($31–$40/£16–£21). AE, DC, MC, V. Sept–May Mon–Fri 11am–11pm, Sat noon–11pm, Sun 5–10pm; June–Aug Mon–Sat 4:30–10pm. T-banen: Stortinget.

Theatercafeen ⓕ INTERNATIONAL   The *New York Times*, with a great deal of justification, listed this cafe as among the 10 most famous on the planet. If you like to eat and drink in opulence, head here for your fix. The last of the grand Viennese cafes in northern Europe, this long-standing favorite was founded a century ago to rival the Grand Café. Each has its devotees, although we like this one better because of its Viennese schmaltz. The cafe attracts present-day *boulevardiers* and businesspeople, and serenades them with a piano and a duet of violins. With soft lighting, antique bronzes, cut-glass lighting fixtures, and Art Nouveau mirrors, it's the type of place that encourages lingering. Menu items are well prepared and traditional, and are adjusted accordingly to get the best flavors out of each season. That might mean fresh asparagus and spring lamb, or in the autumn, breast of wild goose. The fish dishes, including a casserole of fresh mussels, are particularly good. You can also enjoy such traditional Norwegian fare as reindeer with wild mushrooms or Norwegian fjord salmon.

In the Hotel Continental, Stortingsgaten 24. ⓒ **22-82-40-50**. Reservations recommended. Main courses 190NOK–320NOK ($29–$49/£15–£26); 4-course menu 500NOK ($77/£40); 5-course menu 600NOK ($92/£48); openfaced sandwiches 70NOK–90NOK ($11–$14/£5.60–£7.20) at lunch. AE, DC, MC, V. Mon–Sat 11am–11pm; Sun 3–11pm. T-banen: Stortinget.

A Touch of France ⓕ FRENCH   We're always trying to discover new places in Oslo, but we also have restaurants where we return time and time again. One of our "pets" is this most typical of all French bistros. When you take in the Art Nouveau decor, the French posters, the sidewalk tables (in the summer), and the waiters in long white aprons, you'll feel you're back in Paris. A Touch of France is known for serving the freshest oysters in town. Bouillabaisse is also a specialty here, but that grand dish loses something in translation this far north. We often opt for the traditional salt-baked leg of duck, which is served in a savory garlic sauce. On other occasions we've enjoyed a classic calves' liver with mushrooms, spinach, and bacon. After your main course, a dessert cart is wheeled around, loaded with such temptations as crème brûlée or a delectable chocolate-and-almond cake.

Øvre Slottsgate 16. ⓒ **23-10-01-60**. Reservations required. Main courses 175NOK–238NOK ($27–$37/£14–£19). AE, DC, MC, V. Mon–Sat noon–11pm. Bus: 27, 29, 30, 41, or 61.

INEXPENSIVE

Brasserie 45 ⓕ *Kids* CONTINENTAL   After watching an Ibsen play at the National Theater, we always like to head to this nearby restaurant for dinner. Airy and stylish, this second-story bistro overlooks the biggest fountain along downtown Oslo's showplace promenade. The uniformed staff bears steaming platters of ambitious, imaginative cuisine. This is a family business, and the hard-working owners use their own hands, a dogged courage, and a certain discerning taste to treat you to the best of Mother France's kitchen. In recent years they have wandered the globe for inspiration, finding it in such places as Thailand, so you'll find onion soup, chocolate mousse, and smoked moose alongside king prawns in a spicy Thai sauce. The cooks aren't afraid of simplicity—try their grilled barbecued lamb chops with garlic cloves and creamy potatoes au gratin. In summer, end with freshly picked blackberries with ice cream. Families like to come here because of the kids menu, which includes lasagna in a creamy tomato sauce.

Stortingsgaten 20. © **22-41-34-00.** Reservations recommended. Main courses 90NOK–170NOK ($14–$26/£7.20–£14). Fixed-price menu 279NOK–310NOK ($43–$48/£22–£25). AE, DC, MC, V. Mon–Thurs noon–midnight; Fri–Sat noon–1am; Sun 3–11pm. T-banen: Sentrum.

OLD TOWN (GAMLEBYEN/KVADRATUREN)
VERY EXPENSIVE

Statholderens Krostue ⚜ SWEDISH/DANISH   This relatively uncomplicated cellar-level bistro is associated with Statholdergaarden, one of Oslo's most prestigious restaurants (see below). Unlike its more sophisticated sibling, it's open for lunch as well as dinner and features relatively uncomplicated food that's mostly based on traditional Swedish and Danish recipes. The cuisine provides many original and, most of the time, happy combinations of ingredients. Beneath the vaulted Renaissance-era ceiling, you can order *frikadeller* (meatballs), minced veal patties in creamy dill sauce, steak with fried onions, fried eel with potato-and-herb dumplings, and grilled salmon with saffron-flavored noodles. Lunch specialties include platters piled high with Danish or Norwegian ham, herring, boiled eggs, and vegetables, as well as a selection of *smørrebrød* (Danish open-faced sandwiches).

Rådhusgata 11. © **22-41-88-00.** Main courses 240NOK–300NOK ($37–$46/£19–£24); fixed-price menu 400NOK ($62/£32). AE, DC, MC, V. Tues–Sat 11:30am–10pm. Tram: 11, 15, or 18.

Statholdergaarden ⚜⚜⚜ NOUVELLE NORWEGIAN   We know of no grander and more tranquil setting in Oslo for a deluxe restaurant than this restored 17th-century house offering a first floor dining room that still has its original decor. Beautifully laid tables are placed under period stucco ceilings, whose motifs reappear on the china. Come here for that special meal, like asking your partner to marry you. One of Oslo's most historic restaurant settings (the building dates from 1640) has one of its most successful chefs, Bent Stiansen, whose modern interpretation of Norwegian cuisine has attracted the admiration of gastronomies throughout the country. Menu items change frequently, according to what's in season. The best examples include grilled crayfish served with scallop and salmon tartare, and thyme-infused cod with crabmeat mousse and two sauces (a simple white-wine sauce and another based on a rare vanilla bean imported from Thailand). One of our all-time favorite dishes is lightly fried arctic char with sautéed Savoy cabbage and lime beurre blanc (white butter). Don't confuse this upscale and prestigious site with the less expensive bistro Statholderens Krostue (see above), which occupies the building's vaulted cellar.

Rådhusgata 11. © **22-41-88-00.** Reservations recommended. Main courses 292NOK–365NOK ($45–$56/£23–£29); 4-course fixed-price menu 720NOK ($111/£58); 6-course fixed-price menu 872NOK ($134/£70). AE, DC, MC, V. Mon–Sat 6–midnight. Tram: 11, 15, or 18.

EXPENSIVE

Det Gamle Rådhus (Old Town Hall) ⚜ NORWEGIAN   One of the oldest restaurants in Oslo, Det Gamle Rådhus is in Oslo's former Town Hall (1641). This is strictly for nostalgia buffs, as the restaurant is not at all cutting edge. It's there for those wanting to see Oslo the way it used to be, who won't mind that the innovative fires died a long time ago. You'll dine within a network of baronial- or manorial-inspired rooms with dark wooden panels and Flemish, 16th-century-style wooden chairs. In the spacious dining room, a full array of open-faced sandwiches is served on weekdays only. A la carte dinner selections can be made from a varied menu that includes fresh fish, game, and Norwegian specialties. If you want to sample a dish that Ibsen might have enjoyed, check out the house specialty, *lutefisk,* but hold your nose. This Scandinavian dish is made from dried fish that has been soaked in lye and then poached in broth. More to your liking might be smoked salmon (it's smoked right on the premises), a parfait of chicken livers, freshwater pikeperch sautéed in a lime sauce, or Norwegian lamb coated with herbs and baked with a glaze.

Nedre Slottsgate 1. ℂ 22-42-01-07. Reservations recommended. Main courses 210NOK–289NOK ($32–$45/£17–£23); open-faced sandwiches 70NOK–120NOK ($11–$18/£5.60–£9.60); 3-course set dinner 400NOK ($62/£32). AE, DC, MC, V. Mon–Fri 11am–3:30pm; Mon–Sat 5–10:30pm. Kroen Bar Mon–Sat 4pm–midnight. Closed last 3 weeks in July. Bus: 27, 29, 30, 41, or 61.

MODERATE
Stortorvets Gjæstgiveri ✸ NORWEGIAN   This is the oldest restaurant in Oslo, and one of only three buildings to have escaped complete destruction during the many fires that roared through the city during the late 19th century. The present restaurant is composed of a trio of wood-framed buildings, the most antique dating from the 1700s. Originally an inn stood on this spot with stables out back. The inn's upstairs bedchambers with their wood-burning stoves are virtually unchanged since their original construction, although they're now used as private dining rooms. This revered vestige of Oslo's past is one of the principal performance sites during the annual midsummer jazz festival.

This restaurant changes radically as you move through it: Expect a cafe near the entrance; an old-fashioned, charming, and usually packed restaurant in back; and outside dining in good weather. Menu items are traditional, well prepared, and flavorful, and include grilled halibut with beurre blanc sauce; veal with smoked ham and sausage; chicken breast stuffed with spinach and creamed porcini mushrooms; filet of reindeer with a compote of onions and apples; and freshwater trout with arugula and balsamic vinegar. One of the trademark offerings is *lutefisk,* a cod dish so complicated (and with such a high possibility of spoilage) that many lesser restaurants don't even try to prepare it. Here, thanks to automated high-tech kitchen equipment, they sell thousands of portions of it a year, mostly in autumn, when it's at its aromatic best.

Grensen 1. ℂ 23-35-63-60. Small platters and snacks 75NOK–210NOK ($12–$32/£6–£17); main courses 80NOK–330NOK ($12–$51/£6.40–£26). AE, DC, MC, V. Cafe and restaurant daily 3–11pm. Tram: 12 or 17.

3 Brødre ✸ MEXICAN   We used to come here for old-fashioned Norwegian fare, but the cuisine is now south of the border—the U.S. border, that is. "Three Brothers" is named after the glove manufacturers who once occupied this building. The Mexican food here may have lost a bit of its punch traveling so far to the icy north, but this is a longtime favorite with locals. The fare is zesty and well prepared, and you'll get hearty portions at reasonable prices. Here you can fill up on fajitas, including one version made with prawns; or say to hell with your waistline as you dig into double-cheese enchiladas and burritos. The entire street level houses the bustling bar, while a piano bar rests upstairs. Lighter meals, such as snacks and sandwiches, are available on the outside dining terrace in the summer.

Øvre Slottsgate 13. ℂ 23-10-06-70. Main courses 145NOK–260NOK ($22–$40/£12–£21). AE, DC, MC, V. Mon–Sat 4pm–1am. Street-level bar Mon–Sat 11pm–2:30am; piano bar Wed–Sat 5pm–2am. Bus: 27, 29, or 30.

INEXPENSIVE
Engebret Café NORWEGIAN   The Engebret fanatically clings to a fast-fading past, and we hope it lives into another century at least. A favorite since 1857, this restaurant sits directly north of Akershus Castle in two buildings that have been joined

together. The facade of the buildings has been preserved as an architectural landmark. It has an old-fashioned atmosphere and good food, served in a former bohemian literati haunt. During lunch, a tempting selection of open-faced sandwiches is available. The evening menu is more elaborate; you might begin with a terrine of game with blackberry port-wine sauce or Engebret's always reliable fish soup. Main dishes include red wild boar with whortleberry sauce, Norwegian reindeer, or salmon Christiania. For dessert, try the cloudberry parfait.

Bankplassen 1. ℂ **22-33-66-94.** Reservations recommended. Main courses 220NOK–345NOK ($34–$53/£18–£28). AE, DC, MC, V. Mon–Sat 11am–11pm. Bus: 27, 29, or 30.

Mamma Rosa *(Kids* ITALIAN   This is but a lowly trattoria—and no better than it should be—but we like to go here for a change of taste and texture after staring at too many plates of reindeer steak. Established by two Tuscan brothers, this trattoria enjoys popularity that's a good indication of Norwegians' changing tastes. You can order 10 kinds of pizza, fried scampi and squid, rigatoni, pasta Mamma Rosa (three kinds of pasta with three sauces), grilled steaks, and gelato. Frankly, some of the dishes have lost a bit of flavor on the trip this far north. Families frequent this restaurant in large numbers nightly. Children can always find something on the menu.

Øvre Slottsgate 12. ℂ **22-42-01-30.** Main courses 100NOK–215NOK ($15–$33/£8–£17); pizzas 85NOK–120NOK ($13–$18/£6.80–£9.60). AE, DC, MC, V. Mon–Sat noon–11:30pm; Sun 3–10:30pm. T-banen: Stortinget.

Vegeta Vertshus VEGETARIAN   Since 1938, this two-floor diner/cafeteria near the Rådhus has been Oslo's best vegetarian restaurant and is a stronghold of social activism and news of countercultural activities. At street level is a cafe with a buffet of 25 salad dishes and many hot dishes, along with bread, butter, cheese, and coffee. A smoke-free bar downstairs serves a special student buffet Tuesday to Saturday. The kitchen is also proud of its pizza. You can order juices (we had our first glass of beer and carrot here long ago), mineral water, soft drinks, or nonalcoholic wine.

Munkedamsveien 3B. ℂ **22-83-42-32.** Soups and salads 65NOK ($10/£5.20); buffet 150NOK ($23/£12). AE, DC, MC, V. Sun–Fri 11am–9pm; Sat 11am–11pm. Bus: 27.

AKER BRYGGE

Lofoten Fiskerestaurant *✸✸* SEAFOOD   This is Aker Brygge's most appealing—and best—seafood restaurant. Opening onto the waterfront, the interior sports nautical accessories that evoke life on an upscale yacht. In good weather, tables are set up on an outdoor terrace lined with flowering plants. Menu items change according to the available catch, with few choices for meat-eaters. The fish is plentiful, served in generous portions, and very fresh. Look for culinary inspirations from Italy and France, and an ample use of such Mediterranean flavors as pesto. Menu items include grilled halibut with assorted shellfish and a coconut-flavored risotto; grilled filet of tuna with garlicky potato cakes, Parmesan cheese, and a red-pepper cream sauce; and filet of trout poached in white wine and served with a tomato-enriched beurre blanc.

Stranden 75, Aker Brygge. ℂ **22-83-08-08.** Reservations recommended. Lunch main courses 140NOK–265NOK ($22–$41/£11–£21); dinner main courses 179NOK–285NOK ($28–$44/£14–£23). AE, DC, MC, V. Mon–Sat 11am–11pm; Sun noon–10pm. Bus: 27.

Solsiden *✸ (Finds* NORWEGIAN/SEAFOOD   The degree to which this restaurant is known throughout Oslo seems way out of proportion to its size and season (it's been open for 6 months). Part of its fame involves its location within an ugly, cement-sided warehouse opening onto a pier that's directly across the harbor from the bigger, glossier restaurants of the Aker Brygge complex, directly below the imposing bulk of Akershus castle. It's especially appealing on sunny midsummer evenings when sunlight streams onto the pier, while many of the restaurants of Aker Brygge lie in the shadows. The venue features an open kitchen, wide views of Oslo's harbor, the setting sun, and a hardworking staff. Menu items include only fish and shellfish, with no meat of any kind. The highly theatrical house specialty is a platter of shellfish, prepared for a minimum of two diners at a time, artfully draped with seaweed. Norwegian salmon with herb-flavored oil and potato purée is a perennial favorite. Habitués tell us that instead of settling for one of the fancier dishes—grilled tuna with lemongrass and sesame onions—it's best to ask for *dagens fisk*, or the catch of the day.

Søndre Akershus Kai 34. (C) **23-33-36-30**. Reservations required. Main courses 235NOK–292NOK ($36–$45/ £19–£23); 3-course fixed-price menu 400NOK ($62/£32). May–Aug Mon–Sat 5–10pm; Sun 5–9pm. Closed Sept–Apr. Tram: 10 or 15.

WEST END
VERY EXPENSIVE
Bagatelle ✿✿✿ FRENCH/CONTINENTAL   This longtime favorite is the best restaurant in Oslo, although many critics will dispute that. For years we have been won over by the light, modern cuisine, market-fresh ingredients, and imaginative mind of culinary whiz Eyvind Hellstrom.

The quality of service ensures that there are no distractions from the serious business of dining. Wonderfully aromatic seafood is the star of the menu, including the catch of the day, which the chefs often smoke to perfection. Our divine sole arrived steamed in seaweed, giving a tangy aroma of the sea. A "voluptuous" steamed halibut reached celestial levels when it was accompanied by a caviar cream sauce. Meat-eaters are catered to with such offerings as a saddle of reindeer graced with fresh pears and a tangy pepper sauce. Richly flavored was the slow-cooked veal with a sage so fresh you'd think it was just picked in the field. The chef's finely honed classic technique is showcased in a delectable herb-roasted Norwegian rack of lamb.

Bygdøy Allé 3. (C) **22-44-63-97**. Reservations required. Main courses 320NOK–420NOK ($49–$65/£26–£34); 3-course fixed-price menu 750NOK ($116/£60); 5-course fixed-price menu 950NOK ($146/£76); 7-course fixed-price menu 1,150NOK ($177/£92). AE, DC, MC, V. Mon–Sat 6–10:30pm. Bus: 30, 31, 45, 72, or 73.

Magma ✿✿✿ MEDITERRANEAN/CONTINENTAL   This is one of the hottest dining reservations in Oslo. Established in 2000 on a busy boulevard within the city's quietly prosperous West End, on the street level of the Rica Hotel Bygdøy Allé (with which it is not directly associated), it's outfitted in a postmodern, punk-conscious style that might have been inspired by a hip-hop club in London or New York. Expect lots of space, a postindustrial decor of vinyl sofas and banquettes, pillbox-shaped stools, splashy pop art, and the superb cuisine of Norway's chef-of-the-minute, Sonja Lee. Born of Korean and Norwegian parents and one of the most successful culinary entrepreneurs in Norway, she studied in Paris, Monaco, and southern France. Even better, she has assembled a team of hip, young assistants who seem to work beautifully together in the hypermodern kitchens, which, incidentally, are available for visits from any diner who's interested in a tour. Ingredients that go into these dishes are pure and perfect, and are usually based on flavors of the faraway Mediterranean. Try the braised rabbit with tomatoes and olives; homemade ravioli studded with ricotta and Norwegian wild mushrooms; and (direct from the Ducasse kitchens) spit-roasted veal with a gratin of macaroni and veal jus, a real masterpiece.

Bygdøy Allé 53. ⓒ **23-08-58-10**. Reservations required. Main courses 180NOK–220NOK ($28–$34/£14–£18); fixed-price menus: 500NOK ($77/£40) for 5 courses, 600NOK ($92/£48) for 6 courses, 750NOK ($116/£60) for 7 courses, 800NOK ($123/£64) for 8 courses, 900NOK ($139/£72) for 10 courses; tasting menu 950NOK–1,200NOK ($146–US$185/£76–£96) for 10–13 courses. AE, DC, MC, V. Daily 11am–2pm; Mon–Sat 5:30–10pm. Tram: 10, 12, or 15.

EXPENSIVE

Feinschmecker 𝄞𝄞 SCANDINAVIAN   One of our local friends, a savvy food critic, has proclaimed this the best restaurant in Oslo. We're not prepared to agree, but Feinschmecker ranks near the top. One of the most prestigious restaurants in Oslo will entertain you with the style and verve. The dining room's antique furniture and small-paned windows evoke old-time style despite the building's modernity. Menu items change frequently. Dishes are immaculately presented with a high degree of finish, and we found that the quality of materials shines throughout, particularly in such dishes as grilled scallops with crispy potatoes. Even better are the sautéed ocean crayfish tails with apple cider, wild rice, and sun-dried tomatoes, or grilled monkfish with sautéed mushrooms and a morel-enriched cream sauce. A particularly sought-after main course, and rightly so, is rack of Norwegian lamb. For dessert, try the gratin of raspberries, which has been preeminent here since the place opened in the 1980s.

Balchensgate 5. ⓒ **22-44-17-77**. Reservations recommended. Main courses 265NOK–350NOK ($41–$54/£21–£28); fixed-price menu 675NOK ($104/£54); 5-course menu 745NOK ($115/£60); 7-course menu 895NOK ($138/£72). AE, DC, MC, V. Mon–Sat 4:30–11pm. Closed 3 weeks in July. Tram: 12 or 19 to Ilesberg.

MODERATE

Hos Thea 𝄞 *(Finds* SCANDINAVIAN/SPANISH   This century-old building, once a private home, lies in a West End neighborhood 3km (2 miles) south of Oslo's center. The stylish, well-managed restaurant also attracts a loyal crowd of people active in the media and the arts. The waitstaff and chefs share duties, so the person who prepares your meal is likely to carry it to your table as well. Depending on the staff's mood and the season, the superbly prepared menu items might include medallions of veal served with beurre blanc and carrots or breast of tender duck in a delectable red-wine sauce. Ingredients "come from all over," including filets of whitefish flavored in a sauce laced with saffron plucked from the plains of Spain. The venison served came from the north of Norway and was handled delicately and set out with a sauce made of mixed Nordic berries picked in summer.

Gabelsgate 11 (entrance on Drammensveien). ⓒ **22-44-68-74**. Reservations recommended. Main courses 100NOK–300NOK ($15–$46/£8–£24). AE, DC, MC, V. Daily 4:30–11pm. Tram: 10 or 13.

Village Tandoori 𝄞 INDIAN   We spent a lot of time admiring the weavings, paintings, chastened brass, and woodcarvings that adorn the walls of this restaurant, a network of dark rooms that evoke an antique house in the Punjab or Rajasthan regions of India. The food is flavorful, exotic, and extremely good, with a wide variety. We were told that many of the recipes come from someone's mother, or in the case of the lamb tikka marinated in yogurt and spices, someone's grandmother. Those with a carnivorous streak will opt for the Lahore-style lamb marinated in a tantalizing chile sauce or the spicy Punjabi chicken. Delectable prawns come flavored with either paprika or garlic, and the house specialty, for those who want a "taste of everything," is the "village grill," a three-way marriage of prawns, chicken, and lamb.

Bygdøy Allee 65. ⓒ **22-56-10-25**. Reservations recommended only Fri–Sat nights. Main courses 165NOK–235NOK ($25–$36/£13–£19). AE, DC, MC, V. June–Aug daily 5–11pm; Sept–May daily 3–10pm. Tram: 10, 12, or 15.

BYGDØY

Lanternen 𝔾 CONTINENTAL Norwegian yachties, who for some unknown reason claim to have the "most developed" palates in Norway, like this place. So do we. Set close to the arrivals point for the Bygdøy ferry from the quays near Town Hall, within a low-slung white-painted clapboard-covered house from the 19th century, this restaurant is charming, welcoming, and sophisticated. From the windows of its woodsy, modern interior, you'll see about 1,000 privately owned sailboats and motor craft bobbing in the nearby marina, giving the entire venue a distinctly nautical appeal.

Both appetizers and main courses are wisely limited but well chosen and intriguing to the taste buds. On a visit, we launched our repast with a homemade fish soup, while our companions delighted in the chile-flavored steamed mussels flavored with fresh garlic and white wine. Fresh, seasonal, and high-quality ingredients characterize the main courses, which range from poached sole with lobster sauce and shrimp to an herb-marinated filet of lamb. We recommend the baked chicken breast, enlivened with the additions of cured ham and mozzarella, and bound with a Madeira-laced sauce.

Huk Aveny 2. © **22-43-78-38**. Reservations recommended. Main courses 146NOK–229NOK ($22–$35/£12–£18). AE, DC, MC, V. Daily 11am–midnight. Closed 1st 2 weeks of Jan. Bus: 30 or the Bygdøy ferry from the quays near Town Hall.

Najaden (Kids) NORWEGIAN In general, we are not turned on by museum restaurants, viewing them as a mere convenience. But Najaden is better than most dining rooms in this category. In the Norwegian Maritime Museum, this restaurant (the name translates as "mermaid") overlooks a room of sculptures removed from 19th-century clipper ships. The popular lunch buffet offers an elaborate array of freshly prepared fish and meat dishes. You won't get a lot of culinary excitement, but the food is fresh and served in generous portions—and the location is unbeatable when you're sightseeing on Bygdøy. This is very much a family-style atmosphere. Kids enjoy the nautical atmosphere and the casual, often noisy dining room. Also, the buffet is large and generous enough for a child, even for the pickiest of eaters.

Bygdøynesveien 37. © **22-43-81-80**. Reservations recommended. Main courses 198NOK–248NOK ($30–$38/£16–£20); lunch buffet 140NOK ($22/£11), half price for children under 12. AE, DC, MC, V. May 16–Oct 14 daily noon–6pm; Oct 15–May 15 Mon–Sat 11am–3:30pm. Bus: 30. Ferry: Bygdøy.

HOLMENKOLLEN

Frognerseteren 𝔾 NORWEGIAN In some way, this strikes us as the most Norwegian of all the Norwegian restaurants in Oslo. Set within a short hike (or cross-country-ski trek) from the end of Oslo's tram no. 1, the Frognerseteren rests in a century-old mountain lodge. Richly embellished with dragon and Viking-ship symbolism, the building helped define the Viking revival style that became the architectural symbol of independent Norway. There's a self-service section and a more formal sit-down area within several small, cozy dining rooms. Throughout, the place has the aura of an antique ski lodge, and for many Oslovians, it's as much a cultural icon as a restaurant. It's also the centerpiece of several kilometers of cross-country ski trails and a departure point (and destination) for hikers and their families. The chef specializes in succulent game dishes, including pheasant pâté with Cumberland sauce, medallions of reindeer, and filet of elk sautéed in honey and nuts. You can also order poached, marinated, or smoked Norwegian salmon. The chef's specialty dessert is a scrumptious apple cake.

Holmenkollveien 200. ✆ **22-92-40-40.** Reservations recommended. Cafe platters 60NOK–110NOK ($9.25–$17/ £4.80–£8.80). Restaurant main courses 240NOK–295NOK ($37–$45/£19–£24); fixed-price menus 500NOK–750NOK ($77–$116/£40–£60). DC, MC, V. Restaurant Mon–Sat noon–10pm; Sun noon–9pm. Cafe Mon–Sat noon–10pm; Sun noon–9pm. Tram: 1.

FROGNER

Restaurant Le Canard ✸ FRENCH/CONTINENTAL   This deluxe restaurant lies in the suburb of Frogner, just about a kilometer (¾ mile) west of the center. Here you'll encounter a smart, stylish restaurant in one of Oslo's more fashionable neighborhoods. The classically oriented cooking demonstrates first-class workmanship without being showy. The mansion that contains this prestigious restaurant is almost as intriguing as the cuisine. Religious symbols are scattered throughout the building, which was designed in the 1880s by a noted Jewish architect. The always impeccable menu might include a divine grilled lobster with sautéed chanterelles and watercress sauce, a tantalizing carpaccio of smoked scallops, or a perfectly roasted duck—that is, with most of the fat cooked off—that is set off to perfection with a blend of mango and olive *jus*.

President Harbitzgate 4. ✆ **22-54-34-00.** Reservations recommended. Main courses 240NOK–395NOK ($37–$61/ £19–£32); 3-course fixed-price menu 550NOK ($85/£44); 5-course fixed-price menu 770NOK ($119/£62); 7-course fixed-price menu 970NOK ($149/£78). AE, DC, MC, V. Nov–June Mon–Sat 6–11pm; July–Oct Tues–Sat 6–10:30pm. T-banen: Nationaltheatret.

5 Seeing the Sights

Some would be happy to come to Oslo just for the views of the harbor and the Oslofjord. Panoramas are a major attraction, especially the one from Tryvannstårnet, a 120m (390-ft.) observation-tower atop 570m-high (1,900-ft.) Tryvann Hill in the outlying area. Many other attractions are worthy of your time and exploration, too. The beautiful surroundings make these sights even more appealing.

IN CENTRAL OSLO

Akershus Slott og Festning (Akershus Castle & Fortress) ✸✸ *Kids*   It has withstood fierce battles, drawn-out sieges, and endless fires, and architecturally it has changed beyond recognition from what King Haakon V ordered built in 1299 when Oslo was named capital of Norway. The moats and reinforced ramparts were added in the mid-1700s. For several centuries it was not only a fortress but the abode of the rulers of Norway.

Before going inside, take in the grounds that surround the fortress, which was strategically built on the eastern side of the harbor. From the well-manicured lawns there are **panoramic views** ✸ of Oslo and the Oslofjorden. In summer, concerts, dances, even Hamlet-like theatrical productions are staged here.

A fire in 1527 devastated the northern wing, and the castle was rebuilt and transformed into a royal Renaissance palace under the Danish-Norwegian king, Christian IV. Now the government uses it for state occasions. A fortress, or *festning*, with thick earth-and-stone walls is constructed around the castle, with protruding bastions designed to resist artillery bombardment. Forty-minute English-language guided tours are offered Monday to Saturday at 11am, 1pm, and 3pm, and on Sunday at 1 and 3pm.

Festnings-Plassen. ✆ **22-41-25-21.** Admission 40NOK ($6.15/£3.20) adults, 10NOK ($1.55/80p) children, family ticket 80NOK ($12/£6.40). May–Sept 15 Mon–Sat 10am–4pm, Sun 12:30–4pm. Closed Sept 16–Apr. Tram: 10 or 12.

Oslo Attractions

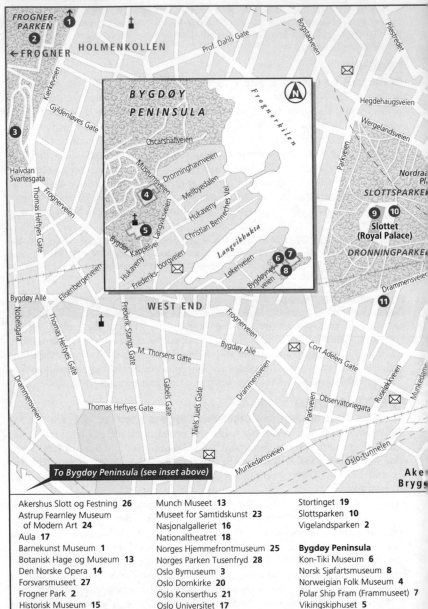

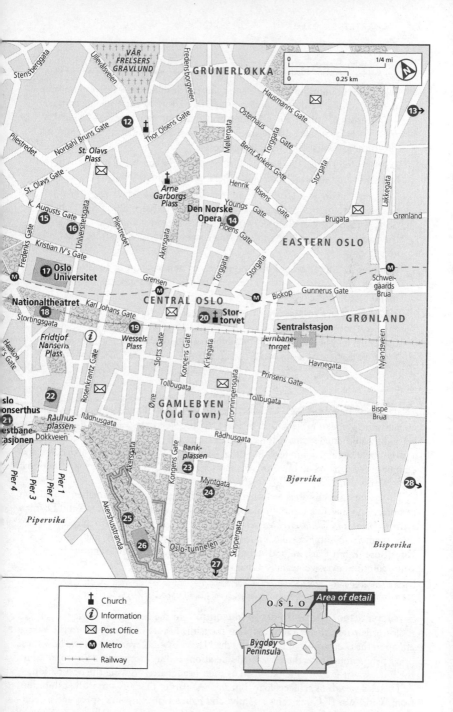

GRÜNERLØKKA

0 ———— 1/4 mi
0 ———— 0.25 km

Stensbergata
Ullevålsveien
VÅR FRELSERS GRAVLUND
Fredensborgveien
Hausmanns Gate
⊠
13→

Pilestredet
Nordahl Bruns Gate
12 †
Thor Olsens Gate
Møllergata
Osterhaus Gate
Bernt Ankers Gate
Fossveien
Storgata
Lakkegata

St. Olavs Plass
⊠
† Arne Garborgs Plass
Henrik Ibsens Gate
Youngs Gate
Brugata
⊠
Grønland

St. Olavs Gate

K. Augusts Gate
15
16
Universitetsgata
Pilestredet
Akersgata
Den Norske Opera 14
Ploens Gate
Storgata
EASTERN OSLO

Frederiks Gate
Kristian IV's Gate
17 Oslo Universitet
Grensen
Torggata
Storgata
Schweigaards Brua
M

Ⓜ

Nationaltheatret
18
Karl Johans Gate
Ⓜ
CENTRAL OSLO
Ⓜ
Biskop Gunnerus Gate
GRØNLAND

Stortingsgata
Fridtjof Nansens Plass
ⓘ
Wessels Plass
19
⊠
20 † Stortorvet
Jernbane-torget
Sentralstasjon
Havnegata
Nylandsveien

Haakon ...'s Gate
Rosenkrantz Gate
Slotts Gate
Koncens Gate
Kirkegata
Prinsens Gate

slo onserthus
22
⊠
Tollbugata
⊠
Dronningensgata
Tollbugata
Bispe Brua

21 estbane-asjonen
Dokkveien
Råthus-plassen-
Rådhusgata
GAMLEBYEN (Old Town)
Rådhusgata

Pier 4 Pier 3 Pier 2 Pier 1
Akersgata
Kongens Gate
Bank-plassen
23
Myntgata
24
Bjørvika
28→

Pipervika
25
26
Oslo-Tunnelen
Skippergata
27↓
Bispevika

† Church
ⓘ Information
⊠ Post Office
– – Ⓜ Metro
+++ Railway

OSLO
Area of detail
Bygdøy Peninsula

Best Oslo Experiences

Enjoying Fresh Shrimp off the Boats   In the morning, head for the harbor in front of the Rådhuset, and buy a bag of freshly caught and cooked shrimp from a fisherman. Although this may not be everyone's idea of a good breakfast—sales begin around 7 or 8am and may end in late morning—shrimp lovers will find Valhalla here.

Experiencing Life on the Fjords   In the summer head for the harbor, where boats wait to take you sightseeing, fishing, or to the beach.

Hanging Out in the Students' Grove   Summer is short in Oslo, and it's savored. Late-night drinkers sit in open-air beer gardens along Karl Johans Gate, enjoying the endless nights. Our favorite spot for a beer and to watch the passing parade is Studenten on the corner of Karl Johans Gate and Universitesgata.

Listening to Street Musicians   Hundreds of musicians flock to Oslo in the summer. You can enjoy their music along Karl Johans Gate and at the marketplace Stortorvet.

Taking the Ferry to Bygdøy   The Bygdøy peninsula offers a treasure trove of attractions including Viking ships, Thor Heyerdahl's *Kon-Tiki,* seafood buffets, a sailboat harbor, and bathing beaches. At the folk museum are old farmsteads, houses, and, often, folk dancing.

Astrup Fearnley Museum of Modern Art *(★) (Finds)*   This is one of those special nuggets art lovers stumble across in their travels, wondering why such a place isn't better known. Actually, this privately funded museum has been around since 1993. In a stunningly designed modern building, some of Norway's leading architects and designers constructed a museum to showcase both Norwegian and international post–World War II art.

The changing exhibitions are often drawn from the museum's permanent collection in storage and traveling international shows, while works from Yoko Ono and Damien Hirst (*Mother and Child Divided (★)*) are on display. This is also your chance to introduce yourself to some locally known Norwegian artists of great stature, especially Knut Rose, Bjørn Carlsen, and Arne Ekeland. Allow at least 40 minutes. If you like your sculptures oversize, wander through the garden.

Dronningensgatan 4. ⓒ **22-93-60-60.** www.af-moma.no. Free admission. Tues–Wed and Fri 11am–5pm; Thurs 11am–7pm; Sat–Sun noon–5pm. T-banen: Stortinget. Tram: 1, 2, 10, or 12. Bus: 27, 29, 38, 51, or 56.

Forsvarsmuseet (Armed Forces Museum)   In the heart of Oslo at the ancient Akershus Fortress, this is a museum that traces the history of Norway from the Viking era up to the occupation of Norway by the Nazis in World War II. It shows how these brave people fought for their eventual liberation, and its location is a bit ironic, since the fortress was used by the Germans as their headquarters during the occupation.

There's a wealth of artifacts here, but the best part of the museum is the exhibitions from World War II. Guns, tanks, bombs, and fighter planes are on display, and a depiction of how the resistance contributed to the final victory for the Allies is particularly moving. Exhibitions also depict the "heavy water" battle in the Rjukan (1943–44), dramatized here as it has been in so many war films.

Give yourself at least 40 minutes to explore, and then head to the on-site cafeteria for some "fortification" of your own.

For a preview of the castle itself, see **Akershus Slott og Festning,** above.

Akershus Fortress, Bygning 62. © **23-09-35-82.** www.mil.no. Free admission. June–Aug Mon–Fri 10am–6pm, Sat–Sun 11am–4:30pm; Sept–May Mon–Fri 10am–3pm, Sat–Sun 11am–4pm. Tram: 1, 2, or 10.

Historisk Museum (University Museum of Cultural Heritage)   From the cold Arctic wastelands to the hot, sunny islands of Asia, this museum—owned by the University of Oslo   is a vast treasure trove, containing everything from a carved *stavkirke* (wooden church) to a 1,000-year history of the coins of Norway. But, if you're rushed for time, skip it unless you're interested in national antiquities, ethnographic exhibitions, or numismatic exhibits. Viking artifacts and a **display of gold and silver** ⋒ from the 2nd through the 13th centuries are in the Treasure House. In the medieval hall, look for the reddish Ringerike Alstad Stone, which was carved in relief, and the **Dynna Stone** ⋒, an 11th-century runic stone honoring the fairest maiden in Hadeland. There's also a rich collection of ecclesiastical art in a series of portals from stave churches. Grant this museum at least 45 minutes.

Frederiksgate 2 (near Karl Johans Gate). © **22-85-99-12.** Admission 40NOK ($6.15/£3.20) adults, 20NOK ($3.10/£1.60) students, free for children under 12. May 15–Sept 14 Tues–Sun 10am–4pm; Sept 15–May 14 Tues–Sun 11am–4pm. Tram: 7, 8, 11, or 17.

Kunstindustrimuseet (Museum of Decorative Arts and Design) ⋒   Founded in 1876, this is one of the oldest museums in Norway and among the oldest applied arts museums in Europe. The museum has been around long enough to acquire many treasures. Since 1876 it has owned the bold, imaginative **Baldishol tapestries** ⋒ from the early part of the 12th century, antique dragon-style furniture, and the royal wardrobe. The collection of 18th-century **Norwegian silver** ⋒, glass, and faience is stunning, and there's also an impressive selection of contemporary furniture and crafts. Visiting craft and design exhibits are on display on the ground floor. The museum also schedules lectures, guided tours, and concerts. Allow yourself an hour here.

Café Solliløkken and the museum shop on the ground floor, the former offering light meals, mostly sandwiches and salads, and some hot Norwegian daily specials (most often fish). All its pastries are homemade.

St. Olavs Gate 1. © **22-03-65-40.** Free admission. www.nationalmuseum.no. Tues–Wed and Fri 11am–4pm; Thurs and Sat–Sun 11am–7pm. T-banen: Stortinget. Bus: 37.

Museet for Samtidskunst (National Museum of Contemporary Art)   We once saw a painting here of a three-headed woman with 14 breasts. It's haunted our memories ever since. Opened in 1990, this collection of works acquired by the state after World War II presents an array of international and Norwegian contemporary art. Previously grouped together in the National Gallery, the works have more room to "breathe" here, in what was once the central bank of Norway. Exhibits change frequently; allot 30 minutes for your visit.

Bankplassen 4. © **22-86-22-10.** www.nationalmuseum.no. Free admission. Tues–Wed and Fri 10am–5pm; Thurs 10am–8pm; Sat 11am–4pm; Sun 11am–4:30pm. Tram: 10 or 12. Bus: 60.

Nasjonalgalleriet (National Gallery) ✿✿✿ This museum houses Norway's greatest and largest collection of art, but let's face it, most visitors flock here to see Edvard Munch's *The Scream,* one of four versions, this one painted in 1893. This painting was stolen in 1994 and, unlike the version taken from the Munch Museum in 2004 (see later), was subsequently recovered.

Munch has a total of 58 of his works displayed here, some of them among his most celebrated, including *The Dance of Life* ✿, *Moonlight* ✿✿, and *Ashes.*

The leading Norwegian Romantic landscape painter Johan Christian Dahl (1788–1857) is in fine form here, as well as Norwegian realist, Harriet Backer, and Christian Krohg, who drew inspiration from sailors and prostitutes.

Scandinavian painting in general is also showcased, especially from neighboring Sweden and Denmark, one salon alone containing works from the golden age of Danish painting.

Although weak compared to some national collections, European painting in general is on parade, with old masters represented ranging from El Greco (a remarkable *St. Peter Repentant*) to Cézanne. All the art displayed was created before 1945, the year Norwegians freed themselves from the Nazi yoke. Allow 2 hours.

Universitesgata 13. ✆ 22-20-04-04. www.nationalmuseum.no. Free admission. Mon, Wed, and Fri 10am–5pm; Thurs 10am–8pm; Sat 10am–4pm; Sun 11am–4pm. Tram: 7 or 11.

Norges Hjemmefrontmuseum (Norwegian Resistance Museum) ✿ If you, like us, are WWII buffs, this museum is a living history book. From underground printing presses and radio transmitters to the German attack in 1940 to the liberation in 1945, the museum documents Norway's World War II resistance activities. Photographs from the Nazi attack on Norway have been printed on black iron sheets, and a cluster of German rifles are shaped to form the symbolic swastika. We are especially moved by the daring underground newspapers, which appeared as early as the summer of 1940 and continued to publish throughout the dark years of the war. Allow about an hour. Outside is a monument dedicated to Norwegian patriots, many of whom were executed by the Nazis at this spot.

Akershus Fortress. ✆ 23-09-31-38. www.mil.no/felles/nhm/start/eng. Admission 30NOK ($4.60/£2.40) adults, 15NOK ($2.30/£1.20) children. Apr 15–June 14 and Sept Mon–Sat 10am–5pm, Sun 11am–4pm; June 15–Aug Mon, Wed, and Fri–Sat 10am–6pm, Tues and Thurs 10am–7pm, Sun 11am–5pm; Oct–Apr 14 Mon–Sat 10am–3pm, Sun 11am–4pm. Tram: 10, 12, 15, or 19.

Oslo Domkirke (Oslo Cathedral) ✿ As cathedrals in European capitals go, this Oslo citadel ranks way down the food chain, but it's worth a visit nonetheless. The main problem with it is that restorers and "redecorators" went to work on it in the 1800s and again right after WWII. Instead of preserving the original interior, they applied new touches. The **pulpit and altarpiece** ✿, however, carved in the late 17th century with lovely motifs of acanthus leaves, are still beautiful. The five-story-tall (we're not kidding) organ dates from the 18th century.

Oslo's 1697 cathedral at Stortorvet (the marketplace) contains works by 20th-century Norwegian artists, including bronze doors and stained-glass windows.

Most visits here take half an hour. A bilingual service (in Norwegian and English) is conducted on Wednesday at noon, and an organ recital is presented on summer Saturdays at 1pm. *Tip:* For one of the best panoramic views in Oslo, go to the nightwatchman's room in the steeple, which was added in 1850.

Stortorvet 1. ✆ 23-31-46-00. Free admission. Daily 10am–4pm. T-banen: Stortinget. Bus: 17.

Rådhuset (City Hall)   Inaugurated in 1950, the City Hall has been called everything from "aggressively ugly" to the pride of Norway. When we first took it in, we agreed with the more critical view. But over the years it's won our hearts with its architectural combination of romanticism, classicism, and functionalism. The whole world looks in on this red-brick building every December when the Nobel Peace Prize is awarded. Its simple brick exterior with double towers houses, among other things, a stunning 25×13m (85×43 ft.) wall painted by Henrik Sørensen and the mural *Life* by Edvard Munch. Tapestries, frescoes, sculpture, and woodcarvings are also on display. Guided tours in English are available. Be sure to check out the astronomical clock and swan fountain in the courtyard. Allow about 20 minutes.

Rådhusplassen. ⓒ 23-46-16-00. Admission 35NOK ($5.40/£2.80) adults, free for children under 12. May–Sept daily 9am–5pm; Oct–Apr daily 8:30am–4pm. Guided tours Mon–Fri at 10am, noon, and 2pm. Tram: 10 or 12.

Stortinget (Parliament)   This yellow brick building, our favorite parliament building in Europe, is a grace note in an otherwise dull urban landscape. Most of its charm is from the outside. The original neo-Romanesque style, constructed from 1861 to 1866, has been retained. Norway hired its finest artists to decorate the building, depicting scenes from the country's history or its daily life. You're shown through on a guided tour and can see where some of the world's most progressive and socially conscious politicians meet. Guided tours lasting 20 minutes are open to the public (there's no need to book ahead).

Karl Johans Gate 22. ⓒ 23-31-35-96. www.stortinget.no. Free admission. Guided tours in English July 1–Aug 15 Mon–Fri 10am, 11:30am, and 1pm; Sept 15–June 15 Sat 10am, 11:30am, and 1pm. Closed Aug 16 Sept 14 and June 16–30. T-banen: Stortinget. Tram: 13, 15, or 19.

IN FROGNER PARK

Vigelandsparken 𝒜𝒜𝒜   It took us a few years to warm to the sculptures of Gustav Vigeland, the most prominent of all 20th-century Norwegian sculptors. But we finally came to dig him and have been returning ever since to see 227 of his monumental sculptures, mostly devoted to the theme of mankind's destiny. The artist worked for a total of 4 decades on this 30-hectare (75-acre) park, but, sadly, died 1 year before his lifetime achievement could be completed.

The chief treasure here is the **Vigeland Monolith** 𝒜𝒜𝒜, a 16m (52-ft.) sculpture composed of 121 colossal figures, all amazingly carved into one piece of stone. The monolith is easy to spot, as it rises on top of the highest hill in the park. Summer lovers often visit it at night, as it's floodlit and somehow seems even more dramatic at that time. The monolith is reached by a circle of steps, upon which are 36 groups of other figures carved in stone by the great artist. The column itself, with its writhing figures, is said to symbolize the struggle of life, which is one of the main themes running through Vigeland's work.

The best of the sculptures lie along a paved axis stretching for 1km (½ mile). These sculptures depict Vigeland's interpretation of life beginning at birth and ending in death. The most famous of these statues, which you'll quickly recognize since it is one of the most reproduced pieces of art in Oslo, is *The Angry Boy (Sinnataggen)* 𝒜𝒜. Allow 2 hours.

Frogner Park, Nobelsgate 32. ⓒ 23-49-37-00. Free admission to park; museum 40NOK ($6.15/£3.20) adults, 20NOK ($3.10/£1.60) children. Park daily 24 hr. Museum June–Sept Tues–Sun 11am–5pm; Oct–May Tues–Sun noon–4pm. Tram: 12.

ON BYGDØY

Located south of the city, the peninsula is reached by commuter ferry (summer only) leaving from Pier 3, facing the Rådhuset (Town Hall). Departures during the day are every 40 minutes before 11am and every 20 minutes after 11am, and a one-way fare costs 20NOK ($3.10/£1.60). The no. 30 bus from the National Theater also runs to Bygdøy. The museums are only a short walk from the bus stops on Bygdøy.

Frammuseet ✮ The world's most famous polar ship, *Fram*, dating from 1892, is displayed in its original condition with its interior and artifacts perfectly preserved. This is the brave little ship that Fridtjof Nanse sailed across the Arctic from 1893 to 1896. The trip made the handsome, fur-coated Viking one of the most renowned polar explorers before setting off on two other explorations, the last ending in 1912. You can spend half an hour here exploring the interior of the ship.

Bygdøynesveien. ℂ 23-28-29-50. www.fram.museum.no. Admission 40NOK ($6.15/£3.20) adults, 20NOK ($3.10/£1.60) children, 80NOK ($12/£6.40) family ticket. Jan 2–Apr daily 10am–3:45pm; May–June 15 daily 10am–5:45pm; June 16–Aug daily 9am–6:45pm; Sept daily 9am–5:45pm; Oct–Dec daily 10am–3:45pm. Ferry: From Pier 3 facing the Rådhuset (summer only). Bus: 30 from the National Theater.

Kon-Tiki **Museum** ✮ *Kids* *Kon-Tiki* is a world-famous balsa-log raft, and in 1947, the young Norwegian scientist Thor Heyerdahl and five comrades sailed it from Callao, Peru, to Raroia, Polynesia (6,880km/4,300 miles). Besides the raft, there are other exhibits from Heyerdahl's subsequent visits to Easter Island. They include casts of stone giants and small originals, a facsimile of the whale shark, and an Easter Island family cave, with a collection of sacred lava figurines hoarded in secret underground passages by the island's inhabitants. The museum also houses the original papyrus *Ra II*, in which Heyerdahl crossed the Atlantic in 1970. Although kids like to be taken here, adults will find it fascinating as well. For those who get really interested, they can read Heyerdahl's account of his adventures in his book, *Kon-Tiki,* published in countless editions around the world (available in the museum shop, of course). Most visits to this museum take about 45 minutes.

Bygdøynesveien 36. ℂ 23-08-67-67. www.kon-tiki.no. Admission 45NOK ($6.95/£3.60) adults, 20NOK ($3.10/£1.60) children, family ticket 95NOK ($15/£7.60). Apr–May and Sept daily 10am–5pm; June–Aug daily 9:30am–5:30pm; Oct–Dec daily 10:30am–4pm. Ferry: From Pier 3 facing the Rådhuset (summer only). Bus: 30 from the National Theater.

Norsk Folkesmuseum (Norwegian Folk Museum) ✮✮✮ *Kids* The greatest thing about this museum is that it allows you to "tour" Norway in just 1 day. From all over the country, museum curators moved 155 buildings from their original sites and, with great difficulty, transported and reassembled them on 14 hectares (35 acres) on the Bygdøy peninsula.

But they didn't stop there. The curators decided to make this open-air folk museum an active, living, breathing entity. To do that, they feature a variety of activities, including horse-and-buggy rides, folk music and dancing by men and women in native dress, traditional arts and crafts, and even Norwegian evenings.

Artisans demonstrate age-old crafts such as pottery, weaving, silversmithing, and candle making. You can purchase these handcrafted products in their workshops. At a Christmas fair held here, some 120 old-fashioned stands sell handmade products, including Christmas ornaments.

Among the old buildings is the **Gol Stave Church** ✮✮✮, moved here a century ago. Dating from 1200—still with no windows—it came from the town of Gol,

224km (139 miles) northwest of Oslo. One of the oldest such museums in the world, the Folk Museum contains many buildings from the medieval era, including the Raulandstua, one of the oldest wooden dwellings still standing in Norway.

Wander the streets of Gamlebyen, or **Old Town** ☆, a reproduction of an early 20th-century Norwegian town. The rural buildings are grouped together by region of origin, and the urban houses are laid out in the form of an old town.

Inside, the museum's 225,000 exhibits capture every imaginable facet of Norwegian life, past and present. Furniture, household utensils, clothing, woven fabrics, and tapestries are on display, along with fine examples of rose painting and woodcarving. Farming implements and logging gear pay tribute to the development of agriculture and forestry. Also look for the outstanding exhibit on Norway's Sami population. After the millennium the museum incorporated the **Bygdo Royal Farm,** cultivated fields and grazing lands that offer hikes along the trails. Allow 3 hours.

Museumsveien 10. ⓒ 22-12-37-00. www.norskfolke.museum.no. Admission 70NOK ($11/£5.60) adults, 30NOK ($4.60/£2.40) children under 17. Jan 2–May 14 and Sept 15–Dec 30 Mon–Fri 11am–3pm, Sat–Sun 11am–4pm; May 15–Sept 14 daily 10am–6pm. Ferry: From Pier 3 facing the Rådhuset (summer only). Bus: 30 from the National Theater.

Norsk Sjøfartsmuseum (Norwegian Maritime Museum) ☆ (Kids)

Norway is justly proud of its seafaring past, a glorious tradition that lives on at this museum, which chronicles the maritime history and culture of the rugged country, complete with a ship's deck with helm and chart house. One gruesome section focuses on shipwrecks. A carved-out tree trunk is said to be the oldest surviving Norwegian boat. The Boat Hall features a fine collection of original small craft. The fully restored polar vessel *Gjoa,* used by Roald Amundsen in his search for the Northwest Passage, is also on display. The three-masted schooner *Svanen* (Swan) is moored at the museum. Built in Svendborg, Denmark, in 1916, *Svanen* sailed under the Norwegian and Swedish flags. The ship now belongs to the museum and is used as a training vessel and school ship for young people. Visits require about 45 minutes.

Bygdøynesveien 37. ⓒ 24-11-41-50. www.norsic-sjofartsmuseum.no. Admission to museum and boat hall 40NOK ($6.15/£3.20) adults, 25NOK ($3.85/£2) children. May–Sept daily 10am–6pm; Oct–Apr Mon–Wed and Fri–Sun 10:30am–4pm, Thurs 11am–6pm. Ferry: From Pier 3 facing the Rådhuset (summer only). Bus: 30 from the National Theater.

Vikingskiphuset (Viking Ship Museum, University Museum of Cultural Heritage) ☆☆☆ (Kids)

A fascinating chapter in Viking history came alive when three Viking graves were discovered in the Oslofjord between 1867 and 1904. If you were important enough in the Viking era, you were buried in a ship, complete with worldly riches and a servant or two to assist you in your afterlife. Your favorite dog or horse was also sacrificed and buried with you.

All the ships, each dating from the 9th century, were buried in blue clay, which preserved them. The *Oseberg* ☆☆ impresses us the most with its dragon and serpent carvings. It required 30 oarsmen to move it through the waters. The grave site, dating from 834, had been robbed when it was unearthed. The gold and gems were gone, but what remained was the largest collection of Viking-era artifacts ever discovered. Apparently, the ship was the resting place of a noblewoman. Many of the queen's burial furnishings are on display.

The finest remaining example of a Viking longship, the *Gokstad* ☆, when unearthed, had also been plundered by grave-robbers in ancient times. Few artifacts were uncovered. This, the largest ship unearthed, could accommodate 32 oarsmen and travel at a speed of 12 knots.

The grave-robbers were greedy, but they left behind bedposts with animal head ornamentation and fragments of a sledge, even a gaming board (early Las Vegas). The most unusual item found was the remains of a peacock, a very exotic creature in the Viking era.

Built around the same time as the *Gokstad,* the *Tune* ship is less impressive. The ship is badly damaged and was not restored.

For kids, the ships here conjure up the legend and lore of the Viking era that flourished in the Middle Ages. Allow about 1 hour.

Tip: In summer, go between 11:30am and 1pm to avoid the crowds.

Huk Aveny 35, Bygdøy. © 22-13-52-80. www.khm.uio.no/english/viking_ship_museum. Admission 40NOK ($6.15/£3.20) adults, 20NOK ($3.10/£1.60) children. Oct–Apr daily 11am–5pm; May–Sept daily 9am–6pm. Ferry: From Pier 3 facing the Rådhuset (summer only). Bus: 30 from the National Theater.

NEAR OSLO

Henie-Onstad Kunstsenter (Henie-Onstad Art Center) 🎨🎨🎨   Norway's
largest collection of modern art is worth the trip to Oslo. The center was inaugurated in 1968 to house a gift of some 300 works of art from Sonja Henie, former skating champion and movie star, and her husband, shipping tycoon, Niels Onstad.

Henie and Onstad had "all the money in the world," as one critic put it, and they set out to acquire paintings by the world's most famous artists. Her collection, beefed up by later additions, virtually spans modern art in the 20th century, from Cubism with Braque to Surrealism with Ernst. We're always drawn to the COBRA Group, with works by its founders, Asger Jorn and Karel Appel. The collection is so vast that it has to be rotated.

When you tire of all that art, you can head downstairs to Henie's trophy room to see her three Olympic gold medals—she was the star at the 1936 competition—and 10 world championships. In all, Henie garnered 600 trophies and medals, all of which are on display.

Besides the permanent collection, there are plays, concerts, films, and special exhibits. An open-air theater-in-the-round is used in the summer for folklore programs, jazz concerts, and song recitals. A top-notch, partly self-service grill restaurant, the Piruetten, is also on the premises. The center lies in a beautiful setting beside Oslofjord, 11km (7 miles) west of Oslo. Plan to spend 2 hours here.

Høkvikodden, Sonja Henlesvie 31. © 67-80-48-80. www.hok.no. Admission 70NOK ($11/£5.60) adults, 28NOK ($4.30/£2.25) visitors ages 7–16, free for children under 7. Tues–Thurs 11am–7pm; Fri–Sun 11am–6pm. Bus: 151, 161, 252, or 261.

Skimuseet (Ski Museum) 🎿 Kids   Founded in 1923, this is the oldest ski museum
in the world—as such, it's for aficionados. Even the royal family of Norway has donated their skis to this museum. At Holmenkollen, an elevator takes visitors up the jump tower for a **panoramic view** 🎿🎿🎿 of Oslo and the fjord, the greatest such vista you are likely to experience in Norway. At the base of the ski jump, the museum displays a wide range of exhibits, which are popular with families. They include a 4,000-year-old pictograph from Rødøy in Nordland, which documents skiing's thousand-year history. The museum also has skis and historical items from various parts of Norway—from the first "modern" skis, dating from about 1870, to a ski dating from around A.D. 600.

The Loftiest Lookout Tower in Scandinavia

Tryvannstårnet at Voksenkollen (© **22-14-67-11**) dazzles you with its panoramic sweep of Oslofjord, with Sweden lying to its east. The gallery is approximately 570m (1,900 ft.) above sea level. A 20-minute walk down the hill returns you to Frognerseteren, and another 20-minute walk down the hill takes you to the Holmenkollen Ski Jump, where the 1952 Olympic competitions took place. It's also the site of Norway's winter sports highlight, the Holmenkollen Ski Festival.

Admission is 30NOK ($4.60/£2.40) for adults or 15NOK ($2.30/£1.20) for children 10 to 15; 9 and under free. Open May to September daily 10am to 5pm; off-season daily 10am to 4pm. Take the T-banen to Frognerseteren (SST Line 1) from near the National Theatre to Voksenkollen (a 30-min. ride). From here, it's a 15-minute walk uphill.

Even if you're not a skier, there is something here for those who dream of exploration. Artifacts from the Antarctic expeditions of Amundsen are on display, as well as the Scott expeditions into the snowy wastelands. You can even see relics of Fridtjof Nansen's slog across the Greenland icecap. Of particular interest is the boat he built from his sled and canvas tent to row him the final 100km (62 miles) to remote Nuuk "at the end of the world." Allow 45 minutes.

Kongeveien 5, Holmenkollen. © **22-92-32-64**. Admission (museum and ski jump) 60NOK ($9.25/£4.80) adults, 30NOK ($4.60/£2.40) children. May and Sept daily 10am–5pm; June–Aug daily 9am–10pm; Oct–Apr daily 10am–4pm. T banen: Holmenkollen SST Line 15 from near the National Theater to Voksenkollen (30-min. ride), and then an uphill 15-min. walk.

PARKS & GARDENS

Marka 🔍🔍, the thick forest that surrounds Oslo, is just one of the giant pleasure parks in the area. You can also take a tram marked HOLMENKOLLEN from the city center to Oslomarka, a forested area where locals go for summer hikes and winter skiing. The ride to the stop at Oslomarka takes only 20 minutes, and there are trains every 30 minutes or so depending on the season. The area is dotted with about two dozen *hytter* (mountain huts), where you can seek refuge from the weather if needed. **Norske Turistforening,** Storgata 3 (© **22-82-28-22**), sells maps with the hiking paths and roads of the Oslomarka clearly delineated. It's open Monday to Friday 10am to 4pm, Saturday 10am to 2pm. Our favorite trail—and you should have this pinpointed on a map—is a signposted walk to **Sognsvannet** 🔍, which is a beautiful lake flanked by forested hills and encircled by an easy hiking trail stretching for 4km (2½ miles). In winter the lake is iced over, but in summer those with polar-bear blood can take a dip. Even in summer, swimming here is like taking a bath in ice water. In lieu of swimming, you might find the banks of this lake better suited for a picnic.

Botanisk Hage og Museum (Botanical Gardens) 🔍 We come here to see the more than 1,000 alpine plants gathered from around the world. Complete with waterfalls, the rock garden is an oasis in the heart of Oslo. It's home to many exotic plants, including cacti, orchids, and palms. We always stop to visit our favorite tree, a "living fossil" from Japan. The Maidenhair Tree was planted in 1870, which is amazing considering how far north Norway is. The tree produces lots of seeds, but they remain unfertilized because the nearest male Maidenhair Tree grows in faraway Copenhagen. There's a museum in the park with a botanical art exhibit. Plan on spending 45 minutes here.

Sars Gate 1. (Ⓒ) 22-85-16-30. www.nhm.nio.no/botanisk/bothage/garden_intro.html. Free admission. Apr–Sept Mon–Fri 7am–8pm, Sat–Sun 10am–8pm; Oct–Mar Mon–Fri 7am–5pm, Sat–Sun 10am–5pm. Bus: 20.

Slottsparken   The park surrounding the Royal Palace (Slottet) is open to the public year-round. The changing of the guard, albeit a weak imitation of the changing of the guard at London's Buckingham Palace, takes place daily at 1:30pm. When the king is in residence, the Royal Guard band plays Monday to Friday during the ceremony. The palace was constructed from 1825 to 1848. Some first-time visitors are surprised at how relatively unguarded it is, without walls or rails. You can walk through the grounds, but can't go inside unless you have an invitation from the king. The statue at the front of the castle (at the end of Karl Johans Gate) is of Karl XIV Johan, who ruled Norway and Sweden. He ordered the construction of this palace, but died before it was finished. Allot about 20 minutes.

Drammensveien 1. Free admission. Daily dawn–dusk. T-banen: Nationaltheatret.

OF ARTISTIC INTEREST

Aula (Great Hall)   Admirers of the work of Edvard Munch, like us, will want to see the Great Hall of the university, where Scandinavia's greatest artist painted murals. We've gone here repeatedly over the years just to look at Munch's depiction of *The Sun,* the mural showing rays gently falling over a secluded Norwegian fjord. Until it moved to larger headquarters at the City Hall, this used to be the site of the Nobel Prize award ceremony. Plan on spending 20 minutes here.

University of Oslo, Karl Johans Gate 47. (Ⓒ) 22-85-95-55. Free admission. June 20–Aug 20 daily 10am–4pm. T-banen: Stortinget.

Munch Museet (Edvard Munch Museum) ★★★   Chances are, the National Gallery (p. 270) will not totally satisfy your Edvard Munch fix. Munch (1863–1944) was Scandinavia's greatest painter and, in an act of incredible generosity, donated this collection to his beloved Oslo. The treasure trove is so vast—1,100 paintings, 4,500 drawings, and 18,000 prints—that it can be shown only in rotation. The curators keep a representative sampling of his works on display at all times, so you can trace his development, as he went from Impressionism to Symbolism.

Love, death, darkness, and anxiety were his major themes. Anxiety was best expressed in his most famous painting, *The Scream,* which has four versions. Uninsured, the Munch masterpiece was valued at $75 million. Fans of Munch's *The Scream* and *Madonna* can once again gaze upon these paintings, which were recovered in the summer of 2006 in good condition.

Most fascinating is a series of self-portraits, which reveal his mind at peak moments of his life. Plan to devote at least 1½ hours.

Tøyengate 53. (Ⓒ) 23-49-35-00. www.munch.museum.no. Admission 50NOK ($7.70/£4) adults, 35NOK ($5.40/£2.80) children. June–Aug daily 10am–6pm; Sept–May Tues–Fri 10am–4pm, Sat–Sun 11am–5pm. T-banen: Tøyen. Bus: 60.

LITERARY LANDMARKS

"Walking Tour 2," below, follows in the footsteps of Ibsen.

Ibsen Museum Theatergoers from around the world can pay tribute to Henrik Ibsen by visiting his former apartment. In 1994 Oslo opened this museum to honor its most famous writer, who lived here from 1895 until his death in 1906. Within walking distance of the National Theater, the apartment was where Ibsen wrote two of his most famous plays, *John Gabriel Borkman* and *When We Dead Awaken*. The museum curators have tried to re-create the apartment (a longtime exhibit at the Norwegian Folk Museum) as authentically as possible. The study, for example, has Ibsen's original furniture, and the entire apartment is decorated as though Ibsen still lived in it. The attraction has been called "a living museum," and regularly scheduled talks on playwriting and the theater, recitations, and theatrical performances take place here. Allow 25 minutes.

Arbinsgate 1. ✆ **22-12-35-50.** www.ibsen.net. Admission 60NOK ($9.25/£4.80) adults, 30NOK ($4.60/£2.40) children. Tues–Sun noon–4pm. Guided tours in English at noon, 1pm, and 2pm. Tram: 13, 15, or 19.

Oslo Bymuseum (City Museum) This museum is the virtual attic of Oslo. Everything that Oslovians didn't throw away is on exhibit—the red coats that the city's first policemen wore, the first fire wagon, relics of the great fire of 1624, the exhibits of the Black Death that swept over in 1348. Housed in the 1790 Frogner Manor at Frogner Park, site of the Vigeland sculptures (see the earlier listing for Vigelandsparken, p. 271), this museum surveys the history of Oslo. It also contains mementos of Henrik Ibsen, from the chair and marble-topped table where he sat at the Grand Café to the glasses from which he drank. Even if you don't like the exhibits, you can enjoy Frogner Park with its streams, shade trees, and lawns ideal for a picnic. If picnics aren't your thing, go for delicious ice cream or pastries served at the on-site Café Mathia. Allow about an hour.

Frognerveien 67. ✆ **23-28-41-70.** www.oslobymuseum.no. Admission 40NOK ($6.15/£3.20) adults, 20NOK ($3.10/£1.60) children. Tues noon–6pm; Wed–Sun noon–4pm. Tram: 12.

6 Especially for Kids

Oslo offers numerous attractions suitable for both children and grown-ups, including a visit to the excavated Viking burial ships at the **Vikingskiphuset** (p. 273) and the Boat Hall at the **Norwegian Maritime Museum** (p. 273), both on the Bygdøy peninsula.

Other sights of special interest to children include the polar exploration ship *Fram* at the **Frammuseet** (p. 272); the balsa-log raft *Kon-Tiki* at the *Kon-Tiki* **Museum** (p. 272); the **Ski Museum** (p. 274), **Lookout Tower** (p. 275) and ski jump at Holmenkollen; the **Norwegian Folk Museum** (p. 272), depicting life in Norway since the Middle Ages; and the ancient **Akershus Castle & Fortress** (p. 265) on the Oslofjord.

Barnekunst Museum (International Children's Art Museum) *Kids* The collection here consists of children's drawings, paintings, ceramics, sculpture, tapestries, and handicrafts from more than 30 countries, some of which would have pleased Picasso. There's also a children's workshop devoted to painting, drawing, music, and dance.

Lille Frøens vei 4. ✆ **22-46-85-73.** www.barnekunst.no. Admission 50NOK ($7.70/£4) adults, 32NOK ($4.95/£2.55) children. Jan–June and Sept–Dec Tues–Thurs 9:30am–2pm, Sun 11am–4pm; July–Aug 15 Tues–Thurs and Sun 11am–4pm. Closed Mon, Fri, and Sat Aug 15–31. T-banen: Frøen.

Norgesparken Tusenfryd *Kids*   This is the largest amusement park in Norway, conceived as a smaller version of Copenhagen's Tivoli. It includes a number of simple restaurants, a roller coaster with a loop and corkscrew, an amphitheater with all-day entertainment by performers such as musicians and clowns, and many games. In the summer there is also a water park. The park is 19km (12 miles) south of the Central Station.

Vinterbro by E-6/E-18/Mossevelen. (C) **64-97-64-97**. www.tusenfryd.no. All-day ticket 195NOK–280NOK ($30–$43/£16–£22) adults, 150NOK–240NOK ($23–$37/£12–£19) children 12–19, 11 and under free. Late Apr to Sept daily 10:30am–8pm. Closed Oct to late Apr. Bus: Shuttle service from Oslo's Central Station daily 9:30am–4pm; final return shortly after park closes. Fare 30NOK ($4.60/£2.40) adults, 20NOK ($3.10/£1.60) children 12–19, 11 and under free.

7 Oslo on Foot: Walking Tours

WALKING TOUR 1   HISTORIC OSLO

Start:	Aker Brygge.
Finish:	Royal Palace.
Time:	2½ hours.
Best Time:	Any day when it's not raining.
Worst Times:	Rush hours (weekdays 7–9am and 5–7pm).

Start at the harbor to the west of the Rådhuset at:

❶ Aker Brygge
This steel-and-glass complex is a rebuilt district of shops and restaurants that was developed from Oslo's old shipbuilding grounds. It has a fine view of Akershus Castle.

Head east along Rådhusplassen, looking to your left at the:

❷ Rådhuset
The Oslo City Hall, built in 1950, is decorated with artwork by Norwegian artists.

Climb the steps at the east end of the square and a small hill to see the:

❸ Statue of Franklin D. Roosevelt
Eleanor Roosevelt flew to Oslo to dedicate this statue.

This area is the heart of the 17th-century Renaissance city. Take Rådhusgata east to the traffic hub of:

❹ Christiania Torv
The yellow house on your left, the Young Artists Association, was once the home of a dreaded executioner. His fee depended on the type of execution performed.

TAKE A BREAK
To the right of the Young Artists Association is **Kafé Celsius**, Rådhusgata 19 ((C) **22-42-45-39**), Oslo's oldest residential house. Today it's a charming arts-oriented cafe that serves tasty food. Sandwich prices start at 90NOK ($14/£7.20). You can also order pasta salads and such dishes as ratatouille or tortellini. On cold days they start up the fireplace. It's open Monday to Saturday 11am to midnight, Sunday 11:30am to 7:30pm.

Continue along Rådhusgata, turning right onto Nedre Slottsgate. Walk to the end of the street. At Myntgata, turn right and pass through a gate. You are now on the greater grounds of Akershus Castle. The first building on the right is the:

❺ Norwegian Resistance Museum
The museum has displays on events related to the Nazi occupation of Norway from 1940 to 1945.

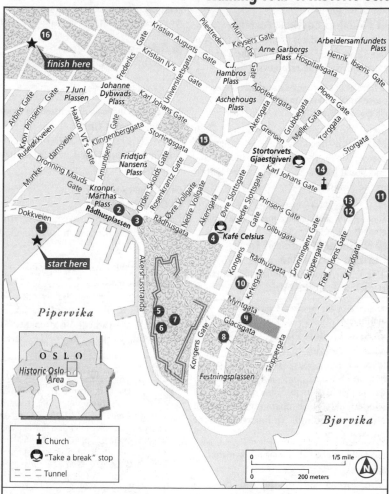

Map legend:

- ✝ Church
- ◐ "Take a break" stop
- – – – Tunnel

| 0 | 1/5 mile |
| 0 | 200 meters |

1 Aker Brygge
2 Rådhuset
3 Statue of Franklin D. Roosevelt
4 Christiania Torv
5 Norwegian Resistance Museum
6 Akershus Castle & Fortress
7 Execution Site
8 National Monument to the German Occupation
9 Grev Wedels Plass
10 Bankplassen
11 Oslo Sentralstasjon
12 Karl Johans Gate
13 Basarhallene
14 Oslo Domkirke
15 Norwegian Parliament (Stortinget)
16 Royal Palace (Slottet)

Also at the site is:

⑥ Akershus Castle & Fortress

The structure dates from 1300 but was rebuilt in the 17th century. Take a guided tour and walk the ramparts.

In front of the Norwegian Resistance Museum, pause on the grounds to look at the:

⑦ Execution Site

Here the Nazis shot prisoners, often Norwegian freedom fighters. There's a memorial to the resistance movement, and you'll have a good view of the harbor in the distance.

Cross the drawbridge to the east, right before Kongensgate, and continue through the castle grounds to the:

⑧ National Monument to the German Occupation

This commemorates Norway's suffering at the hands of the Nazis.

After seeing the monument, turn left (north) into:

⑨ Grev Wedels Plass

This is the site of Den Gamle Logen (Freemason's Lodge). Ibsen wrote poems here in 1850. At no. 9 and Dronningens-gatan 4 is the Astrup Fearnley Museum of Modern Art, with changing exhibits of Norwegian and international art from the postwar period.

Head north along Kirkegata until you reach:

⑩ Bankplassen

This former site of the old Bank of Norway is now the Museum of Contemporary Art (Bankplassen 4), with the state collection of international and Norwegian modern art acquired since World War II. This square was once Oslo's social center. Ibsen staged his first play here in 1851 (at a theater that burned down in 1877).

From Bankplassen, turn right onto Revierstredet and left onto Dronningensgatan. At one time the waterfront came up to this point. Go right

at the Central Post Office onto Tollbugata. At the intersection with Fred Olsens Gate, turn left and walk to the:

⑪ Oslo Sentralstasjon

Trains arrive at Oslo's rail hub from the Continent here and depart for all points linked by train in Norway.

Turn left onto the main pedestrian-only street:

⑫ Karl Johans Gate

The street stretches from the Central Station in the east to the Royal Palace in the west end.

On your right you'll pass the:

⑬ Basarhallene

Boutiques and shops, hawking everything from food to clothing to crafts, fill this huge complex.

Turn right at Kirkegata, heading for the:

⑭ Oslo Domkirke

This 17th-century cathedral resides at Stortorvet, Oslo's old marketplace. Like the City Hall, the cathedral is decorated with outstanding works by Norwegian artists.

 TAKE A BREAK
Old Oslo atmosphere lives on at the **Stortorvets Gjaestgiveri,** Grensen 1 (② 23-35-63-60), on a busy commercial street. This drinking and dining emporium, dating from the 1600s, is often filled with spirited beer drinkers. A beer costs 50NOK ($7.70/£4). It's open Monday to Saturday from 11am to 11pm, Sunday (from Sept–Apr only) 3pm to 9pm.

From Stortorvet, walk west on Grensen until you reach Lille Grensen. Cut left onto this street, returning to Karl Johans Gate. On your left at Karl Johans Gate 22 will be the:

⑮ Norwegian Parliament (Stortinget)

Constructed from 1861 to 1866, it's richly decorated with works by contemporary Norwegian artists.

Continue west along Karl Johans Gate, passing many of the monuments covered on "Walking Tour 2: In the Footsteps of Ibsen & Munch" (see below). Eventually you'll reach Drammensveien 1, the:

⑯ Royal Palace (Slottet)

This is the residence of the king of Norway and his family. Only the park is open to the public.

| WALKING TOUR 2 | IN THE FOOTSTEPS OF IBSEN & MUNCH |

Start:	National Theater.
Finish:	National Gallery.
Time:	2 hours.
Best Time:	Any day when it's not raining.
Worst Times:	Rush hours (weekdays 7–9am and 5–7pm).

The tour begins at Stortingsgata 15, just off Karl Johans Gate near the Students' Grove in Oslo's center, site of the:

❶ Nationaltheatret (National Theater)

Study your map in front of the Henrik Ibsen statue at the theater, where many of his plays were first performed and are still presented. The Norwegian National Theater (℗ **81-50-08-11**), inaugurated in 1899, is one of the most beautiful in Europe.

Facing the statue of Ibsen, continue up Stortingsgata toward the Royal Palace (Slottet). Cut left at the next intersection and walk along Ruselokkveien. On the right, the **Vika Shopping Terraces,** an unattractive row of modern storefronts tacked onto an elegant 1880 Victorian terrace, used to be among Oslo's grandest apartments. During World War II it was the Nazi headquarters.

Continue along this complex to the end, turning right onto Dronnings Mauds Gate, which quickly becomes Lokkeveien. At the first building on the right, you come to:

❷ Ibsen's private apartment

Look for the blue plaque marking the building. The playwright lived here from 1891 to 1895. When his wife complained that she didn't like the address, even though it was one of Oslo's most elegant,

they moved. Ibsen wrote two plays while living here.

Turn right onto Arbinsgate, and walk to the end of the street until you reach Drammensveien. At Arbinsgate 1 is the:

❸ Ibsen Museum

In the first building on the left, at the corner of Arbinsgate and Drammensveien, you'll see an Omega store, but look for the blue plaque on the building. Ibsen lived here from 1895 until his death in 1906. He often sat in the window, with a light casting a glow over his white hair. People lined up in the street below to look at him. The great Italian actress Eleanora Duse came here to bid him a final adieu, but he was too ill to see her. She stood outside in the snow and blew him kisses.

The king of Norway used to give Ibsen a key to enter the private gardens surrounding the Royal Palace. Today, everybody has that privilege.

Turn right on Drammensveien and continue back to the National Theater. Take Karl Johans Gate, on the left side of the theater, and walk east. On your left at Karl Johans Gate 47, you'll pass the:

❹ University of Oslo

Aula, the Great Hall of the university, is decorated with murals by Edvard Munch. The hall is open to the public from June 20 to August 20, daily from 10am to 3pm. For information, call ℗ **22-85-95-55.**

Twice a day Ibsen followed this route to the Grand Café. Admirers often threw rose petals in his path, but he pretended not to see. He was called "the Sphinx" because he wouldn't talk to anybody.

TAKE A BREAK
The **Grand Café**, Karl Johans Gate 31 (© **23-21-20-00**), was the center of social life for the literati and the artistic elite, including Munch. Today a favorite with many visitors, but also with hundreds of Oslovians who appreciate tradition, it is the single most famous cafe in all of Scandinavia (see "Where to Dine," earlier in this chapter). On the far wall of the cafe, you can see Per Krogh's famous mural, painted in 1928. Ibsen, with a top hat and gray beard, is at the far left, and Munch—called the handsomest man in Norway—is seated at the second window from the right at the far right of the window. The poet and playwright Bjørnstjerne Bjørnson can be spotted on the street outside (second window from the left, wearing a top hat), because he wouldn't deign to come into the cafe. You can order food and drink, a big meal, or a snack here.

Returning to the street, note the Norwegian Parliament building (Stortinget) on your right. Proceed left, and turn left onto Lille Grensen. Cross the major boulevard, Grensen, and walk straight to:

⑤ Akersgata

This street was used for Ibsen's funeral procession. Services were conducted at the Holy Trinity Church on June 1, 1906.

Veer left to see the:

⑥ Birthplace of Ibsen's son

On your left, at the corner of Teatergata and Akersgata, is the site of the famous Strømberg Theater, which burned down in 1835. It was also a residence, and Ibsen's son was born here in 1859.

Also on Akersgata is:

⑦ Trefoldighetskirken (Holy Trinity Church)

This church was the site of Ibsen's funeral.

A little farther along Akersgata is St. Olav's Church. Turn on the right side of this imposing house of worship onto Akersveien and go to:

⑧ Damplassen

This small square—one of the most charming in Oslo—doesn't appear on most maps. Norway's greatest poet, Henrik Wergeland, lived in the pink house on the square from 1839 to 1841.

Take a right at the square and head down:

⑨ Damstredet

The antique, wooden houses along this typical old Oslo street are mainly occupied by artists.

Damstredet winds downhill to Fredensborgveien. Here, a left turn and a short walk will take you to Maridalsveien, a busy but dull thoroughfare. As you walk north along this street, look, on the west side, for a large unmarked gateway with wide stone steps inside. Climb to the top, follow a little pathway, and go past gardens and flower beds. Pass a set of brick apartment buildings on the left, and proceed to:

⑩ Telthusbakken

Along this little street, you'll see a whole row of early Oslo wooden houses. Look right in the far distance at the green building where Munch used to live.

Telthusbakken leads to Akersveien. On your left you can see the:

⑪ Gamle Aker Kirke (Old Aker Church)

Enter at Akersbakken, where Akersveien and Akersbakken intersect. Built in 1100, this is the oldest stone parish church in Scandinavia that's still in use. It stands on a green hill surrounded by an old graveyard and a stone wall.

Walking Tour 2: In the Footsteps of Ibsen & Munch

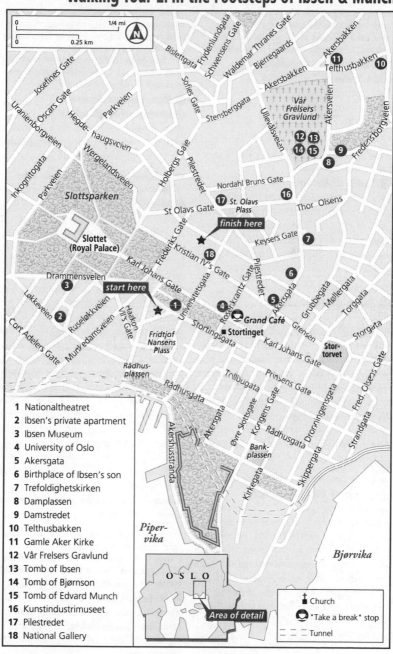

1 Nationaltheatret
2 Ibsen's private apartment
3 Ibsen Museum
4 University of Oslo
5 Akersgata
6 Birthplace of Ibsen's son
7 Trefoldighetskirken
8 Damplassen
9 Damstredet
10 Telthusbakken
11 Gamle Aker Kirke
12 Vår Frelsers Gravlund
13 Tomb of Ibsen
14 Tomb of Bjørnson
15 Tomb of Edvard Munch
16 Kunstindustrimuseet
17 Pilestredet
18 National Gallery

† Church
🛑 "Take a break" stop
– – – Tunnel

A short block from the church along Akersbakken (veer left outside the front of the church and go around a corner), you'll come to the north entrance of the city's expansive burial ground:

⑫ Vår Frelsers Gravlund (Our Savior's Cemetery)

In a section designated the "Ground of Honor" are the graves of famous Norwegians, including Munch, Ibsen, and Bjørnson.

Signs don't point the way, but it's easy to see a tall obelisk. This is the:

⑬ Tomb of Ibsen

His wife, Susanna, whom he called "the cat," is buried to the playwright's left. She died in 1914. The hammer on the obelisk symbolizes his work *The Miner,* indicating how he "dug deep" into the soul of Norway.

To the right of Ibsen's tomb is the:

⑭ Tomb of Bjørnson

The literary figure Bjørnstjerne Bjørnson (1832–1910) once raised money to send Ibsen to Italy. Before the birth of their children, Ibsen and Bjørnson agreed that one would have a son and the other a daughter, and that they would marry each other. Miraculously, Ibsen had a son, Bjørnson a daughter, and they did just that. Bjørnson wrote the national anthem, and his tomb is draped in a stone representation of a Norwegian flag.

To the far right of Bjørnson's tomb is the:

⑮ Tomb of Edvard Munch

Scandinavia's greatest painter has an unadorned tomb. If you're visiting on a snowy day, it will be buried, because the marker lies close to the ground. Munch died during the darkest days of the Nazi occupation. His sister turned down a request from the German command to give Munch a state funeral, feeling that it would be inappropriate.

On the west side of the cemetery, you'll come to Ullevålsveien. Turn left on this busy street, and head south toward the center of Oslo. You'll soon see St. Olav's Church, this time on your left. Stay on the right (west) side of the street. At St. Olavs Gate 1, where Ullevålsveien intersects with St. Olavs Gate, is the:

⑯ Kunstindustrimuseet (Museum of Applied Art)

Even if you don't have time to visit the museum, you may want to go inside to the Café Solliløkken (p. 269).

After visiting the museum, continue along St. Olavs Gate to:

⑰ Pilestredet

Look to the immediate right at no. 30. A wall plaque on the decaying building commemorates the fact that Munch lived here from 1868 to 1875. In this building he painted, among other masterpieces, *The Sick Child.* He moved here when he was 5, and many of his "memory paintings" were of the interior. When demolition teams started to raze the building in the early 1990s, a counterculture group of activists known as "The Blitz Group" illegally took over the premises to prevent its destruction. On its brick-wall side, his masterpiece *The Scream* was re-created in spray paint. The protesters are still in control of the city-owned building, and they are viewed as squatters on very valuable land. It's suspected that if a more conservative government comes into power, officials will toss out the case, throw out the activists, and demolish the building. For the moment, however, they remain in control.

At Pilestredet, turn left. One block later, turn right onto Universitesgata, heading south toward Karl Johans Gate. You'll pass a number of architecturally interesting buildings and will eventually arrive at Universitesgata 13, the:

⑱ National Gallery

The state museum has a large collection of Norwegian as well as foreign art. Two rooms are devoted to masterpieces by Munch.

8 Organized Tours

CRUISES AROUND THE FJORD   Båtservice Sightseeing, Rådhusbrygge 3, Rådhusplassen (© 23-35-68-90), offers a 50-minute boat tour. You'll see the harbor and the city, including the ancient fortress of Akershus and the islands in the inner part of the Oslofjord. Cruises depart from Pier 3 in front of the Oslo Rådhuset (City Hall). They run from mid-May to late August daily on the hour from 10am to 7pm during the high season, less frequently at the beginning and end of the season. Tickets are 100NOK ($15/£8) for adults, 50NOK ($7.70/£4) for children 5 to 15, free for 4 and under.

If you have more time, take a 2-hour summer cruise through the maze of islands and narrow sounds in the Oslofjord. From May to September they leave daily at 10:30am and 1, 3:30, and 5:45pm; the cost is 170NOK ($26/£14) for adults, 90NOK ($14/£7.20) for children. Refreshments are available onboard.

CITY TOURS   H. M. Kristiansens Automobilbyrå, Hegdehaugsveien 4 (© 23-15-73-00), has been showing visitors around Oslo for more than a century. Both of their bus tours are offered daily year-round. The 3-hour "Oslo Highlights" tour is offered at 10am. It costs 260NOK ($40/£21) for adults, 130NOK ($20/£10) for children. The 2-hour "Oslo Panorama" tour costs 190NOK ($29/£15) for adults, 90NOK ($14/£7.20) for children. It departs at 10am. The starting point is in front of the National Theater. Arrive 15 minutes before departure; tours are conducted in English by trained guides.

9 Active Sports

From spring to fall the Oslofjord is a center of swimming, sailing, windsurfing, and angling. Daily excursions are arranged by motor launch at the harbor. Suburban forest areas await hikers, bicyclists, and anglers in the summer. In the winter the area is ideal for cross-country skiing (on marked trails that are illuminated at night), downhill or slalom skiing, tobogganing, skating, and more. Safaris by Land Rover are arranged year-round.

BATHS   The most central municipal bath is **Vestkantbadet,** Sommerrogate 1 (© 22-56-05-66), which offers a Finnish sauna and Roman baths. This municipal bath is near the American embassy, just a kilometer (½ mile) north from Oslo's center. It's primarily a winter destination and is closed in July. Admission is 80NOK ($12/£6.40). The baths are open May to mid-August Monday to Friday 1 to 6:30pm and are reserved Thursday for women only. From mid-August to April the baths are open Monday and Wednesday 1:30 to 6:30pm, Tuesday and Thursday to Friday 1:30 to 7:30pm, and Saturday 10am to 2:30pm. Prices for massages start at 350NOK ($54/£28) for 30 minutes. If you book a massage (© 22-44-07-26), you can use the baths free.

Frognerbadet, Middelthunsgate 28 (© 23-27-54-50), in Frogner Park, is an open-air pool near the Vigeland sculptures. The entrance fee is 67NOK ($10/£5.35) for adults and 30NOK ($4.60/£2.40) for children. It's open mid-May to mid-August, Monday to Friday 7am to 8pm, Saturday and Sunday 10am to 6pm. Take tram no. 2 from the National Theater.

BEACHES   You most likely didn't come to Oslo to go to the beach. Even if you did, you'll find that you often have to swim from a rocky shore. Sun-loving Oslovians, desperate to absorb whatever sun they get on a summer day, often take to whatever remotely resembles a beach. Their few short weeks of summer last until around mid-August, when snow flurries start appearing in the Oslo sky.

Our favorite beach, and the most easily accessible from the center of Oslo, is **Huk,** on Bygdøy peninsula. To reach Huk, take bus no. 30 A—marked BYGDØY—to its final stop. Should you arrive by boat on Bygdøy, follow the signs along Juk Aveny to the beach. Our recommendation is to go over for the day; view the Viking Ship museum, the Folk Museum, and other attractions in the morning; and then head for the beach—preferably with the makings of a picnic—for the early afternoon. In case there are any prudes in your party, be duly warned: Half of the beach is reserved for nudists. The nude beach is on the northwestern side. That same warning should go for all beaches in Norway; along with other Scandinavians, Oslovians like to strip down for the beach.

Once you get here, don't expect a traditional Hawaiian beach. The beach is mostly grass lawns and some smooth rocks that you can lie on to sun yourself like a lizard. If the beach at Huk is overcrowded, as it's likely to be on a summer day, take a 10-minute walk through the forest a bit north of where the bus stops. This leads to the more secluded beach at **Paradisbukta.**

These beaches are our favorites mainly because of their proximity to the center, not because they are great sandy strips. But our secret reason to go there is to people-watch. After a day at the beach, you'll soon agree with a common assessment: The people of Norway are among the handsomest and healthiest-looking in the world.

Our second favorite beach is at **Hovedøya,** on the southwestern shore of the rocky island of Hovedøya. To get here, board boats 92 or 93 leaving from the pier at Oslo called Vippetangen. From late May to mid-August, these boats depart daily from around six in the morning until midnight.

This is the closest island to the mainland and it's wildly popular in summer, as ideal for a picnic as it is for walks. The island is riddled with walking paths, most of which lead to the ruins of a 12th-century Cistercian monastery. Our main reason for liking this beach is its fun-loving atmosphere. It's a wonderful break from too much museum-hopping, and it'll give you a good chance to meet with the English-speaking Oslovians (whose initially icy reserve can melt quickly).

You can also reach a number of beaches on the east side of the fjord by taking bus no. 75 B from Jernbanetorget in East Oslo. Buses leave about every hour on weekends. It's a 12-minute ride to **Ulvøya,** the closest beach to the fjord and one of the best and safest for children. Nudists prefer a section here called **Standskogen.**

FISHING   Good fishing is to be found in the Oslofjord and in the lakes that envelop Oslo. An especially popular "fishing hole" is the vast area of Marka (see "Skiing," below). You can rent canoes from **Tomm Murstad** at Tryvannsvn 2 at Holmenkollen (© **22-13-95-00**) to use for fishing. For information on the nearest place to buy a fishing license, or for more information, contact **Oslomarkas Fiskead-ministrasjon** at Sørkeldalen 914, Holmenkollen (© **40-00-67-68**).

GYMS   Male and female weight lifters call **Harald's Gym,** Hausmannsgate 6 (© **22-20-34-96**), the most professional gym in Oslo. Many champion bodybuilders have trained here, and its facilities are the most comprehensive in Norway. Nonmembers pay 90NOK ($14/£7.20) for a day pass. It's open Monday to Friday from 10am to 9pm, and on Saturday and Sunday from noon to 5pm.

JOGGING   Marka, the forest that surrounds Oslo, has hundreds of trails. The easiest and most accessible are at Frogner Park. A great adventure is to take the Sognasvann train to the end of the line, where you can jog along the fast-flowing Sognasvann stream for an hour or so. **Norske Turistforening,** Storgata 28 (© 22-82-28-00), sells maps outlining hiking trails around the capital, and the staff can give you advice about routes. It costs 110NOK ($17/£8.80).

SKATING   Oslo is home to numerous skating rinks. One of the best is the **Narvisen Skating Rink,** Skikersuppa, Karl Johan (© 95-70-95-05), open daily 11am to 9pm, charging adults 55NOK ($8.45/£4.40) for skate rentals (children 30NOK/$4.60/£2.40). The rink is closed from April to November.

SKIING   A 15-minute tram or bus ride from central Oslo to Holmenkollen will take you to Oslo's winter wonderland, **Marka,** a 2,579km (1,612-mile) ski-track network. Many ski schools and instructors are available in the winter. You can even take a sleigh ride. Other activities include dogsled rides, snowshoe trekking, and Marka forest safaris. There are 14 slalom slopes to choose from, along with ski jumps in all shapes and sizes, including the famous one at Holmenkollen. For information and updates on ski conditions, you can call Skiforeningen, Kongeveien 5 (© 22-92-32-00). The tourist office can give you details about the venues for many of these activities.

TENNIS   The municipal courts at **Frogner Park** are usually fully booked for the season by the locals, but ask at the kiosk about cancellations. **Njårdhallen,** Sørkedalsceien 106 (© 23-22-22-50), offers indoor tennis Monday to Thursday from 7am to 10pm, Friday to Sunday 7am to 8pm. Book your court well in advance. During nice weather you might prefer outdoor tennis at **Njårds Tennis,** Jenns Messveien 1 (© 23-22-22-50), a cluster of courts that are generally open whenever weather and daylight permit.

10 Shopping

THE SHOPPING SCENE

People "born to shop" like Oslo, as it's one of the most shopper-friendly cities of Scandinavia, with traffic-free streets set aside for both window shoppers and serious buyers. The heart of this district is the **Stortorvet,** where more than two dozen shops sell everything from handicrafts to enameled silver jewelry. At the marketplace on Strøget, you can stop for a glass of beer at an open-air restaurant in fair weather. Many stores are clustered along **Karl Johans Gate** and the streets branching off it.

BEST BUYS   Look for bargains on sportswear, silver and enamelware, traditional handicrafts, pewter, glass by Hadeland Glassverk (founded in 1762), teak furniture, and stainless steel.

SHIPPING GOODS & RECOVERING VAT   Norway imposes a 19.4% value-added tax (VAT), but there are ways to avoid paying it. See "Taxes" in "Fast Facts: Norway," in chapter 8. Special tax-free exports are possible; many stores will mail goods home to you, which makes paying and recovering tax unnecessary.

SHOPPING HOURS Most stores are open Monday to Friday from 9am to 5pm, Saturday 9am to 3pm. Department stores and shopping malls keep different hours— in general, Monday to Friday 9am to 8pm, and Saturday 9am to 6pm. Many shops stay open late on Thursday and on the first Saturday of the month, which is called *super lørdag* ("super Saturday"). During the holiday season, stores are also open on Sunday.

SHOPPING A TO Z
ARTS & CRAFTS

Baerum Verk 🅐 *(Finds)* For a unique adventure, head outside of town to a restored ironworks site dating from 1610. Here you'll find more than 65 different shops selling handicrafts and other items, including jewelry and woolens, plus exhibitions and six restaurants. If time remains, visit the ironworks museum on-site and see a smelting production dating from the 17th century. Verksgata 15, Baerum Verk. 🅒 **67-13-00-18.** Bus: 143 or 153.

Kunstnernes Hus 🅐🅐 This is the best place to see and to purchase the latest in cutting-edge Norwegian art. Meaning "The Artists' House" in English, this is an artist-run exhibition hall for contemporary art that first opened in 1930 and since that time has been one of the country's major showcases for the presentation of avant-garde national art. On the ground floor are two well-lit galleries and a reception area, and on the floor above are two more sky-lit galleries. Admission is 40NOK ($6.15/£3.20) for adults and 10NOK ($1.55/80p) for students and ages 7 to 17. Children 6 and under go in free. Hours are Tuesday and Wednesday 11am to 4pm, Thursday and Friday 11am to 6pm, and Saturday and Sunday noon to 6pm. Wergelandsveien 17. 🅒 **22-85-34-10.** T-banen: Sentrum.

Norway Designs 🅐🅐🅐 This is the only store in Norway that came into being as the result of a crafts exhibit. Shortly before it was established in 1957, an exposition of Norwegian crafts went to Chicago and New York, and it attracted a lot of attention. The upscale merchandise here—crystal, pewter, jewelry, and knitwear—emerged from the innovative designs of that exposition. Stortingsgaten 28. 🅒 **23-11-45-10.** Tram: 2, 8, or 9.

BOOKS

Damms Antikvariat 🅐🅐 This is the oldest antiquarian bookstore in all of Norway, in business since 1843. This warm and friendly place is full of history and intrigue, offering a wonderful selection of fiction and travel books. Although they focus mainly on Norwegian titles, you may come across a first edition of a Hemingway or Steinbeck novel. Among some of the more rare treasures, you'll find a page from the *Catholicon,* the first book ever printed with a nonreligious subject matter. Akersgaten 2. 🅒 **22-41-04-02.** T-banen: Stortinget.

Tanum Karl Johan 🅐 This fine bookstore in the center of town is the largest and most comprehensive in Oslo. It offers a vast selection, including many English titles. Karl Johans Gate 37–41. 🅒 **22-41-11-00.** T-banen: Stortinget.

CHINA & CERAMICS

Gastronaut This small and intimate space sells an array of its own exclusive china, glass, and cutlery. The china collections from Spain are simple but elegant, and—to us—a bit pricey, but worth it if you're serious about your table settings. Spanish olive

oils, spices, and specialty foods can also be found here. Bygdøy Alle 56. © **22-44-60-90.**
Bus: 30, 31, or 32.

DELI (FOR YOUR PICNIC)

A Taste of Norway ✹ This place is the most famous deli in Oslo. Quality not
quantity is their self-described motto, and they do live up to their words. You'll find
everything you need to create the perfect outdoor meal. Cured and smoked meats
from all over Europe hang on its walls, along with homemade jams and jellies on their
shelves, a wide array of sharp and mild cheeses, and, as they claim, the best smoked
salmon ✹✹✹ in the world. We love the taste and flavor of it, although we don't agree
with Sean Lennon who claimed that it "is better than world peace." A specialty of the
house is *Fenalnlaar,* cured and seasoned sheep's meat. The only beverage is beer, which
is supplied by a local brewery. For your actual picnic, we suggest you take your food
to one of the beaches, either **Huk** on the Bygdøy peninsula (p. 286) or **Hovedøya**
(p. 286). Tordenskiolds Gate 7. © **22-42-34-57.** T-banen: Nationaltheatret.

DEPARTMENT STORES

GlasMagasinet ✹ Claiming that smaller boutiques tend to charge more, locals
usually head for this big department store, which specializes in unusual home and
kitchen accessories. Since 1739 this has been a leading outlet for knitwear, pewter,
rose-painting, and crystal. Today there are more than two dozen fashion shops alone.
It's the largest outlet in Norway for the glassworks, Hadeland Glassverk ✹✹✹. There's
also a moderately priced coffee shop and a fairly decent restaurant. Stortorvet 9. © **22-
42-53-05.** T-banen: Stortinget. Tram: 11 or 17.

Steen & Strøm ✹✹ The largest department store in Norway, Steen & Strøm specializes in Nordic items, especially for the outdoors. Look for hand-knit sweaters and
caps, hand-painted wooden dishes reflecting traditional Norwegian art, and pewter
dinner plates made from old molds. There's a souvenir shop on the ground floor.
Kongensgate 23. © **22-00-40-00.** T-banen: Stortinget.

FOLK COSTUMES

Heimen Husflid ✹✹ This leading purveyor of modern and traditional Norwegian
handicrafts and apparel carries antique and reproduction folk costumes. More than
three dozen different *bunads* (styles) include different regions of Norway, both north
and south. Hand-knit sweaters in traditional Norwegian patterns are a special item. In
a sweater purchased here, you could even survive the rigors of a winter in Buffalo,
New York. Pewter and brass goods are first rate. It's about a block from Karl Johans
Gate. Rosenkrantzgate 8. © **22-41-40-50.** T-banen: Stortinget. Tram: 7, 8, or 11.

JEWELRY, ENAMELWARE & SILVER

David-Andersen ✹✹✹ This outstanding jeweler, established more than a century
ago, sells enameled demitasse spoons ✹ and sterling silver bracelets with enamel.
They're available in many stunning colors, such as turquoise and dark blue. Multicol-
ored butterfly pins are also popular in gold-plated sterling silver with enamel. David-
Andersen's collection of Saga silver ✹✹ was inspired by Norwegian folklore and
Viking designs, combined with the pristine beauty of today's design. The store also
offers an exquisite collection of pewter items. Karl Johans Gate 20. © **24-14-88-00.** T-banen:
Stortinget.

PEWTER

Heyerdahl ⊛   Want to accessorize yourself like a Viking chieftain or look like an ancient queen? Then visit this place. Between the City Hall and Karl Johans Gate, this store offers an intriguing selection of silver and gold Viking jewelry. There are articles in pewter and other materials, including Viking vessels, drinking horns, and cheese slicers. The store also has an array of woodcarvings depicting trolls, as well as one of Oslo's largest collections of gold and silver jewelry. Roald Amundsensgate 6. ℂ **22-41-59-18.** T-banen: Nationaltheatret.

SHOPPING MALLS

Mall shopping is a firmly entrenched tradition in Oslo thanks to the uncertain weather. When it rains or snows, discerning shoppers have several malls from which to choose.

Paléet ⊛⊛, Karl Johans Gate 37–43, is set on Oslo's most central and most opulent shopping street. The weatherproof complex consists of 45 different shops and boutiques, all of them relatively upscale and flooded with light from skylights. You can purchase candles, incense, sweaters, art, housewares, cosmetics—you name it. Thirteen different restaurants, including burger and beer joints and one serving Indian food, refuel weary shoppers. You can also stop to admire a bronze statue of skating great (and former movie star) Sonja Henie.

Oslo City ⊛, Stenersgate 1, opposite the Central Station, is the biggest shopping center in Norway—loaded with shops and restaurants. Also near the Central Station, **Galleri Oslo,** at Vaterland, has been called Europe's longest indoor shopping street. Businesses are open daily until midnight, including Sunday. A walkway connects Galleri Oslo to the Central Station.

Our favorite place for wandering and shopping in Oslo is **Aker Brygge** ⊛⊛ where we used to see Diana Ross racing by when she lived in this posh district of residential houses. A former shipbuilding yard was redeveloped into a postmodern complex of steel-and-glass buildings. In all, there are nearly 65 shops here, most of them upmarket and many of them fashion boutiques selling the kind of merchandise you see advertised in *Vanity Fair*. There are also 40 restaurants, along with pubs, movie houses, and legitimate theaters. When it's raining, duck into the indoor shopping mall. Even if you don't buy anything, Aker Brygge makes for one of the great strolls of Oslo. The location is right on the harborfront across from the Tourist Information Center at Vestbanen. For more information, dial ℂ **22-83-26-80.**

SOUVENIRS & GIFTS

William Schmidt ⊛⊛   Established in 1853, William Schmidt is a leading purveyor of unique souvenirs. It carries pewter items (from Viking ships to beer goblets), Norwegian dolls in national costumes, woodcarvings—the troll collection is the best in Oslo—and sealskin items, such as moccasins and handbags. The shop specializes in hand-knit cardigans, pullovers, gloves, and caps, and a selection of sweaters made from mothproof, 100% Norwegian wool. Fretgof Namser Plass 9. ℂ **22-42-02-88.** Tram: 10 or 12.

SWEATERS

Oslo Sweater Shop   Some 5,000 handcrafted sweaters are in stock here, close to the Royal Palace. Try them on before you buy. In theory, at least, you can tell the origin of a Norwegian sweater by its pattern and design, but with the increase in machine-made sweaters and the increased sophistication of Norwegian knitwear, the distinctions are increasingly blurred, at least to us. Here, as in virtually every other sweater shop in Oslo, only about 10% of the sweaters are handmade—the remainder are high quality and first rate, but most likely were crafted on an electric knitting machine. Sweaters start at around 900NOK ($139/£72), rising to a maximum of 3,000NOK ($462/£240). Other items include necklaces, pewter ware, souvenirs, and Norway-inspired trinkets. Next to the Clarion Hotel Royal Christiania, Biskop Gunnerus Gate 3. ℂ **22-42-42-25.** Bus: 30, 31, or 41.

11 Oslo After Dark

Oslo has a bustling nightlife that thrives past midnight. The city boasts more than 100 night cafes, clubs, and restaurants, 35 of which stay open until 4am.

Oslo is also a favorite destination of international performing artists in classical, pop, rock, and jazz music. Autumn and winter are the seasons for cabaret, theater, and concerts. There are four cabarets and nine theater stages throughout the city.

For movie lovers, Oslo has a lot to offer. The city has one of the most extensive selections in Europe, with 30 screens and five large film complexes. Films are shown in their original languages, with subtitles.

THE ENTERTAINMENT SCENE

The best way to find out what's happening is to pick up a copy of *What's On in Oslo,* detailing concerts and theaters and other useful information. Oslo doesn't have agents who specialize in discount tickets, but it does have an exceptional number of free events. *What's On in Oslo* lists free happenings as well as the latest exhibits at art galleries, which make for good early evening destinations.

The world-famous **Oslo Philharmonic** performs regularly under the leadership of Mariss Janson at the Oslo Konserthus. There are no Oslo performances between June 20 and the middle of August.

If you visit Oslo in the winter season, you might be able to see its thriving opera and ballet company, **Den Norske Opera.** Plays given at the **Nationaltheatret** (where plays by Ibsen are regularly featured) are in Norwegian, so those who know the language should enjoy hearing the original versions of his plays.

THE PERFORMING ARTS
CLASSICAL MUSIC

Oslo Konserthus 𝒢𝒢𝒢   Two blocks from the National Theater, this is the home of the widely acclaimed Oslo Philharmonic. Performances are given autumn to spring, on Thursday and Friday. Guest companies from around the world often appear on other nights. The hall is closed from June 20 until mid-August, except for occasional performances by folkloric groups. The box office is open Monday through Friday 10am to 5pm and Saturday 11am to 2pm. Munkedamsveien 14. ℂ **23-11-31-11.** Tickets 200NOK–800NOK ($31–$123/£16–£64). T-banen: Stortinget.

THEATER
Nationaltheatret (National Theater) 𝒢𝒢𝒢   This theater at the upper end of the Students' Grove opens in August, so it may be of interest to off-season drama lovers who want to hear original versions of Ibsen and Bjørnson. Avant-garde productions go up at the **Amfiscenen,** in the same building. There are no performances in July and August. Guest companies often perform plays in English. The box office is open

Monday through Friday from 9:30am to 6pm and Saturday 11am to 6pm. Johanne Dybwads Plass 1. © 81-50-08-11. Tickets 150NOK–380NOK ($23–$59/£12–£30) adults, 85NOK–170NOK ($13–$26/£6.80–£14) students and seniors. T-banen: Nationaltheatret. Tram: 12, 13, or 19.

OPERA & DANCE
Den Norske Opera (Norwegian National Opera) 𝕽𝕽   The Norwegian opera and ballet troupes make up Den Norske Opera. The 1931 building, originally a movie theater, was dedicated to the Norwegian National Opera in 1959. It's also the leading venue for ballet—the companies alternate performances. About 20 different operas and operettas are staged every year. There are no performances from mid-June to August. Unlike those for some European opera companies, tickets are generally available to nonsubscribers; seats can be reserved in advance and paid for with a credit card. The box office is open Monday through Saturday from 10am to 6pm (until 7:30pm on performance nights). Storgata 23. © 23-31-50-00. Tickets 160NOK–400NOK ($25–$62/£13–£32), except for galas. Bus: 56, 62, or 66.

SUMMER CULTURAL ENTERTAINMENT
Det Norske Folkloreshowet (Norwegian Evening) performs from July to August at the Norwegian Folk Museum, Museumsveien 10 (© 22-12-37-00 for reservations). The performances are on Tuesday, Wednesday, Friday, and Saturday at 5:30pm. Tickets cost 250NOK ($39/£20) for adults, 50NOK ($7.70/£4) for children (T-banen: Stortinget).

The ensemble at the **Norwegian Folk Museum,** on Bygdøy, often presents folk-dance performances at the open-air theater in the summer. See *What's On in Oslo* for details. Most shows are given on Sunday afternoon. Admission to the museum includes admission to the dance performance. Take the ferry from Pier 3 near the Rådhuset.

SPECIAL & FREE EVENTS
Oslo has many free events, including summer jazz concerts at the National Theater. In front of the theater, along the Students' Grove, you'll see street entertainers, including singers, clowns, musicians, and jugglers.

Concerts are presented in the chapel of **Akershus Castle & Fortress,** Akershus Command, on Sunday at 2pm. During the summer, promenade music, parades, drill marches, exhibits, and theatrical performances are also presented on the castle grounds.

In August the **Chamber Music Festival** at Akershus Castle & Fortress presents concerts by Norwegian and foreign musicians.

The **Oslo Jazz Festival,** also in August, includes not only old-time jazz but classical concerts, opera, and ballet performances.

FILMS
American and British films are shown in English with Norwegian subtitles. Tickets are sold for specific performances only. Many theaters have showings nightly at 5, 7, and 9pm, but really big films are usually shown only once an evening, generally at 7:30pm.

Because of the city's long winter nights, film-going is big business in Oslo. Two of the city's biggest theaters are the **Filmteateret Teletorg,** Stortingsgaten 16 (© 82-03-00-01; T-banen: Nationaltheatret), and **Kinematografer Oslo,** Olav V's Gate 4 (© 82-03-00-01; T-banen: Nationaltheatret). Most tickets cost between 90NOK and

130NOK ($14–$20/£7.20–£10) for adults and are half price for children 10 to 15; 9 and under free. During matinees (usually on Mon and Thurs) the cost is reduced to 70NOK ($11/£5.60) for adults and half price for children.

THE CLUB & MUSIC SCENE
DANCE CLUBS

Bryggeporten Bar & Nattklubb   This place is Alter Brygge's biggest nightclub. Upstairs on Friday and Saturday, a DJ spins sounds ranging from techno to disco. A cover charge is imposed (see below). Downstairs there is no cover, and patrons can relax on the red leather couches, with a round bar in the center, and take in the funky soul music. The minimum age for women is 21, but men must be 23. This is a comfortable place to unwind and have fun. It's open Wednesday to Saturday from 5pm to 3am. Stranden 1. ℂ **22-87-72-00**. Fri–Sat cover 80NOK–100NOK ($12–$15/£6.40–£8). T-banen: Nationaltheatret.

Smuget ✰   This is the most talked-about nightlife emporium in Oslo, with long lines, especially on weekends. It's behind the Grand Hotel in a 19th-century building that was once a district post office. There's an active dance floor with disco music, and a stage where live bands (sometimes two a night on weekends) perform. The clientele—mostly ages 20 to 30—includes artists, writers, rock stars, and a cross section of the capital's night owls. The complex is open Monday through Saturday nights. A restaurant serves Thai, Chinese, Norwegian, Italian, and American food from 11am to 3am; live music plays from 10pm to 3am; and there's disco music from 10pm till very late. Half liters of beer cost 42NOK ($6.45/£3.35); main courses run 93NOK to 210NOK ($14–$32/£7.45–£17). Rosenkrantzgate 22. ℂ **22-42-52-62**. Cover 60NOK–100NOK ($9.25–$15/£4.80–£8). T-banen: Stortinget.

JAZZ & ROCK

Herr Nilsen ✰   This is one of the most congenial spots in Oslo and a personal favorite because it hosts some of the top jazz artists from Europe and America. The space overlooks the courthouse square, and it's the perfect place to be on a snowy evening. The Dixieland music played here evokes New Orleans, and we've been held spellbound by the wonderful musicians booked here. Open Monday to Saturday 2am to 3am, Sunday 3pm to 3am. C. J. Hambros Place 5. ℂ **22-33-54-05**. Cover 50NOK–100NOK ($7.70–$15/£4–£8). T-banen: Stortinget.

Rockefeller/John Dee   With a capacity of 1,200 patrons, this concert hall and club is one of the largest establishments of its kind in Oslo. It's one floor above street level in a 1910 building, formerly a public bath. Live concerts feature everything from reggae to rock to jazz. When no concert is scheduled, films are shown on a wide screen. Simple foods, such as pasta and sandwiches, are available in the cafe. Most of the crowd is in the 18 to 40 age bracket. It's usually open Sunday to Thursday from 8pm to 2:30am, and Friday and Saturday from 9pm to 3:30am. Show time is about an hour after the doors open. Torggata 16. ℂ **22-20-32-32**. Tickets 100NOK–600NOK ($15–$92/£8–£48), depending on act. T-banen: Stortinget.

THE BAR SCENE
PUBS & BARS

Bar 1   Connoisseurs of brandy will love this small cognac-and-cigar bar. You'll find close to 300 different varieties of cognac, plus a selection of the finest whiskeys.

Accompany your libation with something from their wide selection of Cuban and Dominican cigars. You'll find a subdued yet sophisticated post-40 crowd here. Open daily 4pm to 3:30am. Holmensgate 3. © 22-83-00-02. Tram: 22.

Beach Club   This place combines a classic American diner with Norwegian flair. Its large booths and tables are welcoming, and the burgers are great. There is a bar but not much of a social scene, with mostly businessmen having drinks. Mellow lounge music plays every night. Open Tuesday to Saturday 11am to midnight, Sunday and Monday noon to 11pm. Aker Brygge. © 22-83-83-82. T-banen: Nationaltheatret.

Beer Palace   As you might guess, beer is the main draw at this English-style pub, which attracts a 20 to 30 crowd. The atmosphere is intimate and cozy with exposed brick walls and couches in the upstairs lounge. A dartboard and pool table provide entertainment on the first floor. Softly played rock 'n' roll completes the mood. It's open Monday to Thursday 1pm to 1:30am, Friday 1pm to 3am, and Saturday noon to 3am. Holmensgate 3. © 22-83-71-55. Tram: 10 or 12.

Bibliotekbaren (Library Bar)   In a lobby that evokes the Edwardian era, this is a perfect spot for people-watching—that is, middle-aged-people-watching. Sheltered behind racks of leather-bound books, which you can remove and read, you'll feel like you're in a well-furnished private club. There's live piano music at lunchtime, when you can order from a selection of open-faced sandwiches for 60NOK to 80NOK ($9.25–$12/£4.80–£6.40). It's open daily from 10am to midnight; alcohol service starts at 1:30pm. A beer will cost you 50NOK ($7.70/£4); mixed drinks begin at 86NOK ($13/£6.90). In the Bristol Hotel, Kristian IV's Gate 7. © 22-82-60-22. T-banen: Stortinget.

Café Onkel Donalds   Of the many bars and pubs that flourish after dark in Oslo, this is the most artfully designed. Its soaring interior spaces evoke the entranceway to a postmodern opera house, and a network of short staircases will take you from the surging energy of the glossy-looking main bar to a series of more intimate mezzanines. The house special cocktail is an Onkel Donald, a head-spinner combining vodka, peach liqueur, cranberry juice, and sour mash. Lots of romances have credited this bar as their catalyst. It's open Monday to Wednesday 11am to 2am, Thursday to Saturday 11am to 3am, and Sunday noon to 2am. Universitesgata 26. © 23-35-63-10. T-banen: Nationaltheatret.

Etoile Bar   This elegant bar with a Far Eastern motif is attached to Norway's most famous hotel, the Grand. You might see members of Parliament from across the street. The "Star Bar" has views of historic Oslo. Visiting business people mingle at night with a young spirited Oslo crowd. To reach the bar, take the special elevator to the right of the hotel entrance. Beers cost 55NOK ($8.45/£4.40), stronger drinks run from 70NOK ($11/£5.60). The bar is open Monday to Saturday 10am to midnight. In the Grand Hotel, Karl Johans Gate 31. © 23-21-20-00. T-banen: Stortinget.

John's Bar   This unflashy, unglamorous pub enjoys a powerful cachet among the Oslo's hip young denizens. In the case of decor, less is more. When it comes to patrons, you can expect just about anyone or anything: frostbitten fishermen exhausted from hauling in herring from the North Sea, or perhaps a group of grisly bikers in town for some binge drinking. It's open Thursday to Sunday 10pm to 3am. Universitesgata 26. © 23-35-63-10. Tram: 5, 6, or 7.

Limelight   This fashionable bar next door to the Oslo Nye Theater is great for drinks before or after a show. It draws mainly a middle-age crowd and is open daily 6pm to midnight. Beer and mixed drinks cost from 70NOK ($11/£5.60) and up. In the Grand Hotel, Karl Johans Gate 31. © 23-21-20-00. T-banen: Stortinget.

NIGHT CAFES

Lorry   This busy, suds-drenched cafe was established 120 years ago as a working-class bar. Since then, the surrounding neighborhood (virtually across the street from the park that flanks the Royal Palace) has zoomed upward in prestige and price. Now, the cafe's low-slung, wood-sided building is tucked among villas. There's an outdoor terrace for warm-weather dining, but the heart and soul of the place is its Victorian, black-stained interior. Offerings include 130 kinds of beer, 12 of which are on tap. The menu consists of a short list of platters of the day, priced at 100NOK to 200NOK ($15–$31/£8–£16) each, but from around 10:30pm to closing, all everybody seems to do is drink. It's open Monday to Saturday 11am to 3am, and Sunday noon to 1am. Parkveien 12. © 22-69-69-04. Tram: 11.

GAY & LESBIAN BARS

This city of 500,000 has few gay bars. To get information, pick up a copy of *Blick* for 28NOK ($4.30/£2.25), available at most newsstands within the central city, or call Gay/Lesbian Visitor Information, Kongensgate 12, 0153 Oslo (© 22-11-05-09), Monday to Friday 9am to 4pm.

London Pub   This is the most consistent and reliable gay pub in Oslo, with a relatively mature crowd of unpretentious gay men and—to a much lesser extent—women. Set within the cellar of a building a few steps from the prestigious Bristol Hotel, it contains a battered-looking, beer hall–style trio of rooms with two bar areas and a pool table. At its best—during busy periods, usually late in the week—this place can be fun, convivial, and genuinely welcoming to newcomers from faraway places. At its worst, it can be glum and depressing. It's open daily from 3pm to 4am. Another bar, **Chairs,** is upstairs and is a bit more animated and festive than its downstairs cousin. It's open every night from 8pm to 3am. C. J. Hambros Plass 5 (entrance on Rosenkrantzgate). © 22-70-87-00. T-banen: Stortinget.

Sjokoladekoppen Café & the Shu Club   This is a bright addition to Oslo's gay and lesbian scene, with a convivial but somewhat inbred group of old friends and regulars who are usually interested in faces from faraway places. During most of the week it functions as a cafe (its name translates to "the chocolate cup"), but on weekends it expands its venue into that of a high-energy disco, replete with laser lighting, danceable music, and a reputation for attracting the young and the restless from the distant suburbs of Oslo. The cafe is open from 11am to 3:30am daily; the dance club is open Friday to Sunday from 10pm to 3:30am. Kristian IVs Gate 9. ©22-41-66-08 for Café; © 22-41-82-60 for Shu Club. Cover charge in dance club 70NOK ($11/£5.60). T-banen: Stortinget.

12 Side Trips from Oslo

The Oslo area offers a variety of 1-day excursions that are manageable by boat, car, or bus. Except for boat tours of the Oslofjord (see "Organized Tours," earlier in this chapter), getting around is a do-it-yourself activity.

Fredrikstad is in Østfold on the east bank of the Oslofjord. A day trip can be combined with a visit to the port of **Tønsberg** on the west bank by crossing on the ferry from Moss to Horten and then heading south.

The summer resort and ski center of **Lillehammer,** to the north, was the site of the 1994 Olympics.

FREDRIKSTAD ☞
97km (60 miles) S of Oslo

If your busy schedule allows you to visit only one mellow old town along the Oslofjord, make it this one. Lying at the mouth of Glomma River, Fredrikstad is Norway's oldest fortified town. Visitors come here mainly to see the Old Town (Gamlebyen), one of the best preserved in eastern Norway.

King Fredrik II founded the town as a trading post between the mainland of Europe and western Scandinavia. Its characteristic landmarks are the 1880 cathedral and its delicate, silver arch Glomma Bridge, which stretches 824m (2,703 ft.) from end to end and rises 40m (131 ft.) over the water.

ESSENTIALS
GETTING THERE Trains from Oslo's Central Station depart for Fredrikstad about every 2 hours. The trip takes about 1 hour from central Oslo. Call ℂ **81-50-08-88,** or visit www.nsb.no for rail information.

There is frequent bus service daily from Oslo to Fredrikstad, the trip taking 1½ hours. Take Highway E-6 south from Oslo, heading toward Moss. Continue past Moss until you reach the junction at Route 110, and follow the signs south to Fredrikstad. Visit www.nor-way.no for information.

VISITOR INFORMATION The **Fredrikstad Turistkontor** is on Turistsenteret, Østre Brohode, Gamle Fredrikstad (ℂ **69-30-46-00;** www.fredrikstad.no). It's open June 10 to August 18, Monday to Friday 9am to 5pm, Saturday noon to 5pm, and Sunday noon to 5pm. The rest of the year, it's open Monday to Friday from 9am to 4:30pm. You can also rent bikes here, but your driver's license or a credit card number is required as a deposit.

SEEING THE SIGHTS
Fredrikstad was founded in 1567 as a marketplace at the mouth of the River Glomma. **Gamlebyen** ☞ became a fortress in 1663 and continued in that role until 1903, boasting some 200 guns in its heyday. It still serves as a military camp and is the best-preserved fortress town in Scandinavia today. The moats and embankments make for an evocative walk, recalling the days when Sweden was viewed as an enemy and not a friendly country across the nearby border.

The main guardroom and the old prison contain part of the **Fredrikstad Museum,** Tøihusgata 41 (ℂ **69-95-85-00**). At the southwestern end of Gamlebyen is a section of the museum in a former guardhouse from 1731. Inside is a model of the old town and a collection of artifacts, both civilian and military, collected by city fathers over a span of 300 years. It's open May to September, Monday to Friday from 10am to 5pm, Saturday and Sunday noon to 5pm; closed October to April. Admission is 40NOK ($6.15/£3.20) adults, 20NOK ($3.10/£1.60) children 3 to 15, and free for 2 and under.

The cathedral of Fredrikstad, **Fredrikstad Domskirke,** Ferjestedsveien (ℂ **69-30-02-80**), was constructed in 1860 in a flamboyant Gothic Revival style. Its most notable feature is its stained-glass windows by Emanuel Vigeland, the younger and lesser-known brother of Norway's most famous sculptor, Gustav Vigeland. The church was also decorated by other leading Norwegian artists. The Domkirke lies on the western bank of the Glomma opening onto a small park. Open Tuesday to Friday 11am to 3pm; no admission.

Outside the gates of the Old Town stands what remains of **Kongsten Festning,** the fortress of Fredrikstad, which was constructed on Gallows Hill and used by the townspeople as an execution site for criminals. When the Swedes took over the site in 1677, they fortified the stronghold with 20 cannons, underground chambers, passages, and a strong arsenal. Today you can scramble among the embankments, walls, stockades, and turrets, and try to imagine the fortress as it was. An unkempt, lonely spot today, it is always open, charging no admission. To reach it, walk 15 minutes beyond the Gamlebyen drawbridge, turning off Tornesveien at the Fredrikstad Motell & Camping.

WHERE TO STAY

Hotel City ⓕ   With its bars and restaurants, this is more than a hotel, it's an entertainment center. Situated in the town center close to the rail station, this stylish and modern hotel offers well-appointed accommodations. All rooms are furnished with good taste and comfort in mind. Each unit is well maintained and equipped with well-kept bathrooms containing shower units. The fifth floor is known as the "safari floor," where smoking is permitted, and each room is done in a jungle theme with wicker-accented furnishings, tiger-print carpeting, and wall art depicting jungle landscapes and wildlife. The hotel also has two good restaurants, one serving an a la carte international menu, the other with lighter pizza-and-burger fare.

Nygard 44-46, N-1600 Fredrikstad. ⓒ 69-38 56 00. Fax 69-38-56-01. www.hotelcity.no. 110 units. Sept–May 1,450NOK ($223/£116) double; June–Aug 1,100NOK ($169/£88) double. Rates include breakfast. AE, DC, MC, V. Parking 130NOK ($20/£10). Bus: 31. **Amenities:** 3 restaurants; 4 bars; nightclub; sauna; laundry service/dry cleaning; rooms for those w/limited mobility; nonsmoking rooms. *In room:* TV, minibar (in some), hair dryer (in some), Wi-Fi (in most).

WHERE TO DINE

Balaklava Guestgiveri ⓕ NORWEGIAN/INTERNATIONAL   For tradition and atmosphere, this restaurant has no competition in the Old Town. It was built in 1803 as the home of the village priest in a style known in North America as "carpenter Gothic." Today, simple but flavorful meals are served near a massive fireplace in the cellar, or, if the weather's nice, in the outdoor courtyard. The well-prepared fare includes baked salmon with dill sauce, filet of sole with lemon-butter sauce, fish-and-clam casserole with herbs, and an assortment of fresh game dishes in autumn.

Faergeportgaten 78. ⓒ 69-32-30-40. Reservations recommended. 3-course menu 495NOK ($76/£40); 4-course menu 565NOK ($87/£45); 5-course menu 625NOK ($96/£50). AE, DC, MC, V. Summer daily 11am–10pm; winter daily 6–11pm.

Majorstuen *(Kids* INTERNATIONAL   Fresh-from-the-oven pizzas and fresh fish platters draw both locals and visitors to this 18th century house at the edge of Old Town. Its outdoor terrace is one of the most popular places in town during warm weather. Inside are both a pub and a large dining room, attracting a lot of families with small children. The food is unpretentious but plentiful. Among the most popular dishes are filet of beef served with vegetables and salad, Wiener schnitzel, and marinated whale steak in black peppercorn sauce. Majorstuen is the only restaurant in the region that offers whale steak year-round.

Vollportgatan 73. ℂ **69-32-15-55.** Main courses 155NOK–245NOK ($24–$38/£12–£20); pizzas (for 1–4 people) 149NOK–189NOK ($23–$29/£12–£15). AE, DC, MC, V. Sun–Thurs noon–9pm; Fri–Sat noon–10pm.

TØNSBERG ℛ
103km (64 miles) S of Oslo

Tønsberg is Norway's oldest town. Documentation—including the *Saga of Harald Hårfagre,* by Snorre Sturluson—puts the date around 871, when King Harald Fairhair united parts of the country and the Viking town became a royal coronation site.

Don't be completely misled by Tønsberg's age. The town is modern, and if you're willing to hunt and search like a good detective, you can come across its Viking era past. In 3 hours, you can see it all.

The Viking ships *Gokstad* and *Oseberg,* on display in Oslo's Bygdøy peninsula, were discovered at a site near Tønsberg on the western bank of the Oslofjord. King Olav of Vestfold and King Sigrød of Trøndelag, both killed in battle, have their tombs at Haugar.

In the Middle Ages, Tønsberg became a major Hanseatic trading post for eastern Norway, with links to Rostock along the Baltic. In the 1600s it was known as a major port in eastern Norway, worthy of Bergen in the west.

By the mid-1800s, Tønsberg was a port for whalers in the Arctic and Antarctic Seas, rivaling Sandefjord. It was also the headquarters of Svend Foyn, known as the "father of Norwegian sealing and whaling."

Modern Tønsberg is a 104-sq.-km (40-sq.-mile) town with some 32,000 residents. It consists of a historic area filled with old clapboard-sided houses and a commercial center with a marketplace. Foodies around the world seek out the Jarlsberg cheese, which is made here.

ESSENTIALS
GETTING THERE By Train Trains depart for Tønsberg from Oslo's main railway station at intervals of between 60 and 90 minutes from 6am to 11:30pm every day, requiring a travel time of about 90 minutes and a fare of 179NOK ($28/£14) each way. The railway station is in the town center. For information and schedules, call ℂ **81-50-08-88,** or visit www.nsb.no.

By Bus There is no NOR bus service from Oslo.

By Car Take Route 18 south from Oslo via Drammen.

VISITOR INFORMATION Tønsberg **Tourist Information** is at Nedre Langgate 36B, N-3100 Tønsberg (ℂ **33-35-45-20**). It's open in July daily 10am to 5:30pm, and August to June, Monday to Friday 8:30am to 4pm. A little tourist kiosk on the island of Tjøme provides information in July daily from 11am to 5pm. Visit www.visittonsberg.com for information.

SEEING THE SIGHTS
Slottsfjellet, a huge hill fortress near the train station, is touted as "the Acropolis of Norway." That is a gross exaggeration and can lead to unrealistic expectations on the part of a first-time visitor. In its heyday, however, these 13th-century ruins blossomed as the largest medieval fortifications in Norway, attracting the victorious Swedes across the border who came to destroy it in 1503. It has only some meager ruins, and most people visit for the view from the 1888 lookout tower, **Slottsfjelltårnet** (ℂ **33-31-18-72**), rising 17m (56 ft.). It's open May 15 to June 25, Monday to Friday from

10am to 3pm; June 26 to August 20 daily from 11am to 6pm; August 21 to September 15, Saturday and Sunday from noon to 5pm; September 16 to September 29, Saturday and Sunday from noon to 3pm. Admission is 20NOK ($3.10/£1.60) for adults, 10NOK ($1.55/80p) for children.

Nordbyen is the old, scenic part of town, with well-preserved houses. **Haugar Cemetery,** at Møllebakken, is in the center of town, containing the Viking graves of King Harald's sons, Olav and Sigrød.

Sem Church, Hageveien 32 (© **33-36-93-99**), the oldest church in Vestfold, was built of stone in the Romanesque style around 1100. It's open Thursday and Friday 10am to noon; ask at the vestry if it's not open during these hours. Admission is free.

Another attraction is **Fjerdingen,** a street of charming restored houses near the mountain farmstead. Tønsberg was also a Hanseatic town during the Middle Ages, and some houses have been redone in typical Hanseatic style—wooden buildings constructed along the wharfs as warehouses to receive goods from fellow Hanseatic League members.

WHERE TO STAY

Hotel Maritim *Value*   This hotel has long been a local favorite—since 1955, in fact—but the opening of the Quality Hotel Tønsberg (reviewed below) has put it in second place. Operated by a Norwegian seamen's association, it is nonetheless a bastion of modern comfort and convenience—all offered at an affordable price. Located on a square beside the ruins of the Church of St. Olav, the hotel occupies a five-story building that's a 10-minute walk east of the rail station on the main pedestrian street. The rooms, which are frequently renovated, are well furnished and have a color scheme that rivals the spring flowers of Norway. Some of the units are quite large, and each comes with a small bathroom with shower. Fregatten, a good restaurant offering a Norwegian, Japanese, and Chinese cuisine, is on the ground floor. The helpful staff can arrange boat trips or bikes for guests.

Storgata 17, N-3126 Tønsberg. © **33-00-27-00**. Fax 33-31-72-52. www.maritimhotell.com. 34 units. 890NOK–950NOK ($137–$146/£71–£76) double; 1,200NOK–1,400NOK ($185–$216/£96–£112) suite. Rates include parking and continental breakfast. AE, DC, MC, V. Closed Dec 22–Jan 5 and 4 days at Easter. **Amenities:** Restaurant; bar; laundry service; dry cleaning. *In room:* TV, fridge.

Quality Hotel Tønsberg ☆   This hotel—the best in the area—is a member of the Quality chain in Norway. Whenever you see the Quality name, expect a stylish hotel always in the Nordic minimalist style. This one is scenically located along the waterfront at the southern end of town. In spite of its location, it is rather tranquil at night. Its bedrooms are large and most of them open onto views of the fjord. All of them are decorated in pastels and most have carpeting, except for two dozen without carpeting, which are set aside for those suffering from allergies. Each bedroom comes with an immaculately kept private bathroom with shower. Typical Norwegian food is served at the on-site restaurant.

Ollebukta 3, N-3126 Tønsberg. © **800/228-5151** or 33-00-41-00. Fax 33-00-41-01. www.choicehotels.com. 210 units. 1,065NOK–2,105NOK ($164–$324/£85–68) double. Children under 5 stay free in parent's room. Rates include continental breakfast. AE, DC, MC, V. **Amenities:** Restaurant; bar; outdoor heated pool; fitness center; sauna; business center; babysitting; nonsmoking rooms. *In room:* TV, minibar, hair dryer, safe, Wi-Fi.

WHERE TO DINE

Brygga CONTINENTAL/NORWEGIAN   This rustic-looking restaurant with an outdoor terrace opening onto a harbor view is your best choice in town, but, be warned, Tønsberg is not a place for discerning foodies. The Norwegian-style decor includes light gray tones, light-colored woods, and walls covered with modern paintings by local artists. During the week, Brygga feels like a pub, especially when soccer matches are shown on a big-screen TV. The chefs try to please most palates, offering everything from the town's best pizzas to filet of reindeer and moose. We prefer their shellfish dishes, especially their seafood salad studded with shrimp. If you like meat, the chefs will prepare you an excellent beefsteak with béarnaise sauce and a salad.

Nedre Langgate 32. ℂ **33-31-12-70.** Reservations recommended. Main courses 189NOK–250NOK ($29–$39/ £15–£20). AE, DC, MC, V. Daily 11am–10pm.

Himmel & Hav NORWEGIAN/INTERNATIONAL   This minimalist-style cafe, decorated in bright colors, would never be considered for an animal-lovers luncheon. Reindeer and whale steak are on the menu, and the latter dish is named, appropriately or inappropriately (depending on your views), "Free Willy." Less controversial dishes include a surf and turf of filet of beef, sautéed with bacon and served with scampi in a Madagascar pepper sauce. On our last visit we were impressed with the chef's handling of a freshly caught, grilled halibut. During the day, classical or jazz music plays in the adjoining Café del Mar.

Nedre Langgate 32. ℂ **33-00-49-80.** Reservations recommended. Main courses 70NOK–180NOK ($11–$28/ £5.60–£14) at lunch, 210NOK–290NOK ($32–$45/£17–£23) at dinner. AE, DC, MC, V. Daily noon–3:30am.

LILLEHAMMER ✸✸
170km (105 miles) N of Oslo, 364km (226 miles) S of Trondheim

Surrounded by mountains, Lillehammer is one of Europe's favorite resorts and our own choice for many a vacation. The town, at the head (northern end) of Lake Mjøsa, became internationally famous when it hosted the 1994 Winter Olympics. Today the sports sites and infrastructure benefit greatly from the 2 billion-*kroner* investment that the government put into Lillehammer to make it worthy of the games.

Even with all its upgrades, Lillehammer's appeal still lags far behind the popularity of such chic alpine resorts as St. Moritz in Switzerland or St. Anton in Austria. Those great alpine retreats have far more dramatic skiing, an array of first-class and deluxe hotels, fabulous restaurants, and a glittering après-ski life. Compared to them, Lillehammer is just a country town. Yet for many skiers, it has great appeal because of its natural ski conditions. Sadly, "Winter City," as Lillehammer is called, doesn't get much of that famous alpine sunshine.

Even if you're not considering it for a ski holiday, Lillehammer is an attractive venue for summer vacationers, as it has a number of attractions (see below) and a broad appeal for families.

With a population of 23,000, Lillehammer is surrounded by forests, farms, and small settlements. Its main pedestrian street, **Storgata** ✸, is known for its well-preserved wooden buildings.

At the southern end of the Gudbrandsdal valley, Lillehammer was founded as a trading post back in 1827. Over the years, Lillehammer has attracted many artists, such as Jakob Weidemann, who were drawn to its beautiful landscapes and special Nordic light. The most famous artist who lived here was Sigrid Undset, who won the Nobel Prize for literature.

If you're driving into Lillehammer, you may be completely confused by the maze of convoluted traffic patterns, one-way streets, and tunnels. It's better to park as soon as you can and explore Lillehammer on foot. It's easy to navigate and, frankly, there isn't that much to see in the very center once you've walked the Storgata. Lillehammer's greatest attractions, such as its ski slopes and the Maihaugen Folk Museum, lie on the outskirts.

At the peak of summer, the streets, which contain both attractive wood structures and a lot of ugly modern buildings, are full of people shopping, eating, or drinking. In winter skiers take over. Frankly, considering the fame of Lillehammer, many visitors expect a far more beautiful town than they discover here.

What you'll see in Lillehammer is shop after shop, some 250 in all, crowding the Storgata or streets branching off from it. Some of these stores, such as those selling crafts, will be of interest to visitors. Others are merely there to serve the population living in the province—hardware stores and the like.

ESSENTIALS

GETTING THERE   By Train   From Oslo, express trains take about 2 hours and 20 minutes, and local trains take about 3 hours. Depending on the time of year, there are five to eight trains per day. Call ℂ **81-50-08-88,** or visit www.nsb.no for information.

By Bus   Bus trips between Oslo and Lillehammer take about 2½ hours and depart two or three times a day. Visit www.nor-way.no for information.

By Car   Head north from Oslo along E-6.

VISITOR INFORMATION   The Lillehammer Tourist Office is adjacent to the railway station at Torget 2 (ℂ **61-28-98-00;** www.lillehammerturist.no). From mid-June to mid-August it's open Monday to Saturday 9am to 7pm, Sunday 11am to 6pm. Off-season hours are Monday to Friday 9am to 4pm and Saturday 10am to 2pm.

SEEING THE SIGHTS

During the peak summer season, usually June 20 to August 20, the tourist bureau schedules several excursions. These include trips to the **Maihaugen Open-Air Museum (Sandvig Collections)** and voyages on **Lake Mjøsa** aboard the *White Swan of Lake Mjøsa,* an 1850s paddle steamer. Ask the tourist office (see "Visitor Information," above) for a list of activities.

Hunderfossen Familiepark (Hunderfossen Family Park) *(Kids*   Here you'll find a presentation of the most popular Norwegian fairy tales, more than 50 activities for children and adults, a merry-go-round and Ferris wheel, carnival booths, a cafeteria, and a swimming pool. A 12m-tall (40-ft.) troll at the gate welcomes visitors. The park is 12km (7½ miles) north of Lillehammer on E-6.

Fåberg. ℂ **61-27-72-22.** Admission 215NOK ($33/£17) adults, 135NOK ($21/£11) seniors, 200NOK ($31/£16) children 3–13, free for children under 3. May–Sept daily 10am–8pm. Closed Oct–Apr. Bus: Hunderfossen from Lillehammer.

Lillehammer Kunstmuseum (Art Museum)   This art museum is better than most provincial museums in Norway because so many great artists, including Edvard Munch, were inspired by the area. In 1963, it opened as a contemporary museum but later expanded into an annex designed by Snøhetta. To bridge the gap between the two buildings, Bard Breivik, the sculptor, created a sculpture garden using water and stone. In the center of town, the museum displays one of Norway's largest collections of national art. The pieces date from the 1830s to the present. Some of Norway's major artists are represented, but most international visitors seek out works by Edvard Munch, who has four of his paintings, including *Portrait of Ida Roede,* in the collection. This gallery also possesses one of the biggest collections of paintings from the so-called Norwegian Romantic period.

Stortorget 2. (©) **61-05-44-60**. Admission 60NOK ($9.25/£4.80) adults, 50NOK ($7.70/£4) students and seniors, free for children under 16. June 24 to mid-Aug daily 11am–5pm; mid-Aug to June 23 Tues–Sun 11am–4pm.

Maihaugen Open-Air Museum (Sandvig Collections) ⊀⊀   Many Norwegian towns have open-air museums featuring old buildings that have been moved and put on display. This is one of the best of them. This museum consists of 180 buildings, from manor houses to the cottage of the poorest yeoman worker, and there are more than 40,000 exhibits. The houses reassembled here and furnished in 17th- to 18th-century style came from all over the Gudbrandsdal (Gudbrands Valley). Of particular interest is the Garmo Stave Church, built in 1200.

You can also visit 37 old workshops, displaying activities ranging from gunsmithing to wood engraving, and a large exhibit covering Norwegian history from 10,000 B.C. to the present. The museum lies about 10 minutes on foot from the town center, or a 20-minute walk from the train station. Head up Jernbanegata, turn right onto Anders Sandvigs Gate, and then go left up Maihaugvegen following the signposts. The city's concert hall is also at the museum, and two on-site cafeterias serve Norwegian food.

Maihaugveien 1. (©) **61-28-89-00**. Admission 80NOK ($12/£6.40) adults, 40NOK ($6.15/£3.20) children 6–16, free for children under 6. May 18–Sept daily 10am–5pm; Oct–May 17 (indoor museum only) Tues–Sun 11am–4pm. Bus: 007.

Norsk Kjøretøy-Historisk Museum (Museum of Norwegian Vehicle History)
Norway's only vehicle museum illustrates the development of transportation from the first sledges and wagons to modern-day cars. The most intriguing to us are exhibitions of the cars left over from Norway's attempt to build an automobile-manufacturing industry. Most famous of these is the strange "Troll Car," a kissing cousin of Sweden's Saab. The last ones were made in the 1950s and are viewed as collectors' vehicles today. The museum is east of the town center; from the bus stop, head out on Elvegata.

Lilletorvet 7. (©) **61-25-61-65**. Admission 40NOK ($6.15/£3.20) adults, 20NOK ($3.10/£1.60) children 7–14, free for children under 6. June 15–Aug 20 daily 10am–6pm; Aug 21–June 14 Mon–Fri 11am–3pm, Sat–Sun 11am–4pm.

OUTDOOR ACTIVITIES
SKIING   Lillehammer has a 94m (307-ft.) slope for professionals and a smaller jump for the less experienced. The lifts take skiers 457m (1,500 ft.) above sea level up the slalom slope, and more than 402km (250 miles) of marked skiing trails are packed by machines. The Lillehammer Ski School offers daily classes, and several cross-country tours are held weekly. Ask at the tourist office (see "Visitor Information," above) for details.

Hafjell Alpine Center ((©) **61-27-47-06**) was the main venue for Olympic alpine competitions in 1994. It has seven lifts and 20km (12 miles) of alpine slopes. The location is 15km (9¼ miles) north of town. A "ski bus," costing 50NOK ($7.70/£4) one-way and taking 20 minutes, runs here from the center of Lillehammer about six times per day. Lillehammer is also the starting point for 402km (250 miles) of prepared cross-country tracks, 5.8km (3 miles) of which are illuminated.

Lillehammer gears up in December for its winter sports season. In addition to the ski center, there's an admission-free **skating rink,** where you have to bring your own skates. It's open in the winter Monday to Friday from 11am to 9pm, Sunday 11am to 5pm. In the winter you'll also discover festivals, folklore nights, and ski races.

In winter, **Nordseter** is the focal point of two separate slopes—for both the beginner and the intermediate-level downhill skier. It also has a vast network of cross-country ski trails. A lift pass, valid for a full day, costs 150NOK ($23/£12) per person, and ski equipment (either downhill or cross country) rents for 180NOK ($28/£14) per day.

BIKING & HIKING   The best mountain biking and hiking possibilities are from the **Nordseter Hyttegrend (Nordseter Activity Center),** lying 15km (9⅓ miles) northeast of the town center of Lillehammer. Follow the signs to Nordseter at the approach roads to Lillehammer.

Once at this lakefront sporting complex (© **61-26-40-37**), you'll find many options for biking, hiking, boating, hill climbing, and canoeing. From here you can hike to Mount Neverfjell at 1,089m (3,573 ft.). In summer a 21-gear mountain bike rents for 150NOK ($23/£12) per day; a rowboat or canoe for excursions on the waters of lake Nevelvaten rents for 120NOK ($18/£9.60).

Free maps (and advice) are available for anyone who wants to ramble along any of the well-marked hiking trails radiating outward and into the surrounding hills. Likewise, the best biking routes in the area can be plotted for you.

WHERE TO STAY

Radisson SAS Lillehammer Hotel ★★★ (Kids   Set at the halfway point between the open-air museum at Maihaugen and the Olympic Park, this is the best hotel in Lillehammer, opening onto a 3.5-hectare (8½-acre) park. Lying 600m (1,960 ft.) from the main street, it is the most traditional hotel in Lillehammer, having known a previous life as the Lillehammer Hotel. In its latest reincarnation, it is better than ever, a smoothly running and efficient operation with the best facilities in town. A small midrise, it greets you with a fountain at the entrance, a nice touch that sets the tone for the interior. Paintings, paneling, artifacts, and carpeting add to the style of the hotel. Bedrooms are well organized and exhibit the epitome of comfort and taste, with bright fabrics and homey touches throughout, along with well-groomed bathrooms featuring tubs or showers. The drinking and dining facilities are top rate.

Turisthotelveien 6, N-2609 Lillehammer. © **61-28-60-00.** Fax 61-25-73-33. www.radisson.com. 303 units. Sun–Thurs 1,300NOK–1,575NOK ($200–$243/£104–£126) double, Fri–Sat 1,600NOK–1,875NOK ($246–$289/£128–£150) double. AE, DC, MC, V. **Amenities:** 2 restaurants; 4 bars; 2 heated pools (1 indoor); sauna; fitness room; children's programs; 24-hr. room service; laundry service/dry cleaning; nonsmoking rooms; rooms for those w/limited mobility. *In room:* TV, dataport, minibar, hair dryer, Wi-Fi.

WHERE TO DINE

Blåmann Restaurant und Bar MEXICAN/NORWEGIAN   Quesadillas with beef and reindeer may seem like an odd juxtaposition of culinary traditions, but this long-standing favorite more or less succeeds in its offerings (although we've had far better quesadillas than those served here). Housed in an old-fashioned building, it offers views of the river on one side of the restaurant. In summer there is outdoor seating in a "hang" over the Mesna River. Our favorite dish is the mountain trout served in a sour-cream sauce with cucumber salad and potatoes, but we also recommend the delicious hunter's soup made with mushrooms, reindeer, and spices; the breast of ostrich; and the Norwegian lamb. In summer, no dessert tops the "Berry Trip," a mixed-berry medley with homemade ice cream.

Lilletorvet 1. ✆ **61-26-22-03.** Reservations recommended. Main courses 200NOK–310NOK ($31–$48/£16–£25). AE, DC, MC, V. Mon–Sat noon–10:30pm; Sun 2–10:30pm.

Paa Bordet Restaurant ⍟ NORWEGIAN/INTERNATIONAL   This restaurant is housed in a timbered, rustic building dating from 1880. It's long been known locally for its excellent cuisine prepared with quality ingredients. On our visit, we were delighted with the marinated wild salmon and zesty beet root salad. Full-flavored dishes include crispy breast of duck with fresh cabbage, baked apple, and an orange sauce, or roasted filet of elk served with creamed Brussels sprouts. For dessert, try the delightful white chocolate confection with raspberry sorbet.

Bryggerigata 70. ✆ **61-25-30-00.** Reservations recommended. Main courses 185NOK–310NOK ($28–$48/ £15–£25). AE, DC, MC, V. Mon–Sat 6–10:30pm. Closed July.

10

Bergen

While Bergen might be considered boring by Oslo residents, those from Bergen see their city as one of the most underrated in Europe.

We fully agree with the seafaring denizens of Bergen, which gave the world two cultural icons—composer Edvard Grieg and playwright Henrik Ibsen. Bergen is enveloped by majestic mountains, the world's most spectacular fjords, and one of Europe's largest glaciers.

Summer is filled with festivals and all-night parties (the July sun shines all night long), and the staid image of Bergen as a bourgeois, conservative town fades away. However, as one student put it, the party doesn't stop in the winter; it just moves inside.

On even the most rushed of itineraries, try to spare at least 2 days for Bergen. Postpone the urban thrills for when you get to London or Paris. Come to Bergen for its natural beauty, which is still preserved here while it disappears from many parts of the planet.

In western Norway the landscape takes on an awesome beauty, with iridescent glaciers, deep fjords that slash into rugged, snowcapped mountains, roaring waterfalls, and secluded valleys that lie at the end of twisting roads. From Bergen the most beautiful fjords to visit are the **Hardangerfjord** (best at blossom time—May and early June) to the south; the **Sognefjord,** Norway's longest fjord,

immediately to the north; and the **Nordfjord,** north of that. A popular excursion on the Nordfjord takes visitors from Loen to Olden along rivers and lakes to the **Brixdal Glacier.**

On the Hardangerfjord you can stop over at a resort such as **Ulvik** or **Lofthus.** From many vantage points, it's possible to see the **Folgefonn Glacier,** Norway's second-largest ice field. It spans more than 260 sq. km (100 sq. miles). Other stopover suggestions include the summer resorts (and winter ski centers) of Voss and **Geilo.** For resorts in the fjord district, see chapter 11.

Bergen, with its many attractions—good hotels, boarding houses, and restaurants, as well as excellent boat, rail, and coach connections—makes the best center in the fjord district. It's an ancient city that looms large in Viking sagas. Until the 14th century, it was the seat of the medieval kingdom of Norway. The Hanseatic merchants established a major trading post here that lasted until the 18th century.

Bergen has survived many disasters, including several fires and the explosion of a Nazi ship during World War II. It's a town with important traditions in shipping, banking, and insurance, its modern industries are expanding rapidly, and its university is one of the academic jewels of Norway.

1 Orientation

ARRIVING

BY PLANE   Planes to and from larger cities such as Copenhagen and London land at the **Bergen Airport** in Flesland, 19km (12 miles) south of the city. Dozens of direct or nonstop flights go to just about every medium-size city in Norway on such airlines as **SAS** (✆ **91-50-54-00;** www.scandinavian.net).

Frequent **airport bus** service connects the airport to the Radisson SAS Royal Hotel and the city bus station. Departures are every 20 minutes Monday to Friday, and every 30 minutes Saturday and Sunday. The one-way fare is 72NOK ($11/£5.75).

BY TRAIN   Day and night trains arrive from Oslo and stations en route. For information, call ✆ **81-50-08-88.** Travel time from Oslo to Bergen is 8 ½ hours. Visit www.nsb.no for information.

BY BUS   Express buses travel to Bergen from Oslo, Trondheim, Ålesund, and the Nordfjord area. The trip from Oslo takes 11 hours. Visit www.nor-way.no for information.

BY CAR   A toll is charged on all vehicles driven into the city center Monday to Friday from 6am to 10pm. A single ticket costs 15NOK ($2.30/£1.20).

The trip from Oslo to Bergen is a mountain drive filled with dramatic scenery. Because mountains split the country, there's no direct road. The southern route, E-76, goes through mountain passes until the junction with Route 47; it then heads north to Kinsarvik and makes the ferry crossing to E-16 leading west to Bergen. The northern route, Highway 7, through the resort of Geilo, heads to the junction with Route 47 and then south to Kinsarvik. Take the ferry, and go west on E-16.

Visitors with a lot of time may spend 2 or 3 days driving from Oslo to Bergen. Fjords and snowcapped peaks line the way, and you can photograph waterfalls, fjord villages, and perhaps ancient stave churches.

To reduce driving time, motorists can use a tunnel—11km (almost 7 miles), the longest in northern Europe—that goes between Flåm (see chapter 11) and Gudvangen. From Gudvangen, follow E-16 southwest to Bergen.

VISITOR INFORMATION

The **Bergen Tourist Office,** Vågsallmenningen 1 (✆ **55-55-20-00;** www.VisitBergen. com), provides information, maps, and brochures about Bergen and the rest of the region. It's open June to August daily 8:30am to 10pm; May and September daily 9am to 8pm; October to April, Monday to Saturday 9am to 5pm. The Bergen Tourist Office can also help you find a place to stay, exchange foreign currency, and cash traveler's checks when banks are closed. You can also buy tickets for city sightseeing or for tours of the fjords.

CITY LAYOUT

Bergen is squeezed between mountain ranges and bounded by water. The center of the city lies between the harbor, **Bryggen** (check out "Seeing the Sights," later in this chapter), the railway station, and the main square, **Torgalmenningen.**

Like Rome, Bergen is said to have grown up around seven hills. For the best overall view, take the funicular to **Fløien.** The northern section of the city is **Sandviken,** which is filled with old warehouses. The area south of central Bergen is being developed at an incredible rate.

In the center of Bergen, walk on cobblestone streets and explore the quayside, with its medieval houses and the open-air fish market. The center has colonnaded shops and cafes, and in **Gamle Bergen** you can step back in time to the early 19th century.

2 Getting Around

The **Bergen Card** entitles you to free bus transportation and (usually) free museum entrance throughout Bergen, plus discounts on car rentals, parking, and some cultural and leisure activities. Ask for it at the tourist office (see "Visitor Information," above). A 24-hour card costs 170NOK ($26/£14) for adults, and 70NOK ($11/£5.60) for children 3 to 15. A 48-hour card is 250NOK ($39/£20) for adults, and 100NOK ($15/£8) for children 3 to 15. Children under 3 travel or enter free.

BY BUS

The **Central Bus Station (Bystasjonen)**, Strømgaten 8 (© 55-55-90-70), is the terminal for all buses serving the Bergen and Hardanger areas, as well as the airport bus. The station has luggage storage, shops, and a restaurant. City buses are marked with their destination and route number. For **bus information** in the Bergen area, call © **177.** A network of yellow-sided city buses serves the city center only. For information, call © **55-59-32-00.**

BY TAXI

Taxis are readily available at the airport. To request one, call © **55-99-70-10.** A ride from the Bergen Airport to the city center costs around 275NOK ($42/£22). Sightseeing by taxi goes for about 400NOK ($62/£32) for the first hour and 300NOK ($46/£24) for each additional hour.

BY CAR

PARKING   Visitors can park on most streets in the city center after 5pm. For convenient indoor parking, try the **Bygarasjen Busstation** (© **55-56-88-70**), a large garage near the bus and train stations, about a 5-minute walk from the city center. It's open 24 hours a day and charges 15NOK ($2.30/£1.20) per hour. You can park for 24 hours for 75NOK ($12/£6).

RENTAL CARS   You might want to rent a car to explore the area for a day or two. **Budget** (© **800/472-3325** in the U.S.; www.budget.com) maintains offices at the airport (© **55-22-75-27**) and downtown at Storetveitveien 58 (© **55-27-39-90**). Its least expensive car is 700NOK ($108/£56) per day, which includes the 23% government tax, collision-damage waiver, and unlimited mileage. Rates per day are lower for rentals of a week or more.

Hertz (© **800/654-3001** in the U.S.; www.hertz.com) has locations at the airport (© **55-22-60-75**) and downtown at Nygårdsgate 89 (© **55-96-40-70**). For a 2-day rental, its smallest car, a Renault Clio, costs 1,200NOK ($185/£96) per day, including tax, collision-damage waiver, and unlimited mileage.

Avis (© **800/331-2112** in the U.S.; www.avis.com) has branches at the airport (© **55-22-76-18**) and downtown at Lars Hillesgate 20 (© **55-55-39-55**). For a 1-day rental, its smallest car, a Ford Fiesta, costs 1,300NOK ($200/£104) with unlimited mileage. The price includes the 23% tax and the optional collision-damage waiver. Of course, rates are subject to change. The lowest rates are almost always offered to those who reserve their cars from their home country before they leave.

Remember that Norway imposes severe penalties—including stiff fines and, in some cases, imprisonment—on anyone who drinks and drives.

BY FERRY

You can take a ferry across the harbor Monday to Friday from 7am to 4:15pm; they don't run on Saturday or Sunday. One-way fares are 12NOK ($1.85/95p) for adults, and 6NOK ($.90/50p) for children 5 to 15; 4 and under free. Ferries arrive and depart from either side of the harbor at Dreggekaien and Munkebryggen. For information, call © **55-55-20-00.**

BY COASTAL STEAMER

Bergen is the cruise capital of Norway, home to a flotilla of well-engineered ships that carry passengers, cars, and vast amounts of freight up and down the coast. At least 10 of the boats begin and end their itineraries in Bergen and make about 30 stops en route before landing 5 to 6 days later at Kirkenes, far north of the Arctic Circle, near the Russian border. You can book a berth on any one of these ships for short- or long-haul transits, and do a quick bit of sightseeing while the ship docks in various ports.

The most popular tour is a 12-day unescorted northbound cruise—Oslo-Bergen-Kirkenes-Oslo—starting at $2,949 per person based on double occupancy. It's best to book these cruises through the New York City office of the Bergen Line (© **800/ 323-7436** or 212/319-1300; www.norwegiancoastalvoyage.us). The line owns some of the ships and acts as a sales agent for the others. If you're already in Norway, talk to any travel agent. You can make arrangements through Bergen-based **Cruise Spesial-isten,** Lillemarkev 1–3 (© **55-23-07-90**), or with its competitor, **Kystopplevelser,** on Strandkaien 4 (© **55-31-59-10**). Both companies distribute brochures and lots of information concerning the stalwart Norwegian cruise ships that make frequent runs up and down the Norwegian coast.

Other routes head south from Bergen to Stavanger and other ports, and tours go to some of the fjords to the south. For information and reservations, contact the Bergen Line, Cruise Spesialisten (see above), or a local operator, which include **Flaggruten** (© **55-23-87-80**) and **H.S.D.** (© **55-23-87-00**), whose ships usually depart from the Strandkai terminal, on Strandkaien, near the fish market. Faster than many hydrofoils, they go to the inner reaches of the world's longest fjord, the Sognefjord, stopping frequently en route to pick up cargo and passengers, and are worthy vehicles for sightseeing expeditions. Many of them dock at Bergen's inner harbor, near the Stradkaiterminalen.

FAST FACTS: Bergen

Area Code The country code for Norway is **47,** and most land-based telephones within Bergen begin with **55.** (Cellphones, however, are not bound by that general rule and might begin with virtually anything.) In Norway, all telephone numbers have eight digits, the first two of which are usually defined as the "area code." Whether you're dialing a Norwegian telephone from inside or outside of Norway, it's necessary to dial all eight digits.

Banking Bergen has dozens of banks. The most visible is **Den Norske Bank,** Torg Almenning 2 (© **55-21-10-00**). Branches of many of its competitors can be found near the Radisson SAS Hotel Norge on Rådstuplass.

Bookstores One of the best, with a wide range of books in English, is **Norli,** in the Galleriet, Torgalmenningen 8 (② 55-96-28-10). It's open Monday to Friday 9am to 8pm, Saturday 9am to 6pm.

Business Hours Most **banks** are open Monday to Friday from 9am to 3pm, and Thursday until 6pm. Most **businesses** are open Monday to Friday 9am to 4pm. **Shops** are generally open Monday to Wednesday and Friday 9am to 4:30pm, Thursday 9am to 7pm (sometimes also on Fri until 7pm), Saturday 9am to 2pm.

Currency Exchange You can exchange currency at the Bergen Airport. In town you can exchange money at several banks. When the banks are closed, you can exchange money at the tourist office (see "Visitor Information," p. 306).

Dentists Emergency care only is available at **Bergen Legevakt,** Vestre Stromkaien 19 (② 55-56-87-00), from 5 to 10pm.

Doctors For medical assistance, call **Bergen Legevakt,** Vestre Stromkaien 19 (② 55-56-87-00), 24 hours a day. If it's not an emergency, your hotel can make an appointment with an English-speaking doctor.

Drugstores One convenient pharmacy is **Apoteket Nordstjernen** at the Central Bus Station (② 55-21-83-84). It's open Monday to Saturday 8am to 11pm and Sunday 10am to 11pm.

Embassies & Consulates Most foreign nationals, including citizens of the United States, will have to contact their embassies in Oslo (p. 233) if they have a problem. Exceptions to this rule include the **United Kingdom,** which maintains a consulate in Bergen at Øvre Ole Bulls Plass 1 (② 55-36-78-10), and **Canada,** which has a consulate at Asbjørnsen gate 20 (② 55-29-71-30).

Emergencies For the **police,** dial ② **112;** to report a **fire,** call ② **110;** for an **ambulance,** dial ② **113.**

Eyeglass Repair A good optician is **Optiker Svabø,** Strandgaten 18 (② 55-31-69-51).

Hairdressers & Barbers One of the best in town is **Prikken Frisørsalong,** Strandkaien 2B (② 55-32-31-51). It's open Monday, Tuesday, Thursday, and Friday 9am to 4pm, Wednesday 10am to 7pm, and Saturday 9am to 2pm.

Hospitals A medical center, **Accident Clinic (Legevakten),** is open around the clock. It's at Vestre Stromkaien 19 (② 55-56-87-00).

Internet Access Your two best bets are **Accezzo,** next to the Galleriet shopping mall at Torgallmenningen 8 (② 55-31-11-60), and **CyberHouse Internett Café,** Vetrlidsallmenninggen 13 (② 55-36-66-16).

Laundry Try **Jarlens Vaskoteque,** Lille Øvregate 17 (② 55-32-55-04). It's near the Hotel Victoria in a little alley about 45m (150 ft.) northeast of the 17th-century Korskirken church, off Kong Oscars Gate. It's open Monday, Tuesday, and Friday 10am to 6pm, Wednesday and Thursday 10am to 7pm, and Saturday 10am to 3pm.

Libraries The **Bergen Public Library,** Strømgaten (② 55-56-85-00), is open in July and August on Tuesday, Wednesday, and Friday 10am to 3pm, Monday and Thursday 9am to 7pm, and Saturday 9am to 1pm. The rest of the year, it's open Monday to Friday 10am to 8pm and Saturday 10am to 5pm.

Lost Property Various agencies recover lost objects. For assistance, contact the local police station or **Tourist Information** (© **55-55-20-00**).

Luggage Storage & Lockers Rental lockers and luggage storage are available at the **Jernbanestasjonen (railway station),** Strømgaten 1, which is open daily 7am to 11:50pm. The cost ranges from 20NOK to 40NOK ($3.10–$6.15/£1.60–£3.20) per day, depending on the locker's size.

Photographic Needs Go to **Foto Knutsen,** in the Galleriet, Torgalmenningen 6 (© **55-31-16-78**). It's open Monday to Friday 8:30am to 8pm, and Saturday 9am to 6pm.

Police Call © **112.**

Post Office The main post office is on Småstrandgaten (© **55-54-15-00**), 1 block from Torget. It's open Monday to Friday 8am to 5pm, and Saturday 9am to 2:30pm. If you want to receive your mail c/o General Delivery, the address is Poste Restante, N-5002 Bergen. You'll need your passport to pick it up.

Taxes Bergen adds no city taxes to the national value-added tax.

Telephone Public telephones take 1NOK (15¢/8p) coins. Local calls cost 5NOK (75¢/40p), but to an increasing degree, most locals pay for their calls with debit phone cards, available in various denominations at newspaper kiosks and pharmacies. To call abroad, dial © **00**; to call collect, dial © **115.**

3 Where to Stay

Easily found at Vågsallmenningen 1, the **Bergen Tourist Office** (see "Orientation," earlier in this chapter) books guests into hotels and secures accommodations in private homes. More than 30 families take in guests during the summer. The booking service costs 30NOK to 50NOK ($4.60–$7.70/£2.40–£4), depending on the methodologies you ask the staff to use, and prospective guests also pay a deposit that's deducted from the final bill. Double rooms in **private homes** usually cost 380NOK to 450NOK ($59–$69/£30–£36), with no service charge. Breakfast is not served.

The rates quoted for the hotels below include service and tax. Many expensive accommodations lower their rates considerably on weekends and in midsummer. We've mentioned it when these reductions are available, but the situation is fluid, and it's best to check on the spot. All of our recommended accommodations come with private bathrooms unless otherwise indicated.

EXPENSIVE

Clarion Collection Hotel Havnekontoret ★★★   Since 2006, this has become the most sought after address in town. Right on the scenic Bryggen harborfront, the hotel was created from an antique that housed the Bergen Port Authority. The recycling into a first-class hotel of grace and charm has been remarkable. Architects respected the past style, keeping the neoclassicism features and baronic influences from 1919. We prefer to book into one of the tower rooms, because the views over the harbor and the cityscape are spectacular. The six-floor property features rooms with a contemporary, colorful decor, each with a state-of-the-art bathroom with a tub/shower combo. Bedrooms also have all the most up-to-date amenities, including satellite TV with pay movies. The hotel has the best fitness equipment in town, and its buffet restaurant for breakfast and dinner is even patronized by in-the-know locals.

Slottsgaten 1, N-5835 Norway. © 55-60-11-00. Fax 55-60-11-01. www.solstrand.com. 116 units. Mon–Thurs 1,895NOK–2,600NOK ($292–$400/£152–£208) double, Fri–Sun 1,495NOK–2,095NOK ($230–$323/£120–£168) double. AE, DC, MC, V. Parking 100NOK–150NOK ($15–$23/£8–£12). **Amenities:** Restaurant; bar; fitness room; sauna; business center; salon; limited room service; laundry service/dry cleaning; nonsmoking rooms; rooms for those w/limited mobility. *In room:* TV, dataport, minibar, hair dryer.

Clarion Hotel Admiral ☆

This member of the Clarion chain is not as luxurious and well appointed as the just-recommended Clarion Collection Hotel, but it offers first-class comfort in an amazing location—right on the Bergen harbor—with panoramic views of Bryggen and the old wharf. The hotel is minutes from such attractions as the Bergen Fish Market and represents one of the best facelifts of an old building we've seen in Bergen. In 1906 it was one of the largest warehouses in Bergen, with six sprawling floors peppered with massive trusses and beams. In an engineering wonder in 1987, it was miraculously transformed into this modern bastion. Some rooms are small, but others are midsize to spacious, with shiny modern bathrooms with tub/shower combinations. Many rooms lack water views, but the ones that do open onto flower-bedecked balconies.

Christian Sundts Gate 9, N-5004 Bergen. © 55-23-64-00. Fax 55-23-64-64. www.choicehotels.no. 211 units. Mon–Thurs 1,360NOK ($209/£109) double, 1,600NOK–2,500NOK ($246–US$385/£128–£200) suite; Fri–Sun 1,100NOK ($169/£88) double, 1,150NOK–2,550NOK ($177–$393/£92–£204) suite. AE, DC, MC, V. Bus: 2, 4, or 11. **Amenities:** 2 restaurants; bar; business center; limited room service; laundry service/dry cleaning; nonsmoking rooms; rooms for those w/limited mobility. *In room:* TV, minibar, hair dryer, safe.

First Hotel Marin ☆☆ *(Kids)*

This is one of the better first-class hotels in town, rising seven floors in a streamlined format on a steep hillside in a brown-brick building. The hotel gets its name and theme from its location at Bryggen along the waterfront, which, along with the Fish Market, lends itself to the views from several of the bedrooms. Standard doubles are rented, but if you're willing to pay more you'll get a superior double with more space and upgraded amenities. Each room is tastefully and comfortably furnished in stylish Nordic modern with immaculately kept tiled bathrooms with tub/shower combos. Families often book the suites, which come with a separate bedroom with a large double and a living room. One of the suites is equipped as a "princess room," the other as a "pirates room."

Rosenkrantzgaten 8, N-5003 Bergen. © 53-05-15-00. Fax 53-05-15-01. www.firsthotels.com. 152 units. 900NOK–1,450NOK ($139–$223/£72–£116) double; 1,700NOK–2,950NOK ($262–$454/£136–£236) suite. AE, DC, MC, V. Bus: 1, 5, or 9. **Amenities:** 2 restaurants; bar; fitness center; sauna; Turkish bath; limited room service; laundry service/dry cleaning; nonsmoking rooms. *In room:* TV, minibar, hair dryer, Wi-Fi (in some).

Radisson SAS Hotel Norge ☆☆☆

This Radisson SAS is an even better address than the Radisson SAS Royal recommended below. In the city center, near Torgalmenningen, the Norge has been a Bergen tradition since 1885 and continues to be a favorite of local celebrities. The hotel was built in 1962, but was renovated in 2006 and 2007. Rooms are better than ever after these upgrades, with double-glazed windows, bedside controls, and ample bathrooms with showers and, in some cases, bathtubs big enough for two. Our favorites are the ninth-floor units opening onto private balconies overlooking the flower-ringed borders of a nearby park. The hotel's best service and the cuisine (Norwegian and international) are found in the Ole Bull, while

FISH has some of the town's freshest seafood. There's also an on-site piano bar, American Bar. The Contra Bar, on the street level near the reception area, is a leading nightlife venue, and The Metro disco lies in the cellar. Both have separate entrances.

Nedre Ole Bulls Plass 4, N-5807 Bergen. (C) 800/333-3333 in the U.S., or 55-57-30-00. Fax 55-57-30-01. www. radissonsas.com. 347 units. 1,740NOK–2,185NOK ($268–$336/£139–£175) double; from 2,500NOK ($385/£200) suite. Rates include breakfast. Children under 18 stay free in parent's room. AE, DC, MC, V. Parking 150NOK ($23/£12); reserve with room. Bus: 2, 3, or 4. **Amenities:** 2 restaurants; 2 bars, dance club; heated indoor pool; fitness center; sauna; limited room service; babysitting; laundry service/dry cleaning; rooms for those w/limited mobility, solarium. *In room:* TV, minibar, hair dryer, trouser press.

Radisson SAS Royal Hotel ✰✰   This hotel has long been a favorite of ours, as we were here when it opened its doors in 1982, having been built on the fire-ravaged site of an old warehouse that had stood here since 1702. With the passage of the years, it has kept abreast of changing times and decor, although the Radisson SAS Hotel Norge (see above) remains the traditional favorite. Lying right at Bryggen in the center of town, the hotel offers a choice of standard and business class rooms and suites, the latter decorated with locally made arts and crafts, creating one of the coziest ambiences in Bergen. The guest rooms are beautifully maintained, with lithographs and comfortable, upholstered furniture. Although the bathrooms are small, they have tub/shower combinations and phones. The hotel has a nightclub, Engelen, and a pub, Madame Felle, named after a lusty matron who ran a sailors' tavern on these premises during the 19th century. The pub's outdoor terrace, Madame Felle's Promenade, does a thriving business in the summer.

Bryggen, N-5835 Bergen. (C) 800/333-3333 in the U.S., or 55-54-30-00. Fax 55-32-48-08. www.radisson.com. 273 units. 1,550NOK–1,745NOK ($239–$269/£124–£140) double; from 2,045NOK ($315/£164) suite. Rates include breakfast. AE, DC, MC, V. Parking 120NOK ($18/£9.60). Bus: 1, 5, or 9. **Amenities:** 2 restaurants; 2 bars; nightclub; heated indoor pool; fitness center; sauna; limited room service; babysitting; laundry service/dry cleaning; nonsmoking rooms; rooms for those w/limited mobility. *In room:* TV, minibar, hair dryer, trouser press.

MODERATE

Augustin Hotel ✰ *Finds*   The Augustin, the oldest family-run hotel in Bergen, has been in the same family for three generations and is the clear winner in the moderately priced category. The hotel boasts one of the best locations in Bergen—right in the harborfront shopping district—with front rooms that have harbor views. Constructed in 1909 in an Art Nouveau style, the Augustin rises six floors, and in 1995, it more than doubled in size by adding a new wing. Modern rooms in the new wing are equipped with larger showers and tubs, while more traditional and less desirable rooms remain in the old section (they also have showers and tubs). The hotel is decorated with lots of art from well-known contemporary Norwegian artists.

The Altona tavern, once the haunt of Bergen artists and concertmasters in the 17th century, has been creatively integrated into the hotel. The hotel was built on its foundation, and its nostalgic memory is evoked in the hotel's wine cellar, which is open to the public. Even if you're not a guest, we'd recommend a visit to the on-site Brasserie No22, which has some of the best shellfish and meat grills in town. A three-course fixed-price menu costs 295NOK ($45/£24).

Carl Sundts Gate 22-24, N-5004 Bergen. (C) 55-30-40-40. Fax 55-30-40-10. www.augustin.no. 109 units. Mon–Thurs 1,400NOK–1,510NOK ($216–$233/£112–£121) double, from 2,000NOK ($308/£160) suite; Fri–Sun 800NOK–900NOK ($123–US$139/£64–£72) double, from 1,400NOK ($216/£112) suite. AE, DC, MC, V. Bus: 2 or 4. **Amenities:** Restaurant; bar; laundry service/dry cleaning; nonsmoking rooms; rooms for allergy sufferers; rooms for those w/limited mobility. *In room:* A/C, TV, dataport, minibar, hair dryer, iron, trouser press.

Best Western Hotell Hordaheimen   This hotel is a bit staid and not for the rock-around-the-clock crowd, but it's an enduring favorite. Located near the harbor, the hotel has long been a base for young people from nearby districts. It's operated by the Bondeungdomslaget i Bergen, an association that sponsors cultural and folklore programs, and school and civic groups sometimes reserve nearly all the rooms. The five-story hotel was built around 1800 and renovated in stages, recently in 2006, with an additional 30 new rooms scheduled for completion early in 2007. Ongoing refurbishments, as needed, have kept the hotel looking young. The small, simple guest rooms are immaculate, with good beds and tiny bathrooms equipped with tub/shower combinations.

Christian Sundts Gate 18, N-5004 Bergen. ✆ 55-33-50-00. Fax 55-23-49-50. 64 units. Mon–Thurs 1,460NOK ($225/£117) double; Fri–Sun 880NOK ($136/£70). Rates include breakfast. AE, DC, MC, V. Bus: 1, 5, or 9. **Amenities:** Restaurant; lounge; limited room service; laundry service/dry cleaning; nonsmoking rooms; rooms for those w/limited mobility. *In room:* TV, minibar, hair dryer, safe.

Neptun Hotel ☆ *Finds*   The Neptun has a far livelier ambience and decor than the staid Hordaheimen recommended above. It was built in 1952 long before many of its more streamlined and trend-conscious competitors. Its eight-story premises attract lots of business, especially from Norwegians riding the *Hurtigruten* (coastal steamers), who consider it a worthwhile and solid choice in the upper-middle bracket. Each of the bedrooms has a decorative theme related to its name. For example, rooms named after Ole Bull, Nordahl Grieg, Ludvig Holberg, Salvador Dalí, and Joan Miró have photos or artwork commemorating their namesakes' lives and achievements. When you check in, ask the reception staff for a "business" or a "feminine" room, and a decor that more or less corresponds to those parameters will be assigned to you. Units on the fourth and fifth floors are the most recently renovated (in 2006, the same year as an overall upgrade of the lobby and reception areas). About half of the rooms have tub/shower combinations; the remainder contain just showers.

Valkendorfsgate 8, N-5012 Bergen. ✆ 55-30-68-00. Fax 55-30-68-50. www.neptunhotell.no. 145 units. Mon–Thurs 1,525NOK ($235/£122) double, 1,525NOK ($235/£122) suite; Fri–Sun year-round and daily mid-June to mid-Aug 1,155NOK ($178/£92) double, from 1,700NOK ($262/£136) suite. AE, DC, MC, V. Bus: 20, 21, or 22. **Amenities:** 2 restaurants; bar; limited room service; laundry service/dry cleaning; nonsmoking rooms. *In room:* A/C, TV, minibar, hair dryer, iron.

Quality Edvard Grieg Hotel and Suites ☆ *Finds*   We're surprised that this hotel isn't better known considering the quality of its accommodations. Savvy businesspeople know of its charm, but its location away from the center might be off-putting for the casual sightseer. Opened in 1987, this modern, all-suite hotel—Norway's first—lies 19km (12 miles) south of Bergen and 4.8km (3 miles) from the airport. Luxuriously appointed suites are amply sized, with comfortable beds in the rather small sleeping quarters and a separate lounge. The bathrooms are immaculate, with lots of shelf space and tub/shower combinations. The lobby bar is cozy, and patrons can also dance at the Amitra nightclub. Free airport transfers are arranged for arriving and departing guests Monday to Friday from 7am to 10pm.

Sandsliåsen 50, N-5245 Sandsli. ✆ 55-98-00-00. Fax 55-98-01-50. www.choicehotels.com. 153 units. 1,820NOK ($280/£146) suite for 2. Rates include breakfast. AE, DC, MC, V. Free parking. Bus: 30 from the Bergen bus station. **Amenities:** Restaurant; bar; heated indoor pool; fitness center; sauna; bike rentals; laundry service/dry cleaning; nonsmoking rooms; rooms for those w/limited mobility. *In room:* TV, minibar, hair dryer, iron, trouser press.

INEXPENSIVE

Bergen Travel Hotel (Kids)   This is a place to hang your hat for the night and get a good night's sleep for an affordable price—but not a lot more. In the center of Bergen, this five-story building has been a hotel since the 1970s and was renovated in 2005, when it incorporated into its premises a building across the street. Check-in rituals usually involve a kind of nonchalance and an utter lack of fuss. Bedrooms come in various sizes, and each has pale colors and contemporary furniture crafted from dark-grained hardwoods. Some of the accommodations used to be small private apartments, so they can generously accommodate four or more people, making them a family favorite. Bedrooms have wood floors, comfortable but simple furnishings, and four of the units come with small kitchens. Each rental has a small private bathroom with shower, and each is utterly simple and without frills.

Vestre Torgate 20A, N-5015 Bergen. ℂ **55-59-90-90.** Fax 55-59-90-91. www.hotelbergen.com. 63 units. Mon–Thurs 1,080NOK–1,250NOK ($166–$193/£86–£100) double; Fri–Sun 780NOK–1,250NOK ($120–$193/£62–£100) double. Rates include continental breakfast. AE, DC, MC, V. Closed Dec 22–Jan 4. Bus: 2, 3, or 4. **Amenities:** Pub; laundry service/dry cleaning. *In room:* TV.

Comfort Hotel Holberg (✿)   If you're checking into this place in late 2007, look for a thorough renovation of the property, which should make it better than we're claiming here. Set near the Nykirk, a 15-minute walk from Bergen's Fish Market, this seven-story hotel built around 1995 commemorates the life of the late-18th-century writer and dramatist Holberg, "the Molière of the North," one of the most famous writers in Danish and Norwegian letters. (The writer was born in a since-demolished house on the site of the hotel's parking garage.) The hotel's lobby is a testimonial to the author's life, with an informative biography, memorabilia, and photographs of stage productions based on his works. Bedrooms are a modernized reinterpretation of the Norwegian "farmhouse" style, with wood floors, rough-textured half-paneling stained in tones of forest green, and big windows, some of them floor-to-ceiling, that swing open directly onto a view of the quiet residential street below. Bathrooms are tiled, about half of them with tub/shower combinations, with acute angles that make them seem bigger than they actually are.

Strandgaten 190, Pb 1949 Nordnes, N-5817 Bergen. ℂ **55-30-42-00.** Fax 55-23-18-20. www.choicehotels.no. 140 units. Mon–Thurs 550NOK–1,390NOK ($85–$214/£44–£111) double; Fri–Sun 1,495NOK–1,605NOK ($230–$247/£120–£128) double. Rates include breakfast. AE, DC, MC, V. Parking 100NOK ($14/£8). **Amenities:** Restaurant; bar; laundry service/dry cleaning; nonsmoking rooms. *In room:* TV, minibar, hair dryer, beverage maker.

Crowded House   Sometimes guests complain to the tourist office about how basic this place is—and they're right. The only reason to stay here is for the price. This is the simplest and most spartan hotel we'll recommend within Bergen, but scores of college students who have defined it as their temporary home prefer its stripped-down lodgings. Located close to the landmark Mariakirke, it was originally built as a conventional-looking five-story hotel in 1923. It was reconfigured in the 1980s as a "backpackers' hotel" and renamed after a then-popular Australian rock-'n'-roll band. Don't expect luxury or even the "usual" amenities and services, as things are much more barebones than that. Rooms are aggressively plain but well-heated in winter, with washbasins, phones, white walls, carpeting, and relatively comfortable beds. *Note:* All rooms here have telephones, but a percentage of them don't work.

Håkonsgate 27, 5015 Bergen. ℂ **55-90-72-00.** Fax 55-90-72-01. www.crowded-house.com. 33 units (only 1 w/bath). 590NOK ($91/£47) double without private bathroom; 690NOK ($106/£55) double with private bathroom. AE, DC, MC, V. Bus: 5, 9, 20, or 22. **Amenities:** Cafe/bar; common room with TV, communal kitchen.

Park Pension ⚑ *Finds*   This 1890s hotel lies outside the center of Bergen in a part of town that is rapidly gentrifying. We've found that guests can often find accommodations here when the hotels in the city center are fully booked. Of course, the location isn't that far out, as it's only a 10-minute walk from the train and bus stations. This converted four-story town house is in an attractive university area near Grieghall and Nygård Park. The rooms are traditionally furnished, often with antiques. Accommodations vary in size, but all have good beds and adequate bathrooms equipped with tub/shower combinations. A neighboring building (furnished in the same style) accommodates overflow guests. Breakfast is served in the dining room; later in the day sandwiches, small hot dishes, and wine and beer are available.

Harald Hårfagresgaten 35 and Allegaten 20, N-5007 Bergen. © 55-54-44-00. Fax 55-54-44-44. www.parkhotel.no. 33 units. 1,000NOK ($154/£80) double. Rates include breakfast. AE, DC, MC, V. Parking 66NOK ($10/£5.30). Bus: 11. **Amenities:** Breakfast room; lounge; nonsmoking rooms. *In room:* TV, dataport, hair dryer, iron, safe (in some).

P Hotel Bergen *Value*   This cost-conscious, unpretentious hotel occupies the premises of what functioned for many years as a turn-of-the-20th-century hotel that was known for years as the Ambassadeur. In 2006, it was taken over by the P Hotel chain, which performed a few minor upgrades. Everything here is adequate and comfortable, but far from plush. The bathrooms in each room have showers with floor drains rather than tubs. We prefer rooms on the uppermost (fourth) floor beneath the mansard-style roof because of the views over Bergen. Access to these rooms requires climbing an additional flight of stairs above the floor where the elevator ends.

Vestre Torvgate 9, 5015 Bergen. © 55-90-08-90. Fax 55-90-05-84. www.P-Hotels.com. 48 units. 745NOK ($115/£60) double. Rates include breakfast. AE, DC, MC, V. Bus: 1 or 9. **Amenities:** Breakfast room. *In room:* TV.

Steens Hotel—Bed & Breakfast ⚑ *Value*   Those who travel the B&B route are often disappointed how few accommodations there are in Bergen. Among the more established B&Bs, the Steens is the best Bergen has to offer, although there are those who will dispute our claim. This is a stylish 1890 house that has been successfully converted to receive guests. Owned and operated by the same family since 1950, Steens offers great accommodations at reasonable prices. The bedrooms are moderate in size and comfortable, and the bathrooms, though small, are beautifully maintained. The best rooms are in front and open onto a park, and each unit comes with a private bathroom, neatly maintained and equipped with a shower unit. We like the thoughtful, personal touches here, including hot coffee served throughout the day in the public rooms and the Norwegian breakfast, which is more elaborate than a continental breakfast and often includes fresh fruit, yogurt, cereal, and even herring. The location is within a short walk of the bus and rail stations.

22 Parkveien, N-5007 Bergen. © 55-30-88-88. Fax 55-30-88-89. 18 units. www.steenshotel.no. 1,080NOK ($166/£86) double. Extra bed 200NOK ($31/£16). Rates include Norwegian breakfast. AE, MC, V. Bus: 1 or 5. **Amenities:** Breakfast room; lounge. *In room:* TV, dataport.

4 Where to Dine

VERY EXPENSIVE

Kafe Krystall ⚑⚑⚑ *Finds* CONTINENTAL   This is a place for a romantic evening. Thanks to Jugendstil accessories, this intimate restaurant's decor evokes Vienna in the era of Sigmund Freud. Old-fashioned candlelit table settings, jazz music, and the quiet ministrations of a single server (Bergen-born owner Vibeke Bjørvik) create the feeling that you're in a dignified private home. Menu items change every 3 weeks. Our party sampled a menu included a terrine of foie gras and quail served with a port wine sauce; cream of shellfish soup with lobster-stuffed ravioli; roasted turbot served with a risotto of chanterelles and red wine sauce; and filet of lamb with caponata. For dessert, our hearts were won over by the vanilla-and-whisky *panna cotta* topped with chocolate sauce and a serving of lime-marinated raspberries.

16 Kong Oscarsgate. ℂ **55-32-10-84.** Reservations recommended. Fixed-price menus 575NOK–675NOK ($89–$104/£46–£54). AE, DC, MC, V. May–June and mid-Aug to Sept Mon–Sat 6–10pm; Oct–Apr Mon–Fri 6–10pm. Closed July to mid-Aug. Bus: 20, 21, 22, or 23.

EXPENSIVE

Enhjørningen (The Unicorn) ✯✯ SEAFOOD   Part of the charm of this restaurant on the Hanseatic wharf derives from the not-level floors, the low doorways, and the inconvenient access via narrow staircases to its second-floor dining room. Set within one of the old wooden buildings of the Bryggen complex, adjacent to the harbor, it boasts a history and a name that was recorded as early as 1304. After several fires and the removal of lots of rotted timbers, the inn has been restored to its 1700s condition.

You'll sit in one of several old-fashioned dining rooms set railway-style (end-to-end) and outfitted like an early-19th-century parlor with framed oil paintings, usually landscapes. It's usually mobbed, as the staff struggles to maintain order and a sense of gentility amid swarms of diners, especially in midsummer. Choices include a local and good version of fish soup; savory fresh mussels steamed in white wine with cream, curry, and saffron; and *bacalao* (dried cod) served au gratin with a crusty layer of cheese and potatoes. The star offering of the restaurant's limited supply of meat dishes is a "no fish Olsen," a bemused way to describe grilled filet of beef with a pepper-flavored cream sauce. During some seasons, especially at Christmas, they serve the aromatic and distinctively regional *lutefisk*.

Bryggen. ℂ **55-32-79-19.** Reservations recommended. Main courses 275NOK–295NOK ($42–$45/£22–£24); fixed-price menus 490NOK–550NOK ($75–$85/£39–£44). AE, DC, MC, V. Dinner only, Mon–Sat 4–11pm. Closed 2 weeks at Christmas. Bus: 4, 5, 80, or 90.

Finnegaardstuene ✯✯✯ NORWEGIAN/FRENCH   This is one of the leading gourmet restaurants on the west coast of Norway. The foundations of this popular restaurant were laid around 1400, when Hanseatic League merchants used it as a warehouse. Today some of the woodwork dates from the 1700s, and four small-scale dining rooms create a cozy atmosphere. The menu is well thought out, with carefully prepared dishes, and revolves around Norwegian ingredients, especially fresh fish, and classical French methods of preparation. The menu changes with the season and the inspiration of the chef. It might include a warm salad of lobster and sweet beets; grilled duck liver with orange sauce; pan-fried cod with white wine sauce and a puree of lentils; marinated filets of lamb with smoked eggplant and spicy tomato sauce; and filets of venison with juniper berry sauce. An absolutely superb dessert involves caramelized apples served with an apple parfait and apple-flavored sorbet.

Rosenkrantzgate 6. ℂ **55-55-03-00.** Reservations recommended. Main courses 255NOK–285NOK ($39–$44/£20–£23); fixed-price menu 595NOK–895NOK ($92–$138/£48–£72). AE, DC, MC, V. Mon–Sat 6–11pm. Closed 1 week at Easter and Dec 22–Jan 8. Bus: 5 or 21.

Ned's ★★ SEAFOOD/GAME   One of the smallest (36 seats) upscale restaurants in Bergen, this is the best of three dining outlets within what was originally built as a fish market during the late 19th century, and which was gentrified in the 1990s into the Zacchariasbrygge harborfront complex. Intimate, and choice, with an additional 35 seats that spill out during clement weather onto an outdoor terrace, it offers stylish, well-prepared food and a panoramic view of the harbor. Menu specialties change with the seasons. A fish tank from 1889 (which, like the building itself, is protected as a historic monument), reveals some of the night's offerings, including some of the finest lobster—hauled in from the frigid waters of North Norway. The restaurant is heavily praised because of dishes such as smoked cod and leek chowder; medallions of lamb served with wilted spinach and caviar; and roasted filet of cod with white beans, clams, and mussels. For dessert, the chef will often prepare a soufflé (ours was coffee flavored). The waiters are among the friendliest and most helpful we've encountered in Norway.

Zacchariasbrygge 50. © **98-21-99-51.** Reservations recommended. Main courses 235NOK–340NOK ($36–$52/£19–£27); fixed-price menus 440NOK–580NOK ($68–$89/£35–£46). AE, DC, MC, V. May–Aug Mon–Sat 11:30am–11pm, Sun 11:30am–10pm; Sept–Apr Mon–Sat 5–11pm. Bus: 1, 5, or 9.

Restaurant Potetkjeller ★★ *Finds* INTERNATIONAL   Set within a few steps of Bergen's Fish Market, this is one of the oldest, most exclusive, and best restaurants in town. Its oldest feature is an antique flagstone floor (the date of construction is unknown) at the base of a cellar whose vaulted ceiling dates from the mid-1400s. After most of the city's clapboard-sided houses burned to the ground in 1702, the stone-built cellar was used as a dump for the ashes and debris that remained behind. After extensive renovations in the late 1990s, the cellar is now used for additional seating for the restaurant upstairs. (Watch your footing on the floors downstairs, as they're deceptively uneven.) Menu items from the open kitchen change every 2 months, but are likely to include pan-fried king crab salad; oven-roasted halibut with saffron and blue mussels; filets of turbot cooked in a tarragon-flavored bouillon; and a dessert special of baked nectarines with syrup and *semifreddo* (a combination of mascarpone cheese, brandy, espresso, icing sugar, gluten, grated chocolate, and cream). If you opt for wine to accompany your meal, there will be a different wine for each course, selected by the evening's chef. In all, the cellar has 300 different vintages.

Kong Oscarsgate 1A. © **55-32-00-70.** Reservations recommended. Fixed-price menus 395NOK–585NOK ($61–$90/£32–£47) without wine, 695NOK–1,095NOK ($107–$169/£56–£88) with wine. AE, DC, MC, V. Mon–Sat 4–10pm. Bus: 1, 5, or 9.

To Kokker ★ FRENCH/NORWEGIAN   This place is such a classic that we always schedule one meal here on every visit to Bergen, wishing it could be more. To Kokker ("Two Cooks," in this case Norway-born partners Daniel Olsen and Grete Halland) is a favorite with celebrities, including Matt Dillon and Prince Andrew, and local foodies increasingly gravitate here for the chef's well-considered juxtaposition of flavors and textures. Menu items include foie gras; whitebait roe with chopped onions, sour cream, and fresh-baked bread; and reindeer with lingonberry sauce. The 1703 building is adjacent to the oldest piers and wharves in Bergen. The dining room, one floor above street level, has a warmly tinted decor of deep red and soft orange, old paintings, and a solidly reliable staff that works competently under pressure, albeit without a lot of flair.

Enhjørninggården 3. © **55-32-28-16.** Reservations required. Main courses 265NOK–295NOK ($41–$45/£21–£24). AE, DC, MC, V. Mon–Sat 5–10pm. Bus: 1, 5, or 9.

MODERATE

Escalón Tapas Restaurant ⭐ *Finds* SPANISH   Set immediately adjacent to the lowest stage of the Fløibanen cable car, this is a charming, convivial, and unpretentious bar and tapas joint that has consistently won awards as one of the best restaurants of its type in Bergen. The setting lies a few steps down from street level, allowing diners a pavement-level view of the neighborhood outside, or, if they head to the back of the place, a cavelike interior that's cozy, warm, and dotted with mostly Iberian paintings. The staff here recommends that two or—more often—three tapas platters comprise a full meal, depending on your hunger level. The best examples include grilled mushrooms filled with Manchego cheese, Spanish-style potato omelets, meatballs in salsa, scampi in a garlic-flavored wine sauce, tuna marinated in olive oil and capers, and shellfish crepes. As you'd expect, a wide assortment of Spanish wines, as well as hard liquor from around the world, is also available.

Based on the surging success of this restaurant's venue, its management opened a second branch (Lilla Escalón) at Neumannsgate 5 (© **55-32-90-99**) in 2005 with the same tapas-based food choices and basically the same prices. Ironically, despite its name (Lilla means "small"), it's almost twice the size of the original and sits over a cellar that was built in the 18th century for the storage of wine. Lilla Escalón is open daily from noon to 1am.

Vertrlidsalmenningen 21. © **55-32-90-99**. Reservations not accepted. Tapas 45NOK–98NOK ($6.95–$15/£3.60–£7.85); set-price meal consisting of 3 separate tapas dishes 189NOK ($29/£15). AE, DC, MC, V. Sun–Fri 3pm–1am; Sat noon–1am. Bus: 5 or 21.

Holberg-Stuen NORWEGIAN   This is a longtime favorite, and diners come here for old-fashioned flavors, not trendy experiments. One floor above street level, the restaurant was established in 1927 between the harborfront and Ole Bulls Plass. It was named in honor of the 18th-century writer Ludvig Holberg, who divided his time between Bergen and Copenhagen. The setting is much like a tavern, with beamed ceilings, an open log fire, exposed wood, and a vivid sense of Old Norway. The well-prepared dishes include fish soup with fish balls and root vegetables; codfish with pea stew and bacon; and medallions of venison with a puree of peas and blackberry sauce.

Torgalmenningen 6. © **55-55-20-55**. Reservations recommended. Main courses 179NOK–239NOK ($28–$37/£14–£19). AE, DC, MC, V. Mon–Sat 11am–11pm; Sun 2–10pm. Bus: 1, 5, or 9.

Wessel-Stuen NORWEGIAN/CONTINENTAL   Other and better restaurants have opened to successfully challenge this longtime favorite, but the stube still has its habitués, including us. The menu has attempted to keep up with the times, introducing new ingredients and sauces. The chefs can be experimental at times, but they're also soundly grounded in the classics. Meals are likely to include grilled filet of catfish with coriander, garlic, and lime; sea scallops with an orange-flavored basil sauce; and breast of duck with honey-blackberry sauce. Dessert might include a rum-based apple tart with vanilla ice cream.

The restaurant (named for the 18th-c. Danish-Norwegian humorist Peter Wessel) has some of its namesake's framed illustrations and all the trappings of an 18th-century wine cellar. It's decorated in old-tavern style with beamed ceilings, and its adjoining pub is a famous meeting place for locals.

Øvre Ole Bulls Plass 8. © **55-55-49-49**. Reservations recommended. Main courses 98NOK–398NOK ($15–$61/£7.85–£32); fixed-price menu 298NOK ($46/£24). AE, DC, MC, V. Mon–Sat 11am–11pm; Sun 2pm–midnight. Bus: 2, 3, or 4.

INEXPENSIVE

Bryggeloftet and BryggeStuene ⭐ NORWEGIAN   Come here if you're seeking authentic Norwegian flavors. Charming and well managed, this is the most established restaurant along the harborfront, a two-level affair originally built in 1910 as a warehouse. The street-level dining room (known as the Stuene) has low-beamed ceilings, carved banquettes, 19th-century murals of old Bergen, and dozens of clippership models. The Bryggeloftet, upstairs, showcases high ceilings, wood paneling, and a venue that's a bit more formal and less animated. Dinner in either section might include fried *porbeagle* (a form of whitefish) served with shrimp, mussels, and white-wine sauce; roast reindeer with cream sauce; several preparations of salmon and herring; and roast pork with Norwegian sour cabbage. Between September and February, the menu offers *lutefisk*, an old-fashioned Norwegian specialty.

Bryggen 11–13. © 55-31-06-30. Reservations recommended. Main courses 199NOK–350NOK ($31–$54/£16–£28); lunch *smørrebrød* 99NOK–125NOK ($15–$19/£7.90–£10). AE, DC, MC, V. Mon–Sat 11am–11:30pm; Sun 1–11:30pm. Bus: 1, 5, or 9.

Café Hordastova (Value) NORWEGIAN   This elegant cafeteria looks more like a full-service restaurant with its linen tablecloths and upscale cutlery. On the ground floor of Hotel Hordaheimen, this no-nonsense place offers aggressively unpretentious and relatively quick meals. Lunchtime features open-faced sandwiches (*smørrebrød*) and simple platters of the day. Dinner offerings are a bit more elaborate, with carved meats, pepper steak, meatballs, and an excellent version of mushroom soup.

In the Hotel Hordaheimen, Christian Sundts Gate 18. © 55-33-51-13. Main courses, lunch 50NOK–120NOK ($7.70–$18/£4–£9.60), dinner 100NOK–145NOK ($15–$22/£8–£12). AE, DC, MC, V. Sun–Fri 10am–8pm; Sat 10am–6pm. Bus: 21, 22, or 23.

Ristorante Stragiotti ⭐ (Finds) ITALIAN   This is the best Italian restaurant in Bergen. Michele Stragiotti, an Italian native from Piemonte, owns this eatery, a short walk from the Ole Bulls Plass. Stragiotti's is a trimmed-down testimonial to postmodern Italian simplicity. The house specialty is Norwegian beef with your choice of four sauces (mushroom, black peppercorn, tomato, or béarnaise). Expect Norwegian rack of lamb (tender and full of flavor), homemade pastas, freshly caught fish, and lots of scaloppine choices, including a savory version with Gorgonzola cheese. A *grigliata di pesce*, wherein Italian cooking techniques are applied to very fresh Norwegian fish, is particularly appealing.

Vestre Torgate 3. © 55-90-31-00. Reservations recommended. Pizzas 110NOK–152NOK ($17–$23/£8.80–£12); main courses 110NOK–165NOK ($17–$25/£8.80–£13); fixed-price menu 350NOK–450NOK ($54–$69/£28–£36). AE, DC, MC, V. Daily noon–midnight. Bus: 2, 3, or 4.

5 Seeing the Sights

THE TOP ATTRACTIONS

The best way to begin is to take a stroll around **Bryggen** ⭐⭐⭐. This row of Hanseatic, timbered houses, rebuilt along the waterfront after a disastrous fire in 1702, is what remains of medieval Bergen. The northern half burned to the ground in 1955. Bryggen has been incorporated into UNESCO's World Heritage List as one of the most significant cultural and historical re-creations of a medieval settlement, skillfully blending with the surroundings of modern Bergen. It's a center for arts and crafts, where painters, weavers, and craftspeople have their workshops, some of which are open to the public.

Akvariet (Bergen Aquarium) ★★ *(Kids)*   A 15-minute walk from the city center, this aquarium contains the most extensive collection of marine fauna in Europe. Lying on the outer reaches of the Nordnes district, the aquarium offers a panoramic view of the entrance to the port of Bergen. The exceptional marine life here includes seals, penguins, lobsters, piranhas, Norwegian catfish, and even a "bearded" cod. In the outer hall you can dip your hand into the shallow pool (filled with water pumped from the fjord outside) and get up close and personal with the fish. Nine glass tanks, each containing about 62,500 gallons of water, ring the hall. Downstairs, 42 small aquariums house many colorful forms of sea life and illustrates evolutionary development. Kids should enjoy the seal and penguin feeding time, daily at 11am, 2pm, and 6pm in the summer; or, in the winter daily at noon and 4pm. Every hour you can watch the 3-D film *SOS Planet,* as well as Ivo Caprino's film about the Bergen Aquarium. Musical concerts are also performed.

> **Impressions**
>
> *Reaching Bergen we fail to find it particularly attractive. Everything is fishy. You eat fish and drink fish and smell fish and breathe fish.*
> —Lilian Leland, *Traveling Alone: A Woman's Journey Round the World,* 1890

Nordnesbakken 4. © **55-55-71-71.** Admission 120NOK ($18/£9.60) adults, 65NOK ($10/£5.20) children 3–13, free for 2 and under, 260NOK ($40/£3.20) family ticket. May–Sept daily 9am–7pm; Sept–Apr daily 10am–6pm. Bus: 11 from the Fish Market.

Bergen Art Museum ★★★   This expanding art museum possesses one of the most impressive collections in Norway without coming anywhere near equaling the national treasure trove of art in Oslo. In the trilevel Lysverk Building, overlooking Lille Langegard Lake, the museum houses more than 9,000 works of art.

Bergen Billedgalleri is devoted to both Norwegian and international art extending from the 13th to the 20th centuries. The collection is known for its magnificent **Greek and Russian icons** ★ from the 1300s and its **Dutch paintings** ★ from the 1700s. Seek out, in particular, *Birch in the Storm,* a famous painting by J. C. Dahl, as well as *Vardøhus Fortress* by Peder Balke. When the gallery dips into **modern art,** there is a bit of camp, as in their display of poetry and an exhibition by Yoko Ono. The work of Tom Sandberg confirms his reputation as one of Scandinavia's greatest photographers.

We always gravitate to the Rasmus Meyer Collection, featuring paintings from the 18th century up to 1915. It's worth the visit here to gaze upon **Edvard Munch's masterpieces** ★★, especially the trio *The Woman in Three Stages, Melancholy,* and *Jealousy.* Some of the best paintings of the **Norwegian Romantics** also hang here, including works by J. C. Dahl, Harriet Backer, and Nikolai Astrup, the latter known for depicting dramatic landscapes in western Norway. In addition to the art, note the decorated ceiling and wall painting in the **Blumenthal Room** ★ from the 18th century.

The greatest **modern art** ★★ in western Norway is found in the Stenersen Collection. Most of the work, by Norwegian and international artists, is from the 20th century and includes northern Europe's most extensive collection of **Paul Klee's works** ★★.

Rasmus Meyers Allé 3–9. © **55-56-80-00.** Combined ticket to all 3 galleries 50NOK ($7.70/£4). Tues–Sun noon–4pm. Bus: 1, 5, or 9.

Bergen Attractions

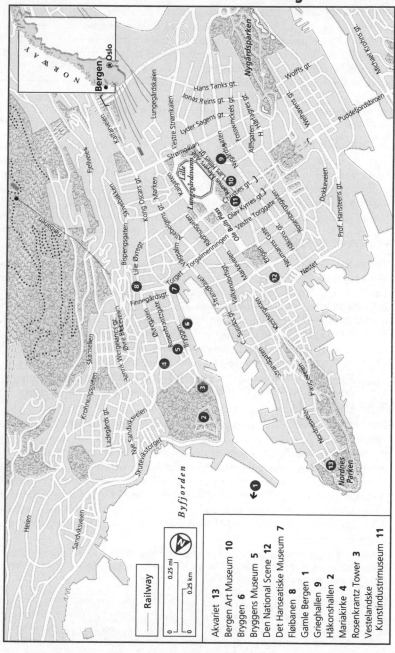

Railway

0.25 mi
0.25 km

Akvariet **13**
Bergen Art Museum **10**
Bryggen **6**
Bryggens Museum **5**
Den National Scene **12**
Det Hanseatiske Museum **7**
Fløibanen **8**
Gamle Bergen **1**
Grieghallen **9**
Håkonshallen **2**
Mariakirke **4**
Rosenkrantz Tower **3**
Vestelandske
Kunstindustrimuseum **11**

Bryggens Museum   This museum was built on the site of Bergen's first settlement, and in digging into the 800-year-old foundation, architects uncovered a treasure trove of medieval tools, pottery, runic stones, and even ancient skulls. Everything they dug up from 1955 to 1972 only enhanced the museum's eventual collection. The museum also illustrates the daily and cultural life of Bergen in the Middle Ages. Call ahead to find out about its regularly changing exhibits, as well as its folk-music and dance performances.

Dreggsallmenning 3, Bryggen. ℂ **55-58-80-10.** Admission 40NOK ($6.15/£3.20) adults, free for children under 16. May–Aug daily 10am–5pm; Sept–Apr Mon–Fri 11am–3pm, Sat noon–3pm, Sun noon–4pm. Bus: 20, 21, 22, 23, 50, 70, 71, 80, or 90.

Det Hanseatiske Museum ⊛   In one of the best-preserved wooden buildings at Bryggen, this museum illustrates Bergen's commercial life on the wharf centuries ago. German merchants, representatives of the Hanseatic League centered in Lübeck, lived in these medieval houses, which were built in long rows up from the harbor. The museum is furnished with authentic articles dating from 1704.

Finnegårdsgaten 1A, Bryggen. ℂ **55-54-46-90.** May–Sept admission 45NOK ($6.95/£3.60) adults; Oct–Apr admission 25NOK ($3.85/£2) adults; free for children under 15 year-round. June–Aug daily 9am–5pm; Sept–May daily 11am–2pm. Bus: 20, 21, 22, 23, or 24.

Fløibanen   For the first time in its 85-year history, the funicular to the top of the 320m (1,050-ft.) Fløien, the most famous of Bergen's seven hills, has upgraded to new cable cars. The two modern carriages featuring glass ceilings and panoramic windows might be new, but the view from the top is still spectacular. The funicular station is a short walk from the Fish Market. Once you reach the station, you can take one of several paths that provide easy walks through a lovely wooded terrain with views of lakes and mountains in the distance. In summer, you can order lunch at the restaurant here, which is open daily and also serves as a tacky souvenir shop.

Vetrlidsalm 23A. ℂ **55-33-68-00.** Round-trip 70NOK ($11/£5.60) adults, 50NOK ($7.70/£4) children aged 4–15. June–Aug Mon–Fri 7:30am–midnight, Sat 8am–midnight, Sun 9am–midnight; Sept–May funicular stops every night at 11pm. Bus: 6.

Gamle Bergen ⊛   This museum offers the opportunity to experience the 18th and 19th centuries, giving you a rare look at small town life with various antique dwellings, different shops, a baker, and even the outlet for the town's local barber and dentist. This collection of more than 40 wooden houses is set in a park. The Old Town is complete with streets, an open square, and narrow alleyways. Some of the interiors are exceptional, including a merchant's living room in the typical style of the 1870s, with padded sofas, heavy curtains, and potted plants. Its old-fashioned, clapboard-sided architecture and evocations of 19th-century domestic life evokes some of the scenes from Ibsen's *A Doll's House*.

Elsesro and Sandviken. ℂ **55-39-43-00.** Admission 50NOK ($7.70/£4) adults, free for children 4–15 and students. Houses mid-May to Aug only, guided tours daily on the hour 10am–5pm. Park and restaurant daily noon–5pm. Bus: 20, 24, 80, or 90 from the city center (every 10 min.).

Gamlehaugen   The king's official Bergen residence was originally occupied in the 19th century by Christian Michelsen, one of the first prime ministers of Norway after it separated from Denmark in 1814. It's open for just a short time each summer. The rambling wood-sided villa lies about 10km (6¼ miles) south of the city, overlooking the Nordåsvannet estuary. Even if you don't know who Michelsen is, a visit here will tell you much about how the upper class lived at the beginning of the 19th century.

The interior is a happy marriage of the once-fashionable National Romanticism and elegant Art Nouveau. Its gardens are open to the public all year, but, as we discovered, the second floor is not. Don't expect the hoopla you might see at Buckingham Palace—the venue is understated, discreet, and (probably for security reasons) aggressively mysterious.

Fjøsanger. © 55-92-51-20. Admission 50NOK ($7.70/£4) adults, 25NOK ($3.85/£2) children 4–15. June–Aug Tues–Sun noon–3pm; Sept–May Sat–Sun only, noon–3pm. Bus: Fjøsanger-bound bus (no. 60) from the Central Bus Station.

Håkonshallen (Håkon's Hall)   Built of local stone, this is the largest secular medieval hall still standing in Norway. While it evokes the Gothic stone halls in England, its glory days as the political and social center of the 13th-century kingdom of Norway are long gone.

Erected between 1247 and 1261, it took its name from its first builder, Håkon Håkonsson. Don't expect to find artistic treasures here: The hall has had a rough life. It was damaged in a 1944 fire caused by the explosion of an overloaded Nazi munitions ship. (The explosion damaged nearly every building in Bergen and sent the ship's anchor flying almost to the top of a nearby mountain.) By 1520 the hall had degenerated to a storage depot, and today is used for musical concerts. Guided tours are conducted hourly; call in advance to confirm.

Bergenhus, Bradbenken. © 55-31-60-67. Admission 30NOK ($4.60/£2.40) adults, 15NOK ($2.30/£1.20) children. Mid-May to Aug daily 10am–4pm; Sept to mid-May daily noon–3pm (Thurs until 6pm). Closed various days in May. Bus: 5.

Mariakirke (St. Mary's Church) 🎯🎯   A short distance from the Fish Market stands Norway's oldest building (12th c.) and best example of Romanesque in the country. The oldest ornament in the church is the altar, but the **pulpit** 🎯🎯 is the richest example of baroque decorative art in the country. A gift from Hanseatic merchants, it has carved figures depicting everything from "chastity" to "naked truth." We like to attend the organ recitals every Tuesday from June 24 to August at 7:30pm.

Dreggen. © 55-31-59-60. Admission 20NOK ($3.10/£1.60) adults, free for children 6 and under. May 22–Aug Mon–Fri 9:30–11am and 1–4pm; Sept–May 21 Tues–Fri 11am–12:30pm. Bus: 9, 20, 21, or 22.

Rosenkrantz Tower   This defense and residential tower was constructed in the 13th century by the governor of Bergenhus (Bergen Castle), Erik Rosenkrantz, and still exudes a spooky aura. Even if you find the setting foreboding, the stunning **panorama** 🎯🎯 of the seaport of Bergen is worth the trek here. Two older structures were incorporated into the tower: King Magnus the Lawmender's keep, from about 1260, and Jørgen Hanssøn's keep, from about 1520. It was rebuilt and enlarged in the 1560s. There are guided tours of the tower and Håkonshallen (see above) about every hour.

Bergenhus, Bradbenken. © 55-31-43-80. Admission 30NOK ($4.60/£2.40) adults, 15NOK ($2.30/£1.20) children 5–15, free 4 and under. May 15–Aug 31 daily 10am–4pm; Sept 1–May 14 Sun noon–3pm. Bus: 1, 5, or 9.

Troldhaugen (Trolls' Hill) 🎯🎯🎯   This can be the most romantic setting in Norway if you arrive just as Edvard Grieg's music is being played at a summer concert from the 200-seat Troldsalen, a concert hall on the grounds. This Victorian house, in beautiful rural surroundings on Lake Nordås, was the summer villa of Grieg and the site where he composed many of his famous works. The house still contains his furniture, paintings, and other mementos. His Steinway grand piano is frequently used at concerts given in the house during the annual Bergen festival, and at Troldhaugen's summer concerts. Grieg and his wife, Nina, a Danish soprano, are buried in a cliff grotto on the estate.

Troldhaugveien 65, Hop. © **55-92-29-92**. Admission 60NOK ($9.25/£4.80) adults, free for children 4–15. Mid-Jan to Apr Mon–Fri 10am–2pm; May–Sept daily 9am–6pm; Oct–Nov Mon–Fri 10am–2pm, Sat–Sun noon–4pm. Closed Dec to mid-Jan. Bus: 23 or 24 to Hop from the Bergen bus station, Platform 20; when you reach Hop exit, turn right, walk about 180m (600 ft.), turn left at Hopsvegen, and follow signs (15-min. walk). Hop is about 5km (3 miles) from Bergen.

Vestlandske Kunstindustrimuseum (West Norway Museum of Applied Art) ★★ *Finds*　This museum is undervisited and unappreciated, but there are treasures inside, including **Ole Bull's violin** ★★. Made in 1562 by the Italian master, Saló, the instrument has a head of an angel carved by Benvenuto Cellini.

Many exquisite pieces are on display, including an impressive collection of Bergen silverware. The Bergen silversmiths of the 17th and 18th centuries were celebrated for their heavy but elaborate baroque designs. Their collection of tankards, for example, is stunning, and many are embossed with floral motifs and or inlaid with silver coins.

The various displays span 5 centuries, the most intriguing of which are devoted to **The Art of China** ★★★. This is one of the largest collections of Chinese applied art outside China itself and includes a series of huge marble Buddhist temple sculptures, silk robes embroidered with dragons, jade, exquisite porcelain, rare textiles, and delicate paintings.

Permanenten, Nordahl Bruns Gate 9. © **55-33-66-33**. Admission 50NOK ($7.70/£4). May 15–Sept 14 daily 11am–5pm; Sept 15–May 14 Tues–Sun noon–4:30pm.

IN NEARBY LYSØEN

To reach the island of Lysøen, 26km (16 miles) south of Bergen, drive or take a bus (from Platform 20 at the Bergen bus station, marked FANA-OS-MILDE) to Sørestraumen on Road 553. Take the Ole Bull ferry across the channel from Sørestraumen, Buena Kai. The round-trip fare is 40NOK ($6.15/£3.20) for adults, 20NOK ($3.10/£1.60) for children 5 to 15, and free for 4 and under. When the museum and villa are open, ferry schedules coincide with the site's hours, and boats depart for the mainland at hourly intervals. The last boat leaves a few minutes after the museum closes.

Museet Lysøen/Ole Bull's Villa　Violin virtuoso Ole Bull's attempt to establish a "New Norwegian Theater" in the U.S. in 1850 may have failed, but he returned to establish the National Theater in Oslo and become a national hero.

Ole Bull had an eye for talent, discovering both Henrik Ibsen and Edvard Grieg. The villa and concert hall built in his honor are now a national monument and are preserved as they were when the musician died in 1880. The building is an architectural fantasy of the 19th century, with a dome, curved staircase, cutwork trim, and gingerbread gables. Bull built 13km (8 miles) of romantic trails that meander around the island, and, if time remains, you may want to walk them.

Lysøen. © **56-30-90-77**. Admission 30NOK ($4.60/£2.40) adults, 10NOK ($1.55/80p) children 4–15. Guided tours early May to Aug Mon–Sat noon–4pm, Sun 11am–5pm; closed Sept to early May. Transportation: See "Organized Tours," below.

ORGANIZED TOURS

For information about and tickets and tours, contact **Tourist Information,** Vågsallmenningen 1 (© **55-55-20-00**). The most popular and highly recommended tour of Bergen is the 3-hour city bus tour. It departs daily at 10am and covers the major attractions, including Troldhaugen and "Old Bergen." It operates May to September and costs 270NOK ($42/£22) for adults, 175NOK ($27/£14) for children 4 to 15. Between mid-May and the end of August, there's an additional daily departure at 2pm.

6 Outdoor Activities

FISHING   In the region around Bergen, anyone can fish in the sea without restrictions. If you plan to fish in fresh water (ponds, streams, and most of the best salmon and trout rivers), you'll need a permit. These are sold at any post office. You'll also need the permission of the owner of the land on either side of the stream. The best fjord fishing, where you can angle for such catches as cod, mackerel, haddock, and coalfish, is offered by **Rjfylke Fjord Tour** (© 91-15-90-48). Twice-daily 2-hour fishing trips depart from Bergen Harbor.

Information and fishing permits, which cost 95NOK to 150NOK ($15–$23/£7.60–£12), are available from **Bergen Sportsfiskere (Bergen Angling Association),** Fosswinckelsgate 37 (© 55-32-11-64). It's open Monday to Friday from 9am to 3pm. **Rjfylke Fjord Tour** (© 911-59-048) offers 2-hour fishing trips departing from Bergen twice daily.

GOLF   The best golf course is **Meland Golf Club,** lying 36km (22 miles) north of Bergen at Meland/Frekhaug (© 56-17-46-00). This is an 18-hole, par-73 golf course with a pro shop, lockers, and changing facilities. The setting is on 90 hectares (225 acres) in the midst of forests, lakes, and mountains. Greens fees Monday to Friday are 375NOK ($58/£30), going up to 475NOK ($73/£38) on Saturday and Sunday.

SWIMMING   The **Sentralbadet,** Theatersgaten 37 (© 55-56-95-70), has a heated indoor pool. An open-air pool whose season is limited to the fleeting Nordic summer is at **Nordnes Sjøbad,** Nordnes. For hours, check with the Bergen tourist office (p. 306). At either pool, adults pay 80NOK ($12/£6.40), children 42NOK ($6.45/£3.40).

TENNIS   Paradis Sports Senter, Highway R1, Paradis (© 55-91-26-00), 6.5km (4 miles) south of Bergen, has five indoor courts, four squash courts, four badminton courts, a health club and gym, and a solarium. It's open Tuesday and Thursday 9am to 10pm, Monday and Wednesday 9am to 11pm, Friday 9am to 9pm, Saturday 10am to 6pm, and Sunday 11am to 9pm.

WALKING   Only 10 minutes away from town by the funicular, several roads and footpaths lead to **Mount Fløien,** an unspoiled wood and mountain terrace with lakes and rivers. The **Bergen Touring Club,** Tverrgaten 4 (© 55-33-58-10), arranges walking tours farther afield and supplies information on huts and mountain routes all over Norway. It also provides maps and advice on where to hike. The office is open Monday to Friday 10am to 4pm (until 6pm on Thurs).

7 Shopping

Shoppers who live outside Scandinavia and spend more than 310NOK ($48/£25) in a tax-free tourist shop can receive a refund up to 18.5% of the purchase price when they leave Norway. See "Fast Facts: Norway," in chapter 8, for details.

THE SHOPPING SCENE

Bargain hunters head to the **Fish Market *(Fisketorget)* 🐟🐟**. Many local handicrafts from the western fjord district, including rugs and handmade tablecloths, are displayed here. This is also one of the few places in Norway where bargaining is welcomed. The market keeps no set hours, but is best visited between June and August daily 7am to 7pm, and September to May every Monday to Saturday 7am to 4pm. Take bus no. 1, 5, or 9.

HOURS   Stores are generally open Monday to Friday from 9am to 6pm (until 8pm Thurs and sometimes Fri), Saturday 9am to 4pm. Shopping centers outside the city are open Monday to Friday 10am to 8pm and Saturday 9am to 6pm. Some food stores stay open until 8pm Monday to Friday and 6pm on Saturday.

SHOPPING A TO Z
ART GALLERIES
Hordaland Art Center and Café *(Kids*)   An artistic focal point of the historic neighborhood that contains it, this is a publicly funded art gallery that puts on as many as 12 different art exhibitions a year. Originally completed in 1742, it served as a school for the children of the local parish for many years. There's a children's play area and an on-site cafe where pastries, sandwiches, and platters are available. Schedules are erratic, varying with each exhibition. Klosteret 17, Nordnes. ⓒ 55-90-85-90. A 5-min. walk from Torgallmenningen.

FASHION
Kløverhuset ⭐⭐   Next to the Fish Market on the harbor, this four-story shopping center has been Bergen's largest and best fashion store since 1923. Bargains include moderately priced and attractively designed knit sweaters, gloves, and Sami jackets. Strandgaten 13–15. ⓒ 55-31-37-90.

Viking Design ⭐   Opposite the Flower Market, this shop has the most unusual knitwear in Bergen—some of its designs have even won prizes. In addition to fashion, there's also a selection of quality pewter produced in Bergen, along with a selection of intriguing Norwegian gifts and souvenirs. Items purchased here can be shipped abroad directly from the store. Strandkaien 2A. ⓒ 55-31-05-20.

GLASSWARE & CERAMICS
Prydkunst-Hjertholm ⭐⭐   This is one of the leading outlets for glassware and ceramics, and purchases much of its merchandise directly from the artisans' studios. The quality goods include glass, ceramics, pewter, wood, and textiles. Gift articles and souvenirs are also available. Olav Kyrres Gate 7. ⓒ 55-31-70-27.

Tibords Interiør Bergen Storsenter ⭐⭐   This outlet has Bergen's best and most extensive collection of glassware, porcelain, and pottery. All the big names are here, including Arabia from Finland, Kosta Boda from Sweden, and Wedgwood from England. Still, this is a true showcase of Scandinavian design. Much of the merchandise is made by local artisans, and the glass, ceramics, and pottery are of the highest quality. The prices, of course, reflect this. Torgallmenningen 8. ⓒ 55-55-33-41.

HANDICRAFTS
In and around **Bryggen Brukskunst** ⭐⭐, the restored Old Town near the wharf, many craftspeople have taken over old houses and ply ancient Norwegian trades. Crafts boutiques often display Bergen souvenirs, many based on designs 300 to 1,500 years old. For example, we purchased a reproduction of a Romanesque-style cruciform pilgrim's badge. Other attractive items are likely to include sheepskin-lined booties and exquisitely styled hand-woven wool dresses.

(*Finds*) Shopping Tour

Norway has a centuries-old tradition of crafts, which undoubtedly developed to help people pass the time during the cold, dark winters when farm families were more or less housebound for months. Some of the major crafts were woodcarving, weaving, and embroidery, and these skills live on today at many local artist and crafts centers. Some of the best areas include Hardanger (around the Hardangerfjord, near Bergen); Song (just north of the Sognefjord, also near Bergen); and Telemark (the district around Skien, within a day's drive from Oslo). For a true, behind-the scenes look at Norway, **Five Stars of Scandinavia,** 2914 Yelm Highway SE, #24, Olympia, WA 98501 (© **800/722-4126;** www.5stars-of-scandinavia.com), will set up a self-guided tour for you, factoring in everything they know about local artisans.

Husfliden ✶✶   Since 1895 Husfliden has been the premier name in Norwegian handicrafts. Top-quality merchandise is sold here, especially hand-woven textiles. The Norwegian sweaters are among the best in town, and there is even a department for national costumes. Many items such as iron bowls and candlesticks are for table settings. Handmade pewter, wooden bowls, hand-woven rugs, and fireplace bellows are other useful items. Well-made, quality wooden toys are also sold here. Vågsallmenningen 3. © 55-54-47-40.

JEWELRY

Juhls' Silver Gallery ✶ (*Finds*)   Next to the SAS Royal Hotel, along the harborfront, Juhls' displays the town's most unusual selection of quality jewelry. The designers are inspired by the constantly changing weather of the far north and, in their words, provide "a cultural oasis in a desert of snow." Bryggen. © 55-32-47-40.

SHOPPING MALL

Galleriet ✶   This is the most important shopping complex in the central Bergen area, with 70 stores offering tax-free shopping. Close to the Fish Market, it displays a wide array of merchandise and features summer sales and special exhibitions. It has several fast-food establishments, too. Torgalmenningen 8. © 55-30-05-00.

8 Bergen After Dark

THE PERFORMING ARTS

Den National Scene ✶✶   September to June is the season for Norway's oldest theater, founded in the mid–19th century. It stages classical Norwegian and international drama, contemporary plays, and musical drama, as well as visiting opera and ballet productions. Engen 1. © **55-54-97-00.** Tickets 200NOK–300NOK ($31–$46/£16–£24). Bus: 2, 3, or 4.

Grieghallen ✶✶✶   The modern Grieg Hall, which opened in 1978, is Bergen's monumental showcase for music, drama, and a host of other cultural events. The stage is large enough for an entire grand opera production, and the main foyer comfortably seats 1,500 guests for lunch or dinner. Snack bars provide drinks and light snacks throughout the performances.

The Bergen Symphony Orchestra, founded in 1765, performs here from August to May, often on Thursday at 7:30pm and Saturday at 12:30pm. Its repertoire consists of classical and contemporary music, as well as visiting opera productions. International conductors and soloists perform periodically. *Tip:* Ticket prices on Thursdays tend to be at the lower end of the range of ticket prices noted below, while those on Friday and Saturday tend to be at the higher end. Consequently, many of Bergen's academic community and its "normal, middle-class music lovers" tend to schedule their concert-going for Thursday throughout the winter. Closed July. Edvard Griegs Plass 1. ℂ 55-21-61-00. Tickets 110NOK–450NOK ($17–$69/£8.80–£36). Bus: 2, 3, or 4.

SUMMER CULTURAL ENTERTAINMENT

Bergen Folklore ⟡   The Bergen Folklore dancing troupe performs from June to August on Tuesday at 9pm. The program, which lasts about an hour, consists of traditional folk dances and music from rural Norway. Tickets are on sale at the tourist office (see "Orientation," earlier in this chapter) and at the door. Bryggens Museum, Bryggen. ℂ 97-52-86-30. Tickets 98NOK ($15/£7.85) adults, free for children 4 and under. Bus: 1, 5, or 9.

FILMS

Bergen has two large movie theaters, **Konsertpaleet,** Neumannsgate 3 (ℂ **55-56-90-83**), and **Forum,** in Danmarkplass (ℂ **55-20-62-48**), which show films in their original versions. The earliest performance is at 11am, the latest at 11pm. Tickets usually cost 85NOK ($13/£6.80).

THE CLUB & MUSIC SCENE

Café Opera   Built in the 1880s, this is a large stone and timber-built structure that was originally conceived as a warehouse, and which functions today as both a restaurant and a cafe. After the kitchen closes, it becomes an animated nightclub that's open Tuesday to Saturday. On Tuesday night there is an open jam session with musicians or poets. On other nights DJs mix depending on their individual tastes. The cafe is host to international DJs and bands on most Fridays and Saturdays. A crowd in their 20s and 30s find this to be one of the more entertaining joints after dark, and though they all drink, talk, and flirt, very few of them actually get up and dance. Engen 18. ℂ 55-23-03-15. Bus: 2, 3, or 4.

Engelen ⟡   This is one of Bergen's more elegant dance clubs, attracting a somewhat conservative crowd in their 40s, 50s, and 60s. That seems to change a bit on Saturday with the arrival of noisy, fun-seeking 20-somethings who tend to make the place a bit more raucous and animated. Light meals are available, but most people just show up to drink. Cocktail drink prices begin at 90NOK ($14/£7.85), or 60NOK ($9.25/£4.80) for a beer. It's open Wednesday to Saturday 10pm to 3:30am. In the Radisson SAS Royal Hotel, Bryggen. ℂ 55-54-30-00. Cover 60NOK–80NOK ($9.25–$12/£4.80–£6.40), free to hotel guests. Bus: 1, 5, or 9.

Kafe Kippers USF ⟡   A favorite rendezvous for artists, this club plays some of the best jazz music in Bergen, attracting a wide age group. Every Friday night they have a live jazz artist performing; otherwise it's the best in "listening jazz." In winter the club holds 80 patrons in snug comfort inside. In summer the on-site outdoor restaurant, Kaien, serving a menu that borrows from cuisines throughout Europe and the world, becomes the largest in Bergen, with 500 seats opening onto fjord waters. Georgenes Cerft 3. ℂ 55-31-00-60. Cover Fri 70NOK–140NOK ($11–$22/£5.60–£11). Bus: 13.

Rick's Café   Sprawling and large enough to hold 1,800 raucous and sometimes slightly drunken persons at a time, this is a labyrinth, with rooms devoted to the after-dark pursuit of cabaret and comedy (there are two small stages for live performances); some serious drinking (on cold winter nights, things can get rather sudsy); or a friendly pickup (no doubt encouraged by the bar's potent cocktails). Attracting a crowd of 20- to 40-somethings, it's open daily from 9am, remaining stalwartly open as a cafe throughout the day, then soldiering on as a bar and nightclub beginning around 5pm and continuing until around 2am, depending on business. Veiten 3. ✆ 55-55-31-31. Bus: 1, 5, or 9. Cover 90NOK ($14/£7.20) after 10pm, by which time as many as five separate bar areas dispense alcohol.

Rubinen   Rubinen is one of Bergen's most popular dance clubs, attracting an over-35 crowd of mostly married couples who intently and, it seems, with great determination come here to whirl their partners across the floor. It features all kinds of music, including country-western, rock 'n' roll, and occasional bouts of Latin, tango, and formal ballroom dancing. Drinks cost from 70NOK ($11/£5.60) to 110NOK ($17/£8.80). It's open Wednesday to Saturday 10pm to 3am, with live music nightly. Rosenkrantzgate 7. ✆ 55-31-74-70. Cover 80NOK ($11/£6.40). Bus: 2, 3, or 4.

THE BAR SCENE

Altona Vinbar   This is one of the oldest and best-known bars in Bergen, attracting a crowd of 30- to 60-year-olds to its location in the Augustin Hotel. Some of the stone walls and the wooden ceiling are original, dating from the 1600s, but you'll find modern sculptures, too. Classical music and elegant drinks, including champagne, cognac, and the best whiskey, are all on the menu. It's open Monday to Thursday 6pm to 1:30am and Friday and Saturday 6pm to 2:30am. Strandgaten 81. ✆ 55-30-40-72. Bus: 2 or 4.

Fotballpuben   This is the biggest sports pub in Bergen, a beer-soaked place with an undeniable affection for football (that is, soccer) and, to a lesser degree, rugby. Feel free to wander through this crowded establishment's labyrinth of inner chambers—joining a 20s-to-50s crowd—whose corners and edges are sometimes upholstered with vinyl padding (installed with a fear of falls from inebriated sports fans?). Live or recorded games are always being played on TVs. The staff prides itself on serving the cheapest beer in Bergen, which is priced from 37NOK to 47NOK ($5.70–$7.25/£2.95–£3.75) per mug, depending on the time of day. It's open Monday to Thursday 9am to 1am, Friday and Saturday 9am to 3am, and Sunday noon to 1am. Vestre Torgate 9. ✆ 55-36-66-66. Bus: 1 or 9.

Kontoret (The Office)   The most frequented pub in the city center, the Kontoret lies immediately adjacent, through a connecting door, to the Dickens restaurant, where platters of rib-sticking English food cost from 190NOK to 220NOK ($29–$34/£15–£18). In the Kontoret, the decor evokes an office from the early 1900s, replete with banged-up manual typewriters and oaken countertops that evoke the green eyeshades and ink-stained printing rituals of an earlier era. The local brew is called Hansa; a half-liter of which costs 57NOK ($8.80/£4.55). It's open Sunday to Thursday 4pm to 12:30am, and Friday and Saturday 4pm to 2am. 4 Kong Olav V Plass. ✆ 55-36-31-33.

9 Side Trips from Bergen

SOGNEFJORD ✮✮✮

If there's only room for one fjord, make it Norway's longest and deepest, **Sognefjord,** a geologic and panoramic marvel. The terrain soars upward from the watery depths of the North Atlantic, and many waterfalls punctuate its edges with spray. The best way to view the fjord involves a full-day jaunt that's possible only between May 18 and September 15. It combines self-guided travel by boat, bus, and rail. Begin by heading to the Bergen harborfront (the Strandkaien), where you'll board a ferry for the 4 ½-hour ride to the fjord-side hamlet of Gudvangen. A bus carries participants on to the town of Voss. After exploring the town, you can board a train to carry you back to Bergen. Many schedule permutations are possible, but the one that's particularly convenient leaves Bergen at 8:30am and returns at 5:15pm. The combined round-trip fare is 785NOK ($121/£63). Details on this and other explorations by public transport are available from the tourist office (see "Orientation," earlier in this chapter).

NORWAY IN A NUTSHELL ✮✮✮

No tour we've ever taken in Norway has the drama and excitement of natural wonder as this 12-hour, scenically captivating preview of the breadth and diversity of landscapes, encapsulating the majesty of fjords and mountains.

Several different transit options operate throughout the day. The one most aggressively recommended by Bergen's tourist office operates year-round. It starts at 8:30am at **Bergen's** railway station. After a 2-hour train ride, you'll disembark in the mountaintop hamlet of **Myrdal,** where you can take in the natural wonders for about 20 minutes. In Myrdal you'll board a cog railway for one of the world's most dramatically inclined train rides. The trip down to the village of **Flåm,** a drop of 870m (2,900 ft.), takes an hour and passes roaring streams and seemingly endless waterfalls.

After a 1-hour stopover in Flåm, where you can have lunch or take a brief hike, you'll board a fjord steamer for a ride along the Sognefjord. You'll reach the fjord-side town of Gudvangen after a 2-hour ride. After 30 minutes in Gudvangen, you'll board a bus for the 75-minute ride to Voss. Here you'll spend 30 minutes before boarding a train for the 75-minute ride back to Bergen. Arrival is scheduled for 8:18pm.

Expect only a rushed overview of each town, as there is more scenery than you can digest in a 12-hour day. The round-trip fare, excluding meals, costs 790NOK ($122/£63) for adults, 345NOK ($53/£28) for children 4 to 15, and free for accompanied children under 4. There are discounts for holders of Eurailpasses or Scanrail passes, and the wide availability of options that, for extra fees, allow you to prolong the experience for up to an additional 2 days, thanks to supplemental overnights at panoramic hotels en route. Our most serious recommendation in this chapter is to have the more prolonged experience instead of a "quickie." For more information, contact Bergen's **Tourist Office** (see "Orientation," earlier in this chapter), or call ✆ **81-56-82-22** (www.norwaynutshell.com).

11

Exploring the Norwegian Coast

The west coast of Norway is the heart of the fjord country (see map, p. 219). It took 3 million years to form the furrows and fissures that give the Norwegian coast its distinctive look. At some points the fjords become so narrow that a boat can hardly wedge between the mountainsides.

Bergen is the best departure point for trips to the fjords. To the south lies the famous Hardangerfjord, and to the north, the Sognefjord, cutting 179km (111 miles) inland. We'll begin our journey in Bergen, heading north by coastal steamer.

1 By Coastal Steamer

Coastal steamers ✦✦ are elegantly appointed ships that travel along the Norwegian coast from Bergen to Kirkenes, carrying passengers and cargo to 34 ports. A total of 11 ships make the journey year-round. Along the route, the ships sail through Norway's more obscure fjords, revealing breathtaking scenery and numerous opportunities for adventure. At points along the way, passengers have the opportunity to take excursions on smaller vessels or sightseeing trips to the surrounding mountains and glaciers.

The chief cruise operator is the **Norwegian Coastal Voyage/Bergen Line,** 405 Park Ave., New York, NY 10022 (© **800/323-7436** or 212/319-1300). Various packages are available. Tours may be booked heading north from Bergen, south from Kirkenes, or round-trip. The 7-day one-way northbound journey costs $670 to $4,381 per person, including meals and taxes. The 12-day round-trip voyage from Bergen to Kirkenes and back to Bergen is $1,100 to $6,538 per person. For information on these and other trips, including air-cruise packages from the United States, contact the Bergen Line.

HAMMERFEST

2,315km (1,438 miles) N of Bergen, 145km (90 miles) N of Alta, 2,196km (1,364 miles) N of Oslo

It's easy to poke fun at Hammerfest as author William Bryson did in *Neither Here Nor There.* He found Hammerfest an "agreeable enough town in a thank-you-God-for-not-making-me-live-here sort of way." Locals are quick to defend how civilized they are, pointing out that they were the first town in Europe to have electric street lighting while Paris and London were still lit by gas.

That Hammerfest is here at all is a sort of miracle. A hurricane flattened it in 1856, and one of Norway's worst fires leveled it again in 1890, the year the town got that street lighting. Hitler ordered that "no building be left standing" during the infamous Nazi retreat of 1945.

But Hammerfest bounced back and, in summer, attracts visitors from all over the world who use it as a base for exploring the North Cape. Arctic hunters enjoy their last few drinks in cozy bars here before setting off on expeditions into an unknown wilderness. If you join them, and if it's a winter night, you just might encounter a polar bear wandering the streets as you wander back to your hotel.

Other communities exist north of Hammerfest, but locals claim that they are villages, not towns. It will be oil, not tourism, "fueling" the economy of Hammerfest for at least for the next 30 years. In 2006, the pumps started sucking oil from the offshore oil wells, which are estimated to possess 195 billion cubic meters (47 cubic miles) of black gold. At present, and running for some 145km (90 miles), the world's longest undersea pipeline goes from the mammoth natural gas fields in the Barents Sea to the small island of Melkøya out in the bay off the coast of Hammerfest.

The Hammerfest area stretches from Måsøy, near the North Cape, to Loppa in the south, the wide region including the rugged coasts along the Arctic Sea.

The city lies 70° 39' 48" north and achieved its town status on July 7, 1789, making it the oldest town in northern Norway. The town was founded because of its natural harbor, something that is equally important today.

A **Meridianstøtta,** or meridian column, stands on the Fuglenes peninsula, across from the harbor. The monument commemorates the work of scientists from Norway, Sweden, and Russia who conducted surveys at Hammerfest between 1816 and 1852 to establish a meridian arc between Hammerfest and the Danube River at the Black Sea. This led to an accurate calculation of the size and shape of Earth.

Today Hammerfest is a modern town with an open and unique atmosphere, where the town's square and harbor are natural meeting places.

ESSENTIALS

GETTING THERE   If you don't take the coastal steamer, you can drive, although it's a long trek. From Oslo, take E-6 north until you reach the junction with Route 94 west. Hammerfest is at the end of Route 94. During the summer there are three buses a week from Oslo. Travel time is 29 hours. SAS has daily flights from Oslo and Bergen to Alta, where you can catch a bus to Hammerfest (Apr–Sept only). For bus information, call **Finnmark Fylkesrederi** (© 78-40-70-00).

VISITOR INFORMATION   The **Hammerfest Tourist Office,** Strandgate (© 78-41-21-85; www.hammerfest-turist.no), in the town center, is open in summer daily from 9am to 5pm, in winter daily 10am to 2pm. The tourist office also organizes boat trips in the area for those who want to go deep-sea fishing and bird-watching. Offerings can change from week to week, but these 3-hour outings require a minimum of eight people, costing 340NOK ($52/£27) per person.

SEEING THE SIGHTS

This is the world's northernmost town of significant size and a port of call for North Cape coastal steamers. Sami from nearby camps often come into town, sometimes with their reindeer, to shop.

The port is free of ice year-round, and shipping and exporting fish is a major industry. The sun doesn't set from May 12 to August 1—and doesn't rise from November 21 to January 23.

For the best panoramic view of the town, we like the zigzag walk up the 72m (240-ft.) **Salen** "mountain." Atop Salen is a 6m-tall (20-ft.) square tower with walls built of gray and blue stones. The old tower was torn down during the war but was restored in 1984. On a clear day you can see the offshore islands. If you arrive at noon, you can order lunch at the on-site **Turistua** (© 78-42-96-00), Salen, which offers a big Norwegian buffet for

200NOK ($31/£16) per person. Although tourists flock here, the name Turistua doesn't come from that. The place was named for a local woman with the last name "Turi."

There is also a Sami "turf hut" here, **Mikkelgammen,** where you can enjoy a Sami meal if you book it 2 days in advance. Guests gather around a campfire for a three-course meal called *bidos.* Naturally, reindeer is the main course of choice. You'll get reindeer soup as well as reindeer meat, followed by Arctic cloudberries in whipped cream. The cost of the meal is 245NOK ($38/£20) per person, followed by a Sami program called *Joik,* including singing (more like chanting) and stories.

You can join the 150,000 others who have joined the **Royal and Ancient Polar Bear Society** (© 78-41-31-00). Apply in person while you're in Hammerfest. Membership costs 160NOK ($25/£13) annually, and the money is used to protect endangered Arctic animals through conservation programs. The Society has moved into a new building next the Coastal Voyager Docks on Havnegata 3. Entrance is 40NOK ($6.15/£3.20). There's a small museum devoted to the hunting heyday of Hammerfest, which lasted from 1910 to 1950, when eagles, arctic foxes, and polar bears were trapped by the English and by German officers during World War II. It's in the basement of the Town Hall, on Rådhusplassen. The center is open June to August, Monday to Friday from 6am to 6pm.

Gjenreisningsmuseet, Söröygatan (© 78-42-26-40), commemorates the cold, bleak years after World War II, when local residents, deprived of most of their buildings, livelihoods, and creature comforts, heroically rebuilt Finnmark and north Norway in the wake of Nazi devastation. Entrance is 40NOK ($6.15/£3.20) for adults, 30NOK ($4.60/£2.40) for students, 15NOK ($2.30/£1.20) for children 8 to 16, and free for children 7 and under. It's open June to September daily from 10am to 3pm; in the off season it's open daily from 11am to 2pm.

Lying a 5-minute walk from the harbor, **Hammerfest Kirke (Church),** Kirkegate 33 (© 78-42-74-70), was consecrated in 1961 and is known for its avant-garde architecture. Unusual for a church, it doesn't have an altarpiece. Instead you get a large and detailed stained-glass window. The altarpiece is found in a hall lying to the right of the main sanctuary. Local carver Knit Arnesen carved the friezes, depicting the history of Hammerfest. Note the chapel across from the church. Dating from 1933, it's the only structure in Hammerfest to survive the Nazi invasion. Admission is free, and the church is open in summer from Monday to Friday 8am to 3pm, Saturday 11am to 3pm, and Sunday noon to 1pm.

WHERE TO STAY
Rica Hotel Hammerfest ⚔   A bit grim and foreboding, the Rica actually offers more comfort than the Quality Hotel Hammerfest (Strandgata 2-4; © 78-42-96-00), although it doesn't have as much character as its competitor. It too opens onto views of the harbor and arguably has a more efficient staff. If you're seeking the best appointed and most spacious accommodations in Hammerfest, ask for a junior suite here. The largest hotel in town was built in the mid-1970s on steeply sloping land and has been regularly spruced up since then. The standard, midsize guest rooms are decorated with Nordic-inspired pastels, but the look is strictly functional. Bathrooms tend to be small and each unit contains a tub/shower combination.

Søröygata 15, N-9600 Hammerfest. © 78-41-13-33. Fax 78-41-13-11. www.rica.no. 80 units. 1,025NOK–1,530NOK ($158–$236/£82–£122) double; 1,665NOK ($256/£133) junior suite. AE, DC, MC, V. **Amenities:** Restaurant; bar; disco; fitness center; sauna; nonsmoking rooms; babysitting; laundry service/dry cleaning. *In room:* TV, minibar, hair dryer, Wi-Fi.

WHERE TO DINE

Odd's Mat og Vinhus ✥✥ NORTHERN NORWEGIAN   Following its opening in 1992, this rustic restaurant was voted the best restaurant in Norway by a Trondheim radio station, and we certainly agree. It's adjacent to the town's largest pier, overlooking the harbor. Inside, every effort has been made to simulate the wild splendor of Finnmark (northern Norway), with the use of roughly textured wood, stone, and many yards of natural hemp knotted into rope curtains. The kitchen opens to the dining room, adding to the cozy feel.

The recipes and ingredients are almost completely derived from northern Norway, with an emphasis on fish and game. You might try filet of carp, partially sun-dried, boiled, and served with mustard sauce and bacon fat, or filet of reindeer, served, raw and chopped, like a tartar, or smoked and thinly sliced, like a carpaccio.

Strandgata 24. ⓒ **78-41-37-66.** Reservations recommended. Main courses 210NOK–290NOK ($32–$45/£17–£23). AE, DC, MC, V. Mon–Thurs 2:30–11pm; Fri 1–11pm; Sat 6–11pm.

Skansen Mat og Vinstue ✥ NORWEGIAN/INTERNATIONAL   This small, intimate restaurant has an open kitchen with a fireplace in the center. Come here for international dishes, which the chefs prepare with "a touch of the Arctic." As good as this place it, it doesn't match the superb viands at the just-recommended Odd's Mat og Vinhus.

The chefs' preparation of reindeer is good, but we prefer the daily fish specials or the tender pepper steak. If you're here on the right evening, you can stick around and dance and drink the night away. The Rica Bar and Disco, also in the cellar of the hotel, is open Friday and Saturday from 10pm to 3am. Admission is 70NOK ($11/£5.60). The minimum age is 20, and beer costs 45NOK to 55NOK ($6.95–$8.45/£3.60–£4.40) per half-liter.

In the Rica Hotel Hammerfest, Sørøygata 15. ⓒ **78-41-13-33.** Main courses 180NOK–265NOK ($28–$41/£14–£21). AE, DC, MC, V. Daily 4–11pm.

HONNINGSVÅG

130km (81 miles) NE of Hammerfest, 2,446km (1,519 miles) NE of Bergen

You have to journey a long way to see **Nordkapp** (North Cape), the most celebrated attraction in Norway. Nearer the North Pole than Oslo, the mighty rock stands at a latitude of 70° 10' 21" N. The attraction is generally viewed from mid-May to the end of July, when the midnight sun does not drop below the horizon.

To the Sami, the North Cape held great religious significance and was a site for sacrifices. The name of North Cape came from the British explorer, Richard Chancellor, who drifted here in 1553. He was looking for the Northeast Passage. Nordkapp is falsely known to be the northernmost point of continental Europe.

The world's northernmost village, the gateway to the North Cape, is a completely modern fishing harbor set in a land of forests, fjord waters, and crashing waterfalls. Only the chapel withstood the village's destruction by Germans in 1944. It's some 80km (50 miles) nearer to the North Pole than Hammerfest, on the Alta-Hammerfest bus route. Honningsvåg is on the southern side of the island of Magerøy, connected to the North Cape by a 35km (22-mile) road.

Note: The attractions and prices around the North Cape have prompted many readers to call the area a "tourist trap."

ESSENTIALS

GETTING THERE   If you don't take the **coastal steamer** (www.coastalvoyage.com), you can reach Honningsvåg by car. From Oslo (a very long trip—about 30 hr. June–Sept), take E-6 north to the junction with Route 95 north. That route leads to Honningsvåg, with one ferry crossing. SAS flies from Oslo or Bergen to Alta; there you can catch a bus to Hammerfest (Apr–Sept only), where you change to another bus to Honningsvåg. For bus information, call **Finnmark Fylkesrederi** (© 78-40-70-00).

VISITOR INFORMATION   The **North Cape Tourist Office,** in the Nordkapphuset (© 78-47-70-30; www.northcape.no), can give you information on sightseeing boat trips, museums, walks, and deep-sea fishing. The office is open June to August, Monday to Friday from 8:30am to 8pm, Saturday and Sunday noon to 8pm; September to May, Monday to Friday 8:30am to 4pm.

A SPECIAL EVENT   The **North Cape Festival,** held for each year for 1 week in mid-June, presents a wide display of local culture. During the festival, participants in the **North Cape March** trek from Honningsvåg to the North Cape and back, a total of around 70km (44 miles).

SEEING THE SIGHTS

Nordkapphallen   This visitor center has a video presentation and museum exhibits. Downstairs you'll find an excellent videograph and a cave with a panoramic window facing the Arctic Ocean. On the way to the cave, you'll see several scenes from the history of the North Cape. Monuments commemorate visits from King Oscar (king of Norway and Sweden) and King Chulalongkorn of Siam (now Thailand), as well as the marking of the "Midnight Sun Road." You might be turned off by the steep entrance price, but the exhibits and the views from within manage to artfully and effectively evoke the meteorological and geological drama of the far North. Call before you visit, since even in high season, hours and days are subject to change. The center is closed between October and March.

Nordkapp. © **78-47-68-60.** Admission 190NOK ($29/£15) adults, 75NOK ($12/£6) children 3–15, 380NOK ($59/£30) family. Apr 1–May 20 daily 2–5pm; May 21–June 16 daily noon–1am; June 17–Aug 4 daily 9am–2am; Aug 5–31 daily noon–midnight; Sept 1–Oct 5 daily noon–5pm. Closed Oct 6–Mar.

Nordkappmuseet   This museum, which could easily be skipped, displays the cultural history of the North Cape, including fishery artifacts and an exhibit that details the effects of World War II on the North Cape. The museum lies at the harbor and town center, a 3-minute walk from the coastal steamer and the North Cape Hotel.

In the Nordkapphuset, Fiskeriveien 4. © **78-47-28-33.** Admission 25NOK ($3.85/£2) adults, 5NOK (75¢/40p) children 6–16, free for children under 6. June 5–Aug 15 Mon–Sat 11am–8pm, Sun noon–7pm; Aug 16–June 4 Mon–Fri noon–3:30pm.

WHERE TO STAY

Rica Hotel Honningsvåg   The North Cape's northernmost hotel is located in the central zone, near the quay. Advance reservations are strongly advised. This five-story, yellow-fronted building was expanded and considerably upgraded in the 1990s. The guest rooms, which have views of the harbor, are functionally furnished with modern but plain pieces. The rooms and bathrooms are a bit small (each comes equipped with a shower), but the beds are comfortable. In this part of the world, you'll happily settle for a roof over your head. Restaurant Carolina (see "Where to Dine," below) is one of the best in town.

Best Offbeat Adventures

- **Dog Sledding:** Traveling over the frozen tundra or through snow-laced forests at the speed of a dog can be one of the great experiences of the Nordic world. You can be a passenger, bundled aboard a sled, or a driver urging on a team of huskies. An outfitter that specializes in the experience, usually as part of midwinter camping trips under a canopy of stars, is **Muir's Tours,** Nepal House, 97A Swansea Rd., Reading, Berkshire RG1 8HA England (© **0118/950-2281;** www.nkf-mt.org.uk). Eight-day, all-inclusive tours are conducted in winter for $1,600/£832 per person. You're given your own team of four to six huskies for this safari. As you ride along, you'll see reindeer along the side of your trail.

- **Observing Musk Oxen:** A remnant of the last ice age, the musk ox had become nearly extinct by the 1930s. Between 1932 and 1953, musk oxen were shipped from Greenland to the Dovrefjell (a national park that's about an hour's train ride south of Trondheim), where about 60 still roam. On a safari you can observe this thriving herd—take along some binoculars—as well as Norway's purest herd of original mountain reindeer. The park, another remnant of the last ice age, is Europe's most bountiful wildflower mountain. Accommodations in or near the park can be arranged through **Borton Overseas** (© **800/843-0602;** www.bortonoverseas.com). Hotel staff members can direct you to where you're most likely to see the herds.

- **Rafting:** Norway's abundant snow and rainfall and its steep topography feed dozens of roaring white-water streams. Experience these torrents firsthand as part of white-water treks downriver. One of Norway's most respected river outfitters is **Norwegian Wildlife and Rafting AS,** Randsverk, N-2680 Vågå (© **61-23-87-27;** www.nwr.no). Based in central Norway, about a 90-minute drive north of Lillehammer, the company has various devices suitable for helping you float, meander, or shoot down the white-water streams, including paddle boards, kayaks, canoes, or inflatable rafts. Trips last from 1 to 8 days.

The hotel also runs an unpretentious grill and offers dancing on Friday and Saturday nights, charging a cover of 10NOK to 15NOK ($1.55–$2.30/80p–£1.20).

Nordkappgata 2–4, N-9750 Honningsvåg. © **78-47-23-33.** Fax 78-47-33-79. www.rica.no. 174 units. 995NOK–1,320NOK ($153–$203/£80–£106) double. Rates include breakfast. AE, DC, MC, V. Closed in winter. **Amenities:** Restaurant; lounge; sauna; dry cleaning; nonsmoking rooms; rooms for those w/limited mobility. *In room:* TV.

WHERE TO DINE

Restaurant Carolina NORWEGIAN   Located in the cellar of the Rica Hotel Honningsvåg, this place is at its most elegant in the winter, when the tour groups are gone. During the summer the smorgasbord is in the dining room, and a la carte dinners are served in the less formal bistro. The cuisine is competently prepared but never exciting; most of the ingredients are shipped in. In the evening music begins at 8pm,

- **Trekking the Fjords:** Two respected U.S.-based outfitters, **Borton Overseas** (© 800/843-0602; www.bortonoverseas.com) and **Five Stars of Scandinavia** (© 800/722-4126; www.5stars-of-scandinavia.com), offer 7- and 8-day treks through Norway, designed to acquaint you with the country's heritage and its thousands of scenic wonders. Amid the cliffs and waterfalls of the fjords, you can participate in point-to-point guided treks that average around 24km (15 miles) per day. En route you'll visit wooden churches, mountain hamlets, and, in some cases, snowfields and slow-moving glaciers. Depending on your budget and your tastes, overnight accommodations range from first-class hotels to simple mountain huts favored by rock climbers and many trekkers.
- **Biking in the Lofoten Islands:** Some of the weirdest and most isolated tundra and lichen-covered rock formations in Norway lie within the Lofoten archipelago, north of the Arctic Circle.

  Berkeley, California-based **Backroads Travel** (© 800/GO-ACTIVE; www.backroads.com) conducts 6-day hiking-and-biking (they refer to them as "multisport") tours of the isolated archipelago at least twice a year, during July and August, with an emphasis on ecology and natural beauty. Washington state–based **Five Stars of Scandinavia** (© 800/722-4126; www.5stars-of-scandinavia.com) offers comparable tours and tends to be cheaper than Backroads. Both operators house their participants in simple mountain huts and lodges.
- **Going on a Moose Safari:** Norway's largest animal, the moose, can weigh up to 600 kilograms (1,323 lb.). These forest dwellers are shy toward people and best spotted at night. If you'd like to go on a moose safari, contact **Daesbekken Villmarksenter** in Finneskogen (© 62-95-48-57; www.villmarksenter.hm.no), east of Oslo, near the Swedish border. Individual visitors can arrange tours from July to September; otherwise, it's strictly group bookings.

and the place is very popular with locals. It's decorated with old-fashioned photographs of Honningsvåg.

In the Rica Hotel, Nordkappgata 2–4. © **78-47-23-33.** Reservations recommended. Buffet 195NOK ($30/£16). AE, DC, MC, V. Summer daily 6–10pm.

A TRIP TO THE NORTH CAPE ★★★

The **Nordkapp (North Cape)** symbolizes the "top of Europe." In prehistoric times the North Cape Horn was a Sami place of sacrifice. The North Cape's name used to be Knyskanes, but in 1553 it was named "North Cape" by the Lord Richard Chancellor of England, who was searching for a sea passage to China. The road to the North Cape is open to traffic from May 1 to October 20.

The first tour ships arrived in 1879. They anchored in Hornvika Bay, and the visitors had to climb 280m (919 ft.) up to the plateau. After the road from Honningsvåg opened in 1956, the flow of tourists turned into a flood. In summer, buses to the North Cape leave daily from outside the tourist office at Fergeveien 4 at Honningsvåg, stop briefly at the ferry terminal across from the Sifi Sommerhotell, and then continue to the visitor center at the North Cape. The one-way passage from Honningsvåg to the North Cape, a travel time of 45 minutes, is 100NOK ($15/£8) adults, 60NOK ($9.25/£4.80) children 3 to 15; free for 2 and under. For more information, call **FFR** (© **78-40-70-00**).

On the road to the Cape is a Sami encampment. It's a bit contrived, but visitors do have an opportunity to go inside one of the tents and come away with an idea of how nomadic Sami used to live.

2 The Fjords

For visitors who'd like to explore the fjords by car, we begin our tour in Bergen. From Bergen, head east on Route 7 to Ulvik.

ULVIK

150km (93 miles) E of Bergen

Ulvik is a rarity—an unspoiled resort. It lies like a fist at the end of an arm of the Hardangerfjord and is surrounded in the summer by misty peaks and fruit farms. It's the beautiful setting that attracts visitors, not an array of attractions. Ulvik's claim to fame? It's where potatoes first grew in Norway. The village's 1858 church is attractively decorated in the style of the region. It's open June to August daily from 9am to 5pm. Classical concerts, often presented by visiting chamber orchestras from other parts of Europe, are offered in summer at the church. When a concert is to be presented, notices are posted throughout the town. Other than the enchantment of the hamlet itself, the real reason to stay here is for the walking and hiking.

ESSENTIALS

GETTING THERE   If you're not driving, you can reach Ulvik by train or bus from Bergen or Oslo. From either city, take a train to Voss, where you can catch a bus for the 40km (25-mile), 45-minute ride to Ulvik. Buses run from Voss daily, five times in the summer, three in the winter. In Ulvik the bus stops in front of the Ulvik church in the town center. There's no formal bus station.

VISITOR INFORMATION   Contact the **Ulvik Tourist Office,** in the town center (© **56-52-63-60;** www.visitulvik.com). It's open May 15 to September 15, Monday to Saturday from 8:30am to 5pm, Sunday 1 to 5pm; September 16 to May 14, Monday to Friday 8:30am to 5pm. The office can arrange excursions, from trips on fjord steamers to bus tours of the Osa mountains.

SEEING THE SIGHTS

A number of do-it-yourself excursions begin at Ulvik; see the tourist office for details. They change seasonally and depend on the weather. Our favorite walk is along the northern tip of the Hardangerfjord, a paradise for hikers. It's home to some 1,000 people and the continent's largest herd of wild reindeer. Mountain trout attract anglers to the area. We've been through this area in July when the cherries ripen, followed in just 3 weeks or so by the most delicious-tasting plums, pears, and apples. It's a great opportunity for a summer picnic, and you can stop and buy fresh fruit and other foodstuffs at one of the roadside farm kiosks.

The Ulvik area offers some of the best walks in the fjord country. These are part of what is known as the **Kulturlandskapsplan** 𝕖 and are divided into four different walks, including the stone-covered grave mounds at Nesheim and Tunheim, the cotter's farm at Ljonakleiv, and a restored country mill in Nordallen in Osa. The tourist office sells a manual, *Heritage Trails of Ulvik,* outlining details on all these walks. The same office will provide information about organized walks on Tuesday and Thursday in summer along forest roads and into the mountains.

WHERE TO STAY & DINE
Moderate
Rica Brakanes Hotel 𝕖𝕖𝕖 There's a famous view of the Hardangerfjord and the surrounding forest from this well-recommended hotel. This is one of the most impressive fjord resorts in the area, although it began modestly in 1860 when it opened as a coaching inn with five bedrooms. Over the years it grew, but the building came to a terrible end when German warships opened fire on it in 1940. When money became available in the postwar era, it was reconstructed and reopened in 1952. With its custom-designed furniture and textiles and stylish interior, it was hailed as Norway's leading fjord hotel. Today all that remains of the original building is one small dining room. The rest of the hotel is airy, sunny, and comfortable. The guest rooms are midsize to spacious and well maintained, with sparkling-clean bathrooms with tub/shower combinations. In the summer, plane rides over the fjords can be arranged, and windsurfing and boat rentals are available.

N-5730 Ulvik. 𝒞 **56-52-61-05.** Fax 56-52-64-10. www.brakanes-hotel.no. 143 units. 1,600NOK ($246/£128) double; 2,500NOK ($385/£200) suite. Rates include breakfast. AE, DC, MC, V. Free parking. **Amenities:** Restaurant; bar; indoor heated pool; 2 tennis courts; fitness center; sauna; nonsmoking rooms; rooms for those w/limited mobility. *In room:* TV, minibar, Wi-Fi.

Inexpensive
Ulvik Fjord Pensjonat 𝕖 *Value* This cozy, family-run hotel in the town center hardly competes with the Rica Brakanes, but has its devotees. The hospitality and home cooking lure guests back each summer, where they wander the extensive grounds and take in panoramic views of the fjord. Ulvik Fjord Pensjonat, constructed in two stages in 1946 and 1977, is one of the finest guesthouses along the Hardangerfjord. The rooms are spacious and pleasantly furnished in regional Norwegian style. All units contain well-kept bathrooms with tub/shower combinations. You'll be welcomed by the Hammer family, who won the Norwegian Hospitality Prize in 1989. Almost 20 years later, the family is still extending the hospitality that brought them acclaim.

N-5730 Ulvik. 𝒞 **56-52-61-70.** Fax 56-52-61-60. www.ulvikfjordpensjonat.no. 19 units, 17 with bathroom. 820NOK ($126/£66) double with bathroom. Rates include breakfast. V. Free parking. Closed Oct–Apr. **Amenities:** Restaurant; bar; lounge; free rowing boat; kids' play area. *In room:* Hair dryer, Wi-Fi.

VOSS 𝕖
40km (25 miles) W of Ulvik, 101km (63 miles) E of Bergen

On the main road between east and west Norway, we know of no better place to stop off than Voss, a famous year-round resort and the birthplace of American football hero Knute Rockne. Positioned between two fjords, Voss is a natural base for exploring the **Sognefjord** to the north and the **Hardangerfjord** to the south, as well as glaciers, mountains, fjords, waterfalls, orchards, rivers, and lakes. Though you won't see actual trolls, revelers still dress in costume for folklore programs.

ESSENTIALS

GETTING THERE   From Ulvik, take Highway 20 to Route 13; then follow Route 13 northwest to Voss. If you're not driving, there's frequent train service from Bergen (travel time is 1¼ hr.) and Oslo (5½ hr.). There are six daily buses from Bergen (1¾ hr.) and one bus a day from Oslo, which takes 9 hours. Call © **56-52-08-00** for the exact time, usually 8am.

VISITOR INFORMATION   The **Voss Information Center** is at Hestavangen 10 (© **56-52-08-00;** www.visitvoss.no). It's open June to August, Monday to Friday from 8am to 7pm, Saturday 9am to 7pm, Sunday 2 to 7pm; September to May, Monday to Friday 9am to 3:30pm.

SEEING THE SIGHTS

St. Olav's Cross, Skulegata, near the Voss Cinema, is the oldest relic in Voss, believed to have been raised when the townspeople adopted Christianity in 1023.

A ride on the **Hangursbanen cable car** (© **56-51-12-12**) will be a memorable part of your visit. It offers panoramic views of Voss and its environs. The mountaintop restaurant serves refreshments and meals. The hardy take the cable car up and then spend the rest of the afternoon strolling down the mountain, which is our favorite walk in the area. A round-trip ride costs 85NOK ($13/£6.80) for adults, 50NOK ($7.70/£4) for children 7 to 15, and is free for children under 6. Entrance to the cable car is on a hillside, a 10-minute walk north of the town center. It's open in summer and winter but closes during May and September to December.

Vangskyrkje   This 1271 Gothic-style stone-built church stands on the grounds of an ancient pagan temple. The church suffered from a 1536 Lutheran Reformation that destroyed much of its original architecture, and what remains is a timbered tower, a Renaissance pulpit, a stone altar, triptych, fine woodcarvings, and a painted ceiling. An aerial attack by the invading Nazis destroyed most of Voss, but the church was relatively undamaged. The church is a 5-minute walk east of the train station.

Vangsgata 3. © **56-51-22-78.** Admission 18NOK ($2.75/£1.45) adults, free for children under 17. Daily 10am–4pm. Closed Sept–May.

Voss Folkemuseum   We've seen bigger and better folks museums than this, but if you have an hour or so in Voss, you should check it out. Almost a kilometer (½ mile) north of Voss on a hillside overlooking the town, this museum consists of more than a dozen farmhouses and other buildings dating from the 1500s to around 1870. They were built on the site by two farm families.

Mølster. © **56-51-15-11.** Admission 41NOK ($6.30/£3.30) adults, free for children 12 and under. May–Sept daily 10am–5pm; Oct–Apr Mon–Sat 10am–3pm, Sun noon–3pm.

WHERE TO STAY
Moderate

Fleischers Hotel ✦✦✦ *(Kids*   This hotel does more than any other to cater to kids, featuring a children's pool with many activities, a playground, and movies. However, it appeals to adults as well, with its peaked, chalet-style roofs and dormers. Built in 1889, the hotel is still run by the founding fathers, the Fleischers. Though it was modernized and expanded (the modern wing has 30 units, all with private showers, toilets, and terraces overlooking the lake), the older rooms still have their charm, including more space. The restaurant serves an a la carte menu; main courses cost 160NOK to 395NOK ($25–$61/£13–£32). In the summer a buffet of local fish and Norwegian specialties is served for 355NOK ($55/£28). The hotel is conveniently located on the lakefront beside the train station.

Evangervegen 13, N-5700 Voss. ℂ **56-52-05-00.** Fax 56-52-05-01. www.fleischers.no. 90 units. 1,020NOK ($157/£82) double. Rates include breakfast. AE, DC, MC, V. Free parking. **Amenities:** Restaurant; bar; lounge; indoor heated pool; 2 saunas; children's activities; limited room service; babysitting; laundry service/dry cleaning; 1 room for those w/limited mobility. *In room:* TV, minibar, hair dryer, trouser press (in some).

Hotel Jarl   Compared to Fleischers, the Jarl, though comfortable and reliable, is a bit of a letdown. In the center of Voss, it's been a durable favorite since its opening in 1972. Maintenance is high here, and all the bedrooms, small to midsize, are tastefully furnished, each with a well-equipped bathroom with tub/shower combo. The chefs prepare a menu of regional specialties and international dishes using high-quality produce, and after dinner you can do a bit of dancing at the hotel's pub and disco.

Elvegata, N-5700 Voss. ℂ **56-51-99-00.** Fax 56-51-37-69. www.jarlvoss.no. 78 units. 1,350NOK ($208/£108) double. Rates include breakfast. AE, DC, MC, V. Free parking. **Amenities:** Restaurant; bar; pub/disco; indoor heated pool; sauna. *In room:* TV, minibar, safe.

Park Hotel Vossevangen ⚝   If you feel that Fleischers is a bit stuffy, you'll find a livelier venue here. On most nights, more is happening here than anywhere else in Voss, which means it attracts a younger crowd. The product of a 1990 merger, this hotel consists of two sections (originally the Park Hotel and the Vossevangen Hotel), joined by a covered passageway. With many of its public and guest rooms overlooking Lake Vossevangen, the guest rooms are attractively furnished and contain well-kept bathrooms with tub/shower combinations. The hotel is family-owned and houses the best restaurant in town, the Elysée (see "Where to Dine," below). Facilities include the Café Stationen, the Pentagon Dance Bar, the Stallen Pub, and the Pianissimo Bar. It's in the town center, about 90m (300 ft.) from the train station.

Uttrågate, N-5701 Voss. ℂ **56-53-10-00.** Fax 56-53-10-01. www.parkvoss.no. 131 units. 1,250NOK–1,650NOK ($193–$254/£100–£132) double. Rates include breakfast. AE, DC, MC, V. Free parking. **Amenities:** Restaurant; bar; lounge; babysitting; nonsmoking rooms; rooms for those w/limited mobility. *In room:* TV, minibar.

Inexpensive

Kringsjå Pension *(Kids)*   This three-story guesthouse in the center of Voss is really a glorified B&B, the best in town, with a slight edge over the Nøring (see below). Some parts were built in the 1930s, while others are more modern. The public rooms are spacious and airy, and the guest rooms are simply and comfortably furnished, with good beds and small bathrooms with tub/shower combinations. A room with four to five beds is ideal for families. The hall bathrooms are well maintained and are also equipped with tub/shower combinations. A generous breakfast is served daily, and other meals are sometimes available but must be arranged in advance.

Strengjarhaujen 6, N-5700 Voss. ℂ **56-51-16-27.** Fax 56-51-63-30. www.kringsja.no. 18 units. 390NOK ($60/£31) per person double; 350NOK ($54/£28) per person family room. Children under 12 get a 50% reduction. Rates include breakfast. AE, DC, MC, V. Free parking. **Amenities:** Lounge. *In room:* No phone.

Nøring Pensjonat *(Value)*   Since 1949 this B&B, or first-class "pension," has attracted frugal travelers from both Oslo and Bergen. Half of its bedrooms face the mountains, and there is a lounge opening onto a terrace, taking advantage of the setting near the river, about a 10-minute walk from the town center. We don't want to oversell this place, but it does provide well-maintained bedrooms—they are small, but comfortable, each with a well-kept bathroom. The staff serves good, hearty breakfasts, plus light meals (with beer or wine) at lunch and dinner.

Uttrågate 41, N-5700 Voss. ⓒ 56-51-12-11. Fax 56-51-12-23. 20 units, 9 with bathroom. 325NOK ($50/£26) per person double without bathroom; 460NOK ($71/£37) per person double with bathroom. Rates include breakfast. AE, DC, MC, V. Free parking. **Amenities:** Restaurant; bar; lounge. *In room:* No phone.

WHERE TO DINE
Moderate
Elysée 𝒢 FRENCH/NORWEGIAN   This is the town's best restaurant (even better food than Fleischers), and dishes are satisfying and based on the freshest ingredients available locally. Menu items include sea scorpion, filet of lamb marinated in honey, and a seasonal game dish, each of which is backed up with one of the best wine *cartes* in the area. For a dessert, nothing's better than the homemade ice cream with fresh berries and a vanilla sauce. The decor of this prestigious restaurant includes *trompe l'oeil* murals based on a modern interpretation of the Pantheon.

In the Park Hotel Vossevangen, Uttrågate. ⓒ 56-51-13-22. Reservations recommended. Main courses 200NOK–280NOK ($31–$43/£16–£22); lunch smorgasbord 300NOK ($46/£24); fixed-price dinner 380NOK ($59/£24). AE, DC, MC, V. Sun–Thurs 7:30am–10am, 1–3pm, and 7–10pm; Fri–Sat 1–11pm.

Fleischers Restaurant 𝒢 NORWEGIAN   The dining room of this landmark hotel, a few steps from the Voss train station, hasn't been altered since the hotel opened more than a century ago. Long the leading restaurant in the Voss area, the Victorian-style Fleischers remains the traditionalists' favorite. Its lunchtime smorgasbord is a lavish array of all-you-can-eat Norwegian delicacies. Specialties include smoked salmon and filet of beef, lamb, pork, and veal. While the food offers a real taste of Norway, you won't get the dash and culinary sophistication of the Elysée.

Evangervegen 13. ⓒ 56-52-05-00. Reservations recommended. Lunch smorgasbord 235NOK ($36/£19); main courses 160NOK–395NOK ($25–$61/£13–£32); summer buffet 355NOK ($55/£28). AE, DC, MC, V. Mon–Sat 1–10:30pm; Sun 1–9:45pm.

Inexpensive
Vangen Café 𝒱𝒶𝓁𝓊ℯ NORWEGIAN   Fleischers and Elysée are wonderful for a special occasion, but this is the place to have your weekly roast reindeer, as well as other traditional Norwegian food such as locally caught fish or freshly made cakes and afternoon snacks. The *dagens menu* (today's menu) is the best value in town. Soft drinks and fruit juices are served, but no alcohol. A 5-minute walk from the train station in the town center, this cafeteria-style outlet is one floor above street level over a small souvenir shop and food market.

Vangen Super-Market, Vangsgata. ⓒ 56-51-12-05. Smorgasbord 40NOK–48NOK ($6.15–$7.40/£3.20–£3.85); *dagens menu* (daily specials) 95NOK–140NOK ($15–$22/£7.60–£11). No credit cards. Mon–Fri 10:30am–6pm; Sat 10:30am–4pm; Sun noon–6pm.

VOSS AFTER DARK
Fleischers Top Spot Nightclub   You'll find this established nightspot in the cellar of the Fleischers Hotel (see above). Bands play nightly for an older, dressed-up crowd. Many people come here just to drink—beer costs 56NOK ($8.60/£4.50). The club is open Monday to Thursday from 9:30pm to 1am, Friday and Saturday until 3am. In Fleischers Hotel, Evangervegen 13. ⓒ 56-52-05-00. Fri–Sat cover 70NOK ($11/£5.60); no cover for hotel guests.

A SIDE TRIP TO THE SOGNEFJORD

The mighty **Sognefjord,** one of the most impressive—and deepest—fjords in the world, stretches for a total length of 205km (127 miles). It spreads its powerful "fjord fingers" as far as **Jostedalsbreen,** the country's largest glacier, and to Jotunheimen, Norway's tallest mountain range. The widest and most dramatic part of the fjord stretches from the coast to Balestrand, from which it grows much narrower.

If you have a choice, opt for a late spring visit, when thousands of fruit trees can be seen in full bloom along both banks of the Sognefjord. The entire district is ideal for skiing, sailing, mountain hiking, and other outdoor activities.

The best way to see the fjord is to take a boat from Bergen operated by **Fylkesbaatane** (© 55-90-70-70; www.fjord1.no/fylkesbaatane). Balestrand is a stopover on the Bergen-to-Flåm line, with departures from Bergen leaving once a day. The journey takes 5½ hours and costs 550NOK ($85/£44) per person.

BALESTRAND

90km (56 miles) N of Voss, 209km (130 miles) NE of Bergen

Balestrand lies on the northern rim of the Sognefjord, Norway's longest and deepest fjord at some 1,308m (4,291 ft.) deep. It's also at the junction of Vetlefjord, Esefjord, and the Fjaerlandsfjord, making it a great place for fjord lovers.

When Esias Tegnèr wrote of the snow-covered mountains and the panoramic Sognefjord in the saga of Fridtjof the Brave, the book brought an array of artists to the area in the mid–19th century. Soon other well-known Scandinavian artists were painting the fjord and mountain landscapes. Their art became so popular that regular visitors started to flock to Balestrand to take in the glories of the area for themselves—and so they have continued to this day.

ESSENTIALS

GETTING THERE   From Voss, continue driving north on Route 13 to Vangsnes and board a car ferry for the short crossing northwest to Balestrand. You can also take a train from Bergen or Oslo to Voss or Flåm, and then make bus and ferry connections north to Balestrand. Bus and ferry schedules are available at the Voss tourist office (© 56-52-08-00) and the Flåm tourist office (© 57-63-21-06). From Bergen there are daily express boats to Balestrand; the trip takes 3½ hours.

VISITOR INFORMATION   The **Tourist Office** (© 57-69-16-17 in winter, or 57-69-12-55 in summer) is in the town center. From June to August it's open daily 8:30am to 10pm; May and September, daily 9am to 8pm; October to April, Monday to Saturday 9am to 4pm.

SEEING THE SIGHTS

The staff at the tourist office can help you plan a tour of the area and put you in touch with local craftspeople. There you can pick up a list of constantly changing excursions and buy tickets for one of the scheduled 1½-day tours, which could include a taxi plane across the **Jostedal Glacier.** If offered, the taxi plane, which costs 800NOK to 900NOK ($123–$139/£64–£72), is the most dramatic ride in the area.

If you're looking for something more spontaneous, we suggest a leisurely stroll and a picnic south along the banks of the fjord. You'll pass many 19th- and early-20th-century homes and gardens along the way. Less than 1km (½ mile) south along the fjord, you'll come to two **Viking Age burial mounds.** One mound is topped by a statue of the legendary King Bele.

You can continue your walk by taking the small ferry that leaves Balestrand and crosses Esefjord to the Dragsvik side. At this point, you can walk for 8km (5 miles) along an old abandon country road that was used in the early part of the 20th century.

Kaiser Wilhelm II, a frequent visitor to Balestrand, presented the district with two statues of Old Norse heroes, King Bele and Fridtjof the Bold. They stand in the center of town. While the English church of **St. Olav** is close to the public, you can still admire this tiny 1897 wooden building from outside.

You can explore the area by setting out in nearly any direction on scenic country lanes with little traffic or a wide choice of marked trails and upland farm tracks. The tourist office (see above) sells a touring map for 70NOK ($11/£5.60). There's good sea fishing, as well as lake and river trout fishing. Fishing tackle, rowboats, and bicycles can all be rented in the area.

Back in Balestrand, near the ferry dock, you can visit the **Sognefjord Aquarium** (© **57-69-13-03**), with its exhibition of saltwater fish and denizens of the deep include Esefjord herring "lip fish," eels, and fierce *Jaws*-like sharks. The exhibition consists of a number of large and small aquariums, both indoors and out on the jetty. The marine environments have been authentically re-created, including the tidal belt at Munken and the sandy seabed around Staken. A man-made model of Sognefjord shows the currents of the fjord and provides an impression of its depth. There is also an audiovisual presentation. The admission of 40NOK ($6.15/£3.20) includes an hour of canoeing on the fjord. It's open from mid-April to May and mid-August to October daily from 10am to 4pm; June to mid-August daily 9:30am to 6pm.

WHERE TO STAY
Moderate
Kviknes Hotel ✦✦   The Kvikne family took over this site in 1877 and has, with each generation since, expanded, altered, and updated, making this a hotel with both old-world charm and modern facilities.

The elaborately detailed building has attracted the likes of politicians and movie stars. Guest rooms vary widely in size and style, and all but a few have fjord views. We go for the units in the original structure, with old-fashioned Norwegian style, flowery fabrics, and spacious bathrooms with tub/shower combinations. Some of these accommodations are furnished with antiques. The less personal rooms are in the annex, where a bland Nordic style prevails. Bathrooms tend to be small to medium in size. The hotel has a large dining room, several lounges, and a dance club. An extensive buffet is served every night; lunches are less elaborate, with brasserie-style meals. Like the cuisine, the chefs are international and use locally grown ingredients whenever possible. Sports such as water-skiing, windsurfing, and fjord fishing can be arranged, or you can take a helicopter flight to the Jostedal Glacier for 750NOK to 850NOK ($116–$131/£60–£68).

Kviknevegen 8, N-6898 Balestrand. © **57-69-42-00.** Fax 57-69-42-01. www.kviknes.no. 200 units. 1,360NOK ($209/£109) double; 1,560NOK ($240/£125) suite. Rates include breakfast. AE, DC, MC, V. Free parking. Closed Oct–Apr. **Amenities:** Restaurant; bar; fitness center; Jacuzzi; sauna; 24-hr. room service; babysitting; laundry service/dry cleaning; nonsmoking rooms; rooms for those w/limited mobility. *In room:* TV, hair dryer.

Inexpensive
Dragsvik Fjordhotell *(Kids)*   Almost a kilometer (½ mile) from Balestrand and 270m (900 ft.) from the ferry quay at Dragsvik, this hotel is a bargain. It lies right on a peninsula of natural beauty and opens onto the magnificent Sognefjord, providing a

magnificent view. The same family has run this place for three generations and built this small guesthouse on a vacation farmland in 1953. Units are comfortable and well maintained, if small. Tiny bathrooms come equipped with tub/shower combinations; doubles in the new wing have the most up-to-date plumbing. Some of the accommodations are in what management calls "fjord cabins," complete with a kitchen, shower, and toilets. Since these might comfortably house anywhere from two to five guests, these are often rented as family units. The large dining room offers a panoramic view of the Fjaerlandsfjord. You can rent bicycles and rowboats from the staff. Bikes cost 100NOK ($15/£8) per half-day, 150NOK ($23/£12) per day. Rowboats cost 200NOK ($31/£16) per half-day, 450NOK ($69/£36) per day.

Dragsvik, N-6899 Balestrand. © **57-69-44-00.** Fax 57-69-44-01. www.dragsvik.no. 19 units. 495NOK–690NOK ($76–$106/£40–£55) double; 590NOK–690NOK ($91–$106/£47–£55) cabin. Rates include breakfast. AE, MC, V. Free parking. Closed Nov–Jan. **Amenities:** Restaurant; bar; limited room service. *In room:* Hair dryer.

FROM BALESTRAND TO FLÅM

The best and most exciting way to approach Flåm is aboard the **electric train from Myrdal** 𝔊𝔊𝔊, which connects with trains from Bergen and Oslo. There Flåm Railway is the steepest place to find railways lines of this adhesion type, where the wheels of the train were designed to grip the tracks more firmly than on a usual rail track. The gradient is 55/1,000 on almost 80% of the line (i.e., a gradient of 1 in 18). The twisting tunnels that spiral in and out of the mountain are manifestations of the most daring and skillful engineering in Norwegian railway history. The electric train follows a 19km (12-mile) route overlooking an 883m (2,900-ft.) drop, stopping occasionally for passengers to photograph spectacular waterfalls. The trip takes 50 minutes. In winter about four or five trains a day make the run to Flåm. In summer, depending on business, service begins at 7:40am and runs throughout the day. Tickets must be purchased in advance. The one-way fare from Myrdal to Flåm is 175NOK ($27/£14).

FLÅM 𝔊

97km (60 miles) SE of Balestrand, 166km (103 miles) E of Bergen

Flåm (pronounced *Flawm*) lies on the Aurlandsfjord, a tip of the more famous Sognefjord. In the village you can visit the old church (1667), with painted walls done in typical Norwegian country style. However, we feel the thrill with Flåm is in the journey rather than in the destination.

ESSENTIALS

GETTING THERE   By **car** from Balestrand, take Route 55 east along the Sognefjord, crossing the fjord by ferry at Dragsvik and by bridge at Sogndal. At Sogndal, drive east to Kaupanger, where you'll cross the Ardalsfjord by ferry, and head south to Revsnes. In Revsnes, pick up Route 11 heading southeast. Drive east until you connect with a secondary road heading southwest through Kvigno and Aurland. From Aurland, take Route 601 southwest to Flåm. The whole trip takes 2 to 3 hours, depending on weather and road conditions.

Bus travel is less convenient. One **bus** a day Monday to Saturday runs between Aurland and Flåm. The trip takes 30 minutes.

From May to September, two **ferries** per day cross the fjord between Aurland and Flåm. The trip takes 30 minutes.

Flåm can also be reached by high-speed **express boats** from Bergen, Balestrand (p. 343), and Leikanger. The boats carry passengers only. In Bergen, call **Fylkesbaatane** (© **55-90-70-70;** www.fjord1.no/fylkesbaatane); the one-way trip costs 600NOK ($92/£48).

VISITOR INFORMATION   The **tourist office** (© **57-63-21-06;** www.visitflam. com), near the railroad station, is open May to September daily from 8:30am to 8:30pm. It also rents bikes for 100NOK ($14/£8).

SEEING THE SIGHTS

Flåm is an excellent starting point for car or boat excursions to other well-known centers on the **Sognefjord** ⑥⑥⑥, Europe's longest and deepest fjord. Worth exploring are two of the wildest and most beautiful fingers of the Sognefjord: the **Næroyfjord** and the **Aurlandsfjord.** Ask at the tourist office about a summer-only cruise from Flåm to both fjords. From Flåm by boat, you can disembark in Gudvangen or Aurland and continue by bus. Alternatively, you can return to Flåm by train.

There are also a number of easy walks in the Flåm district. If time is limited, make that walk along the banks of the **Aurlandsfjord,** leaving the "day-trippers" and the crass souvenirs in the center of Flåm far behind. The setting along the shoreline supports apple orchards, little hamlets, a fisherman's cottage here and there, and farmland where you can sometimes stop in and buy freshly picked fruit.

A map with detailed information is available from the tourist office for 50NOK ($7.70/£4).

WHERE TO STAY

Heimly Pension _Value_   This affordable choice, lying next to Aurlandsfjord, is only 400m (1,312 ft.) from the Flåm railway. It's a cozy, family-run B&B dating from the 1950s and still carrying the aura of that time. Designed in the style of an A-frame chalet, it offers a ground floor lounge where international travelers gather. The small to midsize guest rooms are tastefully and comfortably furnished, with well-maintained private bathrooms with showers. The best views over the fjord are on the two upper floors. A lively pub and a good restaurant serving home-cooked meals lie in an annex across the road.

N-5742 Flåm. © **57-63-23-00.** Fax 57-63-23-40. www.heimly.no. 25 units. 700NOK–900NOK ($108–$139/£56–£72) double. Rates include breakfast. AE, DC, MC, V. Free parking. Closed Dec 24–Jan 2. **Amenities:** Restaurant; bar. _In room:_ No phone.

GEILO ⑥

109km (68 miles) SE of Flåm, 240km (149 miles) E of Bergen, 240km (149 miles) W of Oslo

Most motorists in summer, driving between Oslo and Bergen (or vice versa), have to make a choice—Geilo or Voss? We find that your choice should be made depending on the season. In summer, it's best to head to Voss, with its folkloric activities. In winter, Geilo is best for skiing in the area. Part of the fun of visiting Geilo in winter, as it is in any alpine retreat, is to enjoy the lavish après-ski life of drinking and dining. In that regard, Geilo as a resort ranks higher than any other ski area in Norway, even when pitted against the more famous Lillehammer.

Geilo lies some 792m (2,600 ft.) above sea level in the Hol mountain district. Although it's not strictly in the fjord country, it's included here because it's a "gateway" there en route from Oslo to Bergen. The Geilo area boasts 130km (81 miles) of marked cross-country skiing tracks.

ESSENTIALS

GETTING THERE   From Flåm, motorists return to Aurland to connect with Route 50. It runs southeast through the towns of Steine, Storestølen, Hovet, and Hagafoss. In Hagafoss connect with Route 7 going southwest into Geilo. If you're dependent on public transportation, forget about the meager long-distance bus service and opt for the train connections via Oslo or Bergen. From Oslo, the fare is 600NOK ($92/£48) per person one-way, and the trip takes 3½ hours; from Bergen, it's 600NOK ($92/£48) one-way and takes 3 hours.

VISITOR INFORMATION   The **Turistinformasjonen** office is at Vesleslåtteveien 13 in the town center (© **32-09-59-00**; www.geilo.no). It's open June to August daily from 9am to 9pm; September to May, Monday to Friday 8:30am to 5pm, Saturday 8:30am to 3pm. The town doesn't use street addresses, but everything is laid out easily enough to find.

SEEING THE SIGHTS

The most exciting activity is to book a glacier trek on **Hardangerjøkulen** (1,860m/6,102 ft.) through the tourist office. These are available Monday, Wednesday, and Friday from July 1 to September 15. The tour takes 10 hours and costs 600NOK ($92/£48) per person, including a train ride to and from Finse.

A number of other tours are offered as well: rafting from 700NOK to 825NOK ($108–$127/£56–£66), river boarding (a new high-adrenaline sport involving a white-water trip downstream on a high-impact plastic board-cum-flotation device) from 680NOK to 760NOK ($105–$117/£54–£61), and a 2-hour moose safari for 400NOK ($62/£32). This latter jaunt is offered only on Thursday evening (when the moose can be seen) from July 1 to September 15.

Back in the center of town, you can visit **Geilojorget,** a 17th-century farm, which is open daily in July only from 11am to 5pm. Some old houses, 2 or 3 centuries old, have been moved to the site and are open for guided tours. You can see how farmers lived at the time and visit such buildings as a storage house or cattle barn. Cultural activities such as folk music shows are also presented. On-site is a cafe serving old-time dishes; if you've ever wanted to try a sour-cream cookie, this is the place for you.

WHERE TO STAY & DINE
Very Expensive
Dr. Holms Hotel ✦✦✦   This hotel is like a breath of fresh air, which is exactly why Dr. J. C. Holms, a specialist in respiratory diseases, established the resort in 1909. This is one of the most famous resort hotels in Norway and is our choice when driving across the country between Oslo and Bergen. Here you have convenience (it's near the railroad station), elegance, comfort, and traditional styling all in one.

Since the hotel was freed from the Nazis by the Norwegian resistance in 1945, there have been many changes, including the addition of two wings and a swimming complex. The latest major overhaul took place in 2000, and other smaller improvements have been made to keep the hotel up to date, including new bathrooms with tub/shower combinations in each room in 2006. Original works of art decorate the hotel, and guest rooms, including 11 family rooms, are beautifully furnished in a romantic English style.

Bowl & Dine, the first of the hotel's two restaurants, is a recreation of an American 1950s-style diner, replete with red seats and black-and-white checkered floors. It serves succulent burgers, milkshakes, and pizzas among other dishes. The new brasserie offers more continental fare, specializing in fish and meat dishes with a French accent.

N-3580 Geilo. ℭ **32-09-57-00.** Fax 32-09-16-20. www.drholms.com. 126 units. 1,600NOK ($246/£128) double; year-round 1,850NOK–2,375NOK ($285–$366/£148–£190) suite. Rates include breakfast. Rates may be higher during Christmas and New Year's. AE, DC, MC, V. Free parking. **Amenities:** 2 restaurants; bar; wine cellar; indoor heated pool; children's pool; fitness center; sauna; limited room service; babysitting; laundry service/dry cleaning; library; nonsmoking rooms; rooms for those w/limited mobility. *In room:* TV, minibar.

Moderate

Nye Vestlia Resort ✰✰✰ *(Kids*   While Dr. Holms Hotel has an atmosphere of tradition, this vastly enlarged and modernized hotel offers contemporary comfort, including the best spa between Oslo and Bergen. The building, a contemporary structure, was created from a hotel originally built in the 1960s, and 24 suites, 22 doubles, and 3 luxurious apartments were added. As part of the complex, there are 34 double and family rooms in small cabins surrounding the main hotel building, as well as another 11 but slightly worn-down cabins in idyllic locations in the birch forest with views over Ustedalsfjord and Geilo itself.

Chefs use fresh ingredients from the four corners of the world to compose a menu of traditional Scandinavian food and modern international dishes. Everything from a nine-course gourmet international dinner to a classic mountain buffet is offered.

Some of the best cross-country skiing in the area begins at the doorstep of the resort. In summer, guests go hiking, boating, horseback riding, or golfing, one of the reasons many check in here. This is also the most kid-friendly resort in central Norway, with a ski lift system suitable for kids and a children's ski club. Golf here has also become a sport for the kiddies. The best nightly entertainment is also here, including live dance music almost every evening year-round except Sunday.

N-3580 Geilo. ℭ **32-08-72-00.** Fax 32-08-72-01. www.vestlia.no. 120 units. 1,025NOK–2,600NOK ($158–$400/£82–£208) double including full board (breakfast, lunch, and dinner). AE, DC, MC, V. Free parking. **Amenities:** 3 restaurants; dance bar; indoor heated pool; exclusive spa; golf course; tennis court; fitness center; sauna; playground; babysitting; laundry service/dry cleaning; solarium; rooms for those w/limited mobility. *In room:* TV, minibar.

3 Trondheim to Narvik

To explore the northern Norwegian coast by car, begin your tour in Trondheim.

TRONDHEIM ✰✰✰
684km (425 miles) N of Bergen, 552km (343 miles) NW of Oslo

If you have a day or two to spare after visiting Oslo and Bergen, make it to Trondheim. We often prefer it during "term time," when 25,000 students bring it to vibrant life, biking around town, drinking in the bars, hanging out in the cafes, and listening to the sounds of jazz, often imported from New Orleans.

If you're heading north from here, savor Trondheim, because you're journeying into the wild, which, though civilized to an extent, is hardly tamed, except for Tromsø. If you're arriving in Trondheim from the north, you'll view it as a return to civilization.

After Oslo, Bergen, and Trondheim, the rest of Norwegian cities, including Narvik and Bodø, will become a footnote.

Founded by the Viking king Olaf I Tryggvason in the 10th century, Trondheim is Norway's third-largest city and was the country's capital until the early 1200s. Scenic and pleasant, it's a bustling university center, with expansive avenues created after a fire razed most of the town in 1681. The city lies on the south bay of the Trondheim Fjord, at the mouth of the Nidelven River.

Noted for its timbered architecture, Trondheim retains much of its medieval past, notably the Gothic-style Nidaros Cathedral. Pilgrims came from all over Europe to worship at the shrine of Olaf, who was buried in the cathedral and canonized in 1031.

The city's fortunes declined during the Reformation. Under the Nazi occupation Trondheim became the base of German naval forces in northern Norway, with U-boats lurking deep in its fjord.

Today Trondheim is a progressive city with a rich cultural life, as well as a high-technology center for research and education. Its town center is compact and best explored on foot; most of the historic core of Trondheim lies on a small triangular island surrounded by water but linked via bridges.

Trondheim lies some 684km (425 miles) north of Bergen and 552km (343 miles) northwest of Oslo.

ESSENTIALS
GETTING THERE

BY PLANE   Flights to Trondheim land at **Vaernes Airport** (© 74-84-30-00), lying 32km (21 miles) east of the city center. Most visitors fly here from either Bergen or Oslo. There are also daily connections to and from Copenhagen. Service is provided by **SAS** (© 74-80-41-00; www.scandinavian.net).

Once you arrive at the airport, you can take an airport bus, **Flybussen** (© 73-82-25-00), costing 68NOK ($10/£5.45) for a one-way trip into the center. The trip takes 40 minutes, ending at the rail depot. From the center of Trondheim, buses leave from Erling Skakkes gate daily from 5am to 9pm. Departures Monday to Friday are every 15 minutes, with curtailed departures on Saturday and Sunday. You can also take a taxi from the airport to the center, costing around 480NOK ($74/£38) for up to three people.

BY TRAIN   Two trains a day arrive from Stockholm (trip time: 12 hr.) and three trains per day arrive from Oslo (trip time: 7 hr.) into **Trondheim Sentralstasjon.** A typical fare—say, from Oslo to Trondheim—costs 760NOK ($117/£61) one-way. Trondheim also has links to Bodø if you're heading for the Arctic Circle. This latter trip takes 10 hours, costing around 850NOK ($131/£68) one-way. For rail information, call © 81-50-08-88, or visit www.nsb.no.

BY BUS   Buses from various parts of Norway arrive at the **Rutebilstasjon,** or city bus terminal, adjoining Trondheim Sentralstasjon, where the trains pull in. Trondheim lies at the crossroads of bus travel in Norway, as it is a transportation hub between southern Norway, including Oslo and Bergen, and northern Norway, including the city of Bodø. The most frequented bus route is from Oslo, taking 9½ hours and costing 400NOK ($62/£32) one-way. The more difficult route from Bergen takes more than 10 hours, costing 825NOK ($127/£66) one-way. For information about long-distance buses, contact **Norway Buss Ekspress** (© 81-54-44-44; www.nor-way.no).

BY BOAT   The **Hurtigruten coastal steamer** (© 77-64-82-00) stops in Trondheim. In addition, **Fosen Teraffikklag Kystexpressen boats** (© 73-89-07-00) travel between Kristiansund N and Trondheim, taking 3½ hours and costing 445NOK ($69/£36). Departures are at Pirterminalen Quay in Trondheim.

BY CAR   From Oslo, motorists can take the express highway E-6 north, going via Lillehammer all the way into Trondheim.

VISITOR INFORMATION   Contact the **Trondheim Tourist Office,** Munkegate 19 (© 73-80-76-60; www.trondheim.no), near the marketplace. The staff can also make hotel reservations or arrange for rooms in a private home. Double rooms in private homes cost from 350NOK to 550NOK ($54–$85/£28–£44). From May 21 to June 24, the tourist office is open Monday to Friday 8:30am to 6pm, Saturday and Sunday 10am to 4pm; from June 25 to August 12, it's open Monday to Friday 8:30am to 8pm and Saturday and Sunday 10am to 6pm. From August 13 to August 26, it's open Monday to Friday 8:30am to 6pm, Saturday and Sunday 10am to 4pm; and from August 27 to May 19, it's open Monday to Friday 9am to 4pm Monday to Friday and 10am to 2pm on Saturday.

GETTING AROUND   You can travel all over Trondheim and to outlying areas on city buses operated by **Trondheim Trafikkselskap (Team Traffikk, or TT),** Dronningens Gate (© **81-53-52-30**). Tickets for **single rides** are sold on buses for 22NOK ($3.40/£1.75) for adults, 11NOK ($1.70/90p) for children 4 to 16; children under 4 travel free. If you don't have exact change and offer a bank note that's worth more than the bus fare, you'll receive a credit slip from the driver, which can be redeemed at the TT office or on a later trip. A **day card** for 24 hours of unlimited rides costs 55NOK ($8.45/£4.40) per person.

For a local **taxi,** TrønderTaxi maintains a special, five-digit telephone number (© **07373**) that's in service 24 hours a day. The biggest taxi ranks are found at Torvet, the market square, and also at the central rail station. For local bus information serving the Greater Trondheim area, call © **81-53-52-30.**

Trondheim is a city that's known for its allegiance to all things "green." As such, it maintains a fleet of some 150 red-painted bicycles at bike racks scattered around the city. To secure one, head for the tourist office and pay a fee of 70NOK ($11/£5.60) plus a cash or credit card deposit of 500NOK ($77/£40) in exchange for something that resembles a credit card. After you insert it into a slot on the bike rack, it will release the bike, which you're then free to use for up to five days without additional charge. When you're through with the bike, bring it back undamaged, and your deposit will be returned.

SEEING THE SIGHTS

Nidaros Domkirke (Cathedral of Trondheim) ☆☆☆   Usually the capital city of
a country has the most spectacular cathedral, but not so in Norway. In grandeur, Nidaros dwarfs Oslo Cathedral. Dating from the 11th century, this cathedral is the most important, most historic, and most impressive ecclesiastical building in Scandinavia. It's located in the town center, near the Rådhus. The burial place of the medieval Norwegian kings, it was also the site of the coronation of Haakon VII in 1905, an event that marked the beginning of modern Norway.

Construction actually began on the cathedral in 1070, and some of its oldest parts still remain, mainly from the middle of the 1100s. Following the battle of Stiklestad, King Olaf Haraldson was entombed under the high altar. In time, Olaf became Saint Olaf, and his remains were encased in a gem-studded shrine.

The cathedral has been a victim of fires that swept over Trondheim and was reconstructed each time in its original Gothic style. (The section around the transept, however, is Romanesque.) During the Reformation, the cathedral was looted of precious relics. By 1585, Nidaros had been reduced to the status of a parish church, but around 1869, major reconstruction work was begun to return the gray sandstone building to its former glory.

The west facade is particularly impressive, with its carved figures of royalty and saints. It's especially appealing after dark, when the facade is floodlit (the lights usually stay on every evening until midnight, and it's worth a stroll even if you have to go out of your way). The interior is a maze of mammoth pillars and columns with beautifully carved arches that divide the chancel from the nave. The grandest feature is the stunning **rose window** *. The cathedral's **stained-glass windows** *, when caught in the proper light, are reason enough to visit. Gustav Vigeland, the famous sculptor, carved the **gargoyles and grotesques** * for the head tower and northern transept. A small museum inside displays the **crown jewels** ** of Norway.

Bispegaten 5. © **73-53-91-60**. Admission to cathedral and museum 50NOK ($7.70/£4) adults, 25NOK ($3.85/£2) children. Cathedral and museum May 1–June 10 Mon–Fri 9am–3pm, Sat 9am–2pm, Sun 1–4pm; June 11–Aug 19 Mon–Fri 9am–6pm, Sat 9am–2pm, Sun 1–4pm; Aug 20–Sept 14 Mon–Fri 9am–3pm, Sat 9am–2pm, Sun 1–4pm; Sept 15–Apr 30 Mon–Fri noon–2:30pm, Sat 11:30am–2pm, Sun 1–3pm. Bus: 5, 6, 7, or 9.

Ringve Museum ** *Finds* This is the only Norwegian museum specializing in musical instruments from around the world. Set on the Ringve Estate on the Lade Peninsula, the building originated in the 1740s as a prosperous manor house and farmstead. The mansion was the birthplace of Admiral Tordenskiold, the Norwegian sea hero. The museum today consists of two parts—the museum in the manor house and a permanent exhibition in the estate's former barn. In the barn you can hear the special sound of Norwegian folk instruments; there's even a hands-on exhibition where you can discover the budding musician in yourself. At specific times, concerts are given on carefully preserved antique instruments, including an impressive collection of spinets, harpsichords, clavichords, pianofortes, and string and wind instruments. Also on the premises is an old inn that serves waffles, light refreshments, and coffee.

Lade Alle 60 (3.3km/2 miles east from the center of town at Ringve Manor). © **73-87-02-80**. Admission 75NOK ($12/£6) adults, 25NOK ($3.85/£2) children 7–15, 50NOK ($7.70/£4) students, 150NOK ($23/£12) families. Jan to mid-Apr, open only on Sun 11am–4pm; mid-Apr to mid-May Mon–Fri and Sun 11am–4pm; mid-May to mid-June daily 11am–3pm; mid-June to Aug 5 daily 11am–5pm; Aug 6–Sept , daily 11am–3pm; and Sept 10–Dec 31 Sun 11am–4pm. During opening hours, multilingual guided tours depart at least once per hour, sometimes more frequently.

Stiftsgården When the royal family visits Trondheim today, they live here. With its 144 rooms, it's the largest wooden building in northern Europe, a massive pile in the late baroque style. This buttercup-yellow royal palace near the marketplace was built as a private home by a rich merchant's widow in the 1770s, when Trondheim began to regain its prosperity. The exterior walls were notched together, log-cabin style, and then sheathed with wooden exterior panels. The unpretentious furnishings represent an amalgam of design styles.

Munkegate 23. © **73-84-28-80**. Admission 60NOK ($9.25/£4.80) adults, 30NOK ($4.60/£2.40) children, 100NOK ($15/£8) family. Guided tours every hour on the hour. June 1–Aug 20 Mon–Sat 10am–5pm; Sun noon–5pm. Closed Aug 21 to late June. Bus: 3, 4, 5, 46, or 52.

Sverresborg Trøndelag Folk Museum *** *Kids* This is the best folkloric museum in Norway, and it's filled with farmhouses, cottages, churches, and town buildings, representing everyday life from the region's past 3 centuries. Kids often find this attraction a kind of "Trondheim Disneyworld," but we find it both educational and fun. Standing 5km (3 miles) west of the center, the complex is composed of 60 historic, laboriously dismantled and reassembled buildings, all made from wood and stone, including the first all-brick building in Trondheim (ca. 1780). Among the compound's most intriguing buildings are the 200-year-old barns, many with sod roofs, painted red, and built of weathered natural wood. There's a cafe on the premises, but if you want a good meal, we recommend that you head next door to the celebrated restaurant **Versthuset Tavern** (see "Where to Dine," below), which serves traditional Norwegian dishes. The proudest possession here is Norway's northernmost stave church.

On the grounds of the folk museum, within an antique building hauled in from another part of the province, is a separate museum, the **Sverresborg Ski Museum.** Entrance to the ski museum is included in the price of admission to the Folk Museum, and hours are the same. Tracing the history of skiing in Norway, it contains skis from the 1600s to today, some carved in patterns inspired by the Vikings, and others with fur or sealskin cladding, which prevented them from sliding backwards during cross-country skiing. The museum is also surrounded by a nature park with animals.

Sverresborg Allé. © **73-89-01-00.** Admission 80NOK ($12/£6.40) adults, 30NOK ($4.60/£2.40) children, 195NOK ($30/£16) family ticket, free for children under 5. June–Aug daily 11am–6pm; off season Mon–Fri 11am–3pm, Sat–Sun noon–4pm. Bus: 8.

ORGANIZED TOURS

At the Tourist Office (p. 349), you can purchase tickets for guided tours of the city, lasting 2 hours and taking in the highlights. Departure is from Torvet or Market Square daily at 11am between May 22 and August 27. Adults pay 185NOK ($28/£15), while children under 16 enter free if they're accompanied by an adult.

The tourist office publicizes a 1½-hour sea tour, going along the canal harbor, up the River Nidelven, and out to the fjord. From June 23 to August 18, it leaves Tuesday to Sunday at 2pm, costing 140NOK ($22/£11) for adults and 45NOK ($6.95/£3.60) for ages 3 to 14. From July 3 to August 4, there is an additional departure at 4pm, and from August 21 to September 8, there are tours on Wednesday, Friday, and Sunday at 2pm.

The tourist office also recommends an evening boat tour, lasting 1½ hours, departing every night between June 30 and August 4 at 6pm from the Ravnkloa market. The cost is 140NOK ($22/£11) for adults and 55NOK ($8.45/£4.40) for children ages 3 to 14. Buy your tickets for this and the sea tour (see above) directly on the boat.

EXPLORING NEARBY ISLANDS

You can reach the islands of **Hitra (Ansnes)** and **Frøya (Sistranda)** by fast steamer from Trondheim Monday through Saturday. For more information, ask at the tourist information office in Trondheim.

Hitra is one of Norway's largest islands, with an array of forests, wooded hills, well-stocked lakes, weathered rocks, and small fjords. The island is also known for its large herds of red deer. Other attractions include the **Dolm Church** and **Dolmen town,** a miniature community designed and built by a Dolmoy crofter and fisherman. After you reach Hitra, you might want to visit neighboring Frøya by ferry.

WHERE TO STAY

Many hotels offer special summer prices from mid-June to the end of August. The rest of the year, hotels offer weekend discounts if you stay 2 nights.

Expensive

Clarion Collection Hotel Grand Olav 🏨🏨   This six-story hotel was radically renovated in 2006 and 2007 to a style that the hotel refers to as "modernized rococo." The hotel is adjacent to a building complex that includes elegant boutiques and Trondheim's largest concert hall. The midsize-to-spacious bedrooms are tastefully and comfortably furnished with a certain flair, and the bathrooms are ample in size, with tub/shower combinations and state-of-the-art plumbing.

Kjøpmannsgata 48, N-7010 Trondheim. © **73-80-80-80.** Fax 73-80-80-81. www.choicehotels.no. 106 units. Mon–Thurs 1,645NOK–1,945NOK ($253–$300/£132–£166) double; Fri–Sun 1,075NOK–1,245NOK ($166–$192/£86–£100) double. 1,500NOK–6,000NOK ($231–$924/£120–£128) suite all week long. Rates include breakfast and a light evening meal. AE, DC, MC, V. Parking 147NOK ($23/£12). Bus: 6 or 7. **Amenities:** Small lobby bar; laundry service/dry cleaning; nonsmoking rooms; rooms for those w/limited mobility. *In room:* A/C, TV, dataport, minibar, coffeemaker, hair dryer.

Radisson SAS Royal Garden Hotel ★★★
This glittering extravaganza on the see-and-be-seen circuit is Trondheim's largest and best hotel. It lacks the tradition of the Britannia, but clearly outdistances the "Clarion Sisters" in pure luxury and amenities. Originally built in 1984 to replace a row of waterfront warehouses that had burned down in a fire, it rises on stilts—a glowing, glass-sided jewel-box—abruptly above the Nid River, so close to the water that you can catch salmon from your balcony if you're so inclined. Inside is an intriguing array of angled glass skylights, stone floors, soaring atriums, and plants. The hotel even housed members of the royal family during the 2002 wedding of Norway's Princess Martha-Louise. Rooms are comfortable and tastefully contemporary, outfitted in earth tones, and about half have tub/shower combinations. The most elegant of the hotel's restaurants is the Prins Olavs Grill, named after a ship once owned by the British royal family (original ornaments from the vessel have been used to decorate the dining room). The menu consists of high-quality continental dishes using market-fresh ingredients.

Kjøpmannsgata 73, N-7010 Trondheim. © **73 80 30 00.** Fax 73-00-30-50. www.radissonsas.com. 298 units. Mon–Thurs 1,545NOK–1,900NOK ($238–$293/£124–£152) double; Fri–Sun 1,195NOK ($184/£96) double; 2,500NOK–5,000NOK ($385 $770/£200–£400) suite for 1 week. AE, DC, MC, V. Bus: 1 or 4. **Amenities:** 2 restaurants; bar; indoor pool; Jacuzzi; health club and exercise center; sauna; boutiques; limited room service; laundry service/dry cleaning; solarium. *In room:* TV, dataport, minibar, hair dryer, safe.

Moderate
Britannia Hotel ★★
While the Grand Olav offers dramatic decor and the Royal Garden modern facilities, the Britannia has old-world tradition. This grande dame of Trondheim hotels was built in 1897, and subsequent renovations have kept the place up to high standards. However, there were some badly conceived modernizations made in the 1960s that the hotel could have done without.

The white-stucco structure is graced with a majestic slate-covered dome and a tower evocative of the grand Victorian monuments of England. The Britannia is conservative, stable, and dependable, but lacks a cutting-edge sense of glamour. The renovated guest rooms have wood floors, and the most tranquil (but smallest) "economy" units front the courtyard. In contrast, some of the double rooms are large enough to accommodate two additional guests, while another cluster of units is specifically designed for female guests with such extras as a dressing gown. Half of the 11 suites are duplexes, but all are regal and come in various sizes and decor. A unique feature that sets the Britannia apart from its competitors is a series of "Artists' Rooms," including the boas and gilt-plated "ice" in the Flettfrid Andresen Room (no. 724). Most accommodations are medium-size with tiled bathrooms with tub/shower combinations.

Dronningens Gate 5, N-7001 Trondheim. © **73-80-08-00.** Fax 73-80-08-01. www.britannia.no. 247 units. Mon–Thurs 1,832NOK–2,182NOK ($282–$336/£147–£175) double; Fri–Sun 1,179NOK–1,529NOK ($182–$235/£94–£122) double; year-round 3,028NOK–6,260NOK ($466–$964/£242–£501) suite. Rates include breakfast. AE, DC, MC, V. Parking 200NOK ($31/£16). Bus: 3, 4, 5, or 7. **Amenities:** 3 restaurants; 4 bars; fitness center; sauna; limited room service; babysitting; laundry service/dry cleaning; nonsmoking rooms; rooms for those w/limited mobility. *In room:* TV, minibar, hair dryer.

Scandic Residence   On the market square opposite the Royal Palace, the Hotel Residence, built in 1915 in Jugendstil (Art Nouveau) style, outranks fellow chain member, the Scandic Prinsen (not reviewed here). Accommodations are tastefully decorated, and the units in front open onto the marketplace. Depending on how luxurious you want to live, rooms are "standard" or "superior." The generously sized guest rooms have pale colors, triple-glazed windows, and sturdy, comfortable, tasteful furniture, with big marble bathrooms that offer great shelf space, tub/shower combinations, and, in some cases, bidets.

Munkegate 26, N-7011 Trondheim. ℭ 21-61-47-00. Fax 21-61-47-11. www.scandic-hotel.com/residence. 66 units. Sun–Thurs 952NOK–1,700NOK ($147–$262/£76–£136) double; Fri–Sat 952NOK ($147/£76) double. Rates include breakfast. Children stay free in parent's room. AE, DC, MC, V. Parking 60NOK ($9.25/£4.80). Bus: 3, 4, 5, or 6. **Amenities:** Restaurant; bar; laundry service/dry cleaning; nonsmoking rooms; rooms for those w/limited mobility. *In room:* TV, dataport (in some), minibar, hair dryer, iron, trouser press.

Inexpensive

Thon Hotel Gildevangen ✦ *Value*   One of Trondheim's most architecturally distinctive hotels, the Gildevangen sits behind a dramatic-looking facade of massive, carefully chiseled stone blocks. Originally built in 1910 as an office building and transformed into a hotel in 1930, it suffered water damage during a fire in 2005 and spent much of 2006 and early 2007 renovating its accommodations. The result is a series of clean, upgraded, uncomplicated, and tranquil bedrooms, each of which has a somewhat idiosyncratic floor plan that's a bit different from that of its neighbors. Only breakfast is served here, but from Monday to Thursday a light evening meal is included in the overnight price. Most of the bedrooms have tiled bathrooms with showers and in some rare instances a tub/shower combination. Each room has big windows, generous dimensions, and high ceilings.

Søndregate 22B, N-7010 Trondheim. ℭ 73-87-01-30. Fax 73-52-38-98. www.thonhotels.no. 110 units. Mon–Thurs 1,345NOK ($207/£108) double; Fri–Sun 940NOK ($145/£75) double. AE, DC, MC, V. Bus: 46. **Amenities:** Bar; laundry service/dry cleaning; nonsmoking rooms. *In room:* TV, dataport, minibar, hair dryer.

Thon Hotel Trondheim   This six-story hotel near the market square defines itself as a deliberately simple, relatively inexpensive bed-and-breakfast with medium-size guest rooms and not a lot of supplemental flair and frills. Outfitted with color schemes of "sun-kissed" yellow, many of the rooms contain an extra foldaway bed. The beds are comfortable, and the bathrooms, though small, are equipped with tub/shower combinations. Constructed in 1913, the hotel was renovated and expanded in 1990, with additional small-scale renovations conducted ever since. At press time this hotel contained 131 units, but look for a reduction in this number sometime late in 2007 and early 2008, when the hotel will reduce in size by around 10%.

Kongens Gate 15, N-7013 Trondheim. ℭ 73-50-50-50. Fax 73-51-60-58. www.thonhotels.no. 131 units. 795NOK ($122/£64) double. AE, DC, MC, V. Parking 115NOK ($18/£9.20). Bus from airport stops here. **Amenities:** Breakfast room; self-service laundry; nonsmoking rooms; rooms for those w/limited mobility. *In room:* TV, dataport, minibar, hair dryer.

WHERE TO DINE

Be sure to try the local specialty *vafler medøst* (**waffle and cheese**), sold at most cafeterias and restaurants. Most restaurants will automatically add around a 15% service charge to your bill. If you like the service, it's customary to leave some small change as well.

Expensive

Chablis Brasserie & Bar ✦ FRENCH   This is a casual and informal dining spot serving excellent food. A polished choice, this brasserie/restaurant has deliberately bare tabletops and an artfully rustic brown and white decor. This, coupled with elaborate place settings and lots of sparkling crystal, creates one of the most appealing dining venues in the neighborhood. In summer many diners prefer an outside table. The best dishes include grilled scallops with a mango and lime salad, pan-fried redfish with a fennel compote and puree of root vegetables, and pan-fried breast of duck with asparagus and port wine sauce, and halibut with a chile-and-carrot purée with a lime butter sauce. Always check to see what the catch of the day is.

Øvre Bakklandet 66. ✆ 73-87-42-50. Reservations required. Main courses 235NOK–280NOK ($36–$43/£19–£22); fixed-price 3-course menu 450NOK ($69/£36). AE, DC, MC, V. Daily 5–11pm. Bus: 4, 5, 7, or 52.

Jonathan's ✦ NORWEGIAN/FRENCH   This restaurant, though fine in every way, is far less impressive than the hotel's more elegant Palm Garden. But it's far more affordable, which is why we recommend it. The beautifully prepared food relies on high-quality ingredients. Start with the classic smoked salmon or what is known as "Trondheim caviar" (really carp roe). Main dishes include grilled salmon garnished with shellfish and accompanied by fresh vegetables, veal schnitzel, and grilled steak.

In the Britannia Hotel, Dronningens Gate 5. ✆ 73-80-08-00. Reservations required. Main courses 215NOK–250NOK ($33–$39/£17–£20). AE, DC, MC, V. Daily 5–11pm. Bus: 5, 6, 7, or 9.

Moderate

Havfruen (Mermaid) ✦✦ SEAFOOD   Set amid a cluster of some of the oldest warehouses in town, along the Nidelven River, this is the best fish restaurant in Trondheim— and the most atmospheric. Built around 1800 on the site of a much older warehouse, it's studded with old beams, trusses, and lots of authentic antique charm. Meals are prepared in the open kitchen and served by a staff with impeccable manners and technique. The staff seems to enjoy evaluating and offering advice about the daily fish offerings, some of which are harvested from a large lobster tank. The menu changes seasonally and is based on local fish migration patterns in the frigid waters surrounding Trondheim. You might begin with the creamy fish chowder, the town's best, although other contenders include lobster bisque with ravioli stuffed with lobster and fresh spinach, or poached filets of Arctic char served with an apple-cider vinaigrette. For a main course, you are likely to be won over by the oven-baked halibut with Dauphine potatoes (dipped in egg and breadcrumbs before frying) and a confit of shellfish, or perhaps the pan-fried Norwegian redfish with a tantalizing orange sauce.

Kjøpmannsgata 7. ✆ 73-87-40-70. Reservations required. Main courses 250NOK–290NOK ($39–$45/£20–£23). Set-price menus 455NOK–765NOK ($70–$118/£36–£61). AE, DC, MC, V. Mon–Sat 6pm–midnight. Closed Dec 23–Jan 7. Bus: 5, 6, 7, or 9.

Restaurant Egon AMERICAN   This is one of the friendliest joints in Trondheim and a good place to hang out if you're young. Nothing about this place even pretends to be gourmet or even upscale. It's set in the center of town in an early-20th-century stone building that was originally built as a bank. Within a labyrinth of dark, woodsy-looking pub areas and dining rooms, the restaurant serves the Norwegian equivalent of American-style diner food. There's a beery kind of sudsiness to the place, an appropriate foil for the pizzas that emerge from the open-to-view brick-lined ovens. In summer the venue spills out onto the terrace.

Thomas Angellsgate 8 (entrance on Søndregate). ℂ 73-51-79-75. Pizzas, burgers, salads, and platters 90NOK–210NOK ($14–$32/£7.20–£17). AE, DC, MC, V. Mon–Sat 11am–midnight; Sun noon–11pm Bus: 1 or 4.

Inexpensive

Versthuset Tavern ☆ *Finds* NORWEGIAN   No restaurant in town offers more authentic Norwegian cuisine than this historic eatery, 4.8km (3 miles) south of Trondheim's commercial center and immediately adjacent to the Trøndelag Folk Museum. Built as a private merchant's house in 1739 and later transformed into a clapboard-sided tavern, it's one of the few wooden buildings of its age in this area. Cramped and cozy, it's the town's most vivid reminder of the past, with wide-plank flooring and antique accessories. The most desirable and oft-requested table is directly in front of a fireplace in a side room, and as such it's usually reserved in advance. There's an emphasis on 18th- and 19th-century recipes. Try the *blandet spekemat* served with *flatbrød;* it consists of thinly sliced smoked ham, diced meat, slices of salami, smoked mutton, and garnishes of lettuce and tomato. For a real taste of Norway, opt for the creamy fish soup, the Norwegian-style meatballs (the size of Ping-Pong balls), the pancakes and platters of herring, reindeer steak with red wine sauce, fish cakes, or filets of trout with sesame seed crusts and sour cream sauce.

Sverresborg Allé, at Trøndelag Folk Museum. ℂ 73-87-80-70. Reservations recommended. Main courses 72NOK–265NOK ($11–$41/£5.75–£21). AE, DC, MC, V. Mon–Fri 4–10pm; Sat 2–10pm; Sun 2–9pm. Bus: 8.

TRONDHEIM AFTER DARK

If you're here in late July or early August, at the time of the week-long **St. Olaf Festival,** Dronningensgt 1B (ℂ 73-84-14-50), you can enjoy organ concerts, outdoor concerts, and even opera at the Nidaros Cathedral. The internationally acclaimed **Trondheim Symphony Orchestra** ☆☆☆, Olavskvartalet, Kjøpmannsgata 46 (ℂ 73-99-40-50), presents weekly concerts with some of Europe's most outstanding conductors and soloists. Depending on the event and the day of the week, tickets cost from 90NOK to 400NOK ($14–$62/£7.20–£32).

Bar 3B   Sweaty, shadowy, and candlelit, this is the most extreme of the town's counterculture bars, loaded with clients in their 20s, 30s, and 40s who sometimes proclaim proudly how much they resist hanging out at more mainstream "bourgeois" bars. Within an environment sheathed in colors of blue and black and the occasional mirror, expect a clientele of bikers, tattoo enthusiasts, students, and the routinely disgruntled. Two bars lie on two different floors of this place, and if you manage to strike up some dialogues (and have a drink or two), you might actually have a lot of fun. It's open Monday to Saturday from 2pm to 2:30 or 3:30am, depending on business, and Sunday from 8pm to 2:30am. Brattørgate 3B. ℂ 73-51-15-50.

Den Gode Nabo ("The Good Neighbor") Pub ☆   This is our favorite pub in Trondheim, occupying the cellar of a 250-year-old warehouse. You enter a low-ceilinged labyrinth of rough-hewn timbers and planking, eventually choosing a seat from any of dozens of slightly claustrophobic banquettes, being careful not to hit your head on the timber-built trusses. Before you get too comfortable, however, we advise that you continue walking as deep into the innards of this place as possible to get to the woodsy-looking bar area, where up to 16 kinds of beer on tap cost from 42NOK to 52NOK ($6.45–$8/£3.40–£4.15) per half-liter. During clement weather, the seating options expand outside onto a wooden platform floating on pontoons in the swift-flowing river

Nid. The "pub food" will always include the establishment's best-known dish, the "Good Neighbor fish plate." Priced at 125NOK ($19/£10), it contains heaping portions of vegetables, potatoes, and (usually grilled) fish of the day, accompanied with whatever sauce the chef has conjured up at the moment. You can be a good neighbor at this place every day between 4pm and 1am. Øvre Bakklandet 66. ✆ 40-61-88-09.

FROM TRONDHEIM TO BODØ

North of Mo i Rana (80km/50 miles) toward the Arctic Circle, you'll come to the **Polarsirkelsenteret,** N-8242 Polarsirkelen (✆ 75-12-96-96), on E-6. The center offers a multiscreen show depicting the highlights of Norway, as also houses a cafeteria and gift shop. Many people send cards and letters from here with a special postmark from the Arctic Circle. It's open in May and June daily from 9am to 6pm; July to September daily 8am to 10pm; admission is 60NOK ($9.25/£4.80).

Continue north to Fauske, and then follow Route 80 west along the Skjerstadfjord. Depending on weather conditions, you should reach Bodø in under an hour.

BODØ ✿

750km (466 miles) N of Trondheim, 1,431km (889 miles) N of Bergen, 1,306km (811 miles) N of Oslo

While the city of Bodø is no attraction in itself, its surrounding natural beauty makes it a great place to spend a day or two. This seaport, the terminus of the Nordland railway, lies just north of the Arctic Circle. Visitors come to this capital of Nordland for a glimpse of the midnight sun, which shines from June 1 to July 13. But don't expect a clear view of it. What those tourist brochures don't tell you is that many nights are either rainy or hazy, cutting down considerably on your view. From December 19 to January 9, Bodø gets no sunlight at all.

Bodø is Nordland's largest city, with some 40,000 inhabitants living at the northern entrance to Salt Fjord. Although burned to the ground by the retreating Nazis at the end of World War II, the city dates back to 1816, when it was founded by merchants from Trondheim seeking a northern trading post. In time it became one of the leading fishing centers of Norway, specializing in the drying of cod, and it has also become known for its ship repair yards.

Bodø faces an archipelago rich in bird life, and no other town in the world boasts such a large concentration of sea eagles. From Bodø you can take excursions in many directions to glaciers and bird islands; the most attractive are the Lofoten Islands (p. 362).

ESSENTIALS

GETTING THERE   If you're not driving or traveling by coastal steamer, you can reach Bodø from major cities throughout Norway, usually with connections through either Trondheim or Oslo, on **SAS** (✆ 75-54-48-00; www.scandinavian.net). The airport lies just more than a kilometer (1½ miles) southwest of the city center and is accessed by a bus (it's marked CENTRUMS BUSSEN) that departs at 20-minute intervals every Monday to Friday for 70NOK ($11/£5.60) each way. Passengers arriving on a Saturday or Sunday hire one of the many taxis waiting at the arrivals gate. Bodø is at the end of the Nordland rail line.

Two **trains** a day leave Trondheim for Bodø. The trip takes 10 hours, 20 minutes. Visit www.nsb.no for information.

For **bus** information, contact **Saltens Bilruter** in Bodø (✆ 75-54-80-20). Fauske is a transportation hub along the E-6 highway to the north and Route 80 west to Bodø. From Fauske there are two buses a day to Bodø. The trip takes an hour and 10 minutes. If you take the train from Stockholm to Narvik (north of Bodø), you can make bus connections to Fauske and Bodø, a total trip of 5 hours. Note that if you're taking public transportation, you are likely to pass through Fauske on your way to and from other parts of Norway's far north.

Motorists can continue north from Mo i Rana, our last stopover, until they come to the junction with Route 80 heading west to Bodø.

VISITOR INFORMATION   The **tourist office,** Destination Bodø, Sjøgaten 3 (℃ 75-54-80-00; www.visitbodo.com), is in the town center. It's open January 2 to May 28 and August 28 to December 22, Monday to Friday 9am to 4pm and Saturday 10am to 2pm; May 29 to August 27 Monday to Friday 9am to 8pm, Saturday 10am to 6pm, and Sunday noon to 8pm. The town is relatively flat, and bikes can be rented for 50NOK ($7.70/£4) for 3 hours and 150NOK ($23/£12) for 24 hours.

SEEING THE SIGHTS

Bodin Kirke   Sitting pretty in clover fields, this intriguing onion-domed church can be visited along with a trip to the Norwegian Aviation Museum, which is about 1km (½ mile) northwest of the church. Dating from 1240, the church has seen many changes over the years, including the addition of many 17th- and 18th-century baroque adornments.

Gamle Riksvei 68. ℃ 75-56-54-20. Free admission. June–Aug Mon–Fri 10am–2pm. Closed Sept–May. Bus: 23 from the station.

Bodø Domkirke   As Norwegian cathedrals go, the Bodø Dom ranks low on the totem pole. But when the Nazis bombed their previous church in 1940, locals were eager to open a major place of worship even if they could find no Michelangelo—or the money—to build it. What they came up with is fairly respectable, nothing more. Completed in 1956, this is the most notable building constructed since the German bombers flew over. It features tufted rugs depicting ecclesiastical themes, wall hangings, and a stained-glass window that captures the northern lights. A memorial outside honors those killed in the war. There's also an outstanding spire that stands separate from the main building.

Torv Gate 12. ℃ 75-51-95-30. Free admission. June–Aug daily 9:30am–11:30pm. Closed Sept–May.

Nordlandmuseet (Nordland Museum)   The main building of this museum, in the town center, is one of the oldest structures in Bodø. Here you'll find, among other exhibits, artifacts recalling the saga of local fishermen and artifacts from the Sami culture. There's also a "dry" aquarium, with stuffed fish, along with silver treasure dating from the Viking era. An open-air part of this museum contains more than a dozen historical buildings moved to the site, plus a collection of boats. Part of the exhibit includes *Anna Karoline of Hopen,* the only surviving Nordland cargo vessel.

Prinsengate 116. ℃ 75-52-16-40. Admission 35NOK ($5.40/£2.80) adults; students/children 12 and under free. June 19–Aug 20 Mon–Wed and Fri 9am–4pm, Thurs 9am–8pm, Sat–Sun 11am–4pm; rest of year Mon–Fri 9am–3pm.

Norsk Luftfartsmuseum (Norwegian Aviation Museum) *Kids*   In 1960, the infamous U-2 spy plane made international headlines when it was shot down over the Soviet Union, creating a major diplomatic incident in that Cold War era of "brinkmanship." This museum, shaped like an airplane propeller, takes you on an exciting "flight" of Norway's civil and military aviation history. You're allowed to explore large and small aircraft such as the Spitfire and JU52. Hands-on demonstrations reveal the dynamics of flight. In addition to the exhibition of aircrafts, the museum shows a collection of photographs about the largest predators in the Nordic countries, including lynx, bears, wolves, wolverines, and even humans. The museum was built on the site of a German World War II airfield.

2km (1¼ miles) north of town. Olav V gata. ℂ **75-50-78-50.** Admission 75NOK ($12/£6) adults, 50NOK ($7.70/£4) children under 16. June–Aug Sun–Fri 10am–7pm, Sat 10am–5pm; Sept–May Mon–Fri 10am–4pm, Sat–Sun 11am–5pm. Bus: 23 or marked CITY NORD.

ACTIVE SPORTS

If you'd like to go horseback riding under the midnight sun, **Bodø Hestecenter,** Soloya Gård (ℂ **75-51-41-48**), about 14km (9 miles) southwest of Bodø, rents horses. Buses go there mornings and evenings Monday to Friday, and mornings on Saturday. For more information, ask at the Bodø Tourist Office (see "Visitor Information," above). The cost is 100NOK ($15/£8) for a 45-minute ride.

At the visitor center, you can pick up maps detailing the best hiking in the area. The best area and our favorite is **Bodømarka (Bodø forest),** with its 35km (22 miles) of marked hiking and cross-country skiing trails. For detailed touring, including overnight stays in the forest, contact **Bodø og Omegn Turist-forening (Bodø Mountain Touring Association;** ℂ **75-52-14-13**), which operates a dozen cabins in the forest.

The most up-to-date and well-recommended indoor swimming pool in the region is the **Mørkved Badet** (ℂ **75-55-08-90**), in the hamlet of Mørkved, about 4km (2½ miles) north of Bodø's center. If you want to use it, know that it gives priority to local swim teams and school groups, so public hours are limited to Wednesday from 5 to 10pm, Friday 5 to 9pm, Saturday 9am to 3pm, and Sunday 9am to 4pm. Admission costs 45NOK ($6.95/£3.60) for adults, 25NOK ($3.85/£2) for persons under 18.

A popular man-made attraction, **Saltstraumen Opplevelsesenter,** or adventure center, lies at Saltstraumen, Route 17 (ℂ **75-56-06-55**), and is fun for the whole family. The center gives an in-depth preview through exhibits and artifacts tracing the history of the area and its people from the Ice Age to the coming of the Vikings. An on-site aquarium includes a pond for seals and fish found in regional waters. Admission is 65NOK ($10/£5.20). From May to mid-June it's open daily from 11am to 6pm; from mid-June to late June and from mid-August to late August, it's open daily from 10am to 7pm; from July to mid-August, it's open daily 9am to 8pm; and in September it's open Saturday and Sunday 11am to 6pm.

EXPLORING A SPECTACULAR LANDSCAPE

THE MAELSTROM   From Bodø, you can take a bus to the mighty maelstrom, the **Saltstraumen Eddy** ⍟, 33km (20 miles) south of the city. The variation between high- and low-tide levels pushes immense volumes of water through narrow fjords, creating huge whirlpools known as "kettles." When the eddies and the surrounding land vibrate, they produce an odd yelling sound. Saltstraumen is nearly 3.3km (2 miles) long and only about 167m (500 ft.) wide, with billions of gallons of water pressing through at speeds of about 10 knots. Buses from Bodø run five times a day Monday to Saturday, twice on Sunday. The cost is 65NOK ($10/£5.20) for adults round-trip, half-price for children under 12. A round-trip taxi excursion costs 525NOK ($81/£42) for two passengers.

VISITING A GLACIER   One of Norway's major tourist attractions, **Svartisen Glacier** ⍟⍟⍟, can easily be visited from Bodø. About 161km (100 miles) south of Bodø, the glacier can be reached by car, although a boat crossing over the Svartisenfjord is more exciting. Tours to the glacier on the Helgeland Express, a combination bus-and-ferry excursion, are offered from Bodø several times in the summer (usually every second Sat July–Aug). The cost is 400NOK ($62/£32) for adults, 200NOK ($31/£16) for children under 16. The tours leave Bodø at 1pm and return around 8pm on the same day. You can go ashore to examine the Engaglacier and see the nearby visitor center (© 75-75-00-11). The local tourist office or the local tour operator **Nordtrafikk** (© 75-72-12-00) can provide more information and make reservations. Depending on ice conditions, the visitor center may be able to arrange boat transportation across a narrow and icy channel for a better view.

WHERE TO STAY

The **Bodø Tourist Office** (see "Visitor Information," above) can help you book a room in a hotel. It also maintains a list of local B&Bs and will book you a room for a fee of 18NOK to 27NOK ($2.75–$4.15/£1.45–£2.15).

Many locals within this maritime community, as well as the staff at the Bodø tourist office, will be alert to the schedule of high and low tides on the day of your arrival. The phenomenon occurs four times within any 24-hour period, twice for incoming tides, twice for outgoing tides, with a brief interlude between high and low tides when the waters are almost eerily still.

Expensive
Radisson SAS Royal Hotel ★★   The Royal is by far the finest and most expensive hotel in the area, lying at the waterfront and opening onto panoramic views. A complete renovation of the exterior, bedrooms, and public rooms last occurred in 2000, but there have been minor upgrades annually ever since so that the hotel still looks fresh. The good-size guest rooms are furnished in sleek contemporary style and decorated in a number of motifs, including Japanese, Nordic, Chinese, and British. Rooms have medium-size bathrooms equipped with tub/shower combinations. The Radisson SAS offers some of the best drinking and dining facilities in Bodø, including the Sjøsiden Restaurant, which not only opens onto spectacular views but serves first-rate Norwegian and international cuisine. Live music and dancing are offered every Saturday night in the Moloen Bar. But, the greatest place for a drink is the Top 13 Rooftop Bar.

Storgata 2, N-8000 Bodø. © 800/333-3333 in the U.S., or 75-51-90-00. Fax 75-51-90-02. 190 units. June–Aug 1,095NOK ($169/£88) double, 1,500NOK ($231/£120) suite; Sept–May 1,250NOK ($193/£100) double, 2,250NOK ($347/£180) suite. Rates include breakfast. AE, DC, MC, V. Free parking. **Amenities:** 2 restaurants; 2 bars; lounge; fitness center; sauna; limited room service; babysitting; laundry service/dry cleaning; nonsmoking rooms; rooms for those w/limited mobility. *In room:* TV, dataport, minibar, hair dryer, trouser press, Wi-Fi.

Rica Hotel ★   The Rica is no match for the Radisson SAS, but it's still one of Bodø's best hotels, offering comfort and service with a view of Vestfjorden. Rooms are moderate in size, comfortable, well maintained, and outfitted with large beds, small bathrooms with tub/shower combinations, and large writing desks in most of the units. The hotel has two popular restaurants (see "Where to Dine," below).

Sjøgata 23, N-8001 Bodø. © 75-54-70-00. Fax 75-54-70-55. www.rica.no. 113 units. Mid-June to Aug 17 925NOK ($142/£74) double; Aug 18 to mid-June 1,500NOK ($231/£120) double; year-round 2,000NOK–2,500NOK ($308–$385/£160–£200) suite. Rates include breakfast. AE, DC, MC, V. Parking 75NOK ($12/£6). **Amenities:** 2 restaurants; bar; fitness center; sauna; limited room service; laundry service/dry cleaning; nonsmoking rooms; rooms for those w/limited mobility. *In room:* TV, dataport, minibar, hair dryer.

Moderate
Bodø Hotell *Value*   Opened in 1987, this family-run hotel, located in the town center about 2½ blocks from the harbor, is known for its good value. The bedrooms are modern, and although the bathrooms are small, they are well maintained and come

equipped with shower units. The rooms are a bit small, but there has been an attempt made to give them a homelike feeling of intimacy. Oriental carpeting, swag draperies, writing desks, and art on the walls add to the welcoming ambience.

Professor Schyttesgate 5, N-8001 Bodø. ℂ **75-54-77-00.** Fax 75-52-57-78. www.bodohotell.no. 31 units. Fri–Sat and June 20–Aug 15 daily 680NOK ($105/£54) double; Sun–Thurs 850NOK ($131/£68) double; year-round 750NOK–1,000NOK ($116–$154/£60–£80) suite. Rates include breakfast. AE, DC, MC, V. Free parking. Closed Dec 22–Jan 3. **Amenities:** Lunch restaurant; bar; lounge; sauna; laundry service/dry cleaning; nonsmoking rooms; rooms for those w/limited mobility. *In room:* TV, hair dryer, dataport, Wi-Fi.

Thon Hotel Nordlys This modern hotel rises six floors above Bodø's harbor. Inside there is a collection of valuable contemporary art—some of which is for sale. The guest rooms are contemporary with splashes of yellow, wood floors, and tiled bathrooms with tub/shower combinations. Some of the rooms were specifically tailored to the "female business traveler," with women's magazines and quality beauty products. Groups like this hotel, but we find that the staff is genuinely kind to single travelers as well. Egon, the hotel's restaurant, specializes in robust American and Norwegian fare.

Moloveien 14, N8001 Bodø. ℂ **75-53-19-00.** Fax 75-53-19-99. 152 units. Mon–Thurs 880NOK–1,450NOK ($136–$223/£70–£116) double; Fri–Sun 880NOK ($136/£70) double; 1,600NOK (US$246/£128) junior suite. AE, DC, MC, V. **Amenities:** Restaurant; laundry service/dry cleaning; rooms for those w/limited mobility; nonsmoking rooms. *In room:* TV, minibar, Wi-Fi.

Inexpensive

Norrøna A bit austere, the Norrøna, known as the cheapest lodging in the town center, is run by the nearby Radisson SAS Royal Hotel, which uses it primarily as a bed-and-breakfast. Its prime location in the center of Bodø is one of its chief advantages. The simply furnished guest rooms, though small and plain, are comfortable. Each unit contains a well-kept bathroom with a shower or tub/shower combination. Guests enjoy the same privileges as patrons of the more expensive Radisson SAS Royal Hotel (see above). The hotel operates a British-style pub called Piccadilly.

Storgata 4-B, N-8039 Bodø. ℂ **75-51-90-60.** Fax 75-52-90-61. 87 units. 600NOK–750NOK ($92–$116/£48–£60) double. Rates include breakfast. AE, DC, MC, V. Parking at Radisson and gym. **Amenities:** Bar; lounge; sauna; nonsmoking rooms. *In room:* TV, dataport.

WHERE TO DINE

China Garden CANTONESE Although it doesn't rank with Oslo's Chinese restaurants, this eatery is a welcome change of pace this far north. The cooks really go for that sweet-and-sour flavor with dishes such as prawns or pork laced with garlic and served with black beans., but they also prepare many other standard dishes competently.

Storgata 60. ℂ **75-52-71-25.** Reservations recommended. Main courses 145NOK ($22/£12). AE, MC, V. Sun and Tues–Sat 2–11pm.

Rica Hotel Restaurants NORWEGIAN/INTERNATIONAL Although the Rica is best known for its well-maintained accommodations, it also runs two restaurants (the Spisestuen and Blix) that serve some of the best food in town. You don't get palate-tantalizing excitement here, but the solid, reliable fare uses fresh ingredients whenever available. Usually the Spisestuen serves lunch and the Blix covers dinner, but the arrangement changes depending on the number of bus tours and cruise ships expected. Wherever the meal is served, you're likely to be joined by local residents. Main courses include lasagna, steak, filet of reindeer, fish soup, and fresh local fish. The catch of the day is generally your best bet.

In the Rica Hotel, Sjøgata 23. © **75-54-70-00.** Lunch main courses 135NOK–230NOK ($21–$35/£11–£18); luncheon buffet 200NOK ($31/£16); dinner main courses 220NOK–230NOK ($34–$35/£18–£19). AE, DC, MC, V. Spisestuen daily 11:30am–2pm. Blix Mon–Sat 3–11pm and Sun 2–9pm.

Svendgård NORWEGIAN/INTERNATIONAL Although this restaurant is managed and staffed by employees from Bodø's best-established hotel, the Radisson SAS (see above), it occupies a redbrick building that lies a short walk away from the hotel itself. Inside, within a cream-colored environment that's made cozier by a blazing open fireplace, you'll find a well-trained staff and a tempting combination of Norwegian and international cuisine. You might begin with a carpaccio of venison, grilled scallops served with terrine of oxtail, or fried scampi with a sweet-and-sour sauce. Main courses focus on some of the freshest fish in Bodø, including codfish served with shredded beetroot, and poached anglerfish in a peanut-based satay sauce. End with either the crème brûlée or a parfait made from fresh Arctic berries.

Dronningensgate 26. © **75-52-52-50.** Reservations recommended. Main courses 220NOK–250NOK ($34–$39/ £18–£20). AE, DC, MC, V. Daily 3–11pm.

LOFOTEN ISLANDS ★★★

280km (174 miles) N of Bodø, 1,426km (886 miles) NE of Bergen, 1,250km (777 miles) N of Oslo

Forget the bleak North Cape. For us, this is the most enchanting part of North Norway—and reason enough to come to this bleak wilderness in the first place. Spend only a day in Bodø, but stay here for as long as you can.

The island kingdom of Lofoten, one of the most beautiful regions of Norway, lies 197km (123 miles) north of the Arctic Circle. Its population of 35,000 spreads over large and small islands. Many visitors come just to fish, but the area also offers abundant bird life and flora. The midnight sun shines from May 25 to July 7.

The Lofoten Islands stretch from Vågan in the east to Røst and Skomvaer in the southwest. The steep Lofoten mountain peaks—often called the Lofotwall—shelter farmland and deep fjords from the elements.

The major islands are **Austvågøy, Gimsøy, Vestvågøy, Flakstadøy, Moskenesøy, Vaerøy,** and **Røst.** The southernmost part of Norway's largest island, Hinnøy, is also in Lofoten. Vestfjorden separates the major islands from the mainland of Norway.

In winter the Gulf Stream makes possible the world's largest cod-fishing event, **Lofotfisket,** which takes place between January and March. Arctic sea cod spawn beyond Lofoten, especially in the Vestfjord, and huge harvesting operations are carried out between January and April.

The first inhabitants of the Lofoten Islands were nomads who hunted and fished, but excavations show that agriculture existed here at least 4,000 years ago. The Vikings pursued farming, fishing, and trading; examples of Viking housing sites can be seen on Vestbågøya, where more than 1,000 burial mounds have been found.

From the 14th century on, the people of Lofoten had to pay taxes to Bergen. This was the beginning of an economic dominance lasting for 6 centuries—first executed by the German Hansa tradesmen, and then by their Norwegian heirs.

Harsh treatment of local residents by the Nazis during the World War II played a major part in the creation of the famous Norwegian resistance movement. Allied forces, which landed here to harass the German iron-ore boats sailing from Narvik, withdrew in June 1940. They evacuated as many Lofoten residents as they could to Scotland for the duration of the war.

Today, the Lofotens have modern towns with shops, hotels, restaurants, and public transportation.

ESSENTIALS

GETTING THERE   On the eastern coast of Austvågøy, **Svolvær** is the largest town on the archipelago's largest island. It lacks the charm of the island's other fishing communities, but there is not better refueling stop. The port is a bit dull, but its surroundings of craggy backdrops and sheltered bays form a dramatic Lofoten backdrop. From Bodø, drive east on Route 80 to Fauske. Take E-6 north to Ulvsvåg, and head southwest on Route 81 toward the town of Skutvik. From Skutvik, take the 2-hour ferry to Svolvær. For ferry information and reservations, contact **Lofotens og Vesterålens Dampskibsselskab A/S (DDF;** ✆ **94-89-73-34** to speak with the boat captains themselves, or 81-03-00-00; www.ovds.no) for reservations and information. Passengers without cars pay 70NOK ($11/£5.60) adults and 35NOK ($5.40/£2.80) children 4 to 15 (free for 4 and under) each way for passage to Svolvær from Skutvik. One-way transport of a car with its driver costs 242NOK ($37/£19).

You can fly to Svolvær on **Widerøe Airline** (✆ **75-51-35-00** in Bodø; www.wideroe.no), which has seven flights a day from Bodø.

You can also travel the Lofotens by using a combination of rail, bus, and ferry. Many visitors take a train to Bodø and then transfer to a bus that crosses from Bodø to Svolvær on a ferry. Most bus departures from Bodø are timed to coincide with the arrival of trains from Oslo, Bergen, and other points. Buses also take passengers from elsewhere in Norway to Ulvsvåg and then on to Skutvik, where you can board a ferry to Svolvær. For information on train-bus-ferry connections, contact the **Destination Bodø Office** (✆ **75-54-80-00**). A coastal steamer, departing from Bodø at 3pm daily, also calls at Stamsund and Svolvær.

VISITOR INFORMATION   **Destination Lofoten,** Box 210, N-8301 Svolvær (✆ **76-07-30-00;** tourist@lofoten-tourist.no), is on the harborfront in a big red building right in the middle of town square. It's open January to May 21 Monday to Friday 9am to 3:30pm; May 22 to June 11 Monday to Friday 9am to 4pm, Saturday 10am to 2pm; June 12 to June 24 Monday to Friday 9am to 7:30pm, Saturday 10am to 2pm, Sunday 4 to 7pm; June 26 to August 6 Monday to Friday 9am to 9:30pm, Saturday 9am to 8pm, Sunday 10am to 9:30pm; August 7 to August 27 Monday to Friday 9am to 7pm, Saturday 10am to 2pm; August 28 to December 31 Monday to Friday 9am to 3:30pm.

GETTING AROUND   At the tourist office at Svolvær you can pick up a free pamphlet, *Lofoten Info-Guide,* with information about all ferries and buses throughout the archipelago. All inhabited islands are linked by ferry, and buses service the four major islands, including Svolvær. Motorists can drive the E-10 from Svolvær to the outer rim of Lofoten, a distance of 130km (80 miles). One of the **great drives** 🎯🎯 in the north of Norway, this route will give you a good overall look at the Lofotens.

Our preferred method of getting around the Lofotens is by bike. They can be rented at most of the archipelago's little hotels.

SEEING THE SIGHTS

Lofoten Krigsminnemuseum, Fiskergata 12 (✆ **91-73-03-28**), is the finest museum in the north devoted to the World War II era. There's a little-known collection of 1940s photographs, some of which document the 1941 commando raid on the islands. Also on display is a collection of military uniforms. Admission is 40NOK ($6.15/£3.20) for adults and 20NOK ($3.10/£1.60) for children 5 to 15; free for 5 and under. It's open mid-May to mid-August daily 11am to 4pm. The rest of the year it's open daily from 6 to 10pm.

Daredevils are lured to Svolvær in an attempt to conquer the most daring (and dangerous) climb in the Lofotens, the 40m (131 ft.) **Svolværgeita (Svolværur goat).** This stone column is perched on a hill behind the port and is known for its two pinnacles, which locals have labeled the horns of a goat. There's a 1.5m (5-ft.) jump between the two "horns," which can be fatal if you aren't successful.

One of the most dramatic boat rides in the Lofotens is the short trip into the impossibly narrow **Trollfjord** ✪✪, stretching for 2km (1¼ miles). This is part of the channel that separates the Lofoten island of Austvågøy from the Vesterålen island of Hinnøya. Coastal steamers can barely navigate this narrow passage without scraping the rock walls on either side. One of the most visited sites in the Lofotens, this fjord cuts its way westward from the Straits of Raftsundet, opening onto an idyllic Lofoten landscape, famed as the subject of many paintings.

Trollfjord is the easternmost island in Lofoten and was the scene of the "Battle of the Trollfjord," as related by Johan Bojer in his novel *The Last Viking*. The battle, which took place more than a century ago between fishermen in small vessels and those in larger steamships, was first recorded on canvas by one of its witnesses, the artist Gunnar Berg (1863–93). His painting is on view at the **Svolvær Town Hall.** Ask at the tourist office (see "Visitor Information," above) about linking up with a boat tour of Trollfjord. Departures are from June 10 to August 20, costing 300NOK ($46/£24) per adult, 100NOK ($15/£8) children 4 to 15, and free for 4 and under.

For the best and most scenic walks in the area, take the ferry ride over to the islet of **Skrova.** Here, you can stroll around and leisurely take in the seascapes. Before heading over, pick up a picnic lunch at one of the shops in Svolvær. Ferries leave from Svolvær port every 2 hours, taking only half an hour to reach Skrova and costing 30NOK ($4.60/£2.40) per person.

Another good walk from Svolvær is to the north, heading to the Lille and Store Kongsvatn Lakes. The banks at either lake are perfect to enjoy that packed lunch. You will know you've reached the end of the trail when you come to a power station. If you wish, you can take a path to **Kabelvåg** following the shoreline for most of the way. Or you can return to Svolvær on the same trail you came up on.

RØST & VAERØY: WORLD-CLASS BIRD-WATCHING

Mountains speckled with birds range from Andøy in the north all the way to the southern tip of Lofoten. Many different types of seabirds can be seen during nesting season. The most famous nesting cliffs are at Røst and Vaerøy, remote islands that can be reached by steamer, plane, or helicopter.

On the flat island of **Røstlandet,** the main attraction is the bird sanctuary, made up of approximately 1,000 little offshore islands. The highly prized eider duck is found here. Locals provide small nesting shelters for the ducks and collect eiderdown after the ducklings hatch.

Vaerøy's **Mount Mostadfjell** is the nesting place for more than 1.5 million seabirds, including sea eagles, auks, puffins, guillemots, kittiwakes, cormorants, and others that breed from May to August.

North Vaerøy Church, with its onion-shaped dome, was brought here from Vågan in 1799. The altarpiece, from around 1400, is a late medieval English alabaster relief. It depicts the Annunciation, the Three Magi, the Resurrection, and the Ascension.

WHERE TO STAY & DINE

Destination Lofoten (see "Visitor Information," above) publishes an accommodations guide to the islands and can book accommodations.

In addition to hotels, guesthouses, and campsites, the Lofoten Islands offer lodging in traditional fishing cottages known as *rorbuer*. The larger (often two stories), usually more modern, version is a *sjøhus* (sea house). The traditional *rorbu* was built on the edge of the water, often on piles, with room for 10 bunks, a kitchen, and an entrance hall used as a work and storage room. Many *rorbuer* today are still simple and unpretentious, but some have electricity, a woodstove, a kitchenette with a sink, and running water. Others have been outfitted with separate bedrooms, private showers, and toilets. **Backroads** (© **800/462-2848**) is the best and most convenient outfitter.

In Stamsund

Stamsund Lofoten   This hotel is merely somewhere to rest your head, but it's decent and affordable, located in the heart of town, and offers a view of the harbor. The small guest rooms are simply furnished with good beds, and many have well-kept bathrooms equipped with tub/shower combinations. On the premises are a bar and a restaurant that serves standard Norwegian fare.

N-8340 Stamsund. © **76-08-93-00.** Fax 76-08-97-26. www.stamsund.no. 28 units. 800NOK–1,250NOK ($123–$193/£64–£100) double. Rates include breakfast. AE, DC, MC, V. Free parking. **Amenities:** Restaurant; bar; lounge; nonsmoking rooms. *In room:* TV, minibar, hair dryer.

In Svolvær

Norlandia Royal Hotel   At the crossroads of town, this fully renovated hotel is one of the island's finest choices and vastly superior to the other Norlandia in town (see below). The five-story hotel was constructed in 1974 near the express steamer quay. The bedrooms are midsize and attractively furnished in a modern style, each opening onto views of the distant mountains and the nearby sea. Some floors contain carpeted rooms, the rest offer wood floors. All of the units are equipped with small but efficiently organized private bathrooms with tub/shower combinations. The on-site restaurant, Restaurant Lofoten, is one of the area's best hotel dining rooms.

Sivert Nilsensgata 21, N-8311 Svolvær. © **76-07-12-00.** Fax 76-07-08-50. www.norlandia.no/royal. 48 units. 750NOK–2,000NOK ($116–$308/£60–£160) double; 1,700NOK ($262/£136) suite. Rates include continental breakfast. AE, DC, MC, V. **Amenities:** Restaurant; bar; limited room service; babysitting; laundry service/dry cleaning; nonsmoking rooms; rooms for those w/limited mobility. *In room:* TV, dataport, minibar, hair dryer.

Norlandia Vestfjord Hotel   This is a comfortable but unexceptional place, and not as good as its sister, Norlandia, recommended above. This building was a former warehouse that stored marine supplies and fish. After extensive remodeling, it reopened as this well-managed hotel. The guest rooms are functional and comfortable; ask for one that overlooks the sea. The bathrooms are tiny, with tub/shower combinations. Facilities include a lobby bar and a pleasant restaurant that specializes in fish and steaks. It serves sustaining fare—nothing remarkable.

Fiskergata 46, N-8300 Svolvær. © **76-07-08-70.** Fax 76-07-08-54. www.norlandia.no/vestfjord. 63 units. Sun–Thurs June–Aug 1 1,520NOK ($234/£73) double; summer Fri–Sat 910NOK ($140/£73) double; year-round 1,500NOK ($231/£120) suite. Rates include breakfast. AE, DC, MC, V. Free parking. **Amenities:** Restaurant; bar; limited room service; laundry service/dry cleaning; nonsmoking rooms; rooms for those w/limited mobility. *In room:* TV, dataport, minibar (in some), hair dryer.

NARVIK

301km (187 miles) NE of Bodø, 1,635km (1,022 miles) NE of Bergen, 1,480km (919 miles) N of Oslo

More or less destroyed by invading Nazis during World War II, the rebuilt Narvik can be a bit of an eyesore. But its setting in the midst of panoramic forests, majestic fjords, and towering mountains makes it worth a visit. As an added plus, the midnight sun shines here from May 27 to July 19.

This ice-free seaport on the Ofotfjord is in Nordland *fylke* (country), 403km (250 miles) north of the Arctic Circle. Narvik, founded in 1903 when the Ofoten (not to be confused with "Lofoten") railway line was completed, boasts Europe's most modern shipping harbor for iron ore. It's also the northernmost electrified railway line in the world. It covers a magnificent scenic route, through precipitous mountain terrain and tunnels, over ridges, and across tall stone embankments.

Only 11km (6½ miles) from Narvik, Straumsnes station is the last permanent habitation you'll encounter as you go east. The last Norwegian station, Bjørnfjell, is well above the timberline and about 3 hours from Kiruna, Sweden, some 140km (87 miles) north of the Arctic Circle. You can catch a train at Kiruna to Stockholm. If you're driving from Kiruna to Narvik, take no. 98 heading northwest to E-6 heading southwest toward Narvik.

Narvik looms large in World War II history books, and its port was a graveyard of both men and ships from Germany, Britain, Norway, France, and the Netherlands.

ESSENTIALS

GETTING THERE   From the Lofoten Islands, a car ferry heads to Skutvik three times a day. Follow Route 81 northeast to the junction with E-6, and then take E-6 north to Bognes. Cross the Tysfjord by ferry and continue north on E-6 to Narvik.

The train from Stockholm to Narvik takes 21 to 24 hours. From Stockholm to Narvik, the train costs 875NOK ($135/£70) one-way. There are also two buses a day from Fauske/Bodø (5 hr.). Check www.nsb.no or www.nor-way.no for information.

VISITOR INFORMATION   The **Narvik Tourist Office** is at Kongensgate 26 (© 76-96-56-00;** www.narvikinfo.no). It's open Monday to Friday from 9am to 4pm; June to August it's also open on Saturday from 9am to 2pm.

SEEING THE SIGHTS

To get a good look at Narvik, take the **Gondolbanen cable car** (© 76-96-04-94), whose departure point is located directly behind the Norlandia Narvik Hotel, a 10-minute walk from the town center. The car operates from March to October, and the round-trip fare is 110NOK ($17/£8.80) for adults, 50NOK ($7.70/£4) for children 6 to 15 (free for 5 and under). In just 13 minutes it takes you to an altitude of 640m (2,100 ft.), at the top of Fagernesfjell. Here, you can soak in the impressive panorama of the town or visit the simple restaurant at the tip.

From the peak, you can hike on marked trails that branch out in several directions, all equally impressive. A downhill mountain bike trail also starts near the cable car's final stop. From mid-February to mid-June, and in August and September, the cable operates Monday to Friday from 1 to 9pm and every Saturday and Sunday from 10am to 5pm. From mid-June to the end of July, it operates daily from noon to 1am.

Nordland Røde Kors Krigsminnemuseum (War Museum)   Near Torghallen in the town center, this museum revisits the epic struggle of the Narvik campaign of 1940 and the dreaded years of Nazi occupation. Exhibits detail Germany's battle for Narvik's iron ore and how Nazi forces fought troops from France, Poland, and Norway, as well as a considerable British flotilla at sea. Experiences of the civilian population and foreign POWs are also highlighted.

Kongensgate. ℂ **76-94-44-26.** Admission 50NOK ($7.70/£4) adults, 25NOK ($3.85/£2) children. Mar–June 7 and Aug 21–Sept daily 11am–3pm; June 8–Aug 20 Mon–Sat 10am–10pm, Sun 11am–5pm; Oct–Feb Thurs–Sat 11am–3pm.

Ofoten Museum   A minor museum that can be skipped, the Ofoten Museum displays artifacts and rock carvings tracing the oldest human settlements in the area, going back to the Stone Age. Other exhibits (including a scraper for animal skins and a flint-and-tinder box) show how ancient people lived and worked in the area. Most of the displays are from the 20th century, beginning with the construction of the rail line.

Administrasjonsveien 3. ℂ **76-96-00-50.** Admission 40NOK ($6.15/£3.20) adults, 20NOK ($3.10/£1.60) children 12 and under. June 24–Aug 13 Mon–Fri 10am–3pm, Sat–Sun noon–3pm; rest of year Mon–Fri 10am–3pm.

WHERE TO STAY

These hotels are among the few buildings in Narvik that survived World War II.

Moderate

Quality Hotel Grand Royal ⓖ   The monolithic exterior is a bit off-putting, but Grand Royal is the largest and best equipped lodging in Narvik. It opens onto the main street in the town center, between the train station and the harbor. It was originally named the Grand Royal because the late King Olav was a frequent visitor and his portraits adorn some of the public rooms. The comfortable, good-size rooms are tastefully and traditionally furnished, and all but a handful have been renovated and upgraded. The well-equipped, medium-size bathrooms with tub/shower combinations are the most comfortable in town. The artfully contemporary lobby bar is one of the most alluring cocktail bars in northern Norway. The Royal Blue, the finest restaurant in town, is also here (see "Where to Dine," below).

Kongensgate 64, N-8501 Narvik. ℂ **76-97-70-00.** Fax 76-97-70-07. www.choice.no. 119 units. Mon–Thurs 825NOK ($127/£66) double; Fri–Sat 500NOK ($77/£40) double. Rates include breakfast. AE, DC, MC, V. Free parking. Bus: 14, 15, 16, or 17. **Amenities:** 2 restaurants; 2 bars; sauna; babysitting; laundry service/dry cleaning; nonsmoking rooms; rooms for those w/limited mobility. *In room:* TV, dataport, minibar, hair dryer, safe, Wi-Fi.

Inexpensive

Nordstjernen Hotel ⓥalue   In 1970 the present owner of this hotel opened Nordstjernen on the main street of Narvik to produce a viable alternative to the Grand Royal. Much improved over the years, it's still here, still going strong, and keeping its prices within an affordable range. South of the bus station, the hotel has long been known as one of the best values in the area. Guest rooms are decorated in pastels to offset the winter gloom. Rooms vary in size, but all are comfortable and well maintained. Bathrooms are small and equipped with tub/shower combinations.

Kongensgate 26, N-8500 Narvik. ℂ **76-94-41-20.** Fax 76-94-75-06. www.nordstjernen.no. 24 units. 750NOK–850NOK ($116–$131/£60–£68) double. Rates include breakfast. DC, MC, V. Free parking. Bus: 14 or 16. **Amenities:** Restaurant; lounge. *In room:* TV, hair dryer.

WHERE TO DINE

Royal Blue ⓖ NORWEGIAN   The best restaurant in the region is decorated, appropriately, in strong royal blues. It's the preferred choice of visiting dignitaries, including the king. Service is polite, and the food's delectable. The menu changes seasonally and could include sauna-smoked ham with asparagus or reindeer curry with Brussels sprouts and apricots. Royal Blue is located on the lobby level of the Grand Royal.

In the Quality Hotel Grand Royal, Kongensgate 64. ℂ **76-97-70-00.** Reservations recommended. Main courses 190NOK–400NOK ($29–$62/£15–£32). AE, DC, MC, V. Tues–Sat 5–10pm. Bus: 14, 15, 16, or 17.

12

The Best of Sweden

In the towns and cities of Scandinavia's largest country, you can let yourself be dazzled by the contemporary or wander back to a bygone era. From the castles and palaces in the south to the barren tundra of Lapland, we have combed this vast land of forests, lakes, and glacier-ringed mountains to bring you the best.

1 The Best Travel Experiences

- **Soaking Up Local Culture:** Home to a great cultural tradition, Sweden is acclaimed for its symphony orchestras, theater, ballet (including the renowned Swedish Cullberg Ballet), and opera companies. During the long days of summer, open-air concerts are staged all over the country (local tourist offices can provide details). Many concerts, especially those featuring folk dancing and regional music, are free.

- **Touring the Stockholm Archipelago:** The capital lies in a bucolic setting with more than 24,000 islands (if you count big rocks jutting out of the water). Boats leave frequently in summer from Stockholm's harbor, taking you to Vaxholm and other scenic islands, where you'll find interesting shops and restaurants. See chapter 15.

- **Seeing the Country from the Water:** Passengers glide through Sweden's scenic heartland, between Stockholm and Gothenburg, on a Göta Canal cruise. The route takes you along three of the country's largest lakes and through 58 carefully calibrated locks. The cruise, available between mid-May and mid-September, offers the best of Sweden in a nutshell. See chapter 18.

- **Exploring the Land of the Midnight Sun:** Above the Arctic Circle, the summer sun never dips below the horizon. You have endless hours to enjoy the beauty of the region and the activities that go with it, from hiking to white-water rafting. After shopping for distinctive wood and silver handicrafts, dine on filet of reindeer served with cloudberries, or climb rocks and glaciers in Sarek National Park. See "Swedish Lapland" in chapter 18.

2 The Best Scenic Towns & Villages

- **Sigtuna:** Sweden's oldest town, founded at the beginning of the 11th century, stands on the shores of Lake Mälaren northwest of Stockholm. Walk its High Street, believed to be the oldest street in Sweden. Traces of Sigtuna's Viking and early Christian heritage can be seen throughout the town. See chapter 15.

- **Uppsala:** Sweden's major university city lies northwest of Stockholm. Gamla (Old) Uppsala, nearby, is especially intriguing. It's built on the site of Viking burial grounds, where humans and animals were sacrificed. See chapter 15.

- **Lund:** This town, 18km (11 miles) northeast of Malmö, rivals Uppsala as a university town. It, too, is ancient— Canute the Great founded it in 1020. Centuries-old buildings, winding passages, and cobblestone streets fill Lund; its ancient cathedral is one of the finest expressions of Romanesque architecture in northern Europe. See chapter 17.

- **Jokkmokk:** Just north of the Arctic Circle, this is the best center for absorbing Sami culture. In early February, the Sami hold their famous "Great Winter Market" here, a tradition that's 4 centuries old. You can visit a museum devoted to Sami culture and then go salmon fishing in the town's central lake. See chapter 18.

- **Rättvik:** This great resort borders Lake Siljan in the heart of Dalarna, a province known for its regional painting, handicrafts, and folk dancing. Timbered houses characterize Dalarna's architecture, and on a summer night you can listen to fiddlers. See chapter 18.

- **Visby:** On the island of Gotland, this was once a great medieval European city and Viking stronghold. For 8 days in August, during Medieval Week, the sleepy Hanseatic town hosts an annual festival featuring fire-eaters, belly dancers, and jousting tournaments. Filled with the ruins of 13th- and 14th-century churches and memories of a more prosperous period, Visby is intriguing in any season. See chapter 18.

3 The Best Active Vacations

- **Fishing:** Sweden offers some of the world's best fishing in pristine lakes and streams, and you can even fish in downtown Stockholm. Many varieties of fresh and saltwater fish are available in Sweden's waters.

- **Golfing:** Many Swedes are obsessed with golf. Most courses, from the periphery of Stockholm to Björkliden (above the Arctic Circle), are open to the public, and enthusiasts can play under the midnight sun. Halland, south of Gothenburg, is called the Swedish Riviera, and it's the golf capital of the country. Båstad is the most fashionable resort in Halland, and you can play a game of golf here at two prestigious courses: the **Båstad Golf Club** at Boarp (© **0431/783-70**) and the **Bjäre Golf Club** at Salomonhög (© **0431/36-10-53**), both located right outside the center of Båstad. See chapter 17.

- **Hiking:** The Kungsleden ("King's Trail") might provide the hike of a lifetime. It takes you through the mountains of Lapland, including Kebnekaise that, at 2,090m (6,965 ft.), is the highest mountain in Sweden. This 500km (310-mile) trail cuts through the mountains of Abisko National Park to Riksgränsen on the Norwegian frontier. For more information about this adventure, contact the **Svenska Turistföreningen (Swedish Touring Club),** P.O. Box 25, Amiralitetshuset 1, Flagmansvägen 8, S101 20 Stockholm (© **08/463-21-00**). The club will also provide information about hiking and outdoor venues in any season in each of Sweden's 25 provinces. See chapter 18.

- **Skiing:** In Lapland, you can enjoy both downhill and cross-country skiing year-round. In Kiruna, serious skiers head for the Kebnekaise mountain station, where skiing can be combined with dog-sledding and other winter sports. South of the city of Gällivare, you arrive at Dundret, or

"Thunder Mountain," for some of the finest skiing in the north. The area's best hotel is **Dundret** (© **0970/ 145-60;** www.dundret.se), and its staff possesses all the expertise needed to link you up with both cross-country skiing and skiing on the downhill slopes. Inaugurated in 1955, its chairlift to the top of the slopes was the first of its kind in Sweden.

- **White-Water Rafting:** The best way to profit from the meltdown of Sweden's winter snow involves floating downstream atop the surging waters of the Klarälven River. White-water enthusiasts gravitate to its northern stretches; aficionados of calmer waters move to points near its southern terminus. One of the most respected outfitters for excursions along any length of this historic river is **Vildmark in Värmland,** P.O. Box 209, Torsby SE 68525 (© **0560/14040;**

www.vildmark.se). Established in 1980, and known throughout the region for the quality of its guides, it offers canoe excursions along the northern lengths of the river between April and October, providing canoes, instruction, and all the equipment and excitement you'll need. A 4-day experience covering about 48km downstream (30 miles) costs 5,135NOK ($790) per adult; a 7-day jaunt covering twice that distance costs 6,435NOK ($990) per person. Less structured trips are offered by a competitor in Värmland, in a location 150km (93 miles) north of Karlstad. Here, you can contact **Branäs Sport,** Branäs Fritidsanläggnin, S-680 20 Sysslebäck (© **564/475-70**), an operation that devotes much of its time to the rental of cross-country skis, but also conducts white-water rafting on several nearby streams and rivers.

4 The Best Festivals & Special Events

- **Walpurgis Eve:** One of Europe's great celebrations to welcome spring takes place in Sweden on April 30. Bonfires, songs, festivals, and all sorts of antics herald the demise of winter. The best—and rowdiest—celebrations are at the university cities of Umeå, Lund, Uppsala, Stockholm, and Gothenburg.
- **Stockholm Waterfestival:** In August, much of the city turns out for a week-long festival along the waterfront. Theoretically, the concept behind the festival is water preservation, but entertainment ranges from concerts to fireworks.
- **Drottningholm Court Theater** (Drottningholm): In May, Sweden's cultural highlight is a series of 30 opera and ballet performances presented at this theater, which dates from 1766. The theater's original stage machinery and settings are still used.

Drottningholm Palace (the "Versailles of Sweden") is on an island in Lake Mälaren, about 11km (7 miles) from Stockholm. See chapter 15.
- **Falun Folkmusik Festival:** This annual gathering of folk musicians from around the world at the town of Falun is one of Scandinavia's major musical events. Folkloric groups— many of them internationally famous—perform. Concerts, films, lectures, and seminars round out the events, which usually last for 4 days in July. See chapter 13.
- **Medieval Week** (Gotland): On the island of Gotland, Swedes celebrate the Middle Ages for about a week every August. Visby, especially, swarms with people in medieval garb. Many of them—from the blacksmith to the cobbler—tend market stalls as in olden days. Musicians play the

hurdy-gurdy or the fiddle, and jesters play the fool. A program of some 100 medieval events, from tournaments to a nightly king's procession, is scheduled in Visby. See chapter 18.

5 The Best Museums

• **Royal Warship *Vasa*** (Stockholm): In the Djurgården, this 17th-century man-of-war—now a museum—is a popular tourist attraction and deservedly so. The *Vasa* is the world's oldest known complete ship. It capsized and sank on its maiden voyage in 1628 before horrified onlookers. The ship was salvaged in 1961 and has been carefully restored; 97% of its 700 original decorative sculptures were retrieved. See chapter 15.

• **Nationalmuseum (National Museum of Art,** Stockholm): One of the oldest museums in the world (it celebrated its 210th birthday in 2002), the National Museum houses Sweden's treasure trove of rare paintings and sculpture. From Rembrandt and Rubens to Bellini and van Gogh, a panoply of European art unfolds before your eyes. In addition to paintings, you'll find antique porcelain, furniture, and clocks. See chapter 15.

• **Millesgården** (Lidingö, outside Stockholm): Sweden's foremost sculptor,

Carl Milles (1875–1955), lived here and created a sculpture garden by the sea. Milles relied heavily on mythological themes in his work, and many of his best-known pieces are displayed in what's now a museum. See chapter 15.

• **Göteborgs Konstmuseum** (Gothenburg): This is the city's leading art museum, a repository of modern painting that's strong on French Impressionism. Modern artists such as Picasso and Edvard Munch are also represented, as are sculptures by Milles. See chapter 16.

• **Ájtte** (Jokkmokk): In Sami country, this is the best repository of artifacts of the Sami people. Integrating nature with culture, the museum is the largest of its kind in the world. It depicts how the Sami lived and struggled for survival in a harsh terrain, and shows the houses they lived in and the animals and weapons needed for their livelihood. See chapter 18.

6 The Best Offbeat Experiences

• **Log-Rafting on the Klarälven River:** You can enjoy a lazy trip down the river, winding through beautiful, unspoiled valleys among high mountains, with sandy beaches where you can occasionally swim. There's excellent fishing for pike and grayling. You travel through northern Värmland at a speed of 2kmph (1¼ mph) from the mouth of the Vingängssjön Lake in the north to Edebäck in the south. It takes 6 days to cover the 110km

(68 miles). Overnight accommodations are on the moored raft or ashore. Each raft can accommodate two to five people, and the trips are available from May to August. Participants in the rafting expeditions down the Klarälven River will make their own rafts on the first day of the experience (it can last 1, 2, 3, or 6 days, and incorporate some or all of the river's length). Pine logs are lashed together with rope. Other

offerings include beaver and elk-watching safaris, white-water rafting expeditions, and canoeing. Contact **Vildmark i Farmland,** P.O. Box 209, 68525 Torsby (© **0560/140-40;** www.vildmark.se).

- **Exploring the Orsa "Outback" by Horse & Covered Wagon:** In the province of Dalarna (central Sweden), you can rent a horse and covered wagon (with space for up to five) for a 3- or 5-day trek across the forest and tundra of the Orsa "outback," an almost unpopulated area of wild beauty. For more information, contact **Häst och Vagn Svante Inemyr,** Torsmo 1646, S-794 91 Orsa (© **0250/55-30-14;** http:// itadventure.se/hast.vagn). On-site, they have 18 horses and 60 huskies for dog-sledding tours.

- **Playing Golf by the Light of the Midnight Sun:** In a land where the Sami and reindeer still lead a nomadic life, you can play at the Björkliden Arctic Golf Course, some 240km (150 miles) north of the Arctic Circle (near the hamlet of Björkliden, 97km/60 miles west of Kiruna). The 18-hole course is open between late June and late August only. For information, contact the **Björkliden Arctic Golf Club** at © **0980/400-40.** The rest of the year, contact its affiliate, the Stockholm-based Bromma Golf Course, Kvarnbacksvägen 28, 16874 Bromma, Stockholm (© **08/ 564-888-40**). See chapter 18.

- **Seeing Lapland on a Safari:** On this tour you can explore the last wilderness of Europe and record your impressions on film. You can see Swedish Lapland up close and become acquainted with the Sami people's rich culture. Highlights include visits to old churches and village settlements (usually along a lake), and seeing reindeer. The outdoors outfitter **Borton Overseas** (© **800/843-0602**) offers summer tours of the tundra between May and early September, and winter tours of the snow-covered tundra from January to April. The winter is arguably the most beautiful time to see the tundra.

- **Riding the Rails of the Longest Stretch of Abandoned Railway Track in Europe:** Around 1900, a consortium of logging companies, with the help of the Swedish government, built a railway track running across a 180km (112-mile) stretch of forested wilderness between Dalarna and Värmland, beginning and ending in the hamlets of Perfberg and Venfbro. Trains stopped running along the track in 1967, and today the stretch of rails is part of Sweden's national patrimony. You can ride along these tracks in specially designed foot-pedaled trolleys, in tandem with up to four passengers. Since there's only one track, travel can become inconvenient if you meet up with another trolley headed in the opposite direction. An outfit that's highly experienced in this and many other forms of outdoor activities in the Swedish wilderness, during both summer and winter, is **Dalarnas & Värmlands Äentyrscentrum AB,** Ulfshittan 6, 78196 Börlange, Sweden (© **0243/25-11-07;** www.dalarnasaventyr.se).

7 The Best Buys

- **Glass:** In the deep woods of Småland, Swedish glasswork has helped set the world standard. Glass has been a local tradition since King Gustav Vasa invited Venetian glass blowers to come to Sweden in the 16th century. The first glass was melted here in 1556. The oldest name in Swedish glass, Kosta, was founded in 1742 and is now part of the Orrefors group, the best-known manufacturer. Fifteen major glassworks in Småland, which encompasses Växjö and Kalmar, are open to visitors. Glass is sold at department stores and specialty outlets throughout Sweden.

- **Handicrafts:** Designers create a wide variety of objects in wood, pewter, enamel, tapestry, brass, and even reindeer skins and antlers. Many handicrafts are based on Viking designs, and most objects are in the traditional Sami (or Lapp) style. Shoppers eagerly seek wall textiles, leatherwork, hand-woven carpets, and embroidered items. Swedish cutlery and china are valued for their quality and craftsmanship. Stockholm has the widest selection of shops, and Gothenburg and other towns have specialty outlets.

- **Swedish Design:** Good design and craftsmanship are the hallmarks of Swedish housewares—swinging metal CD racks, wooden chickens on rockers, tea wagons, and more. One of the best places to find products of Swedish design is in the constantly changing display at **DesignTorget,** in the Kulturhuset in the center of Stockholm. It's open daily year-round. See chapter 15.

8 The Best Hotels

- **Grand Hotel** (S. Blasieholmshamnen 8, Stockholm; © **800/223-5652** in the U.S., or 08/679-35-00; www.grandhotel.se; p. 401): Opposite the Royal Palace, this is the most prestigious hotel in Sweden. Well-known guests have included celebrities and Nobel Prize winners. It dates from 1874 and is continuously renovated to keep it in excellent condition. The rooms are luxuriously decorated, and the bathrooms are Italian marble with heated floors.

- **Lady Hamilton Hotel** (Storkyrkobrinken 5, Stockholm; © **08/506-40-100;** www.lady-hamilton.se; p. 408): This is one of Old Town's stellar properties. It's made up of three buildings that have been artfully connected and provide sumptuously furnished accommodations for those who prefer an old-fashioned atmosphere.

- **Victory Hotel** (Lilla Nygatan 5, Stockholm; © **08/506-400-00;** www.victory-hotel.se; p. 409): In the Old Town, this small but stylish hotel was built in 1642. It's famous for the treasure once buried here, part of which can be seen at the Stockholm City Museum. The well-furnished guest rooms typically have exposed beams and pine floors. On a small rooftop terrace, tables are arranged around a fountain.

- **Radisson SAS Scandinavia Hotel** (Sodra Hamngatan 59–65, Gothenburg; © **800/333-3333** in the U.S., or 031/758-50-00; www.radissonsas.com; p. 462): Fashioned in marble and glass with bay windows, this hotel, with innovative styling and beautiful architecture, is more than just a typical chain hotel. Balconies overlook a vast atrium with eye-catching elevators and trees. Amenities include everything from a gym and sauna to a well-equipped health club; the gourmet dining room has a bar.

- **Grand Hotel** (Bantorget 1, Lund; © **046/28-06-100;** www.grandilund.se; p. 509): Since 1899 this has been the prestigious address for those visiting this university and cathedral city. Enlarged and much evolved over the years, it is a citadel of comfort, tradition, and charm for those visiting the southern tier of Sweden.

9 The Best Restaurants

- **Operakällaren** (Operahuset, Karl XII's Torg, Stockholm; © 08/676-58-00; p. 410): This historic monument, part of the Royal Opera Complex, dates from 1787. The chef is a culinary adviser to the king and queen. This is the best place to sample Sweden's legendary smörgåsbord—a groaning table of delectable dishes with an emphasis on fresh fish. All the northern delicacies, from smoked eel and reindeer to Swedish red caviar and grouse, appear on the menu.

- **Paul & Norbert** (Strandvägen 9, Stockholm; © 08/663-81-83; p. 411): With only eight tables on the fashionable Strandvägen, this exclusive restaurant is set in a patrician residence dating from 1873. The most innovative restaurant in Stockholm, it's the creation of German owner Norbert Lang. In winter, the Swedish game served here is without equal in the country. Try the pigeon with Calvados sauce or sautéed sweetbreads in nettle sauce.

- **Wedholms Fisk** (Nybrokajen 17, Stockholm; © 08/611-78-74; p. 414): This classic Swedish restaurant serves some of the capital's finest local food, skillfully prepared with a French touch. Traditional and haute cuisine dishes have been modernized. Each dish seems guaranteed to ignite your enthusiasm, although nothing is showy or ostentatious. The fresh ingredients retain their natural flavor.

- **Gripsholms Värdshus Restaurant** (Kyrkogatan 1, Mariefred; © 0159/347-50; p. 451): If you're seeking traditional Swedish food with French overtones, this is the best dining choice on the periphery of the capital. Local game dishes, including wild grouse, are featured in autumn, and marinated salmon with mild mustard sauce is a year-round favorite. Tastings in the wine cellar can be arranged.

- **Sjömagasinet** (Klippans Kulturreservat, Adolph Edelsvärdsgata 5, Klippan, outside Gothenburg; © 031/773-59-20; p. 466). By far the most interesting restaurant in town, this is one of the finest seafood places on the west coast of Sweden. In a converted warehouse, it serves an array of fresh fish in wonderful concoctions, and the sauces and preparations never diminish the flavor of the seafood. *Pot-au-feu* of fish and shellfish with chive-flavored crème fraîche is worth the trek out of town.

13

Planning Your Trip to Sweden

This chapter gives you many of the details you need to plan your trip to Sweden. Also see chapter 3, "Planning Your Trip to Denmark," which discusses travel to Scandinavia as a whole.

1 The Regions in Brief

GÖTALAND The southern part of Sweden takes its name from the ancient Goths. Some historians believe they settled in this region, which is similar in climate and architecture to parts of northern Europe, especially Germany. This is the most populated part of Sweden, comprising eight provinces— Östergötland, Småland (the "kingdom of glass"), Västergötland, Skåne, Dalsland, Bohuslån, Halland, and Blekinge—plus the islands of Öland and Gotland. The Göta Canal cuts through this district. **Gothenburg** is the most important port in the west, and **Stockholm,** the capital, is the chief port in the east. Aside from Stockholm, **Skåne,** the châteaux district, is the most heavily visited area. It's often compared to the Danish countryside. Many seaside resorts are on both the west and east coasts.

SVEALAND The central region encompasses the folkloric province of **Dalarna** (Dalecarlia in English) and

Värmland (immortalized in the novels of Selma Lagerlöf). These districts are the ones most frequented by visitors. Other provinces include Västmanland, Uppland, Södermanland, and Närke. Ancient Svealand is often called the cultural heart of Sweden. Some 20,000 islands lie along its eastern coast.

NORRLAND Northern Sweden makes up Norrland, which lies above the 61st parallel and includes about 50% of the landmass. It's inhabited by only about 15% of the population, including Sami and Finns. Norrland consists of 24 provinces, of which **Lapland** is the most popular with tourists. It's a land of thick forests, fast-flowing (and cold) rivers, and towering mountain peaks. Lapland, the home of the Lapp reindeer herds, consists of tundra. **Kiruna** is one of Norrland's most important cities because of its iron-ore deposits. Many bodies of water in Norrland freeze for months every year.

2 Visitor Information

In the **United States,** contact the **Scandinavian Tourist Board,** 655 Third Ave., 18th floor, New York, NY 10017 (© **212/885-9700;** www.goscandinavia. com or www.visitsweden.com), at least 3 months in advance for maps, sightseeing

information, ferry schedules, and other advice and tips.

In the **United Kingdom,** contact the **Swedish Travel & Tourism Council,** 11 Montague Pl., London W1H 2AL (© **020/7108-6168**).

You also can try the website **www.visit sweden.com**.

If you get in touch with a travel agent, make sure the agent is a member of the **American Society of Travel Agents** (ASTA). If a problem arises, you can complain to the society's Consumer Affairs Department at 1101 King St., Suite 200, Alexandria, VA 22314 (© **703/ 739-2782;** www.astanet.com).

3 Entry Requirements & Customs

ENTRY REQUIREMENTS

U.S., Canadian, U.K., Irish, Australian, and New Zealand citizens with a **valid passport** don't need a visa to enter Sweden if they don't expect to stay more than 90 days and don't expect to work there. If after entering Sweden you want to stay more than 90 days, you can apply for a permit for an extra 90 days, which as a rule is granted immediately. Go to the nearest *questura* (police headquarters) or to your home country's consulate. If your passport is lost or stolen, head to your consulate as soon as possible.

CUSTOMS

WHAT YOU CAN BRING INTO SWEDEN Foreign visitors can bring along most items for personal use duty-free, including fishing tackle, a pair of skis, two tennis racquets, a baby carriage, two hand-held cameras with 10 rolls of film, and 400 cigarettes or a quantity of cigars or pipe tobacco not exceeding 500 grams (1.1 lb.). There are strict limits on importing alcoholic beverages. However, for alcohol bought tax-paid, limits are much more liberal than in other countries of the European Union.

For a general discussion on what you can take home, see "What You Can Take Home" in chapter 3.

4 Money

For a general discussion of changing money, using credit and charge cards, and other matters, see "Money," in chapter 3.

CURRENCY Sweden's basic unit of currency is the *krona* (plural: *kronor*), written **SEK.** (Denmark and Norway also use *kroner,* but note the different spelling.) There are 100 *öre* in 1 *krona.* Bank notes are issued in denominations of 20, 50, 100, 500, 1,000, and 10,000 SEK. Silver coins are issued in denominations of 50 *öre* and 1 and 5 SEK.

CREDIT & CHARGE CARDS American Express, Diners Club, and Visa are widely recognized throughout Sweden. Discover cards are not accepted. If you see a Eurocard or Access sign, it means that the establishment accepts MasterCard. With an American Express, MasterCard, or Visa card, you also can withdraw currency from cash machines (ATMs) at various locations. Always check with your credit or charge card company about this before leaving home.

ATM NETWORKS PLUS, Cirrus, and other networks connect with automated teller machines throughout Scandinavia. If your credit card has been programmed with a PIN (personal identification number), you can probably use your card at Scandinavian ATMs to withdraw money as a cash advance on your card. Always determine the frequency limits for withdrawals and check to see if your PIN must be reprogrammed for usage on your trip abroad. Also, be aware that most likely you will be able to access only your checking account from overseas ATM machines. Contact **Cirrus** (© **800/424-7787;** www. mastercard.com) or **PLUS** (© **800/843-7587;** www.visa.com) for locations and usage.

Sweden

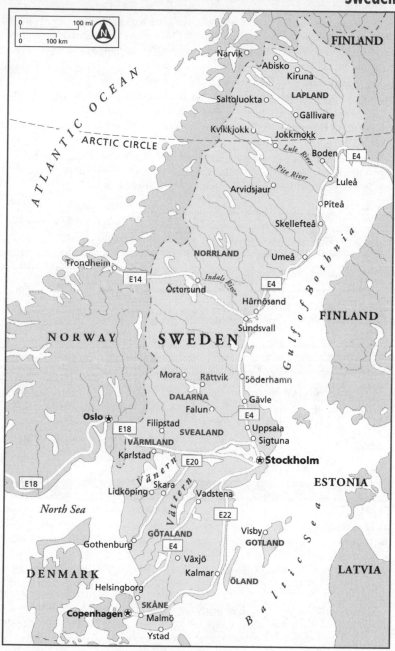

FINLAND

0   100 mi
0   100 km

Narvik

Abisko

Kiruna

LAPLAND

Saltoluokta

Gällivare

Kvikkjokk

Jokkmokk

Lule River

Boden

E4

Pite River

Luleå

Arvidsjaur

Piteå

Skellefteå

NORRLAND

Umeå

ATLANTIC OCEAN

ARCTIC CIRCLE

Trondheim

E14

Indals River

E4

Östersund

Härnösand

Sundsvall

NORWAY

SWEDEN

FINLAND

Gulf of Bothnia

Mora

Rättvik

Söderhamn

DALARNA

Gävle

Falun

E4

Oslo

E18

Filipstad

SVEALAND

Uppsala

VÄRMLAND

Sigtuna

Karlstad

E20

Stockholm

Vänern

ESTONIA

E18

Lidköping

Skara

Vättern

Vadstena

North Sea

E22

GÖTALAND

Visby

Gothenburg

E4

GOTLAND

Växjö

DENMARK

Kalmar

ÖLAND

LATVIA

Helsingborg

SKÅNE

Baltic Sea

Copenhagen

Malmö

Ystad

The Swedish Krona

For American readers   At the time of this writing, $1 = approximately 7.2 SEK. (Stated differently, 1 krona = 13.8¢.) This was the rate of exchange used to calculate the dollar values provided throughout this edition, rounded off to the nearest nickel.

For British readers   At this writing, £1 = approximately 13.7 kronor (or 1 krona = approximately 7p). This was the rate of exchange used to calculate the pound-designated values in the chart below.

Regarding the euro   At the time of this writing, 1€ = 9.25SEK (or 1SEK = .11€).

These monetary relationships can and probably will change during the lifetime of this edition. For more on exact ratios between these and other currencies, check an up-to-date source at the time of your arrival in Sweden.

SEK	US$	UK£	Euro €	SEK	US$	UK£	Euro €
1	0.14	0.07	0.11	75.00	10.35	5.48	8.10
2	0.28	0.15	0.22	100.00	13.80	7.30	10.80
3	0.41	0.22	0.32	125.00	17.25	9.13	13.50
4	0.55	0.29	0.43	150.00	20.70	10.95	16.20
5	0.69	0.37	0.54	175.00	24.15	12.78	18.90
6	0.83	0.44	0.65	200.00	27.60	14.60	21.60
7	0.97	0.51	0.76	225.00	31.05	16.43	24.30
8	1.10	0.58	0.86	250.00	34.50	18.25	27.00
9	1.24	0.66	0.97	275.00	37.95	20.08	29.70
10	1.38	0.73	1.08	300.00	41.40	21.90	32.40
15	2.07	1.10	1.62	350.00	48.30	25.55	37.80
20	2.76	1.46	2.16	400.00	55.20	29.20	43.20
25	3.45	1.83	2.70	500.00	69.00	36.50	54.00
50	6.90	3.65	5.40	1000.00	138.00	73.00	108.00

5 When to Go

CLIMATE

It's hard to generalize about Sweden's climate. Influenced by the Gulf Stream, temperatures vary considerably from the fields of Skåne to the wilderness of Lapland. The upper 10th of Sweden lies north of the Arctic Circle.

The country as a whole has many sunny summer days, but it's not super-hot. July is the warmest month, with temperatures in Stockholm and Gothenburg averaging around 64°F (18°C). February is the coldest month, when the temperature in Stockholm averages around 26°F (−3°C), and Gothenburg is a few degrees warmer.

It's not always true that the farther north you go, the cooler it becomes. During the summer, the northern parts of the country (Hälsingland to northern Lapland) may suddenly have the warmest weather and bluest skies. Swedes claim the weather forecasts on television and in the newspapers are 99% reliable.

What Things Cost in Stockholm

	US$/UK£
Taxi from the airport to the city center	45.00/22.70
Basic bus or subway fare	1.95/1.00
Local telephone call	0.30/0.15
Double room at the Grand Hotel (very expensive)	403.00/203.00
Double room at the Kung Carl Hotel (moderate)	244.00/123.00
Double room at the Långholmer (inexpensive)	150.00/75.60
Lunch for one at Eriks Bakfica (moderate)	30.00/15.10
Lunch for one at Cattelin Restaurant (inexpensive)	8.95/4.50
Dinner for one, without wine, at Operakällaren (very expensive)	104.00/52.40
Dinner for one, without wine, at Prinsens (moderate)	36.00/18.15
Dinner for one, without wine, at Magnus Ladulås (inexpensive)	22.00/11.10
Pint of beer (draft pilsner) in a bar	4.30/2.15
Coca-Cola in a cafe	3.50/1.75
Cup of coffee in a cafe	3.10/1.55
Admission to Drottningholm Palace	7.80/3.90
Movie ticket	11.00/5.55
Budget theater ticket	13.00/6.55

Sweden's Average Daytime Temperatures

		Jan	Feb	Mar	Apr	May	June	July	Aug	Sept	Oct	Nov	Dec
Stockholm	°F	27	26	31	40	50	59	64	62	54	45	37	32
	°C	−3	−3	−1	4	10	15	18	17	12	7	3	0
Karesuando	°F	6	5	12	23	39	54	59	51	44	31	9	5
	°C	−14	−15	−11	−5	3	12	15	11	7	−1	−13	−15
Karlstad	°F	33	30	28	37	53	63	62	59	54	41	29	26
	°C	−1	−1	−2	3	12	17	17	15	12	5	−2	−3
Lund	°F	38	36	34	43	57	63	64	61	57	47	37	37
	°C	3	2	1	6	14	17	18	16	14	8	3	3

THE MIDNIGHT SUN In the summer, the sun never fully sets in northern Sweden; even in the south, daylight may last until 11pm—and then the sun rises around 3am.

The best vantage points and dates for seeing the thrilling spectacle of the midnight sun are **Björkliden,** from May 26 to July 19; **Abisko,** from June 12 to July 4; **Kiruna,** from May 31 to July 14; and **Gällivare,** from June 2 to July 12. All are accessible by public transportation.

Remember that although the sun shines brightly late at night, it's not as strong as at midday. Bring a warm jacket or sweater.

HOLIDAYS

Sweden celebrates the following public holidays: New Year's Day (Jan 1); Epiphany (Jan 6); Good Friday; Easter Sunday; Easter Monday; Labor Day (May 1); Ascension Day (mid-May); Whitsunday and Whitmonday (late May); Midsummer Day (June 21); All Saints' Day (Nov 1); and Christmas Eve, Christmas Day, and Boxing Day (Dec 24, 25, and 26). Inquire at a tourist bureau for the dates of the holidays that vary.

SWEDEN CALENDAR OF EVENTS

The dates given here may in some cases be approximations. Be sure to check with the tourist office before you make plans to attend a specific event. For information on Walpurgis Night and midsummer celebrations, call the local tourist offices in the town where you plan to stay. (See individual chapters for the phone numbers.)

January

Kiruna Snow Festival, Kiruna. The biggest snow festival in Europe takes place in this far northern city under the Northern Lights, featuring dog-sledding and reindeer racing. Call the Kiruna Lapland Tourist Bureau (© **0980/188-80**) for more information. January 24 to 28.

Gothenburg Film Festival, Gothenburg. Entering its 4th decade, this festival attracts film buffs from all over Europe, showing 400 movies often months before their official release. For more information, call the Gothenburg Film Festival at © **0303/339-30-00.** January 27 to February 6.

April

Walpurgis Night ⚑, nationwide. Celebrations with bonfires, songs, and speeches welcome the advent of spring.

These are especially lively celebrations among university students at Uppsala, Lund, Stockholm, Gothenburg, and Umeå. April 30.

May

Drottningholm Court Theater ⚑⚑⚑. Some 30 opera and ballet performances, from baroque to early romantic, are presented in the unique 1766 Drottningholm Court Theater, Drottningholm (© **08/660-82-25;** www.dtm.se), with original decorative paintings and stage mechanisms. Take the T-banen to Brommaplan, and then bus no. 301 or 323. A steamboat runs in the summer; call © **08/587-140-00** for information. Late May to late September.

June

Midsummer ⚑⚑, nationwide. Swedes celebrate Midsummer Eve all over the country. Maypole dances and fiddle and accordion music are typical of the festivities. Dalarna observes the most traditional celebrations. Mid-June.

July

Falun Folk Music Festival. International folk musicians gather to participate in and attend concerts, seminars, lectures, exhibitions, and films on folk music. Events are conducted at various venues; contact the **Falun Folk Music Festival,** S-791 13 Falun (© **023/830-50;** www.falufolk.com), for more information. Mid-July.

Around Gotland Race, Sandhamn. The biggest and most exciting open-water Scandinavian sailing race starts and finishes at Sandhamn in the Stockholm archipelago. About 450 boats, mainly from Nordic countries, take part. Call the Stockholm tourist office for information. Two days in mid-July.

Rättviksdansen (International Festival of Folk Dance and Music), Rättvik. Every other year for some 20 years, around 1,000 folk dancers and musicians from all over the world have gathered to participate in this folkloric tradition. Last week in July.

Stockholm Jazz Festival, Stockholm ⚓. This is a big summer event occurring on the grounds and inside the Modern Art Museum on the island of Skeppsholmen. An outdoor band shell is erected, and members of the audience sit on the lawn to hear top jazz artists from Europe and America. Tickets cost 350SEK to 400SEK ($48–$55/£26–£29) per person. For more information, visit www.stockholmjazz.com. Last week in July for 7 days.

Gay Pride, Tantolunden at Liljeholmsbron, Stockholm. A 1-week event, the largest Gay Pride Festival in the Nordic countries features workshops, concerts, theater, attractions, and a local parade. For more information, call Stockholm Pride at ✆ **08/33-59-55.** July 31 to August 6 (dates can vary).

August

Medieval Week ⚓⚓, Gotland. Numerous events are held throughout the island of Gotland—tours, concerts, medieval plays, festivities, and shows. For more information, contact the Office of Medieval Week, Hästgatan 4, S-621 56 Visby (✆ **0498/29-10-70;** www.medeltidsveckan.com). Early August.

Minnesota Day, Utvandra Hus, Växjöu (Småland). Swedish-American relations are celebrated at the House of Emigrants with speeches, music, singing, and dancing; the climax is the election of the Swedish-American of the year. Call ✆ **0470/414-10** for information. Second Sunday in August.

December

Nobel Day ⚓⚓⚓, Stockholm. The king, members of the royal family, and invited guests attend the Nobel Prize ceremony for literature, physics, chemistry, medicine, physiology, and economics. Attendance is by invitation only. The ceremony is held at the concert hall and followed by a banquet at City Hall. December 10.

Lucia, the Festival of Lights, nationwide. To celebrate the shortest day and longest night of the year, young girls called "Lucias" appear in restaurants, offices, schools, and factories wearing floor-length white gowns and special headdresses, each holding a lighted candle. They are accompanied by "star boys"—young men in white with wizard hats covered with gold stars, each holding a wand with a large golden star at the top. One of these "Lucias" eventually is crowned queen. In olden days, Lucia was known as "Little Christmas." This celebration is observed nationwide. Actual planned events change from year to year and vary from community to community. The best place for tourists to observe this event is at the open-air museum at Skansen in Stockholm. December 13.

6 The Active Vacation Planner

BIKING   Much of Sweden is flat, which makes it ideal for cycling tours. Bicycles can be rented all over the country, and country hotels sometimes make them available free of charge. A typical rental is 200SEK ($28/£14) per day. For more information, contact the **Svenska Turist-föreningen (Swedish Touring Club),** P.O. Box 25, Amiralitetshuset 1, Flagmansvägen 8, S101 20 Stockholm (✆ **08-463-21-00;** www.stfturist.se).

FISHING   In Stockholm, within view of the king's palace, you can cast a line for what are some of the finest salmon in the world. Ever since Queen Christina issued a decree in 1636, Swedes have had the right to fish in waters adjoining the palace. Throughout the country, fishing is an everyday affair; it has been estimated that one of every three Swedes is an angler.

But if you'd like to fish elsewhere in Sweden, you'll need a license; the cost varies by region. Local tourist offices in any district can give you information about this. Pike, pike-perch, eel, and perch are found in the heartland and the southern parts of the country.

GOLFING   After Scotland, Sweden may have more golf enthusiasts than any other country in Europe. There are about 400 courses, and they're rarely crowded. Visitors often are granted local membership cards, and greens fees vary, depending on the club. Many golfers fly from Stockholm to Boden in the far north in the summer months to play by the light of the Midnight Sun at the **Björkliden Arctic Golf Course,** which opened in 1989 some 240km (150 miles) north of the Arctic Circle. For details, contact the **Björkliden Arctic Golf Club,** Kvarnbacksvägen 28, Bromma S-168 74 (© **09/80-40040**). For general information on courses in Sweden, contact the **Svenska Golffoürbundet,** P.O. Box 84, Daneered S-182 11 (© **08/ 622-15-00;** www.golf.se).

HIKING   Sarek, in the far north, is one of Europe's last real wilderness areas; Swedes come here to hike in the mountains, pick mushrooms, gather berries, and fish. The **Svenska Turistföreningen (Swedish Touring Club),** P.O. Box 25, Amiralitetshuset 1, Flagmansvägen 8, S101 20 Stockholm (© **08/463-21-00;** www.stfturist.se), provides accommodations in the area in mountain huts with 10 to 30 beds. The staff knows the northern part of Sweden very well and can advise you about marked tracks, rowboats, the best excursions, the problems you're likely to encounter, communications, and transportation. The company also sells trail and mountain maps.

HORSEBACK RIDING   There are numerous opportunities for overnight horseback trips in such wilderness areas as the forests of Värmland or Norrbotten, where reindeer, musk oxen, and other creatures roam. The most popular overnight horseback trips start just north of the city of Karlstad in Värmland.

Sweden also has many riding stables and schools. Ask about them at local tourist offices. One of the most popular excursions is a pony trek through the region of Sweden's highest mountain, Knebnekaise.

In sites convenient to Stockholm, you might try a ride or two around the rinks at **Djurgårdens ridskola,** Kaknäs, Djurgården (© **08/660-21-11**), or a bit farther afield at **Boügs Gård AB,** in Sollentuna (© **08/96-79-71**), which maintains a complement of Icelandic ponies, which thrive throughout the region's frigid winters. Both sites can help arrange overnight treks through the surrounding fields and forests, even though most of their business derives from rink-riding and improvement of equestrian forms.

One more unusual choice is exploring the *orsa* (outback) by horse and covered wagon. In the province of Dalarna, you can rent a horse and wagon with space for up to five people. The outback is an almost unpopulated area of wild beauty. Rides are available June through August. For more information, contact **Häst och Vagn,** Torsmo 1646, S-794 91 Orsa (© **0481/531-00**).

If you prefer to make your horseback riding arrangements before your departure from the United States, **Passage Tours of Scandinavia,** 235 Commercial Blvd., Fort Lauderdale, FL 33308 (© **800/548-5960** or 954/776-7070; www.passagetours. com), can custom design a suitable tour.

RAFTING   White-water rafting and river rafting are the two major forms of this sport. For white-water rafting, you go in a fast riverboat, the trip made more exciting by a series of rapids. Throughout the country there are both short trips and those lasting a week or so. In Värmland, contact **Branäs Sport AB,** Branäs Fritid-sanläggnin, Gondolvägem 1, S-680 60 Syssleback (© **564/475-50;** www. branas.se).

River rafting is much tamer, because you go gently down a slow-moving river in Sweden's heartland. For information about the best river rafting in Sweden, contact **Kukkolaforsen-Turist & Konferens,** P.O. Box 184, S-953 91 Haparanda (© **922/310-00;** www.kukkolaforsen.se). If you want to try log rafting, we recommend a lazy trip down the Klarälven River. You will travel through northern Värmland at a speed of 2kmph (1¼ mph) from the mouth of the Vinguümngssjoün Lake in the north to Ekshärad in the south, a distance of 110km (68 miles) in 6 days. Overnight accommodations are arranged either on the moored raft or ashore. Each raft can accommodate between two and five people, and the trips are available from May to August. For details contact **Branäs Sverigeflotten,** Klara Strand 66, S 680 63 Likenäs (© **564/402-27;** www.sverige flotten.se).

SAILING & CANOEING Canoes and sailboats can be rented all over the country; you can obtain information about this from the local tourist office. Often hotels situated near watersports areas have canoes for rent.

SWIMMING If you don't mind swimming in rather cool water, Sweden has one of the world's longest coastlines—plus some 100,000 lakes—in which you can take the plunge. The best bathing beaches are on the west coast. Both the islands of Oüland and Gotland have popular summer seaside resorts. Beaches in Sweden are generally open to the public, and nude bathing is allowed on certain designated beaches. Topless bathing for women is prevalent everywhere. If a Swedish lake is suitable for swimming, it's always signposted.

WALKING & JOGGING Sweden is ideal for either activity. Local tourist offices can provide details and sometimes even supply you with free maps of the best trails or jogging paths. In Stockholm, hotel reception desk staff can tell you the best places to go jogging nearby.

7 Health & Safety

For a general discussion of health and insurance concerns, see "Health & Safety" in chapter 3.

Put your essential medicines in your carry-on luggage and bring enough prescription medications to last through your stay. In Sweden, pharmacists cannot legally honor a prescription written outside the country; if you need more of your medications, you have to see a doctor and have a new prescription written.

Sweden's national health-care program does not cover American or Canadian visitors. Medical expenses must be paid in cash. Medical costs in Sweden are generally more reasonable than elsewhere in western Europe.

8 Specialized Travel Resources

A number of resources and organizations in North America and Britain can assist travelers with special needs in trip planning.

FOR TRAVELERS WITH DISABILITIES About two million people in Sweden have a disability; as a result, Sweden is especially conscious of their needs. In general, trains, airlines, ferries, and department stores and malls are accessible. For information about wheelchair access, ferry and air travel, parking, and other matters, your best bet is to contact the Scandinavian Tourist Board (see "Visitor Information," earlier in this chapter). For information on youth hostels with special rooms for those with disabilities, contact **Svenska Turistföreningen,** P.O. Box 25, S-101 20 Stockholm (© **08/ 463-21-00;** www.stfturist.se).

FOR GAY & LESBIAN TRAVELERS

Stockholm is the gay capital of Scandinavia, and Sweden ranks along with Norway, Denmark, and the Netherlands among the most tolerant and gay-friendly nations on earth. Gay marriage is now legal here. The age of consent is almost uniformly the same as for heterosexuals, usually 15 or 16. However, outside Stockholm and Gothenburg, you'll find very few gay bars.

Many gay and lesbian organizations in Stockholm welcome visitors from abroad. Foremost among these is the **Federation for Gay and Lesbian Rights (RFSL),** Sveavägen 57 (Box 350), S-10126 Stockholm

(© **08/501-62-900;** www.rfsl.se), open Monday through Friday from 9am to 5pm. Established in 1950, the group's headquarters is on the upper floors of the biggest gay nightlife center in Stockholm. They also operate a **Gay Switchboard** (© **08/501-62-970**), staffed with volunteers; call daily from 8am to 11pm for information. The biggest event of the year is **Gay Pride Week,** usually held the first week in August. Call or write the RFSL for information.

FOR SENIORS

Visitors over age 65 can obtain 30% off first- and second-class train travel (except Fri and Sun) on the Swedish State Railways. There are also discounts on the ferries crossing from Denmark to Sweden, and on certain attractions and performances. However, you may have to belong to a seniors' organization to qualify for certain discounts. **In Stockholm,** there are discounts on transportation, concert, theater, and opera tickets.

9 Getting There

BY PLANE

See "Getting There" in chapter 3.

THE MAJOR AIRLINES

Travelers from the U.S. East Coast usually choose **SAS** (© **800/221-2350** in the U.S.; www.Scandinavian.net). Another major competitor is **American Airlines** (© **800/433-7300** in the U.S.; www.aa. com), which offers daily flights to Stockholm from Chicago, and excellent connections through Chicago from American's vast North American network. Travelers from Seattle usually fly SAS to Copenhagen and then connect to one of the airline's frequent shuttle flights into Stockholm.

Other airlines fly to gateway European cities and then connect to other flights into Stockholm. **British Airways** (© **800/ AIRWAYS** in the U.S. and Canada; www.

britishairways.com), for example, flies from almost 20 North American cities to London/Heathrow and then connects with onward flights to Stockholm. **Northwest** (© **800/225-2525** in the U.S.; www. nwa.com) also flies at frequent intervals to London, from which ongoing flights to Stockholm are available on either SAS or British Airways. Finally, **Icelandair** (© **800/223-5500** in the U.S.; www. icelandair.com) has proved to be an excellent choice for travel to Stockholm, thanks to connections through its home-port of Reykjavik. It often offers great deals.

People traveling **from Britain** can fly **SAS** (© **0870/6072-7727** in London) from London's Heathrow to Stockholm on any of five daily nonstop flights. Flying time is about 2½ hours each way. Likewise, SAS flies daily to Stockholm from Manchester, making a brief stop in Copenhagen en route. Flight time from Manchester to Stockholm is about 3½ hours each way.

A NOTE FOR BRITISH TRAVELERS

A regular fare from the United Kingdom to Stockholm is extremely expensive, so call a travel agent about a charter flight or special air-travel promotions.

BY CAR

The ferry routes from England to Denmark and from Denmark to Sweden are the most traveled (see "Getting There" in chapter 3), but there are better choices from the Continent.

FROM GERMANY　You can drive to the northern German port of Travemünde and catch the 7½-hour ferry to the Swedish port of Trelleborg, a short drive south of Malmö. This route saves many hours by avoiding transit through Denmark. If you want to visit Denmark before Sweden, you can take the 3-hour car ferry from Travemünde to Gedser in southern Denmark. From Gedser, the E-64 and the E-4 express highways head north to Copenhagen. After a visit here, you can take the Øresund Bridge from Copenhagen to Malmö.

FROM NORWAY　From Oslo, E-18 goes east through Karlstad all the way to Stockholm. This is a long but scenic drive.

FROM DENMARK　The most popular way of reaching Sweden from Denmark is to drive across the new $3 billion Øresund Fixed Link, a bridge and a tunnel, plus an artificial island spanning the icy Øresund Sound between Copenhagen and Malmö. The bridge provides road and rail connections between the Scandinavian peninsula and the rest of Europe, and is the final link in the centuries-old dream of connecting the Continent from its northern tip to its southern toe. In other words, you can now drive all the way in either direction without taking a boat, ferry, or hydrofoil. Car ferries run frequently from Copenhagen to Malmö and from Helsingør in North Zealand to Helsingborg on Sweden's west coast. To reach Stockholm from Malmö, take E-6 north along the coast toward Helsingborg. In the Helsingborg area, turn northeast at the junction with E-4 and continue across southern Sweden. Part of this highway is a four-lane express motorway, and part is a smaller national highway.

BY TRAIN

Copenhagen is the main rail hub between the other Scandinavian countries and the rest of Europe. There are seven daily trains from Copenhagen to Stockholm, and six from Copenhagen to Gothenburg. All connect with the Danish ferries that operate to Sweden via Helsingør or Frederikshavn.

There are at least three trains a day from Oslo to Stockholm (travel time: about 6½ hr.). One of the trains leaves Oslo about 11pm. There are also three trains a day from Oslo to Gothenburg (travel time: about 4 hr.).

RAIL PASSES FOR NORTH AMERICAN TRAVELERS

For information on rail passes, please refer to "Getting There" in chapter 3.

BY SHIP & FERRY

FROM DENMARK　Ferries ply the waters for the brief run from Helsingør, a short drive north of Copenhagen, and Helsingborg, Sweden, just across the narrow channel that separates the countries. The 25-minute trip on a conventional ferry (not a catamaran) begins at 10- to 40-minute intervals, 24 hours a day. Operated by **Scandlines** (© **33-15-15-15;** www.scandlines.dk in Copenhagen), it's one of the most popular ferry routes in Europe. Round-trip passage costs 460DKK ($77/£34) for a car with up to nine passengers; the ticket is valid for up to 2 months. Pedestrians pay 34DKK ($5.70/£2.50) round-trip, regardless of when they return.

FROM ENGLAND Two English ports—Harwich (year-round) and Newcastle-upon-Tyne (summer only)—offer ferry service to Sweden. Harwich to Gothenburg takes 23 to 25 hours; Newcastle to Gothenburg, 27 hours. Boats on both routes offer overnight accommodations and the option of transporting cars. Prices are lower for passengers who book in advance through the company's U.S. agent. For details, call **Sea Europe Holidays,** 6801 Lake Worth Rd., Suite 107, Lake Worth, FL 33467 (© **800/533-3755** in the U.S.; www.seaeurope.com).

FROM GERMANY Stena Line Ferries (© **031/85-80-00;** www.stenaline.com) sails daily from Kiel to Gothenburg. The trip takes 14 hours and costs $308 (£171) for a one-way passage.

10 General-Interest Tours

Sweden's various regions, especially Dalarna and Lapland, offer such a variety of sights and activities that you may want to take an escorted tour. The following tours are just a small sample of what's available. Contact your travel agent to learn about tours.

ScanAm World Tours (© **800/545-2204;** www.scanamtours.com) offers some of the best tours, taking you on Göta Canal cruises or along the lakes, waterways, and into the folkloric district of Dalarna. Minimum tours are for 2 nights, including hotels, costing $295 per person. From here, tours range upward to 7 nights, including hotels, costing $865 per person.

"Gotland Island and the City of Roses" is a cruise on the Gotland Line from Stockholm to Nynäshamn or from Oskarshamn to Visby, including 2 nights at the Visby Hotel or Hotel Solhem. The 3-day tour is available May through September.

Scantours (© **800/223-7226;** www.scantours.com) offers the most diverse tours of Sweden, ranging from Göta Canal cruises to a combined Stockholm and Helsinki jaunt, lasting 5 days and 4 nights.

Passage Tours (© **800/548-5960;** www.passagetours.com) offers trips to both Stockholm and the "Kingdom of Crystal," with stopovers in such glass factories as Kosta Boda and Orrefors. Trips to the port of Kalmar on the Baltic Sea are also included, as well as visits to the island of Öland.

The archipelago that fronts Stockholm's harbor is one of the most frequently visited wilderness areas in Northern Europe, thanks to its convenience to the Swedish capital. One outfitter that can help you appreciate the archipelago's resources in any season is **30,000 Öar** (30,000 Islands), Industrigatan 2A, Stockholm 11285 (© **08/545-52-600;** www.30000oar.se). Owner Bengt Kull will propose a range of activities.

11 Getting Around

BY PLANE

WITHIN SWEDEN For transatlantic flights coming from North America, Stockholm is Sweden's major gateway for Scandinavia's best-known airline, **SAS** (Scandinavian Airlines System). For flights arriving from other parts of Europe, the airport at Gothenburg supplements Stockholm's airport by funneling traffic into the Swedish heartland. In the mid-1990s, SAS acquired **LIN Airlines (Linjeflyg);** it now has access to small and medium-size airports throughout Sweden, including such remote but scenic outposts as Kiruna in Swedish Lapland. Among the larger Swedish cities serviced by SAS are

Malmö, capital of Sweden's château country; Karlstad, center of the verdant and folklore-rich district of Värmland; and Kalmar, a good base for exploring the glassworks district.

During the summer, SAS offers a number of promotional "minifares," which enable one to travel round-trip between two destinations for just slightly more than the price of a conventional one-way ticket on the same route. Children 11 and under travel free during the summer, and up to two children 12 to 17 can travel with a parent at significantly reduced rates. Airfares tend to be most reduced during July, with promotions almost as attractive during most of June and August. A minimum 3-night stopover at the destination is required for these minifares, and it must include a Friday or a Saturday night. When buying your tickets, always ask the airline or travel agency about special promotions and corresponding restrictions.

Those under 26 can take advantage of SAS's special **standby fares,** and seniors over 65 can apply for additional discounts, depending on the destination.

WITHIN SCANDINAVIA The best way to get around the whole of Scandinavia is to take advantage of the air passes that apply to the entire region or, if you're traveling extensively in Europe, to use the special European passes. The vast distances of Scandinavia encourage air travel between some of its most far-flung points. One of the most worthwhile promotions is SAS's **Visit Scandinavia Airpass.** See "By Plane," under "Getting Around," in chapter 3.

BY TRAIN

The Swedish word for train is *tåg,* and the national system is the Statens Järnvägar, the Swedish State Railways.

Swedish trains follow tight schedules. Trains leave Malmö, Helsingborg, and Gothenburg for Stockholm every hour throughout the day, Monday through Friday. There are trains every hour, or every other hour, to and from most big Swedish towns. On *expresståg* runs, seats must be reserved.

Children under 12 travel free when accompanied by an adult, and those up to age 18 are eligible for discounts.

BY BUS

Rail lines cover only some of Sweden's vast distances. Where the train tracks end, a bus usually serves as the link with remote villages. Buses usually are equipped with toilets, adjustable seats, reading lights, and a telephone. Fares depend on the distance traveled. **Swebus** (© 036/290-80-00; www.swebusexpress.se), the country's largest bus company, provides information at the bus or railway stations in most cities. For travelers who don't buy a special rail pass (such as Eurail or ScanRail), bus travel between cities sometimes can be cheaper than traveling the same distances by rail. It's a lot less convenient and frequent, however, except in the far north, where there isn't any alternative.

BY CAR FERRY

Considering that Sweden has some 100,000 lakes and one of the world's longest coastlines, ferries play a surprisingly small part in the transportation network.

After the car ferry crossings from northern Germany and Denmark, the most popular route is from the mainland to the island of Gotland, in the Baltic. Service is available from Oskarshamn and Nynäshamn (call © 0771/22-33-00, Destination Gotland, for more information). The famous "white boats" of the Waxholm Steamship Company (© 08/679-58-30; www.waxholmsbolaget.se) also travel to many destinations in the Stockholm archipelago.

BY CAR

As one of the best-developed industrialized nations in Europe, Sweden maintains an excellent network of roads and highways, particularly in the southern provinces and in the central lake district. Major highways in the far north are kept clear of snow by heavy equipment that's in place virtually year-round. If you rent a car at any bona-fide rental agency, you'll be given the appropriate legal documents, including proof of adequate insurance (in the form of a "Green Card") as specified by your car-rental agreement. Current driver's licenses from Canada, the United Kingdom, New Zealand, Australia, and the United States are acceptable in Sweden.

RENTALS　The major U.S.-based car-rental firms are represented throughout Sweden, both at airports and in urban centers. For a list of U.S. and Canadian car-rental phone numbers, see "Rentals" in chapter 3.

12 Recommended Books

ART & ARCHITECTURE　The most comprehensive survey of Swedish art is found in *A History of Swedish Art,* by Mereth Lindgren (Signum i Lung), published in 1987. In architecture, *Sweden: 20th Century,* edited by Claes Caldenby (Prestel Publishing), offers a current perspective (it was published in 1998).

HISTORY & MYTHOLOGY　*The Early Vasas: A History of Sweden, 1523–1611,* by Michael Roberts (Cambridge), covers one of the most dramatic and action-filled eras in Sweden's long history.

Scandinavian Folk & Fairy Tales, edited by Claire Booss (Avenel), is an extraordinary collection filled with elves, dwarfs, trolls, goblins, and other spirits of the house and barnyard.

BIOGRAPHY　*Sweden in North America (1638–1988),* by Sten Carlsson (Streiffert & Co.), follows the lives of some of the 2% of the North American population of Swedish background—from Greta Garbo to Charles Lindbergh.

Alfred Nobel and the Nobel Prizes, by Nils K. Ståhle (Swedish Institute), traces the life of the 19th-century Swedish industrialist and creator of the coveted awards that bear his name.

Garbo: Her Story, by Antoni Gronowicz (Simon & Schuster), is a controversial, unauthorized memoir based on a long and intimate friendship; it goes beyond the fabulous face, with many candid details of this most reluctant of movie legends.

LITERATURE & THEATER　*A History of Swedish Literature,* by Ingemar Algulin (Swedish Institute), is the best overview on the subject—from the runic inscriptions of the Viking age up to modern fiction.

The Story of Gösta Berling, by Selma Lagerlöf (in various international editions), is the acclaimed work—originally published in 1891—that Garbo filmed.

Three Plays: Father, Miss Julie, Easter, by August Strindberg (Penguin), provides an insight into the world of this strange Swedish genius who wrote a number of highly arresting dramas, of which these are some of the best known.

FILM　*Ingmar Bergman: The Cinema as Mistress,* by Philip Mosley (Marion Boyards), is a critical study of Bergman's *oeuvre* dating from his earliest work as a writer/director in the late 1940s up to *Autumn Sonata.*

Swedish Cinema, from Ingeborg Holm to Fanny and Alexander, by Peter Cowie (Swedish Institute), covers the complete history of Swedish films, from the emergence of the silent era, to the rise of Ingmar Bergman, up to the most recent wave.

PIPPI LONGSTOCKING TALES The world was saddened to learn of the death in 2002 of Astrid Lindgren, the Swedish writer of the Pippi Longstocking tales, who died at the age of 94 at her home in Stockholm. One of the world's most widely translated authors, Lindgren horrified parents but captivated millions of children around the globe with her whimsical, rollicking stories about a carrot-haired *enfant terrible*. In 1999 she was voted the most popular Swede of the century, having produced more than 70 books for young people. The best known is *Pippi Longstocking* (Seafarer Book), first published in 1945.

FAST FACTS: Sweden

Area Code The international country code for Sweden is **46**. The local city (area) codes are given for all phone numbers in the Sweden chapters.

Business Hours Generally, **banks** are open Monday through Friday from 9:30am to 3pm. In some larger cities, banks extend their hours, usually on Thursday or Friday, until 5:30 or 6pm. Most **offices** are open Monday through Friday from 8:30 or 9am to 5pm (sometimes to 3 or 4pm in the summer); on Saturday, offices and factories are closed, or open for only a half-day. Most **stores and shops** are open Monday through Friday between 9:30am and 6pm, and Saturday from 9:30am to somewhere between 1 and 4pm. Once a week, usually on Monday or Friday, some of the larger stores are open from 9:30am to 7pm (during July and Aug, to 6pm).

Camera & Film Cameras (especially the famed Hasselblad), film, projectors, and enlarging equipment are good values in Sweden. Practically all the world's brands are found here. Photographic shops give excellent service, often developing and printing in 1 day.

Dentists For emergency dental services, ask your hotel or host for the location of the nearest dentist. Nearly all dentists in Sweden speak English.

Doctors Hotel desks usually can refer you to a local doctor, nearly all of whom speak English. If you need emergency treatment, your hotel also should be able to direct you to the nearest facility. In case of an accident or injury away from the hotel, call the nearest police station.

Drug Laws Sweden imposes severe penalties for the possession, use, purchase, sale, or manufacture of illegal drugs ("illegal" is defined much as in the U.S.). Penalties often (but not always) are based on quantity. Possession of a small amount of drugs, either hard or soft, can lead to a heavy fine and deportation. Possession of a large amount of drugs can entail imprisonment from 3 months to 15 years, depending on the circumstances and the presiding judge.

Drugstores Called *apotek* in Swedish, drugstores are generally open Monday through Friday from 9am to 6pm and Saturday from 9am to 1pm. In larger cities, one drugstore in every neighborhood stays open until 7pm. All drugstores post a list of the names and addresses of these stores (called *nattapotek*) in their windows.

Electricity In Sweden, the electricity is 220 volts AC (50 cycles). To operate North American hair dryers and other electrical appliances, you'll need an electrical transformer (sometimes erroneously called a converter) and plugs that fit the two-pin round continental electrical outlets that are standard in Sweden. Transformers can be bought at hardware stores. Before using any American-made appliance, always ask about it at your hotel desk.

Embassies & Consulates All embassies are in Stockholm. The Embassy of the **United States** is at Daj Hammarskjölds Väg 31, S-115 89 Stockholm (© **08/783-53-00**); **United Kingdom,** Skarpögatan 6-8, S-115 93 Stockholm (© **08/671-30-00**); **Canada,** Tegelbacken 4, S-103 23 Stockholm (© **08/453-30-00**); **Australia,** Sergels Torg 12, S-103 86 Stockholm (© **08/613-29-00**). **New Zealand** does not maintain an embassy in Sweden, but there is a consulate located at Norrlandgatan 15, 103 95 Stockholm (© **08/506-3200**).

Emergencies Call © **90-000** from anywhere in Sweden if you need an ambulance, the police, or the fire department *(brandlarm).*

Language The national language is Swedish, a Germanic tongue, and there are many regional dialects. Some minority groups speak Norwegian and Finnish. English is a required course of study in school and is commonly spoken, even in the hinterlands, and especially among young people.

Liquor Laws Most restaurants, pubs, and bars in Sweden are licensed to serve liquor, wine, and beer. Some places are licensed only for wine and beer. Purchases of wine, liquor, and export beer are available only through the government-controlled monopoly, *Systembolaget.* Branch stores, spread throughout the country, are usually open Monday through Friday from 9am to 6pm. The minimum age for buying alcoholic beverages in Sweden is 21.

Mail Post offices in Sweden are usually open Monday through Friday from 9am to 6pm and Saturday from 9am to noon. Sending a postcard to North America costs 7.18SEK ($1/50p) by surface mail, 10.5SEK ($1.45/75p) by airmail. Letters weighing no more than 20 grams ($7/10$ oz.) cost the same. Mailboxes can easily be recognized—they carry a yellow post horn on a blue background. You also can buy stamps in most tobacco shops and stationers.

Maps Many tourist offices supply routine maps of their districts free of charge, and you also can contact one of the Swedish automobile clubs. Bookstores throughout Sweden also sell detailed maps of the country and of such major cities as Gothenburg and Stockholm. The most reliable country maps are published by Hallwag. The best and most detailed city maps are those issued by Falk, which have a particularly good and properly indexed map to Stockholm.

Newspapers & Magazines In big cities such as Stockholm and Gothenburg, English-language newspapers, including the latest editions of the *International Herald Tribune* and *USA Today,* are usually available. American newspapers are not commonly available, but in Stockholm and Gothenburg you can purchase such London newspapers as *The Times.* At kiosks or newsstands in major cities, you also can purchase the European editions of *Time* and *Newsweek.*

Passports See "Fast Facts: Denmark" in chapter 3.

Police In an emergency, dial © **90-000** anywhere in the country.

Radio & TV In summer, Radio Stockholm broadcasts a special program for English-speaking tourists, "T-T-T-Tourist Time," on 103.3 MHz (FM) from 6 to 7pm daily. Swedish radio transmits P1 on 92.4 MHz (FM) and P2 on 96.2 MHz (FM) in the Stockholm area. P3 is transmitted on 103.3 MHz (102.9 MHz in southern Stockholm), a wavelength shared by Radio Stockholm and local programs.

The two most important TV channels, STV1 and STV2, are nonprofit. There are three major privately-operated stations—Channel 4, TV3, and TV5, as well as several minor stations.

Restrooms The word for toilet in Swedish is *toalett,* and public facilities are found in department stores, rail and air terminals, and subway (T-banen) stations. They're also located along some of the major streets, parks, and squares. DAMER means women and HERRAR means men. Sometimes the sign is abbreviated to D or H, and often the toilet is marked WC. Most toilets are free, although a few have attendants to offer towels and soap. In an emergency you also can use the toilets in most hotels and restaurants, although in principle they're reserved for guests.

Shoe Repairs Shoe-repair shops rarely accommodate you while you wait. In summer, especially in July, many shops close, but the larger stores in the center of Stockholm have their own repair departments. If all you need is a new heel, look for something called *klackbar* in the stores or shoe departments of department stores. They'll make repairs while you wait.

Taxes Sweden imposes a "value-added tax," called *moms,* on most goods and services. Visitors from North America can beat the tax, however, by shopping in stores with the yellow-and-blue tax-free shopping sign. There are more than 15,000 of these stores in Sweden. To get a refund, your total purchase must cost a minimum of 200SEK ($28). Tax refunds range from 12.5% to 17.5%, depending on the amount purchased. *Moms* begins at 12% on food items, but is 25% for most goods and services. The tax is part of the purchase price, but you can get a tax-refund voucher before you leave the store. When you leave Sweden, take the voucher to a tax-free customs desk at the airport or train station you're leaving from. They will give you your *moms* refund (minus a small service charge) before you wing off to your next non-Swedish destination. Two requirements: You cannot use your purchase in Sweden (it should be sealed in its original packaging), and it must be taken out of the country within 1 month after purchase. For more information, call **Global Refunds** at © **08/545-28-440** in Sweden; www.globalrefund.com.

Telephone, Telex & Fax Instructions in English are posted in public phone boxes, which can be found on street corners. Very few phones in Sweden are coin operated; most require a phone card, which can be purchased at most newspaper stands and tobacco shops. You can send a telegram by phoning © **00-21** anytime.

Time Sweden is on Central European Time—Greenwich Mean Time plus 1 hour, or Eastern Standard Time plus 6 hours. The clocks are advanced 1 hour in summer.

Tipping Hotels include a 15% service charge in your bill. Restaurants, depending on their class, add 13% to 15% to your tab. Taxi drivers are entitled to 8% of the fare, and cloakroom attendants usually get 6SEK (85¢/45p).

Water The water is safe to drink all over Sweden. However, don't drink water from lakes, rivers, or streams, regardless of how clear and pure it appears.

14

Introducing Stockholm

Stockholm is the most regal, elegant, and intriguing city of Scandinavia. It presides over a country the size of California (without the massive population) and believes in high taxes and big government. It is one of the world's most liberal, progressive, and democratic societies, a devotee of such issues as same-sex unions and gender equality.

During World War II, many cities to the south of Sweden were practically razed to the ground, including Berlin and Hamburg. Because of Sweden's neutrality during the war, it was saved from aerial bombardment. Much of what you see today is antique, especially the historical heart, Gamla Stan (the Old Town).

Yet Sweden is one of the world's leading exponents of functionalism, or *funkis*. Some of the world's most innovative architecture appears on its fringes. Swedish fashion and design in glassware, furnishings, and industrial products remain at the cutting edge.

Stockholm also enjoys the most dramatic setting of any capital city of Europe, with 1.9 million people to enjoy it. The city is built on 14 islands in Lake Mälaren, which marks the beginning of an archipelago of 24,000 islands, skerries, and islets stretching all the way to the Baltic Sea. A city of bridges and islands, towers and steeples, cobblestone squares and broad boulevards, Renaissance splendor and steel-and-glass skyscrapers, Stockholm also has access to nature just a short distance away. You can even go fishing in the downtown waterways, thanks to a long-standing decree signed by Queen Christina.

Although the city was founded more than 7 centuries ago, it did not become the official capital of Sweden until the mid–17th century. Today, Stockholm reigns over a modern welfare state.

1 Orientation

ARRIVING

BY PLANE   You'll arrive at **Stockholm Arlanda Airport** (© **08/797-61-00** for information on flights), about 45km (28 miles) north of the city on the E-4 highway. A long, covered walkway connects the international and domestic terminals.

Depending on traffic, the fastest, but not necessarily the cheapest, way to go from the airport to the Central Station within Stockholm is on the **Arlanda Express** train, which takes only 20 minutes and is covered by the Eurailpass. This high-speed line is the finest option for the rail traveler. Trains run every 15 to 20 minutes daily from 5am to midnight. If you don't have a rail pass, the cost of a one-way ticket is 200SEK ($28/£15) for adults and 100SEK ($14/£7.30) for seniors and students (those under 8 ride free). For more information, call © **020/22-22-24.**

A slower (about 40 min.) but cheaper option involves taking a bus from outside the airport terminal building. It takes you to the **City Terminal,** on Klarabergsviadukten, for 95SEK ($13/£6.95).

A taxi to or from the airport is expensive, costing 400SEK ($55/£29) to 500SEK ($69/£37) or more. (See "Getting Around," later in this chapter, for the name of a reputable taxi company.)

BY TRAIN   Trains arrive at Stockholm's **Centralstationen (Central Station; © 07/ 717-57-575** in Sweden) on Vasagatan, in the city center, where connections can be made to Stockholm's subway, the T-bana. Follow the TUNNELBANA sign, which is sometimes abbreviated to merely the capital letter T in blue ink on a white background, enclosed with a blue circle.

Only large towns and cities can be reached by rail from Stockholm's Centralstationen.

BY BUS   Buses also arrive at the Centralstationen city terminal, and from here you can catch the T-bana to your final Stockholm destination. For bus information or reservations, check with the bus system's **ticket offices** at the station (© **08/600- 1000).** Offices in the station labeled BUS STOP sell bus tickets. For travel beyond Sweden, call **Euroline** (© **08/762-5960).**

BY CAR   Getting into Stockholm by car is relatively easy because the major national expressway from the south, E-4, joins with the national expressway, E-3, coming in from the west, and leads right into the heart of the city. Stay on the highway until you see the turnoff for Central Stockholm (or Centrum).

Parking in Stockholm is extremely difficult unless your hotel has a garage. Call your hotel in advance and find out what the parking situation is, as most hotels do not offer parking. However, if you're driving into the city, you can often park long enough to unload your luggage; a member of the hotel staff will then direct you to the nearest parking garage.

BY FERRY   Large ships, including those of the **Silja Line,** Kungsgatan 2 (© **08/22- 21-40),** and the **Viking Line,** Centralstationen (© **08/452-40-00),** arrive at specially constructed berths jutting seaward from a point near the junction of Södermalm and Gamla Stan. This neighborhood is called Stadsgården, and the avenue that runs along the adjacent waterfront is known as Stadsgårdshamnen. The nearest T-bana stop is Slussen, a 3-minute walk from the Old Town. Holders of a valid Eurailpass can ride the Silja ferries to Helsinki and Turku at a reduced rate.

Other ferries arrive from Gotland (whose capital is Visby), but these boats dock at Nynäshamn, south of Stockholm. Take a Nynäshamn-bound bus from the Central Station in Stockholm or the SL commuter train to reach the ferry terminal at Nynäshamn.

VISITOR INFORMATION

The **Stockholm Tourist Center,** Sweden House, Hamngatan 27, off Kungsträdgården (Box 16282), S-10325 Stockholm (© **08/508-28-508),** is open year-round June to August Monday to Friday from 9am to 7pm, Saturday 10am to 5pm, and Sunday 10am to 4pm. Maps, brochures, and advice, are available for free, and tickets to sporting and cultural events, tourist cards, the Stockholm Card, and books are for sale. The staff will also reserve rooms for you, on-site, at hotels and youth hostels.

The largest organization of its kind in all of Sweden is the **Kulturhuset,** Sergels Torg 3 (© **08/508-31-508**). It was built in 1974 by the city of Stockholm as a showcase for Swedish and international art and theater. There are no permanent exhibits; instead, the various spaces inside are allocated to a changing array of paintings, sculpture, photographs, and live performance groups. Kulturhuset also serves as the focal point for information about other cultural activities and organizations throughout Sweden and the rest of Europe. Inside are a snack bar, a library (which has newspapers in several languages), a reading room, a collection of recordings, and a somewhat bureaucratic openness to new art forms. Open Tuesday to Friday 11am to 7pm, Saturday and Sunday 11am to 5pm. No admission is charged.

CITY LAYOUT

MAIN STREETS & ARTERIES Stockholm's major streets—**Kungsgatan** (the main shopping street), **Birger Jarlsgatan, Drottningsgata,** and **Strandvägen** (which leads to Djurgården)—are on Norrmalm (north of the Old Town) and are reserved (with some exceptions) mainly for pedestrians. **Stureplan,** which lies at the junction of the major avenues Kungsgatan and Birger Jarlsgatan, is the commercial hub of the city.

About 4 blocks east of Stureplan rises **Hötorget City,** a landmark of modern urban planning, which includes five 18-story skyscrapers. Its main traffic-free artery is **Sergelgatan,** a 3-block shopper's promenade that eventually leads to the modern sculptures at the center of Sergels Torg.

About 9 blocks south of Stureplan, at **Gustav Adolfs Torg,** are both the Royal Dramatic Theater and the Royal Opera House.

A block east of the flaming torches of the opera house is the verdant north-to-south stretch of **Kungsträdgården**—part avenue, part public park—which serves as a popular gathering place for students and a resting spot for shoppers.

Three blocks to the southeast, on a famous promontory, are the landmark Grand Hotel and the National Museum.

Most visitors to Stockholm arrive at either the SAS Airport Bus Terminal, the Central Station, or Stockholm's Central (Public) Bus Station. Each of these is in the heart of the city, on the harbor front, about 7 blocks due west of the opera house. **Kungsholmen (King's Island)** lies across a narrow canal from the rest of the city, a short walk west from the Central Station. It's visited chiefly by those who want to tour Stockholm's elegant Stadshuset (City Hall).

South of **Gamla Stan (Old Town),** and separated from it by a narrow but much-navigated stretch of water, is **Södermalm,** the southern district of Stockholm. Quieter than its northern counterpart, it's an important residential area with a distinctive flavor of its own and a nostalgic reputation for housing, sometimes in overcrowded squalor, the factory workers of the 19th century's industrial revolution. Fast-growing, with a higher density of new, counterculture bars, stores, and nightclubs than any other district of Stockholm, it emerged around the turn of the millennium as one of the most talked-about districts of the capital. Greta Garbo claimed this island as the site of her childhood home.

To the east of Gamla Stan, on a large and forested island completely surrounded by the complicated waterways of Stockholm, is **Djurgården (Deer Park).** The summer pleasure ground of Stockholm is the site of many of its most popular attractions: the open-air museums of Skansen, the *Vasa* man-of-war, Gröna Lund's Tivoli, the Waldemarsudde estate of the "painting prince" Eugen, and the Nordic Museum.

FINDING AN ADDRESS All even numbers are on one side of the street and all odd numbers are on the opposite side. Buildings are listed in numerical order but often have an A, B, or C after the number. In the very center of town, numbered addresses start from Sergels Torg.

MAPS Free maps of Stockholm are available at the tourist office, but if you want to explore the narrow old streets of Gamla Stan, you'll need a more detailed map. Pocket-size maps with a street index that can be opened and folded like a wallet are sold at most newsstands in central Stockholm and at major bookstores, including **Akademibokhandeln,** Mäster Samuelsgatan 28 (© **08/4021100**).

NEIGHBORHOODS IN BRIEF

As you'd expect of a city spread across 14 major islands in an archipelago, there are many neighborhoods, but those of concern to the average visitor lie in central Stockholm.

We'll begin with the most nostalgic and evocative—and our long-time favorite for sleeping or dining.

Gamla Stan (Old Town) The "cradle" of Stockholm, Gamla Stan lies at the entrance to Lake Mälaren on the Baltic. Its oldest city wall dates from the 13th century. The Old Town, along with the excavated wreck of the *Vasa*, is the most popular attraction in Stockholm. The hotels here are in general the most evocative of 18th-century Stockholm, built in romantic architectural styles, and there are many options for drinking and carousing as twilight falls. The downside of this area is that there are few hotels, and they tend to be expensive; there are, however, dozens of restaurants. Gamla Stan's major shopping street is the narrow Västerlånggatan, reserved almost exclusively for pedestrians, but many artisans' galleries, souvenir shops, and antiques stores abound on its small lanes. Its main square, and the heart of the ancient city, is Stortorget.

Norrmalm North of Gamla Stan, what was once a city suburb is now the cultural and commercial heart of modern Stockholm. Chances are your hotel will be in this district, as the area is generously endowed with hotels in all price ranges; it's also the most convenient location, as it encompasses the City Terminal and the Central Station.

Hotels here are not the most romantic in town, but they're generally modern, up-to-date, and well run.

The most famous park in Stockholm, Kungsträdgården (King's Garden), is also in Norrmalm. In summer, this park is a major rendezvous point. Norrmalm also embraces the important squares of Sergels Torg and Hötorget, the latter a modern shopping complex. Norrmalm's major pedestrian shopping street is Drottninggatan, which starts at the bridge to the Old Town.

Vasastaden As Norrmalm expanded northward, the new district of Vasastaden was created. It's split by a trio of main arteries: St. Eriksgatan, Sveavägen, and Odengatan. The area around St. Eriksplan is called "the Off-Broadway of Stockholm" because it has so many theaters. Increasingly, this district has attracted fashionable restaurants and bars, and has become a popular residential area for young Stockholmers who work in fields such as journalism, television, and advertising.

Vasastaden is slightly more removed from the scene of the action, but it's still a good bet for hotels. In New York City terms, Norrmalm would be like staying in the Times Square area, whereas Vasastaden would be equivalent to staying on the Upper East Side. Hotels in Vasastaden come in a wide range of price categories.

Kungsholmen Once known as "Grey Friars Farm," Kungsholmen (King's Island), to the west of Gamla Stan, is the site of City Hall. Established by Charles XI in the 17th century as a zone for industry and artisans, the island now has been gentrified. One of its major arteries is Fleminggatan. Along Norrmälarstrand, old Baltic cutters tie up to the banks. Stockholm's newspapers have their headquarters at Marieberg on the southwestern tip of the island.

Södermalm South of Gamla Stan, Södermalm (where Greta Garbo was born) is the largest and most populated district of Stockholm. Once synonymous with poverty, this working-class area is becoming more fashionable, especially with artists, writers, and young people. If you don't come here to stay in one of the moderately priced hotels or to dine in one of its restaurants, you might want to take the Katarina elevator, at Södermalmstorg, Slussen, for a good view of Stockholm and its harbor. Admission is 10SEK ($1.40/75p), free for ages 6 and under.

Östermalm In central Stockholm, east of Birger Jarlsgatan, the main artery, lies Östermalm. In the Middle Ages, the royal family used to keep its horses, and even its armies, here. Today it's the site of the Army Museum.

There are wide, straight streets, and it is also home to one of the city's biggest parks, Humlegården, dating from the 17th century.

This is another area of Stockholm that's a hotel district. Östermalm doesn't have quite the convenience of Norrmalm and Vasastaden, but it's still not so far removed from the action as to be called inconvenient. In summer, when visitors from all over the world are in town, this is a good place to hunt for a room. Because Norrmalm and Vasastaden are located close to the Central Station, hotels in those neighborhoods tend to fill up very quickly.

Djurgården To the east of Gamla Stan is Djurgården (Deer Park), a forested island in a lake that's the summer recreation area of Stockholm. Here you can visit the open-air folk museums of Skansen, the *Vasa* man-of-war, Gröna Lund's Tivoli (Stockholm's own version of the Tivoli), the Waldemarsudde estate and gardens of the "painting prince" Eugen, and the Nordic Museum. The fastest way to get here is over the bridge at Strandvägen/Narvavägen.

Skeppsholmen On its own little island, and reached by crossing Skeppsholmsbron, a bridge from the Blasieholmen district, Skeppsholmen is like a world apart from the rest of bustling Stockholm. Although it makes for a pleasant stroll, most people visit it to see the exhibits at the Moderna Museet.

2 Getting Around

BY PUBLIC TRANSPORTATION

You can travel throughout Stockholm county by bus, local train, subway (T-bana), and tram, going from Singö in the north to Nynäshamn in the south. The routes are divided into zones, and one ticket is valid for all types of public transportation in the same zone within 1 hour of the time the ticket is stamped.

REGULAR FARES   The basic fare for public transportation (in Stockholm this means subway, tram/streetcar, or bus) requires tickets purchased from the agent in the toll booth on the subway platform, not from a vending machine. Each ticket costs 20SEK ($2.75/£1.45) and allows travel to points within most of urban Stockholm, all the way to the borders of the inner city. You can transfer (or double back and return to your starting point) within 1 hour of your departure free of charge.

SPECIAL DISCOUNT TICKETS   Your best transportation bet is to purchase a **tourist season ticket.** A 1-day card, costing 60SEK ($8.30/£4.40) for adults and 30SEK ($4.15/£2.20) for children 7 to 17 and seniors, is valid for 24 hours of unlimited travel by T-bana, bus, and commuter train within Stockholm. It also includes passage on the ferry to Djurgården. Most visitors prefer the 3-day card for 180SEK ($25/£13) for adults and 90SEK ($12/£6.60) for children 7 to 17 and seniors, valid for 72 hours in both Stockholm and the adjacent county. The 3-day card is also valid for admission to Skansen, Kaknästornet, and Gröna Lund. Kids up to 7 years of age can travel free with an adult. These tickets are available at tourist information offices, subway stations, and most news vendors. Call © **08/600-1000** for more information.

Stockholmskortet (Stockholm Card) is a personal discount card that allows unlimited travel by bus, subway, and local trains throughout the city and county of Stockholm (except on airport buses). You can take a sightseeing tour with City Sightseeing, where you can get on and off as often as you please. These tours are available daily from mid-June to mid-August. In addition, the card enables you to take a boat trip to the Royal Palace of Drottningholm for half-price. Admission to 75 museums and attractions is also included in the package.

You can purchase the card at several places in the city, including the Tourist Center in Sweden House, Hotell Centralen, the Central Station, the tourist information desk in City Hall (in summer), the Kaknäs TV tower, SL-Center Sergels Torg (subway entrance level), and Pressbyrän newsstands. The cards are stamped with the date and time at the first point of usage. A 24-hour card costs 270SEK ($37/£20) for adults and 120SEK ($17/£8.75) for children 7 to 17 and seniors; a 48-hour card is 420SEK ($58/£31) for adults and 160SEK ($22/£12) for children and seniors; and a 72-hour card is 540SEK ($75/£39) for adults and 190SEK ($26/£14) for children and seniors.

BY T-BANA (SUBWAY)   Before entering the subway, passengers tell the ticket seller the destination and then purchase tickets. Subway entrances are marked with a blue *T* on a white background. For information about schedules, routes, and fares, phone © **08/600-1000.**

BY BUS   Where the subway line ends, the bus begins; therefore, if a subway connection doesn't conveniently cover a particular area of Stockholm, a bus will. The two systems have been coordinated to complement each other. Many visitors use a bus to reach Djurgården (although you can walk) because the T-bana doesn't go here.

BY CAR
If you're driving around the Swedish capital, you'll find several parking garages in the city center as well as on the outskirts. In general, you can park at marked spaces Monday through Friday from 8am to 6pm. Exceptions or rules for specific areas are indicated on signs in the area.

BY TAXI

Taxis are expensive—in fact, the most expensive in the world—with the meter starting at 42SEK ($5.80/£3.05). A short ride can easily cost 120SEK ($17/£8.75). It costs around 200SEK ($28/£15) to reach most destinations within the city limits. Those that display an illuminated dome light can be hailed directly, or you can order one by phone. **Taxi Stockholm** (© 08/15-00-00) is one of the city's larger, more reputable companies. Unlike other Nordic nations, Sweden has not been successful at regulating its taxi industry, a subject that has caused consternation among members of the country's tourist industry. In Sweden, it's best to inquire before you get in a taxi (no matter if it is metered or not) what that price will be. In Stockholm, Taxi Stockholm is among the most fair and reliable of the companies.

BY FERRY

Ferries from Skeppsbron on Gamla Stan (near the bridge to Södermalm) will take you to Djurgården if you don't want to walk or go by bus. They leave every 20 minutes Monday to Saturday, and about every 15 minutes on Sunday, from 9am to 6pm (or later on Sun, depending on business), charging 30SEK ($4.15/£2.20) for adults and seniors; passage is free for children 6 and under.

BY BICYCLE

The best place to go cycling is on Djurgården. You can rent bicycles from **Djurgårds-brons Skepp o Hoj,** Djurgårdsbron (© 08/660-57-57), for about 250SEK ($35/£18) per day. It's open May to August daily from 9am to 9pm.

FAST FACTS: Stockholm

American Express For local 24-hour customer service, call © 08/429-56-00.

Area Code The international country code for Sweden is **46**; the city code for Stockholm is **08** (if you're calling Stockholm from abroad, drop the 0). You do not need to dial 8 within Stockholm, only if you're outside the city.

Babysitters Stockholm hotels maintain lists of competent babysitters, nearly all of whom speak English. There is no official agency; rather, it's a word-of-mouth system. Your hotel reception desk can assist you.

Bookstores For a good selection of English-language books, including maps and tour guides, try **Akademibokhandeln,** Mäster Samuelsgatan 28 (© 08/402-11-00), open Monday to Friday from 10am to 7pm, Saturday from 10am to 4pm, and Sunday from noon to 4pm.

Car Rentals See section 14 in chapter 3. In Stockholm, some of the big car-rental companies include **Avis,** Ringvägen 90 (© 08/644-99-80), and **Hertz,** Vasagatan 24 (© 08/24-07-20).

Currency Exchange There's a currency exchange office, **Forex,** at the Central Station (© 08/411-67-34), open daily from 7am to 9pm. It's fully approved by both the Bank of Sweden and the Swedish tourist authorities, offers some of the best exchange rates in town, and takes some of the lowest commissions for cashing traveler's checks. Several other offices are scattered throughout the city.

Dentists Emergency dental treatment is offered at **Sct. Eriks Hospital,** Fleminggatan 22 (© **08/545-51220**), open daily from 8am to 5pm.

Doctors If you need 24-hour emergency medical care, check with **Medical Care Information** (© **08/320-100**). There's also a private clinic, **City Akuten,** at Apelberg Sq. 48, 1st floor (© **08/545-291-85**).

Drugstores A pharmacy that remains open 24 hours a day is **C. W. Scheele,** Klarabergsviadukten 64 (© **08/454-81-30**).

Embassies & Consulates See "Fast Facts: Sweden," in chapter 13.

Emergencies Call © **112** for the police, ambulance service, or the fire department.

Eyeglasses **The Nordiska Kompaniet,** Hamngatan 18–20 (© **08/762-80-00**), a leading Stockholm department store, has a registered optician on duty at its ground-floor service center. The optician performs vision tests, stocks a large selection of frames, and makes emergency repairs.

Hospitals Call **Medical Care Information** at © **08/320-100** 24 hours a day, and an English-speaking operator will inform you of the hospital closest to you.

Internet Cafe A convenient cybercafe is **Dome House,** Sveavägen 108 (© **08/612-61-10**), open daily 11am to 3am, charging 19SEK ($2.60/£1.40) per hour. **Internet Café Stockholm,** Krukmakargatan 33b (© **08/669-09-99**), open daily 1 to 9pm, charging 20SEK ($2.75/£1.45) per hour.

Laundry & Dry Cleaning **City Kemtvatt,** Drottningsholmsvägen 9 (© **08/654-95-34**), does dry cleaning and also laundry by the kilo for same-day delivery if it's brought in before 10am. It's open Monday through Friday from 7am to 7pm and Saturday from 10am to 2:30pm. Note that the system of coin-operated launderettes is pretty much outmoded in Sweden. The cost for doing laundry is 50SEK ($6.90/£3.65) per kilo (2.2 lb.). Your clothes will be neatly folded as part of the price.

Libraries **The Stockholms Stadsbibliotek,** Sveavägen 73 (© **08/508-310-60**), is the biggest municipal library in Sweden, with 2.5 million books (many in English) and audiovisual materials. It also subscribes to 1,500 newspapers and periodicals (again, many in English). Open June 21 to August 15 Monday to Friday 9am to 7pm, Saturday noon to 4pm. Otherwise, hours are Monday to Thursday 9am to 9pm, Friday 9am to 7pm, and Saturday and Sunday noon to 4pm.

Lost Property If you've lost something on the train, go to the Lost and Found office in the Central Station, lower concourse (© **08/762-25-50**). The police also have such an office at the police station at Kungsholmsgatan 37 (© **08/401-01-00**). The Stockholm Transit Company (SL) keeps its recovered articles at the Klaraostra Kyrkogata 6 (© **08/600-10-00**).

Luggage Storage & Lockers Facilities are available at the Central Station on Vasagatan, lower concourse (© **08/762-25-95**). Depending on the size of your baggage, the cost of storage ranges from 30SEK to 80SEK ($4.15–$11/£2.20–£5.85) per day. Lockers can also be rented at the ferry stations at Värtan and Tegelvikshamnen, at the Viking Line terminal, and at the Central Station.

Police Call © **112** in an emergency.

Post Office The main post office is at Centralstationen 10126 (© **08/781-24-25**), open Monday to Friday 7am to 10pm, and Saturday and Sunday 9am to 6pm. If you want to pick up letters while you're abroad, they should be addressed to your name, c/o Post Restante, Post Center, Central Station 11120, Stockholm, Sweden.

Radio & TV Sweden has two state-owned TV channels and at least five privately owned commercial TV stations. Many private homes and most hotels offer cable connections that bring in such "outside" channels as CNN, MTV, and the BBC. There are three national radio stations, plus a local station for Stockholm that broadcasts on 103.3 MHz (FM).

Restrooms Public facilities are found in the Central Station, in all subway stations, and in department stores, as well as along some of the major streets, parks, and squares. In an emergency, you also can use the toilets in most hotels and restaurants, although generally they're reserved for patrons.

Shoe Repair In the basement of **Nordiska Kompaniet**, Hamngatan 18–20 (© **08/762-80-00**), a leading Stockholm department store, there is a shoe repair place, which also may be able to repair broken luggage.

Taxis See "Getting Around," above.

Telephone, Telex & Fax Instructions in English are posted in public phone boxes, which can be found on street corners. Very few phones in Sweden are coin operated; most require a phone card, which can be purchased at newspaper stands and tobacco shops.

Post offices throughout Stockholm now offer phone, fax, and telegram services. Of course, most guests usually ask their hotels to send a fax. All but the smallest boarding houses in Stockholm today have fax services.

Transit Information For information on all services, including buses and subways (T-bana) and suburban trains *(pendeltåg)*, call © **08/600-10-00**. Or, visit the SL Center, on the lower level of Sergels Torg. It provides information about transportation and also sells a map of the city's system, as well as tickets and special discount passes. Open Monday to Friday 7am to 9pm, and Saturday and Sunday 10am to 9pm.

3 Where to Stay

By the standards of many U.S. or Canadian cities, hotels in Stockholm are very expensive. If these high prices make you want to cancel your trip, read on. Dozens of hotels in Stockholm offer reduced rates on weekends all year, and daily from around mid-June to mid-August. For further information, inquire at a travel agency or the tourist center (see "Orientation," earlier in this chapter). In summer it's best to make reservations in advance, just to be on the safe side.

Most of the moderately priced hotels are in Norrmalm, north of the Old Town, and many of the least expensive lodgings are near the Central Station. There are comparably priced inexpensive accommodations within 10 to 20 minutes of the city, easily reached by subway, streetcar, or bus. We'll suggest a few hotels in the Old Town, but these choices are limited and more expensive.

Note: In most cases, a service charge ranging from 10% to 15% is added to the bill, plus the inevitable 21% *moms* (value-added tax). Unless otherwise indicated, all of our recommended accommodations come with a private bathroom.

BOOKING SERVICES **Hotell Centralen,** Vasagatan (© **08/508-285-08**), on the street level of the Central Station, is the city's official housing bureau; it can arrange accommodations in hotels, pensions (boarding houses), and youth hostels—but not in private homes. There's a 60SEK ($8.30/£4.40) service fee. It's open Monday to Friday 9am to 6pm, and Saturday and Sunday noon to 4pm.

The least expensive accommodations in Stockholm are rooms in private homes. The best way to get booked into a private home is by going to the **Hotell Tjänst AB,** Nybrogatan 44 (© **08/10-44-37** or 08/10-44-57; fax 08/21-37-16). Here Mr. Gustavsson and his staff will book you into a double, private room, without breakfast, from 600SEK ($78/£44), including the reservation fee. There is a 2-night minimum stay requirement. From June 15 to August 15, this agency also can book you into Stockholm's major hotels at a big discount.

Mr. Gustavsson asks that you avail yourself of these bargains only upon your arrival in Stockholm. He's confident of booking you into a room because of his long "secret" list of private addresses; he doesn't answer letters requesting reservations. Hotell Tjänst is open Monday through Friday from 9am to noon and 1 to 5pm. Advance booking is rarely accepted; however, if you're going to arrive in Stockholm on a weekend, when the office is closed, call or fax the office.

NORRMALM (CENTER OF STOCKHOLM)
VERY EXPENSIVE

Grand Hotel 🏵🏵🏵 Opposite the Royal Palace, this hotel—a bastion of elite hospitality since 1874—is the finest in Scandinavia. The most recent restoration was in 2006, which retained the grand and conservatively modern styling of the lobby, added 72 additional bedrooms, and made major changes to the bar and to the grander of the two hotel restaurants. Despite major alterations at roughly 10-year intervals throughout this hotel's life, its old-world style and sense of luxury has always been maintained. Guest rooms come in all shapes and sizes, all elegantly appointed in any of seven different styles. The bathrooms are decorated with Italian marble and tiles, and have heated floors, tubs, and showers. The priciest rooms overlook the water, and we'd recommend that you go for these first. The hotel's ballroom is an exact copy of Louis XIV's Hall of Mirrors at Versailles. Almost as a matter of national pride, the hotel retains an allegiance to the daily presentation, at lunchtime, of a lavish smörgåsbord— one of the very few establishments in Scandinavia that does so. It's a daunting challenge, considering the hard work and expense involved for the hotel's food and beverage team, but it, along with superb service and a sense of imperial charm, remain distinguishing characteristics of this monumental hotel landmark.

Södra Blasieholmshamnen 8, S-103 27 Stockholm. © **800/223-5652** in the U.S. and Canada, or 08/679-35-00. Fax 08/611-86-86. www.grandhotel.se. 380 units. 3,700SEK–4,600SEK ($511–$635/£270–£336) double; from 5,900SEK–13,900SEK ($814–$1,918/£431–£1,015) suite. AE, DC, MC, V. Parking 400SEK ($55/£29). T-bana: Kungsträdgården. Bus: 46, 55, 62, or 76. **Amenities:** 2 restaurants; bar; fitness center; sauna; 24-hr. room service; laundry service; dry cleaning; nonsmoking rooms; rooms for those w/limited mobility. *In room:* TV, dataport, minibar, hair dryer, safe.

Where to Stay in Stockholm

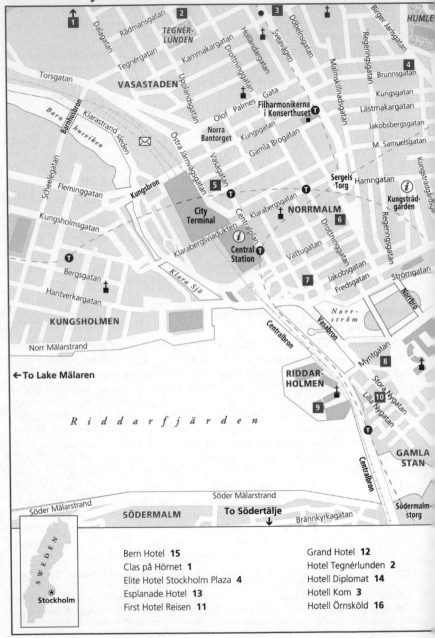

Bern Hotel **15**
Clas på Hörnet **1**
Elite Hotel Stockholm Plaza **4**
Esplanade Hotel **13**
First Hotel Reisen **11**

Grand Hotel **12**
Hotel Tegnérlunden **2**
Hotell Diplomat **14**
Hotell Kom **3**
Hotell Örnsköld **16**

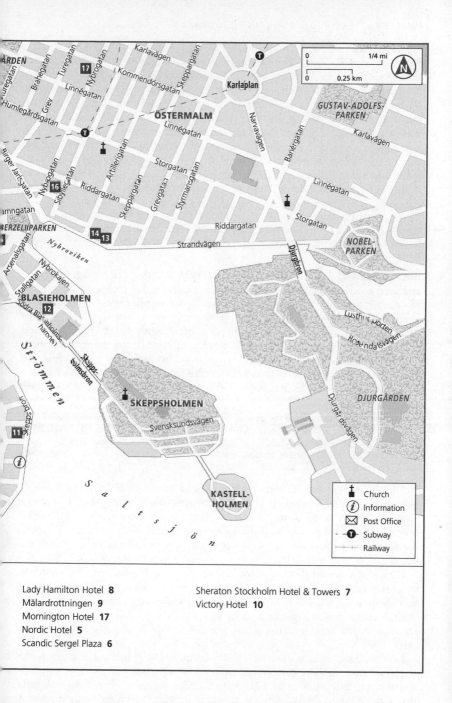

Lady Hamilton Hotel 8
Mälardrottningen 9
Mornington Hotel 17
Nordic Hotel 5
Scandic Sergel Plaza 6

Sheraton Stockholm Hotel & Towers 7
Victory Hotel 10

EXPENSIVE

Berns Hotel *★★* Celebrities often select this as their hotel of choice, but when not hosting rock stars, the Berns can actually be rather subdued. During its 19th-century heyday, beginning in 1863, this was the most elegant hotel in Sweden, with an ornate Gilded Age interior that was the setting for many a legendary rendezvous. In 1989, following years of neglect, it was rebuilt in the original style, and the restaurant facilities were upgraded. Although the dining and drinking areas are usually crowded with sometimes raucous club kids and bar patrons, the guest rooms are soundproof and comfortably isolated from the activity downstairs. Each room offers a good-size bathroom sheathed in Italian marble and neatly maintained shower units. The Red Room is the setting and namesake of Strindberg's novel *Röda Rummet.*

Näckströmsgatan 8, S-111 47 Stockholm. ⓒ 08/566-32-200. Fax 08/566-32-201. www.berns.se. 65 units. 2,600SEK–4,250SEK ($359–$587/£190–£310) double; 3,360SEK–8,600SEK ($464–$1,187/£245–£628) suite. Rates include buffet breakfast. AE, DC, MC, V. Parking 425SEK ($59/£31). T-bana: Östermalmstorg. **Amenities:** Restaurant; bar; sauna; 24-hr. room service; babysitting; laundry service; dry cleaning; nonsmoking rooms. *In room:* TV, dataport, minibar, hair dryer.

Hotel Diplomat *★* The Diplomat is a bit stuffy, but it's a well-managed, discreet, and solid hotel that knows how to handle business clients and corporate conventions. Built in 1911, it retains hints of its original Art Nouveau styling. Public areas are more streamlined. The individually conceived guest rooms are decorated with well-crafted furniture. Many rooms contain bay windows overlooking the harbor; most of the less expensive accommodations face a quiet inner courtyard. Rooms range in size from cramped singles to spacious doubles with sitting areas and high ceilings. Each has good beds and average-size bathrooms, with tiled vanities, bidets, and both tubs and hand-held showers. At least once, take the circular stairs for views of the hotel's antique stained-glass windows.

Strandvägen 7C, Östermalm, S-104-40 Stockholm. ⓒ 08/459-68-00. Fax 08/459-68-20. www.diplomathotel.com. 128 units. Mon–Thurs 2,495SEK–2,895SEK ($344–$400/£182–£211) double; Fri–Sun 1,995SEK–2,395SEK ($275–$331/£146–£175) double; from 3,995SEK ($551/£292) suite. AE, DC, MC, V. Rates include breakfast on weekends. Parking 390SEK ($54/£28). T-bana: Storeplan. **Amenities:** Restaurant; 2 bars; 24-hr. room service; babysitting; laundry service; dry cleaning; nonsmoking rooms; rooms for those w/limited mobility. *In room:* TV, minibar, hair dryer.

Nordic Hotel *★★* *Finds* There's nothing in Scandinavia quite like this hotel, which was voted "The World's Sexiest Hotel" by *Elle* magazine. You're given a choice of a room of "watery calm" in the 367-room Nordic Sea, or "postminimalist luminescence" in the 175-room Nordic Light. Lying on either side of a new square, Vasaplan, the hotel stands adjacent to the express rail link with the airport, or the central rail station.

Each of the two hotels has its own individual design. Nordic Sea, which tends to welcome members of large groups and bus tours, turns to the ocean for its inspiration, and features a 2,400-gallon aquarium and steel walls constructed from ship hulls. Rooms have a certain elegant simplicity with excellent comfort and beautiful bathrooms with tub/showers. These accommodations range in size from extra small to extra large.

Nordic Light, equally modern, equally angular, and positioned just across the boulevard from its more conservative twin, is the more intriguing of the two hotels and the one that tends to be filled with individual clients, often from industries that include the media and the entertainment worlds. The suggestive light patterns

Family-Friendly Hotels

Scandic Sergel Plaza (see below) At "Siggie's Castle," kids can play with toy cars, construct brick buildings, watch a video, and even read a book.

Hotel Tegnérlunden (p. 407) Twenty big, airy rooms are ideal for families on a budget.

Sheraton Stockholm Hotel & Towers (p. 406) This well-run chain has always pampered children. The spacious rooms are comfortably shared with parents.

projected onto the walls of both the bedrooms and the public areas of the Nordic Light re-create the ever-changing patterns of the lights of the north. This hotel is not just about gimmicks; it offers real comfort with rooms boasting the best sound insulation in town. On weekends, after dark, the lobby of the Nordic Light is mobbed with Scandinavian hipsters.

4–7 Vasaplan. ✆ **800/337-4685** in the U.S., or 08/505-630-00. Fax 08/505-630-40. www.nordichotels.se. 367 units in Nordic Sea, 175 units in Nordic Light. 2,140SEK–3,600SEK ($295–$497/£150–£263) double Nordic Sea, 2,760SEK–3,600SEK ($381–$497/£201–£263) double Nordic Light. AE, DC, MC, V. T-bana: Centralen. **Amenities:** Restaurant; 2 bars; steam bath; sauna; some spa treatments; minigym; room service (7am–midnight) at Nordic Sea, 24 hr. room service Nordic Light; laundry service; dry cleaning; nonsmoking rooms; rooms for those w/limited mobility. *In room:* TV, dataport, minibar, coffeemaker, iron, safe.

Scandic Sergel Plaza ★★ *(Kids)* This classic hotel was designed in 1984 as living quarters for parliament members who come into Stockholm from the provinces. Today, its rooms are open to all, and it's an especially inviting choice for families (see "Family-Friendly Hotels," below). The hotel lies at the entrance to Drottninggatan, the main shopping street. The elegant public decor includes 18th-century artwork and antiques. The guest rooms are constantly updated and are beautifully decorated in a tasteful but traditional modern style, using reproductions. Standard doubles have desks, and the suites boast a separate dining area. The best rooms are on the executive floors, with enhanced luxury and services. We like the many extras at this hotel, including the bike rentals and yoga classes.

Brunkebergstorg 9, S-103 27 Stockholm. ✆ **800/THE-OMNI** in the U.S., or 08/517-26-300. Fax 08/517-26-311. www.scandic-hotels.com. 403 units. 2,000SEK–2,600SEK ($276–$359/£146–£190) double; from 4,800SEK ($662/£350) suite. Rates include breakfast. AE, DC, MC, V. Parking 295SEK ($41/£22). T-bana: Centralen. Bus: 47, 52, or 69. **Amenities:** Restaurant; bar; 24-hr. room service; children's playroom; laundry service; dry cleaning; nonsmoking rooms; rooms for those w/limited mobility. *In room:* TV, dataport, minibar, hair dryer, trouser press (in some), Wi-Fi.

MODERATE

Clas på Hörnet ★★ *(Finds)* To escape the blandness that infuses certain Swedish hotels, we like to check in here. Built in the 1730s as a private house, this small, upscale, and very charming inn is less than a kilometer (about ½ mile) north of the commercial heart of Stockholm. Its attention to period detail—its installation was supervised by the curators of the Stockholm City Museum—gives a distinctive country-inn ambience that's enhanced with bedrooms outfitted in the late-18th-century style of

Gustavus III. Each of the bedrooms is outfitted in a different motif, usually with cheerful colors, wide floorboards, antiques, and all the amenities you'd expect from a well-managed and intimate hotel, including medium-size bathrooms with well-kept shower units. Many have four-poster beds.

Surbrunnsgatan 20, S-113 48 Stockholm. © **08/16-51-30.** Fax 08/612-53-15. www.claspahornet.se. 10 units. Mon–Thurs 1,795SEK ($248/£131) double, 2,395SEK ($331/£175) suite; Fri–Sun 1,095SEK ($151/£80) double, 1,995SEK ($275/£146) suite. Rates include breakfast. Parking 200SEK ($28/£15). Bus: 46 or 53. **Amenities:** Breakfast room; lounge; nonsmoking rooms. *In room:* TV.

Elite Hotel Stockholm Plaza ⓡ   This would not be our first choice for a hotel in Stockholm, as it's a bit pricey for what you get. Built on a triangular lot that might remind some visitors of New York's Flatiron Building, this first-class hotel is a well-run choice in the city center. From the time of its construction in 1884 until its complete makeover in 1984, the building had many uses—a run-down rooming house, private apartments, and offices. The light, fresh guest rooms have tiled bathrooms with tub/shower combinations, and we found the staff hospitable.

Birger Jarlsgatan 29, S-103 95 Stockholm. © **08/566-22-000.** Fax 08/566-22-020. www.elite.se. 151 units. 1,340SEK–1,995SEK ($185–$275/£98–£146) double; 2,595SEK–4,595SEK ($358–$634/£189–£335) suite. Rates include breakfast. AE, DC, MC, V. Parking 240SEK ($33/£18). T-bana: Hötorget or Östermalmstorg. **Amenities:** Restaurant; bar; dance club; sauna; room service (7am–11pm); laundry service; dry cleaning; nonsmoking rooms; 1 room for those w/limited mobility. *In room:* TV, dataport, minibar (in some), hair dryer.

Esplanade Hotel ⓡ   This informal hotel, which defines itself as a four-star "hotel garni," lies immediately adjacent to the more expensive and more richly accessorized Diplomat. Respectable and discreet, it attracts representatives from the nearby embassies and others who like its comfortable charm and traditional atmosphere. Constructed as part of the same Beaux Arts architectural complex as the Diplomat in 1910, it was transformed into a hotel in 1954, occupying two floors of a six-story building, the remainder of which are devoted to offices. Many of the rooms are furnished in old-fashioned style. Single rooms are minuscule. Most doubles have double-glazed windows, extra-long beds, and well-kept, decent-size tile bathrooms with tub/shower combinations. Four rooms open on a water view, and the high-ceilinged lounge features a balcony with a view of Djurgården. Breakfast is the only meal served here.

Strandvägen 7A, S-114 56 Stockholm. © **08/663-07-40.** Fax 08/662-59-92. www.hotelesplanade.se. 34 units. Mon–Thurs 2,095SEK–2,295SEK ($289–$317/£153–£168) double; Fri–Sun 1,495SEK–1,695SEK ($206–$234/£109–£124) double. Rates include breakfast. AE, DC, MC, V. Parking nearby 275SEK ($38/£20). T-bana: Östermalmstorg. Bus: 47 or 69. **Amenities:** Breakfast room; lounge; sauna; limited room service; laundry service; dry cleaning; nonsmoking rooms. *In room:* TV, dataport, minibar, hair dryer.

Sheraton Stockholm Hotel & Towers ⓡ Ⓚⓘⓓⓢ   Sure, it's short on Swedish charm, but it's an excellent by other hotel standards, attracting many business travelers and even families. Sheathed with Swedish granite, this eight-story hostelry is within view of Stockholm's City Hall (Rådhuset). The guest rooms are the largest in the city, with one king or two double beds with bedside controls and closets with mirrored doors. A family of three or four can fit comfortably into most rooms. Medium-size tile bathrooms have tub/shower combinations and heated towel racks, and some units have bidets. Most units offer sweeping views of the city, many over Gamla Stan. The restaurants serve market-fresh ingredients deftly handled by a skilled kitchen staff.

Tegelbacken 6, S-101 23 Stockholm. ℂ **800/325-3535** in the U.S. and Canada, or 08/412-34-00. Fax 08/412-34-09. www.sheratonstockholm.com. 462 units. 1,250SEK–2,900SEK ($173–$400/£91–£212) double; from 4,000SEK ($552/ £292) suite. AE, DC, MC, V. Parking 300SEK ($41/£22). T-bana: Centralen. **Amenities:** 2 restaurants; bar; fitness center; indoor heated pool; sauna; 24-hr. room service; babysitting; laundry service; dry cleaning; nonsmoking rooms; rooms for those w/limited mobility. *In room:* TV, dataport, minibar (in some), hair dryer, beverage maker (in suites).

INEXPENSIVE

Hotell Kom *(Value)*   Although still owned by the Swedish version of the YWCA and YMCA, this hotel has been vastly improved and upgraded, and you get good value and a warm welcome here. In a residential neighborhood scattered with stores and private apartments, this small hotel dates from 1972. Rooms, although small, are tastefully and comfortably furnished in the latest Swedish modern. The building itself is well maintained and up-to-date, and many of the rooms open onto good views of the cityscape. Bathrooms are well organized and a bit tiny, but each comes with modern plumbing such as showers. A number of simple and rather small budget rooms are also rented on the ground floor, each with two bunk beds per room. These bargains can accommodate up to four guests.

Döbelnsgatan 17, S-11140 Stockholm. ℂ 08/412-23-00. Fax 08/412-23-10. www.komhotel.se. 128 units. Mon–Thurs 1,795SEK–2,045SEK ($248–$282/£131–£149) double; Fri–Sun 1,220SEK–1,465SEK ($168–$202/£89– £107) double; budget rooms 600SEK ($83/£44) double, 800SEK ($110/£58) quad. Rates include breakfast. AE, DC, MC, V. Parking 190SEK ($26/£14). T-bana: Rådmansgatan. **Amenities:** Breakfast room; lounge; fitness center; sauna; laundry service; dry cleaning; nonsmoking rooms; rooms for those w/limited mobility. *In room:* TV, dataport, minibar, hair dryer, safe, trouser press.

Hotell Örnsköld   Years ago when we were checking out this hotel, we spotted the great Swedish director, Ingmar Bergman, passing through. Only later did we learn that he was checking prop storage and staff housing, which even today are partial functions of this establishment near the Royal Dramatic Theatre. The five-story building that contains this hotel was built in 1910, and the hotel is situated on the second floor. High-ceilinged rooms have simple, contemporary furnishings, and more expensive units are big enough to hold extra beds if necessary. All units contain well-kept bathrooms with shower units. A few cubicle rooms—called "cabins"—are rented for 495SEK ($68/£36); they contain no windows.

Nybrogatan 6, S-11434 Stockholm. ℂ 08/667-02-85. Fax 08/667-69-91. www.hotelornskold.se. 27 units. 1,495SEK–2,195SEK ($206–$303/£109–£160) double; "cabin" 495SEK ($68/£36). Rates include breakfast. AE, MC, V. T-bana: Östermalmstorg. **Amenities:** Lounge; laundry service; dry cleaning. *In room:* TV, dataport, minibar, hair dryer, iron.

Hotel Tegnérlunden *(Rk) (Kids)*   Like a London townhouse hotel, this hidden hotel lies next to a leafy park, unusual for Stockholm, and its best feature is its airy rooftop breakfast room. In spite of a big expansion, the hotel still retains a personal atmosphere. Many of the tasteful, functionally furnished rooms are suitable for families because of their size. They're blissfully quiet, especially those opening onto the rear. The rooms vary in size and shape, and those we inspected were well maintained. The hotel offers comfort but not a lot of style. The bathrooms equipped with shower units are small but beautifully kept.

Tegnérlunden 8, S-113 59 Stockholm. ℂ 08/5454-5550. Fax 08/5454-5551. www.hoteltegnerlunden.se. 102 units. 1,690SEK ($233/£123) double; 2,600SEK ($359/£190) suite. Rates include buffet breakfast. AE, DC, MC, V. Parking 205SEK ($28/£15) in nearby garage. Bus: 47, 53, or 69. **Amenities:** Breakfast room; bar; sauna; laundry service; dry cleaning; nonsmoking rooms; rooms for those w/limited mobility. *In room:* TV, dataport, hair dryer, iron (in some).

Mornington Hotel ⟨ᴋ⟩ With more than 200 rooms, this hotel is just too big to live up to its slogan, "a home away from home." And in 2005, the hotel was greatly expanded, adding dozens of rooms. However, it does have a friendly and helpful staff, and grace notes such as a library, with more than 4,000 volumes, and a small rock garden. Proud of its image as an English-inspired hotel, this efficient modern establishment has a concrete exterior brightened with rows of flower boxes. It was built in 1956 and has been renovated several times. Most rooms (many of which are small) have standard decor, and each unit contains well-kept bathrooms with tub/shower combinations.

Nybrogatan 53, S-102 44 Stockholm. ℂ 800/780-7234 in the U.S. and Canada, or 08/507-33-000. Fax 08/507-33-039. www.morningtonhotel.com. 215 units. Sun–Thurs 2,125SEK–2,525SEK ($293–$348/£155–£184) double, 2,250SEK ($311/£164) suite; Fri–Sat 1,208SEK–1,540SEK ($167–$213/£88–£112) double, 3,300SEK ($455/£241) suite. Rates include buffet breakfast. AE, DC, MC, V. Parking 150SEK–220SEK ($21–$30/£11–£16). T-bana: Östermalmstorg. Bus: 49, 54, or 62. **Amenities:** Restaurant; bar; sauna; 24-hr. room service; laundry service; dry cleaning; nonsmoking rooms; rooms for those w/limited mobility. *In room:* TV, dataport, hair dryer, iron, Wi-Fi.

IN GAMLA STAN (OLD TOWN)
EXPENSIVE

First Hotel Reisen ⟨ᴋᴋ⟩ In the 18th century, this hotel facing the water was the most famous coffeehouse in the Old Town, and in 1819 the Merchant Society took it over and turned it into a nautical style hotel. Today, it's a splendid address with its dark wood, brick walls, and beautiful fabrics, although it doesn't quite match the charm and atmosphere generated by its two competitors nearby, Lady Hamilton and Victory (see below). The three-building structure attractively combines the old and the new. The rooms are comfortably furnished in a modern fashion inspired by traditional designs. Beds are frequently renewed, and the bathrooms are excellent, with deep tubs, massaging showerheads, scales, marble floors, heated towel racks, and phones. Some suites have Jacuzzis, and top-floor accommodations open onto small balconies.

Skeppsbron 12, S-111 30 Stockholm. ℂ 08/22-32-60. Fax 08/20-15-59. www.firsthotel.se. 144 units. Mon–Thurs 2,499SEK–3,299SEK ($345–$455/£182–£241) double, 4,099SEK ($566/£299) suite; Fri–Sun 1,300SEK–1,800SEK ($179–$248/£95–£131) double, from 2,998SEK ($414/£219) suite. Rates include breakfast. AE, DC, MC, V. Parking 395SEK ($55/£29). Bus: 43, 46, 55, 59, or 76. **Amenities:** Restaurant; bar; indoor pool; sauna; 24-hr. room service; laundry service; dry cleaning; nonsmoking rooms. *In room:* TV, dataport, minibar, hair dryer, iron, trouser press.

Lady Hamilton Hotel ⟨ᴋᴋᴋ⟩ *Finds*   Named after Lord Nelson's beloved mistress, this inn combines both Swedish and English history in a building dating from 1470. It's one of the most atmospheric recommendations in the Old Town. During a restoration, owner Majlis and Gunnar Bengtsson found a well from 1300 where today, on a summer day, guests can go for a dip. This hotel lies on a quiet street on Gamla Stan, surrounded by souvenir shops and restaurants. Dozens of antiques are scattered among the well-furnished guest rooms, and most rooms have beamed ceilings. The beds (queen or double) are of high quality. Bathrooms are tiled but vary in size from spacious to small. All have heated towel racks, heated floors, and tub/shower combinations. Top-floor rooms have skylights and memorable views over the Old Town. You'll get a sense of the origins of this hotel when you use the luxurious sauna, which encompasses the stone-rimmed well that formerly supplied the building's water. The ornate staircase wraps around a large model of a clipper ship suspended from the ceiling.

Storkyrkobrinken 5, S-111 28 Stockholm. ℂ 08/506-40-100. Fax 08/506-40-110. www.lady-hamilton.se. 34 units (some with shower only). 2,350SEK–3,000SEK ($324–$414/£172–£219) double; 2,490SEK ($344/£182) triple. AE, DC, MC, V. Parking: 375SEK ($52/£27). T-bana: Gamla Stan. Bus: 48. **Amenities:** Bistro; bar; sauna; room service (7am–11pm); babysitting; laundry service; dry cleaning; nonsmoking rooms. *In room:* TV, dataport, minibar, hair dryer.

Victory Hotel ✮✮ We didn't think we'd find a better hotel than Lady Hamilton until we spent our first night here. It's our most enthusiastic recommendation in Old Town. Named after the naval hero Lord Nelson's flagship, it's an exclusive boutique hotel, and also the flagship of the Bengtsson family's private hotel chain in Old Town. Even the corridors here are museums, as the inn is filled with nautical antiques. In the lobby you can read one of Lord Nelson's heart-rendering original letters to Lady Hamilton, dating from 1801. A small but stylish hotel, the Victory offers warm, inviting rooms, each named after a prominent sea captain. They sport a pleasing combination of exposed wood, antiques, and 19th-century memorabilia. The average-size bathrooms are tiled and have heated floors and shower units; only the suites have tubs. The hotel rests on the foundations of a 1382 fortified tower. In the 1700s, the building's owners buried a massive silver treasure under the basement floor—you can see it in the Stockholm City Museum. There's a shiny brass elevator, but take the stairs, where you'll see one of Sweden's largest collections of 18th-century nautical needlepoint, much of it created by sailors during their long voyages.

Lilla Nygatan 5, S-111 28 Stockholm. © 08/506-400-00. Fax 08/506-40-010. www.victory-hotel.se. 49 units (some with shower only). 2,550SEK–3,600SEK ($352–$497/£186–£263) double; 3,750SEK–6,450SEK ($518–$890/£274–£471) suite. AE, DC, MC, V. Valet parking 395SEK ($55/£29). T-bana: Gamla Stan. Bus: 48. **Amenities:** Restaurant; bar; indoor heated pool; sauna; 24-hr. room service; babysitting; laundry service; dry cleaning; nonsmoking rooms; rooms for those w/limited mobility. *In room:* TV, dataport, minibar, hair dryer, safe.

MODERATE

Mälardrottningen ✮ *(Finds* This yacht-turned-hotel was a hot topic during its heyday, when it was the largest motor yacht in the world at 72m (236 ft.). The yacht was converted into a hotel in the early 1980s and permanently moored beside a satellite island of Stockholm's Old Town. The cabins are cramped and somewhat claustrophobic, and most units have bunk-style twin beds. All units have neatly kept bathrooms with tub/showers. Considering the hotel's conversation-piece status and its location close to everything in the Old Town, it might be worth an overnight stay.

Riddarholmen, S-11128 Stockholm. © 08/545-187-80. Fax 08/24-36-76. www.malardrottningen.se. 60 units. Sun–Thurs 1,250SEK–2,250SEK ($173–$311/£91–£164) double; Fri–Sat 1,050SEK–2,250SEK ($145–$311/£77–£164) double. Rates include buffet breakfast. AE, DC, MC, V. Parking 200SEK ($28/£15) per day T-bana: Gamla Stan. **Amenities:** Restaurant; bar; sauna; laundry service; dry cleaning; nonsmoking rooms. *In room:* TV, hair dryer.

ON LÅNGHOLMEN

Långholmen Hotel Solitary confinement doesn't have to be a bad thing. This former women's penitentiary is now home to a reasonably priced hotel with comfortable but small rooms and is the best place for the single visitor on a budget, with 89 units reserved for solo guests. Accommodations were carved from some 200 cells, creating cramped but serviceable rooms equipped with small showers and toilets. Just 13 rooms are large enough to accommodate two people. The prison was built in 1724 on the small island of Långholmen, and while the last prisoner was released in 1972, you can still learn about the history at the on-site museum. There's also a good restaurant and 24-hour snack bar.

Långholmsmuren 20, S-102 72 Stockholm. © 08/720-85-00. Fax 08/720-85-75. www.langholmen.com. 102 units. Sun–Thurs 1,590SEK ($219/£116) double; Fri–Sat 1,290SEK ($178/£94) double; extra bed 250SEK ($35/£18) per person. AE, MC, V. Rates include breakfast. T-bana: Hornstul. Bus: 4, 40, or 66. **Amenities:** Restaurant; bar; laundry service/dry cleaning; nonsmoking rooms; rooms for those w/limited mobility. *In room:* TV, dataport, hair dryer.

ON SÖDERMALM
EXPENSIVE
Hotel Rival 𝄐𝄐𝄐 *(Finds)*   This is the best and most intriguing place to stay on the rapidly gentrifying island of Södermalm. In many ways, it's our favorite hotel in Stockholm. Originally opened in 1937, this hotel/cafe/bakery/cinema received a new lease on life in 2002, with a lot of the money supplied by Benny Andersson, former member of the musical group ABBA.

The hotel was conceived as a conscious contrast to the Grand Hotel, a grande dame that clings to the *haute* bourgeoisie of imperial Sweden. The Rival could be defined as a sprawling series of nightclubs, bistros, and entertainment lounges, on top of which a network of bedrooms is available for whatever rock star or rock star wannabe happens to be in residence in Stockholm at the time. Bedrooms are partially wood-sheathed, loaded with the electronic equipment you'd need to play CDs or DVDs. Because of the tie-in with ABBA, you'll find a CD of the group's favorite hits in every room. Breakfast buffets, served in a sun-flooded, second-floor room that doubles as the hotel's bistro at lunch and dinner, are appealingly lavish, with wide choices of traditional Swedish food.

Mariatorget 3, S-11891 Stockholm. © 08/545-789-00. Fax 08/545-789-24. www.rival.se. 99 units. Sun–Thurs 1,390SEK–2,890SEK ($192–$399/£101–£211) double; Fri–Sat 1,390SEK–1,990SEK ($192–$275/£101–£145) double. Daily 3,390SEK–5,790SEK ($468–$799/£247–£423) suite. AE, DC, MC, V. T-bana: Mariatorget. **Amenities:** 2 restaurants; 3 bars; gym; 24-hr. room service; laundry service; dry cleaning; rooms for those w/limited mobility; nonsmoking rooms. *In room:* A/C, TV, dataport, minibar, hair dryer, iron, safe.

4 Where to Dine

Split pea soup, sausages, and boiled potatoes are still around, but in the past decade Stockholm has emerged as a citadel of fine dining. Part of this derives from the legendary freshness of Swedish game and produce; part comes from the success of Sweden's culinary team at cooking contests everywhere. Today there are an estimated 1,500 restaurants and bars in Stockholm alone.

Food is expensive in Stockholm, but those on a budget can stick to self-service cafeterias. At all restaurants other than cafeterias, a 12% to 15% service charge is added to the bill to cover service, and the 21% value-added tax also is included in the bill. Wine and beer can be lethal to your final check, so proceed carefully. For a good value, try ordering the *dagens ratt* (daily special), also referred to as *dagens* lunch or *dagens* menu, if available.

NORRMALM (CENTER OF STOCKHOLM)
VERY EXPENSIVE
Operakällaren 𝄐𝄐𝄐 FRENCH/SWEDISH   Opposite the Royal Palace, this is the most famous and unashamedly luxurious restaurant in Sweden. Its promise of world-class French-inspired cuisine has lured us back time and time again, although we dread facing the final bill. Its lavishly elegant decor and style are reminiscent of a royal court banquet at the turn of the 20th century. The service and house specialties are impeccable. Many come here for the elaborate fixed-price menus; others prefer the classic Swedish dishes or the modern French ones. A house specialty that's worth the trip is the platter of northern delicacies, with everything from smoked eel and reindeer to Swedish red caviar. Salmon and game, including grouse from the northern forests, are prepared in various ways. There's a cigar room, too. Dress to impress.

Operahuset, Kungsträdgården. ℭ **08/676-58-00.** Reservations required. Main courses 400SEK–500SEK ($55–$69/ £29–£37); 6-course menu dégustation 950SEK ($131/£69). AE, DC, MC, V. Tues–Sat 6–10pm. Closed Dec 25–Jan 8. T-bana: Kungsträdgården.

Paul & Norbert 🍴🍴🍴 CONTINENTAL In a patrician residence dating from 1873, adjacent to the Hotell Diplomat, this is the finest and most innovative restaurant in Stockholm. Seating only 30 people, it has vaguely Art Deco decor, beamed ceilings, and dark paneling. Chef Norbert Lang prepares a tantalizing terrine of scallops in saffron sauce, and the foie gras is the finest in town. Perfectly prepared main dishes include sautéed medallion of fjord salmon, scallops, and scampi in lobster sauce, and crisp breast of duck with caramelized orange sauce.

Strandvägen 9. ℭ **08/663-81-83.** Reservations required. Main courses 250SEK–310SEK ($35–$43/£18–£23); 9-course *grand menu de frivolity* (chef's menu) 1,100SEK ($152/£80); 5-course fixed-price menu 800SEK ($110/£58); 6-course fixed-price menu 1,000SEK ($138/£73). AE, DC, MC, V. Tues–Fri noon–2pm and 6–10pm; Sat and Mon 6–10pm. Closed Dec 24–Jan 6. T-bana: Östermalmstorg.

EXPENSIVE

Bistro Rival 🍴🍴 *Finds* INTERNATIONAL This hip bistro is the focal point for a series of lesser bars, lounges, and entertainment venues that all flourish, in a congenially cooperative way, within the same (also recommended) hotel. Since the bistro is on the hotel's second floor (and there's a long and narrow balcony on which tables are situated during clement weather), diners can look down on one of the most popular and animated series of bocce games in Sweden. Menu items range from Caesar salad and carpaccio of beef to filet of reindeer and Swedish herring.

In the Hotel Rival. Mariatorget 3 ℭ **08/545-789-00.** Reservations recommended. Main courses 130SEK–245SEK ($18–$34/£9.50–£18); set-price menu 349SEK ($48/£25). AE, DC, MC, V. Daily 4–11:30pm (restaurant), with bar remaining open till between midnight–2am, depending on business. T-bana: Mariatorget.

Divino 🍴🍴 ITALIAN Many local food critics hail Divino as Stockholm's finest Italian restaurant, and we join them in their praise. In a setting attracting an elegant clientele, the restaurant boasts a mammoth wine cellar with some of Italy's best vintages. Too often the antipasti selection is dull in many Italian eateries, but here the chefs work overtime to come up with unusual variations of the classics, including sweetbreads flavored with lemon and fresh thyme, or a tantalizing foie gras with almond foam and figs. Monkfish and lobster are served on one platter and flavored with vanilla bean along with fresh fennel, while sea bass is served with crispy fresh vegetables and truffles. Among the meat and poultry courses, we like the guinea fowl with morels, duck liver, and green asparagus, and the veal entrecôte with prosciutto, sage, and Marsala.

Karlavägen 28. ℭ **08/611-02-69.** Reservations required. Main courses 285SEK–325SEK ($39–$45/£21–£24). AE, MC, V. Mon–Sat 6–11pm. Closed Mon in July. T-bana: Östra Station or Rådmansgatan.

F12 🍴🍴🍴 SWEDISH/INTERNATIONAL Set within the high-ceilinged interior of the Royal Academy of Arts, this is one of the premier restaurants of Stockholm. The decor is ultrasophisticated and hip, with apple-green and lime-colored walls, long, shimmering curtains, and the kind of uncluttered minimalism you might have expected within a fashionable venue in Milan. Since it's near the Swedish parliament and various government ministries, it tends to attract government officials at lunch, but a classier and far trendier clientele in the evening. The menu divides your choices into either "innovative" or "traditional" cuisine. The best traditional choices might

Where to Dine in Stockholm

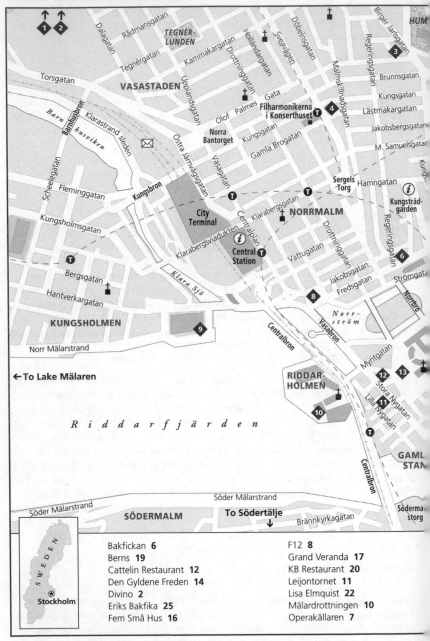

Bakfickan **6**
Berns **19**
Cattelin Restaurant **12**
Den Gyldene Freden **14**
Divino **2**
Eriks Bakfika **25**
Fem Små Hus **16**

F12 **8**
Grand Veranda **17**
KB Restaurant **20**
Leijontornet **11**
Lisa Elmquist **22**
Mälardrottningen **10**
Operakällaren **7**

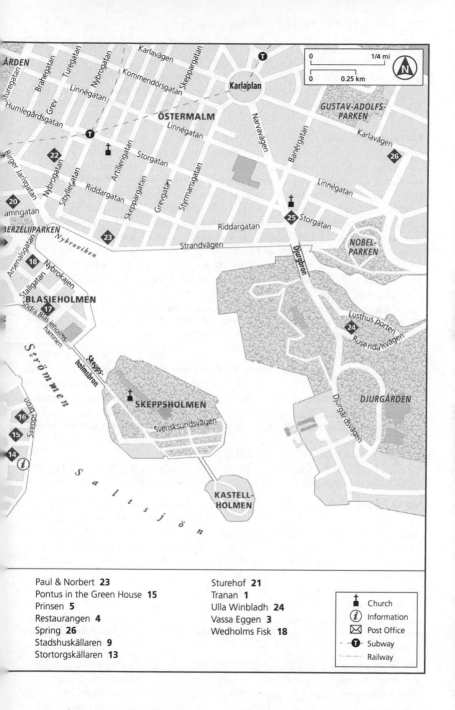

Paul & Norbert **23**
Pontus in the Green House **15**
Prinsen **5**
Restaurangen **4**
Spring **26**
Stadshuskällaren **9**
Stortorgskällaren **13**

Sturehof **21**
Tranan **1**
Ulla Winbladh **24**
Vassa Eggen **3**
Wedholms Fisk **18**

† Church
ⓘ Information
✉ Post Office
-Ⓣ- Subway
┼ Railway

include beef carpaccio with Parmesan and seafood *bouillabaisse* with saffron. "Innovative" choices feature tuna tataki with mango slices and cream; caviar served with cauliflower and white chocolate; and veal with tuna sauce, grapefruit, and licorice.

Fredsgatan 12. (© 08/248-052. Reservations required. Main courses 295SEK–405SEK ($41–$56/£22–£30); set-price menu 995SEK ($137/£73) AE, DC, MC, V. Mon–Fri 11:30am–2pm; Mon–Sat 5–10:30pm. T-bana: Kungsträdgården.

Restaurangen ☆☆ INTERNATIONAL   Come here not for a high-ceilinged decor, whose angularity might remind you of an SAS airport lounge, but for combinations of cuisine that many cosmopolitan Swedes find absolutely fascinating. Owner and chef Malker Andersson divides his menu into "fields of flavor" as defined by unexpected categories. These include, among others, lemon-flavored or coriander-flavored themes, which can be consumed in any order you prefer. If you want a "taste of the lemon," for example, it might appear to flavor fresh asparagus and new potatoes. The chef roams the world, but rather than duplicating classical international dishes, he takes the flavor of one country and combines its traditional dish with the time-honored dish of another country. This fusion can be seen in the tacos combined with foie gras and caviar. Since none of the portions are overly large, a meal here is akin to a series of tapas.

Oxtorgsgatan 14. (© 08/220-952. Reservations recommended. 3-course fixed-price menu 275SEK ($38/£20); 5-course fixed-price menu 375SEK ($52/£27); 7-course fixed-price menu 475SEK ($66/£35). AE, DC, MC, V. Mon–Fri 11:30am–2pm and 5pm–1am; Mon–Sat 5pm–1am. T-bana: Hötorget.

Spring ☆ ASIAN/SCANDINAVIAN   The trendiness of this place never plays second fiddle to the cuisine. East meets West in Johan Lindqvist's showcase of stylish fusion cuisine. The key is not only skill in the kitchen, but a carefully chosen list of ingredients that is fresh and of high quality. The decor is minimalist; blond ash wood from northern Sweden is combined with colorful furniture from Asia. Lots of upwardly mobile young people come here for dishes such as steamed chicken dumplings, Japanese eel with foie gras, poached cod in ginger bouillon with shiitake mushrooms and bok choy, and, for dessert, crème brûlée.

Karlavägen 110. (© 08/783-15-00. Reservations required. Main courses 265SEK–320SEK ($37–$44/£19–£23). AE, MC, V. Mon–Fri 11:30am–2pm; Tues–Sat 6–11pm. T-bana: Östra Station or Rådmansgatan.

Vassa Eggen ☆ *Finds* INTERNATIONAL   This fashionable eatery lies in the center of the city and brings together gastronomic influences from around the world under a beautiful glass-domed dining room. Using only the finest products, the young chefs concoct a cuisine pleasing to both eye and palate. The oxtail tortellini with mascarpone cheese served in a consommé has won raves from Swedish editions of *Gourmet* magazine, while we like the herring with potato purée, char in a creamy lobster juice, brill cooked in brown butter and flavored with horseradish, and chocolate truffle and raspberry sorbet desserts.

Birger Jarlsgatan 29. (© 08/21-61-69. Reservations required. Main courses 115SEK–305SEK ($16–$42/£3.40–£22). Tasting menu 895SEK ($124/£65). AE, DC, MC, V. Mon–Fri 11:30am–2pm and 6–11pm. Closed in July. T-bana: Östermalmstorg.

Wedholms Fisk ☆ SWEDISH/FRENCH   This may no longer be cutting edge, but it still remains the leader of the pack among classic Swedish restaurants. It has no curtains in the windows and no carpets, but the display of modern paintings by Swedish artists is riveting. The cuisine is both innovative and traditional—for example, chèvre mousse accompanies a simple tomato salad, while you can still find classics such as cream-stewed potatoes. You might begin with marinated herring with garlic and *bleak* (a freshwater fish) roe, or tartare of salmon with salmon roe. The chef has reason to be proud of such dishes as perch poached with clams and saffron sauce, prawns marinated in herbs and served with Dijon hollandaise, and grilled filet of sole with Beaujolais sauce. For dessert, try the homemade vanilla ice cream with cloudberries.

Nybrokajen 17. © 08/611-78-74. Reservations required. Lunch main courses 175SEK–225SEK ($24–$31/£13–£16); dinner main courses 265SE–535SEK ($37–$74/£19–£39). AE, DC, MC, V. Mon–Fri 11:30am–11pm; Sat 5–11pm. Closed for lunch in July. T-bana: Östermalmstorg.

MODERATE

Bakfickan ✦ *Finds* SWEDISH   Tucked away behind the Operakällaren, "the Hip Pocket" (its English name), is a chic place to eat for a moderate price. But because it shares a kitchen with the Operakällaren (see above), you get the same food at a fraction of the price. In season, we prefer Swedish specialties such as reindeer and elk; otherwise we like the French oysters with a vinaigrette sauce and black bread, grilled roast rib of beef with Béarnaise sauce, and French chocolate cake.

Jakobs Torg 12. © 08/676-58-00. Main courses 98SEK–245SEK ($14–$34/£7.15–£18). AE, DC, MC, V. Mon–Fri 11:30am–11:30pm; Sat noon–11:30pm. T-bana: Kungsträdgården.

Berns ✦ SWEDISH/INTERNATIONAL/ASIAN   This classic restaurant might have opened in 1860 as a "pleasure palace," but it's changed with the times and looks toward Asia for its new inspiration. Three monumental chandeliers light the main hall, while the plush furniture described by August Strindberg in the Red Room *(Röda Rummet)* is still here. Each day a different Swedish specialty is featured, including fried filet of suckling pig with fresh asparagus, calves' liver with garlic and bacon, or grilled tournedos. More innovative main dishes include cuttlefish with black pasta and tomato sauce, and filet of ostrich with mushroom cannelloni and Marsala sauce.

Näckströmsgatan 8. © 08/566-32-222. Reservations recommended. Main courses 165SEK–350SEK ($23–$48/£12–£26). AE, DC, MC, V. Daily 11:30am–1am. T-bana: Östermalmstorg.

Eriks Bakfica ✦ *Value* SWEDISH   Swedes looking for *husmanskost* (wholesome home cooking) have been coming here since 1979. We always check out the array of daily herring appetizers, but what really attracts us is the tantalizing "archipelago stew," a ragout of fresh fish (it varies daily) prepared with tomatoes and serve with garlic mayonnaise. If you drop in for lunch, ask for Erik's cheeseburger with "secret sauce" (it's not on the menu, so you need to request it).

Fredrikshovsgatan 4. © 08/660-15-99. Reservations recommended. Main courses 120SEK–295SEK ($17–$41/£8.75–£22). AE, DC, MC, V. Tues–Fri 11:30am–midnight; Sat 5pm–midnight; Sun 5–11pm. Bus: 47.

Grand Veranda ✦✦ *Kids* SWEDISH   The Veranda is famous for its daily smörgåsbord buffets, which are artfully (exquisitely, even) laid out in a satellite room off the main dining room. The fame comes for a reason—it's the best smörgåsbord we've had in Sweden and comes at an affordable price. On the ground floor of Stockholm's most prestigious hotel and fronted with enormous sheets of glass, this restaurant opens onto a wide-angle view of the harbor and the Royal Palace. Diners, like the waitstaff, are professional. There are a few rules of smörgåsbord etiquette that you should note: Don't mix fish and meat courses on the same plate, don't mix hot and cold food on the same plate, and keep your visit(s) to the dessert table separate from your trips to the tables containing the other food items. If the buffet doesn't appeal to you, there's an a la carte selection, including filet of reindeer marinated in red wine, or braised wild duck and deep-fried root vegetables served with an apple-cider sauce.

In the Grand Hotel, Södra Blasieholmshamnen 8. ℭ 08/679-35-86. Reservations required. Main courses 125SEK–235SEK ($17–$32/£9.10–£17); Swedish buffet 380SEK ($52/£28). AE, DC, MC, V. Daily noon–3pm and 6–11pm. T-bana: Kungsträdgården. Bus: 46, 55, 62, or 76.

KB Restaurant SWEDISH/CONTINENTAL   This is a traditional artists' rendezvous in the center of town, and while it's not exciting in any way, it offers beautifully prepared comfort food. And we could almost make a meal out of their freshly baked sourdough bread with Swedish butter. We like to begin with salmon trout roe and Russian caviar, and then move on to roasted lamb stuffed with zucchini in a thyme-flavored bouillon. End the meal with a fresh-fruit sorbet in summer or a lime soufflé with orange-blossom honey. There's also an informal bar.

Smålandsgatan 7. ℭ 08/679-60-32. Reservations recommended. Main courses 170SEK–295SEK ($23–$41/£12–£22); fixed-price 2-course dinner 295SEK ($41/£22). AE, DC, MC, V. Mon–Fri 11:30am–11:30pm; Sat–Sun 1–10pm; July daily 5–11pm. T-bana: Östermalmstorg.

Lisa Elmquist 🐟 *Kids* SEAFOOD   It may not be a refined cuisine, but this cafe and oyster bar, amid the food stalls of Stockholm's produce market (Östermalms Saluhall), prepares authentic Swedish food exceedingly well. Families like this place because of its bistrolike atmosphere, its good affordable food, and its no-nonsense format. It's owned by one of the city's largest fish distributors, so the menu varies with the catch. Some patrons come here for shrimp with bread and butter for 112SEK to 193SEK ($15–$27/£8.15–£14). Smoked salmon tartar is served with red onion and sour cream or marinated with a sweet mustard sauce. Fresh boiled lobster also appears on the menu, but at lethal prices. Desserts include a butterscotch tart and a chocolate tart made with white and dark truffles and served with fresh raspberries.

Östermalms Saluhall, Nybrogatan 31. ℭ 08/553-404-10. Reservations recommended. Main courses 70SEK–500SEK ($9.65–$69/£5.10–£37). AE, DC, MC, V. Mon–Fri 11am–5pm; Sat 10am–3:30pm. Closed at 2pm on Sat in July–Aug. T-bana: Östermalmstorg.

Prinsen 🐟 SWEDISH   Since 1897, this restaurant, a 2-minute walk from Stureplan, has been the favorite haunt of artists. Some of them were struggling and unable to pay their bills, and as a result, the walls of the restaurant are hung with many of their works. presented in lieu of payment. Some will tell you that "The Prince" (its English name) is riding on its rich bohemian past, but artists still come here for the satisfying *husmanskost* (home cooking). Seating is on two levels, and in summer tables are placed outside. The cuisine remains fresh and flavorful, a mostly Swedish repertoire with some French inspiration. The sautéed salmon tastes like it was just hauled in from the fjords, and the staff continues to serve old-fashioned favorites such as veal patties with homemade lingonberry preserves. Resisting trends, the cooks serve such classics as a herring platter or *biff rydberg* (beef with fried potatoes and an egg). Later in the evening, Prinsen becomes a local drinking club.

Mäster Samuelsgatan 4. ℭ 08/611-13-31. Reservations recommended. Main courses 199SEK–279SEK ($27–$39/£15–£20). AE, DC, MC, V. Mon–Fri 11:30am–11:30pm; Sat 1–11:30pm; Sun 5–10:30pm. T-bana: Östermalmstorg.

Sturehof 🐟 SWEDISH   This is the most classic French-style brasserie in all of Stockholm, and it's been going strong since the day it opened in 1897. Just as it was beginning to grow stale, it reinvented itself and remains the best spot in central Stockholm for dining at almost any time of the day or night. In summer you can sit out on the terrace and watch Stockholmers pass in parade, or else you can chill out in the lounge with the younger crowd. The dining room is more formal and elegant, with uniformed waiters and stiffly pressed white linen tablecloths. Seafood and shellfish have been a century-long tradition here, and the smoked Baltic herring appetizer is a testament to that. Expect a daily changing menu of *husmanskost,* or try the locally famous *sotare* (small grilled Baltic herring). Herring is king here, and this is one of the few places around still serving boiled salt veal tongue, a local delicacy.

After dinner, if the mood suits, you can drop in to check out **O-baren,** a backroom den with a bar and a dance floor.

Stureplan 2. ✆ **08/440-57-30.** Main courses 100SEK–365SEK ($14–$50/£7.30–£27). AE, DC, MC, V. Mon–Fri 11am–2am; Sat noon–2am; Sun 1pm–2am. T-bana: Östermalmstorg.

Tranan *(Value* SWEDISH   A real local favorite, this 1915 tavern serves very good food and draws a friendly crowd with its affordable prices and the kitchen's deft handling of fresh ingredients. An array of traditional Swedish dishes that often have French overtones is served. Items include filet of beef served with fried potatoes, egg yolk, and horseradish; Swedish meatballs and mashed potatoes; Swedish pork and lard sausage (actually tastier than it sounds) served with mashed potatoes and pickled beets; and herring platters. Later you can go downstairs to enjoy an authentic local bar, where DJs spin the latest hits on Friday and Saturday nights. Patrons must be 23 or older to enter the bar. The area surrounding the restaurant is getting trendier, and as a result, this working-class pub has gone more upscale, attracting young professionals of all sexual persuasions from the neighborhood.

Karlbergvagen 14. ✆ **08/527-281-00.** Main courses 125SEK–295SEK ($17–$41/£9.10–£22). AE, DC, MC, V. Mon–Fri 11:30am–11:45pm; Sat–Sun 5–11:45pm. Cellar bar until 1am. T-bana: Odenplan.

IN GAMLA STAN (OLD TOWN)
VERY EXPENSIVE

Leijontornet ✿✿ SWEDISH/INTERNATIONAL   This is one of Old Town's most stylish and fashionable restaurants, noted for its fine cuisine and quality of service. From the small, street-level bar, where you can order a predinner drink, patrons descend into an intimately lit cellar (the restaurant was built around a medieval defense tower). Dishes often arrive at your table looking like works of art, and some of the country's finest produce appears on the menu. To start we can recommend langoustine on pearl barley with a warm shellfish jelly and juniper-smoked parsnips, or the terrine of Swedish duck liver in apple jelly with hazelnuts in plum marmalade. For an entree, try the seaweed-fried cod with a pea and oyster puree, spider crab, and smoked-shrimp foam. For dessert, we like the dewberry pudding with molasses and a cream cheese mousse, set off with a saffron croustade with buttermilk foam.

In the Victory Hotel, Lilla Nygatan 5. ✆ **08/506-400-00.** Reservations required. Main courses 155SEK–310SEK ($21–$43/£11–£23); 7-course tasting menu 835SEK ($115/£61); 5-course dinner menu 745SEK ($103/£54); 3-course lunch 325SEK ($45/£24). AE, DC, MC, V. Mon–Fri 11:30am–2pm and 6–10pm; Sat 6–10pm. Closed July and bank holidays. T-bana: Gamla Stan.

Pontus in the Green House ✿✿✿ FRENCH/SWEDISH   The most expensive ingredients—Iranian caviar and foie gras and truffles from Umbria—are found here. Set within a building on the western side of Gamla Stan with foundations from the

---

Kids Family-Friendly Restaurants

Grand Veranda (p 415) If you want to introduce your kid to a Swedish smörgåsbord, there is no better place than the ground floor of the Grand Hotel. In this bountiful display, your child will surely find something tempting from the buffet of hot and cold dishes.

Lisa Elmquist (p. 416) Families can dine under a tent at this restaurant, located in the city's produce market, Östermalms Saluhall. The shrimp with bread and butter is a popular choice.

16th century, this is a well-orchestrated and elegant restaurant that attracts some of the most powerful figures in Stockholm. Don't confuse it with a nearby clone, Pontus by the Sea (℃ 08/20-20-95), where the dining experience is roughly equivalent but less popular. Your dining experience might begin with a drink at the ground-floor Greenhouse Bar, where tables and the menu are a lot less elaborate than the those featured upstairs. In the formal restaurant, you'll find a plush-looking late Victorian decor characterized by elaborately crafted banquettes, a monumental and highly ornate bar, touches of scarlet, and a somewhat unresponsive staff. Chef Pontus Frithiof was inspired by two of the grandest and most newsworthy chefs of England, Marco Pierre White and Gordon Ramsay. Their influence is seen in dishes that include barbecued pike-perch with smoked herbs, crayfish terrine, and clams with aioli and fennel; a spectacular version of lamb with two sauces; and crayfish with potato-based paella, saffron, mussels, and shellfish sausage.

Österlånggatan 17. ℃ 08/23-85-00. Reservations required. Main courses in the street-level bar 195SEK–245SEK ($27–$34/£14–£18). Main courses in the upstairs restaurant 340SEK–495SEK ($47–$68/£25–£36); fixed-price menus 340SEK–825SEK ($47–$114/£25–£60). AE, DC, MC, V. Mon–Fri 11:30am–3pm and 6–11pm; Sat 1–11pm. T-bana: Gamla Stan.

EXPENSIVE

Den Gyldene Freden ☆ SWEDISH   "Golden Peace" is said to be Stockholm's oldest tavern, having opened in 1722. The Swedish Academy owns the building, and members, along with artists, lawyers, and poets, frequent the place. The menu boasts good, traditional Swedish cooking and features fresh Baltic fish and game from the forests. Appetizers include a creamy artichoke soup, Jerusalem artichokes with a dollop of caviar, and an especially intriguing consommé of oxtail with tiny ravioli stuffed with quail breast. Dishes such as sautéed duck breast with pickled pumpkin, baked char with a wasabi flavoring, and beef carpaccio with goat cheese toast and citrus salsa also appear on the menu. Different desserts include warm rose hip soup with vanilla ice cream, a "symphony" of lingonberries, and Stockholm's best dark chocolate cake, served with fresh raspberries and coffee ice cream.

Österlånggatan 51. ℃ 08/24-97-60. Reservations recommended. Main courses 135SEK–335SEK ($19–$46/£9.85–£24). AE, DC, MC, V. Mon–Fri 5–11pm; Sat 1–11pm. T-bana: Gamla Stan.

Fem Små Hus ☆ SWEDISH/FRENCH   This atmospheric restaurant draws a *belle clientele* who's happy to savor the master chef's creations and his flair for flavorful marriages of market-fresh ingredients. The name, "Five Small Houses," derives from the five separate cellars that combine to make a series of nine candlelit dining rooms with cellars that date from the 17th century. The cuisine and staff, among the best we've encountered in Stockholm, are worthy of the restaurant's hallowed reputation. Beautifully prepared dishes include platters of assorted herring; filets of fried reindeer with cranberries and port wine sauce; oven-baked salmon with white wine sauce, summer vegetables, and new potatoes; and filets of veal with morel sauce and Gorgonzola. The best ingredients from Sweden's forests and shores are used.

Nygränd 10. ℂ 08/10-87-75. Reservations required. Main courses 250SEK–300SEK ($35–$41/£18–£22); set menus 375SEK–545SEK ($52–$75/£27–£40). AE, DC, MC, V. Daily 5–11pm. T-bana: Gamla Stan.

MODERATE
Mälardrottningen ✿ *finds* SEAFOOD/INTERNATIONAL   While the allure of this restaurant draws from its placement on the deck of a motor yacht, the food is well prepared. Menu items change with the seasons but might include salmon-filet spring rolls with pepper-garlic vinaigrette, pear-and-goat-cheese salad with thyme-flavored honey, and skewered scampi served with Parmesan cheese and pesto and banana chutney. One of the least expensive main courses is a heaping portion of marinated mussels in white wine and butter sauce, served with french fries. More formal dishes include a parfait of chicken livers with an apricot and oregano brioche, prosciutto-wrapped tiger prawns, and grilled Dublin Bay prawns with a fennel-flavored butter sauce.

Riddarholmen. ℂ 08/545-187-80. Reservations recommended. Main courses 105SEK–235SEK ($14–$32/£7.65–£17). AE, DC, MC, V. Mon–Sat 6pm–midnight. T-bana: Gamla Stan.

Stortorgskällaren SWEDISH   There are no culinary fireworks here, but you do get a solid, reliable menu, a cheerful atmosphere, and lots of robust flavors. In the winter this restaurant occupies medieval wine cellars whose vaulted ceilings date from the 15th century, while an outdoor terrace opposite the Swedish Academy opens in summer.

The menu changes often, but could include pâté of wild game with blackberry chutney and pickled carrots, grilled filet of pike-perch served with lime sauce and deep-fried potatoes, chanterelle mushrooms on toast served with strips of smoked reindeer, or a casserole of Baltic fish seasoned with saffron.

Stortorget 7. ℂ 08/10-55-33. Reservations required. Main courses 175SEK–280SEK ($24–$39/£13–£20); fixed-price menus 295SEK–610SEK ($41–$84/£22–£45). AE, DC, MC, V. Mon–Fri 11am–midnight; Sat 11am–11pm; Sun noon–11pm. T-bana: Gamla Stan.

INEXPENSIVE
Cattelin Restaurant ✿ *Value* SWEDISH   This restaurant may not have kept up with the changing times since it opened in 1897, but we still view it as one of the best and most reasonably priced restaurants in Stockholm. The food is good and fresh, and the tab is nothing close to the shockers you'll get elsewhere. Don't expect genteel service—the clattering of china can sometimes be deafening. First-rate menu choices include various preparations of beef, salmon, trout, veal, and chicken, which frequently make up the daily specials. The fixed-price lunch is served Monday to Friday 11am to 2pm. Every Friday night, after meal service ends, the place is sometimes reconfigured into a gay bar and dance club.

Storkyrkobrinken 9. ℂ 08/20-18-18. Reservations recommended. Main courses 159SEK–210SEK ($22–$29/£12–£15); set-lunch menu 75SEK ($10/£5.50). AE, DC, MC, V. Mon–Fri 11am–11pm; Sat 11am–3pm; Sun noon–11pm. T-bana: Gamla Stan.

ON KUNGSHOLMEN

Stadshuskällaren ✿ SWEDISH/INTERNATIONAL   Near the harbor in the basement of the City Hall, this two-in-one restaurant houses the Skänken, which serves lunch only, and the Stora Matsalen, where chefs prepare the annual banquet for the Nobel Prize winners. We sampled a past banquet meal of mountain grouse breast baked in black trumpet mushrooms with caramelized apples, poached onions and broad beans, served with a Norman Calvados sauce and potato cake. Other main-course options include a confit of salmon filet with roasted Jerusalem artichokes, marinated beets, and a lemon emulsion; and grilled turbot with smoked almonds. The Roquefort cheesecake comes with a fig and cherry compote.

Stadshuset. ✆ 08/506-32-200. Main courses 135SEK–235SEK ($19–$32/£9.85–£17); 2-course fixed-price lunch 350SEK ($48/£26); 3-course fixed-price dinner 690SEK ($95/£51). AE, DC, MC, V. Skänken Mon–Fri 11:30am–2pm. Stora Matsalen Mon–Fri 11:30am–11pm; Sat 2–11pm. T-bana: Rådhuset. Bus: 3 or 62.

ON DJURGÅRDEN

Ulla Winbladh ✿ SWEDISH   This is a highly reliable and sought-after staple, thanks to its origins in 1897 as part of Stockholm's World Fair and a name (Ulla Winbladh) that conjures up images of passionate love for most Swedes. It was acquired by its present management in 1994 and occupies a sprawling, stone-built, white-sided pavilion set in an isolated position on the Djurgården. Inside, there's a series of dining rooms, with unusual paintings and a sense of graceful prosperity. There's also an outdoor terrace lined with flowering plants. The menu focuses on time-tested, somewhat conservative Swedish cuisine, always impeccably prepared. Menu items include at least three different preparations of herring; salmon with a terrine of watercress, bleak roe, and asparagus; fish casserole with potatoes and shellfish sauce; Swedish meatballs in cream sauce with lingonberries and pickled cucumbers; and a beautiful version of poached halibut with hard-boiled egg, shrimp, and melted butter.

Rosendalsvägen 8. ✆ 08/663-05-71. Reservations required. Main courses 225SEK–305SEK ($31–$42/£16–£22). AE, DC, MC, V. Mon 11:30am–10pm; Tues–Fri 11:30am–11pm; Sat noon–11pm; Sun noon–10pm. Bus: 47.

Villa Kallhagen ✿ SWEDISH   This restaurant is a lovely, bucolic choice for either lunch or dinner, with crowd-pleasing fare that's market fresh and well prepared. The location, just a 5-minute ride from the city center and near Djurgårdkanalen, is best in summer, when you can enjoy a predinner stroll.

The chef's culinary technique never fails him, and his inventiveness and precision with local ingredients always impresses us. Start with creamy crayfish and fresh chanterelle salad with bleak roe served on fennel bread, and move on to heartier dishes such as fried Baltic herring with Dijon mustard sauce and drawn butter, or the lemon-fried veal with mashed potatoes and a Parmesan terrine.

Djurgårdsbrunnsvagen 10. ✆ 08/665-03-00. Reservations required. Main courses 135SEK–300SEK ($19–$41/£9.85–£22). AE, DC, MC, V. Mon–Fri 11:30am–2pm and 5–10pm; Sat 5–10pm; Sun 11:30am–5pm. Closed in July. Bus: 69 from Central Station.

AT SÖDERMALM

Garlic & Shots MEDITERRANEAN/INTERNATIONAL   We once said we could go for garlic in anything but ice cream, only to be proven wrong by a dessert served here. This theme restaurant follows two strong, overriding ideas: Everyone needs a daily shot of garlic, and everything tastes better if it's doctored with a dose of the Mediterranean's most potent ingredient. The no-frills setting is artfully spartan, with bare wood tables that have hosted an unexpectedly large number of rock stars. Expect garlic in just about everything, from soup (try garlic-ginger with clam) to such main courses as beefsteak covered with fried minced garlic and Transylvania-style vampire steak, drenched in horseradish-tomato-and-garlic sauce. Don't forget the garlic honey ice cream with sweetened green peppercorn strawberries and chocolate-dipped garlic cloves. Wash it all down with garlic ale or beer.

Folkungagatan 84. © 08/640-84-46. Reservations recommended. Main courses 85SEK–300SEK ($12–$41/ £6.20–£22). MC, V. Daily 5pm–1am. T-bana: Medborgarplatsen.

ON LÅNGHOLMEN

Långholmen Restaurant *Finds* INTERNATIONAL Come to this former-state-penitentiary-turned-hotel for an unusual insight into the hardships of the 19th century, and menu items that change with the seasons.

This is hardly prison food—in fact, only market-fresh ingredients are used—and the staff here is clearly dedicated to pleasing your palate. Examples include a carpaccio of shellfish; a combination of lobster and turbot stewed with vegetables in a shellfish bouillon; and tournedos of venison with juniper-berries, smoked ham, pepper sauce, and Swedish potatoes.

From the windows of the old-fashioned dining room, you can still see the high brick walls, small doors, heavy bolts, and bars on the windows, but these are showcased rather than concealed.

Kronohäktet. © 08/720-85-50. Reservations recommended. Lunch main courses 98SEK–168SEK ($14–$23/ £7.15–£12); dinner main courses 175SEK–290SEK ($24–$40/£13–£21); 3-course fixed-price dinner 450SEK ($62/£33). AE, DC, MC, V. Mon–Fri 11:30am–10pm; Sat noon–10pm; Sun noon–7pm T-bana: Hornstul Bus: 4, 40, or 66.

15

Exploring Stockholm

There's no denying that Stockholm is an expensive city, but there are many bargains, and we've done our best to bring them to you. Rapidly evolving, Stockholm's loaded with sights and activities. If the *Vasa* Ship Museum doesn't pique your interest, perhaps the changing of the guard at the Royal Palace or the Gröna Lunds Tivoli amusement park will. Even window shopping for beautifully designed Swedish crafts can be an enjoyable way to spend an afternoon. At night, Stockholm becomes the liveliest city in northern Europe.

1 On Gamla Stan & Neighboring Islands

Kungliga Slottet (Royal Palace) & Museums ☆☆   This is no match for Buckingham Palace, but a visit here offers a look at the daily life of the royal court. Kungliga Slottet is one of the few official residences of a European monarch that's open to the public, and although the king and queen prefer to live at Drottningholm, this massive 608-room showcase remains their official address.

The **Royal Apartments** ☆☆☆, entered on the second floor of the north wing, are the most impressive. Decorated in the 1690s by French artists, they have the oldest interiors of the palace. The lavish **ballroom** ☆☆ is called "The White Sea," and **Karl XI's Gallery** is the venue for official banquets.

In **Rikssalen** (Hall of State), you can see Queen Christina's **silver throne** ☆, a rare piece of silver furniture created for the queen's coronation in 1650. The **Guest Apartment** in the west wing marries rococo and Gustavian classicism. Since the interiors were designed over a period of centuries, expect a hodgepodge of decorative styles, including Louis XVI and Empire.

Second in importance to the state apartments is the **Skattkammaren** ☆☆☆, or Royal Treasury, entered through the south arch. These dark vaults contain the greatest collection of royal regalia in all of Scandinavia, a virtual gold mine when compared to the collections of Oslo or Copenhagen.

The original palace that stood here, destroyed in a fire in 1697, was **Tre Kronor.** Today the Tre Kronor Museum on the ground floor of the palace's northern wing honors its memory. There's more to see at this palace, including the **Slottskyrkan** baroque chapel; **Gustav III's Antikmuseum** ☆, one of Europe's oldest museums; and the **Livrustkammaren** ☆☆ royal armory and Sweden's oldest museum, where **state coaches** ☆☆ and coronation robes, in addition to weapons, are on display.

Royal Guards have been stationed at the palace since 1523, and today military units from all over Sweden take turns standing guard. In summer you can watch the parade of the military guard daily. In winter it takes place on Wednesday and Sunday; on the other days there's no parade, but you can see the **Changing of the Royal Guard** ☆.

Favorite Stockholm Experiences

Exploring Skansen   Wander at leisure through the world's oldest open-air museum (which covers about 30 hectares/75 acres of parkland), and get a glimpse of Swedish life in the long-ago countryside.

Strolling Through Gamla Stan at Night   Walking the narrow cobblestone alleys of the Old Town after dark, with special lighting, is like going back in time.

Taking the Baths   Both men and women are fond of roasting themselves on wooden platforms and then plunging into a shower of Arctic-chilled water.

Watching the Summer Dawn   In midsummer at 3am, you can get out of bed, sit on a balcony, and watch the eerie blue sky. Gradually it's bathed in peach, as the early dawn of a "too-short" summer day approaches.

The changing of the guard takes place at 12:15pm Monday to Saturday and at 1:15pm on Sunday in front of the Royal Palace.

Before you leave, visit the **Royal Gift Shop,** where much of the merchandise is produced in limited editions, including textiles based on designs from the 16th and 17th centuries.

Kungliga Husgerådskammaren. ℂ **08/402-61-30** for Royal Apartments and Treasury, 08/402-61-67 for the Skattkammaren, 08/402-61-30 for Royal Armory, or 08/402-61-06 for Museum of Antiquities. www.royalcourt.se. Entry to the Royal Apartments, Royal Armory, Museum of Antiquities, and Treasury 90SEK ($12/£6.55) adults, 35SEK ($4.85/£2.55) seniors and students, free for children under 7. A combination ticket to all parts of palace is 130SEK ($18/£9.50) adults, 65SEK ($8.95/£4.75) students and children. Apartments and Treasury Sept–May Tues–Sun noon–3pm (closed Jan), June–Aug daily 10am–5pm; closed during government receptions. Royal Armory daily 10am–5pm. Museum of Antiquities mid-Aug daily 10am–4pm. T-bana: Gamla Stan. Bus: 43, 46, 59, or 76.

Riddarholm Skyrkam ✦   The second-oldest church in Stockholm is located on the tiny island of Riddarholmen, next to Gamla Stan. It was founded in the 13th century as a Franciscan monastery, but today is a virtual pantheon of Swedish kings. The last king buried here was Gustav V in 1950. You come here for the royal tombs, as the church is relatively devoid of art. However, it does contain a trio of royal chapels.

Riddarholmen. ℂ **08/402-61-30**. www.royalcourt.se. Admission 30SEK ($4.15/£2.20) adults, 10SEK ($1.40/75p) children 7–18, under 7 free. May 10am–4pm; June–Aug daily 10am–5pm; Sept daily 10am–4pm. Closed Oct–Apr. T-bana: Gamla Stan.

Östasiatiskamuseet (Museum of Far Eastern Antiquities) ✦ *Finds*   You may be going only a short journey to Skeppsholmen, a small island in the middle of central Stockholm, but you're really making a trip to the Far East. The collection of archaeological objects, fine arts, and handicrafts from China, Japan, Korea, and India form one of the finest and most extensive museums of its kind outside Asia.

Among the outstanding displays are Chinese Neolithic painted pottery, bronze ritual vessels, archaic jades, wood carvings, ivory, lacquer work, enamelware, Buddhist sculpture, and Ming blue-and-white wares.

Skeppsholmen. ℂ **08/519-55-750**. www.ostasiatiska.se. Free admission. Tues 11am–8pm; Wed–Sun 11am–5pm. T-bana: Kungsträdgården. Bus: 65 to Karl XII Torg; 7-min. walk.

Stockholm Attractions

Drottningholm Palace and Theater **1**

Gröna Lunds Tivoli **17**

Hallwylska Museet (Hallwyl Museum) **10**

Historiska Museet
   (Museum of National Antiquities) **9**

Kungliga Slottet (Royal Palace) & Museums **6**

Moderna Museet (Museum of Modern Art) **13**

Nationalmuseum (National Museum of Art) **11**

Nordiska Museet (Nordic Museum) **15**

Operahauset (Royal Opera House) **5**

Östasiatiskamuseet
   (Museum of Far Eastern Antiquities) **12**

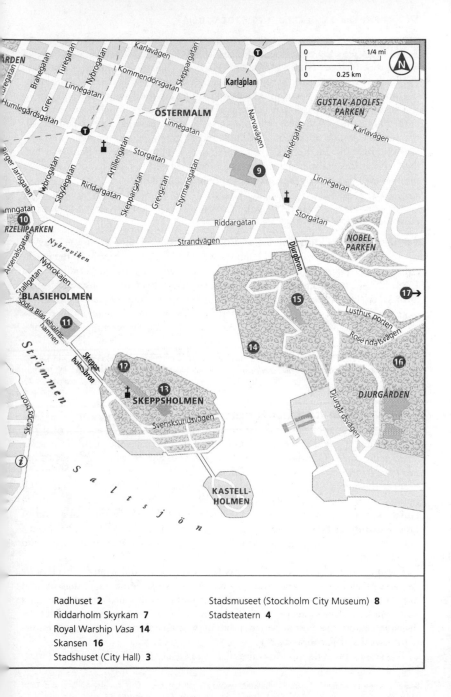

Radhuset **2**

Riddarholm Skyrkam **7**

Royal Warship *Vasa* **14**

Skansen **16**

Stadshuset (City Hall) **3**

Stadsmuseet (Stockholm City Museum) **8**

Stadsteatern **4**

2 On Norrmalm

Hallwylska Museet (Hallwyl Museum) ❀ *(Finds* The rich Countess Wilhelmina von Hallwyl was a collector of almost anything as long as it was valuable and expensive, and she cataloged her acquisitions and left them to the state upon her death.

The catalog of this passionate collector came to 78 volumes, which have been open to the public since 1938. The collection includes classic paintings, rare tapestries, silver, armor, weapons, antique musical instruments, glassware, and umbrellas and buttons (but only the finest ones). On a guided tour you learn historical tidbits, such as the fact that this house had a modern bathroom before the royal palace. Ask about summer evening concerts presented in the central courtyard.

Hamngatan 4. ☎ **08/519-55-599**. www.hallwylskamuseet.se. Guided tours 40SEK ($5.50/£2.90) adults, 20SEK ($2.75/£1.45) children 7–18, free for children under 7. Guided tours in Swedish: Tues–Sun, noon, 1, 2, and 3pm; extra tour Wed 6pm. In English: Tues–Sun 1pm. T-bana: Kungsträdgården.

Kaknästornet (Kaknäs Television Tower) *(Moments* This 1967 tower may be ugly, but the view of greater Stockholm from the top is the best there is. In the northern district of Djurgården stands the tallest man-made structure in Scandinavia—a 152m (499-ft.) radio and television tower. Two elevators run to an observation platform, where you can see everything from the cobblestone streets of Gamla Stan to the city's modern concrete-and-glass structures. A moderately priced restaurant that serves classic Swedish cuisine is on the 28th floor. The view from the restaurant is even better than the food.

Mörkakroken. ☎ **08/789-24-35** or 08/667-2105. Admission 30SEK ($4.15/£2.20) adults, 15SEK ($2.05/£1.10) children 7–15, free for children under 7. Jan–Mar Mon–Wed and Sun 10am–5pm, Thurs–Sat 10am–9pm; Apr and Sept daily 10am–9pm; May–Aug daily 9am–10pm; Oct–Dec Mon–Sat 10am–9pm, Sun 10am–5pm. Closed Dec 24–25. Bus: 69.

Nationalmuseum (National Museum of Art) ❀❀❀ Founded in 1792, the National Museum is one of the oldest museums in the world and Sweden's largest and best museum of world art. The museum grew out of a small collection from Gustav Vasa's collection at Gripsholm Castle. Over the years the collection expanded from bequests, purchases, and even spoils of war.

In all, the museum owns 16,000 art works from the late Middle Ages up to the 20th century, with emphasis on Swedish 18th and 19th century art. The collection of Dutch paintings from the 17th century is rich, and the **18th-century collection of French paintings** ❀❀ is regarded as one of the best in the world. Naturally the museum is a good showcase for Sweden's two most famous artists, Anders Zorn and Carl Larsson.

The first floor focuses on applied arts (silverware, handicrafts, porcelain, Empire furnishings, and the like). First-time visitors, if pressed for time, may want to head directly to the second floor to check out the paintings from northern Europe and a rare collection of **Russian icons** ❀. The museum shows an exceptional number of masterpieces, but the most important room in the museum has one whole wall featuring the **works of Rembrandt** ❀❀.

The museum is at the tip of a peninsula, a short walk from the Royal Opera House and the Grand Hotel.

Södra Blasieholmshamnen. ☎ **08/519-54-300**. www.nationalmuseum.se. Free admission. Tues and Thurs 11am–8pm; Wed, Fri–Sun 11am–5pm. Closed Mon. T-bana: Kungsträdgården. Bus: 2, 62, 65, or 76.

Moderna Museet (Museum of Modern Art) 𝒦𝒦 *Kids*   This former drill house on the island of Skeppsholmen is now one of the greatest repositories of modern art in northern Europe. The museum is especially strong in Cubist paintings, with works by Picasso, Braque, and Léger. We are particularly enthralled by Matisse's *Apollo decoupage* 𝒦 and the celebrated *Enigma of William Tell* 𝒦𝒦 by Salvador Dalí. In all, the present collection includes 5,000 paintings and sculptures, around 25,000 watercolors, and 100,000 photographs, as well as a large number of graphics, videos, and films. As enthralled as we are by the permanent collection, we come for the often stunning temporary exhibitions. Admission to the museum is free, but temporary exhibitions carry a charge.

Musical concerts and the best children's workshops in Stockholm are also presented here. The First at Moderna offers a new exhibition on the first of every month, while Moderna by Night, from 6pm to midnight on Friday, offers food, drinks, entertainment, and art. We also love to patronize the modern espresso bar near the main entrance. *Tip:* Time your visit to have a good and affordable lunch at the self-service restaurant offering views toward Östermalm.

Skeppsholmen. ℂ 08/519-55-200. www.modernamuseet.se. Free admission. Tues–Wed 10am–8pm; Thurs–Sun 10am–6pm. T-bana: Kungsträdgården. Bus: 65.

Historiska Museet (Museum of National Antiquities) 𝒦𝒦   The Viking era lives on here, as more than 4,000 objects and artifacts reveal the lives and travels of these rugged seafarers.

We always head to the **Goldrummet** 𝒦𝒦𝒦 first, a virtual treasure chest of items that, amazingly, date from the Bronze Age. It features Viking silver and gold jewelry, large ornate charms, elaborate bracelets, and a unique neck collar from Färjestaden.

After all this gold, the other exhibitions come as a bit of a letdown. The Gothic Hall holds one of Scandinavia's finest collections of sculpture, church triptychs, and other ecclesiastical objects from the 12th century onward. In the Textile Chamber, fabrics from the Middle Ages to the present are on display.

Narvavägen 13–17. ℂ 08/519-556-00. www.historiska.se. Free admission. May 2–Sept daily 10am–5pm; Oct–May 1 Fri–Wed 11am–5pm, Thurs 11am–8pm. T-bana: Karlaplan or Östermalmstorg. Bus: 47 or 69.

3 On Djurgården

The forested island of Djurgården (Deer Park) lies about 3km (2 miles) to the east of Gamla Stan (Old Town).

Vasamuseet (Royal Warship *Vasa*) 𝒦𝒦𝒦   This 17th-century man-of-war is the most visited attraction in Scandinavia—and for good reason. Housed near the main entrance to Skansen within a cement-sided museum that was specifically constructed for its display, the *Vasa* is the world's oldest complete and identified ship.

On its maiden voyage in 1628, in front of thousands of onlookers, the Royal Warship *Vasa* capsized and sank almost instantly to the bottom of Stockholm harbor. Its salvage in 1961 was an engineering and archaeological triumph. On board were more than 4,000 coins, carpenters' tools, sailors' pants, fish bones, and other items of archaeological interest. Best of all, 97% of the ship's 700 original decorative sculptures were found and are on display alongside baroque carvings. A full-scale model of half of the *Vasa*'s upper gun deck has been built, together with the admiral's cabin and the steering compartment.

Galärvarvsvägen 14, Djurgården. © **08/5195-4800**. www.vasamuseet.se. Admission 80SEK ($11/£5.85) adults. Sept–May Thurs–Tues 10am–5pm; June–Aug Thurs–Tues 8:30am–6pm, Wed 10am–8pm. Closed Jan 1, May 1, Dec 23–25, and Dec 31. Bus: 47 or 69. Ferry from Slussen year-round, from Nybroplan in summer only.

Skansen ✸✸✸   This was the world's first open-air museum in 1891 and presents how Swedes lived. It is also a summer playground for Stockholmers, although it's hardly comparable to the Tivoli Gardens in Copenhagen. Often called "Old Sweden in a Nutshell," this museum features more than 150 reconstructed dwellings scattered over some 30 hectares (74 acres) of parkland. They were originally erected in sites throughout Sweden, from the northern frontier of Lapland to the southern edges of Skåne. Most date from the 18th and 19th centuries.

The exhibits include windmills, manor houses, blacksmith shops—even a complete town quarter that was meticulously rebuilt. Many handicrafts for which Swedes later became noted (glassblowing, for example) are demonstrated. For a tour of the buildings' interiors, arrive no later than 4pm. Folk dancing and open-air concerts, in some cases featuring international stars, are occasionally scheduled in summertime. Check at the Tourist Center for information. There's a lot going on during summer nights (see "Stockholm After Dark," later in this chapter) and many places to eat.

Djurgården 49–51. © **08/442-80-00**. www.skansen.se. Admission 50SEK–80SEK ($6.90–$11/£3.65–£5.85) adults, depending on time of day, day of the week, and season; 20SEK–30SEK ($2.75–$4.15/£1.45–£2.20) children 6–15; free for children 5 and under. Historic buildings Oct–Apr daily 10am–4pm; May daily 10am–8pm; June–Aug daily 10am–10pm; Sept daily 10am–5pm. Bus: 47 from central Stockholm. Ferry from Slussen.

Nordiska Museet (Nordic Museum) ✸✸   This museum showcases preserved items from Sweden's past. The first object you encounter when entering the Great Hall is a mammoth pink-tinted statue of a seated Gustav Vasa. That piece of oak in his forehead was said to have come from a massive tree planted by the king himself.

You almost know what to expect here: 16th-century dining tables, period costumes, dollhouses, textiles, and even an extensive exhibit of tools from the Swedish fish trade.

Djurgårdsvägen 6–16, Djurgården. © **08/5195-6000**. www.nordiskamuseet.se. Free admission. Mon–Fri 10am–4pm; Sat–Sun 11am–5pm. Bus: 44, 47, or 69.

Prins Eugens Waldemarsudde ✸✸   Prince Eugen's (1865–1947) former home and studio, one of the most visited museums in Sweden, is now an art gallery and a memorial to this talented artist, who specialized in depictions of his favorite spots of beauty in central Sweden, earning him the nickname "The Painting Prince."

This lovely three-story mansion on the water was acquired by the prince in 1899, and he lived here until his death. The rooms on the ground floor are furnished just as the prince left them. The prince was not only a painter, but a collector, acquiring works by such great Scandinavian artists as Edvard Munch, Carl Larsson, and Anders Zorn.

Allow time to wander through the gardens with centuries-old trees, enjoying panoramic views of the Stockholm harbor. The park is filled with sculptures by some of the greatest masters of Europe—Carl Milles to Auguste Rodin. While at Waldemarsudde, see the **Old Mill,** a windmill built in the 1780s.

Prins Eugens Väg 6. © **08/545-837-00**. www.waldemarsudde.se. Admission 80SEK ($11/£5.85) adults, 60SEK ($8.30/£4.40) seniors and students, free for children under 19. Tues–Sun 11am–5pm. Bus: 47 to the end of the line.

Thielska Galleriet (Thiel Gallery) ✸✸   It's inevitable to draw comparisons between this world-class gallery and the just-visited Waldemarsudde of Prince Eugen—in fact, the art collection at Thielska surpasses that of "The Painting Prince."

Both of the palatial art-filled mansions at Djurgården were constructed roughly at the same time by architect Ferdinand Roberg.

Ernest Thiel was once a wealthy banker and art collector who commissioned the mansion, drawing upon architectural influences from both the Italian Renaissance and the Far East. Over the years, Thiel began to fill his palatial rooms with great art. However, in the wake of World War I, he went bankrupt and the state took over his property in 1924, eventually opening it as a museum.

Regrettably, we can't see all of Thiel's masterpieces. In a robbery that made international headlines in 2002, many of the finest works were stolen. They were never recovered. Works by Manet, Rodin, Toulouse-Lautrec, and others round out the collection.

Sjötullsbacken 6–8, Djurgården. ✆ 08/662 58 84. www.thielska-galleriet.se. Admission 50SEK ($6.90/£3.65) adults, free for children under 16. Mon–Sat noon–4pm; Sun 1–4pm. Bus: 69.

4 On Kungsholmen

Stadshuset (Stockholm City Hall) ☆☆   Nobel Prize winners are honored and awarded here, and while you won't walk away a winner in the literal sense, you are awarded view of one of the finest examples of modern architecture in Europe. Built in the National Romantic Style, the Stockholm City Hall (Stadshuset), on the island of Kungsholmen, was designed by Ragnar Ostberg and completed in 1923. A lofty square tower rising 100m (328 ft.) dominates the red brick structure. In summer you can climb the tower for what we consider the finest **panoramic view** ☆☆ of Gamla Stan in the area. It bears three gilt crowns, the symbol of Sweden, and the national coat-of-arms. There are two courts: the open civic court and the interior covered court. The Blue Hall is used for banquets and other festive occasions, including the Nobel Prize banquet. About 18 million pieces of gold and colored glass mosaics cover the walls of the **Golden Hall** ☆☆. The southern gallery contains murals by Prince Eugen.

Hantverksgatan 1. ✆ 08/508-290-5. www.stockholm.se/stadshuset. Admission 60SEK ($8.30/£4.40) adults, 30SEK ($4.15/£2.20) ages 12–18, free for children under 12. Tower additional 20SEK ($2.75/£1.45). Apr–Sept daily 10am–4:15pm. City Hall tours (subject to change) June–Aug daily at 10am, 11am, noon, 2pm, 3pm, and 4pm; Sept–May daily at 10am, noon, and 2pm. T-bana: Centralen or Rådhuset. Bus: 3 or 62.

5 On Södermalm

Stadsmuseet (Stockholm City Museum) *(Kids)*   Skip this museum if your time is fading; otherwise give it an hour or so. For architectural buffs, the building may be more intriguing than its exhibits. Constructed in the Italian baroque style, it was designed by the famous Tessin the Elder as the City Hall for southern Stockholm.

The history of Stockholm is presented in stages floor to floor, the first floor depicting Stockholm when it was a great maritime power in the 17th century. On the second floor you can see Stockholm emerging as a multicultural city, when its population soared to more than a million people, causing a housing shortage. Finally, on the third floor, you are shown what a local factory looked like in 1897. Relics of Sweden's first Industrial Exhibition, also from 1897, are also on view.

If you have time, check out the two reconstructed apartments and Torget, a replica of a main square, on the ground floor. There's also a playground for kids and a historical 30-minute slideshow in English daily at 1pm.

Ryssgården, Slussen. ✆ 08/508-31-600. www.stadsmuseum.stockholm.se. Free admission. Tues–Sun 11am–5pm; Thurs 11am–8pm. T-bana: Slussen. Bus: 43 or 46.

6 Near Stockholm

Drottningholm Palace and Theater ✸✸✸   There is no palace in northern Europe as grand and spectacular as this regal complex, which is why it is dubbed the "Versailles of Sweden." The royal family still lives here, on an island in Lake Mälaren, but the royal apartments are guarded and screened off.

Work began on this masterpiece in 1662 by Nicodemus Tessin the Elder (1615–81), one of the most celebrated architects of the 17th century, and it is now listed as a UNESCO World Heritage Site.

Drottningholm needs about 3 hours of your time, but deserves more if you have it. You can explore the palace, Sweden's greatest theater, the magnificent gardens, and even a Chinese Pavilion. The highlight of any tour is the **State Apartments** ✸✸✸, with a spectacular staircase. The apartments dazzle with opulent furniture and art from the 17th to the 19th centuries, painted ceilings, precious Chinese vases, and ornate gold chandeliers.

Queen Lovisa Ulrika's **library** ✸✸ is a work of grand beauty, an excellent example of the Gustavian style by Jean Eric Rehn. After all that grandeur we like to retreat to the **Kina Slott** ✸. The pavilion, on the southeast corner of the park, was constructed in Stockholm in 1753 and later floated downriver to surprise Lovisa on her 33rd birthday.

Allow as much time as you can to stroll through **Drottningholm Gardens** ✸✸✸, checking out the bronze **Hercules Fountain** ✸✸, the water garden, pools, bridges, and islands. **Drottningholm Court Theater** ✸✸✸ is a gem of baroque architecture. The Royal Music Academy and the Royal Opera (founded by Lovisa) presented performances here, and today the theater is complete with the original backdrops and props. Theater buffs can visit the **Theatre Museum,** with exhibits tracing the history of European theater since the 1700s. Between June and July, some two dozen performances are staged. Devoted almost exclusively to 18th-century opera, it seats only 450. Many performances sell out far in advance to season-ticket holders. The theater can be visited only as part of a guided tour, which focuses on the original sets and stage mechanisms.

For tickets to the evening performances, which cost 165SEK to 610SEK ($23–$84/ £12–£45), call ✆ **08/660-82-25.** For more information about the theater, call ✆ **08/759-04-06** or 08/556-931-07, or visit www.dtm.se.

Ekerö, Drottningholm. ✆ **08/402-62-80.** www.royalcourt.se. Palace 60SEK ($8.30/£4.40) adults, 30SEK ($4.15/£2.20) students and persons under 26; theater guided tour 70SEK ($9.65/£5.10) adults, 30SEK ($4.15/£2.20) children 7–18; Kina Slott 50SEK ($6.90/£3.65) adults, 25SEK ($3.45/£1.85) students. All free for children under 7. Palace Oct–Apr Sat–Sun noon–3:30pm; May–Aug daily 10am–4:30pm; Sept daily noon–3:30pm. Theater guided tours in English May noon–4:30pm; June–Aug daily 11am–4:30pm; Sept daily 1–3:30pm. Kina Slott Apr and Oct daily 1–3:30pm; May daily 11am–4:30pm; June–Aug daily 11am–3pm; Sept Tues–Sun, noon–3pm. Lies 11km (6¾ miles) west of Stockholm. T-bana: Brommaplan and then bus no. 301 or 323 to Drottningholm. Ferry from the dock near City Hall.

Millesgården ✸✸✸   This former villa on the island of Lidingö, northeast of Stockholm, is home to Carl Milles's (1875–1955) sculpture garden.

Emigrating to the U.S. in 1931, Milles became a professor of art at the University of Michigan, creating nearly 75 sculptures, many of which are on display around the U.S. today. However, some of the artist's major works are on view here, including his monumental and much-reproduced *Hands of God* ✸✸✸. Sculptures sit atop columns on terraces in this garden, set high above the harbor and the city landscape. Sculptures are copies of his most famous works; the originals are found all over Sweden and the U.S. The site also includes his personal collection of works by other leading sculptors. The villa displays a unique collection of art from both the Middle Ages and the Renaissance, plus rare artifacts excavated in the ruins of ancient Rome and Greece.

Carl Milles Väg 32, Lidingö. © **08/446-75-94.** Admission 80SEK ($11/£5.85) adults, children 18 and under free. May–Sept daily 11am–5pm; Oct–Apr Tues–Sun noon–5pm. T-bana: Ropsten and then a bus to Torsviks Torg or a train to Norsvik. Bus: 207.

7 Especially for Kids

The open-air park Skansen (see above), on Djurgården, offers **Lill-Skansen** for kids. There's a petting zoo with pigs, goats, and horses. Lill-Skansen offers a break from the dizzying (and often tantrum-inducing) excitement frequently generated by a commercial amusement park. A miniature train ride through the park is about as wild as it gets. Lill-Skansen is open daily in summer from 10:30am to 4pm.

Before going to Skansen, stop off at the *Vasa* **Museum** and cap off the evening with a visit to **Gröna Lunds Tivoli** (see "Stockholm After Dark," later in this chapter), which also is on Djurgården.

8 Organized Tours

CITY TOURS   The quickest and most convenient way to see the city highlights is to take one of the bus tours that leave from the Square of Gustaf Adolf, near the Kungsträdgården.

Stockholm Sightseeing (City Sightseeing), Skeppsbron 22 (© **08/587 140 20**), offers a variety of tours, mostly in summer. Tours depart from Gustaf Adolf Torg in front of the Dansmuseet. Panoramic Stockholm, a 1½-hour tour costing 210SEK ($29/£15), purports to show you the landmarks of Stockholm and several waterscapes in record time. This tour is conducted from March 24 to December 31. For Stockholm in a Nutshell, you can take a 2½-hour tour, costing 310SEK ($43/£23), with departures from March 24 to December 17. This tour shows you the highlights of Stockholm, including a sail around the royal park at Djurgården. A more comprehensive tour, the Grand Tour lasts 3½ hours and costs 410SEK ($57/£30). This tour is by both boat and bus. A tour known as Old Town Combination departs June 26 to August 27, lasts 2½ hours, and costs 290SEK ($40/£21). This bus and walking tour offers a guided walking tour through Old Town, with its narrow alleys and tiny courtyards. Finally, from June 26 to August 27, you can go on a 45-minute Horse and Carriage Tour costing 100SEK ($14/£7.30) and departing from Mynttorget by the Royal Palace.

OLD TOWN STROLLS   Authorized guides lead 1-hour walking tours of the medieval lanes of Stockholm's Old Town. These walks are conducted daily from mid-June until late August, departing from the Royal Opera House at Gustaf Adolf Torg. The cost is 90SEK ($12/£6.60). Tickets and times of departure are available from **Stockholm Sightseeing,** Skeppsbron 22 (© **08/587-140-20**).

CANAL CRUISES   Stockholm Sightseeing (© **08/587-140-20**) offers the Royal Canal Tour, March 24 to December 17 daily, every half-hour on the hour. Tours cost 120SEK ($17/£8.75) for adults and 65SEK ($8.95/£4.75) for children 12 and under. Visitors are ferried around the canals of Djurgården.

9 Spectator Sports

Soccer and **ice hockey** are the two most popular spectator sports in Sweden, and Stockholm is the home of world-class teams in both. The major venue for any spectator sport in the capital, the **Stockholm Globe Arena (Globen),** lies less than 6.5km (4 miles) south of central Stockholm. Built in 1989, it's believed to be the biggest round building in the world, with a seating capacity of 16,000. It offers everything from political rallies, motorcycle competitions, and sales conventions to basketball and ice hockey games, tennis matches, and rock concerts. Its ticket office (© **08/ 508-353-00**) sells tickets Monday to Friday 9am to 6pm and Saturday 11am to 4pm for most of Stockholm's soccer games, which are played in an open-air stadium nearby. The Globen lies in the southern suburb of Johnneshov (T-bana: Globen).

Another popular pastime is watching and betting on **trotting races.** These races usually take place on Wednesday at 6:30pm and on an occasional Saturday at 12:30pm in both summer and winter. (In winter an attempt is made to clear snow and ice from the racecourse; slippery conditions sometimes lead to unpredictable results.) Admission to **Solvalla Stadium** (© **08/635-90-00**), which lies about 6.5km (4 miles) north of the city center, is 40SEK ($5.50/£2.90). From Stockholm, take the bus marked SOLVALLA.

For schedules and ticket information, inquire at your hotel or the city's tourist office, or buy a copy of the monthly magazine, *"What's On,"* which is available free at hotels and selected shops throughout the city.

10 Outdoor Activities

GOLF   For those who want to play golf at the "top of Europe," there is the **Bromma Golf Course,** Kvarnbacksvägen 28, 16874 Bromma (© **08/564-888-30**), lying 5km (3 miles) west of the center of Stockholm. It's a 9-hole golf course with well-maintained greens. Greens fees are 150SEK ($21/£11) or 200SEK ($28/£15) on Saturday and Sunday, and golf clubs can be rented.

HORSEBACK RIDING (VIKING STYLE)   Iceland horses—gentle and small— can be ridden at the **Haniwnge Iceland Horse Center** at Hemfosa, 37km (23 miles) south of Stockholm (© **0730/488-885**). For 450SEK ($62/£33), you can ride for 2½ hours; the price includes a picnic lunch. Aside from walking, galloping, trotting, and cantering, the horses have another gait, the *tölt,* a kind of equine speed walk that has no English translation.

SAUNA & SWIMMING   A combination sauna, outdoor heated pool, and children's paddling pool, **Vilda Vanadis,** at Vanadislunden near the northern terminus of Sveavägen (© **08/30-12-11**), is within easy walking distance of the Oden Hotel and the city center. This really is an adventure park, with a variety of attractions, as well as a sauna and a restaurant. The entrance fee is 60SEK ($8.30/£4.40), but once you're inside, the attractions are free. It's open daily May 1 to September 15, from 10am to 8pm.

TENNIS, SQUASH & WEIGHTLIFTING   Aside from tennis at the **Kungliga Tennishallen (Royal Tennishall),** Lidingövägen 75 (© **08/459-15-00** for reservations), you can lift weights and enjoy a sauna and solarium. The center has 16 indoor courts, 5 outdoor clay courts, and 8 squash courts. Tennis courts cost 200SEK to

280SEK ($28–$39/£15–£20) per hour, while squash courts are 30SEK to 210SEK ($4.15–$29/£2.20–£15) for a 30-minute session. The weight room entrance fee is 55SEK ($7.60/£4). The center is open Monday to Thursday 7am to 11pm, Friday 7am to 9pm, and Saturday and Sunday 8am to 9pm.

11 Shopping
THE SHOPPING SCENE
Stockholm is filled with shop after shop of dazzling merchandise—often at steep prices that reflect the high esteem in which Swedish craftspeople are held.

Bargain shoppers should proceed with caution. Some good buys do exist, but it takes a lot of searching. If you're a casual shopper, you may want to confine your purchases to handsome souvenirs and gifts.

Swedish glass, of course, is world famous. Wood items are works of great craftsmanship, and many people like to acquire Swedish functional furniture in blond pine or birch. Other items to look for include playsuits for children, silver necklaces, reindeer gloves, stainless-steel utensils, hand-woven neckties and skirts, sweaters and mittens in Nordic patterns, Swedish clogs, and colorful handicrafts from the provinces. The most famous souvenir to buy is the Dala horse from Dalarna.

SHOPPING STREETS & DISTRICTS   Everybody's favorite shopping area in Stockholm is **Gamla Stan.** Site of the Royal Palace, it even attracts such shoppers as the queen. The main street for browsing is **Västerlånggatan,** site of antiques stores with high prices.

In summer, **Skansen** is fun to explore because many craftspeople display their goods here. There are gift shops (some selling "Skansen glass") as well as individuals who offer their handmade goods at kiosks.

In the **Sergels Torg** area, the main shopping street is **Hamngatan,** site of the famous shopping center **Gallerian,** at the corner of Hamngatan and Sergels Torg, and crossing the northern rim of Kungsträdgården at Sweden House. Big department stores, such as NK and Åhléns, are located nearby.

The **Kungsgatan** area is another major district for shopping, stretching from Hötorget to the intersection of Kungsgatan and Vasagatan. **Drottninggatan** is one long pedestrian mall, flanked with shops. Many side streets branching off from it also are filled with shops. Hötorget, home to the PUB department store, is another major shopping district.

A new shopping district **(SOFO)** has been identified on the rapidly gentrifying island of **Södermalm,** to the south of that island's busy Folkungatan. Streets that have emerged as shopping venues of note include **Götgatan, Kokgatan, Bondegatan,** and **Skånegatan.** Expect a youth-oriented, funky, hipster consciousness within the SOFO district, where there has been an explosion in housing prices on an island (Södermalm) where 60% of all households are single person.

SHOPPING HOURS   Stockholm shops are open Monday to Friday 10am to between 6pm (for large department stores) and 7pm (for smaller, boutique-style shops). Saturday shopping is possible between 10am and somewhere between 1 and 4pm. Once a week, usually on Monday or Friday, some of the larger stores are open from 9:30am to 7pm (July–Aug to 6pm).

SHOPPING A TO Z

AUCTIONS

Stockholms Auktionsverket (Stockholm Auction Chambers) ☆☆☆   The oldest auction company in the world—it dates from 1674—holds auctions 2 days a week from noon to "whenever." You can view the merchandise Monday to Friday from 9am to 5pm. An estimated 150,000 lots are auctioned each year—everything from ceramics to Picassos. Nybrogatan 32. ✆ **08/453-67-00.** T-bana: Östermalmstorg.

BOOKS & MAPS

Akademibokhandeln ☆☆   The biggest bookstore in Sweden carries more than 100,000 titles. A wide range of fiction and nonfiction is available in English. Many travel-related materials, such as maps, are also sold. Mäster Samuelsgatan 28. ✆ **08/402-11-00.** T-bana: Hötorget.

Sweden Bookshop   Whatever's available in English about Sweden can be found at this bookstore above the Tourist Center. The store sells many rare items, including recordings of Swedish music. Slottsbacken 10. ✆ **08/453-7800.** T-bana: Gamla Stan.

CERAMICS

Blås & Knåda ☆ *Finds*   This store features the best products made by members of a cooperative of 50 Swedish ceramic artists and glassmakers. Prices begin at 200SEK ($28/£15) for a single teacup and rise to as much as 25,000SEK ($3,450/£1,825) for museum-quality pieces. Hornsgatan 26. ✆ **08/642-77-67.** T-bana: Slussen.

Keramiskt Centrum Gustavsberg   Bone china, stoneware dinner services, and other fine table and decorative ware are made at the Gustavsberg Ceramics Center. A museum at the center displays historic pieces such as *parian* (a type of unglazed porcelain) statues, based on the work of the famous Danish sculptor Thorvaldsen and other artists. You'll also see hand-painted vases, Toby jugs, examples of Pyro (the first ovenware), and royal dinner services. Visitors can watch potters at work and see artists hand-painting designs. You can even decorate a mug or plate yourself. A shop at the center sells Gustavsberg-ware. Värmdö Island (21km/13 miles east of Stockholm). ✆ **08/570-356-58.** Bus: 422 or 440.

DEPARTMENT STORES

Åhléns City   In the center of Stockholm, the largest department store in Sweden has a gift shop, a restaurant, and a famous food department. We often go here for the makings of a picnic to be enjoyed later in one of Stockholm's city parks. Also seek out the fine collection of home textiles, and Orrefors and Kosta Boda crystal ware. The pewter with genuine Swedish ornaments makes a fine gift item. Klarabergsgatan 50. ✆ **08/676-60-00.** T-bana: Centralen.

Nordiska Kompaniet (NK) ☆☆   A high-quality department store since 1902, NK displays most of the big names in Swedish glass, including Orrefors (see the Nordic Light collection) and Kosta. Thousands of handcrafted Swedish items can be found in the basement. Stainless steel, also a good buy in Sweden, is copiously displayed. Hamngatan 18–20. ✆ **08/762-80-00.** T-bana: Kungsträdgården.

PUB   Greta Garbo worked in the millinery department here from 1920 to 1922. It's one of the most popular department stores in Stockholm; the boutiques and departments generally sell midrange clothing and good-quality housewares, but not the international designer names of the more prestigious (and more expensive) NK.

Massive and bustling, with an emphasis on traditional and conservative Swedish clothing, it offers just about anything you'd need to stock a Scandinavian home. There's also a restaurant. Hötorget 13. © 08/782-1930. T-bana: Hötorget.

FLEA MARKET

Loppmarknaden i Skärholmen (Skärholmen Shopping Center) ⚜ At the biggest flea market in northern Europe, you might find anything. Try to go on Saturday or Sunday (the earlier the better), when the market is at its peak. Free admission Monday to Friday; 15SEK ($2.05/£1.10) Saturday, 10SEK ($1.40/75p) Sunday. Skärholmen. © 08/710-00-60. Bus: 13 or 23 to Skärholmen (20 min.).

GEMS & MINERALS

Geocity ⚜ *Finds* Geocity offers exotic mineral crystals, jewelry, Scandinavian gems, Baltic amber, and lapidary equipment. The staff includes two certified gemologists who will cut and set any gem you select and do appraisals. The inventory holds stones from Scandinavia and around the world, including Greenland, Madagascar, Siberia, and South America. Kungsgatan 57. © 08/411-11-40. T-bana: Hötorget.

GIFTS & SOUVENIRS

Stockholm Tourist Center Gift Shop There are dozens of souvenir shops scattered throughout Stockholm, especially on Gamla Stan, but the merchandise within this official tourism arm of the Swedish government is scrutinized more rigorously for inferior, or nonauthentic, merchandise than any of its competitors. Expect Dalarna horses, embroideries, Viking statuettes, and glassware. Stockholm Tourist Center, Sweden House, Hamngatan 27, off Kungsträdgården © 08/789-24-00. T-bana: Kungsträdgården.

GLASS & CRYSTAL

Nordiska Kristall ⚜⚜ Since 1918, this company has been in the vanguard of Swedish glassmakers. The pick of Swedish glass is on sale here. The company often stages pioneering exhibitions, showcasing its more innovative and daring designs. At this outlet, you get both traditional and modern pieces. Kungsgatan 9. © 08/10-43-72. T-bana: Hötorget.

Orrefors Kosta Boda ⚜⚜⚜ A fabled name in Swedish glass operates this "crystal palace" in the center of Stockholm. Two famous companies combined to form one outlet, with Orrefors focusing on clear vases and stemware, whereas Kosta Boda boasts more colorful and artistic pieces of glass. One of the best-selling items is the "Intermezzo Glass" with a drop of sapphire glass in its stem. 15 Birger Jarlsgatan. © 08/545-040-84. T-bana: Östermalmstorg.

HANDICRAFTS & GIFTS

Brinken Konsthantverk On the lower floor of a building near the Royal Palace in the Old Town, this elegant purveyor of gift items will ship handcrafted brass, pewter, wrought iron, or crystal anywhere in the world. About 95% of the articles are made in Scandinavia. Storkyrkobrinken 1. © 08/411-59-54. T-bana: Gamla Stan.

DesignTorget ⚜⚜ *Finds* In 1994, the government-owned Kulturhuset (Swedish Culture House) reacted to declining attendance by inviting one of Stockholm's most influential designers and decorators, Jerry Hellström, to organize an avant-garde art gallery. In a large room in the cellar, you'll find a display of handicrafts created by 150 to 200 mostly Swedish craftspeople. The work must be approved by a jury of connoisseurs before being offered for sale. The merchandise includes some of the best pottery, furniture, textiles, clothing, pewter, and crystal in Sweden. The organization maintains several other branches, including a store in southern Stockholm at Götgatan 31 ((© **08/462-35-20**). It stocks clothing for men, women, and children, and furniture, with less emphasis on ceramics and handicrafts. In the Kulturhuset, Sergels Torg 3. © **08/21-91-50**. T-bana: Centralen.

Duka   A large selection of carefully chosen crystal, porcelain, and gifts is available in this shop near the Konserthuset (Concert Hall). It offers tax-free shopping and shipping. Kungsgatan 5. © **08/440-9600**. T-bana: Hötorget.

Gunnarssons Träfigurer *★ (Finds)*   This is one of the city's most appealing collections of Swedish carved-wood figures. All are by Urban Gunnarsson, a second-generation master carver. They include figures from World War II, such as Winston Churchill, and U.S. presidents from Franklin D. Roosevelt to Bill Clinton. There's also a host of mythical and historical European personalities. The carvings are usually made from linden or basswood. Drottninggatan 77. © **08/21-67-17**. T-bana: Rådmansgatan.

Svensk Hemslöjd (Society for Swedish Handicrafts)   Svensk Hemslöjd offers a wide selection of glass, pottery, gifts, and wood and metal handicrafts by some of Sweden's best artisans. There's a display of hand-woven carpets, upholstery fabrics, hand-painted materials, tapestries, lace, and embroidered items. You'll also find beautiful yarns for weaving and embroidery. Sveavägen 44. © **08/23-21-15**. T-bana: Hötorget.

HOME FURNISHINGS

Nordiska Galleriet   This store features the finest in European furniture design, including the best from Scandinavia. Two floors hold the latest contemporary furniture. The store can arrange shipment. Nybrogatan 11. © **08/442-83-60**. T-bana: Östermalmstorg.

Svenskt Tenn *★★*   Swedish Pewter (its English name) has been one of Sweden's most prominent stores for home furnishings since 1924. Pewter is no longer king, but the shop now sells Scandinavia's best selection of furniture, printed textiles, lamps, glassware, china, and gifts. The inventory is stylish, and although there aren't a lot of bargains, it's an excellent place to see the newest trends in Scandinavian design. It carries an exclusive collection of Josef Frank's hand-printed designs on linen and cotton. It will pack, insure, and ship your purchases anywhere in the world. Strandvägen 5. © **08/670-16-00**. T-bana: Östermalmstorg.

LINENS

Solgården *★★★*   For the dwindling few who really care about luxury linens and elegant home-ware, such as lace and embroidery, this shop is the finest of its kind in Scandinavia. It was conceived by owner Marianne von Kantzow Ridderstad as a tribute to Gustav III, the king who is said to have launched the neoclassical style in Sweden. Ridderstad designed her shop like a country house, with rough-hewn wood and whimsical furnishings. Each of her linens is virtually a work of art, and the tablecloths are heirloom pieces. You'll cherish the work for its originality and loveliness. Karlavägen 58. © **08/663-9360**. T-bana: Rådmansgatan.

MARKETS

Östermalms Saluhall   One of the most colorful indoor food markets in Scandinavia features cheese, meat, vegetable, and fish merchants who supply food for much of the area, and a red-brick design from the late 19th century that might remind you of a medieval fortress You may want to have a snack or a meal at one of the restaurants. Nybrogatan 31. No phone. T-bana: Östermalmstorg.

SHOPPING MALLS

Gallerian ✿✿✿   A short walk from Sweden House at Kunådgården, this modern two-story shopping complex is, to many, the best shopping destination in Sweden. Merchandise in most of the individually managed stores is designed to appeal to local shoppers, not the tourist market—although in summer that changes a bit as more souvenir and gift items appear. Hamngatan 37. No phone. T-bana: Kungsträdgården.

Sturegallerian ✿✿   In the center of Stockholm, within a venue that was renovated and expanded, this mall has a dazzling array of foreign and domestic merchandise that's sold within at least 60 specialty shops. Summer brings out more displays of Swedish souvenirs and gift items. There are also restaurants and cafes. Sturegallerian opened in 1989, and a year later was named "Shopping Center of the Year in Europe" by the International Council of Shopping Centers. Stureplan. ✆ 08/611-46-06. T-bana: Östermalmstorg.

TEXTILES

Handarbetets Vänner   This is one of the oldest and most prestigious textile houses in Stockholm. It also sells art-weaving and embroidery items. Djurgårdsslatten 82–84. ✆ 08/545-68650. Bus: 47.

TOYS

Bulleribock (Toys) ✿✿   Since it opened in the 1960s, this store has carried only traditional, noncomputerized toys made of wood, metal, or paper. You won't find any plastic toys here. There are no war games that many parents find objectionable. Many of these charming playthings are suitable for children up to age 10. As many as possible are made in Sweden, with wood from Swedish forests. Sveavägen 104. ✆ 08/673-61-21. T-bana: Rådmansgatan.

12 Stockholm After Dark

Djurgården remains the favorite spot for both indoor and outdoor events on a summer evening. Although the more sophisticated may find it corny, this is your best early evening bet. Afterward, you can make the rounds of jazz venues and nightclubs, some of which stay open until 3 or 4 in the morning.

Pick up a copy of *What's On,* distributed at virtually every hotel in town, as well as at the Tourist Center at Sweden House, to see what entertainment and cultural venues are scheduled during your time in Stockholm.

THE PERFORMING ARTS

All the major opera, theater, and concert seasons begin in the fall, except for special summer festival performances. Fortunately, most of the major opera and theatrical performances are funded by the state, which keeps ticket prices reasonable.

CONCERT HALLS

Berwaldhallen (Berwald Concert Hall)   This hexagonal concert hall is Swedish Radio's big music studio. The Radio Symphonic Orchestra performs here, and other high-quality musical programs include lieder and chamber music recitals. The hall has excellent acoustics. The box office is open Monday to Friday noon to 6pm, and 2 hours before every concert. Dag Hammarskjölds Väg 3. ℂ 08/784-18-00. Tickets 50SEK–400SEK ($6.50–$52/£3.65–£29). T-bana: Karlaplan.

Filharmonikerna i Konserthuset (Concert Hall) Home of the Stockholm Philharmonic Orchestra, this is the principal place to hear classical music in Sweden. The Nobel Prizes are awarded here. Constructed in 1920, the building houses two concert halls. One seats 1,600 and is better suited to major orchestras; the other, seating 450, is suitable for chamber music groups. Besides local orchestras, the hall features visiting ensembles, such as the Chicago Symphony Orchestra. Some series sell out in advance to subscription-ticket holders; for others, visitors can readily get tickets. Sales begin 2 weeks before a concert and continue until the performance begins. Concerts usually start at 7:30pm, with occasional lunchtime (noon) or "happy hour" (5:30pm) concerts. Most performances are broadcast on Stockholm's main classical music station, 107.5 FM. The box office is open Monday to Friday 11am to 6pm, Saturday 11am to 3pm. Hötorget 8. ℂ 08/10-21-10. Tickets 100SEK–520SEK ($14–$72/£7.30–£38). T-bana: Hötorget.

OPERA & BALLET

Drottningholm Court Theater 𝓻𝓻𝓻 Positioned on an island in Lake Mälaren, 11km (6¾ miles) from Stockholm, this is the most famous 18th-century theater in the world. It stages operas and ballets with full 18th-century regalia, period costumes, and wigs. Its machinery and 30 or more complete theater sets are intact and in use. The theater, a short walk from the royal residence, seats only 450, which makes it difficult to get tickets. Eighteenth-century music performed on antique instruments is a perennial favorite. The season is from May to September. Most performances begin at 7:30pm and last 2½ to 4 hours. You can order tickets in advance by phone with an American Express card. Even if you're not able to get tickets for an actual performance, you can tour the theater as part of a visit to Drottningholm Palace (p. 430). Drottningholm. ℂ 08/660-82-25. Tickets 165SEK–610SEK ($23–$84/£12–£45). T-bana: Brommaplan and then bus no. 301 or 323. Boat from the City Hall in Stockholm.

Operahuset (Royal Opera House) 𝓻𝓻𝓻 Founded in 1773 by Gustav III (who was later assassinated here at a masked ball), the Opera House is the home of the Royal Swedish Opera and the Royal Swedish Ballet. The building dates from 1898. Performances are usually Monday to Saturday at 7:30pm (closed mid-June to mid-August). The box office is open Monday to Friday noon to 6pm (until 7:30pm on performance nights), Saturday noon to 3pm. Gustav Adolfs Torg. ℂ 08/791-44-00. Tickets 100SEK–680SEK ($14–$94/£7.30–£45); 10%–30% senior and student discounts. T-bana: Kungsträdgården.

THEATER

The theater season begins in mid-August and lasts until mid-June.

Kungliga Dramatiska Teatern (Royal Dramatic Theater) 𝓻𝓻𝓻 Greta Garbo got her start in acting here, and Ingmar Bergman stages two productions a year. The theater presents the latest experimental plays and the classics—in Swedish only. The theater is open year-round (with a slight slowdown in July), and performances are scheduled Tuesday to Saturday at 7pm and Sunday at 4pm. The box office is open Monday to Saturday 10am to 6pm. Nybroplan. ℂ 08/667-06-80. Tickets 120SEK–400SEK ($17–$55/£8.75–£29); student discount available. T-bana: Östermalmstorg.

Oscars Teatern   Oscars is the flagship of Stockholm's musical entertainment world. It's been the home of classic operetta and musical theater since the turn of the 20th century. Known for its extravagant staging of traditional operettas, it was also one of the first theaters in Europe to produce such hits as *Cats* in Swedish. The box office is open Monday to Saturday from 11am to 6pm. Kungsgatan 63. ℂ **08/20-50-00.** Tickets 295SEK–550SEK ($41–$76/£22–£40). T-bana: Hötorget.

LOCAL CULTURE & ENTERTAINMENT

Skansen   Skansen arranges traditional seasonal festivities, special events, autumn market days, and a Christmas Fair. In summer, concerts, singalongs, and guest performances delight visitors and locals alike. Folk-dancing performances are staged in July and August Friday and Saturday at 7pm and Sunday at 2:30 and 4pm. In July and August, outdoor dancing is presented with live music Monday to Saturday from 10 to 11:30pm. Djurgården 49–51. ℂ **08/442-80-00.** Admission 30SEK–120SEK ($4.15–$17/ £2.20–£8.75) adults, 20SEK–50SEK ($2.75–$6.90/£1.45–£3.65) children 6–15 (free 5 and under). Fee depends on the time of the year. Ferry from Slussen. Bus: 44 or 47.

AN AMUSEMENT PARK

Gröna Lunds Tivoli   Unlike its Copenhagen namesake, this is an amusement park, not a fantasyland. For those who like Coney Island–type amusements, it can be a nighttime adventure. One of the big thrills is to go up to the revolving tower for an after-dark view. The park is open daily from the end of April to September, usually from noon to 11pm or midnight. Call for exact hours. Djurgården. ℂ **08/587-501-00.** Admission 60SEK ($8.30/£4.40), 30SEK ($4.15/£2.20) children 4–13, free for children under 4. Bus: 44 or 47. Ferry from Nybroplan.

THE CLUB & MUSIC SCENE
A HISTORIC NIGHTCLUB

Café Opera 🌟🌟   By day a bistro, brasserie, and tearoom, Café Opera becomes one of the most crowded nightclubs in Stockholm in the evening. Visitors have the best chance of getting in around noon during lunch. A stairway near the entrance leads to one of the Opera House's most beautiful corners, the clublike Operabaren (Opera Bar). It's likely to be as crowded as the cafe. The bar is a monumental but historically charming place to have a drink; beer costs 55SEK ($7.60/£4). After 10pm, there is less emphasis on food and more on disco activities. Open daily from 5pm to 3am. At night, long lines form outside. Don't confuse this establishment with the opera's main (and far more expensive) dining room, the Operakällaren. To enter, you must be at least 23 years old. Operahuset, Kungsträdgården. ℂ **08/676-58-07.** Cover 140SEK ($19/£10) after 10pm. T-bana: Kungsträdgården.

DANCE CLUBS & DISCOS

Göta Källare   Stockholm's largest supper club-style dance hall has a reputation for successful matchmaking. Large, echoing, and paneled with lots of wood in *faux-Español* style, it has a terrace that surrounds an enormous tree. The restaurant serves platters of food priced at 119SEK ($16/£8.70). Menu items include tournedos, fish, chicken, and veal. Expect a middle-aged crowd. The live orchestra (which performs *Strangers in the Night* a bit too frequently) plays every night. The hall opens nightly at 10pm. In the Medborgplatsen subway station, Södermalm. ℂ **08/642-08-28.** Cover 130SEK ($18/ £9.50) after 11pm. T-bana: Medborgplatsen.

The Capital of Gay Scandinavia

Copenhagen thrived for many years as a refreshingly raunchy city with few inhibitions and even fewer restrictions on alternative sexuality. Beginning in the mid-1990s, Stockholm witnessed an eruption of new gay bars, discos, and roaming nightclubs. Copenhagen's more imperial and, in many ways, more staid competition made the Danes' legendary permissiveness look a bit weak. Today, thanks partly to the huge influence of London's gay subcultures, no other city in Scandinavia offers more gay-friendly nightlife options as Stockholm. Some of the gay bars and clubs maintain fixed hours and addresses. Others, configured as roving parties, constantly change addresses. Listings for gay entertainment venues appear regularly in *QX*, a gay magazine published in Swedish and English. You can also check out the magazine's website (www.qx. se). And don't overlook the comprehensive website (www.rfsl.se) maintained by RFSL, a Swedish organization devoted to equal rights for gays.

Gay Venues in Södermalm

Looking for a nonconfrontational bar peopled with regular guys who happen to be gay? Consider a round or two on the island of Södermalm at **Sidetrack,** Wollmar Yxkullsgatan 7 (© 08/641-1688; T-bana: Mariatorget). Small, amicable, committed to shunning trendiness, and located deep within a cellar a few blocks from the also-recommended Hotel Rival, it's named after the founder's favorite gay bar in Chicago. It's open Tuesday to Saturday from 6pm to 1am. Tuesday seems to be something of a gay Stockholm institution, but other nights are fine, too. Prefacing the bar is a well-managed restaurant, serving dinner only, Tuesday to Saturday, from 6pm till 1am. (From June till August, dinner is Tuesday to Saturday 8pm till 1am.) Main courses cost from 105SEK to 150SEK ($14–$21/£7.65–£11).

To find a Viking, or Viking wannabe, in leather, a 2-minute walk from the above-recommended Sidetrack, head for **SLM (Scandinavian Leather Men),** Wollmar Yxkullsgatan 18 (© 08/643-3100; T-bana: Mariatorget). Technically, this is a private club. But if you look hot and noncreepy, and if you wear just a hint (or even a lot) of cowhide or rawhide, you stand an excellent chance of getting in if you don't object to paying a "membership fee" of around 100SEK ($14/£7.30). Wednesday, Friday, and Saturday from 10pm to 2am, the place functions as Stockholm's premier leather bar. On Saturday from 10pm to 2am, a DJ spins highly danceable music. It's closed on other nights.

Södermalm's most trend-conscious dining venue is **The Roxy,** a boxy, modern-looking site on the Nytorg 6 (© 08/640-96-55). Funky and whimsical, it has a decor that might have been inspired by a meeting in heaven between the last of the Vienna's Hapsburgs with the design team at SAS. The sofas evoke a Danish airport lounge in 1966, and mismatched crystal chandeliers seem to echo the sounds of a Strauss waltz. Art Deco objets d'art might have been salvaged from a 1930s-era ocean liner, and two or three porcelain incarnations of pink flamingos are strictly from 1950s Miami. Drinks of choice include an Assburner (Jack Daniels with ginger, lime juice, and red-hot chiles); a Razz (raspberry liqueur, vodka, and 7-Up), and a Cosmo spiked with ginger. You can always drop in just for a drink (the crowd tends to be youngish and cute), but if you want dinner, main courses cost from 132SEK to 230SEK ($18–$32/£9.65–£17). The place opens Tuesday to Sunday at 5pm, and closes anytime between 11pm and 1am, depending on business and the night of the week.

Gay Venues on Gamla Stan

At least three gay and lesbian bar/cafes on Gamla Stan lie on the western and eastern edges of Stockholm's Old Town. Dominating (at least in terms of gay business) the quieter and calmer western edge of the island, within a building erected in the 1600s, is **Mandus Bar & Kök,** Österlånggatan 7 (© 08/20-60-55). Depending on the time of day, it evolves from a staid and somewhat prissy cafe into a raucous bar late at night. Thanks to a sophisticated lesbian owner (Joanna), there's a higher percentage of gay women here (about 25% of the clientele) than at of the other bars noted in this section. The place prides itself on its food, with main courses such as tiger prawns, filets of reindeer, and pastas of the day, priced at 75SEK to 98SEK ($10–$14/£5.48–£7.15) at lunchtime, and at 94SEK to 224SEK ($13–$31/£6.85–£16) at dinner.

If you need a caffeine fix and a slice of chocolate cake before all that leather and latex, you might want to drop into Stockholm's most appealing, best managed gay cafe, **Chokladkoppen,** Stortorget 18–20 (© 08/20-31-70; T-bana: Gamla Stan). On the street level of a house erected in the 15th century, across from the Nobel Museum, it's open daily from 9am to 11pm. The staff is charming, and the clientele more gay than not. The consistently most popular item on the menu is a steaming cupful of white hot chocolate, priced at 32SEK (U$4.40/£2.35), which—if you're really hooked on calories—might be accompanied with a slice of white chocolate cheesecake for 34SEK ($4.70/£2.50).

Our remaining selections involve venues that cater to a gay crowd only on specific nights of the week and are subject to change. **Patricia,** Stadsgårdskajen 152 (© 08/743-0570; T-bana: Slussen), is straight most of the week and avowedly gay every Sunday between 7pm and 5am. Sprawling and labyrinthine, with three bars and a good sound system, it's most crowded on Sunday during the summer, much less so in the winter. There's a restaurant on the premises.

Torget, Mälartorget 13 (© 08/20-55-60; T-bana: Gamla Stan), might be the chicest gay and lesbian bar in Stockholm. High-ceilinged, and with a Victorian theme and masses of flowers, it's open every afternoon for food and (more important) for drinks from around 4pm till around 1am. Snacks and platters cost from 85SEK to 179SEK ($12–$25/£6.20–£13).

Finally, for a cozy little bar and restaurant in Gamla Stan or Old Town, head for **Mandus Bar Kök,** Österlångg 7 (© 08/206-60-55; T-bana: Gamla Stan), and the night is yours. The convivial crowd sits talking and drinking wine or beer late into the night.

ROCK & JAZZ CLUBS

Fasching &R&R   This club attracts some of Sweden's best-known jazz musicians. Small and cozy, and well known among jazz aficionados throughout Scandinavia, it is cramped but fun. The venue varies according to the night of the week and the availability of the artists performing. At the end of the live acts, there's likely to be dancing to salsa, soul, and perhaps R&B. The club is open nightly from 7pm to 1am. Kungsgatan 63. (C) 08/534-829-64. Cover 100SEK–250SEK ($14–$35/£7.30–£18). T-bana: Centralen.

Hard Rock Cafe   The Swedish branch of this chain is fun and gregarious. Sometimes an American, British, or Scandinavian rock band presents a live concert; otherwise, rock blasts from the sound system. Burgers begin at 99SEK ($14/£7.20), steaks at 169SEK ($23/£12), and beer at 54SEK ($7.45/£3.95). Open Monday to Thursday 11:30am to midnight, Friday 11:30am to 1am, Saturday noon to 3am, and Sunday noon to midnight. Sveavägen 75. (C) 08/545-494-00. T-bana: Rådmansgatan.

Pub Engelen/Nightclub Kolingen   The Engelen Pub, the Restaurant Engelen, and the Nightclub Kolingen (in the 15th-c. cellar) share a single address. The restaurant, which serves some of the best steaks in town, is open daily 5pm to midnight. Live performances, usually soul, funk, and rock by Swedish groups, take over the pub daily from 8:30pm to midnight. The pub is open Tuesday to Thursday 4pm to 1am, Friday and Saturday 4pm to 3am, Sunday 5pm to 3am. Beer begins at 42SEK ($5.80/£3.05), and items on the bar menu cost 29SEK to 100SEK ($4–$14/ £2.10–£7.30). The Nightclub Kolingen is a dance club nightly from 10pm to about 3am. It charges the same food and drink prices as the pub, and you must be at least 23 to enter. Kornhamnstorg 59B. (C) 08/20-10-92. Cover 50SEK–80SEK ($6.90–$11/£3.65–£5.85) after 8pm. T-bana: Gamla Stan.

Stampen   This pub attracts crowds of jazz lovers in their 40s and 50s. Guests crowd in to enjoy live Dixieland, New Orleans, and mainstream jazz, and swing music from the 1920s, 1930s, and 1940s. On Tuesday, it's rock 'n' roll from the 1950s and 1960s. A menagerie of stuffed animals and lots of old, whimsical antiques are suspended from the high ceiling. It's open Monday to Thursday 8pm to 1am, Friday to Saturday 8pm to 2am. In summer, an outdoor veranda is open when the weather permits. The club has two stages, and there's dancing downstairs almost every night. Stora Nygatan 5. (C) 08/20-57-93. T-bana: Gamla Stan.

A CASINO

Casino Cosmopol   At last Stockholm has a world-class casino and it's installed in the Palladium, a grand old movie house dating from 1918. Housing two restaurants and four bars, the casino is spread across four floors. Guests, who must be at least 20 years old, can play such classic games as American roulette, blackjack, Punto Banco, and seven-card stud. Open daily 1pm to 4am. Kungsgatan 65. (C) 08/781-88-00. Cover 30SEK ($4.15/£2.20). T-bana: Hötorget.

THE BAR SCENE

Blue Moon Bar   Attracting a bevy of supermodels and TV actors, this is both a street-level and basement bar, drawing a chic crowd to its modern decor. Although it's called a bar, it's also a restaurant and a night club, or *nattklubb*, as the Swedes say.

Recorded music is played. Open nightly from 8pm to 4am. Kungsgatan 18. ℂ **08/244700.** Cover 70SEK–80SEK ($9.65–$11/£5.10–£5.85). T-bana: Östermalmstorg.

Cadier Bar ⚘ This bar, positioned on the lobby level of the also-recommended Grand Hotel, is one of the most famous and most plush in Europe. From its windows, you'll have a view of a venue that was lavishly renovated in 2006, as well as Stockholm's harbor and Royal Palace. Light meals—open-face sandwiches and smoked salmon—are served throughout the day and evening. Drinks cost from 130SEK to 140SEK ($18–$19/£9.50–£10), and imported beer 55SEK ($7.60/£4). The bar is named for the hotel's builder. It's open Monday to Saturday 11am to 2am, Sunday 11am to 12:30am; a piano player performs Wednesday to Saturday 9:30pm to 1:30am. In the Grand Hotel, Södra Blasieholmshamnen 8. ℂ 08/679-35-85. T-bana: Kungsträdgården.

Café Victoria The most central cafe in Stockholm becomes crowded after 9pm in winter (7pm in summer). It attracts a varied crowd, many patrons visiting just to drink, but you can have lunch or dinner in an interior section beyond the lively bar area. Main dishes are 180SEK to 265SEK ($25–$37/£13–£19), and a bottle of beer will set you back 50SEK ($6.90/£3.65). Open Monday, Thursday, and Friday to Sunday 11:30am to 3am, Tuesday and Wednesday 11:30am to 1am. Kungsträdgården. ℂ08/ 10-10-85. T-bana: Kungsträdgården.

Gondolen We find Gondolen's architecture as impressive as the view. Part of the structure is suspended beneath a pedestrian footbridge that soars above the narrow channel separating the island of Gamla Stan from the island of Södermalm. The engineering triumph was executed in 1935. The elevator hauls customers (without charge) up the equivalent of 11 stories to the 1940s-style restaurant. The view encompasses Lake Malar, the open sea, and huge areas of downtown Stockholm. You'll pay 86SEK ($12/£6.30) for a whiskey with soda. Open Monday to Friday 11:30am to 1am, Saturday from 4pm to 1am. Stadsgården 6. ℂ 08/641-70-90. T-bana: Slussen.

Icebar ⚘⚘ Finds Located in the Nordic Sea Hotel, this is known as Stockholm's "coolest" bar. This, the world's first permanent ice bar, opened in 2001. Amazingly, the interior is kept at temperatures of 27°F (–5°C) all year. The decor and all the interior fittings, right down to the cocktail glasses themselves, are made of pure, clear ice shipped down from the Torne River in Sweden's Arctic north. If you own one of those fabulous Swedish fur coats, the Icebar would be the place to wear it. Dress as you would for a dogsled ride in Alaska. In the bar you can order any drink from a Bahama Mama to an Alabama Slammer, although you may have to order liquor-laced coffee to keep warm. Be warned that advance reservations are required and tightly controlled, with groups entering and leaving at intervals of about every 40 minutes. A staff member will give you a parka, with a hood, to keep you warm within this architectural, constantly refrigerated oddity. Vasaplan 4–7. ℂ 08/217177. T-bana: Centralen.

Sturehof Since 1897, this pub and restaurant has been one of Stockholm's major drinking and dining venues. In the exact center of the city, it is now surrounded by urban sprawl and is attached to an arcade with other restaurants and shops. It remains a pleasant refuge from the city's congestion and is popular as both an after-work bar and a restaurant. Open Monday to Friday 11am to 2am; Saturday noon to 2am, and Sunday 1pm to 2am. Stureplan 2. ℂ 08/440-57-30. T-bana: Östermalmstorg.

13 Side Trips from Stockholm

Some of Sweden's best-known attractions are clustered around Lake Mälaren—centuries-old villages and castles (Uppsala and Gripsholm) that revive the pomp and glory of the 16th-century Vasa dynasty. You can spend a very busy day exploring Sigtuna, Skokloster Castle, Uppsala, and Gamla Uppsala, and stay overnight in Sigtuna or Uppsala, where there are good hotels. Another easy day trip is to Gripsholm Castle in Mariefred or Tullgarn Palace.

The boat trip from Klara Mälarstrand in Stockholm is popular. It leaves at 9:45am, goes along the beautiful waterway of Mälaren and the Fyris River to Sigtuna—where it stops for 2 hours—and arrives at Uppsala at 5pm. Here you can visit the cathedral and other interesting sights, dine, and then take the 45-minute train trip back to Stockholm. Trains run every hour until 11pm.

SIGTUNA ⋆
45km (28 miles) NW of Stockholm

If time remains after visiting Sweden's present capital, you can head for the environs to see Sweden's oldest town and its first capital. This time warp village—founded in A.D. 980—lies on the shores of Lake Mälaren, northwest of Stockholm, and deserves about 2 or 3 hours.

The best thing here is **Stora Gatan** ⋆⋆, the main street since the Middle Ages. It is lined with pastel-painted, wood-framed buildings from the 1800s. Shops or a cafe along the way are likely to distract you from your stroll, as they do us. This street is believed to be the oldest in Sweden that follows its original route. Traces of Sigtuna's Viking and early Christian heritage can also be seen throughout the town.

ESSENTIALS
GETTING THERE   From Stockholm's train station, take a 45-minute train ride to Märsta. Trains depart at 30-minute intervals throughout the day and evening. In Märsta, transfer to a bus (it will be marked either SIGTUNA NO. 575 or SIGTUNA NO. 570) for an additional 20-minute ride on to Sigtuna. In the summer, boats run to Sigtuna from Klara Mälarstrand Pier in Stockholm and from Uppsala.

VISITOR INFORMATION   For information, contact the Sigtuna Tourist Info office at ✆ **08/592-500-20.**

SEEING THE SIGHTS
In the Middle Ages, Sigtuna was a great place of worship and known for its churches, which are mostly in ruins today. Along Pråstgatan you can still see the ruins of **St. Lars** and **St. Per,** which was Sweden's first cathedral. Nearby stands **Mariakyrkan,** the oldest brick-built building in Sigtuna. Originally a Dominican friars' abbey, it was consecrated back in 1247. After Gustav Vasa demolished the monastery, Maria became a parish church in 1529. We like to come here to listen to the summer concerts. If they are not being presented, settle for the restored medieval paintings on display. It is open daily from 9am to 8pm in July and August (or to 4pm off season).

If you have time, visit the **Sigtuna Museum,** Storogatan 55 (✆ **08/597-838-70**), an archaeological museum that features early medieval artifacts found in the surrounding area. You'll see gold rings, runic inscriptions, and coins, as well as exclusive objects from Russia and Byzantium. You can also skip this one with no harm done. Admission is 20SEK ($2.75/£1.45) for adults, 10SEK ($1.40/75p) for seniors and

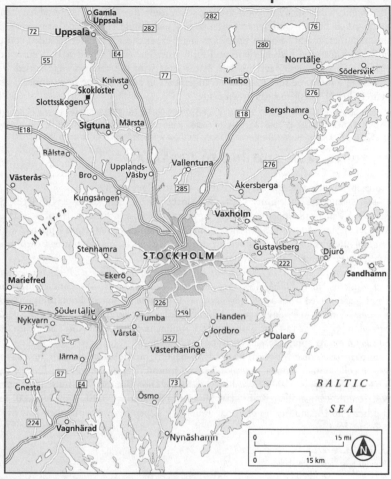

students. Admission is free for those 19 and under. Hours are June to August daily noon to 4pm; September to May Tuesday to Sunday noon to 4pm.

One of the reasons for Sigtuna's resurgence is the **Sigtuna Foundation** (see below), a Lutheran retreat and cultural center founded near the turn of the 20th century and often frequented by writers. It's open to the public daily from 1 to 3pm.

Daily buses and trains connect Stockholm to Sigtuna and Uppsala. From Stockholm, take a train to Märsta, and then a bus for the 10-minute ride to Sigtuna.

WHERE TO STAY & DINE

Sigtuna Foundation 🕊 *Finds*   A stay at this massive building might provide one of your most memorable stopovers in Sweden. Intended as a center where sociological and philosophical viewpoints can be aired, the 1917 structure is more a way of life than a hotel. Over the years, guest lecturers have included the Dalai Lama, various

Indian gurus, and many of postwar Europe's leading theologians. The establishment functions as both a conference center and a guesthouse. There's no proselytizing, although there might be opportunities to share experiences. There are secluded court-yards, lush rose and herb gardens, and fountains. The guest rooms have been refurbished in a bland style, and modern bathrooms with tub/showers were added. To guarantee a room, be sure to make arrangements in advance. The foundation is less than 1.5km (1 mile) from the town center.

Manfred Björkquists Allé 2–4, S-193 31 Sigtuna. ℂ 08/592-589-00. Fax 08/592-589-99. www.sigtunastiftelsen.se. 62 units. 870SEK–1,230SEK ($120–$170/£64–£90) double. Rates include breakfast. AE, DC, MC, V. Free parking. Bus: 570 or 575. **Amenities:** Restaurant; lounge; rooms for those w/limited mobility. *In room:* No phone.

EN ROUTE FROM SIGTUNA TO UPPSALA
Skokloster Castle ℛℛ

From Stockholm, take the train to Bålsta, and then bus no. 894.

The splendid 17th-century castle **Skokloster,** S-746 96 Skokloster (ℂ **018/38-60-77**), is one of the most interesting baroque museums in Europe. It's next to Lake Mälaren, 65km (40 miles) from Stockholm and 50km (31 miles) from Uppsala. With original interiors, the castle is noted for its extensive collections of paintings, furniture, applied art, tapestries, arms, and books.

Admission is 40SEK ($5.50/£2.90) for adults, 20SEK ($2.75/£1.45) for seniors and students, and 20SEK ($2.75/£1.45) for children 7 to 18. Guided tours in English are offered from May daily noon to 3pm; June to August 11am to 4pm; September, Monday to Friday 1pm to 3pm, Saturday and Sunday noon to 3pm; October, Monday to Friday 1pm, Saturday and Sunday noon to 3pm; April, Saturday and Sunday noon to 3pm. Closed November to March.

Skokloster Motor Museum (ℂ **018/38-61-06**), on the palace grounds, houses the largest collection of vintage automobiles and motorcycles in the country. One of the most notable cars is a 1905 eight-horsepower De Dion Bouton. The museum is open year-round. Admission is 50SEK ($6.50/£3.65) for adults, 25SEK ($3.25/£1.80) for children 7 to 14, and free for children under 7. It's open May to September daily from noon to 4pm.

UPPSALA ℛℛℛ
68km (42 miles) NW of Stockholm

Human sacrifices to Norse gods used to take place here, but now it's Sweden's major university city. It appears smaller than it is as you bike by its waterways and past its old cathedral, but it's actually the fourth largest city in this country, and the single most popular day trip from Stockholm.

Not only does it have a great university, but a grand 15th-century cathedral and a lot of tradition and history. Even Queen Christina once held court here, and the church is still the seat of the archbishop, making it the ecclesiastical capital of Sweden.

As for the university, it's got quite a pedigree dating from 1477. With a student population hovering around 30,000, Uppsala is the Oxford of Sweden, lying at the northern tip of Lake Mälaren.

The city is riddled with beautiful green parks and dozens of cafes, most of which are frequented by students. The small Frysiån River runs through the town, and the main square, Stora Torget, leads to a pedestrian shopping district.

Uppsala was also the hometown of the world's most famous botanist, Carl von Linné (1707–78), also known as Carl Linnaeus.

Film buffs know that Uppsala was the birthplace of the great director, Ingmar Bergman (no relation to another great Swede, Ingrid Bergman). The director Bergman used Uppsala as a setting for one of his most classic films, *Fanny and Alexander.*

The best time to visit Uppsala is on April 30, Walpurgis Eve, when the academic community celebrates the rebirth of spring with a torchlight parade. The festivities last until dawn throughout the 13 student "nations" (residential halls).

ESSENTIALS

GETTING THERE   The **train** from Stockholm's Central Station takes about 45 minutes. Trains leave about every hour during peak hours. Some visitors spend the day in Uppsala and return to Stockholm on the commuter train in the late afternoon. Eurailpass holders ride free. **Boats** between Uppsala and Skokloster depart Uppsala daily at 11am and 7:30pm, returning to Uppsala at 5:45 and 11:30pm. Round-trip passage costs 150SEK ($21/£11). For details, check with the tourist office in any of the towns.

VISITOR INFORMATION   The **Tourist Information Office** is at Fyris Torg 8 (*©* **018/727-4800**). It's open Monday to Friday 10am to 6pm, Saturday 10am to 3pm, and Sunday noon to 4pm (July to mid-Aug).

GETTING AROUND   Buses come in from the surrounding suburbs to the center of Uppsala, arriving, along with the trains, at the Central Station. Once you arrive in the center of Uppsala, all the major attractions are within easy walking distance. However, if you're going to explore Gamla Uppsala (see the box below), you need to take bus no. 2 or 54, departing from the Central Station.

SEEING THE SIGHTS

Carolina Rediviva (University Library) *©*   This is one of the greatest of all Scandinavian libraries. At the end of Drottninggatan is the Carolina Rediviva, with more than five million volumes and 40,000 manuscripts, including many rare works from the Middle Ages. The most treasured manuscript is the *Codex Argenteus* or **Silver Bible** *©©©*. Displayed in the exhibit room, it was translated into Gothic in the middle of the 3rd century and copied in about A.D. 525. It's the only book extant in old Gothic script, having been written in silver ink on purple vellum. Also worth seeing is *Carta Marina,* the earliest map (1539) of Sweden and its neighboring countries.

Drottninggatan. *©* **018/471-39-00.** Admission 20SEK ($2.75/£1.45) adults, free for children under 12. Exhibit room June 14–Aug 15 Mon–Fri 9am–5pm, Sat 10am–5pm, Sun 11am–4pm; Aug 16–June 13 Sun 10am–5pm. Bus: 6, 7, or 22.

Linnaeus Garden & Museum *©*   Swedish botanist Carl von Linné (or Linnaeus) developed a classification system for the world's plants and flowers, and his garden and former home are on the spot where he restored Uppsala University's botanical garden. Linnaeus, who arranged the plants according to his "sexual classification system," left detailed sketches and descriptions of the garden, which have been faithfully followed.

Linnaeus was a professor of theoretical medicine, including botany, pharmacology, and zoology, at Uppsala University. You can visit his house, which has been restored to its original design, and an art gallery that exhibits the works of contemporary local artists.

Svartbäcksgatan 27. *©* **018/13-65-40** for the museum, or 018/471-25-76 for the garden. Museum 25SEK ($3.45/£1.80) adults, free for children. Gardens 30SEK ($4.15/£2.20), free for children under 15. Museum June–Sept 15 Tues–Sun noon–4pm. Closed Sept 16–May. Gardens May–Aug daily 9am–9pm; Sept daily 9am–7pm. Closed Oct–Apr. Walk straight from the train station to Kungsgatan, turn right, and walk about 10 min.

Uppsala Domkyrka 🏰🏰 It is said that medieval church builders in Uppsala set out to create a cathedral that would outdo that great Trondheim Cathedral in Norway. In that lofty mission, they did not succeed, but they did create Sweden's most celebrated Gothic building and the country's coronation church for three centuries. It's a notable, elegant building, but a bit soulless, perhaps because of all the fires that have swept through it over the ages.

The largest cathedral in Scandinavia, this twin-spired Gothic structure stands nearly 120m (394 ft.) tall. Founded in the 13th century, it received the most damage in 1702 in a disastrous fire. Among the regal figures buried in the crypt is Gustav Vasa. The remains of St. Erik, patron saint of Sweden, are entombed in a silver shrine, and one of the chapels is filled with 14th-century wall paintings recounting his legend. The botanist Linnaeus and the philosopher-theologian Swedenborg are also interred here. A small museum displays ecclesiastical relics.

Domkyrkoplan 2. ℂ 018/187-173. Free admission to cathedral. Museum 30SEK ($4.15/£2.20) adults, free for children under 16. Cathedral daily 8am–6pm. Museum Apr–Aug daily 10am–5pm; Sept–Mar daily noon–3pm. Bus: 1.

Museum Gustavianum 🏰 *Finds* Across from the cathedral stands the best of this university city's museums. It even houses one of only seven ancient anatomical theaters in the world to get by on natural light. Gruesome public dissections used to take place here. The 1663 theater was lit by a sun-crested cupola, one of the distinctive landmarks of Uppsala today. Gustavianum is Uppsala University's oldest preserved building. Here you can see a number of attractions, none more attention-grabbing than the **Augsburg Cabinet of Curiosities** 🏰🏰, a gemstone-encrusted ebony cabinet gifted to King Gustav II Adolf from the German city of Augsburg in 1632. The museum also includes archaeological and historical exhibitions, which include items from the sarcophagus of Khonsumes, a priest from the 21st dynasty, to student lecture notes from the first term in 1477—the year the university was founded.

Akademigatan 3. ℂ 018/471-75-71. Admission 40SEK ($5.50/£2.90) adults, 30SEK ($4.15/£2.20) students and seniors, free for children under 12. Mid-May to mid-Sept Tues–Sun 11am–5pm; off season Tues–Sun 11am–4pm. Bus: 1, 2, 51, or 53.

WHERE TO STAY

First Hotel Linné 🏰 At the edge of Linnaeus Garden, this is one of the best-managed and most inviting hotels in town. The hotel interior reflects its view of Linnaeus's garden and includes floral patterns and warm red tones. The hotel is especially inviting in winter, when a large open fire blazes away. Rooms feature modern furniture and plumbing, and each unit has a neatly kept bathroom with a tub and shower. One drawback is that the less expensive doubles are a bit cramped.

Skolgatan 45, S-75332 Uppsala. ℂ 018/10-20-00. Fax 018/13-75-97. www.firsthotels.com. 116 units. Sun–Thurs 1,454SEK–1,654SEK ($201–$228/£106–£121) double, from 1,854SEK ($256/£135) suite; Fri–Sat 854SEK ($118/£62) double, from 954SEK ($132/£70) suite. Rates include breakfast. AE, DC, MC, V. Parking 30SEK ($4.15/£2.20). **Amenities:** Restaurant; bar; sauna; limited room service; laundry service/dry cleaning; nonsmoking rooms; rooms for those w/limited mobility. *In room:* TV, minibar, hair dryer, safe.

Radisson SAS Hotel Gillet 🏰 Built in 1972, this attractively designed hotel still holds its own, yet it falls short in comparison to the Scandic Hotel Uplandia (see below). Favored by businessmen, it also attracts parents who are visiting their sons and daughters at the university. The bedrooms are well furnished and spacious, with comfortable furnishings standing on hardwood floors set against a backdrop of pastel walls. The bathrooms are kept up-to-date and equipped with tub/shower combinations.

Gamla Uppsala 🎔🎔

About 15 centuries ago, **"Old Uppsala"** 🎔🎔 was the capital of the Svea kingdom. In its midst was a grove set aside for human and animal sacrifices. Viking burial mounds dating from the 6th century are believed to contain the pyres of three kings.

Nearby, on the site of the old pagan temple, is a 12th-century **parish church,** once badly damaged by fire and never properly restored. Indeed, some people describe it as a stave church that turned to stone. Before Uppsala Cathedral was built, Swedish kings were crowned here.

Across from the church is the **Stiftelsen Upplandsmuseet,** Sankt Erikstoth 10 (© **018/16-91-00**). The open-air museum with reassembled buildings depicts peasant life in Uppland. Free admission. Open all year-round Tuesday to Sunday noon to 5pm.

Gamla Uppsala, about 5km (3 miles) north of the commercial heart of Uppsala, is easily accessible by bus no. 2 or 24, both of which leave frequently from the Central Station.

With its two restaurants, the hotel offers some of the best dining in town. The East West Bistro is for simpler and more affordable fare, while Atlantis World Kitchen features a menu inspired by cuisines from around the world. The restaurant uses high-quality, market-fresh ingredients and has a modern design and cozy ambience.

Dragarbrunnsgatan 23, S-75320 Uppsala. © **018/15-53-60.** Fax 018/68-18-18. www.radissonsas.com. 160 units. 995SEK–1,830SEK ($137–$253/£73–£134) double; 1,990SEK–2,200SEK ($275–$304/£145–£161) suite. Rates include breakfast. AE, DC, MC, V. Parking 170SEK ($23/£12). Bus: 801. **Amenities:** 2 restaurants; bar; indoor heated pool; sauna; room service (7am–11pm); laundry service/dry cleaning; massage; nonsmoking rooms; rooms for those w/limited mobility. *In room:* A/C, TV, dataport, minibar (in some), hair dryer.

Scandic Hotel Uplandia 🎔🎔 Its location may not be glamorous—next to the bus terminal—but this is the best hotel in town. It is more cutting-edge than the Radisson SAS because of its sophisticated aura and high-tech amenities. Construction was in two stages in the 1960s and early 1980s, but architects harmoniously blended it together. Rooms in the older section are just as well appointed and comfortable as in the newer wings, and all units are furnished with renovated, tiled bathrooms equipped with tub/shower combos. There is much use of blond wood. We've found the staff helpful and efficient, and the designers have softened some of the impersonal corners, making for a warm, inviting ambience.

Dragarbrunnsgatan 32, S-751 40 Uppsala. © **800/633-6548** in the U.S., or 018/495-26-00. Fax 018/495-26-11. www.scandic-hotels.com. 133 units. 920SEK–1,935SEK ($127–$267/£67–£141) double, 1,880SEK ($259/£137) suite. Rates include breakfast. AE, DC, MC, V. **Amenities:** Restaurant; bar; sauna; room service (7am–11pm); laundry service/dry cleaning; sauna; fitness room; nonsmoking rooms; rooms for those w/limited mobility. *In room:* A/C (in some), TV, dataport (in some), hair dryer.

WHERE TO DINE

Domtrappkällaren 🎔🎔 SWEDISH Even though this was previously a prison, no other restaurant in Uppsala can compete with this one for charm and atmosphere. It was built in the town center on the ruins of 12th-century cathedral buildings. The

vaulted ceilings and copies of Jacobean paintings in the main dining room complement the low-ceilinged, sun-flooded intimacy of the upper floors. On request, you can
dine in a narrow room, where unruly students were imprisoned in the Middle Ages,
or in one that served as a classroom in the 17th century. The chef invariably chooses
the very finest ingredients, which he handles with a razor-sharp technique, as reflected
by his poached filet of reindeer with a horseradish-flavored zabaglione and his potato
pancakes served with sautéed bits of salt pork and accompanied by lingonberry jam.
A perfect ending to any meal would be the cold cloudberry soup with almond and
caramel sweet bread, or the passion-fruit soufflé with homemade vanilla ice cream.

Sankt Eriksgränd 15. ⓒ **018/13-09-55.** Reservations recommended. Main courses 205SEK–250SEK
($28–$35/£15–£18). AE, DC, MC, V. Mon–Fri 11am–2:30pm and 5–11pm; Sat 5–11pm. Closed Dec 24–26. Bus: 2.

Flustret FRENCH This is a good choice if you're overnighting in Uppsala and
want to combine fine cuisine with entertainment. In a riverside setting near the castle, this pavilion is an exact replica of its predecessor, a demolished Victorian building.
Its spacious ground-floor dining room serves first-rate meals served by one of the best
waitstaffs in town (some of whom are university students). We found nothing on the
menu more elegant and delicious than the lobster soup appetizer. Although the
kitchen relies a bit on the always dependable salmon, the chefs are daring enough to
take on such classic dishes as veal steak Oscar or pheasant Veronique. The most festive dessert is bananas flambé. A dance club on the second floor is open Thursday to
Saturday 3pm to 3am, charging no cover.

Svandammen. ⓒ **018/100444.** Reservations recommended. Main courses 210SEK–250SEK ($29–$35/£15–£18).
AE, DC, MC, V. Thurs–Sat 6pm–midnight. Bus: 24.

Restaurant Odinsborg ⭐ _Value_ SWEDISH Go here if you have a Viking-size
appetite. In a century-old former private house, this restaurant serves strictly old-fashioned Swedish food. The culinary highlight in the Viking-theme dining room is the
smorgasbord. Menu items include excellent preparations of fried herring, marinated
salmon, smoked eel, and whitefish with a dill-flavored butter sauce. You might also try
roasted lamb, chicken filets, or steak. Street addresses aren't used in Gamla Uppsala,
but the restaurant is easy to spot. The smorgasbord is served only from May to August,
attracting far more visitors from abroad than locals. Otherwise, chefs prepare a finely
honed a la carte menu during the cold months.

Near the burial grounds, Gamla Uppsala. ⓒ **018/323-525.** Daily smörgåsbord 165SEK ($23/£12). Main courses
119SEK–199SEK ($16–$27/£8.70–£15). AE, DC, MC, V. Daily noon–6pm. Bus: 2 or 24.

GRIPSHOLM CASTLE ⭐⭐

When the sun is shining on a summer day, and Stockholmers are enjoying their precious few days of good weather, we know of no finer trip than to take a boat (see
below) and leave the city altogether, heading for **Mariefred** ("Marie's Place" in English) and Gripsholms Slott, constructed as a fortress for King Gustav Vasa in 1537 and
one of the best preserved castles in Sweden. A view of the castle can be seen as the boat
arrives at Mariefred, an idyllic little town that invites wandering as you take in its little wooden houses in pastel colors.

To the south of town, Gripsholms Slott eats up a small island in Lake Mälaren with
its massive structures, including four round brick towers and two courtyards. This castle was often used by royals to stash bothersome fellow royals here. Queen Hedvig
Eleonora, reportedly a busybody interfering in politics, was banished here after her
husband's death. The son of Gustav Vasa, King Erik XIV, exiled brother Johan here.

You can visit three floors filled with antiques and objets d'art collected over a period of 4 centuries. The castle is actually a national portrait gallery of Sweden, with paintings that range from the great Gustav Vasa himself to today's ruling king and queen.

During the reign of the 18th-century "actor-king," Gustav III, the **Gripsholm theater** 🏛🏛 was erected here. A ham actor, the king cast himself as the star in both comedy and drama. It is one of the best preserved theaters of its era in Sweden, though not of the magnificence of Drottningholm Theater (p. 438).

Gripsholm Castle is 68km (42 miles) southwest of Stockholm. By **car,** follow E-20 south; you can drive right to the castle parking lot. To get to Gripsholm Castle, take the train from Stockholm central to Läggesta. From Läggesta catch a bus to the center of Mariefred. **Boats** leave from mid-May to September at 10am from Klara Mälarstrand Pier (200SEK/$28/£15 round-trip). The castle is a 10-minute walk from the center of Mariefred.

Even though Gripsholm (📞 **0159/101-94**) was last occupied by royalty (Charles XV) in 1864, it's still a royal castle. It's open May 15 to September 15 daily 10am to 4pm; September 16 to May 14 Saturday and Sunday from noon to 3pm. Closed December 21 to January 1. Admission is 60SEK ($8.30/£4.40) for adults, 30SEK ($4.15/£2.20) ages 7 to 15, free for ages 6 and under.

WHERE TO STAY

Gripsholms Värdshus & Hotel 🏛🏛   Most visitors leave Mariefred in the late afternoon and return to Stockholm at night. But if you have only 1 night to spend in the environs of Stockholm, make it Mariefred, with its lakeside paths, narrow cobblestone streets, and old squares. The place to stay is this hotel, the oldest inn in Sweden, dating from 1609. During the reign of King Karl XI, local townspeople protested at having to house and feed His Majesty's entourage when he was visiting Gripsholms. This led to the creation of this inn, which in 1989 was restored and opened to the public.

A few steps from the village church, the mellow inn is just a 10-minute walk from the castle. Painted a golden yellow and built of wood, it was constructed on the site of an old monastery. Public rooms are filled with art, antiques, timbers, and other artifacts discovered during the renovations. The bedrooms are spacious and airy with wood floors, modern furnishings, and much comfort. Each room is individually decorated and bathrooms are equipped with tub/shower combos, heated floors, and towel racks. The hotel has the best restaurant in the region (see "Where to Dine," below).

Kyrkogatan 1, S-647 23 Mariefred. 📞 0159/34750. Fax 0159/34777. www.gripsholms-vardshus.se. 45 units. 2,190SEK–2,890SEK ($302–$399/£160–£211) double; from 3,690SEK ($509/£270) suite. Rates include breakfast. AE, DC, MC, V. **Amenities:** Restaurant; bar; sauna; 24-hr. room service; laundry service; dry cleaning; 1 room for those w/limited mobility. *In room:* A/C, TV, dataport, minibar, hair dryer, safe, trouser press, Jacuzzi in suites.

WHERE TO DINE

Gripsholms Värdshus Restaurant 🏛   SWEDISH/INTERNATIONAL   Here you get panoramic views and the finest food in town. In summer we always opt for a table on the veranda, which opens onto a panoramic view of Gripsholm Bay. The menu is adjusted to take advantage of whatever is in season. We like the way the chefs can turn out good-tasting Swedish fare based on traditional recipes, but can also segue into modern cooking using a global cuisine for their inspiration.

Breast of guinea fowl has always been served in Sweden, but here it comes with caramelized turnips and a lemon and Szechuan pepper gravy. Grilled halibut is accompanied by a red paprika cream sauce and a basil-flavored ratatouille, while lamb

cutlets are spiced up with a shallot studded mustard sauce. For dessert, try the raspberry mousse parfait. Tastings in the wine cellar can also be arranged.

Kyrkogatan 1. © **0159/34750**. Reservations recommended. Main courses 115SEK–230SEK ($16–$32/£8.40–£17).
AE, DC, MC, V. Midsummer daily noon–10pm; rest of year Mon–Fri noon–2pm, Mon–Sat 6–10pm, Sun 12:30–4pm.

TULLGARN PALACE 🕉

This former royal palace near Trosa in Sörmland is just an hour's drive from Stockholm. You can feast on wild hogs cooked over an open fire, consuming your meal
while being cooled by the breezes from the lake. If you're lucky, your visit can be tied
in with one of the outdoor cultural performances. A picnic is possible beside one of
the dams in the area. At the very least you can enjoy a cup of coffee and a Swedish
pastry in the Stable Café or the Orangery.

The palace occupies a panoramic setting on a bay of the Baltic Sea and was a
favorite of Gustav V (1858–1950), the great-grandfather of Sweden's present king.
The palace dates from the early part of the 1800s. In 1772, Gustav's younger brother,
Fredrik Adolf, turned it into his summer retreat.

The grounds invite exploration with a theater, orangery, sculptured parks, and
ponds. Though the facade is austere, the **palace interiors** 🕉🕉 are filled with riches,
the rooms a hodgepodge of elegant styles—rococo, Gustavian, and Victorian—that
hold their own fascination.

The palace (© **08/551-720-11**) is 60km (37 miles) south of Stockholm. By **car**,
take E-4 south about 60km (37 miles), and turn right at the sign that directs you to
Tullgarns Slott, near Vagnhärad. It's another half kilometer (¼ mile) to the palace.
Getting here by public transportation is extremely inconvenient and not worth the
trouble. You first have to take a train to Södertälje Södra (about 20 min.), and then
wait for a bus to Trosa, which lies 7km (4¼ miles) south of the castle. From Trosa, you
have to take a taxi the rest of the way. You could spend all morning just trying to get
to the castle, so we recommend skipping it unless you have private transportation or
endless amounts of time.

Admission is 50SEK ($6.90/£3.65) for adults, 25SEK ($3.45/£1.85) for students
and children 7 to 18, and free for those under 7. The palace is open to the public on
weekends from June to early September. Guided tours leave the main entrance every
hour from 11am to 4pm.

WHERE TO STAY

Romantik Stadtshotell Trosa 🕉   Come here for some R&R in an inn that is both
a window to the past and a doorway to future, with modern spa-like facilities. The
most charming and historically evocative hotel in the region lies in the heart of Trosa,
a quiet hamlet 7km (4¼ miles) south of Tullgarns Castle. Built in 1867 of yellow-
tinged bricks and set in the center of the town, it was enlarged and modernized in the
early 1990s. Today it provides cozy, comfortable rooms with a hint of the aesthetics of
yesteryear: wood floors and a scattering of antique accessories, always coupled with
color schemes of yellow and green. Bathrooms with shower units are modern and up-
to-date. There's a first-class restaurant on the premises that's open daily, year-round,
for lunch and dinner.

Västra Langgatan 19, S-61921 Trosa. © **0156/17070**. Fax 0156/16696. www.trosastadshotell.se. 44 units. July and
Fri–Sat year-round 1,400SEK ($193/£102) double; rest of year 1,760SEK ($243/£128) double. Rates include breakfast.
AE, DC, MC, V. **Amenities:** Restaurant; bar; spa; Jacuzzi; sauna; fitness center; solarium; massage; nonsmoking rooms;
rooms for those w/limited mobility. *In room:* TV, hair dryer.

WHERE TO DINE

Tullgarns Värdshus SWEDISH/FRENCH   It's not often that you get to dine in a Swedish royal palace without an invitation. Here you can dine in a wing of Tullgarn Palace, or order a picnic lunch to be consumed in the royal park.

The restaurant has its own kind of charm and is a summer-only event. The cooks here don't try to compete with the master chefs in the environs of Stockholm, but they serve substantial, reliable fare, and even a few surprises such as pâté of wild boar. Of course, all those old favorites are here, including salted salmon with cream potatoes.

In Tullgarn Palace, Vagnhärad. (© 08/551-720-26. Main courses 139SEK–239SEK ($19–$33/£10–£17). MC, V. May 15–Aug 29 Mon–Fri noon–2:30pm and 5–7pm; Sat–Sun noon–7pm. Closed Aug 30–May 14.

SANDHAMN, VAXHOLM & THE ARCHIPELAGO OF STOCKHOLM

Stockholm is in what the Swedes call a "garden of skerries," an archipelago with more than 24,000 islands, islets, and rocks merely jutting out of the water. The islands nearest the city have become part of the suburbs, thickly populated and connected to the mainland by car ferries or bridges. Many others are wild and largely deserted, attracting boaters for picnics and swimming. Summer homes dot some of the islands. July is the peak vacation month, when yachts crowd the waters.

You can see the islands by taking a boat trip from Stockholm harbor. If you'd like to stop at a resort island, consider **Sandhamn,** where you'll find shops and restaurants. It takes about an hour to explore the entire island on foot. The beaches at the eastern tip are the best in the archipelago. **Vaxholm,** a bathing resort known as "the gateway to the northern archipelago," also makes a good stopover and is one of our personal favorites. Artists and writers have traditionally been drawn to Vaxholm, and some hold exhibits during the summer, when the tourist influx quadruples the population. The west harbor and the main sea route to the north are filled with pleasure craft.

ESSENTIALS

GETTING THERE   Throughout the year (but more often in the summer), boats operated by several companies depart from in front of the Grand Hotel at Södra Blasieholmshamnen. Most of them are marked VAXHOLM and usually continue to Sandhamn after a stop in Vaxholm. Be sure to ask before boarding.

The trip from Stockholm through the archipelago to Sandhamn takes 3½ hours each way and costs 120SEK ($17/£8.75) one-way. The ferry trip to Vaxholm from Stockholm takes less than 40 minutes and costs 65SEK ($8.95/£4.75) one-way. There are no car ferries. If you plan lots of travel around the archipelago, consider buying an **Inter-Skerries Card** for 490SEK ($68/£36). The card allows 30 days of unlimited travel anywhere within the Stockholm archipelago for much less than the cost of individual tickets.

Vaxholm-bound boats depart every hour during the summer (about five times a day in winter) from the Strömkagen, the piers outside the Grand Hotel. For information, call the steamship company **Vaxholmes Belaget** (© 08/679-5830).

Buses depart from the Central Station daily (unless inclement weather prevents it) every 30 minutes beginning at 6am. The last bus from Vaxholm leaves at 1am. A round-trip fare is 40SEK ($5.50/£2.90; trip time: 1 hr.).

ORGANIZED TOURS

Strömma Kanalbolaget (© 08/587-14000) offers a guided cruise in English through the canals and bays to Sandhamn. Tours depart from June to August at 10am and last

8 hours. The Canal Cruise to Sandhamn costs 265SEK ($37/£19); children under 12 pay 133SEK ($18/£9.70). The company also offers the Thousand Island Cruise through the Stockholm archipelago. From July to August 13, the cruise costs 900SEK ($124/£66) and includes lunch and a two-course dinner. Children under 12 enjoy the same deal for 450SEK ($62/£33).

WHERE TO STAY

Waxholms Hotell   Our favorite pastime here is sitting out on a starry night watching the ships of the archipelago drift by. Built in 1902, this stone hotel, painted bright yellow, lies at the pier where the ferries from Stockholm dock. A substantial, sturdy, and exceedingly comfortable hotel, the Waxholms opens onto views over the bay. Stockholmers come here for a minivacation. The midsize-to-spacious bedrooms are tastefully furnished and modernized, each with a well-kept bathroom with shower unit. Even if you are visiting just for the day, as most people do, this hotel is your best bet for dining and drinking. An informal pub, Kabyssen, is at street level. One floor above is the Waxholm Hotel Restaurant (see "Where to Dine," below).

Hamngatan 2, S-185 21 Vaxholm. ℂ 08/541-301-50. Fax 08/541-313-76. www.waxholmshotell.se. 42 units. 1,125SEK–1,600SEK ($155–$221/£82–£117) double; 2,700SEK ($373/£197) suite. Rates include breakfast. AE, DC, MC, V. Closed Dec 24–Jan 1. Free parking. **Amenities:** 2 restaurants; bar; sauna; babysitting; laundry service/dry cleaning; nonsmoking rooms. *In room:* TV, hair dryer.

WHERE TO DINE
In Vaxholm

Waxholm Hotell Restaurant ⭐ SEAFOOD   Overlooking the water from the second floor of the previously recommended hotel, this dining room is the best place for cuisine in Vaxholm. Fish is the chef's specialty, as seen in dishes such as fried Baltic herring with mashed potatoes, fried perch with a chanterelle sauce with bacon, and an especially good sautéed filet of char dressed up with a grilled shellfish sausage and a mussel sauce. For dessert, try the apple and nut pastry with homemade cinnamon ice cream or the raspberry and buckthorn mousse.

Hamngatan 2. ℂ 08/541-301-50. Reservations required in summer. Main courses 126SEK–297SEK ($17–$41/£9.20–£22). AE, DC, MC, V. Summer daily noon–10:30pm; off season daily noon–9pm. Closed Dec 24–Jan 1.

In Sandhamn

Sandhamns Värdshus ⭐ SWEDISH   This old favorite has been feeding hungry visitors from Stockholm since 1672. The tables have changed, even the boats, but the panoramic vista of the harbor is timeless. The chefs are imaginative and know how to bring flavor to their concoctions. The chef's fish and shellfish casserole is the best we've sampled in the archipelago.

Harbourfront. ℂ 08/571-53-051. Reservations required Sat–Sun. Main courses 145SEK–247SEK ($20–$34/£11–£18). AE, DC, MC, V. Mon–Thurs noon–2:30pm and 5–10pm; Fri noon–2:30pm and 5–10:30pm; Sat noon–10pm and Sun noon–3pm.

16

Gothenburg

Every visitor to Sweden heads to Stockholm, but as any Gothenburger will tell you, "We've got something to show you too." We go to Stockholm for its beauty and regal monuments, but we come to Gothenburg for its attractions and to have fun. It has one of Europe's largest student populations, as is reflected in the *joie de vivre* that permeates the atmosphere here.

Prices are mercifully cheaper than in Stockholm, and the informal, relaxed mood of the people is contagious. Here you can be sucked into the local life and even embraced with enthusiasm as a visitor, not shunned as a stranger. The Göta River runs through the city, and boat trips here are just as delightful as those in Stockholm. You can even go island hopping.

Regrettably, Gothenburg still suffers from its early-20th-century reputation of being a dull industrial center. Those days are long gone, and what awaits you now is a sprawling, youthful metropolis filled with some of the brightest and best-looking people in Europe.

Called the "gateway to northern Europe," Gothenburg is the country's chief port and second-largest city. Canals, parks, and flower gardens enhance its appeal, as do a large number of museums (featuring everything from the world's only stuffed blue whale to modern art) and the largest amusement park in northern Europe. Gothenburg is also a convenient center for excursions to a spectacularly pristine archipelago that's the home of fishing villages, wildlife refuges, and several lovely vacation resorts.

Proud of its links to the sea, and the now declining shipbuilding industry that flourished here during the early 20th century, the city has managed to transform its economic base toward tourism and conventions. Gothenburg boasts one of the largest convention centers in Europe and hosts an annual book fair that's the premier event of its kind in Scandinavia.

Gothenburg received its city charter from Gustavus Adolphus II in 1621. The port contains a shipyard, Cityvarvet, which today is a pale shadow, limiting itself only to repair of ships, not their construction. The city is also the home of Volvo, the car manufacturer (whose plant is about a 15-min. drive from the city center). Despite this heavy industry, Gothenburg's environmental programs have made it a European leader in developing new products and procedures for dealing with waste. We also find it a city with a sense of humor and a decidedly human aspect—locals refer to it as "the biggest small town in Sweden." Today, Gothenburg is an attractive interface between high-tech savvy and old world charm.

A walk down Kungsportsavenyn, known as *Avenyn* (the Avenue), is a Gothenburg tradition, even in winter, when the street is heated by underground pipes so that the snow melts away quickly. There are many outdoor cafes from which to watch the action on this wide, pedestrian thoroughfare.

1 Orientation

ARRIVING

BY PLANE   SAS (℃ 800/221-2350 in the U.S.; www.scandanavian.net) operates 8 to 10 daily flights from Copenhagen to Gothenburg (most of them nonstop) between 7:30am and 11:05pm. (Many Swedes who live on the west coast of Sweden consider Copenhagen a more convenient airport than the one in Stockholm.) SAS also operates 10 to 15 daily flights between Stockholm and Gothenburg, beginning at about 7am and continuing until early evening.

Planes arrive at **Landvetter Airport** (℃ 031/94-10-00), 26km (16 miles) east of Gothenburg. A *Flygbuss* (airport bus) departs every 30 minutes for the 30-minute ride to the central bus terminal, just behind Gothenburg's main railway station. Buses run daily between 5:15am and 12:15am. A one-way trip costs 75SEK ($10/£5.50). A newer airport, Gothenburg City Airport, opened in 2002. Positioned 18km (11 miles) northwest of the city center, it receives mostly low-cost flights, many of them charters, from other parts of Europe.

BY TRAIN   The Oslo-Copenhagen express train runs through Gothenburg and Helsingborg. Trains run frequently on a north-south route between Gothenburg and Helsingborg/Malmö in the south. The most traveled rail route is between Gothenburg and Stockholm, with trains leaving hourly in both directions; the trip takes between 3 and 4½ hours, depending on the train.

Trains arrive at the **Central Station,** on one side of Drottningtorget. Inside the station is a currency exchange bureau and an office of the Swedish National Railroad Authority (SJ), which sells rail and bus tickets for connections to nearby areas. For information, call ℃ 771/75-75-75.

BY BUS   There are several buses from Gothenburg to Helsingborg/Malmö (and vice versa) daily. Trip time from Gothenburg to Helsingborg is 3 hours, Gothenburg to Malmö, 3 to 4 hours. Several buses connect Stockholm and Gothenburg daily. The trip takes 6 to 7 hours. Gothenburg's bus station, at Nils Ericson Platsen, is located behind the railway station. For information in Gothenburg, call **Swebus,** Sweden's largest bus company (℃ 036/290-8000).

BY FERRY   The **Stena Line** (℃ 031/704-00-00; www.stena.se) has six crossings per day in summer from North Jutland (a 3-hr. trip); call for information on specific departure times, which vary seasonally. They also offer a connection from Kiel, Germany, which departs daily from Kiel at 7pm, arriving at 9am the following morning in Gothenburg. Vessels for both of these routes have excellent dining rooms.

From June to mid-August, there's service from Newcastle upon Tyne (England) to Gothenburg twice a week, taking 24 hours. This service is operated by DFDS **Scandinavian Seaways** (℃ 031/65-06-50). There's no rail-pass discount on the England-Sweden crossings.

BY CAR   From either Malmö or Helsingborg, the two major "gateways" to Sweden on the west coast, take E-6 north. Gothenburg is 280km (174 miles) north of Malmö and 226km (140 miles) north of Helsingborg. From Stockholm, take E-4 west to Jönköping and continue west the rest of the way through Borås to Gothenburg, a distance of 470km (291 miles).

VISITOR INFORMATION

The **Gothenburg Tourist Office,** Kungsportsplatsen 2 (© **031/61-25-00;** www.
goteborg.com), is open June 3 to July 23 daily 9am to 6pm; September to May Monday to Friday 9am to 5pm, and Saturday 10am to 2pm.

CITY LAYOUT

The layout of Gothenburg, with its network of streets separated by canals, is reminiscent of Amsterdam—not surprisingly, as it was designed by Dutch architects in the 17th century. Its wealth of parks and open spaces has given it a deserved reputation as Sweden's greenest city.

Some of the old canals have been filled in, but you can explore the major remaining waterway and the busy harbor by taking one of the city's famous **Paddan sightseeing boats** (© **031/60-96-70**). Their circular tour through the waterways and canals of Gothenburg strikes us as one of the most absorbing and intriguing boat tours offered in Scandinavia. *Paddan* is the Swedish word for "toad," and the allusion is to the squat shape of the boats that enables them to navigate under the many low bridges. A Paddan service takes you from the point of embarkation, Kungsportsplatsen (near the Central Station), direct to the Liseberg amusement park. The park is the most popular visitor attraction in the area, attracting some three million visitors annually.

The best place to start sightseeing on foot is **Kungsportsavenyn (the *Avenyn*),** a wide, tree-lined boulevard with many sidewalk cafes. (Take a look at the "Gothenburg" map, later in this chapter.) *Avenyn* leads to **Götaplatsen,** a square that's the city's artistic and historic center. Its centerpiece is a huge bronze fountain with a statue of the sea god Poseidon, sculpted by the great Carl Milles. Gothenburg's old commercial section lies on either side of the central canal. At the central canal is **Gustav Adolfs Torg,** dominated by a statue of Gustav himself. Facing the canal is the **Börshuset (Stock Exchange).** On the western side is the **Rådhuset (Town Hall),** originally constructed in 1672. Around the corner, moving toward the river, is the **Kronhuset** (off Kronhusgatan), a 17th-century Dutch-designed building—the oldest in Gothenburg.

Gothenburg is dominated by its **harbor,** which is best viewed from one of the Paddan boats. The major attraction here is the **Maritime Center** (see "Seeing the Sights," later in this chapter). The shipyards are dominated by the IBM building. Part of the harbor is connected by an overhead walkway to the shopping mall of **Nordstan.**

The most rapid growth in Gothenburg has occurred recently on **Hisingen Island,** now home to about 25% of the town's population. Set across the Göta River (the mouth of which functions as Gothenburg's harbor) from the rest of the city, it's the fourth largest island in Sweden and home of heavy industry, which includes the Volvo factories. In 1966 a bridge was built across the harbor (i.e., the Göta River), connecting—for the first time in history—the island to Gothenburg. Despite its growing population and its heavy industry, Hisingen Island retains wide swaths of uninhabited scrublands and forest, and we've often gone here for summer hikes.

2 Getting Around

The cheapest way to explore Gothenburg (other than by foot) is to buy a **Göteborgspasset (Gothenburg Card).** Available at hotels, newspaper kiosks, and the city's tourist office, it entitles you to unlimited travel on local trams, buses, and ferryboats; most sightseeing tours; and free admission to the city's major museums and sightseeing attractions; discounts at certain shops; free parking in certain centrally located parking lots; and several other extras that usually make the card worthwhile. A ticket valid for 24 hours costs 210SEK ($29/£15) for adults and 150SEK ($21/£11) for children up to 17 years old; a 48-hour ticket is 295SEK ($41/£22) for adults and 210SEK ($29/£15) for children.

BY PUBLIC TRANSPORTATION (TRAM)   A single tram ticket goes for 20SEK ($2.75/£1.45). If you don't have an advance ticket, board the first car of the tram—the driver will sell you a ticket and stamp it for you. Previously purchased tickets must be stamped in the automatic machine as soon as you board the tram.

BY TAXI   Taxis are not as plentiful as we'd like. However, you can always find one by going to the Central Station. **To call a taxi,** dial ✆ **031/27-27-27** or 031/64-40-00. A taxi traveling within the city limits now costs 100SEK to 200SEK ($14–$28/£7.30–£15), although a ride from the center to either of the airports will run up a tab of around 400SEK ($55/£29).

BY CAR   Parking is a nightmare, so a car is not practical for touring Gothenburg. You'll need a car to tour the surrounding area, but there is good public transportation within the city, as well as to many sights. **Avis** (✆ **031/80-57-80**) has a rental office at the Central Station and another at the airport (✆ **031/94-60-30**). Its rival, **Hertz,** also has an office at the center of town at the Central Station (✆ **031/80-37-30**) and one at the airport (✆ **031/94-60-20**). Compare rates and, of course, make sure you understand the insurance coverage before you sign a contract.

FAST FACTS: Gothenburg

Area Code   The international country code for Sweden is **46**; the city code for Gothenburg is **031** (if you're calling Gothenburg from abroad, drop the 0; within Gothenburg, drop the 031).

Bookstores   The biggest and most central is **Akademi Bokhandeln,** Norra Hamngatan 26 (✆ **031/61-70-31**).

Business Hours   Generally, **shops** are open Monday to Friday 10am to 6 or 7pm and Saturday from 10am to 3 or 4pm. Large department stores, such as NK, are also open on Sunday, usually from 11am to 4pm. Most banks are open Monday to Friday from 9:30am to 3pm; and **offices,** Monday to Friday 9am to 5pm.

Currency Exchange   Currency can be exchanged at **Forex,** in the Central Station (✆ **031/15-65-16**), daily 7am to 9pm. There are also currency exchange desks at both Landvetter and Gothenburg City Airport, each open daily 5:15am to 10:45pm.

Dentists   Call the referral agency, Stampgatan (✆ **031/80-78-00**), Monday to Friday 8am to 8pm and Saturday and Sunday 8am to 4pm.

Doctors   If it's not an emergency, your hotel can call a local doctor and arrange an appointment. If it's an emergency, go to **Axess Akuten,** Södra Allégatan 6 (✆ **031/725-00-00**).

Drugstores   A good pharmacy is **Apoteket Vasen,** Götgatan 12, Nordstan (✆ **0771/450-450**), open daily 8am to 10pm.

Embassies & Consulates   Neither Britain nor the U.S. maintains a consulate in Gothenburg; Americans and citizens of Australia, Britain, Ireland, and New Zealand must contact their embassies in Stockholm.

Emergencies The number to call for nearly all emergencies (fire, police, medical) is ℂ **112.**

Eyeglasses Go to **Wasa Optik,** Vasaplatsen 7 (ℂ **031/711-05-35**). It's open Monday to Friday 9am to 6pm.

Hairdressers & Barbers We like the skilled staff at **Salong Noblesse,** Södra Larmgatan 6 (ℂ **031/711-71-30**), open Monday to Friday 9am to 7pm and Saturday 9am to 3pm.

Internet The city library, Stadsbibliotek, Götaplatsen (ℂ **031/61-65-00**), offers free Internet access from a half-dozen stations, although it's best to phone in advance to the English-speaking staff for insights into the library's reservations policies that might be in effect at the time. It's open Monday to Friday 10am to 8pm, and Saturday and Sunday 11am to 5pm (closed on Sun May–Aug). There are also seven or eight computers available for access at Centralhuset (no phone), a service center within Gothenburg's Central Railway Station. They're usually available daily from 9am to 7pm.

Laundry & Dry Cleaning Since most Swedes have access to washing machines of their own, and most hotels make laundry and dry-cleaning part of their service packages, self-service laundromats are hard to find. One that's centrally located, however, close to the Scandic Hotel Europa, is the **Nordstan Service Center,** Lilla Klädpressare 1 (ℂ **031/150300**), which also does dry-cleaning.

Liquor Laws You must be 18 to consume alcohol in a restaurant, but 21 to purchase alcohol in liquor stores. No alcohol can be served before noon. Most pubs stop serving liquor at 3am, except special nightclubs with a license to stay open later. Liquor can be purchased at state-owned liquor shops known as *Systembolag,* but only Monday to Friday 10am to 6pm, and Saturday 10am to 2pm.

Lost Property Go to the police station (see "Police," below).

Luggage Storage & Lockers You can store luggage and rent lockers at the Central Station for 20SEK to 60SEK ($2.75–$8.30/£1.45–£4.40), depending on the size of the luggage.

Photographic Supplies An excellent store is **Expert,** Arkaden 9 (ℂ **031/80-20-70**), open Monday to Friday 10am to 6pm and Saturday 10am to 2pm.

Police The main police station is Polismyndigheten, Ernst Fortells Plats (ℂ **031/739-20-00**), opposite Ullevi Stadium.

Post Office Gothenburg doesn't define any particular branch of its many post offices as preeminent or "central," but a branch of the Swedish Postal Service that's convenient to everything in the city's commercial core is at **Nordstan** (ℂ **031/80-65-29**), a 5-minute walk from the Central Station. It's open Monday to Saturday 10am to 3pm.

Radio & TV Gothenburg has Swedish-language TV broadcasts on TV1 and TV2 (the government-funded stations), as well as TV3 and TV4, which are commercially (i.e., privately) funded. It also receives such British channels as Super Sky and BBC. National radio stations include P1, P2, P3, and P4; Radio Gothenburg broadcasts on 101.9 MHz (FM).

Shoe Repair Try **Mister Minit,** Nordstan (ℭ **031/152-127**). Repairs are made while you wait.

Taxes Gothenburg imposes no special city taxes other than the value-added tax (*moms,* usually calculated at 25%), which applies nationwide.

Transit Information For tram and bus information, call ℭ **0771/41-43-00.**

3 Where to Stay

Reservations are important, but if you need a place to stay on the spur of the moment, try the **Gothenburg Tourist Office,** Kungsportsplatsen 2 (ℭ **031/61-25-00;** www.goteborg.com). There's also a branch of the tourist office in the Nordstan shopping center (no phone), near the railway station. It's open Monday to Friday from 9am to 7pm, Saturday from 9am to 3pm. It lists the city's hotels and boardinghouses, and reserves rooms in private homes. Reservations can be made by letter or phone. The tourist office charges a booking fee of 60SEK ($8.30/£4.40), but if you reserve your own accommodation on the website (www.gothenburg.com), the booking will be free. Double rooms in private homes start at around 200SEK ($28/£15) per person, and breakfast always costs extra.

The hotels listed in the following section as "expensive" actually become "moderate" in price on Friday, Saturday, and during midsummer.

EXPENSIVE

Elite Park Avenue Hotel 🏵   After more than half a century in business, this hotel is once again a prestigious address, though it still lacks a certain character. Built in 1950, and radically renovated in 2005 and 2006 after its takeover by Sweden's Elite Hotel Group, this 10-story contemporary hotel stands as a highly visible fixture on the city's most central boulevard. With a pedigree that attracted, under different ownership, Henry Kissinger, The Beatles, and The Rolling Stones, it recently earned a new lease on life and a shot of additional glamour. Midsize to spacious bedrooms are attractive and comfortable, with tile- or marble-trimmed bathrooms and lots of contemporary comforts. We go for the rooms on the upper floors because they have the most panoramic views of the water and the cityscape. On the premises are a restaurant, The Park Avenue Café, a bistro, and a second branch of a cozy English/Irish pub, the Bishop's Arms, whose clone lies in the cellar of this hotel's affiliate, the also-recommended Elite Plaza. A few steps from the hotel's entrance is an also-recommended nightclub, The Madison, which is loosely affiliated with this hotel.

Kungsportsavenyn 36-38, S-40016 Gothenburg. ℭ 031/727-1000. Fax 031/727-1010. www.elite.se. 318 units. Mon–Thurs 1,715SEK–2,950SEK ($237–$407/£125–£215) double; Fri–Sun 1,095SEK–1,295SEK ($151–$179/£80–£95) double, 2,600SEK–3,700SEK ($359–$511/£190–£270) suite. Rates include breakfast. AE, DC, MC, V. Parking 185SEK–255SEK ($26–$35/£14–£19) per night. Tram: 1, 4, 5, or 6. Bus: 40. **Amenities:** Restaurant; bistro; bar/pub; 24-hr. room service; babysitting; laundry service/dry cleaning; nonsmoking rooms; rooms for those w/limited mobility. *In room:* TV, dataport, minibar, coffeemaker, hair dryer, safe, trouser press.

Elite Plaza 🏵🏵🏵   Equaled in Gothenburg only by the Radisson SAS Scandinavia, this 1889 insurance company was stunningly converted into a superior first-class hotel. During the conversion, each of the major architectural features of this palatial structure were preserved, including the stucco ceilings, mosaic floors, and high ceilings, all of which contribute to a rather formal, but not particularly cozy, collection of bedrooms. The public lounges are adorned with an impressive collection of modern art, and all the midsize to spacious bedrooms and plumbing have been updated to give the building a new lease on life. Lying in the center of town, the hotel is within a short walk of the Central Station and the Opera House. The less formal (and less expensive) of its two restaurants is separately recommended in "Where to Dine," and its breakfast buffet is particularly lavish. Two of our favorite spots in this hotel include the elegant bar area, which is sheathed in wood paneling, staffed with formally dressed waiters, and lined with dramatic, large-scale modern paintings, and its first-rate sauna facilities in the basement.

Västra Hamngatan 3, S-404 22 Gothenburg. ⓒ 031/720-40-00. Fax 031/720-40-10. www.ellte.se. 143 units. Sun–Thurs 2,225SEK–2,925SEK ($307–$404/£162–£214) double, 3,700SEK–18,000SEK ($511–$2,484/£270–£1,314) suite; Fri–Sat 1,395SEK–1,795SEK ($193–$248/£102–£131) double, 2,990SEK–15,000SEK ($413–$2,070/£218–£1,095) suite. Rates include breakfast. AE, DC, MC, V. Tram: 1, 6, 9, or 11. **Amenities:** Restaurant; bar; 2 exercise rooms; 2 saunas; 24-hr. room service; babysitting; laundry service; dry cleaning; nonsmoking rooms. *In room:* TV, dataport, minibar, hair dryer, safe, trouser press (in some).

Hotel Gothia Towers ⓡⓡ   The twin towers of this well-run government-rated four-star hotel, which rise 18 mirror-plated stories above Sweden's largest convention center, were the tallest buildings on the west coast until they was surpassed in the late 1990s by a newer building in Malmö. A total of 410 rooms lie in its Gothia West Tower; the others in its Gothia East Tower. At press time, plans were under discussion for the construction of a third tower, to help service the surging need of hotel space associated with the thousands of visitors flocking to the country's largest convention center. Its brisk, friendly format places it among Scandinavia's best business-oriented hotels. Rooms are comfortable, contemporary, and tasteful. Touches of wood, particularly the hardwood floors, take the edge off any sense of cookie-cutter standardization. Bathrooms are spacious, with sleek, tiled tubs and showers. We gravitate to the rooms on the top three floors of the towers, which are more plush than those at lower levels, featuring enhanced amenities and services. A covered passageway runs from each of the towers directly to the convention center.

Mässans Gata 24, S-402 26 Gothenburg. ⓒ 031/750-88-00. Fax 031/750-88-82. www.gothiatowers.com. 704 units. Mon–Thurs 1,800SEK–2,600SEK ($248–$359/£131–£190) double; Fri–Sun 1,100SEK–1,700SEK ($152–$235/£80–£124) double; 4,100SEK–7,000SEK ($566–$966/£299–£511) suite. AE, DC, MC, V. Tram: 4 or 5. **Amenities:** 2 restaurants; 3 bars; fitness center; sauna; limited room service; laundry service; dry cleaning; nonsmoking rooms; rooms for those w/limited mobility. *In room:* TV, dataport, minibar, coffeemaker, hair dryer, iron, safe, trouser press.

Quality Inn 11 ⓡ   Select this hotel if you're looking for an out-of-the-way hideaway that's very far from the bustle of Gothenburg's downtown scene. Otherwise, be prepared to make your own entertainment within a quiet corner of the city with absolutely no sense of urban edginess.

Facing central Gothenburg from its waterfront position on Hisingen Island, this sprawling red-brick hotel opened in 1992 within the premises of what originated around 1890 as a machinists' shop for the shipbuilding industry. In addition to its hotel facilities, its interior contains a movie theater and a convention center. The newer sections of this hotel are angular and very modern; the antique sections reek of the sweat and hard work of the Industrial Revolution. Views, both from the bedrooms and the endless hallways, sweep out over the harbor and the remnants of the heavy industry that used to dominate both the harbor and the town. Rooms come in a wide range of categories. Even at the lowest level—moderate or standard—the bedrooms are functionally but tastefully furnished. The superior doubles have upgraded furnishings and better bathroom amenities. The most expensive way to stay here is in a luxurious suite; the corner suites are among the finest in town.

Maskingatan 11, Hisingen, 41764 Gothenburg. © **031/779-11-11.** Fax 031/779-11-10. www.hotel11.se. 260 units. June–Aug 990SEK–1,400SEK ($137–$193/£72–£102) double; Sept–May 990SEK–1,700SEK ($137–$235/£72–£124) double. AE, DC, MC, V. Bus: 16. **Amenities:** Restaurant; bar; 24-hr. room service; laundry service/dry cleaning; rooms for those w/limited mobility. *In room:* A/C, TV, dataport, minibar, safe (at additional charge).

Radisson SAS Scandinavia Hotel 𝕽𝕽𝕽 If you want the most modern and spectacular hotel in Gothenburg, check in here. This unusual deluxe hotel surrounds a large greenhouse-style atrium, which seems like an indoor tree-lined city square. It stands opposite the railroad station, and it's one of the best-run and best-equipped hotels in Sweden. Opened in 1986, with extensive renovations completed in 2006, the hotel offers among the finest rooms in town; they're large and luxuriously appointed. Bathrooms are first class, with tub/shower combinations. The fifth floor of the hotel contains the exclusive concierge rooms with extended service and speedier check-ins, and upgraded accommodations are most often booked by the business community.

Södra Hamngatan 59–65, S-401 24 Gothenburg. © **800/333-3333** in the U.S., or 031/758-50-00. Fax 031/758-50-01. www.radissonsas.com. 349 units. Mon–Thurs 1,715SEK–1,965SEK ($237–$271/£125–£143) double; Fri–Sun 1,290SEK–1,965SEK ($178–$271/£94–£143) double; 3,000SEK–4,500SEK ($414–$621/£219–£329) suite. AE, DC, MC, V. Parking 255SEK ($35/£19). Tram: 1, 2, 3, 4, 5, or 7. Bus: 40. **Amenities:** Restaurant; bar; indoor pool; fitness center; sauna; 24-hr. room service; babysitting; laundry service/dry cleaning; nonsmoking rooms; rooms for those w/limited mobility. *In room:* TV, dataport, minibar, hair dryer, safe.

Scandic Hotel Europa 𝕽𝕽 If you're seeking a cozy Swedish inn, check in elsewhere. This is one of the largest hotels in Scandinavia; a big, bustling blockbuster of a building that rises eight bulky stories across from Gothenburg's railway station. Built in 1972 of concrete and glass, the hotel underwent a massive renovation, which added thousands of slabs of russet-colored marble, with additional renovations continuing through 2006. Today it's a member of Hilton International, and the well-trained staff includes dozens of young graduates from hotel training schools. Midsize to spacious bedrooms are outfitted in monochromatic tones of either autumn-inspired browns or pale Nordic tones of blue, and have conservative, modern furniture as well as up-to-date bathrooms equipped with tub/shower combos. The largest and plushest rooms lie on the hotel's second, eighth, and ninth floors.

Köpmansgatan 38, P.O. Box 11444, S-404 29 Gothenburg. © **031/751-65-00.** Fax 031/751-65-11. 452 units. Sun–Thurs 1,650SEK–1,950SEK ($228–$269/£120–£142) double; Fri–Sat 890SEK–1,090SEK ($123–$150/£65–£80) double; 2,500SEK–5,000SEK ($345–$690/£183–£365) suite. Rates include breakfast. AE, DC, MC, V. Parking 150SEK ($21/£11). Tram: 1, 2, 3, 4, 5, 6, 7, 8, 9, or 10. **Amenities:** Restaurant; 2 bars; indoor pool; sauna; limited room service; laundry service/dry cleaning; nonsmoking rooms; rooms for those w/limited mobility. *In room:* A/C, TV, dataport, minibar, hair dryer, safe.

MODERATE

Hotel Best Western Eggers 𝕽 *Finds* For our *kronor,* this inn has more old-fashioned charm and authentic character than any other hotel in town. The third-oldest hotel in Gothenburg was built in 1859, predating the Swedish use of the word to describe a building with rooms for travelers. Many emigrants to the New World spent their last night in the old country at the Hotel Eggers, and during World War II, the Germans and the Allies met here for secret negotiations. Today it's just as good as or better than ever, with stained-glass windows, ornate staircases, wood paneling, and a distinct sense of history. (If you ask, one of the older staff members here will discuss

the role of the hotel as a trysting spot, many decades ago, for Prince Albert, a member of Sweden's Royal Family, and his long-time [then-secret] companion, Lillian.) Rooms vary in size, but they are all individually furnished and beautifully appointed, with large bathrooms equipped with tub/shower combinations. In the hotel dining room, gilt leather tapestry and polished mahogany evoke the 19th century, a perfect backdrop for the classic Swedish dishes served here.

Drottningtorget, SE 40125 Gothenburg. ℂ **800/528-1234** in the U.S. and Canada, or 031/333-44-40. Fax 031/333-44-49. www.hoteleggers.se. 69 units. June 14–Aug 10 and Fri–Sat year-round 1,090SEK–1,500SEK ($150–$207/£80–£110) double; rest of year 1,990SEK–2,240SEK ($275–$309/£145–£164) double. Rates include breakfast. AE, DC, MC, V. Parking 100SEK–130SEK ($14–$18/£7.30–£9.50). Tram: 1, 2, 3, 4, 5, 6, 7, 8, or 9. Bus: 40. **Amenities:** Restaurant; bar; limited room service; laundry service/dry cleaning; nonsmoking rooms. *In room:* TV, dataport, hair dryer.

Hotel Onyxen ℛ *Finds*   This hotel is one of the relatively unknown gems of Gothenburg. We've anxiously watched its prices rise—it used to be featured in budget guides—but it still offers decent value in spite of inflation. Well run and family managed, the hotel is housed in a building from Gothenburg's Belle Epoque days around the turn of the 20th century. Originally it was a many-balconied apartment house until its owners decided to convert it into a good hotel in the 1980s. Recent improvements have modernized it a bit, and we like its sophisticated colors of white and cappuccino. Bathrooms come with shower units and are small but well maintained. There's a residents' pub and cocktail lounge near the lobby, but the only meal served is breakfast.

Sten Sturegatan 23, S-412 52 Gothenburg. ℂ **031/81-08-45**. Fax 031/16-56-72. www.hotelonyxen.com. 34 units. Mon–Thurs 1,590SEK–1,790SEK ($219–$247/£116 131) double; Fri–Sat 1,090SEK–1,290SEK ($150–$178/£80–£94). Rates include breakfast and access to an evening soup-with-fresh-bread buffet served Mon–Sat in the lobby. Parking 120SEK ($17/£8.75). Extra bed 200SEK ($28/£15) for adults and 100SEK ($14/£7.30) for persons under 16. AE, DC, MC, V. Tram: 2, 4, or 5. **Amenities:** Breakfast room; bar; laundry service/dry cleaning; nonsmoking rooms. *In room:* TV, hair dryer, iron, trouser press, Wi-Fi.

Hotel Opera   In high-priced Sweden, this hotel is known for its moderate tariffs. Even though its prices would get you luxurious accommodations in many parts of the world, it remains a most recommendable choice for comfort. From the outside, you'll look at this boxy, white-fronted building and swear that it's part of an architectural whole. But it includes two distinctly different divisions—one with three stories, the other with four—that resulted from the interconnection of two once-separate hotels back in 1994. Rooms come in categories of "recently renovated" (i.e., slightly larger, brightly accessorized units last renovated in 2004) and "not so recently renovated" (usually with decors dating from the mid-1990s), with spaces that are a bit more cramped. Each has a neatly kept bathroom equipped with tub/shower combo.

Norra Hamngatan 38, S-401 26 Gothenburg. ℂ **031/80-50-80**. Fax 031/80-58-17. www.hotelopera.se. 145 units. Sun–Thurs 1,150SEK–1,450SEK ($159–$200/£84–£106) double; Fri–Sat 590SEK–895SEK ($81–$124/£43–£65) double. Rates include breakfast. AE, DC, MC, V. Parking 120SEK ($17/£8.75). Tram 1, 4, 5, 6, 7, 8, or 9.

Novotel Göteborg ℛℛ   Most Novotels are dull and boring, with chain format rooms and cafeteria-like food. But this is an exception, and it's one of our preferred Novotels in the north. The recycling of this red brick Industrial Age brewery was done with style and sophistication, and we've spent several comfortable nights here over the years. This converted building is set on the harborfront 4km (2½ miles) west of the center. It is a stylish hotel run by the French hotel conglomerate Accor. Each plushly carpeted room offers panoramic views of the industrial landscape. The room style is

Swedish modern, with many built-in pieces, good-size closets, and firm sofa beds. Bathrooms tend to be small, but they do have tub/shower combos.

Klippan 1, S-414 51 Gothenburg. © 800/221-4542 in the U.S., or 031/720-2200. Fax 031/720-2299. www.novotel.se. 149 units. Mon–Thurs 1,560SEK–1,690SEK ($215–$233/£114–£123) double; Fri–Sat 940SEK–1,040SEK ($130–$144/ £69–£76) double; 1,890SEK ($261/£138) suite. Rates include breakfast. AE, DC, MC, V. Free parking. From Gothenburg, follow the signs on E20 to Frederikshavn, and then the signs to Kiel; exit at Klippan, where signs direct you to the hotel. Tram: 3 or 9. Bus: 91 or 92. **Amenities:** Restaurant; bar; sauna; room service; laundry service/dry cleaning; nonsmoking rooms; rooms for those w/limited mobility. *In room:* TV, dataport, minibar (in some), hair dryer, safe.

Quality Panorama Hotel *Finds*   Other guidebooks tend to ignore this 13-story hotel, a 10-minute walk west of the center of town, but we consider it a discovery. Even though it is little publicized, it is one of the better choices in the so-called "moderate" category in pricey Sweden. It is spacious with a sense of drama, as evoked by its sky-lit and plant-filled lobby. There is also a balcony-level restaurant serving good and reasonably priced food made with market-fresh ingredients. Each of the midsize-to-large bedrooms was renovated in 2005 and furnished in a comfortable, tasteful style, with soft lighting. The wood floors were cleaned and carpeted, and double glazing was put on the windows. The finest accommodations, and certainly those with a view, are found on the 13th floor. Bathrooms tend to be small and come either with a tub/ shower or just a shower.

Eklandagatan 51–53, S-400 22 Gothenburg. © 031/767-70-00. Fax 031/767-70-70. www.panorama.se. 338 units (some with shower only). Mon–Thurs 1,895SEK–1,995SEK ($262–$275/£138–£146) double; Fri–Sun 990SEK– 1,090SEK ($137–$150/£72–£80) double. Rates include breakfast. AE, DC, MC, V. Parking 95SEK ($13/£6.95). Closed Dec 22–Jan 7. Tram: 4 or 5. Bus: 49 or 52. **Amenities:** Restaurant; bar; Jacuzzi; sauna; limited room service; laundry service; dry cleaning; nonsmoking rooms; rooms for those w/limited mobility. *In room:* TV, minibar, hair dryer, Wi-Fi.

INEXPENSIVE

Hotel Örgryte   Though this long-time favorite lacks character, it's a good, safe choice for an overnight stay. Named after the leafy residential district of Örgryte, where this hotel is situated, this family-owned hotel lies 1.5km (about 1 mile) east of the commercial core of Gothenburg. It was originally built around 1960 and renovated many times since, although the elevator was replaced with a larger and more modern unit in 2006. Rooms were upgraded and outfitted with pastel-colored upholstery and streamlined, uncomplicated furniture that makes use of birch-veneer woods. Most units are medium-size, often big enough to contain a sitting area; bathrooms are rather cramped but do contain tub/shower combinations. Both the exterior and the public areas are not particularly inspired in their design, but overall, the place provides decent, safe accommodations at a relatively reasonable price.

Danska Vägen 68–70, SE-41659 Gothenburg. © 031/707-89-00. Fax 031/707-89-99. www.hotelorgryte.se. 70 units. Sun–Thurs 1,490SEK ($206/£109) double; Fri–Sat 940SEK ($130/£69) double; 1,750SEK–2,125SEK ($242– $293/£128–£155) suite. Rates include breakfast. AE, DC, MC, V. Parking 100SEK ($14/£7.30). Bus: 60 or 62. **Amenities:** Restaurant; bar; sauna; laundry service/dry cleaning; nonsmoking rooms. *In room:* TV, dataport, hair dryer.

Quality Hotel Winn   Chain run but also chain efficient, this no-nonsense but comfortable and affordable four-story hotel lies in an isolated wooded area about 3km (1¾ miles) north of Gothenburg's ferryboat terminal. Functional and modern, its bedrooms are more comfortable than you might imagine from the uninspired exterior. Each is outfitted in pastel shades, with well-kept bathrooms equipped with a tub/ shower combination.

Gamla Tingstadsgatan 1, S-402 76 Gothenburg. © 031/750-1900. Fax 031/750-19-50. www.winnhotel.com. 121 units. June 15–Aug 15 and Fri–Sat year-round 995SEK ($137/£73) double; rest of year 1,425SEK ($197/£104) double.

Rates include breakfast. AE, DC, MC, V. Free parking. Bus: 40, 45, 48, or 49. **Amenities:** Restaurant; bar; indoor pool; sauna; laundry service; dry cleaning; nonsmoking rooms; rooms for those w/limited mobility. *In room:* TV, minibar, hair dryer, Wi-Fi.

Tidblom's Hotel 🟊 *Finds*   This is a good, if offbeat, choice, recommended if you're seeking an off-the-record weekend. It's better for motorists because of its location, although it can also be reached by public transportation. Set 3km (1¾ miles) east of Gothenburg's center, in a residential neighborhood filled with other Victorian buildings, this hotel was built in 1897 as a dormitory for Scottish craftsmen imported to work at the nearby lumber mill. Despite its functional purpose, its builders graced it with a conical tower, fancy brickwork, and other architectural adornments that remain in place today. After stints as a warehouse, a delicatessen, and a low-rent hotel, the building was upgraded in 1987 into a cozy, charming, and well-accessorized hotel. Guest rooms have good, firm beds; ample bathrooms with tub/shower combos; wooden floors; and more flair and character than you'll find at many larger, more anonymous hotels in Gothenburg's center.

Olskroksgatan 23, S-416 66 Gothenburg. ⓒ 031/707-50-00. Fax 031/707-50-99. www.tidbloms.com. 42 units. Sun–Thurs 1,450SEK ($200/£106) double; Fri–Sat 940SEK ($130/£69) double. Rates include breakfast. AE, DC, MC, V. Free parking. Tram: 1, 3, or 6. **Amenities:** Restaurant; bar; sauna; 24-hr. room service; laundry service; dry cleaning; nonsmoking rooms; rooms for those w/limited mobility. *In room:* TV, dataport, minibar, hair dryer, safe.

4 Where to Dine

Gothenburg, as you'll soon discover, is a great restaurant town. It may never compete with the sublime viands of Stockholm, but outside the capital it's one of the best cities in Sweden for fine dining. Grandmother's dishes can still be found, but Gothenburgers today are on the cutting edge of cuisine.

EXPENSIVE

Fiskekrogen 🟊🟊 SEAFOOD   This restaurant offers you a choice of some three dozen fish and shellfish dishes, and is an especially good choice because that fish is prepared very well. One of the most appealing seafood restaurants in Gothenburg occupies a building across the canal from the Stadtsmuseum, in a handsome, internationally modern setting whose sea-green and dark-blue color scheme reflects the shades of the ocean. Fiskekrogen prides itself on a medley of fresh seafood that's artfully displayed and prepared with a zest that earns many loyal customers throughout the city. One of the most appealing aspects of the place is a display of seafood on ice—succulent oysters, fresh lobster, fat crayfish, clams, and mussels. More conventional seafood dishes include poached tournedos of cod with Swedish caviar, asparagus, and an oyster-enriched vinaigrette; and butter-fried halibut with chanterelles, fava beans, truffled new potatoes, and merlot sauce.

Lilla Torget 1. ⓒ 031/10-10-05. Reservations recommended. Main courses 275SEK–365SEK ($38–$50/£20–£27); set menus 645SEK–845SEK ($89–$117/£47–£62). AE, DC, MC, V. Mon–Fri 11:30am–2pm and 5:30–11pm; Sat 1–11pm. Tram: 6, 9, or 11. Bus: 16.

Fond 🟊🟊🟊 SCANDINAVIAN/CONTINENTAL   It's not quite a love affair, but we honestly consider this to be one of the best restaurants on the west coast of Sweden. It truly lives up to its fine reputation and richly deserves its Michelin star. An address patronized by the town's discerning gourmets, this is the culinary domain of Stefan Karlsson, a media darling and winner of several culinary citations. He has chosen an attractive modern backdrop for his restaurant, lying in the Lorensberg sector of town. Light Scandinavian wood furnishings, wall panels, and Italian chairs form a backdrop for the cooking, which shows more finesse than most rival establishments and reflects the personality and style of the chef. In other words, he puts his personal stamp on every dish, each one prepared with market-fresh ingredients.

We always select a table with a panoramic view over the avenue. Memorable dishes include a choice loin of Swedish lamb with wine gravy and a side of sugar-glazed cabbage, cabbage in a mousse with scallops, and deep-fried crayfish with a black pepper glaze and baby carrots with an orange sauce. Desserts are made fresh daily and are meticulously crafted and full of flavor.

Götaplatsen. © 031/81-25-80. Reservations required. Main courses 200SEK–365SEK ($28–$50/£15–£27); 6-course set menu 680SEK ($94/£50). AE, DC, MC, V. Mon–Fri 11:30am–2:30pm; Mon–Sat 5–11pm. Closed 2 weeks at Christmas and 4 weeks in midsummer.

Restaurant 28+ ✲✲✲ INTERNATIONAL/FRENCH   This cozy, intimate, stylish restaurant sits in the pantheon of great restaurants of Gothenburg, enjoying equal rank with Fond. The trio of dining rooms are lit with flickering candles and capped with soaring masonry ceiling vaults. It's the city's hippest culinary venue, featuring main courses that include cooked crayfish with a fennel-flavored *nage* (an aromatic broth), smoked filet of char in a red wine and butter sauce, grilled breast of pigeon, and saddle of reindeer with Jerusalem artichokes and blackberry vinaigrette. We have consistently found that the most imaginative cuisine in Gothenburg is served here. The items taste fabulously fresh, and the food is delicately seasoned. The service is among the city's best.

Götabergsgatan 28. © 031/20-21-61. Reservations recommended. Fixed-price menus 895SEK–945SEK ($124–$130/£65–£69); main courses 345SEK–445SEK ($48–$61/£25–£32). AE, DC, MC, V. Mon–Sat 6–9:30pm (last order). Bus: 40. Tram: 1, 4, 5, or 6. Closed July 1–Aug 21.

Sjömagasinet ✲✲✲ SEAFOOD   The seafood and fish served at the previously recommended Fiskekrogen are hard to top, but somehow the chefs here manage to do just that. Not only that, they have the loveliest restaurant setting in all of Gothenburg. Sjömagasinet is located near the Novotel in the western suburb of Klippan, about 4km (2½ miles) from the center. The building, erected in 1775, was originally a warehouse, and today it retains its low-ceilinged, heavily timbered sense of rustic craftsmanship of a bygone age. Amid dozens of nautical artifacts from the late 19th and early 20th centuries, you can have predinner drinks in either of two separate bars, one of them outfitted in a cozy, English colonial style.

Very fresh seafood is served here, evidenced in the lightly salted cod filled with a truffle-and-cauliflower cream. Our favorite dishes are the *pot-au-feu* of fish and shellfish, served with a chive-flavored crème fraîche, and poached filet of halibut with a warm cabbage salad and potato salad.

Klippans Kulturreservat. © 031/775-59-20. Reservations recommended. Main courses 275SEK–445SEK ($38–$61/£20–£32). AE, DC, MC, V. Mon–Fri 11:30am–2pm and 6–10pm; Sat 5–10pm; Sun 2–8pm in summer. Tram: 3 or 9. From the town center, head west on E3, following the signs to Frederikshavn, and then to Kiel; exit at Klippan and then follow the signs for the Novotel.

MODERATE

A Hereford Beefstouw ✲ *Value* STEAK   The true carnivore may want to skip some of the fancy restaurants recommended above and head here. This is the best and most appealing steakhouse in Gothenburg, with a reputation for expertly prepared Brazilian beef, and a salad bar that's the most varied and copious in town. One of the three separate dining rooms is smoke-free, and all have thick-topped wooden tables, lots of varnished pine, and touches of African oak. The only sauces available to accompany your beef are béarnaise-butter sauce, parsley butter sauce, and garlic butter sauce: the management believes in allowing the flavor of the meat to come through. The largest platter is a 500-gram (18-oz.) T-bone steak. Other platters, such as filet steaks, veal sirloins, and tenderloins, are more reasonably sized. A full list of wines and beers is available.

Linnégatan 5. © **031/775-04-41**. Reservations recommended. Main courses 135SEK–360SEK ($19–$50/£9.85–£26); salad bar as a main course 150SEK ($21/£11). AE, DC, MC, V. Mon–Fri 11:30am–2pm and 5–10pm; Sat 4–11pm; Sun 3–9pm. Tram: 2, 3, 6, 9, or 11.

Bliss Resto 🖈 *Finds* INTERNATIONAL   In its own way, this is one of the hippest and most appealing, dining and drinking spots in Gothenburg, and it's among our four favorite spots in Gothenburg. The staff is charming, and there's a sense of whimsical internationalism to the place. Most patrons range in age from 25 to 40. There are tables set outside during clement weather, zebra-skin upholsteries, great music, and an ambitious cuisine that's entirely composed of tapas. Management usually recommends that five or six of them will create an adequate meal for a party of two. There's a provocative drink menu, and while the bartender might not describe the ingredients, he'll describe the feeling that drinking one or two of them will induce. Tasty tapas and their succulent ingredients change with the season, but might include salmon pastrami with cream sauce, deep-fried prawn cakes with chile dip, spicy chorizo rolls stuffed with lemon-flavored cream sauce, and skewered lamb with wasabi and dill-flavored bouillon. Come here for a drink before or after a meal in another restaurant, or for a full-fledged dining experience.

Magasinsgatan 3. © **031/138555**. Reservations recommended for dinner, not necessary for lunch. Tapas 29SEK–48SEK ($4–$6.60/£2.10–£3.50). AE, DC, MC, V. June–Aug Wed–Thurs 7pm–midnight, Fri–Sat 7pm–2am; Sept–May Tues–Thurs 7pm–midnight, Fri–Sat 7pm–2am. Tram: 6, 9, or 11.

Brasserie Lipp SWEDISH/FRENCH   Now that the real and authentic Brasserie Lipp in Paris has fallen off in its standards, this bistro serves even better fare than the real thing. Located on Gothenburg's busiest avenue, this brasserie was established in 1987, with palate adjustments for Swedish tastes. Its good food is a combination of French and Swedish—for example, escargots in garlic-butter sauce, Lipp's Skagen toast (piled high with fresh shrimp), a tender Swedish entrecôte of beef with Dijon mustard sauce, *choucroute garnie* (sauerkraut with sausage and pork, the most famous dish served at its Paris namesake), and many different kinds of fish, most caught in the waters near Gothenburg.

Kungsportsavenyn 8. © **031/105830**. Reservations required. Main courses 169SEK–265SEK ($23–$37/£12–£19); daily lunch platters 69SEK–75SEK ($9.50–$10/£5.05–£5.45). AE, DC, MC, V. Mon–Fri 11:30am–11:30pm; Sat–Sun 11:30am–midnight. Tram: 1, 4, 5, or 6. Bus: 40.

Cyrano's FRENCH/SWEDISH   Popular and bustling, this long and narrow bistro takes you back to older times in Provence. The woodsy-looking milieu is one of stucco walls, bar tops crafted from extraordinarily thick planks, and Provençal accessories. You can order a half-dozen kinds of pizza (the one with *merguez*, a North African form of spicy sausages, olives, bacon, and mushrooms is especially flavorful), as well as such staples as a tomato, basil, and mozzarella salad; frogs' legs in Pernod sauce; and a succulent chicken marinated in lime. The only drawback is that tables are just a bit too small and close together. However, judging from this place's popularity, very few of the clients seem to mind.

Prinsgatan 7. ℭ 031/143110. Reservations recommended. Main courses 140SEK–295SEK ($19–$41/£10–£22); set-price menu 220SEK ($30/£16). AE, DC, MC, V. Daily 5–11pm. Tram: 6.

Linné Terrassen Kök & Bar SWEDISH One of the best restaurants within its neighborhood, this eatery occupies the outlandish-looking covered deck that disfigured the front of an antique, 19th-century Swedish house. In winter, the venue moves inside to a cozy antique bar that's flanked with a well-appointed network of dining rooms that still retain the panels, coves, and architectural accessories of their original construction. The cookery is predictable and respectable—and we don't mean that as a putdown. Menu items include a goat's cheese mousse with beetroot salad and walnut dressing, a platter of charcuterie and cheeses with cured meats from Sweden and cheeses from Spain, and grilled black Angus sirloin with red wine sauce. Dessert might be a selection of sorbets with marinated strawberries. This place roars into action as a bar and is separately recommended in "Gothenburg After Dark" (see later).

Linnégatan 32. ℭ 031/24-08-90. Reservations recommended. Main courses 125SEK–149SEK ($17–$21/£9.15–£11). AE, DC, MC, V. Mon–Fri 4pm–1am (from 2pm in summer); Sat–Sun 1pm–1am. Tram: 6.

Smaka (Taste) SWEDISH This is a solid and much-visited staple for conservative and flavorful Swedish cuisine within the Vasaplatsen neighborhood, a residential area near the "main downtown campus" of Gothenburg University. You'll enter a blue-painted environment that evokes the dining room within an old-fashioned Swedish farmhouse, which may be a reflection of the cuisine and the patrons, who appreciate the restaurant's old-fashioned agrarian virtue and would probably resist any attempts to change it. Food is served on the bare boards of wide-planked, well-scrubbed pinewood tables, without tablecloths. Begin your meal with filets of sweet pickled herring with browned butter, chopped egg, and dill; or whitebait roe with toast, chopped onions, chopped hard-boiled egg, and boiled potatoes. Main courses include Swedish staples such as meatballs, the size of Ping-Pong balls, served with lingonberries; sautéed filet of pork with fried potatoes; or minced veal steak flavored with herbs and served in a mustard sauce.

Vasaplatsen 3. ℭ 031/132247. Reservations recommended. Main courses 89SEK–195SEK ($12–$27/£6.50–£14). Set-price menu 299SEK ($41/£22). AE, DC, MC, V. Daily 5–11pm. Tram: 13 or 16.

Soho 🦀 INTERNATIONAL The owner of this cozy and well-managed place enjoyed New York City's Soho so much that he named his restaurant in its honor. It's the kind of hip, in-the-know place that publishers use to entertain prospective best-selling authors during the Gothenburg Book Fair, and even during nonconvention moments. The decor is Iberia-inspired, something like the living area of a prosperous hacienda in Spain, even though the thick wood tables and accessories derive from the Czech Republic, India, and Central America. There's a wine bar filling a substantial corner of the place. Here, in winter, up to 40 reds and 40 whites are sold by the glass, priced at 59SEK to 200SEK ($8.15–$28/£4.30–£15). (That number is somewhat reduced in July–Aug.) There's a series of simple platters available at the bar, costing 45SEK to 60SEK ($6.20–$8.30/£3.30–£1.40) each, and more substantial food served in the dining area. Here, menu items include platters with pickled herring and cured salmon served with regional cheese; pasta with strips of veal, mushrooms, goat cheese citrus sauce, and arugula; and creamy blue mussel soup with herb-and-garlic flavored toast.

Östra Larmgatan 16. ℂ **031/13-33-26.** Reservations recommended. Lunchtime main courses 85SEK–150SEK ($12–$21/£6.20–£11); buffet lunch 80SEK ($11/£5.85); main courses 100SEK–225SEK ($14–$31/£7.30–£16). AE, DC, MC, V. Mon–Fri 8am–10:30pm; Sat 10am–11:30pm; Sun 11:30am–4pm. Tram: 1, 2, or 3.

Wasa Allé & Wasa Källare ⓡⓡ SWEDISH/FRENCH/BRAZILIAN/ASIAN
This is one of the most appealing restaurants in Gothenburg, an elegant, even posh, enclave of good times and fine dining that's the culinary focal point of the Wasastan neighborhood, just across the avenue from the "downtown campus" of the University of Gothenburg. Set within what functioned for many years as a pharmacy, the restaurant contains a large and angular bar, contemporary-looking crystal chandeliers, touches of stained glass from its earliest incarnation, and a high-ceilinged sense of grandeur that stands in quirky contrast to the animation at the bar and at the dining tables. Menu items in the restaurant include such favorites as shellfish lasagna with squid, crayfish, and scallops, served with "sugarpea foam" and a confit of tomatoes; and oyster and parsley soup with a sashimi of Swedish fish and shellfish. Menu items are simpler and cheaper in the street-level "Källare," where food, displayed in refrigerated glass cases, is described as Swedish home style and in distinct contrast to the more exotic cuisine served upstairs. Daily platters might include filet of chicken in parsley-flavored wine sauce, roasted elk with chanterelles and mashed potatoes, or Swedish meatballs. Glasses of wine in the cellar cost around 55SEK ($7.60/£4) each. Although service in the restaurant is attentive and fast-paced, when dining in the cellar-level cafe, you'll place your order at the counter and carry it to your table.

Vasagatan 24. ℂ **031/31-31-91.** Reservations recommended in the restaurant, not necessary in the cafe. In cafe, platters 48SEK–75SEK ($6.60–$10/£3.50–£5.50); in restaurant, main courses 225SEK–265SEK ($31–$37/£16–£19); set-price menus 395SEK–695SEK ($55–$96/£29–£51). AE, DC, MC, V. Cafe: Mon–Sat 10am–6pm; restaurant: Mon–Thurs 11:30am–2pm and 5:30–11pm; Fri 4pm–1am, Sat 6pm–1am. Tram: 1 or 3.

INEXPENSIVE
The Bishops Arms BRITISH/SWEDISH The city-wide chain celebrates old England with a Swedish accent. Although this is the largest location, with a wider selection of beer than at any of its siblings, there are clones of its basic format within other members of the Elite Hotel group in Gothenburg. The decor is appropriately woodsy and rustic, with black slate floors. The ceiling showcases the iron beams and brick vaulting of the building's 19th-century construction as the headquarters to an insurance company. There is also lots of stained glass. Note that some of the platters are prepared within the kitchens of the hotel's more expensive main restaurant, thereby providing some high-quality food at "pub grub" prices. The food, though good and filling, hardly taxes the imagination of the busy chefs in back. Menu items include Greek and Caesar salads, shrimp sandwiches, and pork filets in mushroom-flavored cream sauce. Place your food orders at the bar, and a staff member will carry the final product directly to your table. Pints of beer cost 58SEK ($8/£4.25) each.

In the cellar of the Elite Plaza Hotel. Västra Hamngatan 3. ℂ **031/720-40-00.** Main courses 69SEK–195SEK ($9.50–$27/£5.05–£14). AE, DC, MC, V. Fri–Sun 5pm–midnight; Mon–Thurs 5pm–1am.

Café Husaren INTERNATIONAL This former pharmacy/milliner/bank is the best-known and most animated cafe in the Haga district of Gothenburg. The century-old decor includes a reverse-painted glass ceiling conceived in 1890. Place your order for well-stuffed sandwiches, freshly made salads, and pastries, which include the biggest and most succulent cinnamon roll in town. You carry your food to one of the indoor or, in summer, outdoor, tables. The shrimp salad is very good here.

Haga Nygata 24. ✆ **031/13-63-78**. Sandwiches 20SEK–45SEK ($2.75–$6.20/£1.45–£3.30); pastries 12SEK–32SEK ($1.65–$4.40/90p–£2.35). Mon–Fri 9am–8pm; Sat–Sun 9am–6pm. Tram: 3, 6, 9, and 11.

Froken Olssons Café SWEDISH   This is one of the most central coffee shop/cafes places in Gothenburg, less than 2 blocks from the *Avenyn*. It tends to be crowded and noisy at lunchtime. Even though there's a large interior, the crowd overflows onto an outdoor terrace in summer. Pastas, chicken dishes, and hot pies with salad are featured. Baguettes filled with such ingredients as shrimp or ham and cheese are cafe staples. Beer, wine, and exotic coffees are served, but liquor isn't available.

Östra Larmgatan 14. ✆ **031/13-81-93**. Coffee 24SEK ($3.30/£1.75); *dagens* (daily) menu 50SEK–69SEK ($6.90–$9.50/£3.65–£5); hot pies with salad 60SEK ($8.30/£4.40); sandwiches 30SEK–70SEK ($4.15–$9.65/£2.20–£5.10). AE, DC, MC, V. Mon–Fri 9am–10pm; Sat–Sun 10am–10pm. Tram: 1, 4, 5, or 6. Bus: 40.

George Du Wal *Value* GREEK/ INTERNATIONAL   Don't expect anything that's particularly chic—what you get here is simple food from a restaurant that's a member of a national chain. Set in the heart of Gothenburg's commercial core, this is an airy, light-filled space that was established 30 years ago as a cafe. It was reconfigured into a restaurant with surprisingly good and fairly priced food. Service is cheerful, portions are plentiful, and menu items include stuffed vine leaves, succulent grilled chicken on skewers, chicken salads, and homemade pastas.

Kyrkogatan 32. ✆ **031/711-77-11**. Reservations not necessary. Main courses 78SEK–128SEK ($11–$18/£5.70–£9.35). MC, V. Mon–Sat 11am–11pm; Sun 11am–10pm.

Solrosen (Sunflower) *Value* VEGETARIAN   This is the best vegetarian restaurant in Gothenburg. Diners take advantage of the all-you-can-eat salad bar and the unlimited coffee. Beer and wine are also available. The Sunflower blooms in the Haga district, a low-rise neighborhood of 18th- and early-19th-century buildings. You serve yourself at the counter.

Kaponjärgatan 4. ✆ **031/711-66-97**. Main courses 50SEK–130SEK ($6.90–$18/£3.65–£9.50). Daily platters 50SEK–75SEK ($6.90–$10/£3.65–£5.50). AE, DC, MC, V. Mon–Fri 11:30am–1am; Sat 2pm–1am. Tram: 1, 6, or 9.

5 Seeing the Sights

THE TOP ATTRACTIONS

The best way to get your bearings when you set out to see the city is to go to the 120m-tall (394-ft.) **Guldhedens Vattentorn** (water tower), Syster Estrids Gata (✆ **031/82-00-09**). To get here, take tram no. 10 or bus no. 51 or 52 from the center of the city, about a 10-minute ride. The elevator ride up the tower is free, and there's a cafeteria/snack bar on top. The tower is open February to November (and sometimes in Dec) Saturday to Thursday noon to 10pm.

Early risers can visit the daily **fish auction** at the harbor, the largest fishing port in Scandinavia. The auction begins at 7am sharp. Sample some freshly made fish cakes at one of the stands here, and visit the **Feskekörka (Fish Church),** on Rosenlundsgatan (no phone), which is in the fish market. Built in 1874, it's open Tuesday to Friday 9am to 5pm and Saturday from 9am to 1pm (Tram: 3, 6, 9, and 11).

The traditional starting point for seeing Gothenburg is the cultural center, **Götaplatsen,** with its *Poseidon Fountain* ✶✶, sculpted by Carl Milles. This fountain is a powerful symbol of maritime Gothenburg. The trio of buildings here are the **Concert Hall,** the municipally owned **theater,** and the Göteborgs Konstmuseum.

Gothenburg

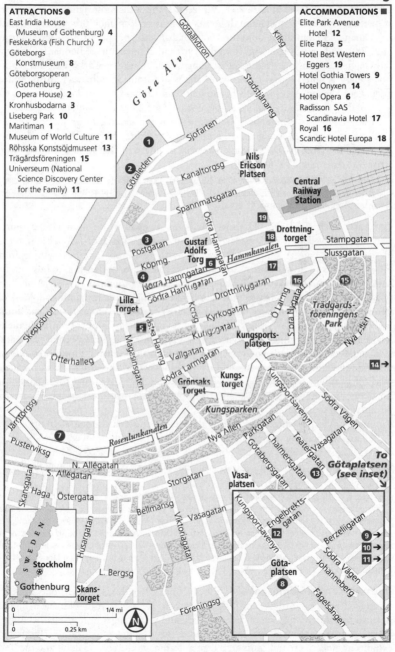

Göteborgs Konstmuseum ✦✦✦   We feel that this is the most significant repository of Swedish art outside Stockholm. It houses an array of 19th and 20th century Swedish art; Dutch and Flemish art from the 1600s; Italian and Spanish art from the 1500s to the 1700s; and French paintings from the 19th and 20th centuries. Bonnard, Cézanne, van Gogh, and Picasso are represented, along with sculpture by Carl Milles and Rodin. The gallery is noted for its collection of the works from Scandinavian artists Anders Zorn, Carl Larsson, Edvard Munch, and Christian Krohg. Of more local interest is the work of the "Gothenburg Colorists," who painted for 20 years beginning in 1930.

Head first for the **Fürstenberg Gallery** ✦✦✦ to see an amazing group of paintings by some of Sweden's leading artists, even works by Prince Eugen. Then wander into the **Arosenius Room** ✦✦✦, where you will see the wit, charm, and humor of the artist Ivar Arosenius (1878–1909).

Götaplatsen. ☎ 031/61-29-80. Admission 40SEK ($5.50/£2.90) adults, 80SEK ($11/£5.85) adult entry to special exhibitions, free for students and children under 20. Tues and Thurs–Fri 11am–6pm; Wed 11am–9pm; Sat–Sun 11am–5pm. Tram: 4, 5, 6, or 8. Bus: 40, 41, or 58.

Liseberg Park ✦✦ *Kids*   Liseberg stands on its own as the most visited tourist attraction in Sweden. It lacks the lavish sense of nostalgic kitsch of Tivoli, but in terms of size, it's the biggest amusement park in northern Europe, with everything from roller coasters and flower gardens to bandstands and ballroom dancing. In business for about 8 decades, it makes more frequent concessions to popular (usually American) pop culture than you're likely to find within Tivoli. Singles and romantic couples stroll frequently along paths flanked with immaculately maintained flower beds, and entire families sometimes make visits here the focal point of their summer holiday. Some of Sweden's best performing artists entertain every summer at Stora Scenen, the park's main stage. An ongoing attraction within the park is the Gasten Ghost Hotel. Adventure rides include the Källerado rapid river, a simulated white-water trip through the wilds of northern Sweden, and the HangOver, the most harrowing roller coaster in northern Europe. The Tornet is a circling observation platform, visible from most points within Gothenburg, which carries its participants, rotating, to dizzying heights above the cityscape, where they remain aloft for up to seven panoramic minutes.

For the younger set there's a children's playground with a circus, a kiddie roller coaster, a fairy tale castle, and a rabbit house. Many Gothenburgers like to come here in summer to eat, as there are at least two dozen dining spots within the park ranging from fast food to steak.

Korsvägen. ☎ 031/40-01-00 or 031/40-02-20. www.liseberg.se for daily programs and times. Admission to park, but not including rides inside the park 70SEK ($9.65/£5.10) adults, free for children under 7. An all-inclusive 1-day pass valid for access to all rides within the park costs an additional 270SEK ($37/£20) per person (no discount for children). Hours and opening days during Apr, May, Sept, and Oct vary wildly, depending on school holidays and advance reservation for school groups. Hours during June are usually, with exceptions, Wed–Tues from 11–10pm. Hours during July–Aug, with exceptions, are usually from either 10 or 11am to between 9 and 11pm. Tram: 4 or 5 from the city.

Röhsska Konstslöjdmuseet ✦✦   Dating from 1916, this is Sweden's only museum of applied art. Some of the artifacts shown here are 1,000 years old. Each floor is devoted to a different epoch of decorative art, and work ranges from the early Chinese dynasties to the modern era that produced the Absolut vodka bottle. Temporary exhibits of modern art and crafts are a regular feature on the ground floor, and the third floor is permanently devoted to East Asian art. Two marble lions from the Ming dynasty (1368–1644) flank the entrance to this National Romantic style building.

Vasagatan 37–39. Ⓒ **031/61-38-50**. Admission 40SEK ($5.50/£2.90) adults, free for students and those under 20. Tues noon–8pm; Wed–Fri noon–5pm; Sat–Sun 11am–5pm. Tram: 3, 4, 5, 7, or 10. Bus: 40, 41, or 58.

East India House (Museum of Gothenburg) Ⓕ   This building was constructed in 1750 as the headquarters, warehouse, and auction room of the East India Company, and houses exotic spices, silks, and fine porcelain. Despite great success in the beginning, the company went bankrupt in 1809.

Taken over by the city, the warehouse was turned into three museums focusing on archaeology, history, and industry. Exhibits highlight artifacts from the heyday of the Swedish Vikings, the harsh working conditions in the textile factories in the early 1900s, and pieces from the "attics" of Gothenburg that include rare antiques, folkloric costumes, a stunning porcelain collection, and period interiors.

Norra Hamngatan 12. Ⓒ **031/61-27-70**. Admission 40SEK ($5.50/£2.90) adults, free for students and children under 20. June–Aug daily 10am–5pm; Sept–May Tues–Sun 10am–5pm (till 8pm on Wed). Tram: 1 or 9. Bus: 40, 58, or 60 to Brunnsparken.

Maritiman Ⓚⁱᵈˢ   This is the largest floating ship museum in the world. Located on the harbor and dedicated to Gothenburg's 19th and 20th-century shipyard and maritime history, this museum consists of 19 ships, boats, and barges, the largest of which is the destroyer *Småland*. Decommissioned from the Swedish navy in 1979, but still equipped with guns and torpedoes, it's the largest of a collection of vessels that require visitors to navigate lots of ramps, staircases, and ladders. Designed to be an authentic maritime experience, the museum includes lightships, steamships, tugboats, and a submarine. The museum includes at least one cafe year-round.

Packhuskajen 8. Ⓒ **031/10-59-50**. www.maritiman.se. Admission 75SEK ($10/£5.50), 30SEK ($4.15/£2.20) children 7–15, free for children under 7. Mar–Apr, Sept–Oct 10am–4pm; May–Aug 10am–6pm; Nov Sat–Sun only 10am–4pm. Closed Dec–Feb. Tram: 5 to Lilla Bommen.

PARKS & GARDENS

Botaniska Trädgården (Botanical Garden) ⒻⒻ   This park is Gothenburg's oasis of beauty and is, in fact, the most dramatic, cultivated bit of nature in western Sweden. The botanical gardens were first opened to the public in 1923 and have been improved considerably over the years. Winding paths stretching for a few kilometers have been cut through the gardens so you can stroll along at leisure. You can wander into a bamboo grove evoking Southeast Asia, or explore a Japanese dale. In spring, the blooming **Rhododendron Valley** ⒻⒻ is one of the most stunning sights in Gothenburg. The splendid **Rock Garden** Ⓕ alone is worth the journey, featuring ponds, rugged rocks, cliffs, rivulets, and a cascade.

Carl Skottsbergsgata 22A. Ⓒ **031/741-11-06**. Free admission to garden; greenhouses 20SEK ($2.75/£1.45), free for children under 17. Garden daily 9am–sunset. Greenhouses May–Aug daily 10am–5pm; Sept–Apr daily 10am–4pm. Tram: 1, 7, or 8.

Slottsskogen ⒻⒻ Ⓚⁱᵈˢ   With 110 hectares (272 acres), this is the largest park in Gothenburg, and it's perfect for a picnic on a summer day. First laid out in 1874 in a naturally wooded area, it has beautiful walks, animal enclosures, a saltwater pool, bird ponds, and an aviary, as well as a children's zoo (open May–Aug). A variety of events and entertainment take place here in summer. There's an outdoor cafe at the zoo, plus restaurants at Villa Bel Park and Björngårdsvillan.

Near Linnéplatsen. Ⓒ **031/365-37-00**. Free admission. Daily 24 hr. Tram: 1 to Linnéplatsen.

Trädgårdsföreningen 🌟🌟 *Kids*   If we lived in Gothenburg, we'd make seasonal visits here, coming in February for the camellias, in March and April for the orchids, in July for the giant waterlilies, and in early July and again in late August when the roses are at their peak. Located across the canal from the Central Station, this park boasts a large rosarium with about 4,000 rose bushes from 1,900 different species. The park's centerpieces include the **Palmhuset (Palm House)** 🌟🌟, an ornate greenhouse whose design was inspired by London's Crystal Palace, and a butterfly house. The city of Gothenburg sometimes hosts exhibits, concerts (sometimes during the lunch hour), and children's theater pieces in the park.

Entrances on Slussgatan (across from the Central Station) and Södra Vägen. © 031/365-58-58. Park 15SEK ($2.05/£1.10) adults, free for children 17 and under, free for everyone Sept–Apr. Palm House 20SEK ($2.75/£1.45) adults, free for children up to age 17. Daily 10am–5pm. Butterfly House is only open for private art exhibitions.

The Gothenburg Opera House (Göteborgsoperan)   It's the pride of Gothenburg, a sprawling, glass-fronted building erected at the edge of a harbor that a century ago was known throughout the world for its shipbuilding prowess. Today, views from this dramatic building encompass what remains of Gothenburg's heavy industry, within a postmodern format that was inspired by an ocean liner. The opera is completely closed during July and August. For information on tickets, which are priced at from 95SEK to 470SEK ($13–$65/£6.95–£34), depending on the venue, call © **031/ 13-13-00.** For information about 90-minute guided tours, which are scheduled on an as-needed basis by an outside tour operator and priced at around 150SEK ($21/£11) per person, call © **031/10-80-00.** For more details, see "Opera & Ballet" under "Gothenburg After Dark," below (Tram: 5 and 10).

ORGANIZED TOURS

A sightseeing boat trip along the canals and out into the harbor will show you the old parts of central Gothenburg, and take you under 20 bridges and out into the harbor. **Paddan Sightseeing Boats** 🌟🌟 (© **031/60-96-70**) offers 55-minute tours, with a brisk multilingual commentary, May to June daily from 10am to 5pm; July to mid-August daily from 10am to 9pm; mid-August to September 3, daily from 10am to 7pm; and September 4 till October 1 daily from 11am to 3pm. Boats depart from the Paddan terminal at Kungsportsplatsen, which straddles the Avenyn in the city center. The fare is 95SEK ($13/£6.95) for adults, 60SEK ($8.30/£4.40) for children 6 to 12, and free for kids under 4. A family ticket (two adults and two children ages 6–12; free for kids under 6) costs 250SEK ($35/£18). We advise you to dress warmly for this trek, since part of the itinerary takes you out into the sometimes wind-lashed harbor. It's usually a good idea, during less than perfect weather, to buy a poncho from the ticket window for around 75SEK ($10/£5.50). Also, be prepared, during passages under some of the low bridges en route, to crouch down in your seat, or even kneel on deck with your head cradled in your arms, to avoid bumping it against the bottoms of the two or three low-lying bridges.

Nya Elfsborg, Fästning (© **031/60-96-70**), is docked in the 17th-century fortress (Fästning) at the harbor's mouth. This boat takes you on a 90-minute tour from Lilla Bommen through the harbor, to and around Elfsborg Fortress, built in the 17th century to protect the Göta Älv estuary and the western entrance to Sweden. It still bears traces of hard-fought sea battles against the Danes. Carvings on the prison walls tell tales of the threats to and hopes of the 19th-century prisoners-for-life. Fortress guides wait for you at the cafeteria, museum, and souvenir shop for a 30-minute tour in English and Swedish. There are five departures per day from mid-May to the end of August. The fare is 130SEK ($18/£9.50) for adults, 70SEK ($9.65/£5.10) for children up to 12 years old.

The meticulously restored *M/S S:t Erik,* originally built in 1881, is available for evening cruises along the waterways of Gothenburg's southern archipelago. For information about tours, check with the tourist office (see "Orientation," earlier in this chapter), or contact **Borjessons Line** (© **031/60-96-70**), which provides excursion packages, brochures, tickets, and timetables. The tour costs 150SEK ($21/£11) for adults and 80SEK ($11/£5.85) for children 6 to 12. Departure times vary widely with the season and with demand.

For a guided 1-hour **bus tour** of Gothenburg, go to the tourist office, or call © **031/60-96-70** for details. Between June and August, city tours are offered between five and seven times daily depending on demand. From September to May, the tour runs only on Saturday twice a day. The fare is 120SEK ($17/£8.75) for adults, 60SEK ($8.30/£4.40) for children and students. Passengers buy their tickets directly aboard the bus, which departs from a clearly signposted spot adjacent to the Stora Theatern.

6 Especially for Kids

At **Liseberg Park** (see above), every day is children's day, with rides and characters (some of them developed in close cooperation with the management of Disney). At least some of the rides, including the merry-go-round and kids' boats, are free for tots.

Your children may want to stay at the amusement park's hotel, in the city center, a shorter walk from the park than any other lodgings in Gothenburg. **Hotel Liseberg Heden,** Sten Sturegatan S-411 38 Gothenburg (© **031/750-69-109;** fax 031/750-69-30; www.liseberg.se), offers discounted summer rates. They include breakfast and coupons for free admission to the amusement park and many of its rides and shows. Between May and September, the discounted rate for double rooms is 960SEK ($132/£70). From October to April, doubles cost 1,060SEK ($146/£77) Friday and Saturday, and 1,430SEK ($197/£104) Sunday to Thursday. The hotel accepts major credit cards (Amex, Diners Club, MasterCard, and Visa). It was built in the 1930s as an army barracks and later functioned as a youth hostel. Today, after tons of improvements, it's a very comfortable first-class hotel. To reach the 179-room hotel, take tram no. 4 or 5 to Berzeliegaten.

Naturhistoriska Museet, Slottsskogen (© **031/775-24-00**), displays stuffed and mounted animals from all over the world, including a stuffed elephant, Sweden's only stuffed blue whale, and lots of big drawers you'll slide open for views of hundreds of carefully preserved insects. It's open June to August daily 11am to 5pm; September to May Tuesday to Friday 9am to 4pm, and Saturday and Sunday 11am to 5pm. Admission is 80SEK ($11/£5.85) for adults, free for children up to 19 years old (Tram: 1, 2, or 6. Bus: 51 or 54 to Linnéplatsen).

There's also a **children's zoo** at Slottsskogen from May to August (see "Parks & Gardens," above).

Kids will love **Restaurang Räkan/Yellow Submarine** (see "Where to Dine," earlier), where seafood platters arrive to the table in battery-powered boats.

7 Shopping

THE SHOPPING SCENE

Many residents of Copenhagen and Helsingør come to Gothenburg for the day to buy Swedish merchandise. Visitors should shop at stores bearing the yellow-and-blue tax-free shopping sign. These stores are scattered throughout Gothenburg.

MAJOR SHOPPING DISTRICTS   Nordstan ✿✿ (www.nordstan.se), with its 150 shops and stores, restaurants, hotels, patisseries, coffee shops, banks, travel agencies, and post office, is the largest shopping mall in Scandinavia. Here you can find almost anything, from exclusive clothing boutiques to outlets for the major confectionery chains. There's also a tourist information center. Most shops are open Monday to Friday 10am to 7pm and Saturday 10am to 6pm; Sunday 11am to 5pm.

Kungsgatan/Fredsgatan is Sweden's longest pedestrian mall (3km/1¾ miles long). The selection of shops is big and varied. Near these two streets you'll also find a number of smaller shopping centers, including Arkaden, Citypassagen, and Kompassen.

Another pedestrian venue, in this case one that's protected from inclement weather with an overhead roof, is the **Victoria Passagen,** which opens onto the Vallgatan, near the corner of the Södra Larmgatan. Inside, you'll find a cafe or two, and a handful of shops devoted to handicrafts and design objects for the home, kitchen, and garden.

At **Grönsakstorget/Kungstorget,** carts are filled daily with flowers, fruits, handicrafts, and jewelry, among other items. It's right in the city center.

The often-mentioned **Avenyn,** with its many restaurants and cafes, has a number of stores selling quality merchandise that has earned for it an enviable reputation as the Champs-Elysées of Sweden.

Kronhusbodarna, Kronhusgatan 1D (© 031/711-08-32), houses a number of small-scale and rather sleepy studios for glassblowers, watchmakers, potters, and coppersmiths, some of whom sell their goods to passersby. They can be visited, if the artisans happen to show up (call ahead to make arrangements). Take tram no. 1 or 7 to Brunnsparken.

The **Haga District** houses a cluster of small-scale boutiques, fruit and vegetable stands, art galleries, and antique shops, most of them in the low-slung, wood-sided houses that were built as part of an expansion of Gothenburg during the early 1800s. Defined as Gothenburg's first suburb, it's set within a short distance of the Avenyn.

SHOPPING A TO Z
ANTIQUES
Antik Hallarna ✿✿   What was originally conceived in the 19th century as a bank is now the site of at least 21 independent antique dealers who peddle their wares in this urban location across the street from the Elite Plaza Hotel. Expect lots of somewhat dusty, small scale collectibles and objets d'art, coins, stamps, and antique watches and clocks. Västra Hamngatan 6. Each of the dealers in this place maintains its own phone number, but the phone of one of the largest dealers is © 031/774-20-30. Mon–Fri 10am–6pm; Sat 10am–2pm. June–Aug Mon–Fri 10am–5pm, closed Sat.

DEPARTMENT STORES
Bohusslöjd ✿✿   This store has one of the best collections of Swedish handicrafts in Gothenburg. Amid a light-grained birch decor, you'll find wrought-iron chandeliers, unusual wallpaper, fabric by the yard, and other items such as hand-woven rugs, pine and birch-wood bowls, and assorted knickknacks, ideal as gifts or souvenirs. In 2006,

incidentally, this outfit celebrated its 100th birthday. Kungsportsavenyn 25. ℭ 031/16-00-72. Bus: 5B or 40.

C. J. Josephssons Glas & Porslin 𝕽𝕽𝕽 This store has been selling Swedish glass since 1866 and has established an enviable reputation. The selection of Orrefors crystal and porcelain is stunning. There are signed original pieces by such well-known designers as Bertil Vallien and Goran Warff. There's a tourist tax-free shopping service plus full shipping service. Korsgatan 12 and Kyrkogatan 34. ℭ 031/17-56-15. Tram: 6, 9, 11, or 41. Bus: 16 or 60.

Nordiska Kompaniet (NK) 𝕽 Because this is a leading and decidedly upscale department store, shoppers are likely to come here first as a one-stop emporium for some of the most appealing merchandise in Sweden. (The Swedish headquarters of the same chain is in Stockholm.) The store's packing specialists will take care of shipping your purchases home for you. More than 200,000 items are available and include Kosta Boda "sculpture" crystal, Orrefors crystal, Rorstrand high-fired earthenware, dolls in national costumes, Dalarna horses, and books about Sweden. Östra Hamngatan 42. ℭ 031/710-10-00. Bus: 40.

DESIGN

Design Torget 𝘒𝘪𝘥𝘴 Assembled into one all-encompassing venue, you'll find at least 40 different purveyors of intensely designed, thought-out items for the kitchen, home, and garden, as well as some children's toys. Vallgatan 14. ℭ 031/774 00 17. Tram: 6, 9, or 11.

EMBROIDERY

Broderi & Garn Virtually every (female) long-term resident of Gothenburg is familiar with this shop: The grandmothers and mothers of many working women here have patronized the place since it was established nearly a century ago. Come here for embroidery yarns, needles, and patterns that incorporate everything from scenes of children playing to replicas of the Swedish flag. The staff will explain the differences between cross-stitching and crewel work. Kits with everything you need to make your own embroidered masterpiece range in price from 100SEK to 2,000SEK ($14–$276/£7.30–£15) each. Drottninggatan 31. ℭ 031/13-33-29.

FASHION

Hennes & Mauritz Established in the 1940s, this is a well-established clothing store for men and women that keeps an eye on what's happening in cutting-edge fashion around the world. The spirit here is trendy, with an emphasis on what makes both genders look chic and youthful for nights out on the town, days in the office, or weekends at the park. Despite its undeniable sense of flair, garments are less expensive than we at first assumed, with lots of low-markup bargains for cost-conscious shoppers. Kungsgatan 55–57. ℭ 031/711-00-11. Tram: 1, 4, or 5.

Ströms This is the most visible men's clothing emporium in Gothenburg, with a history at this location that goes dates from 1886. We've purchased a number of smart items here over the years, some of which still rest proudly in our closets. Scattered over two floors of retail space, you'll find garments that range from the very formal to the very casual, and boutique-inspired subdivisions that contain ready-to-wear garments from the leading fashion houses of Europe. Despite the fact that it is known for men's clothing, it also sells some garments for women and children. Kungsgatan 27–29. ℭ 031/17-71-00. Tram: 1, 2, or 3.

HANDICRAFTS

Lerverk   This is a permanent exhibition center for 30 potters and glass-making craftspeople. We can't recommend any specific purchases because the offerings change from month to month. Although glassworkers are more readily associated with the east coast, on our latest trip we were astonished at the skill, designs, and imaginative products of west coast potters and glassmakers. Västra Hamngatan 24–26. ℂ 031/13-13-49. Tram: 1, 2, 3, 4, or 7 to Grönsakstorget.

8 Gothenburg After Dark

To the Gothenburger, there's nothing more exciting than sitting outdoors at a cafe along the Avenyn enjoying the short-lived summer season. Residents also like to take the whole family to the Liseberg amusement park (see "Seeing the Sights," earlier in this chapter). Although clubs are open in the summer, they're not well patronized until the cool weather sets in.

For a listing of entertainment events scheduled at the time of your visit, check the newspapers (*Göteborgs Posten* is best), or inquire at the tourist office.

THE PERFORMING ARTS

THEATER

The Gothenburg Card (see "Getting Around," earlier in this chapter) allows you to buy two tickets for the price of one. Call the particular theater or the tourist office for program information. Performances also are announced in the newspapers.

Folkteatern   This theater stages productions of Swedish plays or foreign plays translated into Swedish. The season is from September to May, and performances are Tuesday to Friday at 7pm and Saturday at 6pm. Olof Palmes Plats (by Järntorget). ℂ 031/20-38-20. Tickets 125SEK–225SEK ($17–$31/£9.10–£16). Tram: 1, 3, or 4.

Stadsteatern   This is one of the major theaters in Gothenburg, but invariably the plays are performed in Swedish. Ibsen in Swedish may be too much of a challenge without knowledge of the language, but a musical may still be enjoyed. The season runs from September to May. Performances usually are Tuesday to Friday at 7pm, Saturday at 6pm, and Sunday at 3pm. Götaplatsen. ℂ 031/61-50-50. Tickets 185SEK–230SEK ($26–$32/£14–£17) Bus: 40.

OPERA & BALLET

Göteborgsoperan (Gothenburg Opera House) ⭑⭑   This elegant new opera house was opened by the Swedish king in 1994 and was immediately hailed as the most exciting major piece of public architecture in Sweden. Set directly astride the harborfront, with a big-windowed facade whose red and orange trim reminds us of an ocean-going vessel, it features some of the finest theater, opera, operettas, musicals, and ballet performances in Sweden. Its views overlook the water, and there are five bars and a cafe in the lobby. The main entrance (on Östra Hamngatan) leads to a foyer with a view of the harbor; here you'll find the box office and cloakroom. Big productions can be staged here on a full scale. You'll have to check to see what performances are scheduled at the time of your visit. Packhuskajen. ℂ 031/10-80-00, or 031/13-13-00 for ticket information. Tickets 100SEK–450SEK ($14–$62/£7.30–£33). Tram: 5 and 10.

CLASSICAL MUSIC

Konserthuset ☆☆   Ironically, the symphony orchestra of Gothenburg functions as Sweden's national symphony, not its counterpart in Stockholm. And this, the Konserthuset, built in 1935 and noteworthy for its acoustics, is that orchestra's official home. Between September and June, it's the venue for world-class performances of classical music. During July and August, with the exception of two or so outdoor concerts, one of which is conducted on the Götaplatsen, the concert hall is closed. Götaplatsen. ✆ 031/726-53-00. Tickets 270SEK ($37/£20). Bus: 40. Tram: 3 or 5.

THE CLUB & MUSIC SCENE
BARS & NIGHTCLUBS

Berså Bar   There's a lot about this place that might remind you of a sudsy, talkative, neighborhood bar, except that it lies astride one of the busiest intersections in Gothenburg, a prime spot for drop-ins and checking out who and what's going on. There's a dance floor, a brisk big-city feeling to the bar area, and a dining menu where main courses cost from 129SEK ($18/£9.40) to 189SEK ($26/£14). If you happen to engage someone here in a dialogue, ask him or her how to translate this bar's name: even the locals will give different answers, since it was conceived as a deliberate play on Swedish words. The answer you'll usually get is "a cozy and comfortable campsite." Hours are Sunday to Thursday 11am to 1am; Friday and Saturday 11am to 3am. Kungspannplatsen 1. ✆ 031/711-2480.

Glow   In stark contrast to the sprawling size of the Trädgår'n (see below), this nightclub and cocktail lounge is small-scale and intimate. Outfitted in pale colors and attracting a clientele over 30, it's the most popular late-night venue in Gothenburg, sometimes bringing in workers from restaurants around town who relax and chitchat here after a hard night's work. There's a small dance floor, but most visitors ignore it in favor of mingling at the bar. Open daily from 8pm to 5am. Avenyn 8. ✆ 031/10-58-20. Tram: 1, 4, 5, or 6.

Linnéterrassen Kök & Bar   If you linger after your evening meal here, you might be surprised at the way that the bar area of this (separately recommended) restaurant grows increasingly crowded, often surpassing the volume of clients in the restaurant. As such, the place makes a fun and charming bar favored by attractive and usually available singles.

At the bar, you'll find 40 kinds of wine served by the glass, at least 10 beers on draft, 50 single-malt whiskies, and a daunting collection of wines by the bottle. In winter, live jazz is performed every Wednesday and Friday from 7 to 9pm, often to standing-room-only crowds. Linnégatan 32. ✆ 031/24-08-90. Tram: 6.

Oakley's   This is one of the most popular and most visible supper clubs in Gothenburg, a frequently reconfigured long-time survivor of the entertainment industry that has chugged out food and cabaret for as long as anyone can remember. Set within a short walk of the Avenyn, behind the red-and-white facade of what was originally built as a fire station, it offers a changing array of dancers and impersonators who work hard to keep the audience amused. Expect a changing array of musical acts, plenty of musical and show-biz razzmatazz, and imitations of Swedish pop stars that you might not have heard of. Food items derive from around the world and are well-prepared renderings of fish and meat (salmon terrine with champagne sauce, turbot with a wasabi-flavored cream sauce), which are served, supper-club style, at tables within sightlines of a stage. There's an automatic cover charge of 120SEK ($17/£8.75) per person, to which is added the cost of your meal. Main courses cost from around 200SEK to 230SEK ($28–$32/£15–£17) each. The club is open Tuesday to Saturday 7pm to 1am. Reservations recommended. Tredje Långgatan 16. ⓒ **031/42-60-80.** www.oakleys.nu. Tram: 1, 3, 4, or 9.

Park Lane   In this leading nightclub along Sweden's west coast, the dinner-dance room sometimes features international stars. Past celebrities have included Marlene Dietrich and Eartha Kitt. The dance floor is usually packed. Many of the musical numbers performed here are devoted to songs and lighthearted cabaret acts, so even if you don't speak Swedish, you can still appreciate the entertainment. The international menu consists of light supper platters such as crab salad or toasted sandwiches. Beer begins at 50SEK ($6.90/£3.65). Open Tuesday to Saturday 11:30pm to 3am. Elite Park Avenue Hotel, Kungsportsavenyn 36–38. ⓒ **031/20-60-58.** Cover 80SEK–110SEK ($11–$15/£5.85–£8); hotel guests enter free. Tram: 1, 4, 5, or 6. Bus: 40.

Trädgår'n   This is the largest and most comprehensive nightspot in Gothenburg, with a cavernous two-story interior that echoes on weekends with the simultaneous sounds of a restaurant and a dance club. No one under 25 is admitted to this cosmopolitan and urbane venue. Main courses in the restaurant are 170SEK to 270SEK ($23–$37/£12–£20). The restaurant is open Monday to Friday 11:30am to 2pm and Wednesday to Saturday 6pm to 10:30pm. The disco is open Friday to Saturday 11pm to 5am. Cover charge for the disco is 100SEK ($14/£7.30). Allegaten 8. ⓒ **031/10-20-80.** Tram: 1, 3, or 5.

Tranquilo   It's fun, colorful, and Latino, and Gothenburg's newest nightspot. It features a pan-Latino aesthetic of ultrabright colors, all laid out in rectangles of color that manage, despite the ongoing background of salsa and merengue, to look like they were designed by Scandinavians. The place somehow evokes a bar (a singles bar), where a lot of the women could be models. Food, such as tacos, grilled tuna, and desserts, is served throughout the evening, with main courses priced from 165SEK to 235SEK ($23–$32/£12–£17). Try the caipirinhas, which cost around 92SEK ($13/£6.70) each. Food is served daily from 11:30am to 10:30pm, with the bar remaining open between 1am or 3am, depending on business. Kungstorget 14. ⓒ **031/13-45-55.** Tram: 1, 2, or 3.

A CASINO
Casino Cosmopol   In a whimsically ornate Victorian-era building constructed on the harborfront in 1865, this is a palace of amusement, offering games, food, drink, entertainment, and, of course, casino games such as blackjack, poker, Punto Banco, and American roulette. Naturally, there are slot machines—204 in all. The better of the casino's two restaurants is Casanova on the second floor, offering panoramic views of the harbor. The stage next to the Jackpot Bar Bistro, located just beside the games, features occasional entertainment. Guests must be 21 years of age and carry some form of official photo ID. Entrance fee is 30SEK ($4.15/£2.20) for a day pass. Daily 1pm to 4am. Packhusplatsen 7. ⓒ **031/333-55-00.** Tram: 1 or 2.

A DANCE CLUB
Valand/Lilla London   Some Gothenburgers manage to find what they want, gastronomically and socially, within this combination restaurant and dance club on the Avenyn. Many clients move restlessly between the two venues, ordering stiff drinks, pastas, seafood, and steaks at Lilla London, in combination with dancing, drinking,

and flirting at Valand, the dance club located upstairs. On the premises is a small-stakes casino with blackjack and roulette, and a lot of good-looking, sometimes raucous and sometimes available, singles. The minimum age for entry is 25. Main courses at Lilla London are 150SEK to 230SEK ($21–$32/£11–£17). Although Lilla London is open Monday through Thursday 5pm to 1am; Friday and Saturday 4pm to 3am; and Sunday 1pm to 3am, Valand is open only on Friday and Saturday 8pm to 3am. Vasagatan 41. ⓒ 031/18-30-93. Cover 80SEK–100SEK ($11–$14/£5.85–£7.30) for disco after 10pm. Tram: 1, 4, 5, or 6. Bus: 40.

GAY GOTHENBURG

Greta's   Named in honor of Greta Garbo, whose memorabilia adorns the walls of its upper floor, this is the leading gay bar and restaurant in Gothenburg, with a clientele that includes all ages of gay men and lesbians. The larger of the two bars is a wood-topped sinuous affair that fills part of the ground floor with an undulating series of curves. Decor is a mixture of kitsch and new wave, fused in ways that are almost as eye-catching as the clientele. Menu items change at least every season but might include fish and lime soup, lamb filet with mushrooms in a red-wine sauce, breast of duck with potato croquettes, or a creamy chicken stew baked in phyllo pastry. Every Friday and Saturday night from 10pm to 3am, the place is transformed into a disco, and every Saturday night beginning at 1am, there's some kind of show, often drag. Wednesday 6pm to 2am; Thursday 6pm to 1am; Friday and Saturday 6pm to 4am. There's a cover charge of 80SEK ($11/£5.85), but only on Friday and Saturday nights after 10pm. Reservations recommended Friday and Saturday. Main courses run 98SEK to 149SEK ($14–$21/£7.15–£11). Drottninggatan 35. ⓒ 031/13-69-49. Tram: 1, 2, or 3.

17

Skåne (Including Helsingborg & Malmö)

The southernmost province of Sweden, Skåne, always strikes us as its own little country, and because of its greater sunshine and fertile plains, it is also the granary of the country.

Outside of Stockholm, Skåne (pronounced *shok*-neh), especially the emerging city of Malmö, evokes a more continental aura. The long-anticipated bridge between Sweden and Denmark became a reality in 2000, opening up the southernmost corner of Sweden. With three million people living within a 49km (30-mile) radius of the link, the region has the largest population concentration in all of Scandinavia—and it's still growing. An artificial island was constructed halfway across the Öresund to connect 3km (1¾ miles) of immersed railway and motorway tunnels and a 7.7km (4¾-mile) bridge.

Denmark used to govern Skåne before the Swedes reclaimed their beloved southern frontier in 1658. However, Danes still have a large presence, perhaps because it is so easy to reach Malmö from Copenhagen that many Danes simply drive to Malmö for a Sunday lunch or elegant dinner.

Skåne may not have snowcapped mountains or the famous fjords of Norway, but it seems to possess about everything else, including some of Sweden's most varied scenery that ranges from dark forests, scenic waterways, and sandy beaches to ancient ports, medieval cities, and some of the country's stateliest cathedrals (Lund, for example). The beaches are inhabitable only from July to mid-August, and even then the waters are cold to visitors from warmer climes.

Skåne has more castles than any other region in Sweden and is riddled with cobbled streets such as those found in medieval Ystad. Those interested with Vikings can visit several ancient sites and Bronze Age remains.

Skåne is easy to reach. You have a wide choice of flights, either to Malmö's Sturup Airport or to the Copenhagen airport, from which there are frequent hovercraft connections directly to the center of Malmö. Hovercraft also run between downtown Copenhagen and Malmö, and every 15 or 20 minutes, day or night, connections are possible by car ferry from Helsingør, Denmark, to Helsingborg, Sweden. If you're traveling by car, there are ferry routes from Denmark, Germany, and Poland.

Of course, more and more visitors are using Copenhagen as their gateway to Skåne. To do so, rent a car in Copenhagen and drive across the bridge.

1 Båstad ⟨★⟩

179km (111 miles) SW of Gothenburg, 105km (65 miles) N of Malmö

Jutting out on a peninsula surrounded by hills and a beautiful landscape, Båstad is the most fashionable international seaside resort in Sweden and lies 179km (111 miles) south of Gothenburg and 105km (65 miles) north of Malmö.

All the famous international tennis stars have played on the courts at Båstad. Contemporary Swedish players—inspired by the feats of Björn Borg—receive much of their training here. There are more than 50 courts in the district, in addition to the renowned Drivan Sports Centre. Tennis was played here as early as the 1880s and became firmly established in the 1920s. King Gustaf V took part in these championships for 15 years from 1930 onward under the pseudonym of "Mr. G," and Ludvig Nobel guaranteed financial backing for international tournaments.

Golf has established itself almost as much as tennis, and the Bjäre peninsula offers a choice of five courses. In 1929, Nobel purchased land at Boarp for Båstad's first golf course. The bay provides opportunities for regattas and different kinds of boating. Windsurfing is popular, as is skin diving. In summer, sea bathing also is popular along the coast.

The Bjäre peninsula, a traditional farming area, is known for its early potatoes, which are served with pickled herring all over Sweden.

ESSENTIALS

GETTING THERE   By car, head west on Route 115 from Båstad. If you're not driving, you'll find speedy trains running frequently throughout the day between Gothenburg and Malmö. Six buses a day also arrive from Helsingborg; the trip takes 1 hour.

VISITOR INFORMATION   For tourist information, **Båstad Turism,** Kyrkogatan 1 at Stortorget (℃ **0431/750-45;** www.Bastad.com), is open from June 20 to August 7 Sunday to Friday 10am to 6pm and Saturday 10am to 4pm; off season Monday to Saturday 10am to 4pm. You can book hostel rooms here from 135SEK to 170SEK ($19–$23/£9.85–£12) per person, or rent bikes for 70SEK to 90SEK ($9.65–$12/ £5.10–£6.60) per day. They also will provide information about booking tennis courts, renting sports equipment, or reserving a tee time for a round of golf.

GETTING AROUND   You don't need to rely on buses once you're in Båstad, as you can walk around the center of town in about 30 minutes. To reach the harbor and the beach, follow Tennisvägen off Köpmansgatan through a residential district until you come to Strandpromenaden. To your immediate west, you'll see a number of old bathhouses now converted to restaurants and bars. If you don't have a car, you'll need a bus to reach the Bjäre peninsula. From Båstad, bus no. 525 leaves every other hour Monday to Saturday only and runs through the center of the peninsula. If it's a Sunday, you'll have to rely on a taxi. Call ℃ **0431/696-66** for service.

EXPLORING THE AREA

The best sights are not in Båstad itself but on the Bjäre peninsula (see below). However, before leaving the resort, you may want to visit **Mariakyrkan (Saint Mary's),** Köpmansgatan (℃ **0431/78700**). Open daily from 9am to 4pm, it's one of the landmark churches of Skåne. Saint Mary's was built between 1450 and 1500. Inside are many treasures, including a sculpture of Saint Mary and Christ from about 1460 (found in the sanctuary), an altarpiece from 1775, a medieval crucifix, a pulpit from 1836, and various fresco paintings.

Båstad is the site of the **Norrvikens Trädgårdar (Norrviken Gardens)** 🏵🏵🏵, Kattvik (© **0431/369040**), 2.5km (1½ miles) west of the resort's center, the most splendid gardens on the west coast of Sweden. Founded in 1906 by Rudolf Abelin, these gardens have been expanded and maintained according to his plans, embracing a number of styles. One is Italian baroque, with a pond framed with pyramid-shape boxwood hedges and tall cypresses. A Renaissance garden's boxwood patterns evoke the tapestry art of 15th-century Italy; in the flower garden, bulbs compete with annuals. There also are a Japanese garden, an Oriental terrace, a rhododendron dell, a romantic garden, and a water garden.

At Villa Abelin, designed by the garden's founder, wisteria climbs the walls and blooms twice a year. The villa houses shops, exhibits, and information facilities, and there are also a restaurant and a cafeteria on the grounds.

The gardens can be viewed from May 1 to September 1 daily from 10am to between 5pm and 8pm, depending on business and the hour of sunset. Admission is 90SEK ($12/£6.60) for adults, free for children under 15.

THE BJÄRE PENINSULA 🏵🏵

With the time you have remaining after exploring the gardens, turn your attention to the **Bjäre Peninsula** 🏵🏵, the highlight of the entire region, where the widely varied scenery ranges from farm fields to cliff formations. Before exploring in depth, it's best to pick up a detailed map from the Båstad tourist office (see above).

The peninsula is devoted to sports, including windsurfing, tennis, golf, hiking, and mountain biking. It has white, sandy beaches and riding paths, plus at least six different 18-hole courses that are open from early spring. The Båstad tourist office can provide more information.

If you don't have a car, public transport is provided by bus no. 525, leaving Båstad every hour Monday through Saturday. It traverses the center of the peninsula.

The **Skåneleden walking trail** 🏵🏵 runs the entire perimeter of the island and is also great for cycling. However, the terrain is quite hilly in places, so you need to be in fabulous shape.

On the peninsula's western coast is the sleepy village of **Torekov,** a short drive from Kattvik. Here you'll find a bathing beach and pier.

From Torekov, you can take a boat to explore **Hallands Väderö,** an island off the west coast of Sweden. Ferryboats, some of them old-fashioned wood vessels used during part of the year for fishing, make the 15-minute crossing every hour between June and August. From September to May, departures are every 2 hours. The cost is 80SEK ($11) round-trip, with the last departure at 4pm daily. For more information, call Hallands/Väderö Billettkassan (© **0431/36-30-20**).

One of Sweden's few remaining seal colonies exists on **Hallands Väderö.** "Seal safaris" come here to view, but not disturb, these animals. In addition to seals, the island is noted for its rich bird life, including guillemots, cormorants, eiders, and gulls.

OUTDOOR ACTIVITIES

GOLF The region around Båstad is home to six separate golf courses. Two of them accept nonmembers who want to use the course during short-term visits to the region. They include the **Båstad Golf Club,** Boarp, S-269 21 Båstad (© **0431/783-70;** to reach it, follow the signs to Boarp, and drive 4km/2½ miles south of town), and the

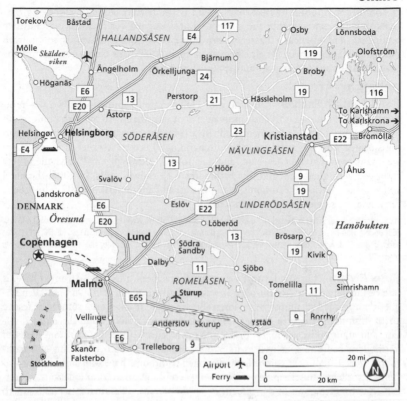

Skåne

Torekov○ Båstad
HALLANDSÅSEN E4 117
Mölle *Skälder-viken* ○ Osby Lönnsboda
○ 119 ○Olofström
Ängelholm Örkelljunga Bjärnum○
○Höganäs 24 ○ Broby
E6 Perstorp 19 116
E20 13 21 Hässleholm
○ Åstorp To Karlshamn→
Helsingør Helsingborg *SÖDERÅSEN* 23 Kristianstad To Karlskrona→
E4 *NÄVLINGEÅSEN* E22 Bromölla
13 ○Höör ○Åhus
Svalöv○ 9
Landskrona○ 19
DENMARK E6 ○Eslöv *LINDERÖDSÅSEN*
Öresund E20 E22 *Hanöbukten*
Copenhagen Lund ○Löberöd 13 Brösarp○
○Södra Sandby 19 Kivik○
Dalby○ 9
Malmö 11 ○Sjöbo
ROMELÅSEN Tomelilla Simrishamn
E65 Sturup 11
Vellinge○ 9 Borrby
Andersiöv Skurup Ystad
E6 9
Skanör Trelleborg 9
Falsterbo
Stockholm Airport ✈ 0 20 mi
Ferry ⚓ 0 20 km

Bjäre Golf Club ⛳, Salomonhög 3086, S-269 93 Båstad (📞 **0431/36-10-53;** follow
the signs to Förslöv, driving 10km/6¼ miles east of Båstad). Newest of the lot is the
New Äppalgårdans Golf Club, Hallansvagen (📞 **0431/22330**). Positioned 3km (2
miles) east of Båstad, it opened in 2006. All three of these golf courses charge greens
fees of around 350SEK ($48/£26) for a full day's play, and golf clubs can be rented for
around 225SEK ($31/£16) per day. Advance reservations for tee times are essential, but
since most of the golf clubs are open to the public, membership in any of them is not.

TENNIS Båstad is irrevocably linked to the game of tennis, which it celebrates with
fervor, thanks to its role as the longtime home of the **Swedish Open.** If you want to
improve your game, consider renting one of the 14 outdoor courts (available Apr–
Sept) or one of the six indoor courts (available year-round) at the **Båstads Malen Tennis Sällskat** (also known as the Drivan Tennis Center), Korrödgatan, S-26922 Båstad
(📞 **0431/68500**). Set about half a kilometer (⅓ mile) north of Båstad's town center,
it's the site of a corps of tennis professionals and teachers who give lessons for 250SEK
($35/£18) per hour. Indoor courts rent for 140SEK ($19/£10) per hour, outdoor
courts rent for 120SEK ($17/£8.75) per hour. And if you really want to immerse
yourself in the spirit of the game, consider renting one of the 98 bunk-style beds
within the establishment's youth hostel, where ultrasimple accommodations are priced

at 135SEK to 175SEK ($19–$24/£9.85–£13) per person. Functional-looking bar-racks-style bedrooms within the compound are designed for between two and five occupants, and often are the temporary home of members of tennis teams from throughout Scandinavia. Originally established in 1929, this club built most of the tennis courts you see today around 1980.

WHERE TO STAY

Hotel-Pension Enehall On a slope of Hallandsåsen Mountain, only a few min-utes' walk from the sea, this cozy, intimate place caters mainly to Swedish families and the occasional Dane or German. Built in 1924 as an elegant private home, it was transformed into this personalized and (charmingly) eccentric hotel in 1960. There are many personal touches here, and the rooms, although small, are adequately equipped with good beds and tiny bathrooms with shower units. In 2006, the hotel added an additional 10 bedrooms, with plans to add another 10 in 2007. The food is tasty, and the service polite and efficient.

Stationsterrassen 10, S-36936 Båstad. (©) **0431/750-15.** Fax 0431/750-14. www.enehall.se. 70 units. 865SEK ($119/£63) double. Half-board 655SEK ($90/£49) per person, double occupancy. Rates include breakfast. AE, DC, MC, V. Free parking. Bus: 513. **Amenities:** Restaurant; bar; sauna; nonsmoking rooms; 1 room for those w/limited mobility. *In room:* TV.

Hotel Riviera Often a favorite venue for conferences, this yellow-fronted hotel is one of the better hotels in the area. It was originally built in 1932 and has been fre-quently upgraded at almost yearly intervals ever since. It takes on a somewhat festive air in summer. Located by the sea, about a kilometer (⅝ mile) from the railroad sta-tion and about 3km (1¾ miles) east of the town center, it offers views from many of its modern bedrooms, as well as its 300-seat restaurant. Both bedrooms and bath-rooms are small, but the comfortably furnished bathrooms have tub/shower combina-tions. Excellent housekeeping results in impeccably clean accommodations. Guests can relax by sitting out in the gardens or on the terrace. The kitchen serves a superb combination of Scandinavian and international food; in season there is often dancing and a live band.

Rivieravägen 33, S-269-39 Båstad. (©) **0431/369-050.** Fax 0431/761-00. www.hotelriviera.nu. 50 units. 890SEK ($123/£65) double. Rates include breakfast. AE, DC, MC, V. Closed Sept–Apr. Free parking. **Amenities:** Restaurant; bar, nonsmoking rooms. *In room:* TV.

Hotel Skansen 🐾🐾 Comfortable, sprawling, and contained within a compound of usually brick-fronted buildings, this hotel is surrounded with six tennis courts, most of them ringed with bleachers, that are home to the annual Swedish Open. A few min-utes' walk from the marina and 5m (16 ft.) from the beach, it was originally built in 1877 as a warehouse for grain and food supplies. Today it incorporates its original building (which is listed as a national monument) with three more recent structures. The interior of the main building has a beamed roof, pillars, and views of the sea. Reno-vated in stages, bedrooms are airy, elegant, and traditionally outfitted with conserva-tive furniture, including good beds with ample private bathrooms containing shower units. In 2006, the hotel added an additional 30 bedrooms.

The in-house restaurant is open daily year-round, but is closed on Sunday in the winter. Set within the oldest of the hotel's five buildings, it serves excellent Swedish and international cuisine. The rest of the year, meals are served only to hotel guests and only by special arrangement. A cafe operates year-round and offers seating in the courtyard during warm weather.

Kyrkogatan 2, S-269 21 Båstad. © **0431/55-81-00.** Fax 0431/55-81-10. www.hotelskansen.se. 170 units. 1,360SEK– 1,560SEK ($188–$215/£99–£114) double; 2,800SEK ($386/£204) suite. Rates include breakfast. AE, DC, MC, V. Free parking. Bus: 513; 5-min. walk. **Amenities:** Restaurant; bar; indoor pool; 6 tennis courts; fitness center; sauna; babysitting; nonsmoking rooms; rooms for those w/limited mobility. *In room:* A/C (in some), TV, dataport, minibar, hair dryer, safe.

WHERE TO DINE

The preceding hotels all have good restaurants, although you should call in advance for a reservation. If you're just passing through, consider dropping in at the **Sol-backens Café & Wåffelbruk,** Italienska Vägen (© **0431/70-200**). This bustling cafe is locally famous, known since 1907 for serving Swedish waffles and other snack-style foods. If the weather is fair, opt for a table on the terrace overlooking the water.

Centrecourten SWEDISH/INTERNATIONAL   In a town as obsessed with tennis as Båstad, you'd expect at least one restaurant to be outfitted in a tennis-lovers' theme. In this case, it consists of a cozy and small-scale dining room with photos of such stars as Björn Borg, a scattering of trophies, old-fashioned tennis memorabilia, and tennis racquets. The best menu items include fresh fish, such as mussels, lemon sole, and cod. House specialties include duck with a bacon flavored purée of potatoes and a brisket of beef with fresh chanterelles and shallots. The eatery also serves the most savory pizzas in town, emerging piping hot from the oven. The cuisine is merely good, but the ingredients are fresh and the flavors often enticing, especially in the seafood selections.

Köpmansgatan 70b. © 0431/75275. Reservations recommended. Pizza 65SEK–85SEK ($8.95–$12/£4.75–£6.20); main courses 110SEK–160SEK ($15–$22/£8–£12). AE, MC, V. Daily noon–11pm.

BÅSTAD AFTER DARK

One good option is **Pepe's Bodega,** Warmbadhuset Hamnen (© **0431/369169**), where spicy food and festive cocktails evoke southern Spain, northern Mexico, or a forgotten corner of South America. It's open Wednesday to Sunday from 5pm to 1am, with food served until 11pm. There's also an on-site disco.

2 Helsingborg ★

230km (143 miles) S of Gothenburg, 559km (347 miles) SW of Stockholm, 63km (39 miles) N of Malmö

Helsingborg likes to call itself Sweden's gateway to the Continent, or even the "pearl of the Öresund." We used to see it as a mere gateway between Sweden and Denmark, but after having spent a lot more time here, we have warmed considerably to its charms. More and more the city is taking great care to make it a more inviting and tourist-friendly destination. There are enough attractions to make for one very busy day of sightseeing before you rush over to Denmark to see "Hamlet's Castle" or head south to sample the more continental charms of Malmö.

At the narrowest point of the Øresund (Öresund in Swedish), 5km (3 miles) across the water that separates Sweden and Denmark, sits this industrial city and major port. Many people from Copenhagen take the 25-minute ferry ride (leaving every 20 min.) across the sound for a look at Sweden.

Of course, what they see isn't "Sweden," but a modern city with an ancient history. In the Middle Ages, Helsingborg and Helsingør together controlled shipping along the sound. Helsingborg is mentioned in the 10th-century Njal's-Saga (an ancient Viking document), and other documents also indicate that there was a town here in 1085. The city now has more than 100,000 inhabitants and the second-busiest harbor in the country. This is the city that introduced pedestrian streets to Sweden, and it has long promenades along the shore of the sound.

Helsingborg (Hålsingborg) rebuilt large, vacant-looking sections of its inner city into one of the most innovative urban centers in Sweden. The centerpiece of these restorations lies beside the harbor and includes an all-glass building, the **Knutpunkten,** on Järnvägsgatan. Contained within are the railroad, bus, and ferryboat terminals; an array of shops similar to an American mall; and a heliport. The sunlight-flooded railroad station is the cleanest, brightest, and most memorable we've seen in Sweden. In addition, many dozens of trees and shrubs have transformed the center city into something like a verdant park, with trees between the lanes of traffic.

ESSENTIALS

GETTING THERE   By Ferry   Ferries from Helsingør, Denmark, leave the Danish harbor every 20 minutes day or night (trip time: 25 min.). For information about ferryboats in Helsingborg, call ℂ **042/18-61-00;** for information on the Danish side, call ℂ **33-15-15-15.** The cost of the ferryboat for pedestrians is 26SEK ($3.60/£1.90) each way or 51SEK ($7.05/£3.70) round-trip. The regular round-trip cost of the ferryboat for a car with up to five passengers is 625SEK ($86/£46). There's a reduction for drivers planning to return to Sweden the same day; in that event, the round-trip fare is 385SEK ($53/£28) **for passage.**

By Plane   The Ångelholm/Helsingborg airport lies 30 minutes from the center of the city, with regular connections to Stockholm's Arlanda airport. There are between two and four flights per day (flying time: 1 hr.). For SAS reservations, call ℂ **0770/72-77-27.**

By Train   Trains run hourly during the day between Helsingborg and Malmö, taking 50 minutes. Trains arrive four times per day on the 5-hour trip from Stockholm, and they also leave Helsingborg twice per day for Stockholm. Trains between Gothenburg and Helsingborg depart and arrive twice a day (trip time: 2½ hr.). Call ℂ **042/10-43-50** for information.

By Bus   Three buses per day link Malmö and Helsingborg. Two leave in the morning and one in the afternoon (trip tine: 1 hr. and 10 min.). Buses leave twice per day from Gothenburg and arrive in Helsingborg in 3¼ hours. Buses to and from Stockholm leave once per day (trip time: 9 hr.). Call ℂ **0200/21818** for more information.

By Car   From Malmö, head north on E-6 for 1 hour; from Gothenburg, drive south on E-6 for 2½ hours; from Stockholm, take E-4 south for 7½ hours until you reach Helsingborg.

VISITOR INFORMATION   The tourist office, **Helsingborg Turistbyrå,** Rådhuset (ℂ **042/10-43-50;** www.helsingborg.se), is open from mid-June to mid-August Monday to Friday 9am to 8pm, and Saturday and Sunday 9am to 5pm; mid-August to mid-June Monday to Friday 10am to 6pm and Saturday 10am to 2pm.

GETTING AROUND   Most of Helsingborg's sights are within walking distance; however, if your legs are tired and the weather less than perfect, you can always take a city bus, numbered 1 to 7. Most buses on their way north pass the Town Hall; those heading south go by Knutpunkten. You can buy tickets on board the buses for 16SEK ($2.20/£1.15). Tickets are valid for transfer to another city bus line as long as you transfer within 1 hour from the time the ticket was stamped. For information, call ℂ **042/10-43-50.**

SEEING THE SIGHTS

Built in 1897, the turreted, Neo-Gothic **Town Hall** (Rådhuset), Drottninggatan 1 (© **042/10-50-00**), has beautiful stained-glass windows depicting scenes from the town's history. The artist, Gustav Cederström, took great pride in the epic history of his hometown and painted these scenes. But, frankly, we like to stop here throughout the day (9am, noon, 3pm, 6pm, and 9pm) and listen to the songs ringing from the 216-foot bell tower. Two memorial stones outside were presented by the Danes and the Norwegians to the Swedes for their assistance during World War II. There is also a sculpture relief representing the arrival of Danish refugees.

In the main town square, the **Stortorget** is a monument commemorating General Stenbock's victory at the Battle of Helsingborg in 1710 between Sweden and Denmark. Today the statue is virtually ignored, as ferry-bound travelers pass it by, but it marked a turning point in Danish/Swedish history. In 1709 the Danes invaded Skåne once again and wanted to take it back. But they were finally defeated the following year in a battle just outside Helsingborg.

Fredriksdal Friluftsmuseum 🌟🌟 *Kids*   If you have time for only one open-air museum in Skåne, make it this one, lying 2km (1¼ miles) northeast of the Helsingborg center in the Fredriksdal district. Built around a manor house constructed in 1787, the park covers 28 hectares (69 acres) of landscaping. Allow yourself at least 2 hours to wander and explore the streets with their old houses, which were moved to this site.

In the rose garden, the most beautiful one we've visited in Skåne, there are innumerous types of roses on display, but we estimate the number to be more than 450. There's also a children's farm and a French baroque style open-air theater, built in 1927, where major cultural performances are staged in the summer months. Check locally to see what's happening at the time of your visit.

Gisela Trapps Vag 1. © **042/104-540**. Admission 60SEK ($8.30/£4.40), free for children 16 and under. June–Aug daily 10am–7:30pm; Sept–May daily 10am–6pm; Oct–May 11am–4pm. Bus: 1 or 7.

Kärnan (The Keep) 🌟   One of the most important medieval monuments in Sweden, and the symbol of Helsingborg, Kärnan rises from the crest of a rocky ridge in the city center. The origins of this 30m-tall (100-ft.) square tower—built in the 11th century—are mysterious; it adopted its present form in the 1300s. Its name translates as "the keep," a moniker related to its original position as the most central tower (and prison) of the once-mighty Helsingborg Castle. The thickness of its walls (about 4m/13 ft.) make it the most solidly constructed building in the region. An object of bloody fighting between the Swedes and the Danes for generations, the castle and its fortifications were demolished in 1679. Kärnan (which was restored and rebuilt in 1894) is the only part of the fortress that remains. Here you can climb the 146 steps for a panoramic terrace that gives you a grand view of Danish Helsingør across the sound.

The easiest way to reach Kärnan is to board the elevator, which departs from the *terrasen* (terrace) of the town's main street, the Stortorget. For 5SEK (70¢/40p) per person, you'll be carried up the rocky hillside to the base of the tower. However, many visitors avoid the elevator, preferring instead to climb a winding set of flower-flanked steps as part of their exploration of the city.

Kärngränden (off the Stortorget). © **042/105-991**. Admission 20SEK ($2.75/£1.45) adults, 10SEK ($1.40/75p) children 8–16. Apr–May Tues–Fri 9am–4pm, Sat–Sun 11am–4pm; June–Aug daily 11am–7pm; Oct–Mar Tues–Sun 11am–5pm. Bus: 1 or 6.

Mariakyrkan (Church of St. Mary)   Rather than a grand cathedral, Helsingborg has this church filled with treasures. It's one of the best examples we know of Danish Gothic architecture and dates from the 14th century. Don't be disappointed as you approach the plain facade; the gems are concealed inside, including a treasure trove of silver in the Vestry and Silver Chamber. Note the intricately carved Renaissance pulpit (1615) and the triptych from 1450, which always catches our eye. If the sun is shining, the modern **stained-glass windows** 𝕲𝕲 are jewel-like. To get here, walk east from the harbor.

Södra Storgatan. ℂ 042/37-28-30. Free admission. June–Aug Mon–Sat 8am–6pm, Sun 9am–6pm; Sept–May Mon–Sat 8am–4pm, Sun 9am–4pm. Bus: 1 or 6.

Sofiero Slott 𝕲𝕲   Before the Swedish royal family moved their summer palace to Öland, they used to spend those precious weeks of sunshine right outside Helsingborg. One of the most famous buildings in southern Sweden, lying 5km (3 miles) north of Helsingborg, this castle was constructed between 1864 and 1865 to be the summer residence of King Oscar II and his wife, Sofia. In 1905 it was bequeathed to their grandson, Gustav Adolph, and his wife, Margareta, who enlarged the site and created some of the most memorable gardens in the country. Their interests supposedly sparked a nationwide interest in landscape architecture. After his coronation, Gustav Adolph spent his last days here, eventually bequeathing Sofiero as a gift to the city of Helsingborg in 1973. In 1993, many of the original gardens were re-created in memory of their designer, Queen Margareta. Today the most visited sites include the 1865 castle, which contains a cafe and restaurant; the rose garden; and the Rhododendron Ravine, with an estimated 10,000 rhododendrons, which are in their full glory in early June.

Sofierovägen. ℂ 042/137-400. Admission 70SEK ($9.65/£5.10) adults, free for children under 12. Daily 11am–5pm. Closed Oct to mid-Apr. Bus: 219 or 221.

SHOPPING

In the center of Helsingborg you'll find a number of shopping possibilities, including **Väla Centrum,** which is one of the largest shopping centers in all of Scandinavia. To reach it, follow Hälsovågen and Ångelholmsvägen north about 6km (3¾ miles; it's signposted), or take bus no. 202 from Knutpunkten. Seemingly everything is here under one roof, including two large department stores and 42 specialty shops, selling everything from shoes to tropical fish.

The best bookstore in town is **Bengt Bökman,** Bredgattan 22 (ℂ 042/10-71-00), with many English-language editions. The best place to buy glass is **Duka Carl Anders,** Kullag 17 (ℂ 042/24-30-20), which carries the works of such prestigious manufacturers as Kosta Boda and Orrefors.

Northwest Scania is known as the pottery district of Sweden. The first Scanian pottery factory was founded in 1748 in Bosarp, 15km (9¼ miles) east of Helsingborg. The city of Helsingborg got its first factory in 1768 and another began manufacturing in 1832. Since then, the tradition has been redeveloped and revitalized, making the area famous far beyond the borders of Sweden.

At a point 7km (4¼ miles) south of Helsingborg, you can visit **Raus Stenkarlsfabrik,** less than a kilometer (½ mile) east of Råå (look for signs along Landskronavagen). It's open May to August Monday through Friday 10am to 6pm, Saturday 10am to 4pm; in the off season, you must make an appointment. Call ℂ 042/26-01-30 for more information.

In Gantofta, 10km (6¼ miles) southeast of Helsingborg, lies **Jie-Keramik** (© **042/ 387-750**), one of Scandinavia's leading manufacturers of hand-painted decorative ceramics, wall reliefs, wall clocks, figures, and other such items. You can visit a factory shop or patronize a cafe on-site. From Helsingborg, drive south to Råå, and then follow the signs to Gantofta. You also can take bus no. 209 from Knutpunkten in the center of Helsingborg. The outlet is open June to August daily noon to 6pm. Off-season hours are daily 10am to 4pm.

If you drive 20km (12 miles) north of Helsingborg to Höganäs, you'll find two famous stoneware factories. **Höganäs Saltglaserat** (© **042/216-540**) has been manufacturing salt-glazed stoneware since 1835. Today the classic, salt-glazed Höganäs jars, with their anchor symbol, are still in production. Everything is made by hand and fired in coal-burning circular kilns from the turn of the 20th century. The shop here is within the factory, so you can see the throwers in action and go inside the old kilns. Open year-round Monday to Friday 9am to 4pm and Saturdays in June, July, August, and September 10am to 1pm. The other outlet, **Höganäs Keramik** (© **042/35-11-31**), is Scandinavia's largest stoneware manufacturer. In the Factory Shop, inaugurated in 1994, flawed goods from both Höganäs Keramik and Boda Nova are on sale at bargain prices. This outlet is open from May to August Monday through Friday from 9am to 6pm, Saturday and Sunday 10am to 5pm. Off-season hours are Monday to Friday 10am to 6pm, Saturday 10am to 4pm, and Sunday 11am to 4pm.

WHERE TO STAY
EXPENSIVE
Radisson SAS Grand Hotel Helsingborg ☾☾☾ This is Helsingborg's grandest hotel, an imposing brick-built pile from 1926 that has been completely modernized without destroying its classic environment. We applaud this chain-run hotel for that, and for turning this golden oldie into one of the best hotels in southern Sweden. The hotel combines high-ceilinged, richly paneled public areas and spacious, well-accessorized guest rooms with elaborate ceiling moldings, old-world decorative touches, and lots of modern comforts and conveniences. The renovated rooms have ample bathrooms with a tub and shower. After all the hustle-bustle of crossing over from Denmark, it's great to work off tension on the nearby jogging track along the Strandpromenaden.

Stortorget 8–12, Box 1104, S-251 11 Helsingborg. © **800/333-3333** in the U.S., or 042/38-04-00. Fax 042/38-04-04. www.radissonsas.com. 164 units. Mid-June to Aug and Fri–Sun year-round 960SEK–1,200SEK ($132–$166/£70–£88) double, 1,590SEK–2,090SEK ($219–$288/£116–£153) suite; rest of year 1,700SEK ($235/£124) double, 2,100SEK–2,600SEK ($290–$359/£153–£190) suite. Rates include breakfast. AE, DC, MC, V. Parking 150SEK ($21/£11). Bus: 7B or 1A. **Amenities:** Restaurant; bar; sauna; 24-hr. room service; laundry service/dry cleaning; nonsmoking rooms; rooms for those w/limited mobility. *In room:* TV, dataport, minibar, hair dryer, iron, Wi-Fi.

MODERATE
Comfort Hotel Nouveau ☾ *finds* This hotel lives up to its namesake and delivers solid comfort. The 1960s building was radically upgraded in the 1990s and is now one of the most desirable choices for an overnight stay. The tastefully decorated building, built of ocher brick and touches of marble, draws on upscale models from England and France, and includes chintz curtains, varnished mahogany, often with wood inlays, and warm colors inspired by autumn. Rooms are nice and cozy—not particularly large, but well maintained, with tasteful fabrics, frequently renewed linen, and small but adequate bathrooms equipped with shower units. As a thoughtful touch, a fresh flower is often placed on your pillow at night.

Gasverksgatan 11. S-250 02 Helsingborg. ⓒ 042/37-19-50. Fax 042/37-19-59. www.choicehotelseurope.com. 95 units. Mid-June to mid-Aug and Fri–Sat year-round 950SEK ($131/£69) double; rest of year 1,520SEK ($210/£111) double; 1,250SEK–1,750SEK ($173–$242/£91–£128) suite. Rates include breakfast. AE, DC, MC, V. Free parking. Bus: 7A or 1A. **Amenities:** Restaurant; bar; indoor pool; sauna; laundry service; dry cleaning; nonsmoking rooms; rooms for those w/limited mobility. *In room:* TV, dataport, minibar, hair dryer, Wi-Fi.

Elite Hotel Mollberg ⓖ   This landmark hotel, arguably, is Sweden's oldest continuously operated hotel and restaurant. It still attracts traditionalists, though trendsetters infinitely prefer the more glamorous Elite Marina Plaza (see below). Although a tavern has stood on this site since the 14th century, most of the building was constructed in 1802. Its elaborate wedding-cake exterior and high-ceilinged interior have long been its hallmarks. Kings, counts, and barons used to check in here, although there aren't too many of those fellows around anymore.

As is typical of a building of this age, bedrooms come in different shapes and sizes, but each has been modernized and furnished in a comfortable, tasteful way, with ample bathrooms complete with a tub or shower. On site is a modern French-style brasserie with special musical evenings, and a rather successful clone of a London pub, the Bishop's Arms, with the town's largest selection of beers and whiskey.

Stortorget 18, S-251 14 Helsingborg. ⓒ 042/37-37-00. Fax 042/37-37-37. www.elite.se. 104 units. 1,295SEK–1,595SEK ($179–$220/£95–£116) double; 2,200SEK ($304/£161) suite. Rates include breakfast. AE, DC, MC, V. Parking 110SEK ($15/£8). Bus: 7A, 7B, 1A, or 1B. **Amenities:** Restaurant; bar; sauna; limited room service; laundry service; dry cleaning; nonsmoking rooms; solarium. *In room:* TV, dataport, minibar, hair dryer.

Elite Marina Plaza ⓖⓖ   This is like a glittering palace at night, its reflection cast in the waters of Öresund. Marina Plaza is Helsingborg's most innovative and most talked-about hotel, and opens onto panoramic views. It's adjacent to the city's transportation hub, the Knutpunkten. The atrium-style lobby overflows with trees, rock gardens, and fountains. Midsize to spacious guest rooms line the inner walls of the hotel's atrium and have a color scheme of marine blue with nautical accessories, as befits its waterfront location. Bedrooms are attractively furnished, offering much comfort, and the bathrooms are state-of-the-art with both a tub and a shower. Even in winter the on-site dining and drinking facilities are the best in town, becoming even more so in summer when the Oceano BBQ opens with grilled meats and entertainment. Guests in the major restaurant, Aqua, can enjoy a first-rate cuisine while taking in views of the boat traffic and harbor life.

Kungstorget 6, S-251 10 Helsingborg. ⓒ 042/19-21-00. Fax 042/14-96-16. www.marinaplaza.elite.se. 190 units. 1,225SEK–1,795SEK ($169–$248/£89–£131) double; 1,575SEK–3,150SEK ($217–$435/£115–£230) suite. Midsummer discounts available. AE, DC, MC, V. Parking 140SEK ($19/£10). Bus: 41, 42, 43, or 44. **Amenities:** Restaurant; bar; pub; sauna; limited room service; laundry service/dry cleaning; nonsmoking rooms; rooms for those w/limited mobility. *In room:* TV, dataport, minibar, hair dryer, safe.

Hotel Helsingborg ⓖ   In the heart of town, this is a lovely old hotel with such luxuries from the past as marble stairs, but it has also kept abreast of the times, updating itself without destroying its classic lines. Of the three hotels that lie along this grand avenue, this one is closest to the city's medieval tourist attraction, the Kärnan. It has a heroic neoclassical frieze and three copper-sheathed towers, and occupies four floors of what used to be a bank headquarters, dating from 1901. The high-ceilinged rooms are pleasantly modernized and flooded with sunlight on many a summer day. They retain a certain Art Nouveau look, with strong colors and many decorative touches. All rooms have been upgraded and renovated, with functional bathrooms equipped with tub/shower combos.

Stortorget 20, Box 1171, S-252 23 Helsingborg. © 042/37-18-00. Fax 042/37-18-50. www.hotelhelsingborg.se. 56 units. 895SEK–1,495SEK ($124–$206/£65–£109) double; 1,100SEK–1,800SEK ($152–$248/£80–£131) suite. Rates include breakfast. AE, DC, MC, V. Parking 90SEK ($12/£6.60). Bus: 7A, 7B, 1A, or 1B. **Amenities:** Restaurant; bar; sauna; laundry service/dry cleaning; nonsmoking rooms; rooms for those w/limited mobility. *In room:* TV, hair dryer, Wi-Fi.

Scandic Horisont   If you'd like to escape the traffic and the hysteria at the center of town, check into this more tranquil choice about a kilometer (½ mile) south of the ferryboat terminal. Hiding behind one of the most striking modern facades in town, this 1985 hotel offers free transportation Monday to Thursday (mainly for the benefit of its business clients) between its precincts and the center of town. Guest rooms are comfortably furnished and well accessorized, and come in various shapes. You can stay here at a moderate price or more expensively if your demands dictate that. Bathrooms are tiled and well maintained, each with tub and shower. A carefully crafted international menu is served at the on-site restaurant, along with Swedish classics.

Gustav Adolfs Gate 47, S-250 02 Helsingborg. © **800/780-7234** in the U.S. and Canada, or 042/49-52-100. Fax 042/49-52-111. www.scandic-hotels.com. 164 units. 960SEK–1,660SEK ($132–$229/£70–£117) double; 2,400SEK ($331/£175) suite. Rates include breakfast. AE, DC, MC, V. Free parking. Bus: 7B, 1B, or 2. **Amenities:** Restaurant; bar; Jacuzzi; sauna; laundry service; dry cleaning; nonsmoking rooms; rooms for those w/limited mobility. *In room:* TV, dataport, hair dryer, Wi-Fi.

INEXPENSIVE

Hotell Linnéa ⋆ *(Finds)*   Conveniently located a few yards from where ferries from Denmark pull in, this is a small hotel that occupies a pink Italianate house, built in 1897. Guest rooms are appealingly outfitted, with comfortable beds and high-quality furnishings that include tasteful reproductions of 19th-century antiques. Bathrooms are small but adequate and come mostly with tub/shower combinations. Only breakfast is served, but many reliable dining choices are close by.

Prästgatan 4, S-252 24 Helsingborg. © 042/37-24-00. Fax 042/37-24-29. www.hotell-linnea.se. 28 units. July–Aug and Fri–Sat year-round 895SEK–1,120SEK ($124–$155/£65–£82) double; rest of year 1,025SEK–1,330SEK ($141–$184/£75–£95) double, 1,400SEK–1,680SEK ($193–$232/£102–£123) suite. Rates include breakfast. AE, DC, MC, V. Parking 110SEK ($15/£7.70). Bus: 7A or 7B. **Amenities:** Breakfast room; bar; laundry service; dry cleaning. *In room:* TV.

Hotell Viking   In the center of town, less than 2 blocks north of the Drottninggatan, this hotel looks more historic, more cozy, and a bit more artfully cluttered than many of its more formal and streamlined competitors. It was built during the late 19th century as a row of shops where the owners usually lived upstairs from their businesses. Today, after a radical remodeling, you'll find a carefully preserved sense of history; a pale color scheme of gray, beige, and ocher; and hands-on management from the resident owners. The individually designed bedrooms are cozy, neat, and functional. Some of the rooms are superior to the regular doubles, and these go first, complete with adjustable beds, a computer, a stereo, and plasma screen TV. Bathrooms are a bit small, but adequately outfitted.

Fågelsångsgatan 1, S-252 20 Helsingborg. © 042/14-44-20. Fax 042/18-43-20. www.hotellviking.se. 40 units. Mid-June to July and Fri–Sun year-round 895SEK ($124/£65) double; rest of year 1,435SEK ($198/£105) double. Rates include breakfast. AE, DC, MC, V. Free parking. Bus: 7A, 7B, 1A, or 1B. **Amenities:** Breakfast room; bar; laundry service; dry cleaning; nonsmoking rooms; rooms for those w/limited mobility. *In room:* TV, minibar, hair dryer, Wi-Fi.

WHERE TO DINE

Gastro ⋆⋆ CONTINENTAL/FRENCH   In the wake of the closure of the two finest restaurants in Helsingborg, this first-class choice has emerged as the best. It's set within a modern, big-windowed building of yellow brick overlooking the city's historic core. Within a room decorated with birchwood veneer, pale tones, and a medley of riveting modern paintings, you can enjoy specialties based on Swedish ingredients, prepared using Mediterranean culinary techniques. Menu items vary with the season, but our favorites are pan-fried scallops with sun-dried and marinated tomatoes, served with a terrine of green peas; or a superb fried breast of duckling with onions, carrots, and prosciutto. Expect lots of fresh fish from the straits of Helsingborg and the Baltic, and lots of savoir-faire from the well-versed, attentive staff.

Södra Storg 11–13. (℃ 042/24-34-70. Reservations recommended. Main courses 120SEK–340SEK ($17–$47/£8.75–£25). AE, DC, MC, V. Mon–Sat 7–10pm. Closed July. Bus: 11.

Pålsjö Krog SWEDISH   For traditional Swedish cooking, we head here in spite of its inconvenient location. A 10-minute drive north of the center of Helsingborg, this yellow wood-sided building was originally constructed around 1900 as a bathhouse beside the beach. In the late 1990s, it was transformed into a cozy Swedish restaurant, the kind of place where local families come to enjoy recipes that haven't changed very much since the end of World War II. Within a large dining room painted in tones of pale yellow and decorated with hints of Art Deco, you'll get food items that include grilled pepper steak, sirloin with béarnaise sauce, poached Swedish salmon with dill sauce, and aromatic local mussels steamed with herbs in white wine. Drinkers and smokers appreciate the cozy aperitif bar near the entrance, where cigars are welcomed and the staff can propose a wide assortment of after-dinner cognacs.

Drottninggatan 151. (℃ 042/14-97-30. Reservations recommended. Main courses 149SEK–218SEK ($21–$30/£11–£16). AE, DC, MC, V. Daily 11:30am–2:30pm and 6–10pm.

SS Swea ☾ SEAFOOD/SWEDISH   Come here for some of the best and freshest fish and shellfish at the port, both of which are presented in a wide-ranging menu appealing to most tastes. This restaurant at Kungstorget is a ship that's furnished like the luxury cruisers of yore. It offers market-fresh food deftly handled by skilled chefs and served in a cozy ambience by a thoughtful waitstaff. Appetizers might range from iced gazpacho to a Greek salad studded with feta cheese. However, most diners prefer one of the fish starters, such as the delectable smoked salmon. Fish platters, which depend on the catch of the day, also dominate the menu. Our juicy flounder, served with bacon-flavored mushrooms, was superb in every way. The meat eater will find comfort in a classic pepper steak with *pommes frites* (french fries). You might also try the filet mignon, laced with Black and White scotch.

Kungstorget. (℃ 042/13-15-16. Reservations required. Main courses 170SEK–255SEK ($23–$35/£12–£19); fixed-price 3-course menu 265SEK ($37/£19). AE, DC, MC, V. Mon–Thurs 6–10pm; Fri 6–11pm; Sat 1–11pm; Sun 1–8pm.

HELSINGBORG AFTER DARK

Helsingborg has had its own city symphony orchestra since 1912. In 1932, its **Concert Hall,** or **Konserthuset,** opened at Drottninggatan 19 (℃ **042/10-42-70**). One of the finest examples of 1930s Swedish functionalism, today the hall is still the venue for performances by the 50-piece orchestra. The season opens in the middle of August with a 10-day Festspel, a festival with a different theme every year. Tickets are available at the **Helsingborg Stadsteater City Theater,** Karl Johans Gata (℃ **042/10-68-00** or 042/10-68-10), which dates from 1817. Today's city theater is one of the most modern in Europe; of course, performances are in Swedish.

With a decor that includes crystal chandeliers and lots of original paintings (which are often rotated with works by various artists), **Marina Nightclub,** Kungstorget 6

(© 042/19-21-00), is set within the Hotel Marina Plaza. It admits only clients 24 or older. It's open Friday and Saturday 11pm till around 5am.

An English-inspired pub that draws a busy and convivial crowd is **Telegrafen,** Norra Storgatan 14 (© 042/18-14-50), where live music, especially jazz, is presented on either of two levels devoted to maintaining a cozy environment for drinking, chatting, and flirting. Live-music enthusiasts should also consider an evening at one of the largest jazz venues in Sweden, **Jazzklubben** ★, Nedre Långvinkelsgatan 22 (© 042/18-49-00). Keynote nights include Wednesday, Friday, and Saturday, when live Dixieland, blues, Celtic ballads, and progressive jazz are featured beginning around 8:30pm. Most other nights, based on a schedule that varies with the season and the whims of the staff, the place functions as a conventional bar.

3 Malmö ★★

285km (177 miles) S of Gothenburg, 620km (384 miles) SW of Stockholm

Now that it's linked to the Continent via Denmark with the bridge over Öresund, Malmö is taking on an increased sophistication. We find each visit more appealing than the one before. Once the staid old capital of Skåne, it is today a vibrant, modern city with a definite youth orientation.

Nothing seems to evoke Malmö's entry into the 21st century more than the avant-garde and controversial **"Turning Torso"** ★★★, rising over the Western Harbor. Sweden's tallest building, rising 190m (624 ft.), consists of nine cubes with a total of 54 floors with a 90-degree twist from base to top. The apartment building is the creation of architect Santiago Calatrava and was inspired by his sculpture of the same name.

If you can, allow at least 2 days for Malmö, Sweden's third largest city. Malmö still doesn't have the attractions of Gothenburg, but the old city, dating from the 13th century, makes a good base for exploring the attractions of western Skåne. Others prefer to use ancient Lund (covered later).

From early days, Malmö (pronounced *mahl*-mer) prospered because of its location on a sheltered bay. In the 16th century, when it was the second-largest city in Denmark, it vied with Copenhagen for economic and cultural leadership. Reminders of that age are **Malmöhus Castle** (see below), the **Town Hall,** and the **Stortorget,** plus several homes of rich burghers. Malmö has been a Swedish city since the end of a bloody war in 1658, when the Treaty of Roskilde incorporated the province of Skåne into Sweden.

ESSENTIALS

GETTING THERE   By Plane   Malmö's airport (© 040/613-11-00) is at Sturup, 30km (19 miles) southeast of the city. It receives international flights from London, plus flights from cities within Sweden and Stockholm (trip time: 1 hr.). Three airlines that serve the airport are **Malmö Aviation** (© 040/660-29-00), **SAS** (© 770/727-727), Flyme (© 02476/270675), and Ryanair (© 0900/2020240), which offers flights to London and points within continental Europe. The city's major international link to the world is Copenhagen Airport at Copenhagen, to which Malmö is connected via the Öresund Bridge.

By Train   Railway service is frequent between Gothenburg and Malmö (trip time: 3½ hr.), and since the construction of the bridge, rail service is now direct, quick, and easy to both central Copenhagen and its airport. From Helsingborg to Malmö (trip time: 45 min.), trains leave hourly. From Stockholm, travel is 4½ hours aboard the high-speed X-2000 train, 6 to 7 hours aboard slower trains. There also is train service between Copenhagen and Malmö. Trains depart from the central railway stations of both cities at 20-minute intervals, stopping en route at the Copenhagen airport. The cost each way between the centers of each city is 90SEK ($12/£6.60).

By Bus   Two buses daily make the 4½-hour run from Gothenburg to Malmö. For bus information, call **Travelshop,** Skeppsbron 10, P.O. Box 211, S-21120 Malmö (© **040/33-05-70**). They specialize in the sale of bus tickets within Sweden and to other points within Europe as well.

By Car   From Helsingborg, motorists can head southeast along E-6 directly into the center of Malmö.

VISITOR INFORMATION   The **Malmö Tourist Office,** Central Station Skeppsbron 2 (© **040/34-12-00;** www.malmo.se), is open as follows: May to September, Monday to Friday 9am to 7pm, and Saturday and Sunday 10am to 5pm; October to April, Monday to Friday 9am to 5pm, Saturday and Sunday 10am to 3pm.

GETTING AROUND   It's easy to walk around the city center, although you may need to rely on public transport if you're branching out to sights on the periphery. An individual bus ticket costs 15SEK ($2.05/£1.10) and is valid for 1 hour. You also can purchase a 200SEK ($28/£15) magnetic card, which offers a slight reduction on the fare and can be used by several passengers at the same time. Individual tickets are sold aboard the bus by the driver. Discount cards can be bought or refilled at the automated vending machines in the Central Station and at other strategic transport junctions throughout the city.

SEEING THE SIGHTS

The **Malmö Card,** which is available from the Malmö Tourist Office, entitles visitors free admission to most of the city's museums during the period of its validity. It also grants free parking and free bus travel within the city limits. A card that's valid for 1 day costs 130SEK ($18/£9.50); one that's valid for 2 days goes for 160SEK ($22/£12); one that's valid for 3 days is 190SEK ($26/£14). An adult who has a Malmö card can be accompanied, with no additional charge, by two children up to 16 years of age.

You have to begin your exploration somewhere, and we find that the best place to do that is around **Stortorget** 🦋, the main square of Malmö, dating from the 1530s. The vast square was more of a market square than it is today. In its center stands an equestrian statue of King Karl X Gustav, who took Skåne back from the Danes. That event in 1658 is also commemorated with a fountain that's one of the most imaginative in Scandinavia and includes a nightingale, the symbol of Malmö.

Bordering the eastern side of the square is the **Rådhuset (Town Hall),** once imbued with a look of Renaissance splendor in 1546. It has undergone major changes over the years, most notably in the 1860s when Helgo Zettervall redesigned the facade in the Dutch Renaissance style, which is more or less what you'll see today. Unless you have official business, the interior cannot be visited except for the cellar restaurant (see Rådhuskällern; p. 503).

Nearby lies **Lilla Torg** 🦋🦋, Malmö's most charming square and the centerpiece of much of its nightlife and cafes. This attractive, cobble-covered square ringed with fine half-timbered buildings dating from the 16th to the 18th centuries looks like a film set. In addition to its desirability as a place to people-watch, many handicraft shops are found here. For many centuries this was the bustling open-air marketplace of Malmö; however, in the early 20th century, a covered market (the sturdy brick-built Saluhallen) replaced the open-air booths and stalls. Today, the Saluhallen houses a small-scale shopping mall with handicrafts, foodstuffs, and a number of restaurants, the best of which are recommended in "Where to Dine," later in this chapter. While on this square, check out the **Form Design Centre** at Lilla Torg 9 (see below).

Malmöhus Slott (Malmöhus Castle) ᏨᏨ   There is so much to see and do here, that we always set aside a minimum of 3 hours. If you're very rushed, skip all but the Konstmuseet, Skåne's great treasure trove of art. This impressive fortress, and Malmö's greatest monument, was founded in the 15th century. The castle is a 10- to 15-minute walk west of the Stortorget and is split into the following divisions:

Konstmuseet ᏨᏨ   These second-floor galleries boast a collection of old Scandinavian masters, especially those from southern Sweden. Notable among the artists is Carl Fredrik Hill (1849–1911), one of Sweden's most revered landscape painters and a forerunner of European modernism. There's also a wonderful series of **Russian oil paintings** ᏨᏨ, created in the 1890–1914 revolutionary period. This is the largest collection of such works outside Russia. Of almost equal intrigue is the museum's collection of **Nordic Art** ᏨᏨ, painted in the volatile 1920s and '30s.

Naturmuseum   This museum hardly stacks up against similar museums in New York or London, but you might give it a look if time remains. It covers the geology of Skåne including its flora and fauna. Its most compelling exhibits are an **aquarium** and a **tropicarium** in the basement.

Stadsmuseum   The city museum is a disappointment. City officials have moved some artifacts from their "attic" to display here, plus, all the exhibits are in Swedish.

Kommendanthuset   Part of the 18th-century arsenal, this member of the museum cluster lies across the street from the castle. Check out what's going on here at the time of your visit, as this house is host to a frequently changing roster of traveling exhibits, many related to photography.

Near Kommendanthuset is the **Teknikens och Sjöfartens Hus** (Science and Maritime Museum). Transportation history from the steam engine to the jet can be traced here.

Malmöhusvägen. ⓒ **040/341 000.** Free admission with Malmö Card. All-inclusive ticket 40SEK ($5.50/£2.90), 10SEK ($1.40/75p) ages 7–15; free 6 and under. Sept–May noon–4pm, June–Aug 10am–4pm.

Sankt Petri kyrka ᏨᏨᏨ   Malmö doesn't possess a great cathedral (for that, you have to travel to Lund [discussed later]), but it does have a grand church, lying a block east of the Rådhuset (see above). Dark and a bit foreboding on the exterior, it is light and airy within. This Gothic church originated in the 14th century, when Malmö was under the control of the Hanseatic League, and was modeled on Marienkirche, a famous church in Lübeck, Germany. Other than the slender pillars and supporting ogive vaulting, the church's most stunning feature is its **Krämarkapellet** ᏨᏨ, or tradesmen's chapel, from the 1400s. Amazingly, the original artwork remains. At the Reformation, the artwork here was viewed as "redundant," and the chapel was sealed off, which, in effect, protected its paintings from the overzealous "restoration" of the reformers. Look for the impressive New Testament figures surrounded by decorative foliage on the vaulted ceiling. Also notice the tall retable from 1611 and an exquisitely carved black limestone and sandstone pulpit from 1599.

Göran Olsgatan. ⓒ **040/35-90-43.** Free admission. Mon–Fri 10am–4pm; Sat 10am–6pm; Sun 10am–6pm.

Malmö Konsthall/Art Gallery One of Europe's largest contemporary art centers, this museum hosts exhibitions of avant-garde and experimental artwork—chicken blood or dung on canvas—but also appreciates the classics of modern art as well. In our view, no other venue in southern Sweden so effectively mingles contemporary architecture with modern paintings. With a rich core of art by both modern masters and cutting-edge painters, it's a visual feast for anyone who appreciates recent developments in painting and sculpture. It's unpredictable what will be on parade at the time of your visit.

S:t Johannesgasse 7. © 040/34-12-93. www.konsthall.malmo.se. Free admission. Daily 11am–5pm (until 9pm Wed).

A NEARBY ATTRACTION

Svaneholm 🏰🏰 Lying 40km (25 miles) to the east of Malmö via E-65, this is an impressive Renaissance castle from 1530. The province of Skåne is known for its castles, and this is the best one to visit while based in Malmö. Many aristocratic families have lived here, but the castle's most colorful character was Baron Rutger Macklean (1742–1816), who introduced crop rotation to Sweden. The castle was partially converted into an Italian-style palace. Today it houses a museum of paintings, furnishings, and tools dating primarily from the 18th and 19th centuries. The establishment is owned by the Svaneholm Castle Cooperative Society Ltd. For information, write **Svaneholm Museum,** S-274 00 Skurup (© **0411/400-12**).

Admission to the castle is 25SEK ($3.45/£1.80) for adults and 5SEK (70¢/35p) for children 6 to 14 years old. It's open May, June, and August Tuesday to Sunday 10am to 5pm; July daily 10am to 5pm; September Wednesday to Sunday 11am to 4pm. The castle is open other times upon request. An on-site restaurant (© **0411/450-40**) serves regional specialties. Reaching Svaneholm is difficult by public transportation; a train from Malmö stops at Skurup, but it's a walk of about 3km (1¾ miles) from there. Therefore, many visitors opt to go by taxi the rest of the way. During the summer, the castle offers free transportation from Skurup, but you must call 1 hour in advance.

SHOPPING

Malmö's main pedestrian shopping street is **Södergatan,** which runs south of Stortorget toward the canal. Nearby, at the 16th-century Lilla Torg, a charming 16th-century antique square, you can visit the **Form Design Centre** (© **040/664-51-50**). It combines a museum-like exhibition space with boutiques selling upscale handicrafts, including Swedish textiles by the yard, woodcarvings, and all manner of other crafts.

Established in 1927, **Juvelerare Hugo Nilsson,** Södra Tullgatan 2 (© **040/12-65-92**), features some of the most famous names in Danish jewelry making, including Georg Jensen, Rauff, and Ole Lynggaard. Jewelry by Finnish designers such as Lapponia is also sold.

You'll find an unusual collection of Nordic arts and crafts at **Älgamark,** Ö. Rönneholmsvägen 4 (© **040/97-49-60**). It carries Viking jewelry (replicas in pewter, bronze, silver, and gold), along with handicrafts from Swedish Lapland. Traditional pendants, bracelets, and knives are also for sale.

One of Sweden's leading furriers is **Mattssons Päls,** Norra Vallgatan 98 (© **040/12-55-33**). Saga mink coats and jackets are the most luxurious buys, but Mattssons has a full range of fine furs at prices lower than you'll see in the United States. In the boutique are fur-lined poplins and accessories, all tax-free for tourists. The store is 5 minutes on foot from the Central Station and the Copenhagen boats.

Finally, if you haven't found what you're looking for in the specialty shops, try **Hansa,** Stora Nygatan 50 (② **040/770-00**). It's a shopping complex with more than 40 shops, cafes, and restaurants. The latest fashions and items for the home are among the many specialties featured here. However, most foreign visitors come by to check out its selection of Swedish souvenirs and handicrafts.

WHERE TO STAY
EXPENSIVE

Hilton Malmö City 🏨🏨🏨   The city's most visible luxury hotel rises 20 stories from a position in the commercial heart of town, making it the third tallest building in Malmö, but hardly competition for the "Turning Torso" (see above). Originally conceived in 1989 as a Sheraton, then transformed into a Scandic Hotel, and now under a member of Hilton International, it boasts sweeping views of the Öresund region from almost all of its bedrooms. The top three floors contain only upgraded "executive level" rooms and suites and a well-engineered health club. Many of its guests are business travelers. The spacious rooms are tastefully and comfortably appointed, with light colors and many electronic amenities. The bathrooms are luxurious and equipped with tub/shower combinations. Suites are the best in town, with kitchenettes and large sitting areas, and some of them have their own Jacuzzi.

Triangeln 2, S-200 10 Malmö. ② **040/693-47-00.** Fax 040/693-47-11. www.hilton.com. 214 units. Sun–Thurs 2,290SEK ($316/£167) double; Fri–Sat 1,190SEK ($164/£87) double; 4,900SEK ($676/£358) suite. Rates include breakfast. AE, DC, MC, V. Parking 95SEK ($13/£6.95). Bus: 14 or 17. **Amenities:** Restaurant; bar; fitness center; sauna; business services; 24-hr. room service; babysitting; laundry service/dry cleaning; nonsmoking rooms; rooms for those w/limited mobility. *In room:* A/C, TV, minibar, hair dryer, iron, Wi-Fi.

Noble House 🏨🏨   Elegance at a moderate price is the keynote here. One of the most modern and up-to-date hotels in town—and certainly one of the most glamorous—is named after the best-selling novel by James Clavell (the former owner was a great devotee of his writings). The comfortable pastel-colored rooms are decorated with copies of early-20th-century Swedish paintings. Because of the four-story hotel's convenient location in the town center, its quietest rooms face the interior courtyard. Each room has a standard hotel-size bathroom with a tub/shower.

Gustav Adolfs Torg 47, S-211 39 Malmö. ② **040/664-30-00.** Fax 040/664-30-50. www.hkchotels.se. 130 units. June 24–Aug 15 and Fri–Sat year-round 995SEK ($137/£73) double, 1,595SEK ($220/£116) suite; rest of year 1,495SEK ($206/£109) double, 2,445SEK ($337/£178) suite. Rates include breakfast. AE, DC, MC, V. Parking 160SEK ($22/£12). Bus: 1, 2, 5, 6, 7, or 8. **Amenities:** Restaurant, breakfast room; bar; sauna; laundry service/dry cleaning; nonsmoking rooms; rooms for those w/limited mobility. *In room:* TV, dataport, minibar, hair dryer (in some), safe.

Radisson SAS Hotel 🏨🏨   This chain-run hotel competes with the Hilton for the same business clientele. This is a viable alternative and is also a suitable choice for vacationers. The Radisson SAS contains tastefully decorated rooms with elegant bathrooms equipped with tub/shower combos. Built in 1988, the seven-story hotel is only a 5-minute walk from the train station, which provides transportation to Copenhagen in only 40 minutes. As an added convenience, the hotel bus stops nearby. If you don't want to go out at night, try the hotel's excellent Thott Restaurant, serving both traditional Swedish dishes and international specialties.

Östergatan 10, S-211 Malmö. ② **800/333-3333** or 040/698-40-00. Fax 040/698-40-01. www.radissonsas.com. 229 units. June 5–Aug 5 1,390SEK–1,690SEK ($192–$233/£101–£123) double; Aug 6–June 4 Mon–Thurs 2,095SEK–2,395SEK ($289–$331/£153–£175) double; year-round Fri–Sun 1,390SEK–1,690SEK ($192–$233/£101–£123) double; from 3,000SEK ($414/£219) suite. Rates include breakfast. AE, DC, MC, V. Parking 160SEK ($22/£12). Bus: 14 or

17. **Amenities:** Restaurant; bar; sauna; 24-hr. room service; babysitting; laundry service/dry cleaning; nonsmoking rooms; rooms for those w/limited mobility. *In room:* TV, minibar, hair dryer, Wi-Fi.

MODERATE

Elite Hotel Savoy *Set immediately across the square from the railway station, this landmark hotel has figured prominently in Malmö history, as its origins date from the 14th century. There is modernization here yet respect for the classic decor. It boasts some of the most plushly decorated accommodations in Sweden. Rooms contain champagne-colored upholstery, cabriole-legged or Chippendale-style furniture, excellent beds, and all the extras of a deluxe hotel. Well-maintained bathrooms come in a wide variety of sizes, with tub/shower combos. In the hotel restaurant, you can order from an international menu, perhaps stopping for a before-dinner beer in the British-style pub, the Bishop's Arms.

Norra Vallgatan 62, S-201 80 Malmö. © **040/66-44-800.** Fax 040/66-44-850. www.savoy.elite.se. 109 units. June 19–Aug 9 and Fri–Sat year-round 800SEK–1,100SEK ($110–$152/£58–£80) double; rest of year 1,700SEK–1,900SEK ($235–$262/£124–£139) double; 2,400SEK ($331/£175) suite. Rates include breakfast. AE, DC, MC, V. Parking 180SEK ($25/£13). Bus: 14 or 17. **Amenities:** Restaurant; bar; fitness center; sauna; limited room service; laundry service/dry cleaning; nonsmoking rooms. *In room:* TV, dataport, minibar, hair dryer, safe, iron.

Hotell Baltzar *(Finds)* Around 1900, an entrepreneur who had made a fortune selling chocolate moved into a private home whose turrets, towers, and fanciful ornamentation evoked a stone-carved confection. Several decades later, when it became a hotel, it expanded into one of the neighboring buildings. Today you'll find a somewhat eccentric hotel with many charming corners and cubbyholes, and a reception area set one floor upstairs from street level. Grace notes include frescoed ceilings (in some of the public areas and also in about 25% of the bedrooms), antiques, and elaborate draperies in some of the public areas. The comfortable, high-ceilinged guest rooms were upgraded with the kind of furnishings and parquet floors that would suit a prosperous private home. The medium-size bathrooms are impeccably maintained and equipped with tub/shower combinations. The location on an all-pedestrian downtown street, about a block south of the heartbeat Stortorget, keeps things relatively quiet inside. Breakfast is the only meal served.

Södergatan 20, S-211 24 Malmö. © **040/665-5700.** Fax 040/665-5710. www.baltzarhotel.se. 40 units. Mon–Thurs 1,300SEK–1,800SEK ($179–$248/£95–£131) double; Fri–Sun 850SEK–950SEK ($117–$131/£62–£69) double. Rates include breakfast. AE, DC, MC, V. Free parking. Bus: 10. **Amenities:** Breakfast room; 24-hr. room service; laundry service/dry cleaning; nonsmoking rooms. *In room:* TV, minibar, hair dryer, safe.

Rica Hotel Malmö *Built in 1914, with many subsequent changes and improvements, this hotel lies on Malmö's main square, facing the Town Hall, a short walk from the railway station. In 2005, most of the guest rooms were rebuilt in a tasteful modern format, with the remainder scheduled for a makeover during 2007. Originally, this hotel was owned by the Salvation Army, which strictly forbade the consumption of alcohol on the premises, but since its sale to the Rica chain, all of that is a distant memory, and there's now a bar adjacent to the lobby. The rooms are generally spacious, but bathrooms tend to be cramped though well maintained with tub/shower combinations.

Stortorget 15 S-211 22 Malmö. © **040/660-95-50.** Fax 040/660-95-59. www.rica.se. 82 units. Mon–Thurs 1,495SEK–1,645SEK ($206–$227/£109–£120) double; Fri–Sun 995SEK–1,095SEK ($137–$151/£73–£80) double. Rates include breakfast. AE, DC, MC, V. Parking 130SEK ($18/£9.50). Bus: 6 or 10. **Amenities:** Breakfast room; lounge; sauna; laundry service/dry cleaning; nonsmoking rooms. *In room:* TV, minibar, hair dryer, Wi-Fi.

Scandic Hotel Kramer ⓕ   A top-to-bottom redesign extended the shelf life of this long-time favorite. On the side of the town's main square, this château-style twin-towered building is one of Malmö's landmark hotels. Built in 1875 and enlarged in the mid-1980s with the construction of a modern wing, it was renovated between 1992 and 1994, and again postmillennium. The rooms were redecorated with an old-fashioned sense of nostalgia. Each has a marble bathroom with a tub/shower, dark paneling, curved walls, and kitschy 1930s-style accessories.

Stortorget 7, S-201 21 Malmö. ⓒ 040/693-54-00. Fax 040/693-54-11. www.scandic-hotels.com. 113 units. Sun–Thurs 1,300SEK–2,250SEK ($179–$311/£95–£164) double; Fri–Sat 1,350SEK ($186/£99) double. Rates include breakfast. AE, DC, MC, V. Parking 190SEK ($26/£14). Bus: 14, 17, or 20. **Amenities:** Restaurant; bar; sauna; limited room service; laundry service/dry cleaning; nonsmoking rooms. *In room:* TV, minibar, hair dryer, dataport.

Teaterhotellet   The only negative aspect of this hotel is its banal-looking 1960s-era facade; it's no uglier than hundreds of other contemporaneous Scandinavian buildings, but it isn't particularly inviting or pleasing. Inside, however, you'll find a cozy, tasteful, and colorful establishment that attracts many repeat clients. Appealing touches include beige and tawny-colored marble floors, lots of elegant hardwood paneling, lacquered walls in neutral tones of pale amber and beige, and spots of vibrant colors in the guest rooms (especially jewel tones of red and green) that perk up even the grayest of Swedish winter days. Rooms are renovated with new furniture, plus restored bathrooms with showers and tubs. Less than a kilometer (about ½ mile) south of the railway station, the hotel is near a verdant park and the Stadsteater. Only breakfast is served, but you can usually get someone to bring you a sandwich and coffee.

Rönngatan 3, S-211 47 Malmö. ⓒ **040/665-58-00**. Fax 040/665-58-10. www.teaterhotellet.se. 44 units. Sun–Thurs 1,300SEK–1,800SEK ($179–$248/£95–£131) double; Fri–Sat 850SEK–950SEK ($117–$131/£62–£69) double. Rates include breakfast. AE, DC, MC, V. Parking 125SEK ($17/£9.15). Bus: 5. **Amenities:** Breakfast room; bar; limited room service; laundry service/dry cleaning; nonsmoking rooms. *In room:* TV, minibar (in some), hair dryer, Wi-Fi.

INEXPENSIVE

Elite Hotel Residens ⓕ *Value*   Though it's not a market leader like its sibling, the Elite Hotel Savoy, this is still a recommendable choice. In 1987, a team of local investors enlarged the beige and brown-sided premises of a historic 1517 inn with the addition of a brick-and-stone structure erected. The interconnected structures provide solid, comfortable, and upscale lodgings near the railroad station. Except for certain corners where an effort was made to duplicate a woodsy-looking men's club, many of the public areas are outfitted in a glossy, modern setup with lots of mirrors, touches of chrome, and polished marble floors. Guest rooms, each renovated between 2006 and 2007, are traditionally outfitted and fairly spacious. They have hardwood floors or wall-to-wall carpeting, well-upholstered furnishings, and, in some cases, Oriental carpets. The medium-size bathrooms are equipped with tub/showers. Windows are large and double-insulated against noise from the urban landscape outside.

Adelgatan 7, S-211 22 Malmö. ⓒ **040/664-48-90**. Fax 040/664-48-95. www.elite.se. 69 units. June to mid-Aug and Fri–Sat year-round 995SEK–1,095SEK ($137–$151/£73–£80) double; rest of year 1,495SEK–1,645SEK ($206–$227/£109–£120) double. Rates include breakfast. AE, DC, MC, V. Parking 180SEK ($25/£13). Bus: 2, 4. **Amenities:** Breakfast room; limited room service; laundry service; dry cleaning; on-site sauna and free access to a nearby fitness club, nonsmoking rooms. *In room:* TV, dataport (in some), minibar, hair dryer, iron, safe (in some).

WHERE TO DINE
EXPENSIVE
Årstiderna I Kockska Huset ⓕⓕⓕ SWEDISH/INTERNATIONAL   The best restaurant in Malmö lies behind a red brick facade on a "perpetually shadowed"

medieval street in the city's historic core. It was built in the north German style in 1523 as the home and political headquarters of the Danish-appointed governor of Malmö, Jürgen Kock. In its own richly Gothic way, it's the most unusual restaurant setting in town, with vaulted brick ceilings, severe-looking medieval detailing, and an undeniable sense of the posh life. Owners Marie and Wilhelm Pieplow have created an environment where the prime ministers of Sweden and Finland, as well as dozens of politicians, artists, and actors, have dined on exceedingly good food. Menu items change with the seasons; the establishment's name, Årstiderna, translates from Swedish as "The Four Seasons." Likely to be featured are scallops and Norwegian lobster "du jour," gin-cured salmon with asparagus and melted, mustard-flavored butter; grilled salted cod with clams and a lemon-flavored beurre blanc; and raspberry and licorice-glazed venison with gravy and a ragout of mushrooms. All of these dishes recommended are prepared with infinite care using the best and most market fresh of ingredients.

Frans Suellsgatan 3. © **040/23-09-10** or 040/70320. Reservations recommended. Main courses 200SEK–355SEK ($28–$49/£15–£26); fixed-price lunch 95SEK–185SEK ($13–$26/£5.95–£14); fixed-price dinner 330SEK–500SEK ($46–$69/£24–£37). AE, DC, MC, V. Mon–Fri 11:30am–11pm; Sat 5–11pm. Bus: 7, 14, or 31.

Johan P ⭑⭑ *Finds* FISH/SEAFOOD   The most appealing seafood in Malmö is prepared and served in this artfully simple, mostly white dining room, whose terraces spill, during clement weather, onto the cobble-covered street on one side, and into the corridors of the Saluhall (food market) on the other. The result is a bustling but almost pristine setting, where the freshness of the seafood is the main draw. Menu items are prepared fresh every day, based on whatever is available within the Saluhallen, and the kitchens are open to view to whoever happens to be passing by. Some of our most memorable meals in Malmö included brimming bowlfuls of this restaurant's fish soups, accompanied with fresh bread and a salad; half-lobster with lemon-flavored mayonnaise; lobster-studded monkfish with vinegar sauce; and grilled veal with morels in white sauce with a compote of onions. Dessert might include a mousse made with bitter white chocolate, served with dark-chocolate madeleines and coffee sauce.

Saluhallen, Landbygatan 3. © **040/97-18-18.** Reservations recommended. Daily specials (lunchtime only) 82SEK ($11/£6); main courses 180SEK–350SEK ($25–$48/£13–£26); 3-course fixed-price menu 375SEK–475SEK ($52–$66/£27–£35). AE, DC, MC, V. Mon–Fri 11:30am–10pm (last order); Sat noon–midnight. Bus: 14 or 17.

Kramer Gastronomie ⭑ CONTINENTAL/FRENCH   This restaurant serves the best food of any hotel dining room in Malmö. There's an upscale, vaguely baroque-looking bar that's separated from the brown and off-white dining room with a leaded glass divider, and an attention to cuisine that brings a conservative, not particularly flashy clientele back again and again. The composition of the fixed-price menus changes every week. The chef is dedicated to his job, personally shopping for market-fresh ingredients. Menu items include shots of shellfish bouillon served with Parmesan chips and cilantro salsa; scallops with grilled tuna and bacon; and char-grilled halibut with glazed turnips, truffle butter, and dill oil. Pastas here are upscale and esoteric, including a version with spinach, crayfish, fried filet of sole, and dill sauce.

In the Scandic Hotel Kramer, Stortorget 7. © **040/693-54-00.** Reservations recommended. Main courses 200SEK–350SEK ($28–$48/£15–£26); 3-course fixed-price menu 340SEK ($47/£25). AE, DC, MC, V. Mon–Fri 5–11pm; Sat 6–11pm. Bar open till 1am. Bus: 10.

Wallman's Salonger ⭑ CONTINENTAL   Malmö's leading supper club and cabaret, painted a heady shade of Bordeaux red, is the most entertaining restaurant in the city—with an entertaining staff as well. It's configured like a dining and supper club, with views over a stage and dance floor upon which members of the staff—each an aspiring actor or at least a candidate for a job in the theater—will sing, dance, and amuse you with an array of songs and cabaret acts. Set menus are identified by names that include "Elvis Presley," "Judy Garland," and "Golden Hits." The finest examples include a catch of the week from the Baltic served with risotto verde and a tomato cassoulet; a cashew, chestnut, and prosciutto tart served with creamy roasted garlic; and an array of steaks, salads, seafood, veal, or pork dishes, plus vegetarian dishes. Dishes are usually flavorful and well prepared, but since most clients are watching the good-looking performers on stage or hitting the dance floor themselves, no one seems especially concerned. An evening here can get a bit pricey, but since it incorporates dining and entertainment, the relatively high tab seem realistic and understandable.

Generalsgatan 1. ✆ **040/74945** for reservations (before 5pm), or 040/970376 after 5pm. Reservations recommended. Mandatory cover charge of 60SEK–100SEK ($8.30–$14/£4.40–£7.30) for bar (i.e., nondining) clients after 8pm; mandatory cover charge of 150SEK–175SEK ($21–$24/£11–£13) for dining clients, depending on the location and sightlines of their table. 3-course fixed-price menus 479SEK–579SEK ($66–$80/£35–£42). AE, DC, MC, V. Wed–Sat 7:30pm–3am. Kitchen closes at 11pm. Closed May to mid-Aug. Bus: 5

MODERATE

Lemongrass ASIAN   When we begin to tire of a Swedish diet, we book a table here. Lemongrass is set in one large, spartan room, with sand-colored walls, clusters of exotic-looking plants and, tufted bunches of the lemon grass for which the restaurant was named. There's a bar where you can wait for your table if you have to and a menu that contains food items from Japan (including sushi), China, and Thailand. A staff member will help you coordinate a meal from disparate culinary styles in ways that you might have expected only in Los Angeles, London, or New York.

Grunbodgatan 9. ✆ **40/30-69-79.** Reservations recommended. Main courses 156SEK–210SEK ($22–$29/£11–£15); 7-course fixed-price menu 365SEK ($50/£27). AE, MC, V. Mon–Thurs 6pm–midnight; Fri–Sat 6pm–1am. Bus: 4.

Rådhuskällern *(Value)* SWEDISH   This is the most atmospheric place in Malmö, located in the cellar of the Town Hall. Even if you don't eat here, at least drop in for a drink in the pub or lounge. The severe exterior and labyrinth of underground vaults were built in 1546; the dark-vaulted dining room was used for centuries to store gold, wine, furniture, and food. Menu staples include halibut with lobster sauce, fried redfish with mango sauce, tournedos of beef with red wine sauce and creamed morels, and roast duck; and there's always an array of daily specials. Although the fare is first rate, it never overexcites the palate.

Kyrkogatan 5. ✆ **040/790-20.** Reservations recommended. Main courses 110SEK–215SEK ($15–$30/£8–£16); set menus 235SEK–325SEK ($32–$45/£17–£24). AE, DC, MC, V. Mon–Thurs 11:30am–2pm and 5–10:30pm; Fri 11:30am–2pm and 5–11pm; Sat 5–11pm. Closed July 1–Aug 21. Bus: 14 or 17.

INEXPENSIVE

Anno 1900 *(Finds)* SWEDISH   The name of this place gives a hint about its decor, which includes lots of antique woodwork and accessories from the heyday of the Industrial Revolution. There's a garden in back that's open during warm weather, and a world-traveled management team that seems to cherish the memories of their youthful heydays in New York City. Menu items derive from tried-and-true *husmannskost* classics: cauliflower soup, roasted pork with onion sauce, braised calf's liver, poached halibut with horseradish sauce, *frikadeller* (meatballs), and fried herring.

Norra Bultoftavagen 7. (℃) **040/18-47-47.** Reservations recommended. Main courses 100SEK–225SEK ($14–$31/£7.30–£16); fixed-price lunch 110SEK–195SEK ($15–$27/£8–£14). AE, DC, MC, V. Mon–Fri 11:15am–2pm; Thurs–Sat 6–11pm. Bus: 14 or 17.

Casa Mia ITALIAN   Venetian gondola moorings ornament the front terrace of this Nordic version of a neighborhood trattoria. Schmaltzy Neapolitan ballads are likely to be playing softly in the background, and your waiter is likely to address you in Italian. You might begin with a steaming bowl of stracciatella alla romana (egg-and-chicken soup) or the fish soup of the house, and then move on to penne with shrimp, basil, cream, and tomatoes; or spaghetti with seafood. Later you can dig into saltimbocca alla romana (veal with ham), roasted lamb with new potatoes, or an array of grilled meats with aromatic herbs. There are about a dozen types of pizzas on the menu, and pastries are offered for dessert. The food is not as good as what's served in a typical trattoria in northern Italy, but the cuisine is a refreshing change of pace. The staff works hard to maintain their Italian bravura amid the snows of Scandinavia.

Södergatan 12. (℃) **040/23-05-00.** Reservations recommended. Pastas and pizzas 67SEK–135SEK ($9.25–$19/£4.90–£9.85); main courses 159SEK–225SEK ($22–$31/£12–£16). AE, DC, MC, V. Mon–Sat noon–11pm; Sun noon–10pm. Bus: 14 or 17.

Restaurant B & B (Butik och Bar) SWEDISH/ITALIAN   This well-managed, relatively inexpensive bistro occupies a corner of the Saluhallen (food market; directly adjacent to the landmark square, Lilla Torget), which provides the fresh ingredients that go into each menu item. Within a simple, old-fashioned setting with glowing hardwood floors, pristine white walls, and a scattering of antiques that evoke the Sweden of long ago, you'll find flavorful, unpretentious food firmly rooted in the traditions of both Italy and Sweden. The menu includes Swedish staples such as Skagen toasts (with shrimp, hard-boiled eggs, and dill-flavored mayonnaise), elk steak with cloudberry sauce, and fried flank steak with roasted potatoes. Italian offerings include saltimbocca, various pastas, and grilled steaks with Mediterranean herbs.

Saluhallen, Landbygatan 1. (℃) **040/12-71-20.** Reservations recommended. Main courses 139SEK–179SEK ($19–$25/£10–£13); fixed-price lunch 65SEK–79SEK ($8.95–$11/£4.75–£5.75). AE, DC, MC, V. Mon–Sat noon–10pm. Bus: 2, 3, 4, 5, or 7.

MALMÖ AFTER DARK

Those seeking cultural activities after dark should get tickets to the **Malmö Symphony Orchestra** ✸✸✸, which is renowned across Europe. It performs at the Konserthus, Föreningsgatan 35 (℃ **040/630-45-06**). The tourist office distributes programs of its upcoming schedule as well as schedules and descriptions of other cultural events.

CAFES & BARS

For serious after-dark pursuits, many locals, especially young people, head for nearby Copenhagen. But for people-watching and chair-sitting, no place in Malmö is more popular than the Lilla Torg, with its plethora of outdoor cafes and restaurants that shelter an attractive mix of locals and visitors. The most popular of the dozen or so watering holes surrounding the square include Victor's and the Moosehead Bar.

At the **Moosehead Bar,** Lilla Torget 1 (℃ **040/12-04-23**), the clientele might seem a bit less concerned with etiquette and social niceties than the patrons of more sedate hangouts in other parts of the square. Its woodsy-looking, brick-lined decor and its emphasis on the biggest animal of the northern forests and tundra might remind you of a college student hangout in Maine, but the dialogues and the language being spoken is pure Swedish. Don't expect gourmet cuisine here: Everybody's favorite meal is a juicy burger made from either beef or moose meat (it's up to you to specify which), accompanied by a foaming mugful of Åbro, the local lager. Barring that, consider ordering a green melon or a pineapple daiquiri, priced at between 79SEK and 104SEK ($11–$14/£5.75–£7.60), depending on the size.

One of the most packed and long-lived hipster bars in Malmö is **Centiliter & Gram (Cl. & Gr.)** ⚡, Stortorget 17 (© **40/12-18-12**). When it was inaugurated in the mid-1990s, it was one of Malmö's hottest restaurants, but since then, although the food is still entirely respectable, it's best known, and most frequently patronized, as a night bar with a clientele aged 25 and up. It occupies an artfully minimalist herb-and-grass-colored space whose focal point is a central bar that rocks with an ongoing stream of electronic, usually house, music. Guests often stay to flirt long after their dishes have been cleared away, extending evenings into prolonged and highly social epics. Main courses cost from 75SEK to 225SEK ($10–$31/£5.45–£16), with an emphasis on salads, pastas, grilled fish and steaks, and light vegetarian fare. Despite the availability of food, the place is genuinely popular because of its bar and the social goings on that revolve around it. The establishment's name, incidentally, derives from wine (which is measured in centiliters) and food (which is measured in grams). Open Wednesday to Saturday 5pm to 3am.

A cozy and highly appealing replica of an Anglo-Irish pub is the **Bishop's Arms,** Norra Vallgatan 62 (© **040/664-48-88**). Located within the Elite Savoy Hotel, it serves generous platters, priced at 100SEK to 160SEK ($14–$22/£7.30–£12) each, of such Anglo and Celtic staples as fish and chips, burgers, buffalo wings, and pepper steaks, as well as some of the coldest beer in town. There's always a congenial crowd. As is common in the U.K., you'll place your drink and/or food order directly at the bar, and then a staff member will carry it to your table. Open Monday to Saturday 4pm to 1am, Sunday 4pm to 11pm (Bus: 4, 5, or 7).

DANCE CLUBS

The hippest and most appealing dance club in the area is **Slagthuset,** Jörgen Köcksgatan 7A (© **040/10-99-31**). It's set within the red-brick premises of what was conceived in the 19th century as a slaughterhouse for cattle and hogs, in a location directly behind the railway station. This high-energy and much-talked-about place now functions as the largest dance club in Scandinavia. Wander freely among crowds of good-looking, sometimes raucous clients through three floors, each with its own bars, dance floor, labyrinth of interconnected rooms, and music. It's open only on Friday and Saturday nights, from 10pm to 5am. Entrance costs 100SEK ($14/£7.30).

Its most visible competitor is **Club Skeppsbron,** Skeppsbron 2 (© **040/30-62-02**). Outfitted for a relatively mature clientele, this nightclub incorporates a restaurant, an outdoor terrace, big windows overlooking a canal, and a mixture of antique nautical paneling with postmodern angularity. It's open only on Saturday nights, from 10pm till 5am, year-round. Entrance costs 100SEK ($14/£7.30).

Dancing is also the rage at the creatively designed **Nightclub Étage,** Stortorget 6 (© **040/23-20-60**). Initially conceived as an upscale bar and restaurant in the late 1980s, this nightspot lowered its prices and began marketing to a mass audience in the early 1990s. Despite its lowered expectations, the bar has not seemed to suffer as a result. It's reached by climbing a circular staircase from an enclosed courtyard in the town's main square. Satellite bars open and close regularly on every floor. The complex is open Monday and Thursday to Saturday 10pm to at least 4am, depending on the crowd. Cover for the dance club ranges from 75SEK to 90SEK ($10–$12/ £5.50–£6.60).

Many love affairs, both long and short, have gotten a boost at the **Malmborgen Compound** Gränden (© **040/12-38-95**), a sprawling antique warehouse on Hamburgsgatan. There's a restaurant within the building's courtyard, where main courses that include pizzas, shish kabobs, and Swedish meatballs with salad cost 98SEK to 162SEK ($14–$22/£7.15–£12), and where food is served daily from 11:30am till 11:30pm. The compound also contains a somewhat nondescript scattering of minor bars and cafes, but its most visible venue is the **Swing Inn,** Stadt Hamburgsgatan 3 (© **040/12-22-21**), where romantic dancing is the norm. Attendees tend to be over 35, and the recorded music is reminiscent of a 1960s variety show. There's a restaurant on the premises serving platters of traditional Swedish food Thursday to Saturday between 10 and 11:30pm. Main courses cost from 125SEK to 185SEK ($17–$26/£9.10–£14). Music and bar activities are scheduled on Thursday 10pm to 1am, Friday 10pm to 3am, and Saturday 10pm to 4am. The cover charge is 80SEK ($11/ £5.85) after 11pm.

GAY & LESBIAN

Gay nightlife in Malmö took a turn for the better thanks to the involvement of Claes Schmidt, creator of such mainstream clubs as the also-recommended Slagthuset (see above). Claes "came out" publicly to the Swedish press in 2003 as a (mostly heterosexual) cross-dresser. Immediately in the wake of this "confession," the local paper sold an additional 20,000 copies (huge by local standards) of the edition that carried the story about his double life. (For more on the story, visit his website www.saralund.se.) In the wake of these confessions, Claes became the most famous cross-dresser in Europe, working occasionally, and dressed as Sara Lund, as a paid consultant at corporate conscious-raising conventions and at universities throughout Scandinavia.

Claes' newest nightclub sensation in Malmö is **Indigo** ★★, 15 Monbijougatan (© **040/611-99-62;** www.rfsl.se/malmo). Indigo is now the most popular cutting-edge nightclub in Malmö. However, it's hard to find. It lies in a former warehouse within a drab industrial neighborhood in the *Triangeln* neighborhood, a 12-minute walk from the Hilton Hotel. You'll climb solid, industrial-strength stairs to the third floor of this brick-built fortress, encountering some amicably punkish people en route. Inside, you'll find a vast and echoing space with enormous dance floors, satellite bars for the city's various drag or leather events. Best known of these is Switch, a twice-per-month drag ball and elegance contest that occurs the second Friday of every month. (Be sure to check the schedule, as it can and often does change according to the whim of whoever's monitoring the event.)

Some weekends, Indigo's a regular, old-fashioned gay bar for regular, old-fashioned Swedes and Danes, other nights, thanks to the welcome flash and flair of Claes, it gets a lot more exotic. In most cases, Indigo is open only on Friday and Saturday nights from 11am to 3am, and usually charges an entrance fee of 50SEK to 70SEK ($6.90– $9.65/£3.65–£5.10).

AN AMUSEMENT PARK

Between May and September, locals, often with their children, and hordes of boisterous teenagers head for **Folkets Park** (People's Park), Amiralsgatan 35 (© **040/ 709-90**), where a battered compound that reminds some visitors of a B-rated Tivoli draw crowds. Children might enjoy the playhouse, small zoo, reptile center, and puppet theater. Restaurants, some devoted to fast food, also dot the grounds, and at random intervals, there might be a live concert from a pop or rock group. Hours are daily from 3pm to midnight in summer, noon to 6pm in winter. Admission is free; however, some performances require an admission price of 50SEK to 110SEK ($6.90–$15/ £3.65–£8.05). Take bus no. 5.

4 Lund ⋆⋆

18km (11 miles) NE of Malmö, 301km (187 miles) S of Gothenburg, 602km (374 miles) SW of Stockholm

The second oldest town in Sweden, Lund is a mellow old place with a thousand-year history. It holds more appeal for us than its rival university city, Uppsala, north of Stockholm, and in some respects is comparable to Cambridge in England.

Medieval streets and a grand cathedral are compelling reasons to visit, but the vibrant student life is even more compelling. But remember, if you're paying a summer visit, the students are away on vacation, so it will be quieter. The most exciting time to be in Lund, as in Uppsala, is on Walpurgis Eve, April 30, when student reveries signal the advent of spring.

Lund is said to be founded in 1020 by Canute the Great, ruler of the United Kingdom of England and Denmark, when this part of Sweden was a Danish possession. However, the city's 1,000-year anniversary was celebrated in 1990 because archaeological excavations show that a stave church was built here in 990. The city really made its mark when its cathedral was consecrated in 1145, after which Lund quickly became a center of religion, politics, culture, and commerce for all of Scandinavia.

The town has winding passageways, centuries-old buildings, and the richness of a university town. Lund University, founded in 1666, continues to play an active role in town life.

ESSENTIALS

GETTING THERE   By Train   Trains run hourly from Malmö (see earlier in this chapter), and the ride is only 15 minutes. Call ✆ 0771/77-77-77.

By Bus   Buses also arrive hourly from Malmö, but they take 30 minutes. Call ✆ 0771/77-77-77.

By Car   From Gothenburg, head south along E-6; Malmö and Lund are linked by an express highway, only a 20-minute drive.

VISITOR INFORMATION   The tourist information office, **Lunds Turistbyrå,** at Kyrkogatan 11 (✆ **046/35-50-40;** www.lund.se), is open June to August Monday to Friday 10am to 6pm and Saturday and Sunday 10am to 2pm; September to May Monday to Friday 10am to 5pm.

SEEING THE SIGHTS

Botaniska Trädgården (Botanical Gardens)   A block east of the cathedral, these gardens contain some 7,500 specimens of plants gathered from all over the world. Clusters of students congregate here, stretching out beneath the trees. Families also use the grounds to enjoy a picnic lunch. Serious horticulturists should visit when the greenhouses are open.

Östra Vallgatan 20. ✆ 046/222-73-20. Free admission. Gardens daily 6am–8pm; greenhouses daily noon–3pm. Bus: 1, 2, 3, 4, 5, 6, or 7.

Domkyrkan (Lund Cathedral) ✮✮✮   This stately old building is magnificent. With this ancient structure, Romanesque architecture in Sweden reached its zenith—in fact, the **eastern facade** ✮✮ of the church is one of the finest expressions of Romanesque architecture in northern Europe. The imposing twin-towered, gray-sandstone cathedral dominates the town. Work began on it in 1080, coming to an end at its consecration in 1145.

The interior is filled with splendor and wonder, especially the **apse** ✮✮✮ from 1130, a masterpiece of Romanesque styling with its Lombard arcading and third tier gallery. The **mosaic** ✮✮✮ of the apse vault, representing the Resurrection, was the creation of Joakim Skovgaard between 1925 and 1927 in the true Byzantine tradition. Look for the elaborately carved 1370 **choir stalls** ✮✮✮ depicting Old Testament scenes. Beneath the seats are grotesque carvings.

Nothing is more dramatic than the remarkable 14th-century **Astronomical Clock** ✮✮✮, which depicts days, weeks, and even the courses of the moon and the sun in the zodiac. The clock was silent for 3 centuries until it was restored in 1923. If you're here at noon or 3pm daily, you'll be treated to a splashy medieval tournament complete with clashing knights and blaring trumpets, and the Three Wise Men paying homage to the Virgin and Child. On Sunday the noon show doesn't begin until 1pm. Finally, head for the **Crypt** ✮✮✮, whose pillars are carved with zigzagging and twisting patterns.

Kyrkogatan. © **046/35-88-80.** Free admission. Mon–Fri 8am–6pm; Sat 1–5pm; Sun 1–6pm. Bus: 1, 2, 3, 4, 5, 6, or 7.

Historiska Museet   Founded in 1805, this is the second-largest museum of archaeology in Sweden, a journey back to the past that takes in artifacts of the Stone, Bronze, and Iron Ages. Collections trace the development of the people of Skåne from antiquity to the Middle Ages. One of the exhibits displayed here is that of the **skeleton of a young man** ✮✮ dating from around 7,000 B.C.—one of the oldest human skeletons found in northern Europe. Most collections from the Bronze Age came from tombs. During excavations in eastern Skåne, a large grave was unearthed; the jewelry and weapons found are on display. The medieval exhibition is predictably dominated by church art removed from Skånian churches.

Kraftstorg 1. © **046/222-79-30.** Admission 35SEK ($4.85/£2.55) adults, 20SEK ($2.75/£1.45) children 12–18, free for children under 11. Tues–Fri 11am–4pm; Sun noon–4pm. Closed Mon and Sat. Bus: 1, 2, 3, 4, 5, 6, or 7.

Kulturen (Museum of Cultural History) ✮✮   After leaving the cathedral, walk across the university grounds to Adelgatan, which the local citizens consider their most charming street. Here you'll find Kulturen, another of Sweden's open-air museums. This one contains reassembled sod-roofed farms and manor houses, a carriage museum, ceramics, peasant costumes, Viking artifacts, old handicrafts, and even a wood church moved to this site from the glassworks district.

It's one of the best organized and maintained open-air museums of Sweden. Opened in 1892, it was able to save some buildings before they disappeared forever. Allow 2 hours to get in the 17th houses, still perfectly preserved today, and a meal at the outdoor restaurant, near several runic stones dug up and brought here.

Tegnérsplatsen. © **046/35-04-00.** Admission 50SEK ($6.90/£3.65) adults, free for children. Apr 15–Sept daily 11am–5pm; Oct–Apr 14 Tues–Sun noon–4pm. Bus: 1, 2, 3, 4, 5, 6, or 7.

WHERE TO STAY

The tourist office (see above) can help you obtain housing in private homes for as little as 225SEK ($31/£16) per person per night.

EXPENSIVE

Grand Hotel ✦✦✦   The Grand has changed over the years, yet has kept its elegant architecture and still remains the number-one choice of discerning visitors to Lund, including the most well-heeled parents of students enrolled at the university. In spite of its fashion and formality, the Grand is not stiff and starched, but invites the office worker in for a beer after a hard day's work or provides a welcoming setting for family feasts. The tone is set by the supremely elegant marble lobby, which almost justifies the hotel calling itself Grand.

The location overlooks the fountains and flowers of a city park. No room is the same, but each is comfortably furnished with a mix of modern and traditional. Many patrons come here to dine even if they aren't staying at the hotel, enjoying the magnificent surroundings as they order traditional Scanian and Swedish cuisine, as well as a carefully crafted selection of international specialties. We are astonished by the wine list, boasting 500 different vintages from some three dozen countries around the world. At the hotel's wine bar, you can sample these exclusive wines either by the glass or the bottle.

Bantorget 1, S-221 04 Lund. ℂ 046/28-06-100. Fax 046/28-06-150. www.grandilund.se. 84 units. June 7–Aug 8 and Fri–Sat year-round 1,015SEK–1,630SEK ($140–$225/£74–£119) double, 3,000SEK ($414/£219) suite; Aug 9–June 6 1,850SEK–2,350SEK ($255–$324/£135–£172) double, 4,300SEK ($593/£314) suite. Rates include breakfast. AE, DC, MC, V. Parking 100SEK ($14/£7.30). Bus: 1, 2, 3, 4, 5, 6, or 7. **Amenities:** Restaurant; wine bar; fitness center; sauna; limited room service; laundry service/dry cleaning; nonsmoking rooms. *In room:* TV, dataport, minibar, hair dryer.

Hotel Concordia ✦   A classic, elegant landmark from 1882, Concordia was originally built as a private home and for many years it was a student hotel. The building today has no sign of its past and has been successfully converted to a government-rated, four-star hotel with comfort, charm, and elegance. Although the public rooms have what is known as a "Lundian character," that style does not extend to the bedrooms. The mostly midsize bedrooms have less character, but boast parquet floors, warm colors, and tiled bathrooms. They have been modernized and are comfortably furnished. The housekeeping here is about the finest in town. The location is only a 5-minute walk south of the railway station.

Stålbrogatan 1, S-222-24 Lund. ℂ 046/13-50-50. Fax 046/13-74-22. www.concordia.se. 64 units. Sun–Thurs 1,520SEK ($210/£111) double; Fri–Sat 950SEK ($131/£69) double; 1,800SEK ($248/£131) suite. Rates include breakfast. AE, DC, MC, V. Parking 75SEK ($10/£5.45). Bus: 1, 2, 3, 4, 5, 6, or 7. **Amenities:** Breakfast room; lounge; fitness center; sauna; business center; laundry service/dry cleaning; nonsmoking rooms. *In room:* TV, minibar, hair dryer, iron, Wi-Fi.

MODERATE

Best Western Hotel Djingis Khan ✦ *(Finds)*   This building looks like an upmarket student dormitory, but it's one of the best hotels in town, though not a rival of the Grand (see above). We found the staff the most helpful in town (they'll help you book flights, order a taxi, or arrange for a shirt to be washed).The midsize bedrooms have sleek modern styling and are comfortably arranged with all the gadgets you'll need. The hotel doesn't quite escape its original function when it was built in the 1970s as employee housing for a local hospital, but the conversion to a hotel in the early '90s was more or less successful. Public areas contain lots of English-inspired dark paneling, Chesterfield sofas, and an ambience that evokes a private men's club.

Margarethevägen 7, S 222 40 Lund. ℂ 800/780-7234 in the U.S. and Canada, or 046/33-36-10. Fax 046/46-33-36-10. www.djingiskhan.se or www.bestwestern.com. 73 units. Sun–Thurs 1,595SEK ($220/£116) double; Fri–Sat 800SEK ($110/£58) double. Rates include breakfast. AE, DC, MC, V. Closed July. Free parking. Bus: 3 or 93. **Amenities:** Restaurant; bar; indoor pool; fitness center; sauna; 24-hr. room service; laundry service; dry cleaning; nonsmoking rooms; rooms for those w/limited mobility. *In room:* TV, minibar, hair dryer, Wi-Fi.

Hotel Lundia ⭐⭐ *(Finds)*   When Jonas Lloyd renovated this long-established property near the railway station, he wanted to combine Swedish modern with Japanese simplicity. Much of the success of this hotel's overhaul is in Lloyd's use of natural materials. Lundia is under the same management as the Grand Hotel (see above) but is hardly a rival, although its interior is graced with winding staircases, white marble sheathing, and large windows. Guest rooms are quite special, with softly curved furniture in birch wood with accents of cherrywood. We were impressed that the raw walls were treated with beeswax glazing. The tasteful, comfortable furnishings rest on floors made of massive oak, each board nailed by hand. Bathrooms represent Nordic design with tiles, Danish-style modern plumbing, and tubs and showers.

Knut den Stores Gata 2, S-221 04. ℂ 046/280-65-00. Fax 046/280-65-10. www.lundia.se. 97 units. Late June to early Aug and Fri–Sat year-round 995SEK ($137/£72) double; rest of year 1,995SEK ($275/£146) double; 2,100SEK–4,100SEK ($290–$566/£153–£299) suite. Rates include breakfast. AE, DC, MC, V. Parking 100SEK ($14/£7.30). Bus: 1, 2, 3, 4, 5, 6, or 7. **Amenities:** Restaurant; bar; limited room service; laundry service/dry cleaning; nonsmoking rooms; rooms for those w/limited mobility. *In room:* TV, dataport, minibar, hair dryer, safe, Wi-Fi.

Scandic Star ⭐⭐   Lying a 20-minute walk from the city center, this hotel, built in 1991, doesn't have the grace and tradition of the Grand, but it's one of the most comfortable hotels in southern Sweden. Though it caters to the individual traveler, and does so exceedingly well, it is often a venue for business conventions. Rock stars and film actors also seem to prefer it over the Grand. What makes it so special is that nearly all the double rooms are configured as minisuites, with separate sitting areas and traditional, conservative furnishings that would fit into a well-appointed upper-middle-class Swedish home. The well-maintained bathrooms come with a shower and tub. The bar in the spacious courtyard has become a town meeting point. No other hotel in Lund matches the public facilities of this one, including a pool. The on-site Garda's Restaurant zealously guards the recipes for the Skåne specialties served.

Glimmervägen 5, PO Box 11026, SE-220 11 Lund. ℂ 046/285-25-00. Fax 046/285-25-11. www.scandic-hotels.com. 196 units. Mid-June to mid-Aug and Fri–Sat year-round 990SEK ($137/£72) double; rest of year 1,650SEK ($228/£120) double; 1,800SEK–4,100SEK ($248–$566/£131–£299) suite. AE, DC, MC, V. Free parking. Bus: 3 or 7. **Amenities:** Restaurant; bar; indoor pool; fitness center; sauna; limited room service; laundry service; dry cleaning; nonsmoking rooms; rooms for those w/limited mobility. *In room:* TV, minibar, hair dryer, iron, safe, Wi-Fi.

WHERE TO DINE
MODERATE
Barntorget 9 ⭐ SWEDISH/CONTINENTAL   Charming and traditional, this restaurant occupies a white-painted, wood-sided structure that, at the time of its construction in the 1860s, contained three separate residences and that later functioned as a bakery, a motorcycle repair shop, and a clothing store. Today, in a much-gentrified form, amid frescoed ceilings, flower pots, and candleholders (up to 120 per night), you'll enjoy a sophisticated medley of ingredients cooked in Swedish, and sometimes vaguely French, ways. The best examples we've enjoyed include marinated mussels and snails in garlic sauce, traditional Swedish meatballs and duck breast with orange sauce, and an old-fashioned Swedish favorite, minced veal with cream-based gravy and mashed potatoes. The restaurant is a very short walk of Lund's railway station.

Barntorget 7–9. ℭ **046/32-02-00.** Reservations recommended. Main courses 215SEK–240SEK ($30–$33/£16–£18). AE, DC, MC, V. Mon–Thurs 6pm–midnight; Fri–Sat 6–11pm. Bus: 2 or 4.

The Living Room ⚅ SWEDISH/INTERNATIONAL   The chefs here believe that when you go out to dine, you have "the right to expect something different," And that's exactly what you get here. We like the way the chefs constantly vary their menu to take advantage of market conditions and the best available produce. There is also a perfectly balanced mix between an inspired international cuisine and traditional Swedish fare. The most frequently ordered dish is a skillet-grilled entrecôte (perfectly tender and full of flavor) served with béarnaise sauce, but there are plenty of other good options, including a juicy grilled trout with root vegetables and a grilled tuna with risotto cooked with a zesty lemon oil. If you arrive for lunch, you can dine lighter fare such as freshly made salads, well-stuffed sandwiches, and delectable burgers. For dessert, the crème brûlée (our favorite) and the blueberry pie are memorable. As its name suggests, the environment is like a laid-back living room filled with sofas.

In the Hotel Lundia, Knut den Stores Gata 2. ℭ **046/280-65-00.** Reservations required Fri–Sat. Main courses 190SEK–295SEK ($26–$41/£14–£22). AE, DC, MC, V. Daily 11:30am–11pm. Bus: 1, 2, 3, 4, 5, 6, or 7.

Ø Bar ⚅ *Finds* INTERNATIONAL   This intriguing restaurant defines itself as a "laboratory for chefs" because of the experimental nature of a menu that changes every week. The venue looks like it might have been designed by a Milanese postmodernist, with blue and ash-white walls and a severe kind of angularity. It's usually mobbed every night with both diners and clients of the convivial bar area. Here you're likely to meet students from the university and their professors, engaged in animated dialogue. If you've been hankering for filet of elk, you'll find the town's best version here. It's enhanced by a sauce made with fresh thyme and a side of apple- and potato-laced muffins. Each night the chef makes a homemade pasta dish with various sauces. The standard of the Swedish kitchen, grilled halibut, comes alive with zesty flavorings of horseradish and lemon oil.

Mårtenstorget 9. ℭ **046/211-22-88.** Reservations recommended. Main courses 95SEK–195SEK ($13–$27/£6.95–£14). AE, DC, MC, V. Daily 11:30am–midnight; bar until 1am or 2am. Bus: 1 or 2.

Staket *Value* SWEDISH/INTERNATIONAL   This old tavern, a favorite with students, serves good food in a step-gabled brick facade that's a historic landmark. Food and drink are offered in the cellar—our favorite place for a rendezvous—but also at the street level dining room. Both areas have their appeals, but fondues are served only in the cellar. Start with the succulent crab cocktail or tasty goulash soup before moving on to the mixed grill of succulent meats or tender tournedos of beef. The desserts, unfortunately, are not worth writing home about.

Stora Södergatan 6. ℭ **046/211-93-67.** Reservations recommended. Main courses 170SEK–205SEK ($23–$28/£12–£15). AE, DC, MC, V. Mon–Thurs 11am–11pm; Fri–Sat noon–midnight; Sun 1–11pm. Bus: 1, 2, 3, 4, 5, 6, or 7.

INEXPENSIVE

Dalby Gästgifveri ⚅ *Finds* SWEDISH   As enticing as Lund is, it's also fun to escape it for a dinner in a neighboring hamlet, especially if that hamlet is an attraction unto itself. If you really want to flatter the pride of the local residents of this small village (pop. 2,000), you'll acknowledge that the village inn, Dalby Gästgifveri, is the oldest of its kind in Skåne. That isn't completely true, however, as the house that contains it has burned to the ground (and was rebuilt) at least twice since 1870. But during excavations conducted on the village church next door, evidence was unearthed that supports the belief that a tavern and inn associated with the church was serving food and drink to passersby in the 12th century. The wood-sided structure is painted in the colors of the Skanish flag (ocher and oxblood red). Within a pair of street-level dining rooms loaded with rustic antiques, you'll enjoy menu items that include smoked eel with lemon sauce, yellow-tomato soup, a Skanish omelet laced with pork and served with lingonberries, and the all-vegetarian corn schnitzels (a form of fritter). The restaurant is a 15-minute drive east of Lund.

Tengsgatan 6, in Lund's suburban hamlet of Dalby. ⓒ **046/20-00-06.** Reservations recommended. Main courses 25SEK ($3.45/£1.80); fixed-price lunch (available Mon–Fri only) 95SEK ($13/£6.95). AE, DC, MC, V. Mon–Tues 11:30am–3pm; Wed–Sat 11:30am–9pm; Sun 1–5:30pm. Bus: 160 from Lund.

Gloria's Bar and Restaurant AMERICAN   On two floors of an old-fashioned building in the historic center of town, this American-inspired sports and Western bar has a crowded and likable bar in the cellar and an even larger bar upstairs. Scattered throughout the premises are photographs and posters of American sports heroes, baseball and football memorabilia, and Wild West artifacts. Draft beer comes in foam-topped mugs. The restaurant serves copious portions of such rib-stickers as hamburgers and steaks, and an array of Cajun-inspired dishes. Various styles of live music are performed between 9:30 and 11:30pm each Thursday. Friday and Saturday feature a disc jockey spinning rock.

St. Petri Kyrkogata 9. ⓒ **046/15-19-85.** Reservations recommended. Main courses 99SEK–249SEK ($14–$34/ £7.20–£18). AE, DC, MC, V. Mon–Fri 11:30am–10:30pm; Sat 12:30–11pm; Sun 1–11pm. Bus: 1, 2, 3, 4, 5, 6, or 7.

LUND AFTER DARK

Most dance clubs in Lund operate only on weekends, when the clientele includes many students from the university. The hottest spot is **Tegnér's Matsalar,** Sandgatan 2 (ⓒ **046/131-333**), which has a dance floor in the basement of the already-recommended **Gloria's Restaurant,** every Friday and Saturday beginning at 10:30pm. Entrance is free. Another option, also open only Friday and Saturday, is the **Palladium,** Stora Södergatan 13 (ⓒ **046/211-66-60**), a beer pub with a college-age clientele. Admission is free.

With its small dance floor, **Basilika,** Stora Södergatan 13 (ⓒ **046/211-66-60**), occasionally hosts live bands from England or other parts of Europe. The big nights here are Friday and Saturday, when a 50SEK ($6.90/£3.65) cover charge is imposed. A final hot spot is **Stortorget,** Stortorget 1 (ⓒ **046/139-290**), which has a nightly DJ and an age requirement (22 and older).

EASY EXCURSIONS

From Lund, you may want to make a side trip to **Dalby Church** ⓖ, 5-240 12 Dalby (no phone), in Dalby, 13km (8 miles) east of Lund. This beautiful 11th-century former bishop's church is the oldest church in Scandinavia; be sure to visit its crypt. Open daily from 9am to 4pm. Several buses a day (nos. 158 and 161) run between Lund center and Dalby.

About a 30-minute drive northeast of Lund (off Rte. 23) is the **Castle of Bosjökloster** ⓖⓖ, Höör (ⓒ **0413/250-48**). Once a Benedictine convent founded around 1080, it was closed during the Reformation in the 16th century. The **great courtyard** is spectacular, with thousands of flowers and exotic shrubs, terraces, and a park with animals and birds. Indoors are the vaulted refectory and the stone hall where native arts and crafts, jewelry, and other Swedish goods are displayed. You can picnic on the grounds or enjoy lunch at a simple restaurant in the garden for 100SEK ($14/£7.30).

The entire complex is open daily from May 1 to September 30 from 8am to 8pm; the museum and exhibition hall inside the castle, daily from 10am to 6pm. Admission is 65SEK ($8.95/£4.75) for adults, seniors, and students; free for children up to age 16. In the park stands a 1,000-year-old oak tree. The castle lies 45km (28 miles) from Malmö and 29km (18 miles) from Lund. From Lund, there's a train link to Höör. Once at Höör, take the "ring bus" marked Bosjökloster, which travels 5km (3 miles) south on Route 23 to the castle.

5 Ystad ⟨★

55km (34 miles) E of Malmö, 46km (28 miles) W of Simrishamn

Time has passed Ystad by, and that's why we like to visit it. Its **Gamla Stan** ★★★ contains an astonishing 300 well-preserved half-timbered antique houses, which you can explore by roaming the cobbled streets. They're scattered about town, but we found the greatest concentration of them on **Stora Östergatan.**

Most of the houses date from the latter 1700s, though **Änglahuset,** on Stora Norregatan, is from around 1630. You can launch yourself into the past by starting at **Stortorget** ★★, the impressive main square of Ystad, which was a big smuggling center during the Napoleonic wars.

As impressive as the main square is, we came upon another square of great charm. **Tvättorget** in the old town is Ystad's smallest square, and it's surrounded by half-timbered houses. It may be hard to find and is reached by walking up a narrow lane called Bäckahästgränd.

At one time in its history, Ystad was much more important than the provincial town you see today. Back in the 17th century, Ystad was known as "Sweden's window to the world." Amazingly, the first automobile in Sweden was driven on the old streets of Ystad. The town also opened Sweden's first bank, and the first building that could be called a hotel.

There is some activity here, with ferries leaving for the Danish island of Bornholm—even to Poland. If you're a fan of the best-selling inspector Karl Wallander crime thrillers—all written by Henning Mankell—you'll know that Ystad is a setting for these suspense tales. If you don't have time to wade through all of Mankell's series, opt for the fourth installment, *The Man Who Smiled.* It's the best and most evocative— and it's translated into English. Devotees of the series can tour the sights associated with the inspector with a volunteer fire brigade every Tuesday and Thursday from July to mid-August. Fans are taken around town on an antique fire engine. The tourist office (see below) will have details.

Devotees of the silent screen know of Ystad as the birthplace of Valentino's "beautiful blond Viking" Anna Q. Nilsson, who was born here in 1890 and whose fame at one time was greater than that of Greta Garbo, a fellow Swede. Some of Nilsson's greatest films were *In the Heart of a Fool* (1921); *Ponjola* (1923), in which she played a boy; and *Midnight Lovers,* finished in 1925, the year of a horseback-riding accident that ended her career. Today she is remembered mainly for appearing in a cameo role as one of the "waxworks" in the 1950 Gloria Swanson classic *Sunset Blvd.*

ESSENTIALS
GETTING THERE   By Train   There are good rail connections between Malmö and Ystad. From Monday to Saturday trains run roughly on the hour between Malmö

and Ystad (trip time: 1 hr.). On Sunday, there are only six daily trains from Malmö. For more information, call © **0771/777-77-77.**

By Bus   There are three daily buses Monday to Saturday from Malmö to Ystad, taking 1 hour. On Sunday, there is only one bus.

By Car   From Malmö, head east on Route 65. For more information, call © **0200/ 218218.**

VISITOR INFORMATION   The tourist bureau, **Ystads Turistbyrå,** St. Knuts Torg (© **0411/577681;** www.ystad.se), is at the bus station in the same building as the art museum (Konstmuseum). It's open from November to May Monday to Friday 9am to 5pm; June to August Monday to Friday 9am to 7pm, Saturday 10am to 6pm, Sunday 10am to 6pm; September to October Monday to Friday 9am to 5pm.

SEEING THE SIGHTS

The focal point of the town is **St. Maria Kyrka,** Stortorget (© **0411/692-00**), which dates to the early 1200s. Each successive century brought new additions and changes. Regrettably, many of its richest decorative features were deemed unfashionable and removed in the 1880s. However, some of the more interesting ones were brought back in a restoration program 4 decades later. The chancel with the ambulatory is late Gothic, and the church spire dates from 1688. Inside, look for the baptismal chapel, with a richly carved German altar from the 15th century. The church is open from June to mid-September only, daily from 10am to 6pm. There is no admission fee.

The **Museum of Modern Art (Ystads Konstmuseum),** St. Knuts Torg (© **0411/ 57-72-85**), in central Ystad includes a small military museum. Permanent exhibits feature mainly art from Denmark and Skåne from the past 100 years. Admission is 30SEK ($3.90/£2.20). The Ystad Tourist Office is in the same building as the museum. The museum is open Tuesday through Friday from noon to 5pm, Saturday and Sunday from noon to 4pm.

The only museum in Sweden in a medieval monastic house is the **City Museum in the Grey Friars Monastery (Stadsmuseet i Gråbrödraklostret),** St. Petri Kyrkoplan (© **0411/57-72-86**). Constructed in 1267, the building is a monument from the Danish era of Ystad. Various antiquities in the museum trace the area's history. The museum is open year-round Monday through Friday from 10am to 5pm, and Saturday through Sunday from noon to 4pm. The admission fee is 30SEK ($3.90/£2.20).

WHERE TO STAY

Hotell Continental ⭐⭐   You wouldn't know it by looking at it, but this landmark lays claim to being Sweden's oldest hotel, having opened its doors in 1829. It was constructed over the site of an old customs house when Ystad was the major port link between Sweden and the Continent. In 1996, a family-owned company took it over and began a program of refurbishing and redecorating that continues to this day. These owners seem to take a personal interest in their guests, many of them arriving by train or by ferry from Europe; the hotel is convenient to both terminals. Marble sheathing in the lobby and gleaming crystal chandeliers add a grace note. The mid-size-to-spacious bedrooms are furnished with sleek modern styling that is both comfortable and tasteful, and the bathrooms are well laid out and equipped with tub/shower combos. Consider the dining room here even if you're not a guest. Chefs prepare Swedish classics and often use regional produce in summer. At breakfast, we requested the most classic Swedish dish—*åggakaka*, a thick pancake with crispy bacon and lingonberries.

Hamngatan 13, S-271 00 Ystad. © 0411/137-00. Fax 0411/125-70. www.hotelcontinental-ystad.se. 52 units. June 21–Aug 4 and Fri–Sat year-round 940SEK–1,190SEK ($130–$164/£69–£87) double; rest of year 1,090SEK–1,595SEK ($150–$220/£80–£116) double. Rates include breakfast. AE, DC, MC, V. Parking 25SEK ($3.45/£1.80). **Amenities:** Restaurant; bar; limited room service; babysitting; laundry service; nonsmoking rooms; rooms for those w/limited mobility. *In room:* TV, dataport, hair dryer.

Hotel Tornväktaren *(Value)*

This is Ystad's best recommendation for those who don't want to check into the more expensive hotels we've recommended. Much of the charm of this simple bed-and-breakfast derives from its hardworking owner, Mr. Roy Saifert. His home is a turn-of-the-20th-century stone-built, red-trimmed structure with a garden, 10 minutes on foot from the railway station. Rooms are outfitted in pastels with lots of homey touches that include frilly curtains, wall-to-wall carpeting, and lace doilies covering painted wooden furniture. Not all rooms have a private bathroom, but we have found that the corridor facilities are adequate. The breakfast served here is generous and home cooked, mostly made to order. Other than a filling morning breakfast, no meals are served.

St. Östergatan 33, S-271-34 Ystad. © 0411/784-80. Fax 0411/729-27. 9 units, 5 with bathroom. 795SEK ($110/£58) double with bathroom; 695SEK ($96/£51) double without bathroom. Rates include breakfast. AE, MC, V. Free parking. **Amenities:** Breakfast room; lounge; nonsmoking rooms. *In room:* TV.

Ystads Saltsjöbad *(Finds)*

This hotel is a classic, made all the more so by its helpful owners, Ann and Kent Nyström, and their helpful staff. Beautifully situated on 4 hectares (10 acres) of forested land beside the sea, this hotel is close to Sweden's southernmost tip. It was built in 1897 by one of the most famous opera stars of his day, Swedish-born Solomon Smith. Designed as a haven for the Gilded Age aristocracy of northern Europe, it consists of three connected four-story buildings with big-windowed corridors, set close to the sands of an expansive beach. The guest rooms are comfortably furnished in turn-of-the-20th-century style. Each unit has a neatly kept bathroom with a tub/shower combination. The clientele changes throughout the year. In the summer, the hotel caters to beachgoers; in the winter, it's often filled with corporate conventions. The neighborhood provides good opportunities for healthful pastimes such as tennis and golf. No menus in town seemed more seasonally aware than those offered here. Fresh produce is delivered several times a day, and the owners insist their local suppliers be "environmentally aware." An international cuisine is married to traditional Swedish fare. Both the main dining room and a smaller, more intimate a la carte restaurant, Apotheket, open onto views of the sea.

Saltsjöbadsgatan 6, S-271 39 Ystad. © 0411/136-30. Fax 0411/55-58-35. www.ystadssaltsjobad.se. 109 units. June 19–Aug 26 1,140SEK–1,220SEK ($157–$168/£83–£89) double; Sept–June 18 1,210SEK–1,300SEK ($167–$179/£88–£95) double; year-round Mon–Thurs 3,500SEK ($483/£256) suite; year-round Fri–Sun 2,200SEK ($304/£161) suite. AE, DC, MC, V. Closed Dec 23–Jan 6. Free parking. **Amenities:** 2 restaurants; 2 bars; cafe; 2 pools (1 indoor); spa; sauna; limited room service; laundry service/dry cleaning; nonsmoking rooms. *In room:* A/C, TV, hair dryer, Wi-Fi.

WHERE TO DINE

Lottas Restaurang INTERNATIONAL   Fans praise this as one of the most popular and bustling restaurants in town; its detractors avoid it because of slow service by a small staff that sometimes seems impossibly overworked. Everyone awards high marks, however, for the well-prepared cuisine. Meals are served in a brick dining room within a century-old building that once functioned as a private home. The menu consists of old-fashioned Swedish cuisine made from fresh ingredients and might include fried and creamed filet of cod with dill-flavored boiled potatoes, pork schnitzels with asparagus and béarnaise sauce, and marinated breast of chicken with roasted potatoes. For dessert, try warm chocolate cake with ice cream.

Stortorget 11. ℂ 0411/788-00. Reservations recommended. Main courses 142SEK–210SEK ($20–$29/£10–£15). AE, DC, MC, V. Mon–Sat 5–10pm.

Restaurant Bruggeriet ✦ SWEDISH/INTERNATIONAL   This novel restaurant was originally built in 1749 as a warehouse for malt. In 1996, a team of local entrepreneurs installed a series of large copper vats and transformed the site into a pleasant, cozy restaurant and brewery. Today they specialize in two "tastes" of beer—a lager and a dark—that are marketed under the brand name Ysta Färsköl. Depending on their size, they sell for 28SEK to 48SEK ($3.85–$6.60/£1.95–£3.35) per mug. Food items seem carefully calibrated to taste best when consumed with either of the two beers. The kitchen doesn't like to experiment and adopts the idea that if it was good enough for grandfather, it is good enough for today's patrons. Those items include fried herring marinated in mustard and sour cream, grilled salmon in a red-wine sauce, Swedish lamb flavored with garlic and fresh herbs, and a tenderloin steak in a brandy sauce.

Långgatan 20. ℂ 0411/69-9999. Reservations recommended. Main courses 138SEK–215SEK ($19–$30/£10–£16). AE, DC, MC, V. Mon 11:30am–2pm; Tues–Fri 11:30am–10pm; Sat noon–midnight; Sun 3pm-8pm.

Sandskogens Vardshus *Finds* SWEDISH   Set about 1.5km (1 mile) east of Ystad's center, this structure was originally built in 1899 as a summer home for the town's mayor. It was converted to a restaurant in the 1930s, and ever since, it has provided local diners with well-prepared Swedish specialties. One of the most popular appetizers in Sweden is a toast served with white bait roe, sour cream, and onions. We like the pot of marinated mussels, freshly caught brill enhanced with a caramelized butter sauce, and gratin of lobster accompanied by a lemon sole. In summer we'd walk a mile for one of the pastry chef's cloudberry parfaits made with golden berries from the Arctic.

Saltsjøvagen, Sandskogen. ℂ 0411/147-60. Reservations recommended. Main courses 110SEK–205SEK ($15–$28/ £8–£15); fixed-price lunch 125SEK ($17/£9.15); fixed-price dinner 225SEK ($31/£16). MC, V. Daily 1–9pm. Closed Jan–Feb.

Store Thor SWEDISH/FRENCH   One of the most reliable lunchtime restaurants in Ystad occupies a series of vaulted cellars that were built as part of a monastery in the 1500s. Several hundred years later, the Rådhus (Town Hall) was reconstructed after a disastrous fire above the monastery's cellars. Today, amid small tables and romantic candlelight, you can enjoy such tasty dishes as shellfish soup with saffron, beef filet stuffed with lobster, and saddle of lamb roasted with fresh herbs.

Stortorget 1. ℂ 0411/185-10. Main courses 98SEK–195SEK ($14–$27/£7.15–£14). AE, DC, MC, V. Mon–Fri 11:30am–2pm and 6–10pm; Sat 6pm–1am; Sun 4–9pm.

6 Simrishamn ✦

630km (391 miles) S of Stockholm, 95km (59 miles) E of Malmö, 40km (25 miles) E of Ystad

If it's a question of Ystad or Simrishamn, make it Ystad. That doesn't mean that this old fishing village is without its charms. Actually, with its cobblestone streets and tiny brick houses, it's one of the most idyllic villages in Skåne. It's also the best center for exploring some of the major attractions of the province, which are found in its environs, including Dag Hammarskjöld's farm, a medieval castle, and a Bronze Age tomb (see below).

Because of its proximity to Ystad, Simrishamn can also be treated as a day trip. At some point, wander down by the harbor where the fishing boats pull in, carrying one of Sweden's greatest bounties of cod, eel, and herring. If you're here in summer, you'll also notice hundreds of tourists eating ice cream while waiting for a ferry to take them to the vacation island of Bornholm in Denmark.

Once you arrive at the southeastern tip of Skåne, you'll find good sandy beaches, especially at **Sandhammaren.**

ESSENTIALS

GETTING THERE   By Train   Ten trains a day (eight on Sat and Sun) make the 45-minute run between Malmö and Simrishamn. For information, call (C) **0771/77-77-77.**

By Bus   Nine buses per day arrive from Kristianstad (four a day on Sat and Sun), and 10 buses per day arrive from Ystad (three on Sat and Sun). From Lund, there are eight daily buses. Tickets can be purchased onboard these buses. Call (C) **0771/77-77-77.**

By Car   From Ystad, our last stopover, continue east along Route 10.

VISITOR INFORMATION   For information about hotels, boardinghouses, summer cottages, and apartments, check with the tourist bureau. **Simrishamns Kommun Turistbyrå,** Tullhusgatan 2 ((C) **0414/819-800**), is open June to August Monday to Friday 9am to 8pm, Saturday 10am to 8pm, and Sunday 11am to 8pm; September to May Monday to Friday 9am to 5pm.

SEEING THE SIGHTS

The chief attraction here is a stroll through its **Gamla Stan** (R), or Old Town, which is the historic core, a maze of fondant-colored tiny cottages that in some ways evokes a movie set. If you're driving, there is parking down by the harbor. As you stroll along, follow Strandvägen to **Sjöfartsplatsen,** which is a garden studded with works of art made from the debris of shipwrecks. On our last visit, we made a surprising discovery when we wandered into **Frasses Musikmuseum,** Peder Morks Väg 5 ((C) **0414/14520**). Here we found the world's most complete collection of Edison phonographs. The museum also has a collection of antique musical curiosities including self-playing barrel organs. It's open June and August on Sunday 2 to 6pm. In July hours are Monday to Wednesday and Sunday 2 to 6pm. Admission is 25SEK ($3.45/£1.80). The chief attraction is **St. Nicolai Kirke,** Storgatan ((C) **0414/41-24-80**). Open June to September daily 10am to 6:30pm, Sunday noon to 6:30pm; October to May Monday to Friday 10am to 3pm, Saturday 10am to 1pm. Originally constructed as a fisherman's chapel in the 12th century, the church literally dominates the town. It's built of chunky sandstone blocks, with a brick porch and step gables. Over the years there have been many additions, with a nave added in the 1300s, although the vault dates from the 1400s. Inside look for the flamboyantly painted pulpit from the 1620s. The pews and votive ships on display were installed much later, in the 1800s. Outside you'll see two sculptures, both by Sweden's greatest sculptor Carl Milles, called *The Sisters* and *Angel with Trumpet.*

The main square and the center of local life is **Storgatan.** The best streets to look at charming 19th-century houses are **Östergatan** and **Stora Norregatan.** Nearly all of them have carved-wood doors and potted plants on their doorsteps.

NEARBY ATTRACTIONS

Backakra ⟨⟨ Located off the coastal road between Ystad and Simrishamn is the farm that Dag Hammarskjöld, the late United Nations secretary-general, purchased in 1957 and intended to make his home. Although he died in a plane crash before he could live there, the old farm has been restored according to his instructions. The rooms are filled with gifts to Mr. Hammarskjöld—everything from a Nepalese dagger to a lithograph by Picasso.

The site is 31km (19 miles) southwest of Simrishamn and can be reached by the bus from Simrishamn marked YSTAD. Likewise, a bus from Ystad, marked SIMRISHAMN, goes by the site. Scheduling your return might be difficult because of infrequent service—check in advance.

Other than the caretakers, the site is unoccupied most of the year, with the exception of 18 members of the Swedish Academy, who are allowed to use the house for meditation and writing whenever they want.

S-270 20 Loderup. ⟨⟨ **0411/52-66-11.** Admission 30SEK ($4.15/£2.20) adults, free for children under 5. June 8–Aug 16 daily noon–5pm; May 16–June 7 and Aug 17–Sept 20 Sat–Sun noon–5pm. Closed Sept 21–May 15.

Glimmingehus ⟨⟨⟨ Don't be scared away when locals warn you that the best preserved medieval castle in Sweden has more than a dozen ghosts. They only come out during the night. Even more than Kivik (see below) and Backakra (see above), this is the chief attraction in the area. Appearing somewhat Gothic, the ancient structure, built between 1499 and 1505, appears much as it did at the time of its construction. Nearly all other such castles in Sweden are in ruins or have been extensively tampered with—so this one is for purists. This majestic edifice was constructed by Adam van Büren for a member of the Danish aristocracy, who demanded strong fortresslike walls but tiny windows. Naturally the fortress had a moat. In time the aristocrats, finding the castle far too austere, moved out and the rats moved in. There were so many rats here at one time that the author Selma Lagerlöf, in her *Wonderful Adventures of Nils,* describes an epic battle between the gray and the black rats.

Hammenhög 276 56. ⟨⟨ **0414/186-20.** Admission 60SEK ($8.30/£4.40) adults, free for children 7–18. Daily 10am–6pm. Closed Nov–Mar. From Simrishamn follow Rte. 10 southwest for 10km (6¼ miles) to the village of Hammenhög and then follow the signs.

Kivik Tomb ⟨⟨ The drive here is worth the journey as it takes you through fields planted with fruit, mainly pears and apples. Before you arrive at a doorway to Sweden's past, we suggest you stop off in the little village of **Kivik,** where the cider is said to taste better than anywhere else in Scandinavia.

Discovered in 1748, this remarkable find, Sweden's most amazing Bronze Age relic, is north of Simrishamn along the coast of Kivik. In a 1931 excavation, tomb furniture, bronze fragments, and some grave carvings were uncovered. Eight floodlit runic slabs depict pictures of horses, a sleigh, and what appears to be a fun-loving troupe of dancing seals.

Bredaror. No phone. Admission 20SEK ($2.75/£1.45). Daily 10am–6pm. Closed Sept–Apr. From Simrishamn follow Rte. 10 northwest to the village of Kivik, at which point the tomb is signposted.

WHERE TO STAY

Hotel Kockska Gården ⟨Value⟩ This unspoiled half-timbered former coaching inn looks like one of those old places in the English countryside. The hotel is built around a large medieval courtyard in the city center. It's an inviting choice, as it has been updated and is now more comfortable than ever. The bedrooms are up to date with tasteful furnishings and soothing pastel colors. The bathrooms, though small, are neatly kept, each with a shower. Breakfast is the only meal served, but there are places to eat within an easy walk of the front door.

Storgatan 25, S-272 31 Simrishamn. ℭ **0414/41-17-55**. Fax 0414/41-19-78. 18 units. 990SEK–1,090SEK ($137–$150/£72–£80) double. Rates include breakfast. AE, MC, V. Free parking. **Amenities:** Breakfast room; lounge; non-smoking rooms. *In room:* TV.

Hotel Svea 🔒 We wouldn't want to check in forever, but for an overnight this is the best choice to recommend in town and also has the finest restaurant (see below). Right on the waterfront, in the town center, Svea was built around the turn of the 20th century. Much of what you see today was rebuilt, modernized, and radically renovated. Many of its well-appointed, conservatively comfortable rooms overlook the harbor; all units have medium-size bathrooms equipped with tub/shower combinations. The hotel's only suite, the Prince Eugen, is named after a member of the royal family of Sweden who stayed here shortly after the hotel was built.

Strandvägen 3, S-272 31 Simrishamn. ℭ **0414/41-17-20**. Fax 0414/143-41. www.hotellsvea.com. 59 units. 1,090SEK ($150/£80) double; 1,690SEK ($233/£123) suite. AE, DC, MC, V. Free parking. **Amenities:** Restaurant; bar; sauna; laundry service; dry cleaning; nonsmoking rooms; rooms for those w/limited mobility. *In room:* TV, hair dryer, safe, Wi-Fi.

WHERE TO DINE

Restaurant Svea 🔒 SWEDISH/INTERNATIONAL   The best restaurant in town lies within the pale yellow walls of the recommended Hotel Svea. The kitchen focuses on fresh fish caught in local waters (of which you get a view from the restaurant windows), but also turns out beef, pork, chicken, and some exotic meats, such as grilled filet of ostrich. Other menu items include strips of smoked duck breast in lemon sauce, filet of fried sole with white wine or tartar sauce, medallions of pork with béarnaise sauce, and a succulent filet of beef with salsa-style tomato sauce.

In the Hotel Svea. Strandvägen 3. ℭ **0414/41-17-20**. Reservations recommended. Main courses 140SEK–215SEK ($19–$30/£10–£16); 3-course menu 210SEK ($29/£15). AE, DC, MC, V. Daily 6:30–10:30am; 11:30am–1pm; and 6:30–10pm. Closed Dec 21–Jan 8.

18

Exploring the Swedish Countryside

After seeing Stockholm, visitors often face a difficult decision about what else to do. Sweden is a large country, and most travelers have tough choices to make. In this chapter we'll focus on the best possibilities, including an excursion on the **Göta Canal,** one of Scandinavia's major attractions. Another trip is to folkloric **Dalarna,** a province that evokes quintessential Sweden. Besides the traditional customs, handicrafts, and festive costumes, the region is important artistically, as two of Sweden's most famous painters, Anders Zorn and Carl Larsson, came from here.

We'll also take a ferry to **Gotland,** Sweden's vacation island, which is known for its cliff formations and wide, sandy beaches. Inhabited since 5000 B.C., Gotland is Scandinavia's most intriguing island, with Visby as its capital.

For the more adventurous, **Swedish Lapland** is an alluring destination and home to the once-nomadic Sami. In one of Europe's last great open spaces, you can see golden eagles soar above snowcapped crags and "listen to the silence." Skiers flock to the area, but the summer miracle of the Midnight Sun shining above the Arctic Circle attracts the most visitors. This area is so vast (some 1,000km/620 miles from north to south) that we've highlighted only the best destinations. Swedish Lapland is also a great place for summer sports—canoeing, river rafting, salmon fishing, hiking, and climbing. Local tourist offices can put you in touch with outfitters who arrange these adventures.

1 The Göta Canal ★★★

In Sweden in summer, everyone seems to take to the water to enjoy the precious days of sunshine before a long, cold winter. The **Göta Canal cruise** ★★★ covers a distance of 560km (347 miles) from Gothenburg in the west to Stockholm in the east, or vice versa. Of course, this actual sail is not entirely on the canal and covers other lakes and rivers as well. The highest loch is more than 90m (295 ft.) above sea level. To break up the sail on the 4-day cruise, captains wisely stop four or five times along the way, but only at the most scenic or intriguing shops. Day trips and cruises also are offered.

The canal was begun in the early 19th century for the purpose of transporting goods across Sweden, thereby avoiding expensive tolls levied by Denmark on ships entering and leaving the Baltic Sea. However, soon after the canal was completed, Denmark waived its shipping tolls, and the railway between Stockholm and Gothenburg was created, allowing for the cheaper and faster shipment of goods across Sweden. The canal became more of a tourist attraction than a means of transportation.

Boats depart Gothenburg heading east along the Göta Älv River. About 30 minutes outside Gothenburg, you'll see the 14th-century **Bohus Fortress.** This bastion played a leading role in the battles among Sweden, Norway, and Denmark to establish supremacy. Bohus Castle and Fortress (Bohus Fästning) was built by order of Norway's Haakon V on Norwegian territory. After the territory was ceded to Sweden in 1658, Bohus Fortress was used as a prison. Climb the tower, **"Father's Hat,"** for what we consider the finest panoramic view of the entire trip. Farther down the river, the boat will pass the town of **Kungälv,** known by the Vikings as Konghälla, whose traditions are 1,000 years old.

As the boat proceeds eastward on the Göta's clear water, the landscape becomes wilder. About 5 hours into the journey, you reach the town of **Trollhättan,** home of one of Europe's largest power stations. The once-renowned Trollhättan Falls, now almost dry, can be seen at their full capacity only in July. Today most of the water is diverted to a series of underground channels to the power station.

After passing a series of locks, boats enter **Lake Vänern,** Sweden's largest lake, with a surface area of more than 2,130 sq. km (831 sq. miles). The trip across Lake Vänern takes about 8 hours. Along the way you'll pass **Lidköping,** home of the famous Rörstrand porcelain. Lidköping received its charter in 1446. North of Lidköping, on the island of Kållandsö, stands **Läckö Slott,** a castle dating from 1298. Originally home of the bishops of Skara, the castle was given to King Gustavus Vasa in 1528 and later presented to Sweden's great hero, Gen. Magnus Gabriel de la Gardie.

Having crossed Lake Vänern, the boats once again enter the canal. A series of locks, including the canal's oldest at Forsvik, carry the steamers to Sweden's second-largest lake, **Lake Vättern.** This lake is famous for its beauty and translucent water, and we find it even more alluring and scenic than noble Vänern itself. At some points, visibility reaches a depth of 15m (49 ft.).

The medieval town of **Vadstena** on the eastern shore of Lake Vättern is our favorite stopover on the Göta Canal trip because it is the most atmospheric and evocative town. Within the town are narrow streets and frame buildings. It's known throughout Sweden for its delicate handmade lace, which you can see by walking along Stora Gatan, the main street. Also worth a visit is the **Klosterkyrkan (Abbey Church).** Built between the mid–14th and the 15th centuries to specifications outlined by its founder, St. Birgitta (Bridget) of Sweden, this Gothic church is rich in medieval art. Parts of the abbey date from 1250.

Another major sight is **Vadstena Castle.** Construction began under Gustavus Vasa, king of Sweden in 1545, but was not completed until 1620. This splendid Renaissance Vasa castle, erected during a period of national expansion, dominates the town from its position on the lake, just behind the old courthouse in the southern part of town. The caretaker told us that the last royalty seen living here was back in 1715. Since those days the castle has been restored in respect to its original architecture.

Boats bound for Stockholm depart Lake Vättern and pass two small lakes, Boren and Roxen. Just south of Lake Roxen you'll find the university town of **Linköping,** site of a battle between Roman Catholic King Sigismund of Poland and Duke Charles of Södermanland (later Charles IX). Charles won the battle and established Linköping as part of Sweden rather than a province of Rome. In the town's main square stands the Folkung Fountain, one of sculptor Carl Milles's most popular works. Northwest of the main square you'll find the cathedral, a not quite harmonious blend of Romanesque and Gothic architecture.

From Linköping, boats enter Lake Roxen and continue their journey northeast by canal to **Slätbaken,** a fjord that stretches to the sea. Steamers then continue along the coast to Stockholm.

The **Göta Canal Steamship Company** offers turn-of-the-20th-century steamers, including its 1874 *Juno,* which claims to be the world's oldest passenger vessel offering overnight accommodations. The line also operates the 1912 *Wilhelm Tham* and the newer—that is, 1931—*Diana.* Passengers can walk, jog, or bike along the canal path, and there are organized shore excursions at many stops along the way.

A lot of hawkers will try to sell these Göta Canal cruises to you, but we've found the most reliable company—and the best deals—come through **Scantours** (© 800/223-7226 or 310/636-4656; www.scantours.net). North Americans can book these tours before leaving home. Cruise costs can vary, but count on spending $1,695 per person, based on double occupancy, for a 6-day package. Discounts are given for early reservations.

2 Dalarna ⓒⓒⓒ

This province offers everything from maypole dancing and fiddle music to folk costumes and handicrafts. Dalarna, which means "valleys," it is sometimes referred to as "Dalecarlia," the Anglicized form of the name.

Lake Siljan, arguably the most beautiful lake in Europe, is ringed with resort villages and towns. Leksand, Rättvik, and Mora attract summer visitors with sports, folklore, and a week of music. From June 23 to 26, the Dalecarlians celebrate midsummer with maypole dancing. In the winter, people come here to ski.

FALUN ⓒ

488km (303 miles) NE of Gothenburg, 229km (142 miles) NW of Stockholm

Our driving tour of the region begins in Falun, the old capital of Dalarna; it lies on both sides of the Falu River. The town is noted for its copper mines; copper revenue has supported many Swedish kings. Just 10km (6½ miles) northeast, you can visit the home of the famed Swedish painter Carl Larsson.

ESSENTIALS

GETTING THERE By Train There is frequent service during the day from Stockholm (trip time: 3 hr.) and from Gothenburg (trip time: 6 hr.). For schedules, call © 771/75-75-75.

By Bus Buses operated by **Swebus** (© 0200/21-82-18) run between Stockholm and Falun either once or twice every Friday, Saturday, and Sunday, depending on the season. Coming from Gothenburg, although the distance is greater, buses arrive twice a day every day of the week, making frequent stops along the way.

By Car If you're driving to Falun from Stockholm, take the E-18 expressway northwest to the junction with Route 70. From here, continue to the junction with Route 60, where you head northwest. Falun is signposted.

VISITOR INFORMATION The **Falun Tourist Office,** Trotzgatan 10–12 (© 023/830-50; www.falun.se), is open from mid-August to mid-June every Monday to Friday 9am to 6pm, and Saturday 9am to 2pm. During summer, from mid-June to mid-August, it's open Monday to Friday 9am to 7pm, Saturday 9am to 6pm, and Sunday 10am to 5pm.

Dalarna

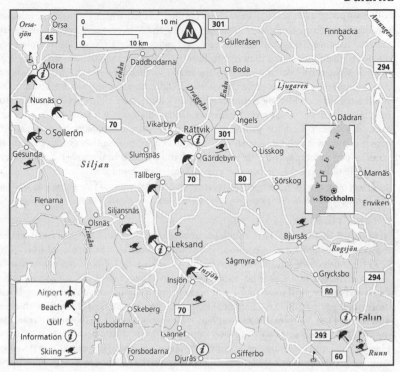

SEEING THE SIGHTS

Before you get down and dirty at some dark pits and mines, head first to the market square, *Stora Torget*, to see the **Kristine Church** (*©* 023/279-10), a copper-roofed structure dating from the mid-17th century (the tower itself dates from 1865). It's open daily 10am to 4pm, and admission is free. It closes at 6pm in summer.

Falun is the site of **Lugnet** (*©* 023/835-00), one of Sweden's largest sports complexes. The Bjursberget ski resort is 20km (13 miles) away.

Carl Larsson-gården ✶✶✶   Carl Larsson (1853–1919) is justifiably acclaimed as Sweden's greatest painter. A 20-minute trip from Falun will take you to a small village, Sundborn, site of Lilla Hyttnas, Larsson's home (now known as Carl Larsson-gården). There are guided tours throughout the day, and English-language tours sometimes are available.

While at the home of the artist, you can also ask about viewing **Carl Larssons porträttsambling** ✶ (a portrait collection donated by Larsson), displayed in the Congregation House next to the local church. The pictures, painted between 1905 and 1918, depict well-known local residents representing many different occupations. To reach the garden, take bus no. 64 from Falun to Sundborn, which is 5 minutes away from Carl Larsson-gården.

Carl Larssons Väg 12, Sundborn. *©* 023/600-53. Admission 90SEK ($12/£6.60) adults, 40SEK ($5.50/£2.90) children 7–17, free for children 6 and under. May–Sept daily 10am–5pm; Oct–Apr by appointment only (call *©* 023/600-69 or 023/600-53 for reservations). Bus: 64 from Falun. Lies 10km (6¼ miles) to the northeast.

Falu Koppargruva ★★★   This copper mine, around which the town developed, was the world's largest producer of copper during the 17th century; it supplied the raw material used for the roof of the Palace of Versailles. Since 1970, when the mine was opened to the public, more than one million visitors have taken the elevator 54m (177 ft.) below the earth's surface and into the mine. Guides take you through old chambers and winding passages dating from the Middle Ages. In one section of the mine you'll see a shaft divided by a timber wall that's more than 195m (640 ft.) high; this may be the world's tallest wood structure. Today the only industrial product of the mine is pigment used for producing Sweden's signature red paint *(Falu Rödfärg)*, which is used not only on virtually all Swedish barns, but on thousands upon thousands of private homes and even commercial and public buildings. Buildings painted this shade of barn red have become virtual symbols of Sweden.

Gruvplatsen. ⓒ 023/78-20-30. Admission 100SEK ($14/£7.30) adults, 50SEK ($6.90/£3.65) children 7–18. May–Sept daily 10am–5pm; Oct–Apr Mon–Fri 11am–5pm, Sat–Sun 11am–4pm. Tours must be booked in advance in winter.

WHERE TO STAY

First Hotel Grand ★   This hotel's impressive spa facilities and overall comfort give it an edge over any other accommodations in the area. This buff-colored hotel 90m (295 ft.) south of the landmark Falun Church was built in 1862, with a modern addition constructed in 1974. The tastefully modern guest rooms are among the best-decorated in town. All have ample-size bathrooms equipped with shower units. If you don't mind paying 200SEK ($28/£15) extra, you can book a Grand Room with a free minibar and pay TV, plus a luxurious bathrobe with slippers. For the most elegant living of all, reserve a suite with its own sauna and large private bathrooms. On site is Harry's Pub and Restaurant, which not only serves good food but might entertain you with jazz, blues, or even a sports evening. The spa is the best in town, with many types of treatments followed by a sauna and a relaxing swim.

Trotzgatan 9–11, S-791 71 Falun. ⓒ 023/7948-80. Fax 023/14143. www.firsthotels.com. 151 units. Sun–Thurs 1,498SEK–1,698SEK ($207–$234/£109–£124) double; Fri–Sat 798SEK–998SEK ($110–$138/£58–£73) double; 2,750SEK ($380/£201) suite. Rates include breakfast. AE, DC, MC, V. Parking 80SEK ($11/£5.85). Bus: 701 or 704. **Amenities:** Restaurant; bar; indoor heated pool; fitness center; sauna; room service (7am–10pm); laundry service; dry cleaning; nonsmoking rooms; rooms for those w/limited mobility. *In room:* TV, minibar (in some), dataport, trouser press.

LEKSAND ★★

48km (30 miles) W of Falun, 267km (166 miles) NW of Stockholm

Leksand is a doorway to Lake Siljan and, in its present form, dates from the early 1900s when it was reconstructed following a fire that razed the community. However, some type of settlement has existed on this site since pagan times.

Many of the old traditions of the province still flourish here. Women occasionally don the traditional dress for church on Sunday, and in June and July the long "church boats" from Viking times may cross the lake carrying parishioners to church. These same boats compete in a church-boat race on the first Sunday in July. Since World War II, a miracle play, *The Road to Heaven,* has been presented here in open-air performances, providing an insight into the customs and folklore of Dalarna. The play runs for 10 days at the end of July.

ESSENTIALS

GETTING THERE   By Plane   You can fly from Stockholm on **Skyways** (ⓒ **0771/ 959-500**); the nearest airport is **Dala-Airport** (ⓒ **0243/645-00**), in Borlänge, 50km

(31 miles) south, from which there is frequent bus and train service to Leksand. Car rentals are available at the airport.

By Train There's a direct train from Stockholm to Mora that stops in Leksand (trip time: 3½ hr.). For reservations and information, call © 771/75-75-75.

By Boat Another way to reach Leksand is by boat on the *Gustaf Wasa* ⚓ (© 010/252-32-92 for information and reservations). Every Monday at 3pm it makes one long trip from Mora to Leksand (through Rättvik). The round-trip fare is 120SEK ($17/£8.75) for adults, 60SEK ($8.30/£4.40) for children 5 to 15, and free for those under 5. Tickets are sold on board. The return is by train.

By Car From Falun, our last stopover, head north on Route 80 to Bjursås, and then go west on a secondary road signposted as SÅGMYRA. Follow the signs into Leksand.

VISITOR INFORMATION Contact the **Leksands Turistbyrå,** Norsgatan 40 (© 0247/79-61-30; www.stab.se), open June 15 to August 10 Monday to Friday 10am to 8pm, Saturday 10am to 5pm, and Sunday 11am to 5pm; rest of the year, Monday to Friday 10am to 5pm, and Saturday 10am to 11pm.

A SPECIAL EVENT Sweden's biggest music festival, **Music at Lake Siljan** ⭐⭐⭐, takes place during the first week of July. There are some 100 concerts covering a wide range of music at venues in both Leksand and Rättvik. Fiddle music predominates. For information, contact **Music at Lake Siljan,** Karlsviks väg 2, S-795 35 Rättvik (© 0248/102-90).

SEEING THE SIGHTS

Leksand's **parish church** ⚓ (Leksands Kyrka) is in the town center, on Norsgatan, near the lake (© 0247/807-60). Founded in the 13th century, it assumed its present form in 1715 and is one of the largest rural churches in Sweden. During renovations in 1971, a burial site was found that dates to the period when the Vikings were being converted to Christianity. The church is open for worship throughout the year, but guided tours (in Swedish and English) are offered only from mid-June to early August. Tours are scheduled Monday through Saturday from 10am to 1pm and 2 to 5pm, Sunday from 1 to 5pm. Admission to the church is free; the tour costs 200SEK ($30/£15) per person.

Nearby, also on Norsgatan, is an open-air museum, **Fräsgården** (© 0247/802-45). The cluster of 18th- and 19th-century buildings (which are part of the museum's collections) features depictions by that period's peasants of Christ and his Apostles in Dalarna dress. The museum is open only from mid-June to mid-August, Tuesday through Friday from noon to 4pm, Saturday and Sunday from noon to 5pm. Admission is 50SEK ($5.75/£3.65) for adults, free for children.

An athletic and health-conscious town, Leksand has ample opportunity for **outdoor sports.** There are downhill skiing facilities at the popular resort **Granberget,** about 20km (13 miles) to the southwest. The town's tourist office can provide information on swimming, cross-country skiing, curling, ice-skating, tennis, and boat rides on Lake Siljan. All are available in or near the town center, depending on the season and weather.

WHERE TO STAY

During the summer, you may find it fun to rent a *stuga* (log cabin) with four beds for 1,900SEK to 4,500SEK ($262–$621/£139–£329) per week. You can use it as a base for exploring all of Dalarna. The **Leksands Turistbyrå,** Norsgatan 40 (© **0247/79-61-30**), will book you one. You also can inquire about renting a room in a private home.

Masesgården *(Finds)* This is one of the most sports-and-fitness-conscious hotels in Sweden. It has a reputation for educating guests about new eating and exercise habits, and a philosophy of preventing disease and depression through proper diet and exercise. Most people spend a week, participating in supervised aerobic and sports regimes, not indulging in conventional spa-style pampering. Beside a sea inlet, with a view of Leksand across the fjord, it's a sprawling compound of low-slung buildings. Guest rooms are soothing and more plush than you might have imagined. Each comes with a well-maintained bathroom equipped with a shower unit.

The daily program includes lectures that stress the link between a healthy body and a healthy soul ("astrological reincarnation and modern lifestyles" is a favorite), and physical disciplines such as tai chi. Theme weeks concentrate on individual subjects, such as meditation and modern yoga, and Reiki healing through applied massage. Other activities include aerobics, sometimes in a swimming pool, and weight training. Classes are conducted in Swedish, but most staff members speak English. This is not a holiday for the faint-hearted. Be prepared to sweat and reevaluate your lifestyle, in ways that might not always be completely comfortable.

Grytnäs 61, S-793 92 Leksand. © 0247/645-60. Fax 0247/122-51. www.masesgarden.se. 34 units, 23 with bathroom. 8,330SEK ($1,150/£608) per person per week in double without bathroom; 8,850SEK ($1,221/£646) per person per week in double with bathroom. Rates include all meals and 30 hr. of supervised sports activities. AE, DC, MC, V. Free parking. **Amenities:** Restaurant; lounge; indoor heated pool; sauna; wellness programs. *In room:* No phone.

Moskogen Motel Moskogen offers very basic and very different types of accommodations, mostly red-painted summer cottages. You don't really have to rough it: the cottages aren't that basic and have a number of facilities. The motel and huts at this "self-service holiday village" make a good base for excursions around the Lake Siljan area. The rooms are well furnished and comfortable, with good beds. Each unit has a tiny kitchen and a neatly kept bathroom with shower unit. A restaurant on the premises serves light lunches and dinners. The Moskogen is 1.5km (1 mile) west of the railway station.

Insjövägen 50, S-793 00 Leksand. © 0247/146-00. Fax 0247/144-30. www.moskogen.com. 49 units. 950SEK ($131/£69) double; 1,350SEK ($186/£99) suite. Rates include breakfast. AE, DC, MC, V. Free parking. Bus: 58. **Amenities:** Breakfast room; bar; 2 heated pools (1 indoor); exercise room; Jacuzzi; sauna; tennis court; laundry service/dry cleaning; nonsmoking rooms; rooms for those w/limited mobility. *In room:* TV, safe.

WHERE TO DINE

Bosporen SWEDISH/TURKISH Most guests dine at their hotels, but this little eatery continues to attract the more independent-minded foodies. This restaurant, 360m (1,181 ft.) west of the railroad station, maintains longer, more reliable hours than any other place in town. Its Istanbul-derived name comes from the Turkish-born owners. The chefs are equally at home in the Swedish and Turkish kitchens. Shish kabobs and Turkish salads are featured, but you can also order fried Baltic herring, sautéed trout, fresh salmon, or plank steak. The cooking is fair and even a bit exotic in a town not renowned for its restaurants.

Torget 1. © 0247/132-80. Main courses 68SEK–225SEK ($9.40–$31/£4.95–£16). AE, DC, MC, V. Summer daily 11am–11pm; mid-Sept to May daily 3–10pm.

RÄTTVIK 🐦🐦

20km (13 miles) NE of Leksand, 275km (171 miles) NW of Stockholm

If we couldn't get in Tällberg because of heavy bookings (a likely possibility in summer), then Rättvik would be a most delightful runner-up.

With some of the best hotels in the district, Rättvik is one of the most popular resorts bordering Lake Siljan. In summer, conducted tours begin here and go around Lake Siljan. Culture and tradition have long been associated with Rättvik; you'll find peasant costumes, folk dancing, Dalarna paintings, arts and crafts, fiddle music, and "church boats"—flamboyantly painted boats in which entire congregations floated for Sunday services. The old style of architecture is still prevalent, and you'll see many timber houses. Carpenters and painters from Rättvik are known for their craftsmanship.

ESSENTIALS

GETTING THERE   **By Train**   You can reach Rättvik by rail. The Stockholm train to Mora stops in Leksand, where you can catch another train for the short trip to Rättvik. Train information in Stockholm is available at the **Central Station** (© 771/75-75-75).

By Bus   Buses to Rättvik operate Friday to Sunday from Stockholm. There's also a bus connection between Leksand and Rättvik. For schedules, call © **0200/21-82-18**.

By Car   From Leksand, head north on Route 70 into Rättvik.

VISITOR INFORMATION   The **Rättvik Tourist Office** is in the train station (© **0248/79 72 10**, www.stab.se). It's open from June 15 to August 10 daily 10am to 7pm, and Sunday 10am to 7pm; from August 11 to June 14 Monday to Friday 10am to 5pm.

SEEING THE SIGHTS

Don't overtax yourself running around taking in the minor attractions of Rättvik. Instead, come here to enjoy nature. For a sweeping view that stretches for many kilometers, drive 5km (3 miles) east of town along the road leading to Falun. Here, soaring more than 24m (79 ft.) skyward, is a red-sided wooden tower, originally built in 1897, called the **Vidablick,** Hantverksbyn (© **0248/102-30**). Be warned in advance that there's no elevator and the stairs are steep. Admission is 25SEK ($3.45/£1.85) for adults, 5SEK (70¢/35p) for children 7 to 15. On the premises are a coffee shop and a souvenir stand. The complex is open only from May 1 to September 6 daily from 10am to 5pm.

Gammelgården 🐦🐦 (© **0248/137-89**) is an antique Dalarna farmstead whose pastures and architecture evoke the 19th century. The Swedes are a bit crazy for their open-air museums, and at this point you may begin to tire of them. If not, take this one in. The hours are erratic—basically, it's open whenever a farm resident is able to conduct a tour—so it's important to phone in advance. Upon prior notification, visits can be arranged throughout the year, but regular scheduling is most likely between mid-June and mid-August daily from noon to 5pm. Admission is 20SEK ($2.75/£1.45). To reach Gammelgården from the center of Rättvik, 1.5km (1 mile) north of town along Route 70, follow the signs pointing to Mora.

You can also visit the artists' village (established by the Swedish artist Sören Erikson) at **Rättviks Hantverksby,** Gårdebyn (© **0248/302-50**).

WHERE TO STAY

Expensive

Hotel Lerdalshöjden ★ *Finds* This hotel has grown and prospered since 1943 when the Stefan Hagberg family took it over when it had just 11 rooms and a kitchen with a wood stove. In 40 years they built up a lively trade. New owners are now installed but they carry on the same high standards of the long ago Hagbergs. We like the panoramic views of Lake Siljan and the distant mountains from its location right next to ski slopes, where it receives visitors year round. Near the top of a hill overlooking Rättvik, the hotel is a 10-minute walk north of the lake. The only remaining part of the original building is the **Lerdalshöjden restaurant** (see "Where to Dine," below). The guest rooms are well furnished and maintained. They have modern accessories and good-size bathrooms equipped with shower units.

S-795 35 Rättvik. © 0248/511-50. Fax 0248/511-77. www.lerdalshojden.se. 95 units. 995SEK–1,050SEK ($137–$145/£73–£77) double; 1,700SEK ($235/£124) suite. Children under 12 stay free in parent's room. Rates include breakfast. DC, MC, V. Free parking. Bus: 58 or 70. **Amenities:** Restaurant; bar; spa; fitness center; sauna; room service (7am–10pm); laundry service; dry cleaning; all nonsmoking rooms. *In room:* TV, trouser press.

Inexpensive

Hotel Gärdebygården *Value* This hotel, off Storgatan in the town center, is a very good value. Opened in 1906, it lies within a short walk of the lake. The hotel has expanded to include a trio of outlying buildings. The comfortable rooms are sedately outfitted, with conservative furniture, but the bathrooms with shower units are very small. Some units have a view of the lake. The big breakfast is almost like a Swedish smorgasbord. Some nights are devoted to communal singalongs and cross-country ski trails and jogging paths are a short distance away.

S-795 36 Rättvik. © 0248/302-50. Fax 0248/306-60. 44 units. 895SEK ($124/£65) double. Rates include breakfast. MC, V. Free parking. Bus: 58 or 70. Closed Oct–May. **Amenities:** Restaurant; bar; laundry service; dry cleaning. *In room:* TV, minibar, hair dryer.

WHERE TO DINE

Lerdalshöjden SWEDISH This summer-only restaurant is the only original section remaining in the turn-of-the-20th-century hotel. It has long been a favorite with lake-district locals. We join them in liking its traditional, tasty Swedish home-style cooking, including fresh fish and beef dishes. Try steak tartare with bleak (a freshwater fish) roe, or fried ptarmigan with red-currant sauce.

If a hungry visitor arrives off season, he or she is often referred to the **Green Hotel** (© **0248/502-50**), signposted from the center of town and lying less than a kilometer (about ½ mile) away. This traditional hotel dates from the 1600s, when it first opened as an inn. Additional rooms were added in the 1960s. With breakfast and dinner included, charges year-round are around 1,000SEK ($138/£73).

In the Lerdalshöjden Hotel. © 0248/511-50. Reservations recommended. Fixed-price menu 350SEK ($48/£26). DC, MC, V. Daily noon–2pm and 6–9pm. Closed Aug 16–June 14.

MORA ★

45km (28 miles) W of Rättvik, 328km (204 miles) NW of Stockholm

This old resort town in Upper Dalarna is a busy place in both summer and winter, and we find it a good base for touring the surrounding area. It is fabled as the town where King Gustav rallied the peasants to form an army to go against Denmark. This history-making event is commemorated every year in the 80km (50-mile) Vasa Race. Mora is also the hometown of the once-celebrated Anders Zorn, who is known mainly today for his paintings of nude women bathing. Between Lake Orsa and Lake Siljan, the provincial town of Mora is our final major stopover in the province.

ESSENTIALS

GETTING THERE   By Plane   You can fly from Stockholm on **Next Jet** (© 08/ 593-631-31); there are two flights per day Monday to Friday, and the flight time is 50 minutes. On Saturday and Sunday there is only one flight per day. The airport (© 0250/301-75) is about 6.5km (4 miles) from the center; taxis meet arriving flights.

By Train   There's direct rail service daily from Stockholm (trip time: 4 hr.). For information and schedules, call © 771/75-75-75.

By Bus   Weekend buses leave from Stockholm's Central Station for the 4¼-hour trip. Contact **Swebus Vasatrafik** at © 0200/21-82-18.

By Boat   The *Gustaf Wasa* (see "Essentials," in the "Leksand" section, above) travels between Mora and Leksand. The boat departs Leksand in the afternoon and leaves Mora at 3pm on Monday. Call © 010/252-32-92 for information and reservations.

By Car   From Rättvik, continue around Lake Siljan on Route 70 to Mora.

VISITOR INFORMATION   Contact the **Mora Turistbyrå**, Strandgatan 14 (© 0250/ 59-20-20; www.siljan.se). It's open from June 15 to August 31 Monday through Friday 10am to 7pm, and Saturday and Sunday 10am to 5pm; September 1 to June 14, Monday to Friday 10am to 5pm.

SEEING THE SIGHTS

Mora is home to a **Santa complex** (© 0250/287-70), which features Santa's house and factory. Visitors can meet Santa and see his helpers making and wrapping presents for children all over the world, and kids can enroll in Santa School and participate in troll and treasure hunts.

Mora also was the hometown of Anders Zorn (1860–1920), Sweden's most famous painter, and all of the town's top sights are associated with him. The first, **Lisselby**, is an area near the Zorn Museum made up of old houses that now are used as arts and crafts studios and boutiques.

Zornmuseet (Zorn Museum) 🅡🅡   The son of a brewer, Anders Zorn was born in Mora in 1860, showing incredible artistic talent at a very young age. He became Sweden's most internationally recognizable artist, in a class with fellow artist Carl Larsson and sculptor Carl Milles.

Zorn spent time in the United States, where he painted portraits of President Grover Cleveland and later President William Taft. As an etcher, Zorn was compared to Rembrandt. Many art critics felt that Zorn surpassed the Dutch master in this genre. Zorn was also an accomplished sculptor, and it is his *Gustav Vasa* that greets Vasalopp's skiers when they arrive in Mora.

Of all the paintings here, we find *Midnight* to be Zorn's masterpiece, although there are those who'll pay millions for his female nudes. In *Midnight* (1891) light played a decisive role with a woman rowing in the shadowless summer light, evocative and eerie at the same time. The same year, the artist painted his second most memorable work. Called *Margit*, it depicts a girl braiding her hair in the rays of light from a small window.

The museum also displays works Zorn collected, including paintings from his chief rival, Carl Larsson, and Prince Eugene. He also gathered a large collection of the rural art and handicrafts of Dalarna.

Vasagatan 36. ℭ **0250/592-310.** Admission 50SEK ($6.90/£3.65) adults, 2SEK (30¢/15p) children 7–15. Mid-May to Aug Mon–Sat 9am–5pm, Sun 11am–5pm; Sept to mid-May daily noon–4pm.

Zornsgården 👁👁 Zorn died here at the age of 60 in 1920, when he was full of new ideas and artistic projects. He and his wife, Emma, did not have any children. When Emma herself died in 1942 during the war, she donated almost all of their entire holdings, both property and art, to the state. The state decided to allow their home to remain as Emma had left it, hoping that it would give future generations an insight into the artistic world and visions of Sweden's greatest painter.

Their former house is large and sumptuous, and they furnished it with exquisite taste, both in furnishings and, of course, in their choice of art. Zorn's love of his native countryside is evident in his paintings, and fortunately, we are able to see many of the unspoiled scenes he painted so long ago. After visiting his former home, we always pay our respects to this great artist by going to his gravesite in Mora Cemetery.

Vasagatan 36. ℭ **0250/592-310.** Admission 50SEK ($6.90/£3.65) adults, 15SEK ($2.05/£1.10) children 7–15. Mid-June to Aug Mon–Sat 10am–5pm, Sun 11am–5pm; Sept to mid-June Mon–Sat noon–5pm, Sun 1–5pm. Full tours of the house are conducted by guides at noon, 1, 2, and 3pm (in summer every 30 min.).

SHOPPING IN NEARBY NUSNÄS

In Nusnäs, about 9.5km (6 miles) southeast of Mora, you can watch the famous Dalarna horse (dalahäst) being made. You're free to walk around the workshops watching the craftspeople at work, and the finished products can be purchased at a shop on the premises. They also sell wooden shoes and other crafts items. **Nils Olsson Hemslöjd** (ℭ **0250/372-00**) is open from June to mid-August Monday to Friday 8am to 6pm, and Saturday and Sunday 9am to 5pm; and from mid-August to May Monday to Friday 8am to 5pm, and Saturday 10am to 2pm. To find Nusnäs, take the signposted main road east from Mora, turning off to the right at Farnas. From Mora, bus no. 108 also runs to Nusnäs.

WHERE TO STAY

Mora Hotell & Spa 👁 In terms of overall facilities and comfort, we'd rate this Best Western the best in town—no surprises, but no disappointments either. The Mora is in the center of town across from the lakefront, a minute's walk from the tourist bureau. Renovations over the years have added sun terraces and glassed-in verandas. The interior is tastefully decorated with bright colors and folkloric accents. All accommodations—mostly midsize bedrooms—have comfortable furniture, including ample bathrooms equipped with shower units. The hotel is known for its Emma Spa, with superb massage, body treatments, steam rooms, and Jacuzzis.

Strandgatan 12, S-792 00 Mora. ℭ **0250/59-26-50.** Fax 0250/189-81. www.bestwestern.com. 141 units. Sun–Thurs 1,368SEK ($189/£100) double, 1,488SEK ($205/£109) suite; Fri–Sat 948SEK ($131/£69) double, 1,038SEK ($143/£76) suite. Rates include breakfast. AE, DC, MC, V. Parking 70SEK ($9.65/£5.10) in the garage, free outdoors. **Amenities:** Restaurant; bar; indoor heated pool; spa; Jacuzzi; sauna; room service (7am–10pm); babysitting; laundry service/dry cleaning; nonsmoking rooms; rooms for those w/limited mobility. In room: TV, dataport, safe, trouser press.

WHERE TO DINE

Terrassen (Value SWEDISH/INTERNATIONAL The finest dining room in the area is a good bet for a meal even if you aren't staying at the hotel. We've always come away filled and satisfied here, although hardly raving about the cuisine, which is of a high standard and reliable—nothing more. Fresh produce is used whenever possible, and fresh fish and Swedish beef dishes are featured. You might begin with herring or a freshly made salad. Service is polite and efficient, and the fixed-price lunch is an exceptional value.

In the Mora Hotell & Spa, Strandgatan 12. ℂ 0250/59-26-50. Reservations recommended. Main courses 80SEK–191SEK ($11–$26/£5.85–£14). Fixed-price lunch 69SEK ($9.50/£5). AE, DC, MC, V. Mon–Sat 6–9pm.

FROM MORA BACK TO STOCKHOLM

From Mora, take Route 70. In Enköping, pick up E-18, which takes you to Stockholm.

3 Gotland (Visby) ★★

219km (136 miles) S of Stockholm, 150km (93 miles) S of Nynäshamn, 89km (55 miles) E of the Swedish mainland

There is no town in all of Scandinavia that evokes the romance and charm of the Middle Ages more than the once-powerful city of Visby.

In the middle of the Baltic Sea sits the island of "Gothland"—the ancient home of the Goths—about 121km (75 miles) long and 56km (35 miles) wide. Swedes go to Gotland—the country's most popular tourist island—for sunny vacations by the sea, whereas North Americans tend to be more drawn to the old walled city of Visby. An investment of a little extra time will reveal that Gotland, with its cliffs, unusual rock formations, bathing beaches, and rolling countryside, is rich territory. If you can visit only one island of Sweden, make it Gotland, even if you have to skip Öland. Buses traverse the island, as do organized tours out of Visby.

From the end of the 12th century and throughout the 13th, the walled city of Visby rose to the zenith of its power as the seat of the powerful Hanseatic merchants and the trade center of northern Europe. During its heyday, 17 churches were built, step-gabled stone houses were erected, and the townspeople lived in relative luxury. Visby was eventually ransacked by the Danes, however, and fell into decline. Sometime late in the 19th century, when Visby was recognized as a treasure house of medieval art, it became a major attraction.

ESSENTIALS

GETTING THERE   By Plane   Visitors can fly **SAS** to Gotland from Stockholm; there are three daily flights, which take about 30 minutes. For information and schedules, call ℂ **0770/72-77-27.** There is no bus service.

By Boat   Those who want to take the boat to Gotland must first go to Nynäshamn; by bus from Stockholm, it's about a 1-hour ride. The last car ferry to Visby leaves at 11:30pm and takes about 3 hours and 15 minutes. In summer there also are five daily connections. You can make reservations through your travel agent or directly with the ferry service, **Destination Gotland,** for cabin or car space. It's wise to book deck space if you plan to travel on a weekend. Call ℂ **0771/22-33-00** in Gotland.

VISITOR INFORMATION   In Visby, contact the tourist bureau, **Gotlands Turist Service,** Skeppsbron 4–6 (ℂ **0498/20-17-00**), open May to August Monday to Friday 8am to 7pm, Saturday and Sunday 7am to 6pm; September to April Monday to Friday 8am to 4pm.

A SPECIAL EVENT   We've attended many festivals in Sweden, but not one of them appealed to us as much as this journey back to the Middle Ages. During the annual **Medieval Week** ★★ in August, Visby once again becomes a Hanseatic town. At the harbor, Strandgatan swarms with people in medieval dress, many of them tending market stalls. You meet the blacksmith, barber, cobbler, and trader. Musicians play the hurdy-gurdy, the fiddle, and the flute; jesters play the fool. Toward nightfall a kingly procession comes into the square. The program has more than 100 such events during the festival, along with medieval mystery plays, masses, choral and instrumental music, tournaments, and displays of horses, as well as archery competitions, fire-eaters, belly dancers, and walking tours of the medieval town.

SEEING THE SIGHTS
IN VISBY ★★

The walled city of Visby is made for wandering and getting lost. The cobbled streets will carry you into many nooks and crannies. UNESCO has proclaimed Visby a World Heritage Site, something that must be carefully preserved for future generations to discover. Mercifully from the middle of May to the middle of August, vehicles are banned in the Alstadt, or Old Town.

The city is a marvel. The most enthusiastic visitors walk the entire perimeter of the walls, the **Ringmurer** ★★★, a distance of 3.5km (2¼ miles). The walls are riddled with medieval gates and towers. There is both a land wall and a sea wall, the latter 5.3m (17 ft.) tall. It was built as a fortification sometime in the late 1200s, incorporating an ancient gunpowder tower, the **Kruttornet** ★. The crenellated land wall is only 6m (20 ft.) high. Amazingly, a total of 27 of the original 29 towers are still standing.

Visby is a good town for walkers, but you may want to take one of the organized tours that are offered in season. Because so many of the sights, particularly the ruins of the 13th- and 14th-century churches, are better appreciated with some background, we recommend the tours that take 2 hours each and cost 85SEK ($12/£6.20) per participant. They're offered only in summer, between mid-June and mid-August. Between mid-June and mid-July, English-language tours are conducted every Wednesday and Saturday at 10am.

In town, you can walk about, observing houses from the Middle Ages, ruined fortifications, and churches. Notable among these is the **Burmeisterska Huset,** the home of the *burmeister,* or the leading German merchant, at Strandgatan 9.

You can stroll down to the old **Hanseatic harbor** (not the same harbor in use today) and to the **Botanical Gardens,** which have earned Visby the title "City of Roses." You'll pass two of the most famous towers in the old wall—the **Maiden's Tower** (a peasant girl was buried alive here for helping a Danish king) and the **Powder Tower** (the oldest fortification in Visby).In the heyday of its power and glory, little Visby boasted 17 churches. Only one today, **Domkyrkan (Cathedral of St. Mary)** ★★, is in use. Found at Kyrkberget, it was dedicated in 1225 and was built with funds collected by German merchant ships. Pope Clement VI in Avignon gave his permission to build the so-called Swertingska chapel in 1349. The church was damaged in four serious fires: 1400, 1586, 1610, and 1744. It attained its status as a cathedral in 1572. The only original fixture left is a sandstone font from the 1200s. The landmarks of Visby are the two towers of the church. The tower at the western front is square, whereas two slimmer ones appear on the east. In the interior, one of the curiosities is the fringe of grotesque angels' faces beneath the pulpit. Hours are daily 8am to 8pm. Free admission. For more information, call ✆ **0498/206-800.**

The ruins of the former **Dominican Monastery of St. Nicholas** are just down the road from Domkyrkan. The church has a rose window cut from a single big stone—it's more than 3m (10 ft.) in diameter. Work began on the monastery in 1230, but it was destroyed by Lübeck forces in 1525. For more information, call ✆ **0498/206-800.**

Another sightseeing recommendation is the impressive **Gotlands Fornsal** ✹✹, the Historical Museum of Gotland, Strandgatan 14 (✆ **0498/29-27-00**), on a medieval street noted for its step-gabled houses. We'd vote this one of the best regional museums in the country—it's certainly among the largest, and you'll need to devote about 2 hours to take in the highlights. The museum contains artifacts discovered on Gotland, including carved stones dating from A.D. 400, art from medieval and later periods, plus furniture and household items. After five floors of exhibitions, and 8,000 years of history, we like to wind down at the on-site cafe and browse through the bookstore. It's open from May 15 to August daily 10am to 5pm, September to May 14 Tuesday to Sunday noon to 4pm. Admission is 60SEK ($8.30/£4.40) for adults, free for children 16 and under.

EXPLORING THE ISLAND

At the **Turistbyrå,** Skeppsbron 4–6 (✆ **0498/201700**), ask what island tours are scheduled during your visit; these daily tours (different every day) are the best way to get a quick overview of Gotland. The price can be as low as 70SEK ($9.65/£5.10) for a brief walking tour or as high as 400SEK ($55/£29) for a complete tour of the island by van.

One thing you can be sure of is that each tour will visit the **Lummelunda Grottan,** Lummelunds Bruk (✆ **0498/27-30-50**), a karst cave formed of limestone bedrock by a subterranean stream. The explored part of the stream cave stretches for 4km (2½ miles) and contains stalactite and stalagmite formations, fossil remains, and subterranean waters. The part of the cave with some of the biggest and most beautiful chambers is open to visitors. It's located 13km (8 miles) north of Visby along Route 149. A bus departs from Österport Visby from June 19 to August 14 daily at 2pm. The cave is open from May to June 25 daily 9am to 4pm, June 26 to August 14 daily 9am to 6pm, August 15 to September 14 daily 10am to 2pm (closed at other times). Visits on your own cost 70SEK ($9.65/£5.10) for adults, 50SEK ($6.90/£3.65) for children 5 to 15, free for children 4 and under.

ISLAND TOURS   An 11-hour bus tour of **northern Gotland** and **Fårö** takes you to the port of Fårösund for the 10-minute ferry ride over the strait. On the excursion around Fårö (Sheep Island), you can see dwarf forests and moors.

Returning to Gotland, the bus takes you to the open-air history museum at **Bunge,** which documents the old peasant culture. That's followed by a tour of the **Blase limestone museum** in Fleringe, which has two restored 19th-century lime kilns.

Another tour takes you to the southern tip of the island to see the legendary "old man of **Hoburgen,**" a rock formation known as a chalk stack. The tour includes the Iron Age village of **Gervide** as well as two 17th-century farms. The bus travels along the windswept shoreline of the west coast.

A DRIVING TOUR   If you are pressed for time, stick to the sights in Visby. But if you have 4 or 5 hours and have rented a car, we have devised this road tour of Gotland that encapsulates the island in a nutshell. Arm yourself with a good road map of Gotland before setting out. If you get lost that's all right, as the island is too small to be lost for long.

From Visby, drive north on Route 149, heading toward the fishing port of **Lickershamn.** Look for a narrow trail along the cliffs. This path leads you to a rock that juts into the water. Known as the *Maiden,* this promontory offers some of the best views on Gotland.

From Lickershamn, continue along Route 149, passing to the towns of **Ire** and **Kappelshamn.** From Kappelshamn, follow Route 149 south to the junction with Route 148 in **Lärbro.** Here, go north on Route 148 to **Fårösund.** The village of Fårösund sits on the shores of the 1.5km-wide (1-mile) Fårösund channel, which separates the small island of **Fårö** from the main island of Gotland. You can take a ferry to Fårö to visit some of the island's superb beaches.

From Fårösund, take Route 148 back to Lärbro. A few kilometers past Lärbro, take Route 146 southwest toward **Slite.** Follow it down the coast to **Aurungs.** Here, go west on a secondary road heading toward **Siggur.** In Siggur, follow signs south to the village of **Dalhem.** The most remarkable sight in Dalhem is the village church, situated just outside town. Its wall paintings and stained glass are the finest on Gotland. Train buffs may enjoy visiting the Railway Museum located in the old train station.

From Dalhem, continue south on the road that brought you to town. Head toward **Roma.** Look for the ruins of Roma Abbey, a Cistercian monastery destroyed during the Protestant Reformation.

Head west from Roma on a secondary road toward Route 140 that runs along Gotland's western coast. You'll pass the villages of **Bander** and **Sojvide** before you reach Route 140. Follow it south to **Burgsvik,** a popular port and resort town. Just east of Burgsvik, visit the small hamlet of **Öja.** Its church boasts a triumphal cross dating from the 13th century.

After visiting Öja, return to Burgsvik. Here you head south, passing the villages of **Bottarvegården** and **Vamlingbo.** At the southern tip of Gotland you'll find **Hoburgen,** with its towering lighthouse. Along with the lighthouse, you'll encounter cliffs, many with strange rock formations, and a series of caves.

Return to Burgsvik to connect with Route 140. Turn off after **Fidenäs,** following Route 142 toward **Hemse.** Outside Hemse, take Route 144 to **Ljugarn,** a small port and resort town on Gotland's east coast. You can visit the small customs museum. Just south of Ljugarn, on a secondary road, is a series of Bronze Age stone sculptures. The seven rock formations, depicting ancient ships, form the largest group of stone settings on the island.

Follow Route 143 northwest from Ljugarn to return to Visby.

SHOPPING

No one goes to Gotland to shop. But, once here, you'll find some pleasant surprises. The most memorable goods available are produced on the island, usually by individual craftspeople working in highly detailed, small-scale productions. Our favorite store is **Yllet,** S:t Hansgatan 19, Visby (© **0498/21-40-44**), where clothing made from wool produced by local sheep is sold in the form of sweaters, scarves, hats, gloves, coats, and winter wear for men, women, and children. We've found that colors here tend to be natural and soft, deriving from the untinted, unbleached fibers originally produced by the sheep themselves. Also, don't overlook the gift shop that's showcased within the island's historical museum, **Gotlands Fornsal,** Strandgatan 14, Visby (© **0498/29-27-00**), where reproductions of some of the museum's art objects are for sale, as well as handicrafts and textiles made on the island.

Gotland is home to dozens of highly skilled, independent artists, who mostly work out of their own houses or studios manufacturing ceramics, textiles, woodcarvings, or examples of metalwork. Their merchandise tends to be marketed by cooperatives— loosely organized networks that publicize and display the works of artists. The artists' work is judged by a panel that decides whether their products are qualified to represent the local art and handicraft scene. Objects are displayed and can be purchased at **Galerie Kvinnfolki,** Donnersplats 4 (© **0498/21-00-51**). Kvinnfolki limits its merchandise to items crafted by women, which includes jam made from local berries, textiles, children's clothing, and a line of cosmetics made on the island from all-natural oils, emollients, and pigments.

WHERE TO STAY

If you should arrive without reservations (not a good idea), contact the **Gotland Resort** (© **0498/20-12-60**). The English-speaking staff will try to arrange for rooms in a hotel or private home in or near Visby. The average rate for accommodations in a private home is 220SEK ($30/£16) per person, per night.

Hotell Solhem It was the setting that first attracted us to this Best Western hotel. Solhem lies in the midst of a beautiful park, Palissadparken, and is the most tranquil choice we found in Visby. The well-run hotel was built in 1987 on a slope overlooking the harbor, a few blocks north of the center. In 1998, its size was doubled, thanks to an addition designed to match the hotel's existing core with ocher-colored walls, prominent gables, a terra-cotta roof, and a vague sense of the seafaring life of the early 19th century. Bedrooms are comfortable and warm, with simple furniture and small bathrooms equipped with shower units. What we like about this place is that the owners have made an attempt to see that no two rooms look alike. Even so, some of them look a bit like an upmarket college dormitory. Some of the rooms house six persons in reasonable comfort, with extra beds costing 350SEK ($48/£25) for adults or 175SEK ($24/£13) for children. If you can, get a room with a view of the water and the flood-lit city walls at night. If not, settle for a garden view; at least try to get one of the 17 rooms with a private balcony.

Solhemsgatan 3, S-621 58 Visby. © **0498/25-90-00.** Fax 0498/25-90-11. www.hotellsolhem.se. 94 units. 890SEK–1,550SEK ($123–$214/£65–£113) double. Rates include breakfast. AE, DC, MC, V. Free parking. Closed Sat–Sun Jan–Feb. **Amenities:** Breakfast room; lounge; sauna; babysitting; laundry service; dry cleaning; nonsmoking rooms; rooms for those w/limited mobility. *In room:* TV, dataport, hair dryer.

Hotel S:t Clemens (*Value*) We've liked this place since we first visited when researching *Scandinavia on $10 a Day.* Thanks to a number of improvements over the years, we still find it cozy. This 18th-century building in the town center has been successfully transformed into a well-run small hotel. It's decorated tastefully in a modern style, with light pastels used effectively. It's open year-round, and the staff is helpful and efficient. In spite of the hotel's age, all of its bathrooms have modern shower and toilet facilities with adequate shelf space. All renovations were carried out with care, so as not to ruin the architecture. No two rooms are identical; your choices range from the smallest single in the shoemaker's old house with a view over church ruins, to a four-bed unit with a sloping ceiling and the greenery of the botanical gardens framing the window. Even the old stable offers rooms for guests with allergies. A homelike atmosphere permeates the whole place, which is comprised of a series of five antique buildings connected by two idyllic gardens.

Smedjegatan 3, S-621 55 Visby. © **0498/21-90-00.** Fax 0498/27-94-43. www.clemenshotell.se. 30 units. 760SEK–1,440SEK ($105–$199/£55–£105) double; 1,650SEK–2,400SEK ($228–$331/£120–£175) suite; additional bed 250SEK ($35/£18) extra. Rates include breakfast. AE, DC, MC, V. Free parking. **Amenities:** Breakfast room; lounge; sauna; nonsmoking rooms; rooms for those w/limited mobility. *In room:* TV, dataport, hair dryer.

Strand Hotel   This former site of the Visby Brewery now houses this Best Western hotel. The 110 rooms are spread across three buildings, which look older than they are. Guests intermingle in the library or the adjoining bar. The comfortable bedrooms are midsize and tastefully modern, and the bathrooms are well maintained with up-to-date plumbing that includes shower stalls. Breakfast is the only meal served.

Strandgatan 34, S-621 56 Visby. ℂ 800/528-1234 in the U.S., or 0498/25-88-00. Fax 0498/25-88-11. www.strand hotel.net. 110 units. 980SEK–1,880SEK ($135–$259/£72–£137) double; 2,800SEK ($386/£204) suite. Rates include breakfast. AE, DC, MC, V. Free parking. **Amenities:** Breakfast room; bar; indoor pool; sauna; babysitting; laundry service; dry cleaning; nonsmoking rooms. *In room:* TV, dataport, minibar, hair dryer.

Villa Alskog ★★ *Finds*   Our favorite nest on the island is this restored 1840 building close to the sandy beaches. It's a delight in every way, offering real old-fashioned Gotland hospitality. Stone fences, open spaces, and a tree-studded landscape evoke an atmosphere of long ago, although there's also an outdoor pool as a modern touch. The decor is traditional Swedish, with bright colors and wood floors. Bedrooms are midsize and beautifully maintained, with comfortable, tastefully furnished modern bathrooms with shower stalls. This is the best place for spa treatments we found on the island, complete with a Japanese hot tub. In the lobby, you can avail yourself of a 24-hour buffet. The food is good and most filling, with lots of Swedish flavor. In a public area, guests have access to a phone, TV, and dataport connection.

Alskog, S-620 16 Ljugarn. ℂ 0498/49-11-88. Fax 0498/49-11-20. www.villa-alskog.se. 30 units. 995SEK ($137/£73) double. AE, DC, MC, V. **Amenities:** Restaurant; bar; outdoor pool; gym; spa; sauna; room service (7am–midnight); laundry service; nonsmoking rooms; rooms for those w/limited mobility. *In room:* No phone.

WHERE TO DINE

Burmeister ITALIAN/INTERNATIONAL   Don't expect too much, and you won't be disappointed here. This large restaurant in the town center offers dining indoors or under shady fruit trees in the garden of a 16th-century house originally built for the wealthiest citizen of Visby. The cuisine is rather standard international, never achieving any glory. The place is incredibly popular in summer, and long lines form—so they must be doing something right. Pizza is the most popular menu choice. After 10pm in summer, the restaurant becomes a dance club; the cover charge ranges from 100SEK to 200SEK ($14–$28/£7.30–£15).

Strandgatan 6, Visby. ℂ 0498/21-03-73. Reservations required. Main courses 155SEK–245SEK ($21–$34/£11–£18); pizzas 99SEK–125SEK ($14–$17/£7.25–£9.15). AE, DC, MC, V. June 20–Aug 5 Mon–Sat noon–4pm and 6–11pm. Disco mid-June to Aug 5 Mon–Sat 10pm–2am.

Gutekällaren SWEDISH   This restaurant and bar in the town center was originally built as a tavern in the early 1600s on foundations that are much older. It was enlarged in 1789, and today is one of the oldest buildings (if not *the* oldest) in Visby. It offers fresh fish and meat dishes, including some vegetarian specialties. You might begin with a delectable fish soup made with lobster and shrimp, and then follow with filet of sole Waleska or roast lamb chops. The dessert specialty in summer is a parfait made of local berries. Cooking here is solid and reliable, with fresh ingredients.

Stortorget 3, Visby. ℂ 0498/21-00-43. Reservations recommended. Main courses 185SEK–240SEK ($26–$33/£14–£18). AE, DC, MC, V. Daily 6–11pm.

Munkkällaren ★ SWEDISH/INTERNATIONAL   This restaurant is one of the best, and you'll recognize it in the center of Visby by its brown wood facade. The dining room, which is only a few steps from the street, is sheathed in white stone, parts of which date from 1100. In summer, the management opens the doors to two more pubs in the compound. The main pub, Munken, offers platters of flavorful *husman-skost* (Swedish home cooking), including *frikadeller* (meatballs). In the restaurant you might begin with escargots in creamy garlic sauce, or toast with Swedish caviar. Specialties include a savory shellfish stew, an ably-crafted salmon-stuffed sole with spinach and saffron sauce, and venison in port-wine sauce. Live music is often performed in the courtyard, beginning around 8pm. After the music stops, a dance club opens Friday to Sunday from 11pm to 2am. Admission to the club is 80SEK to 150SEK ($11–$21/£5.85–£11).

Lilla Torggränd 2, Visby. © 0498/27-14-00. Reservations required in summer. Main courses 128SEK–260SEK ($18–$36/£9.35–£19). AE, DC, MC, V. Restaurant Mon–Sat 6–11pm; pub Mon–Sat 9pm–2am (June 1–Aug 7 noon–11pm).

VISBY AFTER DARK

There's a lot more energy expended on star-gazing, wave-watching, and ecology in Gotland than on bar-hopping and nocturnal flirting. If you want to heat it up after dark, there's a limited offering. The island's premier venue for folks over 40 who enjoy ballroom-style dancing occurs every Saturday night at the **Borgen Bar,** Hästgatan 24 (© **0498/24-79-55**), which contains a restaurant, a dance floor, and music that ranges from the big band era to more modern, supper-club selections. A hipper alternative is the **Munkkällaren,** which was recommended previously as a restaurant and derives at least some of its business from its role as a bar and late-night, weekend-only dance club. It's a good pickup spot. A similar atmosphere is found at **Gutekällaren**, another previously recommended restaurant, whose interior becomes a dance club either 2 or 4 nights a week, beginning around 10pm, for high-energy dancers mostly ages 35 and under. If you happen to be a bit older than 35, you'll still feel comfortable hanging out at the establishment's bar, soaking up aquavit and absorbing the local color.

4 Swedish Lapland ✦✦✦

Swedish Lapland—*Norrland,* to the Swedes—is the last wilderness of Europe. The vast northern land of the Midnight Sun has crystal-blue lakes, majestic mountains, glaciers, waterfalls, rushing rivers, and forests. Lapland covers roughly half the area of Sweden (one-quarter of which lies north of the Arctic Circle).

The sun doesn't set for 6 weeks in June and July, and brilliant colors illuminate the sky. In spring and autumn, many visitors come here to see the northern lights.

Swedish Lapland is a paradise for hikers and campers (if you don't mind the mosquitoes in the summer). Before you go, get in touch with the **Svenska Turistföreningen (Swedish Touring Club),** P.O. Box 25, Amiralitetshuset 1, Flagmansvägen 8, S101 20 Stockholm (© **08/463-21-00**). It maintains mountain hotels and has built bridges and marked hiking routes. The touring club has a number of boats in Lapland that visitors can use for tours of lakes. There are hundreds of kilometers of marked hiking and skiing tracks. March, April, and even May are recommended for skiing. Some 90 mountain hotels or huts (called *fjällstugor* and *kåtor*) are available, with beds and bedding, cooking utensils, and firewood. Huts can be used for only 1 or 2 nights. The club also sponsors mountain stations (*fjällstationer*).

You must be in good physical condition and have suitable equipment before you set out because most of the area is uninhabited. Neophytes are advised to join one of the hiking or conducted tours offered by the Swedish Touring Club. Contact the club for more details.

LULEÅ
931km (578 miles) N of Stockholm

This is the northernmost major town in all of Sweden and can be viewed as a refueling stop and a place for food and shelter. While fire destroyed most of the Old Town, Luleå is not totally devoid of charm. If you have 2 or 3 hours to wander about, you can visit the town's original settlement, which enjoys protection by the UNESCO World Heritage Site.

Our tour north begins in Luleå on the way to Lapland. This port city on Sweden's east coast at the northern end of the Gulf of Bothnia is 113km (70 miles) south of the Arctic Circle. Boats depart from its piers for some 300 offshore islets and skerries known for their flora and fauna.

Luleå has a surprisingly mild climate—its average annual temperature is only a few degrees lower than that of Malmö, on the southern tip of Sweden.

The town of Luleå is a port for shipping iron ore in summer. Its harbor remains frozen over until May. The state-owned ironworks here have led to a dramatic growth in population.

Establishing a city this far north was laden with difficulties. Gustavus Adolphus may have founded the city in 1621, but it wasn't until 1940 that development really took hold. Today, as the seat of the University of Luleå, the town has a population of 70,000 and is liveliest when the students are here in winter, although most visitors (except businesspeople) see it only in summer.

ESSENTIALS

GETTING THERE   By Plane   SAS runs nine flights each weekday between Stockholm and Luleå (two Sat–Sun), which take 1¼ hours. There are six flights each weekday between Gothenburg and Luleå (two on Sat, four on Sun), taking 2¼ hours. For information and schedules, call ✆ **0770/72-77-27.**

By Train   Six trains arrive daily from Stockholm (travel time: 15 hr.); an additional six come from Gothenburg (travel time: 19 hr.). Trains from Stockholm to Kiruna usually deposit passengers bound for Luleå at the railway junction at Boden, 9.5km (6 miles) northwest of Luleå. Here they board one of three connecting trains a day going between Boden and Luleå. Train traffic from Gothenburg to Luleå also necessitates a transfer in Boden. For more information, phone ✆ **0771/75-75-75.**

By Bus   A bus runs between Stockholm and Luleå on Friday and Sunday, taking 14 hours. For further information, call **Swebus** at ✆ **0200/21-82-18.**

By Car   From Stockholm, take the E-4 expressway north to Uppsala and continue northward along the coast until you reach Luleå.

VISITOR INFORMATION   Contact the **Luleå Tourist Office** at Storgatan 43B Luleå (✆ **0920/22-24-75;** www.lulea.se), open in summer Monday to Friday 9am to 7pm, and Saturday and Sunday 10am to 4pm; off season Monday to Friday 10am to 6pm and Saturday 10am to 2pm.

SEEING THE SIGHTS

It is a privilege to visit any town in the north of Sweden that enjoyed its heyday in the 17th century, and this ghost of yesterday doesn't disappoint. Some of the most evocative

and historic architecture in Luleå lies 9.5km (6 miles) north of the modern city in **Gammelstad (Old Town)** <N>, the town's original medieval core and a once-thriving trading center. Its demise as a viable commercial center began when the nearby harbor became clogged with silt and was rendered unnavigable. In 1649, a new city, modern-day Luleå, was established, and the Old Town—except the church described below—fell into decline and disrepair. Today it serves as a reminder of another era and is the site of the region's most famous church, **Gammelstads Kyrka** <N>, also known as Neder Luleå Kyrka (no phone). This is the largest medieval church in the north. Built in 1492, the church is surrounded by clusters of nearly identical red-sided huts, many of which date from the 18th and 19th centuries. The church rented these to families and citizens traveling to Luleå from the surrounding region as temporary homes during holy days.

Gammelstad's other major site is the **Hägnan Museum** (also known as the Gammelstads Friluftsmuseum), 95400 Gammelstad (© **0920/29-38-09**). Consisting of about a dozen historic buildings hauled in from throughout Norrbotten. It's nothing

Finds **The Ice Hotel** ✿✿✿

Since the late 1980s, the most unusual hotel in Sweden is re-created every winter on the frozen steppes near the iron mines of Jukkasjärvi, 200km (124 miles) north of the Arctic Circle. Here, the architect Yngve Bergqvist, financed by a group of friends who (not surprisingly) developed the original concept over bottles of vodka in an overheated sauna, uses jackhammers, bulldozers, and chainsaws to fashion a 60-room hotel out of 4,000 tons of densely packed snow and ice. The basic design is that of an igloo, but with endless amounts of whimsical sculptural detail thrown in as part of the novelty. Like Conrad Hilton's worst nightmare, the resulting "hotel" will inevitably buckle, collapse, and then vanish during the spring thaws. Despite its temporary state, during the long and frigid darkness of north Sweden's midwinter, it attracts a steady stream of engineers, theatrical designers, sociologists, and the merely curious who avail themselves of timely activities in Sweden's far north: dogsled and snowmobile rides, cross-country skiing, and shimmering views of the aurora borealis. On the premises are an enormous reception hall, a multimedia theater, two saunas, and an ice chapel appropriate for simple meditation, weddings, and baptisms.

Available for occupancy (temperatures permitting) between mid-December and sometime in March, the hotel resembles an Arctic cross between an Arabian casbah and a medieval cathedral. Minarets are formed by dribbling water for about a week onto what eventually becomes a slender and soaring pillar of ice. Domes are formed igloo-style out of ice blocks arranged in a curved-roof circle. Reception halls boast whimsical sculptures and rambling vaults supported by futuristic-looking columns of translucent ice.

special—we've seen better compounds in the south—but if you're in the area you might give it a look-see. It's open between June 6 and August 15 daily from 11am to 5pm, depending on the season. Entrance is free. To reach Gammelstad from modern-day Luleå, take bus no. 8 or 9 from Luleå's center.

Adjacent to Gammelstad Bay you'll find some of the richest bird life in Sweden. Ornithologists have counted 285 different species of birds during the spring migrations. The best way to experience this cornucopia of avian life involves following a well-marked hiking trail for 7km (4.3 miles) south of Gammelstad. Signs will point from Gammelstad to the **Gammelstads Vikens Naturreservat** ✿✿. For information about the trail, call the Luleå Tourist Office (see above). The trail, consisting of well-trod earth, gravel, and boardwalks, traverses marshy, usually forested terrain teeming with bird life. En route, you'll find barbecue pits for picnics and an unstaffed, unsupervised 9m (30-ft.) tower (Kömpmannholmen, no phone) that's useful for spying on bird nests in the upper branches of nearby trees. The trail ends in Luleå's suburb of Pörson, site of the local university and a small-scale museum, **Teknykens Hus,** Pörson, 97187 Luleå (✆ **0920/49-22-01**). Conceived as a tribute to the industries that bring employment and prosperity to Norrbotten, it's open daily from 11am to 5pm in summer, and Tuesday to Friday 11am to 4pm in winter. Entrance fee is 50SEK

Everyone wants to know if a stay here is comfortable, and while it's not particularly cozy, it's an experience to be had. Upon arrival, guests are issued thermal jumpsuits of "beaver nylon" whose air-lock cuffs are designed to help the wearer survive temperatures as low as –8°F (–22°C). Beds are fashioned from blocks of chiseled ice lavishly draped, Eskimo-style, with reindeer skins. Guests keep warm with insulated body bags that were developed for walks on the moon. Other than a temporary escape into the hotel's sauna, be prepared for big chills: Room temperatures remain cold enough to keep the walls from melting. Some claim that this exposure will bolster your immune system so that it can better fight infections when you return to your usual environment.

There's lots of standing up at the long countertop crafted from ice that doubles as a bar. Swedish vodka that's dyed a shade of blue and served in cups crafted from ice is served.

Ice Hotel, Marknadsvägen 63, S-981 91 Jukkasjärvi, Sweden. *©* **0980/ 668-00.** Fax 0980/668-90. Doubles cost from 2,240SEK ($309/£164) and suites from 3,040SEK ($420/£222) per day, including breakfast. Heated cabins, located near the ice palace, are available from 2,240SEK ($309/£164) per night, double. Toilets are available in a heated building next door.

From Kiruna, head east immediately along Route E-10 until you come to a signpost marked JUKKASJÄRVI and follow this tiny road northeast for about 2.5km (1½ miles).

($6.90/£3.65) for adults, 30SEK ($4.15/£2.20) for children 5 to 15, and free for those under 5. From Pörson, after your visit to the museum, take bus no. 4 or 5 back to Luleå. Hiking along the above-mentioned trail is not recommended in winter, as heavy snowfalls obliterate the signs and the path.

Norrbottens Museum, Storgatan 2 (*©* **0920/24-35-00**), close to the city center at Hermelin Park, offers a comprehensive look at Norrbotten's history. Exhibits show how people lived in the northern regions over the centuries. The museum has perhaps the world's most complete collection of Sami artifacts. Admission is free. It's open Tuesday through Friday from 10am to 4pm, Saturday and Sunday from noon to 4pm. Take bus no. 1, 2, 4, 5, 8, or 9.

WHERE TO STAY & DINE

Elite Stadshotellet *★★*   This is the finest choice in town. The Stadshotellet is housed in a stately, architecturally ornate, brick-and-stone building that stood here at the turn of the 20th century. With all the improvements over the years, it's still the grandest and most traditional hotel, standing right in the center of town next to the waterfront. The airport bus stops right outside the door at a site near the north harbor. Both the bus and train stations are within walking distance.

The hotel was conceived by "six local gentlemen" in 1897, and they demanded a magnificent facade with excellent stone craftsmanship, spires, and towers. In 1959 a devastating fire swept across the third and fourth floors, and the cut-glass chandeliers came crashing down. To rebuild it in an authentic style, the hotel owners of the time had to import stucco workers from the south of Italy, who also restored the original roof. As late as 2001, The Bishop's Arms, a cozy pub in the English style, was added to keep the hotel abreast of the times. Each room is individually decorated and are also the most spacious in town, especially the large and luxurious suites, with bathrooms in Italian marble. Traditional Swedish fare and zestier Italian specialties are served in the signature restaurant, Tallkotten.

Storgatan 15, S-971 81 Luleå. © 0920/67-000. Fax 0920/670-92. www.elite.se. 135 units. Mon–Thurs 1,495SEK–1,695SEK ($206–$234/£109–£124) double; Fri–Sun 795SEK–995SEK ($110–$137/£58–£73) double; 2,800SEK ($386/£204) suite. Rates include buffet breakfast. AE, DC, MC, V. Parking 100SEK ($14/£7.30). Bus: 1, 2, 4, 5, 8, or 9. **Amenities:** Restaurant; bar; sauna; room service (7am–10pm); laundry service/dry cleaning; nonsmoking rooms; 1 room for those w/limited mobility. *In room:* TV, dataport (in some), minibar, hair dryer.

Hotel Nordkalotten ★★ *Finds*   More than any other, this hotel captures the spirit of the north of Sweden. Set 5km (3 miles) south of the town center, this is the most architecturally intriguing hotel in the region, with charming grace notes. It originated in 1979, when the city of Luleå established a tourist information center on its premises. In 1984, the hotel was acquired by an independent entrepreneur who was lucky enough to secure thousands of first-growth pine logs (many between 600 and 1,000 years old) that had been culled from forests in Finland and Russia. To create the comfortable hotel you see today, he hired well-known Finnish architect Esko Lehmola to arrange the logs into the structural beams and walls of the hotel's reception area, sauna, and convention center. The result, which could never be duplicated today because the raw materials are no longer available, is a hotel where the growth rings of the wood reveal hundreds of years of forest life.

Most unusual of all is a dining and convention room set within what is shaped like an enormous tepee—also crafted from the ancient trees—that's flooded with sunlight from wraparound windows. Guest rooms are outfitted in soothing tones of beige and gray, with conservatively contemporary furnishings, tiled bathrooms with showers, and wall-to-wall carpeting. Double rooms have their own private saunas.

Lulviksvägen 1, S-972 54 Luleå. © 0920/20-00-00. Fax 0920/20-00-90. www.nordkalotten.com. 172 units. Mid-June to mid-Aug 790SEK ($109/£58) double and suite; Fri–Sat year-round 1,330SEK ($184/£97) double and suite; Sun–Thurs year-round 1,813SEK ($250/£132) double and suite. AE, DC, MC, V. Free parking. From Luleå's center, follow the signs to the airport. **Amenities:** Restaurant; bar; indoor heated pool; sauna; laundry service; dry cleaning; nonsmoking rooms; rooms for those w/limited mobility. *In room:* TV, dataport, minibar, Wi-Fi.

FROM LULEÅ TO JOKKMOKK

From Luleå, take Route 97 northwest. Thirty minutes into the trip, you can stop at **Boden.** Founded in 1809, this is Sweden's oldest garrison town. After losing Finland to Russia, Sweden built this fortress to protect its interior from a Russian invasion. Visit the **Garnisonsmuseet (Garrison Museum),** which has exhibits on military history, as well as many uniforms and weapons used throughout Sweden's history. It's open from June to September daily from 11am to 4pm, charging 10SEK ($1.30/£0.75) for admission. It lies at the southwest edge of town. After visiting Boden, continue along Route 97 to Jokkmokk.

JOKKMOKK ☆

198km (123 miles) NW of Luleå, 1,191km (740 miles) N of Stockholm

Surrounded by a vast wilderness, this little community on the Luleå River, just north of the Arctic Circle, is the best center for immersing yourself into the culture of the Sami. It has been their cultural center and trading post since the 1600s.

Jokkmokk, meaning "bend in the river," is also the finest base in Lapland we've found for exploring the great outdoors. For some a car will be vital here, and while bus routes link Jokkmokk to surrounding villages, the system offers service that is too infrequent to be of practical use by the average visitor.

Other than the summer tourists, visitors are mostly business travelers involved in some aspect of the timber industry or the hydroelectric power industry. Jokkmokk and the 12 hydroelectric plants that lie nearby produce as much as 25% of all the electricity used in Sweden. Most residents of the town were born here, except for a very limited number of urban refugees from Stockholm.

ESSENTIALS

GETTING THERE   By Plane   The nearest airport is in Luleå, 198km (123 miles) away (see "Getting There," in the "Luleå" section, above, or call **SAS** at ☏ **0770/727-727**). From Luleå, you can take a bus for the final leg of the journey.

By Train   No trains run between Stockholm and Jokkmokk. However, three trains make the run from Stockholm to Murjek, a town lying 60km (37 miles) to the south of Jokkmokk. From Murjek, you can take one of three buses a day for the final lap into Jokkmokk.

By Bus   There is one scheduled bus per day from Luleå to Jokkmokk, which is timed to meet the plane's arrival. For information, call ☏ **0200/21-82-18.**

By Car   From Luleå, take Route 97 northwest.

VISITOR INFORMATION   Contact the **Jokkmokk Turistbyrå,** Stortorget 4 (☏ **0971/222-50**), open from June to mid-August daily from 10am to 6pm, from mid-August to May Monday to Friday 8:30am to noon and 1 to 4pm.

SEEING THE SIGHTS

At a point 7km (4.3 miles) south of Jokkmokk, you cross the Arctic Circle if you're traveling along Route 45. At a kiosk here, you'll be given a souvenir certificate in case you need to prove to anybody that you're a genuine Arctic explorer.

Jokkmokk is the site of **The Great Winter Market** ☆☆☆, a 400-year-old tradition. It's the best place in Scandinavia to stock up on smoked reindeer meat. Sami from all over the north, including Finland and Norway, come to this grand market held the first weekend of February from Thursday to Sunday. Sami display and sell those precious handicrafts they've been working on during the bitter winter months. Some 30,000 people flock to this market every year. If you're planning a visit, you'll need to make reservations a year in advance.

Salmon fishing is possible in the town's central lake. Locals jump in the river in summer to take a dip, but we suggest you watch from the sidelines unless you like to swim near freezing waters.

Karl IX decreed that the winter meeting place of the Jokkmokk Sami would be the site of a market and church. The first church, built in 1607, was known as the **Lapp Church.** A nearby hill, known as **Storknabben,** has a cafe from which, if the weather is clear, the Midnight Sun can be seen for about 20 days in midsummer.

It is only fitting that Jokkmokk is home to the national Swedish Mountain and Sami Museum, or **Ájtte** ★★★, Kyrkogatan (© **0971/170-70**), in the center of town. This museum (whose Sami name translates to "storage hut") is the largest of its kind; its exhibits integrate nature and the cultures of the Swedish mountain region. One part of the museum is the **Alpine Garden** (© **0971/10100**), which lies close to the museum on Lappstavägen. If you want to learn about the natural environment and the flora of the north of Sweden, this is the place to go. The mountain flora is easily accessible and beautifully arranged. There's also a restaurant and a gift shop. Museum admission is 50SEK ($6.90/£3.65) for adults, free for children 17 and under. The museum is open year-round; in summer, Monday to Friday 11am to 5pm, and Saturday and Sunday noon to 5pm; off season, it closes at 4pm.

WHERE TO STAY & DINE
Hotell Gästis ★ You wouldn't know it from the rather bleak facade, but this hotel is a landmark, dating from 1915 when it was the best, and only, place to stay in the area. It's conveniently located in the exact center of town about 180m (590 ft.) from the rail station. It offers well-maintained rooms with modern furnishings and small bathrooms equipped with shower units. Floors are either carpeted or covered in vinyl. The restaurant serves well-prepared meals, including continental dishes and *husmanskost*. Entertainment and dancing are presented once a week, and the sauna is free for all hotel guests.

Harrevägen 1, S-96 231 Jokkmokk. © **0971/100-12.** Fax 0971/100-44. www.hotell-gastis.com. 27 units. 750SEK–995SEK ($104–$137/£55–£73) double; 900SEK–1,200SEK ($124–$166/£66–£88) triple. Rates include breakfast. AE, DC, MC, V. Free parking. **Amenities:** Restaurant; bar; sauna. *In room:* TV, hair dryer.

A SIDE TRIP TO KVIKKJOKK
Talk about roughing it. We've hiked many parts of the world, and Sarek was one of our toughest challenges. The **Sarek National Park** ★★★, between the Stora and Lilla Luleälv, covers an area of 1,208 sq. km (471 sq. miles), with about 100 glaciers and 87 mountains rising more than 1,770m (5,806 ft.); eight are more than 1,950m (6,396 ft.). The most visited valley, **Rapadel** ★, opens onto Lake Laidaure. In winter, sled dogs pull people through this valley.

In 1909, Sweden established this nature reserve in the wilderness so that it could be preserved for future generations. To take a walk through the entire park would take at least a week, so most visitors stay only a day or two. Although rugged and beautiful, Sarek is extremely difficult for even the most experienced of hikers. There is absolutely nothing here to aid the visitor—no designated hiking trails, no tourist facilities, no cabins or mountain huts, and no bridges over rivers (whose undertows, incidentally, are very dangerous). Mosquitoes can be downright treacherous, covering your eyes, nose, and ears. You should explore the park only if you hire an experienced guide. Contact a local hotel such as **Kvikkjokk Fjällstation** (see below) for a recommendation.

Kvikkjokk is the starting or finishing point for many hikers using the **Kungsleden Trail.** Call the **Svenska Turistföreningen** (© **08/463-21-00**) for information, and also see "Abisko," later in this chapter. One- or 2-day outings can be made in various directions. Local guides also can lead you on a boat trip (inquire at the hotel listed below). The boat will take you to a fascinating delta where the Tarra and Karnajokk rivers meet. The area also is good for canoeing.

WHERE TO STAY

Kvikkjokk Fjällstation   Originally established in 1907 by the Swedish Touring Club, and enlarged with an annex in the 1960s, this mountain chalet offers simple, no-frills accommodations for hikers and rock-climbers. It's also the headquarters for a network of guides who operate canoe and hiking trips into the vast wilderness areas that fan out on all sides. Accommodations are functional, woodsy, and basic, and include eight double rooms, eight four-bed rooms, and two cabins with four beds each. There's a sauna, a plain restaurant, and access to canoe rentals and a variety of guided tours that depart at frequent intervals. The station is open only from February 4 to April 23 and June 17 to September 17. There is no laundry service, but they do offer a washing machine to guests. For information about the Kvikkjokk Fjällstation out of season, call the **tourist information office** in Jokkmokk (129km/80 miles away) at ⓒ **0971/222-50.**

S-962 02 Kvikkjokk. ⓒ **0971/210-22.** Fax 0971-210-39. 18 units, none with bathroom. 310SEK–370SEK ($43–US$51/£23–£27) per person. AE, MC, V. Free parking. Closed Sept 19–Feb 15. **Amenities:** Restaurant; lounge; sauna. *In room:* No phone.

FROM JOKKMOKK TO KIRUNA

After visiting Kvikkjokk, return to Jokkmokk and head north on Route 45 toward Gällivare. Along the way, you'll pass **Muddus National Park** ⊛⊛. You can enter from the town of **Saite.** Although not as dramatic as Sarek (see "A Side Trip to Kvikkjokk," above), this park, established in 1942, is worth a visit. Its 50,417 hectares (121,000 acres) are home to bears, moose, otters, wolverines, and many bird species. The Muddusjokk River flows through the park and over a panoramic 42m (140-ft.) waterfall. Trails cross the park; they're well marked and lead visitors to the most interesting sights.

Continue along Route 45 through Gällivare, toward Svappavaara. In Svappavaara, take E-10 northwest to Kiruna.

KIRUNA

193km (120 miles) N of Jokkmokk, 1,317km (818 miles) N of Stockholm

Covering more than 4,800 sq. km (1,872 sq. miles), Kiruna is the largest (in terms of geography) city in the world. Its extensive boundaries incorporate both Kebnekaise Mountain and Lake Torneträsk. This northernmost town in Sweden lies at about the same latitude as Greenland. The Midnight Sun can be seen here from mid-May to mid-July.

Unless drastic changes are made, Kiruna as we know it may not exist a few years from now. It's in danger of sliding down a hole left by the iron ore mines that put this Arctic outpost on the map a century ago. During World War II, iron ore from the mines here was exported to Nazi Germany. Before the earth swallows it up, Kiruna is going to have to be moved.

Its railway station and new highway will be relocated first. At the moment, the town's inhabitants face no immediate threat from the hole carved out by mines more than a kilometer under their feet. In the years ahead, many houses in the affected area will be loaded onto large trailers and moved to new and safe locations. Some of these buildings will be difficult to move—City Hall, for example, which will have to be cut into six pieces. A similar solution may have to be devised for the town's wood church, dating from 1913.

ESSENTIALS

GETTING THERE   By Plane   SAS (© 0770/727-727) flies twice daily from Stockholm (flight time: 95 min.).

By Train   Two or three trains per day make the 16-hour trip to Gällivare, a major rail junction. From here, you can change trains to Kiruna, a trip of 1½ hours. For schedules and information, phone © 0771/75-75-75.

By Bus   There's also daily bus service between Gällivare and Kiruna. Contact **Länstrafiken** at © 0926/756-80.

By Car   From Gällivare, continue northwest along E-10.

VISITOR INFORMATION   Contact the **Kiruna Turistbyrå,** Lars Janssonsgatan 17 (© 0980/188-80; www.lappland.se), open from June 15 to August 20 Monday to Friday 8:30am to 8pm, Saturday and Sunday 8:30am to 6pm; from August 21 to June 14 Monday to Friday 8:30am to 5pm, Saturday 8:30am to 2:30pm.

SEEING THE SIGHTS

Kiruna, which emerged at the turn of the 20th century, owes its location to the nearby deposits of iron ore.

In summer, **InfoMine Tours** ★★ descended 540m (1,771 ft.) into the earth where you can see the area where 20 million tons of iron ore are dug up every year. Tours leave every hour from 9am to 4pm, with groups forming outside the tourist office (see above). The cost is 220SEK ($30/£16) or 140SEK ($19/£10) for students and children 5 to 15; free for kids under 5. These tickets are available at the tourist office.

Southeast of the railroad station, the tower of the **Stadshus** (© 0980/70-496) dominates Kiruna. The building was designed by Arthur von Schmalensee and inaugurated in 1963. A carillon of 23 bells rings out at noon and 6pm daily. This cast-iron tower was designed by Bror Markland and features unusual door handles of reindeer horn and birch. The interior draws upon materials from around the world: a mosaic floor from Italy, walls of handmade brick from the Netherlands, and pine from the American Northwest. Note also the hand-knotted hanging entitled *Magic Drum from Rautas,* a stunning work by artist Sven (X:et) Erixon. The upper part of the hanging depicts the Midnight Sun. Inside you'll find an art collection and some Sami handicraft exhibits. It's open June to August Monday to Friday 9am to 6pm, and Saturday and Sunday 10am to 6pm; September to May Monday to Friday 10am to 5pm.

A short walk up the road will take you to the **Kiruna Kyrka** ★★, Kyrkogatan 8 (© 0980/678-12), open Monday to Friday from 9am to 6pm, Saturday and Sunday 11am to 4:45pm. This church was constructed like a stylized Sami tent in 1912 (indeed, the dark timber interior does evoke a Lapp hut), with an origami design of rafters and wood beams. Sweden's architects on several occasions have voted it as their country's most beautiful building. Gustaf Wickman designed this unusual church, which has a free-standing bell tower supported by 12 props. Christian Eriksson designed the gilt bronze statues standing sentinel around the roofline. They represent such states of mind as shyness, arrogance, trust, melancholy, and love.

You also can visit **Hjalmar Lundbohmsgården** (© 0980/701-10), the official museum of the city of Kiruna. It's situated in a manor house built in 1899 by the city's founder and owner of most of the region's iron mines, Hjalmar Lundbohm. Many of the museum's exhibits deal with the city's origins in the late 19th century, the economic conditions in Europe that made its growth possible, and the personality of the

Moments **Northernmost Golf in the World** ⭐⭐

Here's how to achieve one-upmanship on your golfing buddies back home: You can play at the northernmost golf course in the world. The **Arctic Golf Course** has only 9 holes, occupying a terrain of mostly thin-soiled tundra with a scattering of birch forest. It's open only from mid-June to mid-August. During that limited period, golfers can play 24 hours per day, as the course is lit by the Midnight Sun. For more information, contact Björkliden Arctic Golf Club, Kvarnbacksvägen 28, Bromma S-168 74 (© **08/5648-8830**). Bromma is a suburb of Stockholm.

entrepreneur who persuaded thousands of Swedes to move north to work in the mines, no small accomplishment we'd say. It's open June through August Monday to Friday from 10am to 6pm; off season, you must phone ahead for opening hours, which could be any day of the week between the hours of 8am and 4pm. Admission is 35SEK ($4.85/£2.55) for adults, 15SEK ($2.05/£1.10) for children 7 to 15, free for children under 7.

WHERE TO STAY & DINE
Moderate
Scandic Hotel Ferrum ⭐   We were immediately won over by this hotel when we found our rooms opening onto the mountains and the Kebnekaise massif in the distance. Run by the Scandic chain, this hotel is named after the iron ore *(ferrum)* for which Kiruna is famous. The six-story hotel was built in 1967 and is one of the tallest buildings in town. Functional and standardized in design, it's one of your best bets for lodging and food. It has two well-run restaurants, Reenstierna and Matsalar. Our favorite spot for socializing in Kiruna is the rustically decorated pub, Mommas, where both the crowd and the beer are compatible.

The staff arranges enough outdoor adventures to challenge an Olympic athlete: dog-sled rides, snowmobiling, Arctic safaris, river rafting, skiing, and fishing. The sauna overlooks Sweden's highest mountain, and you wind down in the relaxation room where on most days a roaring fire greets you. The rooms are modern and comfortably furnished with excellent beds and neatly kept bathrooms with tub/shower combos.

Lars Janssonsgatan 15, S-981 31 Kiruna. © **0980/39-86-00.** Fax 0980/39-86-11. www.scandichotels.com. 171 units. 1,540SEK–1,840SEK ($213–$254/£112–£134) double; 2,400SEK ($331/£175) suite. Rates include buffet breakfast. AE, DC, MC, V. Parking 85SEK ($12/£6.20). Closed Dec 23–26. **Amenities:** 3 restaurants; bar; lounge; casino; gym; sauna; laundry service; dry cleaning; rooms for those w/limited mobility; nonsmoking rooms; solarium. *In room:* TV, dataport, hair dryer, trouser press, Wi-Fi.

Inexpensive
Vinterpalatset (Winter Palace)   This privately owned hotel occupies what was originally built in 1904 as a private home for a prosperous entrepreneur in the iron-ore industry. Radically renovated and upgraded, it includes the much-improved main house, a 1950s-era annex containing four of the hotel's individually designed 20 rooms, a sauna/solarium complex, and a bar with an open fireplace. There's also a dining room, frequented mostly by other residents of the hotel, which serves rib-sticking Swedish food. Rooms are high ceilinged, dignified looking, and outfitted with hardwood floors

and comfortable furniture. Bathrooms are quite small, each with a shower. The King Bore's Bar has an open fireplace.

P.O. Box 18, Järnvägsgatan 18, S-981 21 Kiruna. (℘) **0980/677-70.** Fax 0980/130-50. www.vinterpalatset.se. 20 units. Mid-June to mid-Aug and Fri–Sat year-round 890SEK ($123/£65) double; rest of year 1,420SEK ($196/£104) double. The hotel also has 4 rooms in the annex that are 740SEK ($102/£54) mid-June to mid-Aug and Fri–Sat year-round; rest of year 990SEK ($137/£72). Rates include buffet breakfast. AE, DC, MC, V. Free parking. **Amenities:** Restaurant; bar; sauna; room service (7am–midnight); laundry service/dry cleaning, nonsmoking rooms; Jacuzzi; solarium. *In room:* TV, dataport, hair dryer, Wi-Fi.

ABISKO

89km (55 miles) NW of Kiruna, 1,467km (911 miles) N of Stockholm

Any resort north of the Arctic Circle is a curiosity. Abisko, on the southern shore of Lake Torneträsk, encompasses a scenic valley, a lake, and an island. An elevator takes passengers to Mount Nuolja (Njulla). Nearby is the protected Abisko National Park (see below), containing remarkable flora, including orchids.

ESSENTIALS

GETTING THERE   By Train & Bus   You can get a train to Kiruna (see above). From here, there are both bus and rail links into Abisko. For train information, call (℘) **0771/75-75-75.** For bus information, call **Länstrafiken** at (℘) **0926/756-80.**

By Car   From Kiruna, continue northwest on E-10 into Abisko.

VISITOR INFORMATION   Contact the tourist office in Kiruna (see "Visitor Information" under "Kiruna," above).

EXPLORING THE AREA

Abisko National Park ★★ ((℘) **0980/40-200**), established in 1903, is situated around the Abiskojokk River, including the mouth of the river, where it flows into Lake Torneträsk. The highest mountain is Slåttatjåkka, 1,170m (3,838 ft.) above sea level. Slightly shorter Nuolja, which rises 1,140m (3,739 ft.), has a cable car. The name *Abisko* is a Sami word meaning "ocean forest." The park's proximity to the Atlantic gives it a maritime character, with milder winters and cooler summers than the more continentally influenced areas east of the Scandes or Caledonian mountains.

Abisko is more easily accessible than **Vadvetjåkka National Park,** the other, smaller park in the area. Three sides of Vadvetjåkka Park are bounded by water that is difficult to wade through, and the fourth side is rough terrain with treacherously slippery bogs and steep precipices fraught with rock slides. Established in 1920, it lies northwest of Lake Torneträsk, with its northern limits at the Norwegian border. It's composed of mountain precipices and large tracts of bog and delta. It also has rich flora, along with impressive brook ravines. Its highest mountain is Vadvetjåkka, with a southern peak at 1,095m (3,592 ft.) above sea level.

Abisko is one of the best centers for watching the **Midnight Sun,** which can be seen from June 13 to July 4. It's also the start of the longest marked trail in the world, the Kungsleden.

The **Kungsleden (Royal Trail)** ★★★ is approximately 338km (210 miles) and journeys through Abisko National Park to Riksgränsen on the Norwegian frontier, cutting through Sweden's highest mountain (Kebnekaise) on the way. Properly fortified and with adequate camping equipment, including a sleeping bag and food, you can walk these trails, which tend to be well maintained and clearly marked. Cabins and rest stops (local guides refer to them as "fell stations") are spaced a day's hike

(13–21km/8–13 miles) apart, so you'll have adequate areas to rest between bouts of trekking and hill climbing. These huts provide barely adequate shelter from the wind, rain, snow, and hail in case the weather turns turbulent, as it so often does in this part of the world. At most of the stops, you cook your own food and clean up before leaving. Most lack running water, although there are some summer-only toilets. At certain points, the trail crosses lakes and rivers; boats are provided to help you get across. The trail actually follows the old nomadic paths of the Sami. Those with less time or energy will find the trail broken up into several smaller segments.

We have discovered that the trail is long but relatively easy to walk along. All the streams en route are traversed by bridges. In places where the ground is marshy, it has been overlaid with wooden planks. In summer, locals operate boat services on some of the lakes you'll pass. Often they'll rent you a rowboat or canoe from a makeshift kiosk or collapsible tent that's dismantled and hauled away after the first frost.

During the summer, the trail is not as isolated as you may think. It is, in fact, the busiest hiking trail in Sweden, and adventurers from all over the world traverse it. The trail is most crowded in July, when the weather is most reliable.

For maps and more information about this adventure, contact the local tourist office or the **Svenska Turistföreningen,** the Swedish Touring Club, P.O. Box 25, S101 20 Stockholm (© **08/463-21-00**).

WHERE TO STAY & DINE

Abisko Turiststation Owned by the Swedish Touring Club since 1910, this big, modern hotel, about 450m (1,476 ft.) from the bus station, offers accommodations in the main building, in the annex, and within 28 cabins. Each cabin is made up of two apartments suitable for up to six occupants, and each unit features a kitchen and a private bathroom with a shower unit. From the hotel you can see the lake and the mountains. The staff is helpful in providing information about excursions. The rooms are basic but reasonably comfortable, and some offer exceptional views. A washing machine is made available to guests. Buffet-style Swedish meals are served in the on-site Restaurant Tjuonavagge. Storstugan, also on the premises, is the friendliest pub in town, where guests can chat by the crackling fire.

S-98107 24 Abisko. © **0980/402-00**. Fax 0980/401-40. www.abisko.nu. 77 units, 43 with bathroom; 56 cabin apts. 840SEK ($116/£61) double without bathroom; 980SEK ($135/£72) double with bathroom. Rates include breakfast. Cabin apt 1,080SEK ($149/£79) per night or 7,710SEK ($1064/£563) per week up to 6 occupants. AE, MC, V. Free parking. Closed Sept 20–Feb 28. **Amenities:** Restaurant; bar; sauna. *In room:* TV, minibar, iron/board.

ENDING YOUR DRIVING TOUR

Because Abisko is close to the Norwegian border, you may want to cross into Norway after your tour of Swedish Lapland. If so, just take E-10 west across the border toward Narvik. From Kiruna, trains and buses go to the hamlet of Riksgränsen, the last settlement in Sweden, before continuing for the final, short leg to Narvik. Schedules depend entirely on the weather; for buses, call © **0200/218218;** for trains, © **0771/ 75-75-75.** However, if you'd like to return to Stockholm, follow E-10 east toward the coast, and then head south on E-4 to the capital city.

19

The Best of Finland

Finland offers visitors a tremendous variety of sights and experiences, everything from sophisticated Helsinki to the vast wilderness. To help you decide how best to spend your time in Finland, we've compiled a list of our favorite experiences and discoveries. Below, you'll find the kind of candid advice we'd give our close friends.

1 The Best Travel Experiences

- **Taking a Finnish Sauna:** With some 1.6 million saunas in Finland—roughly one for every three citizens—there's a sauna waiting for you here. Visitors can enjoy saunas at most hotels, motels, holiday villages, and camping sites.

- **Exploring Europe's Last Frontier:** Located in Scandinavia's far north—its northern tier traversed by the Arctic Circle—Finnish Lapland seems like a forgotten corner of the world. Its indigenous peoples, the Sami, have managed to preserve their distinctive identity and are an integral part of Lapland and its culture. Dozens of tours are available through **Nordique Tours,** a subdivision of Picasso Travel, 11099 S. La Cienega Blvd., Suite 210, Los Angeles, CA 90045 (© **800/995-7997;** www.nordiquetours.com).

- **Traversing the Finnish Waterworld:** From the coastal islands to the Saimaa lake district, Finland is one vast world of water. Adventures range from daring the giddy, frothing rapids of the midlands to paddling the deserted streams or swift currents of Lapland. Every major town in Finland has canoe-rental outfitters, and local tourist offices can offer advice on touring the local waters.

- **Wandering Finnish Forests:** Finland has been called one huge forest with five million people hiding in it. In fact, nearly four-fifths of the country's total land area is forested. Walk in the woods, picking wild berries and mushrooms along the way.

- **Discovering Finnish Design & Architecture:** Finnish buildings are among the world's newest—more than 90% have been erected since 1920—but their avant-garde design has stunned the world and spread the fame of such architects as Alvar Aalto. In Helsinki, you can see the neoclassical Senate Square, Eliel Saarinen's controversial railway station (dating from 1914), and the Temppeliaukio Church, which has been hollowed out from rock with only its dome showing. While in Helsinki, you can also visit the University of Industrial Arts—the largest of its kind in Scandinavia—to learn about current exhibits of Finnish design.

2 The Best Scenic Towns & Villages

- **Turku:** Finland's most charming town developed around an ancient trading post. Its castle played a prominent role in Finnish (as well as Scandinavian) history. The national capital until 1812, Turku today is an important cultural center, with two universities. It's also a good base for short cruises of the Turku Archipelago. See chapter 22.

- **Savonlinna:** The commercial and cultural center of the eastern Savo region, one of Finland's most ancient provinces, this town is the center of Lake Saimaa traffic. Filled with attractions, including museums and art galleries, it's also a good center for exploring—often by boat—one of the most scenic parts of Finland. See chapter 22.

- **Lappeenranta:** Founded in 1649 by Queen Christina of Sweden, this town lies at the southernmost edge of Lake Saimaa. It covers a large area stretching from the lake to the Russian border. The commercial and cultural center of South Karelia, it's a spa town and the gateway to the Saimaa Canal. It's filled with attractions and is also a good base for excursions, including visa-free day tours to Vyborg in Russia. See chapter 22.

- **Porvoo:** Situated about 50km (30 miles) northeast of Helsinki (at the mouth of the River Porvoo), this was an important trading center in the Middle Ages. Porvoo has been loved by some of Finland's greatest poets and artists. Old Porvoo, with its lanes and wooden houses—the oldest of which date from the 16th century—is well worth exploring. See chapter 21.

3 The Best Active Vacations

For additional sporting and adventure travel information, see "The Active Vacation Planner" in chapter 20.

- **Bicycling:** Thousands of miles of narrow paths and captivating gravel tracks lead to towns where broad highways are flanked by well-maintained bicycle routes. Local tourist offices can provide maps of the best trails.

- **Canoeing:** Choose from a large variety of waterscapes: coastal waters dotted with thousands of islands, rivers flowing to the sea, or lakes in the Greater Saimaa region. The best coastal areas are the archipelago along the southwest coast, the coast of Uusimaa province, and the Åland Islands. A popular region for canoeing is the lake district; here the lakes are linked in long chains by short channels with strong currents. Together the lakes form a network of routes extending for thousands of kilometers.

- **Fishing:** For those who are skilled, Finland offers the chance to fish year-round. Fishermen here divide their calendar not into months, but according to the fish in season. Sea trout become plentiful as the rivers rise in March and April. May and June are the golden months for pike. Midsummer, when the rapids are at their best, marks the season for Lapland grayling and pike-perch. Also in midsummer, salmon fishermen prepare for the high point of their year. Autumn brings sea trout inshore, along with the "Flying Dutchmen of the Deep"—pike—that stalk the shoals of herring. Even in winter,

Finnish fishermen drill through the ice to catch perch, pike, and trout. Ice fishermen angle for burbot during the dark winter nights, since its roe is regarded as the choicest of caviars.

- **Hiking:** Hiking is a popular form of recreation in heavily forested Finland. Lapland holds its own special appeal, but you can ramble for a day or more even in southern Finland. Outside Helsinki, for example, there are numerous trails in Nuuksio National Park. The provinces of middle Finland have a network of hiking trails that total some 300km (185 miles).

- **Skiing:** The ski season in Finland is the longest in Lapland, from October until mid-May. In northern Finland, south of Lapland, there's good skiing for more than 5 hours a day in natural light, even when the days are short. Numerous ski trails are lit artificially when winter is at its darkest. The peak holiday ski season is just before spring, when there's lots of daylight and sunshine. In southern Finland, skiing conditions are ideal in January and February; in central Finland the best months are December through March; and in northern Finland the best months are December through April.

4 The Best Festivals & Special Events

- **Tar Skiing Race** (Oulu): This cross-country ski race was established more than a century ago and has been held almost every year since then. In March, hundreds of participants from around the world show up to compete on the 76km (47-mile) race-course. See p. 562.

- **Midnight Sun Film Festival** (Sodankylä): Held each June, this is the world's northernmost film festival, featuring works by well-known directors as well as new names in the industry. See p. 563.

- **Kuopio Dance and Musical Festival** (Kuopio): This is Scandinavia's oldest drama festival, held in late June and the first week of July; distinguished performers and troupes from all over the world come to participate. There's a different theme each year. See p. 563.

- **Savonlinna Opera Festival** (Savonlinna): Every year from early July to early August, this festival stages three or four of its own productions and hosts visiting opera companies from abroad. See p. 654.

- **Helsinki Festival:** Beginning in mid-August, international artists come to Helsinki to perform chamber music and recitals, or to present visual arts exhibits, dance programs, film screenings, and theatrical performances, as well as opera, jazz, pop, and rock concerts. See p. 563.

5 The Best Museums

- **Ainola** (Järvenpää, outside Helsinki): This was the home of Finland's famous composer, Jean Sibelius, who lived here for more than half a century until his death in 1957. Along with his wife, Aino (for whom the house is named), he's buried on the property. Situated about 40km (24 miles) from Helsinki. See p. 607.

- **Finnish National Gallery** (Helsinki): The nation's major repository of modern art includes graphics, sculpture, paintings—the widest possible range in the country. Naturally, native-born sons and daughters are emphasized, with the work of Finnish artists dating from the mid–18th century. See p. 603.

- **Gallen-Kallela Museum** (Espoo): On a wooded peninsula, this museum honors the Finnish artist Akseli Gallen-Kallela (1865–1931), who is known mainly for his paintings, especially those from the *Kalevala* ("Land of Heroes"), the Finnish national epic. See p. 608.
- **Mannerheim Museum** (Helsinki): This was the home of Baron Carl Gustaf Mannerheim, marshal of Finland and president of the republic from 1944 to 1946. It has been turned into a museum filled with memorabilia, including his swords, medals, and uniforms, along with his collection of antiques and furnishings. See p. 606.
- **National Museum of Finland** (Suomen Kansallismuseo, Helsinki):

No other museum in the country documents the history of the Finnish people like this one. The tools that shaped ordinary life in the country since the Stone Age are documented here, with exhibits ranging from folk costumes to church art. See p. 606.

- **Seurasaari Open-Air Museum** (Seurasaari): This museum is on an island off the coast of Helsinki (now a national park). Here some 100 authentically furnished and decorated houses have been reassembled—everything from a 1600s church to an "aboriginal" sauna. If you don't have the opportunity to explore Finland in depth, these buildings will help you understand something of Finnish life past and present. On summer evenings, folk dances are presented here to the tunes of a fiddler. See p. 608.

6 The Best Offbeat Experiences

- **Camping Outdoors:** There are about 350 campsites with some 6,300 camp cabins and holiday cottages. If you have an international camping card (FICC), you don't need a Finnish camping card. Campers can buy a family camping card at the first site at which they intend to stay; it costs 5€ ($6.50) for the whole year. Regional tourist offices can provide information about campsites, or write to the **Finnish Campingsite Association,** Mäntytie 7, FIN-00270 Helsinki (© **09/477-407-40;** www.camping.fi). In North America, the card is available from the **Family Campers and RVers Association,** 4804 Transit Rd., Building 2, Depew, NY 14043; (© **800/245-9755;** www.fcrv.org).
- **Experiencing a Finnish Farm:** Despite its role as an industrialized

nation, Finland's roots extend deep into the soil. Several hundred English-speaking farmers have opened their homes to temporary guests, offering a firsthand view of how the country grows such flavorful produce and vegetables. Local tourist offices have information. A well-respected travel expert, **Lomarengas Finnish Country Holidays,** Eteläesplanadi 22C, 3rd Floor, FIN-00130 Helsinki (© **09/576-633-50;** www.lomarengas.fi), compiles an annual booklet with descriptions, map locations, and photographs of scenic farms, antique and modern cottages, and log cabins. Prices for rooms within farms vary, but even the most expensive generally fall in the budget category. It's also possible to arrange rentals of cabins and cottages suitable for two to eight people.

- **Panning for Gold:** In the Lemmenjoki region (near Inari), in Finnish Lapland, there are all-day gold-panning trips along the River Lemmenjoki between mid-June and mid-September. Participants are shown how to wash gold by sluicing and panning. On the return trip you'll stop at Ravadas waterfall, one of the most spectacular sights in northern Finland. For more information, contact **Lemmenjoki Cabins,** Ahkun Tupa, FIN-99885 (© 016/67-34-35).

- **Lighthouse-Watching in the Gulf of Bothnia:** The waters separating Finland from Sweden are dotted with thousands of islands, some of them forested, some of them wind-scoured and rocky, and most of them uninhabited. Between May and August, when the waters are ice-free and the Northern Lights shimmer down upon waters, you might opt for lighthouse-watching cruises that last between 1 and 3 days. The most famous of the lighthouses in the archipelago near Vaasa is the **Valassaaret Lighthouse,** designed by an associate of Gustave Eiffel (Henri Lipart) in the 1890s. Others lighthouses date from the early 1960s. Your exposure to the bird life, marine life, and botany of the Gulf of Bothnia will be unparalleled. For more information, contact **Botnia Tourist,** Vaasanpuistikko 22, FIN-65100 Vaasa (© 06/325-11-25; www.botnia tourist.com).

- **Seeing Lapland on a Safari: Borton Overseas** (© 800/843-0602; www.bortonoverseas.com) will take you on a tour of Finnish Lapland. You experience close encounters with the Sami people and their culture, and get to see one of the last great wildernesses of Europe. You're taken to old village settlements and along lakes, where you can watch herds of reindeer. Summer tours of the tundra are held between May and early September, and in winter it's also possible to traverse the snow-covered tundra on tours between January and April.

- **Taking a Snowmobile Safari:** From the first week of January until mid-April, you can take a 6-day/5-night snowmobile safari; you fly from Helsinki to Ivalo in the north of Finland and back again. At the Saarisellkä Skiing Resort, you first get snowmobile driving lessons and then have the opportunity to go snowmobile trekking through varying winter landscapes. Overnights are sometimes arranged in wilderness huts; safari outfits and all meals are provided. For more information, contact **Nordique Tours,** 11099 S. La Cienega Blvd., Suite 210, Los Angeles, CA 90045 (© 800/ 995-7997; www.nordiquetours.com).

7 The Best Buys

- **Clothing & Textiles:** There's everything from cottons and linens (often in stunning modern fashions such as those by Marimekko) to warm stoles and shawls. Collectors also seek out *ryijy* rugs and *raanu* wall hangings. Many of these goods are displayed and sold at shops along the Esplanade in Helsinki.

- **Glass & Ceramics:** Finland offers a wide variety of stunning designs, ranging from practical everyday items at moderate prices to one-of-a-kind objects designed by well-known Finnish artisans. The best-known factory names (and the best quality) to look for are Arabia for china, or Nuutajärvi, Iittala, and Riihimäki for glass. Their products are displayed in shops throughout the country. Showrooms for both Arabia and Iittala are on the Esplanade in Helsinki. Many

Finnish glass factories can be visited; contact local tourist offices for further information.

- **Jewelry:** Although Finland is not often associated with jewelry making, it has some rare items for sale—especially from the *Kalevala* series based on centuries-old Finnish ornaments. Modern designers working in gold or silver produce many bold and innovative pieces of jewelry, sometimes as settings for Finnish semiprecious stones or combined wood and silver. Lapponia jewelry—sold all over the country—is one example.

- **Wines & Spirits:** Vodka and liqueurs made from local berries are popular, especially the rare cloudberry, the Arctic bramble, and the cranberry. Alcohol is sold at retail through the outlets of Alko, the State Alcohol Company.

8 The Best Hotels

- **Hotel Kämp,** Pohjoisesplanadi 29, Helsinki (✆ **09/57-61-11;** www. hotelkamp.fi; p. 583): One of the most luxurious hotels in the north of Europe, the Kämp brings five-star comforts to the Finnish capital. It was constructed in 1887, but has been dramatically and beautifully restored. A great deal of Finnish history took place under its roof, and the politics of the country, a blend of east and west, continue to thrive on its dramatic premises.

- **Palace Hotel,** Eteläranta 10, Helsinki (✆ **09/13-45-61;** www.palace kamp.fi; p. 586): On the south harbor, this glamorous hotel—known for its scenic 10th-floor dining room—is the city's finest. The accommodations are spacious, with sleek Finnish styling such as dark-wood paneling and built-in furniture. The Palace offers the highest level of personal service, and amenities include three saunas on the 11th floor.

- **Hilton Hotel Kalastajatorppa,** Kalastajatorppantie 1, Helsinki (✆ **09/458-11;** www.hilton.com; p. 590): Set in a bucolic park on the sea, this is a tranquil and luxurious choice. Comprising three buildings with two restaurants, plus two modern glass wings linked by tunnels, it's a cozy retreat. In summer, amenities include a beach with watersports equipment.

- **Hilton Helsinki Strand,** John Stenbergin Ranta 4, Helsinki (✆ **800/445-8667** or 09/393-51; www.hilton. com; p. 590): Opening onto a bay, this deluxe chain member boasts the most dramatic atrium in Helsinki. Some of Finland's top designers were called in to create some of the capital's most tasteful and comfortable guest rooms, often using deluxe construction materials such as marble from Lapland.

9 The Best Restaurants

- **Ravintola Nokka,** Kanavaranta 7F, Helsinki (✆ **09/687-7330;** p. 595): In a 19th-century building, this elegant restaurant is a showcase for the products of Finland. Its chefs dazzle with their prowess with home-grown produce and fresh game. Cheerfully and competently served, the house repertoire of foods, from mallard duck to Finnish cheese, is filled with dishes of high caliber.

- **Chez Dominique,** Richardinkatu 4, Helsinki (✆ **09/612-73-93;** p. 591): One of only two Michelin-starred restaurants in all of Finland, this is a gourmet citadel reigning as Helsinki's "restaurant of the year" with most of the city's newspaper and magazine food critics. Near Esplanadi Park, the first-class restaurant offers French-inspired cuisine using fresh Scandinavian products whenever available.

- **G. W. Sundmans,** Eteläranta 16, Helsinki (© **09/622-64-10;** p. 591): The only restaurant in Helsinki to equal—but not surpass—Chez Dominique is housed in a former mansion. It, too, is Michelin starred. Deluxe French and Scandinavian cuisine is served in elegant surroundings. Succulent dishes native to Finland include grilled sirloin of elk with a rowanberry *sabayon* sauce.

- **Havis,** Eteläranta 16 Helsinki (© **09/6869-5660;** p. 594): Known for its fine seafood, this upscale tavern was established in 1973. Most of its saltwater fish comes from Finnish coastal waters, while its freshwater fish—everything from Baltic crayfish to brook trout—is from Finnish lakes. The restaurant has a beautiful atmosphere and some of the finest service in Helsinki.

- **Palace Gourmet,** in the Palace Hotel, Eteläranta 10, Helsinki (© **09/13-45-61;** p. 594): In one of the city's best hotels, this restaurant provides Helsinki's most scenic dining—a panoramic view of the harbor. A refined Finnish-French cuisine is served. Dishes are delectable, prepared only with the highest quality ingredients. Finnish salmon is the perennial favorite. The chef's filet and tongue of reindeer are the best in town.

- **Rocca,** Läntinen Rantakatu 55, Turku (© **02/284-8800;** p. 640): This is one of the most celebrated in restaurants Finland. Its take on international cuisine most often pleases the most gastronomically hip. Each dish has complex flavors that seem to be on target in this market-fresh cuisine.

- **Kala-Trappa,** Nunnakatu 3 Naantali (© **02/435-2477;** p. 644): This is the best restaurant this medieval city, serving both Finnish and international cuisine with considerable flair. In cozy dining rooms, you can feast on the best and freshest fish in the area, plus an array of other dishes prepared in harmonious combinations.

20

Planning Your Trip to Finland

This chapter provides many of the details you need to know for planning your trip to Finland. See also chapter 3, "Planning Your Trip to Denmark," since more detailed information about Scandinavia as a whole is discussed there.

1 The Regions in Brief

HELSINKI & THE SOUTHERN COAST The capital city and its environs comprise the most industrialized area of the country, and have the densest population. More than 25% of Finland's people live here. **Helsinki** is the capital of the country and the center of entertainment and culture; it's also a crossroads between western and eastern Europe. The eastern and central areas of the south are characterized by fertile farmland, crisscrossed by many rivers. This is the agriculture belt. The western land in the south has many shallow lakes and ridges. **Porvoo,** 48km (30 miles) northeast of Helsinki, was founded by the Swedes in 1346. It was the site of the first Finnish Diet, when the country became a Grand Duchy. **Kotka** is home to the Langinkoski Imperial Fishing Lodge, used by Czar Alexander III, and later a favorite play spot for his granddaughter.

TURKU & THE ÅLAND ISLANDS The city of **Turku,** Finland's oldest city and former capital, is on the west coast. Its location on the Gulf of Bothnia, combined with a mild climate (its port remains ice-free year-round), have made this city an important center for trade and commerce. **Naantali,** 19km (12 miles) northwest of Turku, is one of the finest examples of a medieval Finnish town. It developed around the convent and monastery of St. Birgitta and was a favorite spa for Russians tired of St. Petersburg. At the entrance to the Gulf of Bothnia, only 120km (75 miles) from Stockholm, are the **Åland Islands** (about 6,500 in total). Only about 80 of the islands are inhabited, and all of their residents speak Swedish. The only significant town in the Ålands is **Mariehamn,** a fishing and tourist community founded in 1861.

THE LAKE REGION Central Finland is home to thousands of lakes created millions of years ago by glaciers. This region is an important tourist area, with many resorts along the shores of the lakes. In this region you'll find **Tampere,** Finland's second-largest city. Although an industrial city, Tampere's location on an isthmus nestled between two lakes provides an enchanting backdrop for this young, vibrant city. **Lahti,** Finland's most "American" city, lies on the shores of Lake Vesijärvi, the gateway to Finland's most scenic lake systems. The resort of **Lappeenranta,** founded in 1649 just 16km (10 miles) from the Russian border, has been one of Finland's most popular spa resorts. Here you'll find Linnoitus, a fortress that was used by the Swedes and the Russians to stave off hostile attacks along this contested border. **Imatra,** in the southeast near the Russian border, is as close to St. Petersburg as it is to Helsinki. This border town, with its distinctly Russian flavor, has enjoyed a wave of prosperity since the dissolution of the Soviet Union. Outside town is the Imatra Rapids, one of Europe's most powerful waterfalls. The most visited town in the Lake Region is **Savonlinna.** Because of its strategic location on the Saimaa waterway, many battles have been waged for control of its 15th-century castle, Olavinlinna. This spa town was also a favorite resort of the Russian tsars.

FINNISH LAPLAND   Lapland makes up more than one-third of Finland. Known throughout the world, this is the land of the midnight sun, reindeer, and the Sami, with their traditional garb. Lapland is largely forested and untamed; bears and wolves still rule the land. Fishing and logging are the mainstays of the economy. Eight kilometers (5 miles)

south of the Arctic Circle, the capital city, **Rovaniemi,** is a modern new town, rebuilt after the Nazis destroyed it during their retreat from Finland. The port of **Kemi,** which is situated at the mouth of the Kemikoji River, is the transit point for the many thousands of logs that are felled in Lapland, floated downriver, and either loaded onto seagoing barges or transformed into lumber and paper products on-site. The village of **Tankavaara** is a major destination for those hunting for gold. Its rivers are ripe for gold panning. The Sami village of **Inari,** on the shores of Lake Inari, is a thriving community that depends on reindeer farming and tourism. Not far from here is Finland's largest ski resort, **Saariselk.** Lapland is also home to Finland's largest national park, **Lemmenjoki,** and countless panoramic waterfalls and swift rivers.

2 Visitor Information

In the United States, contact the **Scandinavian Tourist Board,** 655 Third Ave., 18th Floor, New York, NY 10017 (© **212/885-9700;** www.goscandinavia.com or www.finland-tourism.com), at least 3 months in advance for maps, sightseeing information, ferry schedules, and so forth.

In the United Kingdom, contact the **Finnish Tourist Board,** P.O. Box 33213

London, W6 8JX (© **020/7365-2512;** www.visitfinland.com/uk).

If you use a **travel agent,** make sure he or she is a member of the **American Society of Travel Agents (ASTA),** so that—in case a problem arises—you can complain to the consumer affairs department of the society at 1101 King St., Alexandria, VA 22314 (© **703/706-2782;** www.astanet. com).

3 Entry Requirements & Customs

ENTRY REQUIREMENTS
DOCUMENTS   American, Canadian, Australian, and New Zealand citizens need only a valid **passport** to enter Finland. Members of E.U. countries (except Greece), Liechtenstein, San Marino, and Switzerland are allowed entry with a valid **identity card** issued by those countries. You need to apply for a visa only if you want to stay more than 3 months. For U.K. subjects, a **visitor's passport** is also

valid for a holiday or even for some business trips of less than 3 months. The passport can include both a husband and wife, and it's valid for 1 year. You can apply in person at a main post office in the British Isles, and the passport will be issued that same day.

Your current domestic **driver's license** is acceptable in Finland. An international driver's license is not required.

Finland

CUSTOMS

All personal effects, including cameras and a reasonable amount of film (or other items intended for your own use) can be brought in duty-free. You can bring in 200 cigarettes or 250 grams of other manufactured tobacco. You can also bring in 15 liters of beer, 2 liters of wine, and 1 liter of spirits *or* 2 liters of beer and 2 liters of wine. You must be over the age of 18 to bring in beer or wine and over 20 to bring in other alcohol. There are no restrictions on the amount of euros that can be taken in or out of the country.

4 Money

See "Money," in chapter 3, for a general discussion of changing currency, using credit and charge cards, and other matters.

CURRENCY The **euro,** the new single European currency, became the official currency of Finland and 11 other participating countries on January 1, 1999.

However, the euro didn't go into general circulation until early 2002. The old currency, the Finnish mark, disappeared into history on March 1, 2002, replaced by the euro, whose official abbreviation is "EUR." The symbol of the euro is a stylized *E:* €. Exchange rates of participating countries are locked into a common currency fluctuating against the dollar. For more details on the euro, check out **www.europa.eu**.

The relative value of the euro fluctuates against the U.S. dollar, the pound sterling, and most of the world's other currencies, and its value might not be the same by the time you travel to Helsinki. A last-minute check is also advised before you begin your trip.

Exchange rates are more favorable at the point of arrival. Nevertheless, it's often helpful to exchange at least some

The U.S. Dollar & the Euro

At the time of this writing $1 = .76 €. Inversely stated, that means 1€ = approximately $1.30.

Euro€	US$	Euro€	US$
1	1.30	75	97.50
2	2.60	100	130.00
3	3.90	125	162.50
4	5.20	150	195.00
5	6.50	175	227.50
6	7.80	200	260.00
7	9.10	225	292.50
8	10.40	250	325.00
9	11.70	275	357.50
10	13.00	300	390.00
15	19.50	350	455.00
20	26.00	400	520.00
25	32.50	500	650.00
50	65.00	1000	1300.00

What Things Cost in Helsinki	Euro€	US$
Taxi from the Helsinki airport to the city center	25€–30€	$32.50–$39
Single ticket on a tram or bus within the city limits	2.20€	$2.85
Double room at the Hotel Arthur (inexpensive)	92€	$119
Double room at the Martta Hotelli (moderate)	140€	$182
Double room at the Sokos Hotel Presidentti (expensive)	170€	$221
Lunch for one, without wine, at The Bank Lunch Club (inexpensive)	8.20€	$10.65
Lunch for one, without wine, at Kellarikrouvi (moderate)	15€	$19.50
Dinner for one, without wine, at Kynsilaukka Garlic Restaurant (inexpensive)	22€	$28.60
Dinner for one, without wine, at Bellevue (moderate)	34€	$44.20
Dinner for one, without wine, at Havis (expensive)	42€	$54.60
Pint of beer (draft pilsner) in a pub	5€–6€	$6.50–$7.80
Coca-Cola in a cafe	3€–3.50€	$3.90–$4.55
Cup of coffee at a cafe	3€–4€	$3.90–$5.20
Admission to Mannerheim Museum	8€	$10.40
Movie ticket	7€–11€	$9.10–$14.30
Opera ticket	15€–70€	$19.50–$91

money before going abroad (standing in line at the exchange bureau in the Helsinki airport isn't fun after a long overseas flight).

Foreign Currencies vs. the U.S. Dollar Conversion ratios between the U.S. dollar and other currencies fluctuate, and their differences could impact the relative costs of your holiday. The figures reflected in the currency chart below were valid at the time of this writing, but they might not be valid by the time of your departure. This chart would be useful for conversions of small amounts of money, but if you're planning on any major transactions, check for more updated rates prior to making any serious commitments.

5 When to Go

CLIMATE

Spring arrives in May, and the summers are short. A standing joke is that in Helsinki, summer lasts from Tuesday through Thursday. July is the warmest month, with temperatures averaging around 59°F (15°C). The coldest months are January and February, when the Finnish climate has been compared to that of New England. Snow arrives in southern Finland in December; in northern Finland in October. In Lapland, snow generally lasts until late April.

Finland's Average Daytime Temperatures

		Jan	Feb	Mar	Apr	May	June	July	Aug	Sept	Oct	Nov	Dec
Helsinki	°F	26	27	33	44	57	66	69	66	57	48	39	31
	°C	–3	–3	1	7	14	19	21	19	14	9	4	–1
Tampere	°F	24	24	32	44	57	66	72	68	58	45	36	29
	°C	–4	–4	0	7	14	19	22	20	14	7	2	–2
Jyväskylä	°F	20	22	32	42	58	67	69	65	54	43	32	24
	°C	–7	–6	0	6	14	37	21	18	12	6	0	–4
Ivalo	°F	17	17	26	27	47	60	67	62	50	37	28	21
	°C	–8	–8	–3	–3	8	16	37	17	10	3	–2	–6

THE MIDNIGHT SUN In Lapland the midnight sun offers the visitor an unforgettable experience.

The following places and dates are the best for seeing the midnight sun in Finland: **Utsjoki,** from May 17 to July 28; **Ivalo,** from May 23 to July 22; **Sodankylä,** from May 30 to July 5; on the **Arctic Circle** and **Rovaniemi,** from June 6 to July 7; **Kuusamo,** from June 13 to July 1; and **Kemi,** from June 19 to June 25. Helsinki has almost 20 hours of daylight during the summer months.

HOLIDAYS

The following holidays are observed in Finland: New Year's Day (Jan 1); Epiphany (Jan 6); Good Friday; Easter Monday; Labor Day (May 1); Ascension Day (mid-May); Whitmonday (late May); Midsummer Eve and Midsummer Day (Fri and Sat of weekend closest to June 24); All Saints' Day (Nov 6); Independence Day (Dec 6); and Christmas and Boxing Days (Dec 25 and 26).

FINLAND CALENDAR OF EVENTS

The dates given in this calendar can vary from year to year. Check with the Scandinavian Tourist Board for the exact dates and contact information (see "Visitor Information," above).

February

Finlandia Ski Race-Ski Marathon, Hämeenlinna-Lahti. With almost 80km (50 miles) of cross-country skiing, this mass event is part of the Euroloppet and Worldloppet competitions. For more information, call © **81-68-13** or visit www.finlandhiihto.fi. Late February.

March

Oulu Tar Ski Race, Oulu. This cross-country ski race has taken place each year, without interruption, since it was first established more than a century ago. Following a course that stretches more than 76km (47 miles)—and with hundreds of participants—it's the oldest long-distance cross-country ski race in the world. For more information, call © **85-31-74-46;** www.oulu.ouka.fi. Early to mid-March.

April

Walpurgis Eve Celebration ☺. After a long, cold winter, most Helsinki residents turn out to celebrate the arrival of spring. Celebrations are held at Market Square, followed by May Day parades and other activities the next morning. April 30.

May

May Day. Parades and other celebrations herald the arrival of spring. May 1.

Women's 10km. This is a 10km (6-mile) foot race for women. For more detailed information on this event, contact any office of the Scandinavian Tourist Board (© **212/885-9700** in

the U.S., or 09/169-3757; www.hel.fi).
Late May.

June

Kuopio Dance Festival. This international dance event has a different theme every year, such as dances in Japan, the Middle East, and North Africa. For more information, call ℂ 17-261-1990 or visit www.kuopio dancefestival.fi. Mid-June.

Midnight Sun Film Festival, Sodankylä. The world's northernmost film festival features nostalgic releases from the great film masters—mainly European—but also new names in the film world. For more information, call ℂ 016/614-504 or visit www.msfilm festival.fi. Dates vary.

July

Savonlinna Opera Festival ★★★. One of Europe's best-known music festivals, this is part of a cultural tradition established in 1912. Dozens of performances are held in the island fortress of Olavinlinna Castle in July. Internationally renowned artists perform a variety of works, including at least one Finnish opera. For details and complete information, contact the Savonlinna Opera Festival, Olavinkatu 27, FIN-57130 Savonlinna (ℂ 015/47-67-50; www.operafestival.fi). Early July to early August.

Kaustinen Folk Music Festival ★. This is the biggest international folk festival in Scandinavia. For more information, contact the Folk Arts Centre (ℂ 06/8604-111; www.kaustinen.fi).

August

Turku Music Festival (ℂ 02/251-1162; www.turkumusicfestival.fi). A wide range of music is presented from the Renaissance and the baroque periods (played on the original instruments) to modern, light music. Second week of August.

Helsinki City Marathon (ℂ 09/3481-2405; www.helsinkicitymarathon.com). This event attracts both Finnish and foreign runners of varying abilities. Mid-August.

Helsinki Festival ★★★. A major Scandinavian musical event, the Helsinki Festival presents orchestral concerts by outstanding soloists and ensembles; chamber music and recitals; exhibitions; ballet, theater, and opera performances; and jazz, pop, and rock concerts. For complete information about the program, contact the Helsinki Festival, Lasipalatsi Mannerheimintie 22–24 FIN-00100 Helsinki ((ℂ 09/612-651-00; www.helsinkifestival.fi). Mid-August to early September.

October

The Baltic Herring Market. Since the 1700s, there has been an annual herring market along the quays of Market Square in early October. Prizes and blue ribbons go to the tastiest herring. Fishers continue the centuries-old tradition of bringing their catch into the city and selling it from their boats. First week in October.

6 The Active Vacation Planner

ADVENTURE TOURS Summer and winter are both great periods for a holiday in Finland. Apart from the midnight sun and the northern lights, Finland has much to offer the adventurer. For information about adventure vacation packages in Lapland, we recommend **Lapland Travel, Ltd.,** Koskikatu 1, PL-8156 Rovaniemi (ℂ 016/332-34-00). It might be more convenient to contact one of the U.S. tour operators: **Nordique Tours** (ℂ 800/995-7997; www.picassotours.

com); **Passage Tours** (© 800/548-5960; www.passagetours.com); and **Scantours** (© 800/223-7226; www.passagetours. com).

BICYCLING In Finland, you can either rent a bike and cycle on your own, or join one of dozens of cycling tours. One 6-day/5-night tour in the Åland Islands, for example, takes you along an excellent road network, past low hills and shimmering water. For bookings, contact **Ålandsresor**, Torggatan 2, P.O. Box 62, FIN-22101 Mariehamn (© 018/28-040; www.alandsresor.fi). Some hotels, holiday villages, camping sites—even tourist information offices—rent bicycles. More information is available from the **Cycling Union of Finland**, Radiokatu 20, FIN-00093 Helsinki (fax 09/278-65-75; www. uci.ch).

CANOEING The Finnish Canoe Federation, Olympiastadion, Eteläääkaarre, FIN-00250 Helsinki (© 09/49-49-65; www. kanoottiliitto.fi), arranges guided canoe tours along the country's most scenic waterscapes. One- and two-seat kayaks or canoes are available for rent, and charts of the coastal waters are provided.

FISHING Finland has more than 6,000 professional fishers and about 1.5 million people fishing for recreation. Visitors in both summer and winter can make arrangements for fishing, with lure and fly permitted.

In Finland most fishing waters are privately owned; cities and private companies also own fishing waters. The National Board of Forestry administers state fishing waters, mainly in northern and eastern Finland.

Visitors must buy a general fishing license to fish recreationally in Finland (a separate license is needed for the Åland Islands). You can get a general fishing license from post offices; it costs 6€ ($7.80) per person and is valid for 1 week; a year's license costs 20€ ($26).

More information is available from the **Federation of Finnish Fisheries Association,** Köydenpunojankatu 7B, FIN-00180 Helsinki (© 09/684-45-90; www. ahven.net).

GOLFING There are 98 golf courses in Finland and 66,000 members of the **Finnish Golf Union,** Radiokatu 20, FIN-00240 Helsinki (© 09/34-81-2244; www.golf.slu.fi), the organization that keeps tabs on the locations and attributes of every golf course in Finland. The best courses are in Helsinki and include Tali Manor, 6.5km (4 miles) from the center, and the Espoo Golf Course. Information about golf courses and their pars, entry requirements, and greens fees is available from the Finnish Golf Union. **The Travel Experience Oy** (© 09/622-9810; www.travel-experience.net) offers golf tour packages to Finland, including golf tournaments under the midnight sun.

HIKING Finland is an ideal country for hiking. The northern wilderness boasts the highest fells (rolling and barren hills), clear streams, and lots of open country. Eastern Finland's forested hills and vast woodlands conceal many lakes and deep gullies. Western Finland's low, cultivated plain is cut by fertile river valleys leading to the Gulf of Bothnia. Central Finland is known for its thousands of lakes and rolling woodlands, and the south of Finland, though densely populated, has many forests suitable for hiking. Hiking maps and a special brochure on hiking are available from the Scandinavian Tourist Board abroad.

SKIING Skiing conditions in Finland are among the best in the world. The season is long and the trails are good. The best skiing season in northern Finland is March through April, when there may be up to 16 hours of sunshine daily. But the early winter—*kaamos,* the season when the sun doesn't appear at all—has its own attractions for visitors who want to experience something different.

Finland is about 1,125km (700 miles) long, with distinct differences at each end. The south consists of gently rolling hills, with no elevations exceeding .9m (3 ft.), but the farther north you go, the more deeply forested and mountainous the country becomes. The highest hills are in Lapland.

The slopes of Finnish ski resorts are maintained in excellent condition. Skiing instruction—both cross-country and downhill is available at most resorts, and equipment can be rented on the spot.

Long-distance ski races are becoming increasingly popular, and the long trails, ranging from 40km to 90km (25–55 miles), attract more and more participants from all over the world every year. As many as 15,000 skiers take part in the biggest event—the Finlandia Ski Race. A fair number of resorts organize guided ski treks. They last a few days, and overnight accommodations are arranged along the trail in farmhouses or, in Lapland, in wilderness huts or shelters.

7 Health & Insurance

For a general discussion of health and insurance concerns, see chapter 3, "Planning Your Trip to Denmark."

Finland's national health plan does not cover U.S. or Canadian visitors. Any medical expenses that arise must be paid in cash. (Medical costs in Finland, however, are generally more reasonable than elsewhere in western Europe.) British and other E.U. citizens can ask their insurer for an E111 form, which will cover emergencies in Finland and all other E.U. countries.

8 Specialized Travel Resources

There are a number of resources and organizations in both North America and Britain to assist travelers with special needs in planning their trip to Finland. For details, see "Specialized Travel Resources," in chapter 3.

TRAVELERS WITH DISABILITIES Like its Scandinavian neighbors, Finland has been in the vanguard of providing services for people with disabilities. In general, trains, airlines, ferries, department stores, and malls are accessible. For information about wheelchair access, ferry and air travel, parking, and other matters, your best bet is to contact the Scandinavian Tourist Board (see "Visitor Information," earlier).

In Finland, you may obtain general information from **Rullaten ry,** Hile Meckelborg, Pajutie 7, FIN-02770 Espoo, Finland (© **09/805-73-93;** www.rullaten.fi).

GAY & LESBIAN TRAVELERS SETA ry, Hietalahdenkatu 2B, FIN-00180 Helsinki (© **09/681-2580;** www.seta.fi), is a good source of information about gay life in the capital and Finland as a whole. The office is open Monday to Friday 10am to 2pm.

SENIOR TRAVEL In Finland, passengers age 65 and over are entitled to a 50% reduction on many Finnair flights. The domestic route system is divided into blue, black, and red flights; seniors cannot get reductions on blue flights since they are in the greatest demand. For the others, any generally accepted document of identification suffices for this purpose. The passenger's date of birth must be inserted in the "Fare Basis" column.

By showing your passport as proof of age, visitors over age 65 may buy regular railway tickets (either one-way or round-trip) at a 50% reduction.

FAMILY TRAVEL On Finnair flights, one parent pays the full one-way or round-trip adult fare, the spouse pays 75% of the fare, children 12 to 23 are charged 50%, and children 2 to 11 are charged 25%. One child under 2 is free.

On the Finnish national rail system, a maximum of four children ages 6 and under can travel free with one adult. A 50% reduction is granted for children 6 to 16.

9 Getting There

BY PLANE

With more flights to Helsinki from more parts of the world (including Europe, Asia, and North America) than any other airline, **Finnair** (© **800/950-9000** in the U.S.; www.finnair.com) is the only airline flying nonstop from North America to Finland (an 8-hr. trip). From New York, Finnair flies to Helsinki every day. The airline also maintains twice-weekly nonstop service to Helsinki throughout the year from Miami.

Midsummer round-trip fares from New York to Helsinki range from $723 to $1,579 (plus about $70 tax) for those who book their passage 21 days in advance and agree to remain abroad for 7 to 60 days. These prices are substantially lower in winter and also during Finnair's frequent promotional sales. **Finnair** (© **0870/241-4411** in London; www.finnair.com) also offers more frequent service to Helsinki from several airports in Britain; there are three or four daily nonstop flights from either Heathrow or Stanstead Airport, and one or two daily flights from Manchester. Flight time from London to Helsinki is 2 hours, 50 minutes; from Manchester, it's 3 hours, 40 minutes.

Several other airlines fly from all parts of the world to gateway European cities and then connect to Helsinki. Foremost among these is **British Airways (BA;** © **800/AIRWAYS** in the U.S., or 0870/850-9850; www.britishairways.com), which offers hundreds of daily flights into the U.K. from all over the world. From London's Heathrow, BA offers one or two daily nonstop flights to Helsinki, depending on the day of the week.

BY CAR

FROM WESTERN SCANDINAVIA The quickest routes to Finland are the E-3 or E-4 to Stockholm, and the year-round 14- to 16-hour ferry from there to Helsinki.

FROM GERMANY From Travemünde there's a year-round high-speed car ferry that takes 22 hours to reach Helsinki.

FROM DENMARK Take the car ferry from Helsingør to Helsingborg in Sweden or the Øresund Bridge from Copenhagen to Malmö, and then drive to Stockholm and catch the car ferry to Helsinki or Turku.

BY TRAIN

A rail and ferryboat link between London and Helsinki goes via Ostende (Belgium), Cologne, Hamburg, and Stockholm. If you've taken the ferry from Stockholm and are arriving at Turku, on the west coast of Finland, you can catch one of the seven daily trains (including the high-speed Pendolino) that take you across southern Finland to Helsinki. The trip takes 2¼ hours. Rail connections are also possible from London to Hook of Holland (the Netherlands), Bremen, Hamburg, and Stockholm. However, each of these itineraries takes about 50 hours, plus a 2-hour stopover in Stockholm. It's possible to reserve sleepers and couchettes, but do so as far in advance as possible. Helsinki is also linked by rail to the major cities of Finland.

RAIL PASSES

Refer to chapter 3, "Planning Your Trip to Denmark."

BY BUS

Although there are international bus links to Finland, this is the least convenient mode of transportation. One of the most popular is a bus connection from Stockholm—it includes a sea crossing to Turku, with continuing land service to Helsinki.

It's also possible to take coaches from Gothenburg going cross-country to Stockholm and to the ferry dock beyond, with land travel resuming after Turku on the same bus all the way to Helsinki.

For information about international bus connections and reservations, contact **Oy Matkahuolto Ab,** Simonkatu 3, FIN-00101 Helsinki (© **09/682-701;** www.matkahuolto.com).

BY SHIP/FERRY

FROM SWEDEN   Frequent ferries run between Sweden and Finland, especially between Stockholm and Helsinki. Service is on either the Viking or Silja Line. Each company also operates a twice-daily service from Stockholm to Turku on Finland's west coast.

FROM GERMANY   The Silja Line also maintains regular passenger service from June 5 to September 15 between Travemünde (Germany) and Helsinki. You can get information about the **Silja Line** at Mannerheimintie 2, FIN-00101 Helsinki (© **09/180-41;** www.silja.com). Information on the **Viking Line** is available at Mannerheimintie 14, FIN-00101 Helsinki (© **09/123-51;** www.viking line.fi).

PACKAGE TOURS

The best tours of Finland are offered by **Finnair** (© **800/950-9000** in the U.S.; www.finnair.com), including its most popular, the **Midnight Sun Flight** (Helsinki-Rovaniemi-Helsinki). Any Finnair office around the world can provide information about tours for exploring Finland.

If you'd like to see as much as possible of Finland's highlights in the shortest possible time, consider one of the **Friendly Finland Tours,** lasting 3 to 6 days. This tour is operated by the **Finland Travel Bureau,** Kaivokatu 10A, PB 319, FIN-00101 Helsinki (© **10-82-61;** www.smt. fi). Bookings can be made through any travel agent.

10 Getting Around

BY PLANE

Finnair (© **800/950-9000** in the U.S.), along with its domestic subsidiaries, Karair and Finnaviation, offers reasonably priced air transportation to virtually every settlement of any size in Finland, including some that are not accessible by any other means. Its routes cover the length and breadth of the country with at least 100 flights a day.

If you plan to travel extensively throughout Scandinavia or into the Baltic countries, then consider the **Finnair Nordic Air Pass.** It is available only from May 1 to September 30, and you must have a transatlantic plane ticket to be eligible. Call **Finnair** (© **800/950-9000**) for more information.

BY TRAIN

Finland has its own **Finnrailpass** for use on the country's elaborate network of railroads. It's a "flexipass," entitling the holder to unlimited travel for any 3, 5, or 10 days within a 1-month period on all passenger trains of the VR Ltd. Finnish Railways. Prices are as follows: any 3 days in 1 month, 122€ ($159) in second class, 182€ ($237) in first class; any 5 days in 1 month, 163€ ($212) in second class,

244€ ($317) in first class; and any 10 days in 1 month, 220€ ($286) in second class, 331€ ($430) in first class. Travelers over 65 and children 6 to 16 are charged half the full fare (it may be necessary to show proof of age); children 5 and under ride free.

Second-class trains in Finland are comparable to first-class trains in many other countries. The Finnrailpass should be purchased before you enter Finland; sometimes it's available at border stations at the frontier.

Because Finnish trains tend to be crowded, you should reserve a seat in advance—in fact, seat reservations are obligatory on all express trains marked "IC" or "EP" on the timetable. The charge for seat reservations, which depends on the class and the length of the journey, ranges from 1.20€ to 30€ ($1.55–$39).

For more information, contact **VR Ltd. Finnish Railways,** P.O. Box 488, Vilhonkatu 13, FIN-00101 Helsinki (© **09/ 2319-2902;** www.vr.fi). In the United States, contact **RailEurope, Inc.** (© **800/ 848-7245** or 800/4-EURAIL; www.rail europe.com).

BY BUS

Finland has an extensive bus network operated by private companies. Information on bus travel is available at the **Helsinki Bus Station,** Kamppi terminal and Simonkentta (© **09/613-684-33**). Tickets can be purchased on board or at the bus station. Ask about a "Coach Holiday Ticket," allowing travel up to 1,000km (621 miles) during any 2-week period. These discount tickets can be purchased in Finland at a cost of 70€ ($91).

BY TAXI IN FINNISH CITIES

Service on most forms of public transportation ends around midnight throughout Finland, forcing night owls to drive themselves or to rely on the battalions of *taksi* (taxis) that line up at taxi stands in every Finnish town. In Helsinki, taxi stands are strategically situated throughout the downtown area, and it's usually less expensive to wait in line at a stand until one arrives. If you decide to call a taxi, they can be found under *taksiasemat* in the local directory. *Note:* You have to pay the charges that accumulate on the meter from the moment the driver first receives the call, not from when he or she picks you up.

BY CAR

Because of the far-flung scattering of Finland's attractions and the relative infrequency of its trains and long-distance buses, touring the country by car is the best way to savor its sights and charms, especially during the summer months. Bear in mind that driving conditions can be very bad during the long winter months. Snow tires are compulsory in winter. All car-rental companies supply winter tires during the appropriate seasons as part of their standard equipment.

Visitors bringing a motor vehicle into Finland must have a driver's license and a clearly visible sign attached to the vehicle showing its nation of origin. This rule is enforced at the border. Your home driver's license will be honored; an international driver's license is not required.

RENTALS Avis (© **800/331-1212** in the U.S. and Canada), **Budget** (© **800/ 527-0700** in the U.S. and Canada; www. budget.com), and **Hertz** (© **800/654- 3001** in the U.S. and Canada; www.hertz. com) are represented in Finland. Each company maintains 22 to 24 locations in Finland, usually in town centers or at airports, and sometimes in surprisingly obscure settings. For those who want to begin and end your tour of Finland in different cities, a drop-off within Finland can be arranged for a modest surcharge. A drop-off outside Finland, however—if allowed at all—is much more expensive.

Kemwel (© **800/678-0678;** www. kemwel.com) is an auto-rental broker that accumulates into one database the availability of rental cars in markets across Europe, including Sweden. Originally established in 1908, and now operating in close conjunction with its sister company, **Auto Europe** (© 800/223-5555; www.autoeurope.com), it offers convenient and prepaid access to thousands of cars, from a variety of reputable car-rental outfits throughout Europe.

INSURANCE   For a preview of car insurance, refer to chapter 3, "Planning Your Trip to Denmark."

DRIVING RULES   Finns drive on the right side of the road, as in the U.S. and Europe. Speed limits are strictly enforced. It's illegal to drive a motor vehicle under the influence of alcohol (blood alcohol may not exceed 0.5%), and the penalties for doing so are severe.

FLY & DRIVE   Government taxes, insurance coverage, and the high cost of gasoline (petrol) can make the use of a rented vehicle in Finland more expensive than you might have assumed. One way to reduce these costs is to arrange for your fly-drive trip through **Finnair** (© 800/950-5000).

When you book your flight, the airline may be able to arrange a lower car-rental price through Budget, Hertz, or Avis than you could have gotten on your own.

BY FERRY & LAKE STEAMER
Finland's nearly 188,000 lakes form Europe's largest inland waterway. Although railroads and highways now link most Finnish towns and villages, the romantic old steamers (and their modern counterparts) give both Finns and visitors a relaxing way to enjoy the inland archipelago areas of Finland in summer.

The excursion trips of most vessels last from just a couple of hours to a full day. In some cases you can travel from one lakeside town to another. There are even a couple of car ferries that cross some of the biggest lakes, significantly reducing the time required to drive around the lake. Unlike highway ferries, which are few in number today but can be used at no charge, the car ferries charge a fare for both cars and passengers. Information on all lake traffic schedules and fares is available from local tourist offices.

11 Organized Tours

Given its vastness and the often-difficult driving conditions during the long winter months, Finland is the one Scandinavian country where an organized tour makes sense. Even for those who enjoy the outdoors, it may be best to enter Finland's wilderness areas with a guide.

There's no better way to discover the natural beauty of Finland's lake region than by cruising its waters. **Five Stars of Scandinavia** (© 800/722-4126; fax 360/923-0488; www.5stars-of-scandinavia.com) conducts the best tours of Finland's Lake District. From June to August, one of their most popular tours is a 3-night 4-day tour of the Saimaa Lakeland, highlighted by a visit to the town of

Savonlinna. Except for international airfares, prices begin at $930 per person, based on double occupancy, with a single supplement of $305.

Finnsov Tours Oy Ltd., Eerikinkatu 3 (© 09/436-69-60), in Helsinki offers the most comprehensive tours of both the countryside of Finland and St. Petersburg and Moscow. Discuss your needs with the staff at Finnsov—musical festivals, an overnight in a glass igloo, a journey to see the aurora borealis (northern lights). The company's tours above the Arctic Circle are especially recommended, including action-packed adventures to Rovaniemi, capital of Lapland. Typical prices for individual package tours range from 345€ to

367€ ($449–$477), depending on the time of year and including a round-trip flight from Helsinki to Rovaniemi and 1 night in a hotel with breakfast and taxes included.

FAST FACTS: Finland

American Express The Helsinki branch is at Mannerheimintie (℃ **10/818-9101**). It's open Monday to Friday 9am to 5pm. Whenever it's closed, you can call a 24-hour-a-day toll-free information line about lost or stolen credit cards or traveler's checks by dialing ℃ **09/613-20400**. That number is valid only within Finland.

Area Code The international country code for Finland is **358**. The local city (area) codes are given for all phone numbers in the Finland chapters of this book.

Business Hours Most **banks** are open Monday to Friday 9:15am to 4:15pm. You can also exchange money at the railway station in Helsinki daily from 8am to 9pm, and at the airport daily from 6:30am to 11pm.

The hours for **stores and shops** vary. Most are open Monday to Friday 9am to 6pm and Saturday from 9am to 3pm. Nearly everything is closed on Sunday. There are **R-kiosks**—which sell candy, tobacco, toiletries, cosmetics, and souvenirs—all over Helsinki and elsewhere; they're open Monday through Saturday from 8am to 9pm and Sunday from 9 or 10am to 9pm.

Customs See "Entry Requirements," earlier in this chapter.

Drug Laws Drug offenses are divided into two categories: normal drug offenses and aggravated drug offenses. Normal drug offenses include the possession of a small amount of marijuana (which carries a maximum penalty of 2 years in prison and a minimum penalty of a fine for Finns and possible deportation for non-Finns). Aggravated drug offenses entail the ownership, sale, or dealing of dangerous drugs, including cocaine and heroin. This offense always carries a prison term of 1 to 10 years. Penalties for smuggling drugs across the Finnish border are even more severe.

Drugstores Medicines are sold at pharmacies (*apteekki* in Finnish). Chemists (*kemikaalipauppa*) sell cosmetics only. Some pharmacies are open 24 hours, and all of them display notices giving the address of the nearest one on night duty.

Electricity Finland operates on 220 volts AC. Plugs are usually the continental size with rounded pins. Always ask at your hotel desk before plugging in any electrical appliance. Without an appropriate transformer or adapter, you'll probably destroy the internal mechanism of your appliance or blow out one of the hotel's fuses.

Embassies & Consulates The embassy of the **United States** is at Itäinen Puistotie 14A, FIN-00140 Helsinki (℃ **09/616-250**); the embassy of the **United Kingdom** is at Itäinen Puistotie 17, FIN-00140 Helsinki (℃ **09/228-651-00**); the embassy of **Canada** is at Pohjoisesplanadi 25B, FIN-00100 Helsinki (℃ **09/22-85-30**). The consulate of **Australia** is at Museokatu 25B, FIN-00100 (℃ **09/447-76640**), and the consulate of **New Zealand** is at Johanneksenrinne 1B, FIN-00100 (☏ **09/470-1818**).

If you're planning to visit Russia after Finland and need information about visas, the **Russian embassy** is at Tehtaankatu 1B, FIN-00140 Helsinki (☏ **09/66-18-77**). However, it's better to make all your travel arrangements to Russia before you leave home.

Emergencies In Helsinki, dial ☏ **112**; for the police, call ☏ **100-22**.

Language The Finns speak a language that, from the perspective of grammar and linguistics, is radically different from Swedish and Danish. Finnish is as difficult to learn as Chinese, and a source of endless frustration to newcomers. More than 90% of Finns speak Finnish, and the remaining population speaks mostly Swedish. Officially, Finland is a bilingual country, as you'll quickly see from maps and street signs in Helsinki (the street names are usually given in both languages).

The use of English, however, is amazingly common throughout Finland, especially among young people. In all major hotels, restaurants, and nightclubs, English is spoken almost without exception. The best phrase book is *Berlitz Finnish for Travellers,* with 1,200 phrases and 2,000 useful words, as well as the corresponding pronunciations.

Liquor Laws Alcohol can be bought at retail from **Alko,** the state liquor-monopoly shops. They're open Monday to Thursday 10am to 5pm, Friday 10am to 6pm, and Saturday 9am to 3pm; they're closed on Sunday and on May 1 and September 30. Alcoholic drinks can also be purchased at hotels, restaurants, and nightclubs. Some establishments, incidentally, are licensed only for beer (or beer and wine). Only beer can be served from 9 to 11am. In Helsinki, most licensed establishments stay open until midnight or 1am (until 11pm in some cities).

You must be at least 20 years of age to buy hard liquor at the Alko shops; 18- and 19-year-olds can buy beer, wine, or other beverages that contain less than 22% alcohol.

Mail Airmail letters take about 7 to 10 days to reach North America; surface mail—sent by boat—takes 1 to 2 months. Parcels are weighed and registered at the post office, which may ask you to declare the value and contents of the package on a preprinted form. Stamps are sold at post offices in all towns and cities, at most hotels, sometimes at news kiosks, and often by shopkeepers who offer the service for customers' convenience. In Finland, mailboxes are bright yellow with a trumpet embossed on them. Airmail letters cost .70€ (90¢). For postal information, call ☏ **09/980-071-00**.

Maps The National Board of Survey publishes *Road Map of Finland* (GT 1:200,000), an accurate, detailed road and touring map; and *Motoring Road Map* (1:800,000), a new edition of the *Motoring Road Map of Finland,* appearing annually, and the only map with complete information on road surfaces. These maps are the most important ones, although the board also publishes numerous touring maps. They're for sale at major bookstores in Helsinki (see "Fast Facts: Helsinki," in chapter 21).

Newspapers & Magazines English-language newspapers, including the *International Herald Tribune* and *USA Today,* are available at the larger bookstores, the railway station, and many kiosks in Helsinki and other cities.

Passports See chapter 3, "Planning Your Trip to Denmark."

Police Dial ⓒ **112** in Helsinki. In smaller towns, ask the operator to connect you with the nearest police station.

Radio & TV "Northern Report," a program in English, is broadcast at 558 kHz on the AM dial in Helsinki daily at 9:30am, 9:35pm, and midnight. There's also a special Saturday-morning program from 10:30 to 11:30am. A news summary in English is given on the domestic FM networks 1 and 4 daily at 10:55pm. Radio Finland international programs at 100.8 MHz (FM) in Helsinki are presented daily at 5:30, 7:35, 9:30, 11, and 11:30am; at 1:30, 2, 3, 4, 5:05, and 9:35pm; and at midnight, as well as on 94.0 MHz (FM) in Helsinki at 10:30pm. For information and a free publication, *Radio Finland,* about radio programs in foreign languages, call ⓒ **09/148-01** in Helsinki.

Restrooms Most public restrooms are in terminals (air, bus, and rail). Hotels usually have very clean toilets, as do the better restaurants and clubs. Most toilets have symbols to designate men or women. Otherwise, *naisille* is for women and *miehille* is for men.

Safety Finland is one of the safest countries in Europe, although with the arrival of desperately poor immigrants from former Communist lands to the south, the situation is not as tranquil or as safe as before.

Taxes A 17% to 22% sales tax is added to most retail purchases in Finland. However, anyone residing outside the E.U., Norway, or Finland can shop tax-free in Finland, saving 12% to 16% on purchases costing more than 40€ ($52). Look for the TAX-FREE FOR TOURISTS sticker that indicates which shops participate in this program. These shops give you a voucher covering the tax, which you can cash when you leave the country—even if you bought the items with a credit or charge card. The voucher and your purchases must be presented at your point of departure from the country, and you are then reimbursed for the amount of the tax. You're not permitted to use these tax-free purchases within Finland. Your refund can be collected at an airport, ferry port, or highway border point.

Telephone, Telex & Fax To make **international calls** from Finland by direct dialing, first dial the international prefix of 990, 994, or 999, then the country code, then the area code (without the general prefix 0), and finally the local number. For information on long-distance calls and tariffs, call ⓒ **0800/909-99.**

   To place calls to Finland, dial whatever code is needed in your country to reach the international lines (for example, in the United States, dial **011** for international long distance), then the country code for Finland **(358),** then the area code (without the Finnish long-distance prefix 0), and finally the local number.

   To make long-distance calls within Finland, dial 0 to reach the long-distance lines (the choice of carrier is at random), the area code, and the local number. (Note that all area codes in this guide are given with the prefix 0.) For phone number information, dial ⓒ **02-02-02.** Besides phone booths and hotels, calls can be made from local post and telephone offices.

You can send faxes and telex messages from your hotel (at an additional charge).

Time Finnish Standard Time is 2 hours ahead of Greenwich Mean Time (GMT) and 7 hours ahead of U.S. Eastern Standard Time (when it's midnight in New York, it's 7am in Finland). While Finland is on "summer time" (Mar 28–Sept 26), it is 3 hours ahead of GMT.

Tipping It's standard for **hotels and restaurants** to add a service charge of 15% and usually no further tipping is necessary. In restaurants, it's customary to leave just small change. **Taxi drivers** don't expect a tip. However, it's appropriate to tip **doormen** at least 1€ ($1.20), and **bellhops** usually get 1€ ($1.30) per bag (in most Finnish provincial hotels, you normally carry your own luggage to your room). At railway stations, **porters** are usually tipped 1€ ($1.30) per bag. Hairdressers and barbers don't expect tips. **Coat check charges** are usually posted; there's no need for additional tipping.

21

Helsinki

The Helsinki that greets today's visitor is one of the most vibrant and prosperous cities in the world, with one of the highest standards of living and the world's highest literacy rate.

Locals still refer to Helsinki as "a big village," but it is hardly the country town it was only decades ago. With all its bays, inlets, and offshore islands, Helsinki is almost surrounded by water—or at least you may think so. Water does envelop Helsinki on three sides, and it grew up around a natural harbor overlooking the Gulf of Finland.

The half million people you see walking about—at least in summer—are the best educated, the best clothed, the best fed, and the best housed on earth.

Helsinki may stand at the doorway to Russia, but its cultural links are firmly in Scandinavia. It was originally founded in 1550, halfway between Stockholm and St. Petersburg, on orders of the Swedish king Gustavus Vasa, who established it as a buffer zone between Sweden and what was at the time called "the Russian menace."

A city of wide streets, squares, and parks, adorned with sculpture, Helsinki was one of the world's first planned municipalities and is noted for its 19th-century neoclassical architecture. Because the city is relatively compact, most of it can be explored on foot.

From the capital of an autonomous Grand Duchy of Russia, Helsinki was transformed in 1917 (the year of the Russian Revolution) into the capital of the newly independent Finland. Today it's not only a center of government but the nation's intellectual capital, with a major university and many cultural and scientific institutions. Although Helsinki is also a business and industrial center (most major Finnish firms have their headquarters here), and the hub of Finland's transportation networks, the city is relatively free of pollution.

Allow at least 2 or 3 days to absorb some of the culture and cityscape created by these vibrant, progressive people.

1 Orientation

ARRIVING
BY PLANE　The Helsinki-Vantaa Airport (© **020/014-636**), which receives flights from more than 21 airports within Finland and from more than 30 airports worldwide, lies 19km (12 miles) north of the center of town, about a 30-minute bus ride. Special buses to the airport leave from the City Terminal at Asemaukio 3, and stop at the Air Terminal at Töölönkatu 21 (near the Scandic Hotel Continental) at 20- to 30-minute intervals every day between 5am and midnight. Tickets cost 5.20€ ($6.75) each way. A slightly less expensive, but also less comfortable, option involves taking public bus no. 415, 451, or 615, which departs from the Central Railway Station two

or three times an hour between 5:30am and 10:20pm. The price is 3.60€ ($4.70) each way.

A conventional taxi ride from the airport to the center of Helsinki costs about 25€ to 30€ ($33–$39) each way; you'll be assured of a private car shared only by members of your immediate party. A slightly cheaper alternative is to hire a special yellow taxi (℡ 09/0600-555-555) at the airport terminal, which might be shared by up to four separate travelers; the cost is 21€ ($27) per person.

On your departure, note that the airport requires passengers on domestic flights within Finland to check in 30 minutes before flight time. Passengers on flights to other points in Europe usually must check in between 45 and 60 minutes before take-off, and passengers bound for any of the former regions of the Soviet Union or anywhere in North America usually need to check in between 1 and 2 hours in advance.

BY TRAIN   The Helsinki Railway Station is on Kaivokatu (℡ 06/0041-902 for train information). See "Getting Around," in chapter 20, "Planning Your Trip to Finland," for more information. The station has luggage-storage lockers costing from 2€ to 4€ ($2.60–$5.20), depending on the size. The lost-luggage department is open daily from 6:30am to midnight.

BY BUS   Bus transit into and within Helsinki is divided into three separate terminals, the largest of which is the **Kamppi Terminal,** which occupies two floors of a six-story building in downtown Helsinki that's otherwise devoted to a shopping arcade. The Kamppi Terminal is the home base of bus nos. 102 to 205, and site of most of the suburban outbound buses headed in the direction of Espoo. Smaller and less visible, often used mainly by commuters, the **Elielinaukio Terminal** is home base of bus nos. 206 to 345, most of which head out at regular intervals in the direction of Espoo, and also bus nos. 360 to 474 going in the direction of Vantaa.

There's also the **Railway Square Bus Terminal,** home base of buses nos. 611 to 742 headed to Vantaa. For information about bus, tram, and subway routes within Helsinki, call ℡ 0100/111 every Monday to Friday 7am to 7pm, Saturday 9am to 5pm. Alternatively, you can address questions in person at the upper level of the Rautatientori subway station, where maps, tickets, and Helsinki Cards are readily available, either free or for sale. See "Getting Around" in chapter 20 for more information. If you're arriving from Stockholm, you can either ride a ferryboat all the way to Helsinki, or you can take a ferry aboard either the Viking or the Silja Line to Turku on the west coast of Finland, and then, at Turku, you can board one of about 20 daily buses that make the 2½-hour run to Helsinki.

BY CAR   Helsinki is connected by road to all Finnish cities. If you arrive at the port of Turku on a car ferry from Sweden, you can take the E-18 express highway east to Helsinki. See "Getting Around," below, and in chapter 20 for information about car rentals.

BY FERRY   Most of the terminals that service the dozens of ferryboats coming in and out of Helsinki's harbor arrive at and depart from terminals that line the perimeter of Helsinki's South Harbor (especially on the small island of Katajanokka), and to a lesser degree, selected areas of Helsinki West Harbor. Regardless of their exact location, most are within easy walking distance of the center, just a short walk from Market Square (Kauppatori), and accessible via tram nos. 2 and 4. In its role as a maritime force to be reckoned with, Helsinki offers access to dozens of sea routes to other points within Scandinavia and Europe. In addition, as many as 200 different cruise ships, some of them among the finest and most upscale in the world, drop anchor in Helsinki during the course of an average summer. For general information about the port of Helsinki and information about what specialized services you should contact, call the Port of Helsinki (© 09/173-331; www.portofhelsinki.fi/english).

To Stockholm: Over the years, some of the options for maritime transits between Helsinki and Stockholm have grown in numbers and degrees of luxuriousness. The **Viking** and **Silja Lines** carry the highest volume of passengers and operate the greatest number of ships. For information in Helsinki, contact Silja Line (© **09/18-041;** www.silja.com) or Viking Line (© **09/12-351;** www.vikingline.fi).

To Germany: There's maritime transit at least once a day between Helsinki and Lübeck/Travemünde aboard **Finnlines** (© **09/251-0200;** www.ferrycenter.fi). Transit requires 36 hours each way. There's also daily service between Hanko, a port that lies within a 90-minute drive from Helsinki, and Rostock, a Baltic port within what used to be known as East Germany, aboard **Superfast Ferries** (© **09/2535-0640;** www.superfast.com).

To Estonia: Between May and September, there are as many as 38 ferryboat departures per day from these terminals to **Tallinn,** capital of Estonia, a waterborne journey that, depending on the boat, takes between 1 and 4 hours. The fastest boats, hydrofoils, operate only on relatively calm seas and only between April and November. The largest of the lines servicing Tallinn include **Eckerö Line** (© **09/228-8544;** www.eckeroline.fi), the **Linda Line** (© **09/228-8544;** www.lindaline.fi), and **Tallink** (© **09/649-808;** www.tallink.fi). *Note:* Don't think you can jump on a ferryboat for a spontaneous excursion to Estonia. At press time, despite the fact that Estonia is a semiautonomous nation, visas were mandatory and required applications submitted days or even weeks in advance, preferably from the Estonian embassy or consulate in your home nation.

VISITOR INFORMATION

The **Helsinki City Tourist Office,** Pohjoisesplanadi 19, FIN-00100 Helsinki (© **09/ 169-37-57;** www.VisitHelsinki.fi), is open from May 2 to September 30, Monday to Friday 9am to 8pm and Saturday and Sunday 9am to 6pm; off season, Monday to Friday from 9am to 6pm and Saturday from 10am to 4pm. **TourShop-Helsinki,** a service at the Helsinki tourist office, is your best bet for booking tours once you reach the city. The tourist office sells event, air, bus, and cruise tickets, and the money-saving Helsinki Card. Hotel packages and guide bookings are also available here.

CITY LAYOUT

MAIN ARTERIES & STREETS   Helsinki is a peninsula, skirted by islands and skerries. The main artery is the wide and handsome Mannerheimintie, named in honor of the former field marshal. East of Mannerheimintie, opening onto Kaivokatu, is the Helsinki Railway Station. Toward the harbor is Senaatintori, crowned by the landmark cathedral. Designed by Carl Ludwig Engel, this "Senate Square" also includes the government and university buildings.

Continuing east is a bridge crossing over a tiny island—Katajanokka—dominated by the Eastern Orthodox cathedral. Back across the bridge, sticking close to the harbor, past the President's Palace, is the most colorful square in Helsinki, the Kauppatori (Market Square)—see it early in the morning when it's most lively. From the pier here, it's possible to catch boats for Suomenlinna, fortified islands that guard the sea lanes to Helsinki. The sea fortress celebrated its 250th anniversary in 1998.

The great promenade street of Helsinki—Esplanadi (Esplanade; which is divided into two parallel avenues, the Etaläesplanadi [south] and the Pohjoisesplanadi [north], separated with a statue-and flower-dotted green strip in the middle)—begins west of Market Square. Directly north of the Esplanade and running parallel to it is Aleksanterinkatu, the principal shopping street.

FINDING AN ADDRESS Street numbers always begin at the south end of north-south streets and at the eastern end of streets running east-west. All odd numbers are on one side of the street and all even numbers on the opposite side. In some cases, where a large building houses several establishments, there might be an A or B attached to the number.

MAPS The best city maps of Helsinki contain a highly detailed and alphabetized street index, and can easily be carried in your pocket. Such maps are sold at nearly all bookstores and many news kiosks in the central city, including Helsinki's major bookstore, **Academic Book Store,** Keskuskatu 1 (at the corner of the Pohjoisesplanadi; © 09/121-41).

NEIGHBORHOODS IN BRIEF
Helsinki is divided roughly into districts.

The Center The historic core stretches from Senaatintori (Senate Square) to Esplanadi. Senate Square is dominated by the Lutheran cathedral at its center, and Esplanadi itself is an avenue lined with trees. At one end of Esplanadi, the wide Mannerheimintie, extending for about 5km (3 miles), is the main road from the city center to the expanding suburbs. The section south of Esplanadi is one of the wealthiest in the capital, lined with embassies and elegant houses, rising into Kaivopuisto Park.

North of Center If you'd like to escape the congestion in the center of town, especially around the rail terminus, you can follow the main artery, Mannerheimintie, north. This section of Helsinki lies between Sibelius Park in the west and a lake, Töölönlahti, in the east. It has a more residential feel than does the area in the center, and several fine restaurants are located here. Those driving cars into Helsinki prefer this section.

Kruununhaka & Hakaniemi The district of Kruununhaka is one of the oldest. Helsinki was founded in 1550 at the mouth of the Vantaa River, but was relocated in 1640 on the peninsula of Vironniemi in what's known as Kruununhaka today. This section, along with neighboring Hakaniemi, encompasses the remaining buildings from 17th-century Helsinki. The waters of Kaisaniemenlahti divide the districts of Hakaniemi and Kruununhaka.

The Islands Helsinki also includes several islands, some of which are known as "tourist islands," including Korkeasaari, site of the Helsinki Zoo. The main islands are linked by convenient ferries and water taxis.

Called the "fortress of Finland" and the "Gibraltar of the North," Suomenlinna consists of five main islands, all interconnected, and is the site of many museums. You can spend a day here exploring the old fortifications. Seurasaari, another island, has a bathing beach and recreation area, as well as a national park and the largest open-air museum in Finland. One of the islands, tiny Kustaanmiekka, is the site of our longtime favorite restaurant (Walhalla) where you might want to enjoy lunch while exploring the Suomenlinna fortress and museums. Prior to our most recent visit to Helsinki, we had assumed that the grim, windswept fortifications of Suomenlinna were frequented only by non-Finnish tourists. Quite the contrary: Many Helsinki residents ferryboat over at weekly intervals, winter and summer, for meditative walks, reading, and personal reflection.

Espoo Many workers in Helsinki treat Espoo as a bedroom suburb. Actually, since 1972, when it received its charter, it has been the second-largest city of Finland, with a population of 220,000 and a recent expansion of its museum scene.

Tapiola Another "suburb city," Tapiola was founded in 1951, providing homes for some 17,000 residents. This "model city" greatly influenced housing developments around the world with its varied housing, which ranges from multistory condo units to more luxurious one-family villas. The great Finnish architect, Alvar Aalto, was one of its planners.

2 Getting Around

Helsinki has an efficient transportation network, which includes buses, trams, a subway (metro), ferries, and taxis.

BY PUBLIC TRANSPORTATION

DISCOUNT PASSES   Visitors to Helsinki can purchase the **Helsinki Card,** which offers unlimited travel on the city's public buses, trams, subway, and ferries; a free guided sightseeing tour by bus (conducted daily, year-round); free entry to about 50 museums and other sights in Helsinki; and free ferryboat access and entrance to the Suomenlinna Fortress. It also includes discounts on access to the airport via the Finnair airport bus transfer and discounts at selected restaurants and shops. The Helsinki Card is available for 1-, 2-, or 3-day periods. The price of the card for adults is 29€ ($38) for 1 day, 42€ ($55) for 2 days, and 53€ ($69) for 3 days. A card for children (age 7–16) costs 11€ ($14) for 1 day, 14€ ($18) for 2 days, and 17€ ($22) for 3 days. The cards can be bought at approximately 50 sales points in the Helsinki area, including the Helsinki City Tourist Office, the Hotel Booking Center (see "Where to Stay," later in this chapter), travel agencies, and hotels. For further information, check with any Finnish Tourist Board worldwide or the Helsinki City Tourist Office, Pohjoisesplanadi 19 (© **09/169-37-57**).

You can also buy a Tourist Ticket for travel within Helsinki over a 1-, 3-, or 5-day period. This ticket lets you travel as much as you like within the city limits on all forms of public transportation except regional buses to far-flung outlying townships that include Espoo, Kauniainen, and Vantaa. A 1-day ticket costs 6€ ($7.80) for adults, 3€ ($3.90) for children 7 to 16; a 3-day ticket costs 12€ ($16) for adults, 6€ ($7.80) for children 7 to 16; and a 5-day ticket costs 18€ ($23) for adults, 9€ ($12) for children 7 to 16. Children under 7 travel free. Tickets can be purchased at many places throughout Helsinki, including the Helsinki City Tourist Office and transportation service depots, such as the Railway Square Metro Station, open Monday to Thursday 7:30am to 6pm and Friday 7:30am to 4pm.

BY METRO/BUS/TRAIN The City Transport Office is at the Rautatientori metro station (© **09/472-24-54**), open Monday to Thursday 7:30am to 7pm and Friday from 7:30am to 5pm. The transportation system operates daily from 5:30am to 1:30am. A single ticket, valid for rides on any city bus or tram, costs 2.20€ ($2.85) for adults, 1.10€ ($1.45) for children 3 to 15, and free for 3 and under. Transfers are allowable within 1 hour of your initial boarding, and the penalty for persons caught riding without a valid ticket is around 70€ ($91).

BY FERRY   Ferries depart from the eastern end of Eteläesplanadi (no terminal) heading for the offshore islands of Suomenlinna and Korkeasaari (Zoo).

BY TAXI

You can find taxis at taxi stands or hail them on the street. All taxis have an illuminated yellow sign: TAKSI/TAXI. The basic fare costs 6€ ($7.80) and rises on a per-kilometer basis, as indicated on the meter. Surcharges are imposed in the evening (6–10pm) and on Saturday after 2pm. There's also a surcharge at night from 10pm to 6am and on Sunday.

A taxi from the Helsinki-Vantaa Airport to the center of Helsinki costs 30€ to 35€ ($39–$46), and the ride generally takes 30 to 40 minutes. Call © **09/251-5330.** An airport taxi shuttle service is available for individual travelers to any point in the greater Helsinki area, costing anywhere from 45€ to 55€ ($59–$72). The van is shared by a maximum of eight passengers. Call © **09/251-5300.**

BY CAR

Driving around Helsinki by car is not recommended because parking is limited. Either walk or take public transportation. However, touring the environs by car is ideal.

CAR RENTALS   The major car-rental companies maintain offices at the Helsinki airport (where airport surcharges apply to car pickups) and in the center of town. Most new visitors prefer to take a taxi to their hotel and then rent a car after becoming oriented. Try **Avis Rent-a-Car,** Hietanienenktu 6 (© **09/44-11-55**), **Budget Rent-a-Car,** Malminkatu 24 (© **09/686-65-00**), or **Hertz,** Mannerheimintie 44 (© **0800/11-22-33**).

PARKING   Helsinki has several multistory parking garages, including two centrally located facilities that almost always have an available space: **City-Paikoitus,** Keskuskatu (no numbered address; © **09/686-9680**), and **Parking Eliel,** adjacent to the railway station (© **09/686-9680**).

BY BICYCLE

You can rent a bicycle (and simultaneously contribute to the ecological health of the environment) by contacting **Greenbike,** Bulevardi 32, entrance via the Albertinkatu (© **050/404-0900**), at rates that range from 11€ to 15€ ($14–$20) per day. A worthy competitor, charging roughly the same rates, are the bike rental facilities within the **Nordic Fitness Sports Park,** Mäntymäentie 1 (© **09/4776-9760**). With the rentals comes a booklet, issued by the Helsinki Tourist Office, showing three distinctly different routes through and around the city. These routes include the orange (city center), the blue (seafront), and the green (city parks) routes, ranging in length from 17km to 37km (11–23 miles) and that require between 2½ and 4½ hours each, respectively. The Helsinki Tourist office can also put you in contact with reputable tour operators who specialize in 2-night/3-day packages that focus exclusively on bicycle tours through the vast terrains of rural Finland.

FAST FACTS: Helsinki

American Express The Helsinki branch is at Arkadienkatu 2, 00100 Helsinki (© 09/613-204-00), and is open Monday to Thursday 9am to 5pm and 9am to 4pm on Friday. Whenever it's closed, you can call an active 24-hour-a-day toll-free information line about lost or stolen credit cards or traveler's checks at © 0800/11-46-46. That number is valid only within Finland.

Area Code The country code for Finland is 358. In most instances, the city code for Helsinki is 09, but in some rare instances it might begin with 010 or 020. For calls to Helsinki from outside of Finland, after dialing the country code, you'll usually drop the first "0" in each of the above-noted city codes.

Babysitters Every hotel in Finland has a list of English-speaking employees, such as maids, who, with advance notice, can babysit your child. The rate in Helsinki is about 8.50€ ($11) per hour, per child, perhaps less in certain provincial towns. Although hotels are the main procurers of babysitters throughout Helsinki, there are alternatives. During daytime hours, if you're a devoted shopper, the well-respected Stockmann department store, Aleksanterinkatu 52 (© 09/1211), offers a free babysitting service every Monday to Friday 10am to 7pm and Saturday 9am to 6pm.

Bookstores The most famous bookstore in Finland—and the best stocked, with thousands of English titles—is Helsinki's Academic Bookstore, Keskuskatu 1 (© 09/121-41). Technically, it's one of the many separate departments within Helsinki's largest department store, Stockmann's.

Business Hours Most banks are open Monday to Friday 9:15am to 4:15pm. Most businesses and shops are open Monday to Friday 9am to 5pm and Saturday 9am to 2pm. Larger stores are usually open until 7pm Monday to Friday and as late as 6pm on Saturdays. With a few exceptions (noted below), nearly everyplace is closed on Sunday. Many shops in the center of Helsinki are open until 8pm on certain nights, especially Monday and Friday, and in midsummer, when daylight seems to go on, some shops remain open till as late as 9pm.

R-kiosks, which sell candy, tobacco, toiletries, cosmetics, and souvenirs are open Monday to Saturday 8am to 9pm and Sunday 9 or 10am to 9pm.

Currency Exchange You can exchange dollars for euros at virtually any bank and in most cases, at the reception desk of your hotel; however, you're likely to get better rates at banks. You can also exchange money at the railway station Monday to Friday 9am to 6pm, and at the airport daily 6am to 11pm.

Dentists Go to Oral, Erottajankatu 5A (© 010/400-3000). It's open Monday to Friday from 8am to 8pm. Outside of those hours, dial © 0600/97070.

Doctors To summon a physician in an emergency, dial © 112. For private medical advice that's available 24 hours a day, dial © 10-023. To summon a doctor to your hotel room, contact **Mehiläinen**, Runeberginkatu 47A (© 010/414-4444 or 010/414-4266).

Drugstores The **Yliopiston Apteekki**, Mannerheimintie 96 (© 09/41-57-78), is open 24 hours daily.

Embassies & Consulates The embassy of the United States is at Itäinen Puistotie 14A (© **09/616-250**); the embassy of Canada is at Pohjoisesplanadi 25B (© **09/228-530**); and the embassy of the United Kingdom is at Itäinen Puistotie 17 (© **09/2286-5100**). Citizens of Australia and New Zealand should go to the British embassy.

Emergencies Dial © **112** for medical help, an ambulance, police, or in case of fire.

Eyeglasses One of the best and most conveniently situated opticians—where you can get new glasses or contact lenses in about a day—is the optical department at **Stockmann department store,** Aleksanterinkatu 52 (© **09/1211;** tram: 3b). One floor above street level, it's open Monday to Friday from 9am to 8pm and Saturday from 9am to 6pm.

Helsinki Helpers Between June and mid-September, the streets in the center of Helsinki are patrolled by a corps of 20-something Helsinki Helpers, identified by their green uniforms. They're conspicuously on hand to dispense advice and information about how to cope with everyday life in Helsinki and maps.

Hospitals An emergency hospital for tourists is the Helsinki University Central Hospital, Meilahti Hospital (for both medical and surgical care), at Haartmaninkatu 4 (© **09/4711**). For 24-hour information about health services, call © **09/10023** (within Finland only).

Internet Access Finland, by some estimates, is the most computer friendly (and cellphone-friendly) country in the world. Consequently, virtually every hotel in Helsinki offers at least one Internet station for the use of its guests, and almost every hotel in town offers Internet connections, wireless or hard-wired, for the use of its guests. In addition, there are lots of Internet stations available for pay on the city streets. The most prominent of these includes the Library "Kirjasto 10" within a branch office of the city's post office at Elielinaukio 2G (© **09/ 3108-5000**). There are also Internet terminals offered to users without charge at the main office of the Helsinki Tourist Office, Pohjoisesplanadi 19 (© **09/ 169-3757**).

Laundry Laundries and dry cleaners are scattered strategically throughout the city, but two that are especially central include Rööperin pesulapalvelut, Punavuorenkatu 3 (© **09/622-1146**), and Easywash, Topeliuksenkatu 21 (© **09/ 406-982**). You can either do it yourself, or you can pay a per-kilo charge to have it done for you.

Liquor Laws The legal age for drinking beer and hard liquor throughout Finland is 18. Many nightclubs and dance clubs, however, admit only "well-dressed" (and nonrowdy) patrons, and sometimes insist that they appear to be 24 or older. Age limits (or even the appearance of age limits), however, usually don't apply to pubs. Laws against drunken driving are rigidly enforced in Helsinki.

Lost Property The Lost Property Office is at Punanotkonkatu 2 (© **09/189- 3180**) and is open year-round, Monday to Friday 8am to 4:15pm.

Luggage Storage & Lockers These facilities are at the Central Station on Kaivokatu. The staff offers both lockers with keys and an employee-staffed area where you get a ticket for your luggage. The charge is 2.50€ ($3.25) per bag. The service operates daily from 5:30am to midnight.

Mail For post office information, call 📞 **0800/171-00**. The main post office in Helsinki is at Mannerheiminaukio 1A (📞 **0200/71000** for information). It's open Monday to Friday 7am to 9pm, Saturday to Sunday 10am to 6pm. If you don't know your address in Helsinki, have your mail sent to you at FIN-00100 Poste Restante (general delivery) in care of the main post office. At this Poste Restante, you can pick up mail (after presenting your passport) Monday to Saturday 8am to 10pm and Sunday 11am to 10pm. You can buy stamps at the railway station post office Monday to Friday 7am to 9pm, Saturday 9am to 6pm, and Sunday 11am to 9pm. Yellow stamp machines outside post offices take 1€ ($1.30) coins.

Police In an emergency, dial 📞 **112**. Otherwise, dial 📞 **100-22** for information about the precinct nearest you. Central headquarters for the Helsinki police is at Pieni Roobertinkatu 1-3 (📞 **09/1891**).

Radio & TV Radio Finland (📞 **09/148-01**) broadcasts news in English every day on the national YLE-3 network at 9:55pm. The external service of the Finnish Broadcasting Company has daily programs in English, which can be heard on 103.7 MHz (FM) Monday to Friday at 7:30, 9:30, 11, 11:30, and 2am, at 1:30, 3, 4, 5, and 9:30pm, and at midnight. Radio One features the BBC World Service News daily at noon (in winter, broadcasts are at 11am). Helsinki has two TV channels. Programs from abroad, such as those from the United States and Britain, are broadcast in their original languages, with Finnish subtitles.

Restrooms There's a centrally located public toilet at Sofiankatu 2. Otherwise, many locals use cafe toilets (where you should at least order a cup of coffee or a soft drink) or make use of the public facilities at transit terminals.

Taxes Throughout Finland there's a value-added tax of between 6% and 22% on all goods and services. Most hotels carry a surcharge of 6%, but nearly everything else a visitor is likely to buy in Finland is taxed at between 20% and 22%, depending on the object.

Telephones and Telephone Enquiries For information and number inquiries, dial 📞 **118** or 📞 **020202** in Helsinki. If you're thinking about calling home (providing you're not calling collect) and want to know the cost, dial 📞 **0800/909-99**.

As mentioned previously, Finland has one of the highest cellphone-to-resident ratios of any country in the world, and Nokia, a leading manufacturer of cellphones, is, not surprisingly, based in Finland. As a result, there are very few, if any, coin-operated public phones in Helsinki, or anywhere else in Finland. (The few that remain tend to be located within the city's main railway station.) Consequently, you might be wise to limit your phone needs to within your hotel room, always remembering that surcharges on long-distance calls from hotels anywhere in the world are likely to be daunting. If in doubt, it might be wise to stick to e-mails from the (often free) Internet terminals at many hotels.

For local calls within the city of Helsinki, you don't need to dial the area code (09).

You can send faxes from most hotels. If your hotel does not have a fax machine, go to one of the larger hotels and ask someone on the staff to send your fax. You'll be billed for the transmission, and probably a surcharge, too.

Transit Information See "Orientation," earlier in this chapter.

Weather Summers in Helsinki are often sunny, but the weather is rarely uncomfortably hot. The best weather is in July, when the highest temperature is usually about 69°F (30°C). Midsummer nights in Helsinki are greatly extended (at this time Lapland is bathed in the midnight sun). In winter, temperatures hover between 21°F and 27°F (–6°C to–3°C).

3 Where to Stay

There's a big choice of accommodations in Helsinki. The trick is to find something that suits your budget. As elsewhere in Scandinavia, Finland isn't cheap. Your best bet with hotels is to plan as far in advance as possible and take advantage of any discounts that might be offered. Even an expensive hotel sometimes offers a few moderately priced rooms, but they are usually booked quickly and are difficult for the average visitor to get. In Helsinki, peak rates are charged in the winter because most of the major hotels depend on business travelers to fill their rooms.

Note: Taxes are included in the rates given here, and many hotels also include breakfast. Unless otherwise indicated, all our recommended accommodations below come with a private bathroom.

A ROOM IN A HURRY **Hotellikeskus** (Hotel Booking Center), Rautatieasema (*©* **09/ 2218-1400;** hotel@helsinkiexpert.fi), in the heart of the city within the central hall of the railway station, is open year-round, Monday to Friday 9am to 7pm, Saturday 9am to 6pm, Sunday 10am to 6pm. Tell them the price you're willing to pay, and an English-speaking employee will make a reservation for you and give you a map and instructions for reaching your lodgings. Hotellikeskus charges a booking fee of 5€ ($6.50). You can also book a room online, in advance of your arrival, without paying a booking charge, by visiting www.helsinkiexpert.fi.

IN THE CITY CENTER
VERY EXPENSIVE

Crowne Plaza Helsinki 🟥🟥🟥 In 2005, this former Hesperia Hotel had a major face-lift and now, as the Crowne Plaza, packages contemporary style, a hardworking staff, and a glossy, marble-sheathed lobby in stories. Rooms are slick, with all the modern conveniences and comforts you'd expect from a luxury hotel. Dining options include the gourmet-conscious Maccu restaurant and the pop brasserie Fidel, which offers burgers and cocktails.

Mannerheimintie 50, FIN-00260 Helsinki. *©* 09/2521-0000. Fax 09/2521-3999. www.crowneplaza-helsinki.fi. 349 units. 255€–302€ ($332–$393) double; 317€–695€ ($412–$904) suite. AE, DC, MC, V. **Amenities:** 2 restaurants; 2 bars; health club; spa; car rental desk; 24-hr. room service; laundry service/dry cleaning. *In room:* A/C, TV, minibar, safe, Wi-Fi.

Hotel Kämp 🟥🟥🟥 More visitors from the United States and Japan stay here than at any other hotel in Finland, joining the ranks of politicians and rock stars. Originally built in 1887, with a newer wing added in the 1960s and a radical upgrade

Where to Stay in Helsinki

Crowne Plaza Helsinki **1**
Helka Hotel **3**
Hilton Helsinki Strand **7**
Hotel Anna **17**
Hotel Arthur **9**
Hotel Kämp **14**
Hotelli Finn **12**
Klaus K. Hotel **5**
Martta Hotelli **6**
Palace Hotel **16**
Radisson SAS
   Plaza Hotel **8**
Rivoli Jardin **15**
Scandic Hotel Marski **13**
Seurahuone Helsinki **11**
Sokos Hotel Presidentti **2**
Sokos Hotel Torni **4**
Sokos Hotel Vaakuna **10**

- - - - Ferry
―――― Railway

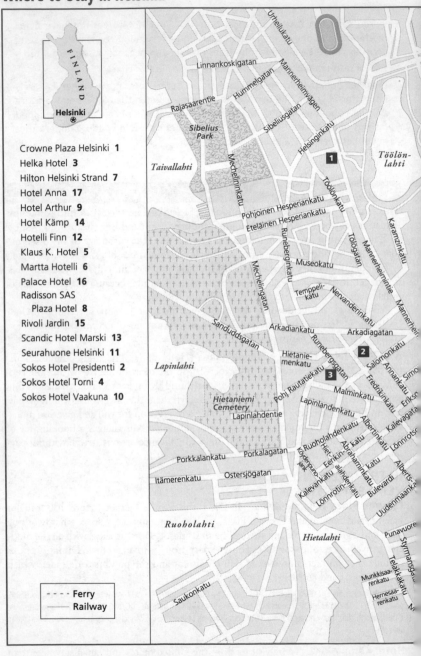

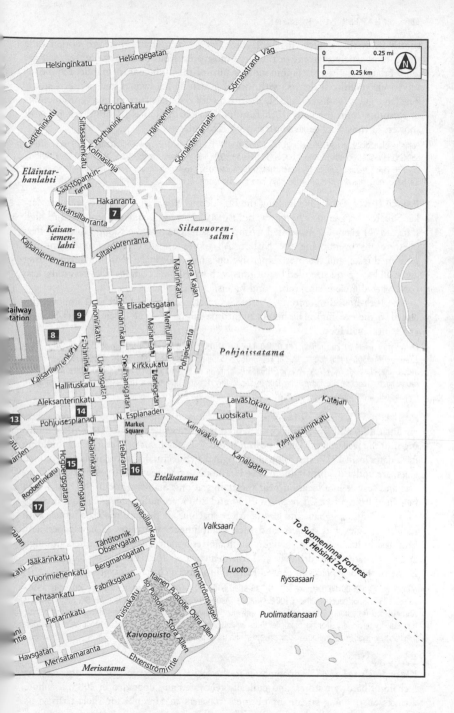

Helsinginkatu
Helsingegatan
Sörnasstrand Väg
Castréninkatu
Agricolankatu
Siltasaarenkatu
K.Porthanink
Hämeentie
Kolmaslinja
Sörnäistenrantatie

Eläintar-
hanlahti

Säästöpankin-
ranta
Hakanranta
7

Pitkänsillanranta
Kaisan-
niemen-
lahti
Siltavuorenranta
Siltavuoren-
salmi

Kaisaniemenranta

Nora Kajan
Maurinkatu

Railway
station
9
Snellman nkatu
Elisabetsgatan
Meritullirkatu
Unioninkatu
Fredrikinkatu

8
Mariankatu
Snellmansgatan

Pohjaissatama

Kaisaniemenkatu
Hallituskatu
Kirkkokatu
Mariegatan

Aleksanterinkatu
Unionsgatan
14

13
Pohjoisesplanadi
N. Esplanaden
Market
Square
Laivastokatu
Katajan

Luotsikatu

katu
varden
Fabianinkatu

Kanavakatu
Mariikasarinkatu

Hogbergsgatan
15
Kaserngatan
Eteläranta
16
Eteläsatama
Kanalgatan

Iso
Roobertinkatu
17

Laivasillankatu
Valksaari

To Suomenlinna Fortress
& Helsinki Zoo

katu
atan
Tähtitornik
Observgatan
Luoto
Ryssasaari

Jääkärinkatu
Bergmansgatan
Vuorimiehenkatu
Fabriksgatan
Ehrenströmsvägen

Tehtaankatu
Itäinen Puistotie Östra Allén
Puolimatkansaari
Pietarinkatu
Puistokatu
Iso Puistotie · Stora Allén

ni
ntie
Kaivopuisto

Havsgatan
Merisatamaranta
Ehrenströmintie
Merisatama

shortly before its "rebirth" in 1999, the hotel lies behind an ornate red stone facade that's immediately adjacent to the city's most prestigious boulevard. Public areas are appropriately opulent, a combination of turn-of-the-20th-century grandeur and conservatively traditional decors, with lots of glistening hardwoods and polished stone. The large guest rooms are lavishly outfitted with elaborate curtains and reproductions of furniture from the early 19th century. Each bathroom is beautifully kept, with showers or tubs. Service, as you'd expect, is superb.

Pohjoisesplanadi 29, FIN-00100 Helsinki. (© **09/57-61-11.** Fax 09/576-11-22. www.hotelkamp.fi. 179 units. 410€– 550€ ($533–$715) double; 800€–3,000€ ($1,040–$3,900) suite. Weekend packages available. AE, DC, MC, V. Parking 35€ ($46). Tram: 1, 3, 7, or 11. **Amenities:** 2 restaurants; bar; nightclub; fitness center; sauna; 24-hr. room service; babysitting; laundry service/dry cleaning; nonsmoking rooms. *In room:* A/C, TV, minibar, hair dryer, safe.

Palace Hotel 🌟🌟   Overlooking the Presidential Palace, just a few steps from Market Square, this gem of a hotel was built in 1952 and subsequently renovated to high standards of glamour. Associated within the same chain as the Kämp Hotel, it offers guest rooms overlooking the harbor. All rooms are decorated with elegant but restrained taste, and the most expensive ones have balconies. Most units have sitting areas; all have good-size tiled bathrooms with tub/shower combos. The best units also come with double basins, robes, and bidets.

The 10th-floor dining room, Palace Gourmet, is a preferred luncheon stopover (it's closed in the evening). The hotel's nighttime dining area, La Cocina, offers Spanish and continental food.

Eteläranta 10, FIN-00130 Helsinki. (© **09/13-45-61.** Fax 09/65-47-86. www.palacekamp.fi. 39 units. Mon–Thurs 235€–350€ ($306–$455) double; Fri–Sat 130€–250€ ($169–$325) double; 350€–610€ ($455–$793) suite. Rates include breakfast. AE, DC, MC, V. Parking 30€ ($39). Tram: 3B or 3T. **Amenities:** 2 restaurants; 2 bars; indoor pool; sauna; limited room service; babysitting; laundry service/dry cleaning; nonsmoking rooms. *In room:* A/C, TV, dataport, minibar, hair dryer, safe.

Radisson SAS Plaza Hotel 🌟🌟   Two of Finland's most renowned architects, Pervin Imaditdin and Ilmo Valjakka, adapted this former Renaissance-style office building into the well-run pocket of posh it is today. In the heart of Helsinki, the building itself dates from 1917, and some of its original architectural features, including stained glass, are under the protection of the Helsinki City Museum. You get first-class comfort and service in a location near the train stations. Standard rooms, each of which benefited from a face-lift between 2004 and 2006, are rather small, coming in a trio of styles: Nordic, Italian, and classic. More spacious are the business class rooms, with handsome lines and designs, and such complimentary features as newspapers and breakfast buffets. Lit by a skylight, the main restaurant, Pääkonttori, offers nostalgia and a first-rate menu of Italian and continental specialties. The library bar, Lasibarri, is one of the best places in central Helsinki to have a cozy rendezvous.

Mikonkatu 23, FIN-00100. Helsinki. (© **09/775-90.** Fax 020/123-4704. www.radissonsas.com. 291 units. 195€– 235€ ($254–$306) double; 600€–1,100€ ($780–$1,430) suite. Rates include breakfast. AE, DC, MC, V. Tram: 3. **Amenities:** 2 restaurants; 2 bars; nightclub; health club; 4 saunas; business services; limited room service; babysitting; laundry service/dry cleaning; rooms for those w/limited mobility; nonsmoking rooms. *In room:* A/C, TV, dataport, minibar, hair dryer, iron, beverage maker, private sauna (in some), trouser press.

EXPENSIVE

Klaus K. Hotel 🌟   Originally built in the 1950s as the seven-story headquarters for a chain of hardware stores, and radically renovated and upgraded in 2005, this hotel attracts an ongoing stream of business travelers in Helsinki for short-term visits. There's a lot about this hotel to like. The staff is charming, and the hotel, in addition to housing people, has cozy bars, restaurants, and a nightclub. The rooms are high-ceilinged and airy, but not particularly stylish or cutting edge. Thanks to a location a 5-minute walk from the uphill end of the North and South Esplanades, it's central to virtually everything in Helsinki. One thing we like the most about this place involves an intriguing association with decorative themes from the Finnish national epic, the *Kalevala*, as seen in the granite bas-reliefs that flank the entrance to the hotel, and the decor of the separately recommended nightclub, Ahio.

Bulevardi 2-4, 00120 Helsinki. ⓒ 020/770-4700. Fax 020/770-4730. www.klaushotel.com. 139 units. 137€–250€ ($178–$325) double; 350€ ($455) suite. AE, DC, MC, V. Tram: 4, 7, or 10. **Amenities:** 3 restaurants; 2 bars; nightclub; babysitting. *In room:* TV, minibar, safe, Wi-Fi.

Rivoli Jardin ⓕ *Finds*   This is one of the best family owned boutique hotels in Helsinki in a neighborhood that's convenient to everything in the city center. This small-scale, well-managed, and stylish address lodges lots of business travelers. Guest rooms, although a bit small, are comfortable, each renovated in 2005. They're mono-chromatically outfitted in pale colors and have either wall-to-wall carpeting or hand-woven Oriental rugs over hardwood floors. Bathrooms are attractively tiled, usually with tub/shower combos. A hideaway bar serves sandwiches and drinks. Breakfast, the only meal served, is available in a greenhouse-inspired winter garden.

Kasarmikatu 40, FIN-00130 Helsinki. ⓒ 09/68-15-00. Fax 09/65-69-88. www.rivoli.fi. 55 units. 237€ ($308) double; 335€ ($436) suite. Rate includes breakfast. AE, DC, MV, V. Free parking. Tram: 10. **Amenities:** Bar; sauna; limited room service; babysitting; laundry service/dry cleaning; nonsmoking rooms; rooms for those w/limited mobility. *In room:* A/C, TV, dataport, minibar, hair dryer.

Scandic Hotel Marski ⓕ   Despite its somewhat stern appearance (resembling a bulky and anonymous-looking office building), this hotel is one of the best in Helsinki, conveniently located in the city's commercial core opposite Stockmann's department store. Originally built in 1962 and much renovated since, it offers comfortable rooms outfitted with unusual textures, modern furniture, and good beds. Units within the hotel's original core are roomier (and hence at the higher end of the below-noted price scales) and somewhat better decorated. Some are within a neighboring annex connected by a passageway to the hotel's original core. Each of the rooms has dark wood furnishings, adequate work space, and patterned fabrics. Bathrooms throughout have neatly kept tub/shower combos. About 10 rooms boast a private sauna.

Mannerheimintie 10, FIN-00100 Helsinki. ⓒ 09/680-61. Fax 09/64-23-77. www.scandic-hotels.com. 289 units. Sun–Thurs 235€–265€ ($306–$345) double; Fri–Sat 116€–136€ ($151–$177) double; 465€ ($605) suite. Rates include breakfast. AE, DC, MC, V. Parking 17€ ($20). Tram: 3B, 3T, or 6. **Amenities:** Restaurant; cafe; bar; fitness center; sauna; limited room service; laundry service/dry cleaning; nonsmoking rooms; rooms for those w/limited mobility. *In room:* A/C, TV, minibar, hair dryer, safe, Wi-Fi.

Sokos Hotel Presidentti ⓕ   Built in 1980 and renovated in 2006 and 2007, this hotel stands in the commercial center of Helsinki, close to Finlandia Hall, Parliament House, and the railway station. Relentlessly modern, and very busy with groups, it boasts lots of drinking and dining facilities. The guest rooms are warm, comfortable, modern, soundproofed, and outfitted with color schemes of pale blues and beige. The bathrooms tend to be small, but come equipped with tub/shower combos and heated towel racks. Airport taxis depart from here directly for the airport.

The hotel's largest, and most visible, restaurant is the Restaurant Sevilla, which offers Iberian food. Also on site is a nightclub, the Presidentti Club.

Eteläinen Rautatiekatu 4, FIN-00100 Helsinki. ⓒ **020/1234-608.** Fax 09/694-78-86. www.sokoshotels.fi. 494 units. Mon–Thurs 170€–205€ ($221–$267) double; Fri–Sun 106€–124€ ($138–$161) double; 335€–685€ ($436–$891) suite. Rates include buffet breakfast. AE, DC, MC, V. Parking 28€ ($36). Tram: 3B or 3T. **Amenities:** 2 restaurants; bar; indoor pool; sauna; limited room service; babysitting; laundry service; dry cleaning; nonsmoking rooms; rooms for those w/limited mobility. *In room:* TV, dataport, minibar, hair dryer, trouser press.

Sokos Hotel Torni ⓡ Rising to a height of 14 stories, the Torni was the first "skyscraper" built in Helsinki (1931) and many irate locals demanded that it be torn down. Nevertheless, it prospered and has become the number-one choice for visiting celebrities. The recently renovated rooms are contemporary, with big windows and carpeting. The finest units are those in the tower, but all the rooms are average in size, with double-glazed windows; bathrooms are fully tiled with tub/shower combos.

Yrjönkatu 26, FIN-00100 Helsinki. ⓒ **020/1234-604.** Fax 09/433-671-00. 151 units. Sun–Thurs 258€ ($335) double; Fri–Sat 119€–258€ ($155–$335) double; 338€–398€ ($439–$517) suite. Rates include breakfast. AE, DC, MC, V. Parking 20€ ($26). Tram: 3, 4, or 8. **Amenities:** Restaurant; 2 bars; sauna; limited room service; laundry service; dry cleaning; nonsmoking rooms. *In room:* A/C, TV, minibar, hair dryer, safe, Wi-Fi.

Sokos Hotel Vaakuna ⓡ *Kids* Built for the Helsinki Olympics in 1952 and still going strong, this centrally located, curve-sided Helsinki hotel lies atop a local landmark, the Sokos department store. Some of the rooms overlook the main rail terminal and its bustling square. Despite frequent renovations, the interior remains deliberately configured as a period piece of what Finland's superb sense of design looked like in the 1950s. The buffet breakfast is served on the 10th floor rooftop terrace. Guest rooms are midsize to spacious, with well-maintained bathrooms with a tub or shower. There is no charge for a child under 5 sharing a room with a parent using existing bedding. Many residents of Helsinki visit this hotel for its restaurants, known for their regional and international cuisine.

Asema-Aukio 2, FIN-00100 Helsinki. ⓒ **020/1234-610.** Fax 09/433-771-00. www.sokoshotels.fi. 270 units. Sun–Thurs 225€–250€ ($293–$325) double; Fri–Sat 117€–125€ ($152–$163) double; 265€–650€ ($345–$845) suite. Rates include buffet breakfast. AE, DC, MC, V. Tram: All trams to rail station. Parking 22€ ($29). **Amenities:** 2 restaurants; bar; business center; sauna, limited room service; babysitting; laundry service; dry cleaning; nonsmoking rooms; rooms for those w/limited mobility. *In room:* TV, hair dryer, minibar, Wi-Fi.

MODERATE

Martta Hotelli ⓡ *Finds* This is a great choice for those who shun big hotels. Less than 1km (½ mile) north of the main train station, in a quiet residential area, this cozy hotel is owned by a women's organization (formerly a radical feminist group that supported Finland's educational advancement). The hotel was built in the late 1950s on land bequeathed by a wealthy donor. Strictly functional but comfortable, it accepts both men and women. The small guest rooms have a no-nonsense Finnish design, but the bathrooms are adequate and contain tub/shower combos. The restaurant on the upper floor serves breakfast and lunch.

Uudenmaankatu 24, FIN-00120 Helsinki. ⓒ **09/618-74-00.** Fax 09/618-74-01. www.marttahotelli.fi. 44 units. 140€–165€ ($182–$215) double; 180€ ($234) suite. Rates include breakfast. AE, DC, MC, V. Closed: Dec 22–Jan 1. Parking: 8€ ($10). Tram: 3T. **Amenities:** Restaurant; sauna; limited room service; dry cleaning; nonsmoking rooms. *In room:* TV, hair dryer, Wi-Fi.

Seurahuone Helsinki ⓡ The origins of this hotel began in 1833, when it opened in cramped and not particularly grand premises that it quickly outgrew. In 1913, it moved into a five-story Art Nouveau town house that was custom-built to house it across the street from Helsinki's railway station. Since then, it has been expanded, most recently in 2006, as part of a series of comprehensive upgrades, one of which included a new wing. Rooms are moderate in size, mostly with twin beds, along with combination bathrooms (both showers and tubs). The public rooms are often crowded, thanks to this hotel's role as host for meetings of many public organizations.

Kaivokatu 12. FIN-00100 Helsinki. ℂ **09/691-41**. Fax 09/691-40-10. www.hotelliseurahuone.fi. 118 units. Sun–Thurs 197€–227€ ($256–$295) double; Fri–Sat 127€–157€ ($165–$204) double; 350€–400€ ($455–$520) suite. Rates include breakfast. AE, DC, MC, V. Tram: 3B, 3T, or 4. **Amenities:** Restaurant; bar; limited room service; laundry service; dry cleaning. *In room:* TV, minibar, hair dryer, safe.

INEXPENSIVE

Helka Hotel *(Value*   Owned by the Finnish version of the YWCA, this 1928 hotel is a budget oasis in a sea of expensively priced hotels. In the heart of the city, close to the train station, and rising six floors, it's a serviceable, affordable choice, without being any great style setter. Guest rooms are generally spacious and sparsely furnished, and come with a private bathroom with shower attached. Double windows cut down on the noise. The on-site restaurant is recommended for its good Finnish and international dishes and its reasonable prices.

Pohjoinen Rautatiekatu 23A, Helsinki 00100. ℂ **09/613-580**. Fax 09/441-087. www.helka.fi. 150 units. 102€–159€ ($133–$207) double; 185€–250€ ($241–$325) suite. Rates include breakfast. AE, DC, MC, V. Tram: 1, 2, 3B, 3T, 6, or 7, Metro: Kamppi. **Amenities:** Restaurant; bar; sauna; limited room service; laundry service; rooms for those w/limited mobility; nonsmoking rooms. *In room:* A/C, TV, dataport, minibar, hair dryer.

Hotel Anna *(Value*   In a residential neighborhood, this well-run and affordable hotel was converted from a 1926 apartment building that survived World War II Russian bombardment. Convenient to shopping and museums, the hotel retains a lot of its original charm, even though it was practically rebuilt in 1985, with additional upgrades completed in 2002, including the recent installation of an upgraded ventilation system. The small to midsize bedrooms are comfortably decorated.

Annankatu 1, FIN-00120 Helsinki. ℂ **09/616-621**. Fax 09/602-664. www.hotelanna.fi. 64 units. 115€–160€ ($150–$208) double; 205€ ($267) suite. Rates include breakfast buffet. AE, DC, MC, V. Parking 12€ ($16). Tram: 3B, 3T, or 10. **Amenities:** Breakfast room; sauna; room service 7–10am; laundry service; nonsmoking rooms. *In room:* A/C, TV, minibar, hair dryer, safe, Wi-Fi.

Hotel Arthur *(Value*   A large and well-maintained establishment, the Arthur is owned and operated by the YMCA, who named it after Arthur Hjelt, the long-ago founder of that organization's Finnish branch. Originally built in 1906, with additional space added in 2006, it lies within a 4-minute walk from the railway station in a quiet neighborhood. The rooms are decorated in a functional, modern style, offering cleanliness and comfort instead of soul and character. Both bedrooms and bathrooms (which have tub/shower combos) are a bit cramped but well maintained—stay here for reasons of economy.

Vuorikatu 19, FIN-00100 Helsinki. ℂ **09/17-34-41**. Fax 09/62-68-80. www.hotelarthur.fi. 161 units. Mon–Thurs 114€–134€ ($148–$174) double; Fri–Sun 92€–112€ ($120–$146) double; 250€ ($325) suite. Rates include breakfast. AE, DC, MC, V. Parking 14€ ($18) Tram: 1, 2, 3, 6, or 7. **Amenities:** Restaurant; bar; sauna; limited room service; laundry service; dry cleaning; nonsmoking rooms; rooms for those w/limited mobility. *In room:* TV, minibar (in some), hair dryer, safe (in some), Wi-Fi.

Hotelli Finn   This is a well-run, functional hotel, built shortly after World War II. It occupies the top two floors (fifth and sixth) of a centrally located office building. It prides itself on being the cheapest hotel in Helsinki and accommodates a scattering of summer visitors, dockworkers from northern and western Finland, and a handful of businesspeople from neighboring Baltic States. Rooms are small and just slightly better than the average college dorm lodgings, but the price is right. Units with private bathrooms have neatly kept shower units. Breakfast, which costs an additional 6€ ($7.80), is served in the rooms, and on the ground floor of the same building, under different management, are three separate restaurants.

Kalevankatu 3B, FIN-00100 Helsinki. ℭ **09/684-43-60.** Fax 09/684-436-10. www.hotellifinn.fi. 27 units, 18 with bathroom. 70€ ($91) double without bathroom; 85€ ($111) double with bathroom. AE, DC, MC, V. Tram: 3, 4, 7, or 10. **Amenities:** Lounge. *In room:* TV.

NORTH OF CENTER

Hilton Helsinki Strand ൙൙൙   This is one of our preferred modern hotels in Helsinki. Set at the edge of the water behind a bay-windowed facade of beige and brown brick, it has the most dramatic atrium in the capital, festooned with plants and featuring glass elevators. An octagonal shape is repeated throughout the hotel's design. The rooms, each renovated in 2005, were conceived by some of Finland's best talent and decorated with local designs, including hand-woven wall hangings and in some cases, parquet floors. Marble from Lapland was used extensively. Half the well-furnished guest rooms provide views of the harbor. The spacious units have medium-size bathrooms with robes, toiletries, and tub/shower combos.

John Stenbergin Ranta 4, FIN-00530 Helsinki. ℭ **800/445-8667** in the U.S., or 09/393-51. Fax 09/393-532-55. www.hilton.com. 192 units. 175€–400€ ($228–$520) double; 550€–1,100€ ($715–$1,430) suite. Rates include breakfast. AE, DC, MC, V. Parking 20€ ($26). Tram: 3B, 3T, 6, or 7. **Amenities:** Restaurant; bar; indoor pool; sauna with exercise room/gym, massage service; 24-hr. room service; babysitting; laundry service/dry cleaning; nonsmoking rooms; rooms for those w/limited mobility. *In room:* A/C, TV, minibar, hair dryer, safe, Wi-Fi.

WEST OF CENTER

Hilton Hotel Kalastajatorppa ൙൙   Translated from Finnish, the tongue-twisting name of this hotel means "cottage of the fisherman." It's certainly no cottage, but it is close to the water, and just 5km (3 miles) northwest of the city center. Located on a ridge of land between two arms of the sea, this pair of marble- and granite-faced buildings was designed to blend in with the surrounding landscape of birch and pines. The core of the hotel dates from 1937, and the newer sections contain some of the most modern convention facilities in Finland. The facility was upgraded in 2005. The guest rooms (last updated in 1998) are in either the main building or a seashore annex that provides panoramic views of the water. Outfitted with wood paneling and hardwood floors, units are tasteful, understated, and comfortable, with adequate bathrooms with tub/shower combinations.

Kalastajatorpantie 1, FIN-00330 Helsinki. ℭ **09/458-11.** Fax 09/458-12211. www.hilton.com. 238 units. 145€–370€ ($189–$481) double; 520€–1,000€ ($676–$1,300) suite. Rates include breakfast. AE, DC, MC, V. Free parking outside, 12€ ($16) inside. Tram: 4. **Amenities:** Restaurant; 2 bars; indoor pool; sauna; gym/exercise facilities; 24-hr. room service; laundry service; dry cleaning; nonsmoking rooms; rooms for those w/limited mobility. *In room:* A/C, TV, minibar, hair dryer, safe, Wi-Fi.

4 Where to Dine

Restaurants bring variety to their menus with typically Finnish dishes, many of which marry Scandinavian recipes (especially Swedish) with influences from Russia and the Baltic. Although Scandinavian-style smörgåsbords are increasingly rare, a worthy replacement is the "Helsinki Menus." Offered by about 15 of the city's most visible restaurants, they tend to focus on traditional Finnish food that's composed of fresh and usually Finnish ingredients, compiled into flavorful and often nostalgic combinations that really reflect the nation's traditions and bounty. As the economic fortunes of Finland have increased in recent years, chefs from other parts of Europe, especially France, have rushed in to fill the need for sophisticated culinary products.

IN THE CITY CENTER
VERY EXPENSIVE

Chez Dominique ✶✶✶ FRENCH/INTERNATIONAL   One of only three Michelin-starred restaurants in Finland, this gourmet citadel is glossy, elegant, famous, and undeniably posh. In 2006, it moved into new headquarters, with 56 seats and a contemporary decor outfitted in earth tones, on Richardinkatu in the heart of town. The restaurant is the culinary showcase for Hans Välimäki, one of Scandinavia's most outstanding chefs. From first-class, market-fresh ingredients to the elegant decor, Chez Dominique represents dining at its finest in Helsinki. The only restaurant that rivals it is the also-recommended G. W. Sundmans (see below).

Appetizers are creative and imaginative, the best examples including a terrine of foie gras with a duck confit and a side of shallot ice cream, and slightly smoked tuna with a gratin of Granny Smith apples. Main dishes include roasted turbot with garlic sauce and a potato risotto, medallions of lamb with sautéed chanterelles, and lobster tortellini with vanilla and anise sauce.

Richardinkatu 4. ✆ **09/612-73-93.** Reservations required. Main courses 38€–50€ ($49–$65); prix-fixe menus 79€–130€ ($103–$169). AE, DC, MC, V. Mon–Fri 11:30am–2pm; Mon–Sat 6–10pm. Closed July. Tram: 10.

G. W. Sundmans ✶✶✶ SCANDINAVIAN/FRENCH   We like this place more than Chez Dominique. The elegant setting is a restored Empire-style mansion overlooking the harbor, a few steps from Market Square. Tiled stoves and paintings on the ceiling evoke Finland of the 19th century. The main restaurant, which is divided into five rooms, lies on the second floor. (At street level within the same building is the also-recommended, and considerably less expensive, Sundman Krog.) Chef Jarmo Vähä-Savo and his staff prepare light, contemporary fare, using the best raw materials available. There's also a celebratory feeling to the cuisine, as you enjoy such dishes as fried sweetbreads with asparagus and pickled chanterelles, or foie gras with a compote of figs. One of the fixed-price offerings, the Menu Skandinavia, features such dishes as sugar-cured salmon with fennel, risotto with chanterelles and local cheese, and apple pie with cardamom ice cream.

Eteläranta 16. ✆ **09/622-64-10.** Reservations required. Main courses 32€–35€ ($42–$46); prix-fixe menus 64€–79€ ($83–$103). AE, DC, MC, V. Mon–Fri 11am–2:30pm and 5–10:30pm; Sat 6–10:30pm. Tram: 1, 2, 3T, or 4.

La Petite Maison ✶✶ FRENCH   A bit less expensive than the above-recommended Chez Dominique, and in the eyes of its fans a bit cozier and more accessible, this restaurant occupies two intimate dining rooms on a street that's listed in most of the architectural guides to Helsinki as the one that showcases more Art Nouveau buildings than any other street in town. Inside, you'll find an open kitchen, a bar area loaded with the fruits of a Finnish harvest, and elaborate arrays of crystal and silver. The chef, the *maître d'hôtel,* and most of the staff here derive from France and permeate their menus with dishes steeped in the traditions of that country. Depending on the season and the whim of the chef, meals might include house-style tuna *niçoise,* hunters-style filet of beef with seasonal mushrooms, and a well-prepared confit of duckling. The wine list is one of the most sophisticated in town, always with several all-organic choices, and desserts are always freshly made and always include at least one selection based on chocolate, such as the dark chocolate flan with peach sorbet.

Where to Dine in Helsinki

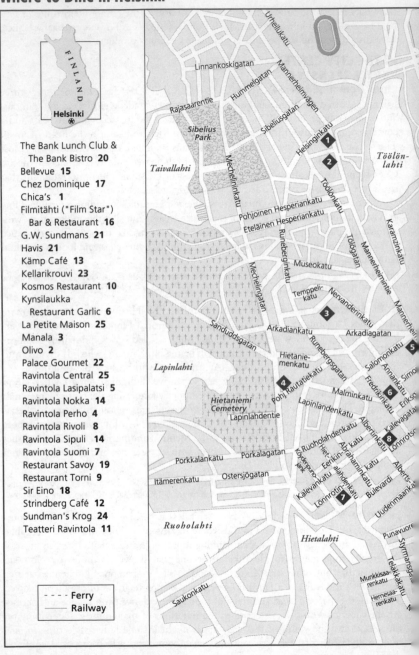

The Bank Lunch Club &
  The Bank Bistro **20**
Bellevue **15**
Chez Dominique **17**
Chica's **1**
Filmitähti ("Film Star")
  Bar & Restaurant **16**
G.W. Sundmans **21**
Havis **21**
Kämp Café **13**
Kellarikrouvi **23**
Kosmos Restaurant **10**
Kynsilaukka
  Restaurant Garlic **6**
La Petite Maison **25**
Manala **3**
Olivo **2**
Palace Gourmet **22**
Ravintola Central **25**
Ravintola Lasipalatsi **5**
Ravintola Nokka **14**
Ravintola Perho **4**
Ravintola Rivoli **8**
Ravintola Sipuli **14**
Ravintola Suomi **7**
Restaurant Savoy **19**
Restaurant Torni **9**
Sir Eino **18**
Strindberg Café **12**
Sundman's Krog **24**
Teatteri Ravintola **11**

---- Ferry
········· Railway

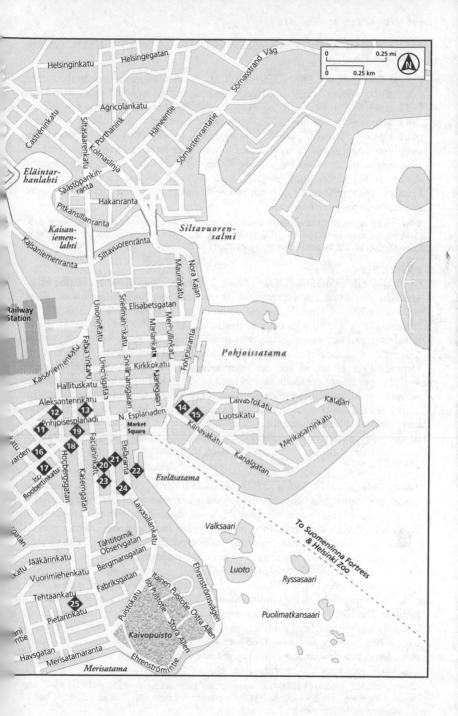

Huvilakatu 28. ✆ 010/270-1704. Reservations recommended. Prix-fixe 61€–89€ ($79–$116). AE, MC, V. Mon–Sat 6–10pm. Tram: 3B or 3T.

Palace Gourmet ✿✿ FINNISH/FRENCH   With a panoramic view of the harbor from the 10th floor of the Palace Hotel, this is one of the most acclaimed restaurants in Helsinki and has been offering exquisite cuisine combined with excellent service and a unique ambience since 1952. It has wood paneling, large windows, and—to a trained eye—an excellent postwar Finnish design. Its wine cellar is one of the best in the country, having won many awards. Only set-price menus are available and might, according to what's in season, include roasted halibut with a vanilla-flavored garlic mousse and tarragon sauce; poached asparagus with smoked ham or celery-and-Parmesan soup; grilled rolls of perch filet with parsley sauce; and filet and tongue of reindeer with rowanberry mousse.

In the Palace Hotel, Eteläranta 10. ✆ 09/13-45-61. Reservations required. Prix-fixe lunch menus 41€–94€ ($49–$113); prix-fixe dinner menus 65€–94€ ($78–$113). AE, DC, MC, V. Mon–Fri 11:30am–3pm and 6pm–midnight. Closed for lunch July and the first 2 weeks of Aug. 3B. Bus: 16.

EXPENSIVE

Havis ✿✿ FINNISH/SEAFOOD   Named after the heroic female statue (the Havis Amanda) that stands a few steps from its entrance, this upscale tavern is the finest seafood restaurant in Helsinki. Located across the boulevard from Market Square, it has vaulted ceilings covered with nautical frescos and an appealing sense of solidly established calm and well-being. Established in 1973, and having moved into its present quarters in 2004, the restaurant prides itself on serving seafood primarily from Finland. Depending on the season, you can enjoy such delights as perch soup with a perch-stuffed crepe, roasted tuna with avocado and citrus, glow-fried whitefish prepared over an open fire with a puree of green peas and carrot sauce, and mushroom lasagna with parsley sauce. Dessert changes with the whim of the chef, but might include a strawberry consommé with Pernod-flavored strawberry sauce. The service is impeccable.

Eteläranta 16. ✆ 09/6869-5660. Reservations required. Main courses 18€–45€ ($23–$59); 3-course prix-fixe lunch 29€ ($38), prix-fixe dinner 42€–53€ ($55–$69). AE, DC, MC, V. Daily 11:30am–3pm and 5–11:30pm. Tram: 1, 2, 3T, or 4. Bus: 16.

Kämp Café ✿ CONTINENTAL/INTERNATIONAL   The best part about this upscale and rather posh bistro involves its sense of humor and (dare we say it) realistic evaluation of its own clientele. In 2005, when the dining public did not come out in droves, it deliberately revamped its own image from ultraposh bastion into an upscale and elegant, but not stratospherically expensive, bistro—the kind of place where you'll be comfortable and well fed but not intimidated. It occupies much of the street level of the historic core of Helsinki's most elegant and most historic hotel. Amid a decor inspired by the 19th-century style of the Russian Empire, it opens onto a view of an imperial-looking bar (the Kämp Club). You can always order from the bar menu in the Kämp Club, but since we found the tables here cramped and rather uncomfortable, we prefer the dining room. Here, very polite staff members will haul out, among others, a parfait of duck liver with port wine jelly, platters of fried pike-perch (zander) with whitefish roe sauce, grilled entrecôte of veal with *diablo* sauce, and a "pavlova" meringue with fresh raspberries.

Pohjoisesplanadi 29. ✆ 09/5761-1204. Reservations required. Main courses in the bar 12€–22€ ($15–$29); main courses in the dining room 22€–36€ ($29–$49); 4-course prix-fixe menu 52€ ($68). AE, DC, MC, V. Mon–Fri 11:30am–midnight; Sat 5pm–midnight. Tram: 1 or 7.

Ravintola Nokka 🍴🍴 FINNISH This is one of the top five restaurants of Helsinki, outpaced only by such choices as G. W. Sundmans and Chez Dominique. In a late-19th-century brick building below the Helsinki Culinary Institute, immediately fronting the harbor, the restaurant is the cheapest member of a respected chain that includes some of the best-known dining venues in Helsinki. You might be happiest here if you explore its rambling interior before actually sitting down for a meal. There's a cozy bar area (which specializes in Calvados, carrying nearly 50 brands) near the entrance and at least three additional dining areas, most of which feature a sweeping view over one of the most high-tech kitchens in Finland. The chefs fan out across Finland to get their raw ingredients: Arctic char from Pyhämaa, duck from Alhopakka, fresh fish from western Finland, lamb from Bovik, and snails from Porvoo. Their Helsinki Menu is one of the town's best, beginning with mallard duck consommé with goose-liver mousse, followed by reindeer fawn steak in herb sauce, Finnish cheese, and lingonberry ice cream with warm caramel sauce. On the a la carte menu, main dishes reflect an astute mingling of flavors: whitefish with crayfish foam and a parsley sauce, or roast deer seasoned with juniper and rosemary.

Kanavaranta 7F. ② 09/687-7330. Reservations required. Main courses 18€–29€ ($23–$38). Prix-fixe menu 56€–58€ ($73–$75). AE, DC, MC, V. Mon–Sat 11:30am–midnight. Tram: 4.

Restaurant Savoy 🍴🍴 FINNISH/INTERNATIONAL In an office building near the harbor, this restaurant's decor exemplifies Finnish modernism. In 1937 Finland's greatest architect, Alvar Aalto, designed every detail of the place, even the lighting fixtures. Few other restaurants in Finland celebrate the memory and tastes of the nation's greatest national hero, Marshal Mannerheim. It proudly serves his favorite drink—a Marskin Ryyppy (a schnapps made with vodka, aquavit, dry vermouth, and dry gin). It justifiably declares its *vorschmack* (an appetizer made of minced beef, lamb, and Baltic herring that's simmered for 2 days and served with baked potatoes and sour cream) as the best in town. Other specialties include a terrine of venison with cranberry sauce, cold cucumber soup with char-grilled tuna and watercress, and peppered roast veal with roasted sweet peppers and a goat-cheese mousse.

Eteläesplanadi. ② 09/684-402-10. Reservations required. Main courses 36€–42€ ($47–$55); 3-course prix-fixe menu 72€–89€ ($94–$116). AE, DC, MC, V. Mon–Fri 11:30am–2pm and 6–10pm. Closed Dec 23–Jan 7. Tram: 3B.

MODERATE

Bellevue RUSSIAN Close to Market Square and the Uspenski Orthodox cathedral, the Bellevue has been an enduring favorite since 1917 because of its good cooking and its nostalgia for all things tsarist and Russian. You can dine in a long, corridor-like dining room or in one of the smaller, cozier side rooms. Herring, still served Russian style, is always a good appetizer, as are blinis and caviar. The chicken Kiev, filet of beef with herb-flavored butter, and pot-roasted bear steak (limited by the fact that Finland allows only 70 bears killed per year) are highlights on the menu. For dessert, try a flaming *baba* cake. Russian wine is served.

Rahapajankatu 3. ② 09/17-95-60. Reservations recommended. Main courses 17€–65€ ($22–$85); prix-fixe lunch 35€ ($46). AE, DC, MC, V. Mon–Fri 11am–midnight; Sat 5pm–midnight. Closed Sun. Tram: 4.

Kellarikrouvi FINNISH/SCANDINAVIAN This restaurant, built in 1901, was originally a storage cellar for potatoes and firewood for the apartment house above it. Since 1965, it has been a cozy restaurant, the first in Finland to serve beer from a keg. Enjoy it at the street-level bar (where you can also dine if you like) before descending a steep staircase to the vaulted labyrinth of the cellar. Here, depending on which room within the vast place you opt for, the ambience can be noisy and animated—especially on weekends—or relatively subdued. Your dinner might begin with a terrine of perch followed by pork cutlets with a potato-and-cheese gratin, grilled kidneys in a mustard-cream sauce, reindeer steak with game sauce and roasted potatoes, or fried cubed salmon with root vegetables and whisky sauce. Dessert might consist of a Bavarian-style cream puff stuffed with cloudberries.

Pohjoinen Makasiinikatu 6. © 09/686-07-30. Reservations recommended for dinner. Main courses 15€–28€ ($20–$36); prix-fixe lunch (11am–2pm) 15€–36€ ($20–$47). AE, DC, MC, V. Mon–Fri 11am–midnight; Sat 4pm–midnight; Sun (upstairs section only) 2–10pm. Tram: 3B.

Kosmos Restaurant *&* FINNISH

If you want traditional Finnish cuisine without a lot of innovative continental touches, this is your place. Near the center of Helsinki's main street, Mannerheimintie, this restaurant is known throughout Finland as a gathering place for artists, writers, and television personalities. The decor is 1930s and simple, and the menu specialties include grilled whitefish, smoked eel, fried Baltic herring, mutton chops with a creamy herb sauce, and chicken in cherry sauce. Light meals, such as open tartare sandwiches, *vorschmack,* and *borscht,* are also available. In the summertime, you can order "deep-fried" strawberries for dessert; pears drenched with a chocolate-cream sauce are also delicious. The special lunch is served until 3pm.

Kalevankatu 3. © 09/64-72-55. Reservations recommended. Main courses 14€–30€ ($18–$39); prix-fixe lunch 25€ ($33). AE, DC, MC, V. Mon–Fri 11:30am–midnight; Sat 4pm–midnight. Tram: 3B, 3T, or 4. Bus: 17 or 18.

Ravintola Lasipalatsi *&* FINNISH/CONTINENTAL

Only a handful of other restaurants in Finland, such as the Savoy, are so clearly and closely linked to a specific architect and a specific period. Built in 1935, this restaurant sweeps in a gentle, glass-covered curve along the junction of the two busiest boulevards in Finland, about a block from the railway station. It was originally conceived as a site for the care and feeding of visitors to the eagerly awaited Helsinki Olympic games of 1940. Today, it's loaded with a mass of diners from everywhere, with just a whiff of formality and grandeur from the uniformed staff. Service, though well meaning, isn't particularly coherent or organized. Menu items include *vorschmack,* fried pike-perch with a sauce made from a combination of Finnish cheeses; and grilled wild salmon.

Mannerheimintie 22. © 020/7424-290. Reservations recommended. Main courses 16€–29€ ($21–$38); prix-fixe menu 40€–42€ ($52–$55). AE, DC, MC, V. Mon–Fri 11am–10:30pm; Sat noon–10:30pm; Sun 5–10pm. Tram: 3B, 3T, or 4.

Ravintola Rivoli *&* FRENCH/FINNISH

The dining room is an Art Nouveau fantasy set in a labyrinthine room with upholstered banquettes. One of its subdivisions is named "Fish Rivoli," and from its separate menu you can order some of the finest seafood dishes in the city. In both dining rooms, you can enjoy such fare as filet of perch with herb butter, and grilled salmon with mustard sauce. At lunchtime, special *husmanskost* is offered, featuring such dishes as onion soup and grilled rainbow trout. The management also operates an adjoining pizzeria.

Albertinkatu 38. © 09/64-34-55. Reservations recommended. Main courses 13€–40€ ($17–$52). AE, DC, MC, V. Mon–Fri 11am–midnight; Sat 5pm–midnight; Sun 1–5pm (buffet). Closed Sat June–Aug and bank holidays. Tram: 6. Bus: 14.

Ravintola Sipuli *&&* FINNISH/CONTINENTAL

Set within five rooms of what was originally built in the 19th century as a warehouse, this restaurant takes its name from the gilded onion-shaped domes of the Russian Orthodox Uspenski Cathedral, which rises majestically a short distance away (Sipuli translates as "onion"). While renovating its premises for its new role as a restaurant, a team of architects thoughtfully added a skylight within the upstairs dining room that provides an upward angle of the cathedral. This, coupled with red brick walls, intricate paneling, and thick beams, creates coziness and charm.

Don't assume that the amiably battered street-level bistro is all that there is to this restaurant. Feel free to explore the upstairs dining rooms that showcase a more intricate, and more expensive, series of dishes than those offered within the street-level bar, where simple lunches are served. Upon every visit we fall under the bewitching spell of the chef, who is an expert at creating robust flavors. He always uses the finest of ingredients from stream and field, and Finnish products when available, as seen in his smoked filet of pike-perch served with a salmon mousse and reindeer meat that has been carefully butchered and shaped as noisettes.

Kanavaranta 7. (09/622-9280. Reservations recommended. Lunchtime buffet in street-level bar 8.20€ ($11) per person; main courses in upstairs restaurant 28€–39€ ($36–$51). AE, DC, MC, V. Lunchtime buffet in street-level bar Mon–Fri only 11am–3pm. Upstairs restaurant daily 3–9:30pm (last order). Closed Sat–Sun mid-Sept to mid-May. Tram: 2 or 4.

Ravintola Suomi FINNISH   In 2005, what had been a humble and unpretentious neighborhood restaurant went dramatically upscale, throwing away its flavorful, house-made repertoire and infusing traditional Finnish cuisine with a welcome sense of chic. The result is a dining room outfitted in a streamlined, woodsy-looking venue that's very pleasing, and some old-fashioned Finnish cuisine with postmodern twists. Examples include a terrine of white-tailed deer with an herb-flavored mustard sauce and dark rye bread, smoked filet of elk with a game-flavored pepper sauce, and such vegetarian specialties as a mushroom-and-barley-flavored risotto with carrot sauce. Dessert might include blueberry pie with Arctic brambleberry ice cream and wild raspberry sauce, or perhaps a selection of Finnish cheeses.

Lonnrotinkatu 13. (09/680-3780. Main courses 25€–30€ ($33–$39). AE, DC, MC, V. Mon–Fri 11am–2:30pm and 5–10:30pm; Sat 4–10pm. Tram: 6.

Restaurant Torni FINNISH   The Sokos Hotel Torni (see "Where to Stay," earlier in this chapter) throws all its culinary energies into this showcase of Finnish cuisine. In a pastel-colored Art Nouveau dining room on the hotel's street level, a crew of formally dressed waiters serves specialties from the forests and streams of Finland. The best examples include baked snow grouse with game sauce, and breast of wild duck with port wine and ginger sauce. The refined cuisine is prepared with admirable products from all over the country.

In the Sokos Torni Hotel, Kalevankatu 5. (09/43360. Reservations recommended. Main courses 21€–31€ ($27–$40); 4-course prix-fixe menu 56€ ($73). AE, DC, MC, V. Mon–Fri 11:30am–10:30 pm; Sat 5–11pm. Tram: 3, 4, or 10.

Sir Eino FINNISH/CONTINENTAL   This is a warm, wood-paneled bar and grill that offers reasonably priced food within an otherwise rather expensive neighborhood. Know in advance that at least two-thirds of this rather large dining and drinking emporium is devoted to the bar area, and that you'll have to walk what seems like a very long and shadowy distance to reach the dining room. (It's actually behind the bar, so if you're confused, just keep walking.) Once you're here, main-course salads, priced at around 12€ ($16), are very appealing for light appetites, and a spit-roasted half-chicken is one of the specialties of the house.

Eteläesplanadi 18. (09/8568-5770. Reservations not necessary. Main courses 14€–25€ ($18–$33). AE, DC, MC, V. Tues–Thurs 4–10pm; Fri–Sat 4–11pm. Tram: 3B or 3T.

Sundman's Krog Ⓟ *Value* FINNISH   This is a cozy and relatively affordable bistro that occupies the street level of the same historic home that houses G. W. Sundmans. The food is flavorful and devoid of fussy continental overtones. The buffet, set within the hull of an antique wooden rowboat, is laden with herring, local cheeses, and salads. *Note:* The fried herring from this buffet is best consumed with a smear of herring roe, sour cream, chopped onions, and a liberal dose of black pepper. Other dishes might include pike-perch with crayfish sauce, gratin of herbed whitefish with tomato-flavored risotto, and peppered noisettes of reindeer with chanterelle sauce.

Eteläranta 16. Ⓒ 09/6226-4120. Reservations recommended. Main courses 19€–25€ ($25–$33); prix-fixe menus 38€–47€ ($49–$61). AE, DC, MC, V. Mon–Fri 11am–11pm; Sat noon–11pm; Sun 1–11pm. Last order accepted at 9:45pm.

Teatteri Ravintola INTERNATIONAL   The management of this very popular, sprawling complex of bars, nightclubs, and restaurants compares it to "a Caribbean cruise ship, in that we've got almost everything, and we're almost never closed." There's a deli and takeout service near the entrance (open daily from 9am), two bars, and a well-managed restaurant whose menu includes the cuisines of Cuba, Asia, India, and Italy, with frequent changes and reinventions. The Teatteri Bar attracts business folk relaxing after work, while the Clock Bar sports a blazing fireplace and R&B music. One flight above street level, Teatteri Clubbi, hosts a dancing crowd ages 35 to 50 and is open Wednesday to Saturday, from 10pm to 4am. Entrance is usually free, except on Friday and Saturday nights, when there's a cover charge of 8€ ($10).

In the Svenska Theater, Pohjoisesplanadi 2. Ⓒ 09/681-11-36. Main courses 16€–31€ ($21–$40); 3-course prix-fixe menus 35€–40€ ($46–$52). AE, DC, MC, V. Food service Mon–Thurs 11am–11pm; Fri–Sat 11am–midnight; closed Sun Sept–May, otherwise Sun 1–10pm. Bar service Mon–Sat 11am–2am; Sun (June–Aug only) 2pm–1am. Tram: 1 or 7.

INEXPENSIVE

The Bank Lunch Club and The Bank Bistro FINNISH/INTERNATIONAL *Value*   This high-ceilinged area that originally functioned as the lobby of a bank offers at least four different food stations and one of the most cost-conscious lunches in town. There's nothing glam or pretentious about it; all you'll see are office workers surging in from across this high-tech, high-rise neighborhood selecting lunches from, among others, pasta, sushi, and wok-fried dishes prepared to order. Since it's open only Monday to Friday for a relatively short 3-hour stretch, diners throughout the rest of the day tend to spill into the cozier and certainly less frenetic bistro. There, amid wood paneling, bentwood furniture, and a high-tech, metro-urban decor, you'll find a more sophisticated array of dishes that might include snails with garlic sauce, tomatoes stuffed with a tapenade of olives, and whitefish served with chanterelle-studded risotto. During warm weather, ask at the bistro if *kesakeitto* is available. This national summer soup of Finland sells during the warm-weather months for 8€ ($10).

Unioninkatu 20. Ⓒ 09/1345 6260. Reservations not accepted. Lunch Club buffet 8.20€ ($11) per person; Bistro main courses 18€–22€ ($23–$29). AE, DC, MC, V. Lunch Club Mon–Fri 11am–2pm; Bistro Mon–Fri noon–11pm; Sat 4–11pm. Tram: 3B or 3T.

Filmitähti ("Film Star") Bar & Restaurant *Kids* INTERNATIONAL   Food here is well prepared and cheerfully served within an environment that makes even newcomers appreciate the rich history of Finnish filmmaking. And although the candy-cane decor of bubble-gum red and white might evoke *Sunset Blvd.,* the food derives from places more widespread than just L.A. Yes, there are burgers and big, meal-sized salads on the menu, but items that might be more difficult to come by in Hollywood include reindeer sausages, grilled Arctic char, Szechuan-grilled whitefish with fruit curry and pineapple salsa, and pizzas piled high with, among other ingredients, elk meat, reindeer salami, blue cheese, and cranberries. There's also a children's menu where main courses cost 7€ ($9.10) each. The venue is light, whimsical, and fun, and the food is surprisingly good.

Erottajankatu 4. ✆ 020/770-4712. Reservations not necessary. Main courses 11€–21€ ($14–$27). AE, DC, MC, V. Daily noon–midnight. Tram: 3T.

Kynsilaukka Restaurant Garlic ✿ *Finds* INTERNATIONAL   Its name translates from medieval Finnish as "garlic," and that's exactly what you'll get here. The restaurant prides itself on its use of more than 20 pounds of Spanish garlic every day. You'll dine within a pair of cozy and consciously rustic dining rooms, perhaps preceding your meal with a garlic martini (chilled gin served with a clove of vermouth-marinated garlic) or a pint of garlic-flavored beer. Menu items are influenced by the cuisine of Russia, as seen in the grilled gratin of vegetables with garlic and sour cream, pike balls in garlic-flavored cream sauce, and filet steak with garlic and red-wine sauce. Desserts include cloudberry crepes with ice cream, which can be rendered more or less garlicky depending on how much garlic marmalade you add.

Frederikkatu 22. ✆ 09/65-19-39. Reservations recommended. Main courses 11€–24€ ($14–$31); prix-fixe lunch 13€ ($17). AE, DC, MC, V. Mon–Fri 11am–11pm; Sat–Sun 1–11pm. Tram: 3B or 3T.

Manala FINNISH/INTERNATIONAL   In a residential neighborhood several blocks west of the Crowne Plaza Hotel, this restaurant prides itself on both its cuisine and the collection of 19th-century Finnish paintings that line its walls. There's a popular bar with an outdoor terrace, which you'll see as you enter. You can enjoy such specialties as fresh fish, sautéed reindeer, grilled chicken with garlic potatoes on a hot iron grill, and a wide range of pizzas. The chef is well known for his homemade Finnish bread, served with a homemade cheese pâté. Virtually every night of the week the late-night bar attracts lots of actors and musicians, and on Friday between 11pm and 4am, there's live Finnish-style dance music.

Dagmarinkatu 2. ✆ 09/580-77707. Reservations recommended. Main courses 11€–22€ ($14–$29); pizzas 8€–10€ ($10–$13); prix-fixe menu 27€–29€ ($34–$38). AE, DC, MC, V. Mon–Fri 11am–4am; Sat–Sun 2pm–4am. Tram: 4, 7, or 10.

Ravintola Central *Kids* FINNISH/INTERNATIONAL   Known and recommended by many of the residents of the upscale residential neighborhood that contains it, this is a warm and woodsy-looking bar and tavern that serves generous portions of rib-sticking food in a friendly setting. No one will mind if you drop in just for a drink (many patrons seem to view it as their favorite "local"), but if you want to stay for a meal, you can watch the food preparation in the open kitchens. Menu items waver between an appreciation for Finnish nostalgia and more exotic influences from outside Scandinavia. Examples include at least a dozen kinds of pizza, including a version studded with strips of reindeer filet, grilled steak with a brandy-peppercorn sauce, and pike-perch with lobster stuffing. Every Friday, the menu features fresh steamed mussels, served with a white wine sauce and french fries. Children's platters go for around 6€ ($7.20) each.

Pietarinkatu 15. ✆ 09/636-483. Pizzas 8.50€–11€ ($11–$14); main courses 9€–21€ ($12–$27). AE, DC, MC, V. June to mid-Sept Mon–Sat 2–11:30pm, Sun 2–10:30pm; mid-Sept to May Mon–Sat noon–10:45pm, Sun noon–9:45pm. Tram: 3B or 3T.

Strindberg Café CONTINENTAL   Named after one of Sweden's greatest playwrights, a short walk from the Swedish Theater, this is a warm and convivial rendezvous point that's usually packed, especially on weekends. Its street level houses a cafe and a pastry shop, but its heart and soul lies upstairs, where a conservatively modern setting contains a colony of comfortably upholstered chairs and sofas and a big-windowed dining room. Menu items contain an appropriate mixture of comfort food and modern continental. Examples include a savory version of Finnish *vorschmack*, grilled calf's liver with cream sauce and sage, filet of reindeer with rösti potatoes and goat cheese, and double filets of Baltic herring filled with smoked salmon and boiled new potatoes. Consider baked Alaska with rhubarb for dessert.

Pohjoisesplanadi 33. (℃ 09/681-20-30. Main courses in upstairs restaurant 17€–27€ ($22–$35); sandwiches and pastries in street-level cafe 4.50€–11€ ($5.85–$14). AE, DC, MC, V. Mon–Sat Cafe 11am–1am; restaurant 12–2:30pm and 6–10:30pm. Tram: 1, 7, or 10.

NORTH OF CENTER
EXPENSIVE

Olivo &*& MEDITERRANEAN   In 1998, the culinary experts at one of Helsinki's most sophisticated modern hotels threw out their longtime roster of prestigious but dull restaurants and focused all their attention, and their enormous resources, on this well-appointed charmer. Set on the hotel's lobby level, it specializes in cuisine from around the edges of the Mediterranean, a medley of North African, Greek, French, and Italian dishes that, as a whole, contribute to one of the most exotic and sophisticated menus in Helsinki. You'll find some succulent salads and pastas (black tagliatelle with squid ink, tomatoes, garlic, and shellfish) inspired by the traditions of Italy, as well as grilled jumbo prawns wrapped in bacon and served with shellfish and tomato sauce, and warm carpaccio of reindeer with Parmesan cheese. Otherwise, the venue is based purely on olive oil and Mediterranean traditions.

In the Scandic Continental Hotel, Mannerheimintie 46. (℃ 09/4737-2207. Reservations recommended. Main courses 12€–30€ ($16–$39); prix-fixe menus 35€ ($46). AE, DC, MC, V. Mon–Fri 11:30am–3pm and 6–11:30pm; Sat 4–11:30pm. Tram: 4, 7, or 10.

INEXPENSIVE

Chica's TEX-MEX   This is the least expensive and most popular of the limited number of Mexican restaurants in Helsinki. We'll be frank: The food served here is not the equal of any decent Mexican place in the American Southwest, but it comes as a welcome respite when you've had too many herring balls in cream sauce. The decor evokes the colors of the Mexican desert, accented with shades of green, yellow, and blue, and there's lots of exposed wood and a bar with comfortable sofas, which is worth visiting for a margarita even if you don't plan to have dinner afterward. Menu choices include seven kinds of fajitas, enchiladas, stuffed chiles, and a barbecue platter that everyone seems to like. The place was founded by an entrepreneurial Finn after visiting New Mexico and Arizona, so it has a distinctive American touch.

Mannerheimintie 68. (℃ 09/49-35-91. Reservations recommended for dinner. Main courses 9€–20€ ($12–$26). AE, DC, MC, V. Mon–Thurs 11am–11pm; Fri 11am–midnight; Sat noon–midnight; Sun 1–11pm. Tram: 3B or 3T.

Ravintola Perho &* FINNISH/CONTINENTAL   Owned and managed by the Helsinki Culinary School, this is the only restaurant of its kind in Finland. Completely staffed by students and trainees, it offers a comfortable modern setting and a cuisine that's professionally supervised (though not necessarily prepared) by the teaching staff. Diners can usually choose either large or small portions of virtually any dish.

Perfect Picnics

To buy all the foods you want for a picnic, head for the delicatessen on the street level of **Stockmann department store,** Aleksanterinkatu 52 (© 09/ 1211). (See "Shopping," later in this chapter, for more information.) At this deli, you'll find several types of smoked or marinated carp, whitefish, perch, or salmon along with marinated terrines of reindeer, and perhaps cloudberry or lingonberry preserves (sold in small jars), which can be thickly spread on fresh-baked herb bread. You'll also find little bottles of wine and Arctic liqueurs. The deli is open Monday to Friday 9am to 9pm and Saturday 9am to 6pm. Tram: 3B, 3T, 4, 6, or 10. With your picnic basket, you can head for the national park on the island of Seurasaari, the best spot in Helsinki for a family outing.

Menu items include smoked whitebait with mustard sauce, a terrine of smoked reindeer, and glow-fried Arctic char with creamed asparagus and herbed potatoes. There's also a version of "Finnish pasta," served with salmon, cream, and herbs. Many diners find the youthful enthusiasm of the staff charming. The cuisine depends on the culinary lesson of the day.

Mechelininkatu 7. © 09/580-78-66. Reservations not accepted. Main courses 10€–20€ ($13–$26). AE, DC, MC, V. Sept–May Mon–Sat 11am–11pm; Sun noon–4pm. Closed June–Aug. Tram: 8.

THE ISLANDS

Gallery Restaurant Wellamo FINNISH/FRENCH/RUSSIAN   Established on a quiet residential island (Katajanokka Island) central to the rest of town, this is a charming, well-managed and completely unpretentious restaurant with a loyal clientele. Paneled and outfitted in textured shades of off-white and brown, it features flickering candles and a revolving series of for-sale paintings by local artists. Menu items include selections from Russia, Finland, and France, and are thus more exotic than those offered at many of Wellamo's competitors. Examples include lamb soup; snails a la bourguignonne; grilled *bruschetti* served with pickled cucumber, honey, and sour cream; mussels Provençal with aioli and chips; bouillabaisse with aioli; whitefish a la Russe; and a sauté of rabbit, elk, and mutton. The restaurant is well known for its herring. During the evening hours, you're likely to hear the sounds of a live pianist.

Vyökatu 9. © 09/66-31-39. Reservations recommended. Main courses 12€–21€ ($16–$27). AE, MC, V. Tues–Fri 11am–2pm and 5–10pm; Tues–Sat 5–10pm; Sun 1–8pm. Tram: 4.

Restaurant Walhalla ⚔ *Finds* FINNISH/INTERNATIONAL   On the fortified island many historians view as the cradle of modern Finland, this restaurant provides a cheerful and historic insight into Finnish cuisine and culture. Open only in summertime, it requires access by ferryboats, which depart from Helsinki's harbor adjacent to the Havis Amanda statue at intervals of every 30 and 60 minutes, depending on the time of day, daily from 9am to 11pm. The return trip to the center of Helsinki occurs at equivalent intervals daily between 9:30am and 11:30pm. Round-trip fares are 5.50€ ($7.15) per person. Once you land on Kustaanmiekka Island, walk for about 5 minutes to a series of brick-and-granite vaults in the center of the Viapori

Midsummer Dining above the Ramparts of 18th-Century Helsinki

Dining at **Särkänlinna Restaurant** ✦✦✦ is more cultural than culinary. Getting here requires a 12-minute transit by ferryboat from Helsinki's "mainland," a walk across an otherwise barren island in the middle of Helsinki's harbor, and a wobbly climb up a winding flight of 18th-century stairs.

The configuration of the dining room is more than a bit bizarre. In 1924, a well-known architect, Oiva Kallio, designed a wood-sided simulation of a long and narrow railway car, and perched it atop the defensive 18th-century ramparts of an island, Särkkä, that functioned as a military outpost to the much larger fortifications on neighboring Suomenlinna. Today, between mid-May and mid-September, you catch a ferryboat that departs at 20-minute intervals every day between 4 and 9pm. The 5€ ($6.50) per person round-trip cost of the boat is billed along with the cost of your meal.

Menu items reflect the best of Finland and include a tartare of salmon with potato cakes and roe mousse, a ceviche of whitefish with tomato consommé and basil-flavored sorbet, fried filets of reindeer with deep-fried blue cheese, and a starter platter of Baltic delicacies.

Why, you might ask, does the floor slope gently within this restaurant? It reflects the floor plan of the original ramparts, where a deliberate slope was factored in as an aid to sailors and soldiers who had to roll cannonballs from their storage area down to the waiting cannon. Main courses cost 20€ to 33€ ($26–$43). AE, DC, MC, V are accepted. Open mid-May to mid-September nightly from 5:30 to 10pm. Advance reservations required.

---

fortress. There's a simple pizzeria on the premises that operates daily from noon to 8pm (June–Aug only), but the preferred spot is the more formal restaurant that's set atop a panoramic terrace. The menu focuses on traditional Finnish specialties such as salmon soup, filet of reindeer, fried snow grouse, and different preparations of salmon, lamb, pike-perch, and duck. The cooking is competent in every way and the ingredients first-rate, although the setting might outshine the food offerings.

Kustaanmiekka Island, Suomenlinna. (© **09/66-85-52.** Main courses 26€–32€ ($34–$42); prix-fixe menu 38€–46€ ($49–$60). AE, DC, MC, V. Daily 6–9pm (last order). Closed mid-Sept to Apr. Bus: Water bus from Market Sq. to Kustaanmiekka, priced at 5.50€ ($7.15) round-trip per person.

5 Seeing the Sights

Helsinki is filled with many activities, from exploring museums and enjoying a Finnish sauna to taking a summer cruise through the archipelago or sampling a Finnish *seisovapöytä* (smörgåsbord). If your time is limited, though, be sure to visit the **Mannerheim Museum,** the **home of Sibelius,** the **Seurasaari Open-Air Museum,** and the **Suomenlinna Fortress.** For those with more time and money, Helsinki offers a number of specialty shops. For an overview of Finnish products, visit Stockmann, Helsinki's largest department store (see "Shopping," later in this chapter).

IN THE CITY CENTER

Eduskuntatalo (Finnish Parliament)   One of the world's most enlightened and progressive governing bodies assembles here. Near the post office, this 1931 building of pink Finnish granite houses the 200 members of the one-chamber parliament. Forty percent of members are women, one of the highest proportions of female legislators in the world. Members meet in the domed interior of Parliament Hall, which is decorated with sculpture by Wäinö Aaltonen. The architect, J. S. Sirén, chose a modernized neoclassic style in celebration of the new republic. Visits involve lots of stairclimbing and as such is not recommended for everyone.

Mannerheimintie 30. ℭ 09/4321. Free admission. Tours Sat 11am and noon, Sun noon and 1pm; July–Aug also Mon–Fri at 1pm. Tram: 3B or 3T.

Finnish National Gallery 𝄢𝄢𝄢   Finland's largest selection of sculpture, painting, and graphic art is displayed at this museum. The Finnish National Gallery is host to three semiautonomous museums: the Ateneum Art Museum, the Kiasma (Museum of Contemporary Art), and the Sinebrychoff Art Museum (Museum of Foreign Art).

Ateneum Art Museum 𝄢𝄢   Housing the largest collection of fine art in Finland, this museum displays the works of mostly Finnish artists produced between the mid-1700s and 1960. It also contains a scattering of paintings and sculpture by non-Finnish artists from the 19th and 20th centuries. Except for international art connoisseurs, the Finnish artists displayed here aren't known by the general public, so a visit here will be a discovery.

Kaivokatu 2. ℭ 09/17-33-6401. www.ateneum.fi. Admission 6€ ($7.80) adults, 4€ ($5.20) students and seniors, free for children under 18. Supplemental fee for special exhibits 8€ ($10) adults; 6.50€ ($8.45) for students and seniors; free for persons under 18. Tues and Fri 9am–6pm; Wed–Thurs 9am–8pm; Sat–Sun 11am–5pm. Tram: 3B, 3T or 6.

Kiasma (Museum of Contemporary Art) 𝄢𝄢   Under the administration of the Finnish National Gallery (see above), this is Helsinki's most experimental major museum. An American architect, Steven Hall, designed the radically innovative building, every aspect of which was conceived for the display of art produced since the 1960s. The art that's celebrated within this place might be either electronic or tangible, musical or performance oriented. Exhibitions change frequently within an environment where the "permanent collection" occupies a smaller percentage of floor space than any other museum in Finland. The name of the museum (*chiasma* is defined in medical dictionaries as the crossing point of optic nerves) suggests Finland's special ability to achieve crossovers between the worlds of fine art and high technology.

Mannerheiminaukio 2. ℭ 09/173-365-01. Admission 6€ ($7.80) adults, 4€ ($5.20) students and seniors, free for those under 18. Free admission Fri 5–8pm. Tues 9am–5pm; Wed–Sun 10am–8:30pm. Tram: 3B or 3T.

Sinebrychoff Art Museum (Museum of Foreign Art) 𝄢   Part of the Finnish National Gallery (see above), this museum was built in 1842 and still displays its original furnishings. It houses an extensive collection of foreign paintings from the 14th century to the 19th century and has a stunning **collection of foreign miniatures** 𝄢𝄢. There is also an impressive array of porcelain. Temporary exhibitions, usually presented without any additional charge, have in the recent past included a stunning collection of antique *charkas* (elaborate silver or silver-gilt vodka or schnapps chalices) from Russia.

Sinebrychoff, Bulevardi 40. ℭ 09/17-33-6460. Admission 6€ ($7.80) adults, 4€ ($5.20) students and seniors, free for persons under 18. Free admission Fri 5–8pm. Tues and Fri 10am–6pm; Wed–Thurs 10am–8pm; Sat–Sun 11am–5pm. Tram: 6.

Helsinki Attractions

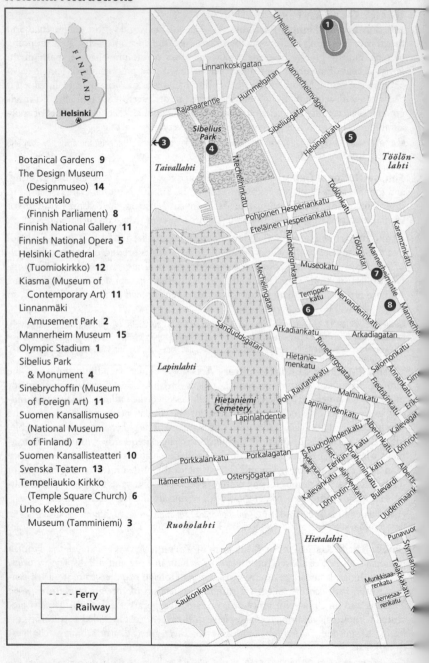

Botanical Gardens **9**
The Design Museum
(Designmuseo) **14**
Eduskuntalo
(Finnish Parliament) **8**
Finnish National Gallery **11**
Finnish National Opera **5**
Helsinki Cathedral
(Tuomiokirkko) **12**
Kiasma (Museum of
Contemporary Art) **11**
Linnanmäki
Amusement Park **2**
Mannerheim Museum **15**
Olympic Stadium **1**
Sibelius Park
& Monument **4**
Sinebrychoffin (Museum
of Foreign Art) **11**
Suomen Kansallismuseo
(National Museum
of Finland) **7**
Suomen Kansallisteatteri **10**
Svenska Teatern **13**
Tempeliaukio Kirkko
(Temple Square Church) **6**
Urho Kekkonen
Museum (Tamminiemi) **3**

- - - - Ferry
——— Railway

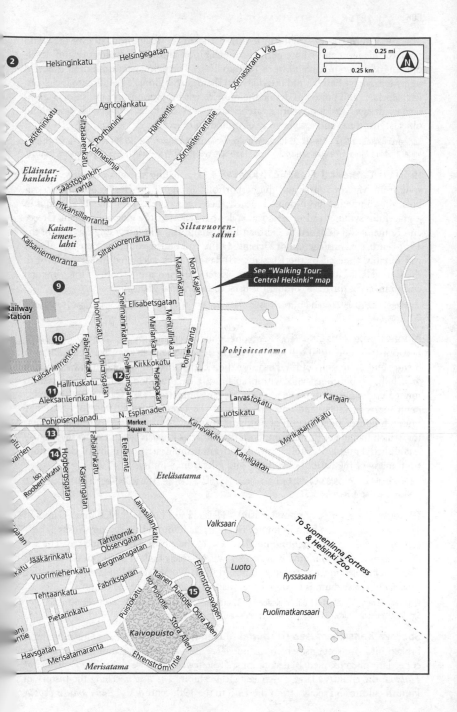

See "Walking Tour: Central Helsinki" map

The Design Museum (Designmuseo) Students of design from all over the world flock to this museum, whose permanent exhibition chronicles the history and development of design in Finland from 1870 to 2002. The permanent exhibition is beefed up by temporary Finnish and international theme exhibitions. The museum is elegant, well stocked, and poised to define the most recent innovations in Finnish or Scandinavian design. Fashion, fabrics, architecture—it's all here, along with household objects, furniture, and a wide array of utilitarian objects.

Korkeavuorenkatu 23. ✆ **09/622-0540.** www.designmuseum.fi. Admission 7€ ($9.10) adults, free for children under 14. Mon 11am–6pm (June–Aug only); Tues 11am–8pm year-round, Wed–Sun 11am–6pm year-round. Tram: 10.

Helsinki Cathedral (Tuomiokirkko) 🛦 Dominating the city's skyline, a short walk from Market Square and the harborfront, is one of the city's most visible symbols, a monumental green-domed cathedral erected between 1830 and 1852. Built in a gracefully symmetrical neoclassical style that reflected the glory of ancient Greece and Rome, it was designed by German-born architect Carl Ludvig Engel as part of the 19th-century reconstruction of Helsinki (a fire had destroyed most of the city after it was forcibly annexed by the Russians). Today the rites celebrated inside conform to the Evangelical Lutheran denomination. Extensive renovations, both to the cathedral and to its crypt, in 1998, brought it back to its original grandeur.

Unioninkatu 29 ✆ **09/2340-6120.** Free admission. Mon–Sat 9am–6pm; Sun noon–6pm; Sun services 10am. Closed Oct. Tram: 1, 2, 3B, or 3T.

Mannerheim Museum 🛦🛦 Anyone who's fascinated by the history of Europe between 1900 and 1950 will love this place. In its own subtle ways, it reflects the early history and aspirations of the Finnish nation better than anything else in Helsinki. A gracefully proportioned villa within an upscale neighborhood otherwise devoted to foreign embassies, it functioned as the elegant home of Baron Carl Gustaf Mannerheim, marshal of Finland and president of the republic from 1944 to 1946. The museum houses his collection of European furniture, Asian art, and personal mementos, which include uniforms from both the Imperial Russian army and the then newly established Finnish Republic, swords, an astonishing array of military decorations from many of the nations of Europe, and gifts from admirers.

Kalliolinnantie 14. ✆ **09/63-54-43.** Admission (including guided tour) 8€ ($10) adults, free for children under 12. Fri–Sun 11am–4pm. Tram: 3B or 3T.

Olympic Stadium (Olympiastadion) Helsinki was host to the Olympic Games in 1952; a tower remains from its impressive sports stadium, and an elevator whisks passengers up to the top for a **panoramic view** 🛦🛦 of the city and the archipelago. The stadium, 2km (1¼ miles) from the city center, was originally built in 1940, but the Olympic Games scheduled for that year were canceled when World War II broke out. The seating capacity of the stadium is 40,000, larger than any other arena in the country.

Paavo Nurmi tie 1. ✆ **09/44-03-63.** Admission 2€ ($2.60) adults, 1€ ($1.30) children under 16. Mon–Fri 9am–8pm; Sat–Sun 9am–6pm. Closed during athletic competitions. Tram: 3B, 3T, 4, or 10.

Suomen Kansallismuseo (National Museum of Finland) 🛦🛦 This museum is broken into five sections, which include *The Treasure Trove,* presenting the museum's collections of coins, medals, decorations, silver, jewelry, and weapons; *The Prehistory of Finland,* the country's largest archaeological exhibit; *The Realm,* telling the history of Finnish culture and society from the 13th to the 19th centuries; *A Land and Its People,* presenting rural life in Finland before industrialization; and *The Past Century*, showing independent Finland and its culture in the 20th century.

Highlight of the *Treasure Trove* is the **Silver and Jewelry Room** 𝄞𝄞, with some stunning goldsmith work and a display of fashionable jewelry dating back to the Renaissance era. An amazing piece is an **elkhead soapstone** sculpture 𝄞𝄞 from the Stone Age is found in *Prehistory of Finland*. In *The Realm* you discover such treasures as the **oldest preserved ecclesiastical wood sculpture** 𝄞𝄞 in Finland, and the **Drawing Room of Jakkarila Manor** 𝄞, with wall coverings, art, ceiling paintings, and a flamboyant rococo style dating from the 1760s. From St. Petersburg **the throne of the Russian emperor** 𝄞𝄞 was brought to Finland in 1809.

Mannerheimintie 34. ⓒ **09/4050-9544.** Admission 6€ ($7.80) adults, 4€ ($5.20) students, free for children under 18, and free for all on Tues from 5:30–8pm. Tues–Wed 11am–8pm, Thurs–Sun 11am–6pm. Tram: 4, 7A, 7B, or 10.

Temppeliaukio Kirkko (Temple Square Church) 𝄞𝄞   This "Church of the Rock" is about 2 blocks west of the National Museum in the Töölö residential district west of Mannerheimintie. Only the domed copper roof and a circular curtain wall of granite blocks are visible from outside. It was designed by two architect brothers, Tuomo and Timo Suomalainen, who were inspired by the shape of Helsinki's archipelago. They chose a rocky outcrop rising some 12m (40 ft.) above street level. The interior walls were blasted from bedrock, and the church's low-rise format and ecosensitive design appealed to residents of neighboring apartment buildings. Its interior is flooded with light from a circular skylight that rings the lower edges of the low slope of the dome. Because of its superb acoustics, the church is often used as a concert hall.

Lutherinkatu 3. ⓒ **09/234-05920.** Free admission. Daily 10am–5pm year-round. Closed during special events. Sun services 10am in Finnish and 2pm in English. Tram: 3B or 3T.

Urho Kekkonen Museum (Tamminiemi)   This site celebrates the accomplishments of Urho Kekkonen (1900–86), who served as president of Finland longer (1956–1982) than anyone else. Built in 1904 in the *Jugendstil* (Art Nouveau) style, the site today is a testimonial to the survival of Finland against the Soviet menace, and a testimonial to the man who helped make that happen. Of particular interest is a view of the most famous sauna in Finland. A log-sided, old-fashioned building with a wood-fired stove, it hosted several pivotal diplomatic meetings, including some with Nikita Khrushchev. The sauna can be visited only between June and August. Finnish-language tours depart at 30-minute intervals throughout opening hours; an English-language tour is conducted every day at 1:30pm. Otherwise, you can borrow an English-language cassette and player for a self-guided tour.

Seurassarrentie 15. ⓒ **09/4050-9650.** Admission 5€ ($6.50) adults, 4€ ($5.20) students and seniors, free for children under 18. Mid-May to mid-Aug daily 11am–5pm; otherwise Wed–Sun 11am–5pm. Bus: 24 from Erottaja bus stop, adjacent to the Swedish Theater and Stockmann department store.

NEAR HELSINKI

Ainola 𝄞𝄞   Few countries seem as proud of a native composer as Finns are of Jean Sibelius, who lived within this log building for more than half a century. He named the house after his wife, Aino, and lived here from 1904 until his death in 1957; he and his wife are buried on the property. Avant-garde at the time of its construction, the house was designed by Lars Sonck, who also designed the summer residence of the president of Finland. The wooden interior of Ainola is lined with books and some surprisingly modern-looking furniture. Järvenpää is 39km (24 miles) from Helsinki.

Favorite Helsinki Experiences

Enjoying a Finnish Sauna   Regardless of where you've bathed before, you haven't been cleansed to the core until you've experienced a Finnish sauna. Whether used for giving birth to babies or entertaining Russian ambassadors, the sauna is often looked upon with almost religious awe, and an enormously high percentage of private Finnish homes and apartments have one.

Hearing a Sibelius Concert   To listen to the work of Finland's greatest composer, Jean Sibelius, is a moving experience. This sensitive, vulnerable artist achieved a universal melodic language. In his lifetime, Sibelius and his music became the symbol of Finland.

Cruising the Archipelago   Since Helsinki is the capital of a country of 188,000 lakes, it, too, is best seen from the water. On a warm summer day, take a cruise through the archipelago; you'll pass innumerable little islands and navigate around many peninsulas.

Taking an Overnight Cruise to Tallinn, Capital of Nearby Estonia   Arranging a visa for a visit to Estonia, across the water, is time-consuming and requires planning prior to your arrival in Helsinki. But once you're there, the rich, once-forbidden majesty of this capital of the Baltic republic opens before you, at prices, at least for souvenir goods, that you'll find surprisingly low.

Ainolantie, in Järvenpää. ✆ **09/287-322.** Admission 5€ ($6.50) adults, 2€ ($2.60) students, 1€ ($1.30) children 7–16. May–Sept Tues–Sun 10am–5pm; closed Oct–Apr. Bus: From Platform 1 of the Helsinki Bus Station, follow the Helsinki-Hyryla-Järvenpää route to where the road forks at a sign saying AINOLA; from there, it's a 4-min. walk to the home. Train: Järvenpää station.

Gallen-Kallela Museum 𝕽𝕽   On a wooded peninsula in a suburb of Helsinki, this museum is dedicated to the great Finnish artist Akseli Gallen-Kallela (1865–1931), who built his studio here between 1911 and 1913, calling it his "castle in the air." Gallen-Kallela had a restless, fanciful personality, and his reputation is based mainly on his paintings, especially those inspired by the *Kalevala* (Land of Heroes). This Finnish national epic, first published in 1835, derived from a much older oral tradition that originated during the Middle Ages in Karelia, one of the provinces that Finland lost to the Russians after World War II. The museum houses a large collection of his paintings, graphics, posters, and industrial design products. Beside the museum is a cafe in a wooden villa dating from the 1850s.

Tarvaspää, Gallen-Kallelantie 27, Espoo. ✆ **09/541-33-88.** Admission 8€ ($10) adults, 4€ ($5.20) students, free for children under 18. Tues–Sat 10am–4pm; Sun 10am–5pm. Tram: 4 to Munkkiniemi; then walk for 2km (1¼ miles) along the clearly signposted seaside pathway.

ON NEARBY ISLANDS
ON SEURASAARI
Seurasaari Open-Air Museum 𝕽𝕽   One of the largest collections of historic buildings in Finland, each moved here from somewhere else, lies on the island of Seurasaari, a national park. Representing the tastes and evolution of Finnish architecture through

the centuries, the collection includes a 17th-century church, an 18th-century gentle-man's manor house, and dozens of oddly diverse farm buildings. There's also an old-fash-ioned "aboriginal" sauna.

The verve associated with this collection of historic, free-standing buildings is most visible during the summer months, when you can visit the interiors, and when an unpretentious restaurant serves coffee, drinks, and platters of food. Although the buildings are locked during the winter months, you can still view the exteriors and explore on foot the park that surrounds them. A stroll through this place in the win-tertime is not as far-fetched an idea as you might think; the park is favored by strollers and joggers even during snowfalls.

Seurasaari Island. 🕐 **09/405-096-60.** Admission 5€ ($6.50) adults; 4€ ($5.20) students and seniors, free for per-sons under 18. May 15–31 and Sept 1–15 Mon–Fri 9am–3pm and Sat–Sun 11am–5pm; June 1–Aug 30 daily 11am–5pm. Closed Sept 16–May 14. Bus: 24 from the Erottaja bus stop, near Stockmann department store, to the island. The 5km (3-mile) ride takes about 15 min. and costs 2€ ($2.60) each way.

ON SUSISAARI & KUSTAANMIEKKA

Suomenlinna Fortress 🎯🎯   This 18th-century fortress (🕐 **09/684-18-80**) lies in the Baltic's archipelago on seven islands, five of which are interconnected with bridges, that guard the maritime approaches to Helsinki. With their walks and gardens, cafes, restaurants, and old-frame buildings, the islands are one of the most intriguing outings from Helsinki. Originally built in the mid–18th century, when Finland was a part of Sweden, the fortress was named "Sveaborg" by the Swedes and later became known by the Finns and Russians (who assumed control in 1808) as Viapori. After Finland became an independent country, the fortress acquired its present name, Suomenlinna, which means "the fortress of Finland." It served as a working part of the nation's defenses until 1973. A complete visit to this site requires at least 4 hours for a full inves-tigation.

You can take a ferry from Market Square to Suomenlinna year-round beginning at 6:20am daily. The boats run about once an hour, and the last one returns from the island at 1:45am. The round-trip ferry ride costs 2€ ($2.60) for adults and 1€ ($1.30) for children 5 to 15; free for kids under 5.

The island has no "streets," but individual attractions are signposted. During the peak summer months (June–Sept), Suomenlinna maintains two information kiosks, one at Market Square (by the departure point for the Suomenlinna ferryboat), and a second on the island itself (near Tykistölahti Bay). The latter kiosk serves as the start-ing point for guided tours—offered in English—of the fortress, with a focus on its military history. Tours are scheduled between June and September, daily at 10:30am and 1pm. From mid-April to May, and from September to early December, they're offered on a limited basis (only Sat–Sun at 1:30pm). They cost 6.50€ ($8.45) for adults and 3€ ($3.90) for children 5 to 15; free for kids under 5. The rest of the year, the guided tours, which must be reserved in advance, are offered on an as-needed basis and priced at around 150€ ($195) for up to 16 participants.

THE MUSEUMS OF SUOMENLINNA

A number of minor museums on either Susisaari or the connected island of Kustaan-miekka can be explored if you have the time.

Coastal Artillery Museum   Set within the thick walls and vaulted ceilings of an area of the Suomenlinna fortress originally built to store gunpowder, this museum contains exhibits that show how Finland defended itself from foreign aggression dur-

---

Fun Fact **Did You Know?**

- Helsinki is famed for its architects, but it was a German, Carl Ludvig Engel, who laid out the present inner city.
- Two brothers designed Temppeliaukio Church from solid rock; it occupies nearly a whole block, but from the street only the dome is visible.
- The Havis Amanda fountain scandalized the city when it was placed in Market Square in 1908, but now it's Helsinki's symbol.
- The major boulevard, Esplanadi, was once a political dividing line—Finns walked on the south side and Swedes on the north.
- Wäinö Aaltonen caused an uproar in 1952 when his nude statue of Paavo Nurmi, the champion runner of the 1920s, was unveiled.
- Sixty-six percent of the world's icebreakers are built in Finnish shipyards, and 30% of the world's luxury cruise liners are made in Turku.
- The origins of the name "Finland" derives from French sailors during the Middle Ages, who defined the cold, usually icebound harbors of the region, and the swampy wetlands around the country's lake district as "le fin des landes" (the end of the land).

---

ing World Wars I and II. Opened in 1948, the museum traces the stages in the defense of Finnish shores from prehistoric times to the present. The weapons for defending the coastline now include missiles, motorized artillery, and turret guns. Also on display are equipment for directing fire, range finders, and a marine surveillance camera. Newer technology is represented by close-range missiles and a laser range finder.

Kustaanmiekka. ☎ 09/181-452-95. Admission 4€ ($5.20) adults, 2€ ($2.60) children. May 12–Aug daily 10am–6pm; Sept daily 11am–4pm; otherwise closed.

Ehrensvärd Museum   This historical museum includes a model ship collection and officers' quarters from the 18th century, as well as displays based on Suomenlinna's military history. The museum bears the name of Augustin Ehrensvärd, who supervised construction of the fortress during the late 18th century.

Suomenlinna B40. ☎ 09/684-18-50. Admission 3€ ($3.90) adults, 1€ ($1.30) children 7–17, free for children under 7. Apr and Oct Sat–Sun 11am–4pm; May–Aug daily 10am–5pm; Sept daily 11am–4pm. Closed Nov–Mar.

Submarine Vesikko   The relatively small-scale (250 tons) submarine *Vesikko* was built in Turku in 1933 for the Germans, who used it for mostly experimental purposes. In 1936, the Germans sold it to the Finns, who based it in Suomenlinna's shipyard throughout most of World War II. During that war, the submarine successfully torpedoed (and sank) the much larger (4,100-ton) Russian ship *Vyborg*. The Paris Peace Treaty of 1947 forbade Finland to have submarines, so all except the Vesikko were scrapped. The Vesikko was opened as a museum in 1973.

Tykistölahti, Suomenlinna. ☎ 09/181-46238. Admission 4€ ($5.20) adults, 2€ ($2.60) students, seniors, and kids 7–17. Mid-May to Aug daily 11am–6pm; otherwise closed.

ON KORKEASAARI

Helsinki Zoo   A collection of northern European animals, including a herd of wild forest reindeer, wolverines, northern owl species, and many other mammals and birds from Europe and Asia, can be found here. We especially like the way the zoo houses its animals and birds in large natural enclosures—not prison cells. A tropical house contains plants from southern climes that Finns have never seen before. On site is a good cafe with a summertime terrace.

Korkeasaari Island. ℂ **09/169-5969.** Admission by water bus, 10€ ($13) adults, 4€ ($5.20) children; by bridge, 5€ ($6.50) adults, 3€ ($3.90) children 5–12; free for kids 4 and under. The Helsinki Card (see "Getting Around," earlier in this chapter) covers admission to the zoo as well as free rides on the ferry and water bus. May–Sept daily 10am–8pm; Oct–Feb daily 10am–4pm; Mar–Apr daily 10am–6pm. Water bus: From Market Square and Hakaniemen-ranta in front of the Merihotelli. Bus: 16 (year-round) to Kulosaari, and then walk less than 1.5km (1 mile) via Mustikkamaa Island to the zoo; or take no. 11 (summer only) from the Herttoniemi subway station.

PARKS & GARDENS

Botanical Gardens   These gardens, a 5-minute walk from the Central Station, feature shrubs and flowers, herbs, ornamentals, Finnish wildflowers, and indigenous trees and bushes. The greenhouses reopened after extensive renovations, making them better than ever. However, unlike the rest of the gardens, they are closed on Monday.

University of Helsinki, Unioninkatu 44. ℂ **09/91-91-24-453.** Admission 4€ ($5.20) adults, 2€ ($2.60) children 7–12, free for children under 7. Apr 1–Sept 30 Mon–Fri 7am–8pm, Sat–Sun 9am–8pm; Oct–Mar 31 Mon–Fri 7am–5pm, Sat–Sun 9am–5pm.

Pihlajasaari Recreational Park   A popular attraction favored by bird-watchers and joggers, this park is made up of two small neighboring islands filled with sandy beaches—it's a summer playground for the city. A restaurant and a cafe are in the park.

Pihlajasaari Island. ℂ **09/63-00-65.** Admission 4€ ($5.20) adults, 2€ ($2.60) seniors and children 5–12, free for kids 4 and under. Daily 24 hr. Motorboat leaves from the end of Laivurinkatu May to mid-Oct daily at 9am, 9:30am, and then at hourly intervals until 8:30pm, depending on weather.

Sibelius Park & Monument   Called *Sibeliuksen puisto* in Finnish, this park was planned to honor Jean Sibelius, Finland's most famous composer. The grounds are not manicured, but are maintained in a somewhat natural state. Old birch trees shade park benches, and rocky outcrops divide the landscape. The park was meant to reflect the rugged natural beauty of Finland, as inspired by Sibelius's work *Finlandia*. At one side of the park is the monumental sculpture, Eila Hiltunen's tribute to Sibelius, the genius whose music is believed to embody the soul of Finland. The monument was unveiled in 1967, a decade after the composer's death; Sibelius is depicted at the peak of his powers and his career.

Mechelininkatu. Free admission. Daily 24 hr. Bus: 24.

ARCHITECTURAL HIGHLIGHTS

Hvittträsk 🕫🕫, in Luoma, Kirkkonummi (ℂ **09/405-096-30**), the studio home of architects Eliel Saarinen, Armas Lindgren, and Herman Gesellius, was built of logs and natural stone, and ranks among the most remarkable architectural creations of its time. The artistic unity of the house with its forest surroundings was a remarkable

---

Impressions

I became aware at once of the translucent, transparent, pure, elusive, clean, and clinical quality of Helsinki. I began to hate the almost paralyzing perfection of modern buildings, equipment, accommodation, accessories, service.

—James Kirkup, *One Man's Russia*, 1968

The Building of Finland

Finland's architectural heritage before the 20th century incorporates Swedish, Russian, and Viking motifs into buildings that often seem to arise from the human subconscious as interpreted by Scandinavian mythology. More than in any other nation, Finland's identity is intimately associated with its postwar architecture.

The architectural landscape of Finland is relatively young—more than 90% of the country's structures were built after 1920. Part of this is because of Finland's ongoing struggle to survive during the many years it swung back and forth between the orbits of the often-violent regimes of Sweden and Russia. Much of the destruction during the 20th century was initiated by Nazi Germany, to a somewhat lesser degree by the Soviet Union. In some cases, however (as occurred in such "lost" provinces as Karelia, which was painfully ceded to the Soviets after World War II), it was the Finns who burned their buildings.

At least some of the impetus for postwar rebuilding came from the government's passage of the "Arava System," which, in an attempt to honor the sacrifices of Finns during the war, offered state-subsidized loans to construct houses. So many utilitarian objects were created and so many homes were built between 1940 and 1958 that Finns refer to this period as "The Age of Heroic Materialism." Everything from armaments to medicine were marshaled into programs designed for the good (and the survival) of the Finnish nation.

In many cases, the signature of the individual architect could rarely be discerned in the typical private home. Throughout Finland, many dwellings were designed as a simple cube, warmed with a centrally located stove (often wood-burning) and capped with a steeply pitched roof that sheltered a high attic suitable for conversion into additional bedrooms.

Alvar Aalto (1898–1976), an architect whose comfortably minimalist and sometimes eccentric designs are now intertwined with the Finnish aesthetic,

achievement. Today it's used as a center for exhibits of Finnish art and handicrafts. A first-rate restaurant, Hvittäsk (© **09/297-60-33**), is open Tuesday to Thursday noon to 8pm and Friday to Monday noon to 6pm.

Admission to the center is 6€ ($7.80) for adults, 2.50€ ($3.25) for children 5 to 15; free for kids under 5. It's open daily from 10am to 7pm. To get there, take bus no. 166 from the Central Bus Station, Platform 62, and then walk about 2km (1¼ miles). Or take the train to Luoma, and then walk about 2km (1¼ miles). By car, follow the Jorvas motorway about 20km (12 miles), turn off at the Kivenlahti exit, drive about 5km (3 miles) toward Kauklahti, and then follow the Hvittäsk signs.

Tapiola, a notable model community, is in Espoo, 10km (6 miles) west of Helsinki. This garden city, from the pre–World War II era, is filled with parks, fountains, handsomely designed homes and apartments, shopping centers, playgrounds, schools, and churches. In the center of Tapiola is a large office building with a self-service cafeteria became an important visionary in the postwar rebuilding of Finland. His work was already known to connoisseurs, thanks to his designs for the Finnish Pavilions at the Paris World's Fair of 1937 and the New York World's Fair of 1939.

A noteworthy (and pragmatic) moment in Aalto's career included designing a series of standardized wood-sided homes partially prefabricated in a Finnish lumber yard. By 1943, during an unexpected lull in the hostilities of World War II, 14 two-family homes designed by Aalto were completed, launching him into a postwar career that shifted his focus from classicism to functionalism and that continued at a fast pace throughout the 1950s and 1960s.

Since then, Aalto has been referred to as "a vitalist to whom nothing human was alien." Bold but tasteful, he developed the Finnish preference for exposed wood and free forms into undemonstrative, functional, and nurturing buildings that are noteworthy for their cost-effectiveness, comfort, and sense of style. Important commissions often incorporated fieldstone and red brick, poured concrete and, later, large expanses of white stone, marble, or plaster. Noteworthy buildings include such monuments as the Säynätsalo Town Hall (completed in 1952); the Sunila pulp mill, which included a new town (Kotka) to house its workers; some of the buildings on the campus of the University of Jyväskylä (completed in 1966); the main building of Helsinki University in Otaniemi (built between 1955 and 1964); and Finlandia Hall, Helsinki's main symphonic concert hall, completed in 1971. Other commissions included hospitals, libraries (such as the one at Viipuri), and private homes, some filled with the distinctive laminated wood furniture for which he and his wife, Aino (who died in 1949), eventually became world famous.

on top (a good choice for lunch). To reach Tapiola, go to stop no. 52 or no. 53 near the Central Station. From either stop, take any bus marked TAPIOLA.

ESPECIALLY FOR KIDS

Helsinki has many activities for children, beginning with the opportunity to travel around on the ferryboats and water buses that link the city's islands and attractions. The Helsinki Card (see "Getting Around," earlier in this chapter) entitles them to free admission or reduced rates at a number of attractions. We've noticed that children like the Traditional Helsinki by Sea boat tours (see "Organized Tours," below), the Helsinki Zoo, the Pihlajasaari Recreational Park, Suomenlinna Fortress, the model-ship collection in the Ehrensvärd Museum, the submarine Vesikko on Susisaari Island, the outdoor Olympic Stadium, and many other sights and excursions.

Linnanmäki Amusement Park Linnanmäki, 3km (2 miles) north of Helsinki, is a fun fair of splashing fountains, merry-go-rounds, Ferris wheels, restaurants, cafes, and theaters. Founded in 1950 by the Children's Foundation to raise money to care for the thousands of children orphaned by World War II, Linnanmäki is still raising money for a new generation of children. The amusement park has 37 different rides.

Linnanmäki. ✆ 09/77-39-91. www.linnanmaki.fi. Day pass for adults and children 25€ ($33) or 3.50€–5€ ($4.55–$6.50) each ride; free for children 5 and under. Mon–Fri 4–10pm; Sat–Sun 1–9 or 10pm. Closed Sept–Apr. Tram: 3B or 3T.

WALKING TOUR **CENTRAL HELSINKI**

Start:	Senate Square.
Finish:	Helsinki Railway Station.
Time:	Allow 3 hours, not including museum and shopping stops.
Best Times:	Any day it's not raining.
Worst Times:	Rush hours (Mon–Fri between 8–9:30am and 5–6:30pm), because of the heavy traffic.

The tour begins at:

❶ Senate Square

You'll find the square in front of the monument to the Russian tsar Alexander II, erected in his honor shortly after the annexation of Finland. Helsinki's most historic and beautiful square was designed in the early 1800s at the height of the Russian Empire's fascination with the architectural glories of ancient Greece and Rome. The designer was Berlin-born Carl Ludvig Engel, who created other public buildings in St. Petersburg.

On the north side of the square is the:

❷ Lutheran Cathedral

Featuring triplicate statues of saints, it has four small cupolas ringing its central dome. As you face the cathedral, the Senate, capped by a low dome and graced by six Corinthian columns, is on your right. Opposite the cathedral, on the south side of the square, stand the ocher facade and Ionic columns of a house from 1762 that was redesigned by Engel.

Leaving the square, ascend the steeply inclined Unioninkatu, skirting the right-hand (western) edge of the square. The street was dedicated to the tsar in 1819 and, because of its difficult terrain, was considered extremely expensive at the

time of its construction. The elegantly graceful building opposite the western facade of the cathedral is the:

❸ Library of the University of Helsinki

Some critics consider this the most beautiful of the many buildings created by Engel. Admire its rhythmically repetitive Corinthian pilasters and columns.

Continue uphill. At the northwestern corner of the cathedral's rear side rises the spire of the:

❹ Russian Orthodox Church of the Holy Trinity

Designed by Engel in 1827, it has an ocher-colored facade and an artfully skewed Orthodox double cross placed above its doorway.

After passing Kirkkokatu, turn right (east) onto Rauhankatu, where you'll see the statue called:

❺ Dawn

This statue of a young girl is set onto a porphyry base near the corner. The gray-fronted modern building serving as the statue's backdrop contains the printing presses and engravers' shops for banknotes issued by the Bank of Finland.

Continue east on the same street, passing an ornately neoclassical building with a trio of wise

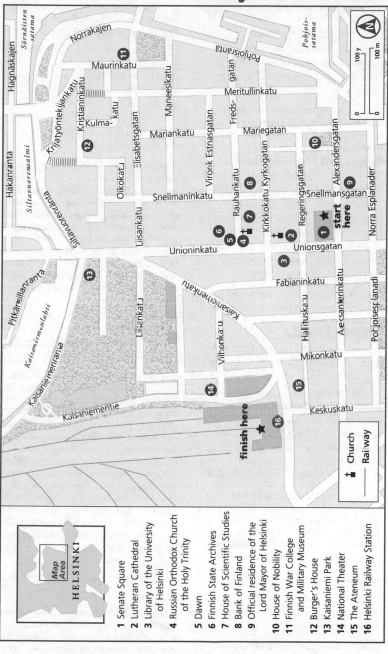

Walking Tour: Central Helsinki

1 Senate Square
2 Lutheran Cathedral
3 Library of the University of Helsinki
4 Russian Orthodox Church of the Holy Trinity
5 Dawn
6 Finnish State Archives
7 House of Scientific Studies
8 Bank of Finland
9 Official residence of the Lord Mayor of Helsinki
10 House of Nobility
11 Finnish War College and Military Museum
12 Burger's House
13 Kaisaniemi Park
14 National Theater
15 The Ateneum
16 Helsinki Railway Station

women set on its pediment. This is the storage space for the:

❻ Finnish State Archives

Originally designed in 1890, over the course of time the archives were greatly expanded with annexes and underground vaults.

At the corner of Snellmaninkatu, turn right. The russet-fronted temple with four Corinthian columns and a single acanthus leaf at the pinnacle of its pediment is the:

❼ House of Scientific Studies

Just below its heraldic plaques is a heroic frieze cast in solid bronze, paying homage to the generosity of Alexander II, who promised to retain the internal laws and religion of Finland after its 1809 annexation. For many years the frieze was the largest bronze casting in Finland. The building was erected in 1891.

Across Snellmaninkatu is a somber gray building set above a steep embankment—the central headquarters of the:

❽ Bank of Finland

The bank was designed in 1892 by Bohnsted, a Russian-German architect. In front of the bank stands a statue of the Finnish statesman J. V. Snellman, the patriot whose life was devoted to raising the Finnish language to the same legal status as Swedish. Snellman was also responsible for making the Finnish *markka* the official currency of the country, thereby replacing the Russian *ruble*.

Continue to walk downhill along Snellmaninkatu, skirting the eastern edge of the cathedral's outbuildings. Shortly, you'll reenter Senate Square. Proceed to the bottom of the square, and turn left onto Aleksanterinkatu. At no. 14 on that street, behind a russet-colored 1823 facade, is the:

❾ Official Residence of the Lord Mayor of Helsinki

This structure stands next door to the Theater Museum at Aleksanterinkatu 12.

Continue walking east along Aleksanterinkatu. In a short time, you'll enter a small gate dotted with a handful of birch trees. Behind the trees rises the neo-Venetian facade of the:

❿ House of the Nobility

Originally a private club and the reunion hall of the Finnish and Russian aristocracy, the House of Nobility was completed in 1861. Walk along Aleksanterinkatu, crossing Mariankatu, and continue toward the harbor. Some of the buildings along the harbor date from the 1760s and are among the oldest in Helsinki.

At the waterfront, turn left onto Meritullintori, skirting the edge of the harbor. A sweeping vista of the Russian Orthodox Uspenski Kathedralen (cathedral) comes into view. At this point, the street changes its name to Pohjoisranta and continues to follow the harbor. Continue along this street to the third intersection, Maneeskikatu, where the quay will widen into a formal park ringed with Art Nouveau buildings, some of the finest in Helsinki. Facing the park, notice on your left the redbrick neo-Victorian building, the:

⓫ Finnish War College & Military Museum

The college was originally constructed as a barracks in the 1880s.

Turn left onto Liisankatu. Completed in 1813, the street honored the Russian tsarina Elisabeth (Liisa is the Finnish version of Elisabeth).Take the second right, turning uphill onto Meritullinkatu. Cross (but don't turn onto) Kulmakatu. At this point, Meritullinkatu becomes a pedestrians-only walkway for residents of the surrounding apartment buildings. At the dead end, turn left and negotiate a narrow, elevated sidewalk high above the street running below (Kristianinkatu). One block later, cross (but don't turn onto) Kulmakatu. A few paces later, at Kristianinkatu 12, you'll see the simple stone foundation and ocher-colored clapboards of the:

⓬ Burger's House

Helsinki's oldest remaining wooden house, dating from the early 1800s, now accommodates a small museum.

A few steps later, Kristianinkatu dead-ends at a pedestrians-only sidewalk, Oikokatu. Go right (downhill), descending two narrow flights of concrete stairs heading toward the lake. At the bottom you emerge onto a busy avenue,

Siltavuorenranta; turn left and notice the stylish bulk of the Scandic Hotel Continental rising across the water. Walk along the curving embankment for a while, coming to the tramway and car traffic hub of Unioninkatu, which you should cross. You'll then enter:

⑬ Kaisaniemi Park (The Company Keeping Park)

This tract of waterfront land, beloved by residents of Helsinki, was a marshy bog-land until the 1830s, when it was drained and opened as Helsinki's first park. The park contains the Botanical Gardens of the University of Helsinki, which date from 1833.

Walk through the park, flanking the water on your right, and then follow the natural left-bending southward curve of the park's main path. (Don't cross any of the railroad tracks.) After exiting from the park, your path becomes Läntinen Teatterikuja, in a neighborhood of Art Nouveau apartment buildings. Follow the street for a block through the theatrical headquarters of Finland. On your left stands the:

⑭ National Theater

Vaguely reminiscent of the opera house in Vienna, the National Theater features decorative sculptures on its facade—note especially the representation of bears. The theater was designed by the architect Tarjanne in 1902.

Across the square, immediately opposite the National Theater, is:

⑮ The Ateneum

The Finnish National Gallery, designed by Hoijer and completed in 1887, is the best art museum in Finland.

On the western side of the square (to your right as you face the Ateneum) is one of the most famous public buildings in Europe, the:

⑯ Helsinki Railway Station

Designed by Eliel Saarinen in 1916, the station includes sculptures evocative of the monumental works of Pharaonic Egypt. It has been copied endlessly ever since by avant-garde set designers of plays and films such as *Batman*.

After such an exhausting tour, you'll want to:

TAKE A BREAK
From the railway station, head directly south until you reach Pohjoisesplanadi, site of a number of cafes. Our favorite is **Aino**, Pohjoisesplanadi 21 (© **09/62-43-27**). Named after a pivotal female character within the Finnish national epic, the *Kalevala*, it sits beside a pulsating street lined with shops near the Market Place. In addition to ordering food and drink here, you'll find it great for people-watching.

6 Organized Tours

CITY TOURS   For a sightseeing trip without a guide, catch tram no. 3T, which takes you past 35 major city buildings and monuments. The 45-minute trip is available only in summer. You can board tram no. 3T in front of the railway station or at Market Square Monday through Saturday from 6am to 1am and Sunday from 7:30am to 1am. The tram departs regularly at intervals ranging from 5 to 15 minutes. During rush hour, you might have difficulty finding a seat. A ticket costs 2€ ($2.60), 1€ ($1.30) for children under 13.

Open-top Tours (© **050/430-2050**; www.opentoptours.com) offers a hop-on, hop-off sightseeing tour around Helsinki on an open double-decker bus, with 11 stops throughout the city. Departures are from Unioninkatu 30 next to the Tourist Information; tickets cost 22€ ($29). Tickets are valid for 24 hours and can be purchased on the bus.

Helsinki Expert (© **09/2288-1600**; www.helsinkiexpert.fi) offers a special audio city tour introducing you to the major attractions. Tours depart from Esplanade Park and Katajanokka Terminal, costing 23€ ($30) for adults or 11€ ($14) for ages 7 to 16.

HARBOR TOURS   For a waterside view of Helsinki and its nearby islands, contact **IHA-lines Oy** (© **09/6874-5050;** www.ihalines.fi), which offers two 1½ hour tours costing 14€ ($18) for adults or 24€ ($31) for a family ticket. One tour explores Helsinki and its fortresses around Suomenlinna, another the eastern archipelago. Food is served aboard, and a luncheon buffet costs 11€ ($14) for adults, 5€ ($6.50) for children 5 to 13, and free for kids under 5.

7 Spectator Sports & Outdoor Activities

Major sports events take place at the Olympic Stadium, Paavo Nurmi tie 1 (© **09/44-03-63**), described under "Seeing the Sights," earlier. In summer, soccer games between Finland and other European countries are scheduled. Check *Helsinki This Week,* which lists the events taking place at the stadium at the time of your visit. Take tram no. 3B, 3T, 4, or 10.

JOGGING   Finns are just as fond of jogging as Americans or Canadians. The best paths are close to Olympic Stadium and in Kaivopuisto Park (the southern part of Helsinki). There are also some good jogging trails around Hesperia Park, which is convenient if you're staying at a hotel in the city center.

SAUNAS & BEACHES   Most hotels (at least the better ones) have a sauna. If you want to sample a Finnish sauna and your hotel doesn't have one, the reception desk can direct you to the nearest sauna that's open to the general public.

Traditionally every Finnish city had a wood-heated public sauna. The only wood-heated public sauna remaining in Helsinki is the **Kothiharjun Sauna,** Harjutorinkatu, near the Sörnäien metro station (© **09/753-15-35**). Open Tuesday to Friday 2 to 8pm and Saturday 1 to 7pm.

If you're in Helsinki in the summer, you'll find the best beaches at Mustikkamaa, Uunisaari, Pihlajasaari, Hietaniemi, and Seurasaari. There's also a popular beach on Suomenlinna; you might combine a trip to the beach with a visit to Suomenlinna fortress. However, if you're from a warmer climate, you may find the waters of the Baltic, even in July, too chilly for your tastes.

TENNIS   The best bet for playing tennis in Helsinki is to travel 5.5km (3½ miles) northwest of the railway station to the Pitäjämäki district. Here the **Tali Tennis Center,** Kutonokuja 4, Pitäjämäki (© **09/55-62-71**), welcomes visitors. Built in 1967, this is the largest, most modern, and most popular tennis complex in Helsinki. The center maintains 19 indoor tennis courts and 11 outdoor courts. Depending on the time of day and season, indoor courts cost 12€ to 20€ ($16–$26) per hour; outdoor courts are almost the same price at 11€ to 20€ ($14–$26) per hour. The use of outdoor courts is severely limited by the weather and the seasons. You can rent a free tennis racquet and buy tennis balls once you're there. Take bus no. 14, 39, 248, 241, or 261 from the center of the city. The tennis center is open daily from 6am to 11pm, but call first to see if the courts are available.

8 Shopping

Finland has taken a bold, creative lead in the highly competitive world of interior design. Search out ceramics and glassware (Arabia is famous), hand-woven articles, hand-carved wood, jaunty fashions, and rugs.

Textiles and jewelry also bear the distinctive stamp of Finland, and toy stores brim with educational toys for each stage of a child's development. Souvenir possibilities include decorations made from reindeer skin, costumed dolls, baskets, and pungent berry liqueurs made from yellow cloudberries, cranberries, and Arctic brambleberries. Of course, you'll find all your sauna needs here as well.

THE SHOPPING SCENE

Most stores are open Monday to Friday 9am to 5pm and Saturday 9am to 2pm. Sometimes stores stay open until 4pm on Saturday, especially in the summer.

SHOPPING AREAS   The major shopping neighborhoods are in the center of the city. They include *Esplanadi,* which offers the finest of Finnish design—but at high prices. Even if you don't buy anything, it's a delightful street for promenading in summer. Airline offices, banks, and travel agencies share the street with shops filled with the best of Finnish crafts, as well as a number of art galleries.

Esplanadi leads from the commercial heart of town all the way to the waterfront. Bordering the water is **Market Square** (Kauppatori), an open-air market selling produce, fish (both raw and ready-to-eat), handcrafted souvenirs, and some of the most magnificent berries (including glorious blackberries from the Finnish forest) we've ever seen. Most of the vendors are in place during daylight hours, between April and October, Monday to Saturday.

The other main shopping section is called simply **Central,** beginning at Esplanadi and extending to the famous Helsinki Railway Station. Many of the big names in Finnish shopping are here, none more notable than the Stockmann department store. Many shopping complexes are also situated in this district, including the Forum. One of the main shopping streets here is **Aleksanterinkatu,** which runs parallel to Esplanadi, stretching from the harbor to Mannerheimintie.

Other shopping streets, all in the center, include **Iso Roobertinkatu** and **Bulevardi,** lying off Esplanadi. Bulevardi, starting at the Klaus Kurki Hotel, winds its way to the water. Two recent additions to the shopping scene include **Kamppi,** or the Kamppi Shopping Mall, in the heart of the city, and a smaller but choice competitor **Hakkoniemin Kauppahalli.** The former devotes four of its floors to shops; the remainder—especially the lower floors—are the domain of the city's new bus station. The latter contains about 20 shops, most of them stylish and upscale.

TAX REFUNDS   Tax-free shopping is available at stores that display EUROPE TAX-FREE SHOPPING signs in their windows. It's available to all visitors who reside outside the European Union. The value-added tax (usually 16%) on articles bought in these shops is refunded to you when you leave Finland. The minimum tax-free purchase varies from country to country.

Most of the large department stores and shops can ship your purchases directly to your home address. That way you avoid having to file a claim at Customs. If you take the merchandise with you, ask for a check for the tax amount. This check can be cashed at the airport or harbor where you depart. The savings, which come to about 12% to 16%, apply to both cash and credit- and charge-card purchases. However, if you use your purchased goods before leaving Finland, you won't get a tax refund. Most international cards, such as American Express and Visa, are accepted at major shops, but always ask beforehand.

If you have any questions about tax-free shopping, contact **Europe Tax-Free Shopping (Finland) Ltd.,** Salomonkatu 17A (✆ **09/613-296-00**).

Shopping for Finnish Design

This is, after all, the nation that pulled itself up, architecturally speaking, by its own bootstraps after its 1918 independence from the Russians. It has been argued that a sense of the Finnish nation was assisted during its birth process by staggeringly brilliant designers and architects (Saarinen, among others), who brought a new definition of utilitarianism and modernism to the world at large. Conveniently, the Helsinki Tourist Office provides a "Design District Helsinki" map. It lays out the location, within a relatively condensed neighborhood, of at least 100 shops, each selling objects (housewares, clothing stores, jewelry) that were influenced by the nation's 20th-century tradition of brilliant modernist designs in every imaginable arena.

SHOPPING HOURS   Most stores are open Monday to Friday 9am to 6pm and Saturday 9am to 1pm. A new government regulation allows shopping on Sunday in June, July, August, and December. As a result, Forum and Stockmann are open during those months on Sunday noon to 4pm.

SHOPPING A TO Z
BOOKS
Academic Bookstore ★★★   Sprawling over two floors crammed with books in many languages, this store (judging from the number of titles in stock) could be the largest bookstore in Europe. It offers many English-language books, along with a number of travel aids. It also has the finest stationery department in Finland and sells greeting cards as well as high-quality gift and hobby articles. If you're here on a Friday, you can attend a literary get-together in the store, which brings together writers and members of the reading public. All of Finland's major authors and leading politicians, plus many foreign writers (including Kurt Vonnegut and Norwegian actress Liv Ullmann), have attended these meetings. The building, with large sky-lit windows and Carrara marble slabs, was designed by Aalto. In Stockmann's department store, Keskuskatu 1. ✆ 09/121-41. Tram: 3B.

DEPARTMENT STORES
Stockmann ★★   Helsinki's largest department store is also Finland's finest and oldest. Its main entrance is on Aleksanterinkatu, with other entrances on Keskuskatu, Pohjoisesplanadi, and Mannerheimintie. Stockmann has the most diversified sampling of Finnish and imported merchandise of any store: glassware, stoneware, ceramics, lamps, furniture, furs, contemporary jewelry, clothes and textiles, handmade candles, reindeer hides—a little bit of everything. Purchases made through the store's Export Service entitle you to a full and immediate 18% deduction, and you don't have to carry your purchases home with you. Aleksanterinkatu 52. ✆ 09/1211. Tram: 3B.

FASHION
Annikki Karvinen ★   Ms. Karvinen became famous for her sophisticated and subtle choice of colors, and for elevating *poppana* (Finnish cotton) into the stellar peaks of fashion. All *poppana* fabrics are hand woven, and Ms. Karvinen has adapted the same style to velvet, silk, and viscose for more formal and more expensive fashions.

She designs jackets for both indoors and outdoors. In addition, her outlet offers table-cloths, bedspreads, and other household items for sale. Pohjoisesplanadi 23. © 09/681-17-50. Tram: 3B.

Marimekko ⚘ Ever since the early 1960s, when Jacqueline Kennedy was photographed wearing Marimekko outfits, the name has been familiar to Americans. Meaning "Mary's frock," Marimekko offers a large variety of prints in vivid colors. This is the company's flagship store, a three-storied marble womb flooded with sunlight, with an emporium of men's fashion in the cellar. The company, founded in 1951 by Armi Ratia, and radically reorganized in the early 1990s, now includes a collection of unusually textured fabrics sold by the yard for decorating homes and offices, and housewares. Equally important are the dresses, suits, coats, bags, interior accessories, and many other goods that are sold here, including Marimekko's famous striped T-shirts and dresses. The inventory of shirts and colors changes with the season. Pohjoisesplanadi 31. © 09/686-02-40. Tram: 3B.

Ril's Concept Store ⚘ This women's boutique highlights the designs of Kuopio (Ritva Lisa Pohjolainen), who is currently enjoying international attention from the fashion industry—and giving Marimekko some serious competition in the process. The designer creates innovative, daring styles, only for women, for business and social engagements; Kuopio designs are favored by various female members of the Finnish government and the media. Pohjoisesplanadi 25. © 09/17-45-00. Tram: 3B, 3T, or 4. Bus: 18.

Tarja Niskanen This is the most famous milliner in Finland, known for designing attractive headgear that protects women from the rigors of the Finnish winter. Don't expect delicate designs here—the emphasis is on warmth. Heavy-duty designs made from chinchilla, mink, fox, leather, or velvet range in price from about 75€ ($98) for a velvet hat to around 2,000€ ($2,600) for something made from sable. Pietarinkatu 10. © 09/62-40-22. Bus 14.

FURNITURE

Artek ⚘⚘⚘ The roots of this shop date from 1935, when it was established by Alvar Alto (the greatest design luminary to come out of Finland) and three of his colleagues. Inside, you'll find meticulously crafted reproductions of Alto's distinctive bentwood and laminated chairs, tables, wall units, and lamps, the originals of which forever changed the use of industrial materials for home furnishings. Each of the designs is ferociously patented, and although they're distributed at other furniture stores in Finland, they each bear the Artek label. Because in some ways the shop is a showcase for the Finnish national aesthetic, and because its floor space is so large, it's also the venue for exhibitions of arts, crafts, and designs from other countries. 18 Eteläsplanadi. © 09/6132-5277. Tram: 4 or 10.

Skanno This family enterprise, dating from 1946, has long been a big name in home furnishings and textiles; it continues to offer the best designs of the past along with innovative 21st-century ones. One of its most famous designs is the novel sofa, the Kameleleonitti, or chameleon, which can be stripped of its cover and given a new one. A visit to Skanno will help explain why Finland is one of the world leaders in modern design. Porkkalankatu 13G. © 09/612-9440. Tram: 8, Metro: Ruoholahti.

GIFTS

Anne's Shop Opposite the Temppeliaukio Church, this shop offers tax-free shopping. It also has some of the finest gifts in town, including Finnish knives, wood and ceramic products, dolls and hats from Lapland, wool sweaters, reindeer skin, and jewelry. Fredrikinkatu 68. No phone. Tram: 3B or 3T.

Kiseleff Bazaar Hall (Kiseleffin Talo) This shopping quarter in the old center of Helsinki, between the cathedral and Market Square, contains 21 small, specialized shops that sell lots of unique gifts. Here you can find handicrafts, souvenirs, old-fashioned toys, antiques, sauna accessories, knives, and Christmas decorations. Aleksanterinkatu 28, with another entrance at Unioninkatu 27. No phone. Tram: 3B, 3T, or 4.

GLASS, PORCELAIN & CERAMICS

Hackman Shop Arabia 🌟🌟 *Finds* This shop assembles under one roof the products of some of the world's most prestigious manufacturers of household porcelain and art ceramics. Most of the goods are made by Arabia and its affiliated group, Iittala, which is famous for, among other things, glass. Located in the center of Helsinki's most prestigious shopping district, it inventories first-rate household goods by Finland's leading designers. The multilingual staff can arrange for any of your purchases to be mailed home.

Arabia was established in a suburb of Helsinki in 1873. Today its ceramic factories are among the most modern in the world. Arabia's artists create their own works, sometimes in highly collectible limited editions.

Although most visitors buy their goods at the company's main store, Hackman Shop Arabia maintains a small museum and a spacious discount sales area at its factory 5km (3 miles) east of the center at Hämeentie 135 (© **0204/39-35-07**). Here discontinued styles and slightly imperfect seconds are available at significant reductions off the regular prices. To reach the suburban factory, take tram no. 6 to the end of the line or, between June and mid-September, take Arabia's special bus (it's hard to miss, since it's covered with Arabia signs) from a point near the main store. Pohjoisesplanadi 25. © **0204/39-35-01**. Tram: 3B.

HANDICRAFTS

Aarikka This shop carries one of Finland's best selections of design-conscious gifts, wood and silver jewelry, and wood toys. Unusual household utensils, fashioned from wood, are also available. Pohjoisesplanadi 27. © **09/65-22-77**. Tram: 3B.

Artisaani 🌟🌟 *Finds* Near Market Square, Artisaani is a cooperative of about 20 artisans who sell their own arts and crafts direct from their country workshops. Ceramic sculptures; pottery; glassware; gold, silver, and bronze jewelry; leather goods; printed fabrics; and other textiles are displayed. Unioninkatu 28. © **09/66-52-25**. Tram: 3B.

Ryijypalvelu A well-stocked second-floor shop specializing in *ryas* (Finnish woven goods) is operated by the Women's Organization of the Disabled War Veterans' Association to raise money for Finland's veterans with disabilities. You can also buy kits for producing the same rugs at home for about one-third the price. Abrahamink 7. © **09/66-06-15**. Tram: 6.

Suomen Käsityön Ystävät (Friends of Finnish Handicrafts) 🌟🌟 *Finds* Suomen Käsityön Ystävät was founded in 1879 to develop and preserve the traditions of Finnish handicrafts. Some of the designs are more than a century old, and others, introduced by well-known Finnish artists, are fresh and contemporary. If you want to save money and produce something with your own hands, you can purchase complete rug and embroidery kits. Here you can see a permanent exhibit of museum-quality *ryijy* tapestries. Textiles, table linens, towels, and gift items, such as shawls and embroidered work—including early-20th-century Jugendstil patterns—can be purchased here. Shipping service is available. Runeberginkatu 40. ℂ 09/612-60-50. Tram: 3B or 3T.

JEWELRY

Kalevala Koru Founded in 1937, this store is owned by the Association of Kalevala Women in Finland, whose aim is to preserve the best cultural traditions of a long-ago Finland. They accomplish this through educational programs and through sales of the most authentic reproductions of traditional designs and styles they can find. The name of their organization is derived from the *Kalevala,* the Finnish national epic.

The store sells both traditional and modern jewelry in bronze, silver, and gold. Many of these pieces are based on originals uncovered in archaeological excavations that date from the 10th and 11th centuries. Each is produced by some of Finland's foremost artisans, and copies of Sami jewelry are also sold. The store cooperates with the Finnish National Museum. Unioninkatu 25. ℂ 020/761-1380. Tram: 3B.

KNIVES

Marttiini Oy Some connoisseurs consider the knives sold within this factory outlet to be the finest within a nation known for the quality of its precision steel. The array of scary-looking knives is fascinating to anyone interested in hunting, fishing, or even in regular kitchen use. Deriving from a factory based in Finnish Lapland (in Rovaniemi), they're priced from 19€ ($24) for a serviceable all-purpose blade to 150€ ($195) for a Finnish machete, capable of doing some real damage, engraved with traditional Sami motifs. The shop faces the city's Lutheran cathedral and displays its products behind glass like works of art. Aleksanterinkatu 28. ℂ 0403/110605. Tram 3B.

MUSIC

Digelius Music This store has the best selection of Finnish folk music and jazz in the country, as well as one of the largest offerings in Europe (around 10,000 titles) of folk music from Asia, Africa, the Americas, and Europe. The store provides mail-order service to customers worldwide. Laivurinrinne 2. ℂ 09/66-63-75. Tram: 3B or 3T.

Fuga This is one of the best music stores in Helsinki, with classical recordings from all over Europe, as well as folk and a smattering of jazz. One of the two Nuotio brothers can offer advice. Kaisaniemenkatu 7. ℂ 09/700-182-51. Tram: 2, 3B, or 6.

SHOPPING COMPLEXES

Forum Shopping Center Covering an entire block, the Forum includes 150 shops, restaurants, service enterprises, and a seven-story atrium—making it the number-one shopping center in Finland. You'll find a wide array of merchandise here, including art, gold, jewelry, food, decorating items, clothing, yarn, leather, records, glasses, rugs, watches, and sporting goods. Mannerheimintie 20. No phone. Tram: 3B, 3T, 7A, or 7B.

Itäkeskus Shopping Complex This complex of shops and restaurants opened in 1992 in a residential suburb a 15-minute subway ride east of Helsinki's center. It has some resemblance to an American shopping mall, but the emphasis is on Scandinavian and Finnish merchandise. You'll find at least 240 shops, including about 20 kiosks and food stalls. Itäkeskus 5. ℂ 09/343-10-05. Metro: Itäkeskus.

Kämp Galleria This is Helsinki's most desirable shopping arcade, with a cluster of about 50 aggressively upscale shops, set close to the newly developed Hotel Kämp. Pohjoisesplanadi 33. No phone. Tram: 3B or 3T.

9 Helsinki After Dark

Postmillennium, Helsinki has seen an explosion of nighttime possibilities. Friday and Saturday nights are impossibly overcrowded, so if you plan to go out, you need to show up early at a club, or you may not get in. The older crowd sticks mainly to bars in popular first-class hotels.

Nearly all theatrical performances are presented in Finnish or Swedish. However, music is universal, and the Helsinki cultural landscape is always rich in music whatever the season. The major orchestral and concert performances take place in Finlandia Hall (see "Classical Music & Concerts," below). Operas at the Finnish National Opera are sung in their original languages.

Your best source of information—virtually your only source, other than Finnish newspapers—is a little magazine called *Helsinki Guide,* distributed free at most hotels and at the tourist office. It has complete listings, not only of cultural events, but of practically anything that's happening in the Finnish capital—from the Baltic herring market to bodybuilding contests.

THE PERFORMING ARTS

THEATER

Suomen Kansallisteatteri (Finnish National Theater) 𝓰𝓰𝓰   The Finnish National Theater enjoys international fame because of its presentations of the classics of Finland and many other countries; each play, however, is performed in Finnish. The theater itself, one of the architectural gems of 19th-century Helsinki, was established in 1872 and stages about 10 premieres a year. Läntinen Teatterikuja 1. ☎ 09/173-313-31. Tickets 20€–26€ ($26–$34). Tram: 3B.

Svenska Teatern (Swedish Theater) 𝓰   If you speak Swedish, you might want to attend a performance at the horseshoe-shaped Swedish Theater, which has been presenting plays since 1866. The theater is in the absolute center of Helsinki, opposite Stockmann department store. The theatrical season begins in early September and runs through May. The box office is open Monday from noon to 6pm, Tuesday to Friday noon to 7pm, and Saturday 1 hour before the performance. The theater is closed on Sunday. Norra Esplanaden 2. ☎ 09/616-214-11. Tickets 15€–45€ ($20–$59) Tram: 3B.

OPERA & BALLET

Finnish National Opera 𝓰𝓰𝓰   The ballet and opera performances of the Finnish National Opera enjoy international fame. Operas are sung in their original languages. The original Finnish National Opera was built in the 1870s as a Russian garrison theater, but in 1993 the opera house moved to its new home. The ticket office is open Monday to Friday 9am to 6pm and Saturday 3 to 6pm. On performance nights, the ticket office stays open until the performance begins. The opera and ballet season runs from September to June. Helsinginkatu 58. ☎ 09/403-022-11. Tickets 15€–70€ ($20–$91). Tram: 3B.

CLASSICAL MUSIC & CONCERTS

Helsingin Kaupunginorkesteri (Helsinki Philharmonic Orchestra) 𝓰𝓰𝓰   The oldest symphony orchestra in Scandinavia performs from September to May in the gracefully modern Finlandia Hall, designed by Alvar Aalto of white Carrara marble. Just a short distance from the town center, it's the musical nerve center of Finland, offering between 70 and 80 on-site concerts a year, plus a grinding assortment of foreign engagements in Europe, the U.S., Japan, and South America. They're also the world's premier and most-respected interpreters of works by Finnish natives Sibelius and Rautavaara. The box office is open Monday to Friday 9am to 4pm and all concerts begin at 7pm. For tickets and information, call ℰ **600/900-900.** Finlandia Hall, Karamzininkatu 4. ℰ **09/402-41.** Tickets 15€–35€ ($20–$46) adults, 10€–25€ ($13–$33) students. Tram: 3B.

THE CLUB & MUSIC SCENE
NIGHTCLUBS/CABARET
Baker's   Although it's been reconfigured, redecorated, and reincarnated many times since it was established in 1915, Baker's is the most deeply entrenched, long-lived drinking and dining complex in Helsinki. It sprawls across three floors, and on busy nights is crammed with nightclubbers—many of them single. The place sometimes gives the effect of an upscale railway station, where food and drink are dispensed with gusto, dance music plays, and the roulette wheel of a small-stakes casino whirs. Most people come for the cafe, open daily from 7am to 4am, or for the bar, open Monday to Saturday 11am to 2am. If you're hungry, a restaurant (which can be reached through the rest of the complex or from a separate entrance on Kalevankatu 2) serves fish dishes, such as salmon, and meat dishes, such as grilled steaks, Monday to Saturday from 11am to 1am. A la carte items cost 12€ to 30€ ($16–$39). If you want to dance, a club supplies hot music, sometimes Latin-derived, Friday and Saturday from 10pm to 4am. Patrons must be at least 24 to enter. Mannerheimintie 12. ℰ **09/612 63 30.** Cover 2€ ($2.60) includes coat check. Tram: 3B.

Storyville   One of the busiest and most active live music venues in Helsinki was named after the fabled red-light district of New Orleans and, as such, focuses on a menu of Creole and Cajun specialties. It occupies the street level and cellar of a building in the heart of town and has an open-minded policy that offers full restaurant service to anyone who wants it, but doesn't pressure anyone into dining. Full meals average 25€ ($33) each. More important, live music—blues, New Orleans–style jazz, Dixieland, rock, or funk—is heard nightly from 10pm to between 2 and 3am, depending on the crowd. Museokatu 8. ℰ **09/40-80-07.** Cover 6.50€–9€ ($8.45–$12). Tram: 4, 7, or 10.

ROCK
Tavastia Club   The most visible emporium for rock 'n' roll is Tavastia, a battered, all-purpose room whose venue changes with every rock group that performs. Don't expect any semblance of a regularly maintained schedule, as everything is very iffy, depending only on the ability of management to book acts from Finland and abroad, and then on that group's ability to show up on time. It includes everything from heavy metal to blues and soul, with good representation from punk-rock bands from the U.K. Expect an audience that's loaded with Finnish students in their early twenties Local newspapers, plus flyers distributed in counterculture sites throughout the city, publicize this place's upcoming events. Urho Kekkosenk 4–6. ℰ **09/694-85-11.** For a schedule of upcoming events, visit www.tavastiaklubi.fi. Cover 7€–25€ ($9.10–$33). Tram: 4 or 7.

DANCE CLUBS
Club König   This is a smoky, cramped, and usually convivial nightclub, which features two distinctly different types of music, U.S.- and U.K.-derived disco from the

'70s, '80s, and '90s, plus Finnish pop. Each of these musical genres blares from speakers at opposite ends of a large and sometimes rambunctious cellar. As you'd expect, dual bars positioned at opposite ends of the room dispense enough alcohol to keep everyone if not exactly in harmony, at least able to tolerate the dissonance. Club-goers range in age from 25 to 55, and many of the regular barflies here seem to have known one another forever. Beer costs 5€ ($6.50) per glass. It's open Wednesday to Saturday 9pm to 3:30am. Mikonkatu 4. ℂ 09/856-85740. Cover 7€ ($9.10) on Fri and Sat nights. Tram: 3B or 3T.

Kaarle XII (a.k.a. Kalle)   This is a tried-and-true nightclub where a congenial crew of locals gets together, gets rowdy, sometimes drinks too much, and often tries to flirt with newcomers. Some of them, according to management, even met their future partners here. The most crowded nights, when lines form outside, are Thursday, Saturday, and, to a lesser degree, Friday. Named in honor of a long-deceased Swedish king, the club contains a street-level pub, an upstairs dance club, and a total of six bars. The decor is plush, albeit a bit battered, and nostalgic. It's open Thursday through Saturday from 8pm to 4am. Beer costs 4.80€ ($6.25) per mug. The only food service here is sandwiches dispensed at the bars. Must be 24 or older to enter. Kasarmikatu 40. ℂ 09/612-99-90. Tram: 3B.

Onella   Three different musical venues might be playing simultaneously within different areas of this nightclub: glam rock, disco-disco, and "Suomi (Finnish) pop." This is a mammoth emporium, holding up to 1,000 late-night partyers, most of them in their 20s. Set within a 5-minute walk from the rail station, it's a high-energy place that seems to be much gossiped about within Helsinki offices the next day. Its biggest competitor, the one whose allure and venue is the most akin to it, is Kaarle XII (Kaale). Open Sunday to Tuesday 11pm to 4am; Wednesday to Saturday 10am to 4am. Must be 22 and older to enter. Fredrikinkatu 48. ℂ 09/586-8011.

Presidentti Club   Many of the clients of this glossy, hard-surfaced nightclub are business travelers, often occupants of the hotel that contains it, and as such, not particularly familiar with other nightlife venues within Helsinki. But the drinks are strong, the music is up-to-date, and you'll usually be able to at least strike up a dialogue within this bar and dance club if you work hard enough. Most of the men here wear jackets, even though they're not required, and there's some kind of live music performed nightly beginning around 10pm. It's open Tuesday to Saturday from 9pm till around 2am. A whiskey with soda costs 7€ ($9.10). In the Sokos Hotel Presidentti, Eteläinen Rautatiekatu 4. ℂ 020/1234 608. Cover 8€–14€ ($10–$18). Tram 3B or 3T.

Studio 51   This is a glittery disco evocative of New York's Studio 54 in its 1970s heyday. Drawing a clientele aged 20 to 40, it also has a VIP lounge. There is no cover unless a special band has been imported for the evening's festivities. Otherwise, you get music spun by a DJ. Open Wednesday to Saturday 10pm to 4am. Fredrikinkatu 51–53. ℂ 09/612-9900. Tram: 3 or 4.

THE BAR SCENE
PUBS
Beetroot   It's dark, cozy, and popular with the under-30 crowd, and it's known for serving the cheapest beer, 3.80€ ($4.95) a glass, on a street that's loaded with competition. Inside, it evokes a battered living room. A DJ spins tunes here every Wednesday to Saturday beginning around 9pm. It's open every night from 3pm to 3am. Iso Roobertinkatu 10. ℂ 044/088-8699. Tram: 10.

Corona Bar for Billiards   Although it has one of the largest collections of pool tables in Helsinki (nine of them, plus a snooker table, each positioned into a high-energy cluster at the back of the premises), most of the hip young people who gravitate here don't really bother with them. Gathered at the bar near the entrance are lots of actors and writers, most of them under 35, enjoying the raffish and sometimes raucous ambience that might remind you of an urban scene in Los Angeles or New York. Pints of beer cost from 4.50€ ($5.85); sandwiches are available if you're hungry. If you are interested in playing pool, a table rents for 6.50€ to 9.20€ ($8.45–$12) per hour, depending on the time of day. *Caution:* Some Finns are avid gamblers, so be alert to the possibility that your friendly billiards game with a local might be riskier than you imagined. The place is open daily from 11am to 2am. Eerikinkatu 11. © 09/64-20-02. Tram: 1.

O'Malley's Pub   This cramped, gregarious pub one of the most popular in Helsinki—evokes the spirit, legend, and lore of Ireland. Bar snacks are available, although they appear to be an afterthought to an evening devoted to drinking, more drinking, and animated conversation. O'Malley's is open Monday to Saturday 4pm to the unusually early hour (at least for Helsinki) of 11:30pm. Live music, usually from an Irish-derived rock band, is presented 2 nights a week, often Wednesday and Thursday. In the Sokos Hotel Torni, Yrjönkatu 26. © 09/1234 604. Tram: 3B.

BARS

Ahio Club   It's stylish, it's hip, and it attracts scads of some of the best-looking 20- and 30-somethings in Helsinki. Set on the street level of an also-recommended hotel, it features at least two bars and a layout that seems to shelter you within a series of caves. Best of all, it boasts a decor based on the myths and legends of early Finland. There's a modernized version of a primeval fire pit, as described in the national epic poem of Finland, *Kalevala,* and a repetitive oval-shaped motif that symbolizes the half-dozen eggs that the goddess of the air broke upon her knee during the creation of the world. Come here for a good time, and know in advance that the average Finn will be flattered if you show at least a cursory understanding of the *Kalevala* and its aesthetic and literary implications. Entrance is free, and a glass of beer costs around 5.50€ ($7.15). It's open Sunday to Thursday 4pm to midnight, Friday to Saturday 4pm to 4am. In the hotel Klaus K., Bulevardi 2–4. © 020/770-4700. Tram: 4, 7, or 10.

Atelier Bar *Finds*   On the top floor of the famous old Sokos Hotel Torni (see "Where to Stay," earlier in this chapter), site of many well-documented episodes of espionage during World War II, this is one of Helsinki's most famous bars, yet many visitors never find it. It welcomes many local artists and writers who don't seem to mind the cramped space. The walls are decorated with original paintings, some of them by regular patrons. Take the elevator up as far as it will go, and then you navigate a narrow iron staircase. Drinks cost 8€ ($10), and beer prices begin at 5.50€ ($7.15). It's open Monday to Saturday 2pm to 1am and Sunday from 2pm to midnight. In the Sokos Hotel Torni, Yrjönkatu 26. © 09/1234 604. Tram: 3, 4, or 10.

Kola Bar   This is our favorite punk-oriented cafe/bar in Helsinki. Funky, amiably battered, and set within a pair of high-ceilinged rooms, it's accented with op-art wallpaper, plastic tables, and earthy colors. Paintings on display can usually be bought directly off the walls, and every Wednesday, Friday, and Saturday, beginning at 9pm, DJs work the crowd. Beer costs 3.50€ ($4.55), espresso 1.80€ ($2.35), and sandwiches—the only form of food sold—4€ ($5.20) each. Open daily noon to 2am. Helsinginkatu 13. © 09/694-8983. Tram: 3B.

Palace Roof Bar Now a fashionable bar in a fashionable hotel, this 11th-floor room actually dates from the 1960s, when part of its interior was originally designed as a men's restroom. Those memories are all but forgotten today in this charming little bar with glowing paneling, nautical accessories, and a sprawling outdoor terrace overlooking the harbor. Special cocktails include Singapore Slings. Drinks cost 8€ ($10). The bar is open between May and September, every Monday to Friday 5pm to midnight. On the 11th floor of the Palace Hotel, Eteläranta 10. ℭ 09/13-45-61. Tram: 3B. Bus: 16.

CASINOS

Several Helsinki nightclubs have small-stakes casinos—usually just a roulette wheel with an attractive croupier and a deliberately low maximum bet. For more serious action, head directly for the only bona fide casino in Finland.

Grand Casino Helsinki With enough distractions to amuse and divert gamblers and nongamblers alike, this is the only full-scale casino in Finland. Built in the 1920s, and renovated frequently since then, it offers games that include slot machines (at least 300 machines), roulette, blackjack, poker, and *sicbo,* a "throw the dice" game whose origins lie deep within ancient China. The cover charge is minimal: A day ticket that includes cloak room service costs 2€ ($2.60); otherwise, there are no costs involved other than what you opt to put at risk on any of the games of chance. On the premises there are two bars, a restaurant, and a cabaret-theater where young women in glittery costumes strut their stuff along with magic acts and *chansons* or *lieder* in a barrage of languages. Showtime is usually every Wednesday to Saturday at 7:30pm. A four-course prix-fixe menu, which includes access to the show, costs between 60€ to 80€ ($78–$104), depending on what you order. The casino lies adjacent to the train station. Residents of the European Union must present an official ID card; residents of countries outside the European Union must present a valid passport. Dress codes inside are casual: jackets and ties for men are not required. Open daily noon to 4am. Mikonkatu 19. ℭ 09/680-800. Tram: 1, 2, 3, 6, or 7.

GAY & LESBIAN NIGHTLIFE

Con Hombres This is the newest and most glossy-looking gay bar in Helsinki, evolving at press time into the entertainment center its owners envisioned it as being, with plans for an on-site disco (Fri–Sat night beginning around 10pm), and a bar whose theme involved frequent DVD playbacks of everybody's favorite talent contest, the Eurovision Song Contest of years past. Open daily 2pm-2am. Eerikinkatu 27. ℭ 09/586-5550. Drinks around 6€–9€ ($7.80–$12) each; cover for the disco 3€ ($3.90). Tram: 7.

Don't Tell Mamma It's the biggest gay nightclub in town, but not always the most fun. Depending on the night of the week, various rooms within this duplex establishment might be animated and crowded, or not even open, depending on the crowd and the whims of the security staff on the night of your visit. Frankly, we found the place a bit glum and, as such, recommend that you limit your visits to Friday and Saturday nights. It's open Monday to Saturday 9am to 4am, Sunday noon to 4am. Iso Roobertinkatu 28. ℭ 09/676-315. Tram: 3T.

Lost & Found Its staff and its owners are self-admittedly gay, a percentage of its clients are gay, and it defines itself as endlessly tolerant about the gender preference, lifestyle habits, or nationality of anyone who happens to saunter in. But ironically, most of its clients are heterosexual, and many of them swear that this place is their favorite neighborhood bar. It sprawls over two floors, each with a busy bar area. From

September till May, it's open nightly from 6pm till around 4am, but between June and August, it's open nightly from 8am till 4am. Annankatu 6. © **09/680-10-10.** Coat check 2€ ($2.60); beer around 4.80€ ($6.25). Tram: 1 or 4.

Nalle Pub   Established during the early 1990s, this was the premier lesbian bar in Helsinki, with a devoted following and a reputation as a rendezvous site for the country's tightly knit network of gay women. Recently, a scattering of well-behaved gay men have also been patronizing the place, but overall, the venue is predominantly a spot maintained by women and aimed at women. Set about a kilometer (½ mile) north of the city's commercial core, within a rapidly gentrifying neighborhood (the Kallio District) once dominated by blue-collar factory workers, it's open daily from 3pm to 2am and has a TV set, video games, a large bar area, recorded music, and a strong sense of community. Cover charge Friday and Saturday 1.50€ ($1.95). Kaarlenkatu 3–5. © **09/701-55-43.** Tram: 3, 3B, or 3T.

Stuff   Most of the clientele at this dark but accommodating bar are gay men, and although the energy level might be a bit lower than you might prefer, it's viewed as an important link in the small-scale world of Finnish gay life. You'll almost certainly be able to strike up a conversation with someone here, at least after the second drink, and if you can't, there are DVDs playing here and there, and both video games and an Internet station to distract you. It's open daily from 3pm to 2am. Eerikinkatu 14. © **09/ 60-88-26.** Tram: 3B, 4, 7, or 10.

10 Side Trips from Helsinki

PORVOO (BORGÅ) 😊😊
48km (30 miles) NE of Helsinki

This colorful hamlet gives visitors a look at what a small town in this area was like a century or so ago—it's the second-oldest town in Finland. Simply strolling the Old Quarter, shopping for handicrafts, art, paintings, chocolates, exotic mustards, and smoked fish is a charming way to spend an afternoon. The town is especially appealing in the weeks before Christmas, when it goes out of its way to evoke an endlessly cheerful Finland of long ago.

Founded by Swedish settlers in 1346 at the mouth of a river, Porvoo was already an important trading center in the Middle Ages. Ships commandeered by member cities of the Hanseatic league unloaded then-exotic delicacies here, including wine, dried fruits, and spices, and loaded up on local products that included dried fish, butter, timber, tar, and flax. Even before the town was given its charter, the Swedes maintained a wood fortress on a hill that helped control river and sea trade for several centuries. After Sweden relinquished Finland to Russia, Porvoo was the site of the first Finnish Diet in the early 19th century, when Tsar Alexander I made the little country a semiautonomous grand duchy.

Today, the village and its environs boasts a half-dozen art galleries, pottery and jewelry studios and shops, a gamut of antique stores and secondhand shops, and in addition to the separately recommended cathedral, a half-dozen historic churches or chapels. *Tip:* The town's most famous culinary product is a cylinder-shaped tart, usually consumed at breakfast or with afternoon coffee, that was the favorite pastry of Finland's national poet, J. L. Runeberg. It's widely available in cafes and pastry shops throughout Porvoo.

ESSENTIALS

GETTING THERE   The best way to get to Porvoo is aboard either the M/S *King* or the MS *J. L. Runeberg,* which operate from May 15 to September 1 and depart from and return to Market Square in Helsinki daily. A round-trip requires about 3 to 3¼ hours each way, with a round-trip ticket priced at 32€ ($42) for adults and 15€ ($20) for children 3 to 12; under 3 free. En route, you'll have sweeping views over Helsinki's archipelago. For bookings and inquiries, contact **J. L. Runeberg** (© **019/524-33-31**). Alternatively, buses depart from Helsinki's main bus terminal four or five times a day for Porvoo, requiring about an hour for the transfer, and charging between 8€ and 11€ ($10–$14) per person, each way. For more information about bus transit, contact the Porvoo tourist office, or call © **019/6893-600.**

VISITOR INFORMATION   The Porvoo Tourist Office is at Rihkamakatu 4, SF-06100 Porvoo (© **019/520-23-16;** www.porvoo.fi). In summer, it's open Monday to Friday 9:30am to 4:30pm, and Saturday and Sunday from 10am to 4pm. After September 1, hours are Monday through Friday from 9:30am to 5pm and Saturday from 10am to 2pm. The Porvoo Association of Tour Guides offers walking tours of the old town every summer between late June and early September, every Monday to Friday at 2pm. Priced at 6€ ($7.80) per adult, and free for persons under 17, they last for about an hour and originate in front of the tourist office.

SEEING THE SIGHTS

If you arrive in Porvoo by boat, you'll get a good view of the old merchants' houses and warehouses along the waterfront—most dating from the 18th century.

Albert Edelfelt's Studio Museum   One of Finland's most famous painters was born in Porvoo in 1854 and, even after his move to the then-center of the art world (Paris), he made it a point to return to his home town every summer for the rest of his life. In 1883, he built a small studio for himself near what's known as Haikko Manor (see below), where he worked every summer throughout most of his adult life. Many of his famous paintings were created here, including portraits of the Russian Imperial family, which hang today in the art gallery of Haikko Manor Hotel. You'll recognize this cozy and historic artistic shrine by the artist's initials "A. E.," which are displayed near the entrance.

Edelfeltinpolku 3. © 019/ 577-414. Admission 3€ ($3.90) adults, includes multilingual guided tour. Free for children under 16. June–Aug Tues–Sun 10am–4pm; May 15–31 and Sept 1–9 Tues–Sun 10am–2pm.

Cathedral of Porvoo   The most venerable building in Porvoo is its cathedral, the oldest parts of which date from the late 1200s. Some visitors refer to it as "the unluckiest building in Finland." Ravaged, rebuilt, and plundered repeatedly during its tormented life by, among others, the Danes and the Russians, and damaged by aerial bombardment in August 1941, it became a cathedral in 1723 when Porvoo was defined as an administrative headquarters for the local church.

Tragedies within this building continued in ways that seemed relentless. On the night of May 29, 2006, the cathedral was ravaged by fire, which was started as a deliberate act of vandalism that was widely condemned throughout Scandinavia. At press time, because of the fire, all ceremonies within the cathedral had been canceled. The fire did not cause much damage to the actual structure of the church because the ceiling did not collapse. However, the church was badly damaged by smoke and water. Some windows were broken and chandeliers fell down. Repair works have started, but local authorities estimate that it will be several years, at least, before the church's interior can be visited once again by members of the general public.

For the purposes of getting a better understanding of Porvoo, however, the church stands prominently on what looks like a verdant country lane in the town center, surrounded by antique stone and clapboard houses. As such, the church is often sought out by day-trippers from Helsinki as a symbol of the sufferings of Finland itself. Kirkkotori. ⓒ 019/661-12-50.

Porvoo Historical Museum   Set within the country-baroque red brick premises of Porvoo's Old Town Hall, which was built in 1764, this museum celebrates the role of Porvoo as a mercantile trading center throughout the sometimes tormented history of what's known today as Finland. Inside, you'll find exhibitions that focus on clothing, jewelry, toys, glass, vehicles, and collections of Finnish Art Nouveau furniture and ceramics. There are also artworks from the prehistoric period and the Middle Ages, and exhibitions that relate the various tragedies, including the fire of 1760, when two-thirds of the small town's approximately 300 buildings burned to the ground in a single day.

Vanha Raatihuoneentori. ⓒ 019/574-7500. Admission 5€ ($6.50) adults, 1€ ($1.30) ages 7–17. Free for persons under 7. May–Aug Mon–Fri 10am–4pm, Sun 11am–4pm; Sept–Apr Wed–Sun noon–4pm.

WHERE TO STAY
Haikko Manor (Hotelli Haikon Kartano) ⓐⓐ   What you'll see when you first arrive at this resort is a grand neoclassical manor house flanked by a sprawling series of modern, two-story wings that contain additional bedrooms and a full-service spa. All of it lies on 14 hectares (35 acres) of steeply sloping and heavily forested oceanfront property 7km (4⅓ miles) southwest of Porvoo.

The site was established as a farm in 1362, but the manor house as you see it today dates from 1913. It was rebuilt after a fire by members of the von Etter family, who were famously associated, through family links and friendship, with the brother of the last of the Romanoff tsars.

The more expensive accommodations are antique-loaded, high-ceilinged lodgings within the manor house; the more reasonably priced accommodations are comfortable and very tasteful units within the modern wings. On-site spa, sauna, and hydrotherapy facilities are extensive and comprehensive. Spa treatments last for between 30 and 90 minutes each, and cost from 30€ to 80€ ($39–$104). Most require reservations a day or two in advance.

Haikkoontie 114, 06400 Porvoo. ⓒ 019/57601. Fax 019/5760-767. www.haikko.fi. 227 units. 180€–240€ ($234–$312) double; 315€–375€ ($410–$488) suite. Rates include breakfast. AE, DC, MC, V. From the center of Porvoo, take bus no. 2. **Amenities:** Restaurant; bar; 2 tennis courts; spa; bike rentals; limited room service; laundry service/dry cleaning; on-site museum and art gallery. *In room:* A/C, TV, minibar, hair dryer, safe, Wi-Fi.

WHERE TO DINE
Wanha Laamanni (The Old Judge's Chambers) ⓐ *finds* FINNISH   The best restaurant in town occupies a barnlike antique building a few steps downhill from the Porvoo Cathedral. It was originally built in 1790, on much older foundations, as a private house with interconnected stables. Today it retains the architectural quirks of its original construction (out-of-kilter floors, low doorways, awkwardly narrow staircases, working fireplaces) and a late 18th-century decor. During clement weather, many diners opt for tables within the building's farm-style courtyard, but if you do, try to at

least duck inside to see the interior's meticulously hand-painted wallpaper whose design was inspired by 16th century originals. The chef turns out many excellent Finnish specialties such as whitefish filets marinated with an essence of spruce sap and served with a mustard sauce, duck livers with truffle oil and marinated mushrooms, and chicken filets with fig sauce and peasant-style potato cake. The wine list is among the most comprehensive in town.

Vuorikatu 17. Ⓒ 019/523-04-55. Reservations recommended. 3-course lunch (winter only) 25€ ($33); main courses 19€–29€ ($25–$38). AE, DC, MC, V. Daily 10:30am–11pm. Closed 2 days at Christmas.

KOTKA
134km (83 miles) E of Helsinki

The **Langinkoski Imperial Fishing Lodge** ✮✮✮, Langinkoski (Ⓒ **05/228-1050**), about 5km (3 miles) north of Kotka, was the imperial fishing lodge of the Russian tsar's family, the summer retreat for Alexander III from 1889 to 1894. This log house on the River Kymi offers an insight into how the last of the Romanovs spent their summers before they met violent deaths during the Russian Revolution. Near the Langinkoski Rapids (for which it was named), the lodge is open from May to August daily from 10am to 7pm; during September and October, it's open Saturday and Sunday from 10am to 4pm. Admission is 4€ ($5.20) for adults, 2€ ($2.60) for persons 7 to 17. Free for children under 7.

The tsar chose a spot in Finland's premier salmon-fishing area to build the lodge on property consisting of half a dozen small islands connected by bridges. Its deliberately unpretentious architecture was in the Finnish style of hand-hewn pine logs, far removed from the grandeur of the family's 900-room palace outside St. Petersburg. On the grounds of the fishing lodge is a small Russian Orthodox chapel built during the early 1800s by monks from the Valamo monastery, and within the lodge are photographs of the imperial family.

Information is available from the **Kotka Tourist Office,** Keskuskatu 6 (Ⓒ **05/234-44-24;** www.kotka.fi/matkailu), open from June to August Tuesday to Friday 9am to 7pm and Saturday 10am to 7pm; from September to May Monday to Friday from 9am to 5pm. If you drive, Kotka is a 2-hour trip from Helsinki. Five buses leave Helsinki daily, traveling to Kotka in 2 hours. Once at the bus station at Kotka, you can take bus no. 12, 13, or 14 to the lodge at Langinkoski.

22

Exploring the Finnish Countryside

Since Finland is so vast and often diffi-cult to explore, particularly because of wintry weather most of the year, we've focused on just a few places of interest: **Turku and the Åland Islands,** a driving tour through the scenic **lake region,** and a summer driving tour to **Finnish Lap-land.**

1 Turku & the Åland Islands

If you have only one Finnish town to visit outside Helsinki, make it Turku. Finland's former capital is its oldest town (founded about 1229), with close ties to Sweden. Swedes affectionately call it Åbo, and perhaps regret its loss. A town with proud tra-ditions, Turku was the former center of Finland's spiritual, secular, and commercial life until Russia made Helsinki the capital.

In the Middle Ages, trade and seafaring were the main occupations of the people of Turku. A university was founded in 1640, adding to the town's prestige. Tragedy struck on September 4, 1827, when Turku suffered the biggest fire ever to ravage a Scandinavian town. Following the fire, the Academy of Turku, the first university in Finland, was moved to Helsinki. But after Finland became independent, a Swedish-language university, Åbo Akademi, was founded in Turku, which thereby regained some of its lost prestige.

Turku makes an ideal gateway for visiting the Åland Islands, an archipelago in the Baltic, midway between Sweden and Finland. Many Swedes come to the Ålands for their summer vacations.

The islands are relatively autonomous; the inhabitants have their own parliament and government, their own flag and culture, and even their own postage stamps.

During the era of its world-famous shipowner Gustaf Erikson, Åland (pronounced *Oh*-lant) boasted the largest fleet of sailing ships in the world. Its traditions as a mar-itime "nation" are ancient.

TURKU
164km (102 miles) W of Helsinki, 155km (96 miles) S of Tampere

On the western coast, at the confluence of three rivers, the seaport of Turku (Åbo in Swedish) is the oldest city in Finland and was once the most important city in the country; it was both an ecclesiastical center and a trade center. In addition to the cathedral, the city acquired a citadel in the late 13th century, making it a power player by the standards of the Middle Ages. Turku's cultural and financial power was assured when the king of Sweden, who then ruled over Finland, made Turku the seat of gov-ernment and installed his representative here.

In the 17th century, an academy was established in Turku, and in 1808, Russia conquered Finland and moved its capital to Helsinki, which was closer to St. Petersburg and theoretically easier to administer. In 1827, a fire destroyed many of Turku's old wood buildings.

But Turku bounced back, becoming not only a major port and industrial city but also a university town, with both a Swedish and a Finnish Academy. It was rebuilt by Carl Ludvig Engel, who designed Helsinki, with stone-and-brick buildings, a grid plan, and wide streets.

The legendary long-distance runner, Paavo Nurmi (1897–1973), known as "The Flying Finn," was the most famous son of Turku. He won a total of nine gold and three silver medals in three different Olympics.

ESSENTIALS

GETTING THERE   If you're driving from Helsinki, head west along E-3 all the way. If you're not driving, Turku is easily reached by either train or bus from Helsinki; many trains and buses make the trip every day (trip time: about 2¼ hours). The Turku train station is on Ratapihankatu 37; for RAIL information, call ℂ **0600-41-900.** The bus station is on Aninkaistentulli 20 (℃ **0200-4000**).

Turku can also be reached by ferry from Stockholm; every morning and evening a ferry leaves Stockholm for the 12-hour trip to Turku. For information, call the **Silja Line** in Turku (℃ **0600-174-552**).

VISITOR INFORMATION   Contact the **Turku City Tourist Office,** Aurakatu 4 (℃ **02/262-74-44**), open Monday to Friday 8:30am to 6pm and Saturday and Sunday 9am to 4pm.

A **Turku Tourist Ticket** entitles you to unlimited travel on the city's buses within a 24-hour period. It costs 4.50€ ($5.85) and can be purchased at the City Tourist Office.

SEEING THE SIGHTS

Aboa Vetus 👁👁 **& Ars Nova** 👁   These are twin museums under one roof, Ars Nova devoted to modern art and Aboa Vetus Finland's most intriguing archaeology museum. Both museums are housed in the Rettig Palace by the Aurajoki River in the former private residence of a tobacco factory owner. The Aboa Vetus museum, an eerie look into the depths of a town block from the Middle Ages, was discovered by accident in the 1990s during renovation work. The streets of the old town were dug out from a depth of 7m (23 ft). You can walk through these centuries-old streets and take a peek into the homes.

In contrast, the other museum, Ars Nova, couldn't be more modern. The permanent collection of some 500 paintings, mostly donated by the Matti Koivurinta Foundation, features works by Finnish artists and international legends such as Max Ernst.

Itäinen Rantakatu 4-6. ℃ 02/250-05-52. www.aboavetusarsnova.fi. Admission 8€ ($10). Daily 11am–7pm. Closed Mon mid-Sept to Mar. Bus: 4.

Forum Marinum 👁   Legend, sea history, and a real maritime atmosphere prevail at this fleet of museum ships moored on the River Aurajoki. You can climb aboard and do everything but go sailing. Our favorite here is the beautiful three-masted bark *Sigyn,* which was launched from Gothenburg in Sweden in 1887. A 1902 sailing ship, *Suomen Joutsen* (Swan of Finland), was actually built in France but used by the Finnish navy during its War WWII battles with Russia. Finally, you can check out the mine layer, *Keihässalmi,* and the corvette *Karjala,* to see what Finland used to battle the Russian Bear in the 1940s.

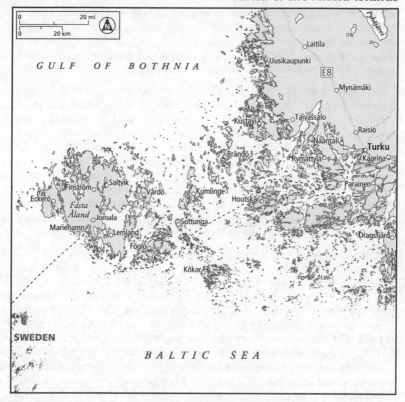

In an old restored granary you can visit the maritime exhibitions, including scale models, a hydrocopter, 1940s torpedoes, and multimedia displays.

Linnankatu 72. © **02/282-95-11.** www.forum-marinum.fi. Admission 12€ ($16) adults, 7€ ($9.10) children 5–12, free for kids 4 and under. May–Sept daily 11am–7pm; off season Tues–Sun 10am–6pm. Bus: 3.

Luostarinmäki Handicrafts Museum
The outdoor compound housing this handicraft museum is a collection of little 18th-century cottages on a hillside, about a 5-minute walk from the city center, south of Vartiovuori hill near the Open-Air Theater. This is the only part of Turku that escaped the fire of 1827, and 18 original structures now make up the working museum. You can watch a potter, goldsmith, bookbinder, and makers of wigs, gloves, and combs as they ply their trades. Displays of Finnish arts and crafts of all types can be seen.

On Luostarinmäki (Cloister Hill). © **02/262-03-50.** Admission 4€ ($5.20) adults, 2€ ($2.60) children 5–12, free for 4 and under. Apr 15–Sept 15 daily 10am–6pm; Sept 16–Apr 14 Tues–Sun 10am–3pm. Bus: 3.

Sibelius Museum
This is the most extensive music museum in Finland, with more than 350 musical instruments from around the world on display. At a beautiful site overlooking the River Aurajoki, a few steps from the cathedral, the museum is named in honor of Jean Sibelius, the most revered composer in Finland, although he neither lived nor worked in Turku. Music lovers can sit in a small concert hall and listen to

the works of the master every day or at concerts held on Wednesday evenings at 7:30pm from September to May. The Wednesday concerts sell out early, so stop by in the morning to buy your ticket.

Bishopsgatan 17. ☎ 02/215-44-94. Admission: museum 3€ ($3.90) adults, free 18 and under; concerts 7€ ($9.10) adults, 3€ ($3.90) children. Tues–Sun 11am–3pm, Wed also 6–8pm. Bus: 1.

Taidemuseo ✲✲ This is the second most important art museum in the country. Built in 1904 in both the Art Nouveau and the Finnish National Romantic style, it is a repository of some 4,000 pieces of art, mainly from the 19th and 20th centuries. Chief honors here go to Akseli Gallen-Kallela (1865–1931), Finland's national painter who is represented by 30 works from the national epic, the *Kalevala*. One of his most reproduced works, painted in a realist style when he was only 20, is *The Old Woman and the Cat*. Helene Schjerfbeck (1862–1946) is acclaimed for her portraits, and Victor Westerholm (1860–1919) is the most honored painter from the Åland Islands. Works from other Nordic countries and international graphics are also exhibited.

In Puolalapuisto Park, Aurakatu 26. ☎ 02/262-71-00. Admission 6€ ($7.80) adults, 3.50€ ($4.55) students, free ages 15 and under. Tues–Fri 11am–7pm; Sat–Sun 11am–5pm. Bus: 3.

Tuomiokirkko ✲✲✲ The "mother" of the Lutheran Church of Finland, this Gothic cathedral from the 1200s is the greatest medieval monument in the country. Built on the banks of the Aura River, this imposing brick-built structure is dedicated to the Virgin Mary and Finland's first bishop, St. Henrik. Buried in the vaults lie bishops, warlords, and even one queen, Karin Månsdotter, wife of King Erik XIV of Sweden.

Since its partial destruction by fire in 1827, the cathedral has been completely restored. The massive west tower rises to a height of 102m (335 ft.), the work of C. L. Engel, the famous German architect. Engel also designed the pulpit.

The cathedral contains no grand treasures, although there are beautiful stained-glass windows. Found in the South Gallery is the finest cathedral museum in Finland, the **Tuomiokirkkomuseo** ✲✲, with its collection of relics and liturgical artifacts dating from the Middle Ages. The medieval wood sculptures are most impressive, as are the models depicting different stages of the Dom's construction. We like to come here on a Tuesday evening when the cathedral features live music.

Tuomiokkotori 20. ☎ 02/261-71-00. Admission: cathedral free; cathedral museum 2€ ($2.60) adults, 1€ ($1.30) children 5–15, under 5 free. Cathedral daily 9am–5pm; cathedral museum Apr 16–Sept 15 daily 9am–8pm; Sept 16–Apr 15 daily 9am–7pm. Bus: 25.

Turun Linna ✲✲✲ Massive and proud, Turku Castle dates from 1280, when it was built on a small island at the mouth of the River Aura, 2.4km (1½ miles) southwest of the city center. This is the largest medieval castle in Finland, and once the entire nation was ruled from here.

After buying your tickets in the entrance hall, you can visit the **Porter's Lodge** with Finland's first **secular murals** ✲ dating from 1530. A stunning array of **medieval wooden religious sculptures** ✲✲ is to be seen in a room called Sture Church, which the citizens of Turku used as a house of worship from the 1480s. In the Nun's Chapel hangs the single-most famous artwork in the castle, a **14th-century portrait of the Virgin** ✲ by the Master of Lieto. In the **King's Hall,** look for Albert Edelfelt's celebrated painting of *Duke Karl Insulting the Corpse of Klaus Fleming* ✲, painted in 1878.

The Outer Castle houses the **Historical Museum of Turku** ✲✲. Its chief exhibit is a stunning **miniature castle model** ✲✲✲, depicting the castle in the heyday of Duke Johan and his duchess holding court. The collection in the museum includes

Turku

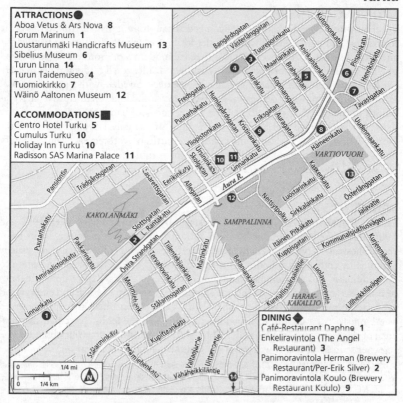

antiques, some dating from the 17th century, along with porcelain, tapestries, silver work, pewter, glass, costumes, and even flapper dresses from the 1920s.

Note: There are stairs, stairs, and more stairs throughout this monument, some of which are slippery and narrow.

Linnank 80, Keskusta. ℰ **02/262-03-00.** www.nba.fi/en/turku_castle. Admission 6€ ($7.80) adults, 3.50€ ($4.55) children 5–15, under 5 free. Apr 16–Sept 15 daily 10am–6pm; Sept 16–Apr 15 Tues–Fri and Sun 10am–3pm, Sat 10am–5pm. Bus: 1.

Wäinö Aaltonen Museum ⟨⟩

Wäinö Aaltonen (1894–1966), one of the most prominent sculptors of his day, began his career on Hirvesalo, a city-owned island on the eastern bank of the Aurajoki River. Many statues by the sculptor are placed on the streets of Finlánd and Turku. The permanent collection consists of works of art purchased by Turku since 1937, including sculptures, paintings, graphics, and drawings. In all, the collection totals some 4,500 works, but about half of which are in public offices, hospitals, schools, and other buildings in Turku. The museum also owns a permanent collection of Finnish paintings, sculptures, and other art, and presents temporary exhibitions as well.

Itäinen Rantakatu 38. ℰ **02/262-08-50.** Admission 4€ ($5.20). Tues–Sun 11am–7pm. Bus: 7, 15, or 17 from Market Sq.

SHOPPING IN TURKU

Sylvi Salonen Oy   Set astride the main pedestrian thoroughfare of Turku, this is the town's best and most comprehensive outlet for Finnish and Scandinavian handicrafts and gifts. They're densely packed into a cheerful modern storefront on the street level of what otherwise functions as an office building. Inside, you'll find examples of every handicraft made within Finland and, to a lesser extent, Sweden, with a special emphasis on sweaters, knitwear, kitchenware, carved beechwood and birch, creative interpretations of the (Swedish-derived) Dalarna horse, hats and handbags crafted from very dense felt, and carved and hand-painted replicas of virtually every lighthouse in the Nordic world. There are also many examples of artfully textured *ryas,* contemporary hand-woven tapestries and/or wall hangings, which rival the complexities and intricacies of rustic Persian and Turkish carpets.

Yliopistonkatu 26. Ⓒ **02/278-2300.**

WHERE TO STAY

Centro Hotel Turku ⍟ *(Value*   Built in stages by a local family between 1972 and 1986, this is the best boutique hotels in Turku, thanks to the insistence, by its owners, of showcasing hip trends in modern Finnish design and contemporary art, usually executed by craftspersons under 30, within its rooms. The most recent renovation to its minimalist and comfortable bedrooms occurred in 2006. Expect decors in both public areas and bedrooms that include angular lines and lots of birch and cherrywood veneers. No meals are served here other than breakfasts, but these are copious, served as a Finnish-style buffet from a food service station in the lobby. Note that the presence of this hotel isn't immediately visible, as it's set within a quiet but obscure-looking courtyard a very short walk from the commercial heart of town.

Yliopistonkatu 12. FIN-20100 Turku. Ⓒ **02/469-0469.** Fax 02/469-0479. www.centrohotel.com. 62 units. Mon–Thurs 99€–111€ ($129–$144) double; Fri–Sun year-round and daily during midsummer 78€–90€ ($101–$117) double. AE, DC, MC, V. Bus: 4. **Amenities:** Breakfast room; laundry service/dry cleaning. *In room:* TV, hair dryer, Wi-Fi.

Cumulus Turku *(Kids*   Set on a prominent street corner in the town center, this is a solid, uncomplicated, middle-bracket hotel with a hard-earned reputation for comfort among business travelers. It was built in the mid-1960s, but all of its monochromatically beige or pale blue-gray rooms were renovated in 2005. You'll register within a modern, wood-paneled lobby that's permeated with a sense of business-oriented functionalism, in the center of which is a small bar area whose only staff member doubles as the receptionist. It shares some of its facilities, including its restaurant (The Armada) with the also-recommended (and more richly accessorized) Holiday Inn next door, but this hotel is less expensive, a bit less formal, and more relaxed about accommodating boisterous children (there's even a third-floor children's playroom). The elevators here reach only the fourth floor, and clients on the uppermost (fifth) floor climb a flight of additional stairs.

Eerikinkatu 30, FIN-20100 Turku. Ⓒ **02/218-1000.** Fax 02/218-1399. www.cumulus.fi. 108 units. Mon–Thurs 105€–114€ ($137–$148) double; Fri–Sun year-round and during midsummer 71€–98€ ($92–$127) double; 180€–189€ ($234–$246) suite. Rates include breakfast. Outdoor parking free, nearby indoor parking 8€ ($10). AE, DC, MC, V. Bus: 4 or 90. **Amenities:** Restaurant; lobby bar; babysitting. *In room:* TV, hair dryer, iron, Wi-Fi.

Holiday Inn Turku   We define this as the best of the town's middle-bracket hotels. More richly accessorized, and somewhat more stylish, than its neighbor, the also-recommended and slightly less expensive Cumulus Turku, this hotel was built in 1997 and upgraded and renovated in 2005. Perks associated with a stay here include a sun-flooded, crescent-shaped stone-floored lobby, and comfortable midsize bedrooms outfitted with color schemes of soft russets and browns. Its in-house bar and restaurant (Hemingway's and the Brasserie Armada) are shared with the clients of the immediately adjacent Cumulus Hotel.

Eerikinkatu 28. FIN-20100 Turku. © 02/338-211. Fax 02/338-2299. www.restel.fi/holidayinn. 299 units Mon–Thurs 120€ ($156) double; Fri–Sun year-round and daily during midsummer 103€ ($134) double. Rates include breakfast. Outdoor parking free, nearby indoor parking 8€ ($10). AE, DC, MC, V. Bus: 4 or 90. **Amenities:** 2 restaurants; bar; indoor pool; sauna; limited room service; babysitting; laundry service/dry cleaning. *In room:* TV, minibar (in some), safe (in some), Wi-Fi.

Radisson SAS Marina Palace ⋒⋒⋒   This is the most appealing, stylish, and comfortable modern palace hotel in Turku. Built in 1973 and radically upgraded in 2006 when it was acquired from another chain by Radisson/SAS, it occupies a prime position beside the Aurajoki River. Although it's in the heart of town, you'll get the impression of being far from the noise and traffic of an urban center. Bedrooms are plush and very large, outfitted in cool, neutral colors and subdued but carefully thought-out contemporary Finnish designs, with whimsical touches of *faux-baroque* gilt and scarlet. The uniformed staff is kind, helpful, and informative. TV sets in the rooms are flat-paneled and technologically cutting-edge, and there are enough mirrors to make the lodgings look even brighter and more spacious than they already are.

Linnankatu 21, FIN-20100 Turku. © 02/1234-710. Fax 02/1234-711. www.turku.radissonsas.com. 184 units. Mon–Thurs 135€–155€ ($176–$202) double; Fri–Sun 110€–130€ ($143–$169) double; 300€–350€ ($390–$455) suite. AE, DC, MC, V. Bus: 4. **Amenities:** Restaurant; bar; 3 saunas; exercise room; limited room service; babysitting; laundry service/dry cleaning. *In room:* TV, minibar, safe, hair dryer, iron, Wi-Fi.

WHERE TO DINE

Café-Restaurant Daphne ⋒ *Value* SCANDINAVIAN   Between 1947 and 1984, Göran Schildts, one of Finland's most respected writers, sent reports back to Helsinki about what he discovered on his voyages on the waters of the Baltic, the Mediterranean, and the canals of France aboard his two-masted schooner, the *Daphne*.

The building that contains this restaurant, named after Schildts's *Daphne*, was built as a warehouse in 1936. Immediately adjacent to Turku's maritime museum, it overlooks a marina from its location about 1.6km (1 mile) southwest of the commercial core of Turku. There's an outdoor terrace, lots of delectable pastries, and self-service buffets laden with tempting hot and cold foods, including an admirable collection of herring.

In the Forum Marinum, adjacent to Forum Marinum, Linnankatu 72. © 02/282-9505. Reservations not necessary. Access to the soup and salad buffet 6.50€ ($8.45) per person; access to the soup, salad, and hot buffet 12€ ($16) per person. AE, DC, MC, V. Mon–Fri 11am–2:30pm; Sat 11am–5pm. Cafe daily 11am–6pm (till 7pm June–Aug). Bus: 1.

Enkeliravintola (The Angel Restaurant) FINNISH   There's a theme associated with this restaurant (dining in heaven), which you might find charming or cloying, depending on your point of view about the afterlife. It's a worthy restaurant with an amusing theme, good food, and lots of insights into the Finnish aesthetic. It occupies an antique wood-sided house a short walk uphill from the commercial core of Turku, within a warren of artfully old-fashioned dining rooms loaded with depictions of angels. There are also a quintet of ceramic stoves that in midwinter throw off a gentle heat. Our favorite dining room is replete with depictions of saintly icons.

Menu items continue the angel theme with fried perch with stewed spinach known as "The Kitchen Angels' Favorite," Greek salads known as "Piece of Heaven," and fried salmon with chanterelles and new potatoes identified as "Cupid's Hit."

Kauppiaskatu 16. © 02/231-8088. Reservations recommended. Main courses 18€–22€ ($24–$29). AE, DC, MC, V. Tues–Sat 11am–10pm; Sun 11am–6pm. Bus: 3.

Panimoravintola Herman (Brewery Restaurant Herman/Per-Erik Silver) ★★
SCANDINAVIAN   Why Herman? And why Per-Erik Silver? Because in the lore and legend associated with nearby Turku Castle, beer, and lots of it, was part of the motivation that kept feudal Finland going, and Herman was the traditional name of whatever brewmaster kept the hops percolating. This restaurant, one of the most famous in town, occupies the solid brick premises of what was built in 1849 as a sailcloth factory and, because of the gleaming copper vats and pipes of its self-contained brewery, Herman seemed like an appropriate name. Its owner, Per-Erik Silver, rivaled only by the owner of the also-recommended Rocca, is one of the two most famous restaurateurs in Turku, thanks to frequent TV appearances and cookbooks authored in his name.

Beer is brewed on the premises, and the place was voted as Finland's Restaurant of the Year in 2003. Menu items are creative and in some cases, inspired. The best examples include a combination, on the same plate, of ginger-marinated salmon with melon and salmon tartare; grilled whitefish with creamed morels and buttered spinach; grilled filets of beef with roasted paprika, pineapple, and herb-potato cake; and a platter piled high with both braised knuckles and filets of lamb with thyme sauce. Dessert might be an oven-baked chocolate pudding with an orange salad, or a rhubarb soufflé with strawberry sorbet.

Läntinen Rantakatu 37. © 02/230-3333. Reservations recommended. Main courses 22€–26€ ($29–$34); prix-fixe menus 35€–58€ ($46–$75). AE, DC, MC, V. Mon–Fri 11am–10:30pm; Sat 2–10:30pm; Sun 2–8:30pm. Bus: 1.

Panimoravintola Koulu (Brewery Restaurant Koulu) SCANDINAVIAN
Everyone in Turku seems to harbor some deep-seated memory, often from their childhood, about this place. Somber, solid, stone-built, and monumental, it retains an aura of dour civic-minded responsibility from when it functioned, during the early 20th century, as Turku's schoolhouse, where many of the city's elderly residents learned to read and write.

All of that changed when a local brewery transformed the vast and drafty premises into a dining and drinking compound. It changes radically throughout the course of any given day. At midday, it offers one of the most frugal dining bargains in Turku, where clients serve themselves from an austere, buffet-style dining room high on the second floor. After dark, it's reconfigured as a more expensive restaurant, where candlelit tables are arranged unexpectedly along the drafty sides of what were originally conceived as very high ceilinged, wide hallways. And at any time of the day or evening, up to five kinds of freshly brewed beer, whose composition, density, and color changes according to the season, are likely to be flowing.

Menu items range from bar snacks (bratwurst with sauerkraut on a bun) to more elaborate fare (steak with guacamole; pasta with mushrooms and a chile-flavored dill sauce), depending on where you sit. Beer, probably because it's brewed on-site, is relatively cheap. And many evenings, live music reverberates through the rooms.

Eerikinkatu 18. © 02/274-5757. Reservations not necessary. Bar snacks 11€–20€ ($14–$26); main courses 17€–20€ ($22–$26); lunch buffet 8€ ($10) per person. Buffet Mon–Fri 11am–2pm; a la carte dishes and bar snacks daily 11am–midnight; bar daily 11am–2am (till 3am Fri–Sat). Bus: 1 or 4.

Rocca ★★★ INTERNATIONAL   This, rivaled only by the also-recommended Brewery Restaurant Herman, is the finest and most prestigious restaurant in Turku, and one of the most celebrated in Finland. And whereas Herman is a bit earthier and less pretentious, there's no mistaking the fact that this one is *haute, grande,* and posh.

Cold Snows, Hot Barbecue

Tired of too constant a diet of Scandinavian food? Consider gathering the ingredients for a hot picnic at Turku's latest restaurant rave, **The Rib Shack,** which some define as the funkiest and hippest take-out restaurant in town. You'll find its glistening tile-sheathed premises astride a traffic roundabout on the southwest edge of town, within what once functioned as a gasoline station. Here, under the scrutiny of Jerome and Anna van Breemen (he's Dutch, she's Finnish, they're savvy restaurateurs, and they're both beautiful), you'll find sacks of aromatic beech and applewood and an American-style pit smoker that they imported, incongruously, from Indiana. That, coupled with a set of sizzling grills and high-octane charm, combine into the kind of barbecue you might have hankered for in Nashville.

How have the Finns reacted to this all-American obsession for slow-cooked, deep-spiced meat? Though dubious at first, civic and church groups now regularly order the stuff by the kilo for consumption after their meetings, and many of the town's hotels recommend the place to their guests as an after-hours substitute for room service. Steaming and mouth-watering portions of barbecued pork, salmon, chicken, beef, or shrimp, suitable for between one and two persons, cost between 12€ and 15€ ($16–$20) each, and succulent side dishes (baked potatoes, corn on the cob, ranch-style beans, side soups and salads, and garlic bread) cost from 3€ to 4€ ($3.90 $5.20) per person. Order ribs online from your laptop by visiting www.ribs.fi; by calling **02/251-0001;** or by actually schlepping out to its premises, 3km (1¾ miles) southwest of Turku at **The Rib Shack, Askalstentie 20, Mäntymäki** (bus no. 13 heads here from the town center). Hours are Monday to Saturday 4 to 10pm, Sunday 2 to 8pm. They accept American Express, MasterCard, and Visa.

Even the artwork (menus, logos, and paintings) evokes a kind of stylish Parisian whimsy. It occupies a red-brick structure originally built in the 19th century as a warehouse—a place that long ago grew accustomed to the glare of TV cameras during interviews with its owner, Antti Vahtera.

Come here to see and be seen among a mixture of trend-conscious minimalism, social prestige, and gastronomic hip. The a la carte selections are elegant and tempting, including tasty dishes such as scallops marinated with ginger and chili, served with mangos and tomato salad; an assortment of cold (i.e., marinated and/or smoked) fish "a la Rocca"; and a whole fried filet of veal with morel-bacon potatoes and parsley sauce. Dessert might include a milk chocolate parfait with peach soup, or one of the most appealing assortments of cheese in the region. And the wine list is fabulous.

Läntinen Rantakatu 55. © **02/284-8800.** Reservations required. Main 16€–27€ ($21–$35). Prix-fixe menus 32€–75€ ($42–$98). AE, DC, MC, V. Mon–Fri 11am–3pm; Tues–Sat 5–11pm. Bus: 1.

TURKU AFTER DARK

The Nightclub and Dining Complex at the Sokos Hamburger Bors Hotel   A

richly accessorized compound of dining and drinking options in the heart of Turku has enough venues and hideaway cubbyholes to appeal to virtually anyone. The hotel itself is a seven-story, 409-room behemoth that rises from the town center. The complex opens daily at 11am for the lunch crowd and then continues with after-work libations and early-evening flirt-fests till between 11pm and 4am, depending on the individual establishment and the night of the week. There's even a dance club, open nightly from around 9pm, charging 5€ ($6.50) on Friday and Saturday, and demanding that clients be at least 22 years of age.

Because the place is so fluid and multifaceted, we advise you to wander freely, stopping at whatever bar, banquette, or watering hole appeals to you en route. (Some are red velvet and bordello-style, others are stainless steel and high-tech. Most can be a lot of fun.) The best bet for a cost-conscious meal within its premises is the **Shamrock Café/Oscars Place,** a faux Irish burger and steak hangout, where a woodsy-looking bar attracts the young and available, and where burgers, lasagna, and roasted duck with honey sauce come configured as main courses priced at 12€ to 24€ ($16–$31) each. Kauppiaskatu 6. ⓒ **02/337-3800.** Bus 1, 3, 13, 28, 32, and 42.

The Old Bank Public House ⍟   Set behind a massive granite facade from the turn of the 20th century, this is one of Turku's most visible and most popular after-work bars. The baronial premises that contain it were originally conceived in 1902 as the headquarters for a bank, with richly carved woodwork, elaborate ceilings, and stained glass. Beer costs from 5€ to 8€ ($6.50–$10) a mugful, and the bartenders will cheerfully provide a menu that lists more than 200 brands of beer, more than 20 of which are on tap. Sandwiches, snacks, and salads range from 4.50€ to 5.50€ ($5.85–$7.15). Open Monday to Tuesday noon to 1am, Wednesday and Thursday noon to 2am, Friday and Saturday noon to 3am, and Sunday 4pm to 1am. Aurakatu 3. ⓒ **02/274-57-00.** Bus: 3.

A SIDE TRIP TO NAANTALI ⍟⍟

The people of this town resisted change so successfully in the 17th century that today Naantali remains a fine example of a medieval Finnish town. Naantali, 19km (12 miles) north of Turku, takes its name from a convent and monastery of St. Birgitta, called "the Valley of Grace," which moved to the coast in 1443. The convent was rich and the little town prospered until the Reformation brought an end to the religious house.

Today you can stroll through narrow lanes lined with wood houses still on their original sites. In Medieval times, each house had its own name on a plaque over the door. Some of these plaques have survived, and the houses are known by their original names. The present buildings of the Old Town date from the late 18th and early 19th centuries.

After the Reformation, Naantali declined until the town became a popular health resort after a spa was established in 1863. It was particularly popular with Russians, who preferred it over St. Petersburg This tradition has been revived recently at a spa hotel (see below).

ESSENTIALS

GETTING THERE   The easiest way to reach Naantali is to take a bus (nos. 11 or 110) from Turku; buses run every 15 minutes, require 20 minutes for the trip, and cost 3.70€ ($4.80) each way. The most romantic way to go is aboard S/S *Ukkopekka,* sailing from the River Aurajoki in the center of Turku, with departures from June 10 to August 8 daily at 10am and 2pm. A return ticket costs 20€ ($26) or 10€ ($13) for children 3 to 14. An archipelago buffet is offered for 13€ ($17). For more information, call **Höyrylaiva Osakeyhtiö,** Linnankatu 38 (ⓒ **02/515-33-00;** www.ukkopekka.fi).

VISITOR INFORMATION   The **Naantali Tourist Service,** Naantalin Matkailu (© **02/435-98-00**), is open Monday to Friday 9am (Sat 10am) to 6pm and Sunday 10am to 3pm from mid-June to mid-August. Otherwise it's open by 9am to 4:30pm Monday to Friday only. Internet access is available here for 1€ ($1.30) for 30 minutes.

SPECIAL EVENTS   The **Naantali Music Festival** (© **0600/10800;** www.naantali music.com), an international music festival, is held here in mid-June; the main concerts are presented in the 15th-century Convent Church, with vesper hymns sung at 8pm. Tickets in general range from 10€ to 30€ ($13–$39) and are sold through the tourist office.

SEEING THE SIGHTS
The main attraction of Naantali is its **Old Town** ✸✸✸, one of the best preserved in all of Finland. The town grew up around its Convent of the Order of St. Birgitta in the 1400s. Today, many artists occupy the restored homes, and the narrow, cobblestone streets with one- or two-floor wood-built houses are among the most photographed in Finland. Many of the houses now function as small art galleries.

The most interest in the Old Town centers on the **Naantali Museum,** Katinhäntä 1 (© **02/434-53-21**), where you can visit three old wood houses with outbuildings in the heart of the Old Town. Admission is 2€ ($2.60). The museum is open only from May 15 to August, daily noon to 7pm.

All that remains of the **Naantalin Luostarikirkko,** Nunnak, Keskusta (© **02/437-54-32**), is the Convent Church, completed in 1462 and renovated a number of times since, including the addition of a tower in 1797. Exhibits in the church's collection of relics include the brown worn by nuns when they took their vows and a Gothic tabernacle for the Reserved Sacrament. Charging no admission, the church is open in May daily 10am to 6pm; June to August daily 10am to 8pm; and September to April Wednesday noon to 2pm and Sunday at noon.

Our favorite spot here is **Kulturanta** ✸✸✸, the summer residence of the president, which we find one of the most beautiful places in all of Finland, with its stone castle and more than 3,500 flowering rose bushes. The location of this massive granite villa, ornamental gardens, and extensive park is on the island of Luonnonmaa. The castle, designed by Lars Sonck, was built in 1916 and is clearly visible from Naantali Harbor across the bay. The residence can't be visited, but the landscaped grounds are open. Guided tours of the gardens are conducted Tuesday to Sunday from June 27 to August 13, leaving at 2pm from the main gate, costing 6€ ($7.80) or 3€ ($3.90) for ages 4 to 14.

Muumimaailma (Moominworld) is a Disney-like park reached by a footbridge from Naantali to Kailo Island (© **02/511-111;** www.muumimaailma.fi). On a sunny day, it's a great place for a picnic. If you didn't bring food, there is a snack bar. The theme park includes a beach, sporting activities, a theater, a miniature golf course, and a Pirate's Fort and Snork's Pancake Factory, where you can fry your own pancake and select your favorite topping. The characters and stories for the park are based on the writings of Tova Jansson, one of the leading children's writers. The park is open daily from mid-June to mid-August, costing 16€ ($21) for a 1-day pass.

WHERE TO STAY
Naantalin Klypyla Spa (Naantali Spa Hotel) ✸✸✸   This is one of only three full-service spas in southwestern Finland, and a mecca for those seeking "the cure" in a modern, low-key, and demurely charming environment. Built in 1984, and renovated

several times since then, it's a sprawling, three-story building positioned in the verdant countryside within a 20-minute walk from Naantali's historic core. Public areas are airy, uncluttered, flooded with sunlight, and filled with plants, lattices, and references to ancient Greece and Rome. Expect a clientele that's about equally divided between corporate conventioneers (there's usually about three conventions occurring within this place at any given time), retirees, stressed-out urbanites, and a scattering of vacationers.

About 140 of the hotel's 350 accommodations are aboard a glistening, well-scrubbed yacht (the *Sunborn*), which is permanently moored to a pier beside the hotel, and which is connected to the main body of the hotel by a series of glass-enclosed catwalks. Inside this "floating palace," everything glistens, and everything looks like it was polished an hour or so prior to your arrival. Accommodations are relatively large and actually rather opulent, replete with nautical artifacts, rich paneling, and deep upholsteries. Accommodations within the adjacent "brick and mortar" hotel are spacious and very comfortable. Overall, this is an extremely well-run and, for a short stay, a rather intriguing hotel, staffed with an intelligent and hardworking crew who take infinite care at soothing ruffled feathers.

Matkalijantie 2, FIN-21100 Naantali. © 02/44-550. Fax 02/857-790. www.naantalispa.fi. 350 units. 152€–172€ ($198–$224) double; 172€ ($224) suite. Wide range of packages available, discounts for stays of 2 days or more. Rates include breakfast. AE, DC, MC, V. Free parking. **Amenities:** 5 restaurants (2 of which lie off-site, in the center of historic Naantali, and some of which are seasonal); 2 cafe/bars; comprehensive spa facilities with exercise areas, saunas, hydrotherapy, massage, and beauty treatments; babysitting; laundry service/dry cleaning. *In room:* TV, minibar (in most), safe (in most), hair dryer, iron.

WHERE TO DINE

Kala-Trappa ✸✸ FINNISH/INTERNATIONAL This is the best restaurant in Naantali, with a history that's deeply tied into the drama of the town and a reputation so solid that most of the civic charities of Naantali, including the Rotarians, select it regularly as the site of their monthly meetings. Set within a wood-sided cottage just uphill from the harbor, it contains a warren of paneled and very cozy dining rooms, each outfitted with nautical accessories (maps and marine charts, antique compasses, photos, and scaled-down models of yachts).

Their pizzas are wafer thin with savory toppings. Some dishes attempt exotica, including chicken breast with a fruity salsa. Their fresh fish, based on the catch of the day, is prepared with flawless technique. Some of their meat and poultry dishes are flavored in harmonious combinations.

Nunnakatu 3. © 02/435-2477. Reservations recommended. Main courses 18€–22€ ($23–$29) Mon–Fri 11am–11pm; Sat noon–midnight; Sun noon–10pm.

Uusi-Kilta ✸ SCANDINAVIAN It boasts the most panoramic location of any restaurant in Naantali, a headland at one end of the town's harbor within a wood-sided house that was originally built around 1880. During clement weather, most of the tables on the wraparound terrace are filled with chattering or sunbathing diners; the rest of the year, the venue moves inside, to a pair of severely dignified dining rooms accented with a substantial-looking mahogany bar. The chefs turn out a well-balanced menu of contemporary and market-fresh ingredients with harmonious combinations of flavors including luscious desserts. The best items include fried cod with a gratin of olives; fried filets of perch with herb butter; linguine with giant crabs; carpaccio of beef; reindeer calf's liver; and lemon-flavored scallops on a skewer with rosemary.

Mannerheiminkatu 1. © 02/435-1066. Main courses 14€–19€ ($18–$24). AE, DC, MC, V. Daily noon–10pm year-round.

Wanha Kaivohuone ✸✸ SCANDINAVIAN   On the town's outskirts, this first-class restaurant is owned and operated by the Naantali Spa in a yellow-sided antique building that's so photogenic it's often used by Helsinki-based fashion photographers as the background for photo shoots. Built late in the 19th century under the region's Russian administration, it now functions during midsummer as an evening supper club. The restaurant is a frequent venue for senior citizens who want first-class cuisine served with fresh ingredients. The menus are seasonally adjusted and could include cream of parsnip soup with a confit of wild duck; smoked filet of whitefish with a ragout of vegetables and balsamic beurre blanc; a divine filet of venison with chanterelle-studded potatoes; and a velvety crème caramel with seasonal berries.

Because the dining times or even days are subject to change, contact the Naantali Spa Hotel (see above) for exact times.

Nunnakatu 7. ✆ 02/44-55-999. Reservations recommended. Fixed-price menus 35€ ($46). AE, DC, MC, V. May–Aug daily (call ahead for hours). Off season Fri–Sat for dinner (call for hours).

THE ÅLAND ISLANDS

The Ålands, off the west coast of Finland between Turku and Stockholm, form an archipelago of 6,500 islands, islets, and skerries. The total land mass is about 1,320 sq. km (510 sq. miles), with 805km (500 miles) of roads, yet it's the water that you remember (the sea stretches in all directions). Most of the islands are not inhabited (there are only some 27,000 residents scattered throughout the archipelago), but an estimated one million tourists visit the Ålands each year.

The islands form on odd geopolitical entity, with its heart belonging to Sweden (locals speak Swedish) but its land mass under the control of the Finns, who have granted islanders many semi-autonomous privileges. Ålanders fly their own flag over their own parliament and issue their own national stamps.

Åland comes from a word in the Old Norse language that meant "water island," and the English word "island" is also derived from the same word. The archipelago was settled some 6,000 years ago by seal hunters; large burial cairns can still be seen. During the Viking Age, the islands were the most densely populated part of Scandinavia.

From medieval times until the early 19th century, Åland was part of Sweden; in 1809, however, Sweden lost both Åland and Finland to Russia. After the fall of the czar in 1917, Åland petitioned the king of Sweden to be allowed to rejoin Sweden, but Finland objected. In 1921, the matter was settled by the League of Nations, which gave Finland sovereignty over the chain but protected Swedish culture and left Swedish as the official language. Today the residents of Åland are still more Swedish than Finnish, and the young men of the islands are exempt from serving in the Finnish armed forces.

ESSENTIALS
GETTING AROUND   Most of the inhabited islands are connected by a series of bridges, causeways, and ferry services. Except for the MS *Kumlinge,* fares are not charged on the local car-ferries unless you travel the complete route from end to end. "Road ferries" are always free, since they serve as road extensions among the islands.

The largest island, 48km (30 miles), **Mainland,** is home to about 90% of the population. The island has dark coniferous woodland, much farmland and pastureland, fishing ports, and rocky fjords. The mainland is also known for its old fortresses and 11 medieval churches, the oldest dating from the 12th to the 15th century.

The second-largest settlement, **Eckerö,** is the westernmost municipality in Finland. It was once a stop on the mail route between Sweden and Imperial Russia.

Other major islands of interest include:

Kumlinge: This has a 15th-century church and is served by a ferry line from Långnäs; the crossing takes 2 hours.

Vårdö: This is the closest settlement to the Åland mainland, only 5 minutes away. The southern part of the island is lush vegetation.

Brändö: The ferryboat from Långnäs (the same one that serves Kumlinge) also goes to this island, a municipality of some 1,000 islands. The largest of these islands are connected by causeways and bridges.

Föglö: Some 600 residents live on these clusters of islands, some of which are linked by bridges and causeways. Föglö, the largest of the island municipalities, is about 30 minutes from the Åland mainland.

Sottunga: From Långnäs, there's a 1½-hour ferry trip to Sottunga. Once here, you'll find only 150 residents in what's the smallest municipality in the Ålands.

Kökar: A rather bleak landscape. The remains of a 2,500-year-old Bronze Age community have been found at Karlby. Kökar is reached on a 2½-hour ferry crossing from Långnäs.

MARIEHAMN

The capital of the Ålands, Mariehamn is the only real town in the archipelago, with a population of 10,700. Founded in 1861, Mariehamn was named after the empress of Russia, Marie Alexandrovna, wife of Alexander II. It lies on an isthmus with harbor facilities, and thousands of linden trees line its streets. The people here have always looked to the sea for their livelihood—that is, before the days of tourism.

The town is small, so buses are not required to follow a specific route. However, there is a bus that runs from the harbor to the center of town, a distance of 3.2km (2 miles).

ESSENTIALS

GETTING THERE   Finnair (℗ 600/14-01-40; www.finnair.com) offers four daily flights from Helsinki (trip time: 1 hr.) and four from Turku (trip time: 30 min.). The Mariehamn **airport** is 3.2km (2 miles) north of the center of town. There is year-round **bus service** from both Helsinki and Turku, traveling via the interisland ferries.

The Viking Line runs **seagoing ferries** from Stockholm to Turku, with a stop en route at Mariehamn, and the Silja Line also makes the 6½-hour trip from Stockholm to Mariehamn. There is usually one ship per day on each line. For prices, tickets, and information, contact the **Viking Line** (℗ 018/262-11; www.vikingline.fi in Mariehamn) or the **Silja Line** (℗ 018/167-11; www.silja.com in Mariehamn).

VISITOR INFORMATION   The **Mariehamn Tourist Information Office,** Storagatan 8, FIN-22100 Mariehamn (℗ 018/240-00), is open June to August daily 9am to 6pm; September to May Monday to Saturday 10am to 4pm.

ATTRACTIONS IN TOWN

Ålands Museum ⓡ **& Ålands Konstmuseum**   If you have any interest in the history of the Ålands islands, this is the place to come. At the eastern end of the harbor between the Town Hall and Parliament, the museum traces the history of the islands beginning with the early settlers 5,000 years ago. There's even a Stone Age replica boat made of seal skin.

In the same building, hanging exhibits are presented in the less-intriguing art museum, displaying the works of local painters. There is one artist, however, that deserves to be singled out. Joel Pettersson (1892–1937), known for his landscapes of island scenes, was hailed as "the Van Gogh of the Ålands."

Öhbergsvägen. 𝄐 **018/250-00**. www.aland-museum.aland.fi. Admission 3.50€ ($4.55) adults, 2€ ($2.60) children 7–15. Tues 10am–8pm; Wed–Mon 10am–4pm. Closed Mon Sept–May.

Museum Ship *Pommern* ✶

Near the Maritime Museum is the four-masted bark *Pommern*, built in 1903 in Glasgow, and one of the few remaining sailing ships in the world. The ship is unique in that it's still in its original condition as a cargo ship; all other such existing ships have been rebuilt into something else over the years. Just before the outbreak of World War II, the *Pommern* made her last journey from Hull to her homeport of Mariehamn, where she was anchored at the outbreak of World War II. After temporary service as a granary, the ship was eventually donated to the town to become a museum.

Storagatan. 𝄐 **018/531-421**. www.pommern.aland.fi. Admission 5€ ($6.50) adults, 3€ ($3.90) children 5–12, free for kids 4 and under. July daily 9am–7pm; May–June and Aug daily 9am–5pm; Sept–Apr daily 10am–4pm.

Sjöfartsmuseum

You've got to love the sea and sailing to appreciate this flotsam-and-jetsam museum of nautical oddities—everything from figureheads from old boats to ships in a bottle. Exhibits trace Åland's great sailing-ship era, but we are not overly impressed. In the center is the re-creation of a sailing vessel with mast. Chances are you'll give this museum no more than half an hour.

Storagatan. 𝄐 **018/199-30**. www.sjofartsmuseum.aland.fi. Admission 5€ ($6.50) adults, 3€ ($3.90) children 6–12, free for kids 5 and under. July daily 9am–7pm; May–June and Aug daily 9am–5pm; Sept daily 10am–4pm; Oct–Apr Mon–Fri 10am–4pm, Sat–Sun noon–4pm.

WHERE TO STAY

Ålandhotel Adlon   This popular, well-managed hotel, set beside the harbor, is one of the first buildings that passengers who arrive by ferryboat see. Built in 1973 and renovated in 2006, it offers well-maintained and contemporary-looking midsize bedrooms, each with a parquet floor, comfortable bed, and a writing table. The best-accessorized of the bedrooms are on the uppermost (fourth) floor; and because of somewhat bigger bathrooms, they're known as "spa" rooms. There's a busy and popular sports bar, and immediately adjacent, a pizzeria. In the same chain, but within the town center, is the Adlon's sister hotel, the somewhat more plush Savoy Hotel, with 85 rooms whose doubles rent for 115€ to 135€ ($150–$176), and whose in-house restaurant, the Bistro Savoy, is separately recommended in "Where to Dine," below.

Hamngatan 7. FIN-22100 Mariehamn. 𝄐 **018/153-00**. Fax 018/150-45. www.alandhotels.fi. 54 units. 110€–130€ ($143–$169) double. AE, DC, MC, V. **Amenities:** Pizzeria; sports bar; limited room service; laundry service/dry cleaning. *In room:* TV, minibar (in some).

Hotel Arkipelag ✶

This is the most upscale and prestigious hotel in Mariehamn, a four-story, modern palace that was originally built in 1974 and renovated many times since. Bedrooms are comfortable, with earth-toned color schemes. Set in the town center, it's a sedate and well-managed address, where upscale business travelers and dignitaries from the Finnish mainland stay. The president of Finland has been a guest on occasion.

Strandgatan 31, FIN-22100 Mariehamn. 𝄐 **018/240-20**. Fax 018/243-84. www.hotelarkipelag.com. 86 units. 142€ ($185) double; 195€ ($254) suite. Rates include breakfast. Free parking. AE, DC, MC, V. **Amenities:** Restaurant; 3 bars; indoor and outdoor pools; exercise room; 2 saunas; limited room service; babysitting; laundry service/dry cleaning; small-stakes casino. *In room:* TV, minibar, Wi-Fi.

Hotel Cikada   This hotel originated as a five-room guesthouse in 1968, when a writer from the Finnish mainland wrote a novel, *The Cricket (Cikada)*, in one of the bedrooms. Later, when the hotel expanded into the summer place you see today, the owners adopted the book's title as the name. It lies a very short walk from the ferryboat terminal, immediately adjacent to the museum ship *Pommern,* near a cluster of trees that helps to shelter it from the industrial section of the nearby harborfront. About a third of its comfortable bedrooms, each with a color scheme of wine-red, off-white, or brown, have their own narrow loggias.

Hamngatan 1. FIN-22100 Mariehamn. ℂ 018/163-33. Fax 018/17-363. www.cikada.aland.fi. 84 units. 69€–96€ ($90–$125) double. Rates include breakfast. Free parking. AE, DC, MC, V. Closed Oct–Apr. **Amenities:** Restaurant; bar; indoor and outdoor swimming pools; 2 saunas; limited room service. *In room:* TV.

WHERE TO DINE

Bistro Savoy SCANDINAVIAN   Set in the center of Mariehamn, on the street level of a well-known hotel, this is one of the town's best restaurants, with a cozy setting, well-prepared food, and a contemporary, mostly wooden decor that spills onto a veranda that's glassed in for all-weather dining. The best menu items include grilled scallops with a purée of red peppers; a soup made from Jerusalem artichokes and cheddar cheese; peppered beef with a pepper-flavored cream sauce; and fried breast of duck with a raspberry-ginger sauce and a fondant of celery.

In the Ålandhotel Savoy, Nygatan 10. ℂ 018/15400. Main courses 12€–20€ ($16–$25). AE, DC, MC, V. Mon–Fri 10:30am–2pm and 6–9:30pm; Sat 6–10:30pm.

Restaurant Nautical ⊛ SCANDINAVIAN   Set within the same building as the Åland Maritime Museum, immediately adjacent to the museum ship *Pommern,* this is our favorite restaurant in Mariehamn, thanks to a richly paneled decor inspired by the interior of a private yacht. Fresh seafood is a specialty here, with many different variations of herring, and skillful preparations of the restaurant's signature dish, pikeperch or perch served with either dill-flavored or crayfish sauce. As an appetizer, try the slightly salted marinated salmon with horseradish sauce, or a steaming bowl of shellfish soup.

Hamngatan 2. ℂ 018/199-31. Lunch main courses 9.50€–14€ ($12–$18); dinner main courses 22€–25€ ($29–$33). AE, DC, MC, V. Mon–Fri 11am–10:30pm; Sat 5–10:30pm. Closed last week in Feb.

2 The Lake Region

Saimaa, an extensive lake district in eastern Finland, has thousands of islands and straits and lots of blue water. It's a land of small villages, vacation centers, and welcoming people, wrapped in the peace and quiet of the wilderness.

From Lappeenranta, one of the centers of the Finnish lake region, you can book cruises lasting anywhere from 2 hours to 2 days in the southern part of Lake Saimaa, or take a cruise to the Saimaa Canal and see the Russian border. In this region, you can do everything from fish with a seine and cook your catch over a campfire to windsurf.

Savonlinna lies in the center of the Saimaa lake district in southeastern Finland, between Haapavesi to the north and Pihlajavesi to the south. From here you can take a boat trip to other towns on Lake Saimaa.

Tampere, Finland's second-largest city, is also set in a geographic area of numerous lakes. A center of culture, tourism, and commerce, Tampere and its surrounding Pirkanmaa region are known for its vast waterways and forests.

The Lake Region

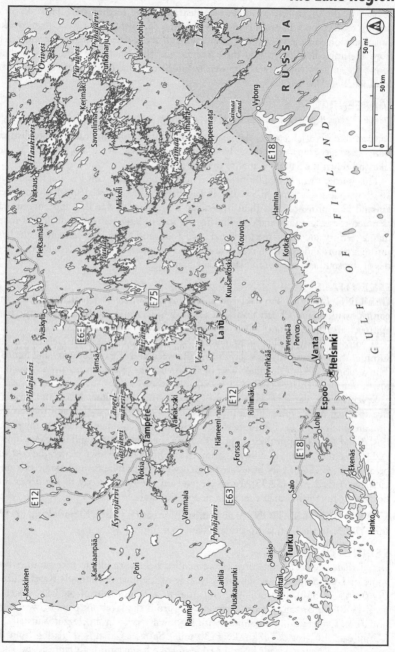

Each of the major centers in the lake district can be reached from Helsinki on a driving tour. Allow a minimum of 4 days up to a complete week (if you plan to take day excursions on the lakes). You can explore all these cities by making a wide arch from Helsinki, heading first to the east near the Russian border and then circling across the country with a final stopover in Tampere. From Tampere, it's an easy drive south back to Helsinki.

LAPPEENRANTA ⍟

138 miles (222km) NE of Helsinki, 10 miles (16km) W of the Russian border

Lappeenranta is a lake town, the heart of Lake Saimaa and the eastern lake district. Both passenger ships and private boats sail from the harbor of Lappeenranta to the lake and down the Saimaa Canal to the Gulf of Finland.

This border town of 60,000 people between two different cultures was founded in 1649 by Queen Christina of Sweden. It was fortified first by Sweden, which governed Finland as a province, and then by Russia. Since World War II, Lappeenranta has assumed increasing importance following the loss of large parts of Karelia. For more than a century and a half, the town had been a spa, and today Lappeenranta is the best summer resort and excursion center in eastern Finland. A bright, modern town, it nestles at the southern edge of the large Lake Saimaa.

ESSENTIALS

GETTING THERE   From Helsinki, head northeast on E-4 to Lahti, where you connect with Route 12 east until you reach the junction with Route 6 for the final approach to Lappeenranta.

If you're not driving, Lappeenranta can be reached by plane from Helsinki; in the summer there are two flights a day during the week and one on Saturday and Sunday. The airport lies 2km (1¼ miles) west of the town center; there is no airport bus into town, but a taxi charges 10€ ($13) to take you there.

Seven trains a day leave Helsinki for Lappeenranta (trip time: 4 hr.), and there are five to seven daily express buses from Helsinki. The railway station and the bus station are side-by-side, a 20-minute walk south from the commercial heart of town. Bus nos. 3 and 4 travel from there to points within the town center, and if a client hires a taxi from either the bus or railway station to any hotel in the town center, the cost will be around 8€ ($10). City buses are painted white with blue trim. A single ride on a city bus costs 2.25€ ($2.95). Fares are paid on the bus, directly to the driver, but because of the town's small size, most people just walk.

VISITOR INFORMATION   The Tourist Information Office, Kievarinkatui (© 05/ 667-788), is open Monday to Friday 10am to 4:30pm.

SEEING THE SIGHTS

Better than any of the museums recommended below, we like to take summer boat tours of **Lake Saimaa** ⍟⍟. The most visible of the boat operators is **Karelia Lines** (© 05/45-30-380). Between June and August, a 2-hour tour of the lake, priced at 14€ ($18) per person, departs every evening from the lakefront piers between 6:30 and 7pm. On board is a restaurant, with sit-down service by an elegant waitstaff

You can also visit the 48km-long (30-mile) **Saimaa Canal** ⍟⍟, dating from the mid-1850s. The canal leads from the edge of Lake Saimaa through Finnish and Russian territory to Vyborg, the former capital of Finland's lost province of Karelia. Built during the 19th century, the canal is famous for its changing elevations and the complicated series of locks that makes navigation possible. Boat trips and cruises can be arranged through the tourist office (see above).

The **Lappeenranta Outdoor Marketplace** 🎭🎭 is the most colorful in eastern Finland, with everything from fresh produce and berries from the swampy wetlands around Lappeenranta to cheese and "Finnish fast food" (sandwiches, sausages, wok-fried rice dishes). Between June and August, it operates daily from 7am to noon from a location on Kievarinkatu near the junction of the Sammonkatu, very close to the Hotel Cumulus Lappeenranta, about a block from the town's main street (Valtakatu). Vendors operate from beneath tented protection from the rain or from within boxy-looking kiosks.

Between September and May, the market is conducted at that location only Saturday and Sunday 7:30am until around 1pm. The lakefront area of Lappeenranta is active every summer evening with additional purveyors of handicrafts and fast food and, to a lesser degree, Friday and Sunday evenings during clement weather in spring and autumn.

This also a cultural town, with **summer concerts** held in the parks and **summer theater** at Linnoitus Fortress (see below). Cavalrymen dressed in traditional skeleton tunics and red trousers (the uniform worn in 1922) ride in the fortress and harbor area in summer. **Guard parades and evening tattoos** (outdoor military exercises performed by troops) are held several times during the summer months.

IN THE FORTRESS

Linnoitus 🎭🎭, the fortress of Lappeenranta, on Kristiinankatu, was begun by Sweden and continued by Russia as a link in its chain of defenses. The entire chain fell into disuse after the Peace of Turku in 1812, when that part of the country known as "Old Finland," including Lappeenranta, was reunited with other Finnish territory. The fortress was turned over to the town in 1835, and the defenses slowly deteriorated; restoration began in 1976. There are pottery and other handicraft shops in the fortress area. The location is a 5-minute walk west of the town center.

The following attractions—the Orthodox church, the South Karelian Museum, the South Karelian Art Museum, and the Cavalry Museum—are all located inside or near the fortress. The old orthodox church, or **Ortodoksinen kirkko** 🎭, Kristiinankatu (no phone), was completed in 1785, but only the high and narrow nave belongs to the original building. The most valuable icon here is the 200-year-old *Communion of the Holy* 🎭, found in the middle of the north wall. The Orthodox Church of Finland owes its allegiance to the Ecumenical Patriarch of Constantinople. Admission is free, and the church is open from June to mid-August Tuesday to Sunday 10am to 5pm.

The **Etela-Karjalan Museo (South Karelian Museum),** Kristiinankatu 15 (© 05/616-22-55), is located at the northern end of the fortress in the 19th-century artillery depot. Museum displays include a model of the former Finnish town of Viipuri (Vyborg). The model features the city as it was at midday on September 2, 1939, at the outbreak of World War II, complete with models of people, cars, ships, and trains. When Finland was forced to give Vyborg to the Russians, many artifacts from that ancient city were transferred here. The textile department of this museum is worth visiting since it has examples of traditional Karelian folkloric clothing. Admission is 5€ ($6.50) for adults, 4.50€ ($5.85) for students, and free for children 15 and under. The museum is open June to August Monday to Friday 10am to 6pm and Saturday and Sunday 11am to 5pm. In winter it's open Tuesday to Sunday 11am to 5pm.

The **Cavalry Museum,** Kristiinankatu 2 (© **05/616-22-57;** www.lappeenranta.fi. museof), is in the oldest building in Lappeenranta, the former guardhouse of Linnoitus by the town gates, built in 1772. The history of the Finnish cavalry from the *hakkapeliitat* (the cavalry in the 1618–1648 war) until modern times is depicted through uniforms, guns, and items related to horse care. The museum is open June to August only, Monday to Friday 10am to 6pm and Saturday and Sunday 11am to 5pm.

Outside the fortress, the **Wolkoff House Museum,** Kauppakatu 26 (© **05/616-22-58;** www.lappeenranta.fi/museot), which opened in 1993, was a Russian-born merchant family's home with interiors and furniture from the 1890s to the 1960s. The house was built in 1826, and the Wolkoff family lived here from 1870 to 1983. The interiors are shown only on a guided tour. Admission is 4€ ($5.20) for adults, 3€ ($3.90) for students, and free for children 15 and under. It's open June to August Monday to Friday 10am to 6pm, Saturday and Sunday 11am to 5pm. Off-season hours are only on Saturday and Sunday 11am to 5pm.

WHERE TO STAY

Hotel Cumulus Lappeenranta   Set on the town's main street, near the tourist office and the outdoor market, this four-story 1982 hotel is clean, unpretentious, and firmly planted in the consciousness of local residents as a solid, respectable, middle-bracket hotel. Bedrooms, outfitted in white with touches of green and filled with comfortable contemporary furnishings, were renovated in 2004. The main venue for on-site dining is the Huviretki tavern, open daily for lunch and dinner, which is supplemented by a bar (Hemingway's) that's outfitted with memorabilia associated with the writer.

Valtakatu 31, FIN-53100 Lappeenranta. © **05/677-811.** Fax 05/677-8299. www.cumulus.fi. 55 units. Sun–Thurs 118€ ($153) double; June–Aug and Fri–Sat year-round 85€ ($111) double. Rates include breakfast and free evening access to the sauna and swimming pool. Free parking. Bus: 3. **Amenities:** Restaurant; bar; indoor pool; sauna; limited room service, laundry service/dry cleaning. *In room:* TV, minibar (in some), Wi-Fi.

Scandic Patria Lappeenranta (★   During the 1980s, the outmoded and relatively uncomfortable grande dame of Lappeenranta hotels was demolished and rebuilt, reopening in 1991 in a concrete-and-glass sided format that had nothing to do with the original design. Each of the cozy, big-windowed units inside was upgraded and redesigned once again in 2006, when management added cherry-veneer paneling to some of the surfaces of the bedrooms and inaugurated a color scheme of blue and white. Clients here tend to be just a bit more artsy than what's attracted to some of this hotel's nearby competitors, including a scattering of music-industry and show-biz types. The in-house restaurant, Messikukko, serves a combination of Finnish and Mediterranean (mostly Spanish and Greek) food, and the lobby bar draws a crowd of both local residents and hotel guests. The hotel maintains a pair of saunas on its fifth (uppermost) floor.

Kauppakatu 21, FIN-53100 Lappeenranta. © **05/677-511.** Fax 05/451-24-41. www.scandic-hotels.com. 132 units. Mon–Thurs 130€–145€ ($169–$189) double; Fri–Sat and daily during midsummer 105€–120€ ($137–$156) double; 260€ ($338) suite. Rates include breakfast. AE, DC, MC, V. Bus: 6. Free parking. **Amenities:** Restaurant; bar; 2 saunas; indoor Jacuzzi; limited room service; laundry service/dry cleaning. *In room:* TV, hair dryer, Wi-Fi.

Sokos Hotel Lappee (★★   This, rivaled only by the also-recommended Scandic Patria Lappeenranta, is the best-accessorized and most upscale hotel in town. Set in the town center, close to Town Hall and a 4-minute walk, past other buildings, to the lakefront, it rises three stories in a design that was radically upgraded between 2005 and 2007. Rooms come in color combinations of soft reds, golds, and wheat tones, with comfortable contemporary furnishings. This hotel has the most comprehensive sauna complex (five separate units) in town, the biggest and most appealing indoor pool (40m/131 ft. long), and its most comprehensive collection of dining, drinking, and nightlife facilities, which include the evening-only Casanova restaurant, serving Finnish and Mediterranean food, the Piccolo Lobby bar for drinks and snacks, and the Nightclub Doris. It's open only on Friday and Saturday from 10pm till 4am, charging 5€ to 15€ ($6.50–$20) for entrance whenever there's a live band playing. There's even a separate bar and snack bar within the hotel's above-mentioned sauna compound that operates only during hours of peak usage.

Brahenkatu 1, FIN-53100 Lappeenranta. © **05/678-61.** Fax 05/678-65-45. www.sokoshotels.fi. 204 units. Mon–Thurs 129€–146€ ($168–$190) double; midsummer and Fri–Sat year-round 86€–104€ ($112–$135) double. Rates include breakfast. AE, DC, MC, V. Free parking. Bus: 1. **Amenities:** Restaurant; cafe; nightclub; indoor pool; exercise room; sauna complex with 5 different saunas and its own bar/snack bar; limited room service; laundry service/dry cleaning. *In room:* A/C, TV, minibar (in most), safe, Wi-Fi.

Summerhotel Karelia Park *(Value* Lying 2km (1¼ miles) west of the town center at the edge of Lake Saimaa, this hotel was built in 1972 to provide housing for local students. It continues to function as a residence for students today, but between June and August, its four floors are transformed into a conventional hotel. Rooms are small and a little battered, but reasonably comfortable and the most affordable in the area. There is a simple restaurant serving beer and two saunas on-site. Otherwise, it's basic and efficient. Isolated in a forest, it provides many walking paths in the region and a cluster of swimming beaches beside the lake.

Korpraalinkatu 1, FIN-53810 Lappeenranta. © **05/452-84-54.** Fax 05/453-04-05. 90 units. 29€ ($38) per person in a double. Rates include breakfast. MC, V. Closed Sept–May. Free parking. Bus: 5 or 6. **Amenities:** Restaurant; 2 saunas. *In room:* TV (in some), no phone.

WHERE TO DINE

Local eateries are very limited in scope. For more formal first-class dining, visitors patronize the restaurants of the top-recommended hotels above.

Majurska FINNISH The most famous cafe in Lappeenranta, Majurska is situated at an old fortress 450m (1,500 ft.) from the town center. Long a local favorite because of its homemade cakes and pies, the kitchen makes good use of seasonal berries and fruits, and also comes up with some good quiche-like creations with cheese and onion. For lunch, many Finns order a piece of pie or cake plus good tea or coffee. There's no meat, no fish, and no lunchtime platters. In the same building are several art exhibits and small handicraft shops.

Kristiinankatu 1. © **05/453-05-54.** Cakes or pies with coffee or tea .50€–.60€ (65¢–80¢). No credit cards. June–Aug daily 10am–8pm; Sept–May daily 10am–5pm.

Tassos GREEK/INTERNATIONAL Established by Finns who appreciated their holidays in Greece almost 30 years ago, this is a centrally located restaurant that hotel concierges tend to recommend to clients who don't want to dine in-house. There's a worthy selection of Greek staples here, including both lamb and vegetarian versions of *moussaka, stifado* (a well-seasoned stew made from pork and beef), and *souvlaki.* The most popular dish on the menu, according to the hardworking staff, is a succulent version of pepper steak, whose cream-based sauce is an appropriate foil for your choice of potatoes and vegetables.

Valtakatu 41. © **05/67-86-565.** Reservations recommended for dinner. Main courses 15€–30€ ($20–$39). AE, DC, MC, V. Mon–Fri 11am–11pm; Sat noon–11:30pm. Bus: 1, 3, or 5.

SAVONLINNA ⟨ℜ⟩⟨ℜ⟩⟨ℜ⟩
336km (209 miles) N of Helsinki, 230km (143 miles) N of Lappeenranta

This is the most romantic town in Finland. Lorded over by one of northern Europe's most dramatic castles, it is also the site of the country's famous opera festival. Set on two islands between Lake Haapavesi and Lake Pihlajavesi, Savonlinna also enjoys the most dramatic "waterspace" of any town in Finland. It lies on seven islands, but over the centuries that has been obscured by bridges and landfills.

Founded in 1639, Savonlinna is the oldest town in eastern Finland. Its major attraction, the castle of Olavinlinna (see below), dates from 1475, built to protect what was then the eastern border of Sweden. The town slowly expanded to the islands around the castle.

The area around the town, forming part of the Saimaa waterway, has more lakes than any other area in Finland. Because of its strategic location, Savonlinna has been the scene of many battles. In its heyday, wealthy families from St. Petersburg used Savonlinna as a holiday and health resort.

The old spa familiar to czarist Russia burned in 1964—only a few czarist villas were spared. However, the Kylpylä Hotelli Casino, on Kasinonsaari (see below), attracts spa lovers to the area today.

ESSENTIALS
GETTING THERE   From Lappeenranta, drive 35km (22 miles) northeast on Route 6 to Imatra. After passing by the city, continue on Route 6 to Parikkala and the junction with Route 14, which will take you northwest into Savonlinna. If you're not driving, there are three to five flights a day from Helsinki (trip time: 50 min.). For reservations in Helsinki, call **Finnair** (© **0600/140-140**). The airport lies 25km (16 miles) northeast of the city center. An airport taxi shuttle meets arriving flights, the 20-minute trip costing 10€ ($13) one-way, whereas a private taxi ranges from 20€ to 25€ ($26–$33). Most visitors arrive by train from Helsinki; a trip via Parikkala takes more than 5 hours. At Parikkala you have to change to a smaller regional train or else a connecting bus. One-way rail fares from Helsinki cost 48€ ($62). Trains arrive at the Savonlinna-Kauppatori in the center of town. There is an express bus service running several times a day from Helsinki to Savonlinna, taking 5 to 6 hours and costing 48€ ($62) for a one-way ticket. For train or bus fares, check with the terminus in Helsinki.

VISITOR INFORMATION   The **Savonlinna Tourist Service,** at Puistokatu 1, FIN-57100 Savonlinna (© **015/517-510**), is open daily from June to August 9am to 5pm, but during the Opera Festival, it remains open until 8pm. From September to May, it is open Monday to Friday 9am to 5pm.

SPECIAL EVENTS   The **Savonlinna Opera Festival** ⟨ℜ⟩⟨ℜ⟩⟨ℜ⟩, traditionally held in July in Olavinlinna Castle, is a world-class cultural event. For information, contact the Savonlinna Opera Festival Office, Olavinkatu 35, FIN-57130 Savonlinna (© **015/ 476-750;** www.operafestival.fi). Tickets range from 27€ to 207€ ($35–$269).

SEEING THE SIGHTS
Olavinlinna Castle (Castle of St. Olof) ⟨ℜ⟩⟨ℜ⟩⟨ℜ⟩ (© **015/531-164;** www.olavinlinna.fi), a three-towered medieval fortress founded in 1475, is the city's major attraction. Situated on a small island in the middle of Kyronsalmi Straits, it's reached by a rotating bridge. Located at the eastern end of Linnankatu, the triangular-shaped castle boasts

30m-tall (98-ft.) towers that provide a spectacular **panoramic vista** *๕๕๕* of the Finnish lake district.

One-hour guided tours (30€/$39 per person) take you through the vast corridors of the castle, with its spooky halls, stone-built rooms, and lookout towers.

To the left of the castle entrance is a small **Castle Museum** *๕*, displaying artifacts found in the castle or related to it. Even more intriguing is the **Orthodox Museum** *๕๕* on the right, a splendid treasure trove displaying Russian icons and other valuable church plates and vestments. The summer opera festival is held here. Admission is 5€ ($6.50) for adults, 3.50€ ($4.55) for students and ages 7 to 17, and free for kids 6 and under. From January 2 to May 31, hours are daily 10am to 3pm; June 1 to August 15 daily 10am to 5pm; and August 16 to December 31 daily 10am to 3pm.

Other attractions include the **SS** *Salama* (© 015/571-4710; www.savonlinna.fi/museo/museumships.htm) museum ship, built in Vyborg in 1874; it's the only steam schooner in Finland—and perhaps in the world. The ship is docked in Riihisaari and is open May 15 to September 3, Tuesday to Sunday 11am to 8pm. Admission is 5€ ($6.50) adults, 2€ ($2.60) students, 1€ ($1.30) ages 7 to 16, and free kids 6 and under.

Retretti, in Punkaharju (© 015/775-22-00; www.retretti.fi), is an art center that opened in 1982 in a grotto about 22km (14 miles) south of Savonlinna. It includes a concert hall, and during the opera festival in Savonlinna, chamber-music concerts are presented here. Exhibits vary from year to year since the artwork is on loan. The center can be reached by boat from the Marketplace in Savonlinna, or by bus from the Savonlinna bus station. Admission to the art center is 15€ ($20) for adults, 12€ ($16) for seniors, 9€ ($12) for students, 5€ ($6.50) for children 5 to 15, and free for children 4 and under. The center is open from the end of May until the end of August, daily from 10am to 5pm (in July it stays open until 6pm).

SIDE TRIPS FROM SAVONLINNA

At least 10 different lake steamers use Savonlinna's harbor as a midsummer base. Beginning around 9am and continuing until about midnight, a sightseeing cruise boat departs hourly. Cruise rates range from 10€ to 13€ ($13–$17) for adults and 5€ ($6.50) for children 5 to 15; free for under 5. The tourist office (see above) can provide schedules and details.

The SS *Heinävesi* travels regularly to **Punkaharju,** 25km (16 miles) southeast of Savonlinna. Departures are daily at 1:30pm from June 13 to August, costing 13€ ($17) for adults and 5€ ($6.50) for children 3 to 12; free for under 3. At Punkaharju, you can also do some sightseeing, visit a summer art exhibit, explore a typical holiday village, and enjoy a leisurely lunch at a restaurant in the holiday village or at **Punkaharjun Valtionhotelli State Hotel** (© 020/744-3440), with 24 rooms located in the main building or in a nearby villa.

At Punkaharju, Lake Puruvesi is divided by a long Ice Age ridge that extends for 7.2km (4½ miles), forming a causeway between the Puruvesi and Pihlajavesi lakes. This "thread" has been turned into a national park, one of the most famous and most photographed spots in Finland. Although you can also reach Punkaharju by bus or train, boat travel is certainly the most scenic.

Kerimäki kirkko (© 015/578-9111; www.kolumbus.fi/kerisrk), 22km (14 miles) northeast of Savonlinna and connected by Route 71, has the largest wood church in the world. Built in 1847, the church is large enough to accommodate 5,000 worshippers and is a masterpiece of carpentry with its pews, columns, galleries, tie-beams, arches, domes, and lanterns. According to the ground plan, it's a short-armed double cruciform church. The altarpiece was painted by Aleksandra Såltin in 1890. The organ, which has a registration of 20 stops and was constructed by the Kangasala organ factory, was mounted in 1894. The church is mostly visited during the Opera Festival, when it hosts concerts. At that time, buses run between the center of Savonlinna and the rural village of Kerimäki. The church is open June to August Monday to Friday 9am to 8pm, Saturday 9am to 6pm, and Sunday 11am to 8pm. To climb the adjacent bell tower, adults pay 5€ ($6.50).

WHERE TO STAY

Kylpylä Hotelli Casino (Spa Hotel Casino) ☆☆☆ This is Savonlinna's most upscale and most prestigious hotel, the temporary home to divas who select it as their home during their midsummer opera gigs and a clientele that is concerned with keeping their appointments at the in-house spa. Set on one of the islands that comprise the land mass of Savonlinna, and connected via a bridge to the town's railway station, it is neither antique (it was built as an all-new entity in 1969) nor associated with any casino (Savonlinna hasn't had one since the heyday of the tsars). What you'll find is a modern, conservative, and discreetly upscale hotel that was most recently renovated in 2006. Rooms are outfitted in tones of pearl gray and white.

Kasinonsaari, FIN-57101, Savonlinna. © 015/73950. Fax 015/272-524. www.spahotelcasino.fi. 80 units. Mon–Thurs 129€ ($168) double; Fri–Sun 102€ ($133) double; opera season (July) 162€ ($211) double. Rates include breakfast. AE, DC, MC, V. Free parking. Bus: 1, 2, or 3. **Amenities:** 2 restaurants; spa; indoor pool; sauna complex; baby-sitting; laundry service/dry cleaning. *In room:* TV, minibar, Wi-Fi (in some).

Savonlinna Seurahuone Built in stages between 1956 and 1989, with renovations to the rooms completed in 2006, this hotel occupies a central position immediately in front of Savonlinna's summer-only marketplace. It has well-maintained, contemporary, and comfortable bedrooms, many with views over the lake. It's reputation for fair, middle-bracket value attracts many business travelers. Its in-house entertainment facilities (the Restaurant Mefisto and the Tamino Bar and Nightclub) attract local residents as well as hotel guests.

Kauppatori 4. FIN-57130 Savonlinna. © 015/5731. Fax 015/273-918. www.savonlinnaseurahuone.fi. 83 units. Mon–Thurs 110€ ($143) double; Fri–Sun 94€ ($122) double; opera season (July) 165€ ($215) double; 152€–178€ ($198–$231) suite. Rates include breakfast. AE, DC, MC, V. Outdoor parking free; indoor parking 11€ ($14) extra. Bus: 1, 2, or 3. **Amenities:** 2 restaurants; cafe/bar; nightclub; exercise facilities; 2 saunas; limited room service; baby-sitting (summer only); laundry service/dry cleaning. *In room:* TV, minibar, Wi-Fi (in some).

WHERE TO DINE

Majakka (The Lighthouse) ☑ᵥₐₗᵤₑ FINNISH/SEAFOOD This is one of the busiest and most popular independent restaurants in Savonlinna, a civic institution that has thrived within this centrally located spot since the mid-1960s. Within a woodsy, partially paneled decor that's dotted with miniature models of sailboats and rowboats, you'll get good value and very reliable, down-home Finnish cuisine. Enduring culinary staples at this place include pan-fried vendace, a whitefish species from the nearby lake, served with root vegetables and creamy herbed potatoes; and a "Majakka Special," with grilled filets of pork, beef, and grilled chunks of "cottage sausage," all drenched with Madeira sauce and served with creamy potatoes and vegetables.

Satamakatu 11. © 015/531-456. Main courses 13€–22€ ($16–$29). AE, DC, MC, V. Mon–Thurs 11am–11pm; Fri–Sat 11am–midnight. Bus: 1, 2, 3, or 4.

Piatta INTERNATIONAL   Set on the lobby level of an also-recommended hotel, with windows that look out over the fresh fruits and vegetables of Savonlinna's outdoor market, this restaurant is crowded every day at lunch and dinner with locals as well as hotel guests. The decor evokes an old-fashioned Finnish (or Swedish) tavern, with lots of exposed wood paneling, a jolly bar near the entrance, and a list of food items that includes everything from salads and pizzas to beef liver with fried onions and gooseberry-flavored sorbet. In July, during opera season, this restaurant is supplemented with the opening, by the hotel, of an additional restaurant, Othello, which serves basically the same menu.

In the Savonlinna Seurahuone Hotel, Kauppatori 4. © 015/5731. Sandwiches, pizzas, and pastas 7€–13€ ($9.10–$17); platters and main courses 14€–21€ ($18–$27). AE, DC, MC, V. Mon 11am–10pm; Tues–Fri 11am–11pm; Sat noon–11pm; Sun noon–8pm. Bus: 1, 2, or 3.

3 Tampere 🖈

172km (107 miles) N of Helsinki, 155km (96 miles) NE of Turku

Located on a narrow isthmus between two lakes (Lake Näsijärvi and Lake Pyhäjärvi), Tampere is Finland's second-largest city (pop. 203,000), and is primarily an industrial center; however, it remains one of the cleanest, brightest cities in Scandinavia, and is filled with parks, bodies of water, museums, art galleries, theaters, and statues, including some by Wäinö Aaltonen.

A vibrant young city with a university and a growing technology industry, Tampere is the site of one of Scandinavia's major attractions, an outdoor theater (Pyynikki) with a revolving auditorium. Tampere's Swedish name is *Tammerfors*.

ESSENTIALS

GETTING THERE   From Jyväskylä, continue driving southwest along E-4 (also E-80), which has signs directing you all the way to Tampere. If you're not driving, you can reach Tampere by air, train, or bus. **Blue 1** (© **0600-25831;** www.bluel.com) offers flights from both Copenhagen and Stockholm. Most visitors, who are already in Helsinki, fly to Tampere on one of several daily flights from Helsinki aboard **Finnair** (© **0600-140-140**). A train leaves Helsinki nearly every hour for Tampere (trip time: 2¼ hours); five buses a day make the 2½ hour trip from Helsinki. For bus schedules and fares, call **Matkahuolto Oy** (© **0200/40-00;** www.matkahuolto.fi). From June 3 to August 17, boats run between Tampere and Hämeenlinna in the south. If you're visiting Hämeenlinna, you might want to take the 8-hour boat trip to Tampere. The one-way fare is 65€ ($85). For schedules and information, contact **Finnish Silverline** (© **03/212-4803;** www.finnishsilverline.com).

VISITOR INFORMATION   The **City Tourist Office,** Verkatehtaankatu 2 (P.O. Box 487), FIN-33101 Tampere (© **020/716-6800**), can help arrange sightseeing tours, provide maps, and offer miscellaneous information. The office is open June to August Monday to Friday 8:30am to 8pm, Saturday 8:30am to 6pm, and Sunday 11am to 6pm; September to May Monday to Friday 8:30am to 5pm.

SPECIAL EVENTS   The **Tampere Choir Festival** has been held in alternate years during the second week in June since 1975, while the **Tampere International Theater Festival** has been Finland's only festival of professional theater, held during the second week of August, since 1969. The **Tampere Jazz Happening,** Finland's best modern jazz festival, opens the first week of November. Consult the tourist office for specific dates, which vary from year to year.

WHAT TO SEE & DO
SEEING THE SIGHTS

Tampere, obviously, doesn't compete with Helsinki in the number of attractions, but there's still enough to keep you busy here for at least 2 days.

Lenin Museum This curious museum lies in the Tampere Workers Hall, where the first meeting between Lenin and Stalin took place in 1905. Lenin paid a number of secret visits to Finland, and this museum contains mementos of his life and work. On site is the most bizarre gift shop in all of Finland.

Hämeenpuisto 28. ⓒ 03/276-8100. www.tampere.fi/culture/lenin. Admission 4€ ($5.20). Mon–Fri 9am–6pm; Sat–Sun 11am–4pm. Bus: 2, 3, 15, 16, 24, 26, or 27.

Moominvalley *(Kids)* This museum contains original fairy-tale illustrations by Tove Jansson's *Moominfigures* in 40 dioramas and two "Moominhouses."

Hämeenpuisto 20. ⓒ 03/716-6578. www.tampere.fi/muumi/English. Admission 4€ ($5.20) adults, 1€ ($1.30) children 4–17, free for children 3 and under. Tues–Fri 9am–5pm; Sat–Sun 10am–6pm. Bus: 16 or 25.

Tampere Art Museum This museum has no permanent home, but rather floats from hall to hall. However, we suggest you seek it out for what are the best temporary art exhibitions in Finland. The permanent collections include paintings, sculpture, drawings, graphics, regional art, and the city's art collection.

Veturiaukio 4. ⓒ 03/716-5341. Admission 4€ ($5.20) adults, 1€ ($1.30) children 16 and under. Tues–Sun 10am–6pm. Bus: 16.

Tuomiokirkko *(★★)* The gray-granite Tampere cathedral, built between 1902 and 1907, is the finest example of the Finnish National Romantic style. The towering spires and the piers holding up the vaulting evoke the Gothic style of the Middle Ages, but the stunning interior is one of the best examples in Finland of Art Nouveau. The cathedral contains many pieces of art, including *The Wounded Angel* and *The Garden of Death* by Hugo Simberg (1873–1917). The artist was the most famous Symbolist in Finland, and his style is best evoked by the large murals *The Garland Bearers*.

Tuomiokirkonkatu 3. No phone. Free admission. May–Aug daily 9am–6pm; Sept–Apr daily 11am–3pm. Any bus to train station.

THEATER

Pyynikki Summer Theater *(★★★)* About 1.6km (1 mile) from the center of Tampere, this outdoor theater (the first in the world) has a revolving auditorium and seats 836. The plays are presented in Finnish, and a free summary of the plot is available in English (though it's not really necessary). It's imperative to reserve tickets in advance. Plays are presented from mid-June until the end of August.

Postilokero 246. ⓒ 03/216-03-00. www.pyynikinkesateatteri.com. Tickets 10€–30€ ($13–$39). Bus: 12.

ORGANIZED TOURS

From June to August, a daily guided tour of the city leaves at 2pm from in front of the **City Tourist Office,** Verkatehtaankatu 2 (ⓒ **020/716-68-00**), costing 13 € ($17) for adults, 4 € ($5.20) for children 7 to 16, and free for children 6 and under. The trip lasts 2 hours, and the commentary is given in English.

From June 2 to August 2, Tampere is the meeting point for two popular lake cruisers, including the Finnish *Silverline,* which has a good restaurant. Information is available from **Laivayhtioiden Tilauskeskus (Boatlines Booking Center),** Verkatehtaankatu 2 (ⓒ **03/212-48-04**).

The Lake District's Greatest Adventure Park

Särkänniemi 𝒦𝒦𝒦 is set on 10 hectares (25 acres), meaning there's a lot to see and do here. Lying 1.5km (1 mile) west of the city, it sits on a headland jutting out into Lake Näsijärvi. After entering the park, we suggest, for orientation purposes, you mount the **Näsinneula Observation Tower,** which at 168m (551 ft.) is the highest in Finland, offering one of the area's best **panoramic views** 𝒦𝒦.

The chief artistic treasure of the adventure park is the **Sara Hildén Taidemuseo** 𝒦𝒦, a striking avant-garde piece of architecture that competes with the paintings it showcases inside. The Sara Hildén Foundation owns the greatest modern art collection outside Helsinki, with works by such international artists as Léger, Giacometti, Paul Klee, Picasso, and Miró. Near the observation tower, the museum also presents a changing array of international works. The foundation was established in 1962 by the world-class art collector Sara Hildén, whose collection focuses mainly on postwar art. The museum stands in beautiful lakeside surroundings, and some of its sculpture is displayed on the shores of Lake Näsijärvi next to the museum. You can enjoy views of the water at an on-site cafe.

At the **Dolphinarium,** the dolphins give five daily performances, while at the nearby **Children's Zoo,** kids on a common playground can mingle with tamed domestic animals and take pony treks or rides in donkey-pulled carriages. The **Aquarium** houses some 2,000 creatures of the sea from 200 different species, as well as a seal pool, with feeding times daily at 11am and 4pm. On the ground floor of the Aquarium, you can see a tank with mangrove trees and rainbow-hued fish. At the **Planetarium,** there's a 25-minute show (in both English and Finnish) daily at noon and 2pm.

Of course, local families come here for the **amusement park,** which features nearly three dozen carnival-like rides, of which the Tornado Super Roller-Coaster is the most popular. Most rides cost 5€ ($6.50) each.

A 5€ ($6.50) admission includes entrance to the Adventure Park, the Sara Hildén Taidemuseo, the Observation Tower, and the Children's Zoo. Attractions such as the Dolphinarium, Aquarium, and Planetarium cost 5€ ($6.50) each.

To get to **Särkänniemi,** take bus no. 4 from the train station. The park (© **0207/130-212;** www.sarkanniemi.fi) is open in summer Sunday to Friday noon to 9pm and Saturday noon to 10pm, with off-season hours adjusted monthly.

WHERE TO STAY

Cumulus Koskikatu   This middle-bracket hotel is one of the town's most respected, attracting residents with its restaurant, the Huviretki, and the bar, the Hemingway Pub. Midsize bedrooms are outfitted in pastel tones, and are furnished with conservatively modern pieces that are comfortable and completely appropriate for the many business clients who opt to stay here. You'll find the hotel at the edge of Koskipuisto Park, near the river in the center of town.

Koskikatu 5, FIN-33100 Tampere. © **03/242-41-11.** Fax 03/242-43-99. www.cumulus.fi. 230 units. Mon–Thurs 151€–179€ ($196–$233) double; Fri–Sun 92€–120€ ($120–$156) double. Rates include breakfast. AE, DC, MC, V. Parking 11€ ($14). Bus: 1, 16, or 18. **Amenities:** Restaurant; pub; indoor pool; 2 saunas; (in summertime only) children's playroom; limited room service; laundry service/dry cleaning (Mon–Fri only). *In room:* TV, minibar (in some), safe (in some), Wi-Fi.

Scandic Rosendahl ⋆⋆

Tampere's most architecturally dramatic modern hotel lies about 2km (1¼ miles) south of the town center, within a forest at the edge of Lake Pyhäjärvi. Built in 1977 and most recently renovated in 2006, it boasts a softly angled design of mirrored walls, polished stone, and lacquered ceilings, making it the most avant-garde hotel in town. Bedrooms are comfortable, well-upholstered, and quiet. There's a pier in front of the hotel where cruise ships making a tour of the lake or the transit from Tampere to Hämeenlinna sometimes stop. The town's famous outdoor theater, Pyynikki, is nearby.

Pyynikintie 13. FIN-33200 Tampere. © **03/244-1111.** Fax 03/2441-2211. www.scandic-hotels.com. 213 units. Mon–Thurs 96€–107€ ($125–$139) double; Fri–Sun 79€–88€ ($103–$114) double; 245€ ($319) suite. AE, DC, MC, V. Bus: 21. **Amenities:** Restaurant; bar; pub; indoor pool; children's pool; golf simulator; 3 outdoor tennis courts; squash courts; wellness compound with 4 saunas and exercise equipment; miles of cross-country ski and hiking trails; laundry service/dry cleaning facilities. *In room:* TV, minibar, Wi-Fi.

Scandic Tampere City Hotel ⋆

A reliable and long-enduring favorite, this seven-story hotel was originally built in 1932, and nearby doubled in size with the addition of a new wing after its acquisition by the Scandic chain after the turn of the millennium. Set behind a pale ocher facade in the heart of town, immediately across from the railway station, it offers comfortably furnished bedrooms, some of which overlook the surrounding town and others that front a soaring atrium with splashing fountains and potted plants. The in-house restaurant, the Piazza Food Factory, remains busy throughout the day and evening with clients from outside the hotel.

Hameenkatu 1, FIN-33100 Tampere. © **03/244-61-11.** Fax 03/46-21-11. www.scandic-hotels.com. 263 units. Mon–Thurs 170€–185€ ($221–$241) double; Fri–Sun 111€–126€ ($144–$164) double; 241€ ($313) suite. Rates include breakfast. AE, DC, MC, V. Parking 12€ ($15). Bus: 4 or 27. **Amenities:** Restaurant; bar; children's playroom; limited room service; laundry service/dry cleaning. *In room:* TV, minibar, beverage maker, iron, safe, Wi-Fi.

Sokos Hotel Ilves ⋆

Set within the heart of Tampere, this hotel is more plush and up-to-date than the also-recommended Sokos Hotel Tammer (see below). It's also one of the tallest buildings in town. Rooms were renovated in 2006, leaving a mostly monochromatic color scheme in the conservatively contemporary bedrooms, which range from midsize to spacious.

There's a nightclub and disco on the premises, the Ilves Bar and Nightclub, which attracts lots of local residents and hotel guests every Wednesday to Saturday from 9pm until at least 4am. Entrance for hotel guests is free at any time, entrance for nonresidents ranges from free to as much as 8€ ($10), depending on the night.

Hatanpäänvaltatie 1, FIN-33100 Tampere. © **020/123-4631.** Fax 03/5698-6263. www.sokoshotel.fi. 336 units. Mon–Thurs 120€–175€ ($156–$228) double; Fri–Sun 110€–150€ ($143–$195) double; 310€–610€ ($403–$793) suite. Rates include breakfast. AE, DC, MC, V. Parking 14€ ($18). Bus: 1. **Amenities:** Restaurant; bar; nightclub; indoor pool; 4 saunas; limited room service; babysitting; laundry service/dry cleaning. *In room:* TV, minibar, safe, hair dryer, Wi-Fi.

Sokos Hotel Tammer ⋆

Because it has been frequently ripped apart and renovated, you might not immediately realize that this is the oldest hotel in town. It was for years considered the most glamorous hotel in town—a designation that is no longer accurate—but public and private areas were renovated with sensitivity, taking care to preserve its Art Deco detailing. Before passing into the reception area, you'll pass beneath the dramatic, five-story-tall archway that soars nearly to the roofline. Bedrooms are high-ceilinged, large, and comfortably furnished, many opening onto views of the town. Furnishings are in a sleek Nordic style, and each room is individually designed. The private bathrooms are tiled, sometimes with a shower but often with a tub/shower combo. An outdoor terrace offers pleasant views of the sea.

Satakunnankatu 13, FIN-33100 Tampere. © 020/123-46-32. Fax 03/5697-6266. www.sokoshotels.fi. 87 units. Sun–Thurs 149€–210€ ($194–$273) double; Fri–Sat 99€–125€ ($129–$163) double; 230€–265€ ($299–$345) suite. Rates include breakfast. AE, DC, MC, V. Free parking. Bus: 5. **Amenities:** Restaurant; bar; 2 saunas; limited room service; laundry service/dry cleaning. *In room:* TV, minibar, coffeemaker (in some), trouser press.

Victoria (*Value*   This is usually cited as the least expensive of the major hotels of Tampere. Built in 1972 in a location close to the railway station, it has been spruced up at almost yearly intervals. Each of the cozy and comfortable bedrooms is outfitted in pastel colors with lots of exposed wood. Other than breakfast, no meals are served here, but there's a very small lobby bar.

Itsenaisyydenkatu 1, FIN-33100 Tampere. © 03/242-51-11. Fax 03/242-51-00. www.hotellivictoria.fi. 71 units. Mon–Thurs 134€ ($174) double; Fri–Sun 89€ ($116) double. Rates include breakfast. AE, MC, V. Closed Dec 22–Jan 8. Free parking. Bus: 1. **Amenities:** Bar; indoor pool; laundry service/dry cleaning. *In room:* TV, minibar (in most), hair dryer.

WHERE TO DINE

Astor (*★* CONTINENTAL   This contemporary-looking restaurant offers a cozy setting, sophisticated and attentive service, and savory cuisine. Set in the heart of town, and favored by the city's business and academic community, it's the kind of place where romances are likely to blossom. The best menu items include filets of Baltic herring with mustard sauce; whitefish mousse with red currant sauce; creamy crayfish or cream of forest mushroom soup; and pan-fried breast of duck with and orange-and-ginger-flavored sauce. Dessert might include a parfait of Arctic blackberries. There's a piano bar on the premises.

Aleksis Kiven Katu 26. © 03/260-5700. Reservations recommended. Main courses 17€–25€ ($22–$33). Prix-fixe menus 35€–42€ ($46–$55). AE, MC, V. Mon 11am–midnight; Tues–Thurs 11am–1am; Fri–Sat 11am–2am; Sun 2–10pm. Bus: 1.

Finlaysonin Palatsi FINNISH/INTERNATIONAL   Built as a palace in 1899, this is now an elegant restaurant with a number of dining rooms and cozy private rooms. In summer, an outdoor dining facility is open in the surrounding park. The chef attempts to use local products wherever possible. The fish dishes, such as salmon and whitefish, are excellently prepared, as are the game specialties. Begin with such classic Finnish appetizers as cold smoked whitefish with a red cabbage strudel, or a smoked reindeer salmon roll. One of the best dishes is a roasted filet of pike-perch with a white truffle sauce. Try the cloudberry ice cream.

Kuninkaankatu 1. © 03/260-5770. Reservations recommended. Main courses 15€–26€ ($20–$34). Prix-fixe menus 34€–48€ ($44–$62) AE, DC, MC, V. Daily 11am–2am. Bus: 1, 2, or 3.

Hella & Huone (*★★* (*Finds* CONTINENTAL   This restaurant is set to the immediate north of Tampere's Talo Park, in the heart of town, and the food is lavishly fussed over, professionally prepared and presented, and relatively ambitious. With just 33 seats and a small staff, you can be sure you'll get all the attention you deserve. You'll never know in advance what might be on the menu, as it depends on the mood of the chef and the availability of the ingredients, but fresh fish, shellfish, and game dishes are likely to crop up whenever they're in season, and the chef is proud of what the kitchen manages to do with duck, lamb, and turbot. A recent meal here featured pâté of foie gras in puff pastry with braised green tomatoes and chutney, cream of morel soup, roasted pheasant with whortleberry sauce, an array of French cheeses, and poached pears in vanilla syrup.

Salhojankatu 48. ⓒ **03/253-2440.** Reservations recommended. Main courses 20€ ($26) each; 4-course prix-fixe menu 43€ ($56). AE, DC, MC, V. Tues–Sat 6–9:30pm. Bus: 1

Knossos GREEK Popular, a bit claustrophobic, and lined with souvenirs from the island of Crete, this Greek tavern is cozy, convivial, and evocative of many of the clients' previous vacations in the Mediterranean. Between introductory shots of beer or ouzo, you might be tempted by a platter piled high with *meze* (warm and cold Greek appetizers that include stuffed vine leaves and hummus); salads studded with black olives, herbs, and chunks of goat cheese; fried calamari; or all-vegetarian or lamb versions of moussaka.

Koskikeskus 2. ⓒ **03/223-8899.** Main courses 17€–25€ ($21–$33). AE, MC, V. Mon–Sat 11am–11pm; Sun noon–6pm. Bus: 5

Plevna Brewery Pub and Restaurant FINNISH In 1820, an investor from Scotland founded a cotton mill in Tampere. About 60 years later, his heirs built the brick-sided weaving hall in which this restaurant is located. Today, it's a rollicking, sometimes raucous, assembly of diners and drinkers who appreciate the large mugs of very fresh beer priced at 5.40€ ($7) for a half-liter. There's a warren of rooms containing the bar facilities, and a separate set of dining rooms where food seems to have been specially contrived to go well with the suds. Examples include creamy salmon soup, fried filets of perch with honey-flavored *crème fraîche*, filets of butter-fried herring, "brewmaster's steaks" (braised in beer), and pork schnitzels. The restaurant is named after a battle in the Balkan town of Plevna, in which some of the workers from the mills lost their lives.

Itäinenkatu 8. ⓒ **03/260-1200.** Main courses 10€–24€ ($13–$31). AE, MC, V. Mon–Thurs 11am–1am; Fri–Sat 11am–9:30pm; Sun 11am–11pm. Bus: 1, 5.

4 Finnish Lapland

Above the Arctic Circle, Lapland comprises one-third of Finland, the country's northernmost, largest, and most sparsely populated province, which is why it's often called "The Last Wilderness in Europe."

Although Lapland has four seasons, some people refer to eight seasons a year. In the summer, the vegetation sprouts flowers and bears fruit all within 3 months because the sun doesn't set for weeks on end. In Utsjoki, in the northernmost part of Lapland, starting in the middle of May, the sun doesn't set for nearly 70 days. If summer, with its midnight sun, is an extraordinary experience, then so is the polar night, the twilight time of the year, when there is never true since the sun glows softly on the horizon.

The period during October and November, when there's no sun, is called *kaamos*. Winter is the longest period of the year, but it includes the night light show—the aurora borealis. After the polar night comes the dazzling spring snow, when skiing is great until May, when the sun gives twice as much light as it did in the dead of winter.

Lapland is an area of great forests, and jobs in forestry and agriculture are the most common occupations here. Finland's longest river, the Kemijoki, runs through the area, and its lower reaches are terraced with seven hydroelectric plants. Lapland also has western Europe's largest artificial lakes, Løkka and Porttipahta.

Despite human intrusion, this is still a land of bears, wolves, eagles, and wolverines. However, the animal that symbolizes this land is the reindeer, and there are more than 300,000 here.

North of the Arctic Circle, the **Arctic Road** ✯✯✯ lies as far north as the roadless tundras of Alaska, Greenland, and Siberia. However, it provides easy access to the diverse scenery of the north.

As early as the 1930s, visitors from all over Europe traveled north in their cars, heading for Petsamo, the end point of the Arctic Road at that time. Today, the Arctic Road is an adventure, stretching for more than 998km (620 miles). It starts near the Arctic Circle at Rovaniemi and passes through central and northern Lapland as it heads toward the Arctic Ocean and eastern Finnmark, on the very edge of Europe. Extensive areas along the road have been protected and preserved.

ROVANIEMI
834km (518 miles) N of Helsinki, 287km (178 miles) S of Ivalo

Our summer driving tour begins in Lapland's capital, Rovaniemi, which is best reached by flying from Helsinki. Once here, you can rent a car and tour Lapland (summer is the best time, as winters can be rough).

When the Nazis began their infamous retreat from Lapland in 1944, they burned Rovaniemi, the gateway to Lapland and a prime rail and communications center, to the ground. But with characteristic Finnish *sisu* (suggesting courage and bravery against overwhelming odds), Rovaniemi bounced back and became a completely modern town, designed largely by Finland's greatest architect, Alvar Aalto, who created roads shaped like reindeer antlers.

Eight kilometers (5 miles) south of the Arctic Circle, Rovaniemi is at the confluence of two significant Finnish rivers, the Kemijoki and the Ounasjoki. This capital of Finnish Lapland goes back some 8,000 years, and the settlement at Rovaniemi was mentioned in documents in the 1400s. As a tourist and travel center, Rovaniemi has excellent road, rail, and air connections. Highway 4, which passes through the city, stretches from southern Finland to Inari in Lapland. You can drive to northern Norway on the Great Arctic Highway and to Kiruna, Sweden, and Narvik, Norway, by following the North Calotte Highway. If you arrive by plane, you'll probably take a bus into Rovaniemi, although a reindeer-drawn *pulkka* would be more colorful.

Regardless of when you come, you'll surely escape the heat. In July, the hottest month, the temperature is likely to be around 50°F (10°C); however, you won't escape the mosquitoes from the swampy tundra.

ESSENTIALS
GETTING THERE There are daily flights from Helsinki (trip time: 1 hr.). The airport lies 8km (5 miles) north of the center of town, and yellow minivans, costing 5€ ($6.50) per person, will take you into town. Their departures are timed to coincide with the arrival of flights. For airport information, call the **Finnair** desk at the airport (© **016/36-36-700**). Four trains a day depart from Helsinki for Rovaniemi, taking 10 hours for the trek north. The train station is at Rantakatu; for rail schedules, call © **0600/41900.**

GETTING AROUND Rovaniemi is the bus center for northern Finland, and buses fan out from the station to Lapinkävij to all major communities north of Rovaniemi.

For schedules, call © **0200/4060.** Bus no. 8 is the town's most serviceable bus, hitting all the attractions and hotels of Rovaniemi before continuing on to Santa's Village and the Arctic Circle. The one-way fare is 3.50€ ($4.55) per person.

VISITOR INFORMATION The **Rovaniemi Tourist Information** office, Rovankatu 21, FIN-96200 Rovaniemi (© **016/346-270**), is open June to August Monday to Friday 8am to 6pm and Saturday and Sunday 10am to 4pm; September to May Monday to Friday from 8am to 8pm. In December, it's also open Saturday and Sunday 10am to 2pm.

SEEING THE SIGHTS

Administrative and Cultural Center ☆☆ "The architect's job is to give life a more sensitive structure," wrote architect Alvar Aalto in 1955. This is exactly what he did when he created this elegant trio of buildings, which draws devotees of his designs from all over the world.

The cultural complex, **Lappia-Talo,** Hallituskatu 11, was the last of Aalto's buildings to be completed here, having opened in 1975. The first building, the library, **Kirjasto** ☆☆, Hallituskatu 7 (© **016/322-2463**), opened in 1965. The house has a valuable Lappish collection, and temporary art exhibitions are staged in its Lappinica Hall. Admission is free and it's open Monday to Thursday 11am to 8pm, Friday 11am to 5pm, and Saturday 11am to 3pm.

A third building, **Kaupungintalo** ☆☆, Hallituskatu 7 (© **016/322-2288**), is the most famous government building in northern Finland. Aalto completed it in 1988 as the finishing touch of the administrative and cultural center. This Town Hall consists of several divergent wings, and it's dominated by the council chamber, which evokes crystal because of its "folded" wall surfaces. The entrance wall of the hall is a distance echo of Aalto's famous theme of Northern Lights. Admission free; the Town Hall is open Monday to Friday 8am to 4pm.

Arktikum ☆☆☆ This is the best museum in all of Scandinavia that's devoted to the people and the culture of region. An avant-garde, underground construction, which mimics an ice tunnel, shelters two exceptional museums that demonstrate living conditions for the people, especially the Sami, who live north of the Arctic Circle.

Almost daily, a show features the Northern Lights in the **Polarium Theater. The Provincial Museum of Lapland Exhibitions** ☆☆ is a fascinating re-creation of Sami culture, with folklore costumes, small-scale models of Rovaniemi from 1939 to 1944, and an award-winning exhibition called "The Survivors," illustrating life in Lapland from prehistoric times to today.

The Arctic Circle Centre Exhibitions ☆☆☆ take you to the top of the world, offering a rare insight into these northern people and their flora and fauna. You learn such things as the number of words Inuits have for snow, and see the equipment they use for catching seals. The exhibitions also trace the tremendous natural wealth of the region while addressing risks involved in exploiting them.

It'll take at least 2 hours, which can include lunch at the **Arktikum Restaurant** (© **016/322-3263**), where all the food is prepared using fresh local produce. The 10€ ($13) luncheon buffet is the best in town. You can also order a la carte items, such as sautéed reindeer, costing from 16€ to 17€ ($21–$22). An on-site gift shop sells handmade souvenirs.

Pohjoisranta 4. © **016/322-3260.** Admission 8€ ($10) adults, 7€ ($9) students and seniors, 5€ ($6.50) ages 7–15, free 6 and under. Family ticket for 2 adults and 2 children 20€ ($26). Aug Tues–Sun 10am–8pm; Sept–Nov Tues–Sun 10am–5pm; Dec–July daily 10am–6pm. Lies 1km (½ mile) north of city center.

Napaiiri: The Arctic Circle ✮✮ All visitors want to visit the Arctic Circle, the southernmost line at which the Midnight Sun can be viewed. Bus no. 8 runs from the center of Rovaniemi to this location, 8km (5 miles) north of Rovaniemi on the Rovaniemi-Sodankylä highway. Don't think the Arctic Circle is permanently fixed, as it can shift several yards or meters daily. At this point, the sun never sets in midsummer, nor does it ever rise in the pitch black of midwinter. The **Arctic Circle Marker** is found here.

Napaiiri is also the site of **Santa Claus Village** (see "Shopping," below), the most commercialized center of all of Lapland. Thousands of letters from children all over the world are mailed to the **Santa Claus Main Post Office,** FIN-96930, Arctic Circle. You can also send a postcard home with an official stamp from Santa Claus himself. Next to the post office, you can join a line of kids waiting to meet Santa.

Other than the shopping complex, with its restaurants and cafes, the big attraction here is **Santapark** ✮ (© **016/333-0000;** www.santapark.com), lying at Syväsenvaara Mountain 2km (1¼ miles) west of the Rovaniemi airport. A free Santa train runs in summer between Santa Claus Village and Santapark. The park lies inside a cave in the mountain. Once inside, you're greeted with elves baking gingerbread and, yes, yet another Santa.

Entertainment includes a sleigh ride, a Christmas carousel, and a multimedia theater. There's also a cafeteria and a store. The train stops at a reindeer park for visitors to enjoy a ride on one of Santa's herd. A family ticket costs 50€ ($65); otherwise, adults pay 20€ ($26), children 3 to 15 pay 15€ ($20), free for under 3. From midsummer to mid-August, hours are Tuesday to Saturday 10am to 4pm. The park also reopens in late November to mid-January Tuesday to Sunday 10am to 4pm.

Rovaniemen Kirkko This Evangelical Lutheran parish church was built in 1950 to replace the one destroyed during the war. Designed by the architect Bertel Liljequist, it stands on the same spot where three previous churches had stood. The interior is quite beautiful, noted for its wall and ceiling decorations, wood carvings, and the best altar fresco, *Fountain of Life* ✮✮, by Lennart Segerstrale.

Kirkkotie 1. © 016/335-511. Free admission. Daily 9am–9pm. Closed Oct to mid-May.

Lapland Safaris & River Cruises

In the very short summer, white-water rafting, river cruises, fishing in local rivers, and trips to reindeer and husky farms can be arranged, while winter visitors can opt for snowmobiling, skiing, or sled safaris.

There are several tour operators. One of the best is **Arctic Safaris,** Koskikatu 6 (© **016/340-0400;** www.arcticsafaris.fi). The largest and best-known agency, offering tours of the vast Lapland area, is **Lapland Safaris,** Koskikatu 1 (© **016/331-1200;** www.laplandsafaris.com).

Prices depend on what you want to do or see. A 3-hour summer tour costs around 70€ ($91), while short trips on the river cost 20€ ($26). In winter, the price of the safaris are far more expensive, a snowmobile safari, for example, ranges from 100€ to 150€ ($130–$195). About 2 to 4 hours of husky or reindeer sledding costs from 100€ to 150€ ($130–$195).

SHOPPING

Lauri-Toutteet oy *, Pohjolankatu 25 (© **016/342-25-01**), is a log cabin in the center of town that houses workshops where craftspeople turn out both modern and traditional decorative pieces using such items as reindeer antlers and the gnarled roots of pussy willows. The store's cafe is a permanent sales exhibit, featuring curly birch products, wool and leather goods, jewelry, and Puukko knives. Open Monday to Friday 9am to 6pm.

The Trading Post, Route 4 (© **016/356-20-96**) at Santa Claus Village at the Arctic Circle, might be corny and overly commercialized, but it has some of the country's best handicrafts shops. On the two floors of elegant shops, you'll find cloudberry jam, engraved horn-handled knives, birch and pinewood children's toys, beautifully detailed hand-knit sweaters, and the best hand-woven Finnish tablecloths and textiles. There are also pieces of regional jewelry fashioned from silver and a semiprecious form of feldspar called spectrolite (found only in parts of Russia, Canada, and Finland).

One store sells Saga mink coats for perhaps half the price of similar coats in North America (excluding the Customs duty). Always popular among visitors is a certificate you can buy to prove that you've been north of the Arctic Circle; if you mail postcards from here, they'll receive a special Arctic Circle postmark. There's also an outdoor cafe for summertime Midnight Sun watching. Hours are daily in summer 8am to 8pm; off season daily 10am to 5pm. Bus no. 8 runs here from the center of Rovaniemi.

WHERE TO STAY

Rovaniemi has the finest hotels in northern Finland, although many tend to be expensive unless you book at a summer discount or weekend rate. Private homes that accept paying guests are the best bargain. For the most part, these homes are quite modest (don't expect a private bathroom). Ask at the tourist office for further information.

City Hotel   Comfortable, unpretentious, and recently renovated in 2006, this is a serviceable and well-managed hotel a few steps north of the town center. Its newest rooms are on the uppermost (fourth) floor. The in-house restaurant, the Monte Rosa, is recommended separately in "Where to Dine," below.

Pekankatu 9, FIN-96200 Rovaniemi. © **016/330-01-11**. Fax 016/311-304. www.cityhotel.fi. 92 units. Mon–Thurs 120€ ($156) double; Fri–Sun 99€ ($129) double. Rates include breakfast. AE, DC, MC, V. Free parking. **Amenities:** Restaurant; pub; limited room service; laundry service/dry cleaning. *In room:* TV, minibar, hair dryer.

Hotelli Aakenus   This small-scale inn is run by a local family (unlike other Rovaniemi hotels that are chain-run) and located about a .5km (1/3 mile) west of Town Hall at the edges of Rovaniemi's "urban sprawl." The small bedrooms are simple but comfortable, each of which was renovated and upgraded in 2005. Nothing here is luxurious, but the staff works hard, the prices are reasonable, and everything is well maintained.

Koskikatu 47, FIN-96200 Rovaniemi. © **016/342-2051**. Fax 016/342-2021. www.hotelliaakenus.net. 45 units. Mon–Thurs 70€ ($91) double; Sat–Sun 66€ ($86) double. AE, DC, MC, V. **Amenities:** Restaurant; bar; sauna. *In room:* TV, Wi-Fi.

Rantasipi Pohjanhovi *   This is the oldest hotel in town and the one with the most flair, built in 1936 when Rovaniemi was a logging-town outpost with a bright future ahead of it. Enlarged and virtually rebuilt in 1947, with another major renovation completed in 2004, this hotel offers a disco, a stylish and top-rated restaurant, recommended separately in "Where to Dine," below, and comfortably contemporary-looking bedrooms, each outfitted with well-chosen Finnish fabrics. It's popular with convention groups.

Pohjanpuistikko 2, FIN-96200 Rovaniemi. ☏ **016/33-711**. Fax 016/313-997. www.rantasipi.fi. 212 units. Mon–Thurs 138€–146€ ($179–$190) double; Fri–Sun 95€–103€ ($124–$134) double; 190€ ($247) suite. Rates include breakfast. AE, DC, MC, V. Free parking. **Amenities:** Restaurant; cafe; karaoke bar; large indoor pool; sauna complex; car rental desk; business center; hairdresser/salon; limited room service; travel agency. *In room:* TV, minibar, iron, Wi-Fi.

Sokos Hotel Vaakuna 𝕽   Stylish and well managed, with a pair of separately recommended restaurants that draw in substantial numbers of nonresidents, this hotel rises five pink-toned floors above the town center. You'll register within a lobby sheathed with slabs of Finnish granite before heading up to the rooms, which were each renovated in 2005. The staff is helpful and accommodating, and there's a zesty energy about this place that isn't present in some of its more staid competitors.

Koskikatu 4, FIN-96200 Rovaniemi. ☏ **020/123-4695**. Fax 016/332-21-89. www.sokoshotels.fi. 159 units. Mon–Thurs 94€–160€ ($122–$208) double; Fri–Sun 94€–140€ ($122–$182) double; 220€ ($286) suite. AE, DC, MC, V. Parking 5€ ($6.50). **Amenities:** 2 restaurants; bar; nightclub; 2 saunas; limited room service; laundry service/dry cleaning; nonsmoking rooms. *In room:* TV, minibar.

WHERE TO DINE

Amarillo TEX-MEX   This is one of two restaurants in the Sokos Hotel Vaakuna, and offers everything from nachos, fajitas, and grilled T-bone steaks to grilled filets of lamb, spicy fried chicken, and juicy burgers, all in a Western-inspired ambience.

In the Sokos Hotel Vaakuna, Koskikatu 4. ☏ **020/123-4695**. Main courses 10€–23€ ($13–$30). AE, DC, MC, V. Mon–Thurs 11am–midnight; Fri 11am–2am; Sat noon–2am; Sun noon–1am.

Fransmanni Restaurant 𝕽 FRENCH/CONTINENTAL   This, the second of the Sokos Hotel Vaakuna's two restaurants, is grand, French, and rather formal. The menu lists well-prepared Gallic creations such as snails flavored with garlic and Roquefort cheese; cream of salmon soup; an herb-laden chicken casserole; and filets of reindeer with dark honey sauce.

In the Sokos Hotel Vaakuna, Koskikatu 4. ☏ **020/123-4695**. Reservations recommended. Main courses 14€–28€ ($18–$36). AE, DC, MC, V. Mon–Thurs 11am–midnight; Fri 11am–2am; Sat noon–2am, Sun noon–1am.

Monte Rosa FINNISH   It's warm, paneled with woods from Finnish forests, and priced appropriately for it's location in one of the town' recommended middle-bracket hotels. Examples of enduringly popular items include cream of chanterelle soup; Caesar salad with chunks of grilled chicken; grilled Lappish lamb with chanterelle sauce; and reindeer filets with juniper-berry or chanterelle sauce. There's a luncheon buffet every Monday to Friday from 11:30am to 2:30pm, when many of the town's office workers select from the wide array of meats (three kinds), fish, and salads. During clement weather, additional dining space opens on an outdoor terrace.

In the City Hotel, Pekankatu 9. ☏ **016/330-01-11**. Lunch buffet 9€ ($12) per person; main courses 15€–25€ ($20–$33). AE, DC, MC, V. Mon–Fri 11am–10:30pm; Sat–Sun 1–10:30pm.

Restaurant at the Rantasipi Pohjanhovi Hotel 𝕽𝕽 FINNISH/CONTINENTAL   Other restaurants in Rovaniemi might be flashier and follow culinary and decorative trends a bit more closely, but when asked where they'd want to celebrate a rite of passage, most residents come here. It's relatively formal, with crisp white napery, but it isn't staid. Windows look out over one of Lapland's most evocative rivers, and food is superb, drawing upon game, fish, and produce from the surrounding region, some of it provided by individual local hunters and fishermen. Reindeer, ptarmigan, trout, and snow grouse are always reliable bets, often accented with berries culled late during the region's brief summers.

In the Rantasipi Pohjanhovi Hotel, Pohjanpuistikko 2. © **016/33 711**. Reservations recommended. Main courses 18€–29€ ($23–$38). AE, DC, MC, V. Daily 11am–3pm and 6–9:30pm.

Sky Ounasvaara Panorama Restaurant *ℛℛℛ* LAPPISH/INTERNATIONAL
Lying 2km (1¾ miles) east of the town center, this restaurant is on the second floor of the Sky Hotel Ounasvaara, offering panoramic views from its perch on Ounasvaara Hill. The furnishings of the restaurant have been kept simple in order not to detract from the grand vistas and virgin forest outside.

A Finnish gourmet society consistently names this restaurant as one of the top 19 in the country, and it also holds the Chaine des Rotisseurs plaque. The restaurant also has the Foyer Bar and a panoramic roof terrace for watching either the Midnight Sun or the northern lights.

Begin your meal with salmon roe or champagne-flavored asparagus soup with asparagus ravioli. For a main course, we especially like the Lake Inarinjärvi whitefish flavored with a star anise-spiced crayfish sauce or the Arctic char roasted in almond oil and served with a zesty dark orange sauce. For dessert, nothing beats the coconut lime crème brûlée with bits of pineapple and coconut. The restaurant's set menus are the best in Lapland.

Although it's far from the city center, you can also stay here overnight in one of the 71 well-furnished bedrooms, renting for 145€ ($189) in winter for a double or 75€ ($98) in summer. The accommodations are spacious and well furnished, and many of them are equipped with bathtubs (unusual for Lapland) and their own sauna. If you're staying over for a while, you might ask about cabin rentals, each of which has two separate bedrooms, making them ideal for families.

The restaurant lies next to the **Ounasvaara Ski Center** (© **016/369-045**; www.ounasvaara.net), with 123km (76 miles) of cross-country skiing tracks, plus six downhill slopes and three ski jumps.

Ounasvaara, FIN-96400. © **016/335-33-11**. Fax 016/318-789. www.laplandhotels.com. Reservations recommended. Main courses 13€–24€ ($17–$31); prix-fixe menus 38€–54€ ($49–$70). AE, DC, MC, V. Daily 11am–10pm.

ROVANIEMI AFTER DARK
The great cultural center of Lapland is **Lappia-Talo** *ℛℛℛ*, Hallituskatu 11 (© **016/322-2495**), designed by Alvar Aalto in 1975. One of the town's architectural wonders, this concert hall and convention center houses the world's northernmost professional theater, the Rovaniemi Theater Company. It is also the venue for the Lapland Music School and the Chamber Orchestra of Lapland. It's closed from June to August, but if you're in Rovaniemi at other times, check to see what's playing.

For livelier action, head for the **Onnella Disco** *ℛ*, Poromiehentie (© **016/775-9492**), the largest and newest in Lapland, with a trio of bars and three separate dance floors. Music features Finnish pop, house and garage, and even 1970s and 1980s disco. Open Wednesday to Saturday 9am to 4am, Onnella charges a cover of 8€ ($10) on Friday and Saturday nights.

Index

THE NEW TRAVELOCITY GUARANTEE

EVERYTHING YOU BOOK WILL BE RIGHT, OR WE'LL WORK WITH OUR TRAVEL PARTNERS TO MAKE IT RIGHT, RIGHT AWAY.

To drive home the point,
we're going to use the word "right" in every single sentence.

Let's get right to it. Right to the meat! Only Travelocity guarantees everything about your booking will be right, or we'll work with our travel partners to make it right, right away. Right on!

Here's a picture taken smack dab right in the middle of Antigua, where the guarantee also covers you.

The guarantee covers all but one of the items pictured to the right.

For example, what if the ocean view you booked actually looks out at a downright ugly parking lot? You'd be right to call – we're there for you. And no one in their right mind would be pleased to learn the rental car place has closed and left them stranded. Call Travelocity and we'll help get you back on the right track.

Now, you may be thinking, "Yeah, right, I'm so sure." That's OK; you have the right to remain skeptical. That is until we mention help is always right around the corner. Call us right off the bat, knowing that our customer service reps are there for you 24/7. Righting wrongs. Left and right.

Now if you're guessing there are some things we can't control, like the weather, well you're right. But we can help you with most things – to get all the details in righting,* visit **travelocity.com/guarantee.**

*Sorry, spelling things right is one of the few things not covered under the guarantee.

I'd give my right arm for a guarantee like this, although I'm glad I don't have to.

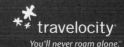
travelocity
You'll never roam alone.